Ethics of Liberation

A book in the series
LATIN AMERICA OTHERWISE
Languages, Empires, Nations
A series edited by
Walter D. Mignolo, Duke University
Irene Silverblatt, Duke University
Sonia Saldívar-Hull, University of Texas,
San Antonio

ENRIQUE DUSSEL

Ethics of Liberation

IN THE AGE OF GLOBALIZATION AND EXCLUSION

Translated by
EDUARDO MENDIETA, CAMILO PÉREZ BUSTILLO,
YOLANDA ANGULO, AND NELSON MALDONADO-TORRES
Translation edited by Alejandro A. Vallega

Duke University Press
DURHAM AND LONDON
2013

© 2013 Duke University Press
All rights reserved
Printed in the United States of America
on acid-free paper ∞
Designed by C. H. Westmoreland
Typeset in Adobe Garamond Pro
by Tseng Information Systems, Inc.

LIBRARY OF CONGRESS
CATALOGING-IN-PUBLICATION DATA
Dussel, Enrique D.
[Etica de la liberación en la edad de la globalización
y la exclusión. English]
Ethics of liberation : in the age of globalization and
exclusion / Enrique Dussel ; translation edited by Alejandro A.
Vallega ; translated by Eduardo Mendieta . . . [et al.].
p. cm. —
(Latin America otherwise : languages, empires, nations)
Includes bibliographical references and index.
ISBN 978-0-8223-5201-3 (cloth : alk. paper)
ISBN 978-0-8223-5212-9 (pbk. : alk. paper)
1. Liberation theology. 2. Christian ethics—Catholic authors.
3. History—Philosophy. 4. Social ethics. 5. Knowledge,
Theory of. 6. Internationalism. I. Vallega, Alejandro A.
II. Title. III. Series: Latin America otherwise.
BT83.57.D8713 2012
170—dc23   2011053092

TO RIGOBERTA MENCHÚ,
woman, Mayan Indian, farmer, of brown-skinned race,
Guatemalan

TO THE ZAPATISTA ARMY OF NATIONAL LIBERATION,
which reminds us of the ethical path almost lost in the mountain
(new Holzwege), whose steps we have followed in the construction
of this philosophical work

TO KARL-OTTO APEL,
who dared to dialogue with the philosophers of the South,
inspiring us theoretically

TO GUSTAVO ALBERTO DUSSEL (1936–76),
dean of the Faculty of Physics and Mathematics of the University
of Buenos Aires in the time of the Rector Rodolfo Puiggrós, who
died in his youth in the sadness of political persecution

TO JOHANNA,
who daily made possible this long book

But no *living being* believes that the shortcomings of his existence have their basis in the *principle* of his life [*Prinzip seines Lebens*], in the *essence* [*Wesen*] *of his life*; everyone believes that their basis lies in circumstances external to his life. *Suicide* is against nature.

—KARL MARX, *Vorwärts!*,
no. 63, August 7, 1844, Paris

Je pense, donc je suis [from Descartes, *La discours de la méthode*] is the cause of the crime against *Je danse, donc je vie.*

—F. EBOUSSI BOULAGA,
La crise du Muntu, 56

Contents

About the Series

Latin America Otherwise: Languages, Empires, Nations is a critical series. It aims to explore the emergence and consequences of concepts used to define "Latin America" while at the same time exploring the broad interplay of political, economic, and cultural practices that have shaped Latin American worlds. Latin America, at the crossroads of competing imperial designs and local responses, has been construed as a geocultural and geopolitical entity since the nineteenth century. This series provides a starting point to redefine Latin America as a configuration of political, linguistic, cultural, and economic intersections that demands a continuous reappraisal of the role of the Americas in history, and of the ongoing process of globalization and the relocation of people and cultures that have characterized Latin America's experience. *Latin America Otherwise: Languages, Empires, Nations* is a forum that confronts established geocultural constructions, rethinks area studies and disciplinary boundaries, assesses convictions of the academy and of public policy, and correspondingly demands that the practices through which we produce knowledge and understanding about and from Latin America be subject to rigorous and critical scrutiny.

Ethics of Liberation is the English-language translation of *Ética de la liberación en la edad de la globalización y de la exclusión* (1998), which followed Dussel's *Philosophy of Liberation* (1977) and has been followed by the recently published (in Spanish) *Política de la liberación* (2007). A condensed version of *Philosophy of Liberation* can be found in *Twenty Theses on Politics*, which was published by Duke University Press in 2008.

If there is a thread that runs through Enrique Dussel's work and life, it is his concern for unveiling the logic of oppression and exclusion that lies at the very foundation of the modern colonial world as we know it today. As a Latin American philosopher, Dussel stands in for the two pillars of this type of critique who had searched for a conception of life that, when implemented in the state and the economy, would not build a system based on the exploitation and exclusion of human beings. Those two pillars were Bartolomé de las Casas, who witnessed Spanish excesses in the colonies of Indias Occidentales, and Karl Marx, who witnessed in England the excesses of the industrial bourgeoisie in the heart of Europe.

Las Casas wrote during the very beginnings of the modern colonial world, and Marx wrote at the moment of its consolidation, when the Industrial Revolution made possible both the expansion of Europe all over the world and Europe's encroachment within every existing civilization. Dussel, on the contrary, dwells within the history of the first European colonies in the New World, today called "Latin America." Dussel, being aware of this distinction, entitled the first chapter of *Philosophy of Liberation* as "Geopolitics and Philosophy," in which he stated that it is not the same when studying philosophy in Spain, Germany, England, or Latin America. Here, *Ethics* designates a basic universal attitude of human existence in society, the historicity of the modern colonial world founded on a racism, sexism, and power differential. *Ethics* is also a reflection on how a basic attitude of human existence cannot be one that is dictated from a single experience. Philosophical ethics needs its own geopolitics. And that is what Dussel has also made clear in his debates with European philosophers such as Karl-Otto Apel, Jürgen Habermas, and Paul Ricoeur.

In this regard, a geopolitics of knowledge stands at the very foundation of the Latin America Otherwise series.

WALTER MIGNOLO

Editor's Foreword to the English Edition

The publication in English of Enrique Dussel's *Ethics of Liberation* marks a long-awaited event. First of all, as those acquainted with the philosophy of liberation and particularly with Dussel's major role in its development worldwide know, this philosophy sets out with the situation and engagement of the excluded, silenced, oppressed, the "wretched" of the world. Its aim is to articulate new possibilities for humanity out of and in light of the suffering, dignity, and creative drive of those peripheral lives; a task that only has become more urgent and poignant with the struggle to resist and find alternatives to the dominating exploitative globalization of the world, its peoples, and resources. Thus, given that the philosophy of liberation is founded on these ethical insights, *Ethics of Liberation* is the work in Dussel's corpus that grounds all other works: it is the crucial cornerstone for the philosophy of liberation.

A second important characteristic of this translation is that, unlike many of the other major works of the most important figures in world philosophies, this translation was ultimately edited in direct collaboration with the author. Dussel collaborated with the correcting of the translation down to the last manuscript sent to the press. As a result, the translation includes certain neologisms and explanations from the author himself that do not appear in the original, and that will certainly be of interest to those scholars working on Dussel's thought. To name one crucial moment: in this translation, adding to the Spanish edition, Dussel begins to use the term "goodness claim" in direct association with "the good," "*to agathon*," and "*das Gute*." In terms of his choices in terminology, he chooses to refer to issues of embodiment by using the word "corporeality," and with regards to the possibilities of ethical experience in their concrete undergoing he uses "fulfillment" rather than "realization." All of these terms indicate distinct ways of articulating, situating, and undertaking the question of ethics. Last, the quotations from other sources used by Dussel are often his own translations from originals, or specifically chosen translations from Spanish translations. We have decided to keep these and translate them directly into English, in order to preserve the thematic emphasis and interpretative weight of the author's choices. The alternative would have been to replace Dussel's choices with standard English translations, which would have taken away part of the interpretative inflection of the author's voice.

Enrique Dussel began writing *Ethics of Liberation* in October 1993 and completed it in 1997. The first edition was published in 1998 and was soon followed by four editions (1998, 2000, 2002, and 2006). The preparation of this voluminous work took eight years and involved four translators. As a result the manuscript we had was tortuous, and at times translations were simply incomplete. In addition, often the choices of translation for terminology did not match. The translation was then recovered and brought to its present form, thanks to the effort of those listed below, without whom this version would have been impossible to publish. Although the translators at times referred to the various editions of the *Ethics*, the present translation refers to the latest edition published by Trotta in 2006.

I must thank Reynolds Smith and Miriam Angress at Duke University Press for their excitement and support. Also, I want to thank Justine Keel for her careful editorial work on the manuscript. I must also thank the editors of Duke University Press who so diligently worked on the project, particularly Maura High and Christine Dahlin. I am grateful to the College of Arts and Sciences at the University of Oregon and to the philosophy department's office manager, T. K. Landázuri for their support in the last stages of the project.

ALEJANDRO A. VALLEGA
December 2010

Preface

We are confronted by the overwhelming yet contradictory reality of a
"world system" in crisis five thousand years[1] after its inception, which has
globalized its reach to the most distant corner of the planet at the same time
that it has paradoxically excluded a majority of humanity. This is a matter
of life and death. The human life invoked here is not a theoretical concept,
an idea, or an abstract horizon, but rather a *mode of reality* of each concrete
human being who is also the absolute prerequisite and ultimate demand
of all forms of liberation. Given this framework it should not be surprising
that *Ethics* is an ethics grounded in an avowed affirmation of life in the face
of the collective murder and suicide that humanity is headed toward if it
does not change the direction of its irrational behaviour. *Ethics of Liberation* seeks to think through this real and concrete ethical situation in which
the majority of contemporary humanity is immersed, philosophically and
rationally, as we hurtle toward a tragic conflagration on a scale that is unprecedented in the biological trajectory of the human species.

The themes explored here are of such dimensions that I can only seek to
place them for descriptive purposes in an architectural framework of categories of analysis that will take shape as the result of an ethical "process" of
construction. Our point of departure is a world system of globalized exclusion whose exploration requires the critical assimilation of the thought of
numerous contemporary thinkers who have been selected because they are
most relevant to the argument. Future works will explore such problems as
the *grounding of the principles* of the ethical framework set forth here, as well
as the concrete treatment of the most critical liberation struggles waged by
emerging sociohistorical subjects seeking recognition within civil society in
each country and on a global scale.

Contemporary ethics at the end of the twentieth century and at the beginning of the third millennium has some "problematic knots" that must be disentangled—*aporiai* or dilemmas that we will address fully and polemically—while undertaking to analyze them from the perspective of the ethics of liberation. Two spheres of debate are particularly lively in this context. In the first place, the debates that proceed from (a) the denial that a normative ethics can be developed that is based upon a rationality with empirical validity given that its deployment would be grounded at the level of mere value judgments—a position maintained by the school of analytical metaethics (since G. Moore's *Principia Ethica* in 1903), among others— all the way to (b) the affirmation of a utilitarian ethics of "the greatest happiness for the greatest number." I will explore the first, continuing with Habermas's discourse, with reference to the supposed existence of normative claims (which are not merely subjective judgments but instead have at least the intention of satisfying claims of rightfulness). But I will also attempt to go further by attempting to demonstrate the possibility of developing an ethics grounded in factual, empirical, and descriptive judgments. I will incorporate the contributions of utilitarianism, which has been so criticized by the metaethics of the philosophy of language and formalist moralities (including that of John Rawls), thereby retrieving the material aspect of the drives toward happiness, although I will demonstrate the inconsistency inherent in this approach in terms of the claim that seeks to ground a universal material principle with sufficient validity.

Second, I will situate the ethics of liberation with regard to a debate that is still in progress and which has confronted (c) the ethics of communitarianism, inspired by history and values, in the face of (d) formal ethics (particularly discourse ethics). I will incorporate both of these for varying reasons but will situate them at distinct moments of the architectural process of *Ethics of Liberation*. I will include the communitarian ethics (of Alasdair MacIntyre, Charles Taylor, or Michael Walzer) at the material level of my ethical architecture. In this way I seek to articulate the contributions of this school within a redefined horizon that will facilitate the transcendence of its particularistic incommensurability and open it up to a universalism of *content* beyond the merely historical, hypervalues, or the authenticity of a specific cultural identity. The practical truth of its content will thus enable a claim of universality. In a similar fashion I will also incorporate aspects of proceduralist and formalist moralities (ranging from Emmanuel Kant up through Karl-Otto Apel to Jürgen Habermas, in particular), but this will be accomplished through a radical reconstruction of their function in the overall ethical process. Their transformative incorporation will help clarify the moment of "application" of the ethical material principle.

We will also engage philosophical perspectives such those of (e) pragmatism (as reflected in thinkers running the gamut from Charles Sanders Peirce to Hilary Putnam) or (f) system theory (Niklas Luhmann); I will draw from these what is necessary in order to define (g) a third principle: that of feasibility, inspired by the thought of Frank Hinkelammert.

In this way the goodness claim (with reference to the subject of the norm, action, microphysics of power, institution, or ethical system) is attained as the end result of a complex process wherein the content of truth, intersubjective validity, and ethical feasibility have the effect of producing or enabling the fulfillment of "the goodness claim" (*das Gute*). In a definitive sense "the good" person is a concrete ethical subject, but only once this subject has brought "goodness" into action upon a normative basis. This summary overview of the landscape we are about to explore concludes part I of this book, and it might appear that we have already exhausted the central themes of ethics in general. Nonetheless, it is only in part II of this book where the ethics of liberation as such begins to undertake the development of its own theses.

In fact it is upon the basis of the assumed "goodness claim" of norms, acts, microstructures, institutions, or ethical systems that victims appear as the concretion of the effects of their application, according to the mechanism that Max Horkheimer defined as one of "material negativity." My point of departure here is from the perspective of the victim, such as Rigoberta Menchú (a woman, of Maya Quiché indigenous origin, brown-skinned, Guatemalan . . .). "Goodness claim" becomes inverted and is dialectically transformed into "evil" because it has produced a victim such as her. This is also the point at which the analysis of the great critical or "accursed" philosophers begins, such as Marx; those of the first Frankfurt school: Max Horkheimer, Theodor Adorno, Herbert Marcuse, Walter Benjamin; and also Friedrich Nietzsche, Sigmund Freud, Emmanuel Levinas, and so on. In this way, it is such ethical-material critiques that set the philosophies of negation into motion.

Suddenly, the consensus-building attributes of discursive reason that could not bring to bear its basic norms because the affected participants are always empirically and inevitably in asymmetry, can now be "applied" thanks to the symmetrical intersubjectivity of the victims who have joined together in a community of victims. New and unexpected problems emerge at this point, which have been dealt with by Jean Piaget or Lawrence Kohlberg, but in a new light following the reinterpretation undertaken by Paulo Freire. It is in this context that I formulate for the first time the epistemological question of the "third" criterion for the demarcation of the *critical* social sciences (superseding the position expressed in this regard by Karl Popper, Thomas Kuhn, P. Feyerabend, or I. Lákatos, and hoping also thereby to clarify certain ambiguities of "critical theory"). I also highlight meanwhile how Ernst Bloch evidenced for us the positive meaning of yearning with hope for the possibility of utopia, from the perspective of the symmetrical intersubjectivity of the victims.

This is the path by which we arrive at the most critical moment in the architecture of the ethics of liberation, after the fall of the Berlin Wall in 1989, as I seek to give a contemporary meaning to long-standing debates played out by Rosa Luxemburg, Antonio Gramsci, José Carlos Mariátegui, and so many others. My purpose is to lay the basis for new horizons of strategic and tactical ethical reasoning grounded in the metaethics of liberation. These reflect complex processes of articulation among the victimized billions of the world system, who emerge as critical communities with critical activists at their core. Their expressions include the new social, political, economic, racial, environmental, gender-based, and ethnic movements that emerged during the last quarter of the twentieth century. These are struggles for the recognition of victims who *transform* the character of previous liberation movements, which this *Ethics* seeks to legitimize and to provide with a philosophical grounding. My hope is that *Ethics of Liberation* could provide these movements with some guidance as to ethical criteria and principles for the unfolding of the praxis of liberation from the perspective of the victims, as they confront the effects of oppressive norms, acts, microstructures, institutions, or ethical systems in the context of everyday life, in the present historical moment, instead of postponing their application to some later moment when the revolution has arrived.

It might seem to some that this is an endeavor limited to the elaboration of an ethics of "principles." In fact, although my emphasis here is on criteria and principles, this is an ethics that is nonproceduralist in character, grounded in daily life and the dominant models prevalent in that context, and which seeks to encompass the nonintentional negative effects (the production of victims) resulting from every kind of autonomously organized and regulated structure. This ethics develops a material ethical discourse that is content-based and formal (and intersubjective in its validity) and that takes empirical feasibility into account, always seeking to approach issues from the perspective of the victims at all possible levels of intersubjectivity. Jürgen Habermas pointed out to me at a meeting in St. Louis in October 1996 that he did not expect very much from the normativity of ethics;[2] I wouldn't expect much either if I believed that the only cause that motivates the demands that set processes of liberation of the victims into motion were of a purely ethical character. My approach instead is that such motivations include affective drives that are deeply rooted in the critical superego of the oppressed, and that are often nonintentional in character, grounded in social contexts and cultural values, and in historical and biographical causes and factors, and in the impetus of principles such as responsibility and solidarity. Ethical philosophy expresses these in an articulated, structured, and rational manner that incorporates such non-proceduralist structures of this kind that are *always implicit*. To make them explicit is our philosophical responsibility. The enunciation of principles has a dynamic complementary relationship to play with respect to actions undertaken that seek liberation, by helping deconstruct false or incomplete contrary arguments, and by developing arguments in favor of such liberation processes.

I don't expect very much in terms of this ethics' explicit theoretical normative capacity, but I continue to believe that it can play a strategically necessary role in another dimension, which is especially important in collective learning processes where critical consciousness can be developed as part of the political, economic, and social organizing efforts of new emerging social movements in civil society.

I began to write this book in October 1993, twenty years after a bomb set by right-wing extremists partially destroyed my house and my study in Mendoza, Argentina, and drove me into exile in Mexico, where I have lived ever since. At that time I was writing *Towards an Ethics of Latin American Liberation*.[3] This was an ethics that took the affirmation of "exteriority" as its point of departure, and which, beyond Heidegger, was inspired by Latin America's popular struggle. The present work takes the next step with respect to that initial effort and is characterized by a greater emphasis on issues of negation and materiality, with a much more elaborately constructed rational architecture of principles. My current approach is not only different because it comes twenty years later, but principally because during the intervening period the overall historical context has changed, and a new perspective has matured within me, at the same time as the discourse of ethics in contemporary philosophy has been transformed.

In the first place, the above-mentioned ethics was qualified as "*towards an ethics.*" This book, instead, is an ethics as such. Second, my initial work was denominated as "of *Latin American* liberation." Now, I seek to situate myself in a global, planetary horizon, beyond the Latin American region, beyond the Helleno- and Eurocentrism of contemporary Europe and the United States, in a broader sweep ranging from the "periphery" to the "center"[4] and toward "globality."[5] Third, as is evident, in the seventies I took my point of departure from the philosophers most studied during that period: the last stage of the work of Martin Heidegger, Paul Ricoeur, Hans-Georg Gadamer, the first Frankfurt school, the contributions of Jacques Derrida, Emmanuel Levinas, and many others. Now, we must take into account not only these philosophers, but also, in particular, more recent developments in philosophy in the United States and Europe—as I have already indicated above. In addition, at that time the debate that my initial efforts at an ethics of liberation were grounded in had come out of the context of the Latin American reality I was immersed in, from the perspective of groups of activist scholars with whom I was engaged, and from my critical rereading of texts. Now, out of world reality and from some personal dialogues with philosophers of "the center," the reflections have reached new pertinence. In the fourth place, the fall of the Berlin Wall in November 1989,[6] the collapse of the Soviet bloc, the electoral defeat of the Sandinistas in Nicaragua in 1990, and increased pressures on the Cuban Revolution through the U.S. blockade have together implied a series of setbacks for alternative models of social order that once nourished the hopes of people around the world in the possibility of a path out of their misery. All of this has contributed to a generalized sense of disenchantment and even desperation among the oppressed, and to the virtual disappearance of critical thinking among philosophers.

The Cold War is over, and along with it the geopolitics of bipolarity. At the same time the United States' indisputable military hegemony has been restored, and the dictates of U.S. foreign and economic policy and culture have been globalized. The crisis of revolutionary utopias causes many to give up entirely the search for alternatives to the contemporary global system, and the metaphysical dogma of neoliberalism à la Friedrich Hayek (the new "grand narrative" and the only "utopia" acceptable to the powers that be) consolidates its domination. The prevailing judgment amid the "public opinion" that is dominant in philosophical circles assumes that "liberation" must give way to functional, reformist, "feasible" acts. But despite this, and contrary to what many claim, it seems as if the ancient suspicion of the necessity of an ethics of liberation from the perspective of the "victims,"[7] of the "poor" and their "exteriority" and their "exclusion," has reaffirmed its relevance amid the terror of a harrowing misery that destroys a significant portion of humanity at the end of the twentieth century,[8] together with the unsustainable environmental destruction of the Earth.

The ethics of liberation does not seek to be an ethics for a minority, nor only for exceptional times of conflict and revolution. It aspires instead to be an ethics for everyday life, from the perspective and in the interests of the *immense majority of humanity excluded by globalization* throughout the world where the current historical "normality" prevails. The philosophical ethics most in fashion, the *standard* ones, and even those that have a critical orientation with a claim to being postconventional in character, are in fact themselves the ethics of minorities (most emphatically of hegemonic, dominating minorities; those that own the resources, the words, the arguments, the capital, the armies) that frequently and quite *cynically* can ignore the victims, those most affected, who have been dominated and excluded from the "negotiating tables" of the ruling system and from the dominant communities of communication. These are victims whose rights have not been advocated or vindicated, who go unacknowledged by the *ethos* of authenticity, who are coerced by the dominant legality, and with a claim to legitimacy that demands recognition.

In any event, *Ethics of Liberation* does not supplant my previous effort, which includes themes, explored in five volumes, that I will not repeat here.[9] Instead my emphasis here is on updating and where necessary reformulating and radicalizing the previous work, and on developing new, more fundamental aspects of its argument, clarifying, expanding, and retracting some of its elements in response to certain critiques of its approach. But because this is deliberately a work of *synthesis*, the themes to be addressed cannot be explored in all of their detail; instead I will only outline a "process" (in six specific moments or dimensions) and *situate* the "place" of the matter dealt with within the overall architectural framework of my approach. A full analytical exposition would require much greater space than is possible in a single work of this character. The themes that are "outlined" in this fashion can be studied in greater detail in other works of mine and in the works of colleagues to whom I will refer. Only in some cases will my exposition of these cases be more detailed, when it concerns questions that I deal with for the first time.

On the other hand, I have included in this book discussions of the work of numerous contemporary philosophers of ethics. I do this not because of some kind of purism of bibliographical scientificity, but instead because my purpose is to grapple with the thinking of relevant authors in order to incorporate their contributions to the discourse of the *Ethics of Liberation*, and to pursue the logic of its approach by "bringing water to the mill" of my central arguments from other sources. Frequently, as *Ethics* seeks to produce a double effect of developing an overall architecture and of subsuming the reflections of contemporary ethicists, it may seem that we have lost our path along the way. I ask for the reader's patience in order to discover and pursue the driving thread of the discussion that is developed through the efforts of the authors whose work is explored here. In any event, many themes remain open for further exploration and study in the future. The research program of a fully developed critical ethics is developed initially only in broad strokes; other works in the tradition of the philosophy of liberation should complete it. I hope that colleagues and students will help to fill these necessary gaps.

I would like to emphasize that when I refer in this work to the concept of the "Other" I will situate myself *always and exclusively* at the anthropological level. It is too simplistic to pretend to refute *Ethics of Liberation* by misunderstanding the theme of the Other as that of a nonphilosophical problem—by suggesting, for example, that it is theological in character, as in the case of the work of Gianni Vattimo or Ofelia Schutte. In my approach, the Other is understood as being the other woman/man: a human being, an ethical subject, whose visage is conceived of as the epiphany of living human reality in bodily form (corporeality). The approach to the concept of the Other that I rely upon in this work is exclusively a matter of rational, philosophical, and anthropological significance. In the context of *Ethics*, the only Other that could be referred to in the most absolute terms would be something like an Amazonian tribe that has never had *any contact* with any other contemporary civilization, which is a very rare phenomenon. The freedom of the Other—following in this aspect the approach of Maurice Merleau-Ponty[10]—cannot be an absolute unconditionality, but instead is always a quasi-unconditionality with reference or "relative" to a context, a world, a concrete reality, or a feasibility. In *Ethics* the Other will not be denominated either metaphorically or economically with the label of the "poor." Now, inspired by Walter Benjamin, I will refer instead to the subject of *Ethics* as a "victim," a concept that is both broader and more exact.

The Fifth Congress of the Afro-Asiatic Association of Philosophy was held in Cairo in December 1994. There we organized an International Committee of the Third World in order to deal with South-South philosophical dialogue. This book seeks to contribute to the continuation and deepening of these dialogues in the context of the twenty-first century.

It should not be forgotten that the ultimate framework or context for *Ethics* is the process of *globalization*; but, unfortunately and simultaneously, this process also necessarily implies the *exclusion* of the great majority of humanity: the victims of the world system. My reference to the current historical age as one of globalization and exclusion seeks to capture the double-edged movement that the global periphery is caught between: on the one hand, the supposed modernization occasioned by the formal globalization of finance capital ("fictitious" capital as Marx characterized it); but, on the other hand, the increasing material, discursive, and formal exclusion of the victims of this purported civilizing process. *Ethics* seeks to provide an account of this contradictory dialectic, constructing the categories and the *critical* discourse capable of enabling us to reflect in philosophical terms regarding this self-referential performative system that destroys, negates, and impoverishes so many at the beginning of the twenty-first century. The threatened destruction of the majority of humanity demands an *ethics of life* in response, and it is their suffering on such a global scale which moves me to reflection, and to seek to justify the necessity of their liberation from the chains in which they are shackled.

I presented this work as a master's-level course at the Escuela Nacional de Estudios Profesionales (ENEP Aragón) of the National Autonomous University of Mexico (UNAM), for which I am grateful. I am also grateful for the support provided by the UNAM's Department of Graduate Studies. I also presented it at the Philosophy Department of the Universidad Autónoma Metropolitana (UAM-Iztapalapa), various portions of it in Spain (Madrid, Valencia, Murcia, Pamplona, Cadíz, the Canary Islands), as well as in Haiti, Cuba, Argentina, Colombia, Peru, Bolivia, Paraguay, Guatemala, Costa Rica, Brazil, the United States, Canada, Germany, Switzerland, Italy, Norway, Sweden, Egypt, the Philippines, among other settings. My students at the UNAM participated actively in this work, especially those who encouraged it and criticized it creatively, including Marcio Cota, Germán Gutiérrez, Silvana Rabinovich, Juan José Bautista, Pedro Enrique Ruiz, and many others. Debates with Karl-Otto Apel, Paul Ricoeur, Gianni Vattimo, Richard Rorty, Franz Hinkelammert, and others preceded and accompanied the writing of this book. I am very grateful for the corrections to the text made by my friends Raúl Fornet-Betancourt, Eduardo Mendieta, Michael Barber, Hans Schelkshorn, Mariano Moreno, and James Marsh. Last, I want to express publicly my acknowledgment of two institutions, the Universidad Autónoma Metropolitana and Mexico's National System of Researchers, because the research that made this book possible is the fruit of the support provided to me as professor of the faculty of the university and as a member of Level 3 of the National System of Researchers.

Introduction
World History of Ethical Systems

[1] This introduction is neither an anecdotal description nor a simple history. It is instead a proposal with philosophical intent,[1] in which the historical *contents* of "ethical systems" are analyzed following a historical sequence that in some way, and always partially, conditions *ethical material and formal moral* levels[2] as well as ethical criticism (which in turn has *negative* and *positive* aspects).[3] Empirically, neither in the present, nor in Europe, nor in the United States,[4] is an absolutely postconventional morality possible.

I will try only to "situate" the ethical problematic within a global horizon, in order to remove it from the traditional interpretation that has been merely Helleno- or Eurocentric, in order to open up the discussion beyond contemporary Euro–North American philosophical ethics. The entire discussion is merely indicative—neither exhaustive nor even sufficient—in order to show how we might expand our questioning toward broader panoramas of "globalism."[5]

The content of a cultural ethical life should not be confused with philosophical formalism[6] as such and insofar as it is taken as the method that originated in Greece (although with acknowledged antecedents in Egypt and with parallel processes in India and China). The contents of Greek culture should not, therefore, be identified with philosophy formally or as such. Mythical texts[7] such as those of Homer or Hesiod can be studied as philosophical examples, taking notice of their contents of ethical life, while other narratives, such as that of the Egyptian *Book of the Dead*, Semitic or Hebrew texts, the Upanishads, or those by Lao Tzu, are discarded because they are not formally philosophical (ignoring them as mere mythical, literary, religious, or artistic examples). It is not generally noted that the properly philosophical aspect of Greek thought is not the mythical expression of the "immortal soul" or the "eternity" and "divinity" of the *physis*, but instead the formal philosophical method, because the Hellenic "immortal soul" and the Egyptian Osiris's "resurrection of the flesh" are both cultural propositions of *contents* of ethical life, which may, or may not, be treated philosophically, but which are not intrinsically philosophical. For this reason we can broach here "philosophically" mythical texts of all the cultures of the history of humanity, which are of great importance for the interpretation of the ethical contents of contemporary ethical life (and which will have, in addition, pertinence to the formal development of ethics itself).

[2] This is to say, time was needed in order to be able to reach a degree of civilizing complexity sufficient to allow the "ethics systems" and "moral aspect" to achieve levels of more abstract *universality*,[8] and to arrive in this way to evolutionary and growing levels of *criticism*. The historical evolution of the "interregional system," which I want to describe in four stages (see table 1), is not a mere complementary example. It constitutes a central thesis: the "ethical lives" of humanity develop around and out of an Asiatic-Afro-Mediterranean system,[9] which from the sixteenth century becomes, for the first time, a "world system." On the other hand, the maturation of these ethical lives slowly reached levels of sufficient development to allow an "ethics" that was increasingly aware of its universality (from the Egyptian-Mesopotamian period up through the second scholastic period of the sixteenth century with Francisco Vitoria, in the eighteenth century with Kant, and in the twentieth century with Apel or Habermas), and, at the same time, "ethical-critical" categories of great radicalism (from those mythically developed from the period of slavery in Egypt and the Hammurabian ethics of justice, up to Bartolomé de las Casas in the sixteenth century, Marx in the nineteenth, and the ethics of liberation today).

[3] In my interpretation,[10] the first moment of a history of ethical historical systems occurs in the area between the north of Africa and the Middle East (Egypt and Mesopotamia), in what I call stage I of the interregional system (§I.1), which will have a profound later impact. In an uninterrupted form, for more than fifty centuries, a particular content of ethical life would, in some way, survive up to the end of the twentieth century. During this time, the ethical-critical categories that I want to formalize had already begun to gestate materially.[11] Continuing toward the East, across the Pacific Ocean, in the *extreme orient of the Orient*, we arrive at a disconnected fragment of the Asiatic-Afro-Mediterranean interregional system: the Amerindian high cultures, which ought to be an extension of the interregional system (not in the Neolithic, but in the Paleolithic) — this is their place in the history of humanity (§I.2). The second moment in the history of ethical systems, a new stage in the Asiatic-Afro-Mediterranean system (§I.3), unfolded among the peoples of the Euro-Asiatic steppes, who used

Table 1. The Four Stages of the Interregional System That Unfolded as a World System after 1492

Stage	Diachronic Name of the Interregional System	Poles around a Center[a]
I	Egyptian-Mesopotamian (from 4th millennium BC): §I.1	Without center: Egypt and Mesopotamia
II	"Indo-European" (from 200 BC): §I.3	Center: Persian region, Hellenic world (Seleucidic and Ptolemaic) from 4th century BC
		Eastern extreme: China
		Southeastern: Indian kingdoms
		Western: Mediterranean new world
III	Asiatic-Afro-Mediterranean (from 4th century AD): §I.4	Center of commercial connections: Persian region and Tarim, then the Muslim world (from 7th century AD)
		Productive center: China
		Southwestern: Bantu Africa
		Western: Byzantine-Russian world
		Extreme West: Western Europe
IV	"World system": §§I.5–6	Center: Western Europe. Today, United States (after AD 1492) and Japan (from 1945 to 1989 with Russia)
		Periphery: Latin America, Bantu Africa, Muslim world, India, Southwestern Asia, Eastern Europe
		Semiautonomous: China and Russia (from 1989)

a. The "center" is only a zone of contacts in stages II and III; in stage IV it is the proper "center" of a periphery (Modernity).

to be called Indo-Europeans (and who originated in the region to the north of the Black Sea, the Caucasian mountains, and the Caspian Sea as far as Mongolia). In a third stage (§I.4), we find ourselves with an interregional system hegemonized by the Muslim world. This system occupied the "central" region where the different poles of the system connected: China (the first pole, in the Northeast); India (the second pole, in the Southeast); and the Byzantine Empire and Russia, which served as a wall bounding this regional culture, which was secondary and peripheral to Latino-Germanic Europe (the third pole, to the West). Slowly, from the seventh century AD, the Muslim ethos spread from the center (to Spain and Marruecos in the Atlantic and as far as Mindanao in the Pacific; see map 1).

This way of interpreting history prepares us for an understanding of

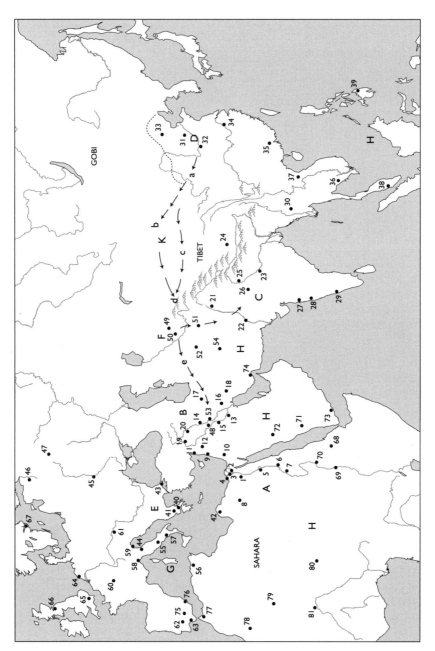

Map 1. Relevant cities of the Asian/Afro-Mediterranean system in different periods.

A. *Egypt and Eastern Mediterranean:* (1) Memphis, (2) Heliopolis, (3) Sais, (4) Alexandria (E), (5) Abydos (Thinis), (6) Thebes, (7) Elephantine, (8) Ammonion (Temple of Amon), (9) Sidon, (10) Jerusalem, (11) Antioch, (12) Aleppo (H)

B. *Mesopotamia and Persia:* (13) Ur, (14) Assur, (15) Babylon, (16) Susa, (17) Ecbatana, (18) Persepolis, (19) Edessa, (20) Nisibis

C. *India:* (21) Harappa, (22) Mohenjo-Daro, (23) Benares, (24) Lhasa, (25) Delhi (H), (26) Agra (H), (27) Bombay, (28) Goa (G), (29) Calcutta, (30) Pagan

D. *China and the Asiatic Southeast:* (31) Anyang, (32) Loyang, (33) Peking, (34) Nanking, (35) Canton (G), (36) Angkor, (37) Hanoi, (38) Malaya (H), (39) Mindanao (H)

E. *Part of the Greek Culture:* (40) Athens, (41) Thebes, (42) Cyrene, (43) Byzantium, (44) Ravenna, (45) Kiev, (46) Novgorod, (47) Moscow

F. *Center of the Ancient System:* (48) Seleucia (E), (49) Samarkand (H), (50) Bukhara (H), (51) Kabul (H), (52) Tus (H), (53) Baghdad (H), (54) Seistan (H)

G. *Latin-Germanic World:* (55) Rome, (56) Hippo, (57) Naples, (58) Genoa, (59) Venice (E), (60) Paris, (61) Vienna, (62) Seville (H), (63) Cadiz (A, H), (64) Amsterdam, (65) London, (66) Edinburgh, (67) Stockholm

H. *Part of the Ethiopian-Muslim World:* (68) Aksum, (69) Khartum, (70) Meroe, (71) Mecca, (72) Medina, (73) Aden, (74) Hormuz, (75) Cordoba (G), (76) Granada (G), (77) Ceuta, (78) Marrakesh, (79) Taza, (80) Agades, (81) Timbuktu

K. *The Silk Route:* (a) China, (b) Zungaria, (c) Tarim, (d) Turan, (e) Juzjan

NOTE: A capital letter in parentheses (e.g., A, E, G, H) indicates that the city also belonged during some other period to another ethos or culture (e.g., Alexandria [A4], Seleucia [A4], and Venice [G59] were also of Greek culture, indicated by E; Aleppo [A12], and Samarkand [F49] were also Muslim, indicated by H).

the phenomenon of "Modernity" from another historical horizon, which allows us with full awareness to criticize the ideological periodization of history as ancient, medieval, and modern history, a view that is naively Hellenocentric and Eurocentric.

§I.1. Origin of the Interregional System: Afro-Bantu Egypt and the Semites of the Middle East

[4] I will situate myself in the most ancient of the life worlds that has relevance for our theme.[12] Against custom, I will not set out from Greece[13] (since my view is not Hellenocentric), because what will after be known as classical Greece was in the fourth millennium BC a barbarian world, peripheral, colonial, and western merely with respect to the east of the Mediterranean, which, from the Nile to the Tigris, constituted a nuclear civilizing "system" of this region of union between Africa and Asia.[14]

The black, *Bantu African* world (*kmt* in Egyptian), today to the south of the Sahara, is one of the origins of Egyptian culture—one of the columns of the Neolithic revolution.[15] In the eighth millennium BC the then-humid Sahara was crossed by rivers and was inhabited by numerous Bantu farmers. From the sixth millennium, when the process of the drying up of the rivers and desertification began,[16] many Bantu peoples emigrated toward the Nile. (The cultural influence of the regions east of the Nile will come much later.) High Egyptian culture has deep and numerous roots in Upper Egypt. Great tombs can be found from the fifth millennium BC, between the second and third fall in the Sudan. The concept of divine monarchy "is found among the peoples of central and southern Africa, and even in the south of Ethiopia."[17] The Bantu peoples who were inhabitants of Upper Egypt unified the region of the Nile from the South. For this reason theirs were the first centers of the fourth millennium BC.[18] These (probably next to Abydos), and later Thebes, are all found in the "black" South.[19] The pharaoh of the Second Dynasty, Aha, established the city of Memphis in the Nile delta, where the capital of the ancient empire would be located in 2800 BC. In the city of Heliopolis, theogonies began to be rationalized in the schools of the sages (as in the *edduba* of Mesopotamia, the much later academy of Plato, and the Calmecac in Mexico): in the beginning there were the primordial waters (Nun), from where there emerged Atum-Re (the sun), which shaped the Air (Shu) and Fire (Tefnut), from which came the Earth (Geb) and the Sky (Nut). All of this took place two thousand years before the pre-Socratics—or Jaspers's "Axial Age" (*Achsenzeit*). In Hermopolis, Thot (or Tautes, Hermes, etc.) was the creator-organizer[20] of a new "rationalization"; Ptah (the god of Memphis)[21] was now the universal creator, but this creation issued from his Heart (Horus) and through the medium of language, the word, *logos*,[22] *nous*: Thot,[23] who creates everything out of wisdom, is therefore before the creation of the universe.

[5] Thot (a person and a god, like the Quetzalcóatl of the Nahuas) was also the wise inventor of writing, of the sciences, of wisdom. Plato wrote, "The story is that in the region of Naucratis in Egypt there dwelt one of the old gods of the country, the god to whom the bird called Ibis is sacred, his own name being Theuth. He it was who invented number and calculation, geometry and astronomy, not to speak of draughts and dice, and above all writing. Now the king of the whole country at that time was Thamus."[24]

Aristotle himself acknowledges, like Plato in the *Republic* (in which Plato describes an Egyptian town in ideal terms, following his trip to Sais, the great metropolis of Athens in the delta of the Nile), that the Egyptian sages were the originators of the wisdom of the Greeks themselves:[25] "Hence when all the discoveries of this were fully developed, the sciences which relate neither to pleasure nor yet to the necessities of life were invented, and first in those places where men had leisure [*eskhólasan*]. Thus the mathematical sciences originated in the neighborhood of Egypt,[26] because there the priestly class was allowed leisure [*skholázein*]."[27]

The cosmos and humanity have an order or universal law: *Maat*, which is "truth" or universal "natural law" in a practical sense. "*Maat* was the key to the Egyptian view of ethical behavior. . . . *Maat* is right order in nature and society, as established by the act of creation, and hence means, according to the context, what is right, what is correct, law, order, justice, and truth. *Maat* was a guide to the correct attitude one should take to others."[28]

I point to all of this in order to begin to break with the Hellenocentric perspective. Indeed, the daily life of Egypt was woven around the cult of its dead and the ancestors, who came from the South, of the Bantu and black peoples. The culmination of this ethical life was already found in the Egyptian high culture of the fourth millennium BC, when life was organized around such a cult. The "affirmation of life" went through one of its possible paths:[29] earthly life is valuable, and so is corporeality; for this reason the dead reassume corporeality (resurrects)[30] after empirical death, in order to no longer die. The individual principle of the person (*Ka*),[31] which is written with a proper, unique name ("singularity" [*Einzelheit*]: "Osiris N"), survives death. The "flesh" is valuable, has meaning; it is mummified, it is perfumed, and resurrects for all eternity. All of this opens up a horizon of concrete ethical norms of great carnal, historical, communitarian positivity. Facing the final judgment, the person, the Ka, says, "I have not done falsehood against men. . . . I have not made hungry. . . . I have not laid anything upon the weights of the hand balance. . . . I have not been rapacious. . . . I have not destroyed food supplies. . . . I have propitiated God with what he desires; I have given bread to the hungry, water to the thirsty, clothes to the naked and a boat to him who was boatless. . . . 'You have caused him to come,' say they about me. 'Who are you?' they say to me."[32] Concrete, individual human existence, with its *own name*, responsibly lived and historically open to the light of judgment[33] of Osiris,[34] constitutes the real "carnality" (in its materiality)[35] of the life of the human subject as supreme ethical reference: to feed, to give to drink, to clothe, to house . . . the hungering, thirsty, naked, flesh abandoned to the inclemency of weather.[36]

[6] First Bantu Africa, then the Egyptian Mediterranean, and now another creative center of ethical life appeared—the Sumerian, Mesopotamian, Semitic world—which made up the second cultural column. In the eighth millennium BC in Anatolia,[37] and afterward, in the fourth millennium BC, in cities such as Uruk, Lagash, Kish, and Ur, an ethical life was born that was rationalized in legal codes that reached Uruinimgina (reigned 2352–2342 BC)[38] and Gudea (reigned 2144–2124 BC). These constituted an impressive development: the codes always included laws in favor of the weak, poor, and foreigners. In the Hammurabi Code (Hammurabi lived 1792–1750 BC),[39] in force in antiquity, we read: "At that time, Anu and Bel called me, Hammurabi, the exalted prince, the worshiper of the gods, to cause justice to prevail in the land, to destroy the wicked and the evil, to prevent the strong from oppressing the poor."[40] It would be worth doing a commentary on this magnificent code (ethical procedural), where judges and witnesses in the midst of a world full of anomie, pillage, brutality, and injustice guarantee justice and hereditary property. For this reason, the legislator can announce in the epilogue "that the strong might not oppose the poor, and that they should give justice to the orphan and the widow,[41] in Babylon, the city whose turrets Anu and Bel raised.[42] Let any oppressed man, who has a cause, come before my image as king of righteousness! Let him read the inscription on my monument!"[43] I want to make it very clear that an ethics of the fulfillment of the needs (food, drink, cloth, habitat . . .) of life affirms the unitary dignity of the ethical-corporeal subject. The ethical-mythical nucleus of the resurrection of the flesh makes carnality positive, and real needs become ethical and critical criteria—which transcend the concrete Babylonian ethical life, and that for that reason they are also applied to the "exteriority," with respect to the "foreigner," for example.

[7] Between Mesopotamia and Egypt there is an intermediary zone, that of the Aramaic, Phoenician, Punic, Hebrew, and Moabite peoples. They had the advantage of being able to compare the concrete ethical conceptions of both high cultures, and to produce an extremely critical symbiosis. The Phoenicians launched themselves upon the sea and reached Greece (Kadmos, son of Agenor, and his sister Europe, both Phoenicians, were the founders of Thebes), to the north of Africa (Carthage was one

of its colonies), and to Spain. In addition, I should mention the 'Apiru (Hebrews),[44] in the time of the reign of the kingdom of Amarna, under Egyptian hegemony. The 'Apiru were mercenaries, illegals, fugitives, refugees, semibarbarians, and farmers in the mountains of Palestine, and prone to rebellion, who struggled for their autonomy and organized into tribes (according to the model of retribalization). In other words, the heroic narrative told in Exodus is not situated historically in mythical Egypt,[45] but in Palestine; it would consist of a movement of semislaves, under the domination of the Philistines (Indo-Europeans, masters of iron) of Amarna, who liberated themselves in the thirteenth century BC: "Jonathan defeated the garrison of the Philistines which was at Geba; and the Philistines heard of it. And Saul blew the trumpet throughout all the land, saying 'Let the Hebrews hear.'"[46]

[8] In this way there began a slave struggle for liberation that will become epic in the mythical narrative of Moses,[47] which can be treated rationally and philosophically as a specific "model of praxis" in the global history of concrete systems of ethical life. We should then read with new eyes a quasi-symbolic text, such as this: "And the Egyptians were in dread of the people of Israel. So they made the people of Israel serve ['avodah] with rigor, and made their lives bitter with hard service ['avodot], in mortar and brick, and in all kinds of works ['avodot], in the field."[48] This text concerns the point of departure of an "ethical-critical paradigm": the slaves (dominated victims, or excluded persons), through a diachronic process of struggle, will reach political, economic, cultural liberation in a "promised land." This group leans toward a future utopia, in the midst of the crisis of the Egyptian-Mesopotamian interregional system.[49] The posterior rereading of this text, through the centuries, establishes a type of specific liberating rationality in planetary history, which I seek to *formalize* philosophically.

We can conclude that the systems of ethical life of the interregional system in its first stage, though of great complexity and maturity, did not formulate theoretical ethical systems that still justify great empires.

§I.2. Cultures without Direct Links to the System: The Mesoamerican and Inca Worlds

[9] Here we should deal with India (the third column of the Neolithic revolution,[50] which flourished on the margins of the Indus river as far as the Punjab from 2500 BC), and China (the fourth column,[51] next to the Yellow River, which originated about 2000 BC); both cultures are prior to the appearance of the horseman and the mastering of iron. In order not to overextend the discussion, I simply indicate their "place" within a general

history of the Neolithic, which moves from the west to the east—a direction contrary to Hegel's ideological proposal.

However, I will linger briefly on the originary cultures of the American continent, given that the "place" in world history of these peoples should not be situated simply in the context of the "discovery" of America ("invasion," from the Indian perspective) by Columbus in 1492. On the contrary, such a historical place is located in the east of the Far East, more than forty thousand years ago, when the last glaciers receded, and *Homo sapiens* entered the hemisphere through Alaska, passing over the Bering Strait, and began to migrate southward in waves. The originary American inhabitants proceeded from Asia, from Siberia and the region that borders with the Pacific, as much in their races as in their languages. It is clear that in America there emerged an autonomous creative-cultural activity—I do not accept the "diffusionist" position. Nonetheless, since the Neolithic period there were frequent contacts with the Polynesians, who in their transoceanic voyages arrived at the coast of America. In any event, they did not form part of the interregional system of the Asiatic continent.

If the Euro-Asiatic steppes are an area of contact (figure 1, I), the Pacific Ocean (II) (with its Polynesian cultures) must be considered, as I have said, another area of contact. In a global vision of ethical lives, reductionistic naiveté, in the style of Alfred Weber,[52] for instance, cannot be repeated. In the history of the *ethos*, the ethical vision of the Aztecs, Mayas, Chibchas, and Incas, at the very least, should always be included.

[10] From Alaska to Tierra del Fuego the universe is interpreted through a "dual" principle. It is not the "One" of Plotinus or Lao Tzu,[53] but the "Two" of the *tlamatinime*:[54] the Ométeotl of the Aztecs,[55] the she/he Alom-Qaholom (Mother/Father) of the Mayas, the she/he Tocapo-Imaymana Viracocha of the *amautas* among the Incas,[56] the "twins" of all the cultures from the Great Lakes and prairies of North America as far as the Caribs and Tupi-Guarani and the Alakaluf of southern Patagonia.[57] This dual principle establishes an ethical understanding that is dynamic, dialectical, but for this reason no less tragic, necessary, and entirely regulated by divine forces.

The Mesoamerican culture (Mayan-Aztec) is the fifth nucleus of high culture. In it there are many times: the "other time" prior to that of the gods, with different moments, until the birth of the Sun (product of divine immolation), which inaugurates the "time of the Sun."[58] During the time of the sun, the "time of the human being" manifests itself only with the "fifth Sun."[59] The human world is situated in the middle of "two spaces," between heaven and the nether worlds (like the Dur-Anki sanctuary of Mesopotamian Nippur).[60] Divine forces, humans in their dreams,[61] and the magicians with their rites, can *pass* from human space-time to "other" times (prior, simultaneous, or future) and spaces (inferior or superior). In

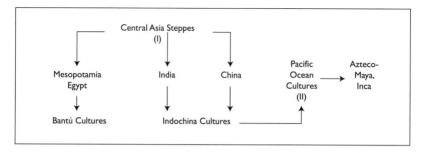

Figure 1. The great Neolithic cultures (the "six columns") and areas of contact from west to east.

Darcy Ribeiro wrote, "What we had in mind with the design of the paradigm regarding rural rudimentary states . . . were the city-states that first reflect a fully urban life, based upon agricultural irrigation systems and collectivist socio-economic systems, prior to 4000 BC in Mesopotamia (Halaf); between 4000 and 3000 BC in Egypt (Memphis, Thebes); in India (Mohenjo Daro) around 2800 BC, before 2000 BC in China (Yang Shao, Hsia); and much later . . . in the Andean Highlands (Salinar and Gallinazo, 700 BC, and Mochica, AD 200); and in Colombia (the Chibcha or Muisca civilization, 1000 BC)" (1970, 61). Ribeiro forgot to mention the Aztec-Mayan Mesoamerican world. For instance, the Zacatenco-Copilco, next to the Tezcoco Lake (now a suburb of Mexico City), flourished in 2000 BC, but its classic age lasted from AD 300 to 900; the Yucatanean-Aztec area (Teotihuacan III was reigning in AD 700); and, from AD 400 to 800, the Tiahuanaco of the Bolivian Titicaca.

NOTE: The arrows do not indicate any necessarily direct relation among the cultures (this would be a diffusionist thesis), but they simply provide a direction in space and a posteriority in time, which in some cases may be a direct relation (as among some Polynesian and some urban Amerindian cultures).

all of these worlds with their "other" space-times dwell beings that have "bodies," but of "light" matter, which is invisible to our human sensibility, ours being of "heavy" matter. This is a universe that is immensely more complex than the visible one, which is inhabited by gods-forces, organized, ritualized, and expressed in myths, and made into calendars. Astrology rationalizes the future; the hermeneutics of phenomena (omens) discover the meaning of the present; the theogonies (interpretations based on astronomical observations and farming cycles) or "protophilosophies" rationalize cosmic forces in relation with the social or political institutions (a type of cosmopolitanism), all with reference to "other" space-times and their mutual and corresponding "passages" toward and from the human world.

[11] In the Inca-Quechua culture (the sixth nucleus of high culture in

the extreme east of the East), the universal moral conception of the empire — ruling over hundreds of particular cultures — was expressed in a paradigmatic manner with three formal imperatives: *Ama lulla, Ama kella, Ama sua* (Thou shalt not lie, Thou shalt not cease to work, Thou shalt not steal).

The meaning of these moral demands would take us very far. In fact, they refer to a universal negation of a nongeneralizable maxim,[62] which systematizes a practical understanding of existence. Sebastiano Sperandeo explained to me, during the holiday of the Inti Raimi in 1994 in Quito, that the first commandment establishes the practical requirements of the norms that regulate intersubjective relation: "Ama lulla" (Thou shalt not lie), rules the claim to transparent and authentic sincerity. The second commandment, "Ama kella" (Thou shalt not be lazy, you ought to work), includes the poietic norms with respect to cosmoecological relations — because here "work" is an activity that reproduces the universe; this commandment also indicates participation in the co-responsible reproduction of life, in order to keep death in abeyance. One must keep disciplined control and remain active. The third commandment, "Ama sua" (Thou shalt not steal), rules over the economic and political relations proper to the empire; it has nothing to do with private good, but instead indicates that to take possession of something not produced leads to disequilibrium, a damage, a negation (*kajta*) that must be repaired.

It is a matter of an ethical "synthesis" of a high degree of abstract moral rationality.

Among the Aztecs, to take an example, ethics (the *tlacahuapahualiztli*: "art of breeding and educating humans") contained principles of great humanism:

> Even if he were poor and lowly,
> Even if his mother and his father were the poorest of the poor . . .
> His lineage was not considered, only his way of life mattered . . .
> The purity of his heart,
> His good and humane heart . . .
> His stout heart . . .
> It was said that he had God in his heart,
> That he was wise in the things of God.[63]

Setting out from "customs" (*huehuetlamanitiliztli*)[64] — which juridically reached a high degree of precision, with codes of law and courts of justice, always among the Aztecs — the *tlamatinime* rationalized a unitary doctrine about the meaning of human, individual, and communitarian praxis.

[12] All of this deserves special study, since it constitutes the *ethos* still contemporary to millions of indigenous peoples in the Latin American continent, in the popular mestizo culture and especially among the farmers. To end this section, I would like to focus on one aspect: the ethical Nahuatl

concept of *macehual*. For the Aztecs, Quetzalcóatl had offered blood from his body in order to resurrect the bones of the fifth human race, thus giving birth to the present race of humans. In this way each human being is a "deserved" (*macehual*);[65] he or she is a being that has received her or his being gratis from the sacrifice of the Other. This "being deserving" from and by alterity puts the human being in a state of debt, but not because of a prior failure (as is the case among the "Indo-Europeans": the *prôton kakón*, or the *Schuld* [guilt] of Kierkegaard), but instead as an originary affirmation of life that is given and received freely. In this way "macehuality" is a "mode of existence": to live positively out of the undeserved and freely given that originate in "alterity." Justice for the members of the community is an act of required gratefulness.

§I.3. The "Indoeuropean" World: From the Chinese to the Roman Empire

[13] Let us return to the Asiatic-African-Mediterranean continent.[66] I want to refer here to customs or ethical lives different from the Egyptian-Mesopotamian system, already noted, of stage I of the interregional system. These ethical lives are a new evolutionary stage of great complexity, of enormous heterogeneity among its components, but with a certain constant ontology that I hope to foreground: the Grounding, the Identity of all differences, the ultimate reference to the world (cosmological, anthropological, ethical) is in these cosmovisions (and even philosophies) the affirmation of an absolute horizon of the real as the "One." In this way the affirmation of life answers to a different logic than the one already discussed in section I.1.[67] In the Euro-Asiatic steppes,[68] from Mongolia to north of the Black Sea, horse riders, at first masters of bronze and then of iron, worshipers of celestial, masculine, Uranic gods,[69] controlled from north to south the farming (related to the "mother earth"), urban peoples of the cultures of Anatolia, the Nile, the Euphrates and Tigris, from the Indus to the Yellow River.[70] They organized the first great empires, cultures, or "views of the world," such as those of the Hindus in India, the Persians in Iran, the Greek and Romans in the Mediterranean, the Buddhists from Nepal, and by indirect influence, the Taoists and Confucianists in China.[71]

The fact that temporal life, between empirical birth to death, was negatively considered by these cultures has relevance for ethics. Empirical birth is a "fall" (because of a failure or fault prior to empirical birth), and empirical death is interpreted as a "birth" to true life. This leads to a negative ethical judgment of corporeality, sexuality; it is domination of the woman; negativity of plurality, of historicity, and last, the justification of all domination and exclusion of slaves, servants, farmers, "castes," or exploited social strata. Masculine celibacy and feminine virginity are requirements and

preconditions of a "contemplative," theoretical life, frequently escaping social and political responsibility. The victim, the poor, the excluded do not
appear as interpellators within the horizon of these systems of ethical life.
"Liberation" is considered exclusively as "liberation of the soul" from the
prison of the body, of matter, of plurality, from pain, and the "original sin"
(*próton kakón*).[72]

[14] Let us consider Plotinus (AD 204–70), in his *Enneads*, as the representative figure of a certain type of view of the world (as *content* of ethical
life). In fact, in Alexandria,[73] the Roman and Greek traditions converged;
Antioch was the gateway to the steppes and the contacts with the "Silk
Route" to China; through the Red Sea, China could be reached. If the
"Indo-European" peoples had begun their expansion, thousands of years
previously, from a center north of the Caspian Sea, Alexandria then became a place for something like a synthesis or confluence of these different
traditions; so now the center was in the south. This city had a very central
position in the Asiatic-African-Mediterranean interregional system, and
the *Enneads* are something like the philosophy of that historical system.

For Plotinus, the first, absolutely ontological point of departure is the
"One": "Anything existing after the First must necessarily arise from the
First . . . it must be authentically a unity . . . it may be described as transcending Being. . . . The One-First is not a body . . . the principle cannot
be a thing of generation [*agénnetos*]."[74] Already centuries before, Heraclitus
had declared: "When you have listened, not to me but to the Law [*Logos*],
it is wise to agree that all things are one [*hén*]."[75] The originary One is the
Ahura Mazda (the Wise lord) of Zoroastrianism of the Iranian Zarathustra
in the times of the Persian king Darius.[76] This notion will be preserved as
the positive principle of Manicheanism. One of the most ancient books of
India, the *Rig Veda*, speaks to us of the One:

> At first was neither Being nor Non-being . . .
> There was no death then, nor yet deathlessness; of night or day there was
>   not any sign.
> The One breathed without breath, by its own impulse.
> Other than that was nothing else at all.[77]

Later this will be the Brahman of the Upanishads: "It is true that the
braham is Everything."[78] In the Tao Te Ching of Lao Tzu, classic expression of Taoism, we read:

> The principle [Tao] that can be expressed is not the enduring and unchang-
> ing principle. The name that can be named is not the enduring and un-
> changing name. (Conceived of as) having no name, it is the Originator of
> heaven and earth. . . . Therefore the sage, in the exercise of his government,
> empties their minds, fills their bellies, weakens their wills, and strengthens

their bones. He constantly (tries to) keep them without knowledge and without desire, and where there are those who have knowledge, to keep them from presuming to act (on it). Where there is abstinence from action, good order is universal.[79]

[15] The second moment is plurification, division (*diremption* or *Entzweiung*, as Hegel put it), and the fall of the One into multiplicity: "Multiplicity (*to plêthon*) is a falling away from the one, infinity (limitlessness) being the complete departure, an innumerable multiplicity, and this is why the unlimit is an evil and we evil at the stage of multiplicity."[80] In this way the soul of the universe, which is one, falls into a body; and the body, because it is matter, is the origin of evil in the human being.[81]

The body is evil, then, because it is material. Birth is "death" to the true divine life. Heraclitus himself reminds us: "Immortals are mortal, mortals are immortal: (*each*) lives the death of the other, and dies their life.[82] It is delight, or rather death, to souls to become wet . . . we live their (*the soul's*) death, and they (*the souls*) live our death."[83] For Plato similarly, the "soul" of the world is more ancient than the body;[84] the soul "was not born [*agéneton*],"[85] it is immortal[86] and eternal.[87] Empirical birth is a "fall" into a "body [*sôma*]"[88] that is a "prison [*sêma*]."[89]

In the *Bhagavad-Gita*, part of the great poem *Mahabharata*, we read: "Finite, they say, are these [our] bodies [indwelt] by an eternal embodied [self]—[for this self is] indestructible, incommensurable. Therefore fight, oh, Bharata. Who thinks this [self] can be a slayer, who thinks that it can be slain, both these have no [right] knowledge: it does not slay nor is it slain. Never is it born nor dies; never did it come to be nor will it ever come to be again: unborn, eternal, everlasting is this [self], primeval. It is not slain when the body is slain."[90]

For Buddha, similarly, plurality, corporeality, the I as singularity, are the origin of suffering that must be overcome: "This is the truth of the cause of pain: that craving which leads to rebirth, combined with pleasure and lust, namely the craving for sensual pleasure, the craving for existence, the craving for nonexistence."[91] To "want," "love," "desire" fixes one to plurality and prevents the return to the one of being. One must not love anything!

For Mani, the prophet of Sasanidan Iran, the body is the participation in the perverse principle (*Ahriman*): "Then Adam looked at himself and cried. He raised his powerful cry like the roar of a lion, pulled at his hair, beat his chest and exclaimed: cursed be they who have shaped my body, they who have chained my soul; cursed be they the rebellious ones who have enslaved me!"[92] Anthropological dualism, with its corresponding contempt for the body, sensibility, the passions, and sexuality will later penetrate the Gnostic-Roman traditions, Latin Manicheanism, the Albigensians and Cathars, until it culminates with Descartes and Kant.[93] The liberation of woman takes into account this long history of the life worlds in order to develop a new position.

[16] In a third moment, from the prison of the body, ethics is an ascetic ascent, a negation of the negation.

Plotinus explains in the following way the point of departure: "In the intellectual, then, they [individual souls] remain with the All-Soul, and are immune from care and trouble. . . . This state long maintained, the soul is a deserter from the totality; its differentiation has severed it; its vision is no longer set in the intelligible; it is a partial thing, isolated, weakened, full of care, intent upon the fragment, severed from the whole, it nestles in one form of being."[94] Ethics, that is to say, is now in its entirety an ascending "return" toward the One (*Enneads*, II, 9, 6).[95]

This act of return is the *dialektiké* of the ascent toward the Idea of the Good in Plato, the *bios theoretikós* of the exercise of the *noûs* in Aristotle,[96] the *apátheia* of the Stoics, and the *atharaxia* of Epicurus,[97] the *gnosis* of the Gnostics, the "wisdom" of the Manichean monks, the final *ecstasies* of the Buddhist monk by means of which he is freed from samsara (eternal return to the *ensomatosis* [incorporealization] or recorporealization of the soul)[98] into the state of nirvana, and the *vita contemplativa* as human perfection in the Latin medieval. Plotinus writes: "The purification consists in isolating the soul, not leaving her to join the things[99]; not to look at them any more; not to have any more strange opinions to his (divine) nature. As for the separation (the ecstasy) it is the condition state of the soul that one does not find any more in the body, as the light that one does not find already in the gloom."[100]

It is thus that from Greece and Rome to the Persians, from the empires of India and Taoist China, an ontology of the absolute as One, a dualist anthropology of the superiority of the soul over the body (which is always in some way the cause of evil), establishes an ascetic ethics of "liberation" from material plurality as a "return" to the originary one. This is the movement of Neoplatonic ontology, and later of German idealism, especially of Hegel's *Logic*.[101] This is the logic-ethics of the Totality.

[17] Empirical death is, for this ethical view of the world, the "birth" to true life. Earthly life is a time negated by pain and suffering. To deserve a death that liberates the human being from the "eternal recurrence" of reincorporealization it is necessary to fulfill the "natural law" (*physikón nómon*), to live in accordance with the "order," with the institutions, such as those of the "castes," with the established ethical order, with the status quo. Confucius wrote:

> The ancients who wished to illustrate illustrious virtue throughout the kingdom, first ordered well their own States. Wishing to order well their States, they first regulated their families. Wishing to regulate their families, they

first cultivated their persons. Wishing to cultivate their persons, they first rectified their hearts. Wishing to rectify their hearts, they first sought to be sincere in their thoughts. Wishing to be sincere in their thoughts, they first extended to the utmost their knowledge. Such extension of knowledge lay in the investigation of things. Things being investigated, knowledge became complete. Their knowledge being complete, their thoughts were sincere. Their thoughts being sincere, their hearts were then rectified. Their hearts being rectified, their persons were cultivated. Their persons being cultivated, their families were regulated. Their families being regulated, their States were rightly governed. Their States being rightly governed, the whole kingdom was made tranquil and happy.[102]

This is a formal morality that consolidates the existing ethics; it justifies institutionality, political organization, the economy, pedagogy, and domination in the genders (of the male over the female). There is no principle of materiality or negativity that can subvert the "order" in the name of the victims, the poor, exploited, or excluded. Thus, in a bureaucratically institutionalized China run by mandarins with a Confucian ethics, the Celestial Empire of the Rising Sun will not have any internal contradictions that may launch it toward new moments of future ethical life. The eternal return of the "Same." At the end of the twentieth century other relevant currents have developed out of these traditions. In these "ethical paradigms" is formulated a respect for life on earth, especially in the Hindu ethical life, an ontological *ecophilia* (point of departure for ecology) from which we can still learn a lot.

One last reflection. Was it not the case that this second stage of the interregional system, of intense institutionalization (thanks to the horse and to iron) and of growing domination, produced an immense social and economic stratum, an entire world of victims, oppressed, impoverished farmers, marginalized and poor (what Toynbee called, with too much ambiguity, the internal and external proletariat), who will end up rebelling against their condition of slavery and humiliation, brandishing a critical ethics that advocated the transformation, the dignity of the ethical subject, and justice? Was not this perhaps the reason for the proposal of primitive Buddhism (against the system of Hindu castes),[103] of Christianity and Islam?

§I.4. The Byzantine World, Muslim Hegemony, and the East: The European Medieval Periphery

[18] We will now study stage III of the interregional system of the Asiatic-Afro-Mediterranean continent.[104] If we place ourselves in the year 300 BC, in the previous stage of the system, we could contemplate the dy-

nasty of the western Tsin (AD 265–317) in China, fully Confucian, and with the will to dominate the entrance to the Silk Route to the West. We would also see transition from the Sakas to the Gupa in India;[105] a Sasanida Persian empire with Sapor II (AD 309–79); a decadent Rome in the time of Diocletian—besieged by the Germans. In any event, the Indo-European ontology and the dualist ethical life were firmly established in stage II of the interregional system.[106]

The fundamental event of stage III of the interregional system (which imposed itself hegemonically in the "central" regions from the fourth century AD onward and lasted until 1492) consisted of a profound transformation of the ethical-mythical nucleus itself (that is to say, the hegemonic validity of its ethical-critical categories). The view of the world in the first stage of the interregional system, the Egyptian-Mesopotamian-Semitic one, made itself present again, although bringing about by itself an expansive universalizing development (through Christianity as well as Islam), perhaps, as noted above, because of the unbearable situation of the oppressed of the empires. The ethical critique by the small, oppressed, and enslaved people under the power of those who dominated the techniques of war and agriculture, with horse and iron (the Philistines and their symbolic warrior Qoliat, in the times of Amarna) was reformulated in a peripheral region of the Roman empire, propitious for exploited and excluded ones. The Oriental Roman and Hellenic world (the Greek-Macedonian, the Seleucid, and Ptolemaic) became the Byzantine world; the Persian world and the north of Africa (at that time already Christianized) became Muslim. Since the region of the Turan Tarim[107] is the key to the "contacts" of the entire Asiatic-Afro-Mediterranean system, whoever controlled this geographical horizon also controlled the totality of the entire commerce of the "system." First it was the Persians, for a short time the Byzantines, and finally the Muslims (Arabs, Turks, and Mongolians). This "central" region of the system was replaced only in the fifteenth century, by the Hispanic Atlantic (with the development of the first "world system," as we will see). Western Germanic continental Europe remained isolated from the seventh century AD with the Muslim expansion. It is this "continentalization" of the center of Europe and even of the Latin Mediterranean, without contact with the "center" of the interregional system, that appears, in a merely Eurocentric and provisional perspective, under the name of the "Middle Ages."

[19] The Semitic "ethos" (Jewish, Christian [never European], and Muslim, all of which originated around the Syrian-Arabic dessert, from Palestine to Mecca) began to occupy a strategic position.[108] Centuries later, during the maturity of the third stage of the interregional system, Maimonides, the great Jewish intellectual of the caliphate of Hispanic Cordoba (who died in Cairo in 1204) wrote:

Inasmuch as the Christian community came to include those communities [the Greeks and the Syrians], the Christian preaching being what is known to be, and inasmuch as the opinions of the [Platonic] philosophers were widely accepted in those communities in which philosophy had arisen, and inasmuch as a king rose who protected religion—the learned of those periods . . . saw that those preachings are greatly and clearly opposed to the philosophic opinions. Thus there arose among them this science of *kalâm* [interpretation]. They started to establish premises that would be useful to them with regard to their belief and to refute those opinions that ruined the foundations of their Law. When thereupon the community of Islam arrived and the books of the [Aristotelian] philosophers were transmitted to it, then were also transmitted to it those refutations composed [by the Greek Fathers] against the books of the [Platonic] philosophers. . . . There is no doubt that there are things that are common to all *three of us*, I mean the *Jews, the Christians, and the Moslems*: namely, the affirmation of the temporal creation of the world.[109]

In the crisis of the Roman Empire—invaded by the Germans from the outside, and characterized by increasing slavery and exploitation of the masses within—from its Oriental-Greek region (which has nothing to do with the future "Western" culture), a critical ethics that originated from the victims, the poor, the excluded, and the slaves themselves[110] gained strength among those marginal and oppressed groups. The ethical criteria already formulated, among many others and contradictorily, by Egyptians and Babylonians develops with clarity: human "corporeal carnality" (*basar* in Hebrew, *sárx* in Greek)[111] and not the Indo-European soul, is the ultimate reference: "For I was hungry and you gave me food, I was thirsty and you gave me drink, I was a stranger and you welcomed me, I was naked and you clothed me, I was sick and you visited me."[112] Carnal corporeality and its *needs* (hunger, thirst, homelessness, nakedness, illness . . .) as criteria, and the *community* as economic intersubjective instance, constitute what is relevant: "And they devoted themselves to the apostles' teaching and fellowship, to the breaking of bread and prayers. . . . And all who believed were together and had all things in common; and they sold their possessions and goods and distributed them to all, as any had need."[113]

[20] This experience will be reread for centuries, always awakening a utopian *yearning*, a "principle of hope" (well analyzed by Ernst Bloch).[114] These criteria, categories, and principles, expressed by a mythical reason, unleash a process of growing rationalization and of continual hermeneutical rereadings. We can see it centuries later, in texts such as that of the *Koran*, in the most ancient *shuratas* of Mecca: "Did He not find you an orphan and give you shelter? And find you lost and guide you? And find you in want and make you to be free from want? Therefore, as for the orphan, do not oppress

him. And as for him who asks, do not chide him."[115] This is an ethics of the poor, the oppressed, the marginalized, and the barbarians.

Tatian, in his *Address to the Greeks* (AD 170–72) writes: "Be not, O Greeks, so very hostilely disposed towards the Barbarians, nor look with ill will on their opinions. For which of your institutions has not been derived from the Barbarians. . . . To the Babylonians you owe astronomy; to the Persians, magic; to the Egyptians, geometry; to the Phoenicians, instruction by alphabetic writing. Cease, then, to miscall these imitations [*mímésis*] inventions [*euréseis*] of your own."[116] We cannot leave untranscribed the following text, filled with naiveté and enthusiasm, which adheres to the new critical ethics of existence:

> But with us there is no desire of vainglory. . . . Not only do the rich among us pursue our philosophy [*filosofousi*], but the poor enjoy free instruction; for the things which come from God surpass the requital of worldly gifts . . . for I do not attempt, as is the custom with many, to strengthen my own views by the opinion of others, but I wish to give you a distinct account of what I myself have seen and felt. So, bidding farewell to the arrogance of Romans and the idle talk of Athenians, and all their ill-connected opinions, I embraced our barbaric philosophy [*barbárou filosofías*]. . . . These things, O Greeks, I Tatian, a disciple of the barbarian philosophy, have composed for you. I was born in the land of the Assyrians, having been first instructed in your doctrines, and afterwards in those which I now undertake to proclaim. . . . I present myself to you prepared for an examination [*anákrisin*][117] concerning my doctrines.[118]

It should come as no surprise, then, that Justin, a Palestinian philosopher, affirmed carnal corporeality (from the ancient myth of Osiris of the "resurrection of the flesh") against the "immortality of the soul": "Plato affirms . . . that the soul is immortal [*athanaton*], because if it is immortal it is clear that it must be uncreated [*agenetos*] . . . , while [we opine] that the soul dies."[119] The origin of this ethical understanding is African, Oriental, Asiatic, and has nothing to do with Europe or the West![120]

[21] In AD 330, Constantinople was founded, which centuries later would have a million inhabitants. In the year 425 the university was organized (with ten chairs in Latin and Greek language, others of rhetoric, one of philosophy, several of theology, and two of law).[121] The Greek church fathers juxtaposed theology as wisdom to Greek philosophy as *theological* wisdom.

With Heraclius (AD 610–41), the Byzantines recovered all of Mesopotamia. In the year 1203, through treason, the Crusaders occupied Byzantium. Until 1453, Byzantium was the wall that held back the Turks from the Latino-German Europe (the extreme West, without geopolitical importance until that moment).

In AD 860, northerners swept down from the Baltic, traveling along rivers as far as the Black Sea, until they reached the walls of Byzantium. Thus was born Russian culture, from Kiev to Smolensk and Novgorov; the nation was occupied by the Mongolians in 1237, and only in 1480, with the Moscow of Ivan II the Great, did Russia defeat the Golden Horde, thus beginning its expansion in the sixteenth century across the frozen tundra of the North toward the Pacific. Thus was constituted the Russian empire of the Tsars.

The Semitic world of the Arabs of the desert,[122] thanks to Mohammed (his escape to Mecca took place in the year AD 622/1 AH), expanded rapidly through the pacified Byzantine Empire—and for this reason without great resistance. Bostra was conquered in 634, Jerusalem in 637, Alexandria in 643; the Muslim invasion of Spain took place in 711 and reached Pontier in 732. From the Indus valley to north of the Pyrenees, including the Balearic Islands, Sicily, and Crete—with a Muslim presence also in Corsica and Sardinia, in the Adriatic and the south of Italy—Islam dominated the Mediterranean. With the Oamyades caliphates (661–750), first, the Abbasids (750–1258) and, later, Abderraman (from 800) in Cordoba, the center of the Asiatic-African-Mediterranean interregional system would be reconstituted for approximately five hundred years; these were the times of glory for the intercontinental capital, Baghdad, founded in 762 and taken by the Mongols in 1258.[123]

[22] Everything, or almost everything, that someone like Max Weber labeled the European medieval or Renaissance "internal" factors in the genesis of Modernity, had been accomplished with resources from the Muslim world, centuries earlier. Ferdinand Braudel tells us that the letters of a Jewish merchant in Cairo (1095–99) demonstrate that the Muslims already knew about "every method of credit and payment, and every form of trade association (disproving the too facile belief that these were invented later by the Italians)."[124] An extensive economic network of markets existed, with monetary instruments that allow the management of stage III of the interregional system. Agricultural products were commercialized (a hundred thousand camels were used only for the commerce in fruit products); this led to the milling of cereals (there were water and wind mills already in the year 947 in Seistan, a city near the Indus River, while in Basrah the current of the Tigris was used to move wheels of floating mills).[125] The Muslim caravans that linked China and India with the Mediterranean were made of up to six thousand camels. All of this gave impetus to several industries. The carpets of Bukhara used the Hindu blue or red dyes that came from India passing through Kabul, ending up in Morocco and Marrakesh. Coral from the north of Africa made it to India; slaves bought in Ethiopia, iron brought from India, along with pepper and spices were distributed through the entire "system." Sugar cane and cotton from

the Asiatic Southeast, and the silkworm, paper, and compass from China, were other products of the market. Indian numbers (later called "Arabic," with zero) and gunpowder also came from India. In Cordoba, the caliph Al-Hakan II (961–76) had as many as 400,000 manuscripts (and forty-four volumes of catalogues), while Charles V of France (son of John the Good) had only 900 manuscripts during the same period.

The vizier of Khorasan, at the beginning of the tenth century, sent "missions to all the countries to ask for copies of the customs of all the Courts and all the ministries, in the Greek empire, in Turkestan, in China, in Iraq, in Syria, in Egypt, in Zenjan [India], Zabol, and Kabul. . . . He studied them carefully and selected those he judged best to enforce on the court and administration of Bukhara."[126]

In science, the advance was even greater. In the year 820 a treatise of algebra by Mohamet Ibn-Musa was published (which, translated in Europe in the sixteenth century, meant an advance in the mathematics of the time). In optics, astronomy, chemistry, pharmaceutics, and medicine, the Muslim world was about four hundred years ahead of peripheral Europe.

[23] I want to touch last on my theme. In its ethical view of existence, the Muslim experience is Semitic (and for that reason, although there are novelties, it still moves within the Egyptian-Mesopotamian, Jewish, or Christian tradition).[127] With respect to *falasifa* (philosophy), this had among the Arabians a very particular development.[128] Al-Kindi (born in Kufa, Syria; died in the year 873/260 AH), that is to say, 402 years before Thomas of Aquinas, used philosophical texts that Syrian Christians had translated from the Greek.[129] This was in fact an authentic Arabic philosophical "Enlightenment," which developed from Al-Kindi, passing among many through Al-Farabi[130] and Ibn Sina,[131] culminating with Ibn-Rushd.[132] All of them defend the rights of reason before faith. I am of the opinion that it is with them that is properly born what we today call in a secularized fashion "philosophy." Before that, historically it was "rational wisdom" with *theological intention* (as much among the Greeks as among the fathers of the Byzantine Church).[133] The Christians, from the second century onward, juxtaposed the Greek philosophers as theologians (Christian) with theologians (Greek). For this reason, as we saw, Tatian can be called a "barbarian philosopher"; that is to say, "non-Greek lover of wisdom (theologian)." The debates concerning the resurrection or the immortality of the soul, the eternity or creation of the cosmos, predetermination or freedom of the will, and so on are controversies between two "theologies," from the resources of the worlds of quotidian life in confrontation with each other.

[24] I am of the opinion that it is the Muslim who could know both prior discourses (those of the Greeks, the Jews, and the Christian Hellenists and the precision and *formal* rigor that made possible Aristotle's *Orga-*

num—which has little to do with the Neoplatonic *theologies*), who could thus perceive *for the first time* the autonomy of a *formal philosophical* horizon that is properly rational (the *Aristotelian* logic and metaphysical categories, not so much the Platonic ones) with respect to the Koran, held by the believers as *material* and positively revealed. Thus is born the *kalam* proper, or the use of philosophy as hermeneutical method in the development of a rational discourse constructed out of the "revealed" text and, at the same time, as autonomous cultivation of a secularized philosophy as such.[134]

This explicit and formal distinction is also not given among the worshipers of the Upanishads, in Buddha, or in Confucius, since these were wisdoms that incorporated, without negating or differentiating autonomously, myths or theologies—they could not be secularized formally. Complete secularization will be "modern," but the beginning of their differentiation will be the fruit of the Enlightenment of the Arabian philosophy from the ninth century onward.

[25] Al-Gazzali,[135] an exception among the Islamic thinkers, rejected philosophy as the autonomous use of reason and dogmatically affirmed an exclusively revealed theology. Thus is born irrationalist, orthodox, and fundamentalist thought.

I would like to expand on the theme of the Muslim world in order to refute the reasoning of those who opine that Modernity is the product of an exclusively "internal" process of medieval Europe, but I would overshoot the limits that I have imposed for this work of ethical synthesis.

In a non-Eurocentric exposition we should give space here for the description of the *Chinese* world (which will always be the extreme eastern pole of the interregional system, and that will extend its influence to Thailand and Indochina, reaching the Mongols in 1211), the *Hindu* (with the Gupa until AD 525; in the year AD 1205 the Muslim sultanate of Delhi is established, which falls into the hands of the Great Mongol in 1526), that of Malacca (occupied by the Muslims until 1420), as far as the *Philippines* (where the Muslims also arrived, in Mindanao, in the fifteenth century). In addition, from the southeast of the interregional system, we would have to include sub-Saharan Africa (from the east, with the ports of Mogadishu or Mombasa, to the kingdoms of Monomotapa in the south or Abyssinia in the north, going across the savannah toward the west, as far as the kingdoms of Mali, Songai, and Ghana, and then down the western coast to Zaire, what is now the Congo).

[26] In turn, so-called medieval Europe is an interpretation "from within" (a provincial or Eurocentric perspective), which would have fallen into an "intermediate" time (middle-eval), between the fall of the Roman Empire and Modernity. Instead, if we consider this period from the standpoint of its relationship with the Asiatic-Afro-Mediterranean interregional

system we will be able to observe that in a first moment, continental German Europe was connected with the Mediterranean and formed part of the western Roman empire. In a second moment, due to the Arabic expansion in the seventh century, Latin-German continental Europe loses contact with the eastern Mediterranean and, for that reason, with the interregional system. With the fall of the Latin world there emerged simultaneously the holy German empire (in AD 800 Charlemagne is consecrated emperor). This is perceived "from within" Europe as an epoch of feudal isolation and separatism. It is important to consider that this feudalism "inward" is a consequence of the loss of the "outward" link through the eastern Mediterranean (now in Muslim hands). It is the German Europe, which matures, protected from the Muslim expansion by the Byzantine Empire. The third moment corresponds to the attempt at a relinking with the interregional system, and this explains the Crusades (1095–1291), which had as a consequence the reincorporation of continental Europe with the Mediterranean (this is the beginning of the Middle Ages, but not yet the beginning of Modernity, as we will see) through such Italian cities as Venice, Amalfi, Naples, Pisa, and Genoa. We are in the thirteenth century, the classical age of scholastic philosophy in Paris, Oxford, Bologna, Prague, and Salamanca. Since the invasion of Constantinople by the Turks in 1453, many Greek thinkers immigrated to Italy, which produced the phenomenon of the Hellenic Italian intellectual renaissance.

Latin-Germanic Europe for this reason has not ceased being a secondary, regional, and peripheral culture of the Muslim world, since as late as 1532 the Turks were still at the walls of Vienna. Nothing *from within itself* presages a new age or any future splendor. It is in nothing superior to the Muslim world;[136] on the contrary, it maintains a very complex relationship of inferiority, isolation, a true "*finis terrae*" (the extreme West of the Asiatic-African-Mediterranean continent), at great commercial disadvantage with respect to the Muslim "central" areas of the third stage of the interregional system.[137]

[27] In this second part of the introduction, from the historical horizon articulated above, we study the question of Modernity. In fact, there are two paradigms of Modernity.[138]

a. The first paradigm, from a Eurocentric horizon, states that the phenomenon of Modernity is *exclusively* European; that it develops out of the Middle Ages and later on diffuses itself throughout the entire world.[139] Weber situates the "problem of universal history" with a question asking "to what combination of circumstances the fact should be attributed that in *Western civilization*, and in Western civilization only,[140] cultural phenomena have appeared which (as *we*[141] like to think) lie in a line of development having *universal* significance and validity."[142] Europe had, according to this paradigm, exceptional *internal* characteristics that allowed it to supersede, through its rationality, all other cultures. No one expresses this thesis of Modernity philosophically better than Hegel: "The German Spirit is the Spirit of the new World. Its aim is the realization of absolute Truth as the unlimited self-determination [*Selbstbestimmung*] of Freedom—*that* Freedom which *has its own absolute* form itself as its purport [*ihre absolute Form selbst*]."[143] What draws attention here is that the Spirit of Europe (the German spirit) is the absolute Truth that determines or realizes itself through itself without owing anything to anyone. This thesis, which I will call the "Eurocentric paradigm" (in opposition to the "*world* paradigm"), is the one that has imposed itself not only in Europe and the United States, but also in the entire intellectual world of the world periphery. As I have said, the "pseudo-scientific" division of history into antiquity (as antecedent), the medieval age (preparatory epoch), and the modern age (Europe) is an ideological and deforming organization of history. Philosophy and ethics need to break with this reductive horizon in order to open themselves to the "world," the "planetary" sphere. This is already an ethical problem with respect to other cultures.

Chronology has its geopolitics. Modern subjectivity develops spatially, according to the Eurocentric paradigm, from the Italy of the Renaissance to the Germany of the Reformation and the Enlightenment, toward the France of the French Revolution.[144] This concerns central Europe.

[28] b. The second paradigm, from the planetary horizon, conceptualizes Modernity as the culture of the *center* of the "world system"[145] of the first world system—through the incorporation of Amerindia,[146] and as a result of the *management* of said "centrality." In other words, European Modernity is not an *independent*, autopoietic, self-referential system, but, instead, is "part" of a world system: its *center*. Modernity, then, is planetary. It begins with the *simultaneous* constitution of Spain with reference to its "periphery" (the first periphery, properly speaking, namely, Amerindia: the Caribbean, Mexico, and Peru). *Simultaneously*, Europe (in a diachrony that has its premodern antecedents: the Renaissance Italian cities and Portugal) will go on to *constitute* itself as "center" (as superhegemonic power that from Spain passes to Holland, England, and then France . . .) over a growing "periphery" (Amerindia, Brazil, and the slave-supplying coasts of Africa, Poland in the sixteenth century,[147] the consolidation of Latin Amerindia, North America, the Caribbean, and Eastern Europe in the seventeenth century;[148] the Ottoman Empire, Russia, some Indian kingdoms, parts of Asia, and the first regions penetrated by Westerners in continental Africa until the first half of the nineteenth century).[149] Modernity, then, would be for this planetary paradigm a phenomenon proper to

the *system* "center-periphery." Modernity is not a phenomenon of Europe as *independent* system, but of Europe as "center." This simple hypothesis absolutely changes the concept of Modernity, its origin, development, and contemporary crisis; and thus, also the content of belated Modernity or post-Modernity.

[29] Furthermore, I sustain a thesis that qualifies the one preceding: the centrality of Europe in the world system is not the sole consequence of an internal superiority accumulated during the European Middle Ages over against other cultures. Instead, it is also the effect of the simple fact of the discovery, conquest, colonization, and integration (subsumption) of Amerindia (fundamentally). This simple fact will give Europe the determining *comparative advantage* over the Ottoman-Muslim world, India, or China. Modernity is the fruit of this happening, and not its cause. Subsequently, the *management* of the centrality of the world system will allow Europe to transform itself in something like the "reflexive consciousness" (modern philosophy) of world history, and the many values, discoveries, inventions, technology, political institutions, and the like that are attributed to itself as its exclusive production, are in reality the effect of the *displacement* of the ancient center of stage III of the interregional system toward Europe (following the diachronic way of the Renaissance to Portugal as antecedent, toward Spain, and later toward Flanders, and England). Even capitalism is the product, and not cause, of this juncture of European planetarization and centralization within the world system. The human experience of 4,500 years of political, economic, technological, cultural relations of the interregional system will now be hegemonized by Europe—which had never before been a center, which during its best times had got to be only a periphery. The slippage takes place from Central Asia toward the Eastern and Italian Mediterranean, or more precisely toward Genoa, toward the Atlantic. With Portugal as an antecedent, it begins properly in Spain, and in the face of the impossibility of China's even attempting to reach, through the Orient (the Pacific), Europe and thus integrate Amerindia as its periphery. Let us look at the premises of the argument.

§I.5. Unfolding of the World System: From "Modern" Spain of the Sixteenth Century

[30] Let us consider the unfolding of world history starting from the rupture, due to the Ottoman-Muslim presence, of stage III of the interregional system—which in its classic epoch had Baghdad as its center (from AD 762 to 1258)—and the transformation of the interregional system into the first *world* system, whose center would situate itself, up to the present, in the North Atlantic region. This change of center of the system has its

prehistory from the thirteenth through the fifteenth century AD, before the collapse of stage III of the interregional system, but the change *originates* properly in 1492 with the new stage IV of the world system. Everything that had taken place in Europe was still a moment of *another* stage of the inter-regional system. Which state originated the unfolding of the world system? My answer is, the one that could annex Amerindia, and from it, as a spring-board or "comparative advantage," go on to accumulate, toward the end of the fifteenth century, a previously nonexistent superiority.

a. Why not China? The reason is very simple, and I would like to ex-plain it at the outset. It was impossible for China[150] to discover Amerindia (a nontechnological impossibility, that is to say, empirically possible but not possible for historical or geopolitical reasons). China had no interest in attempting to reach Europe because the "center" of the interregional sys-tem (in stage III) was in the East, either in Central Asia or in India. To go toward a completely "peripheral" Europe? This could not have been an ob-jective of Chinese foreign commerce.

As it happens, Cheng Ho, between 1405 and 1433, was able to make seven successful voyages to the center of the system of the time (he trav-eled to Sri Lanka, India, and as far as eastern Africa).[151] In 1479 Wang Chin attempted the same, but the archives of his predecessor were denied him. China closed on itself and did not attempt to do what Portugal was under-taking at that very moment. Its internal politics—perhaps the rivalry of the mandarins against the new power of the eunuch merchants[152]—prevented its move into foreign commerce. Had China undertaken such a move, how-ever, it would have had to depart *toward the West* in order to reach the cen-ter of the system. The Chinese instead went toward the East and reached Alaska and, it appears, even California, and still further south, but when they did not find anything that would be of interest to its merchants, and as they went further from the center of the interregional system, they aban-doned the enterprise. For geopolitical reasons, then, China was not Spain.

[31] However, we still need to ask ourselves, in order to refute the old "evidence," which has nevertheless been reinforced since Weber: Was China culturally *inferior* to Europe in the fifteenth century? According to those who have studied the question,[153] China was neither technologically[154] nor politically,[155] nor commercially, and not even in its humanism,[156] inferior. There is a kind of mirage in this question. The histories of Western sci-ence and technology do not take strictly into account that the European "jump," the technological *boom*, begins to take place in the sixteenth cen-tury but that it is only in the seventeenth century that it shows its multiply-ing effects. The *formulation* of the modern technological paradigm (in the seventeenth century) is confused with the origin of Modernity, and it leaves no time for the crisis of the medieval model. It is not noticed that the sci-

entific revolution — to talk with Thomas Kuhn — departs from a Modernity that has already begun, antecedent, a fruit of a "modern paradigm."[157] It is for that reason that, in the fifteenth century (if we do not consider the later European inventions), Europe does not have any superiority over China. Needham allows himself to be bewitched by this mirage, when he writes: "The fact is that the spontaneous autochthonous development of Chinese society did not produce any drastic change paralleling the Renaissance and the scientific revolution of the West."[158] To speak of the Renaissance and the scientific revolution[159] as being *one and the same event* (one from the fifteenth century, and the other from the seventeenth) demonstrates the distortion of which I speak. The Renaissance is still a European event, of a peripheral culture in stage III of the interregional system.[160] The scientific revolution is a product of the formulation of the modern paradigm, which needed more than a century of Modernity in order to attain maturity. Pierre Chaunu writes: "Towards the end of the fifteenth century, to the extent to which historical literature allows us to understand it, the far East as an entity comparable to the Mediterranean . . . is not in any way inferior, at least superficially, to the far West of the Euro-Asiatic continent."[161] Let me repeat: Why not China? Because China found itself in the farthest East of the interregional system, because it looked to the center: to India in the West.

[32] b. Why not Portugal? For the same reason. That is, because it found itself in the farthest point of the West of the same interregional system, and because *it also looked, and always did, toward the "center"*: toward the India of the East. Cristobal Colón's proposal (to attempt to reach the center through the West) to the king of Portugal was as insane as it was for Colón to claim to have discovered a new continent (since he *only and always* attempted, and could not conceive another hypothesis, to reach the center of stage III of the interregional system).[162]

As we have seen, the Italian Renaissance cities are the farthest point of the West (peripheral) of the interregional system that, after the Crusades, articulated anew continental Europe with the Mediterranean. The Crusades (which failed in 1291) ought to be considered a frustrated attempt to connect with the center of the system, a link that the Turks ruptured. The Italian cities, especially Genoa (a rival of Venice, which had a presence in the eastern Mediterranean), attempted to open the western Mediterranean toward the Atlantic, in order to reach the center of the system by going south, around Africa. The Genoese placed all their experience in navigation and the economic power of their wealth at the service of opening for themselves this path. It was the Genoese who occupied the Canaries in 1312,[163] and it was they who invested in Portugal and helped the Portuguese develop their navigational power.

Once the Crusades had failed, Europeans could not count on the expansion of Russia through the steppes (the Russians, advancing through the frozen woods of the North, reached the Pacific and Alaska in the seventeenth century);[164] the Atlantic was the only European door *to the center of the system.* Portugal, the first European nation, already unified in the eleventh century, transformed the Reconquest[165] against the Muslims into the beginning of a process of Atlantic mercantile expansion. In 1419, the Portuguese discovered the Madeiras; in 1431, the Azores; in 1482, Zaire; in 1498, Vasco de Gama reached India (the center of the interregional system). In 1415, Portugal occupied the African-Muslim Ceuta; in 1448, El-Ksar-es-Seghir; in 1471, Arzila. But all of this is the *continuation* of the interregional system whose connection was through the Italian cities: "In the twelfth century when Genoese and the Pisans first appeared in Catalonia, in the thirteenth century when they first reach Portugal, this is part of the efforts of the Italians to draw the Iberian peoples into the international trade of the time. . . . As of 1317, according to Virginia Raus, the city and the part of Lisbon would be the great center of Genoese trade."[166] A Portugal with contacts in the Islamic world, with numerous sailors (farmers expelled from intensive agriculture), with a money economy, in "connection" with Italy, opened peripheral Europe once again to the interregional system. But it did not stop being a periphery because of this. Even the Portuguese could not claim to have moved from this position, since although Portugal could have attempted to dominate the commercial exchange in the sea of the Arabs (the Indian sea),[167] it could never claim production of the commodities of the East ("china" or porcelain, silk fabrics, tropical products, the sub-Saharan gold, and so on). In other words, it was an intermediary and always peripheral power of India, China, or the Muslim world.

With Portugal we are in the antechamber, but still neither in Modernity nor in the world system (stage IV of the system that originated, at least, between Egypt and Mesopotamia).

[33] c. Why does Spain begin the world system, and with it, Modernity? For the same reason that it was not possible in China and Portugal. Since Spain could not reach the center of the interregional system in Central Asia or India, it could not go toward the East through the south Atlantic (around the coasts of western Africa, to the cape of Buena Esperanza [Good Hope], discovered in 1487) since the Portuguese had already anticipated them, and thus had exclusive rights. Spain only had one option left: to go toward the center, to India, through *the Occident*, through the West, by crossing the Atlantic Ocean.[168] Because of this, Spain "bumps" into, "finds without looking," Amerindia, and with it the entire European "medieval paradigm" enters into crisis (which is the paradigm of a peripheral culture, the westernmost point of stage III of the interregional system), and

thus inaugurates, slowly but irreversibly, the first *world* hegemony. This is the only world system that has existed in planetary history, and this is the modern system, European in its center, capitalist in its economy. *Ethics of Liberation* intends to situate itself explicitly (is it perhaps the first practical philosophy that attempts to do so "explicitly"?) within the horizon of this modern world system, taking into consideration not only the center (as has been done *exclusively* by modern philosophy from Descartes to Habermas, thus resulting in a *partial*, provincial, regional view of the historical ethical event), *but also* its periphery (thus producing a *planetary* vision of the human experience). This historical question is not informative or anecdotal. It has a philosophical sense that is *strictu sensu*! I have already treated the theme in another work.[169] In that work I showed Colón's existential impossibility, as a Renaissance Genoese, of convincing himself that what he had discovered was not India. He navigated, according to his own imagination, close to the coasts of the fourth Asiatic peninsula (which Heinrich Hammer had already represented cartographically in Rome in 1489),[170] always close to the Sinus Magnus (the "great gulf" of the Greeks, territorial sea of the Chinese), when he transversed the Caribbean. Colón died in 1506 without having passed the horizon of stage III of the interregional system.[171] He was not able to supersede subjectively the "interregional system—with a history of 4,500 years of transformations, beginning with Egypt and Mesopotamia—and to open himself to the new stage of the world system. The first person to suspect a *new* continent was Americo Vespucci, in 1503, and therefore, he was existentially and subjectively, the first "modern," the first to unfold the horizon of the "Asian-Afro-Mediterranean system" as world system, which incorporated for the first time Amerindia.[172] This revolution in the *Weltanschauung*, of the cultural, scientific, religious, technological, political, ecological, and economic horizon is the *origin* of Modernity, seen from the perspective of a world paradigm and not solely from a Eurocentric perspective. In the world system, the accumulation in the center is for the first time accumulation on a world scale.[173] Within the new system, everything changes qualitatively or radically. The very medieval European "peripheral subsystem" changes internally as well. The founding event was the discovery of Amerindia in 1492.[174] Spain was ready to become the first modern state;[175] through this discovery it began to become the center of its first periphery (Amerindia), thus organizing the beginning of the slow shifting of the center of the older stage III of the interregional system (Baghdad of the thirteenth century), which had from peripheral Genoa (the western part of the system) begun a process of reconnection, first with Portugal and now with Spain—with Seville to be precise. Genoese Italian wealth suddenly flowed into Seville. The "experience" of the eastern Renaissance Mediterranean (and through it, of the Muslim world, of India and even China) is thus articulated with the imperial Spain of Carlos V (who reaches the central Europe of the bankers of Augsburg, the Flanders of Amberes, and later, Amsterdam, followed by Bohemia, Hungary, Austria, and Milan, and especially the kingdom of the Two Sicilies,[176] of the region around southern Italy, namely Sicily, Sardinia, the Baleares, and the numerous islands of the Mediterranean). But because of the economic failure of the political project of the world empire, Carlos V abdicated in 1557: the path was left open for the world system of mercantile, industrial, and, today, transnational capitalism.

[34] Let us take as an example a level of analysis from among the many that may be analyzed — I would not want to be criticized as being a reductive economist, because of the example I have adopted. It is not coincidence that twenty-five years after the discovery of the silver mines of Potosí in high Peru and the mines in Zacateca in Mexico (1546) — from which a total of eighteen thousand tons of silver were shipped to Spain between the years 1550 and 1660[177] — Spain, thanks to the first shipments of this precious metal, was able to pay for the great armada that defeated the Turks in 1571 in Lepanto, among the many campaigns of the empire. This victory led to the dominion of the Mediterranean as a connection with the center of the older stage of the system. However, the Mediterranean had died as the road of the center toward the periphery on the West, because now the Atlantic was structuring itself as the center of the new world system![178]

Wallerstein writes: "Gold and silver were desired as precious goods, for consumption in Europe and even more for trade with Asia, but it was also a necessity for the expansion of the European economy."[179] I have read, among the many unpublished letters of the General Indian Archive of Seville, the following text of July 1, 1550, signed in Bolivia by Domingo de Santo Tomás: "It was four years ago, to conclude the perdition of this land, that a mouth of hell[180] was discovered through which every year a great number of people are immolated, which the greed of the Spaniards sacrifice to their god that is gold,[181] and it is a mine of silver which is named Potosí."[182] The rest is well known. The Spanish colony in Flanders would replace Spain as a hegemonic power in the center of the recently established world system — it liberated itself from Spain in 1610. Seville, the first modern port (in relations with Amberes), after more than a century of splendor would cede its place to Amsterdam[183] (the city where Descartes wrote his Le Discours de la Méthode in 1636, and where Spinoza lived).[184] Amsterdam was a naval, fishing, and crafts power, from where agricultural exports flowed, with great expertise in all branches of production, and it would, among many things, bankrupt Venice.[185] After more than a century, Modernity already showed in this city, a metropolis with a definitive physiognomy: its port, the canals that as commercial thoroughfares reached the houses of the bourgeoisie, the merchants (who used their fourth and fifth floors as store rooms, from which boats could be directly loaded with cranes); a thousand details of a capitalist metropolis.[186] From 1689 on, England would challenge it, and would end up taking over Holland's hegemony—a dominance that England, however, would always have to share with France, at least until 1763.[187]

[35] Amerindia, meanwhile, constitutes the fundamental structure of the first Modernity. From 1492 to 1500 about 50,000 square kilometers were colonized (in the Caribbean and mainland, from Venezuela to Panama).[188] In 1515 this number reached 300,000 square kilometers with about three million dominated Amerindians. By 1550, more than two million square kilometers were colonized (which is a greater area than the whole of Europe of the center), with more than twenty-five million (a low figure) of indigenous peoples subjugated,[189] many of whom were integrated to a system of work that produces value (in Marx's strict sense) for the Europe of the center (in the *encomiendas, mitas, haciendas*, and so on). We also must add, from 1520 onward, plantations with slaves of African provenance (about fourteen million of them in the region, including Brazil, Cuba, and the United States, until slavery ended in the nineteenth century). This enormous space and population would give to Europe, center of the world system, the *definitive comparative advantage* with respect to the Muslim, Indian, and Chinese worlds. It is for this reason that in the sixteenth century "the periphery (Eastern Europe and Hispanic America) used forced labor (slavery and coerced cash-crop labor [of the Amerindian]). The core, as we shall see, increasingly used free labor."[190] For the goals of this philosophical work, it is of interest to indicate solely that with the birth of the world system, the "*peripheral* social formations"[191] were also born (see figure 2): "The form of *peripheral* formation will depend, finally, at the same time on the nature of the accumulated precapitalist formations and the forms of external aggression."[192] These were, at the end of the twentieth century, the Latin American peripheral formations,[193] those of the African Bantu, the Muslim world, India, the Asian Southeast,[194] and China; to which one must also add part of Eastern Europe before the fall of existing socialism.

§I.6. Modernity as "Management" of Planetary Centrality and Its Contemporary Crisis

[36] We have thus arrived at the central thesis of the two halves of this introduction. If Modernity was the fruit of the "management" of the centrality of the first world system, and this is our hypothesis, we now have to reflect on what this implies.

One must be conscious that there are at least, in origin, two Modernities.

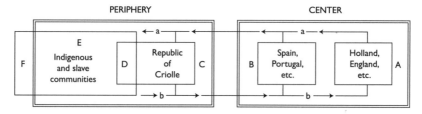

Figure 2. An example of the center-periphery structure in the "center" and "periphery" (colonial Latin America, eighteenth century).

NOTE: Arrow a represents the control and export of manufactured goods; arrow b, the transfer of value and exploitation of labor. A: power of the "center"; B: semiperipheral nations; C: peripheral formations; D: exploitation of Amerindian labor or slaves; E: indigenous communities; F: ethnic communities that have retained a certain exteriority to the world system.

See Dussel 1983a, vol. I, pt. 1, 223–41.

a. In the first place, Hispanic, humanist, Renaissance Modernity was still linked to the old interregional system of Mediterranean and Muslim Christianity.[195] In it, the management of the new system would be conceived from the older paradigm of the III interregional system. That is, Spain *managed* centrality as domination through the hegemony of an integral culture, language, and religion (and thus, the evangelization process that Amerindia will suffer); as military occupation, bureaucratic-political organization, economic expropriation, demographic presence (with hundreds of thousands of Spaniards or Portuguese who will forever inhabit Amerindia), ecological transformation (through the modification of the fauna and flora), and so on. This is the World Empire project, which, as Wallerstein notes, failed with Carlos V.[196]

[37] b. In the second place, there is the Modernity of Anglo-Germanic Europe, which began with Amsterdam, and which frequently passes as the *only* Modernity (this is the interpretation of Sombart, Weber, Habermas, or even the postmoderns, which produced a reductionist fallacy that occluded the meaning of Modernity, and, thus, the sense of its contemporary crisis). This second Modernity had to accomplish or increase its efficacy through *simplification*, in order to be able to "manage" the immense world system — which suddenly opened itself to tiny Holland,[197] which, from being a Spanish province, now situated itself as the center of the world system. It had to carry out an abstraction, favoring the *quantum* to the detriment of *qualitas*, thus *leaving out* many valid variables (cultural, anthropological, ethical, political, and religious variables; factors that were valuable even for the European of the sixteenth century) that would not allow an adequate, "factual,"[198] or technologically possible management of the world system.[199]

This *simplification* of complexity[200] encompassed the totality of the "life world" (*Lebenswelt*), the relationship with nature (a new technological and ecological position, which is no longer teleological), subjectivity itself (a new self-understanding of subjectivity), and community (a new intersubjective and political relation); as a synthesis, a new economic attitude would establish itself (capital's practical-productive position).

[38] The first Hispanic Renaissance and humanist Modernity produced a theoretical or philosophical reflection of the highest importance, one that has gone unnoticed in so-called modern philosophy (which is only the philosophy of the second Modernity). The theoretical-philosophical thought of the sixteenth century has contemporary relevance because it is the first, and only, system of thought to live and express the originary experience of the period of the constitution of the first world system. Thus, out of the theoretical "recourses" that were available (the scholastic-Muslim-Christian and Renaissance philosophy), the central philosophical ethical question that was obtained was the following: "What right has the European to occupy, dominate, and *manage* the cultures that have recently been discovered and militarily conquered, and that are now in the process of being colonized? From the seventeenth century on, the second Modernity did not have to question its conscience (*Gewissen*) with these questions, which had in fact already been answered: from Amsterdam, London, or Paris (in the seventeenth century and from the eighteenth century onward), Eurocentrism (a superideology that would establish the valid legitimacy, without possible opposition, of the domination of the world system) would *no longer* be questioned, until the end of the twentieth century—and this by liberation philosophy, among other movements.

I have touched on this question in another work.[201] For now, we will remind ourselves only of the theme in general. Bartolomé de las Casas demonstrates in his numerous works, using an extraordinary bibliographical apparatus, and grounding his arguments rationally and carefully, that the constitution of the world system as European expansion in Amerindia (in anticipation of the expansion in Africa and Asia) does not have any right; it is an unjust violence, and cannot have any ethical validity:

> The common ways mainly employed by the Spaniards who call themselves Christian and who have gone there to extirpate those pitiful nations and wipe them off the earth is by unjustly waging cruel and bloody wars. Then, when they have slain all those who fought for their lives or to escape the tortures they would have to endure, that is to say, when they have slain all the native rulers and young men (since the Spaniards usually spare only the women and children, who are subjected to the hardest and bitterest servitude ever suffered by man or beast), they enslave any survivors. . . . Their reason for killing and destroying such an infinite number of souls is that

the Christians have an ultimate aim, which is to acquire gold, and to swell themselves with riches in a very brief time and thus rise to a high estate disproportionate to their merits. It should be kept in mind that their insatiable greed and ambition, the greatest ever seen in the world, is the cause of their villainies.[202]

In the time since then, philosophy no longer formulated this problematic, which nonetheless showed itself unavoidable at the origin of the establishment of the world system. For the ethics of liberation, this question is today still fundamental.

[39] In the sixteenth century, then, new philosophical questions were established out of the old philosophical paradigm, from the new colonial praxis of domination, but the formulation of the *new paradigm* had not yet occurred. The origin of the new paradigm, however, should not be confused with the origin of Modernity. Modernity begins more than a century before (in 1492), the moment in which the paradigm, adequate to its very own new experience, was formalized — to speak again with Kuhn. If we note the dates of the formulation of the new modern paradigm, we see that it took place in the first half of the seventeenth century.[203] This new paradigm corresponded to the exigencies of *efficacy*, technological "feasibility" or governmentality of the management of an enormous world system in expansion; it was the expression of a necessary process of *simplification* through the "rationalization" of the life world of the subsystems (economic, political, cultural, religious, etc.). "Rationalization" as indicated by Werner Sombart,[204] Ernst Troeltsch,[205] or Max Weber,[206] is *effect* and not cause. On the other hand, the effects of that *simplifying rationalization*, undertaken in order to *manage* the world system, are perhaps more profound and negative than Habermas or the postmoderns imagine.[207]

The corporeal Muslim-medieval subjectivity is *simplified*: subjectivity is postulated as an *ego*, an I, about which Descartes writes: "Accordingly this *I*—that is, the soul by which I am what I am — is *entirely* distinct from the body, and indeed is easier to know than the body, and would not fail to be whatever it is, even if the body did not exist."[208] The body is a mere machine, *res extensa*, entirely foreign to the soul.[209] Kant himself writes: "The human soul should be seen as being linked in the present life to two worlds at the same time: of these worlds, inasmuch as it forms with the body a personal unity, it feels but only the material world [*materielle*]; on the contrary, as a member of world of the spirit [*als ein Glied der Geisterwelt*] it receives and propagates the pure influences of immaterial natures."[210] This dualism — which Kant would apply to his ethics, inasmuch as the "maxims" ought not to have any empirical or "pathological" motives — is posteriorly articulated through the negation of practical-material reason, which is replaced by instrumental reason, the one that will deal with technical, technological *management* (a *more geometric* reason)[211] in the *Critique of Judgment*. It is here that the conservative tradition (such as that of Heidegger) continues to perceive the *simplifying* suppression of the organic complexity of life, now replaced by a technique of the "will to power" (in the critiques elaborated by Nietzsche). Galileo, with all the naive enthusiasm of a great discovery, writes: "Philosophy is written in this grand book, the universe, which stands continually open to our gaze. But the book cannot be understood unless one first learns to comprehend the language and read the letters in which it is composed. It is written in the *language of mathematics*, and its characters are triangles, circles and other geometric figures, without which it is humanly impossible to understand a single word of it; without these, one wanders about in a dark labyrinth."[212]

[40] Heidegger already said that the "mathematical position"[213] before entities is to have them already known, "ready-to-hand" (in the axioms of science, for example), and to approach them only in order to use them. One does not "learn" a weapon, for instance, but instead one learns to make "use" of it, because one already knows what it is: "The *mathemata* are the things insofar as we take cognizance of them as what we already know them to be in advance, the body as the bodily, the plant-like of the plant, the animal-like of the animal, the thingness of the thing, and so on."[214] The "rationalization" of political life (bureaucratization), of the capitalist enterprise (administration), of daily life (Calvinist asceticism or Puritanism), the decorporealization of subjectivity (with its alienating effects on living labor, criticized by Marx, as well as on its drives, as analyzed by Freud), the nonethicalness of every economic or political gestation (understood only as technical engineering, etc.), the suppression of practical-communicative reason, now replaced by instrumental reason, the solipsistic individuality that negates the community, are all examples of the diverse moments which are negated by *simplification*, apparently necessary for the management of the centrality of a world system that Europe found itself in the need of perpetually carrying out. Capitalism, liberalism, dualism (without valorizing corporeality), and so on are *effects* of Europe's management of the function given it by its role as center of the world system. They are effects that have constituted themselves into systems that end up totalizing themselves. Capitalism, the mediation of exploitation and accumulation (the effect of the world system), was later transformed into an *independent system* that from its own self-referential and autopoietic logic can destroy Europe and its periphery, and even the entire planet. This is what Weber observes, but reductively. That is to say, Weber notes part of the phenomenon but not the horizon of the world system. In fact, the formal procedure of *simplification* that makes the world system *manageable* produces formal rationalized subsystems that later on do not have internal standards of self-regulation

of their limits within Modernity, which could then be redirected at the service of humanity. It is in this moment that there emerge critiques from within the center (and from out of the periphery, such as is mine) against Modernity itself. Now one attributes to *ratio* all culpable causality (as object "understanding," which is set through disintegration), from Nietzsche to Heidegger, or with the postmoderns—this culpability will be traced back as far as Socrates (Nietzsche), or even Parmenides himself (Heidegger). In fact, the modern *simplifications* (the dualism of an *ego-soul* without a body, teleological instrumental reason, the racism of the superiority of one's own culture, etc.) have many similarities with the *simplification* that Greek slavery produced in the second interregional system. The Greek *Weltanschauung* was advantageous to the modern man—not without complicity does the modern subject resuscitate the Greeks, as did the German Romantics.[215] The subsumptive superseding (*Aufhebung*) of Modernity will mean the critical consideration of *all* the simplifying reductions produced since its origin—and not only a few, as Habermas imagines. The most important of these reductions, after solipsistic subjectivity, without community, is the negation of the corporeality of a said subjectivity—to which are related the critiques of Modernity by Marx, Nietzsche, Freud, Foucault, Levinas, and the ethics of liberation, as we will see throughout the length of this work.

[41] Because of all of this, the concept that one has of Modernity determines, as is evident, the claim to its fulfillment, or the type of critique one may formulate against it (such as that of the postmoderns). In general, every debate between rationalists and postmoderns does not overcome the Eurocentric horizon. The crisis of Modernity (already noted by, as I have frequently noted, Nietzsche and Heidegger) refers to internal aspects of Europe. The peripheral world appears to be a passive spectator of a thematic that does not touch it, because it is "barbarian," "premodern," or simply, still in need of being "modernized." In other words, the Eurocentric view reflects on the problem of the crisis of Modernity solely with the European–North American moments (and now, the Japanese), but it minimizes the periphery. To break through this reductivist fallacy is not easy. I will attempt to indicate the path toward its surmounting.

If Modernity began at the end of the fifteenth century, with a Renaissance premodern process, and from there a transition was made to the properly modern in Spain, then Amerindia forms part of Modernity from the moment of the conquest and colonization (the *mestizo* world in Latin America is the only one that is as old as Modernity),[216] since it was the first "barbarian" that Modernity needed in its self-definition. If Modernity enters into crisis at the end of the twentieth century, after five centuries of development, it is not a matter only of the moments detected by Weber and Habermas, or by Lyotard or Welsch;[217] we will have to add the critical moments from a "planetary" description of the phenomenon of Modernity.

[42] If we situate ourselves within the planetary horizon, we can distinguish at least the following positions in the face of the formulated problematic.

a. In first place, on the one hand, there is the "substantialist" *developmentalist*[218] (quasi-metaphysical) position that conceptualizes Modernity as an *exclusively European* phenomenon, which *expanded from the seventeenth century on* through all the "backward" cultures (situating the Eurocentric position in the "center" and modernizing in the "periphery"); Modernity in this view is a phenomenon that must be concluded. Some of those who assume this first position (for example, Habermas and Apel), defenders of reason, do so critically, since they think, thanks to a new structure of critical questions,[219] that European superiority is not material, but formal. On the other hand, there is the conservative "nihilist" position, which negates Modernity's positive qualities (see Nietzsche or Heidegger, for instance) and which proposes more or less an annihilation without exit. The postmoderns take this second position (in their frontal attack on "reason" *as such*; with differences in the case of Levinas),[220] although, paradoxically, they also defend parts of the first position, from the perspective of a developmentalist Eurocentrism.[221] The postmodern philosophers are admirers of postmodern art, of the *media*, and although they theoretically affirm *difference*, they do not reflect on the origins of these systems that are the fruit of a rationalization proper to the *management* of the European "centrality" in the world system, before which they are profoundly uncritical; because of this, they do not have possibilities of attempting to contribute valid alternatives (cultural, economic, political, etc.) for the peripheral nations, or for the peoples or great majorities who are dominated by the center and/or the periphery.[222]

[43] b. In the second place, we defend another position, from out of the periphery, one that considers the process of Modernity as the already indicated rational "management" of the world system. This position attempts to recuperate what is redeemable in Modernity, and negates domination and exclusion in the world system. It is then a project of liberation of a periphery negated from the very beginning of Modernity. The problem is not the mere superseding of instrumental reason (as it is for Habermas) or of the reason of *terror* of the postmoderns; instead, it is the question of the overcoming of the world system itself, such as it has developed for the last five hundred years. The problem is the exhaustion of a civilizing system that has come to its end.[223] The overcoming of *cynical-managerial reason* (planetary administrative), of capitalism (as economic system), of liberalism (as political system), of Eurocentrism (as ideology), of machismo (in erotics),

of the reign of the white race (in racism), of the destruction of nature (in ecology), and so on presupposes the liberation of diverse types of oppressed and/or excluded. It is in this sense that the ethics of liberation defines itself as transmodern (since the postmoderns are still Eurocentric).

At the end of the present stage of civilization two absolute limits of the "system of five hundred years" (as Noam Chomsky calls it) become apparent.

a. These limits are in the first place, the ecological destruction of the planet. From the very moment of its inception, Modernity has constituted nature as "exploitable" object, with the increase in the rate of profit of capital[224] as its goal: "For the first time, nature becomes purely an object for humankind, purely a matter of utility; ceases to be recognized as a power for itself."[225] When the earth is seen constituted as an "exploitable object" in favor of *quantum*, of capital, capital that can defeat all limits, all boundaries, there manifests the "great civilizing influence of capital," and capital now reaches finally its insurmountable limit, where it itself is its own limit, the impassable barrier for ethical-human progress. We have arrived at this moment: "The universality towards which it irresistibly strives encounters barriers in its own nature, which will, at a certain state of its development, allow it to be recognized as being itself the greatest barrier to this tendency, and hence will drive towards its own suspension."[226] Given that for Modernity nature is only a medium of production, nature fulfills its fate of being consumed and destroyed. In addition, the by-products of that destruction accumulate upon the Earth, until it jeopardizes the reproduction or survival of life itself. Life is the absolute condition of capital; its destruction destroys capital. We have arrived at this state of affairs. The "system of five hundred years" (Modernity or capitalism) confronts its first absolute limit: the death of life in its totality, through the indiscriminate use of an anti-ecological technology constituted progressively through the sole criterion of the *quantitative* "management" of the world system in Modernity: the increase in the rate of profit. But capital cannot limit itself. Thus comes about the utmost danger for humanity.

[44] b. The second limit of Modernity is the destruction of humanity itself. "Living labor" is the other essential mediation of capital as such; the human subject is the only one that can "create" new value (surplus value, profit). Capital that defeats all barriers requires incrementally more absolute time of work; when it cannot supersede this limit, it augments productivity through technology—but this increase decreases the importance of human labor. It is thus that there is *superfluous humanity* (disposable, unemployed, excluded). The unemployed do not earn a salary, money; but money is the only mediation in the market through which one can acquire commodities in order to satisfy needs. In any event, work that does not

create employment increases unemployment. Thus, the numbers of needy people and those not solvent increase—as much in the periphery as in the center.[227] It is poverty, poverty as the absolute limit of capital. Today we know how misery grows across the entire planet. It is a matter of a "law of Modernity": "Accumulation of wealth at one pole is, therefore, at the same time accumulation of misery, the torment of labor, slavery, ignorance, brutalization and moral degradation at the opposite pole."[228] The modern world system cannot overcome this essential contradiction. The ethics of liberation reflects philosophically from this planetary horizon of the world system, from this double limit that configures the terminal crisis of a civilizing process: the ecological destruction of the planet and the extinction, in misery and hunger, of the great majority of humanity. Before this prospect, of two coimplicating phenomena of such planetary magnitude, the projects of many philosophical schools seem naive and even ridiculous, irresponsible, irrelevant, cynical, and complicitous; the projects of so many philosophical schools (as much in the center, but even worse yet in the periphery, in Latin America, Africa, and Asia), closed in their "ivory towers" of sterile Eurocentric academicism. Already in 1968 Marcuse wrote, referring to the opulent countries of late capitalism:

> Why do we need liberation from such a society if it is capable—perhaps in the distant future, but apparently capable—of conquering poverty to a greater degree than ever before, or reducing the toil of labor and the time of labor, and of raising the standard of living? If the price for all goods delivered, the price for this comfortable servitude, for all these achievements, is exacted from people far away from the metropolis and far away from its affluence? If the affluent society itself hardly notices what it is doing, how is it breeding terror and enslavement, how is it fighting against liberation in all corners of the globe?"[229]

In this way Modernity confronts the impossibility of its subsuming the populations, economies, nations, cultures it has been attacking since its origin, that it has excluded from its horizon and cornered into poverty. This is the whole theme—the exclusion of African, Asian, and Latin American alterity and their indomitable will to survive. I will return to this theme, but for now I want to indicate that the globalizing world system reaches a limit inasmuch as it excludes the Other, who resists, and from whose affirmation the negation of the critique of liberation originates.

§I.7. The Liberation of Philosophy?

[45] Given the landscape outlined in the foregoing paragraphs, the ethics of liberation must first of all undertake a reflection regarding the geopolitical implantation of philosophy itself, on the extent to which it is situated[230]

in the center or in the periphery. In effect, it seems as if a *philosophy of "liberation"* (genitive objective: its theme) requires the liberation *of "philosophy" itself* (genitive subjective: the subject that is active and at the same time that is activated) as its point of departure. Throughout history, at least since the Greeks, philosophy has frequently been bound to the engines of power and ethnocentrism. Nonetheless, it is true that there have always been philosophic counterdiscourses of greater or lesser critical density, and it is with this counterhegemonic[231] tradition that I would identify my own work. In previous examples of ethnocentrism (such as that of China, the Aztecs, Hindu civilization, Christianity, or Islam) the pattern tended to be that one culture situated itself as superior to other cultures: the ethnocentrism was essentially of a "regional" character. In the context of Modernity, the European variant of ethnocentrism was the first "global" ethnocentrism (Eurocentrism has been the only global ethnocentrism thus far known to history: with it, universality and European identity became fused into one; *philosophy must be liberated* from this reductionist fallacy). Under such circumstances, when the philosopher belongs to a hegemonic system (be it Greek, Byzantine, Islamic, or medieval Christian, and particularly in the modern period), his or her world or ethical system has the claim of presenting itself as if it were equivalent to or identical with the epitome of the human "world"; while the world of the Others is that of barbarity, marginality, and nonbeing. Let us take an example as the guiding thread of our discussion in this context.

Charles Taylor has written a classic work, *Sources of the Self: The Making of the Modern Identity*.[232] He explains his intention in this work as follows: "This is what I am trying to do from now on. But this is not something which is simple. . . . often it will precisely involve articulating that which has remained implicit. . . . But there is an extraordinary resource available to make this possible, which is history itself, given that the articulation of modern forms of comprehending that which is good must thus be an historical task."[233] The historical review that Taylor undertakes is "a combination of the analytical and the chronological."[234] This implies analyses of the evolution of the contents of the modern *Self* from the perspective of its historical origins and "*sources*." His choice of a methodology for the exposition of his ideas is inspired in philosophical texts, has been derived from the Greek philosophers, and is focused exclusively on European thinkers. All of this might appear obvious or a secondary matter without special circumstances.

[46] a. In effect, I would like to refer *methodologically* to the manner in which Taylor attempts to carry out his analytical history of the development of modern identity taking into account the *sources* of the self. The virtually exclusive raw materials for his enterprise are the works of philosophers[235] (Plato, Augustine, Descartes, Locke . . .), who are analyzed from within

their own discourses. His work is a kind of philosophical history written from within philosophy itself.[236] It is a magisterial effort, erudite, characterized by a creative way of arriving at novel conclusions, albeit limited to an "intraphilosophical" exploration that lacks a history, an economics, or a politics. This methodological limitation will prevent the author from arriving at more critical conclusions. Within this context it would appear as if capitalism, colonialism, and the continuous recourse to violence or military aggression had no importance at all.

b. A second aspect I would like to explore is that Taylor takes Plato as his point of departure for his reconstruction of modern identity. In doing so he reproduces a long-standing tradition in Western philosophy: the Greeks are taken not only at the point of departure for the formalization of philosophy, but also as a privileged example useful for analyzing the concrete contents of their own ethnicity, in this case that of the articulation of ethics directed toward the good (*agathón*). This implies a *Hellenocentrism* that has grave consequences. Taylor's desired end for the reconstruction of the concept of the *Self* [237] would have been better served if he had explored Egyptian or Mesopotamian sources (as I have demonstrated in the first part of this introduction). But Taylor has recourse instead to Plato, thereby falling prey to the Hellenocentrism mentioned above. Paul Ricoeur had already demonstrated in his book *The Symbolic of Evil* [238] that the tragic myth of Prometheus (which Plato repeats with his doctrine of *ananke*) is radically opposed to the "Adamic myth," which suggests the structure of "temptation" as a dialectical process engaging free wills in contention (and it is certainly within the Adamic tradition that we should situate the "sources of the modern Self"). Taylor's Hellenocentrism completely distorts his research.

c. The third aspect of Taylor's methodology that I will mention is how for him, as for Hegel—who in this regard was the first philosopher to explore the issue [239] —the original diachronic process of Modernity can be tracked in a linear manner in terms of a succession from Augustine to Descartes to Locke, and so on. Such a seamless transition from Augustine (a thinker whose context was that of a Latin Mediterranean periphery of the Greek Hellenistic world) to Descartes (in seventeenth-century Amsterdam, at the center of the world system) would demand many explanations that are of no interest to Taylor. His interpretation of modern identity in this *Eurocentric*, regionalistic manner, without regard for the global meaning of Modernity, and by excluding Europe's own *periphery* as an additional relevant "source" for the constitution of the modern *Self* as such,[240] renders him incapable of discovering "certain" innovative aspects of "modern identity" and of the "sources of the self."

[47] These philosophers appear to have ignored the fact that the prob-

lem of "universality" has been posed in the context of Modernity in a manner *that has no precedent*. "Eurocentrism" is precisely characterized by the assumption that historical expressions of European *particularity* in fact constitute moments of *abstract human universality in general*. This reflects the singularity of European particularity as the first such identity that *in fact* became global, as the first concrete human expression of universality.[241] *Modern* European culture, civilization, philosophy, subjectivity, and so on thereby became identified as equivalent to the human universal abstractions of culture, civilization, philosophy, and subjectivity in general, *without further qualification*. But in fact, many of the most important achievements of Modernity were not exclusively European creations, but are instead the results of a continuous dialectic of impacts, effects, and responses between the European center and its periphery. This includes what might be described as the constitutive process, which has culminated in modern subjectivity as such. The *ego cogito*, as we have seen, has a direct relationship with a protohistory of the seventeenth century, which is reflected in Descartes's ontology, but which does not emerge from a void. The *ego conquiro* (I conquer) is its predecessor, as a "practical ego." Hernán Cortés's[242] conquest of Mexico in 1521 precedes *The Discourse on Method* (published in 1637) by more than a hundred years, as I have noted. Descartes studied at La Flèche, a Jesuit college belonging to a religious order which at that historical moment had extended itself throughout the American continent, Africa, and Asia; furthermore, as noted above, Descartes settled in 1629 in an Amsterdam that was at the center of a new world system. Nonetheless, the "barbarian" Other was not considered then to be part of the necessary context for all meaningful reflection regarding subjectivity, reason, or *cogito*.[243]

At the beginning of this section I quoted a statement by Max Weber that reflected his Eurocentrism. The question that should have been posed was: is it not the case that the chain of circumstances made it possible for certain cultural phenomena to be produced uniquely on European soil that, *contrary* to what has always been assumed and represented, and given Western Europe's conquest of a position *at the center* of the *world system*, provided it with comparative advantages that enabled the region to impose its system of domination over the rest of the cultures of the world, and in addition to impose its own culture upon them with universal claim? This question justifies a brief excerpt from Taylor:

> This [possessive individualism] is in effect merely an example within the context of a more generalized process through which certain practices of Modernity have been imposed, frequently in a brutal manner, *beyond their places of origin*. As to some of these, the process appears to have been part of an irresistible dynamic. Clearly the practices of technologically oriented

science contributed towards the technological advantage enjoyed by the nations where they were developed. This, combined with the consequences of the new-found emphasis upon the disciplinary movement which I described earlier, *gave European armies a marked and increasing military advantage over non-Europeans during the 17th century* up through the mid-20th century. And this, when combined with the practical economic consequences that we describe as capitalism, enabled the European powers to establish global hegemony for a certain period.[244]

As I discussed previously, according to Taylor, this comparative advantage only begins to take hold in the seventeenth century. This historical interpretation reflects a "substantialist"[245] approach, but in this case economic, technological, and military dimensions are alluded to but are absent in his book's subsequent analysis.

[48] Habermas falls into the same pattern. In effect, as he writes regarding critical counterdiscourses, he reflects a precise form of Eurocentrism; in *The Philosophical Discourse of Modernity* he writes:[246] "The change in paradigm from a rationality centered upon one subject to one based upon a communicative reasoning may be encouraging as we reinitiate *that counterdiscourse* [*Gegendiskurs*] which from the beginning has been *immanent* to Modernity. . . . This is a different way out which enables us to take into account, pursuant to different premises, the reasons for the self-criticism that Modernity has been undertaking in contradiction *with itself.*"[247] The new critique of reason undertaken by the postmodernists eliminates this counterdiscourse which is *immanent* (*innewohnenden*) to Modernity itself, which will very soon be "two hundred years old (!), which is what I am seeking to commemorate with these lectures."[248]

Modern Europe has created "the spiritual presuppositions and material bases of a world in which that mentality has usurped the place of reason — this is the true nucleus of a criticism that has been made of reason since Nietzsche. But who but Europe could wrest from its *own* [*eigenen*] traditions the penetration, the energy, and the will of vision and fantasy?"[249]

These texts clearly reflect Eurocentrism and also display the developmentalist fallacy.[250] In the first place, Habermas situates the origin of this counterdiscourse at a specific historical moment, that of Kant (which is why he refers to the two hundredth anniversary of this supposed advent). And so, if we approach history from a global perspective, anchored in a non-Eurocentrist vision of Modernity, this counterdiscourse in fact is more than five hundred years old: it was first heard on the island of Hispaniola in the Caribbean in 1511, when António de Montesinos assailed the injustices being committed against the indigenous peoples of this region, and echoed from there to the halls of the University of Salamanca, deepening the theoretical and practical labor of the critique initiated by Bartolomé de

Las Casas in 1514, and thereafter, when this nascent counterdiscourse was reflected in the lectures of Francisco de Vitoria (compiled in his seminal work entitled *De indiis*). Once again, as is typical among philosophers from Central Europe, the sixteenth century is irrelevant, and Latin America is simply absent from their mental landscape.

[49] Furthermore, since Modernity, from my perspective, is a global phenomenon, it was precisely this counterdiscourse, and none other, that had the possibility of arising in the context of European critical reason, as it opened itself up and constituted itself with and from the perspective of the alterity that was being dominated and exploited: from within the Other who it was thought had been hidden by European domination, which always sought to negate it. But this counterdiscourse, which is European in terms of its geographical implantation, is also a consequence within the European center of the dominated periphery. Bartolomé de Las Casas would not have been able to formulate and articulate his critique of the Spanish conquest of the Americas if he had not himself lived in the periphery and heard the cries and witnessed the tortures to which indigenous people were being submitted. It is that Other who is the actual origin of this counterdiscourse that took root in Europe. It is evident that Europe, as the visible point of the iceberg, possessed the cultural, economic, and political hegemony[251] necessary in order to *manage* this critique from the "centrality" of its system, which then monopolized humanity's ideological capital (as Pierre Bourdieu would describe it), which had the capacity to channel "information" as power. It is because of this that it became the most privileged site in the world for the discussion of global as well as philosophical issues (thereby constituting what we have come to know as modern philosophy). But this intellectual production, when it is counterhegemonic, even within European philosophy (for example, as in the cases of Montaigne, Pascal, Rousseau, or Marx), is not solely European: neither in terms of its origin nor its significance. Furthermore, the periphery has also had its own currents of intellectual and philosophical production (for example, Francisco Xavier Clavijero, 1731–87[252] in Mexico, who was a contemporary of Kant), whose own counterdiscourse was unintelligible to Europe, since it presupposed a much richer antihegemonic global vision or horizon, despite the scarcity of its provincial or regional *(re)sources*. Clavijero was unable to publish his works in Spanish in Mexico and had to publish them in exile in Italy. The cultures of the periphery were kept isolated from the world and from one another, and were connected only through Europe, where they were reinterpreted through the logic of the "center." As a result, "European" philosophy is not an exclusively European product but instead a *production of humanity that has been situated in Europe* as a center, which includes the contribution of the cultures of the periphery that have engaged it in an essential co-constitutive dialogue.

[50] To say that this counterdiscourse is *immanent* to Modernity would only be acceptable if Modernity were redefined on a global scale. In that case, Modernity must be understood to include its peripheral alterity. Modernity would then encompass all of the following: (1) its hegemonic core; (2) the *dominated* peripheral colonial world, as part of the "world system"; and (3) the sectors of the world that have been *excluded* from this system, as its exteriority. The alternative is to define Modernity exclusively from the perspective of a European horizon, and to contend that this counterdiscourse is also an *exclusively* European product. In that case, the periphery itself must make itself European in order to be able to criticize Europe, because it must employ a European counterdiscourse in order to demonstrate Europe's contradictions to itself, sunken amid its impotence to contribute anything new to the discussion, and condemned to negate itself in any case in the process.

If, to the contrary, this counterdiscourse is reconceived as a dialectical result of a critical dialogue from the perspective of alterity (which includes the affirmation of alterity, then, as a principle grounded in the negation of negation: an *analectical* moment), it is not possible to describe it as *exclusively and intrinsically* European, and even less persuasively as something unique which only Europe can "extract from its *own exclusive traditions*," or give continuance to. Instead, it is quite possible to affirm that it is from *outside of Europe* that this counterdiscourse can be developed most critically, and not as the continuation of an alien or *uniquely* European discourse, but rather as the next step in a process of critical labor upon which the periphery has already left its stamp within the counterdiscourse produced in Europe and through its *own* peripheral *discourse*. Indeed, almost as a matter of course, when the discourse at issue is not Eurocentric it is already virtually a counterdiscourse in itself, built upon the basis of that which is peripheral or dominated within the world system, and grounded in the affirmation of the exteriority of the excluded.

This is why the study of thought (traditions and philosophy) in Latin America, Asia, and Africa is not a task that is anecdotal or parallel to the study of philosophy *as such* (which would be that which is European in character) but instead involves the *recovery* of a history that incorporates the counterdiscourse that is nonhegemonic and that has been dominated, silenced, forgotten, and virtually excluded—that which constitutes the alterity of Modernity. Kant (a key hegemonic philosopher), or later Marx (a counterdiscourse within Europe) and Clavijero (an excluded philosopher from the periphery) will be studied in the future as exemplifying two faces of the same epoch of human thought. Certainly Kant, because of his hegemonic context (situated empirically in Europe, in the cities of the Hanseatic region), has produced a critical philosophy that is the match of the best of its equivalents on a global scale, and which can be considered to be the point of departure for all philosophy throughout the world for the last two hundred years. Kant, in the strictest sense, is not exclusively a European thinker, but instead one who had the capacity (because of his historical, political, economic, and cultural context) to devise a critical philosophy of *global* relevance. But the philosophical thought of Clavijero, which until now has had only regional importance (in a peripheral, dominated region),[253] and which has been all too quickly forgotten by many, even in the Mexico of his origin, is the "other face" of Modernity, and, because of this, has an equivalent "global" relevance. Kant and Clavijero are part of the sphere of philosophical strivings within the same global horizon, fragmented by lines that demarcated the center, the periphery, and zones of exclusion during the eighteenth century. Future histories of philosophy will have a new *global* vision of philosophy and will delve more deeply into currently unexamined aspects, which will uncover key elements of the *joint configuration* of a global set of themes in the periphery (which also produced a peripheral and critical philosophy of its own, grounded in the affirmation of its excluded exteriority) and in the center of the world system (which produced a philosophy of the European center, which up until the present has been identified with philosophy "as such"). The philosophy of the center and that of the periphery (identified with those oppressed by or simply excluded from the world system) are two sides of the same philosophical coin in Modernity, and its counterdiscourses (both in the center as in the periphery) are the heritage of philosophers throughout the world, not just of Europeans.

[51] This is an essential point of departure for my philosophical project as a whole. The *Philosophy of Liberation* is a counterdiscourse, a critical philosophy born in the periphery (from the perspective of the victims, the excluded), which has the intention of being relevant on a global scale. It has an *explicit* consciousness of its peripheral and excluded character, but at the same time it has the intention and commitment of embracing and engaging the complexity of the world as a whole. It has emerged from, and is committed to pursuing a conscious confrontation with, European or North American schools of philosophy (both postmodern and modern, proceduralist and communitarian, etc.), which confound and even identify their concrete European origins with their unrecognized function as "philosophies of the center" throughout the last five hundred years. A clear differentiation in the study of philosophies of European origin between those concretely grounded in European identity as such (the European *Sittlichkeit* itself); those originating in Europe's function as "center" in the world system; and those of truly universal character in the strictest sense, would produce an awakening of European philosophy from the deep sleep in

which it has been submerged since its modern origins, five hundred years after the birth of Eurocentrism.

It is necessary to be *explicitly* conscious of this ever-present "horizon" of the colonial or barbarous Other, and of the cultures in an asymmetrical, dominated, "inferior,"[254] excluded position, as an essential, permanent *source* or resource in the joint configuration and constitution of the identity of the "modern self." The failure to consider this Other in the constitution of the "modern self" in effect nullifies Taylor's historical analysis, given its Eurocentric character. From such a truncated analysis the only thing that can emerge is one aspect of the modern self that revolves around its own center. This is something quite distinct from the dialectically constituted Modernity reconstructed from the perspective of its negated alterity ("situated [*gesetzt*]" in the Hegelian sense of a non-self-identified,[255] alienated being), from the perspective of the other face of the coin of Modernity.[256]

[52] I had intended to close this section, which is already too long, with a survey of current philosophical thinking in the world of the periphery,[257] but will instead summarize certain illustrative aspects here in an abbreviated manner. What I have written in previous sections regarding the contributions of Asia (§§I.1–I.3 and, in part, §I.4) and regarding the Islamic world (§I.4) serves to outline the exploration of fundamental aspects of philosophy in the historical era that predates Modernity. For its part, in the context of Modernity, the problematic of Bantu Africa is prototypical, while Latin America has a kind of intermediate specificity.[258] In contrast, contemporary Asia has an ancient philosophical profile at its roots.[259] It is impossible to encompass all of this complexity in this book, so I have decided to focus on one aspect of the debate regarding the philosophy of the periphery: the contemporary dimensions of "African philosophy."[260]

[53] Some have reminded us that Egyptian-Bantu philosophy lies at the origins of Greek philosophy,[261] although more recent stages of this process of reflection are focused on the "peripheral self" of African philosophy subsequent to the era of colonial emancipation—from 1945 to the present.[262] Students of this process agree with the description of its first moment as that of "ethno-philosophy"—Tempels,[263] for example, sets forth an ontology of "vital forces" where the "dogmatic employment of the fundamental principles of Western philosophy"[264] is evident; while the work of Kagame[265] marks an advance toward an emphasis on the African origins of this overall process of implantation. The second moment could be understood as that of "philosophic sagacity,"[266] which seeks to recover the traditions of African popular wisdom, although the strictly philosophical dimensions of this thought are the subject of debate. The third moment (in a nonchronological sense) is that of "ideological philosophy,"[267] which includes the theoretical production of the leaders of Africa's process of colo-

nial and national liberation.[268] The fourth moment could be described as the "professional philosophy" of Africa.[269] We must then add a fifth moment, of African critical philosophy,[270] which is of greatest interest to us here. Among all the recent work in this vein, I focus on one specific example because of its suggestive depth of reflection regarding the theme of human existence in the world of the periphery of Modernity, a reflection whose point of departure is excluded alterity understood as a form of resistance: Eboussi Boulaga's *The Crisis of "Muntu": African Authenticity and Philosophy*.[271]

[54] Eboussi Boulaga, like all critical philosophers from the periphery, situates himself in the face of Modernity—undertaking a critique that appears to be very similar, on the surface, to that of the postmodern philosophers[272]—from a "point of departure" quite distinct from that of European/North American philosophy: "The polarity between the dominator and the dominated has repercussions in all of the spheres where the contradiction repeats between those who exist and those who do not, and of those who have with respect to those who do not. The vanquished are defined by their privations, which proclaim the superiority of their master as their negation. . . . Philosophy thereby takes upon itself the trappings of an allegory regarding the Power of the conqueror, among its many other activities and objects."[273] The *Muntu*[274] negates itself and is always found in asymmetry[275]—"in this sense the lowest, most abject, perverse or incapable white person is always superior."[276] But when the African seeks to affirm his or her exteriority he or she has no exit available, and even less so if he or she turns to Western philosophy: "Logically the negation of the negation of itself occupies the space of the empty affirmation of the self, in search of its attributes, as well as those of human beings in general, along the paths of freedom, the ideology of development, as well as those of the State and of efficiency."[277]

Here, Eboussi Boulaga undertakes an ontological description of unequalled interest (which could not be carried out by a "foreign"[278] anthropologist), exposing what could be described as the analysis of excluded African alterity through its transformation into positive criticism, and drawing upon some ad hoc philosophical images and categories that he has created. Let us stop for a moment to focus on certain aspects of his exposition, which he himself highlights as those that are most risky:[279] "That which is real is that which preserves that *which is original*, within. . . . That which is real is that which preserves *the original* within itself along with that which has its origin in the hierarchical and the genealogical. That which is real is that which preserves *the original* as its destiny in a reintegrated form."[280] The "real" (and the sacred) is a referent for that which is "original" both in the past and in the present, the "vital force" that is expressed through the "word,"[281] the "name," the "verb," the "language," the "custom," "ethnicity,"[282] the "individual."[283] The "real" is the excluded, exterior and prior to the peripheral self of the oppressed, which has an "order," "hierarchy," and "genealogy" of its own, which can direct us back to the original: "Succeeding generations determine and assess the place of individuals according to the extent to which they are closer or farther from the distance that separates them from their origin or which reflects these origins in the present and makes them contemporary through their representation. . . . Authenticity is nothing but the permanent authorization of origin; it is the permanence of original force."[284]

This is why "tradition" becomes "mediation," which "symbolically" unifies the genealogical plurality and the universal "harmony" that becomes contemporary through "knowledge" (Odera Oruka's *Philosophic Sagacity*): "Knowledge is the celebration of the vital force of reintegration. Knowledge is the knowledge of the symbolic self of things which enables connection and mediation."[285] The "system," the entirety of the universe, lives in time marked by "periodicity" and "rhythm":

> Time passes and returns, the force that expands and begins again manifests the eternity of Power in its incessant emanation and expansion from its origin. . . . Periodicity is the substantial time of things. . . . Everything is alternation and rhythm. . . . Rhythm is vital. . . . It is rhythm which produces ecstasy, that flowing out of one's self that is identified with the vital force. . . . It would not be exaggerated to affirm that rhythm is the *architectural framework of the self*, which for the human being of the civilization for which this philosophy is expounded, is the most fundamental experience, which eludes all of the trappings of malign genius [as Descartes would put it], which remains free of all doubt, and which is *Je danse, donc je vie* [I dance, therefore I am alive].[286]

This expression could in fact perfectly summarize all of *Ethics of Liberation*, as an ethics of the body and its reality and an ethics of life, as we shall see in what follows. It is through "assimilation" that the individual "imitates" the original or the authentic, which confers an "analogical" property upon it. Existence becomes a "metaphor" of that which is original through "representation" and "substitution." Through the function of the seer, and the "*divination*" of individuals, their contemporary imaginary becomes identified with their primordial nature and vainly seeks to annihilate the individual, the demoniacal, evil, illness, the Enemy in general, reintegrating this target into the harmonious order of the primordial: "Since the paradise of innocence is a dream, the ontologies of force and global systems are the ontologies and systems of human irresponsibility."[287] This great African philosopher comes to a conclusive judgment: "The global system reveals the misery of its content which drives it towards sterility, to the monotonous repetition of empty and grandiloquent affirmations."[288]

[55] What are the implications of such a reflection? What is the character of a philosophical reflection undertaken from this perspective of African material alterity? Eboussi Boulaga, with rigorous precision, clearly confronts this problem. Such an experience of life cannot be negated irresponsibly (and this is what critical ethnophilosophy must reconstruct in depth); it is not viable, either, to return to the source of the original in the past in a folkloric manner, with the claim that it is more ancient than that of Europe, and that a predatory Europe seized upon it for inspiration; but it is not possible either to simply adopt the modern project: "The circle of the dialectic negates the pathetic, and the problematic that is represented in the consciousness of the *Muntu* which is torn between *two worlds*, pulled between the past and the present, and not knowing how to reconcile them. This rhetorical theme which is rich with accompanying effects is not thought expressly. The *Muntu* is one and so is the world. Together they constitute the unity of multiple contradiction. Their unity is in fact nothing but a *process of unification*."[289]

Meanwhile, we have to prepare the way. We must dismantle the philosophy that has been "institutionalized" in the "symbolics of domination,"[290] which in Africa is, itself, and in the first place, the "effective exercise of power and domination."[291] This philosophy is the concrete expression of an "authoritarian" practice that accords a privileged status to Greece as European and discredits other cultures; which legitimizes colonialism and justifies European particularism as if it were universal: "*Philosophy* is one of the symbols and institutions which the West has transported beyond its bounds and has offered up as a means to assimilate others."[292] Eboussi Boulaga's task is that of an authentic project directed at the liberation "of philosophy." The point of departure of the debate is the "linguistic question":[293] "Everything begins when the *Muntu* experiences the shipwreck of its word drowned in insignificance, in the possibility of non-meaning. This comes about when it can still speak but can no longer make itself understood, like an animal that growls or a barbarian who sputters."[294] What we must do is to take tradition as our point of departure (thereby recovering in part the intention of North American communitarianism), but understanding it as a "critical utopia" which can only be attained through its transcendence.[295] It is necessary to use and reuse philosophy, but comprehending it as a medium to "become free." But this is not yet a reality: "The *Muntu* passes its time becoming conscious of what has passed, and as to what *the violence of history has made of it*. It passes time understanding the uselessness of apologetics, and through them, of abstract universality. Nobody is convinced by its discussion, and in any case it is still not heard with seriousness, because what is denied to it, what is stolen, is its tongue. It is nothing but a barbarian."[296] Philosophy, and ethics in particular, thus must *free themselves from "Eurocentrism"*[297] in order to become empirically, materially, and factually global from the perspective of the affirmation of its excluded alterity, in order now to enable the deconstructive analysis of its "peripheral self." Hegemonic philosophy has been the fruit of a process of rethinking the world through the lens of domination. It has not attempted to be the expression of a truly global experience, and much less of a process of reflection undertaken from the perspective of those excluded from the world system; it has been trapped instead in a regional perspective with claims of universality (through the negation of the particularity of other cultures). This is why in the histories of philosophy in common use it is only the Greco-Roman world that is highlighted at stage II of the history of the interregional system; and in stage III, only a small part of the Islamic world (and nothing of the wisdom of the East); in Modernity, only Europe is left standing. Until now, the "hegemonic philosophical community" (European and North American)[298] has not accorded any recognition to the philosophical discourses of the worlds that today constitute the periphery of the world system. And this *recognition of the dignity* of other discourses of Modernity *outside of Europe* is a practical task that the ethics of liberation seeks to render inevitable, visible, and peremptory. Such recognition of the discourses of the Other, of the victims who have been oppressed and excluded, is in fact the first constitutive moment of the ethical process which is necessary in order to undertake the liberation of philosophy.

PART I

Foundation of Ethics

[56] In part I, we enter fully into the exposition of the *foundation*[1] of this *Ethics of Liberation*. It concerns an ethics of life, from out of its negation in actuality. The argumentative strategy will always be to analyze each one of the *necessary*, but not *sufficient*, moments until a level of complexity is reached where *sufficiency* would seem to be given. However, as we will see, the complete sufficiency of the ethical validity of the praxis, individual or communitarian, and its ultimate consequences, institutional and historical, can never be reached fully, given that it would encompass the totality of human actions in the entire history of the world.

I will analyze the necessary moments of ethics, that is, the material or content aspect of ethics (figure 3) in chapter 1, the formal or procedural aspect in chapter 2, and ethical feasibility as process in chapter 3. In this way, I will have presented the *foundations*, or the process of the construction of the "established order": the *"goodness claim"* (A). In part II, we will arrive at the proper point of departure for the ethics of liberation: for ethics as material critique in chapter 4, the system now appears as dominant. Thus is opened a new path to a new antihegemonic *consensual validity* from alterity in chapter 5. All of this culminates in the praxis and the institutional transformation or construction of a new ethical life in chapter 6, a critical feasibility that, by necessity and sufficiency, will always be a process of liberation.

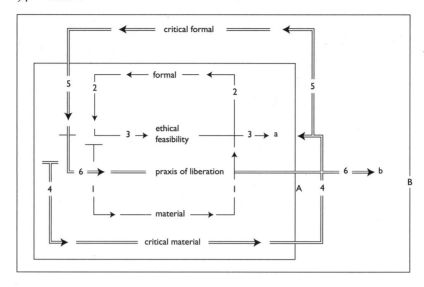

Figure 3. The six moments of the architechtonic of an ethics of liberation.

NOTE: *Fundamentals*: 1: ethical-material aspect; 2: moral-formal aspect; 3: ethical-procedural feasibility; a: the current ethical project: "goodness claim." *Ethical critique, antihegemonic validity and praxis of liberation*: 4: critical ethical-material aspect; A: the ruling ethical system (including the postconventional), which appears before critique as the "Totality"; 5: antihegemonic critical moral-formal aspect; 6: ethical-critical feasibility or praxis of liberation (construction of a new ethical system); b: project of liberation; B: future new ethical system.

CHAPTER I

The Material Moment of Ethics
Practical Truth

[57] This is an ethics of life; that is to say, human life is the content of ethics. For this reason, I want to forewarn the reader, here and at the outset, about the meaning of a material ethics or ethics of content.[1] The project of an ethics of liberation unfolds in in its own way from the exercise of an ethical critique (which I present in chapter 4), where the negated dignity of the life of the victim, oppressed or excluded, is affirmed. Chapter 1, on the material content of ethics, is certainly the most difficult part of my discussion and the one that will raise the most suspicions. I present it not because I want to ground a Darwinist or naturalist[2] (neo-Aristotelian, communitarian, axiological, or any other) material ethics but because it is necessary to clarify on behalf of the victims, of the dominated or excluded, the material aspect of ethics, in order to ground it well and to be able to take the critical step from it (chapters 4–6). I am aware that I could be criticized as "rationalist" or "foundationalist," "vitalist," "irrationalist," or "materialist." However, my position is different from all of those positions.

In this chapter, I attempt to indicate some elements—only *some*—of a universal principle of all ethics, especially of critical ethics: the principle of the obligation to produce, reproduce, and develop the concrete human life of each ethical subject in community. This principle claims universality. It is actualized through cultures and motivates them from within, as well as the values or the different ways of accomplishing the "good life," happiness, and so on. But none of these instances is ever the universal principle of human life. The principle penetrates them all and moves them to their self-fulfillment. Cultures, for instance, are particular modes of life, modes that are moved by the universal principle of human life of each subject in community from within. Every norm, action, microstructure, institution, or cultural ethical life always and necessarily has as its ultimate *content* some moment of the production, reproduction, and development *of the human life* in the concrete. The limit act that would seem not to have life itself as content—suicide—is in no way an exception. The suicide, in the first place, cannot justify ethically his absolute self-negation; nor can he ground on suicide a posterior ethical act or a social order, given that he negates himself as a subject of every posterior action. Furthermore, if, exhausted, hopeless, or suffering, one were to "take one's life," one would be presupposing one's life always, since it is precisely because concrete life has lost meaning that this person seeks to extinguish it—unlivable life grounds the possibility of negating life: suicide. I will return in a future work to this grounding, against the cynic who claims to justify death, thus committing a performative contradiction. For now, I want to "situate" the structural place of the question. But grounding "against cynics," when these claim to ethically justify death, it is necessary to show, from the absolute dignity of human life, the injustice or perversity that determines the negated existence of victims. My ultimate intention is to justify the struggle of victims, of the oppressed, for their liberation: reason is only "the cunning of life" of the human subject—and not the inverse—and, as such, we use it and defend it before the necrophiliacs (the lovers of the death of victims, the oppressed, the impoverished, of women, nonwhite races, peoples of the South, Jews, the old, street children, the future generations, and so on). For this reason, I recommend, in order to understand the importance and sense of this material, or its ethical content, that one first read chapter 4, which is the initial critical theme of this ethics of liberation. In fact, in chapter 1 the possibility of negating what is negated is grounded *affirmatively* as the origin of the material critical process of ethics, which will be described in part II, on ethical critique. After reading chapter 4, the importance of the *positive* material ethics that we now describe will be understood better.

[58] It is a matter of following a long path, but from its correct "beginning" (the *Anfang* of Hegel or Marx), in this case, through its content. I will present the *material*[3] moment of ethics, which, contrary to Kant, has a universality that I will show in its moment. Kant writes: "All practical principles that presuppose an *object* (matter)[4] of the faculty of desire as the determining ground of the will are, without exception, empirical and can furnish no practical laws."[5] Practical laws are universal, and it would seem that the "appetitive faculty" is necessarily particular, egoistical. In another, earlier text Kant expresses it even more clearly: "To preserve one's life is a duty,[6] and besides everyone has an immediate inclination to do so. But on this account the often anxious care that most people take of it[7] still has no inner worth and their maxim has no moral content."[8] It is a matter, precisely, of the question of the criterion and the material principle of ethics,

as much because of its content (the conservation of human life) as because of the inclination, the drive, or affectivity that tends toward their conservation. I will show that the so-called inclination (*Neigung*), "appetitive faculty," or "desire" can also have universality.[9] But, in addition, as we will see, the human affective-evaluative system acts while fulfilling the indicated material principle of ethics, which is both necessary and universal. We will see in due course that the mere "material" dimension (spelled with "a" in German) is not sufficient for the fulfillment of the "goodness claim" of the maxim, act, institution, or system of ethical life. Other criteria or ethical-moral principles will be necessary for their fulfillment, such as the areas of consensuality of moral validity or the feasibility of mediations, in order to effectively reach "goodness."[10] It is a matter of the articulation of numerous criteria and principles of ethics, and of the construction of many categories that are frequently defined unilaterally.

Moreover, we will have to pass beyond the reductionistic dualism (of Descartes, Kant, or the "Enlightenment") that situated in a hypothetical "soul" what ethics is needed in order to present its theme and that, because of its dualistic "metaphysical anthropology," deformed from the outset all possible posterior analysis. But, in addition, having fixed our attention on "consciencism," we have lost the entire level of the self-organizing process of life, including even the processes of self-regulated social life, which are not discovered by conscience since it is a matter of structures that are partly nonintentional.

§1.1. The Human Cerebral Cognitive and Affective-Appetitive System

[59] Ethics should give importance to those self-organized or self-regulated processes of life, since the modern, exaggerated, and unilateral importance of "consciencism" results in the loss of the organic corporeality of ethical existence. Consciousness does not need to always intervene, but it is determinative in "critical" intervention, and corrects nonintentional negative or perverse effects. For this reason, I will make a quick propaedeutic detour into a topic of extreme currency, which, paradoxically, has only recently begun to awaken the attention that it deserves among philosophers.[11] It concerns the empirical studies of the biology of the brain that will allow us, without falling into reductionism or into ethical naturalism or Darwinism, to recuperate the dimension of the *corporeality* with organic processes that are highly self-referential — hence left to the side by the formal moralities — in order to frame more strictly the not always valid claims of material ethics.[12] We should take into account the difference, always present even in the long run, between the neurological "fact" and the reflexive "fact"

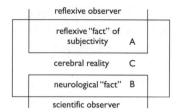

Figure 4. The neurological and reflexive "facts" of subjectivity.

NOTE: "Fact" A is constituted from the standpoint of the psychological, psycho-analytical analysis or quotidian experience of reflection, as when I say, "I am tired." "Fact" B is constituted from observations of the neurobiological sciences. Asymptotically, fact A will never be fact B. Were this identification to be produced, one would "subjectively" feel as electrical the electric current that is produced when the synapses of a neuron or nerve cell "communicate" with another: this is empirically impossible. However, both "facts" A and B are aspects of one and the same "reality" C. In this way, it is not neurological naturalism to claim that real life (C) — neurologically observable (B) — is the criterion of truth (in A). The material fact B is the "carrier" of the psychological or reflexive fact. This real life, in its production, reproduction, and development, always requires, in turn, for its concrete fulfillment, the formal and moral principle. "Truth" becomes "valid" only via recourse to formal intersubjectivity. The moment of formal morality intervenes not because of an ethical defect but instead because of the necessity for the valid application of the material principle, without which there would be no ethical goodness, as we will see.

of subjectivity, although the second is materially "carried" by the first (see figure 4).

Humberto Maturana[13] proposes three degrees of "organic units" of life.

a. The *unity of the first degree* is given in the living cell. All physical matter that constitutes our corporeality is as old as the universe (more than thirteen billion years).[14] All the living cells of our corporeality, which are products of reproductive divisions of living cells, are part of a *continuum* that has been living since the origin of life on the earth (about four billion years ago).[15] We are a moment of autopoietic life: "By realizing what characterizes living beings in their autopoietic organization, we can unify a whole lot of empirical data about their biochemistry and cellular functioning. The concept of autopoiesis, therefore, does not contradict these data. Rather[, it] . . . stresses that living beings are *autonomous* entities."[16] The metabolism of *internal* dynamics of the cell (autopoietic and autonomous) reacts to the *environment* through its mitochondria and membranes, its boundaries, inaugurating a process of autogenesis.

b. The *unity of the second degree* is produced in metacellular organisms (multicellular, from mushrooms to the higher mammals). Metacellular ontogenesis is a process of cellular phylogenesis. Evolution consists in perturbations that are conserved autopoietically through adaptation.[17] The appearance of the nervous system allows the organism then to "expand the dominion of possible behavior when it grants the organism a tremendously versatile and plastic structure,"[18] which grants it, in turn (through the system of sensorimotor coordination), a greater mobility.[19]

c. The *unity of the third degree* is fulfilled in social phenomena (from beehives to the higher primates). Ants "communicate" by continually passing one another nourishing chemical substances (trophallaxis). Higher animals use interactive behaviors of the gestural, postural, or tactile type. The unity of the third degree, which includes ontogenetic and phylogenetic behaviors of greater complexity, is the "linguistic dominion among participant organisms."[20] Let us look at this with greater attention.

[60] Gerald Edelman[21] describes in neurological-scientific terms the functioning of the brain. The brain, the internal moment of human corporeality, is a "selective recognition system"[22] that proceeds on the basis of interconnected neural groups. In the first place, in the same way as the immune system or the evolutionary process of the species, the cerebral nervous system acts through selection,[23] starting from the universal criterion of becoming permanent and enabling reproduction and development, to nurture the life of the human subject, and this from the plant level to the most heroic and sublime cultural or ethical levels. Antonio Damasio tells us in his *Descartes' Error* that "several hours after a meal your blood sugar level drops, and neurons in the hypothalamus detect the change; activation of the pertinent innate pattern makes the brain alter the body state so that the probability for correction can be increased; you feel hungry, and initiate actions to end your hunger; you eat, and the ingestion of food brings about a correction in blood sugar,[24] this time an increase, and the appropriate neurons place the body in the state whose experience constitutes the feeling of satiety."[25] As the reader might imagine, this is a radical simplification of an immensely bigger process (a trillion times more complex). In any event, all of this is part of the functions that are fulfilled by the brain—as functions of ethical corporeality, which we are dealing with here. That is to say, the brain is the organ directly responsible for the human subject's "continuing to live," via reproduction and the development of the human life of the organism, of the communitarian and historical corporeality of the ethical subject.

[61] Let us now look at the functions of the brain as nonintentional, self-organized, and self-regulated processes of life, which *always act as a whole*, although a few of these functions refer more directly to some internal organs that frequently constitute "circuits," where the currents of neural information "enter," "exit," or "return" in diverse mutually implicated movements.

The stimulus (or simply the perception of reality)[26] of the external world

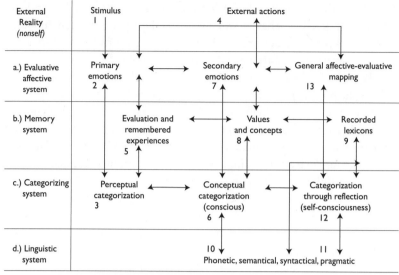

Figure 5. Some moments or higher functions of the brain.

NOTES:

   1. The moments (functions) are situated
      a. In the brain, principally in the limbic system and in the base of the brain (the oldest organs in the evolutionary process of the brain).
      b. In different cerebral regions (especially in regions with "mappings").
      c. Principally in the thalamus-cortical region (frontal, parietal, temporal).
      d. In the most recent cortical region, especially in the Broca and Wernicke regions.
      e. With self-organized corporeality.
   2. Moments 9 through 13 develop at the end of the evolutionary process of the higher species.

(moment 1 in figure 5) makes itself present through a signal that is received by the brain, through specialized neural receptive and transmitting mediations that bring about as a result, after other moments, a "perceptual categorization" (moment 3)[27] through selective recognition, adaptive to the reproduction of the life of the organism, as noted earlier. In this way, "maps"[28] or structures of groups of neurons begin to form that react in similar ways in the future, although never in the same way, before a "memory" or a "new recall." Once there are enough maps, the brain can begin a more complex function, called "global mapping": "A global mapping is a dynamic structure containing multiple local maps with entries and exits (both motor and sensory) that are able to interact with non-mapped parts of the brain."[29]

[62] What is most important for the goals of an ethics is that the process follows a "path" that includes not only the thalamocortical region (a recent formation in human evolution and unique because of uncommon cerebral development of the genus *Homo*), but also, before that, the limbic system and the base of the brain (the oldest, already present in insects and reptiles, for example): "Categorization always occurs in reference to internal criteria of value and this reference defines its appropriateness. Such value criteria[30] do not determine specific categorizations but they constrain the domains in which they occur. . . . [T]he bases for value systems in the animals of a given species are already set by evolutionary selection."[31]

To put it in another way: in order to construct its object,[32] the process of categorization requires "passage" through the "evaluative-affective" system (essentially constituted by the limbic system and the base of the brain, as already noted), where some of its organs are the hypothalamus, the ganglia, the hippocampus, and the thalamus, which give the "green light" (or "red light") to the categorizing process that follows. What cause requires such a "circuit" through the affective-evaluative system (moment 5 of figure 5)? It is a matter of having to "determine," "confirm," and "judge," no less, the manner in which, or how, the categorized "allows" or "opposes" the continuation or growth of the life of the organism, of the corporeality as totality, of which the brain itself is only a functional part. The human brain holds this criterion as a fundamental "criterion of truth." When an insect or a mammal perceives through its senses another animal, for example, it "perceives-evaluating" that animal as "dangerous" or as "mediation" for the survival of the organism in question (it must make the distinction between "enemy" or "nourishment," for example). If it did not have this evaluative capacity, the individual would die, and if all specimens lost this capacity, they would disappear as a species. It is a question of life or death.[33] What is positively "worthy" (the norm or the maxim that is judged—by a judgment of fact)[34] is what allows the reproduction of life. "Value"[35] (here the evaluation by judgment that coordinates what is to operate from the criterion of truth) is no more than the fact that such mediation (the object or judgment in question) allows survival, that is, what is "kept" by memory in the repertoire of past experiences in certain neural groups, which can be "recalled" again, "remembered," in order to accept or not accept these stimuli (in an intuitive fashion, without explicit judgment, and in nonhuman species not at all syntactically or linguistically).[36] If this neural "memory" is wrong in its recall of the affective evaluation, the organism (the insect or the mammal) could be destroyed, as already noted, by things, organisms, or other *real* moments, the "danger" of which it was not aware at the time.[37]

[63] This is something new and important: the exercise of the affective-

evaluative system (moments 2 or 5) (the evaluation beforehand of the same explicit and abstract "value judgment," of the same subject or predicate of "judgment of fact" of instrumental reason, even) is an originary constitutive moment of the very act of theoretical-practical and empirical capturing, par excellence, of categorization: "No selectively based system works value-free. Values are necessary constraints on the adaptive working of a species. . . . Undoubtedly, these value systems also underlie the higher-order constructions that make up individual aims and purposes. *We categorize on value*.[38] . . . Science has turned out to be eminently practical, as it must be, given its service to the verifiable truth."[39] With the "matter" of the perceptual categorization (moment 3), the human brain accomplishes a second function: "*conceptual* categorization":

> The brain areas responsible for *concept formation* contain structures that categorize, discriminate, and recombine the various brain activities occurring *in different kinds of global mappings*. . . . They must represent *a mapping of types of maps*. . . . The frontal cortex is a prime example of a conceptual center in the brain.[40] Given its connections to the basal ganglia and the limbic system, including the hippocampus, the frontal cortex also establishes relations subserving the *categorization of values* and sensory experiences themselves. In this way, conceptual memories are affected by values[41]—an important characteristic in enhancing survival.[42]

Just as the affective-evaluative system constitutes a moment of the process of categorization, conceptual categorization reorganizes the system of values,[43] ordering them, in turn, also on the basis of the criterion of the reproduction and development of the life of the human organic subject (in order to be simultaneously subsumed in linguistic-cultural criteria) (moment 8).

[64] For its part, the "primary consciousness" of something (in level 6) is reached, at least, by the degree of evolution of the higher mammals, which have a sufficient limbic system and conceptual memory, and a neural connection that connects the cortex with the thalamus. This allows the "continual reentrant signaling between the value-category memory and the ongoing global mappings that are concerned with perceptual categorizations in real time."[44] "To be conscious" of this as "nourishment" (or as a "poison") supposes that one is able to make the distinction between "self" (not yet an "I") and the "nonself," and to have the capacity to confront what faces the organisms with the memory of what is itself remembered (Edelman's *remembered present*). What is most relevant for philosophy in Edelman's work is his neurobiological explication of self-consciousness.

In fact, self-consciousness (level 12)—which seems now to be a phenomenon present initially, in some fashion, in some higher species—

presupposes in turn language (level 11 of figure 5)—situated mainly in the Broca and Wernicke cortical regions—which is not identified with the function of conceptual categorization and which presupposes it.

The upright posture of the higher primates[45] allowed *Australopithecus* to accelerate the evolutionary process, which culminated in the species *Homo sapiens*. First came the development of the regions of the brain where phonetic capacities resided, the epigenetic products of learning from memory, which allowed humans to increase and remember a lexicon that had meaning, a semantic process with perceptive-conceptual content: "Meaning arises from the interaction of value-category [8] memory with the combined activity of conceptual areas [6] and speech areas [10]."[46] For Humberto Maturana, language is not a primary mode of operation of the nervous system.[47] On the contrary, it is an ad hoc subsystem, phylogenetically developed by *Homo sapiens* (which developed the cerebral cortex through evolution) in order to name and communicate a global perceptual world that without any language would not allow the management of "objects" in different and analytical manners.

[65] The *human* "unity of the third degree"—of Maturana—is then given in language, since this is not only a neurological or genetic moment, but also a cultural product.[48] The hominids, to which group we belong, have existed for more than fifteen million years; *Homo habilis* existed four million years ago. In this time, "learned behavioral cooperation and coordination" was developed through language, which granted the resources to creatively accumulate an indefinite quantity of new distinctions among "objects" that would not be able to be manipulated without language—in the first place the distinction between environment and language: "We find ourselves in this convergence, not as the origin of a reference or in reference to an origin, but as a mode of continuous transformation in the development of a world of language that we build with other human beings."[49]

Syntax (not only genetic), as well as the process of conceptual categorization, produces complex structures of relations of neural groups that establish their rules out of a spoken, phonetic practice (long before that of writing; I am thinking now of Jacques Derrida).[50]

[66] Self-consciousness can be obtained when corporeality, because of the higher functions of the brain, the so-called mind, can be comprehended and named (and now in a more radical fashion than in the mere "consciousness") as a "self"[51] (or an "us") clearly distinct from the "nonself" and the "you," "he," "she," or "they." Thus emerges the possibility of the reflection and self-reference of the subject (the "self") on itself ("oneself"), as the subject becomes conscious of its knowing as a conscious subject and of belonging to a community of speakers that is different from "its" merely given reality, from out of a past horizon, lexically remembering inasmuch as it is

.the resource of the language of a community, overflowing into the future as a historical project: "Higher-order consciousness adds socially constructed selfhood to this picture of biological individuality. The freeing of parts of conscious thought from the constraints of an immediate present and the increased richness of social communication allow for the anticipation of future states and for planned behavior. With that ability come the abilities to model the world, to make explicit comparisons, and to weigh outcomes; through such comparisons comes the possibility of reorganizing plans."[52]

[67] Here I want to touch on a theme that is of great importance to ethics and it concerns the already mentioned evaluative-affective cerebral system. This is, in fact, the complex cerebral subsystem examined in the writings of James and Lange, and Cannon and Bard (published in 1929), and described by the "Papez circle" (from 1937 onward).[53] I want to foreground in this cerebral system the simple "sensations" (such as those of "pain" or "pleasure")[54] of the "primary and secondary emotions," as Damasio calls them in his work.[55]

In the first place, stimuli can cause "pain" or "pleasure."[56] It is necessary to recall that these sensations are not emotions; they are products of stimuli that irritate or hurt, that soothe or produce agreeable states, that is to say, they sensitize the receptive cells, in a pleasurable or painful manner. Certain substances, *endorphins*, for example, can inhibit the sensation of pain; others, such as caffeine, can disinhibit sensations in general. In principle (that is to say, as fundamental objective state), what leads to the reproduction of life produces pleasure; pain as a system of warning announces death, ultimately. In order to ground the ethical validity of this criterion, and also the exceptions or conflicts that are present in the application of its corresponding principle, which Kant understood only as the exclusive expression of egoism (egoism that is confused with the nature of inclinations), it will be necessary to have recourse to other criteria or principles, as I will show in chapter 2. To perceive in the corporeal state the result of pleasure or pain constitutes the complex phenomenon of the emotions.

The perception of a stimulus can produce, for example, the "emotion" of "fear"—moment 2 of figure 5 (due to the evaluation of some possible "dangerous" moment of such a stimulus), which can be followed by an action (moment 4) because of an innate capacity (such as that of the child's strong embrace of her mother, which reminds us of the primate, clinging to the fur of its mother) or the fruit of learning (as getting ready to act in defense of life): "Such features, individually or conjunctively, would be processed and then detected by a component of the brain's limbic system, say, the amygdala; its neurons' nuclei possess a dispositional representation,[57] which triggers the enactment of a body state characteristic of the emotion of fear."[58] These "body states" affect the entire structure of corporeality (at the endochronological, chemical, neurological, muscular, psychological, and other levels), thus constituting the "basic mechanism" of the primary emotion. This process involves what Levinas describes as "subjectivity" and "psychicness," which are not cognitive, representative, or eidetic moments.

[68] The "secondary emotion" (moment 7 of figure 5) is a "reflex experience of the primary emotion," which can produce an accelerated heartbeat, blushing, tense muscles, and overactive endocrinal glands, as well as affect the immune system. In this case, there is an actualization (by different *mappings*) of what stimulates; it is submitted to an internal evaluation—which does not always "pass" through the cortical region of consciousness—producing a corporeal effect: "Emotion is the combination of a *mental evaluative process*, simple or complex, with *dispositional responses to that process*, mostly *toward the body proper*, resulting in an emotional body state, but also toward the brain itself . . . resulting in additional mental changes."[59] As can be observed, secondary emotions incorporate the cortical process of categorization and the ordering of the emotions themselves, while evaluating them. This is a matter of the higher functions of the brain that we denominate "mental."[60]

In addition, *emotions can be felt* (moment 13 of figure 5) through the "process of continuous monitoring" of the effects caused by corporeal states in the viscera, muscles, and other parts of the body, a result of the "mapping" executed by the cerebral subcortex or cortex. To "feel" is a reflection on the "emotion" (its object). In this way, "the essence of sadness or happiness is the combined perception of certain body states with whatever thoughts they are juxtaposed to, complemented by a modification in the style and efficacy of the thought process."[61] Emotions such as those of happiness, sadness, fear, or disgust correspond to "body states," and can in turn be "felt" as joy or anguish, which are linked to emotions by "signals" that threaten the body, just as do euphoria, melancholy, and panic.[62]

[69] Finally, we can speak of a *"background feeling"* that is even more radical:[63] "I call it *background feeling*," writes Damasio, "because it originates in 'background' body states rather than in emotional states. . . . The feeling of life itself. . . . A background feeling corresponds instead to the body state prevailing *between* emotions."[64] When we are asked, "How do you feel?" or "How are you?," we generally respond, "Very well!" What exactly corresponds to what we implicitly refer to as the "we find" or "we feel" very well? It is a *general feeling*, which reflects corporeality as a totality, since "the background state of the body is *monitored* continuously."[65] If someone is "deprived of the possibility of feeling actual bodily states, especially those that concern fundamental feeling,"[66] it is called *anosognosia*.[67] A general state of satisfaction (a *"background feeling"*) ought then to be distinguished from the feeling of happiness or enjoyment and the sensation of pleasure.

All of this is related to the goal set by corporeality in its different levels with reference to the preservation, reproduction, or development of the life of the human subject. If we add cultural "evaluations" (those of an Egyptian culture are different from Greek, Aztec, Spanish, or modern European culture, etc.), we would have a new "general evaluative feeling" (moral or ethical consciousness)[68] that "monitors" (subsumes) all existence, not only at the visceral level of corporeality but also at the cultural-historical level of this corporeality in a state of linguistic self-consciousness as a social actor of cultural values (incorporated cerebrally in the most developed and recent areas of the linguistic cortical lobes, perfectly linked with the limbic system and base of the brain, producing a complex unity of the different evaluative-affective orders).[69] The neurologist Damasio concludes: "I do not see emotions and feelings as the intangible and vaporous qualities that many presume them to be. Their subject matter is concrete, and they can be related to specific systems in the body and brain, *no less so than vision or speech*. Nor are the responsible brain systems confined to the subcortical sector. Brain core and cerebral cortex work together to construct emotion and feeling, no less so than in vision."[70]

[70] Now we can consider again Kant's proposal. Speaking of the "determining ground [*Bestimmungsgrund*]" of the will, he denies that it may be affective or empirical. At the same time, Kant reduces all affectivity to "pleasure [*Lust*]," and for this reason he concludes: "A principle that is based only on the subjective condition of receptivity to a pleasure [*Empfänglichkeit einer Lust*] or displeasure (which can be cognized always only empirically and which cannot be valid in the same way for all rational beings) can indeed serve as *maxim* for the subject who possesses this receptivity but not as a *law* even for him (because it is lacking in objective necessity, which must be cognized a priori)."[71] That is, the evaluative-affective cerebral system [level a of figure 5] would have no "objective necessity" for Kant. It does have it, instead, in the actual neurobiological description of the system of practical-theoretical categorization [level c]. From the point of view of the brain, both systems have the same objective necessity: they respond, in the first place, to the requirements of human life (the first objective necessity); in the second place, they articulate the linguistic-cultural and historical level; and in the third place, as we will see, they respond to the higher and cultural universal requirements of a critical ethics (integrated to the functions of the limbic system or the base of the brain, next to the frontal lobe of the cortex). Dualism and Kantian formalism (as well as Cartesianism and so many other modern, purely formal, ethical systems) have dealt a bad hand to ethics. The negation of the "body" in favor of the decorporealized "soul" (from the Greeks up to modern ethics) speaks to us of a very specific tradition, following a mythical path of the resurrection of the flesh with the Egyptian Osiris, or the Semitic or Muslim tradition, and culminates in the neurobiological sciences that allow us to recover the unity of

the corporeal, within which the higher functions of the brain require that we highlight definitively the extremely ambiguous simplification in ethics of a substantial independent "soul."[72]

[71] The ethics of liberation needs a unitary understanding of the human being. John Searle[73] notes that it is necessary to avoid false alternatives, since neither naively materialist monism nor dualism is any longer acceptable. The unitary affirmation of corporeality that rejects dualism, all the same, cannot affirm behaviorist or physicalist materialism. Since the brain is situated in a *sui generis* stratum of reality, the solution ought to be different from these traditional ones. Maurice Merleau-Ponty wrote: "It would be better to say that bodily functioning is integrated with a level which is higher than that of life and that the body has truly become a human body."[74] The most complex functions of the human brain (the secondary emotions, happiness, conceptual categorization, linguistic competence, and self-consciousness that allow the autonomy, freedom, and responsibility of the historical and ethical-cultural subject) *subsume* the mere physical-vital functions of the less developed brains of prehuman animals.

In the same way, Xavier Zubiri, in a description of "feeling intelligence" or "intelligent feeling," in explicit reference to cerebral functioning and in order to avoid dualisms when dealing with the theme of "feelings," writes: "Man has feelings, feeling himself in reality. For that reason the animal certainly has *affections*, modifications of its vital tone, but no animal has feelings. . . . It is not that in man there is, on one side, sensible appetites, and on another rational appetites, but instead that there is nothing more than a feeling state, that is the tone [*tonic*] of reality."[75] Heidegger, for his part, who can be accused of many things, never fell into dualism, although he did not analyze sufficiently the "anterior" and "posterior" of the world (as Levinas will show). The "being-in-the-world" of "Da-sein"—the ontological human subject—opens itself to this world as "understanding" (*Verstehen*),[76] which should not be confused with either Kant's pure reason or Hegel's dialectical reason. It is a "mode" of grasping the totality of the existential experiences of human life as a whole: "my world," "our world." From the totality of the "experiences" of the brain as cognitive capacity what presents itself as real consideration (what Heidegger called "interpretation" [*Auslegung*]) can be categorized. I do not wish to make forced comparisons, but I simply want to indicate that Heidegger has avoided dualism.[77]

[72] To conclude, I want to return to some reflections by Maturana. In fact, for this neurologist the last level of development can be called the ethical: the relationship that is given in the linguistic medium among organisms in a community that have reached, through reflexive consciousness, express recognition of the autonomy and freedom before the Other (experienced as an *other* transsystemic subject), as *another* ethical subject: "That is why everything we said in this book, through our knowledge of our

knowledge, implies an ethics that we cannot evade. . . . This is the biological foundation of social phenomena: without love, without acceptance of others living beside us, there is no social process and, therefore, no humanness. Anything that undermines the acceptance of others, from competency to the possession of truth and onto ideological certainty, undermines the social process because it undermines the biologic process that generates it."[78] We have gone from a mere biological nature or prelinguistic sociality to ethics. Is this perhaps another case of the "naturalist fallacy"? George E. Moore critiqued evolutionism, Spencer's for example,[79] because it claimed to "go" from within the evolutionary process to the ethical as such, that is to say, from biological evolution follows "*the corollary that conduct gains ethical sanction.*"[80] I, instead, with contemporary neurobiology, affirm that in fact evolution produces the cerebral conditions that allow the possibility of grounding dialectically and materially the ethical phenomenon (which is established at the level of the "higher mental" functions of the brain, in well-determined linguistic and cultural processes, and from a material universal principle that Moore could not discover because of his axiological intuitionism).[81]

[73] In order to end this part of the discussion, I want to "make an argumentative experiment" that departs from neurological studies: it concerns the so-called naturalist fallacy. This fallacy, reinterpreted within the Fregean-Russellian tradition, as exercises of formal, abstract, and instrumental reason, justifiably indicates how from judgments of fact, normative judgments cannot be deduced by means of a logical-analytical derivation. I think this objection now loses its force. For to attempt the "passage" by means of a material (in German, *material*) grounding from a judgment of facts to a normative judgment in a concrete level, under the exercise of what I will call practical-material reason,[82] would indeed turn into a reductionistic fallacy.[83] In this case, it is no longer an analytical *deduction* but a dialectical *grounding* through contents. This requires the development of other logical material aspects generally poorly studied. In fact, since the evaluative-affective system is a constitutive moment of the cerebral functioning, a system that fulfills the requirements of the reproduction and development of human life, it performs continuously the "passage" from constative, descriptive judgments or judgments of fact ("this is poison") to "ought-to-be" judgments ("*I must* not eat this"). This is a necessary and obligatory mediation for the living "being" in danger of killing itself deliberately (we are always speaking here of the *human* "being"). In the same way, if I say, "I am thirsty," this is a descriptive statement. The human being, as living entity, needs to drink potable liquids in order to live. If it could not drink any liquids, it would die. The cerebral evaluative system, as warning system, judges the situation of "thirst" as a "threat" of extinction

of life, and it enunciates, "I *must*[84] drink liquids," in order to survive. Inasmuch as this requirement is subsumed within an evaluative system, which is also and always rational, ethical-cultural, the vital human descriptive statement turns normative: it is a duty.[85] Said in another way: the limbic system, the base of the brain, and the frontal area of the cortex fulfill cerebral functions, functions that regulate the survival, reproduction, and development of the life of the human being. Its activity consists in determining the evaluative hierarchization itself, and to apply what "ought to be" for the sake of the reproduction and development of the life of the ethical subject. This is a matter of a strict normative, "ethical" "ought-to-be" (which is nothing else than the other face of the description of the "being" or the reality of the living human). The limbic system applies universal, and not merely fixed, prescriptions (not merely plant-form prescriptions or merely related to animal stimuli, but also strictly ethical ones: self-conscious, linguistic, free, responsible, cultural, historical), which intrinsically constitute the process of conceptual categorization and the possibility of the formation and evaluative ordering (ordered by the compatibility of the mediations from the criterion of survival, of the reproduction and development of human life), as a communitarian linguistic moment. This "ought-to-be" has a strictly ethical structure (because it is a *human* cerebral evaluative system), since it was formed with the simultaneous participation of the higher "mental" functions that have subsumed the merely "animalistic" evaluative system (stimulaic or specifically instinctual) into the *human system in general, and, concretely, a system, of ethical-cultural values*[86] in particular that are at the base of the feelings, sentiments, moral consciousness, and self-conscious, linguistic and responsible volitions (without ever ceasing to have a cerebral rooting). The reality of the human life of the ethical-cerebral subject has, in its neural evaluative-affective system, a permanent vigilance of requirements, obligations, an "ought-to-be" that internally incorporates motives, and that integrates itself constitutively in all the activities of the practical and theoretical levels of all possible behavior.[87] But with this I do not want to suggest that self-responsible ethical consciousness could supply the complex self-organized mechanisms of the life of the human-cerebral corporeality, but that it ought to act correctively in critical moments. That is to say, we should not forget that human life includes also always, as one of the dimensions for survival, reason as its "cunning."

§1.2. Utilitarianism

[74] Proceeding ahead with my argument, I will attempt to traverse the discourse of a unilateral material ethics. For that reason, we should look at some aspects of the Anglo-Saxon material ethics tradition. After the end of

the seventeenth century, England defeated military Holland, and although France became a continental power,[88] London, Glasgow, Manchester, and Edinburgh replaced Amsterdam as a mercantile "hegemonic center" of the world system. The Anglo-Saxon world would have the capacity to "manage," backed by continental Europe, the respective Latin American, Asiatic, African, and Eastern European peripheries. A "reduction" took place (a simplification that rationalized some complex aspects of reality and privileges while excluding others), in which the subject was no longer considered an immaterial "ego" (proper to continental rationalism), but instead was seen as a corporeality reduced to a mere empirical subjectivity oriented by the means-ends calculus and geared toward the control of happiness, which was secured by the "reproductive drives" of the system as an effect of the consumption of the preferences of the buyer in the market.[89]

"Empiricist" philosophy criticized continental rationalism (Descartes or Spinoza, as well as Leibniz and Wolff), dismissing it as "metaphysical"[90] and proposed a utilitarian ethics. This ethical current is interesting especially because it contains a certain recuperation of corporeality. Bentham wrote: "The question is not, can they reason? Nor, can they talk? But can they suffer?"[91] Today, in the global periphery, the majority of humanity suffers in its membranes (in the stomach's mucous membrane because of hunger, in the skin because of cold, etc.) the traumatic effects of an unjust, nonintentional ethical-economic structure. This passage from the level of sensibility to that of economic objectivity, through ethical consideration, is a daring one but is precisely the way in which the utilitarians dealt with the theme.

[75] It would seem, in fact, that ethics has something to do with "happiness" or "unhappiness," such as it was perceived by Marx in 1835, when he was a youth of seventeen years, living in Trier: "Experience acclaims as happiest [(der) Glücklichste] the man who has made the greatest number of people happy [die meisten glücklich]."[92] This theme is touched on again at the end of volume 1 of *Capital*, when this youth—now an adult in London (the "center of the world system")—formulates the law of capitalist accumulation just as it is expressed in the *critical* science of economics, which concerns the fundamental contradiction in the last days of Modernity: "Accumulation of wealth at one pole is, therefore, at the same time accumulation of misery, agony of toil, slavery, ignorance, brutality, mental degradation, at the opposite pole."[93] For this reason, the "unhappiness" (misery, torment, brutalization) of the victim, of the oppressed, of the excluded, is one of the central themes of *Ethics of Liberation*.

The origins of utilitarianism[94] can be traced back to Richard Cumberland, Anthony Shaftesbury, and Francis Hutchenson, and more recently to Adam Smith (in Presbyterian, mercantile, industrial Scotland).[95] The entire utilitarian analysis begins with certain clear abstractions and reductions, such as the possession of goods as private property (which stabilizes society in peace and allows the institutionalization of the happy enjoyment), self-love coming from an individualist understanding (which has abandoned the community), the sympathy of the moral sense (which sacralizes the status quo without conscience), and, last, altruistic benevolence.

[76] Utilitarianism consists in a neostoicism (and even a non-Epicurean hedonism)[96] that reduces the management of pure individual subjectivity to the control of the means directed toward an end, by means of an instrumental calculus that situates ethical experience with reference to the passions as the ultimate point of reference. It allows a certain disciplined empirical rationalization of decisions, actions, and their consequences. This consequentialist neostoicism[97] is a position even more coherent than that taken by the Dutch in their metropolitan bourgeoisie. The ethical order is *simplified* to the maximum in order to control rationally military strategy as well as economic and political *business*, both internal and *colonial*. The "Self"[98] objectifies the system and disengages itself from it in order to be able to dominate it with greater efficacy. This is an abstract exercise of instrumental reason. Solipsistic empiricists control their object universally, since they consider only the subject inasmuch as this feels the secured mediation toward an end (happiness) that distances pain; this manageable decision will take the place of the just, prudential act of the ancients.[99]

[77] John Locke performed a systematic *demolition* of the continental rationalist edifice. His simplification is even more radical. Possessive individual subjectivity[100] only has ideas, and these are not innate; everything depends on experience, sensation, and reflection on them. In the final analysis, with respect to the theme that concerns us, he writes in *A Treatise on Human Understanding*: "Good and evil . . . are nothing other than pleasure or pain, or that which produces pleasure or produces pain."[101]

Purely subjective corporeality—without objective parameters, neither rational nor communitarian—measures all objects. Still, for this entire philosophical tradition, including the transcendental observer who conceived the "design" of "God's hand" that regulates Adam Smith's market of supply and demand—"divine providence"—there continues to be a certain external reference to the moral order that efficiently reconciles egoistic individual behavior and the common, social good. The autonomy of the empirical subject, however, is not yet complete. Mandeville had already asked about the problem of whether moral judgments were expressions of feelings (happiness): how could they then be more than the mere expressions of egoism? In turn, Hutcheson had affirmed that "the best nation is that which produces the greatest happiness for the greatest number, and the worst is that which occasions misery in like measure."[102]

[78] David Hume,[103] who rejected divine providence in order to build the foundation of the ethical validity of action in pure secularized subjectivity, affirmed that moral judgment cannot be grounded on any argumentation of reason,[104] but only on sentiments, passions, and feelings.[105] From this radical dualism, which is reductive from both sides, subjectivity is ethically determined exclusively by pleasure or happiness (the goal of the action) and by the passions or feelings (as means), without any intervention by reason, political authority, or religion.[106] Affectivity is the foundation of the new morality. Hume attempted, from another angle and to close the circle, to distinguish between the descriptive "is" and the prescriptive "ought" that will remain in the history of ethics—although reinterpreted with extreme logical-formal reductionism by Frege or Russell—as the "naturalist fallacy." Hume formulated it thus: "I am surprised to find [in other systems of morality], that instead of the usual copulations of propositions, *is* and *is not*, I meet with no proposition that is not connected with an *ought*, or an *ought not*. This change is imperceptible; but is, however, of the last consequence. For as this *ought*, or *ought not*, expresses some new relation or affirmation, 'tis necessary that it should be observed and explained; and at the same time that a reason should be given; for what seems altogether inconceivable, how this new relation can be a deduction from others, which are entirely different from it."[107]

[79] After Hume, we arrive at Jeremy Bentham, who, taking into account a suggestion by William Paley, explicitly set the utilitarian current in motion. He presented, as a "fundamental axiom," that "it is *the greatest happiness of the greatest number that is the measure of right and wrong*."[108] Let us take another formulation of this axiom by Bentham: "Nature has placed mankind under the governance of two sovereign masters, *pain* and *pleasure*. It is for them alone to point out what we ought to do, as well as to determine what we shall do."[109] This is the "principle of utility."[110] Pleasure and pain are the ultimate instance of "all of our *judgments* and all of the *determinations of life*."[111] For this reason, "the principle of utility subordinates everything to these two motives."[112]

Years later, John Stuart Mill reformulated the thesis: "The creed which accepts as the foundation of morals *utility* or the *greatest happiness principle* holds that actions are right in proportion as they tend to promote happiness; wrong as they tend to produce the reverse of happiness."[113] In the face of some objections,[114] Mill retreated from some of his positions and reduced its scope: "It must be admitted . . . that utilitarian writers in general have placed the superiority of mental over *bodily pleasures*[115] chiefly in the greater permanency,[116] safety, uncostliness, etc., of the former—that is, in their circumstantial advantages rather than in their intrinsic nature."[117]

In any event, what utilitarianism intends is to define "an *only and first criterion* or universal ethical *principle*," which, from Aristotle to Reice, is not demonstrable,[118] as are all first principles:[119] "To be incapable of proof by reasoning is common to all first principles, to the first premises of our knowledge, as well as to those of our conduct."[120] We are speaking then of a "criterion of morality."[121] Mill shows the type of proofs (not by apodictic demonstration, but dialectically, as Aristotle might say) that have to be provided in order to be able to ground such a universal principle or criterion.[122] It is on this level that "happiness" is proposed as a universal end: "Happiness is the sole end of human action, and the promotion of it the test by which to judge all human conduct; from whence it necessarily follows that it must be the criterion of morality."[123] This is a "criterion" determined by a happiness that is reached as the fulfillment of the preferences of consumption, by the selection of utility (determined by the "desire" of the buyer), within the capitalist market, as we will see.[124]

Utilitarianism is extremely complex and contains at least four dimensions: (1) a *moment of pleasure*, as the criterion of the fulfillment of needs (subjective, pulsational); (2) a moment of *utility*, or the criterion of efficacy of the action as good insofar as it is the fulfillment of a means toward an end (happiness) (determined by instrumental rationality); (3) a *consequentialist moment*: an act is good always depending on its consequences (as an ethics of responsibility); and (4) a *social effect*, because of the fulfillment of the happiness of the majority. At the beginning of the century, the first objection against utilitarianism was made, as already noted, by George Moore, with his analytical intuitionism.[125] John Rawls, for his part, challenged utilitarianism because of the requirements of his own formalist and liberal argument.[126] An exposition and appropriate critique would take us far. I will highlight only a few aspects relevant for my exposition.

[80] The first difficulty consists in the *ambiguity* of the hedonistic meaning of the concept of happiness; when precision is required, neither Bentham nor Mill can clarify its content from the qualitative point of view (whether the concept is corporeal or mental, egoistic or communitarian; even more so when conflicts or contradictions appear in its application, etc.). A second problem presents itself in the *empirical impossibility* of a strictly hedonist calculus, now quantitative (relating to its duration, intensity, purity, proximity or distance, and efficacy, according the preferences of an individual, and up to what point it is identical, or not, to that of others, etc.). Empirically, it is impossible to do such a calculus within objectively precise parameters. A third problem presents itself in the passage from the individual to the collective. Is what is good (happiness) for one good for all? Is what causes collective happiness also the cause of happiness for each person? Could there be an extremely developed society (happy?) based on slavery, or under a military dictatorship, or under a Stalinist regime of real

socialisms, that could claim to have reached a high level of welfare without respect for the free participation of the affected, nor recognizing in each their dignity as human beings?

One last difficulty: happiness, which is the end that the calculus of instrumental reason aims at, is reached through consumption, or the satisfaction of the preferences of the buyer in the market, by means of the capitalist distribution of goods (something always proposed by utilitarians). There is then an abstract and perverse circle: capital is the absolute a priori condition for the fulfillment of the ethical end (happiness). The horizon from which happiness acquires meaning is not analyzed sufficiently. For utilitarianism, happiness (or pleasure) does not convey a relation to a material objective universal criterion of the production, reproduction, and development of the human life of each human subject. The objective mediations possessed by use (of a house, for example) or consumption (a piece of bread) are the conditions of possibility for the fulfillment of subjective preferences (happiness). But the existence of such mediations, insofar as they are "commodities," possesses a logic that utilitarianism ignores. This is made clear by the fact that utilitarian ethics always operates within a distributionist economics, where the "value"[127] of a product (commodity) is exclusively constituted by the "desire" or "preferences"[128] of the *buyer* (potential consumer, if he or she is solvent), always forgetting that the "product" was already produced by a "producer" (the laborer), whose "happiness" (or "unhappiness," which is of particular interest in *Ethics of Liberation* as empirical alienation and as origin of ethical-critical consciousness) means the fulfillment of "needs" (with respect to the "use value" of the product) and not only of "preferences," which could never be discovered by utilitarianism.[129] That is to say, utilitarianism moves within the abstract circle of instrumental reason, where the goal is happiness, and where the means to reach it are formally calculated, but always within the horizon of the capitalist market. A universal material principle of ethics is not discovered; only the mere subjective happiness (albeit material) of the consumer is considered.

[81] It should be recognized that utilitarianism, which has a progressive agenda, extends the criterion of "pain" or "unhappiness" of the unjust consequences produced by economic institutions right up to the periphery of the modern "world system" and with some reference to the working class in general. Pain and unhappiness (when they are the product of an unfair distribution) would be indicators pointing to ethical demands in "facts."[130]

We have to take into account that the subjective material criterion of utilitarianism can also be thought of as a "model of impossibility,"[131] which could be approximately formulated as an imperative in the following way: "Promote the necessary economic institutions so that happiness is the effect in the *totality*[132] of the population of the country." This would be a utopia—the expanded utilitarian utopia—which, while attempting an effective empirical feasibility, would fall into what I will call a "utopian illusion." In fact, *it is impossible* (not a logical but an empirical impossibility) that the totality of a population could be really and completely happy within the present economic system. In capitalism, objective wealth is accumulated (thus allowing the owners of capital to obtain subjective happiness) in the hands of a few, while augmenting the "poverty" of the majority (that is to say, "pain" and "unhappiness").[133]

The criterion of "the greatest happiness of the greatest number," thought from the horizon of the capitalist political economy, refers exclusively, as I already suggested, to the moment of economic "distribution" through the market[134] (since it could not discover the importance of "production" or the producing subject as the "unhappy" one, given the capitalist horizon from which it sets out). In this case, majorities (who are the "unhappy" ones, the laborers, the poor) ought to receive an equal quantity and quality of goods (which produce "happiness") as those who dominate, who are the "happy" ones.[135] But this is impossible in capitalist society. Utilitarianism does not discover the contradiction of its utopia since it does not recognize the essence of capital. But, at least, it makes sense when it indicates a relationship between economics and ethics.

[82] In fact, a crucial year for observing the transition from "ethics" to "economics," which is the ethical objective-institutional dimension in its properly material determination[136] (and which is of especial interest to us), is 1764, when Adam Smith, the Scottish moralist, visited France and discovered the growing French economy. It is known that economics as a science grew out of ethics (as we see in the development of the "treatise on justice" in Aristotle's *Nicomachean Ethics* or the scholastic books on *De jure et justitia*). Smith, in his work *The Theory of Moral Sentiments* of 1759, was always inspired by neostoical, Anglo-Saxon ethical principles, starting from subjective compassion for the suffering of others ("sympathy") in his reflections on "benevolence": "*This universal benevolence, how noble and generous soever*, can be the source of no solid happiness to any man who is not thoroughly convinced that all the inhabitants of the universe, the meanest as well as the greatest, are under the immediate care and protection of that great, benevolent, and all-wise Being, who directs all the movements of nature; and who is determined, by his own unalterable perfections, to maintain in it, at all times, *the greatest possible quantity of happiness*."[137] Thus wrote Smith the ethicist. Smith the economist, in 1776, would write: "It is not from the benevolence of the butcher, the brewer, or the baker that we expect our dinner, but from their regard to *their own interest*. We address ourselves, not their humanity but to their self-love, and never talk to them

of our own necessities but of their advantage."[138] In fact, this position concerns the attempt to supersede the contradiction enunciated by Mandeville: the egoism of each individual—thanks to the market as a place of reconciliation—promotes common advantage. Such egoism occurs in the "state of nature," when every product belonged to its producer; but in the "second state of nature" (English capitalism raised to an atemporal natural model) an inequality develops between the agents of the production of goods (when the wealthy buy the labor of the poor)—goods that produce "pleasure" and "happiness" in consumers, also in an unequal fashion.[139] Smith does not take note that egoism is the ideal model required by the competition of the market place. The only thing that Smith has done is to propose existing capitalism as a model as if it were "natural."

At this precise moment, we can make a transition from the principles of ethics in general to concrete *economic political institutions*, given that if "morality in general," as Bentham notes, "is the art of directing the action of men in such a way that they produce the greatest sum of possible happiness,"[140] then "happiness ought to be the *object* of the legislator."[141] When one reads with care the critique of the principles of asceticism and sympathy, and the response to the objections to Bentham (about the different types of pleasures and pains[142]—pains considered as sanctions—and the circumstances that determine the sensibility of the actors, etc.), one arrives at the conclusion that the utilitarian "idea of happiness" is a "subjective-material criterion" that points to the ethical goodness claim not only of acts, but also of institutions, especially of economic ones. That is to say, utilitarianism claims to arrive at the real or "feasible"[143] possibility of applying directly to concrete institutions the criterion of "happiness" in order to determine their "goodness" in general (because they produce happiness).

[83] This utilitarian principle was, from a certain point of view, progressive,[144] as I noted above, and perhaps this accounts for the fact that Bentham's doctrine was frequently referred to by the Latin American emancipators at the beginning of the nineteenth century—Bentham himself considered going to Mexico to spend his last days there, in order to carry out his principles of legislation. His friendship with Benardino Rivadavia from Rio de Plata and with Francisco de Paula Santander from the Gran Colombia, and the fact that José del Valle in Guatemala used his principles in the promulgation of the laws of 1825,[145] will not come as a surprise if we are aware that Bentham held the opinion that "the colonies only benefit the ruling few at the disadvantage of the subjected majority, as much in the [Iberian] peninsula as overseas."[146] Only social democracy with adequate economic legislation could fulfill the interests (the "happiness") of the majority. Mill had a similar opinion on these matters.[147] Here it can be seen how utilitarianism, in the hands of the emancipators of the periph-

ery, could be transformed into a theory of neocolonial emancipation.[148] In other words, the periphery experienced "emancipation" only from Spain or Portugal, before falling into a new neocolonial dependence on Bentham's England (and later the United States of the intuitionists, emotivists, analytics, communitarians, etc.). Utilitarianism indicates the *importance of one aspect of the subjective material criterion*, namely, happiness (the moment that contemporary formal moralities reject out of hand); but it is not yet able to define a criterion that subsumes other material aspects of ethics, such as values, the logic of drives, and so on, that could be grounded or developed as a universal ethical principle; for us, this criterion will be concrete "human life."

§1.3. Communitarianism

[84] In 1945, the United States became the hegemonic, central power of the capitalist world. Since 1989, after the dissolution of the Soviet Union, it has exercised a world military domination without precedent, and the analytical philosophical tradition and ethical emotivism used to rule hegemonically. In the face of these, and the liberalism of political theory, or universalistic formalist rationalism (in particular that of the second Frankfurt school)—and always as a critique of Modernity—there began in the United States and Canada a return to the historical reconstruction of "cultural traditions" (in this case, the Euro-American), that is, from concrete "ethical life" (inspired by concepts such as the Aristotelian *ethos* or the Hegelian *Sittlichkeit*).

In order to understand the "communitarian" movement, it is necessary to situate it as an internal reaction to Anglo-Saxon North American philosophy.[149] It is not understandable in Latin America or other cultural horizons, where, in contrast, a traditional Aristotelian school has never ceased to maintain a presence. The same could be said of Arabic thought, where Aristotle remains present in the rereading of the great philosophers of the Muslim past, from Al-Kindi to Ibn Rushd or Ibn Arabi.

The position of the communitarians depends on the need (and this is a feature that can be incorporated into an ethics of liberation because of the generalized ignorance of the dignity of the peripheral systems of ethical life demonstrated in the philosophies of the "center") to take into consideration another material moment, or moment of "content," or moment of ethics than the one considered by the utilitarians—namely, the *history of cultural traditions*—so as to be able to understand why the formalists (whether analytical formalists, emotivists, liberals, or neo-Kantian rationalists) have "emptied" their formal analysis of ethical content. In doing this, the formalists have entered into an irreversible crisis of concrete ethical "meaning," given that they have passed too quickly to an abstract level without analyzing the conditions of their point of departure. When communitarians recuperate the history of systems of ethical life, some of them, however, fall into opposite extremes: either affirming the incommensurability of each "life world" and ignoring a universal material principle, or not taking into account the material moment that the utilitarians had already noted.[150] The communitarians propose two fundamental theses. The first is that "at any fundamental level no rational debate between, rather than within, traditions can occur."[151] And the second: "Given that each tradition will frame its own standpoint in terms of its own idiosyncratic[152] concepts, and given that no fundamental correction of its conceptual scheme *from some external standpoint is possible*, it may appear that each tradition must develop its own scheme in a way which is liable to preclude translation from one tradition to another."[153]

[85] We will see how the ethics of liberation can accept that every debate, conflict, or struggle arises out of a determined tradition — and that it cannot be in any other way. Kant and Habermas themselves also had to set out from their own traditions (even though they were postconventional). However, an ethics of liberation cannot share the conclusion that communitarians arrive at. This is because an ethics of liberation establishes — from the standpoint of the universal material principle of the reproduction and development of the life of each human subject in community, as long as adequate formal conditions are also given — a dialogue among traditions that can be transformed through "external" interpellations (this is the whole theme of critical exteriority) and "internal" ones (from the indicated material principle). The conclusions of this dialogue are reached because we have passed from a *necessary* moment (of setting out from the particular history of a tradition) without understanding that *this is not sufficient* to displace or exclude intercultural and critical dialogue.

Furthermore, without being interested primarily in the economic aspect of the reproduction of the life of the human subject (although indicating the importance of survival in the context of linguistic-cultural symbols and values), communitarianism grounds itself by accepting as a fact, and entering fully into, the political-economic horizon of late capitalism and its cultural historical *ethos*. This is accomplished through reinterpreting what is still relevant in Aristotle (via MacIntyre), or in the position of Hegelian "ethical life" (via Taylor), or by making use of the material principles of different institutional "spheres" in order to clarify the problems of justice (via Walzer). Communitarians, then, occupy a proper place within the contemporary North American panorama of the ethics of content that Latin American, African, or Asiatic philosophy can study with sympathy — given the need to expose the illegitimate hegemony of the Eurocentric ethos, which claims universality.[154] At the same time, communitarianism ought to be superseded from the perspective of a universal material principle[155] and in an intercultural dialogue that is redefined in non-Eurocentric terms.

a. Alasdair MacIntyre

[86] MacIntyre presents his position in *A Short History of Ethics*.[156] He protests, with reason, that "moral philosophy is often written as though the history of the subject were only of secondary and incidental importance. This attitude seems to be the outcome of a belief that moral concepts can be examined and understood apart from their history. . . . Moral concepts are embodied in and are partially constitutive of forms of social life."[157] His entire critique of Anglo-Saxon formal moralities (and, later, of German ones) is grounded in the following argument: "Traditional European society [Locke, Hume, Moore, Stevenson . . .] inherited a moral vocabulary from the Greeks[158] and Christians. . . . But the subsequent disruption of the traditional forms of social life that resulted from the emergence of individualism . . . and capitalism caused the reality of social life to diverge so much from the norms implicit in the traditional vocabulary, that all of the connections between duty and happiness gradually dissolved."[159] Thus MacIntyre insists that analytical-emotivist moralities "could only have success if the moral concepts were ahistorical,"[160] and for this reason concludes: "One of the virtues of the history of moral philosophy is to demonstrate for us that this is not true and that moral concepts themselves have a history. To understand this is to liberate one's self from all forms of false absolutist pretension."[161]

[87] In *After Virtue: A Study in Moral Theory*, MacIntyre continues with the same theme and carries out again a frontal critique against the loss of meaning (as described by Max Weber) that accompanied Modernity. In order to do this, he carries out neither a destruction in the Heideggerian sense, nor a Habermasian reconstruction, but instead a real demolition of contemporary ethics from the standpoint of those of the past. In the first place, he shows the fallacies of emotivism (mainly of Stevenson)[162] and their source (Moore's intuitionism).[163] In the second place, he asks about the cause of the failure of the Enlightenment project,[164] which leads him to study the original moment of fracture: "A central thesis of this book," he writes, "is that the breakdown of this project provided the historical background against which the predicaments of our own culture can become intelligible. To justify this thesis it is necessary to recount in some detail the history of that project and its breakdown."[165] The entire Enlightenment project (meaning mainly Kant) floated on a teleological and theological understanding of existence that gave meaning from below (without its

being perceived)[166] to the project of formal morality; that is to say, it still drew from an *ethos* that allowed it to think reductively without losing the sense of daily ethical existence. Utilitarianism[167] already does not make this assumption and shows its definitive break in the position of Gewirth.[168] Everything will end up being reduced to a "managerial effectiveness";[169] having begun with a very narrow conception of "experience,"[170] it culminates in the lack of "interpretative capacity" of the social sciences.[171] Contemporary ethics, in MacIntyre's view, has lost its sense: "A key part of my thesis has been that modern moral utterance and practice can only be understood as a series of fragmented survivals from an older past."[172] Having arrived at this point MacIntyre does not think, as Nietzsche or Weber did, that we will have to sink into nihilism, but instead he undertakes a reconstruction. In order to accomplish this, he proposes a program of large reach that ought to begin with the study of Aristotle himself,[173] with his notion of *héxis*, character, virtue (the subjective material content of ethics) from the *eu zén* ("good life for man"), *télos*, *eudaimonia*.[174] He shows how the return to the Stoics, which occurred in the Anglo-Saxon tradition, means that "virtues are now not to be practiced for the sake of some good other, or greater, than the practice of virtue itself. . . . [T]he Stoic virtue of self-command [is instead required,] which enables us to control our passions when they distract us from what virtue requires."[175]

He concludes by indicating that to Modernity's fragmented vision of life—according to the Weberian interpretation—it is necessary to oppose a unified experience of existence *in the tradition*.[176] But which tradition? Will it be the tradition of liberal justice (in the style of Rawls or Nozick)?[177] Once again we find ourselves in need of having to know about the content of what we are speaking about.

[88] This uncertainty explains the title of MacIntyre's second work: *Whose Justice? Which Rationality?*[178] the target of which is now North American liberalism. As in Taylor,[179] MacIntyre's Eurocentric vision traverses four successive traditions: from Homer to Aristotle, from the Arabians and Jews to Aquinas, from the Scottish Aristotelian Calvinist tradition to Hume, arriving finally at North American liberalism.[180] If his earlier work had specifically faced up against emotivism or analytic philosophy (hegemonic in the seventies), now he undertakes an attack against liberalism (especially because of the impact that John Rawls's *A Theory of Justice* had during the eighties). His argument begins with a valid observation: "The parallels between this understanding of the relationship of human beings in the social and political realm and the institution of the market, the dominant institution in a liberal economy, are clear."[181] Liberals are not concerned with the content of "the good life" of each citizen. Liberals are interested in the formal framework of "fairness" that allows each person

to pursue his or her preferences. The questions are: "What are my wants? And how are they ordered?"[182] MacIntyre, with reason, shows that this is a matter, in fact, of a historical *tradition* that counts with citizens who share the same preferences within a well-determined horizon: "Liberalism, like all other moral, intellectual, and social traditions of any complexity, has its own problematic internal to it, its own set of questions which by its own standards it is committed to resolving."[183] Here, as I noted above, MacIntyre reaches the conclusion that there exists nonetheless a "logical incompatibility and incommensurability"[184] among traditions. That is to say: "Each tradition can at each stage of its development provide rational justification for its central theses in its own terms, employing the concepts and standards by which it defines itself, but there is no set of independent standards of rational justification by appeal to which the issues between contending traditions can be decided."[185] This conclusion, which may be interpreted as that of a relativist,[186] cannot satisfy us, since it shows only one aspect of the question.

b. Charles Taylor

[89] The philosophical project of Charles Taylor, a Canadian philosopher,[187] is similar to MacIntyre's, although since Taylor studied Hegel in depth[188] he depends on Hegel in a certain way in his project. (Further ahead, I will present some of Hegel's critique of Kant; specifically, his critique of formal morality via material ethics, in one of its threads.)

Taylor presents a material ethics[189] in a universalistic axiological "style."[190] The historical intention of his book *The Sources of the Self* is to show the origin, content, and identity crisis of the modern self. But this self-understanding cannot come from a mere abstract formal morality. In order to achieve self-understanding, a description of ethical life in general must first be articulated, since such understanding can only be constructed from a horizon aligned with intuitions toward the good—the "hypergoods" that presuppose a moral ontology based, ultimately, on the respect for life.[191] There are "strong evaluations" that lie at the base of respect for others and the sense of self-dignity. Taylor thus carries out a certain abstract analysis of the ethical structure—this *Ethics of Liberation* will contribute in turn, and beyond Taylor, strong arguments toward the defense of the universality of material ethics, but it will attempt also to include formal morality as a *procedure of application* of the universal material principle.[192]

Taylor argues that everything that has been thus far indicated has not been taken into account by Modernity, because Modernity has fallen into "disenchantment," a "dissipation of our sense of the cosmos." Hence, in concrete terms, there is a "quest" (to use MacIntyre's term) for a "rearticu-

lation of existence" with "ordinary life." The rediscovery of the "identity of
the modern self" presupposes the acknowledgment and affirmation of the
historical moral sources of Modernity, which are implicit but still operative: the deism of the Christian God, the self-responsibility of the person
as subject, and the Romantic belief in the goodness of nature. But as these
sources are not known or have been forgotten, Modernity enters into crisis.
In order to awaken an operative ethical "motivation," we would have to
count on aesthetic impulse. It is not rational argument that can move on
to the fulfillment of the good life, but aesthetic narrative, expressed in the
tradition of a *pathos* such as that of Schiller, Nietzsche, or Benjamin. Taylor
concludes: "The intention of this work was one of retrieval, an attempt to
uncover buried goods through rearticulation—and thereby to make these
sources again empower, to bring the air back again into the half-collapsed
lungs of the spirit. There is a large element of hope. It is a hope that I see
implicit in Judeo-Christian theism . . . and its central promise of a divine
affirmation of the human."[193]

[90] In Taylor's later book *The Ethics of Authenticity* the theme is deepened, reaching new results. The three "malaises" of Modernity (individualism, the primacy of instrumental reason or of technological capitalism, and
the despotism of the system),[194] produce a "loss of meaning," an "eclipse of
ends," and a "loss of freedom" in bureaucratized society. But in the midst
of so much "disarticulation," there opens up an "ideal of authenticity." The
original source of authenticity—born of a "disengaged rationalism" of a
self that must think reflexively from within itself (a child of the Romantic
period) as an "atomism of the community"[195]—is the "inwardness" of a
self-determined and autonomous will that attempts to be true to itself.[196]
This authenticity is "dialogical,"[197] emerging from "significant others,"[198]
where identity with respect to those others is affirmed as much as is difference. This difference emerges out of a common horizon: "Our identity requires recognition by others."[199] Consequently, being "denied recognition
can be a form of oppression."[200] This conclusion allows Taylor to elaborate a beautiful description of authenticity as a right to creation, discovery,
originality, and opposition to the ruling norms of a society.[201] He avers:
"A fragmented society is one whose members find it harder and harder to
identify with their political society as a community. This lack of identification may reflect an atomistic outlook, in which people come to see society
purely instrumentally."[202]

The theme of "the universal recognition of difference"[203] is taken up in
Taylor's essay "The Politics of Recognition,"[204] where we find a more concrete political agenda. In this work, Taylor broadens the horizon of Modernity.[205] He writes of "a continuing dialogue and struggle with significant others,"[206] and now this philosopher of the "center"—though from a

peripheral region, Quebec—exclaims: "There are other cultures [!] . . . that have, in other words, articulated their sense of the good, the holy, the admirable. . . . [I]t would take a supreme arrogance to discount this possibility *a priori*. . . . But what the presumption requires of us is not peremptory and inauthentic judgments of equal value, but a willingness to be open to comparative cultural study of the kind that must displace our horizons in the resulting fusions. What it requires above all is an admission that we are very far away from that ultimate horizon from which the relative worth of different cultures might be evident."[207] In fact, there is no cultural "common ultimate horizon," but there is a universal material principle that is internal to every and all cultures. Taylor does not see this. It is not a "horizon"; it is a *mode of reality*: human life itself.

From these preoccupations that are of so much interest to us, Taylor elaborates a critique of Habermas's philosophy, taking on Habermas's claim to have constructed an empty universalistic formalism, which in fact is supported by a (material) concrete historical horizon of specific orientations of the good, of a modern European "good life," with substantive contents: "It seems that they [formalists such as Habermas] are motivated by the strongest moral ideals, such as freedom, altruism, and universalism. These are among the central moral aspirations of modern culture, the hypergoods which are distinctive to it. . . . They [the formalists] are continuously incapable of coming clean about the deeper sources of their own thinking."[208] This comment is, in a way, a "repetition [*Wiederholung*]" of Hegel's and Heidegger's critique of Kant: the subject is always already existing in an "ethical life" (Hegel's *Sittlichkeit*) or a "world" (Heidegger). Since Taylor does not discover a universal material principle, he is only partly right. In any event, we should not forget that these historical analyses are *necessary* but not *sufficient*, as we will see.

c. Michael Walzer

[91] The Jewish philosopher Michael Walzer, in his main work, *Spheres of Justice*,[209] clearly adopts the position of material ethics, but includes the historical socioinstitutional moment: "The best account of distributive justice is an account of its parts: social goods and spheres of distribution. . . . A given society is just if its substantive life is lived in a certain way—that is, in a way faithful to the shared understandings of the members."[210] As in the case of the utilitarians, marginalist economists, and so many other North American ethical movements, he is addressing the question of an ethics of "distributive" justice, which takes for granted "capitalist *production*."[211] This taking for granted of capitalist production can be seen, furthermore, because taking "an account of its parts" makes it difficult to take a critical

position in the face of the "totality" of the distributive system as such.[212] Walzer develops a progressive ethical critique out of the horizon of the North American economic and political system, accepting it as point of departure and putting it in question as "totality." But an ethics of liberation will not be able to set out from that "dominating" horizon, to use Walzer's terms, since its concrete applications in each sphere will not make a lot of sense in a peripheral society of capitalism that is globalized (at the level of a distributive market of goods) and excluding (at the level of the production, of employment, and the consumption of the great impoverished majorities).

[92] If "the aim of political egalitarianism is a society free from domination" (an aim that as a regulative idea may be shared by an ethics of liberation), writes Walzer, "[his] purpose in this book is to describe a society where no social good serves or can serve as a means of domination."[213] From this position, Walzer can criticize the utilitarians, because the "planners" of the distribution of the goods that generate happiness would have a "dominating" power.[214] How can we overcome this type of domination? A text by Pascal helps us to get started: "Tyranny consists in desiring domination, universal and beyond its order [La tyrannie consiste au désir de domination, universel et hors de son ordre]."[215]

In this way, Walzer determines some "orders" or "spheres" of distribution, of actions and institutions in whose horizon are exercised analogical types of justice,[216] with respect to specific "social goods."[217] "Complex equality" requires that no *dominant goods* (such as monopoly or "dominance") of one sphere should be imposed on other spheres.[218] Walzer discusses different themes in the eleven chapters of the book. In chapters 2 ("Membership"), 5 ("Office"), and 11 ("Recognition"), he touches on the problems of inclusion, hierarchization, and exclusion—I think that the ethics of liberation, with its category of alterity, exteriority, or exclusion, reaches more critical horizons, although it does draw on some important points from Walzer, which will be taken into account. In chapter 8 ("Education"), Walzer shows the concrete, ethical, and pedagogical conditions that are required for integration into other, different spheres—conditions that are far from the critical-liberating intuitions of a Paulo Freire. In chapters 3 ("Security and Welfare") and 7 ("Free Time"), Walzer analyzes aspects of the subjective appropriation of goods, although the reality of misery and poverty are not confronted. In chapters 4 ("Money and Commodities") and 6 ("Hard Work"), which are extremely critical of some aspects of capitalism, he seems not to penetrate past its horizon.[219] Last, Walzer presents the three spheres of family (chapter 9: "Kinship and Love"), the church (10: "Divine Grace"), and the state (12: "Political Power"). As can be seen, Walzer's description does not aim to be systematic, but remains at the level of suggestions of a material ethics: "We are (all of us) culture-producing creatures; we make and inhabit meaningful worlds. Since there is no way to rank and order these worlds with regard to their understanding of social goods, we do justice to actual men and women by *respecting their particular creations.*"[220]

[93] In this way, pluralism in "complex equality" would be affirmed: "What a larger conception of justice requires is not that citizens rule and are ruled in turn, but that they rule in one sphere and are ruled in another—where "rule" means not that they exercise power but that they enjoy a greater share than other people of whatever good is being distributed."[221] It would seem that Walzer admits that justice must accept "spheres" where some can "enjoy a greater share [of goods] than other people"; that is to say, domination is inevitable, but it is only localized and not generalized in some spheres, mutually compensating one another, because the dominator in one "sphere" may be dominated in another. Have we not contradicted the initial intention to reach an order "without domination," and yet concluded that domination is inevitable and for that reason has to be distributed in different plural orders so that they may mutually counter one another? It is very different to affirm (as an ethics of liberation does) that in fact there is always some domination—which has to be superseded at the very moment it is discovered, as we will see in chapter 4—than it is to affirm that since domination is inevitable, it must be "managed" in the best way possible (which is what Walzer would argue), and for this reason must be compensated by other shared and equalizing dominations within the set of all the spheres.

As we have seen, communitarians defend the importance of material aspects in their approach to the ethical question: history, the concrete good of a given culture, and the different spheres of justice, within which the authentically ethical good ought to be situated in accordance with its content (materially). All of this is necessary, but being necessary does not make it materially *sufficient*,[222] nor does it exclude the formal. In defense of this position, I noted that it is not to be rejected, because it recognizes a constitutive material moment of the ethical life of the general good, of the content of a good, of an act, of an institution, and so on.

§1.4. Some Ethics of Content or Material Ethics

[94] Before reflecting on the universal material principle of ethics, we should consider, if only briefly, some other system of material ethics.[223]

Aristotle proposed a theory of *eudaimonia* (the Greek term does not refer simply to a utilitarian or teleological happiness, as in Weber), which should be considered typical of material ontological ethics: "To us it is clear from what has been said that happiness is among the things that are prized and perfect. It seems to be also from the fact that it is a first principle [*arkhé*]; for it is for the sake of this that we all do all that we do, and the first [*arkhé*] principle and cause [*aítion*] of good [*agathôn*] is, we claim, something prized and divine [*theîon*]."[224] The *Nichomachean Ethics* is not merely an ethical treatise in the common sense; it is a chapter in fundamental ontology. The peculiar mode of acting of the human being in the world (it should not be forgotten that "acting" is *érgon*, from whence comes *enérgeia*, that is the actuality of activity of the human being) takes the form of *praxis*, but in order to be "accomplished" (perfect) it must be adequate to virtue: "If this is the case, the human good turns out to be the activity of the soul in accordance with virtue, and if there is more than one virtue, in accordance with the best and most complete. But we must add 'in a complete life.'"[225] The *eudaimonia* or the "human good" is neither produced (technically), nor is it represented (theoretically) or chosen (by liberation). It is the ontological a priori as "ought-to-be"; it is the constitutive horizon itself of the "com-prehension" of being, from which (practical principle) possibilities open up and one is selected. The ultimate reference is "life," the human "good life" par excellence: "Verbally there is very general agreement; for both the general run of men and people of superior refinement say that it is happiness, and identify living well and faring well with being happy."[226] It should be understood, however, that Aristotle could not overcome historical determination; above all, he lacks critical consciousness with respect to his Hellenocentrism. Here I should repeat everything I said in §I.3 (on Indo-European "ethical lives"), given that Aristotle, from an enslaving *ethos*, analyzes in the last instance the *eudaimonia* as the divine contemplation in the sense of "leisure" (*skholé*): "If happiness [*eudaimonia*] is activity in accordance with virtue, it is reasonable that it should be in accordance with the highest virtue; and this will be that of the best thing in us. . . . [T]he activity [*enérgeia*] of this in accordance with its proper virtue will be perfect happiness [*eudaimonia*]. That this activity is contemplative we have already said."[227] This supreme "good life" could be lived only in the Greek *polis*, because barbarians, Asiatics, or slaves were not humans in a strict sense. This is an ontological material ethics (with formal elements, as we will see below), but still regional, particular. Aristotle defines a good life that lays claim to universality, but he falls nonetheless into a conventional particularism that will need to be overcome.

[95] In the same way, for Thomas Aquinas, whose material ethics is communitarian, human beings reach their "complete fulfillment [*beatitudo*]" in the common good: "One should not cease to consider that the common good [*bonum commune*] according to the adequate understanding is preferable to one's mere good, since any part is ordered by drive to the good

of all [*bonum totius*]. It is a sign, for example, that the hand is raised in order to stop a hit, preserving thus the life of the heart and the head, in the same way that each man should be considered as part . . . and tends as ultimate good the good of the whole . . . and in this consists the whole of *beatitudo*.[228] . . . . He who desires something, desires because of the common good [*bonum commune*], because it is his own good, since it is the good of the entire universe [*bonum totius universi*]."[229] For the medieval philosophers, *beatitudo* (the Aristotelian *eudaimonia*) consisted objectively in the good (ultimately, God himself as a person, as what is shared in the kingdom of God). It is wealth, formally or subjectively, in its possession or use (distributively obtained): enjoyment. All the Muslim or Christian philosophers practiced a material ethics—with monological, formal precritical elements. In any event, the medieval universalism of Germanic-Latin Christianity (like that of the Roman-Byzantine world or the corresponding Islamic world) does not cease to be the particularism of Europe, a secondary and peripheral culture (as we saw in §I.4), which nonetheless claimed an effective universality. This is characteristic of material ethics that are naive (not critical) and regionalist; they still fall into the particularistic fallacy.

[96] Hegel, for his part, is a modern philosopher who consciously set out to subsume formal (Kantian) morality into an ethical life (*Sittlichkeit*) of contents, ultimately with a global intent (which nonetheless ends up negating itself in an absolute idealism, which in a way is, according to Schelling's critique, a self-consciousness that thinks itself without real content). Hegel should be treated after Kant, but for systematic reasons I will now analyze his ethical position. In fact, Hegel's first critique of Kant is an ethical critique.[230] Hegel had studied a rigid, scholastic theology in Tübingen, and for this reason was impacted by the pedagogical rebellion of the young Schiller, who in 1795 published *The Aesthetic Education of Man*. Of Kant, he had read *Religion within the Limits of Reason Alone* and the *Critique of Practical Reason*. Hegel found inspiration in Schiller for an understanding of "reason [*Vernunft*]" as the vital faculty of synthesis, while "understanding [*Verstand*]" determines its object, dissects it, and kills it. Hegel writes in his essay "The Spirit of Christianity and Its Fate" that, "in the kingdom of God, Christ shows to his disciples not the overcoming of laws, but rather the fulfillment of them, not as mere fidelity to duty but as sanctioned by another justification, in which justice is realized more perfectly."[231] For the young Hegel, still a theologian, Kant is the Old Testament of the formal law (Morality [*Moralität*]), whereas Jesus is the New Testament, the "sublation" (*Aufhebung*) of the unilateral in the *pléroma* (the future "ethical life" [*Sittlichkeit*]). There is not only universal formal law, but also, and to the same degree, inclination (to fulfill it), love, "synthesis [*Synthese*]": "The

most comprehensive principle can be called a tendency to do what the laws command, unity of inclination [*Neigung*] and law, through which it loses its form as law; this accord with inclination is the *pléroma* of the law. . . . Similarly, this tendency, a virtue [*Tugend*], is a synthesis in which law loses its universality (which Kant thus always calls it objective), the subject its particularity, and both their opposition [*Entgegensetzung*]."[232] In this text of 1797, we already have the definitive Hegel (and in him, in some way, the intuitions of Taylor and MacIntyre). The objective law that obliges *from outside* is subsumed by the synthesis of the subject-object (as community or concrete people) and is now "second nature."[233] What in "morality" obligates, in "ethical life" (*Sittlichkeit*), is accomplished by love, by drive, by *ethos*: "Agreement [*Übereinstimmung*] is life, and inasmuch the relation of the different: love."[234] That is to say, "The kingdom of God . . . is a living community,"[235] and not a separate individual determined by an objective law that kills. Many aspects of this could be highlighted, especially the Hegelian critique of the impossibility of the effective universalization of the maxim without contradictions,[236] and the empirical impossibility of the adequate "application"[237] of principles, but I am giving just a general overview of the themes.[238] In any event, we know that the mature Hegel of the "ethical life [*Sittlichkeit*]" will appear later, in the *Phenomenology of Spirit* (in part 6), especially in the *Philosophy of Right* (in secs. 142 ff.), in the *Encyclopedia* (in secs. 513 ff.), and in all of his *Lectures* (on the philosophy of world history, the philosophy of religion, aesthetics, and the history of philosophy), in which he deals with different material aspects of world history (where he considers cultural "contents" genetically). Hegel proposes a concept of the cultural-historical *ethos* to which all the contemporary material ethics cannot cease to refer.[239] In contrast to the premodern philosophers, Hegel is clearly conscious of world history, but he interprets it Eurocentrically (his alleged universality is nothing more than the dominating imposition of the European particularity; it exemplifies a particularly bad solution of material universalism in ethics). For this reason, in the end, the "World Spirit" (*Weltgeist*) represents concrete universality, each time taking only one people or state (in order to abandon it when it has fulfilled its instrumental function) as "vehicle" (*Träger*) of the fulfillment of the Spirit in "this world."[240] It is a material ethics of Eurocentric domination:

> The nation to which is ascribed a moment of the Idea in the form of a natural principle is entrusted with giving complete effect to it in the advance of the self-developing self-consciousness of the world spirit [*Weltgeist*]. This nation is dominant [*herrschende*] in world history during this one epoch, and it is only once that it can make its hour strike. In contrast with this its absolute right of being the vehicle [*Träger*] of this present stage in the world spirit's development, the spirit of the other nations are without rights, and

they, along with those whose hour has struck already, count no longer in world history.[241]

To Hegel we owe, in any event, the attempt to recuperate the history of the systems of ethical life as the place in which practical life is lived factically. It is a necessary horizon, but not a sufficient one.

[97] Axiology, for its part, reminds us of another aspect of a material ethics, also necessary. In fact, Kant's *Critique of Pure Reason* influenced the Baden school, which went on to develop the notion of values.[242] Some of its representatives were Windelband, Rickert, and Lask. Even Franz Brentano[243] busied himself with ethics, which is why his disciple Edmund Husserl elaborated an axiological ethics.[244] Dietrich von Hildenbrand,[245] and principally Max Scheler,[246] in their turn, presented complete treatises of axiological ethics following the phenomenological method. Nicolai Hartmann, following a unique ontological line, also wrote a monumental axiological ethics.[247] Francisco Romero and Roberto Hartman[248] became well-known representatives of the axiological movement in Latin America.

Kant wrote that means have a "conditioned value" (*einen bedingten Wert*) with reference to the human person, which is the only "absolute value" (*absolute Wert*).[249] Heidegger, commenting on Nietzsche, indicated that "value is the condition of the increase of life" (*Steigerung des Lebens*).[250] Mediations have value insofar as they are actual possibilities for life;[251] that is to say, values are the condition of the dominion that life has over *becoming*.[252] It is evident that there are no values[253] without cultural intersubjectivity, and for this reason they constitute an essential part of the content of a historical-concrete ethical life.[254]

Max Scheler confronted Kant while attempting to ground a *material* ethics of values that did not set out from the formal *factum* of the law that commands, but instead from an "emotive-intuitive intention [*Fühlen*]," which captures values. He asks: "Are there no material ethical intuitions [*materiale ethische Intuitionen*]?"[255] To which he responds: "We designate as a priori all those ideal units of meaning and those propositions that . . . are self-given [possess *Selbstgegenbenheit*][256] by way of an immediate intuitive *content* in the absence of any kind of positing [*Setzung*] of subjects that think them and of the real nature of those subjects. . . . Intuition of this kind, however, is *essential intuiting* [*Wesenschau*] or *phenomenological experience*."[257]

[98] For Scheler, "the identification of the a priori and the formal is a basic error of the Kantian doctrine."[258] Scheler introduced a wedge between the *mundus intelligibilis* and the *mundus sensibilis* (the Kantian dualism, without superseding it), namely, the "emotive intention" (*intentionale Fühlen*). In the end, he was not able to situate this horizon within reality, tending toward a certain Platonism of values. Speaking neurobiologically,

without expanding too much on the particulars, I can say that values are now known to be implanted cerebrally in the evaluative centers (as already indicated), and, for that reason, also in the historicocultural intersubjectivity of peoples. Today, the ethics of liberation can subsume axiology as a material structure (a priori with respect to the individual who is ontogenetically educated in the phylogenetic intersubjectivity of concrete historical peoples), where the mediations of the criterion and the material-ethical principle of the reproduction and development of the life of each subject in community (biocultural life and ethics) are hierarchized. Values do not in the last instance ground actions or institutions; mediations have "value" (norms, institutions, etc.) that make possible within the practical plexus (including discursive communication) the reproduction and development of the life of the human subject (which is the material universal foundation of ethical-cultural values).

In the same way, the hermeneutics of ethical symbols or myths, such as is carried out by Paul Ricoeur in the *Symbolism of Evil*,[259] is another *material* path of ethics, inasmuch as it discovers the concrete, historical, narrative structure of the intersubjective ethical life of cultures—for example, Greek or Semitic. In some way, following Freud and Jung, Ricoeur proposes the hermeneutics of symbols and historical myths of peoples as a collective unconscious—it is another aspect of material ethics.

Martin Heidegger's existential analytics constitutes what we could call an "ontological-material ethics," whose ultimate "content" is the "comprehension of being [*Seinsverständnis*]."[260] "Being-in-the-world" out of a "pro-ject" (*Entwurf*) as "potentiality-for-Being" ("as an ought-to-be")[261] indicates exactly the concrete facticity of the human being who is always immersed in the historical ethical life of a people. This "com-prehension of being" is also practical; it is that of a dialectically unfolded horizon, rooted in the past, which opens up (the "opening") from the future the possibilities of the present.[262]

[99] To conclude, let us consider some proposals by Xavier Zubiri,[263] who—like López Aranguren[264]—radically defends a material ethics or an ethics of reality in the strong sense. Like no other philosopher that we have looked at so far, Zubiri departs from a clearly neurobiological doctrine: "Man has *cerebrally* an intellective openness to stimuli as reality. . . . [T]he cerebral and the intellective constitute nothing other than one and the same activity."[265] Zubiri, a philosopher from Madrid, sets out from elemental matter and passes through corporeal and biological matter, until he arrives at "organic living matter."[266] Given its cerebral organicity, the living being can simply feel by means of stimulation, or, in the same stimulus, as it actualizes the thing through intellection, a *prius* reality arises forth (what is "its own" of the thing, ratified as prior to intellection). In Zu-

biri, one must distinguish mere feeling through stimuli (which I will call stimulaic-perceptive categorization), from intelligent feeling (or feeling intelligence):[267] "What we first of all learn is precisely stimuli . . . what warms does not consist in *being-warm* [the stimulus as stimulus], but instead in *to be–warm*. . . . This is not learned through stimuli; rather, it is apprehended *really*. It is stimulus, but it *stays* in my apprehension as *being* warm. This mode of staying is the new formality: it is not formality of the stimuli, but formality of reality."[268] An animal can "feel the warmth of the sun" as a sign, which links it instinctively and immediately to a response. A human being similarly "feels the warmth of the sun" but is capable of realizing in such a stimulus the apprehension "the sun is warm": "That is, the stimulating warmth stays in my apprehension as something that is *already* warm. . . . This moment of the *already* expresses that what stimulates stays in the apprehension as something that *is* stimulating, *before* it stimulates and precisely in order to be able to stimulate. This is what I have often called the moment of the *prius*."[269] The transition from mere categorization of stimuli to conceptual categorization begins through this feeling intellection. The real thing actually present, accomplished by millions of neural sets, is referred to retroactively (as recollection, the "remembered present") as "warm sun," as a sphere from which the "I feel-the-warmth-of-the-sun" announces a constitutive reference: the "warmth-of-the-sun" belongs to the sun inasmuch as it is real, "its own," and the "feeling" that I feel (what includes not just a consciousness of the sun, but also a self-consciousness of its being felt by me, myself) does not immediately "trigger" a response (as when an animal is stimulated) but instead is "retained" without a response yet: "Intelligence emerges, then, in its function of apprehending reality, precisely and formally, through the *suspension of the pure feeling*, and at the moment of this suspension of the stimulaic character of the stimulus."[270] This "suspension" of the merely stimulaic response, from the apprehension of the "before" or the *prius* of the real ("warm-sun"),[271] grounds the entire process of posterior higher cerebral functions. The human being apprehends its reality "in the act of living, defined as *self-possession* of its reality."[272] The answers to the "possibilities"—and not mere stimuli—are the fruit of decisions. Mere substantivity (of living beings) transforms in the "suprainstance": "Reality is presented [to the human being] in this formality that we call *good*."[273] That human good is not solely "real"; it is also the product of a process of "self-fulfillment."[274] And inasmuch as this process is accomplished in *myself*, "to belong to me is a formal and positive moment of my reality. And precisely because it is so, I am a person."[275] Zubiri affirms, finally, that complete "fulfillment" (the "*colmar*" [filled to the brim]: *beo* in Latin, *beatitudo*: filled, fulfilled) of human reality is happiness:[276] "Because man is an animal of realities he is constitutively a moral animal; because he is a moral animal, he is an animal of goods, and man's most ultimate and radical good within his parameters is precisely his own happiness."[277]

I could expand farther on this topic, since the philosophers who ground themselves on the material aspect of ethics are numerous, but those already noted are enough, as I already noted, to indicate the material aspects of the ethics that we should now subsume from a more radical material universal principle.

§1.5. The Criterion and Universal
Material Principle of Ethics

[100] This is certainly the most complex and difficult section of this ethics. To say this does not mean that this section is the most relevant or the most indicative of the specificity of *Ethics of Liberation*. Furthermore, in this section I begin an argumentative process that will be developed in the following chapters.[278]

Here we will reflect on the criterion of practical truth or the framework of reference for the determination of adequate mediations for the production, reproduction, and development of the life of each human subject in community. Human beings access the reality that they confront every day from the ambit of their own lives. Human life is neither a goal nor a mere mundane-ontological horizon; human life is *the mode of reality* of the ethical subject (that is, not that of a stone, of a mere animal, or the Cartesian angelic "soul"), which gives content to all of its actions, which determines the rational order and also the level of its needs, drives, and desires that constitute the framework within which ends are fixed. The "ends" (with reference to Weberian formal instrumental reason) are "put in place" by the exigencies of human life. This is to say, insofar as the human being is a living entity, it constitutes reality *as objective* (for practical or for theoretical reason) in the exact measure in which it is determined as the mediation of *human* life. If it confronts something, in fact, empirically and daily, it does so *always* and *necessarily* as that which is, in some way, extracted from the "medium" that constitutes our environment as what leads to the life of the ethical subject. The life of the subject delimits it within certain fixed parameters that it cannot exceed under threat of death. Life is suspended, in its precise vulnerability, *within certain limits* and requiring *certain contents*: if the temperature of the earth rises, we will die of heat; if we cannot drink water because of the desiccation of the planet—as has happened to sub-Saharan peoples—we will die of thirst; if we cannot feed ourselves, we will die of hunger; if our community is invaded by a stronger community, we are dominated (we will live, but in degrees of alienation that are measured from a life lived almost animalistically to the point of extinction itself, as is the case with the indigenous peoples after the conquest in America). Human life marks limits, it normatively grounds an order; it has its own requirements. It also posits contents: food, housing, security, freedom and sovereignty, values and cultural identity, spiritual fulfillment (higher functions of the human being, which constitute the most relevant *contents* of *human* life) are *needed*. Human life is an ethical *mode of reality*.

In this last section of chapter 1, I present three questions: (1) the criterion of practical truth or the *content* of every ethics, (2) the material and *universal* principle of ethics, and (3) the problematic of the *application* of the material ethical principle.

a. The Material Universal Criterion of Practical Truth

[101] I wish to develop this issue, taking as a guiding thread, for the moment, Marx's discourse. In fact, the young Marx of 1844 already had "intuitions," which were not yet the future "categories" of the mature Marx of the *Grundrisse*,[279] but they are strong, clear, definitive "intuitions" of an ethics of content. Indeed, Marx places the *material*[280] in opposition to the merely *formal*[281] in Hegel. For Hegel the only movement of interest is that of self-consciousness as "science of the subject," which proceeds by the subsumption of one and another form or "object" of "experience" until absolute knowledge is reached: "From the one point of view the entity [*Dasein*] which Hegel *supersedes* [*aufhebt*] in philosophy is therefore not *real* religion, the *real* state, or *real* nature, but religion itself already as an object of knowledge, i.e., *dogmatics*; the same with *jurisprudence, political science* and *natural science*."[282] For Hegel, "reality" is "the subject knowing itself as absolute self-consciousness."[283] These are magnificent arguments that have not lost their currency and that show the knowledge Marx had of Hegel. Faced with this absolute consciousness of thought that thinks itself, as absolute emptiness, as "boredom [*Langweile*] [and] longing for a content,"[284] Marx observes: "Real [*wirkliche*], corporeal [*leibliche*] man, man with his feet firmly on the solid ground . . . is directly a *natural being*. As a natural being and as a living [*lebendiges*] natural being he is on the one hand endowed with *natural powers, vital powers* [*Lebenskräften*] — he is an *active* natural being. These forces exist in him as tendencies and abilities — as *instincts* [*Triebe*]. On the other hand, as a natural, corporeal, sensuous, objective being he is a *suffering* [*leidendes*], conditioned and limited creature, like animals and plants. That is to say, the *objects* of his instincts exist outside him."[285] Before Hegel, Marx attempts to recover the "real," but the human real that Marx is interested in is "material" (*material* with "a") reality, reality of "content."[286] To accomplish this Marx must recover a strong anthropological emphasis lost

by modern idealism (from Descartes to Kant),[287] that of a human being defined in the first place by its corporeality as "living" being, vulnerable, and for that reason affected by "needs." Marx describes this question in two previous pages:

> Physically man lives [*lebt*][288] only on . . . products of nature, whether they appear in the form of food, heating, clothes, a dwelling, etc. *The universality of man* appears in practice precisely in the universality which makes all nature his *inorganic* body–both inasmuch as nature is (1) his direct means of life, and (2) the material, the object, and the instrument of his life activity. . . . Man *lives* [*lebt*] on nature—means that nature is his *body* [*Leib*], with which he must remain in continuous interchange if he is not to die. . . .[289] *Life activity, productive life* itself, appears to man in the first place merely as a *means* of satisfying a need—the need to maintain physical existence. Yet the productive life is the life of the species. It is life-engendering life.[290]

[102] Against Hegel, for whom the supreme human act is the thinking that produces the thinking that thinks itself (formally), now what produces human life with self-consciousness is real human life, from its corporeality, which has needs; it is not so among animals: "The animal is immediately one with its life activity.[291] It does not distinguish itself from it. It is *its life activity*. Man makes his life activity itself the object of his will and of his consciousness.[292] He has *conscious life activity*. It is not a determination with which he directly merges. *Conscious life activity* distinguishes man immediately from animal life activity."[293] Marx is far from a simplistic materialism (physical) (*materiell* with an "e"). On the contrary, it is a matter of the human being that produces his physical, spiritual,[294] and cultural life, in its "content" (*material* with an "a"): "An animal forms objects only in accordance with the standard and the need of the species to which it belongs, whilst man knows how to produce in accordance with the standard of every species, and knows how to apply everywhere the inherent standard to the object. Man therefore also forms objects in accordance with the laws of beauty."[295] That material criterion on which ethics is grounded, the reproduction and development of human life, is universal, and furthermore is not solipsistic but communitarian. It concerns a "community of life" (*Lebensgemeinschaft*):

> Thus the *social*[296] character is the general character of the whole movement. . . . Activity and enjoyment, both in their content [*Inhalt*] and in their *mode of existence*, are *social*: *social* activity and *social* enjoyment. The *human* aspect of nature exists only for *social* man; for only then does nature exist for him as a *bond* with *man*[297]—as his existence for the other [*für den andren*] and the other's existence for him [*des andren für ihn*]—and as

the life-element [*Lebenselement*] of human reality [*menschlichen Wirklich-keit*]. Only then does nature exist as the *foundation* [*Grundlage*] of his own *human* existence. . . . Not only is the material[298] of my activity given to me as a social product (as is even the language in which the thinker is active): my *own* existence is social activity, and therefore that which I make of my-self, I make of myself for society and with the consciousness of myself as a social being. My *general* consciousness is only the *theoretical* shape[299] of that of which the *living* shape[300] is the *real* community, the social fabric, although at the present day *general* consciousness is an abstraction from real life and as such confronts it with hostility.[301]

Or as Moses Hess put it in his neglected article "On the Essence of Money": "*Life* is exchange of productive *vitality*. Each individual person behaves here as conscious and as conscious practical individual in the sphere of exchange of its *social life* [*gesellschaftlichen Lebens*]. . . . Each behaves with the social body [*Gesellschaftkörper*] as a singular member. . . . Each dies when it is isolated from the others. Its *real life* consists solely in the mutual exchange of their productive *vitality*, only in mutual interaction, only in connection with the social body."[302] Life is the supreme referent; nonetheless it can be sacrificed for life itself in community: "The person offers consciously his individual life as sacrifice for the *communal life*, if a contradiction be-tween both emerges.[303] . . . Love is more powerful than egoism."[304] I could, through these and many more texts that it would be excessive to cite, con-clude that the *universal material criterion* with which Marx could have de-veloped an ethics can be enunciated in the following, approximate, way: the one who acts humanly[305] has as content in the act, always and neces-sarily, some meditation for the self-responsible production, reproduction, and development[306] of the life of each human subject in a *community of life*, as the material fulfillment[307] of the needs of his or her cultural corpore-ality (the first among them being the desire of the other human *subject*),[308] having as ultimate referent all of humanity.

[103] This material criterion is, at the same time, a criterion of *practical* and theoretical *truth*.[309] Every statement, judgment, or speech act has as its ultimate "referent" human life. This ethics seeks to ground itself in empiri-cal judgments that are descriptive of fact—and not simply on judgments of value. We find ourselves at the level of descriptive statements or judgments, judgments of fact, which have their own consistency:

> Judgments of fact whose *criterion is truth, is life and death*[310] are at the same time constitutive judgments of *objective* reality. . . . *Objective* reality is not something that is given independently of the life of the human being. It is the life of the human being, when it succeeds in preventing death, which maintains reality as *objective* reality. For this reason in suicide its reality is

Table 2. Different Levels to Be Considered

1. The Real, the Sphere of the Life of the Ethical Subject	2. World of Cultures and of the Intercultural	3. Horizon of Means-Ends
Practical-material or originating ethical reason	Hermeneutical, ontological reason	Instrumental, strategic, scientific reason
Statements or judgments of fact, material, ethical, normative judgments	Normative, evaluative statements	Judgments of fact
Practical truth	Cultural values	Efficacy of means-ends

Note: The three levels, laid out in the three columns, are (1) order of reality, of the human life of the subject (universal); (2) ontological-cultural order (materially particular); (3) order of mediations (instrumental reason).

> dissolved,[311] and in the collective suicide of humanity, reality dissolves definitively. . . . [T]he *objectivity* of reality does not antecede human life, but it is as much its product as it is presupposition.[312]

We must, in the first place, begin by differentiating certain moments and different types of rationality, or statements, in order to be able to make the distinctions that we need to have present in the later presentation of this whole *Ethics of Liberation*.

[104] For now I wish only to indicate the difference between the mode of reality of "*human* life" (level 1),[313] from the ontological-hermeneutical horizon that opens as the sphere of the particularity of a culture (level 2).[314]

In MacIntyre as much as in Taylor, to take two concrete examples, the material sphere is exclusively situated at level 2 (of table 2). Taylor does not show clearly how each culture (level 2) is *a mode* of making concrete "*human* life in general*" (level 1); he considers only the "particularity" of each culture, without discovering the universal sphere of human life from which all cultures are particular instances, configured *from within* by the *material universal* criterion of the need to produce, reproduce, and develop *human* life as such (in all of humanity and forever). That is to say, Taylor only discovers a particular ontological-cultural reason (hermeneutical-valuational reason). I also affirm the importance of material rationality, but as a dimension of the reality of the concrete life of each human being (level 1 of the table). It is from this constitution of the peculiar mode of reality, as "*human* life," that the subject accesses objective reality through "practical-material reason" (and also through the "ethical-originary reason"), presupposed in the thought of Marx or Freud, and of many other critics, as we will see in chapter 4.

In the material aspect of ethics, descriptive statements make a *practical truth claim* (with respect to the reality of the production and reproduction of the life of the human subject as human) and a *theoretical truth claim* (with respect to reality in general, as abstraction or second moment of truth that, mediated, refers ultimately to this life). We will return in §2.5 to this theme, when I address the validity claim of formal morality, and distinguish it from the claim of practical truth, not merely of rightness, of statements.

[105] Max Weber has accustomed us to a certain classification of social action, at four levels:

> Social action, like all action, may be oriented in four ways. It may be: (1) *instrumentally rational* [*zweckrational*], that is, determined by expectations as to the behavior of objects in the environment and of other human beings; these expectations are used as "conditions" or "means" for the attainment of the actor's own rationally pursued and calculated ends;[315] (2) *value-rational* [*wertrational*], that is, determined by a conscious belief in the value for its own sake of some ethical, aesthetic, religious, or other form of behavior, independently of its prospectus of success; (3) *affectual* (especially emotional), that is, determined by the actor's specific affects and feeling states; (4) *traditional*, that is, determined by ingrained habitation.[316]

Actions that accomplish means as "means to ends" have to do with "statements of fact" (level 3 of table 2) that are formally an exercise of instrumental reason, and in certain cases scientific reason. For Weber "judgments of value" are mere subjective statements, grounded in values; values that are given culturally without the possibility of rational foundation. In Weber, ethics does not develop out of "statements of fact" and cannot have rational, and for that reason, scientific consistency.

Ethics of Liberation argues that "judgments of fact" in relation to the life or death of the ethical subject can be enunciated. These are not the *formal* judgments of fact of instrumental reason that proceed from the means-ends calculus, but instead are judgments with reference to the production, reproduction, or development of human life, which are material (but not material in the Weberian sense) and from which ends and values can be judged critically. Let us take, for instance, this statement:

1. John is eating.

This is a descriptive statement, a "judgment of fact" as an exercise of "practical-material reason." When we name "John,"[317] which is the name of a human subject, we are differentiating him in the set of the existing entities from both inanimate things and animals. We are, because it concerns a name, *recognizing* him as a concrete subject, with his own identity, unique and exclusive to that subject. In addition, his reality is revealed (in an act

Table 3. Recognition of the Ethical Subject

Object Form of knowledge	Individual (concrete needs)	Person (formal autonomy)	Subject (individual particularity)
Intuition (affective)	Family (love)		
Concept (cognitive)		Civil society (rights)	
Intellectual intuition			State (solidarity)

Note: See Honneth 1992, 46.

of "practical-material truth") as living reality ("John eats to live") and as living *human* reality (that is, as a self-conscious, autonomous, free subject):

2. John, who is a self-responsible living human subject, is eating.

[106] As can be seen, a certain type of "recognition" is at the base of each one of the criteria or conditions of possibility that we enunciate in this *Ethics*. Axel Honneth has studied the question of recognition in Hegel. We can appreciate the complexity of what we are considering in table 3.

"John" is recognized[318] as a member of a family, of a civil society, of a state. The "eating" of this subject (familial, personal, citizen) is mediation for life in general, but specifically for his life as a human subject. It is not animal "swallowing," but a gastronomic act. This subject eats "something" that he has bought, produced himself, or stolen. In this way, I consider it a simple act of licit eating of a dinner in a restaurant, or the eating of a farmer, or the eating of someone who has obtained food illegally and, therefore, is eating with a guilty conscience. All of this is always and inevitably included in the "judgment of fact" (on the human being as a subject who needs to reproduce his or her life by eating), which is not only an abstract calculus of a means toward an end of instrumental reason, but rather is equally a reflection on the subject of the act,[319] and for that reason, a moment of practical-material reason, inasmuch as it refers to life that actualizes the reality of "this *human subject* who is eating" from an even more radical horizon. It is a matter of a "judgment of fact" that is neither instrumental nor formal, merely, but rather a "judgment" or statement of reality, that is, material, inasmuch as it is a statement on a living subject as human. But, in addition, practical-material reason can subsume or determine whether an end, a judgment of fact of instrumental reason or of cultural value, can "refer" or not to the possibility of the production, reproduction, or development of the life of this human subject in community. Hinkelammert writes:

> Life is the possibility to have ends, but it is not an end itself. . . . No action calculated by a means-ends rationality is rational if in its consequences it eliminates the subject that sustains that action. This circle we can call the

reproductive rationality[320] of the subject. This refers to the conditions of possibility of human life. This fundamental rationality imposes itself upon us as necessary, because the means-ends calculus as such does not reveal the effects on these conditions of the possibility of human life. To the light of means-ends rationality something might appear perfectly rational; however, to the light of the reproductive rationality of the *subject* it can appear perfectly irrational.[321]

And he adds a little later:

> Therefore, it concerns a *judgment of compatibility* between two rationalities,[322] in which reproductive rationality passes judgment on means-ends rationality. Its *criterion of truth* cannot but be life or death. The problem is to know if the fulfilment of means-ends oriented action is compatible with the reproduction of the life of *the subjects of life*. What is confirmed as true is the compatibility, and what is confirmed as error is a performative contradiction between both rationalities.[323]

Let us take a step forward.

b. The Universal Material-Ethical Principle

[107] At this juncture, I offer an overview, not an exhaustive analysis, of the "transition" from descriptive statements to normative ones. The entire problematic of a possible dialectical-material *grounding*—not of an abstract and formal "deduction"—of "normative judgments" starting with "judgments of fact" about life constitutes just this. Once again, I point out that the "naturalist fallacy" that Hume indicated in his *Treatise of Human Nature*, is situated at an abstract, logical-formal level.[324] My account, instead, situates itself at a material level (of practical-material reason), which requires new logical developments. Is it possible, materially and concretely, to make *explicit* normative statements from descriptive statements?

The material criterion that I presented in the preceding section refers only to a purely descriptive aspect. Now we need a material principle that is strictly ethical, of obligation or ought-to-be, which can serve as mediation between the descriptive criterion and its critical application. This is the whole problem of the possibility of making explicit *from* the material criterion (of the production, reproduction, and development of human life) a demand, an obligation, or a properly ethical ought-to-be. It concerns the question of the "transition" from the mere descriptive *criterion* (the "being" in a concrete and material sense, as *human* life) to the, properly speaking, normative *ethical material principle* (the "ought-to-be"), which is not logically situated at the same abstract or formal level of the so-called naturalist fallacy, because in this case it would be an impossible or inappropriate deduction. In fact, the naturalist fallacy defines as erroneous the deduction of a demand or *normative material principle* of ethics (which would be a "judgment *of value*") from a means-ends descriptive *formal criterion* (which would be for Weber, and many others, the only type of "judgment of fact"). I situate myself, as I note frequently above, within the sphere of a particular type of judgment of fact (which refers to *human* life in the concrete and as an exercise of practical-material reason). I make these clarifications in order to leave the way open for a theoretical development that allows the reconstruction of material and critical ethics (which the positivist analytical metaethics of philosophical liberalism, discourse ethics, or the neoliberal formal economics of Hayek have negated for diverse reasons).

[108] In the empiricism of Hume, the level of the "is," the descriptive statement ("judgment of fact"), is connected to the ethical "ought-to-be," which is the only object of the sentiments. For me, the "ought-to-be" that is attempted has "reference" to a human dimension present from the beginning. Moore situates himself at the same level of the "judgment of value" of Weber. The later interpretation, Fregeian-Russellian, is concerned with the impossibility of this deduction at an exclusively logical-formal level (of instrumental reason). My argument, meanwhile, runs along another level (the concrete, or material), which sees every major descriptive premise as having an ethical aspect, because it is *human* life, free and responsible, to which I always refer); and for that reason, my argument has another point of departure and of arrival. No one can deny that every statement that refers to the facts of the *living human* being, inasmuch as "living" and inasmuch as "human," ought to be considered as merely descriptive; examples are eating and drinking as needs and the expression of cultural and culinary arts, running as something done in order to move from one place to another and as sport, clothing oneself as a means to conserve warmth and for fashion, inhabiting a place in order to protect oneself from the weather and to experience it as architecture, thinking, speaking, painting, symbolizing, and so on—doing all these things as a living entity and humanly. On the other hand, no one can deny that the *human* being as subject, in the first place, has his or her life, although this might be lived most of the time under the auspices of self-organized institutions, under a certain self-conscious control (as higher neural-cerebral function). Responsibility for one's acts, for one's life, is a consequence not only of consciousness but also of self-consciousness. In the second place, the living human is originally constituted by an intersubjectivity that constitutes the human being as a communicative subject (in a community of life and of linguistic communication). Co-responsibility is another consequence. And, in the third place, as another dimension, the living *human* is a subject that from his or her origin participates in a cultural world (of symbols, values, but also of norms,

prescriptions, etc.). All of this bespeaks a necessary relation to the *human* mode of *being in living*; that is to say, the responsibility of the production, reproduction, and development of life itself in an individual human subject. It would seem then that every descriptive statement of constitutive moments of the human living reality *as human* always includes, necessarily (because it is a *human* subject and nothing else) and from its origin, a responsible self-reflection that "gives" its own life to the demand, the obligation to conserve it—even more so if we consider that the motivation of the pure specific instinct has transformed into cultural moments. These demands, *implicit* ethical obligations, or ought-to-bes are made *explicit* in normative statements, since human beings have lost certain instinctual moments (very present in animals) as an effect of their historical-cultural behavior. In fact, linguistic communitarian behavior, with costumes and institutions regulated by values, has subsumed instinctual evolution, and such behavior has developed culturally. Ethical normativity comes to replace the behavior of the animal species; history replaces and supersedes many genetic stages of evolution. Human free and self-reflexive spontaneity opens an immense horizon to decisions that are not based on stimuli but lie between the "security" of instinct and the pure "arbitrariness" of a freedom without limits; ethics "frames" a behavior regulated by rational duties, obligations, and demands (that have as material parameter the line that separates life from death).

[109] Obligations are not identical to the necessity of physical laws or animal instincts, instead, they are defined socially, by a frame delimited by more or less constant institutional tendencies of nonintentional acts, or monologically or intersubjectively by demands proper to the free, human being, which are socially regulated, because every human act, *qua human*, has as a specific constitutive moment the exercise of *self-consciousness*. From this opens up the possibility of autonomous self-responsibility;[325] responsibility by means of which the human being "takes charge" (or can intervene "correctively"—but also unfortunately, destructively—with full or explicit "conscience") of the mediations, possibilities, or actions that are requirements of fulfillment of *one's own* human life, in community, and, as ultimate explicit horizon, of all humanity. Life is under its own responsibility. This is what is proper and exclusive to the *mode of reality* of human life: *to have it under one's own responsibility*. Humans are the only living entities that are self-responsible. For this reason, they are the only living beings that live ethically. The ethical character of human life is one's self-responsibility for persevering in life. This constitutes *being human as a subject* (sub-ject: the "I" thrown "under," by the act of reflection "about" oneself), without for that reason negating all the moments of vital self-organization or social self-regulation. This self-conscious, self-referential "reflection" (of *human*

life *on* its own life, and taking "charge of it" as subject)[326] is exactly the moment in which human life becomes the responsibility of the human subject: *ante festum*, as an absolute a priori condition, because life is already there *always* (for the subject), to be constituted through self-responsibility as action and ethical project; *in festum*: because we cannot cease to find ourselves with it, inevitably, and to recognize ourselves and the other as the living alter ego; and *post festum*: as memory of what we have done toward the development or destruction of our lives or as future project. To be subject means exactly that my (our) own "*being*," my (our) life, is given to me (to us) from solidaristic responsibility *as an "ought-to-be,"* and this in a necessary and simultaneous way.

From the statement "John, who is a self-responsible living human subject, is eating" (statement 2, presented above) the following normative judgment can be made explicit, materially, as an exercise of practical-material reason:

3. John, who is a self-conscious living being, *ought* to continue eating.

If he did not eat, he would die, and since he is self-responsible for his life, the decision to not eat *ought to be* judged suicide. But suicide is ethically unjustifiable.

[110] That is to say, the production, reproduction, and development of the life of each *human* subject is itself a *fact* (about which "judgments of fact," or "descriptive statements" can be made; and not merely those of instrumental or analytical-formal reason), which are "imposed" on the will itself (the drive level of humanity as a species, of the community, and to each ethical subject) by its inevitable self-reflexive constitution. Human life is not only given spontaneously, but its conservation and development is also imposed on us as an "obligation." This is to say, the statement "*There is* human life" can make *explicit* (rationally, reflexively, and practical-materially) the ethical *ought-to-be* (which can be formulated as a "normative statement" or "ethical judgments of reality"),[327] with a claim to practical truth, in the deontic demands of producing, reproducing, and developing the life itself of the ethical subject. The demand of the *ought-to-live* of life itself can be made *explicit* from the *living reality* of the human subject, precisely because *human* life is reflexive and self-responsible, taking into account the autonomous and solidaristic will it engages in order to be able to survive. Herein lies the weakness, but at the same time the need of ethics, at its deontic level, as normative! If humanity were to lose this ethical consciousness—and it would seem that it is losing it, as can be seen in the insensibility in the face of killing the other, in the face of the misery of the majority of its members in the South of planet Earth—it could plunge into collective suicide.[328] *Living* thus turns from being a *criterion* of practical truth into being an ethical *demand*, or *obligation*: the *ought-to-live*.

Put another way, the "transition" from the material judgment of fact to a normative judgment is produced by practical-material reason, which makes the ethical "demand" *explicit* in biological-cultural self-reflexivity. The "demand" is the responsible self-binding that the will (from the "id" through the "ego") imposes on the subject ("self") out of the "responsibility" to live. The "id-ego" coerces ethically the living, extant "self" in order to prevent it from dying, and to compel it to survive: the "id" is imposed on the "self" (drive, affectivity, life itself as motor) through the "I." This self-decision is imposed, furthermore, as "will to live" (ob-ligation),[329] otherwise the I would disintegrate and would lose the "sense" of life: it would remain in a situation of anomie, of panic before a *vacuum*, of suicide. For this reason, the material principle of ethics is grounded on the universal material criterion already discussed.

If we return to the argumentative example already enunciated, we could retrace it and develop it in the following manner:

2a. John, who is a responsible *human* living subject, is eating.

2b. To live, it is necessary to eat.

2c. If John ceases to eat, he would die.

3a. As self-responsible for his life, he ought not to stop eating, or he would be guilty of suicide. *Ergo*

3b. John ought to continue eating.

The decisive moment is the "transition" from statement 2c (biological need) to 3a (ethical "demand"). It is a dialectical transition because it is a material grounding, or *making explicit*, that is performed by practical-material reason that can comprehend or capture rationally the *necessary relation* between the *natural need* to eat-in-order-to-live and the *ethical* responsibility of the subject who is commanded or who "ought" to eat-in-order-not-to-die. This "ought" is grounded as an *ethical* and material requirement (inasmuch as life is given to put the subject "in charge" of the ethical, rational, and instinctual subject him- or herself, within the requirements of the criterion of truth, and also, although as mediation, concretely from the values of culture, and so on, no longer from the human species' merely animal survival instinct, which has certainly been weakened by civilization. Here the ethical "ought," as a self-responsible norm that binds and commands, comes to subsume the exigencies or laws of instinct—the "natural"[330] requirements of nonhuman living beings. Ethics does not concern only (though it does to an extent), or fundamentally (instead of derivatively), the valorative sphere of subjective judgments (or cultural intersubjective) of value. Ethics fulfills the urgent requirement of the survival of a self-conscious, cultural, self-responsible human being. The ecological crisis is the best example: the human species may decide to "correct" ethically or self-responsibly the nonintentional negative effects of devastating technological capitalism so that the species as a whole will not continue on its road toward collective suicide. Humanity's ethical consciousness may transform in a short period at the *last moment* when the species is at risk of becoming extinct, given that the self-organized controls of its corporeality either pass through the corrective of self-conscious responsibility (and critical, of the "ought-to-be") or run out of resources, because (as I noted above) the animal instinct will not be able to prevent collective suicide.

Hence, I propose the following initial description of what I will call the *universal material principle of ethics*, the principle of corporeality as a "sensibility" that contains the instinctual, cultural-valorative (hermeneutical-symbolic) order of every norm, act, microphysical structure, institution, or system of ethical life, from the criterion of human life in general: the one who acts ethically[331] *ought* (as an obligation) to produce, reproduce, and develop self-responsibly the concrete life of each human subject, in a *community of life*, and inevitably out of a cultural and historical "good life"[332] (from the subject's way of conceiving happiness, with a certain reference to values and to a fundamental way of comprehending being as an ought-to-be, and for that reason also making a *rightness* claim) that is shared instinctually and solidaristically, having as ultimate reference all of humanity. In other words, this is a normative statement that makes a *practical truth claim* and, further, *a universality claim.*[333]

[III] This material principle of ethics includes the point of departure and contains the "matter" (*Inhalt*) of all posterior moments (formal-procedural, of feasibility, critical or of liberation). It constitutes the ethical *content* of all praxis and of every project of future development; it cannot be rejected, superseded, or left to the side under any condition. Out of this, is imposed the facticity of the ethical quotidian world as such. It is not a mere particular or "pathological" horizon that may be abandoned in order to be lifted to an a priori horizon of transcendental principles—as is the case in the ethics of Kant or Apel. Nor does it consist exclusively in the incommensurable horizon (as it is for the postmoderns) or the historical-cultural one (as it is for the communitarians). But, still, although it is the *necessary* point of departure that is presupposed always already by every ethics or morality, it should not be forgotten that it is not a *sufficient* horizon, since we must, for establishing validity, feasibility, or ethical critique, take recourse to *other principles* of codetermination.

I have to add that everything that I have presented here is always situated within a concrete historical and cultural horizon. But this should not move us to accept as a background question, What is the concrete content of a "good life"? Or, in what way may we *interpret* the content of happiness, the total evaluation of the structure of values, or in the last instance, the "comprehension of being" concretely and historically? The unavoidable and ethically relevant issue is, instead, that no one (not even the member of a society of postconventional late capitalism) can act without having in mind a *cultural-linguistic concrete way* of institutionalizing the ethical demand of the production, reproduction, and development of human life *in general* (this is the position of Taylor and Habermas). This claim or demand is absolutely *universal* (and now I articulate my position with respect to that of Taylor and Habermas). These are the a priori material presuppositions of every human act. But, because of the *transcultural moment* of the ethical criterion and principle of production, reproduction, and development of the life of the human subject (pre- or transontological), we may now pass ethical judgment on a culture (its ends and values) *from "within" and according to "its" logic and identity*.[334] In this sense, the principle is universal.

[112] I will offer a detailed formulation of the *discourse of the grounding*[335] of this material principle of ethics below. A *positive* and material grounding, such as I have merely sketched, is needed. But a *negative*, or *ad absurdum*, grounding is also and equally needed, to demonstrate the impossibility of its opposite. In this case, the argument will not take on the skeptic who puts in question reason in general; it will argue against the cynic who pretends to justify an *ethical* order grounded in the acceptance of death, killing, or collective suicide, as when a Friedrich von Hayek justifies the elimination of those who are defeated by "competition" in the market — the only possible economic, formal-rational horizon, the principle of death that, generalized, puts humanity as such in danger. *The impossibility* of arguing ethically without performative contradiction in favor of an order where the norm, action, microstructure, institution, or ethical system proposes the development of an ethical order based on death, killing, or collective suicide (Heidegger's "being-unto-death" or Freud's "*thanatos* principle"?) will have to be demonstrated. Every act of the human subject, inevitably and without exception, is a concrete way of fulfilling the requirement of the production, reproduction, or development of human life, from whose grounding can be developed ethical orders that open up as concrete alternatives for the development of life (better and possible concrete projects of the "good life").[336] The argumentative strategy of grounding ought to follow the direction shown by Wittgenstein: "If suicide is [ethically] allowed then everything is allowed. If anything is not allowed then suicide is not allowed. This throws a light on the nature of ethics, for suicide is, so to speak, the elementary sin. And when one investigates it it is like investigating mercury vapour in order to comprehend the nature of vapors. Or is even suicide in itself neither good nor evil?"[337] The claim of this type of grounding would be to show that no ethical norm, human act, microstructure, just institution, or system of ethical life may contradict the enunciated principle. It is a universal principle, which may be improved in its formulation, but is not *fal-*

sifiable—even taking into account the uncertainty of finite reason, because if it were falsifiable we would lose the ethical grounding of falsifiability, of reason itself; we would fall into an originating and abysmal performative contradiction. The groundings of other subaltern principles and norms of concrete actions can be falsified from this principle. This is the principle of "practical truth" par excellence.

From a material principle of ethics, such as we have initially defined in an *abstract level*, the material ethics studied in this chapter (utilitarianism, communitarianism, the ethics of values, of happiness, etc.) behave as spheres of lesser universality, as particular, necessary, and pertinent *material aspects* (although analyzed differently), but not sufficient, for they should always be grounded in the material principle I have presented.

c. The "Application" of the Material Principle

[113] We can now move to the question of the "application" of the material principle to a norm, action, microstructure, institution, system of ethical life, and so on. In the whole ethical tradition (explicitly since Aristotle), this question has concerned the theme of "prudence (*phronesis*)," or the virtue of practical reason.

In fact, the merely "stimulaic" categorization and valorization of animals "trigger" or prompt a response in a necessary way: instinctively, specifically, immediately—with some exceptions among the higher species. There is then a response or "application" without mediation: the instinct for the reproduction of animal life "applies" to the stimuli, in a necessary manner (from an immediate perceptive-evaluative dimension proper to the species), the neurocerebral criteria of life. There is no distance between the stimulaic categorization and the response—at least until the higher species, as I have said. There exists then an *immediate* or instinctual *material* application of the biological principle.

In the *human* being a *space* opens up between (a) the conceptual categorization, the conscious valorization, the responsible and self-conscious linguistic process, and (b) the possible response. This is the "space" of self-consciousness, freedom, responsibility, and autonomy, which "gives time" to the process of the *application* of the universal material principle of ethics for the elective rational grounding of the norm to be executed in the action. It is a matter of the *necessity* of another principle that codetermines the material principle, which I will call the *moral formal principle* or the principle of practical-intersubjective discursive rationality of the agreement that reaches, from the *truth of the material principle, validity* through argumentation, rational (and effective) grounding of the ends, values, and means to be accomplished. Private and monologically veritative *phronesis* (not necessarily solipsistic) is articulated (not negated but subsumed or transformed) in the discursive intersubjectivity of the validity of formal morality. Habermas indicates correctly, challenging Heinrich's position[338] as well as Blumenberg's,[339] that "if we assume that the reproduction of social life [*die Reproduktion des gesellschaftlichen Lebens*][340] is tied not only to the conditions of cognitive-instrumental dealings with external nature . . . and we assume that socialization depends just as much on the conditions of the intersubjectivity of understanding [*Verständigung*] among participants in interaction, then we also have to reformulate the naturalistic concept of self-preservation [*Selbsterhaltung*]."[341] Evidently, the conception I have proposed in this chapter is not naturalistic but instead presupposes the integration of consensual intersubjectivity, discursive rationality—but equally, the instinctual and affective order of desire—within the process of the production, reproduction, and development of the concrete and communitarian life of an ethical, *human* subject. But this means that we are already moving into chapter 2.

CHAPTER 2

Formal Morality
Intersubjective Validity

[114] This is an ethics of life. Human life in its rational dimension knows that life,[1] as being in a community of living beings, is ensured through the participation of all. Linguistic communication is an essential dimension of human life, and rational argumentation is a new "cunning" of life. In this sense modern morality has contributed a new modality only partially known beforehand: the procedures of formal morality for obtaining intersubjective validity or universality. If the aspect of content (or material) of ethics, which is delimited by the *criterion of practical truth* ("intensive" universality), grounds the material principle of ethics, then the formal aspect of morality, in relation with *the criterion of validity*, grounds the procedural principle of the universality ("extensive" or intersubjective) of the moral consensus. My thesis here entails, as will be seen in chapter 3, that the practical truth of content of the action must be adequately articulated with intersubjective validity constituting, from a concrete "feasibility," a complex unity in which each aspect determines the other in different ways and constitutes what can be denominated the norm, the action, the praxis, the structures of the ethically "good" subject. The "goodness claim" thus has, at least, a "material" and a "formal" component. The "formal" aspect, which I will treat in this chapter, consists in the classic question of the application and the mediation, or "subsumption," of the "material" moment.

[115] As I have said, in premodern ethical philosophy some consideration was given, albeit not much, to the formal procedure for obtaining validity, but it was a generally private or monologic treatment. Aristotle addressed the question in the book on *phronesis* in *Nicomachean Ethics*. In the first place, for Aristotle, practical reason and theoretical reason are not identical: "Socrates, then, thought the virtues were rules or rational principles [*lógous*]

(for he thought they were, all of them, forms of scientific knowledge), while we think they *involve* a rational principle."[2] In this way, Aristotle criticizes the fall into reductivism of identifying general rationality with scientific reason and he proposes in addition a specific type of practical rationality. In fact, the concrete practical judgment that allows one to perform an action (what Kant will call "maxim"), Aristotle calls *hypolepsis*.[3] This norm is arrived at as a "conclusion" of a "practical syllogism"[4] that departs from the material principle. It is then a question of "applying" the said principle (for Aristotle the "good life" in general will be the source of all content) to the concrete empirical case: "What is best, is of such and such a nature, whatever it may be (let it for the sake of the argument be what we please); and this is not evident except to the good man; for wickedness perverts us and causes us to be deceived about the starting-point of action. Therefore it is evident that it is impossible to be practically wise [*phrónimon*] without being good."[5]

In turn, it is understandable that, for Aristotle, the formal act of applying the principle through which the concrete norm (*hypolepsis* or maxim) gains "validity" — qua conclusion of a rational argument — should be exercised monologically (therein resides its contemporary importance), given that it subsumes the material aspects (the principle of practical truth, the virtues, inclinations, or emotions) of the formal process (the judgment, the practical syllogism) in order to make a goodness claim. What is chosen is rationally argued (*according to reason*) morally;[6] at the same time it has an ethically grounded content.[7]

The contemporary relevance of Aristotle consists precisely in this unity or articulation of the *material* and the *formal*, although it has, as is evident, premodern limitations. But, for this reason, it has not fallen prey to some of the limitations of a dualist Modernity, which we must overcome. Aristotle is a universalistic conventionalist, and a philosophical ontologist.

In fact, materially, Aristotle integrates emotions (nowadays we would say the achievements of psychoanalysis) with practical rationality in the formal-material act of the "choice [*proaíresis*],"[8] which is defined in the following way: "Choice is desiderative thought [*orektikòs noûs*] or intellectual desire [*órexis dianoetiké*]."[9]

This all concerns the order of "truth [*alétheia*] in agreement with right desire [*oréxei tê orthê*],"[10] of the "practical truth according to reason [*alethê metà lógou praktikén*],"[11] which constitutes "the good praxis as fully realized [*hê eupraxia télos*]."[12] The material moment (of rationality and practical truth, the emotions and the ontological-ethical contents) is indissolubly united with the formal moment (of the moral validity of the chosen maxim), but, it is evident, only reaches a precritical and private validity (prepragmatic, we might say today). Aristotle still has a ways to go, but he can still teach us much today, given the many material or formal reductionisms that in practice invalidate most contemporary, European or North American philosophical proposals in ethics or morality.

[116] In the same way, Thomas Aquinas referred to this theme in his treatise *Prudentia*, contributing the concept of freedom, which was unknown by the Greeks. As for the Greeks, "the ultimate *télos* [onto-material] cannot be subject to any choice,"[13] which fixes what is impossible or possible, given that what "we do is only possible [*possibilium*] for us,"[14] which is situated between "the impossible [*impossibile*]" and the "illusory [*velleitas*]"[15] (which is to claim to do the impossible).[16] The possible is procedurally and formally elected in a monological way, but taking into account the ontological-material condition: "By [ethical] conscience is applied comprehension of principles . . . to the particular act that is under examination."[17] That is to say, by means of the "conscience" (where, in this period, the entire question of formal morality, or moral argumentation for establishing the validity of a norm, was concentrated, whether individual or political—the latter, however, as the exercise of "political prudence" performed solipsistically only by the prince), the particular maxim is dialectically subsumed with a universality claim into the horizon of ethical life.[18] But the originality of this historical moment of philosophical thought consists, formally or morally, in the fact that the moment of the selection of the maxim counts with a greater autonomy, independence, "separation" or distance due to "freedom." If the end is imposed "*absolutely* [*absolute*],"[19] the "possibilities" instead must be argumentatively and rationally compelled.[20] What is chosen (the maxim) is materially (with reference to happiness, the emotions, or the "good life") a "desired judgment [*intellectus appetitivus*]," and formally (with reference to a solipsistic, prudent validity) a "judged desire [*appetitus intellectivus*]."[21]

Before Modernity, the question of truth (*verum*) included without differentiation reference to the content (the reference to a reality, the content or materiality of ethics) and the possible acceptability of the item in question by the community of the arguers (validity, the formality of morality).[22] We must now delve into this difference.

§2.1. The Transcendental Morality of Immanuel Kant

[117] We enter here into the path of modern morality properly speaking, which is carried out by different traditions in the process of the simplification in the *management* of the world system which I discussed in §I.6. Descartes wrote little on morality[23] that does not go beyond a "provisionary morality." Malebranche in his *Traité de Morale* reminds us of the Stoic-Augustinian tradition, in which love is still the backbone virtue.[24] In

the same way in the ethics of Spinoza: "The intellectual love of the mind towards God is that very love of God whereby God loves himself, not insofar as he is infinite, but insofar as he can be explained through the essence of the human mind regarded under the form of eternity,"[25] which coincides with the *conatus esse conservandi.* Wolff sustains, already entering ambiguously into the question of validity, that "the perfection of the moral life consists in the consensus of the free acts of all and with natural things."[26] Leibniz, for his part, within his metaphysical rationalism, does not abandon happiness as an ethical point of reference,[27] but, above all, proposes a society of spirits with God,[28] which will have a long inheritance (in Kant, Hegel, Marx, and Apel).

Königsberg was a mercantile city of the Hanseatic League, and had been integrated into the Baltic and North Sea systems since the Middle Ages. Pietism had made itself strongly present, and, although that practice required the fulfillment of the Kingdom of God in this world, it was still marked by Calvinist asceticism. Kantian morality was the one best suited to that double requirement. What is better than a morality that, in negating desires, supports itself in the virtue and the fulfillment of pure duty, and that will leave to God, after death, the payment in happiness for what is deserved—though not enjoyed—for the virtue performed in this life? I am not speaking ironically; this is a conviction that has emerged after a careful study of Kant.[29]

The young Kant (1746–59), a rationalist in the Wolffian and Leibnizian vein,[30] shows no relevant originality (other than in light of the later Kant). When in 1759 he names Hamann and Hume (whom he probably began to read in 1756) in a letter, he begins a period, not properly empiricist, in which he attempts to integrate empiricist ethics into his own philosophical discourse. This attempt will end up negating the material or "moral sentiment" level in favor of the "first principles of judgment," which are known only by the "pure intellect [*intellectum purum, reinen Verstand*]."[31] This transitional stage lasts until 1770, when in a definitive way he proposes the hypothesis of a modern formal morality, splitting it from a material ethics of the "good." This material ethics, in turn, with the visit of Adam Smith to France during these years (in 1764), will give origin to *the most material* of the practical horizon: the philosophy of economics and economic-political science. Two hundred and more years after that split, I will attempt to reflect on the need to reestablish the unified or imbricated nature of both levels: ethics and economics. Both are *necessary (but not sufficient)* for an ethics of liberation.

[118] Indeed, the empiricists and Rousseau allow Kant to awaken from the empty rationalist dream. But he was never able to integrate the material, emotive aspect of ethics, because the empiricists themselves had defined the

"moral feelings" reductively—as we saw in §1.2. Kant never had within his reach a notion that would allow him to articulate the rational moment with human sentiments,[32] with the ontological and historical-cultural level, and with the *life of each human subject* in general. He presupposed a dualist conception, of the negation of the body, of the irrationality (and for this reason exclusively as egoism) of the feelings, which he could not integrate with the rationalist horizon of the "perfect life."[33] For this reason, the only possible exit he offered was the transcendental, a formal horizon he had difficulty reintegrating into the whole material moment in the a priori determination of the human act. In 1762, Kant still reminds us of the rationalist tradition that, as in the Middle Ages, affirmed the perfect as the *bonum*, although abstractly or formally and not because of its "material" (*material*) content (*Inhalt*): "The rule: perform the most perfect [*vollkommenste*][34] action in your power, is the first *formal ground* [*formale Grund*] of all obligation to act."[35] The "formal" in morality is the obligation[36] to do a perfect act, regardless of its content. Kant modified the meaning of the Wolffian "obligation [*Verbindlichkeit*]" and with this he began to sketch the difference between the hypothetical and the categorical.[37]

But, immediately, he showed that he was making problematic this integration of the "material" with an empty, rationalist formulation: "And just as, in the absence of any material [*materiale*] first principles, nothing flowed from the first formal [*formalen*] principles of our judgment of the truth, so here no specifically determinate obligation flows from these two rules . . . unless they are combined with indemonstrable material [*materiale*] principles of practical cognition."[38] In this passage, Kant situates exactly the possible unity between the formal and the material; for this reason, the question of the application of the abstract, "formal" principle in concrete material begins to be formulated in this way. Here, "formal" still has a rationalist sense of coordination, of the empty, of the abstract, of the universal. He continues to show his preoccupation with how to integrate the empiricist "material" when he writes: "It is only recently . . . that people have come to realize that the faculty of representing the *true* is *cognition*, while the faculty of experiencing the *good* [*Gute*] is *feeling* [*Gefühl*]."[39] This opinion is repeated in 1765: "The distinction between good and evil [*des Guten and Bösen*] in actions, and the judgment of moral rightness, can be known, easily and accurately, by the human heart through what is called sentiment [*Sentiment*]. . . . The attempts of Shaftesbury, Hutchenson, and Hume, although incomplete and defective, have nonetheless penetrated furthest in the search for the fundamental principles of all morality."[40]

[119] What is important for us now in this rereading of Kant is that he had explicit consciousness of the need for a formal-material connection, but this notion will be discarded, because in this period the "material" was

still defined in an ambiguous manner, with almost exclusive reference to the sentiments seen as irrational inclinations. It is precisely here where the ethics of liberation departs from Kant and reconstructs universally and rationally the material level. After this point, for Kant, the material, practical, empirical level would concern only the whimsical, the corporeal that is irrelevant for morality, the particular that is never universal, which can never be a criterion to determine a priori the good from the bad. In 1770, Kant had already sketched the "transcendental" level, as a way to supersede the erroneous dilemma between rationalism and empiricism: "*Moral philosophy*, therefore, insofar as it furnishes the first *principles of judgment*, is only cognized by the pure understanding and itself belongs to pure philosophy. Epicurus, who reduced its criteria to the sense of pleasure [*Gefühl der Lust*] or pain, is very rightly blamed, together with certain moderns, who have followed him to a certain extent from afar, such as Shaftsbury, and his supporters."[41] Kant defines clearly that "matter [*material, Stoff*] (in the transcendental sense), that is the *parts*, . . . are here taken to be *substance*,"[42] while "form . . . consists in the coordination, not in the subordination, of substances."[43]

The empirical, the corporeal, the moral sentiments are the material. The pure, the methodical, the creative procedure are the a priori formal.[44] Thus, little by little, we arrive at the *Groundwork of the Metaphysic of Morals* of 1785: "All rational cognition is either *material* and concerned with some object,[45] or *formal* and occupied with the form of the understanding and of reason itself and with the universal rules of thinking in general, without distinction of objects."[46] Finally, in the *Critique of Practical Reason* of 1788, Kant dismisses definitively all possible material principles of moral validity: "All the inclinations together (which can be brought into a tolerable system and the satisfaction of which is then called one's own happiness) constitute regard for oneself [*selbstsucht*] (*solipsismus*)."[47]

[120] The question lies in how to develop the entire sphere of formal, universal validity, and Kant will do it in a new way—from which the ethics of liberation has a lot to learn. Kant sought to accomplish this by departing exclusively from a *single, unique* principle.[48] Furthermore, all morality begins with the groundwork of this principle. This option (necessary once the moral sense of the material—*material* with "a" as "content"—is denied) requires that we begin our discourse from a practical principle, thus imposing its inverted architecture on later formalism, up through our own days:[49]

> Practical reason . . . does not have to do with objects for the sake of *cognizing* them but with its own ability to *make them real*.[50] . . . [I]t follows that a critique of the analytic of reason, insofar as it is to be a practical reason (and this is the real problem), *must begin* from the *possibility of practical principles* a priori . . . , and only then could the last chapter conclude this

part, namely the chapter about the relation of pure practical reason to sensibility and about its necessary influence upon sensibility to be cognized a priori, that is, about *moral feeling*.[51]

Indeed, everything then departs from the formal practical principle where the universal proceduralism of the moral validity of the act to be realized begins to be delineated: "All maxims have . . . a *form*, which consists in universality [*Allgemeinheit*]; and in this respect the formula of the moral imperative is expressed thus: that maxims must be chosen as if they were able to hold as universal laws of nature."[52] Kant then specifies his sphere of moral reflection. It concerns the concept of "validity [*Gültigkeit*]" and not of the "good [*das Gute*]" (although he also deals with the latter, in a derivative and weak sense), in order to designate what morality intends. The "as if [*als ob*]" indicates "in such a way," "in such a fashion," that is to say, the *procedure* that has to be necessarily fulfilled so that the maxim gets to "count [*gelten*]." And thus we arrive at the categorical imperative:

> [a] You should [b] act [c] in such a way that [d] you could will that the maxim of your volition [e] should at the same time become [f] a principle of universal law.[53]

[121] For the purposes of my rereading I want to foreground some particular aspects. Inasmuch as the categorical imperative "forces itself upon us of itself as a synthetic a priori proposition,"[54] we ought to consider the following: (a) the *subject* (you), who synthesizes ("I connect" [*verknüpfe*])[55] and refers what is synthesized to the solipsistic apperception (potentially self-conscious consciousness); (b) the *object* (*Gegenstand*), what is synthesized, or the act to be done in the future; (c) the *procedure* ("in such a way" [*so*]), which ultimately consists in the commandment (and which will be developed by discourse ethics), *how* one has presupposed when thinking about how one ought to act; (d) the *matter* or empirical content of the act, which ought to be "known," this being a matter of ethics (in a concrete ethical life);[56] (e) the *synthesis*: the properly rational subsumptive activity or validity ("that is always valid [*gelten*]")—that is to say, the moment in which, having procedurally *tested* that the maxim is generalizable and for that reason is "valid" in all cases and without contradiction within its proper horizon (problems of *material* evaluation), it achieves potential acceptability by all humanity (in the last instance), namely, universality (taking into account *all* that is materially "good" for each one). This is placing the maxim as a coordinated part (matter as substance) within a universal totality (within the order); finally, we must consider (f) the *form* of the act. Only at this point does the maxim become universal law (it has been subsumed within formal universality, where its content is no longer important because it now only matters with respect to the maxim's validity

as such). The valid is acceptable inasmuch as it is universal, with reference to intersubjectivity, and it does not matter any longer as content.[57] The essential moment is that indicated in (c) and (e), that is to say, the "procedural" aspect of the "application" (the classical *applicatio*, the *Anwendung*), for which Kant formulates a new, and always solipsistic, procedural imperative.[58]

In fact, Kant has to presuppose material ethics as a *hypothetical scenario*[59] (if [*ob*] . . . in the case that [*wenn*]), otherwise, the "application" of the principle would turn out to be impossible: "Everyone does, in fact, appraise action as morally good or evil by this rule.[60] . . . If the maxim of the action is not so constituted that it can stand the test as to the form of a law of nature in general, then it is morally impossible."[61] What has taken place, in reality, is that the "hypothetical scenario" is in fact the detailed reconstruction of the material sphere or of the content of ethics, without which formal morality is not possible. Such a "proof" is not formal; it is absolutely *material*.[62]

§2.2. The Neocontractualist Formalism of John Rawls

[122] In the 1950s, North American philosophy had reached a position similar to that of Kant's in 1770. Just as Kant confronted the dilemma between formal, rationalist thought and empiricism, during the fifties the opposition between intuitionism (with some analytical philosophers among the intuitionists) and utilitarianism was also formulated. Before this double challenge, John Rawls opted not for a transcendental philosophy, as Apel was to do, but instead for a moral, political, *formal*, procedural philosophy, which takes off from a hypothetical model that is built on the historical experience of North American progressive liberal tradition.

In fact, from the time of his oldest, programmatic articles,[63] in his first stage, Rawls shows an argumentative strategy that in substance will not change. Since he has the path to the material already laid out (by utilitarianism), and directed toward the a priori affirmation of principles (by intuitionism), he discovers in "game theory" (the "game of bartering") a hypothetical model similar to the Kantian one: the participants of the game, in a renewed contractualist model such as that of Locke or Rousseau, could in an ideal situation (of a game) make decisions without any *material* determination that could deviate their judgments, thus constituting a formal theorem of the theory of rational choice. What is important in our reading is to consider with attention how, having once denied the material aspect of ethics as a point of departure (the inevitable problem of all formalisms), we are required to construct irresolvable hypothetical scenes, which will then always have to be corrected in order to attempt to recuperate step by step, but never adequately, the materiality denied at the outset. In principle, all the participants of the game are rationally egoists (they have approximately equal needs and an equal capacity to guarantee they will not be dominated by others, and are not greedy),[64] and they undertake to make proposals until they arrive at a unanimous agreement concerning the substantive (or material)[65] fundamental principles of an ideally just society. "*Justice as fairness*" is the fundamental subjective attitude to which the participants commit themselves beforehand, seriously and honestly (they commit themselves to "play clean": *fair*), having accepted the benefits, to fulfill the duties that are assigned by the different practices. In fact, the concept of "*practices*" is fundamental—later, they will be the "institutions"—the forms of activities structured by norms that define tasks, functions, movements, and so on. "Justice as fairness" is played at all levels, but especially within the "practices" (institutions) of a society.

[123] In 1967, in his second stage, Rawls resorts to the artifice of the "veil of ignorance" and changes Pareto's simple principle of preferability for the "difference principle," as the fundamental reforms of his first proposal.[66] The "veil of ignorance" is a hypothetical, analytical recourse, with no feasibility. What is it necessary to forget? The "positions of the participants in society." But also language? It does not seem so, because then no one would be able to make offers in the "games of bartering." If each one comes to the "game" with his or her own language, the worker will have a language proper to the working class, of the popular neighborhoods; the aristocrat, a refined language. Would we have to forget all the different nuances of the different cultural levels of language? Which and who has stipulated the rules for this forgetfulness? In short, the supposed "game" cannot be applied empirically; it is a merely hypothetical staging and, moreover, tautological.[67]

[124] In his third stage, Rawls publishes *A Theory of Justice*,[68] where he organizes his entire argument on the notion of the "*original position*":[69] "The idea of the original position is to set up a fair procedure so that any principle agreed to will be just. The aim is to use the notion of pure procedural justice as a basis of theory."[70] This intention is impossible to fulfill. A merely formal position can never enunciate material principles, by definition, unless this materiality entered into the process surreptitiously, without being noted. And this is what takes place. In fact, the two principles that are to be decided on, or at least the second one, have clear *material* determinations, materiality that, as the popular song says, "I forgot to forget you!" What he "forgot to forget" is that the participants are North American liberals who set out from the suppositions of the capitalist system.[71] The universalistic arrogance of Rawls is impressive: he believes that what is valid in the United States is universal (valid for all humanity, for an

African Bantu community, an Indian tribe, or a Latin American or Asiatic peripheral country), at least in his version of 1971. As a foreigner to that philosophical community, I can only be astonished by the magnitude of such a simplification.

Rawls analyzes three levels: "We may . . . distinguish between a single rule (or group of rules), an institution (or a major part thereof), and the basic structure of the social system as a whole."[72] The "impartiality principle,"[73] which is the one Rawls is interested in, is situated in all three levels, but mostly in the second, which consists of "formal justice," or of *"fairness"* that is nothing else but the "adherence to principle" (first level), and honest fidelity or "obedience to the system" (third level) in institutions.[74] Therefore, the principles or rules give origin to both the "basic structure" of society as well as its institutions, which also have to do with "justice as fairness." To begin, let us see how Rawls formulates the two principles:

> The first statement of the two principles reads as follows:
>
> *First*: each person is to have an equal right to the most extensive basic liberty compatible with a similar liberty for all.
>
> *Second*: social and economic inequalities are to be arranged so that they are both (a) reasonably expected to be to everyone's advantage, and (b) attached to positions and offices open to all.[75]

[125] The theme has been the focus of many studies.[76] For the goals of my reading in this *Ethics of Liberation* I want to propose a different type of reflection. In fact, the first principle could be taken to summarize the "liberal" position of Rawls. It is about the right to freedoms; it is therefore formal, or the condition of possibility of all other rights; it has absolute priority over the second principle.[77] This is the horizon of "democratic equality."[78] What is of interest for my reading is mainly the second principle, which is properly material, of the "social and economic" level. Here I must propose a first consideration. If in the first principle we speak of "equality," in the second we admit a priori (since it would be a result of the "original position") *"inequalities."* The unsuspecting reader will ask herself: Why are political or formal "equalities" admitted and at the same time *economic* and social "inequalities" proposed? Should we not have to formulate, at least in principle, an *economic* and social equality as point of departure? No reasons are given for this *fundamental contradiction* in Rawls's whole argument—in general, the critics of Rawls do not touch this question (which indicates that they accept these inequalities a priori). But the issue is even graver, since arguments are given in order to prove how such inequalities are "natural." Let us, for example, look at the following: "The distribution of income and of wealth *does not have to be equal*, but must nonetheless be advantageous to all."[79] Why does it not "have to be equal"? Rawls never

responds to the question directly, although he does tangentially,[80] for example, when he explains: "The least favored [are] those persons whose *class and family origin* is more disadvantaged than that of others, whose natural endowments might permit them to live less well, and those for whom *luck and good fortune* has been adverse during the course of their lives. . . . It seems *impossible* to avoid a certain arbitrariness as we seek to effectively identify the least favored group."[81] Rawls has a special blindness when attempting to comprehend that it is one thing to have the "fortune" to be born in a family more or less well off (this is pure chance), but another thing that there are *historical and social structures* (not natural) in which we must be born, and which are perfectly analyzable and determinable by the *critical* social sciences.[82] "The difference principle gives some weight to the considerations singled out by the principle of redress. This is the principle that undeserved inequalities call for redress; and since inequalities of birth and natural endowment are underserved, these inequalities are to be somehow compensated for."[83]

[126] As can be seen, it is recognized that these inequalities are undeserved. Why does Rawls not state explicitly that they are *unjust*? Because this judgment would devastate something "that the veil of ignorance did not forget": that the most fortunate are North American wealthy liberals, and poorer people should not "envy" them. It is my opinion that if the inequalities are undeserved (to have an undeserved disadvantage is to be a *victim*), and if for this reason they require compensation according to Rawls, then these inequalities are unjust even for him (or he would not conclude that they need compensation of any kind). Without giving any other reasons, he writes: "No one deserves his greater natural[84] capacity nor merits a more favorable starting place in society.[85] But it does not follow[86] that one should eliminate these distinctions. . . . *The natural distribution is neither just nor unjust*; nor is it unjust that persons are born into society at some particular position. *These are simply natural facts.*"[87] This fallacy seems to resemble Aristotle's claim to demonstrate that slaves are "slaves by nature [*physéi doûlos*],"[88] against the explicit opinion of the Sophists. If Aristotle was for reasons of "content" (ethical life or materially) one who supported slavery (without critical consciousness), the same may be said of Rawls with respect to his North American capitalist liberalism. A Latin American, from a dependent, peripheral, and dominated capitalism, has no option but to reveal this as a "fallacy of formalism": it lacks critical criteria and principles with respect to the content (material) that it presupposes and to which *one in fact has recourse*, but without consciousness. Rawls's formal purity is radically deformed by numerous material a prioris that remain unthought. The Achilles's heel of Kant's formalism consisted in a reductionistic understanding of the inclinations or emotions of corporeality

in general; the weakness of some formalisms of the twentieth century will consist of a blind articulation, with the capitalism of the center (liberal, social democratic, etc.) from which these formalisms set out, justifying it as nature or as "the best of all (effectively possible) worlds," and whose unilaterality posteriorly invalidates the entire argumentation—although I will be the first to subsume the positive, formal contributions of those formalisms that have to be taken into account.[89]

[127] If these principles, especially the second, constitute the basic structure of society, the a priori, always-already-presupposed "inequality," as an ontological inequality, transcendental or of nature, will determine and justify all the "inequalities" of content (material and specifically economic). Since the "institutions" are linked to this "basic structure," each one will reproduce this "inequality." And since "justice as fairness" is nothing more than obedience to the constitutive rules of the basic structure and the institutions (which carry in their heart these "inequalities"), it can now be understood (beyond the reason derivable from Pareto) that everything can work perfectly if the "worst off " (to use the euphemism for the victims, the dominated, and excluded) are not "envious." "Now I assume that the main psychological root of the liability to envy is a lack of self-confidence in our own worth combined with a sense of impotence."[90] When the workers killed in Chicago on May 1, 1886, when the indigenous movements today in Latin America, when the oppressed and excluded possess the courage to struggle for the recognition of their own dignity and for just vindication, attempting to change the unequal structures *within which we are born*, the authority of Nietzsche is invoked to characterize this as resentment. If the clarification is made that this speaks only for the United States, the words may sound less harsh in the ears of the "structurally" impoverished majorities of the south of the planet under the military domination of Rawls's country (United States). But even in the United States, one would like to hear the reflection of *black Americans, Hispanics*, the *homeless*, and so many minorities conscious that this being "worst off " is not natural but *historical*. Formalism turns into an ideological philosophy of the ruling system, into a philosophical reflection that departs from the dominating, hegemonic "ethical life" (and ethnicity), but which conceals, like Kant, its supposed "content" (materials).

[128] In the face of criticism, Rawls modified many of his positions, attempting to open up his thought beyond the North American borders, toward a *well-ordered society* that could get past the grounding of the political order in a basic common moral understanding. In his last work, *Political Liberalism*,[91] he attempted, with little success, to go beyond the horizon of the political imaginary of the liberalism of his own country. For this reason, he attempts, going beyond "justice as fairness" (a subjective attitude that

makes the liberal, democratic system possible), to express another intersubjective principle that would give *unity to the well-ordered system of law* without the already indicated basic ethical unity: the *"overlapping consensus."*[92] This is about a political consensus of all the participants, based on adherence to principles, which supersedes the mere solidarity of the ethnic community (unity of ethical life), the empty fulfillment of a contract imposed externally (pure formal contractualism), or the cold tolerance of embattled dogmatic positions (of universal religions). This social consensus will accept in a "well-ordered society" the *reasonable pluralism* of different public positions, as a system of honest cooperation (when there is a "clean game": *fair*), which gives security and stability through the generations (creating a tradition or inculcation of respect for the Other), on the basis of the recognition of persons as free and equal, from a shared view of a minimal, comprehensive doctrine of a democratic society and culture that has a basic structure built on moral foundations, from justice as fairness. All these issues will be taken up when I construct a "politics"—as a specific "front" of liberation— given that they contribute greatly toward the organization of a state of law.

Other criticisms can be made. Some of these include criticisms regarding Rawls's solipsism (from the different positions taken by the community of communication); his reductive conception of reason as merely instrumental and not communicative (nor ethical-critical, as I will show in chapter 4); his prelinguistic focus on consciousness; his lack of knowledge of the ontological order (for example, in the case of Aristotle, who reduces it to the psychology of means-ends); his capitalism of the free market[93] as a continuously unspoken presupposition, but expressed as if it "were in the nature of things"; and so on.

To conclude, I can say that it concerns a study about formal justice, since "our topic is the theory of justice and not economics."[94] I, in turn, set out from the opinion that ethics, in its integral sense, requires a strong concept of justice—not merely formal—and, therefore, it includes equally a philosophy of economics, in its fundamental sense (as practical-technological philosophy, as we will see in future developments of this ethics of liberation). This is not a matter of presenting some "economic problems," but instead of the ethical-practical grounding of economics as such—which has a material aspect, and includes equally a formal aspect.[95] Formalism cannot then present (from its criteria and principles), and least of all, criticize or put materially in question, the capitalist economic system that it already presupposes a priori (as an unknown condition of possibility), because it inadvertently serves as justification at the moral-formal level.

§2.3. The "Discourse Ethics" of Karl-Otto Apel

[129] The year 1968, the time of the first postwar economic crisis in Europe (and especially in Germany), and because of the student movements, was also a year of great ruptures in philosophy. The "first" Frankfurt school,[96] critical, from the Heideggerian, Weberian, Marxist, and Freudian horizons, as I will show in chapter 4, gave way to the "second" generation of the Frankfurt school—pragmatic, but no longer critical. The philosophy of the second Frankfurt school is a fin-de-siècle one, social-democratic, of a Europe of late capitalism, and builds a bridge to Anglo-Saxon thought (with North American pragmatism and the *linguistic turn*). The ethics of liberation has much to learn from discourse ethics, albeit it must mark now clearly its differences.

Without question, Karl-Otto Apel is an original thinker, who captured the different levels of a profound transformation of contemporary philosophy. His traumatic experience as an eighteen-year-old volunteer in the Nazi army (Emmanuel Levinas was in the concentration camp at Stammlager during the same five years) transformed him into an avowed rationalist[97] and a sensitive, nonrigorist ethicist with a great sense of historical responsibility. In any event, he remained determined by his tradition. In fact, as a student of history in the line of Ranke and Dilthey, he specialized in literature, but in the end dedicated himself to philosophy with Erich Rothacker, with whom he studied the philosophy of existence, defending his doctoral thesis "*Dasein* and Knowing: A Theoretical-Cognitive Interpretation of Martin Heidegger's Philosophy."[98] Already in the 1950s he began his readings of the Anglo-Saxon current (beginning with Charles Morris);[99] this was a novelty in Germany. He presented all of this in his professorial thesis in 1963.[100] His theme was the philosophy of language, from an anthropological horizon, not yet ethical. From a Heideggerian-Gadamerian hermeneutical position, he reconciled the metaphysics of Wittgenstein and Heidegger himself.[101] When his friend and student Jürgen Habermas was accepted as a member of the Institute for Social Research in Frankfurt in 1956, Apel raised his own political consciousness too.[102] The discovery of Charles Sanders Peirce would have a decisive importance in his work,[103] allowing Apel to critique Kant's solipsism.[104] From 1967 to 1972, Apel developed the definitive position that would be expressed in a programmatic way in the last essay in his *Transformation of Philosophy*, where he brought together the works in which his new itinerary can be observed: "the *a priori* of the community of communication and the grounding of ethics."[105] It is the postulation of the "community of communication" as the transcendental and ethical[106] presupposition of all language, argumentation, and possible discourse. Little by little, in discussing analytical philosophy and epistemology, Apel opened up the whole thematic of types of rationality, and defined the thematic of the possibility of an "ultimate grounding of ethics"[107]—a theme that I will explore further in a work that will come after this *Ethics*, which will deal with principles. In the same way, setting out from the *pragmatic turn*[108]—as "transcendental pragmatics—Apel formulated the whole theme of a "transcendental semantics" in debate with the semanticist intentionalism, that is, with reference to the *intentional state* of the second Searle,[109] which definitively addresses the question of truth.[110]

In the decades of the sixties and seventies Apel's opponents were situated in a Popperian reductionistic epistemology or in a philosophy of language after the fashion of the first or last Wittgenstein, who had made the *linguistic turn*. After this period, Apel engaged in polemics against those who, having discovered the pragmatic, in Apel's opinion, return to a precommunicative position. Since the mid-eighties, his work has turned more toward a confrontation with postmodern thought—Derrida, Lyotard, and especially Rorty, who appear to him to be radical opponents of rationality. Since 1989, he and I have engaged in a dialogue, which underpins the writing of *Ethics of Liberation*.

[130] I want to indicate (a) positively, the levels on which ethical philosophy has to be "transformed" according to Apel—levels that the ethics of liberation can subsume—in order to (b) critically indicate why Apel had to take "refuge" in a pure and formal transcendental level, from where (c) it would be *impossible* to "descend," having decided to exclusively follow a formal path,[111] to the concrete and material (spelled with "a" in the German) history of the ethical content that distresses human beings today (the majority of whom are the same distressed groups as always, though their numbers have increased geometrically because of the technological-economic destructive process of late capitalism at the end of Modernity, which began five hundred years ago).

a. The first "transformation" that philosophy underwent at the hands of Apel is the passage from "solipsism" in the manner of Kant toward a "community" always already presupposed,[112] which opens up the problematic of intersubjectivity; the ethics of liberation has radicalized this thesis with a counterproposal, of a "community of life" (in §1.5) in the "antihegemonic critical community" (chapter 5). The second transformation is the reflexive subsumption of the "paradigm of consciousness" (from the Cartesian *ego cogito* up to the "understanding of being" of Heidegger) in a "linguistic paradigm" (the *linguistic turn*) of which I have already spoken. The third transformation is the passage from the level of mere linguistic-syntactic-semantic analysis to the "pragmatic paradigm" that begins with Austin[113] or Searle.[114] This transformation allowed Apel to accomplish subsumptive critique of analytical ethics and its criticisms of ethics. The fourth transformation, which presupposes the prior, consists in the transformation of positivist objectivism into a consensual fallibilism in which validity, however, is simply identified (although in a different way than in Habermasian consensualism) with the dimension of truth.[115] The fifth transformation situates morality (the ethics of discourse) as a presupposition (Peirce's "logical socialism," partly transformed) of every community of communication (even the scientific one), and for that reason morality is, first, philosophy.[116]

b. Why did Apel, as Kant did in his own way, have to take refuge in the "transcendental" level? It is my opinion that he did so because he must not have noticed the importance of the fertile soil of an ethics of content, of material, with which he had some contact during his studies with Rothacker (through Heidegger). But Apel passed from Heideggerian ontology to the philosophy of the *linguistic turn*, and he approached its later discovery of ethics in debate only with the epistemological or linguistic philosophy and with reference to the institution of argumentation. Apel never entered into a serious debate with the ethics of content, or material (he did so tangentially, and only at the culturalist level of the communitarians). His idea of the ethics of content is reductive:

> Discourse ethics is post-Kantian and deontological inasmuch as it formulates the question about the binding *Ought* [*Gesollten*] for all *prior* to the Platonic-Aristotelian (and once again utilitarian) question about the *telos of the good life*, or, for instance, the *happiness* of the individual or community. Discourse ethics acts this way not because it undervalues the problem of the *good or perfect* life, or that of the well-being of the community, nor because it does not consider it a problem of ethics, but instead . . . inasmuch as it is a critical-universalistic ethics, neither does it want to nor can it dogmatically prejudice the happiness telos of individuals and communities. Instead it must *leave it to their discretion*.[117]

Apel gives a reductive interpretation of the material sphere (the content) of ethics, as if it were only a cultural, particular, or merely ontological horizon — as condition of possibility. He does not discern that all cultures, as well as the postconventional modern one, are *concrete modes* to historically organize (but without ever exhausting) the "reproduction and development of life in each human subject in community," as we saw in the previous chapter. Scheler's or Rothacker's values, as well as Heidegger's "comprehension of Being," are always moments of a given culture. But the universal material or content principle of ethics, as I have defined it, constitutes all cultures from within their universality, as a mode of reality of the human subject who develops cultures as the sphere within which "human life is possible." The ontological is equally the horizon that unfolds human life as it confronts reality and constitutes it as "totality" (the "world") of mediations for life. In short, the theme has already been treated. In the face of a reductionistic interpretation of the material principle, there is no other possibility for practical universality besides its deontic, formal, or empty dimension—if one seeks to depart from "one" principle. This principle would not be empty if its function were to apply the norm consensually or to argue within the sphere delimited by the material principle. For an ethics of liberation, the intersubjective formal rules of practical argumentation have sense as procedure for the application of norms, mediations, ends, and values of cultures, which are generated from the horizon of a "material universal principle" that is preontological and properly ethical.

[131] Once we have dismissed the possibility of the existence, and with it the grounding, of a material principle, then morality must confront those that formally negate its possibility. The first question cannot be other than the following: How is an ethics possible "in the age of science?"[118] From a positivistic or analytical-epistemological formal horizon, Apel proposes in the first place, pragmatically, an argumentative strategy that attempts to salvage philosophy as such: "It seems to me that here I have shown, *via negationis et eminentia,* that the *self-reflexivity,* performed in a linguistically responsible manner—that is to say, in performative statements and implicitly self-referential propositions—of thought and its truth claim, presents the genuine *paradigm* of *philosophical rationality.*"[119] It is from this *philosophical rationality* that we can seek to ground ethics. Dismissing the material aspect of real life, Apel is left with only one way to ground his ethics (from the "basic norm" "inward"): "self-reflection" in the face of the skeptic.[120] From this level, he will be able to "deduce" (to ground or decide) *all the remaining norms* of ethics and "practical life"—fundamental norms or grounded ones, from "part A" or "part B." In this way, we can depend exclusively on only *"one"* universal, formal, and a priori principle. One of the first and most complete formulations or descriptions given by Apel of the different moments of this basic norm is the following:

> Who argues has *in actu* testified, and with that recognized, that reason is practical, that is, responsible for human action, in the same way that *ethical claim* of reason, as well as its *truth claim,* can be and ought to be satisfied through *arguments*; in other words, that the ideal rules of argumentation in a, in principle limitless, community of communication, of *persons that recognize each other reciprocally,* represent normative conditions of the possibility of a decision on claims of ethical validity through the formation of a consensus. For this reason, with respect *to all the ethically relevant questions of practical life,* is possible . . . to arrive, in principle, to a consensus, and that in praxis one would have to aspire to that consensus.[121]

Apel furthermore clarifies what the function of this norm is:

The essence of the *basic norm of ethics* resides in the fact that because it is, in a certain sense, inexhaustible source [!] of the generation of ethical norms, it has the character of a *methodological principle*, a principle that only under the frame-work conditions of possible questions referred to concrete situations . . . can be brought to the realization of its normative power.[122]

As can be seen, from *"one" single norm* of universal validity may be deduced the ethical validity of *all the remaining ones*. All of the development of ethics (once the basic norm has been grounded) figures in this deduction or "application" of the basic norm.

[132] From the beginning of the discovery of ethics as transcendental presupposition, Apel saw the need for a mediation between the basic norm of *discourse ethics* (part A) and the "life world" (*Lebenswelt*) (part B). This is the whole "problem of the application [*Anwendungsproblem*]" in "time in-between [*Zwischenzeit*], in which the conditions of the application are not yet given."[123] For this reason, he reaches out for an *ethics of responsibility*,[124] in order to be able to be a posteriori responsible for the effects on those "affected" by the "agreements," which have been discursively reached.[125]

The question of the "application," or of the descent from the grounding of the basic norm by self-reflection, as the *inexhaustible* source of all possible normativity, is then absolutely central. But it is here where, from the outset, with the original path of access to the material (or the content of ethics) blocked, it is impossible to take any significant step forward (that is, to think *concrete* problems from ethical normativity). Apel is very clear, as I have noted, about the necessity of a "*mediation* between (a) the formal principle of universality and grounding and (b) the *material situational* norms."[126] In order to move forward on this he will go on to discover a chain of necessary norms in order to ground concrete, material norms. In that reflexive process he begins to find insurmountable difficulties. On several occasions, Apel makes confessions along these lines: "I must admit that the elucidation of the reasons that have led me to distinguish between a grounding part A and a grounding part B of the ethics of discourse *is still not completely clear*."[127] Let us look at the development of this question. I could summarize the matter by saying that Apel "jumped" from the concrete to the transcendental in order to obtain a fundamental basic norm. From that point, he must now "descend." Apel takes the criterion of application of the basic norm from Habermas. This is the formal, universal principle. The problem can be formulated thus: the fundamental distinction for Habermas between "morality" (universal) and "ethics" (concrete), although it sets out from Kant, is used in order to optimize the real or procedural conditions of the application (*Anwendung*) of the principle of universality, through the agency of the real consensual community, whose principle Habermas formulates in the following way: "All rational beings should be able to desire that which has been morally justified. . . . The *D* principle provides: The only norms which are *valid* are those which have been accepted *by all those accepted* as virtual *participants* in a practical discourse."[128] This principle is mediated by the procedure "U," which assumes in practical discourses the role of a rule of argumentation: "The foreseeable consequences and results of the general following of valid norms for the fulfillment of the interest of each one ought to be accepted freely by all."[129] For Apel, the principle "U" of Habermas is a necessary criterion, but it is not sufficient in order to arrive at the application at the concrete, material, historical level as the principle of the grounding of real norms, given that it considers, with reason, that the necessary conditions of symmetry between the arguers (even in a state of rights, for example, or because of the inequality among the members of different classes, sexes, races, etc.)[130] are not always given in concrete-historical conditions. However, it is possible to deduce a universal obligation to transform the asymmetrical reality in order to be able to argue in the future (when the symmetrical conditions are obtained): "It is necessary, in relation with the ultimate grounding of the principle of ethics, to consider *not only* the basic norm of the consensual grounding of norms (acknowledged in the counterfactual anticipation of the relations of ideal communication), *but also at the same time* the basic norms of historical responsibility, of the preoccupation for the preservation of the natural conditions of life and the historical-cultural accomplishments of the real, factually existing in this moment, community of communication."[131]

[133] To accomplish this, Apel proposes a principle of complementarity or of extensionality (*Ergänzungsprinzip* "E") or principle of action ("which functions as a regulative idea for the approximating fulfillment of the conditions of application of U"),[132] which is formulated proximally thus: "The one who argues has also already necessarily accepted the *obligation* to help to supersede the difference—in the long term, and approximately— through the transformation of real relations."[133] This principle is situated at the level of what I will call the "liberation principle" (a notion that will be presented in §6.5), but essentially in our case not only formally, but also from the requirements of a material ethics and of feasibility, as we will see. Apel attempts now to "supersede the separation that exists between ethical-discursive rationality [formal] and strategic rationality [of feasibility], and also the separation between deontic and teleological ethics";[134] that is to say, Apel sees the need to reintegrate the entire sphere of material ethics. But now it is too late. And, furthermore, he only accomplishes a juxtaposition, because he is never going to be able to formally and coherently deduce an ethics of responsibility (which should have material principles and motivations in order to bring about the desired symmetry), setting out from a discourse ethics.

For Apel, then, "the basic norms of historical responsibility"—which is the obligation to change the real conditions of asymmetry—cannot use the "basic norm of grounding" because, as I have said, there exist asymmetrical conditions. That is, "the conditions of the applicability of an ethics of the ideal community of communication . . . *are not yet given, in any way whatsoever.*"[135] And, since the situational and contingent conditions are not given[136] (the symmetry and the real participation of all the possible affected in their interests),[137] it is necessary to resort, as I have noted repeatedly, to an "ethics of responsibility" of a Weberian type, in order to create the conditions of equality and symmetry.[138] This ethics of responsibility does not count on norms that can be deduced or grounded in the ethics of discourse, but only on strategic or instrumental norms. Thus, we fall into a contradiction, given that the ethics of discourse will have to wait and develop confidence, since it lacks its own resources in order to concretely accomplish the symmetry between the real arguers, in a purely strategic and instrumental, frequently cynical, ethics.[139] It no longer counts on those resources because it has from the outset placed incorrectly the problem of material ethics (which would have granted it adequate access: *ante festum* to the material grounding of the basic norm of content, and, *post festum*, to the proper way to its application—a question that I will deal with at the end of this chapter and in chapter 5). In fact, for Apel this is the whole question of the relations between formal, discursive reason and strategic reason:[140] "This is inferred from the fact itself that strategic rationality (means-ends) can never show as ultimately *valid* the *ultimate end* of the action."[141]

[134] For Apel, then, since material ethics is only egoistic affectivity, cultural values, or the strategic level, the material level is completely dismissed with respect to the grounding of a universal ethics. He is aware, however, that the possibility of lying—not telling the truth—cannot be negated rigorously, for example (modifying the example proposed by Kant),[142] in order to protect a friend whom someone wants to kill. However, Apel cannot deduce or ground such a decision from the position of discourse ethics, but only, as I have noted, from the strategic level of feasibility in an ethics of responsibility. This principle of complementation is an "emancipatory content, and, so to say, the formal-utopian principle,"[143] since it creates the requirement or responsibility of the historical transformation of institutions with an aim to reach symmetry among its participants in the future. Apel indicates, last, that this entire procedure is restricted by a "principle of conservation":[144] "The *survival* of the real community of communication—for example, of humanity as it faces the ecological crisis—and the preservation of the "rational reality" of our cultural tradition constitutes the *necessary condition*[145] or the proposed actualization of the ideal community of communication. . . . [T]his last goal provides the principle of conservation with its meaning."[146] That is to say, here survival (biological and cul-

tural) is deduced from the principle and is a condition of possibility of argumentation, where argumentation constitutes the point of reference that cannot be gone beyond, and not vice versa. That is to say, what for me is a fundamental, universal, material, ethical principle (the reproduction and development of the life of each human subject in community), for Apel is only a "deduced condition." But is not the life of each human subject not only the real, absolute condition of the arguer but first and foremost the *content* of the truth of the act itself of argumentation? Is not argumentation a condition (and not the grounding) of the survival of each subject? Do we not argue in order to reproduce and develop the life of the human subject, or do we simply live as a condition to be able to argue as the ultimate limit that cannot be exceeded? Or is it that we fulfill both hierarchizable ends, as simultaneous and mutually determining dimensions?[147]

Intersubjectivity gains "validity," but without a "truth content" it could not produce a consensus; the life (survival), in the reference of "truth," is the "content" (it is to live, as Ernst Bloch would say, in happiness, with joy; as actualization of the cultural, historical, ethical moments of this living), but without intersubjective consensus it would not have moral validity or it would be fragile, and in the long term unsustainable.

Finally, Apel proposes the "self-catching-up principle,"[148] which reminds us that whoever interprets history always already occupies a place in it and must be self-critical in order not to fall into a performative contradiction. History must be reconstructed, *first of all*, normative-rationally (as development that tends to eliminate asymmetries so that the argumentative basic norm can be applied), before any other reconstruction is undertaken.[149] Material ethics, instead, proposes that one has to reconstruct simultaneously and systematically both the positivity of the institutions and ethical lives that have developed the life of the human subject (especially at a cultural and economic level), and the critique of the structures that make impossible the reproduction or development of the life of each human subject in the community.

§2.4. The Formal Morality of Jürgen Habermas

[135] Throughout the thought of Habermas, the latest proponent of the Frankfurt school, there is continuity with respect to a theme of profound political sensibility: the "public sphere (*Oeffenlichkeit*), or the intersubjective validity of argumentation "free of coercion" as a democratic institution of legitimation. This notion unifies Habermas's work, which is organized around the hard nucleus of reestablishing the ethical sense of the mere "external" level of the political or the law, as when Kant writes: "Just as law in general has as its only object that which is *external* [*äußerlich*] to one's ac-

tions, law strictly speaking, that is that which is not mixed with any ethical considerations, is that which demands nothing but *external* bases for the determination of conditions of choice."[150] Habermas attempts to reconcile the public or political level (which is external) with the ethical. We find two periods in the development of Habermas's philosophy, which are starkly defined around a political crisis (the leftism of the student movement of 1968) and a theoretical crisis (the systematic subsumption[151] of the philosophy of the *linguistic turn*).

a. The first period (the last phase of the "first" Frankfurt school) began when Habermas joined the Institute for Social Research as Adorno's assistant in 1956, and with his first works on student politics in Frankfurt, and could be said to have culminated in the appearance of *Towards a Reconstruction of Historical Materialism*[152] (when Habermas was already fully into the second period).[153] The problematic of this moment (to simplify its great richness), is demarcated, on one front, by the methodological debate already began by Adorno against Popperian positivism, in particular.[154] From a dialectical or ontological position, instrumental reason is criticized. Habermas's central work of this period is *Knowledge and Human Interest* (1968). Liberation philosophy learned a lot from this first Habermas. On a second front, there is a dialogue with Marxism, which at that time had a great tradition in Germany (and the world). Habermas's central philosophical work in this thematic is his *Theory and Praxis* of 1963.[155] I wish to focus on a point, in order to illustrate an early reduction in Habermas's thought: a certain difficulty in discovering the sense and universality of what we have called the material aspect (of content) of ethics. In fact, his interpretations, from his earliest work onward, indicate a reduction of Marx's fundamental intuition, and this because, from the beginning, he never "practiced" political economy:[156] "In the advanced capitalist countries, the standard of living—even among the broadest sectors of the population—has risen so far that the interest in the emancipation of society can no longer be expressed immediately in economic terms. *Alienation* has shed its most economically evident form."[157] As the reader can imagine, in the face of the misery in Latin America, Africa, and Asia (85 percent of contemporary humanity), such considerations do not make any sense. In a later text, he writes again on his views on political economy: "The situation is somewhat different in *political economy*. In the eighteenth century it entered into competition with rational natural law and brought out the independence of an action system held together through functions and not primarily through norms. . . . Economics as a specialized science has broken off that relation. Now it too concerns itself with the economy as a subsystem of society and absolves itself from questions of legitimacy."[158]

[136] Habermas always refers to sociology (a social science that, since

Weber, always locates itself at a formal level), but he systematically leaves by the side political economy, which would have required of him that he reflect on the material aspect of ethics. Let us look at this question, setting out from a key case: How does Habermas treat Marx? Frequently, in an indirect fashion, but rarely in a textual fashion. When he does do so, he even makes mistakes of interpretation. Let us take two examples. The first one, from *Theory and Praxis*,[159] refers to a passage in Marx's *Grundrisse*, where Marx writes: "But to the degree that large industry develops, the creation of *real wealth* comes to depend less on labour time and on the *amount* of labour employed than on the power of the agencies set in motion during labour time, whose 'powerful effectiveness' is itself in turn out of all proportion to the *direct* labour time spent on their production, but depends rather on the general state of science and on the progress of technology, or the application of this science to production."[160] Habermas claims to show that there is a contradiction in Marx in his labor value theory. We should not forget, however, that Marx's text refers to "fixed capital."[161] It is not a matter of a "revisionist" text, but of the use of a category that Marx in 1858 had not yet finished developing.[162] Contrary to what Habermas thinks, Marx shows that the law of value is fulfilled, given that the machine (science or technology) consumes in its use (circulating value of fixed capital) less time value than would have been consumed in terms of "labour capacity,"[163] in the production of the use value itself.[164] Machines, science, and technology do not create exchange value; they merely transfer or save exchange value: they allow the production of more use value at the same time as labor (or equal use value with less exchange value). In no way are they, as Habermas thinks,[165] "sources *of exchange* value"—which is what is of interest to Marx. That is to say, the "creation of real wealth [use value] comes to depend less on labour time." One can't see where there is a contradiction. Let us consider another example. Habermas wants to demonstrate that "Marx is assuming something like a nature in itself. It is prior to the world of mankind. . . . 'Nature in itself' is therefore an abstraction, which is a requisite of our thought . . . Kant's 'thing-in-itself' reappears under the name of a nature preceding human history."[166] What Habermas is referring to is *German ideology*:

> So much is this activity, this unceasing sensuous labour and creation, this production, the foundation of the whole sensuous world as it now exists that, were it interrupted only for a year, Feuerbach would not only find an enormous change in the natural world, but would very soon find that the whole world of men and his own perceptive faculty, nay his own existence, were missing. Of course, in all this the priority of external nature remains unassailed, and all this has no application to the original men . . . but this differentiation has meaning only insofar as man is considered to

be distinct from nature. For that matter, nature, the nature that preceded human history, is not by any means the nature in which Feuerbach lives, it is nature which today no longer exists anywhere (except perhaps on a few Australian coral islands of recent origin) and which, therefore, does not exist for Feuerbach either.[167]

[137] This question, which would seem secondary and merely a matter of terms, brings us directly to the "material" question of ethics to which I wish to refer. In fact, Marx indicates explicitly the opposite of what Habermas makes him say. Marx criticizes Hegel's position that "nature" is merely a negative moment that counts only in the process of sublation (*Aufhebung*) of self-consciousness, of the thinking that turns back on itself until it reaches Absolute Knowledge. "Nature" as such does not count for Hegel. Marx needs to show that nature exists "in itself" (from itself), in order to refute Hegel's absolute idealism, but exactly what is of interest to Marx (against the naive or cosmological-metaphysical materialists and the posterior *standard* positivist Marxists) is nature as the "matter" (*material*, with "a": content)[168] of work (as culture, as economics) because mere "nature before human history"—and here Marx is being ironic, and Habermas apparently misses the irony—is of no interest to either Feuerbach or him, or to the ethics of liberation. Marx points to some moments of a material ethics: "The *objects* of his instincts exist outside [*außer*] him, as *objects* independent of him; yet these objects are *objects* that he *needs*. . . . Hunger is a natural *need* [*Bedürfnis*]; it therefore needs a *nature* outside itself,[169] an *object* outside itself, in order to satisfy itself, to be stilled. . . . The sun is the *object* of the plant—an indispensable object to it, confirming its life."[170] It is here where we can consider that for Habermas the material aspect (*material*, with "a," or "content [*Inhalt*]") (of ethics) in Marx consists only in work, in physical-animal (*materiell*, with "e") survival, and does not have in mind the universal ethical principle of the reproduction and development of the life of the human subject, which Marx always has as the horizon of his political economy (preontological[171] and ethical). Habermas quotes Marx's statement: "As a basis for the formation of use values, thus as useful labor, then, labor is a condition which is *independent* of all social formations characteristic of *human* existence [*unabhängige Existenzbedingung des Menschen*], and is thus a perennial natural necessity which serves to mediate the metabolic relationship between humanity and nature, and which thus serves to mediate *human life* [*menschliche Leben*]."[172] I think Habermas is not aware of the importance of the text that he quotes, one that in the ethics of liberation is transformed in a fundamental thesis. In fact, Marx is referring to nothing else than the always already presupposed *a priori universal* criterion, which "puts forth" and "criticizes" ends, values, cultures, economic systems, and ontological horizons,[173] and is the *interior* moment at all these levels. In the

first place, it always refers to "human life"—and not merely to animal or physical life, that is to say, referring to the higher functions of the mind (for Marx, consciousness, self-consciousness, and freedom), and of the culture and economic systems. "Human life" is reproduced and developed in the dialectical relation of the human being with nature (the living and its "environment," not merely physical nature). The relation of the life of the real human subject within that "environment" cannot be merely contemplative, expressive, or passively linguistic: it ought to be active, it must be a *real* relation. In this fundamental and necessary sense, work is, in turn, the *actualization* of the condition[174] of human existence independent of every social formation, in which consists "metabolism." It is life as the preontological absolute condition (if the ontological is a historical system) of existence or human reality in general: universal, the "content" of the ethical act from "practical-material reason" or "originary ethics," from which this radical reason can enunciate "ethical judgments of reality" on the ends themselves (and its judgments of fact) and the values of cultures (and its judgments of value). This level is not merely that of the "transcendental conditions of the possible object of experience,"[175] but the content of reality itself, as vitality (*Lebendigkeit*), as the mode of reality out of which the human subject moves as the "possible." It is human life and not mere nature, according to Marx: "A man is not only a natural being, but a *natural human being* [*menschliches Naturwesen*]; given that he exists for himself . . . and must confirm his own existence through his own action both in his being and his knowing.[176] Thus human objects are not natural objects as they might first appear, nor are human senses equivalent to the direct, objective, *human* sensibility or human objectivity. Nature is not directly adequate as a substitute for the *human being* either objectively or subjectively."[177]

[138] On the other hand, Habermas now and again, in his different works, criticizes Marx's point that the act of work cannot sufficiently give an account of "interaction," and for that reason he falls into "productivism." He does not notice that Marx is placing himself at a more fundamental level: what is of interest to Marx is a *material, universal criterion of the life of the human subject*, beyond every culture or economic system (and with respect to which cultures, economic system, values, and ends as in Weber are "ways" of bringing about the "reproduction and development of *human* life"). Work, relations of production, capital as a system ("totality"), and the economy itself (as activity and as "science") are moments of a process of the "reproduction and development of human life" ("survival" of the human subject) that materially roots, because of its "content," all of human ethical life.

During this period, Habermas therefore criticizes Marx from the point of view of a dialectical vision of interaction, situating Marx in a way that reduces him to the horizon of instrumental reason (here productivist).[178]

In turn, I think that Habermas—in this period from the position of the ontological dialectic, and later from the pragmatics—has not attended to Marx's fundamental intuition regarding the material aspect (of ultimate *content*) of a *universal* ethics, which proposes the criterion of the reproduction and development of the life of each human subject in community as the content and always presupposed condition of the possibility of human reality as such. Ends and values can be "put forth" and "judged" from *within* cultures themselves (as projects of the "good life") from this horizon of reality, in which operates a practical-material or ethical-originary reason, which discovers the first requirements or fundamental duties; happiness and virtue may be reached, as well as the other moments of ethics. It is my opinion that Charles Taylor also did not arrive at this understanding.

[139] b. In his second period, Habermas's perspective is already evident in his essay of 1976, "What Is Universal Pragmatics?"[179] In it, Habermas takes up Apel's theses of the 1970s, a theme also of later works from *The Theory of Communicative Action*[180] onward, especially those on discourse ethics.[181] In this period, the interlocutors change. First, on the philosophical front, we see the analytic philosophers of the *linguistic turn* before whose appearance on the scene, Habermas shows, a transformation of a solipsistic and abstract paradigm into one of pragmatics had to occur, as well as the metaphysical thought of Dieter Heinrich[182] and postmodern irrationalism.[183] Second, on the political front, the grounding of social democracy, of the state of law,[184] had to shift from formal rationality, for Europe and Germany in particular. The third front is the properly ethical problematic of the Apelian tradition, which confronts material ethics (such as that of Taylor)—and, in even greater detail, formal ethics (as in those of analytical formalists or Rawls)[185]—where we see that Habermas is unable to integrate the material moment (and even less that of Marx's economic sphere, or Freud's psychoanalysis), and for that reason will definitively lose the already diminished critical force of the last stage of the first generation of the Frankfurt school. I will focus on this third moment, namely the discourse ethics of Habermas.

[140] In *Moral Consciousness and Communicative Action*, we find one of the broadest texts on the moral theme properly speaking,[186] which was written under MacIntyre's critical pressure,[187] and where Habermas's intention is to broach the theme of a grounding of morality—toward the end of the essay, against Apel,[188] he declines to offer an "ultimate" grounding. In the first place, the prior work of Strawson allows him to start from a phenomenological description (not merely formal) of a phenomenon that is also of great interest to the ethics of liberation: "The indignation with which we react before injuries . . . in cases in which they injure the integrity of others";[189] where it is demonstrated, in a description that ought to be participative, that performative ethical attitudes and sentiments (such

as culpability or the consciousness of duty), that the empiricist skeptic cannot reject, are something different from mere "affectively neutral judgments of the relations between means and ends."[190] Following Toulmin,[191] Habermas undertakes a demolition in group of many studies of analytical morality. In the first place, Habermas rightly shows that it is necessary to "explain the meaning of *moral truth*,"[192] distinguishing the validity claims of *descriptive statements* (constatives or assertives, which would be something like Weber's "judgments of fact") from those of *normative statements* (prescriptive and practical, which would have to be distinguished from Weber's "value judgments").[193] The first have a claim to truth; the second, a rightness claim[194] (or a claim to "moral truth"). For this reason the analytical formalist George Moore is mistaken when he pretends to compare "good" to "yellow." In fact, in 1903 Moore criticized the material ethics of the utilitarians in this precise theme: "This, then, is our first question: What is good? And What is bad? and to the discussion of this question (or these questions) I give the name of Ethics."[195]

Moore took the wrong path, as we have seen, of identifying descriptive predicates ("yellow") with normative ones ("good").[196] Despite repeated failures, subjectivist solutions were tried, but as Habermas notes, "Toulmin has observed that the subjectivist response to the failure of Moore's objective ethics and that of others is simply the reverse of the same coin. Both sides flow from the same false premise regarding the validity of the truth [*Wahrheitsgeltung*] of descriptive statements . . . due to the fact that normative statements . . . cannot be proven by applying the same rules as those apt for descriptive statements."[197]

[141] Habermas judges that both types of statements have to be distinguished from emotional or subjective statements (which express preferences, convictions, pleas, desires, or inclinations).[198] Ayer[199] identified them in a confused way. In the same way, Hare,[200] taking a prescriptivist position, states that when they are studied by metaethics, [only imperatives and statements of personal experience or intention are shown to have any validity] — hoping thereby to prove that it is impossible to argue about, or make any validity claim for, moral pronouncements.[201] For Habermas analytical metaethics is skeptical, not cognitivist. The moral quotidian world remains entirely devalorized from a scientist or objectivist point of view.[202] Habermas will attempt to show that it is a rational task to prove the validity claim of normative statements or moral decisions aimed at bringing about agreements — which is what the entire question of the "grounding" in the context of communicative acts consists of. One must then differentiate a descriptive statement:

1. Iron is magnetic.
It is true that iron is magnetic.

From a normative statement:

2. One should not kill.
It is commanded that no one be killed.

Their objectivity is different, since "the claims of normative validity evidently mediate a reciprocal dependency between speech and the social world which does not exist, however, in the relationship [1] between speech and the objective world."[203] Attempting to show this difference, Habermas intends to develop a grounding principle of every practical discourse (or of normative statements), which is the principle of communicative, pragmatic universality. Integrating the positions of Kurt Baier[204] and Bernard Gert,[205] normative statements ought to be universally[206] and publicly arguable in order to reach a "rationally valid formation of the moral judgment," thus arriving at the "principle of discourse ethics" (D): "Only those norms can claim to be valid [gilt] that meet (or could meet) with the approval [Einverständnis] of all affected [Betroffenen] in their capacity *as participants in a practical discourse*."[207] This principle "D" needs, in order to be able to be *applied*,[208] a "bridge principle [Brückeprinzip]" that is not monological[209] and also not fictitious, as in the case of Rawls's "original position."

The principle "U" concerns the *real* argumentation of those affected in their needs, about which a discursive demonstration must be undertaken: "[Every] valid norm has to fulfill the following condition: (U) *All* affected can accept the consequences and the side effects its *general* observance can be anticipated to have for the satisfaction of *everyone's* interests (and these consequences are preferred to those of known alternative possibilities for regulation)."[210] Here is where the formal touches the material: "Needs [Bedürfnisse] and wants are interpreted in the light of cultural values [kulturelle Werte].[211] Since cultural values are always components of intersubjectively shared traditions, the revision of the values used to interpret needs and wants cannot be a matter for individuals to handle monologically."[212] How do we know that need X determines the ethical demand of summoning the affected to a discussion? Are the affected summoned in a situation of symmetry? Who, and with what ethical criterion, discovers such needs, and with which principle is the process "produced" that culminates in symmetry? These and many other material problems are not resolved by Habermas.

[142] Finally, what is the material or the ethics of content for Habermas? It is at this level where value judgments are found. Let us consider the following:

If we define practical issues as issues of the good life [guten Lebens], which invariably deal with the totality of a particular form of life [das Ganze einer individuellen Lebensform] or the totality of an individual life history, then ethical formalism is incisive in the literal sense: the universalization principle acts like a knife that makes razor-sharp cuts between evaluative [*evaluative*] statements and strictly normative ones,[213] between the good [*das Gute*] and the just [*Gerechte*].[214] While cultural values may imply a claim to intersubjective[215] acceptance, they are so inextricably intertwined with the totality of a particular form of life that they cannot be said[216] to claim formative validity in the strict sense.[217]

Habermas can only consider one relation (between morality and ethics), while the ethics of liberation considers five relations (see figure 6). Let us look at the matter in greater detail.

For Habermas the value judgment is fixed; it seems as though it cannot be criticized. The only relation that Habermas can analyze is the passage from the dogmatic level of the value judgment (b) to the normative statement (a), with intersubjective, rational, argued validity (relation 1 in figure 6); it must be a conservative morality, although an enlightened one. The ethics of liberation can analyze a second relation (relation 2): from *critical* normative statements (c)[218] it can put into question valid, moral discursive agreements (a).[219] But, and this is even more important, the victims, the oppressed (d), can put into question discursively (relation 5) the ruling value judgments (b), now judged by them as oppressive and dominating.[220] Critical ethics may also be able to argue with a claim to scientific or enlightened validity (c) (relation 4), utilizing critical statements and developing realist and possible projects; from where, materially or according to its contents, it may put into question ruling value judgments (b) (relation 3). Critical ethics concerns "an inversion of values" (*Unwertung*) of which Nietzsche could not convincingly explain either the ethical sense or the practical rationality at play.[221] It is an entire ethical "continent" that discourse ethics ought to discover (though then it would cease to be Kantian, and for that reason I think that such a discovery is already impossible). It

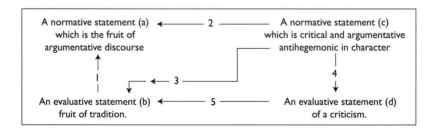

Figure 6. Relations between the formal-moral level and the ethical-material.

NOTE: Relationship 1: the only one indicated by Habermas. Relationships 2 through 5: those suggested by an ethics of liberation.

is not a matter exclusively of a morality or ethical life, but of a morality, ethical life, and criticality that is procedural or diachronically articulated, without exclusions; it is a new ethical project and a new architectonic, as we will see.

[143] Habermas cannot—because of their content, in light of the requirements of the reproduction and development of the life of the human subject—adequately analyze what value judgments are, nor their type of rationality, nor even argumentative or material, critical, discursive rationality. This is because he posits an absolute abstraction, as an exclusion of all contents in morality: "[Deontological ethics] deals not with value preferences but with the normative validity of norms of action."[222]

For the ethics of liberation, normative statements can be value judgments (with a rightness claim because of their material content of value), ethical in a strong sense (with a practical truth claim),[223] or merely moral (with a formal validity claim). It is not so for Habermas: "To that extent discourse ethics can properly be characterized as *formal*, for it provides no substantive guidelines [*inhaltlichen Orientierungen*][224] but only a procedure [*Verfahren*]: practical discourse."[225] In the second place, as with Apel, the material is only the cultural ("totality of a particular form of life"), the hermeneutical ontological, and Habermas is not able to transcend to this level. There are texts that seem to suggest it: "To be sure, cultural values too transcend de facto behavior. They congeal into historical and biographical syndromes of value orientations through which subjects can distinguish the *good life* from the reproduction of mere life [*nackten Lebens*]."[226] Unfortunately, this "life" as such is *only* biological, plant-animal life. This is not about "*human* life" as an absolute condition of possibility and content, a universal criterion with respect to which each culture is a mode of its reproduction, and, for that reason, cannot discover the ethical-material requirements, the "ought-to-be" that "human-life" involves in its own content (which is not found in the formal-logical sphere of the so-called naturalist fallacy).[227]

Habermas, in a long polemical text against Dieter Henrich,[228] touches the question of the reproduction of the life of the human subject practically, in a manner very similar to how I have defined it in the previous chapter. But Habermas does not notice that it concerns the entire problematic of an ethics of content: "A process of self-preservation that has to satisfy the rationality conditions of communicative action becomes dependent on the integrative accomplishments of subjects who coordinate their action via criticizable validity claims. . . . Unlike instrumental reason, communicative reason *cannot* be subsumed *without resistance* under a blind self-preservation."[229] Here Habermas does not know how to articulate the intersubjective, formal-moral principle of discourse ethics with an ethical-material principle of a critical ethics. He juxtaposes them, rejects the second, and cannot think through their articulation.

[144] In the third place, Habermas treats at length the grounding of the "only"[230] formal principle of discourse ethics. In contrast, I have also shown the path toward a grounding of a material principle of every possible ethics. His reductionistic view of the material level forces him to accept with Apel that "moral theories of the Kantian type are specialized. They focus on questions of *justification*, leaving questions of *application* unanswered."[231] He comments, "Any ethics that is at once deontological, cognitivist, formalist, and universalist ends up with a relatively narrow conception of morality that is uncompromisingly abstract. This raises the problem of whether issues of justice can be isolated from particular contexts of the good life."[232] The "energetic abstraction" performed by discourse ethics is not only "energetic" but also reductionistic at the level of contents, and it is for that reason the second moment is unfeasible; he doubts "whether it is reasonable to hope that the insights of a universalist morality are susceptible to translation into practice. . . . How can political action be morally justified when the social conditions in which practical discourses can be carried on[233] and moral insight can be generated and transformed do not exist but have to be created?"[234] Since discourse ethics cannot appeal to an "objective teleology" (another reduction of the ethical-material level that in any event would have to be defined in a nonteleological manner), nor "make restitution for the injustice and pain suffered by previous generations . . . if we cannot at least promise an equivalent to the day of judgment and its power of redemption. Is it not obscene for present-day beneficiaries of past injustices to expect the posthumous consent of slain and degraded victims to norms that appear justified to us in light of our own expectations regarding the future?"[235] For Habermas, ethics cannot "make any kind of substantive contribution,"[236] therefore "moral philosophy does not have privileged access to particular moral truths [*moralischen Wahrheiten*].[237] In view of the four big moral-political liabilities of our time—hunger and poverty in the third world, torture and continuous violations of human dignity in autocratic regimes, increasing unemployment and disparities of social wealth in Western industrial nations, and finally the self-destructive risks of the nuclear arms race."[238] Habermas has formulated some of the themes that concern the ethics of liberation. The only difference is that because discourse ethics is merely formal, it cannot enter into a rational-philosophical debate concerning content. It is not so with an ethics of liberation, as we will see. There is then in Habermas consciousness of the problems and of the impossibility of treating them because the procedural moral function articulated to a material ethics is that of the application of contents, and if they have been limited previously, as is the case with discourse ethics, then it remains like an empty logic.

[145] In the fourth place, when discursively grounding a norm, a "motivational anchoring of moral ideals" is lacking: "The post-conventional differentiation between morality and ethics meant the loss of backing by cultural self-understandings, and by life-world certainties in general."[239] This is partially compensated by the formation of the will in a rule-of-law state. The ethics of liberation, instead, since it does not lose contact with the level of content, but also since it adds a profound solidarity with life to anti-hegemonic critical intersubjectivity (to be examined in chapter 5), never loses the "backing of cultural evidence"—although it does frequently keep a critical attitude when this "evidence" is alienating, an attitude nourished by projects of liberation that are always material.

In the fifth place, and given the impossibility of formulating concepts such as "universal justice, normative rightness, moral point of view with independence from the perspective of a *good life*," discourse ethics confronts a greater difficulty: "Noncontextual definitions of a moral principle, I admit, have not been satisfactory up to now. Negative versions of the moral principle seem to be a step in the right direction. . . . [They] refer negatively to the damaged life instead of pointing affirmatively to the good life."[240] Habermas's suspicion will be analyzed in detail in chapter 4, when I present the material origin of the critique from the proposed negation of a "good life" and the life in general of each human subject. Habermas formulates the problem proximally, but he has to drastically reduce his architectonic in order to be able to analyze his intuition with any breadth. In fact, it will be by the negation of the positive principle of material ethics (in Marx, Freud, Levinas, and others) that critique is possible, but for that we have to affirm beforehand the *universality* of the material principle (which is impossible for Habermas).[241] Again, not using a material principle makes it impossible for him to discover ethically the impossibility of the reproduction and development of the life of each human subject in community, in this or that concrete ethical system, as contents.

In the sixth place, favoring Hegel's view, rather than Kant's: "Practical discourses do disengage problematic actions and norms from the substantive ethics [*Sittlichkeit*] of their lived contexts, subjecting them to hypothetical reasoning without regard to existing motives and institutions."[242] The ethics of liberation, setting out affirmatively from the material level (not only cultural but also the universal sphere of the reproduction and development of human life in general), although it confronts concrete material problems, critically and problematically (from an antihegemonic intersubjectivity, moments 2 and 3 of figure 3)—and for that reason has already lost naive validity of the hegemony, in the style of Gramsci—does not therefore cease to experience "the effective motives and the ruling institutions" (although they need to be rejected, superseding them while transforming them).

[146] In the seventh place, the ethics of liberation cannot accept from Habermas the proposal of "the primacy of what is morally right [*Richtigen*] or obligatory over what is ethically desirable or preferable,"[243] although it does not accept the contrary, from Taylor, either.[244] It is necessary to articulate both aspects, subsuming them positively,[245] as codeterminations without "primacies": what is desirable materially (as mediation of life) ought to be given simultaneously with the intersubjectively valid.

Finally, Habermas, placing himself at stage 6 of Kohlberg's ethical consciousness, proposes (like Apel) a postconventional ethics.[246] The intersubjective community of those who have reached the postconventional stage, which is ruled exclusively by "universal ethical principles,"[247] runs the risk of losing, as we have seen, evaluative-cultural motivations; it should undertake the formation of a will that can, through a rigorous learning process, develop something like a "superego," whose content would be these formal universal principles. The ethics of liberation, once again, cannot subsume only the positive aspects of this formal universalistic intersubjectivity, but in addition will imbricate it with an ethical consciousness (a *Gewissen* and not a mere cognitivistic *Moralbewußtsein*) that departs from a cultural *ethos*, before which it situates itself *critically* (having lost its naive attachment). All of this is accomplished in such a way that as the ethics of liberation subsumes its material aspects; it transforms them, reconstituting them into a moment of a new "development," from the universal, material, ethical principle as a requirement of the reproduction and *development* of the "life of the human subject" in general. The *critical*[248] postconventional ethical life does not cease to take into account the concrete culture of the oppressed and excluded—from which it departs materially—but situates itself critically even with respect to discourse ethics insofar as discourse ethics is not critical. For example, when discourse ethics confronts "late capitalism," it does not know how to criticize it as capitalism. It does not propose a "*critical* postconventional ethical life," but a formal "postconventionality" *within* the hegemony of the ethical life of the culture and system of the north of our planet without explicit consciousness of its complicity.

At the end of *Moralbewußtsein und kommunikatives Handeln*, and contradicting partly all that he has expressed, Habermas quotes Horkheimer: "What is needed, to go beyond the utopian character of Kant's idea of a perfect constitution of humankind, is a materialist theory of society."[249] But a "materialist" (with "a") theory requires an ethics of content that Habermas has declared from the outset impossible. And in saying farewell to a material ethics, Habermas said a definitive farewell to the *critical* thought of the first Frankfurt school.

[147] To close this section, I turn to Albrecht Wellmer. In his work *Ethics and Dialogue*, he presents numerous objections from within discourse ethics. Let me consider two important ones; in the next section I will deal

with some others. Wellmer notes that in a *real* situation it is not possible to accomplish the analysis of the possible consequences of an act (Habermas's "U" principle):

> It evidently makes no sense to assume that, under nonideal conditions for reaching agreement, we should be able to solve our real moral problems by trying to achieve *real* consensuses. Where the possibility of reaching agreement ends [which is the point of departure of an ethics of liberation], the only course that remains open to us is to consider what rational and competent people *would* say. . . . But if, in the course of every moral reflection (which must ultimately always be monologic in nature), we had to reach a decision on the question of whether the consequences and side-effects arising for each individual from the universal observance of a norm . . . could be accepted without coercion by all, *then we should never be able to arrive at a fully justified moral judgment.*[250]

But the greatest of all possible critiques is the one that would disarticulate the entire project of Apel and Habermas: "I should like to . . . [question] the sense in which presuppositions of argument can have a universally understood moral content."[251] Which is to say, "the obligation not to suppress any argument, which is grounded in the validity-orientation of speech, has no *direct* consequences for the question of when and with whom I am obliged to argue,"[252] and this because "obligations to rationality refer to the acknowledgment of arguments, moral obligations to the acknowledgment of persons."[253] This brings us to the issues explored in the following section.

§2.5. The Criterion of Validity and the Universal, Formal Principle of Morality

[148] I have already indicated that the ethical function of the basic norm of formal morality is that of grounding and applying in concrete terms the norms, ethical judgments, decisions, normative statements, and different moments of material ethics.[254] Without the fulfillment of the basic norm of formal morality, ethical decisions have no communitarian and universal "validity." What they have, instead, could be an effect of egotism, solipsism, or violent authoritarianism. As in the previous chapter, I first present the "criterion" and then the "principle" of moral validity, and will close by referring to the problematic of the application, for the first time addressing the "feasibility" or "fulfillment" of the principles enunciated.

To begin with, it is necessary to distinguish between the material criterion of ethics (of "practical truth"), to which I first referred in §1.5a, and the formal criterion of morality (of intersubjective "moral validity"). In fact, it needs to be noted that when Habermas refers to normative statements (in their only dimension of claim to "normative rightness"), he indicates that it is a matter of a "validity claim *analogous to the claim to truth*":[255] "It would be erroneous, though, to equate the moral 'truth' [*moralische 'Wahrheit'*][256] of normative statements with the assertorial validity of propositional statements, a mistake made by intuitionism and value ethics. Kant does not make this mistake. He does not confuse theoretical with practical reason. As for myself, I hold the view that normative rightness must be regarded as a claim to validity that is analogous to a truth claim."[257] I think this formulates well enough the problem that I wish to analyze. I will show, however, that the question is even more complex than discourse ethics supposes, given that we will not situate ourselves only in the horizon of a formal morality. In the first place, (a) following the path already opened by Wellmer, I will differentiate questions referring to the truth of mere formal claims of validity of all possible statements or "speech acts" from the Habermasian consensualist position on truth; this will allow us to define strictly the *criterion of validity*. In the second place, (b) no longer identifying truth and validity within the accomplishments hitherto gained, I now coincide with Habermas in distinguishing between descriptive or assertorial (of theoretical reason) and normative (of practical reason) statements. In this way, I will be able to differentiate between the question of practical or ethical truth (of material content) — superseding even Wellmer, who cannot overcome a certain formalism — and the moral (formal) validity claim, which will allow me to define the *universal, formal, moral principle*. I wish to show, then, that a practical-material reason, with an aspect that I have also called ethical-originary reason, is not the same as formal or discursive practical-moral reason (which, because it is "moral" already, is no longer merely "logical" or theoretical, because the validity of a descriptive statement is not identical to that of a normative one). The *ethical* "truth claim," with practical reference to content (because of the imperative to fulfill material requirements), is not identical to the formal, *moral* "validity claim" (because of the requirement to fulfill the rules of intersubjective consensus). Discourse ethics, especially in Habermas's consensualist position, confuses the claims differentiated in level (a). Intuitionist metaethics confuses the differences at level (b). Both formalisms reject, in the end, the possibility of a not merely consensual practical truth.

a. The Intersubjective Criterion of Validity

[149] Let us see how Wellmer formulates the question:

Insofar as we have really become convinced of something in common, we are able to speak of a *rational* consensus. Thus it can appear as if a *rational* consensus is necessarily also a "true" one. But this is only the way it looks from the point of view of those who are actually involved in the situation:

if *I* have reasons for agreeing, then this *means* precisely that I consider a validity claim to be *true*. But the truth does not *follow* here from the rationality of the consensus, it follows from the appropriateness of the reasons which I can advance for validity claims, and I need to have convinced myself that these reasons are in fact appropriate *before* I can speak of the rationality of the consensus.[258]

This requires from us, at least, that we distinguish the question of truth from the problematic of validity. In this sense, Wellmer adds: "It is only from the point of view of those involved in the situation that consensual rationality appears to be identical with truth. But this cannot mean that the rationality of the consensus is an additional *reason* for it being true.[259] . . . The fact that I hold something to be true with good reason cannot be an additional reason for the truth of the thing I hold to be true, at least not for *me*. . . . [T]he fact that a consensus exists, even if it were arrived at under ideal conditions, cannot be a *reason* for the truth of the thing that is held to be true."[260] With this Habermas's position is frontally criticized, which takes truth to be extreme consensuality.[261] And for this reason, Wellmer writes with reference to his teacher from Frankfurt: "But this thesis would be void of any substantial content. Consensus theory as a substantial theory of truth stands and falls with a *formal* characterization of the rationality of consensuses; but precisely this formal condition of rationality renders it false. If, on the other hand, we take the step that suggests itself in the light of what we have seen here [in the arguments presented by Wellmer], and try to understand the concept of *rationality in nonformal terms*, then consensus theory stands revealed as empty of content."[262] This conclusion is what I want to problematicize, because if it is accepted that a purely consensual theory of truth is ambiguous, I do not think that for this reason a theory of validity linked to another "nonformal" truth would be "revealed empty of content." In that case, we would have to differentiate a theory of truth (not formal) from a theory of validity (formal), where we would have in turn, in any event, to show the decisive importance of the latter, and the need of its articulation with the former. Apel would seem to propose a thesis in this sense, when, following Husserl, he writes: "An example that clarifies the fundamental point of this position could be the following: first I enunciate the following judgment: 'The wall that is behind me is red,' then I turn around and verify so: my adjacuative intention has been fulfilled by the *evidence* that was given by the *phenomenon*."[263] But, definitively, Apel categorically rejects that the "consensus ought to depend on the objective truth[264] of judgments" or that "the concept of truth does not depend on consensus";[265] leaning in the end, always within a formal-consensual conception, to propose that "all available criteria of truth" are not sufficient alone to ground the "intersubjective validity of consensus."[266] For this reason, we must know how to integrate them. That is, truth and validity are identified. In the meantime we may affirm with Wellmer: "The truth claim of the empirical statements implies the reference[267] of these statements to a reality that, up to a point, is *independent* of language."[268]

[150] What is Apel speaking about when he says that there is a "reference" to a "reality that is *independent* of language"? If the concept of *truth* refers us to reality[269] (from a monological, subjectivist position, always constitutively communitarian), the concept of *validity* in turn refers us directly to intersubjectivity. If truth entails reference in some way to reality (a reality shared with others in a community of life),[270] validity entails a reference to the acceptability of other participants in the community of what is "held-to-be-true"; that is, it entails a relation to a possible intersubjective agreement.

Discourse ethics has creatively elaborated the moral levels of the validity claims of statements, in what could be termed an advance in the formulation of the principle of universality, but within the narrow horizon of a merely formal or consensual concept (with variations) of truth. As we saw in §§2.2–2.4, this is due to the fact that it is beholden to a reductive understanding of material content.[271] By contrast, if the universal material or content level is not negated, the concept of intersubjective validity gains precision and significance. It is not simply that from an original solipsistic position we can arrive at the "true" in order to *afterward* seek "consensuality" by intersubjective acceptance; rather, the position of intersubjectivity in the actualization of the real as truth (vertical arrow a of figure 7) has already *before* been constituted from intersubjectivity (as much cerebrally, linguistically, and culturally, as historically) (horizontal arrow b), but in a formally differentiated manner (not a confused or conflated one, as in the case with Habermas). Every actualization of the real (true) is always already intersubjective; and all intersubjectivity (validity) entails "reference" to a veridical presupposition. But they are categorically different. Truth is fruit of the monological (or communitarian)[272] process of "referring to" the real from intersubjectivity (the statement has thus a truth claim); *validity* is the fruit of the process of attempting to have what is monologically held to be accepted intersubjectively (or in a communitarian manner) as truth (the statement has thus a validity claim).

[151] With validity as consensuality (formality of discourse), the argument is accepted and produces agreement, or consensus. It concerns the *criterion of intersubjectivity*. Consensuality is reached from the truth of the argument, but the truth of the argument is impossible, in turn, without *previous* consensuality.[273] Furthermore, truth, even if it had a monological origin in some empirical cases,[274] always has a claim or a quest for a consensus in order to become an intersubjectively verified statement, and this

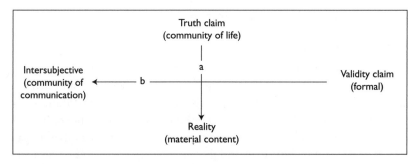

Figure 7. Different levels of the truth and validity claim.

claim or quest is located in a historical tradition (quotidian or scientific). That is to say, intersubjectively (formally or procedurally), there is no truth in the full sense without a prior validity: (a) *ante festum*, given that existence in the form of intersubjective agreements of the issues to be verified is an absolute condition of its possibility; (b) *in festum*, without dialogicity in the intrinsic production of new arguments in the veridical act itself (which constitutes the verifying character of the consensus); and (c) *post festum*, without the intersubjective acceptability that allows new progress in the quest for truth. I believe that with this I have defended myself against Wellmer's challenge: "It does not necessarily follow from the fact that reasons show themselves within the context of a finite rational consensus to be sufficiently good reasons that they will prove themselves *in the long term* to be sufficiently good reasons; then the undisputed reassuring function of consensuses is not adequate to sustain the heavy burden of a consensus *theory* of truth."[275] Truth, as well as validity, is finite, historical, fallible, falsifiable, or verifiable at different levels. A nonexclusively consensual, formal doctrine of truth allows, as we will see, an analysis of greater complexity.

[152] On the other hand, and simultaneously and referentially (because of its materiality), there is no validity without truth: (a) *ante festum*, given that the *new* truthfully grasped content, if still not yet intersubjectively accepted, is what moves us to try invalidating the old valid agreement. This constitutes dissent,[276] from whence rises the new validity; (b) *in festum*, because being-in-agreement takes place only when it is about *something*: what-is-held-to-be-true, which is what grants proving force to the argument in order to produce the intersubjective assent; and (c) *post festum*, because from the *true or valid content* the memory of a community of communication (quotidian, scientific, etc.) can be historically given. There is no serious validity without a truth claim (because of the *material* determination of content, and *as reference to reality*, regardless of how it is to be defined); there is no truth in the full sense without a validity claim (because of

a *formal* or intersubjective determination, and *as reference to a community*). Truth and validity are formally distinct, as much for their reference (the real or the intersubjective) as for their exercise of a different type of rationality (one is material and the other formal-discursive).

The criterion that we are analyzing is, in the first instance, and defined analytically, a criterion of intersubjective validity. All argumentation has simultaneously a double reference: on one hand, it is an instrument of verification (in the broad sense); on the other, of validation. Marx used to say "one is an order of investigation and the other of exposition." The first reference is to truth (and can be monological or communitarian, and not solipsistic); the second refers to validity (and concerns the rhetorical procedure of the correct expression for the intersubjective community). Monologically (or in community, if it is a community of researchers) the argument allows us to state descriptively or assertively a real aspect of the real (verification, in the broad sense); but it equally allows that the other participants of the community accept intersubjectively for themselves, individually or in a group, the same true statement (validation in the broad sense).

I can then conclude these short reflections by saying that the *criterion of validity*, still abstractly, is the claim to establish the actual *intersubjectivity* of veridical statements as agreements rationally accomplished by a community. It is the procedural or formal criterion par excellence.

The ethics of liberation for this reason proposes that we need to define an intersubjective (formal-consensual) moral *criterion of validity* that is articulated with the *criterion of practical truth*[277] of reproducing and developing human life (material, of content). Both criteria are, in turn, as we will see, different forms of a third criterion: the *criterion of feasibility*, subsumed from the previous ethical-moral principles, although it constitutes a new moment in which the unity of the materiality of content with valid consensuality is given, forming, only at this moment, ethical life[278] properly speaking: namely, the "goodness claim."

b. The Universal Moral Principle of Validity

[153] Now we have to pass from the criterion to the formal, moral principle. The themes open up new possibilities, given that even if we are in agreement with discourse ethics with respect to the differentiation between merely descriptive or assertive statements and normative ones, I will propose in this a new internal distinction between normative material statements (with a practical truth claim) and formal moral ones (with a moral validity claim). Even Wellmer will not be able to accept this reclassification. The only thing that I am doing is applying the distinction already argued in the last two chapters.

To take up a theoretical challenge, although the example is premodern (and for that reason without enough development at the formal or procedural level of validity), let us consider a classic text in which we can discern the complexity of the theme that I wish to broach. Aristotle wrote:

> What affirmation and negation are in thinking, pursuit and avoidance are in desire; so that since moral excellence is a state concerned with choice, and choice is deliberate desire, therefore both the reasoning must be true and the desire right, if the choice is to be good, and the latter must pursue just what the former asserts. Now this kind of intellect [*diánoia*] and truth [*alétheia*] is practical [*praktiké*]; of the intellect which is contemplative, not practical, not productive, the good and the bad state are truth and falsity (for this is the function of everything intellectual); while of the part which is practical and intellectual the good state is truth in agreement with right desire [*alétheia homológos té orthê*].[279]

[154] In the first place, with Habermas—and against metaethics, as I indicated above—we must distinguish between descriptive or assertive statements and normative ones.[280] Moore confuses these two types of statements (also, see table 4):

1. This table is *yellow*.

or

2. To do justice is *good*.

"Here the predicative structure of [*it*] *is good* fulfills a different logical function than does the expression *it is yellow*."[281] The different variations of metaethics were skeptical before different aspects of normative statements insofar as they were measured, in some fashion, from the point of departure of descriptive or scientific statements. Habermas's argument for the refutation of this identification circles always around the same problem: assertive statements of type 1 have truth claims with reference to the state of affairs in the objective world, while normative statements of type 2 have a rightness claim with respect to the social world, to the ethical life of a concrete or cultural context.

Since Habermas accepts a consensualist doctrine of truth, the only difference, in his understanding, is the difference of the claims: of truth (qua validity) in one, and rightness in the other. For this reason, he writes: "But if normative sentences do not admit of truth in the narrow sense[282] of the word 'true,' that is, *in the same sense*[283] in which descriptive statements can be true or false, we will have to formulate the task of explaining the meaning of 'moral truth'[284] or, if that expression is already misleading,[285] the meaning of 'normative rightness' in such a way that we are not tempted to

Table 4. Types of Statements

Descriptive Statements	
(Analytical-Formal Theoretical Reasoning or Consideration of Material Contents)	
b.1 Normative statements	b.2 Ethical feasibility: the ethical and moral practical reason subsume strategic and instrumental reasoning
b.1.1 Material ethical (with practical truth claim; material practical reason)	
b.1.2 Moral-formal (with moral inter-subjective validity claim; moral-formal discursive reason)	

Note: The formal level (b.1.2) (denominated by Rawls and Habermas as "just") is not placed in opposition to the same level of ethics or of "the good" (*das Gute*) (b.2), but rather to the level of the material (b.1.1) (the "truly practical"). The ethical originary reasoning, which recognizes the Other as equal, plays itself out within the two domains of b.1.

assimilate the one type of sentence to the other. We will have to proceed on a weaker assumption, namely that normative validity claims are *analogous to truth claims*."[286] As can be seen, Habermas continually hesitates before identifying rightness with moral truth (as is consistent with the consensualism of theoretical validity-truth). "Moral truth" would be what is discursively valid, which also ought to have "normative rightness," and which entails a reference to the particularity of the normative structures of the concrete ethical life of a culture (of even the postconventional ones), that is, "conformity" with cultural values. It would be something like a conservative, discursive rationalism.

[155] I, for my part, and by contrast—since I have intended to defend "contents" (not "metaphysical" contents in the practical sense, but real, falsifiable, historical ones, and never because of an uncritical "agreement") in the material moment of ethics, from a "criterion of truth" (the reproduction and development of the life of the human subject, universally, and constituting from within all cultures)—have the possibility of speaking of *"practical* truth" in a strict sense, not just of "rightness" with respect to a concrete cultural *ethos* (that is certainly always given simultaneously, because the reference of the ethical, material, universal principle inevitably has a historical, cultural *root*). In this position, normative statements can also have a *rightness claim* since they are value judgments (with respect to the institutions and the values of a culture), and they possess simultaneously, from within both and as an internal critical principle, a *practical truth claim*,[287] not only with respect to the objective, physical world, merely natural or living (plant or animal),[288] but also to the properly human qua human: inasmuch as the subject is a living human subject. The "reality"

to which this type of statement makes reference is not only or principally physical, plant or animal reality as such, but instead exclusive and properly a human reality (inasmuch as it is the concrete "human life" of each ethical subject, as described in chapter 1), of which we are reflexively self-conscious and for that reason reasonable, and which depends on us. From here the statement

3. Human beings are living entities; if we want to live and not commit a collective suicide . . .

can be made explicit, as use of practical-material reason, and not as an analytical, logical-formal deduction:

4. We ought to fulfill the necessary mediations in order to live; we ought not to let ourselves die, we ought not to kill, we ought to feed the hungry in solidarity, and so on.

Statement 4 directly entails a relation with the material-ethical criterion and principle, and makes a *practical* truth claim, while serving as a ground for discursive decisions or for every grounded normative statement. This is because life is the absolute condition and constitutive content of human reality; and since said life is "under our communitarian responsibility" (because of the self-consciousness of human development), it is imposed upon us[289] as an imperative to take care of it, to conserve it. Thus, the practical judgment

5. This person X killed person Z with act Y

is a descriptive statement on which can be made explicit or grounded—situating ourselves at another level than the so-called naturalist fallacy and thereby overcoming the formal-analytical judgment (that is, ascending to a material sphere where communitarian co-responsibility is constitutive of ethical subjectivity)—the following statement:

6. Since this X person is responsible for person Z,

and for this reason

7. This person X *should not have* killed Z with an act Y.

Or, in another way:

8. This person X when he or she killed Z committed a *bad* act Y.

This making explicit or grounding are legitimate because person X—because of the communitarian and solidaristic responsibility that he or she has for the life of the other human subject, and because of the unavoidable participation presupposed in a community of life—is always responsible for the life of Z. The requirement to use the argument just outlined as a ground has a universal, "practical truth" claim, and also a claim of "rightness" (but not only of rightness).[290] This "practical truth" ought to be differentiated from the mere "analytical truth" of descriptive statements of physical, or natural objects (which falls into the naturalist fallacy at the instrumental, logical-formal level), and even of observational statements about human beings insofar as these are natural beings, since these can remain at a level of mere descriptive intention. Only anthropological statements referring directly to self-reflexive human determinations and relating to the production, repro-duction, and development of the human life of each subject in community are of the material and concrete type (objects of practical-material reason) on which can be founded the free, self-conscious, responsible ethical *obli-gations* or *requirements*, with reciprocal recognition and co-responsibility for the lives of all. This would require many clarifications and a different logical development than that supposed by the so-called naturalist fallacy, and would be the object of future expositions where I will deepen what I simply *indicate* here.

[156] Let us now take a decisive step. Material normative statements that make a practical truth and rightness claim should be differentiated from properly formal or moral normative statements that make a validity claim as such. Thus, when I say:

> 9. This norm N is not morally valid, because although I am affected by it, I cannot participate symmetrically in the corresponding discussion.

The opposition here is not against the possible "content" of the adopted decision but against the "form" of reaching the moral consensus, against its "validity." I am, for example, violently excluded. For this reason, it is cru-cial to differentiate the "*veridical* content" from the "form in which *validity* is reached." Both have *practical obligations* or *requirements*; some are *ethi-cal* (material), others, discursive *moral* (formal) ones. Both *are necessary* in order to reach the full ethical content of the decision of the concrete or final practical-normative judgment that unleashes the properly "fulfilling" process of the ethical feasibility of the act that can have a goodness claim (which I present in chapter 3); but both are different and not sufficient separately. For Habermas and analytical metaethics all of this is formulated in a different way. For Habermas, since he has identified *truth with validity*, the "content" of practical "truth" disappears; as it does also for intuitionist, emotivist, analytical metaethics, since they claim that the only valid truth is *formal truth*, which is no more than *intelligibility* with sense;[291] whence the difficulty of the possible existence of a practical, material, real truth. The difficulty is found in the "practical" and "material" dimensions of practical truth (which differentiate practical truth from the purely analytical or for-

Table 5. The Place of Ethical-Originary Reason

Practical truth claim from the community of life	1. Practical-material reason
Theoretical truth claim from the community of life	2. Theoretical reason
Recognition of the Other as equal	3. Ethical-originary reason
Validity claim from the community of communication (subsumes level 2)	4. Discursive reason

malist conception of truth, but do so only intralinguistically, confusing "intelligibility claim" with "truth claim" or "validity," as we will see ahead).[292]

[157] Wellmer, for his part, sees a subtle distinction, which gives us the opportunity to broach the deeper theme of this section. In fact, and this is a point I already suggested in the previous section, he writes: "Obligations to rationality [*Rationalitätforderungen*] are concerned with arguments regardless of who voices them, whereas moral obligations [*moralische Verpflichtungen*] are concerned with people regardless of their arguments."[293] My position agrees with Wellmer's, but I develop the theme in such a way that it will end up opposing Wellmer's conclusions. I have indicated that the acknowledgment of the ethical subject *as equal*[294] is an exercise of ethical-originary reason (level 3 of table 5), prior to the use of discursive reason as such (level 4). In order to seriously argue, it is necessary to have acknowledged the Other as equal, in such a way that discursive reason presupposes a type of ethical rationality that is even more radical, thereby intrinsically constituting argumentation as communicative act (not only as rational, abstract, theoretical act).[295] In fact, if truth and validity were the same thing (levels 1, 2, and 4 of table 5), then the *requirements of moral validity* (always with reference to an identity in the ideal speech situation or in the ideal community of communication *in the long run*) could be *directly* grounded on veridical, argumentative requirements (of "content," I would say: level 2 identified with level 4). And this because the validity claim contains universal moral demands—as Habermas shows in the formulation of principle "U" (which is different from the formulation of the basic ethical norm by Apel) and its later developments, such as Kant's imperative (although modified): "So that this holds universally, you *shall* morally proceed in this way." The question is, Why *should* you? Apel would respond: because it is a prerequisite of the "seriousness" in the arguing. But this conceals the moment of the use of ethical-originary reason (which recognizes the other arguer *as equal*; a use that is not argumentative; that is, level 3 of table 5 is not level 2, nor is it level 4).

Like Wellmer, I do not accept the consensual doctrine of truth, and for that reason I must differentiate the material requirements (level 1) and logical-argumentative requirements of truth (level 2) from the moral-intersubjective requirements of the validity of normative statements (level 4). But, unlike Wellmer, I will distinguish the use of practical-material reason[296] from the use of purely theoretical reason,[297] and at the same time introduce the use of ethical-originary reason, which fulfills what Wellmer calls "moral obligations [that] are concerned with people."[298] This determines that (a) theoretical reason, in its veridical aspect (level 2), ought[299] to accept the best argument and to fulfill the material[300] and logical requirements of argumentation; and (b) ethical-originary reason (in the sense that I gave it above) ought[301] to reach the "recognition" of the Other subject as an equal ethical subject in the community of life,[302] *before* he or she is recognized as a participant of the community of communication, in order to situate this subject afterward, who has the dignity of subjects, as a participant of the rational, intersubjective community because an *origin* of possible arguments. Here, once again, (c) it is necessary to situate ourselves at a level different from that taken in the so-called naturalistic fallacy, by moving procedurally or formally (although in relation with the material exercise of practical reason, and not remaining reductively in the mere logical-formal, analytical level of theoretical reason of the naturalistic fallacy, which is situated in level 2 of table 5, abstractly considered). In fact, if we depart from a mere descriptive statement such as

10. I say that Juan is not arguing now,

we refer, first, in this speech act, to the propositional moment inasmuch as it is intelligible (level 2 of formal, theoretical reason), and, following the act, the *recognized* human subject as such (Juan), with proper dignity of an ethical subject (discovered by ethical-originary reason; level 3). The propositional content has a truth claim (because of its matter, since Juan is a living human, an object of practical-material reason, who can argue, and gives evidence that he is doing so; level 1 and 2). This proposition also has a validity claim (with its intersubjective reference, of discursive rationality), inasmuch as I presuppose that this truth is acceptable by all other participants in the community of communication (and I am ready to give reasons before whoever would not accept the truth of this statement). From the mere propositional content of a descriptive statement of "what is" (abstract level 2) a deontic "ought-to-be" cannot be analytically deduced, because we would be placing ourselves exclusively at the formal-abstract level of the Fregean-Russellian logic of intelligibility sense.[303] However, if we think of the speech act at a pragmatic level, to "argue" inasmuch as it is a human act (the speaking of who communicates, etc.) is now subsumed "pragmatically" from the perspective of the recognition of the Other as equal, in a communicative relation (level 4), and for that reason from an explicit intention to reach an intersubjective consensus, formally considered as the exercise of the right of the interlocutor to participate in the discussion. The "is" of the arguing now allows making explicit or grounding the "ought" of the arguing, as a practical requirement of discursive reason. Thus, we could have the following example:

> 11. I observe that Juan is not arguing because he has been violently excluded from the discussion, although he is affected by the decisions taken in relation to some aspect necessary for the reproduction of his life.

The argument could continue materially in the following way:

> 12. In order to reach the validity of the decisions (given that they are invalid because of the exclusion of a person), *ergo*
> 13. Juan *ought* to participate in the argumentation.

This participation is the condition of validity for the practical decisions of the community of communication, and for that reason, it is also a right and a moral "obligation" if Juan is affected in some of his needs, about which we argue. To not allow him to participate would be discursively (morally) reproachable. Because of all of this, for Juan it is a discursive *ought* to have to argue (in order to defend his life or to reach the validity claim to which all aim; if they admitted having consciously excluded someone who is explicitly affected, they would performatively contradict themselves). The "ought-to-argue" is grounded as an *obligation* in reference to the moral "mode" or procedure that was used in order to reach validity (I do not refer here to the "ethical" content of what is being discussed, of what is stated). Violence is irrational (and even antimoral) because it does not respect the autonomy, the equality of the Other, and the Other's right to participate. It is this recognition of the Other as equal that grounds the moral requirement to "have" to argue. Wellmer insists:

> Obligations to rationality refer to the acknowledgment of arguments;[304] moral obligations to the recognition of persons.[305] . . . If the will to truth is identical in meaning with the will to achieving rational consensuses, then universal norms of a genuine cooperation on equal terms with *all* others are indeed built into the validity orientation of speech from the outset.[306]
> . . . It is only if we *presuppose* a strong version of consensus theory as providing a criterion of truth that we can interpret elementary obligations to rationality *directly* as an obligation to direct our efforts toward the achievement of a rational consensus on controversial issue.[307]

Distinguishing, as Wellmer does, among different argumentative requirements (of truth because of content, of validity because of its procedural claim to consensuality), we nonetheless have to accept that the *moral* obligation to argue is grounded, as I have said, on the recognition of the Other arguing subject as an autonomous subject and of *equal* dignity. The procedural criterion of argumentation becomes a moral principle of validity, when others and oneself are recognized as equal moral subjects, when they are made into participants in the argumentation, solidaristically, inasmuch as they are ethically affected in their basic needs.

At the material level, there is *knowledge* (material intelligibility, or knowledge of content by theoretical or practical-material reason) of the truth of arguments; at the formal level of moral validity there is knowledge of arguments from the moral obligation assumed due to the required *recognition* of intersubjectively situated ethical subjects (as a moment of discursive reason). *From the criterion of intersubjectivity, we proceed by way of the grounding* (not by a mere analytical deduction, but by means of the use of practical-material reason, continued by ethical-originary reason, and articulated with discursive pragmatic reason) *of the principle of moral validity*, inasmuch as it is an act of a human being as a human being (now inasmuch as "moral subject"). If we argue intelligibly, as members of a community of communication, we ought to be responsible for our argumentation as mediation (of material truth) of the reproduction and development of our lives as human subjects respecting the other members of the community as equals. While we are affected by what is argued about, in order to defend our life and our dignity we should all struggle similarly to reach formal validity (previously, struggle for recognition), thus being responsible for our arguing (formally), and accepting for the same reason the arguments of the Other, because we have also already recognized the other arguers as equal. Now argumentation turns into a moral obligation.[308]

[158] In this way, descriptive statements about the human life of ethical subjects can be made "explicit" and "developed" as normative statements, containing moral obligations that for Wellmer are not constitutive, but which for me are, because argumentation itself is an act of another human being, and operates within ethical requirements as a quest for the acceptability of the Other with regard to the way in which arguments are proposed. The description of the conditions of possibility of the moral exercise of the validity of the arguing act of the human being—these conditions being analyzed as moral requirements of the type I have described—constitutes what I will now name the *moral principle of universal validity*. This is neither the only, nor the first, nor even the last principle. This is to say, it is a *necessary* principle but not a *sufficient* one, *pace* the opinion of discourse ethics. This principle can be defended against the skeptics.[309]

I will attempt to propose a description of the principle redefining Apel's formulation of the basic norm, taking from it the merely formal, and adding to it, as a codetermination, the reference to practical truth and recognition as always presupposed. The moral, formal, universal principle could be formulated, without pretending to exhaust all of its possible determinations and only considering some aspects, in the following way: He or she who argues with a practical validity claim, from the reciprocal recognition of all the participants as equal, who for that reason maintain symmetry within the community of communication, has always already a priori accepted the procedural moral requirements by means of which all the affected (affected as regards either their needs or the consequences of the argumentation, or because ethically relevant questions[310] are dealt with) ought to be able to factually participate in the argumentative discussion, and is disposed to arrive at an agreement without any coercion other than that of the better argument, framing such a procedure and decision within the horizon of the orientations that flow from the ethical-material principle I have formulated.[311]

[159] Someone could object that, at bottom, I have repeated almost verbatim the description of the principle of universality, Apel's basic norm, and Habermas's "D" and "U" principles. However, the differences are enormous. Now the universal, formal, moral principle (because it must be able to be applied in all cases, always, without exception, and at least with this as a claim) is the *procedural or formal mediation of the material ethical principle*. All of this concerns a universal norm for the "application" of the content (as practical truth or as mediation for the production, reproduction, and development of the human life of each ethical subject) of the normative statement. The mere criterion of formal intersubjective validity has been raised to being a requirement or moral principle of "application."

But, is its concrete application impossible, given that, in fact, the required symmetries are never given historically, as Apel and Habermas recognized? We will see that the ethics of liberation can apply its principle by constructing a critical symmetry in the midst of situations of hegemonic asymmetry (an issue that I will deal with in chapter 5). This moral principle of validity, as I have redefined it, broadens and deepens the principle of Kantian universality and of discourse ethics, and gains in the possibility of application, without losing any of its positive, universal, or rational aspects. The ethics of liberation does not need an ethics of responsibility or a principle of complementarity (from instrumental or strategic reason, in the last instance, cynical); rather, it sets out from criteria that are, as we will see shortly, the development of the principles that I have been presenting in growing complexity. It will be the dominated and excluded themselves, the victims, asymmetrically situated in the hegemonic community, who will be in charge of constructing a new symmetry; it will be a new real, historical, critical, consensual community of communication.[312] Paradoxically, at least, this is my claim: the ethics of liberation carries out the presuppostions of discourse ethics without contradictions, but from a more complex architecture, because it can reach out to the resources of a material ethics or ethics of content, which discourse ethics has abandoned. By virtue of the material-ethical principle, we can discover material *contents*, and not only the *form* of discourse; these contents in turn can yield general ethical orientations (which Habermas must renounce), with which we can reach a procedural, empirical, concrete intersubjective validity, without falling into pure formalism or empty proceduralism.

c. The Application of the Principle of Moral Validity

[160] An account should be given here of the ethical "object," which Kant named the "object of practical knowledge . . . which is made real [*wirklich gemacht*]."[313] In my case, since I have reconstructed the entire material level, I will proceed in a completely different way from Kant, as the following chapter makes clear.

In fact, if the application of the ethical-material principle is carried out by means of the moral principle of formal validity, then a "synthesis" between the material and formal has been produced. The "decision" of the ultimate norm, moral judgment, or concrete normative statement, and the "fulfillment" or real integration of the selected judgment in the carrying out of the human act or praxis (institution, historical structure, values, etc.) is the unity of the material (the mediation with "practical truth" based on the principle of the reproduction and development of the life of the human subject) and the formal (the autonomous symmetrical, free, and responsible participation of each affected subject) that, only now, constitutes from real feasibility what we can denominate the "goodness claim," the ethical life in effect. As I have already noted, the formal moment (the valid; Rawls's "just"; Habermas's consensual or true) is not opposed to practical unity (the goodness claim, feasible and valid-practical truth, etc.) at its same level, but rather is found in another level of complexity.[314]

The moral principle of validity consists of deontic requirements of a procedure of application of ethical, material contents that ought to be clearly distinguished from its theoretical grounding.[315] Its effective application opens up a path toward chapter 3, since it concerns synthesizing or uniting the ethical content (with its practical truth claim)—going from its formal, consensual proceduralism (with its moral validity claim)—with a norm (or maxim), act, microstructure, institution, system of ethical life, that can carry a "goodness claim,"[316] or that can be judged for the first time under the predicate "good," in an empirical, real, concrete ethical sense.

In the medieval tradition the *moralitas* of an act consisted in the transcendental relation of the human act with the norm (*lex*), which constituted the human act as "good [*bonum*]." We have gained much with respect to this precritical tradition (regarding the level of validity), thanks to the contributions of Modernity: materiality or content entails a reference to the reality of the life of each human subject universally (as practical truth); formalism relates to the intersubjectivity of free, autonomous, and consensual agreements (with universal validity). But still missing is the whole complex diachronic of the concrete mode through which the act (norms, structures, institutions, etc.) will be effectively carried out, taking into consideration its circumstances and its consequences (in the short and long term), that is to say, its "feasibility." This takes us beyond the theme of this chapter on *formal* validity, and brings us to a new moment: that of *ethical feasibility*.

CHAPTER 3

Ethical Feasibility and the "Goodness Claim"

[161] This is an ethics of life. It is now a matter of the empirical feasibility of this life. The mediations of the feasibility of the reproduction of human life are performative systems of greater or lesser complexity (such as agriculture, education, or the state); when these become autonomous or totalize they can cease to fulfill their end. We proceed, then, to the last step in the description that presents what I have called the *foundation* of ethics. The "foundation," paradoxically, has to be deepened in direct proportion to what is to be built on top of it.[1] The properly *critical* part of the ethics of liberation will come, however, in chapter 4 onward, but the "foundation" is predetermined from that critical part. To achieve this it was necessary to develop, as we have observed in another ethics, the positive material moment. I also had to positively *subsume* the communitarian intersubjective moment (that of discourse ethics, for example). Now I can attempt a synthesis of these moments (of the material moment of ethics, and the formal moment of morality), from the perspective of the feasibility of both, and thus reach the *real unity*, or synthetic unity, of the ethical life properly speaking: the "goodness claim" of this *Ethics*. Ethical life is procedurally and diachronically constructed, from the grounding or deliberate choice of the practical judgment or norm up to the *feasible* ethical possible fulfillment of the act, the institution, the historical-cultural systematic structures, and so on, passing in this way from the a prioris of the norm or maxim in the intention of the agent to the fulfillment of ethical empirical life. That is to say, if (a) I referred to the dimension of practical truth (from the demands for the *reproduction and development of the life of each human subject in community*, and where normative statements have a *practical truth claim*) in the material aspect; if (b) it was a question of the horizon of the formal ratio-

Table 6. Material, Formal, and Feasibility Dimensions of Ethical Life

a. *The material*: the practical truth of practical-material reasoning, originary ethics, with regard to the reproduction of the life of the human subject: with "truth claim": the *"truthful"* b. *The formal*: the intersubjective validity of discursive reason, of declaratory statements with claim of validity: the *"valid"*	c. *The ethically feasible*: that which is agreed upon is assessed in terms of its feasibility through the application of instrumental strategic reasoning: *the feasible*, technically and economically possible, etc., and is framed by the bounds of the material and formal principles, and brought about through the application of ethical feasibility, a process of "application" or realization fashioned through the act, institution, or the system of ethics: the *"goodness claim"*

nality of valid agreements (from the *demands of symmetrical participation*, and where the normative statements have a *validity claim*) in the formal aspect; now, (c) I will describe the process of the construction of the *ethically feasible*, where the "goodness claim"[2] is made—of the norm, microstructure, institution, or system of ethical life actually achieved. This claim would come from *demands of ethical feasibility* in the concrete and effective fulfillment of the act, taking into account contextual situations and also the consequences of its fulfillment. It involves framing instrumental and strategic reason (which is subsumed by practical-material, ethical-originary, and discursive reason) from the standpoint of practical truth and moral validity (see table 6).

[162] The grounding of an ethics of liberation then transverses at the very least the following:

a. The *ethical-material moment* of contents, affirming material universality, of neurocerebral basis, of hermeneutical-cultural and historical concretion, of the life or death of the ethical subject. This is the horizon of the exercise of practical-material and ethical-originary reason with reference to normative statements (grounded on judgments of fact) with a practical truth claim.

b. The *moral-formal, procedural moment* of intersubjective and communicative moral validity that is fulfilled in the symmetry of the affected participants; it is the horizon of the exercise of discursive reason with reference to normative statements with a universal validity claim.

c. The ethical-processual *moment of possible feasibility* (which is not merely procedural, but of process, or processual), that in a first moment is the exercise of formal instrumental and strategic reason, with reference to judgments of fact; in a second moment it is an articulation with this exercise of the ethical-material and moral-formal principles, yielding as a result the maxim or norm of an act with a "goodness claim," which fulfills the conditions of being "good," the "legitimate" institution, the existing cultural system (*Sittlichkeit*).

Since ethical life is produced "processually" ("becoming"), we cannot leave aside the thought of the north part of the American continent, given that from Alaska (inhabited by a number of indigenous peoples) to Tierra del Fuego (where the disappeared Alakaluf Indians lived, who originated in the Asian Far East), the experience of the "process" of the "becoming" toward the future seems to be a common life experience of white, mestizo, and Afro-American races that came (or were violently brought) there afterward. For this reason, we will reread some theses of pragmatism that, like the philosophy of liberation, is sensitive to the "diachrony" of evolving and historical reality.

§3.1. The Pragmatism of Charles S. Peirce

[163] In 1901 and 1902, a North American philosopher[3] gave a series of lectures to some colleagues in Edinburgh, the Gifford lectures, in which he claimed to have discovered an original philosophy for his country, namely pragmatism.[4] The philosopher's name was William James, and he found himself in the same awkward situation in which Latin American philosophers, ninety years later, find themselves today.[5]

Pragmatism is the philosophy of the United States. Its first antecedents can be traced back to 1867, two years after the end of the Civil War, that is at the origin of the unity of the United States, of the industrial "North" and the slave-owning "South." Some twenty years later, in 1898 (just over a century ago, and it is necessary to remember it), the United States began its imperial expansion in Puerto Rico, Cuba, and the Philippines. Today, it is the global, hegemonic military power—exercising a monopoly of coercion that has *never* been exercised in the same way before by any nation on planet Earth—a geopolitical novelty that causes panic in those who may suffer its "power." It is the center itself of the "Center" of the world system in the stage of late capitalism and postmodern culture.[6] The "Americanism" of the North American republican New Right is the fundamentalist extension of "Eurocentrism." Because of all of this I think that a return of the great philosophical theses of pragmatism is salutary, but this return will not be possible if the pragmatism of the *North* does not open up to a necessary dialogue with the impoverished, exploited, and excluded *South* . . . not without ethical responsibility in the neoliberal globalization that the United States promotes in the world system. The *we Americans*, as Richard Rorty says, defend not only respect for incommensurability or incommunicability, but also equally defend a certain irresponsibility with respect to the Others that is cruelly oppressed. Is this dialogue between North and South not one of the central philosophical tasks of the twenty-first century now under way?

[164] Pragmatism has four pillars: the founders of its first period, Charles S. Peirce (born 1839),[7] William James,[8] George H. Mead,[9] and John Dewey (died 1952).[10] Their lives cover a century, a period in which the influence of pragmatism was hegemonic throughout the entire country (going from the first works of Peirce, in 1867, to the death of Dewey). Due to the upheavals of the Second World War some European philosophers, including members of the Vienna Circle (formed by Moritz Schlick, Otto Neurath, Friedrich Waismann, and Kurt Gödel, among others) and Rudolf Carnap, emigrated to North America, and, together with some American thinkers, they promoted analytic philosophy, discarding pragmatism as nonrigorous.[11] With Quine—who studied with Carnap in Prague—there began a reaction,[12] and today we observe that many are rediscovering pragmatism (among them Richard Bernstein, Hilary Putnam, and Richard Rorty).[13] The ethics of liberation is informed by motivations similar to those of pragmatism. Frequently, when I lecture on the Latin American philosophy of liberation, North American colleagues will tell me that my theses are very similar to those of pragmatism. For this reason I wish here only to outline the similarities and the differences of these two philosophical movements.

[165] Peirce was without a doubt the most original pragmatist. In 1903, this enigmatic philosopher expressed the generative intuition of his philosophy with a hermetic and plurivalent formulation: "Category the First is the Idea of that which is such as it is regardless of anything else. . . . Category the Second is the Idea of that which is such as it is as being Second to some First, regardless of anything else. . . . [I]t is *Reaction*. . . . Category the Third is the Idea of that which is such as it is a being a Third,[14] or Medium, between a Second and its First."[15] This is a philosophy of mediation—of *Betweenness*[16]—in which the immediate is never given to us since it is always mediated:

> 1. We have no power of Introspection, but all knowledge of the internal world is derived by hypothetical reasoning from our knowledge of external facts.
>
> 2. We have no power of Intuition, but every cognition is determined logically by previous cognitions.
>
> 3. We have no power of thinking without signs.
>
> 4. We have no conception of the absolutely incognizable.[17]

This declaration of war against Descartes is a recuperation of many moments left to the side by modern European philosophy. "American" thought[18] erupts creatively. Since it is not possible to operate from the immediate, every form of knowledge and action finds itself already determined by the mediation (*Thirdness*):[19] mediation of the knowing of an object by the intersubjectivity of interpreters as an agreement (through a sign as *representamen*); mediation of knowing by the scientific community;[20] mediation of knowing from (and not only "by") the linguistic horizon (from the icons, indexes, symbols);[21] mediation of knowing as a process (as verification of the laboratory),[22] not only by deduction or induction but also by abduction (as the hypothesis that ought to be verified diachronically); mediation of all knowledge by the future (the counterfactual anticipation of the coincidence of truth and reality *in the long run*);[23] and mediation of the theoretical by the practical, from the horizon of the ethical, as "socialist logic,"[24] by history and "common sense."

[166] I want to underscore this last aspect, which is fundamental in my rereading of pragmatism for the ends of an ethics of liberation. Let us consider a famous text from Peirce: "He who would not sacrifice his own soul to save the whole world, is illogical in all his inferences, collectively. So the social principle is rooted intrinsically in logic."[25] Theoretical reason (logic, for instance) is a second moment of practical reason (in which one can decide "to sacrifice one's own soul," or one's own life: practical truth). To which Peirce adds as commentary: "Now, it is not necessary for logicality that a man should himself be capable of the heroism of self-sacrifice. It is sufficient that he should recognize the possibility of it, should perceive that only that man's inferences who has it are really logical, and should consequently regard his own as being only so far valid as they would be accepted by the hero. So far as he thus refers his inferences to that standard, he becomes identified with such a mind. This makes logicality attainable enough."[26]

To ponder carefully this relation (of the grounding of norms that can lead one even to "give one's life," as a sacrifice, as point of departure for logical inferences) would lead us far. But we must at least indicate the theme. Peirce is ready to unite the ethical will of the scientist with "evolutionary love," an *éros* that moves the undefined community that is always realizing itself in order to stay consistent, as "evolution," with the process of the universe itself.[27] This is the entire problematic of the coimplication of practical truth and moral validity, from the processual reality of the corporeality of the life of the cultural, historical, and human subject. In any event, the ethics of liberation has always affirmed, as did Peirce, that logic (overcoming the "reductionistic fallacy" of analytical or positivist philosophy from Frege to Popper), and even ontology, presupposes ethics.[28] Let us look at all of this more closely, and refer back to the radical source of the formalist positions (epistemological positions that fell into the "reductionistic fallacy" — to name them as Apel does — or into moralities that claim no more than validity) and those of "content" (material ethics, as point of departure). Here, we find ourselves with the "uncircumventable [*nicht-hintergehbar*]" moment or where one's "spade bends backward,"[29] to use Wittgenstein's metaphor.

The theme is a familiar one. Kant proposed a "thing-in-itself" or the unknowable *noumenon*:[30] "We can only come to know phenomena, but never things in themselves [*der Dinge an sich selbst*]. . . . Beyond such phenomena we have to admit that there is something which is not a phenomenon, that is, things in themselves, since they can never be known [*bekannt*] in themselves."[31]

[167] The young Peirce, from his earlier period,[32] decidedly opposes the unknowability of the "thing in itself." Kant thinks that the thing in itself is unknowable; Peirce is of the opinion that it is partially knowable in each cognitive act, and fully *in the long run*. That is to say, and this is not noted frequently in some interpretations (even that of Apel, because he makes the same presupposition), we find in Peirce a kind of identity between "knowability" and "reality." Kant thinks the same way in this regard, that the "reality" of the thing is identical to its "knowability."[33] Let us consider an 1868 text by Peirce: "Ignorance and error can only be conceived as correlative to a real knowledge and truth, which later are of the nature of cognitions. Over against any cognition, there is an unknown but *knowable reality*; but over against all possible cognition, there is only the self-contradictory. In short, *cognizability* (in its widest sense) and *being* are merely metaphysically the same, but are synonymous terms."[34]

We have then four moments that *in the long run* ought to become identical: reality = being = truth = intersubjective validity. Reality[35] is partially and validly known initially by a community; which increases indefinitely through investigation,[36] which captures partially but incrementally the truth, in the sustained effort of a future identity: "The opinion that is fated to be ultimately *agreed*[37] to by all who investigate, is what we mean by the *truth*, and the object represented in this opinion is the *real*."[38] This is a historical fallibilism that tends toward a future identity, given that the truth is "that to a belief in which belief would tend if it were to tend indefinitely toward absolute fixity."[39] Or, to put it another way: "Thought, controlled by a rational experimental logic, tends to the fixation of certain opinions, equally destined, the nature of which will be the same in the end, however the perversity of thought of whole generations may cause the postponement of the *ultimate fixation*."[40] In Apel's words: "We can and we must assume the regulating idea that a scientific community of interpretation and experimentation, without limits and working under ideal conditions, should be able in the long run, in truth, to arrive at an intersubjectively valid opinion, that is to say, an opinion which cannot be refuted by anyone upon the basis of the criteria of truth which are available."[41]

As can be seen, truth is identified with validity (a position criticized by Wellmer and already treated in §2.5), and in this consists the consensual theory of truth: intersubjective consensuality that operates equally as ethical exigency in the manner of a "logical socialism." From this regulative horizon we may understand the "pragmatic maxim." In fact, the "objects" of knowledge are presented from a practical horizon to a community of investigators and are known because of their practical consequences: "Consider what effects, which might conceivably have practical bearings, we conceive the object of our conception to have. Then, our conception of these effects is the whole of our conception of the object."[42]

[168] Here we come to a long parenthesis, which I hope you will grant me, that refers to the theory of truth of a Spanish philosopher who is not very well known: Xavier Zubiri. Zubiri in fact makes a distinction among three types of truth.[43]

a. In the first place, he defines *"real* truth," as a mere cerebral actuality of the real[44] in millions of neural groups, through perceptual and conceptual categorization, which are linked to lexical-linguistic and self-conscious activities: "Truth is reality *present* in intellection in as much as it is really present in itself. Hence, the first and radical truth of sensory intellection . . . is precisely ratification of the *from-itself* [*de suyo*], ratification of reality proper. *Ratification* is the first and radical form of the truth of sensory intellection. This is what I call *real truth*."[45]

Something real is simply "actualized" in the brain; the real is prior to this actualization in the "feeling intellection." "The real" is not *independent* (second act) of the act of cognition (first act). On the contrary, the act of cognition (of cerebral subjectivity) is what is discovered as independent a posteriori to the real. The real is what is of/from *itself* (*de suyo*), a *prius* captured as what is given *before* and without relation, inasmuch *as real,* to the act of cognition. The real (reality) and knowability (being) are not identical. To be real is one dimension, while being known is another. The real is not what is knowable, but rather the substantive thing that exists *from itself.*[46] *Reality* is what is captured of the real as what is *from itself* of that which is real; in the cerebral actualization reality is, precisely, what is "accepted" as the "anteriority" of the *from-itself* of the real. *Truth* (which is not and can never be, nor be identified with, *reality*),[47] on the contrary, entails an "original reference" to the reality of the real: it is ratification.[48]

b. The truth of a judgment, instead, is the reference to the actuality of the real affirmed as "a thing *among others.*" That referentiality of the reality of the thing to other things is the "apophantic" of intellection.[49]

c. Thus we arrive at a third type of truth. Let us take, for example, a text by William James, in which he writes: "The moment pragmatism asks this question, it sees the answer: True ideas are those that we can assimilate, validate, corroborate and verify. False ideas are those that we cannot. That is the practical difference it makes to us to have true ideas; that, therefore, is the meaning of truth, for it is all that truth is known as. This thesis is what I have to defend. The truth of an idea is not a stagnant property inherent in it. Truth *happens* to an idea. It *becomes* true, is *made* true by events. Its verity *is* in fact an event, a process: the process namely of its verifying itself, its veri-*fication*. Its validity is the process of its valid-*ation*."[50]

[169] William James is here thinking of an "idea" and a "process." Zubiri touches on the theme in another way, since he places himself at a third level, namely, where "reason" is an intellective "march" from the reality of things in the "field" *toward* the "world."[51] The "passage" from "apophantic" affirmation to "worldly" rationality is carried out by "experience." Zubiri formulates here the question of the method (which is the "testing of reality") of "veri-fication" (*com-probación*).[52] This third level concerns then "*rational* truth." The *quest for what has been sketched* or surmised (Peirce's hypothesis or abduction) from the "apophantic" toward the "truth" as *encounter* and *fulfillment*[53] allows us to discover "truth *as encounter*: this is the essential goal of rational intellection."[54] Here we touch on the intuition of the question about truth in pragmatism. In fact, Zubiri's rational truth is the fulfillment of a quest as authentification, veridicalness, and verification (of the "apophantic" affirmed as the sketched, postulated, hypothetical [*abduction*] toward the world as grounding). Zubiri treats here the theme of "the essence of truth as encounter."[55] Verification is "*attempt*": "The dialectic of adequacy is a progressive attempt of verification."[56] What is verified? "What is sketched [hypothetical problem] is what is verified, something that takes us from the world to the field."[57] To verify is to ground the field in the world (see arrow x of the figure in note 51);[58] the verified is what is of the field from the world (arrow y of the figure). From which: "Verification is dialectical not only because of its moment of progressive adequacy, but also and more radically because of its intrinsic character: it is a march of the verifiable and the unverifiable towards new sketches. It is the *suggestion-sketch* dialectic. Rational intellection is to proceed by sketching in and through a suggestion, and a stepping back from the sketch to the suggestions of new sketches. *This is the dialectic of a sensory reason.*"[59] Verification is "fulfillment,"[60] that is to say, a "historical success": "Since the fulfillment of possibilities is what formally makes up the essence of the historical, it is the case that the character of rational truth inasmuch as it is success is what formally constitutes the essence itself of what is *historical in this truth*."[61]

Let us consider from this horizon the "pragmatic maxim" to which I referred before this discussion of Zubiri's position. In fact, the "*object* of our conception"—wrote Peirce in the text cited above—is "conceived" (in its content) from the *practical* "effects" that are produced in the temporal process: "effects" of laboratory experiments or of practical actions—of a linguistic community with intersubjective validity. This occurs in such a way that the totality of the consequences of the object is what constitutes its intersubjective "meaning" with procedural validity *in the long run.*

[170] I will return to this topic in the next section in order to enlarge on the theme I have begun, that is, the distinction between descriptive or normative statements of practical truth, to explore it as a process of fulfillment in historical time—as material content of truth and with intersubjective-linguistic validity. In any event, the fundamental intuitions of pragmatism can be fully subsumed by an ethics of liberation, but with a difference: if pragmatism thinks preferentially from the experience of a scientific community, from the natural sciences (from Darwinism, for example), and from North American *common sense*, the ethics of liberation thinks primarily from the experience of the practical-political community,[62] from the critical social sciences (its critique of global political economy, for example), and from the oppressed or excluded of the periphery, as well as those in the center. If William James underscores cognitive action as *verification*—of "truth" as something generated by a *theoretical* process[63]—the ethics of liberation instead focuses on the transformative praxis as *liberation*—where "practical truth" qua moment of the *ethical* and *political* process has a greater reference to praxis than it does in pragmatism itself. And, furthermore, I draw attention to the fact that pragmatism could not discover the phenomenon of Eurocentrism,[64] because it interpreted the United States as the full Western fulfillment of Europe—in the long path from the East toward the West of universal culture, just as Hegel had conceived it. It did not take as its departure point the periphery, the dominated, the excluded, the poor, women, the races discriminated against. Cornel West's project of a "prophetic pragmatism"[65] would like to supersede the narrowness of this reductionistic interpretation—which thinks of everything in terms of New England, of academic approaches, or of the "common sense" of the white, Protestant, bourgeois male, a minority but a hegemonic group, and in power[66]—invoking not only postmodern critique but also Marxism for that new development of pragmatism. Given these new categorical horizons, I think that a dialogue in the near future between pragmatism and the philosophy of liberation would be extremely fertile. I, in turn, will take up the fundamental theses of pragmatism when the discourse and the architectonic of the ethics of liberation require it.[67]

§3.2. The Pragmatic Realism of Hilary Putnam

[171] The analytical or positivist tradition did not criticize only naive metaphysical thinking; it also negated the possibility of scientific rigor in every normative ethics (because these ethics are made up of "value judgments" or "normative statements," which are considered incompatible with such rigor). Ayer writes: "Value judgments . . . , to the extent that they are not scientific, are not, literally speaking, meaningful, because they are simple expressions of emotion that cannot be classified as either true nor false."[68] When attempts are made to demonstrate that "normative ethical concepts are irreducible to empirical concepts,"[69] what is in fact implied is that ethical philosophy is impossible, at least as it is understood by the ethics of liberation. It is for this reason that I must now indicate the way to deal with this difficult question and to understand the relationship among three terms—reality, truth, and validity[70]—in the critical thought of Putnam's pragmatism—a project around which I would like to develop my critique of the "reductionistic fallacy" (as it is named by Apel) of the Tarskian position.

Putnam shows very well how the "formalized language L"—in Tarski's case—from a "metalanguage ML," should establish a "criterion of truth" (criterion W or convention T) that ends up being only a "criterion of intelligibility." Tarski's "true" is not the "classical true."[71] Putnam refuses then, among others, the Tarskian claim to speak of the "true in general" in the determined case of the "true of a determined language L,"[72] given that it is a matter of an abstraction of the ordinary language of a formalized artificial environment that circumvents "semantic antinomies" (and of course, pragmatic antinomies too).[73] "Correspondence" is established between two terms within the horizon of a defined language, in which neither can claim to be reality:

"Snow is white" is true if and only if snow is white.

This logical-semantic tautological expression is exclusively directed to the development of a theory of "meaning-sense" (with an intelligibility claim) that attempts to respond to the question "What is it to understand a sentence?"[74] "According to Tarski, Carnap, Quine, Ayer, and similar theorists, knowing these facts [such as 'snow is white'] is the key to understanding the word 'is true.' In short, to understand *P is true*, where P is a sentence in quotes, just 'disquote' P—take off the quotation marks[75] (and erase 'is true')."[76]

[172] What becomes of the relationship between a term in the statement and the other terms (the "object" or "thing")? Putnam explains Tarski's position with a new example: "There is a description D such that 'D is an

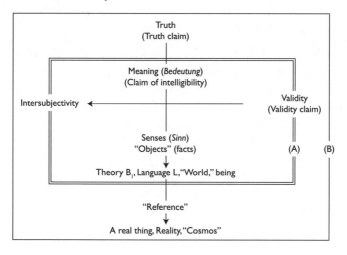

Figure 8. Levels of language and of "reference" to the real.

NOTE: Cristina Lafont's excellent work *Reason as Language* (1993) describes the debate on this topic. As Donald Davidson (1990) tells us: "This is the right moment to look for help as to the distinction between meaning and reference. The problem, we are told, is that questions of reference generally resolve extralinguistic facts, but not questions of meaning" (41).

electron' is provable in B_1, and *this* could be true (for a suitable B_1)[77] even if there are no electrons!"[78] In this case the concept of "true" is merely linguistic or *intratheoretical*: "truth" is intelligibility, and now demonstrability from a theory B_1.

Putnam wants to recover, on the contrary, in some way, "the belief that there exists a world" such that there is "warranted assertibility"[79] to this belief. The Tarskian horizon (A of figure 8)[80] is not sufficient for a "realist conception of truth"[81]—that would have to be situated in horizon B. I think that the analytic or positivist position gave preeminence to the "truth" or the horizon of "language L" (A), above the ordinary language of the world of common sense (B). Carnap himself shows this: "The sense [*Sinn*] of a proposition is grounded in the extent to which it can express something factual. . . . If a (pseudo) proposition does not express a (thinkable) fact, then it has no meaning and is only a proposition in an apparent, initial sense. If a proposition expresses something factual, then it undoubtedly expresses meaning; more specifically, it is truthful if it expresses something factual, and is false if it does not do so."[82] This has to do with the horizon of the meaning-sense (intelligibility) of a proposition in the sphere of a determined abstract language (A in figure 8). In a certain way, we would have here an "analytical notion of truth."[83] But, as Cristina Lafont has shown, there is a long tradition where preeminence has been granted to "meaning above reference,"[84] beginning with Hamann, passing through Humboldt, and concluding with Heidegger.[85]

[173] But—and this will be one of the virtues of Putnam's analysis— where we are situated, whether in a predefined (formal) language or in the quotidian world of ordinary language, things are always complex. In fact: "There are 'external facts,' and we can *say what they are*. What we *cannot* say—because it makes no sense—is that the facts are *independent of all conceptual choices*."[86] And this because—in the example given by Putnam—"if I chose Carnap's language, I must say that there are three objects" but "if I chose the Polish logician's language . . . I must say that there are seven objects."[87] For Putnam there can be different definitions of the objects of the world according to the various "conceptual schemas," types of language, out of which and from which the world is represented. He repeats: "What is wrong with the notion of objects existing 'independently' of conceptual schemes is that there are no standards for the use of even the logical notions apart from conceptual choices. . . . To talk of 'facts' without specifying the language to be used is to talk of nothing."[88] Which leads him to conclude: "*Given* a language, we can describe the 'facts' that make the sentences of that language true and false in a 'trivial' way—using the sentences of that very language; but the dream of finding a well-defined Universal Relation between a (supposed) totality of *all* facts and an arbitrary true sentence as an arbitrary language, is just the dream of an absolute notion of a fact (or an 'object') and of an absolute relation between sentences and the facts (or the objects) 'in themselves.'"[89]

Now we can ask Putnam the question that he himself asks with respect to his own position: "How can one assure oneself that this is not sheer linguistic idealism?"[90] Putnam thinks that among the available languages or "conceptual schemas" is also found ordinary language or "common sense"—whose reconsideration originated the whole reflection of this "second Wittgenstein,"[91] which is frequently discredited because allegedly it does not contain enough "criteria of truth" (compared with those of the "objects" of science). Putnam rejects that there are "intrinsic properties" in things, and leans to thinking—against the opinions originating in the seventeenth century—that there is a "projection" of the common sense in what we could call "objects" of quotidian life (chairs, tables, ice cubes).[92] Putnam's effort is directed at "working out the program of preserving commonsense realism while avoiding the absurdities and antinomies of metaphysical realism in all of its familiar varieties."[93] Let me now develop a series of proposals of interest to an ethics of liberation, taking off from Putnam's distinction between "strict disposition" and "*ceteris paribus* disposition."

[174] I am of the opinion that there are three spheres or "dimensions"

of real things:[94] (a) the *macro* horizon of the entire physical universe (galaxies, astronomical systems, etc.), the "scientific" access to which is recent (via "theories" and instruments of observation, such as the telescope);[95] (b) the horizon of *common sense*, where "things" or "objects" of the quotidian world are detectable "normally" by the biological parameters of our neurological "receptive" system[96] — these "things" or "objects" being denominated by the accords of intersubjective cultural-historical language; and (c) the *micro* horizon, atomic, molecular, observable only by "theories" and scientific instruments (such as the microscope), which supersedes the horizon of *normal* "observability" of the natural neurological human systems; these are "objects" (neutrons, protons, electrons, etc.) recently constituted. All three horizons (a, b, and c) can be *real*, but the parameters or "conceptual schemas" that constitute them are many. "Common sense" moves in horizon b (although amplified by scientific information in the culture of the contemporary man of the street).

[175] Putnam, as in an obstacle course, proceeds by working through some of the obstacles, but I think he is not able to overcome the last one. In fact, Putnam comments accurately: "One can 'solve' just about *any* philosophical problem either by saying that the objects in question don't really exist, or by saying that the statements in question don't really have a truth value. If one is desperate enough or daring enough, one can say that 'truth' itself is a projection."[97] With this Putnam has indicated (and attempts to work out) the obstacles of idealism (a), skepticism (b), or radical subjectivism (c). But this is not all, for in the practical sphere there are still other obstacles. "Rejecting the spectator point of view [the disinterested point of view], taking the agent point of view [as does pragmatism or the ethics of liberation] towards my own moral beliefs and recognizing that *all* of the beliefs that I find indispensable in life must be treated by me as assertions which are true and false. . . . [It] is not the same thing as lapsing back [d] into metaphysical realism about one's own moral beliefs any more than taking this attitude towards one's beliefs about commonsense material objects or towards causal beliefs or mathematical beliefs means lapsing back [e] into metaphysical realism about common sense objects."[98] With magisterial hand, Putnam indicates his position (which I share with him from the perspective of the philosophy of liberation), recuperating also the points of view of moral common sense, and with reference to beliefs, but rejecting the naive metaphysical attitude in morality with respect to real "objects." He adds: "It also does not require us to give up our pluralism or our fallibilism: one does not have to [f] believe in a *unique best* moral version, or [g] a *unique best* causal version. . . . [W]hat we have are *better or worse* versions, and that *is* objectivity."[99] At the end of the day, we face the last obstacle, and for that reason we will pay special attention to Putnam's reflec-

tion: "We are forced to recognize with William James that the question as to how much of our web of beliefs reflects the world 'in itself'[100] and how much is our 'conceptual contribution' [makes no sense]."[101] Confronting this last obstacle, Putnam asks: "Are we not returning towards a complete irrationalism?"[102] He answers from the perspective of his wife, Ruth Anna Putnam:

> Ruth Anna Putnam, following the line of John Dewey [or Marx], appeals at this point to the notion of a *need*. It is because there are real human needs, and not merely desires, that it makes sense to distinguish between better and worse values, and, for that matter, between better and worse. . . . Here Dewey, like Goodman, tells us that human needs also do not pre-exist, that humanity is constantly redesigning itself, and that we *create* needs. Once again, many will feel the sense of vertigo, or worse, the sense of falling into a bottomless pit. Our notions—the notion of a value, the notion of a moral image, the notion of a standard, the notion of a need—are so intertwined that none of them can provide a "foundation" for ethics. That, I think, is exactly right.[103]

Here Putnam "bumps into" the last obstacle, where one's "shovel bends back" (where the argument reaches its limit), and in my opinion he is wrong in his answer. He has reason to affirm that there is no value or a moral image that can be a "foundation." But the *necessities*, the needs of the life of the human subject as such, which can be recreated in their modalities, cannot be created in their *ultimate* content, which is linked to life as such. Eating can be done in many ways, and culinary arts (or the capitalist food market) can introduce new foods, fashions, and tastes. But to "eat" is necessary, and the person who does not eat (in the broadest sense, even if the "food" is intravenous fluid) will die. Death is the limit of all the needs not fulfilled, and death "preexists" them in its fundamental content. This preexistence of *human life* with respect to the ethical subject him- or herself (who is self-conscious and for that reason self-reflexively responsible for the life in his or her charge) is the ultimate criterion of all value, moral images, and modalities that acquire not only the needs but also the conceptual schemas, theoretical frameworks, cultural structures, and so on that can satisfy them and allow one to live! Referring to an example in the context of translation from a foreign language, Putnam presents the following case:

> So what do we in fact do? I think that in actual translation we start out with assumptions as to what the speaker *wants* or *intends*, at least in many situations. After hours without food,[104] we assume he wants food;[105] after hours awake, he may want to sleep (especially if he is rubbing his eyes); etc. We also assume that his "reliability" in the abstract sense of truth-probability is not unconnected with his functional *efficiency*. If a speaker accepts a

sentence S whenever he is looking at *water*, and he reaches for the water in question whenever he is deprived of water and accepts S, then S might mean "there's water" or "there's something to drink."[106]

[176] This is precisely the case in which my "shovel bends back" on the ultimate level of truth-reality (and even validity, since we intersubjectively are "coming to an agreement" about the fact that the man in Putnam's example "needs to drink"). Contrary to what I tried to show in §1.5, Putnam asserts: "We must come to see that there is no possibility of a 'foundation' for ethics, just as we have come to see that there is no possibility of a 'foundation' for scientific knowledge, or for any other kind of knowledge."[107] Paradoxically, Putnam has inverted the problem: for the analytical or logical positivist philosophers the normative-ethical statement is a value judgment, and, for that reason, it lacks scientific validity. For Putnam, both the ethical statement and the scientific now lack decisive grounding. Both find themselves in the same situation of having to "recognize."[108] But if this is so, it is because what is "indispensable *for the life*" of the human subject is the ultimate *uncircumventable criterion of truth* on which "one's shovel buckles." This is the essential intuition of pragmatism and one with which the ethics of liberation is in agreement, but the ethics of liberation takes it to its ultimate consequences, not for theoretical or academic motives alone but also because the majority of humanity faces the risk of death, from hunger, exclusion, and so on. If my arguments are weak then we will have to discover better ones, by a fallibilism that I accept and I need, as Putnam himself puts it:

> The heart of pragmatism, it seems to me—of James's and Dewey's pragmatism, if not of Peirce's[109]—was the insistence on the supremacy of the agent point of view. If we find that we must take a certain point of view, use a certain "conceptual system," when we are engaged in practical activity, in the widest sense of "practical activity," then we must not simultaneously advance the claim that it is not really "the way things are in themselves" [referring to macro objects, or the common sense of micro, as discussed above . . .]. Our *lives* show that we believe that there are more and less warranted beliefs about political contingencies, about historical interpretations, etc.[110]

Since "life" has here a "weak" sense (I would say nonpragmatic), it is forgotten that life itself is the real par excellence (the mode of our reality to which truth "refers"), with respect to which truth in a pragmatic sense has ultimate reference. The "life" we are charged with, to live with self-consciousness and self-responsibility, is both the point of departure—as the mode of reality from which the macro, micro, and common-sense "objects" are constituted—and the point of arrival, what truth and validity "refer to" (linguistically and intersubjectively) in order to reproduce and develop life. This "human life" is a *practical* point of reference, in the sense that it grounds or constitutes the ethical ends and values of intersubjective, linguistic, cultural, and material existence. The life of the human subject, from its receptive parameters (from the neurological to the cultural), constitutes the "objects" of its truth, as practical and theoretical mediations of survival, of the reproduction and development of the life of the human subject itself. Science and common sense (and here especially economic science with a material sense, and not purely formal as in the case of neoliberalism, given that it must displace itself in the *prius* of the need-reproduction-consumption parameters of the worker), have to do with this reproduction and development of the human needs[111] of the life of the ethical subject that *preexist* all creation and recreation of the *modes*, or "fashions" in the style of Dewey, of accessing, managing, fulfilling them.

[177] From this the Tarskian problem may now be made explicit thus: *Snow is white* is "true" if, and only if, snow is "really" white.

In the first place, and only considering the subject of the statement, that the "object" *snow* is a *real* "thing" means that—in the order of "objects" of common sense, of ordinary language (in an intersubjective and linguistic fashion therefore), of a "world" of constitution of the meaning-sense (of intelligibility), and with possible certainty of phenomenological evidence (I say: "Snow is white," and I turn my head and "see" it)—this (deistically or referentially) real is cerebrally "actualized" as given *from itself*; that is, the real is captured as a *prius* in its own actualization: real "snow."

In the second place, we would have to show the apophantic moment of "it is white"—that is to say, in the judgment proper.[112] But, in fact and practically, when it is stated as a speech act—inasmuch as the speaker is an agent and *in real life*, as a communicative act (with its illocutionary moments and its propositional content)—the statement "I say that *snow is white*" is integrated in some way into a *practical* plexus at the "horizon" of the real (for example, because "snow is white," it reflects the sun's rays and blinds our eyes in the high mountains, when we go climbing in Mendoza, Argentina; it has "sense," insofar as in some fashion it makes *reference* to a danger to the reproduction of the life of human agents, who are engaged in the activity of mountain climbing and who are blinded by the brightness of the sun). The "object" appears and is "judged" as a moment in the totality of the praxis of the "human life," and inasmuch it is integrated with the practical plexus it appears as *this* "object" and not as another. It is in this sense that normative statements can be of "*practical* truth" ("I must cover my eyes with dark lenses when mountain climbing"), and human life itself (as the real to which the statements refer) is the "criterion of truth" of "actualization," of judgments and the processes of verification of all the "ends," "values," "objects," and "facts" or "acts" of the world (whether scientific or quotidian in the sense of common sense). All of this must be investigated further.[113]

To conclude this section, a very central one to this ethics of liberation, I would like to offer one last reflection. In sum, what the tradition of the philosophy of the *linguistic turn* teaches us, and what is useful and *necessary* (and for this reason must be subsumed) but not *sufficient* (and for this reason must be contextualized), is that access to the real is always linguistically mediated. From Hamann and Humboldt onward, however, it has been noted that if the "world" is opened up from a *particular language*, relativism is an inevitable consequence. Richard Rorty's position[114] in our times is the most dramatic expression of this. Each "linguistic world" (that of Frege or of Tarski's "language L") presupposes a *criterion of meaningfulness* or sense (with an intelligibility claim) that must manifest itself also because of its internal coherence—Donald Davidson is right about this.[115]

[178] Thus we arrive at the agreement that there are at least three levels in question: (a) that of the meaning or sense coherence of the linguistic "world" (*formal* from Frege to Davidson, and *ontological* from Humboldt to Heidegger); (b) that of the valid intersubjectivity of agreements of a community of communication (from Peirce to Apel or Habermas); and (c) that of the attempt to "open up" to the problematic of "referentiality" toward the real, real "objects," or "things" (from Kripke to Putnam and the ethics of liberation itself): "Given that learning, the possibility of revision, is inherent to a given praxis—that is to say, in inductive and not deductive contexts (such as those of mathematics or jurisprudence, for example)—*designating expressions are used referentially*. For it is on the basis of the *referential use of designating expressions* that we encounter the presupposition of *something* that has to be *discovered*[116] and not *legislated*, that is, *something* in relation to which our knowledge must be self-correcting."[117]

In the face of (a) the relativism of the incommensurability or incommunicability of each linguistic world, of a concept of truth as merely what is "*understandable*" or intelligible[118]—which in ethics leads to a relativism that is more or less skeptical and antiuniversal, and which as we have indicated can have two variants, one that is formalist (that of the analytics) and another that is ontological-culturalist (that of Humboldt or Heidegger)—(b) Apel attempts to salvage universalism by means of a pragmatic reflection coming from a consensual theory of truth—which in ethics leads to a formalism without any content whatsoever, and consequently to its own inapplicability. For its part, (c) the "referentialist" current attempts to salvage the ethical validity of pragmatic common sense but is not able yet to discover "that" to which it "refers" in a convincing fashion—it trips up as it jumps over the last obstacle. I think that the ethics of liberation, at the moment of the analysis of the fundamental structures, can affirm a *claim* and *criterion* of universal *truth* (from the reproduction and development of the life of the human subject in general) — fulfilling thus the "referentialist" attempt — which includes the cultural moments (here also with a *rightness claim* because it is practical truth) of all the possible "linguistic worlds" (even the formal ones, though aware that these are "abstract reductions"[119] that must be resuscitated in the *context* of the real in order to reach practical truth). The ethics of liberation can at the same time subsume all that is positive in discourse ethics with respect to the intersubjective *claim* and *criterion of validity* (truth as consensus, and which having to have "reference" to a material content is now applicable and does not lose its universality even in the intercultural dialogue). And can also affirm the *claim* (or condition of communication) of intelligibility and the *criterion of meaningfulness* (truth as understandability) of meaning with coherence, and also with respect to common sense and as linked to the plexus of action (such as has been proposed by pragmatism since its inception, and which the ethics of liberation claims to be its full development, as will be seen below).

§3.3. The Functional or Formal "System" of Niklas Luhmann

[179] I am particularly interested in the Luhmannian formulation of the "social system,"[120] because it leads us to the clear definition of the concept of "totality" as "system" on which I must count in part II (the critical part) of this *Ethics*. I will not present the richness of the Luhmannian vision, but only that which is important for my argument. In fact, few like Luhmann have made the theoretical decision and coherence of arriving without major contradiction to a description of the autopoietic, self-referential "social system" without a subject or possibility of it. Luhmann's system is about an ontological-sociology that reminds us of Tarski's "language L," but now as a "system S." In both cases the intelligibility claim (linguistic in the first, functional or sociosystemic performative in the second) makes reference to the meaning of action with a certain "sense" (*Sinn*), which as much in Husserl as in Frege (and even Heidegger) is what gives place, what "situates" the functional "part" in the "whole" (the "object," "fact," "entity" or "function" in the "world" of a Heidegger, or in the "system" of Luhmann). Habermas asks himself: "It may be that 'linguistically generated intersubjectivity' and 'self-referentially closed system' are now the catchwords for a controversy that will take the place of the discredited mind-body problematic."[121] Habermas attempts a critique from the perspective of intersubjective linguistic-discursive validity (which I consider of great interest in the sense that it is impossible for a system, without subjects, to arrive at a self-

regulation without any intervention of discursive reason). But, and this is what is of interest to us right now, Habermas cannot radically critique Luhmann, because he does not count with the material or content level, with reference to a nonconsensualist "practical truth" claim, because Habermas is a formalist, albeit in his own way.

In order to understand the Luhmannian theory it is necessary to take charge of the history of sociology—in one of its versions. Luhmann follows his teacher Talcott Parsons.[122] Anthony Giddens comments on Parsons: "Durkheim's ideas in fact, for better or worse, are much more complex than those contained in *The Social System* [by Parsons]. Durkheim argued that there are . . . primary modes of exchange characterized by situations where the interests of the actors involved can drive them to differences with respect to the moral imperatives of their *collective conciousness*."[123] Parsons, because of his understanding of "social order," tends to functionalize all anomie and conflict.[124] This stand is taken to its furthest point by Luhmann who, departing from mechanical cybernetics (a system that is self-regulating), knows that "living" organisms steer the system by self-organized autopoiesis in a more complex fashion than do mechanical systems, thus reducing successfully the complexity of its "environment" (*Umwelt*). The specificity of the "social system" consists in that it self-referentially autoregulates itself by virtue of the production of a "meaning-specific strategy [*sinnspezifische*]."[125]

[180] I will begin with an example. What is the status for Luhmann of each one of the "differentiated systems" that occur within the "social system" as a set? The answer is, they are independent from one another. Each subsystem—as is required by the *formalist* abstract reduction—autoregulates itself autopoietically. The same process takes place with the "economic system"—we could also take as examples the judicial, political, religious, or educational systems. In fact, the "economic system" has for Luhmann a binary *code* by which it organizes itself: "pay/not to pay" ("to have money/not to have money"),[126] which is what allows the "sense" of the moments of the system to be constituted. The *program* of the system is made explicit in the "prices" that self-regulate the instances of payment and economic expectations in general. The self-referential moment, based on such a code and program, communicates internally through money—from which Habermas extracts the concept for his own "critical theory." "Money"[127] is the universal mediation of *communication* in the closed space of the economic system. Since there is a lack of money and commodities, two mechanisms emerge: the market and competition.[128] The "market" (there are different levels of market) self-referentially autoregulates itself (always keeping in mind the cybernetic metaphor) by means of prices. "Competition" in the market is not a discursive or self-conscious moment,

but instead, avoiding all direct interaction (of possible subjects), is an *auto-poietic mechanism*.[129] The economic system (like every other system) does not depend on other subsystems (such as the political, the religious, etc.); they are all autonomous. We have here, precisely, a *formalist* conception of the economy, exclusively capitalist, and self-referential,[130] where the needs for life of the human subject[131] are reduced to the mere "environment" (that is, the "outside" of a systematic consideration). Let us now look at the question as a whole.

The "paradigm change" that is proposed by Luhmann with respect to earlier theories of systems is supported by the following transformations: (a) we will not speak any more of "part and whole" but instead of "system and environment":[132] (b) within open systems (not those that are closed) there are no "parts," but instead an internal "system differentiation"[133]— through the formation of the subsystems of economics, politics, and law, and so on, as we already saw above; and (c) what is in the last instance rele-vant in the new paradigm is that the system is autopoietic, self-referential, and self-organizing.[134] From this there emerges the central critical ques-tion: How can "self-referential closure create openness"[135] and "dynamic stability" with its environment?[136]

[181] From the beginning of Luhmann's systematic reflection, we can observe the use of certain conceptual presuppositions: "The following con-siderations assume that there are systems. . . . But, at least in systems theory, they [scientific statements] refer to the real world. . . . Thus we must first work out a systems theory that has a real reference to the world. Because it claims universal validity [*Anspruch universeller Geltung*] for everything that is a system, the theory also encompasses systems of analytic and epistemic behavior."[137] Luhmann speaks frequently of "reality [*Wirklichkeit*]." This "reality" maintains a constitutive relation of systematic self-referentiality: it concerns a real "world."[138] The "system/environment" or totality of all the systems/environments (given that every system can also function as the en-vironment of the others) would be reality.[139] The "system" posits its "limits" against the "environment [*Umwelt*]."[140] This is to say "Boundaries cannot be conceived without something beyond [*dahinter*]; thus they presuppose the reality of a beyond and the possibility of transcendence."[141]

The matter has its difficulties. Luhmann writes that "reality can be treated as sense";[142] and since "sense" is a moment of the "world," we have once again "world" with "reality."[143] When Luhmann identifies "world di-mensions—namely objectivity (*realitas*),[144] temporality, and sociality—as fitting within the cosmos or the subject's structure of consciousness,"[145] he falls into a formalism in which he confuses the system (formal) with the real (the material).

"The human being," for his part, "may appear to himself or to an observer as a unity, but he is not a system,"[146] and even more clearly: "The statement that persons belong to the environment of systems does not contain an evaluation of the significance of persons for themselves or for others. It only revises the overestimation implicit in the concept of subject, namely, the thesis that consciousness is the subject of everything else. The environment, not *the subject, underlies* social systems, and *underlies* means only that there are preconditions for the differentiation of social systems (e.g., persons as bearers of consciousness) that are not differentiated with the system."[147] This uncoupling of social systems and psychic systems (which in reality are human subjectivity, of neurocerebral constitution), where these are reduced to an environment, would produce a radical separation between "system" and "ethics" (the latter does not constitute a system for Luhmann), between the formal and material spheres of the reality of ethics.[148]

The system, in its process of differentiation into subsystems, will auto-adapt to the environment through selection, decreasing the complexity of the environment, and increasing its complexity through a process of autopoietic self-organization: self-referentiality,[149] irreversible in time, in which it must react with speed, because the impossibility of reproduction quickly produces the dissolution (entropy) of the system.[150] All this concerns the "self-referentiality of being."[151]

[182] The central problem that is important for my interpretation here is that of "double contingency," or of the self-referentiality of the ego and the alter ego. My critique (presented in chapter 4) explodes this self-referentiality, from the heteroreferentiality of the Other, which appears *outside* all "expectation" (*Erwartung*). The social phenomenon of "double contingency" is indicated in the following way: "The self-referential circle is decisive: I will do what you want if you do what I want. In a rudimentary form, this circle is a new unity that cannot be reduced to either of the participating systems."[152]

Or, put another way:

> Thus an *indeterminacy created by prediction* emerges within the meta-perspective of double contingency. However routine and expected a behavior may become, if the ability to predict this behavior is used to motivate complementary behavior, then that may become a motive to change the predictable behavior in order to remove the basis for the prediction and uncouple the connective behavior based on it. If ego knows that alter knows that ego is concerned with predicting alter's behavior, then ego has to consider the effect of this anticipation. This cannot occur as improved foresight because that would only reintroduce the problem. . . . Openness to new conditioning rests on the same condition as negativity, namely, on the doubling of contingency: ego experiences alter as alter ego. But along

with the *nonidentity of perspectives*, ego also experiences the *identity of this experience* on *both* sides.[153]

The "expectation" of the action of the Other frames the contingent possibilities (not necessary but possible ones) within the medium of "trust [*Vertrauen*]" that this expectation guarantees positively, or of "distrust" that this expectation excludes in its anticipation. Within the sphere of this self-referential circle, the "social system" is constituted, in which the psychic system of each agent functions as an environment. Within the horizon of the double contingency, actions are improbable, and their possibilities, open. Each agent has a double reference: toward itself (in figure 9, number 1), and in this sense it observes (arrow a) itself (A) as a specific actor in the social system and for the other social actor (2), and in this second possibility the alter ego is an object (arrow b) of observation (B: the alter for the ego). Vice versa, the alter ego is now for the ego (3, for c in reference to A^1: the ego for the alter) an external observer outside its social function, and for itself (4) observer (d) of its own social functionality (B^1). As can be observed, A is not A^1, nor is B, B^1. In the self-referential social system such a difference is mutually constituted and does not entail a major difficulty. However, as we will see in chapter 4, the difference of B as object of observation of the ego as itself, from B^1, insofar as it is the experience of itself of the other, would constitute—for example in Levinas—the entire problem of the irreducible alterity of the Other to every possible "totalization" (systematic functionality). The alter ego in B becomes a "subject-object" (the Other)—not merely an alter ego "B: *equal to the I*, merely 'there,'" but instead an alter ego "*another than the I* and never equal; B is not equal to B^1." This irruption of the Other beyond every functionality in the "double contingency" will grant the possibility of the *critical* moment, something absolutely impossible for Luhmann, given that the social system, being self-referential, allows contingency, openness, and interpenetration,[154] but never irruption of the "subject" of the Other—of the psychic system as

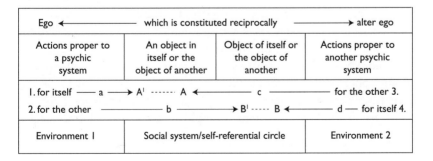

Ego ⟵	which is constituted reciprocally	⟶ alter ego	
Actions proper to a psychic system	An object in itself or the object of another	Object of itself or the object of another	Actions proper to another psychic system
1. for itself —— a ⟶ A^1 ------ A ⟵ —— c —————— for the other 3.			
2. for the other ——————— b ——————— ⟶ B^1 ---- B ⟵ —— d —— for itself 4.			
Environment 1	Social system/self-referential circle		Environment 2

Figure 9. Self-referential circle of "double contingency."

autonomous: that is to say, as a self-reference without regard to the social system itself nor from the dignity of that social system as recognized by the postulation of its self-responsible self-consciousness—and for that reason also is it unclear why a system comes to its end and, diachronically, how it originates. Luhmann is concerned with showing how the social system *remains*, responding to an environment of great complexity. The *irruption* of the alterity of the Other, which is critical of the social system, the *extinction* and *origination* of such a system are heteroreferential moments that Luhmann does not formulate clearly, and that are of extreme importance to an ethics of liberation.

[183] On the other hand, referring to "a special environment of the social systems": the "human being" (I cannot write this without a certain irony or tragic affirmation) is not an internal constituent of the system, but rather is only an "environment." However, Luhmann makes reflections that he does not advance, and that pertain to the "material" problem of ethics. Thus, speaking of the "organic reproduction" and the "psychic reproduction," which have to do with "life"[155] and with "consciousness," he writes: "Autopoiesis *qua* life and *qua* consciousness is a presupposition for forming social systems, which means that social systems can actualize their own reproduction only if they can be sure that life and consciousness will continue. . . . For life and consciousness, self-reproduction is possible only within a closed system."[156] This indicates that, for instrumental reason, only the autopoietically formal systems—which have life as condition but not as material criterion and ethical principle—take charge of life. That is to say, capital should be in charge of the life of the workers. Furthermore, as can be observed, here life only means a biological and naturalist dimension, which is exclusively "organic reproduction." The issue offers us great possibilities within the Luhmannian horizon that remains an understanding of the "social system" without subjects, within a paradigm of consciousness and from the perspective of instrumental reason. I will show in chapter 4 the coherence of this position, and the reason for the impossibility of being able to have a *critical* consciousness within this theoretical-social framework. And for this reason it becomes justifiably the target of the objection that it is "apt to take over the legitimating functions of power, until now exercised by the reigning positivist consciousness."[157] Luhmann, in our vision, reveals himself better than anywhere else in the following text: "Thus economic theory is needed (or else it would not be a useful theory) to keep a cool head with respect to the difference between rich and poor. . . . Some people would like to mount a simplistic attack here using ethics."[158]

§3.4. The "Feasibility" of Franz Hinkelammert

[184] At this moment of the ethics of liberation we face the theme of the fulfillment of the norm for what is true (practically and materially) and valid (formally). It concerns the question of feasibility, of the concrete conditions or circumstances of its effective *possibility*. A norm or praxis that is *impossible* (logically, empirically, or factically) is one that cannot be fulfilled. Thus we enter into a field little explored by contemporary material ethics and formal moralities. We will have to analyze the groundings of the criterion and the principle of the feasibility of praxis. To accomplish this we will examine an important Latin American thinker.

Because of his long experience in Latin America, I consider Franz Hinkelammert a Latin American, although he is an economist of German origin who studied in Münster and Berlin,[159] where he obtained a doctorate in economics with a specialization on the countries of eastern socialist Europe. He has been in Latin America since the 1960s, when he came to Chile in the period of Frei and Allende; in Chile he became one of the theorists of the Unidad Popular (Popular Unity), a democratic revolution cut short by the violence orchestrated by the United States, in accord with the geopolitical decisions of Henry Kissinger. Hinkelammert's work *Critique of Utopian Reason*,[160] written a year before the beginning of perestroika, anticipated the causes of the collapse of real socialism. In it, he carried out a critique on a strictly theoretical level of the bureaucratic planning of Stalinist type (accepting the Popperian argument, but showing its closed conclusion). At the same time, and with the same logic, he criticized the principles of the neoliberal postulate,[161] showing its inconsistency, as accepted by many today.[162] Hinkelammert was ahead of his times, but he is left outside the "great debate" because he writes in Spanish, and because his reflections begin with the people who have historically been excluded.

[185] Our author is not an easy read. His conversation is with conservative thought (in the style of Peter Berger, with his model of perfect plausibility),[163] today's ruling neoliberalism (Friedrich von Hayek or Milton Friedman, with their model of perfect competition),[164] Stalinist bureaucracy (Kantorovich, with a model of perfect planning),[165] and anarchism (with its project of the ethical perfection of subjects, which makes any type of institution unnecessary).[166] Epistemologically, Hinkelammert sets out from and confronts Karl Popper. His critique could be titled "With Popper, beyond Popper" or "The Misery of Antiutopianism." This theme is the point of departure in contemporary debate: John Rawls, Jürgen Habermas, and Karl-Otto Apel, to name just three philosophers, depart from "transcendental models"—in the terminology of Hinkelammert—models of which their authors do not have explicit consciousness of the logic of their

construction. The "originary position" of Rawls as well as the "transcendental community of communication" or the "ideal one" of Apel or Habermas are "transcendental models." The *logic of construction* of such models, which Hinkelammert criticizes, has not yet been studied. These empirically impossible models[167] nonetheless perform the role of regulative ideas.

The impossible has a special place at the epistemological and practical level. Hinkelammert puts forward a universal epistemological principle: the "general empirical principle of impossibility." This principle, already formulated by Max Weber and Karl Popper, and used also by Karl Marx, opens the sphere of the empirical sciences and of actions from the horizon of the "possible," especially in the science of economics[168] and politics[169] (and also in philosophy). From the beginning, Hinkelammert juxtaposes Marx to Weber, given that for Marx "bourgeois society is impossible"[170] because it cannot reproduce conveniently the human life of the worker, while for Weber "socialism is impossible"[171] because it seeks to eliminate mercantile relations. For Popper, socialism is impossible, because perfect knowledge, which presupposes perfect planning, is impossible (because infinite in its content and speed of transmission).[172] The discernment and delimitation of these "impossibilities," and everything that is deduced from them, is the topic of the critique of utopian reason: "The critique of utopian reason is not the rejection of the utopian but only of its transcendental conceptualization. It runs into the discussion about the categorical frameworks within which social thought is elaborated."[173]

[186] For the goals of an ethics of liberation, we find ourselves in a third moment of the *Process*: the material and formal discursive moments of ethics now enter in a new movement, namely of possible "feasibility." Let us see how Hinkelammert analyzes it. The argument is very concentrated,[174] and for this reason I will give a step-by-step account of it. In the first place, he writes: "Reality transcends experience, from which arises the need to have access to reality transforming it into *empiria* by means of universal concepts. Thus is constituted the knowing subject of empirical sciences."[175] Because the knowing subject is a finite being (not an infinite intelligence postulated by Kant as much as by Popper, and for that reason limited within a horizon of impossibility) and living (situated within the sphere of the possibilities limited by its mortality), all reality *opens* up as possibilities for action, from a project of life.[176] It is practical reason that collides with its "impossibilities" in action when pursuing the reproduction of life.[177] But knowable reality (insofar as it is knowable, but not for *now* totally known) always transcends our cognitive capacities. For the living-practical being to be able to actively manage reality, which is partly transcendent, he or she must hypothetically surpass both effectively observed and experimental situations through the medium of universal con-

cepts (transcendental, or for logical positivism, "metaphysical").[178] *Empiria*, empirical facts or the "state of things [*Tatsache*]" is a construct[179] that is posterior to the confrontation with reality that transcends the knower.[180] If reality coincided with *empiria* we would have the situation indicated in Marx's "If essence and appearance coincided, then there would be no need for science."[181] The "objective fact" reflects the limitations of the knowing subject, and the space between what is observed and the unobserved real[182] opens up the sphere of the hypothetical that is occupied by theories.[183] But in these theories not everything is hypothetical. It is not hypothetical that reality transcends what is observable (this is the first "fact" that grounds all science), and that universal concepts constitute the *empiria* of the sciences. But since the knowing subject is an acting-living subject, empirical objects are *constituted* from the open horizon of the "possible" for human life, from the principle of the impossibility of choosing death: "The knowing subject is the name of the reflexive capacity of the acting [and living][184] subject that reflects on his capacities of [living] action by means of universal concepts."[185] And here is where Hinkelammert, suddenly, introduces in an innovative way the problem of "feasibility": "This acting [and living] subject with reflexive capacities, who yearns for the totality of reality[186] but for whom it is impossible to reach it, is the subject of *technology* that refers to the exteriority of the human being. Then, all empirical knowledge is, in the last instance, technological knowledge, and the *criterion of truth*[187] is, in the last instance, its ability to be transformed into technology."[188]

[187] This requires some explanation in order to prevent misunderstanding. It should be underscored that, again, this thinking touches many aspects of Peircean pragmatism, but it is different from it for the same reasons that I indicated in §3.1: "Pure science aims at general theories and, for that reason, at the set of all the *possible ends*, while applied science aims at specific theories, although both are technologically oriented."[189] Reality is in fact observed (*objective* reality) inasmuch as it is integrated in some manner as a medium or end for the reproduction of the life of the actor, since: "The subject of the natural sciences . . . directs himself to the external world of humanity in *function of ends of actions*.[190] When in his action he collides with impossibilities[191] expressed in terms of principles of impossibility, this acting subject, departing from them, reflects on the sphere of all technologically possible ends. In this way, he anticipates the totality [of reality] by means of universal concepts and infinite technological processes, transforming reality into the *empiria* of the acting subject."[192] For Galileo it was "technologically possible" to see the phases of Venus because of the recently invented telescope.[193] But there emerges before us another reductionistic variable of feasibility: "When selecting the ends to be realized, there appears the lack of means for their fulfillment as the *material*

determination of every choice. . . . There appears now an economic universe that conditions all the realizable ends because of the need to inscribe them in the social product of the economy. That is to say, all possible ends have *material conditions of possible*. . . . Technically possible projects turn [or do not turn] economically possible."[194]

But, in addition and as we have already noted, the acting subject puts forward ends in order to reproduce life:

> The practical subject cannot act unless it is a *living subject*. One has to live in order to be able to conceive ends and to undertake them. . . . To live is also a project[195] that has its own conditions of possibility and fails if it does not achieve them.[196] . . . The decision about ends is a decision about the achievement of the project of life of subjects, and it is not exhausted by a formal means-ends relation [as was the opinion of Max Weber]. . . . Not all technically conceivable ends and materially realizable means according to a means-ends calculus [of instrumental reason] are also feasible:[197] only that subset of ends that are integrated to a project of life is feasible.[198]

Here Hinkelammert touches explicitly the theme of how the universal material principle of ethics judges the possibility (ethical feasibility) of the mere criterion of technical-economic feasibility: "Ends that are not compatible with the maintenance of the life of the subject itself fall outside feasibility.[199] . . . Ends outside this feasibility can be realized, but their fulfillment implies the decision to end a project of life that encompasses all the specific projects of ends.[200] It is a decision for suicide."[201] And now Hinkelammert argues, just as I argued against Putnam: "In order to live one has *to be able to live*, and for that one has to apply the criterion of the *fulfillment of the needs* to the selection of ends."[202] The entire construction of the capitalist economy (and practically all the material ethics and formal moralities of Europe and the United States) does not distinguish clearly between satisfying "needs" (eating, clothing, housing, culture, etc.) and satisfying "preferences" (within the plurality of market "choices," of fashions, etc.): "The satisfaction of needs," underscores Hinkelammert, "makes life possible; the satisfaction of preferences make life agreeable. But, in order to be able to be agreeable, before anything else, it has to be possible. . . . To recognize human needs or to deny their satisfaction in the name of preferences makes all the difference now days."[203]

[188] I think that with this the whole question of "feasibility" has been inductively formulated; I will devote the last section of this chapter to this topic, which is the last chapter of part I of this book, which is concerned with the *foundations* of the *process* of the ethics of liberation, to which we will return in chapters 5 and 6, when I will deal with the whole problem of alternatives or antihegemonic projects—the whole question of the ethically

feasible utopia[204] as a project of liberation. In any event, Hinkelammert has opened for us the path toward a material universal ethics—against the pragmatic formalism of Apel and Habermas—but, in addition, he has shown the problem of the constitution of the empirical "object" in a way that differs from Western Marxism's approach to the question—from Lukács,[205] passing through Marcuse, and showing once again the reductionism in the question of the "productivist paradigm of mere labor" as a model of theoretical constitution of knowledge.[206] For Marx life is not an end[207] but a mode of the reality of the subject that opens up the sphere from which ends are "posited." Hinkelammert, beyond communitarian material ethics (such as that of MacIntyre or Taylor), indicates that it is reproductive reason (what I have called "practical-material reason," or "originary ethics") that "posits" (or "rejects") ends or values; that is to say, reproductive reason grounds through its *content* (hence, material) strategic, instrumental, and even discursive reason (inasmuch as the formal sphere of validity must also set out from "practical truth");[208] this is also the reason that constitutes the horizon of knowledge of the empirical objects (even theoretical ones), insofar as these are "possible" from the sphere of the living subject of action. And, as in no other ethics (not utilitarian, communitarian, or discourse ethics, and especially not analytical metaethics, etc.), Hinkelammert opens up the discussion on "feasibility." Why can he and not others open up such a discussion? Because he redefines in a rational, universal and *material* manner (as an ethics of content) the entire problematic of the fulfillment of praxis and institutions. And because in the ethics thought from the "capitalist center" (even in "late capitalism") the decided norms *can be obviously accomplished* because actors are technologically and economically capacitated to realize them. On the other hand, in the world of peripheral capitalism, many adequate norms, grounded materially and formally, are not "feasible" because of technological underdevelopment, and due to economic inability (due to the structural transfer of value to the center of the system), or to the lack of political autonomy (given the neocolonial situation), and so on. In the end, "feasibility" of the chosen, decided, judged, grounded as "good," just, adequate . . . is *impossible to be fulfilled for lack of "feasibility."* An ethics of liberation begins here a chapter that is essential. "Verum et factum convertuntur," as Vico defined it. However, between "verum" (material and practical truth) and the "factum" (fulfilled praxis) is found the "mediation" of the *"factibilitas"*; between the "ought" (what is first decided) and the "to be fulfilled" (the last in the action) comes the "ability" that, as a bridge (frequently broken), is a condition of the "operabilia."

§3.5. The Criterion and the Ethical Principle of Feasibility

[189] The horizon of "feasibility" leads to the last instance of the fulfillment of the practical "object." This is the entire question of the *critique of instrumental reason*, on one side, and of the *critique of utopian reason*, on the other, as we will see. Even theoretically, through the scientific instruments of observation, the relationship between human beings and nature is mediated by civilizational development, which establishes the *technological* conditions of possibility of the constitution of objects (the telescope of Galileo, already mentioned). In the same way, *practically*, the object (the norm, action, institution or the system to be worked) is constituted by certain *technological* conditions of possibility.[209] "Civilizational development"—as Darcy Ribeiro put it[210]—makes *possible* today acts that before were *impossible*. The frame of possibilities has broadened. In the same way, possible actions in late and central capitalism are still *impossible* in peripheral capitalism, not only because of the inferior degree of technological development, but also because of the degree of exploitation (structural transfer of value).

This is to say, if we restrict the technological factor and if in addition we take into account that natural resources are *scarce*, we discover a second condition of possibility: the economic one.[211] Both conditions (technological and economic) constitute conditions of possibility of the feasibility of a practical object to be fulfilled in the near future. It is here where instrumental reason and judgments of fact, judgments of abstract calculus, define a space of validity, as Max Weber explains in a text that I have already quoted in part: "Social action, like all action, may be . . . : (1) *instrumentally rational* [*zweckrational*], that is, determined by expectations as to the behavior of objects in the environment and of other human beings; these expectations are used as 'conditions' or 'means' for the attainment of the actor's own rationally pursued and calculated end."[212]

The ethical problem takes shape when this formal sphere of means-ends becomes autonomous, is totalized, when what *can be done* with "efficacy" (technically and economically) determines what is used as the *ultimate criterion* of theoretical "truth" and "validity." When this happens, one falls into a formal absolutization, in the error indicated by Horkheimer, Adorno, or Marcuse, namely, giving priority to "instrumental reason"—as we will see in chapter 4. Marx called this *inversion* "fetishism": things are taken as ends (mediations of feasibility), and persons as mediations (the life of the subject and its free autonomous participation). For us, this instrumental reason ought to be framed within the requirements of practical truth (reproduction and development of the life of the human subject) and inter-

Table 7. Different Levels of Ethical Impossibility, Possibility, Feasibility, or Operability, in Light of the Fulfillment of Acts and Their Institutional Consequences

a. Logical impossibility
b. Logical possibility: empirical impossibility
c. Empirical possibility: technical impossibility (nonfeasibility)
d. Technical feasibility: economic impossibility, etc.
e. Economic possibility, etc.: ethical impossibility
f. Ethical possibility: principle of operability
g. Effective process of realization
h. Short- and long-term consequences (institutionality)
i. Process of legitimation and legal coercion

subjective validity (full egalitarian participation in practical argumentation by those affected) and positively subsumed within action. These already analyzed principles overdetermine the *criterion of feasibility* and subsume transforming it into a *principle of operability or ethical principle of feasibility*. In this way, for example, the market (the medium or technical-economic institution of feasibility of the competition among production, exchange, and consumption) can be allowed as a self-regulating mechanism (only in appearance), but equally, it will have to be framed within the requirements of a *possible* plan (as the intrinsic rational criterion of technical-economic feasibility) in order to reach greater efficacy when it is subsumed from the ethical material and moral formal principles already enunciated above (see also table 7). Let us look at this complex and new question.

a. Criteria of Feasibility: Instrumental Reason and "Efficacy"

[190] It is now a matter of returning to the relation "being human–nature." At the beginning (see §1.1), the human being emerges from nature through the biological process of evolution of life. This *"human* life" is the absolute material condition of the existence and ultimate content of universal ethics (the criterion of life or death, or of *practical truth*). Now, nature returns, no longer as constitutive of "human *nature*," but as the material nature with which the human being is in relation in order to be able to *really* live, that is, as a medium of *being able* to fulfill a norm, act, institution, ethical system, and so on. Nature fixes certain *frames* of possibility: not everything is possible. Kant names this type of rationality that must take into account the requirements of nature "the faculty of judgment [*Urteilskraft*]":[213] "In the family of the higher faculties of knowledge there is, however, a mediation between understanding and reason: it is the *faculty of judgment*."[214] For Kant, the subject faces nature empirically, "as if"

nature were organized teleologically. From whence a moral imperative can be defined that allows the "synthesis" of the practical "object," to which I referred at the end of §2.1; I will now pick up and continue the argument from that point: "The rule of the *faculty of judgment* under laws of pure practical reason is this: ask yourself whether, if the action you propose were to *take place*[215] by a *law of the nature* of which you were yourself part, you could indeed regard it as possible through your will. . . . If the maxim of the action is not so constituted that it can stand the test as to the form of a *law of nature* in general, then it is morally *impossible.*"[216] As can be seen, at issue is the "possibility" or "impossibility" of a moral act that must comply hypothetically with the natural material conditions for their effective fulfillment. What takes place is that, *really* (and not hypothetically as is for Kant), we are always members of a realm of nature (inasmuch as we are living beings) and we have to take into account the "law of nature" (for example, we have to eat in order not to die, in order not to commit suicide).[217]

[191] The *criterion of feasibility* could in principle be defined in some of its moments in the following way: who proposes to carry out or transform a norm, act, institution, and so on, cannot leave out of consideration the conditions of possibility of its objective, material and formal, empirical, technical, economic, political, and so on fulfillment, such that the act will be *possible* taking into account the laws of nature in general, and human laws in particular. It is a matter of choosing the adequate or efficacious mediations for determined ends. The criterion of abstract truth (theoretical and technical) refers to these ends; its validity is judged by the formal "efficacy" of the compatibility between the means and the end, calculated by instrumental-strategic reason. The person who does not fulfill this empirical-technological requirement attempts an *impossible* act. That is to say: "No project can be fulfilled if it is not materially possible, and the will never can substitute material conditions of possibility."[218]

Strategic-instrumental reason has an irreplaceable function within ethics. It deals with the "means-ends" of human action. However, when the mere "criterion of feasibility" claims to rise as "absolute principle," it falls into numerous reductions, fetishistic abstractions, which were already pointed out by Horkheimer, Adorno, and Marcuse. But just because one may fall into fetishism is not a reason to discard the proper and subaltern function of instrumental reason. At issue is, precisely, the *efficacious* "feasibility" of human action, which is useful and necessary, but not sufficient.

In the first place, it is evident that the logically impossible is not feasible. Some theoretical models are logically impossible, inconsistent, such as the "model of the market of perfect competition," in the style of Hayek. A perfect market means that there is no monopoly on the part of any of the competitors. But any difference (greater capital, better technology, more information, etc.) ought to be considered as a type of monopoly. If there is no difference and complete equality, with a perfect knowledge transmitted at infinite speed at all points, there can be no competition whatsoever. Such a model is impossible. For something to be empirically feasible, it should not be logically contradictory (possibility b in figure 9). But what is logically possible can be empirically impossible (for example, the *perpetuum mobile*; a mechanism that given an original impetus acquires indefinite inertia, encountering no resistance, so remains in motion indefinitely). The utopian models (for example, perfect planning, which is not logically inconsistent, but is empirically impossible)[219] allow the opening up of horizons of new possibilities (such as in the examples given, where the spheres of thermodynamics or the calculus of possible, approximative, and minimal planning open up, etc.).[220] But what is empirically possible (the whole explanatory sphere of the sciences starting from judgments of abstract facts)—area c of figure 9—can be technically impossible[221]—area d. Given the lack of material resources of the planet earth, not everything that is technically possible is also economically.[222] But, and this last is the most grave, not everything that is technically or economically feasible (and even politically, and ideologically, etc.) is ethically and morally possible, "acceptable"—level f of figure 9. It is here where we make the transition from the criterion of abstract feasibility to the ethical principle of concrete feasibility, which I have called the "principle of operability" or "ethical feasibility."

[192] Indeed, the criterion of feasibility is defined by the empirical-technological and economic-historical possibility of the so-called circumstances, of contextually *being able* to fulfill something: the end can be achieved exclusively by certain means, chosen by means of a calculus used in a specific way. Calculability and formal efficacy are requirements of its validity. It is a *being able hic et nunc*.[223] This level of the criterion is strictly a moment of strategic-instrumental reason, of means-ends.

We find ourselves within the horizon that Max Horkheimer addressed in his *Critique of Instrumental Reason*: "The contemporary crisis of reason is characterized [by the fact that] no specific reality can appear *per se* to be rational; since *when emptied of their content*, all fundamental notions become equivalent to their mere *formal* wrappings. Reason also becomes formalized once it becomes subjective."[224] Theoretical or technical truth ("self-reference" to the "being" of the system, as in Luhmann, and not to the "reality" of the life of the subject, which would be a mere "environment") has sense insofar as it is abstract. It is the "efficacy" of instrumental reason. When this reason becomes autonomous or totalized, notes Herbert Marcuse in *One-Dimensional Man*, "the totalitarian universe of technological rationality is the ultimate transmutation of the idea of reason."[225]

The validity reached by these pronouncements of feasibility is achieved within the technological and scientific community, but this validity cannot claim to be a last point of reference for ethics. Theoretical-technological "truth" (efficacy) and instrumental "validity" are purely formal, as Max Weber indicated. When technical feasibility is established in a situation of market scarcity, under the criterion of competiveness, of efficacy of instrumental rationality, the possibility of the reproduction and development of the life of the human subject can be negated. Descriptive statements or abstract statements of fact, or means-ends (efficacy, competiveness), indicate the necessity of continuing our ethical discourse toward the sphere where these may be properly situated in accordance with ethical and moral principles already presented.

b. The Principle of Ethical Feasibility or Operability

[193] The principle of *ethical* feasibility determines the sphere of *what can be done* (*feasibility*: what it is technically and economically possible to carry out) within the horizon of (a) what is ethically *allowed to be done*, and from there to (b) what needs necessarily *to be put into operation*. This horizon includes all acts with ethical feasibility (*operability*). It is not simply what *can be done* (even if it does not respond to ethical requirements), nor is it merely what is confusingly presented as *needed-to-be–put-into-operation*.[226] Ethical demand, in the last instance, concerns that which is deontic: it requires doing that which cannot-not-be-done because of the requirements of life and moral intersubjective validity.

Thus, for instance, objects (those that satisfy, commodities) of the market in "preferences" are *allowed* to be acquired or consumed; the objects of "basic needs" are ethically due: there is a right prior to the market that determines the absolute requirement that they be able to be consumed (although the mediations of their feasibility, of their possession for consumption, have to be determined). The ethical subsumes what is merely feasible.

In the same way, the principle of ethical impossibility[227] frames the principle of logical-empirical and technical possibility, going from the ethical-material and moral-formal principles. The principle of ethical impossibility is an orienting, material and formal principle. Here, instrumental reason and strategic reason are subsumed within the horizon of practical-material, ethical-originary reason as the ethical-orienting reason with respect to instrumental and strategic reason. The latter mediate the empirical feasibility of the former. Without instrumental-strategic reason, ethical-discursive[228] reason falls into utopian illusions (since it could commit itself to the impossible). Without ethical-discursive reason, strategic-instrumental reason falls in the perversity of formal fetishized self-referentiality (which makes absolute the means-ends rationality, the efficient feasibility that can turn against the life of the human subject or against his or her free, necessary participation).

[194] Let us see how to move from the criterion to the principle of ethical feasibility. Let us begin with a "statement of fact" such as the following:

This hungry human being is begging.

Its technical, economic, and so on feasibility must be considered. Perhaps someone will object, in the example given, that it would be better to find him a job, or to transform the system that because of its effects produces victims, than to give him alms. But given that one has money to give, one thought that some alms could be given to the beggar. Whatever the result of the discussion, one may arrive at the following conclusion:

It is feasible to give alms to the hungry.

It is still *possible* to frame this act going from a concrete "empirical judgment" that has now to answer the question: Is the reproduction of the subject's life possible or not in accordance with the semantic content of the descriptive statement? If the answer were affirmative we would have a new descriptive judgment (statement of fact 2 of figure 10).

3. To give the hungry person alms allows (is "compatible with") the reproduction of his life [concrete judgment of fact].

This intersubjective agreement is the end of an argumentative process of discursive reason, in which the following statement achieves validity:

We have decided to give alms to this hungry person.

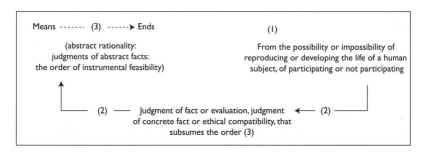

Figure 10. Subsumption of the order of feasibility within ethical judgment.

NOTE: See table 8. In section 1.1 this judgment (2) is denominated "evaluation"; "value" is the object or judgment being evaluated (3), which can be "prioritized" by the greater or lesser need for its fulfillment of the criterion of truth or importance in the reproduction of the life of the ethical subject (1) (in the universal "hierarchy of values," beyond that of any culture or "cultural values").

Since the conditions or possibilities are given and evading it would be irresponsible, then on the prior statement can be grounded[229] the following normative statement:

> *We ought* to give alms to the hungry person.

The "object" (the possible act required by a normative statement) would thus be constituted by a true-practical, valid-moral, feasible, and imperative statement. That is to say, the means-ends judgment (arrow 3 in figure 10) is rational in the full sense (that is to say, ethical) only when it is subordinate, as formal or abstract mediation, to the criterion of the death or life of the ethical subject (statement 2).[230] Instrumental rationality, with a claim to means-ends efficacy through a calculus, must submit to ethical or "normative judgment," that is, it must be subsumed or framed within the concrete order of the possibility of the production, reproduction, and development of the life of the human subject (arrow 2 of the figure) through the argumentative symmetrical participation of the affected.

[195] Because of all that has already been said, I would attempt a first definition of the principle of operability, merely indicative or partial, approximately in the following way: one who ethically performs or decides a norm, action, institution or systematic ethical system, *ought to*[231] comply (a) with the conditions of logical and empirical (technical, economic, political, cultural, and so on) feasibility, which is to say, that it is really *possible* at all these levels, going from the frame of the (b) *requirements*, which are (b1) the ethical-material requirements of practical truth, and (b2) discursive moral-formal requirements of validity, along a spectrum that goes from (b.i) ethically *allowed* acts (that are only "possible" but do not contradict the ethical or moral principles) to (b.ii) acts that *must* be done (that are ethically "necessary" for the fulfillment of the *basic* human needs — or formal, out of respect for the dignity of every ethical subject until the effective and symmetrical participation is achieved of those affected by the decisions taken).

This principle (whose ultimate deontic moment is found in b.ii) is ethical and *universal*, insofar as it defines as necessary, for every human act that claims to be human and *feasible*, that is, *operable*, to have to respond to the fulfillment of the life of each recognized subject as equal and free (to what is ethical), and to take into account the physical-natural and technical requirements included within the possibilities that grant to actors the development of civilization in each period and in concrete historical situations. Only the norm, the act, the institution, and so on that fulfill this "principle of ethical feasibility" or "operability" are not only *possible* but, making a *goodness claim*, also just, ethically and morally adequately *good*. The ethical subject who performs this act can make, substantively, a "goodness claim"—with reference to which the norm, acts, institutions, and so on, are said to be analogically "good." The whole debate between the communitarians (who have a reductionistic concept of the ethical) and discourse ethics (purely formal), which juxtaposed the "good [*das Gute*]" (the supposedly material) to the "just [*right*]" (the apparently formal), defined these opposites inadequately. In reality, the opposition is between practical truth (material) and intersubjective validity (formal), and between what is intersubjectively decided (to execute what has been material-formally agreed upon) and what is feasibly "possible." Only the realization of the possible (feasible) following the integral ethical procedure (that is, ethically) will constitute the "goodness claim." I will remark in passing that the problematic of a "goodness claim" has not been touched by either communitarians or discourse ethics.

Feasibility, then, determines the *management* of the meditations, that is to say, the *"being able" to realize* its (monological or communitarian) projects (material: of life, and formal: with symmetrical participation). "Management" of the meditations are involved in the micro or macro institutions of "being able to" (to make and do).

[196] Taking a different tack, the grounding of this principle of operability (or ethical feasibility) ought take the form of an argument against the extreme anarchist, the voluntarist, or unreal utopian, with their simplification and mistaken judgment with respect to mediations, which leads them to fall into an illusion or "mirage" when they judge as "possible" (feasible) what is "impossible." Thus, the anarchist argues: if all the subjects of a community were ethically perfect, no institution would be necessary.[232] And this is so, because although every institution regulates or disciplines the action in a certain direction in order to reach a certain relative efficacy (feasibility) in the fulfillment of certain ends, it never ceases to include a certain type of discipline. Every institution (in the light of the perfect system) can always and inevitably be interpreted as a disciplinary, repressive, or perverse instance (thus opines the anarchist). *Ergo*: all institutions must be eliminated. This negation of the negation is carried out by means of direct action.

What takes place, empirically, is an attempt to carry out an "impossible act": by direct action to eliminate every existing institution, given that these would be the origin of every domination or injustice. But, empirically, the attempt is to realize an impossible model in concrete existence (one that presupposes that everyone is ethically perfect, and for that reason not in need of institutions). This leads the unreal utopian (who must not be confused with the utopian who acts according to certain feasible utopias, as we will see in chapters 5 and 6) to fall into a dangerous "unrealism," ethical voluntarism, failing to consider the real conditions of feasibility. Contradicting him- or herself, this utopian attempts to eliminate the perverse mediations in the name of *perfect* mediations (which are impossible for finite beings, the human condition being what it is), which leads to a factual contradiction: the unreal utopian uses direct action (an institutional mediation that attempts to make feasible the sought-after impossible ideal) — which has as its apparent end a perfect feasibility — in order to eliminate every imperfect mediation. The product is the death of innocent subjects who embody institutions (against the material-ethical principle), and the death of the suicidal anarchist utopian. Voluntaristic utopianism against the realism of feasibility precipitates into two extremes: in vanguardism (where the "illuminated" decide for the others, for the masses, for the "ignorant" peasants, and "barbarians" of the Peruvian highlands in the eyes of the Sendero Luminoso; which goes against intersubjective moral validity), and anti-institutionalism (against historical, realistic, and ethical feasibility). The utopian anarchist, in the name of *perfect* institutionality (performatively self-contradictory), performs an antiethical irrational crime, such as assassinations carried out by the Khmer Rouge against their "urban society," or those perpetrated by the Sendero Luminoso, where pure and simple violence replaces arguments: unhinged irrationalism against finite feasibility in the name of an infinite, perfect, immediate feasibility, without mediations, absolute: the realm of death imposed in the name of the realm of freedom. Nothing is further from an ethics of liberation.

[197] It will be seen, however, in chapter 6, that when ethical-possible transformations are necessary, the praxis of liberation will have to be executed, and at that moment, will confront conservative antiutopianism. In this way here, in the name of the ethical feasibility of the ethics of liberation, I oppose anarchist illusions, and later, in the name of necessary and possible transformations, I will oppose the conservative antiutopianism (in the style of Karl Popper). A "critique of utopian reason" frames the limits of instrumental reason within its possible and ethical feasibility: against the capricious "illusion" of the anarchist, against the "fixist" domination of the conservative, and against the instrumental reductionism of the abstract reason of "efficacy" and calculus (the false utopia of the happy life by mediation of Weber's rational technology or, once again, of Popper's "fragmentary engineering").

In this last sense, the cynic subordinates the instrumental actions that are solely feasible (that can be done) to those that are ethically possible (that are allowed or that ought to be done). Mere "factical being able" can serve as grounding to instrumental reason (one acts *thus* because *this* "can be" done factically), but it is opposed to the maxim of practical-material, ethical-originary or discursive reason. "To be able to" is in the mediation a condition of possibility of the fulfillment of an act, but not an intrinsic ethical criterion; it is a pure criterion of feasibility.

Furthermore, if we introduce feasibility in time, the notion of "sustainability" becomes clear. The cynic reaches "success" in the short term (coinciding with the "immediatist," or holding that competition is a criterion of discernment, which is always in the "short run," since in the "long run" the branch of capital or the concrete corporation would have been destroyed by this immediate competition). What is factically possible, within the ethical, ought to be "sustainable" in the long run of the reproduction and growth of human life on the planet Earth. The criterion of sustainability ought to be once again the life of the future generations in the long run and not the "survival" of capital in the competition of the market.

So that "to be able" to do can be a condition of *ethical mediation*, instrumental-strategic reason ought to be ordered according to ends (material and universal formal) and values (cultural) *set* by practical-material, ethical-originary, and discursive reason, which frames the mere "being able to" within what is ethically "allowed" or "ought to be done"—what allows the reproduction and development of the life of the human subject inasmuch as he or she is a free participant who acts in a condition of symmetry. But this "allowing to" or "obligation" as duty does not depend solely on mere judgments of value as cultural validity (which only have a *rightness claim* that is relative to each historical-valuing horizon, as is Habermas's opinion), but which also responds, as I have noted frequently, to material universal principles of practical truth and moral formal validity: normative judgments that are grounded in concrete "judgments of fact" on ends— which subsume the formal "judgments of fact" (means-ends) of instrumental reason and that judge them as meditations for human life. A statement of feasibility, of efficacy, that responds to the means-ends calculus (as *formal* judgment of fact), makes the claim to be fulfilled within a horizon of scarcity; a normative statement of ethical feasibility makes the claim to be fulfilled technically and economically with practical truth and intersubjective validity. As the claim (or condition) of intelligibility, the claim (or condition) of feasibility is a *formal condition of possibility* of the ethical judgment, of the "goodness claim": it has a meaning-sense of "efficacy," but not the efficacy of a calculus, not merely quantitative, or formal, in the manner of Weber, but rather an efficacy that is subsumed within the sphere of concrete "content" of material reality (as a mediation to be achieved, which allows the reproduction and participation of the living human as an autonomous ethical subject in community).

But, as I have already indicated, the means are scarce; when there is a contradiction or lack of means we will have to have a criterion of discernment, of hierarchization or priority setting. Among the operable ones (those with ethical feasibility), the *necessary* mediations for the life of subjects and for the participation of those affected by the agreements will have to be given priority. This ethical material and moral formal criterion *before* what is feasible will allow us to overcome a fetishistic use of mere instrumental reason, feasibility in terms of pure efficacy of the systematic calculus (in the manner of Luhmann), and will always allow us to introduce the criterion of practical truth and intersubjective validity (with its universal material ethical and formal moral principles), as an *internal orienting* or *framing* of feasibility itself. This notion allows us to place ethics exactly with respect to the empirical sciences, of nature or society, to technology, to institutions, and to strategic-instrumental rationality. As we will see, these questions were not sufficiently clarified in the "first" generation of the Frankfurt school (still critical because it made reference to material contents) nor in the "second" one.

As I have already indicated, a broad treatment of this question would require an entire critique of instrumental and utopian reason, a question that, in any event, I will take up again in the chapters ahead, and that is here only discursively anticipated.

c. The Process of the "Application" or Realization of the Ethical "Goodness Claim" and Its Consequences

[198] We have seen in different moments of this *Ethics* the problems of "application" (for example, in §§1.5c, 2.5c), and we will return to them later (in §§4.5c, 5.5c, and 6.5c). In each instance application grows diachronically more complex. In the first instance, the application of the material principle (§1.5c) takes care of the formal moral principle: what is validly agreed by intersubjective validity is what is decided a priori, about which a consensus has to be achieved. In the second instance, the valid now has to be judged as possible or framed within real feasibility. The application of the material (by ethical overdetermination) and formal (by recourse again to intersubjective agreements concerning ethical operability or feasibility) principles brings to an end the phase of the *foundation* of *ethics* (or "*Ethics* I"). As can be seen, in this phase we are dealing with the ultimate "application." We will have to once again take up the need to arrive intersubjectively to a final valid agreement about how, when, where, and with what means—in short, under what circumstances, with ethical feasibility, a norm, act, institution, or system operates with a "goodness claim."

As we have seen, what has been selected as "operable"—that is, as having technical-ethical feasibility—plays the function of the a priori that now has to be "realized" in praxis (the norm that rules an action, the institution, the system of ethics, etc.). The procedure of realization has to assume a formal mediation, and this consists in complying effectively with the requirements already defined by compliance with the formal moral principle (defined in §2.5b), which in the "front" or "field" of political liberation we will call the "principle of democracy." That is to say, in the "process" of the realization of praxis we will have to take into account the symmetrical, active, and *constant* participation of those affected—integrating always, as "advisers," the experts, scientists, technicians, those with experience, and so on.[233]

The "application" or subsumption of the judgment of feasibility (of fact), within the order of the grounding, is then a dialectical and diachronic movement through which the abstract or formal is framed or judged from a concrete or material order.[234] To judge the compatibility or incompatibility, or "references" (the question of "practical truth"), of the means-ends order with respect to the life of the subject (which is the criterion of truth qua ultimate *reality*) is to establish the grounding of the material and formal principles as frameworks of the order of feasibility. This is an exercise of a type of rationality that should not be confused with other types:[235] the material-practical or ethical-originary reason (moment 1 of table 8), whose concrete and material "judgment of fact" of compatibility (between the judgment of fact of abstract feasibility and the concrete possibility of the reproduction of life) is the proper act of the so-called moral or ethical conscience[236]—the act of application traditionally fulfilled by prudence, the Aristotelian *phronesis*[237]—which we now (thanks to Apel's and Habermas's contributions) always have to consider as a potential act of a possible discursive community that reaches intersubjectively valid agreements concerning this compatibility. But, in contrast to discourse ethics, the formal intersubjective discursive act reaches validity not only because it fulfills *formal* deontological requirements, but, also and not secondarily, because it is *materially oriented* by the criterion of the life or death of the practical truth of arguing subjects themselves, according to the universal material principle (covered in §1.5). Now we must *concretely, hic et nunc,* argue against Wellmer's arguments.[238]

[199] To take an example, let us consider how Kant resolves this complex question. I touched[239] on Kant when he dealt with the conditions of feasibility without which the "maxim of the action . . . is morally impossible."[240] Now that we know how the maxim is possible, we turn to the question of knowing how to fulfill the *object* of practical reason: "To be an object [*Gegenstand*] of practical cognition so understood signifies, therefore, only the relation of the will to the action by which it or its opposite would *be made real* [*wirklich gemacht*], and to *appraise* whether or not something is an object of *pure* practical reason is only to distinguish the possibility or impossibility of *willing* the action by which, if we had the ability to do so (and experience [*Erfahrung*] must judge about this), a certain object would be *made real*."[241] The difficulty[242] that Kant has in resolving this question resides in that he reckons only with the formal principles. For this reason, he has to make do by conceiving of two "concepts" (that

Table 8. Diverse Levels of Analysis of "Fundamental" Ethics (*Ethics* I)

Moments	1. Ethical (Material)		2. Moral	3. Axiological	4. Analytical or Instrumental	5. Ethical
	a. material-practical reason	b. ethical originary reason				
I. Types of rationality	material-practical reason	ethical originary reason	discursive reason	hermeneutical strategic reason	theoretical or instrumental reason	feasibility ethical reasoning
II. Criterion	of truth (a)	of recognition	of validity (a)	of value	of sense or efficacy	of real feasibility
III. Principle	universal ethical-material (b)	ethics of equality	moral, formal, universal	axiological or strategic		of ethical feasibility
IV. Opposing at the foundation	the cynic who justifies death	the cynic who justifies inequality	the skeptic			the utopian anarchist or conservative traditionalist
V. Type of judgment or statement	factual judgment (a), normative statement (b)	factual judgment (a), normative statement (b)	factual judgment (a), normative statement (b)	value judgment, value statement	judgment of fact, abstract or formal	judgment of fact (a), or normative (b)
VI. With respect to life	life of the ethical subject (practical)	the Other equal	rational accord (practical)	medium value (practical)	means-ends (theoretical-technical)	feasibility of the good
VII. Claim types	truth claim	truth claim	validity claim	rectitude claim	theoretical or technical truth claim	feasibility and goodness claim
VIII. Types of interest	material	of recognition	emancipatory	strategic, hermeneutical	performative or of efficiency	ethical realization

Note: Compare with tables 2 and 9 (pp. 96, 212) and figures 7 and 10 (pp. 145, 191).

of the good and evil, which is a false problem, because neither good or evil can be such) that would constitute a priori the object (the act to be realized), and that are "applied" thanks to the "faculty of pure practical judgment"[243] that, in turn, cannot be moved (motivated) by any affectivity or inclination whatsoever (it is always egotistical)[244] but instead only out of pure duty and respect for the universal law. Furthermore, the morality of the act, purely a priori, can only consider the "pure intention," but never the consequences of the act—that can never be the theme of philosophical-moral reflection. Let us see how we can resolve this problematic from the presuppositions that I have presented.

In the first place, in contrast to Kant (and also Habermas and Apel), what has been "decided" a priori to be fulfilled, with technical-economic feasibility, reaches *ethical* possibility when it is submitted to the material "judgment" of practical-material or ethical originary reason (see level 1 of table 8). In the second place, the chosen norm is applied (that it be feasible and compatible with the life of the subject) through practical and formal intersubjective argumentation (discursive reason) regarding ultimate validity, *in the process itself of the fulfillment* of praxis. This brings us into the last aspect of the practical "process" of the fulfillment of the norm, action, institution, ethical life, and so on.

[200] The "good" act (institution, system, etc.) with a "goodness claim," carries consequences, and these—as Peirce held correctly with respect to the "concept of the practical object"—allow us to know the act. In this sense, there would be no contradiction between an ethics of conviction or correct intention and another of responsibility for the consequences. An ethics of conviction with correct intention (the a priori of the materially and formally accomplished decision) ought to be equally integrated, as necessary, *but not sufficient,* to an ethics of responsibility (which complies now with the principle of feasibility a posteriori, with reference to the foreseeable effects of technology or politics, or with respect to the economy), which is equally necessary, *but not sufficient.* In this case, an ethics of responsibility is not merely "complementary" (as is the case with Apel), since in the ethics of liberation, with the same material, formal, and feasibility, principles will "judge" the consequences (in the short and long term) and with the same reasons that allow it to constitute the ethical object and to realize it, being now able to correct diachronically the consequences in accordance with the concrete requirements that may present themselves.

For Max Weber this presents an aporia: an ethics of conviction or (excluding) an ethics of responsibility. But, at the same time, it is a unity in tension: an ethics of conviction and ethics of responsibility. Excluding one or the other, as much as forcing them together, is the result of not knowing either the universal material principle (a critique anticipated by Marx from the perspective of a reason that reproduces life, which I will analyze in chapter 4) or the formal intersubjective principle (Habermas's critique from the perspective of discursive reason). In fact, with respect to the material, Weber has sunk into the quagmire of cultural values—as some of the North American communitarians have done, and Popper, or Habermas with his normative statements with an exclusive rightness claim; with respect to the *formal* Weber has fallen into the technical-economic means-ends calculus of a mere instrumental reason. From this extremely reduced and insufficient (defectively defined) horizon of categories, he falls into aporias and simplistic articulations. He denies that the ethics of conviction (of correct intention) has anything to do with scientific objectivity, with the empirical world of judgments of fact. But, at the same time, he attempts to show that mere ethics of responsibility, of the calculus of consequences compatible with science, cannot cease to act with evaluating conviction in the practical sphere of politics or in charismatic transformation, for example. The ethics of conviction consists only of judgments of value, of taste, which are subjective, culturally relative, exempted of any possible means-ends calculus (normative statements with a rightness claim, as in Habermas); in sum, it is an ethics immersed in the polytheism of sundered spheres and values in conflict.[245] For Weber, what is "material" is reductively identical to value, ignoring the universal material principle of the ethics of liberation.

The concept of "substantive [*material*] rationality," on the other hand, "is full of ambiguities," says Weber. It defines "certain criteria of ultimate ends, whether they be ethical, political, utilitarian, hedonistic . . . and measure[s] the results of the economic action, however formally 'rational' in the sense of correct calculation they may be, against these scales of 'value rationality' or *substantive* goal rationality."[246] On the contrary, the "formal" is exclusively the abstract means-ends relation of instrumental rationality (with descriptive statements), ignoring the universal formal principle proposed partially by discourse ethics: "A system of economic activity will be called 'formally' rational according to the degree to which the provision for needs, which is essential to every rational economy, is capable of being expressed in numerical, calculable terms, and is so expressed. . . . The concept is thus unambiguous."[247] Both horizons thus find themselves within the narrow horizon that I have called instrumental reason, which consists of abstract judgments of fact or merely cultural judgments of value,[248] which are enunciated from a paradigm of prelinguistic solipsistic conscience.

[201] It might seem that in the end the solution of the ethics of liberation is very similar since it articulates an ethics of conviction of a correct intention with the feasible calculability of an ethics of responsibility, but in fact it is totally different to the Weberian solution. When the axiological reason of values from the universal criterion of life-death of practical truth (which is grounded in concrete, empirical judgments of fact, which

are however the source of the grounding of normative ones, and which are compatible with scientific rationality), as we have seen in chapter 1, and when mere formal instrumental reason, with technical-economic feasibility, empirical or scientific, is subsumed from this material reason with a criterion of universal practical truth but, in addition, from a communitarian discursive reason that also reaches validity through rational argumentation (as seen in chapter 2), then the articulation of the ethics of conviction with the ethics of responsibility does not appear in the mere concrete voluntaristic and even cynic vocation of the politician or charismatic leader (as Weber might argue), but instead is articulated in the intrinsic subsumption of universal material and formal rationality, relying on a principle of ethical feasibility (seen in chapter 3) that truly synthesizes them. We can appreciate and take into account all the details of the Weberian analysis; but from new types of rationality (not only of instrumental reason) and ethical principles (mere action referred exclusively to values), we will supersede his theoretical dualism and notion of voluntaristic juxtaposition.

In evaluating the consequences that will always be "transformed," in terms of an ethics of responsibility, the three fundamental principles (material, formal, and of feasibility) already enunciated will have to continue being *applied*.

[202] One last clarification. The concrete application of the three principles (material, formal, of feasibility) do not have to, in any way whatsoever, stay in the order in which I have systematically and pedagogically presented them. It will vary as different applications come into play. One may set out from a judgment of fact of feasibility (efficacy), in order to intersubjectively decide (formal principle), seeking to determine if it is compatible with the material principle. Or one may follow another sequence, knowing that once the process has begun, in the life of an ethical subject or of a society, the principles may be applied with infinite variations.

The act, the institution, the system of ethical life, and so on realized with all the criteria and principles, only now and for the first time, can be called and justified as "good," or as having a "goodness claim." The justified "good" (*das Gute*, good) is thus an act, an institutional set of acts, or ethical-cultural totality that effectively integrates as a condition of possibility and constitution its ethical materiality, moral formalism and concrete operability (ethical feasibility). Its opposite is the "bad," "wrong," or "evil" (*das Böse*) act (institution, system, etc.), and not what is right; nor is it the practical true or material. What makes a goodness claim, what is "good" or has "goodness" in no way is indefinable as Moore held, nor is it the mere incarnation of values (as is for Scheler or Husserl), nor is it simply the normatively valid (as it was for Apel or Habermas), nor the "just" (Rawls). It is something far more precise and complex.

In a strict and ultimate sense, a norm or a maxim cannot be judged perfectly "good." One may make an act with a "goodness claim," a claim that can be publicly defended, that one has seriously fulfilled all the conditions of possibility. In any event, it is not the norm that can be true practically, normatively valid, or feasible. The norm is "part" of a whole to which the predicate "good" corresponds. Only to the *human act*—and with reference to the subject or ethical agent, the "good" person—can be attributed the "goodness claim."[249] In this sense Aristotle says that "life [*hò bíos*] is praxis [*prâxis*] and not production [*poíesis*]."[250] Only praxis can have a "goodness claim" (substantively the agent who carries it out; or the norm directed at its realization; or the institution developed by repetition in social time; or the ethical system as ultimate complex of praxis in a historical moment). It is in this last sense that Hegel in his *Philosophy of Right* defined "ethical life": "Ethical life [*Sittlichkeit*] it is the good become alive [*lebendige Gute*]. The good endowed in self-consciousness with knowing and willing and actualized by self-conscious action, while on the other hand self-consciousness has in the ethical realm its absolute foundation [*Grundlage*] and the end which actuates its effort."[251]

[203] Thus, if a system of ethical life (or an institution) performs an act with a "goodness claim," it is only in relation to the human act or with the ethical subject itself, that in the final analysis it is "good." For this reason we may conclude that "good" is an *integral* predicate that includes at least the three components that I have analyzed throughout part I of *Ethics of Liberation*. To repeat, *an act is "good"* when the following three cases apply:

a. In the first place, it realizes the *material component* (the ethical principle) of practical truth, (a1) reproducing and developing the life of the subject, in community, with a universal practical truth; (a2) always within a given culture (complying with the requirements of a "good life" and the "values," even in the case of Apel or Seyla Benhabib's modern "postconventional ethical life"), from the understanding of being (the ontological foundation of its historical "world"), in a subjective state of happiness (that includes the whole apparatus of the affective-instinctive life of the subject, as we will see in the case of Freud), with a rightness claim.[252]

b. In the second place, it realizes the *formal component* (the moral principle) of intersubjective validity, (b1) fulfilling what has been argumentatively agreed upon within a communitarian symmetry, with public validity; (b2) and, equally, in accord with the responsible monological ethical conscience, with personal validity.

c. In the third place, it realizes the *feasibility component* (the instrumental principle), (c1) considering calculatingly with instrumental rationality the empirical, technological, economic, and so on, conditions of possibility framed a priori within the ethical requirements, with conviction and a claim to sincerity or correct intention; (c2) and simultaneously analyzing the possible a posteriori consequences (being aware that in the long term every act is a component in the last instance of world history),[253] with a claim to honest responsibility.

An absolutely or perfectly "good" act is *empirically impossible*, just as an absolute judgment on the goodness of any act is also impossible. An intelligence, a will, or a psychic-corporeal system with infinite capacity operating at infinite velocity would be needed—to use Popper's expression. Every act has a "goodness claim" when it fulfills the three enunciated universal conditions, principles within the *frame* of possibility in which many acts are possible. The *frame* of what is ethically allowed (including what is a duty) is immense, but it has precise universal criteria and principles. This is a pluralism that is not relativistic, but rationally universalistic. Within this frame, an active, respectful, democratic, nonrigorist tolerance that attempts to reach validity through the autonomous acceptance of the other is possible. Concrete uncertainty is not bashful of universality.

The "goodness claim," the good, as norm, act, microstructure or institution are subsumed within historical ethical systems (the Hegelian *Sittlickeiten*)—social orders with an ethical structure—as the relative unintentional self-regulation of the life of all ethical subjects that live within its horizon. This, for Aristotle, is the good as a "system" in the *ethos* or character of a people. I have thus concluded an initial description of the *foundation* of ethics ("*Ethics* I"), with which the majority of philosophers conclude their analysis. But I have only just *begun*. I have constructed only the foundations of an architectural from which I will proceed to the development, the critical building of an ethics of liberation, to which I devote part II of this volume.

PART II

Critical Ethics, Antihegemonic Validity, and the Praxis of Liberation

[204] In part I of this book I addressed, though only descriptively, the positive aspects of themes such as truth, validity, the intention or possibility of bringing about "right," that which is "good" or a "goodness claim" itself. It might seem as if everything has been demonstrated that could be expected of such an ethics. But nonetheless from the deepest reaches of the ostensible good (or goodness claim) of the dominant social order there appears a face, many faces, who clamor for life at the very edge of death. These are the faces of the unintentional victims of the dominant system that makes this goodness claim. Now, suddenly, from the standpoint of these victims, truth begins to reveal itself as a nontruth, that which is valid as invalid, the feasible as that which is in fact unviable, and thus that which had the intention or possibility of being "good" can now be interpreted as "unjust" or "evil." To render this kind of judgment of the system of ethics that I have described as "evil"—as "absolute Evil" (*als absolut Böses*), in Adorno's sense[1]—appears now as the negative moment of the exercise of ethical-critical reason.

If we attempt to go back to the historical beginnings of a critical-ethical reason of this kind we would perhaps have to go all the way back to the origins of humanity itself. Any action, institution, or system of ethics is "laid down" as something that has occurred, something that has been done, as a past reality that is produced and "reproduces" itself. To this extent, such an act is the point of departure for any future action; but at the same time it is also "opaque," that which it hides, what it disciplines and begins to limit, oppress, and dominate: this is the two-faced nature of any institution. The distance between that which is "given" and that which is to come ("development"), but which is "impeded" by that which is "habitual," demands knowledge of how to deconstruct what is given so that something new can be brought about. Such a de-construction is a negative, critical process. There are written testimonies of analogous processes going back at least five thousand years—as we saw in §I.1 in Egypt and Mesopotamia—as the ethical prephilosophical experience of a material critical reason with reference to the victims produced by the established system of economic "control" (by the Egyptian pharaohs and their ruling class, which dominated all the valley of the Nile, or of the kingdoms of Mesopotamia).[2] This tradition persists in the history of the peoples of Semitic culture—in part, Egyptian, Mesopotamian, Hebrew-Jewish (by means of the commentaries of the Talmud, and conserving part of the Egyptian-Mesopotamian memory, from the Gnostics to the Kabbalah)—in diverse critical currents, messianic and millenarian Christian and Muslim, which persist all through the European Middle Ages, and reemerge among many others, in the thought of Jacob Böhme as well as in the positivist philosophy of Schelling.

It is not surprising then that, in the very heart of that enlightened and capitalist Europe which is the center of the world system, it would be among others the great Jewish philosophers (Marx, Freud, Bergson, Hermann Cohen, the members of the first Frankfurt school, Rosenzweig, Levinas, Derrida, etc.) who would remind modern culture of the contradiction posed from within by its own victims. But also, among many other experiences of exclusion and exteriority, this ethical-critical thought would develop equally in Latin America as a response to the violent repressions imposed by the military dictatorships (applying the region's own version of a "National Security Doctrine" imported from the United States with guidance from the CIA) from the 1960s onward, under the name of the philosophy of liberation. Critical reason thereby subscribes to this millennial tradition. It is an ethical experience that manifests its presence from within the symbolism and the myths of historical communities who endeavor to explain their situation with prephilosophical views of the world as their points of departure. Nonetheless, and this is what I shall attempt to demonstrate, when philosophy assumes the burden of this millennial tradition (a philosophical-categorical apparition of recent vintage), the tradition manifests itself as a new moment of reason with a claim to universality, and not as a moment of blind faith or irrationality.[3]

[205] Symbolically, in the mythical tradition of the theogonal hierarchies of the Memphis school of ancient Egypt, other divinities can be found together with Ptah, the creator of the universe, such as Horus, the heart-of-love, or Thot, the word-that-is-wisdom. The multiple original components of this school of thought and belief do not provide us with a basis to discern a primordial unity in this mythical world. Instead we find triads, octads, eneads: multiplicity.[4] By contrast, in the first Iron Age em-

pires,[5] the "One" is the ontological horizon,[6] where "the being is the same as the *logos* or the thought." Being coincides with Reality, and Reality is what is Conceivable.[7] Critical-ethical reason can emerge with philosophical precision only when it has achieved an original separation (not separation [Hegel's *Entzweiung*] from "being" itself) of "thought/being"[8] and "reality," a separation that has only recently been granted a precise philosophical charter.[9] The only ethics worthy of the name[10] (here, *Ethics* II, or the ethics of liberation, the latter as the developed expression of a critical ethics, as we shall see) is that which is capable of critically judging[11] the "totality" of a system of ethics. To attempt to situate oneself before an empirical system of ethics, grasped as a totality, and endeavor to judge it—an act of *Urteilskraft*—is something appropriate for a strictly critical ethics. What enables one to situate oneself from the standpoint of the alterity of the system, in the world of everyday life of prescientific common sense, but without ethical complicity, is the ability to adopt the perspective of the victims of a given ethical system. Such victims—without, for now, going into their specific situations—stand out in plain view in any system from the vantage point of a critical-ethical consciousness. For a consciousness that is complicit with that system, the victims are a necessary, inevitable moment, a functional or "natural" aspect—like the slaves in Aristotle's polis or the "least favored" in socioeconomic terms in Rawls's second principle. For the critical consciousness, which cannot emerge except from a very specific ethical position, and by means of the exercise of a new type of rationality (critical-ethical)[12]—among other aspects this "critical positioning" places the actor who assumes it in the same kind of danger as that confronted by a hostage[13] in the face of potentially coercive actions inflicted by the ethical system concerned—the victims are recognized as ethical subjects, as human beings who are not able to reproduce or develop their lives, who have been excluded from participation in the discussion, who are affected by a situation akin to death (in whatever sense, and there are many, of varying depth or drama).

[206] In the light of the simple presence of the victims as victims, an inverted relationship occurs in the context of the exercise of critical-ethical reason (an impossible *Kehre* for Heidegger): the dominant system of ethics, which to a naive consciousness (whether scientific, or occupying the function of political or economic authority, or even part of the moral elite of a system, such as Nietzsche's "priestly race") was the measure of "good" and "evil," becomes in the presence of its victims, in systemic terms, something perverse ("evil"). This gets into the whole question of "fetishism" in Marx, the "inverted values" of Nietzsche, Freud's discovery of the repressive "super-ego," the "exclusionary" society of Foucault, Adorno's "negative dialectics," and Levinas's "totality"—to name only a few of those we will

examine in the following chapters of this book. The system of ethics (the "good," or the "goodness claim") now has become inverted into the "evil" and causes death, in some aspect or at some level of their existence, in the victims of pain, suffering, unhappiness, or exclusion. Critical-ethical reason is a more developed moment of human rationality than those already analyzed; it subsumes material reason (because it assumes it affirmatively, as a way to discover the dignity of the subject and the impossibility of reproducing the life of the victim), formal reason (because it also assumes this in its perception of the exclusion of the victim from the possibility of arguing in his or her own defense), and reason concerning feasibility (because it interprets the conceivable mediations of the dominant system of ethics as "nonefficient" management for life, which at some level produce the death of the victims).

This negative material-ethical judgment is possible, as I have said, from the positive sphere of the affirmation of the life of the human subject, as an ethical principle and criterion, and also from the standpoint of the recognized dignity of the subject, which is denied to the subject when he or she is reduced to a victim. This double affirmation is an exercise that precedes what I have called a material-practical and originating aspect of ethics, a necessary moment, included in and prior to its own negativity (an "analectic" moment, as I have called it).

The ethical judgment of negative practical critical reason is transsystemic, and if the system of the "comprehension of being" (in the Heideggerian sense)[14] is ontological, it would then be pre- or transontological: a judgment that proceeds from the reality[15] of the negated life of the victims, in reference to the ontological totality of a given ethical system. In this sense I have suggested that beyond (*jenseits*) "being" (if "being" is the foundation[16] of the system) there is still the possibility of affirmation of the reality of the victims.[17] What we are dealing with here is the alterity of the other "as other" distinct from the system. This is the alterity of the victim as oppressed (e.g., as a class) or as excluded (e.g., as poor), since the exteriority of "Exclusion" is not identical to that of "Oppression."

In part II of this book, therefore, the issue is not a critical theory—even though I will seek to demonstrate how it originated and how and why it ceased to be truly critical in the second Frankfurt school—but rather that of a theory of ethical criticism (in the genitive objective mode), which I am convinced has not yet been adequately developed. This is a metatheory constructed through the analysis of the exercise of critical practical reason from the standpoint of the historical praxis of the victims and from that of the critical philosophies of the nineteenth and twentieth centuries, those of the "great critics," or those we might characterize as the "damned philosophers."

[207] Ethical criticism, paradoxically, is that which uncovers the strongest and most realistic sense of the "evil" being analyzed. Leibniz asked him-

self about this matter (but using a categorical labyrinth that caused him to lose both the sense of the question and ultimately the answer itself): "But we must also resolve the most speculative and metaphysical objections which have been mentioned, and which touch on the cause of evil. We must therefore ask: what is the origin of evil? *Si Deus est, unde malum?, si non est, unde bonum?*"[18] From this point onward, in order to clearly and radically define our terms, "evil"—not in the intrasystemic sense, a subject that must be addressed in the context of part II of this *Ethics*, and which would be something like the "ontic" or intrasystemic evil—that is, the "original evil,"[19] which is fundamental, or which, in the ontological sense, is revealed by ethical-critical reason in the phenomenon of the "totalization" of the system, indifferent to the feasibility of the reproduction and development of the life and argumentative autonomy of the victims. The system of ethicity that prevails undergoes a total inversion in the eyes of the critic ("that which is upside-down is set upright"). "Ethical-ontological evil" is revealed by the critic when the Luhmannian system, the Hegelian identity, the Heideggerian world, Hayek's market, and that consciousness that is the "I think" of Modernity close in upon themselves, and can no longer reveal or recognize the alterity and autonomy of its victims. Concretely, we are speaking here of the myth of Modernity as the concealment of the Other.[20] That which was a totality has become a closed system, a system of death, which has become paranoid and walks heroically toward collective suicide, like the Nibelungs before Attila, the defeated Nazis before the Allies, humanity in the face of ecological catastrophe, or Latin American governments in the face of foreign debt that was "invented"[21] and that is unpayable. Bergson writes exactly of this, though in an intuitive and critical manner, still without sufficient categorical instruments, in his book *Les deux sources de la morale et la religion*:

> One of the results of our analysis has been to distinguish carefully, in the social domain, between the *closed* [*clos*] and the *open* [*ouvert*]. The *closed society*[22] is one in which its members act toward one another in a manner characterized by indifference to other human beings,[23] always prepared to attack or defend themselves, restricted in this manner to a combative stance. . . . *The open society*[24] is one that embraces a principle that encompasses all of humanity. It is dreamt of, from time to time, by elite souls, and brought about in practice in each moment of creativity, by a greater or lesser transformation of the human being, which makes it possible to surmount difficulties that were until that moment insurmountable.[25]

And in the dramatic words of that giant antipositivist philosopher (opposed to Comtian positivism), writing at the beginning of the twentieth century, but with extraordinary contemporary resonance (at the dawn of the twenty-first century, in the face of the analytical and positivist philosophers of the linguistic turn): "Humanity cries out, almost buried under the weight of the progress which humanity itself has produced. But we do not understand enough that our future is dependent on our own efforts. It is up to us to determine whether we want to continue living."[26] This cry is, in the strictest sense, precisely that of an ethics of liberation.

[208] Kant himself suspected something similar, but it was impossible for him to come up with an adequate response: "But it is soon evident that a natural order whose law was to destroy life itself, through the application of the same principle whose determination was to magnify the production of life, would be contradictory and could not subsist as such an order; as a result that principle cannot materialize itself in reality as a universal natural law."[27] In the same manner, for Kant, "pleasure" and "pain" are merely the motivations of an egotistical subjectivity: "For example, he or she who, wishing to eat bread, has to conjure up a mill. But in practice the precepts underlying one's appetite cannot ever be considered universal,[28] because the determining motive of this hunger is rooted in the sensations of pleasure and hunger, which it cannot be universally assumed are always directed towards the same objects."[29] The pain[30] of the corporeality or bodily reality of the victims, as we shall see, is precisely the primary material origin (which is surely equivocal and uncertain) of all possible ethical criticism, and of that critical empirical judgment ("This does not permit the reproduction of the life of the subject") and, subsequently (with intervening moments that we must analyze), of the ultimate critical "normative judgment" ("This system is evil, unjust, because it makes the reproduction of the life of the victims impossible") — the second moment of figure 11.

It should not be assumed that a critic of a given system of ethics must

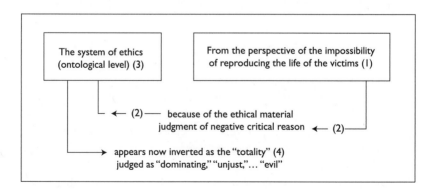

Figure 11. The "negative" ethical-material judgment of critical practical reason.

NOTE: Compare this figure with figures 10 and 12 on pp. 191 and 211 (especially moments 2, 3, and 4, which are properly critical).

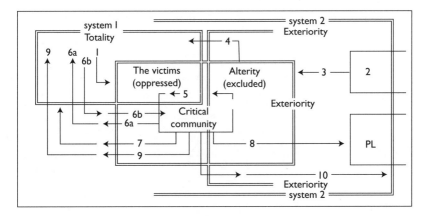

Figure 12. A model of critical praxis: Dialectics of affirmation-negation of critical ethics.

NOTES: The Arabic numbers match those in the text. Simplicity has to do with truth, and unnecessary complexity produces confusion. But when complexity is demanded by the nature of the subject itself, excessive simplifications also produce confusions.

System 1 is the affirmation of the prevailing ethical system. Moment 1: originary negation (subsumption or alienating exclusion); 2: radical ethical affirmation of material and formal principles; 3: critical ethical consciousness of the victim's own negation; 4: negative ethical judgment of system 1; 5: self-interpellation within the community of victims; 6a: interpellation directed toward the dominant sectors of system 1; 6b: militant commitment of the "organic intellectual." *Critical community* comprises emergent sociohistorical actors. Moment 7: dialectical-hermeneutical understanding or scientific explanation of the "causes" of the negation at issue; 8: construction or dialectical affirmation of alternatives. PL: anticipated project of liberation. Moment 9: negation (deconstruction) of the real negation of system 1; 10: affirmative liberating construction of system 2.

In the text, the ten "moments" of figure 12 are referred to simply as moment 1, etc.

always be a critic of its totality (the criticism can be partial) or that he or she must necessarily be an advocate of a revolutionary solution (for processes of this kind, though never impossible a priori, are of an exceptional character, arising only occasionally in a period of several centuries, since under normal circumstances the transformations that occur of norms, actions, or institutions are partial, concrete, and become evident in the flow of life from one day to another).[31] The ethics of liberation is an ethics of everyday life.

[209] In this second part, I therefore describe three new levels of the process in which we are engaged (see table 9 and figure 12).

At the first level of analysis (the theme of chapter 4) moment 1[32] is the

Table 9. Various Levels of Critical Liberation Consciousness

Critical Moments	6. Critical Ethical		7. Antihegemonic or Critical-Discursive
I. Types of rationality	a. critical reason (practical-material)	b. preoriginary ethical-critical reason	critical discursive reason (formal)
II. Criterion	of critical truth (a)	of critical recognition	of critical validity (a)
III. Principle (b)	material, ethical-critical (b)	ethical alterity	moral-critical, formal (b)
IV. Opponent in the formulation	conservative	conservative	dogmatic (hegemonic or vanguardist)
V. Type of (a); judgment or statement	judgment of fact (a); critical normative statement	judgment of fact (a); critical normative statement	critical judgment of fact (a); valid normative-critical statement (b)
VIa. Negation of	the "goodness claim" of the system	the Other as victim	the "validity" of the system
VIb. From the perspective of	impossibility of the life of the victims	recognition of the alterity of the Other	intersubjective exclusion of the victims
VII. Types	critical practical truth claim	critical practical truth claim	critical intersubjective validity claim
VIII. Types of interest	ethical-material critical	ethical-alternative critical	critical discourse

Note: The numbering of the indicated "moments" continues the numbering begun in table 8. All of the "moments" specified in this table have "negative" and "positive" levels.

occurrence of the actual original and empirically demonstrable *negation*[33] (alienation in the strongest sense of the term) of the victims (the slavery of the slave, the effective subsumption of the worker's salaried labor by capital, women as the sexual objects of patriarchy, etc.), where their suffering is the real effect of their material (and even formal) domination or exclusion, as a living contradiction of the *affirmation* of the prevailing (and henceforth dominant) ethical system. Critical ethics as such, understood as an exercise of ethical criticism, initiates its dialectical movement from moment 2, which is the radical ethical affirmation of the life that has been (materially) denied to the victims, as expressed by their desire and struggle to live and from the perspective of the recognition of the dignity of the victim as embodying an Other whom the system denies. This is the place, moment 3, from which victims are understood to have a critical-ethical consciousness,[34] arising from the pain of their immolated bodies, the *nega-*

8. Axiological Critical	9. Of Critical Feasibility	10. Liberation, Ethical Feasibility
critical hermeneutical reason	instrumental, strategic, or analytical reason	liberation reason
criticism of values	of critical, technical, or strategic feasibility	
axiological critical	strategic-instrumental and analytical	of liberation, critical-ethical feasibility
conventional in attitude or ingenuous	the "efficient" within the terms of the prevailing system	antiutopian, conservative
judgment of critical value (*Umwertung*)	judgment of critical fact or critical ends-means	judgment of fact, normative-critical statement (b)
mediations of the prevailing values	ultimate "efficiency" of the prevailing system	the reality of the system (of construction)
the nonvalue of prevailing values	destruction of the life of the victims	possible utopia of the life of the victims
critical rightness claim	theoretical-technological truth claim	ethical-transformative, feasible claim
critical-practical herme-neutical	theoretical, technical, strategic critics	ethical liberatory

tion of their lives and of the asymmetrical or excluded position expressed in their discursive nonparticipation.[35] But it is at this point, moment 4, that the negative critical-ethical judgment can be directed at the norm, action, institution, or ethical system, revealing them to be perverse, unjust, "evil," because they are the cause and origin of the victim's status as such. This is, in sum, the critical-ethical judgment itself.

At the second level (the focus of chapter 5), we find the victims constituting themselves as a community, in a formal intersubjective antihegemonic discourse, which critically *negates* and interpellates[36] the victims themselves as part of their own process of acquiring a *critical consciousness*, and who direct themselves initially (moment 5) to the other victims who have not yet acquired such consciousness (an originary intersubjective interpellation that generates solidarity)[37] and (moment 6) which is then secondarily directed to those capable of acting upon and expressing solidarity with the victims, even though those activated might belong to another strata within the system (a subsequent interpellation [6a]) which fosters a militant collaboration that manifests itself as a co-responsibility for the cause [6b], which also results in an expansion of the community of those who adopt a new critical stance in the face of the system[38] that expresses itself in praxis). Moment 7 occurs as the victims progressively become conscious of the causes of their negation; these causes are analyzed dialectically and explained scientifically by them and by their co-responsible collaborators (experts, scientists, philosophers, political activists and leaders, etc.), a process of theoretical-practical *conscientization* that is undertaken both in a material and formal manner.[39] As a result it is possible, in moment 8, to construct dialectically feasible alternatives that are *affirmative* in character, as an exercise of utopian reason (of that which is possible, against that of conservative and anarchist reason).

At a third level (the subject of chapter 6), moment 9 occurs when the systematic negations of the victims (as described in moment 1),[40] are themselves negated in a deconstructive manner by ethically[41] feasible transformative actions. In moment 10, new instances (norms, actions, institutions, systems) are positively constructed according to ethically feasible criteria, from the perspective of alternatives that have been analyzed, in the process that constitutes the praxis of liberation in its strictest sense.

CHAPTER 4

The Ethical Criticism of the Prevailing System
From the Perspective of the Negativity of the Victims

[210] This is an ethics of life. The negation of human life is now our subject. The clearest and most definitive point of departure for the entire framework of criticism that I have developed is the relationship produced between the negation of the corporeality, the *bodily reality* (*Leiblichkeit*) reflected in the suffering of the victims, of all those dominated (as workers, indigenous people, African slaves, or exploited Asians in the colonized world; as the bodily reality of women, of those who are not white, of the future generations who will suffer the effects of ecological destruction; all of the elderly without a place in a consumer society, children abandoned in the streets, all those excluded because they are foreigners, immigrants, or refugees, etc.), and the process by which the victims become conscious of this negation. This chapter seeks to address the material contradiction between such negation and the consciousness it produces. At the first level we have original empirically founded negativity, which appears to be a "*natural* fact," and which is not accompanied by any kind of critical-ethical consciousness: "For years and years we harvested the *death* of our people in the fields of Chiapas; our children *died* because of a force that was unknown to us; our men and women walked in the long night of ignorance which laid a shadow over our steps. Our communities walked *without truth* or understanding. Our steps moved forward without having a clear destination, we simply lived and *died*, without more."[1]

At the second level, we move from the stage of "nonconsciousness," of ingenuousness, to that of "critical-ethical consciousness":

> The oldest among the elders of our *communities*,[2] our *people*, spoke words that came to us from very far away, from a time when our lives did not exist

yet, from a time when our voice was still silenced. And it was *truth* that walked in the words of the oldest among the elders of our *people*. And we learned in those words that the *long painful night* of our communities came from the hands and words *of the powerful,*

> that our *misery* was wealth for a few,
> that a house had been built for the powerful
> upon the bones and dust of our ancestors and our children,
> and that our footsteps were barred from entering it,
> and that the abundance of its table was filled with the *emptiness* of our stomachs,
> and that its luxuries were bred by our *poverty,*
> and that the power of its roofs and walls was raised over the *fragility* of our bodies,
> and that the wellbeing which filled up its spaces flowed directly from our *death,*
> and that the wisdom that resided there had been nourished by our *ignorance,*
> and that the peace that enveloped it meant *war* for our people.[3]

[211] All of this flows from an "empirical fact" with material, corporeal, bodily content and expression, which is that of negation at the level of the production and reproduction of the life of the human subject, as the most critical dimension of a material ethics. But the victims "learn" (from the critical-ethical consciousness of the elders) that the affirmation of the values of the "established system" or of the project of a *good life* conceived by the powerful is by the same stroke the negation or condemnation to a *life of misery* for the poor.

The next stage is that of the formulation of a *negative* judgment of this project of domination as that which produces the poverty or unhappiness[4] of the dominated or excluded victims. The "truth" of the system is thereby negated from the perspective of the "impossibility of the life" of the victims, because of how it makes them unable to continue living. The truth of a dominant norm, act, institution, or system of ethics is negated as a totality, *because* of its negative effects.

It is only at this point that we can begin to perceive the specificity of an ethics of liberation. Before, it would have been difficult to understand what it proposes.[5] I hope that now it will be clear that the "fact" of being a victim, which has been judged from a critical-ethical perspective, for example, with reference to the poverty[6] produced by peripheral capitalism (in the current phase of the globalization of capitalism as a world system), is not an "immediate" or primary fact (which then would have had to be located with what I addressed abstractly in chapter 1). First I had to affirm the truth, validity, and feasibility of the goodness claim, the supposed "good," of the norm, action, institution, or ethical system at issue. Only now, in light of the already defined nature of the criterion and material principle (of the ethical duty to reproduce and develop the life of the human subject, in the context of a community of life, in a specific cultural context, assuming the achievement of subjective happiness as part of the objective conditions of justice intended, in the final analysis, for all of humanity), is it possible to reveal a fact that is evident on a massive global scale: at the dawn of the twenty-first century, the majority of humanity was a "victim" in one form or another of profound structures of domination or exclusion, and immersed in "pain," "unhappiness," "poverty," "hunger," "illiteracy," and "subordination." As stated in a newspaper, "Poverty on a global scale reached 400 million more people within the last 5 years. Currently 1.5 billion inhabitants of the world are desperately poor and more than 1 billion survive with daily incomes of less than a dollar, even in the developed countries, according to the United Nations."[7]

[212] The utopian project of the prevailing world system, which is becoming globalized (in economic, political, and even erotic terms), is revealed (in the light of its own claims of freedom, equality, wealth, and property for all, and of others of its myths and symbols)[8] as being in contradiction with itself, given that the majority of its possible participants have become victims deprived of the ability to satisfy the needs that this same system has proclaimed as rights. It is only then, from the perspective of the *affirmative character* of the criterion of truth and of the material-ethical principle of the reproduction and development of the life of the ethical subject that the *negative effects* reflected in the death, misery, and oppression of their bodily reality due to alienated labor, the repression of the unconscious and of the libido, especially of women, the lack of political power of these subjects in the face of institutional power, the prevalence of inverted values, the alienation of the ethical subject,[9] and so on, acquire a resonant *ethical sense* of their own. The "Other" that I have insisted upon so often in previous works appears here to be other than that of the kind of "normal" ethics I expounded upon in chapters 1–3. The prevailing system, as an entity that is "natural," legitimate, *appears now* transfigured, in the face of ethical-critical consciousness, and that of Horkheimer's negative system, into the "disciplinary institutions that exclude" in Foucault's micropower, and into Benjamin's "empty time." This is why the "good" norm, act, institution, or ethical system formally or intersubjectively loses its validity, or hegemony (in Gramsci's terms). Critical-ethical consciousness produces an "inversion"[10] (Nietzsche's *Umwertung der Werte*, Marx's "fetishism"), a practical and ethical "transfiguration" that is not simply theoretical.

In this manner, *Ethics of Liberation* subsumes the critical stances of the "great critics" (Feuerbach, Schopenhauer, Nietzsche, Horkheimer, Adorno, Marcuse, and particularly Marx, Freud, and Levinas), and the Latin American experience, to the extent that they criticize the aspects of Modernity and modern reason that foster tendencies toward domination. But *Ethics of Liberation* is equally capable of defending the *universality of reason* as such, and especially of ethical-critical reason, for which nothing is forbidden, against the irrationality of some of these critics (for example, Nietzsche or the postmodernists). It is also capable of defending the universality of life, of corporeality, and so on, within a greater overall complexity.

This multidimensional movement of affirmation, negation, subsumption, and development is possible (albeit impossible for the rational formalism of discourse ethics or for postmodernist irrationalisms), because, although it proceeds from the affirmation of material, formal, and feasible principles that have been enunciated, it can still situate itself *outside, before, or in a transcendental position*[11] with respect to the prevailing system, and with respect to the truth, validity, and feasibility of the supposed "good" and "goodness claim," because it adopts as its own the alterity of the victims, of the dominated, the place of the excluded as outsiders, in a position that is critical and that seeks to deconstruct the "dominant validity" of the system, now revealed as *dominating*: capitalism, patriarchy, racism, and so on. It is this positioning that enables us to judge the "goodness claim" of the system that victimizes as, in fact, dominating, exclusionary, and illegitimate. In this way, although we have explored the importance of the material ethics of authors such as MacIntyre or Taylor, now we can proceed to question them *from the perspective of the victims and of those who have been dominated*. The alterity of the victims reveals the material system of values, and the culture responsible for the pain unjustly borne by the oppressed, and the substantive "content" of the alleged "good"[12] (which I described in another work[13] as the *principium oppressionis*) to be illegitimate and perverse.

§4.1. Marx's Critique of Political Economics

[213] I have spent a great deal of time working on the texts of Marx,[14] but now I would like to focus on the theme of the relationship between positivity and negativity in his thought, and the "explanation" of the cause of the negativity of the victim, in order to better understand what I propose in terms of the foundations necessary for the exercise of critical-ethical reason. As a post-Hegelian leftist, Marx had to undertake a criticism of the purely *negative* philosophy of latter-day Hegel.

This attempt to recover Hegel's original "positive"[15] thought—which led Marx, as a result of his choice of a critical-ethical option, to discover the importance of the economy (after a point of departure rooted exclusively in law and philosophy) and to refer back to actual *positive*, material *substance* as the necessary launching point for serious "criticism"[16]—by the post-Hegelian philosophers of the Left took a certain amount of time, and began publicly in 1841, during the Berlin lectures in which the old and forgotten Schelling criticized the "negativity" of Hegel during his last phase.[17]

In effect, the Schelling of the *Philosophy of Revelation* ushered in a tradition of critical affirmation[18] in philosophy, in which thinkers ranged from Feuerbach and Marx to Levinas and the ethics of liberation. If for Hegel being and thought were identical, Schelling's perspective was quite different:[19] "Hegel returned to *the most negative things of all* [*Allernegativiste*] that can be thought of, headed towards the concept free of all subjective determination. This concept is, for him, pure being itself."[20]

This being of the *"philosophy of identity"*—which was an initial stage in the thought of Schelling, who taught this very subject to Hegel at Jena—deals only with the pure *essence* of a thing, but says nothing about its "real" existence;[21] it is purely tautological, with the pure subject quickly becoming an absolutely empty subjectivity.[22] By contrast, "*positive* philosophy is a historical philosophy [*geschichtliche Philosophie*]."[23] Schelling's 1841 lectures were attended by Bakunin, Kierkegaard, Engels, Feuerbach, Burckhardt, Savigny, Ranke, and von Humboldt, among hundreds of others. It was there that Schelling declared: "That which is the origin [*Anfang*] of all thought, is not yet itself thought."[24] "The beginning of *positive* philosophy is that every act of thinking presupposes Being."[25] But in the final instance, what Schelling wanted to show is that before being looms reality, as a necessary prior assumption of thinking and being, when he affirms, from the perspective of creationist doctrine: "The divine consists of being the master of being [*Herrsein über das Sein*], and it is the principal function of philosophy to pass from pure being [*tò ón*] to the master of being [*Herrn des Seins*]."[26]

For Schelling, therefore, there was a creative source of being that emerges from nothingness,[27] and which becomes manifest in history by means of a "positive revelation," and as a "source of knowledge [*Erkenntnisquelle*],"[28] "which should not be represented as an unfounded knowledge, and instead what we must acknowledge is that it is the most well-founded knowledge of all."[29] The issue then, following an old tradition, is to begin the philosophical discourse from the absolute itself.[30] Beginning with the Neoplatonists,[31] Schelling referred to the doctrine of Nicholas de Cusa regarding the *contractio Dei*,[32] which is found in the mystical tradition of the Jewish Kabbalah[33] and promulgated by Jacob Böhme. Schelling, by accepting the original contradiction in the absolute itself ("the other absolute"),[34] no longer accepted the idea of an absolute identity, and defended the idea of a nonidentity between being and thought, and of the same being and reality of the absolute, that operates as a creative source from the depths of nothingness.

[214] Feuerbach[35] meanwhile was able to grasp a philosophical proposal for how to go beyond Hegelian thought—a transcendence he had attempted for years.[36] In the first place, he undertook a criticism of Hegel's reflections on religion, proposing that ultimately the discussion of God as the origin of ethical problems must be resolved in a new way. If the divine is a manner of projecting anthropological self-interpretation onto the infinite, "theology [must then] be transformed and dissolved into anthropology," he wrote in paragraph 1 of his *Fundamental Principles of the Philosophy of the Future* (1843).[37] In the prologue of this work he wrote: "The philosophy of the future has as its mission to take philosophy from the realm of separated souls to that of *living* and incarnate souls; and to make philosophy descend from the beatitudes of divine thought without any [material] needs to that of human misery."[38] This is why he wrote that the "identity of thought and being is the expression of the divine character of reason."[39] Feuerbach was attempting to transcend that assumed equivalence and to make the passage to alterity through sensibility: "That which is real [*das Wirkliche*] in its reality, or as something real, is real as an object of the senses. Truth, reality, sensibility are all identical. Only that which can be sensed is a truthful and real being."[40]

Beyond being as it has been thought is the reality that can be sensed. Sensibility, on the other hand, is best expressed by the bodily reality of another human being, such as that of the reality lived in an erotic relationship, said Schelling, in an insight that is a forerunner of those of Buber and Levinas: "The real dialectic is not the monologue of a solitary thinker with his or herself, but rather the dialogue between you and me.[41] Absolute philosophy used to say . . . : I am the truth. Human philosophy says, to the contrary: even while lost in thought, even to the extent that I am a philosopher, I am a human being in the face of an another human being [*Mensch mit Mensch*]."[42] The positive character of the exteriority of nature from Hegelian being in Schelling as the master of being was now situated and defined in terms of the reality that can be sensed beyond the horizons of thought.

[215] Kierkegaard,[43] for his part, reflected upon this kind of positive exteriority in another manner, since from the Danish thinker's perspective it was only in the third stage that identity, or that which is merely universal, can be transcended. The first stage, that of the "aesthetic-speculative," is situated at the level of the "system": "a system and a closed whole is one and the same thing, since when a system has no end it is not a system."[44]

This is why "the idea of a system is that of a subject which is at the same time an object, the unity of a moment when Thought and Being are identical. . . . This pure identity is tautological, because the word *Being* does not mean that a person who thinks is, but only that that person is a thinker. We do not want to be unjust and label this objective direction a divinization of the atheistic and pantheistic being itself, but instead to perceive it as part of an incursion into the *comic*."[45] In the aesthetic-ontological contemplative stage (that of the *comic*, before which we have to maintain a stance of "irony"—though not Rorty's kind) the concrete human[46] being is a negated moment of world history as a totality. This level is one step below that of the ethical stage, that of the *tragic*, in which the individual appears with personal responsibility in the face of the law that obliges a certain conduct, and which the individual commits himself or herself to comply with, but "the ethical is in itself that which is general, and under this title is applicable to all. . . . The individual sins from the moment when he or she reaffirms his or her individuality in the face of the general, and can only become reconciled with the general by recognizing it. The tragic hero soon brings the combat to a close by complying with the infinite movement and then finds security in the general."[47]

The third "stage" is the "*pathetic*,"[48] which transcends that of the ethical, and which presupposes a radical affirmation, a leap beyond the tragic, and beyond "Hegel and Goethe [since they] have sought to restore classicism by situating the individual once again in *totality*."[49] The Kierkegaardian affirmation situates itself in the place of the victims, that of the "poor existent individual human being."[50] *Beyond* the universal, and beyond totality and being, one encounters the Other, the one in whom it is possible to believe. This is a faith anchored in a space which surpasses that of ontological rational understanding, a transontological transcendence which is in-comprehensible by either aesthetic or ethical reason: "It is that which is related to what the absolute paradox, that of the absurd and incomprehensible can, must, and wants to be; it has to do with the passion for maintaining the dialectical *distinctiveness* of incomprehensibility.[51] . . . The incomprehensible, understood in this way, has behind it, in time, the explanation that comes from on high."[52]

Kierkegaard developed Schelling. Beyond the idea of being as that which is known emerges the reality of personal existent individuality: "All knowledge with respect to *reality* is pure possibility; the only *reality* regarding which an existing being does not possess an abstract knowledge is that of his or her own, the fact that exists; it is this reality which constitutes his or her absolute interest."[53] Kierkegaard was speaking to us about critical rebellion against the prevailing system of ethics, from the standpoint of the pathos of our own individual existence, which transcends the totality of the concept of existence itself. For him it was a rebellion against Danish Lutheran Christendom (not Christianity), which had ceased to be Christian from his perspective; but he was not only a religious critic—he was equally critical of economic conditions. The critic sets forth from the standpoint of the incomprehensible toward the universality of the prevailing ethical system. Kierkegaard cries out in protest from the suffering in pathos of irreducible individuality.[54]

[216] Within the same post-Hegelian tradition, we depart from the positive criticism of Schelling—against him, but within the same horizon[55]—and go to Feuerbach, and the critical-ethical reason of a young German entrepreneur from Barmen enters history. This young man wanted to establish a branch of his father's factory in Manchester, in Calvinist Scotland, but hand in hand with a young woman who was an Irish Catholic worker—who would have imagined it?—had sufficient critical-ethical consciousness to publish an exemplary ethical work in 1845: *The Condition of the Working Class in England*, which documents the life of the victims of the emergent capitalist system in the very heart of the world system. In the prologue to this book, Marx wrote: "The condition of the working class is the concrete grounding and *point of departure* [*Ausgangspunkt*] for all contemporary social movements, because it is the highest and the most visible summit of our constitutive *misery* [*misère*]."[56]

It is Engels, already old, who wrote the following, against the *standard* interpretations of materialism: "According to the materialist conception,[57] the moment of determination in the last instance[58] of history[59] [is] the production and reproduction of immediate life [*unmittelbaren Lebens*], in a double sense: on the one hand, the production of the means and instruments necessary for life (the objects necessary for *nourishment, clothing, and housing*)[60] and, on the other hand, the production of human beings themselves."[61] In this text we can understand that, in the final instance, neither the economy nor even production itself is the point of departure of the "content" of the ethical system he proposed. Production is the material moment of the economy, and it is rational to the extent that it results in products or satisfactions that have human needs as their basis, and life itself as an ultimate reference or instance. Historically, it was Engels who motivated the journalist, failed academic, and radical petty bourgeois critic named Karl Marx to discover the precise epistemological level of abstraction where the most adequate critical-ethical reasoning should be exercised: that of *criticism* of the nascent political economy. Economics was not the field in which Marx was initially a specialist, but he elected it as the most relevant space within which to develop his critical-ethical discourse.[62]

I referred to Marx in §1.5a of this book. His critical-ethical consciousness manifested itself before his essay on the working class, and was ex-

pressed in a metaphor of the "eye,"[63] when, during the period of the political critiques of Christendom, freedom of the press was infringed: "The
free press is like *the open eye* of the spirit of the people, the incarnated self-
confidence of a people, the nexus between them expressed in words . . . ,
the incorporated culture which sheds light upon the spiritual essence of
material struggles and idealizes their rough material form."[64] The Marx of
this historical moment considered the "free press" to be the political victim of a Christian state.[65] He still thought at that point that "communism
was a dogmatic abstraction."[66] But shortly thereafter he discovered another
kind of victim in the "poor peasants."[67] His exile in Paris enabled him to
enter into direct contact for the first time with the industrial world. There
he came to know leaders of workers' struggles such as Leroux, Blanc, and
Felix Pyat,[68] and was able to immerse himself in their secret societies.[69]
There he discovered directly the *first affirmation*: the desire to live the life
of, and struggle for the rights of, the French working class. It was there that
his life first became linked with historical movements of workers. This is
how he discovered the victims of the system that must be affirmed in their
dignity and negated in the negation, according to the dialectical categories
of positive and negative: "In Germany there is no class which possesses the
weight, the rigor, the daring, and the intransigence necessary to transform
itself into the negative[70] representative of all society. . . . Where does the affirmative[71] possibility of German Emancipation lie then? In the formation
of a class . . . whose universal *suffering* [*Leiden*[72]] impresses upon it a universal character."[73] As a universal victim, or as a victim of the system as such,
its liberation signified the system's total "dissolution [*Auflösung*]": "There
where the proletariat proclaims the dissolution of the *previous universal
order*, it does nothing but profess the secret of its own existence, since it is
in itself the concrete expression of the dissolution of this universal order."

[217] The victims critique this order and proclaim its dissolution and the
necessity of its disappearance: this is a critical-ethical judgment par excellence of the system as a totality (moment 4 in our framework), given that
the positive existent character of the system is the secret of its own negation (through the vehicle of its victims): "When the proletariat calls for
the *negation* of private property, it does nothing more but raise up to the
level of a *societal principle*[74] what society has made a principle of its own,
what appears to be concretized in society itself, without its intervention,
as the *negative* product of this society. The proletariat thus finds itself to be
aided by this same right in the process of giving birth[75] to a new world."
In Germany, where the industrial world is still very backward, the "only
liberation [*Befreiung*] that is possible as a practical matter is a theoretical
liberation," and because of this "philosophy is the head of this emancipation, and its heart is the proletariat.[76] Philosophy will only be able to realize

itself by means of the abolition of the proletariat, which will not be possible to achieve without the *fulfillment of philosophy* [*Verwirklichung der Philosophie*]."

Korsch and Lukács accorded a great deal of importance to the text I have just quoted, akin to that of Marx's famous "Eleventh Thesis" of the *Theses on Feuerbach*.[77] In these *Theses* Marx makes clear that his is not a "contemplative materialism,"[78] nor one merely theoretical in character, like that of Feuerbach—appropriate for an intrasystemic, ontic theory—but rather that of a *praxis*, of "critical-practical revolutionary activity."[79] A theory intended to unfold in such a way as to analyze (both scientifically and otherwise) the causes of the alienation of the system's victims,[80] and to arrive at the conclusion that the "truth" of the prevailing system of ethics, to the extent that it is a cause of their negation, in fact becomes an "untruth."[81]

At this point I think it can be understood that what Marx intended was the articulation of philosophy within a *critical-ethical* horizon (moment 7 of our framework), and not merely an analytical or dialectical system of contemplation within and from the inside of the prevailing system.[82] To "interpret" the world from an exclusively theoretical posture presupposes the acceptance of the given system from within its own horizons. But critical ethics instead proposes "transformation" (moment 10, as a praxis of liberation or action that is transformative of norms, actions, institutions, ethical systems, etc.), and adopts the perspective of the victims and has a critical-ethical consciousness as its driving force (moments 5 through 8 of figure 12, our framework). This approach does not imply the abandonment of all philosophy but rather implies that the theoretically expressed complicity with the system that produces victims must be surpassed and must be replaced by a commitment in praxis with these victims, in order to place the analytical resources of critical-ethical philosophy (which is the fullest "fulfillment of philosophy") at the service of the analysis of the causes of their negation and of the transformative (liberatory) struggles of the oppressed or excluded. Marx, in Paris, *situated himself definitively* in the "place" of his exercise of critical philosophy. But there was still yet another moment to come in his precise calculation of the epistemological level of his critique. It was in Paris that he received Engels's short essay *Outline towards a Critique of Political Economy*,[83] which enabled him to find the specific kind of discourse he needed to develop (moment 7 of the framework). It would be a theoretical critique (in terms of the analysis of the causes of the negation of the victims) coordinated with a critical-ethical intersubjective consciousness already initiated by their social movements (moment 5). Marx understood that this critique had to be articulated at a level of abstraction that would permit a precise, relevant, effective, irrefutable, and deconstructive theoretical and analytical attack on the prevailing ethical system in Europe.

It is worth recalling that the ethical aspect of his critique in the fullest sense does not take as its point of departure the *affirmative* character of human life, but rather its *negation*: the inability to continue living, a matter that nonetheless demands a *positive* horizon that I "demonstrated," deistically,[84] in chapter 1 of this book. Today, in the peripheral world (of dependent capitalism in Africa, Asia, Latin America), as in that of Paris in 1844 (the historical moment of crisis sharpened by the presence of marginality in laissez-faire capitalism), what we need to do is reflect ethically and philosophically upon life *from its negation*, in its most urgent expression: that of the *poverty* of its vast majorities: "The poverty of the human being [*Armut des Menschen*] takes on . . . a human significance, which is inherently social as well. Poverty is the passive link[85] that enables each person to sense another as a need [*Bedürfnis*], to find the greatest wealth in the other human being.[86] The worker's poverty becomes greater [*ärmer*] with the greater production of wealth that he or she creates.[87] Human beings had to be reduced to such *absolute poverty* [*absolute Armut*][88] so that their internal wealth could then be illuminated."[89] Poverty is the impossibility of achieving the production, reproduction, and development of human life, but it is also both the absence of the fulfillment of human needs and the origin of critical consciousness. In effect, when Marx undertook his process of self-education in the study of economics in Paris, he readily discovered the exclusion and exteriority in which the victims of the system are to be found, and the need to situate himself there with new "eyes" (the eyes of criticism):

> The existence [*Dasein*] of capital becomes [the worker's] existence, becomes his or her *life* itself, and determines the *content of his or her life* [*Inhalt seines Lebens*],[90] in a manner different from that which could have been. This is why [bourgeois] political economy pays no heed to the unemployed worker, to the worker situated as a human being *outside of* [*ausser*] the relations of production. The . . . beggar, the unemployed worker, the hungry, the miserable, and the criminal are *figures* which do not exist for it, but only *for other eyes*,[91] those of the doctor, judge, gravedigger, the debt-collector, etc., *figures* [*Gestalten*] who lurk *outside* [*ausserhalb*] the range of its vision.[92]

Marx's theoretical analysis is that of a jurist, philosopher, and apprentice economist who began to develop his critical ethics from the "exteriority" of the victims.[93] From then until his death forty years later, Marx would be faithful to his task as a critical theoretician (moment 7), articulated with the British front of workers' liberation, and with that movement in Europe as a whole, committed to seeking explanations for the causes of the negation (moment 1) of the victims. He was not able to do much with regard to the formulation of *affirmative* alternatives (socialism; moment 8); or with respect to the deconstruction of the system (moment 9), nor in terms of the construction of a new system (system 2 of figure 12), although he attempted to participate in this task through his active collaboration with the First International.

[218] Let us see how Marx situated himself in the critical moment in terms of the negation, defulfillment, and alienation of the worker. His criticism was centered on the concrete modes by which capitalism institutionally negates human life. Here we have to understand the meaning of the need to undertake the passage from the positive descriptive moment of a material critique to that of negative material criticism. In effect, Marx's *critical* perspective is nothing more than that of the concrete recognition of the *nonfulfillment* (the negation) of the positive material criterion which has been indicated. This is to say that the critic (victim, militant, philosopher, political leader, economist, and others) exercises this kind of criticism when he or she applies a negative ethical judgment that negates or contradicts a positive criterion. As Wellmer has argued,[94] Marx renders a judgment of the capitalist system on an ethical basis rooted in the system's negations, and from the perspective of that which is denied by its inherently nongeneralizable proposition: from the perspective of the imperative that forbids the negation of the life of each and every human subject living in community. Capitalism is unjust (and alienates) because it negates the life of the worker-subjects (making the fulfillment of their lives impossible).

The Marx of 1844 still did not clearly understand what capital is, and for this reason he focused his critique on the institution of private property, as the assumed cause of the alienation or institutional negation of the human life of the worker. And because the critical moment cannot be a priori, but must be a posteriori, the material-ethical alternative must also unfold from the point of departure of an affirmative critique in terms of *the affirmative reproduction of the life of the human subject*, which can at a subsequent moment reveal its own negation. This is evident in the 1844 manuscripts: "The degree to which the fulfillment [*Verwirklichung*][95] of the demands of labor[96] implies the denial of the worker's own fulfillment [*Entwirklichung*] is evident, since he or she is ultimately denied in this sense all the way to the extreme of dying of hunger [*Hungertod*]."[97] In effect, what is contrary to human life is death itself. If the criterion upon which material ethics is based is the reproduction of human life, death is its negation. We are thereby confronted with a dialectic between the fulfillment of life and the denial of the fulfillment of life as death: "Objectification reaches such an extreme that it implies not only the loss of the objects most necessary *for the worker's life*, but even for his or her work itself. . . . The worker puts *his or her life* into the object of his labor [. . . but] *the life* which he or she has lent to the object confronts the worker as if it were an alien and hostile thing."[98] Workers "put" their lives into the products of their labor, but they never recover their lives. To the contrary, an object that has been thus invested is transformed into a monster that seeks to attack or dominate the workers: "*Dead* [*tote*] [99] capital always moves onward at the same pace and is indifferent to actual individual activity. . . . The worker *bears the suffering in his or her existence*[100] while capitalism is fulfilled through the profit of its *dead* [*toten*] [101] Mammon. With respect to the worker who appropriates nature through his or her labor, this appropriation is expressed as a form of alienation, his or her efforts as an activity for and by others, and *vitality* [*Lebendigkeit*] as a *sacrifice of human life* [*Aufopferung des Lebens*]."[102]

This process is even clearer in another text from this same period: "My labor [outside of the capitalist system] would be an expression of life [*Lebensäuserung*], and thereby a pleasure within life. Pursuant to the assumptions of private property it is the alienation of life [*Lebensentäusserung*], with the result that I work *in order to live* [*um zu leben*],[103] in order to create a means of living for myself. My work is not life."[104] This is to say that Marx now judged the capitalist system as alienating, unjust, as a system of victimization that promotes a form of human sacrifice, and as a historical structure *that denies the life* of the workers, and which denies their fulfillment, oppresses, impoverishes, and kills. And it is because it kills the life of the human subject that it is understood to be a perverse and unjust system: "This *material* [*materielle*] [105] private property, which is immediately apprehensible by the senses, is the material and sensory expression of alienated human life [*entfremdeten menschlichen Lebens*]."[106] How would it be possible to render the judgment that a system (or its corresponding theoretical framework) is perverse, unjust, and "evil," unless we have the antecedent factual statement capable of demonstrating that it negates the production, reproduction, and development of the concrete life of each human subject?

[219] Now I focus on Marx in the context of London and will observe how he analyzed the performative system at issue (the capital in the abstract),[107] which produces the *original negation* of the victims, of the proletariat, and how he explained the central moment of negation (alienation) in its ultimate (material) *content*, with respect to the production, reproduction, and development of the life of the human subject[108] within that system. I reiterate here my earlier assertion: I believe that Marx *selected the economy as his focus as a logical outcome of a previous critical-ethical choice*, and his *critique of political economy* is, precisely, the exercise of critical-ethical reason at a relevant epistemological material level.

The critical-categorical ethical "explanation" (that of the definitive Marx from August 1857 until his death, including the "four editions" of *Capital*)[109] of the system that causes the *negation* of the proletariat, the victims with whom Marx established a specific kind of co-responsibility, begins methodically with a description that situates itself in the sphere where it maintains a kind of *logical precedence* ("ontological" for Hegel, "other-worldly" for Schelling), with respect to the totality (of capital in the style of Lukács or Marcuse, but without being perceived in this way by them), *prior to* the signing of the labor contract and of the existence of capital in itself, from the perspective of the following extreme (analyzed in historical terms in the sole context of the question of "original accumulation"), *positive* situation: "Non-objectified labor, without value, conceived of *positively*, or negatively in relation to itself[110] . . . the subjective existence of labor itself. Labor . . . as an activity . . . which is the *living source of value* [*die lebendige Quelle des Werts*]."[111]

Critical ethics has its origin in this "positive" moment. The subjectivity of the worker as an activity is that which is the "creative source" of all possible value or wealth. It means, secondarily, the affirmation of life, because the worker's very person, his or her bodily reality, is a *living* subjectivity: "An objectivity which is not separated from his or her person [*Person*], but rather solely an objectivity which coincides with his or her immediate corporeality [*Leiblichkeit*].[112] . . . Nonobjectified labor . . . , labor as *subjectivity* [*Subjektivität*]. . . . Since it is supposed to exist for only a fixed period, *as something which is alive* [*lebendig*], it can exist only *as a living* subject."[113]

[220] Marx radically initiated his discourse on this theme[114] in the first chapter of his *Manuscripts of 1861–63*, "The Transformation of Money into Capital," and again in his *Manuscripts of 1863–65*, which would in turn be transformed into chapter 2 of the 1866 edition of *Capital*, and section 2, chapter 4 of the 1873 edition: "Our possessor of money would have to be so fortunate as to discover within the sphere of circulation, in the market, a good whose use value possessed in turn the singular [positive] characteristic of being a *source of value* [*Quelle von Wert*]; whose effective consumption could itself be then *an objectification of labor*, and thus an act implying *the creation of value* [*Wertschöpfung*]."[115] It is only from the perspective of its affirmative character (which also includes that of the dignity inherent in its "incarnation" in bodily form, "the living personality [*lebendigen Persön-lichkeit*]")[116] that the full meaning of the concept of "negation" in the first instance can be understood as a condition of the possibilities of capital itself: "The worker posited *as noncapital* [*Nicht-Kapital*] is as he is: . . . non-objectified labor, conceived of *negatively* . . . , neither a raw material nor an instrument of labor, nor the primitive form of an eventual product . . . *living labor* [*lebendige Arbeit*] . . . total dispossession, objectivity unclothed, the purely subjective existence of labor. Labor as *absolute poverty* [*absolute Armut*]: poverty understood not as deprivation, but as *complete exclusion* [*völliges Ausschliessen*] from wealth in the most objective terms."[117]

Categorically speaking, the *pauper ante festum*[118] is to be found, in her or his antecedent exteriority, and absolute negativity, before capital itself, its "system" or totality (of "being" and of the "comprehension of being"); these *paupers* have nothing beyond their own living personal corporeality, nor beyond their own empirical materiality (the point of departure and arrival for Marx's "ethical materialism"). Marx's *critique* thus flows from the initial negation of the victim: the future creator of wealth *possesses nothing*; or possesses only "an objectivity which is in no way exterior to the immediate existence of the individual himself": [119] he or she is a poor naked corporeality,[120] is "nothing,"[121] or antecedent negativity, the fruit of the abandonment of the "rural community" now immersed in an alien urban "social" relation.

[221] This *ante festum* negativity is followed by the description of the *original negation* (the essential *in festum* negativity), which demonstrates that the poor person, who is the positive "creative source" of all wealth, becomes implicated in the perverse circle of ontological alienation: "becomes thus a presupposition [*vorausgesetz*] of capital,[122] and on the other hand presupposes capital in turn."[123] The poor are thereby transformed from peasants into poor residents in the city, their precapitalist conditions of rural subsistence destroyed, with no choice but to sell their bodies into labor, or die, in a process of coercion that contractualists such as Rawls seem to forget. The labor contract thus has an *apparent form* endowed with *fairness* (equity), in a supposed expression of the balance of the rights of liberty, equality, and property.[124] In reality, all of this is marked by constitutive coercion, inequality, and poverty. Once the unequal, unjust, ethically perverse contract is made (and here the *untruth and nonvalidity* of the prevailing juridical world begins to manifest itself), the most tragic moment described by Marx, that of *subsumption* (*Subsuntion*) (the definitive *concept* of the young Marx's *intuitive* exploration of labor "alienation"), emerges with all of its force. The "subsumption of the labor process" is alienation itself, the most concrete *negation* of all, and one that is not merely ideological in character.[125] The "creative source of wealth" (a dignified person who fixes his or her own limits) is melded into the product forged by his or her labor, as if transformed into its mediation: a process of "inversion" in the strictest sense. The valorization of value is the "being" and "foundation" of a system that lives off the life of the worker, in a totalizing ontology: "The labor process manifests itself within the machinery of capitalist production in terms of the process of attributing value to its products, with value itself defined *as the end*, and [labor] itself reduced *to a means*."[126] Marx referred back explicitly to Kant,[127] in arguing that the worker's personhood is treated as a means, and the means (the process of the attribution of value to capital) as an end. This is the inversion expressed in the phenomenon of commodity fetishism. The co-responsible analysis of the theoretician himself now pos-

sesses the argumentative tools necessary to carry out the "critical-ethical judgment of capital" *in the strictest sense*.[128] This inversion, which is the *ethical negation in the first instance*, is essential for the reproduction of capital itself, and is the driving force of the social relation of domination which it gives rise to, and has its fullest expression in the process of "subsumption": "This formal subsumption [*formelle Subsumiren*] of the labor process itself [into capital], this process whereby it is taken under its control, is in essence one whereby the worker, as worker, ends up being under the supervision and control of capital and of the capitalist."[129]

[222] This *"formal* subsumption" is ethically significant, since capital (the totality in this context) controls the salaried worker by means of his or her "cooperation,"[130] by means of the "social division of labor"[131] (and in these examples the worker is still the "owner" of the labor process as an irreplaceable specialist). But it was because of the *"material* subsumption"[132] of the labor process itself, by means of its machinery, that the worker ended up under the capitalist's control: "It is not only the *formal* relation (the *formal* subsumption) that is thus modified, but the labor process itself. On the one hand the capitalist mode of production—which now manifests itself as a *sui generis* mode of production—creates a modified shape of *material* [*materiellen*] production. On the other hand the basis of the development of capitalist relations is configured by this modification of the material shape."[133] Living labor is *formally* subsumed in capital—to the extent that it produces surplus value—and this is so in a *material* sense—to the extent that it is the machinery, not the worker, that commands the production process—and the worker is completely dominated by capital;[134] it is only in this case that we can speak of a *"real* subsumption."

The concept of "subsumption" marks the *ethical* moment par excellence of "alienation" or "transubstantiation"—terms used with deliberate irony by Marx—the transformation of living labor into salaried labor (the process of totalization from the perspective of the exteriorization of the subjectivity of the worker),[135] the *negation in the first instance of the victim* of capital, as a kind of incorporation (intratotalization) of the "exteriority" of living labor into the "totality" of capital. All of this is possible because of the discovery (and construction) of the *most critical category* of the entire theoretical-explanatory analysis of capital that Marx undertakes from the perspective of critical *ethics*: the deep, essential, and simple category of "surplus value" (relative to the superficial, and more complex category of "profit" when it is analyzed as a phenomenon).

[223] Now the task is to take the *material-critical criterion*[136] seriously, to explain the cause of the impossibility of the production and reproduction of the human life of the victims of capitalism: the workers, the working class. The theme of surplus value enables Marx to situate the "place" where

the death of the victim is produced within the system of the categories of bourgeois political economy, in a manner that is essential, abstract, and unavoidable for the rational scientific argumentation of his era (and still valid in ours).

Marx did not imagine in December 1857—when he formulated *for the first time* the category of "surplus value [*Mehrwert*]"[137]—that in 1871,[138] when he was preparing the second edition of *Capital*, he would distinguish between the concepts of value as such[139] and exchange value, which would enable him to grasp the matter with much greater clarity. In effect, value is "undifferentiated human labor, labor which is abstractly human . . . in which abstractly human labor is objectified or materialized."[140] Value is human life transformed into an objective reality. Marx now had[141] an economic category (one that was at the same time one of a material anthropological nature)[142] upon which another "economic" category was constructed, and which at the same time was of a "critical-ethical" character and carried *negativity* within it. It is not a simple productive "value" but a "value which is not paid for": "The salary form, then, erases all traces of the division of the work-day between necessary labor [which makes possible the reproduction of the value of the wages paid] and *surplus labor*, between the labor which was *paid* and *unpaid* [*unbezahlte*]. All labor appears as if it were *paid* labor."[143]

[224] It was here that Marx found the *secret* or *mystery* of all capital, of capitalism, bourgeois society (and of Modernity), in his search for a scientific explanation consistent with his research project (moment 7 of figure 12: that of critical-theoretical analysis which is co-responsible with the victims). The victim suffers the consequences of the unpaid character of the labor attributable to all the wealth accumulated by those who have benefited in the prevailing system of ethics (corresponding to system 1 in figure 12). In the surplus time of surplus labor, the worker *creates* an "additional value"[144] "*out of the nothingness" of capital*, and its "*creative source [schöpferische Quelle]*" is not the "foundation [*Grund*]" of capital (the value of the wage) but the very creativity of the subjectivity of the corporeality of the person of the worker him or herself, who by *objectifying his or her life*, will never recover it. This "objectification" of the life of the victim, which is accumulated in capital and which is not recovered as a "subjectification" in the worker, is the critical-ethical theme at the heart of all of Marx's work: "This is why the economy, despite its mundane and pleasant surface appearance, is truly a *moral science*, the *most moral* of all of the sciences."[145] If the overall objective, articulated to the victims, and as the co-responsible co-[l]laboration of the scientist, is to give an analysis of the causes of the suffering and death, the result is an argument that connects the origin (the original negation of the victims, the *first moment* of the framework, namely,

the impossibility of the life of the victims) to the conclusion (the accumulation of capital as the product of the alienated life of the victims), which is to say:

> The accumulation of capital thus implies, by the same token, the increase of the proletariat.[146] The law . . . chains the worker to capital with shackles stronger than those which Haphaestus used to fetter Prometheus to the rock. This law produces an *accumulation of misery* [*Akkumulation von Elend*] proportional to the accumulation of capital. The accumulation of wealth at one end, at the same time is reflected in the *accumulation of misery, the torments of labor, slavery, ignorance, brutalization, and moral degradation*[147] at the opposite pole, that is, where the class is found that produces its own product as capital.[148]

If this is not ethics, then that word has lost all meaning.

[225] This conclusion permits the ethical "comprehension" of the fulfillment of capital as the denial of the fulfillment of the worker, and of the accumulation of capital as that of unpaid labor: *a critical-ethical judgment par excellence.* Capital itself, and the prevailing ethical system become inverted and appear now in their fetishistic form; the same occurs with political economy and its complicit ethical or moral philosophies, as the self-affirmation of capital as if it were the self-creating source of profit.

From the perspective of the reproduction of the life of working people, capital has become contradictory in nature, because, although it is efficient at attributing value to the value of capital, it is nonetheless *inefficient at reproducing the life of its victims,* who today are the majority of humanity. The problem of the impossibility of life as such on Earth if we continue within capitalist frameworks (the ecological problem is also anthropological in its implications, as we shall see) refers us back to the *critical-ethical principle of feasibility.*[149] And since Marx, to the first level of material impossibility (the extinction of life) is now added another: it is capital itself that is *impossible*; it is not empirically feasible *in the long run,* in that the inherent tendency to a declining rate of profit carries within it the seeds of its own destruction. When this *impossibility* blossoms is when *crisis* emerges[150] (once essential but now destabilizing in its effects). The strongest capital (of the individual, group, or "central" nations) will implement compensatory measures against labor (intensifying its exploitation)[151] *in the competition* against other weaker[152] sources of capital; and thereby expelling graver contradictions toward its peripheries. A critical-ethical philosophy can thus emerge in the peripheral regions of misery (Latin America, Africa, Asia, and Eastern Europe). This is the horizon defined by the process of the globalization of Modernity,[153] within which the ethics of liberation emerges and which, with difficulty but not impossibility, aspires as well to be understood in the contemporary "centers" of the United States and Western Europe.[154]

[226] Marx repeatedly undertakes an analysis of the causes of the negation of the victims (a study that he left unfinished in his tormented life as
an intellectual in poverty), seeking always to break out of the academic
ivory tower, but instead committing himself, to the extent to which he
was able, with social movements (communities of critical communication
among the excluded, and among those situated asymmetrically with respect to the centers of power, among all those dominated and victimized)
that were emerging as "historical subjects."[155] The expert, the social scientist, the philosopher (moment 6), who had been moved to a posture of
co-responsibility by the interpellation of the victims,[156] become a critical-
ethical consciousness that returns the victims' "interpellation" to them after
processing it analytically and rationally, employing the best theoretical "resources," in order to co-[l]laborate with them in the enlargement of this
"historical subject" (moments 7 and 8) as an "antidominant community"
of victims, who need this argumentation in order to achieve a *new* order of
validity beyond that of the validity of the system of domination. This subject must now equally begin to imaginatively and rationally produce future
alternatives to capitalism, articulated to these "historical actors" (the revolutionary political party, the organization of the First International, etc.).
This is a matter of the exercise of *ethical-utopian reason*, and I should set out
the issues with regard to Marx, as well as all that is involved in a concrete
social-historical project, from the horizon of the "realm of freedom" and of
"communism" (as a regulatory idea), in order to lay the conditions for the
feasibility of a "socialist"[157] revolution.

All of this is built upon the original *affirmation* or *recognition* of the dignity of the victim, since "work is the substance and immanent measure
of values, but itself has *no value*,"[158] it has "dignity"[159] instead; and intersubjective consciousness, the self-consciousness of struggle for a more just
society with responsibility and hope that transform themselves, from the
place of that *affirmation* or *responsibility*, making possible the emergence of
a new historical subject, the "phantom that haunts Europe."[160]

Marx criticized Adam Smith. Today he is criticized in turn by Hayek and
others. The contemporary task of ethics is therefore not simply to reiterate
Marx's critique, but rather to carry out the critique of his critics, a question which I will address later in the context of the economic "front" of the
ethics of liberation.

To conclude this section, I want to present evidence of the ethical *pathos*
that animated all of Marx's critical-theoretical enterprise, which is reflected
dramatically in the following: "All of the time that I could have dedicated
to labor I had to reserve for my theoretical work, to which I have sacrificed
my health, my joy in living and my family. . . . If we were animals we could
then naturally turn our backs on the *suffering of humanity* in order to dedicate ourselves to saving our own skin. But I would have felt myself to be

unpractical if I had died without at least completing the manuscript of my book."[161]

§4.2. The "Negative" and the "Material" in Critical Theory: Horkheimer, Adorno, Marcuse, and Benjamin

[227] Within the broad tradition that we can describe as "Western Marxism"—initiated by Lukács[162] and Korsch[163]—the Frankfurt school is critical, a direct predecessor of the philosophy of liberation, which developed in the heart of the crisis of late Modernity within capitalism's central core. Horkheimer wrote shortly before his death (1972), in the prologue to Martin Jay's book on the Frankfurt school, about the underlying intentions of that first group of young Jewish[164] critical intellectuals: "Their enterprise was only successful because of the help provided by Hermann Weil and the intervention of his son Felix,[165] which resulted in the gathering together of a group interested in social theory and with varied academic backgrounds, convinced that the formulation of the *negative* in an era of transition was more meaningful than their academic careers. What most united them was their emphasis on *a critical perspective on existing society*."[166] These lines reflect the defining characteristic of the thought of the members of the Institute of Social Research in 1923: the negativity[167] of social criticism.[168] To this we must add, from Martin Jay: "To appeal to an *entity outside of this world* [*ein ganz Anderes*] had an original philosophical-social impetus. It led finally to a more *positive* assessment of certain metaphysical tendencies, because the *empirical whole is a nontruth* (Adorno). *The hope* that the horror of this world would not have the last word is certainly a nonscientific wish."[169]

This means that from the perspective of the victims an ambit of exteriority[170] is opened up that situates the totality of the world as a "nontruth." In effect, between Marx and the Frankfurt school we have the Bolshevik Revolution (and its Stalinist failure), the sociohistorical works of Max Weber and the philosophy of Lukács (read under the influence of Heidegger, and criticized), to which we must add Sigmund Freud[171] and the social revolution in Germany of 1918 and 1919, in which several members of the school's founding circle participated. The group was a secular community of thinkers of Jewish origin, at the beginning very close to German social democracy and to the country's nascent Communist Party. They were philosophers and social scientists connected with social actors (the victims who are the point of departure for their thought: the educated and critical German Jewish community and the German proletariat, which was engaged in the process of "integration") who were able to discover a common enemy (in the "dominant social relations":[172] authoritarian family relations, industrial instrumental capitalist society, and later, German Nazism), but for whom it was difficult to affirm a truly liberatory sense of history—precisely because of the ambiguity of the "social subject" to which they were most closely linked before their exile (1933) and after the return of some of them to Germany, after the war (1946). This small group of researchers was able to maintain its financial autonomy for more than two decades—which granted them a certain space of critical independence, but, perhaps, on the other hand, implied the absence of a concrete social commitment.[173] The return of some members of the group gave the school a deserved prestige. Marcuse, who initially remained in California, became the theoretician of the New Left, of the movements of '68. Latin America's philosophy of liberation—and my own book *Towards an Ethics of Latin American Liberation* (the first volumes of which appeared in 1970)—is indebted to them for some initial philosophical suspicions: they enabled me to politicize ontology,[174] but, from the beginning, I found a lack of *positivity* in their work, an insufficiently clear *exteriority*, as we shall see below.

[228] The question posed by the members of the Frankfurt school was not so much how to elaborate a *positive* theory of society, that could at the same time be critical, but rather more precisely, how does one exercise, or what are the conditions necessary for, a theoretical, interdisciplinary *negative critique* of society, and in order to achieve this, how does one discover how various theories of society could be *criticized*? It was not so much the *content* of the theory at issue that interested me in the first instance (it always matters, nonetheless), but rather above all *how* to undertake this critique (what *method* to use), or what the conditions of possibility were of the *critique* itself. In this way, I understood Marx's *Capital* not primarily as a work of economic theory but above all as a *critique* of political economy.[175] The name given to the Frankfurt school's approach, "critical theory," tends to cause misunderstandings. In reality it is a "theory" about the conditions of possibility of "doing" social criticism. Because of this, I will address at least seven topics relating to this issue of the conditions of possibility of the "criticism" of society and of traditional theories about it: (1) *the point of departure* of the criticism, which is, from the victims; (2) the criticism of the prevailing or dominant *system*; (3) some reflections about *critical reason* itself; (4) the specific kind of *articulation* of critical theory with the "praxis of liberation"—a term coined by Horkheimer, as we shall see; (5) the problem of the *historical social subject* with this critical theory; as well as (6) the *philosophy of history* that this movement presupposes; and last, as a bridge toward the theme of the following section, (7) the structure of the *materiality* and *libidinal negativity* of the whole theme centered on the victims.

[229] I will address these seven topics together in a summary fashion, taking a text by Horkheimer as a guiding thread directly linked to all of these questions.[176] In effect, in 1937, Horkheimer explicitly addressed the

first topic in an essay with the promising title "Traditional Theory and Critical Theory."[177] After describing his understanding of what "traditional theory" is—reviewing the then prevailing state of epistemology from Poincaré to Weber,[178] he arrived at the key moment when he wrote: "What traditional theory permits itself to admit without elaboration as prevailing [*vorhandenen*], its *positive*[179] role in a functioning society . . . [,] is what is questioned by *critical thinking* [*kritischen Denken*]. The goal that this seeks to arrive at, that is, a situation founded in reason,[180] is based upon *present misery* [*Not der Gegenwart*].[181] But this misery does not provide in itself the image of how to surpass it.[182] The theory set forth[183] by critical thinking does not labor in service to an already prevailing reality [*vorhandenen Realität*]:[184] it expresses nothing but its secret."[185] The misery of the victims is thus the point of departure.[186] The victims (misery) cannot be revealed without a previous affirmation of their materiality (understood as their "corporeality" and "content"),[187] which the first Frankfurt school, via Marx and Freud, never lost sight of:[188]

> Through the contradictory movement of historical eras and progressive and reactionary forces, this process [of critical thinking] *preserves, elevates and unfolds human life*.[189] In the given historical forms of society, the excess portion of consumer goods produced . . . directly benefits *only a small group of persons*, and these *conditions of life* [*Lebensverfassung*] are also reflected in thought. . . . Despite the *material* [*materielle*] conveniences provided by class society, each one of its forms was finally revealed to be inadequate. *Slaves, serfs, and citizens*[190] shook off the yoke. . . . [I]n those critical moments[191] the desperation of the masses was decisive at least in passing, penetrating the conciousness,[192] and transforming itself into an objective.[193]

It is evident that the "criticism" Horkheimer spoke of here is different from the mere critique of theory, as, for example, in Kantian philosophy, since this is not sufficient, because "the critical recognition of the categories that *dominate life* [*Leben beherrschenden*] in society also contains their condemnation."[194] As we shall see, Horkheimer defined for himself a complete theoretical task or object. What he made clear at this point is that negative materiality is the point of departure, and that life is the necessary reference in terms of content. Because of this, and this is essential, Horkheimer situated the theme explicitly within the *practical* sphere (but, unfortunately, not yet one that was specifically ethical). In attempting to define the type of rationality and discourse that is constitutive of critical theory *as a critique*, he touched upon everything I have set out systematically to this point (in terms of both material rationality and negativity).[195] Adorno effectively indicated how the point of departure of the critique continued to be present in the system as the epitome of "the dangerous": "That [bourgeois] *rationality* trembles before what persists threateningly just *below the surface of the sphere of its dominion* and which grows proportionately with its own power. . . . This is why it had to displace its origin towards a formal thinking[196] separated from its *content*; this was the only way that it could exercise its *domination* [*Herrschaft*] over *the material*."[197]

[230] The second topic (2), the criticism of the system of domination (system 1 of figure 12), follows an argumentative strategy in which the prevailing system is defined as a totality that becomes an "irrational organism" from which "one must be emancipated":[198] "An action that is directed towards this emancipation,[199] has as its objective the transformation [*Veränderung*][200] of the order,[201] [and] could very well take advantage of the theoretical work[202] as it is carried out within the assumptions of the prevailing reality [*bestehenden Wirklichkeit*]."[203] A first aspect of this is the whole question of the criticism of the prevailing system, the critique of the "ontology"—an ontology which for the Frankfurt school had a pejorative Hegelian and Heideggerian connotation.[204] The "critical-theoretical work" of the "organic intellectual," of the victims, had to employ the best resources of the experts, social scientists, philosophers, and so on, of the system, in order to articulate itself effectively in the process directed by the victims from within. An important percentage of the works produced by the members of the school are testimony to this. The most important is Adorno's *Negative Dialectics*: "This book seeks to free dialectics from its *positive* nature as such, without losing the least bit in terms of its precision."[205]

On the other hand, "the structure of critical behavior, whose purposes go beyond those of dominant social praxis [*herrschenden gesellschaftlichen Praxis*]," confronts the constituted "facts" of the prevailing totality, causing them to lose their "character as mere facticity."[206] And this because "the material [*materielle*] and intellectual activity of man will always have something external [*äusserlich*] to it; that is, nature as the sum of all the factors not yet dominated in each era. . . . But if to this we add the circumstances that depend solely on man himself . . . this exteriority [*Äusserlichkeit*][207] is not only a suprahistorical category . . . but the sign of a lamentable impotence whose acceptance would be antihuman and antirational."[208] Negativity understood now as domination, as exclusion, as the production of the nonincluded (the victims), because of the "fragmented character[209] of the social whole,"[210] which must demand the nonacceptance of that "exteriority"—which will become a critical-ethical principle—as if it were a natural "fact":[211] as, for example, there are always losers in competitions, and this is inevitable (the contrary is empirically impossible) within the paradigm of the total market as identified by Hayek. The issue is a matter of asking oneself if this formal paradigm has not denied the materiality of human life from the beginning as a criterion of truth. It is here where the first Frankfurt school unleashed all of its critical efforts, since an alienating ontology reifies all of its founded, functional, internal, ontic moments. The criticism of the system as "one-dimensional,"[212] the criticism of "instrumental reason,"[213] the critique of positivism,[214] the critical essays on aesthetics and on mass culture at various levels,[215] and especially the criticism of Nazism,[216] are all facets of the same problem: the dominating and massifying oppression *of the prevailing totality*, of the bureaucratized liberal capitalist industrial society, of the culture of Modernity in crisis, which annihilates the possibility of an authentic life for the individual and that of a transformative creativity. All of these "critiques" will have to be taken up again when the need arises for them within the discourse of the ethics of liberation.

[231] On the third topic (3), I must address the kind of rationality that constitutes *critical reason* itself. This "critical reason" is both material and negative in character, and presupposes a prevailing totality, a victim of that totality, and the victim's negative reflection upon this totality. Douglas Kellner, speaking of Marcuse, explains:

> Critical reason is a subversive principle because it submits the existing state of things to the rigors of judgment. Reason demands a *rational order of life* and criticizes the prevailing *irrational conditions* which do not satisfy its demands. The ability of reason to *direct human life and social practice* presupposes that the mind has access to norms and concepts that provide the bases upon which to criticize the existing state of things, as well as the ideal which ought to be brought about in social life. *Critical reason* presupposes an autonomy of the subject and the capacity to uncover *truths* that can transcend and *deny* the given society, with the objective of altering the *irrational* reality until it becomes harmonious with the demands of reason.[217]

Marcuse attempted to discover in the Hegelian vision of the French Revolution what "should make of it [the world] a rational order."[218] "Critical reason" is the rational moment of the "radical act": "The *radical act* conforms to its necessary [*notwendige*] essence,[219] for the act, as well as for the environment within which it is brought to fruition. When this occurs it turns [*wendet*] toward necessity [*Not*], transforming some-thing that has become absolutely *intolerable* and putting in its place that which is necessary [*notwendige*] in itself, that which can subsume [*aufheben*] the intolerable."[220] In any case, for the Frankfurt school, critical reason is dialectical reason at the service of negativity, at a material and practical level, and is clearly distinguished from instrumental reason. Nonetheless, new determinations of this are needed.

Regarding the fourth topic (4), a theory that is critical is one that *articulates* itself to the victims (it is all a question of theory and of praxis),[221] since critical thought knows of the impossibility of absolute knowledge (the thought capable of embracing all of reality), of absolute organization (the state or technique that dominates everything real), or of the absolute market, and this is so because such categories are negated by a *sui generis* "experience [*Erfahrung*]."[222] This "experience" is not that of Hegel in the *Phenomenology of the Spirit*, an experience of the negativity of the sensed object in the process of its involuted ascent toward the Spirit. No. It is "the proletariat [that] *experiences* [*erfährt*]" that contradiction.[223] The point of departure is the "experience" of the victim: "Unemployment, economic crisis, militarization, governments founded upon terror, the general conditions of the masses[224] are all based . . . upon the conditions in which production is carried out."[225] But, and this is something that the ethics of liberation has always understood clearly:[226] "The situation of the proletariat is not a guarantee of adequate [*richtigen*] understanding either. Even if the proletariat experiences in itself the absurdity of *the persistence and increase of misery and injustice*. . . . For the proletariat as well as the world has a surface appearance which is different."[227] This is why it is necessary to accept that the victims themselves, alone, cannot carry out a sufficiently analytical and explanatory criticism against the system (moment 7 in figure 12): "The theoretician, whose activity consists of accelerating developments that might lead to a society without injustice, may find himself in opposition to opinions that prevail, precisely, in the proletariat. If such a possibility of conflict did not exist, theoretical work would be unnecessary. . . . The mission of the *critical theorist* [*kritischen Theoretikers*] is to reduce the discrepancy between his comprehension and that of *oppressed* [*unterdrückten*] humanity for which he thinks."[228] His or her mission is to articulate him- or herself intimately with the very social praxis of the oppressed: "Theory, to the extent that it transforms itself into a real force, as the self-consciousness of the subjects of a great historical revolution, transcends the mentality which is characteristic of dualism. . . . All the theories which emerge should be attributed to the taking up of practical positions."[229] And even more emphatically: "The essential connection of theory with its times does not lie, however, in the correspondence of parts isolated from the construction of history in phases . . . but rather in the continuous transformation of the theoretical judgment of the facts regarding a given society, a judgment which is conditioned by its *conscious relationship with historical praxis*."[230] All of this merits greater exploration in this book's forthcoming chapters. But to leave this theme for now, another, more prescient quote: "A science that, as the expression of some imaginary independence, perceives the formation of praxis, which it serves, and which is inherent to it, as something that is beyond it, and which is satisfied by the separation of thought and action, has already re-nounced its humanity."[231] An erroneous articulation of theory and praxis not only denies the possibility of a *critical* theory, but also denies equally "a *praxis of liberation* [*Praxis der Befreiung*]."[232]

[232] Nonetheless, Horkheimer did not linger long enough to explore how the victims come to ethically discover their negative situation (moments 2 and 3 of our framework).[233] He situated himself—as did Levinas and so many others—in the place, and from the "perspective" of the philosopher-critic, and not properly that of the victim *him- or herself*.[234] How can the victim achieve an everyday form of critical consciousness, which could be *naive* with respect both to critical theory and at the same time to the *origin* and *foundation* of critical theory? In the sixties in Argentina, we used to characterize as "spontaneism" the "attitude of ecstatic veneration of the creative forces of the proletariat,"[235] which undoes the critical intellectual's analytical and dialectical obligations—even though we were criticized for being acritical populists.[236] But, on the other hand, Horkheimer was not conscious either of the possible "vanguardism"—the opposite extreme[237]—into which he fell when he wrote about the need to "confront the proletariat itself in the name of its true interests [*wahren Interessen*]."[238] What are the conditions of possibility for discovering, analyzing, and structuring those "true interests" as a realizable project, in the absence of discursive participation, and of the intersubjectivity that can produce validity, on the part of the victims themselves? As to these matters, was it a lack of concrete experience or an excess of Hegelianism on the part of the Frankfurt school that prevented it from taking the "exteriority of the Other" seriously, and the possibility of constructing a *new project of liberation*[239] from the basis of the victims' transontological reality (reality II)? As can be observed, and taking the expression in its most serious meaning, this is the whole matter of the "truth" (and "validity") of the victim, which puts into question the "untruth"[240] (and "nonvalidity") of the prevailing social system.

[233] But this brings us to the fifth topic (5), regarding the definition of who the *historical social subject* or agent is, to whom the Frankfurt school reattached itself. Perhaps the "sociohistorical subjects" referred to are the response to the following question: "Revolutionary ethics bears witness in this way to the collision and conflict between two historical rights: on one side, the right of that which is existing, the established community upon which the life and perhaps also the happiness of individuals depends; on the other side, the right of that which could be and perhaps should be, because it might be capable of diminishing pain, misery, and injustice."[241] In effect, the new historical subjects emerge as a result of acquiring consciousness of "new rights,"[242] in the name of which the prevailing rights become

perceived as dominating and *illegitimate* in the eyes of the victims whose consciousness has been transformed. My intention here is not to conjure up images of social "subjects" of a metaphysical character, who would exist as some kind of eternal substance. I am referring instead to concrete communities or agents with explicit consciousness of a situation in which they have been dominated. The Frankfurt school discovered some of those to whom it became articulated historically: a community of Jewish revolutionary youth, the European proletariat, citizens dominated by mass culture, all of whom suffered various different kinds of domination analyzed by "critical theory" in its varied dimensions. Nonetheless, either because of Nazi repression, the experiences of exile, or because of the transformations of late capitalism in the postwar period, its possible sociohistorical subjects were gradually "diluted." Even during the period of the first Frankfurt school, Habermas wrote that its "addressees [*Adressaten*]" had been lost: "In the advanced capitalist countries the living standards have risen so much, and among such extensive layers of the population, that the interest in social emancipation can no longer find immediate expression in economic terms. *Alienation* has lost the economically evident form of *misery* [*Elend*]. . . . The proletariat has been dissolved *in terms of its essence* as a proletariat."[243] The ethics of liberation, situating itself among the victims of contemporary history (initially from the perspective of the peripheral world of capitalism in its process of globalization), is proof that, disgracefully, such "misery" is on the increase among billions of human beings, and that therefore such "addressees" exist and constitute the majority of humanity.

[234] With regard to the sixth topic (6), we should ask ourselves: what is the philosophy of history proposed by the Frankfurt school? Or put another way: is some kind of concrete continuity possible among what Benjamin described as "messianic moments," of such a kind that they could be constitutive of a "tradition" in sociohistorical terms? Does an authentic history of liberatory acts have any meaning? Or, even, does all of the praxis of liberation end up being nothing but a sublime but always tragic story of defeated messianic pessimism? Was Habermas correct when he wrote: "Benjamin's antievolutionist concept . . . is very pessimistic when it comes to judging the probability that these kinds of isolated incursions that undermine the *constant recycling of the same* could somehow join together into *a tradition* and not just fall into oblivion."[244] Walter Benjamin in effect conceived of history as traversed by two "arrows"[245] in permanent tension with each other. The first is that of "historical time"—that of everyday life: continuous, empty, quantifiable, the "eternal recycling of the same [*das Immerwiedergleiche*]," that of mere survival, of reproduction, of law and myth, of the system's domination, that supposedly tends "towards [ultimate] happiness."[246] The second arrow that cuts across this "profane

order"[247] is that of "messianic time" that erupts and "leaps" in the form of the new, like creation and redemption.[248] In his "Theses on the Philosophy of History" Benjamin enigmatically wrote that "the first [kind of time] has no theoretical armor. Its procedure is additive. It provides a mass of facts that fill up the homogenous and empty spaces of time."[249]

This is the time characteristic of the prevailing system.[250] Within it arises "progress," whose mystification has been promoted not just by the bourgeoisie but by social democrats (and even common Marxists): "Advances in the domination of nature are recognized, but not the regressions in society. The technocratic features that we find later in fascism are already evident here.[251] Progress, as characterized in the minds of social democrats, was in the first place the advance of humanity itself. . . . In the second place it was an unending progress. . . . In the third place, it was essentially always advancing."[252]

Benjamin's critical thought flowed from the presupposition of a *prevailing system* in order to deny it from the standpoint of its victims,[253] which would enable him to move on to a complete reinterpretation of history: "The class that struggles, that is reduced to submission, is the *subject itself* of historical knowledge. In Marx it appears as the last class to be enslaved, as the avenging class that will carry to its conclusion *the labor of liberation in the name of all the vanquished generations*."[254] This "subject" that struggles does so "because it has been disgraced by the suffering it has endured";[255] it feels pain because its life has been seized as "booty" by the victors: "Those who have been victorious up to the present march in the triumphant procession in which today's rulers tread over the [corpses] of those who now lie buried in the earth."[256] To reconstruct history from among the vanquished "means to appropriate a *memory* just as it flashes in the instant of danger. Historical materialism[257] has the duty of fixing an image of the past exactly as it presents itself in an improvised manner to the historical subject at the moment of danger.[258] The tradition[259] *of the oppressed* teaches us that the rule is the *state of exception* in which we live."[260]

When the victim becomes concious[261] is when the discontinuous erupts into the repetitive history of the same; this is messianic time: "The consciousness of causing the continuum of history to jump is characteristic of revolutionary classes at the moment of their action. The great [French] Revolution introduced a new calendar.[262] . . . The Time-Now [*Jetztzeit*],[263] which like a model of messianic time summarizes the history of all humanity in an enormous abbreviation, coincides in capillary fashion with the figure which that history composes in the universe";[264] "It is a tiger's leap into the past.[265] . . . Within this structure it recognizes the tell-tale sign of a messianic blockage of what is to come next, or put another way: of a revolutionary conjuncture in the struggle in favor of the oppressed past."[266] The victim who becomes conscious, who erupts with a revolutionary praxis, produces a rupture of "continuous time." He or she erupts "remembering" (the liberatory "anamnesis"), "commemorating"[267] other liberatory-messianic moments of past history. Benjamin insists a great deal on this critical reconstruction of history:[268] "Only a humanity which has been redeemed can find an adequate and opportune fit for its history";[269] "I have turned my face towards the past. Where we see a chain of facts, he sees one ongoing catastrophe that tirelessly piles ruin over ruin, dumped at his feet";[270] "History is the object of a construction whose place is not constituted by homogenous empty time, but *a time which is full, the Time-Now [Jetztzeit]*";[271] "Historicism affirms the eternal image of the past; the historical materialist instead affirms an *experience* which with him is unique. . . . He is man enough to make the *continuum* of history *jump.*"[272]

This strong sense of time, of the moment when the victims become conscious, of the collaboration of "organic intellectuals"—as Gramsci would express it—of the deconstructive and constructive praxis of liberation, is messianic time as something new, as "development," "as each second was for him the small door through which the Messiah might enter."[273] The critical historical reinterpretation or anamnesis, is "memory," is the recollection of struggles, because "the Messiah comes not only as a redeemer, but as the one who vanquishes the Anti-Christ":[274] there is a struggle against the prevailing order inherent here. In any case, Benjamin would never clarify exactly how "messianic time" becomes transformed into "*historical* time" of the messianic community or movement itself—is this impossible or contradictory?

[235] In the same manner, in distant[275] California, two philosophers exiled from Nazism engaged in a dramatic dialogue (of an apparently pessimistic character) regarding the results of the theoretical revolution of the *Aufklärung* (Enlightenment). Our ears, accustomed to exile, seem to hear the song of Ernesto Cardenal, a sufferer from Central America in the background:

> By the rivers of Babylon
> There we sat down
> And there we wept
> As we remembered Zion.
> Looking at the skyscrapers of Babylon . . .
> A Babel armed with Bombs. Devastating!
> Blessed are those who take your children
> —the creatures of your laboratories—
> and smash them against the rocks![276]

The dialogue between Horkheimer and Adorno is not *only* (although it is certainly also) a *text* or an argument, but it is also a cry, a protest, and an exercise of critical-ethical reason at the philosophical level. This led Habermas to the need to warn that the "reader should not let himself be seduced by the rhetorical character of the exposition."[277] This warning could lead us to believe that the text is a matter of "pure" rhetoric. Because of this I must demonstrate the *rational argument* at the core of this exchange between the two philosopher-critics I am commenting upon here.

[236] The initial question is: Who is the victim to whom the argument is connected? It is from this *con-text* that the exchange must be "read." Its subject matter is the suffering of the "concentration camps," which permits the conclusion that "the Enlightenment is totalitarian [*Aufklärung ist totalitär*]"[278]—this sounds strange to the ears of Erhard's Germany, but is acceptable today to the ears of a Nicaraguan, of the black Africans of South Africa, of the Palestinians in the Israeli-occupied territories,[279] or of the *homeless* in New Delhi . . . or New York. It is a *rational*[280] criticism that tends to underline the most *negative* aspects of the "prevailing system," not exclusively because of pessimism, but rather in order to criticize the irresponsible optimism of those who considered only the most positive aspects of modern reason—which would be precisely the tendency of the "second" Frankfurt school.[281]

Critical reason, with its claim of universality, proceeded to carry out its criticism of the philosophy of history of the Enlightenment; a merciless critique of modern quantitative "progress" and of bourgeois "instrumental reason." As Horkheimer and Adorno wrote, refuting Kant: "The Enlightenment [*Aufklärung*], in the broadest sense of a thought in continuous *progress*, has always pursued the objective of freeing human beings from fear and converting them into dominators [*Herren*]. But the whole illuminated [*aufgeklärte*] Earth shines under the sign of a triumphant misadventure."[282] How could we summarize *with clarity* the astonishing *rational argument* of these critical philosophers? I think there is an Ariadne's thread available, and it is that which was indicated in the "critical model" that I proposed above (figure 12). In effect, in the origin of all this is the negation of "life," now reduced and repressed under a pathological, fetishistic, suicidal totality:[283] "By means of the subordination of *all life* to the demands of its preservation [*Erhaltung*], the minority which commands guarantees the *survival* [*Fortbestand*] of all, together with its own *security* [*Sicherheit*]."[284] The "originary negation" of the victims (moment 1 of our figure) is a necessary condition for the "self-preservation [*Selbsterhaltung*]" of the system as a disciplined negation (a reflection inspired by, and correcting[285] the tradition of Schopenhauer,[286] above all as interpreted by Freud) of pleasure, of hedonism, of life. The "civilizatory system" as such produces an inevitable contradiction—made necessary in all cultures—between what I will describe here as the "instincts of reproduction"—which in the face of the horrors of death and war, and in order to distance ourselves from them, produce the institutions that "repress" life[287]—and the "instincts of pleasure" — that permit us to confront pain and death in order to achieve happiness, but which can endanger "security." For Horkheimer and Adorno, "enlightened reason" was the pathological, mythical, and *reductionist expression* of the base instincts that ensure the survival of the system. The reduction of *all reason* to one which is *merely reproductive* of itself, or to an "instrumental reason" that is positivist, antiethical, metaphysical, and formalist, is the philosophical justification of terror:

> (a) *Conatus esse conservandi primum et unicum virtutis est fundamentum*[288] constitutes the true motto of all Western civilization. . . . (b) Whoever confides in life [*Leben*] directly, without a *rational* [*rationale*] relationship with *self-preservation* [*Selbsterhaltung*], falls back again into the prehistoric era according to the judgment of the Enlightenment and of Protestantism. . . . (c) But the more the process of *self-preservation* is carried out through the bourgeois division of labor, the more such progress demands the *self-alienation* [*Selbstentäusserung*] of the individuals affected, who must then adapt themselves in body and soul to the demands of a technical apparatus. . . . (e) Positivism, in sum, which has not come to a stop even in the face of the most cerebral thing that could be imagined — thought — has even corralled the last intermediary instance between individual action and the social norm. . . . (f) The exclusivity of the logical laws derived from this uniqueness of function, in the final instance of the *coercive character* [*Zwangscharakter*] *of self-preservation*, which (g) always culminates again in the choice between *survival* [*Ueberleben*] and *decadence* [*Untergang*].[289]

This text sets forth all of the rational argumentation laid out in the entire work, a reasoning that I have divided into seven parts in order to make some brief comments.

[237] In effect, (a) extrapolates from Spinoza's venerable expression "*conatus esse conservandi*"[290] — the Aristotelian *boulesis*, the medieval *intentio*, or the Heidegerrian *Sorge* — the ontological moment *par excellence*, love of being as the "*fundamentum*" (the Hegelian *Grund*), as the *negative* of the West.[291] This *conatus* or impulse (drive, instinct) toward the *fundamentum* of the totalized totality, of the prevailing system, brings about the (en)closure of life as a necessary correlation to the mere "self-preservation" *of the system*. It is *necessary, but not sufficient* to preserve the system. The bare "preservation" of the system — without creativity, growth, or development of human life in general — is that of "the society in which we live *as a necessary evil* [*das schlechte Bestehende*]."[292] "Instrumental reason" is the reason that *controls* (*manages*) this *conatus esse conservandi*. This is how Horkheimer wrote about this in the *Critique of Instrumental Reason*: "This species of reason can be described as a reason which is subjective. It is a reason concerned essentially with means and ends."[293]

But there was for Horkheimer a material reason as well, which has to do

with human life (and which had been overlooked by Habermas and Apel):
"An objective theory of reason. This aspired to the development of a vast
system or hierarchy of everything that exists, including man and his ends.
The *kind of rationality of the life* of a man could be determined according
to its degree of harmony with this totality. . . . This concept of reason *did
not ever exclude subjective reason* but considered it to be a limited and partial expression of a wider rationality, vaster, from which could be deduced
criteria which could be applied to all things *and to all living beings*."[294] We
have come a long way from irrationalism. But the critique of instrumental
reason must begin with the assumption of the burden of an ethical-material
and negative reason. Discursive reason is also necessary, but at another
level, and if it forgets about the level of practical-material reason it becomes
complicit with the system that dominates and which is therefore no longer
critical, which is exactly what has happened.

[238] This is why (b), whoever addresses the issue of the relationship
between material reason and life, beyond the bounds of the mere self-
preservation of the system,[295] is judged to be premodern or Nazi in character. Analytical positivism and philosophical linguistics frequently deny
(criticize) critical reason because it is ethical, metaphysical, "holistic," and
so on. This is how they become capable of justifying terror. We must instead
defend life from the standpoint of universal critical reason and on behalf of
the victims.

The pleasure (c) of attempting to surpass happiness, of putting one's security at risk in order to create something new, is thus negated.[296] The material
reason that is capable of considering the relationship between the ends of
formal action and the reproduction of the life of all (not just that of the
purely performative system) is negated as enunciating "value judgments"
merely, reflecting nonscientific and nonrational tastes; pure emotion, sentiment, prehistory. In this way the self-preservation of the system kills.

This kind of self-preservation (d) is not a philosophical product. It is the
fruit of the bourgeois system, which "rationalizes" and disciplines the body
for this "self-preservation process" (of capital, Marx would say) as a result
of the division of labor, which produces "alienation"—that of living labor in
Marx, of values in Nietzsche—of the drives discovered by Freud, and so on.

Formalism (e), which is positivist-philosophical in character but found
equally in other fields of knowledge (such as Hayek's neoliberalism), is the
rational instrumental management that marks out an "abstract horizon"
(for example, Tarski's "language L"; or the capital that attributes value to
capital by taking the worker as its fetishized measure) and confuses it with
the reality of life, constituting it as a "system" (in the style of Luhmann):
"The Enlightenment gives a priori recognition as matters of being and becoming only to those things which can be reduced to a single unit: its ideal

is the system, from which everything and anything can be deduced."[297] In this way, "individual action and the social norm" are disarticulated. It becomes a matter of a formal solipsism, without content (f), or any criterion other than the normativeness of its practical enunciations. Nothing remains but Weberian relativism (or its Habermasian equivalent if our emphasis is on "contents") with the rightness claim regarding values imposed, on the other hand, by the "coercive character of self-preservation," of the security of the system of domination, in sum, of the elite.

The calculating reason (g) has at its end the sole criterion of the "survival and decline" of the prevailing system, and immolates both nature and humanity in its name, in a suicidal manner. Its vision is quasi-tragic, but if it does not confront the looming crisis with a variety of realism that is apparently pessimistic, it can fall into an optimism that is complicit with the claim of "fulfilling Modernity" without having criticized it first, or of negating only from the standpoint of an irrationalism that does not awaken any hope in the victims, nor any rational possibility of justifying their own praxis of liberation (which, as we shall see, is the postmodern position presciently denied by Horkheimer and Adorno).

[239] This opens up for us, finally, and as a transition to the next section, the seventh topic to which I have dedicated continuous attention (7):[298] the victims are revealed from the standpoint of their material libidinal corporeality—since this critique negates the system for its repressive character with respect to the materiality of the victims—which makes it necessary to undertake a criticism of the repressive asceticism of bourgeois morality. Adorno himself came to write:

> The somatic component brings back to one's awareness the fact that pain should not be and must be transformed. *Suffering is something transitory.* The point at which the *specifically materialist* [*Materialistische*] and the *critical* [*Kritische*] converge is the praxis[299] that transforms society: to suppress suffering or alleviate it. . . . All of the actions of the species refer to physical preservation. . . . [T]he dispositions with which society rushes headlong towards its annihilation, are at the same time absurd[300] and twisted efforts at self-preservation and directed unconsciously against suffering.[301] . . . The *telos* of the new [social] organization is the negation of physical suffering in every single one of its members.[302]

This demanded a return to Freud. The Frankfurt school would incorporate his somatic-drive or pulsatory approach to this kind of critique. Marcuse's conclusion in *Eros and Civilization* is similar to that of Adorno: "It is not those who die, but those who die before they ought to and wish to, those who die in agony and pain, who are an accusing cry against civilization. . . . A human being can die without anguish if he or she knows that what they love is protected from misery and oblivion."[303] In effect, the turn toward Freudian psychoanalysis, which was eminently critical,[304] was necessary in order to be able to handle the materiality of the victims' subjectivity. If we were "souls" there would be no critical thinking, and no injustices, nor victims. The repressed bodily reality of the labor alienated by capital, as Marx explained it, is the same "bodily reality" now repressed by a superego that alienates the drive (*Trieben*) of the libidinal structure under the *imago Patris* analyzed by Freud in the context of the bourgeois authoritarian family.[305] Horkheimer exhorted the members of the Institute for Social Research to explore the dialogue between the works of Marx and Freud, as in his work "Egoism and the Liberation Movement."[306] But the crisis with Fromm produced an internal controversy. Only Marcuse's *Eros and Civilization*[307] explored the question within the critical horizon of the Frankfurt school, and against "revisionist" approaches such as that of Fromm,[308] and as a criticism of the unflinching notion of the bourgeois personality. In this book, Marcuse creatively reworked his youthful reflections on hedonism,[309] and managed to preserve the "critical" sense of psychoanalysis, demonstrating that Freud maintained an irresolvable contradiction between a repressive civilizing process (expressed first in the reality principle and later in the death principle), and the libido, which is motivated by the pleasure principle: "The hypothesis of the death instinct and its role in civilized aggression sheds light on one of the most neglected enigmas of civilization: it reveals the hidden unconscious link which binds the *oppressed* to their oppressors, *soldiers* to generals, and *individuals* to their masters. The total destructions which marked the progress of civilization had their abolition dangling in front of them, and were marked by the instinctive consent to the executioners provided by their *instruments and human victims*."[310]

[240] If the civilizational reality principle presupposes a certain degree of repression of the libido (as the disciplined postponement of desire to permit the diversion of energy into labor), as a "principle of activity"[311] in each historical system, the surplus labor that produces surplus value in capitalism also produces with it a "surplus repression." In ontogenetic and filogenetic terms, this "surplus repression" is handled by means of the internal projection of the "superego," which is imposed imperatively through punishment (understood as the learned anticipation of pain in order to avoid death) and guilt (as the self-responsible memory of that pain), and as moral norms that repress the "surplus" libido generated by the historical system of domination. All of this provides us with a philosophical-ethical material that has no substitute: "The primary instincts refer to life and death[312]— that is, to organic matter as such. And they also bring organic and inorganic matter back together again, and later with the highest level of mental manifestations. In other words . . . this unity has ontological implications."[313]

Civilization inhibits these sexual and aggressive primary instincts, as a regression toward death (the Nirvana principle).[314] It is from this position that Marcuse formulates his judgment regarding the decline of Western culture, which begins when Plato conceives of *lógos* as the domination of the instincts,[315] a tradition that culminates in Hegel: "The ego comes to be free, but if the world has the *character of negation*, the liberation of the ego depends on its *recognition and acceptance* as the master—and that recognition can only be accorded by another ego, another self-conscious subject. . . . The aggressive attitude towards other subjects: the satisfaction of the ego is conditioned by its *negative relationship* with another ego."[316] The possibility of liberation is played out in the opening left us by the "established reality principle" by means of fantasy (imagination) and of utopia such as the "great rejection":[317] the aesthetic dimension provided by the transformation of sexuality into *éros*.[318] Marcuse closes with a quote from a text by Benjamin: "The conscious desire to break with the continuity of history belongs to the revolutionary classes at the moment of acting."[319]

[241] In any case we will see in §4.3 how Marx asked himself, against Ricardo and Rodbertus, whether the question for him in the "theory of rent" was, how to save the "law of value" (since both thought it inapplicable to the case,[320] and with this for Marx all of the economy became irrational). In the same way, I will seek to demonstrate how an ethics of liberation cannot affirm a "death principle" as the original constitutive criterion of human libido (as Freud and Marcuse claim) *as such*,[321] since the "life principle" can provide a foundation for all of the moments of that libido, and the drive structure that is needed (although fragmented and always in tension, in a contradiction that is unsurpassable but manageable[322]), in reference to the reproduction and development of the individual and historical life (in both economic and cultural terms) of the human subject. I believe that, in light of the interpretative hypotheses that I have relied upon (the moments indicated in figure 12), some texts that are very complex and sometimes opaque have been clarified somewhat; at least this has been my hope. In conclusion, I could still cite from one of Horkheimer's last texts: "Critical theory . . . has no specific instance but the interest . . . in the suppression of social *injustice*. This *negative* formulation constitutes, when taken to the level of an abstract expression, the *materialist content [materialistische Inhalt]* of the ideal concept of reason. In a historical period like the one we are living in true[323] theory is not so much *affirmative* as *critical*."[324] This is, explicitly, the science, philosophy, and critical ethics, or ethics of liberation, that I propose to develop on a global scale, articulated clearly and analytically to "subjects," some of whom are longstanding and others who are emerging before our critical eyes, and who will certainly disappear once their historic moment has passed.

§4.3. The Dialectics of Drive

[242] Now I must address fully what has been thought "opaque," what is apparently "other" than reason, and constitutive of the libidinal material base (the fiery horses of which Plato spoke) that motivate and above which reason (the Auriga) moves. My project here, far from that of irrationalism, is that of a *practical material critical reason* (already set forth *positively* in chapter 1 and in §§4.1 and 4.2 of this book), and which is exercised in a manner that takes into account the ethical principle of the demands of the reproduction and development[325] of the life of the human subject. I have explored the mystical depths of human history where the original Egyptian deity Ptah brought about Creation through the intermediation of Horus (the "heart") and Thot (the "word").[326] For his part, Plato emphasized the importance of love for the Good. Aristotle meanwhile defined the human being as "a living being [*zoón*] who possessed *lógon*"; in such a way that reason (*lógos*) emerged from within the horizon of the living being, of "life," and as an internal moment.[327] The entire period of the Latin-German Middle Ages was traversed by intellectualist currents (Dominicans such as Thomas Aquinas) and voluntarists (Franciscans such as Duns Scotus).

In order for an ethics of liberation to be workable it must integrate both of these levels in such a way that the *materiality of the drives* is articulated with material rationality (which is the question of "practical truth"), discursive formality (the intersubjective "validity"), and the "feasibility" and "negativity" of instrumental and practical critical reason. In effect, now we will immerse ourselves in the tradition that opens up a horizontal category of drives that is affective and erotic, to the minimum but necessary degree that will help us better understand this "material" aspect of critical ethics. From the beginning, I address the ontological effort of Schopenhauer's "will to live," which later divides into the repressive reproductive faculty of happiness associated with Apollo and the Dionysian faculty of creative pleasure in Nietzsche. I approach Schopenhauer here, understanding his effort to be an ontological criticism of the axiology of culture (Nietzsche), and seeking culmination in the instincts of self-preservation submitted to the dominion of the death principle, which exercise their own power over the hedonistic instincts or pleasure principle within the framework of the subjectification of cultural institutions (Freud).

a. The "Will to Live" in Schopenhauer

[243] The nonidentical character of being and thought in Hegel (and his disciples) is the condition that makes possible a criticism in the strongest sense (the material is never solely that which is thought of, and the nega-

tion of the being [of the prevailing system] presupposes that being is not the ultimate reality, since from beyond the being it is possible to discover the reality of the victim). Let us begin, then, our path through all this with Schopenhauer, who although he denied his Hegelian origins, nonetheless proposed a new ontological identity: being as will.[328] In truth, for the tormented anti-Hegelian thinker victims are all those living beings who find the origins of suffering and pain (the central concern of Buddhism) in their own bodily realities, and who suffer because of their frustrated "will to live," which in the final analysis is the egotism correspondent to the *principium individuationis*. In his first writings, Schopenhauer indicated that the "cognitive ego is incapable of knowing itself,"[329] but is capable of knowing "desire" itself[330] by means of a kind of "intellectual intuition,"[331] in a process of introspection "into" its own corporeality (until it arrives at the "thing in itself" beyond the "world as representation"): "True criticism must limit the *most conscious part*[332] of empirical consciousness. . . . This is how humanity can obtain its highest level of self-consciousness, and thereby attain the golden age of philosophy and fulfill the imperative of the temple at Delphos: *gnothi seautón* [*know thyself*]."[333] It is necessary to go beyond the "surface appearance" of empirical consciousness (the Platonic *dóxa*, Hinduist *maya*, or the Kantian "pure appearance [*reinen Schein*]")[334] toward an ontological order. The "will" is the "thing-in-itself," the "*realissimum*": "When we seek to attribute to the world of body [*Körperwelt*], which we know by means of the maximum representation of reality [*Realität*], we attribute the reality to it which is characteristic for each of our bodies, since it is the most concrete reality that we know of. . . . But if the world of body is to be something more [*etwas mehr*] than our mere representation of it, we must agree that beyond [*ausser*] our representation of it, it exists in itself and in terms of its own intimate essence, the same way we can immediately find it within ourselves in terms of our *will* [*Willen*]."[335]

[244] This "will" is "sensed" intuitively in the pain of one's own body as the negative expression of pure "blind love," where solidarity with all of the cosmos (beyond the "world as representation," beyond the subject-object of knowledge[336] is nonetheless "experienced." Schopenhauer indicated the relationship between will and life: "Where there is will [*Willen*] there is life [*Leben*]. It therefore follows that the will to live [*Willen zum Leben*] always has a life assured with it, and while it lights the fire within us our existence is assured."[337] The "will to live" (the *conatus essendi* of Spinoza) is the being that moves from the cosmic to the bodily levels of reality (a part of that cosmos, which as a differentiation of the "*objectification of the will* [*Objektivierung des Willens*]"), which has been put into multiplicity by the *principium individuationis*. This individualizing "desire" is what produces pain and suffering due to the unpleasantness and tedium of the repetition of the

same, or the fear-inducing risk of losing, in day-to-day existence, what one desires, an infinite and contradictory dispersion,[338] given the impossibility of ever satiating the infinite desire of the will.[339] Egotism[340] is thus the ontological tendency of "individuality" as the "will to live," of preserving life. The state, thanks to its powers of "punishment," can externally discipline this natural evil.[341]

"Compassion [*Mitleid*]" in the face of the suffering of others is an ethical attitude, capable of surpassing that of egotism, and can be expressed either as justice or as "philanthropy [*Menschenliebe*]." But it must be understood that this "compassion" is nothing but the understanding that the alien Other is nothing of the kind: "Multiplicity and division are associated only with the simple phenomenon in itself; and it is oneself and the same being which manifests itself in everything which lives. [. . . This] constitutes the very essence of the phenomenon of compassion. . . . . This would be, then, the metaphysical basis of ethics, and means that an individual would be capable of recognizing him or herself directly in another, as if the other were his or her true self."[342] "Compassion" enables us to free ourselves from suffering. But isn't it impossible to avoid pain as such? Schopenhauer tried to show us the way: "to deny our will"; to overcome the "will to live" by means of the *self-repression of the will* (*Selbstaufhebung des Willens*), by means of a *contemplative life*. This can be done in two ways: through aesthetic ecstasy,[343] or through the saintliness of the ascetic that Schopenhauer never sought to emulate in his own life; this last option permits a definitive escape through the attainment of the state of Nirvana,[344] which enables one to reach eternal peace.

Nevertheless the generalized state of most vulgar human beings trapped in *maya* is tragic, painful, and without easy exits. Schopenhauer's philosophy of history is absolutely pessimistic and negative, but characterized by an ontological negativity that is regressive, involutionist, quietistic, and conformist—his thought has the surface appearance of being critical but in fact is nothing but a superficial criticism that in the end does not touch the reality of the origin of the pain that is the product of the ethical evil at issue. Schopenhauer's pessimism is salvageable in part in the face of the optimisms[345] of "progress" characteristic of the Modernity that dominates us (that of its capitalist "centers" and oppressor classes), but it would be important to distinguish his particular brand of pessimism from that which justifies the domination of the historical victims by situating the evil, the pain, and the misery of their bodily realities at an ontological level that is a preethical given.

As a result of this kind of logic, the victims of this historical stage of domination are immobilized in the face of a supposedly inevitable pain, unable to negate the injustice and the suffering that are in fact the products of human actions and institutions. This is so because by failing to distinguish between *ontological pain*, which is the reflection of natural conditions (a virus that invades the body, an unexpected earthquake, or death), and the suffering that is an effect of human actions and institutions,[346] this kind of pessimistic thinking dehistoricizes and ontologizes such actions, institutions, and their consequences, thereby acting as a terrifying ideological machinery. The apparent critic has become reactionary.

b. The "Will to Power" in Friedrich Nietzsche

[245] Nietzsche[347] transforms Schopenhauer's "world as representation"—which was abstract and stuck at the level of the constitution of the theoretical object—into an ahistorical world that is divided up between and ruled by Apollonian reproductive instincts, on the one hand, and the Dionysian creative instincts, on the other. Nietzsche opposes Hegel and the German academics (from Winckelmann and the Romantics onward, as we shall see), who interpreted the reconciliation between "being" and "appearance" as the essential note of "classical Greek" thought. For the young Nietzsche, "the tragic" (before and superior to the "Socratic rationalization") had its origin in Dionysian vitality, as an affirmation of plural "appearance" without any claim of unity, and from the perspective of the pain of the tragic hero: "It is an indisputable tradition that Greek tragic theater in its most ancient form had as a single focus the suffering of Dionysus and that during a long period of its existence, the only hero on stage was in fact Dionysus."[348] To free the expression of the Dionysian spirit is to unleash creativity, life, diversity. To deny the Dionysian is to take the path of Apollo, to dissolve appearances in the "unity of reason" as understood by Socrates. The path associated with Apollo is the disciplinary world of the ascetic-repressive values of Hellenistic culture, later inherited by that of the Semitic-Christian and Germanic-Modern (the "truth") worlds. The later Nietzsche transformed the Dionysian into the category of the "human-being-who-transcends-himself [*Übermensch*]": Zarathustra (Nietzsche) who positions himself as the Anti-Christ opposite, no longer the Socrates of philosophy, but the masochistic[349] "Christ."[350] By employing a "genealogical method" he discovers four possible levels of criticism: the criticism of ethics, of religion, of philosophy (as naive "metaphysics"), and of art (though no longer of music, after his distancing from Wagner).

Nietzsche discovers that the ultimate motivation of *morality* is the instinctive-egotistical search for happiness,[351] which is sublimated in altruistic moral acts of a hierarchical and ascetic character, which are valued and disciplined according to either the Socratic-Platonic rationalized system of violence or that of Christian masochism, and finally that of the functionality of modern society. Consider for example the opposition between "pleasure" and "happiness":

> The cause of pleasure is not the satisfaction of the will . . . but the fact that the will seeks to advance [*vorwärts*]. . . . The idea of someone who is happy [*Glückliche*] is an idea characteristic of a herd of sheep.[352] We have to separate out two different forms of pleasure [*Lustarten*]: that of anesthetizing ourselves into sleep [happiness] and that of victory [pleasure itself]. Those exhausted want rest, yawns, peace, silence: this is the kind of *happiness* offered by religions and by nihilist philosophies.[353] A human being in the face of a prehuman represents a great deal of power, not an increase in happiness. How can anyone suggest that I have ever aspired to happiness?[354]

For Nietzsche, Western *metaphysics* (in its negative sense, as for Heidegger), with its central ideas (the soul, the "self," freedom, and God),[355] has arisen as a product of the search for *security* and for *fear of death*: it expresses base instincts of survival.[356] Those who control the system *ensure safety* for themselves, in fear of pain (by means of the threat of "punishment") and of death, protected by a violent order erected in the name of justice, law, and civilization (see also figure 13).

[246] In such a situation, *art* is the only alternative left, which, although it frequently falls into the system of *rationalization*, still contains a Dionysian possibility within: "In such communities, *intellectual progress* is dependent upon individuals who are disconnected from each other, and who are much more insecure and morally weaker [*moralisch-schwächeren*]; these are the men who try out new things and, in general, seek variety.[357] *Pleasure* is a sentiment of power (which presupposes displeasure). . . . Pain is implicit in every *pleasure* [. . . and] the will to create, to assimilate, etc."[358] This is to say that the base reproductive instincts,[359] which distance pain and death with the force of a "phobia," mnemonically repeat through the social and historical institutions the norms, acts, and ethical systems that have been successful at *avoiding pain*. For Nietzsche, it is this avoidance and this happiness which is perverse, boring, and cowardly. It is worth noting here that the *apátheia* of the Stoics and the *ataraxia* of the Epicureans, as well as the masochism of the Nietzschean "Christ" respond to this definition of happiness. The instincts of pleasure[360] confront pain and death in order to attain that which is strongly desired (sexual, political, artistic, creative desires, etc.). Paradoxically, by reaching for the desired through pleasure one must run the risk of confronting the possibility of pain, by exceeding the bounds of the norm, by placing oneself in danger, everything that enables one to confront suffering and even death, all of which in fact spurs the "development"[361] of life. This is why "the point of view grounded in value [*Wert*] is the point of view that involves conditions of

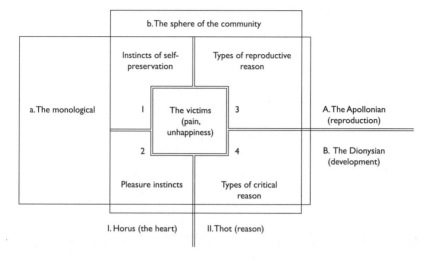

Figure 13. Articulations of the pulsational and rational dimensions in the life of the human subject.

NOTE: See thesis 17 in appendix 2. Any kind of unilaterality that claims exclusive primacy over other moments falls into various different kinds of pathology. For example, egoism is the prioritization of a (the monological individual) over b (the community), in its extreme form in the prioritization of 1a over 1b; (also over 2, 3a, and 4: negatively, the traditional "slavery" to one's passions; positively, Nietzsche's inversion, which privileges 2 over 3 in general). Rationalism is the exclusive prioritization of II over I. *Civilizational surplus-repression* is the prioritization of 3b over 2a (in one of its possible dimensions; there is also exclusionary prioritization over 3a and 3b [acritical conservatism]). *Anarchism* is the exclusionary prioritization of 2–4 over 1–3. Habermasian *discursive reason* is situated only at 3 (I also propose a variant of critical discursive reason in 4b). Evidently Nietzsche defends the exclusionary priority of B (principally 2) over A (principally 3). Kant is situated almost exclusively at 3. Utilitarianism confuses 1 with 2 (happiness with pleasure). For its part, the reference to the pain of a victim (a) or of a group (b) sets into motion the totality of these dimensions (principally but not exclusively from 4). In this way, the "suffering" of a woman in a sexist society defies the sexist-pulsational 2 (a and b), the sexist-pulsational 1 (a and b), and the sexist-ideological 3 (a and b), and sets into motion all of the moments charted here so that they can reconstitute themselves in relation to the possibility of overcoming the negativity in the victim. For example, in 2 the male must transform his sadistic sexuality so that he can achieve a mutually pleasurable symmetry whose point of departure is the recognition of the dignity of the other sexual subject, and so on. The wealth of possible references becomes apparent when it is understood that each dimension represented is *necessary but not sufficient.*

preservation and growth with regard to complex structures of varying duration in the life that is becoming."[362] If we take account of what has been won in this attempt, we can conclude that there is clarity with respect to the "originary negativity":[363] the *principium individuationis* or Apollonian order. The victims in this case are the repressed, those who were Dionysian Aryan lords in *The Origins of Tragedy*, whom Christian civilization seeks to transcend [*Übermenschen*]. But the victims become conscious[364] that they have to break free from the "sickness of the chains" of happy reproduction, of the "rationalized system of functionality," "of authority," of "guilt," and the resentment of the "virtues of being in the herd." This system is the fruit of a "will to power [*Wille zur Macht*]"[365] — in the first sense — of the weak who have produced structures of repression, and who have imposed the "I," "moral conscience [*Gewissen*]," the "language," the grammar, the "metaphysics."[366] This is where the critique of the Apollonian and of Christian-masochist thought must be carried through to its conclusion.[367] Nietzsche proceeds from here to occupy a central place in the tradition of the "great critics." His is the attitude of "nihilism" in the face of *ratio* and cruelty; this is the moment of criticism,[368] of *negativity* with respect to that which is given: the "will to nothing [*Wille zum Nichts*] has been transformed into the lord [*Herrn*] of the will to life."[369] To forget the "past" that oppresses, it is necessary to produce the "dissolution of the subject,"[370] by means of the experience-decision of the "eternal repetition of the same,"[371] in order to live out the creative Dionysian pleasure of the present in negation of the prevailing values. To this end, and in the final instance,[372] once again negatively, because of the inversion "of" what was trapped in the old system, the "will to power" — in its second sense — "transmutes the values [*Umwertung*]," which now culminate, but this time positively, as the "placement of new values [*neue Wertsetzung*],"[373] a transformation of values. This is the "will to power," which is innovative *before* the Apollonian in Greece, but now is *subsequent*, and erupts again in the person of "the-human-being-who-transcends-himself [*Übermensch*]," Zarathustra, the aesthetic creator.[374] Ultimately, when Nietzsche tries to explain how the "will to power"[375] *of the strong, of the dominators*, imposes itself historically, his ideas run aground in works such as *Beyond Good and Evil* (from section 259 onward) and *The Will to Power* (from section 86). Nietzsche had fallen into a new "metaphysical fetishization of the notion of the will to power,"[376] even according to some of his most benevolent interpreters.

[247] Let us stop nonetheless and consider three fundamental negative themes that Nietzsche explores in *The Genealogy of Morals*, because of their importance for Freud, the focus of the next section of this book. As we have seen, according to Nietzsche there are two kinds of human beings,

the "lords" (artists and aristocrats), who are *active*, affirmative, aggressive, and creative; and their counterparts, the slaves, who are purely negative and *reactive*, who triumph without vanquishing, as a result of the three mechanisms explained in the three essays of this work. In the first place is the mechanism of resentment. The weak dominate through resentment as a result of the "*vis inertiae* of habit,"[377] topologically displacing reactive forces and inverting the typology of values. Everything occurs between reactive forces, which impede and destroy each other, with vengeance, impotent in admiration, respect, or love: this is what impotence means for Nietzsche. But what happens to the active forces negated in the person who is resented? They are introjected into their own subject. Thus we have, in the second essay, the theme of a bad moral conscience (*Gewissen*). The inversion of values is introjected into the dominated subject(ivity) by means of discipline, punishment, and memory: "It is because of this idiosyncracy that an *adaptive ability* was invented, that is to say a secondary-level activity, a *reactiveness* [*Reaktivität*], and life has even been defined in this context as an internal adaptation. . . . But by doing so, the essence of life goes without recognition, which is the *will to power* [*Wille zur Macht*], and the elemental preeminence of spontaneous, aggressive, conquering, rebellious, transforming forces is also neglected."[378] And whoever does not bend to these demands now has a "bad conscience," a return unto themselves of the forces that were not fulfilled (topologically) and the change of direction in the typology of these forces as a masochistic self-destructive introjection (as a self-inflicted pain), with the corresponding fiction, because of the construction of a "debt-fault [*Schuld*]" (a pathological feeling of responsibility and its correlative guilt, because of the impossibility of its fulfillment), that unites the herd of the slaves. This is what culture consists of, and in particular that of Modernity. And all of this is founded, ultimately, on an ascetic ideal—one that Nietzsche lived concretely in his Lutheran home and in his Germany, educated within Calvinist pietism, as Weber would demonstrate, in its moment at the origin of capitalism—which is the theme of the third essay. Thanks to the construction of a "world of the beyond,"[379] the body and pleasure are denied in the "here and now" by a "will to nothingness" that annihilates the creative instincts. We could say that Nietzsche elaborated a critique of Kantian criticism. While Kant could not put truth itself into question, "the will to truth demands a critique; it is necessary to put into doubt the value of truth itself."[380]

[248] We can see then ultimately that Nietzsche profoundly transforms Schopenhauer. The "will to live" that was for the latter the origin of all pain,[381] as a result of its determination by the *principium individuationis*, has now become the "will to power": the "will to live as power" (as feasibility, as "how to" live, operate, do . . .). This "will to power" does not

negate all of life, since it "splits up" as if in a *Diremtion*, an originary *Ent-zweiung*. The negation is given in the "Apollonian" and conservative Christian order of the ascetic ideal of the exclusive affirmation of the instincts of self-preservation.[382] Meanwhile, in the order dominated by the pleasure instinct, the will to live expresses itself creatively and vividly. This is why it is necessary to negate the repressive values of the ascetic-priestly class[383] — because they are the ones who make it impossible to live—through the creative action of the *Übermensch*. In any case the "rational" has been situated exclusively in an order that has to be transcended as intrinsically perverse:[384] similar to that of the world *as representation* (reason is only ontic-objective understanding [*Verstand*]) in Schopenhauer—and there is no critical reason, but rather only the ontological "intuition" of being as will; either as the repressive order of *Socratic reason* or its Apollonian or other variants in Modernity (reason as "instrumental reason" or as a fixated affirmation of dominant values), that coincide with the civilizational-reproductive instincts that are necessarily repressed (in the "Christ" who crucified himself because of his affinity for the pleasure of pain)[385]—in the face of which there is no critical reason, nor drives of worthy self-preservation, but only a critical will: "the inversion of values [*Umwertung der Werte*]." Nietzsche's victims (the lords forced into submission, the nobles, the Aryans, heroes such as Carlyle or the "antimoderns," the Dionysians who should have passed through the subterranean world of orgiastic popular cults, persecuted by the Hellenists, having lost the prestige of the theatrical representation of tragedy, or those persecuted by Christian orthodoxy) will be freed like Zarathustra, "human-beings-who-transcend-themselves [*Übermenschen*]," only if they are transformed into subjects of the exercise of the positive "will to power," which is aggressive and creative. Nietzsche's oppressors (the weak, Hellenistic Socratics, Semitic-Christians, and modern Europeans) are the resentful victims of yesterday (since all "current value" is the objectification of past resentment). The material criterion of ethics (as I presented it in §1.5 of this book) falls into a kind of aporia and mistakenly self-destructs: life is the repetitive mortal instinct,[386] or is an irrational Dionysian violence[387] that is to be found "beyond good and evil": that is, beyond ethics. Is this the last word of the complex instinctual order?

[249] Here I would like to address a philosophical-historical question. Nietzsche (and also Heidegger, Gadamer, and Habermas), like many others of the contemporary generation of world philosophers (in Latin America as well), suffered because of the "Romantic distortion" of the interpretation of the achievements of the "Greeks" (and of Hellenism in general). A true inversion, an invention, is produced in Germany, but also in England and France,[388] after the defeat of the Turks in 1683 (and the arrival of the Muscovites at the Black Sea). Central and northern Europe begin to construct a fantastic tale (into which Charles Taylor falls) that still entangles us in its

webs. The great promoters of this story were, among others, the German Romantics. Prussian Germany needed a heroic self-understanding on a global scale, in the culturally valid European mode of anti-Semitic racism. At the University of Göttingen,[389] Winckelmann began the process, which was brought to its apogee by Goethe, Herder, and later Schlegel. Of these the most influential was Wilhelm von Humboldt, the Prussian minister of education, founder of the University of Berlin (which would be the new model for all Germany, especially for its *Socratic* system of "seminars") and of the *Gymnasium* (high school in the spirit of Germanic Hellenism). This is how the hypotheses about Indo-German languages arose, united to Aryan racism (which was inspired by Darwin), as well as hypotheses about the unilineal character of universal history (such as Hegel's *Heilsgeschichte*),[390] all of which was taught and learned around the core of a central science in Prussian political ideology: the *Altertumswissenschaften*. It is understandable then that when Nietzsche—the student of such great teachers of this "science" as Ritschl, who went from Bonn to Leipzig, or Erwin Rodhe—dared to criticize the *Prussian dogma* (the "Greco-German syndrome") of the quasi-divine reconciliation of the truth of *lógos* in Socrates, in favor of the Dionysian (multiple, vital, chaotic), the influential philologist Wilamowitz would exert all his influence to distance the young Nietzsche from a German academic career.[391] Paradoxically, could it be that the later Nietzsche might have attempted to reconstruct a theoretical position more acceptable to the "Prussian bureaucracy" of the strong, the powerful, the nobles, and the Aryans? "It is impossible for a man not to have in his blood the qualities and preferences of his parents. . . . This is the problem of race. . . . In our era which is so democratic, or better, so plebeian, education and culture must consist, above all, of the art of dissembling one's origin and the plebeian atavism in one's soul and body."[392]

[250] Racism extended throughout Europe (including England and France) and the United States. From the time of the Romantics it was thought that tropical climates were not conducive to the development of civilizations (recall Kant's *Anthropology*) and left racial stigmas that could not be overcome. Worst of all, Nietzsche rose up against the Greek romantic dogma from within the same romantic horizon he was rebelling against. But what if the cult of Dionysus was Egyptian and not Greek?[393] If Athens was an Egyptian colony of Sais,[394] and Thebes Phoenician, that is to say, Semitic? And what if Europa the daughter of Kadmos, was also Phoenician?[395] What if philosophy itself (for example the *lógos* as apophantic reason) is present in the text of Memphis about three thousand years before Christ?[396] Even then the young Nietzsche would have to start all over. His historical hypotheses were too weak, too ideological, too Hellenocentric.

There is nothing innocent about romantic Hellenocentrism, since it established the "Greco-German Prussian" axis, which expanded first with

Bismarck and then with Hitler, but also still persists in all of contemporary European culture and in the United States—since "Americanism" is just the latest chapter of Eurocentrism, which passing from "the East towards the West," crossed the Atlantic and arrived at the shores of the Pacific. We must deconstruct this "political ideological syndrome," which persists also in Habermas's modern optimism, in his claim of going all the way to the absolute origin of the "West,"[397] only to disembark in the Dionysian (which is actually Egyptian, but with claim of authentic Hellenism) in Nietzsche or in Parmenides with Heidegger. Hellenocentrism (which claims that Greece is the cultural origin of the West, that it owes nothing to the Egyptians and Semites—when Greece was nothing but the *dependent* and *peripheral* Western part of the cultures of the Middle East, until the expansion led by Alexander the Great) is the basis for Romantic, Prussian, and racist Germanocentrism, and reconstructs the ancient humanist and mercantilist Eurocentrism that began in 1492—not before. Europe is the "center" and the "end" of universal history in the Hegelian ontology. Neither Nietzsche, nor Heidegger, nor Habermas, to cite just a few, are able to transcend ontological Eurocentrism (nor its foundation, Germanocentric Hellenocentrism). For its part, the teaching of philosophy is the quintessence of such Hellenocentrism throughout the world (even in the universities of Africa, Latin America, and among the most influential elites of Asia). Is it possible for philosophical reflection to go beyond the original Greek horizons? An ethics of liberation on a global scale must first "liberate" philosophy from Hellenocentrism, or there will be no *global* philosophy in the future, in the twenty-first century. To speak as Feuerbach did in 1842, I am tempted to say that one of the *principles of the philosophy of the future* should be to not fall into Helleno-, Germano-, or Eurocentrism, but rather to have from the beginning a *global* perspective and horizon.

[251] Returning to the subject of this section, it is important to indicate that the ethics of liberation seeks to formulate the *contents* of materiality and negativity in such a way that it would be necessary to redefine the entire logic of the instincts, drives, passions, and sentiments, which, from the perspective of the *broadening* of the concept of "reason" that I have just analyzed, would permit a more complex and realistic articulation of the moments needed to arrive at the full discovery of the real suffering of the victims.

c. The "Death Principle" in Sigmund Freud

[252] The Freud[398] that concerns us in the next few pages, in order to continue forward with the argument already set forth, serves to problematize Nietzsche's conclusions, but is perhaps still trapped, in 1920, in

Schopenhauer's framework. Freud defines two key moments in the instinctual order: (a) the instincts related to the self-preservation of life (and its respective "reality principle [*Realitätsprinzip*]" and "death principle [*Todesprinzip*]," which also include the instincts of aggression,[399] and (b) the instincts of pleasure or "sexual instincts [*Sexualtriebe*]"[400] (and its "pleasure principle [*Lustprinzip*]"[401] or *éros*). The Freudian solution of the dialectical relationship between these two moments is one characterized by tension, coinciding in its ultimate speculative hypothetical explanation[402] with the pessimism of Schopenhauer, and is contrary to Nietzsche, since it is inclined to give priority to the "death principle": "What we evidently cannot hide is that we have come unexpectedly to the door of Schopenhauer's philosophy, a thinker for whom death is the *authentic result* and, thereby, the end[403] of life, whereas meanwhile the sexual drive is the corporeal expression of the will to live [*Willens zum Leben*]."[404] For Freud the reproduction or preservation of life through the introjection of social institutions into the psychic organism, governed by the death principle, appears to win out over the will to live. In effect, the mere reproduction of life, when it denies all creative possibilities inherent in the will to live, takes *the foundations of the patriarchal* (sexist) *pathology* of Hellenistic and Western European culture as its final ontological horizon. I believe that this problematic touches the heart of the Freudian perspective. Let us situate ourselves therefore at the very frontiers of psychoanalysis, taking Freud's approach as a given:[405] (a) from the perspective of the psychoanalytic theory of culture,[406] and (b) from the standpoint of its formulation of the issue of ethical consciousness (the question of the "superego" [*Über-Ich*]).[407]

[253] In 1920, Freud wrote in *Beyond the Pleasure Principle* that there is a tendency toward stability [*Tendenz zur Stabilität*][408] in human beings that is connected to an "instinct of self-preservation [*Selbsterhaltungstriebe*]" managed by the consciousness as a "reality principle," which results in "the postponement of satisfaction [*Aufschub der Befriedigung*] and the renunciation [*Verzicht*] of some of the possibilities of attaining it, [which] compel us to patiently accept *nonpleasure* [*Unlust*], by means of an obligatory, circuitous route [*Unwerge*], in order to return to pleasure [*Lust*]."[409] This means that the "repression of the possibilities of pleasure [*die Verdrängung einer Lustmöglichkeit*]"[410] is inherent in human culture, but that this repression also serves to distance the terror (differentiated from other emotions such as mere fear or anguish) of "losing one's life [*Lebensgefahr*]."[411] Cultural institutions, as products of the instincts of self-preservation, are able to communicate a sense of security with regard to the habitual, peaceful, and constant reproduction of life—Nietzsche's "happiness," or the peace of the Stoics, understood as the "avoidance of displeasure" or the "absence of tension." They do this to the extent that they reproduce the actions

that have successfully avoided pain and death. The arrival at this state of feeling in ourselves to be "masters of the situation [*zu Herren der Situation*]"[412] means one has gone through a traumatic process[413] through which the "unconscious [*Unbewusstes*]" has been repressed. The psychoanalytical task is that of the application of the "hermeneutic art [*Deutungskunst*],"[414] by which "resistances [*Widerstände*]" are "brought back to consciousness [*Bewusstwerdung*]"[415] through "memory [*Erinnerung*]," which thus makes possible the "reproduction [*Reproduktion*]" or faithful reconstruction of the undesirable content that has been repressed, by means of the "return of the repressed [*das Verdrängte . . . zu wiederholen*]." The "nucleus of the ego [*Kern des Ichs*]" appears: "Our task is to achieve the admission [*Zulassung*] of that displeasure by calling upon [the intervention of] the reality principle."[416] Freud thus discovered in the context of his therapeutic experience that there "is truly an obsession with repetition [*Wiederholungszwang*][417] that goes beyond the pleasure principle itself[418] . . . and which appears to be more primitive, elemental, and instinctual than the pleasure principle which it comes to substitute for."[419]

Freud accepts the continuing sway of Nietzsche's Apollonian tendencies and that of the Schopenhauerian "self-subsumption [*Selbstaufhebung*]" of the will to live, which I will call "instincts" or "drives of self-preservation," and which Marcuse would characterize in addition as expressive of the possibilities of a phenomenon of "surplus repression."[420] The repressive trauma of a civilizational process leaves the "pleasure principle out of the game." But the question is: "How is the instinctual connected with the obsession by repetition . . . ? An instinct would then be in effect an internal force [*Drang*] within the living organism of reproduction [*Wiederherstellung*] [which reflects] a prior state [*eines früheren Zustandes*]."[421]

[254] Freud thus correctly defines the characteristics of the reproductive drive, which when it closes upon itself pathologically tends to return to its origin, negating life in order to achieve the peace of an inorganic state (or that of the security of a mother's breast). Mere institutional cultural repetition without creative development becomes an "obsession with repetition." We would then be immersed in a pathological case that is due to a fetishized institutionality. For Freud, a culture of mere preservation or repetition is a structure dominated by the "death instinct." It is characteristic of such instincts of cultural self-preservation that they embody a desire to "return to the past." This "return to an earlier state"[422] is related to Nietzsche's ontological conception of the "eternal return of the same." Freud thus counterposes the existence of the "impulses of conservative nature [*der konservativen Natur*]" to those of the "impulses of transformation [*Veränderung*] and development [*Entwicklung*]."[423] These "conservative instincts" are opposed to "others that impel the formation of new ones and

progress [itself] [*zur Neugestaltung und zum Fortschrift*]."[424] Paradoxically, although Freud attributes the congenital pathology of all culture to these conservative instincts that "have a tendency toward regression [*Regression*]," he nonetheless affirms that "we must attribute all of the successes of organic evolution to them."[425] This is why he writes, from a vision like Schopenhauer's, centered on the primacy of the interests of reproduction over that of the development of life: "To think that the goal of all life is a state never previously attained, would be in contradiction with the conservative nature of instincts."[426]

From which he concludes: "The end of all life is death [*Das Ziel allen Lebens ist der Tod*].[427] And on the same basis: the nonliving was once alive."[428] This formulation manifests the logic of pure reproduction, which ultimately involves death. But to this logic Freud tentatively seeks to oppose still, through the "sexual drive [*Sexualtriebe*]" something like the "authentic instinct for life [*Lebenstrieb*]," which would be that which drives the human being who transcends him or herself (the *"Übermensch"*).[429] Freud reflects in the face of this: "For myself, I do not believe in such an internal drive and I see no way of keeping alive this beautiful illusion [*Illusion*]."[430] That is to say, Freud believes that the pure self-preservation of life is what is most real in human existence. In the end he vanquished Schopenhauer, since all of the pretended instincts or drives of transcendence, creativity, or Nietzsche's Dionysian ideal are only a "neurotic phobia": "The advances which take place in the development of a neurotic phobia, a disturbance which is nothing more than a form of attempted flight in the face of instinctive satisfaction, provide us with the model of genesis of this apparent instinct of *perfecting* [*Vervolkommnungstriebes*]; an instinct that, nonetheless, we cannot attribute to human beings."[431] So the "death instincts [*Todestriebe*]," as "ego instincts [*Ichtriebe*]," are opposed to the "life instincts" or to the "sex drive" that impel the "progress of life [*Lebensfortsetzung*]."[432] The first, because of their sadistic and aggressive aspects, have a tendency toward the "annihilation of the object," and ultimately "to constantly replenish internal excitations (the Nirvana principle [*Nirwanaprinzip*])."[433] The second do not play a major role according to Freud: "The pleasure principle appears to be at the service of the death instincts."[434] In *The Ego and the Id*, Freud continues to elaborate the same theme, but coming closer to ethical questions, such as the issue already articulated by Nietzsche, regarding the "unconscious feeling of guilt [*unbewussten Schuldgefühls*]."[435] Culture's institutional repression in the name of the reproductive self-preservation of life, is introjected into the ontogenetic psychic apparatus: "An internal differentiation within the same ego, which we label as the *superego* [*Über-Ich*].[436] The ideal of the ego.[437] When the intensity of the Oedipus complex is greatest (ontogenetically) as well as the speed with which it is repressed (phylogenetically) (under the influence of authority, religion, teaching, and reading), it reigns more severely over the ego as a moral conscience [*Gewissen*].[438] We then discover that the repressed drives are themselves the basis of feelings of guilt."[439] Guilt guarantees reproduction. But it is the preservation of life that is essential: "The *superego* dominates [*herrscht*] as a kind of culture underneath the death instinct.[440] We can picture this as the *ego* being found under the dominion of the death instinct, mute but still powerful, and which wants to attain peace by silencing the disturbance wrought by *éros*, pursuant to the indications of the pleasure principle."[441] The *development* of life expressed by *éros* has been repressed.

[255] In his two definitive works on culture — *The Future of an Illusion* and *Civilization and Its Discontents*[442] — Freud radicalizes his stance, as when he affirms that "each individual is virtually an enemy of civilization [*ein Feind der Kultur*],"[443] until "the human being. . . senses the sacrifices that civilization imposes upon him as an intolerable weight,"[444] since it "appears that all civilization must base itself upon the coercion [*Zwang*] and oppression of the instincts [*Triebunterdrückung*]."[445] Up until this point Freud's voice is that of the critic of mere preservation. The renunciation of incest, cannibalism, homicide, which are soon institutionalized as *taboos*, permits "the coercive imposition of work [*Arbeitszwang*]":[446] "The favored classes enjoy the benefits of civilization, but so too do the oppressed [*Unterdrückten*] who participate in such satisfactions . . . as a fragment of the totality."[447] Freud has lost the Nietzschean distinction between "happiness" (toward which the instincts of self-preservation should tend: happiness as security and peace, now under the sway of the death instinct)[448] and "pleasure,"[449] and he identifies the one with the other. At the same time, since cultural institutions are the product of repressive forces of civilization understood as an expression of the death instincts, they are intrinsically perverse (Freud shows here a certain anti-institutionalism). This is why, although all that "we can expect of life is happiness," as a "simple fulfillment of the pleasure principle,"[450] the suffering that besets us negates that "claim of happiness [*Glücksanspruch*],"[451] which is sought after repeatedly through various different "means to avoid suffering."[452] Freud concludes: "The design of attaining happiness which is imposed upon us by the pleasure principle[453] is unreachable [*ist nicht zu erfüllen*], but nonetheless we must not—and cannot—abandon our efforts to come as close as possible to its fulfillment."[454] A certain *pathos* of resignation seems to take possession of Freud, now an old man: "Eros and *anánke* became the parents of human civilization . . . carrying out an ever more perfect *domination*."[455]

[256] Through the coercion of work and sexuality, one arrives at an "adequate distribution of the libido [*Verteilung der Libido*],"[456] accompanied by an impressive amount of aggression: "Aggression is introjected, internal-

ized [*introjiziert, verinnerlicht*], back into the place where it came from: it is directed against the ego itself, incorporating itself into a part of it, which in its expression as the *superego* is in opposition to the remainder, and assumes the function of a moral consciousness . . . lodged in its interior, as a kind of military garrison within a conquered city.[457] The *superego* tortures the sinful ego."[458] Freud confronts this negative reality in a spirit that remains critical, as ever, but without enthusiasm: "I lack the necessary disposition to set myself up as a prophet before my contemporaries, leaving me no remedy but to expose myself to their reproaches for not being able to offer them any consolation whatsoever. Because, at the end, they all seek nothing else: the most frantic revolutionaries have the same zeal as the most pious believers."[459] Liberation implies either fanaticism or blind faith. The self-regulated preservation of life and of the cultural system appears to have been triumphant. For victims—when they are hungry, naked, and homeless, traumatized by the oppression visited on their tortured bodies, those of the periphery, indigenous people, the working class, the marginalized, the exiled, women, those who are nonwhite—these questions are matters of life or death. For them the Freudian horizon closes up again at the end without hope and without alternatives.

Nonetheless, Freudian thought is certainly highly "critical," since it judges Western Modernity as a repressive instinctual order, dominated by the death instinct. We could review each step of figure 12 from the perspective of this diagnosis: the psychocultural negation in the first instance as a form of institutional repression (moment 1); the overall critique of culture and reproductive morality as such (moment 4); the neurotic's awakening to the repressions that have caused his or her suffering (moment 5); the hermeneutical scientific "explanation" of the causes of the psychic alienation of the members of modern Western culture by an annihilating "superego" (moment 7); the therapeutic project seeking to overcome these repressions (moment 8); and most particularly, through therapy, the individual deconstruction of repressive pathology (moment 9), and finally the tentative indication of a possible path for the configuration of a behavior capable of transcending neurosis under the impetus of the death instinct (moment 10). But it is here once again where the lack of an explicit diagnosis of the "pathologies of cultural communities" (that of Western Modernity, with the surplus repression appropriate to a capitalist society) demonstrates the need to transcend the same limits of psychoanalysis.

[257] In table 10 I propose a framework for how to reformulate the Freudian approach and its categories in order to subsume it within the ethics of liberation, differentiating and transforming its classifications in a manner that should be kept in mind throughout the exposition that follows.

Now I must articulate the distinctions already advanced by Schopen-

Table 10. Toward a Reconstruction of the Categorical Instinctual
Framework: The Instincts of Life (in the Presence of the Life Principle)

Types of Instincts	Spheres Where These Instincts Are Expressed
1 Instincts of self-preservation *(anánke)* (the reality principle, or principle of the "reproduction of life")[a]	
1.1 Instincts of aggression (with respect to the living, intra- and extraspecific) 1.1.1 Attack (positive) 1.1.2 Resistance, defense (negative)	1.a individual, monological
1.2 Productive instincts (before nature) 1.2.1 Destruction (of what is ancient: the past) 1.2.2 Construction or production (of the new: the future)	1.b Communitarian (specific)
2 Pleasure instincts *(éros)* (principle of the "development" of life)	
2.1 How to satisfy physical needs (food, clothing, housing)	2.a Narcissistic *(éros* as such)
2.2 Before human beings (eroticism as such) (Oedipus)	2.b. Alterity *(agápe)* The Liberation Principle (Osiris-Moses)[b]

Notes: As may be observed, I did not place the Freudian "death principle" here. The overall reformulation of the theoretical framework that I have proposed has the intention of building its categories from the point of departure of the *instincts of life*. The so-called death principle is the ultimate foundation of all pathology, and because of this it is a deviational tendency of the repressed organic drives. Freud proposed the death instinct, as such and without warning, as the horizon for the "*pathology* of cultural communities" (*Die Unbehagen in der Kultur*, chap. 8, end; chap. 9, 269). This judgment could be extended to the ultimate foundational principles of the Hellenic world, which was also European in terms of its patriarchal core. "Freudian pessimism [consists of] seeing how separated the human being is from nature and the instincts; it is also expressed in considering history itself as a neurosis" (Brown 1967, 112).
a. Now *anánke* is necessity, repetition, security but not the "death principle"; this is reserved to its role as the basis of all possible pathology, when "reproduction" negates liberatory "development."
b. This level will be fleshed out in figure 13, and includes Levinas's position.

hauer, Nietzsche, and Freud. In effect, all civilizations (or "cultures," in the Freudian or German sense) can be interpreted as constituting an institutional horizon within which determinations are produced in the human psyche; these determinations in turn constitute a "disciplined" subjectivity. Even at the neurological level—given that the evolution of the cerebral cortex over the course of millions of years has permitted the emergence of phenomena such as consciousness, language, and self-consciousness[460]—the structural tendencies, drives, or instincts that have been *reconstructed from the inside* continue being intrinsically cultural and institutionalized. This is why at the first level (*anánke*)[461] (1 in table 10), the instincts of life in general demand types of instincts or drives of self-preservation, which contain inherent tendencies toward security and repetition within given historical cultural institutions, that have a place in cerebral evolutionary development. The first of these is language, which enables the possibility of "intersubjective agreements" with their own tendency toward instituting happiness." This level is governed by the "reality principle," always historical and concrete, and redefined as the "principle of action" by the Marcuse of *Eros and Civilization*, since the repression borne by the psyche in the bourgeois culture of capitalism has a degree of surplus repression of its own—which regulates the instincts of aggression (1.1.1 in table 10) or defense (1.1.2), of construction (1.2.2) or destruction (1.2.1), in order to achieve satisfaction, albeit by a roundabout path, which is delayed but guaranteed. By means of work (which is disciplined in the body and subsumed in historical systems of production) satisfactions are produced in order to reach a necessary level of foreseeable consumption. If we surpass at this initial level (1) the mere solipsistic prelinguistic paradigm of the constitution of human instincts, we can accept that at the individual (1.a) or community level (1.b) the self-regulation of social systems as a form of institutional cultural self-preservation still permits a "monological" or "ethnocentric" attitude that cannot be closed necessarily as a totality.

[258] On the other hand, the autonomy should be preserved of the instincts of pleasure (*éros*) (2 in table 10), which reminds us of the Nietzschean creative capacity, but which are susceptible of falling into an autoerotic "narcissism" (2.a). Marcuse's liberatory exit, by means of fantasy, aesthetics, Orpheus with his "song," are quite similar to Nietzsche's Dionysian alternative. I cannot fail to include in this interpretation the innovative pleasure instincts, though I am well aware of the fact that they can become "totalized" equally easily under the death instincts. I believe that in the end there is a final "window" available to us—which I analyze shortly in the context of the work of Levinas—which proposes a drive of alterity (*le désir*), and which transforms mere *éros* into *ágape*;[462] this is an opening inclined toward the Other *qua Other* (not as in the case of the utilitarian common good of level 1.b in table 10). We must then round into the final laps of our exploration, and if we situate ourselves in terms of a point of departure at the place of the victims (at the center of reference of figure 13), who suffer in a twofold manner all of the repressions indicated by Freud, then we must start all over again. Upon the suffering body of the exploited victim, where his or her drives are subjected to a surplus repression pursuant to the demands of the happy self-preservation[463] of the hegemonic members of the cultural system, we find the nonintentional effects of the institu-

tional order: the pain, the unhappiness (which the utilitarians had hoped to avoid), and the surplus repression of the dominated victims (for example, slaves subjected to slavery, the proletariat under capitalism, women under patriarchy, or nonwhite groups under the domination of racism, etc.). In the same way, such victims of the dominant sectors of the system are victims because of the negation of their pleasure instinct (like Horkheimer's Ulysses, lashed to the mast of the ship, who hears the "siren songs" but not the "deaf" and exhausted rowers, who feel no pleasure at all).

Who could "open" themselves—and how, on what instinctual-drive basis—to the pain of the victims who were not already moved to Schopenhauerian pity, which is ultimately a masochistic solidarity with those who are unavoidably suffering determined by the *principium individuationis*? Are there any drives among these (those of self-preservation or of development by means of pleasure, fantasy, or aesthetics)[464] that would enable us to create something ethically new without becoming trapped by the "eternal return of the same"? In effect, the dialectics of totality (of "the same") and of the Other open up a path for us from which we could reconstitute all of the discourse advanced thus far.

§4.4. "Sensibility" and "Alterity" in Emmanuel Levinas

[259] When I began to turn to Levinas in *Toward a Latin American Philosophy of Liberation* (1970) I was, as part of that effort, able to move beyond the Heidegger of *Being and Time*. Without setting aside that perspective, I will now proceed with my argument from within the drive framework. Levinas's[465] initial approach, as a critic from the standpoint of phenomenology, was to situate himself outside of the purely ontological order. Of Lithuanian Jewish origin, his mother tongues were Russian and Lithuanian, but he was educated in French Strasbourg and German Freiburg. Levinas endured five traumatic years in a Nazi concentration camp, whose imprint was left on his real, vulnerable corporeality. He was a *victim* of the Jewish Holocaust in the very heart of Modernity. He was also a survivor who dedicated his most mature work in the following manner: "In memory of those beings closest to me among the six million murdered by the Nazis, together with millions upon millions of human beings of all faiths and nations,[466] victims [*victimes*] of the same kind of hate of other human beings, and of the same kind of anti-Semitism."[467] And then he peculiarly enters into the discourse we have been discussing so far and writes:

> The ego [*moi*] exists separately from pleasure [*jouissance*], that is to say, as a state of happiness ["*heureux*"], and can satisfy its pure and simple being to happiness itself as a state of good feeling [*bonheur*]. It exists in an overt sense, as a state over that of being in a general sense. But in a state of desire

[*Désir*] the being of the ego [*moi*] still appears in a superior moment, and can still sacrifice [*sacrifier*] happiness [*bonheur*] itself to its desire [*Désir*]. It thereby finds itself beyond the limits of the situation, at the edge or pinnacle of being because of the happiness it enjoys and because of what it desires (truth and justice). It is above and beyond being in itself. The state of *desiring* produces an inversion in the classical notion of substance.[468]

This "desire [*Désir*]" is a creative drive,[469] but one that is found beyond the mere Dionysian instinct and that transcends it completely.[470] Levinas begins his classic work:

> The Other who is metaphysically desired is not equivalent to the other which is a bread to be eaten. . . . *Metaphysical desire* [*désir métaphysique*] is characterized by an overwhelming tendency toward *something else*, toward something which is *absolute* in its otherness. . . . At the base of desire, depending upon its sense of the everyday, lies necessity [*besoin*].[471] Metaphysical *desire* does not aspire to any kind of return, since it is a *desire* for a country where we were never born. . . . Metaphysical desire does not rest upon any previous inheritance. [This is] a *desiring* which cannot be satisfied. . . . Desires which can be satisfied do not at all resemble the metaphysical *desire* which, when its satisfaction is denied or amid the exasperation of nonsatisfaction and of *desire*, amount to voluptuousness itself. . . . It is like goodness — the *desired* does not fulfill, and instead deepens it. . . . *To desire* [*désir*] without satisfaction, which, precisely, accepts distancing and the alterity [*alterité*] of the Other.[472]

And still more clearly: There is "the possibility that the Other might appear as the object of necessity [*besoin*][473] although it preserves its alterity, or better yet, the possibility of enjoying the Other . . . ; this simultaneity of *necessity* [*besoin*] and of *desire* [*désir*], of concupiscence and of transcendence, . . . constitutes the originality of eroticism, which in this sense is definitively supremely *equivocal*."[474]

[260] This "metaphysical desire" is the "drive of alterity," which cuts across the horizon of psychologism, of the "world" in the sense conceived by Heidegger, of the "system" as defined by Luhmann, of totality itself, and it penetrates all the way to the intimacy of the Other. It is a creative force to the extent that it *moves toward an exit*[475] from "the same," and beyond achieved happiness:

> In the *Cantique des colonnes*, Valéry speaks of a desire without defect [*désir sans defaut*]. He refers, undoubtedly, to Plato, who, in his analysis of pure pleasures, discovered a hope that was not conditioned by any previous deprivation. Let's explore once more this term *desire* [*désir*]. For a subject who is inclined toward him or herself, who according to the Stoic formula is

characterized by *ormé* or the *tendency to persist in his or her own being*,[476] or for whom, according to the Heideggerian formula, *is consuming his or her existence in the very course of that existence*; for a subject who is also defined by a self-referential concern and who in happiness [*bonheur*],[477] is realized in his or her own self, we oppose the *desire of the Other* [*Désir de l'Autre*], which has its origin in a self which is satisfied, and in this sense is independent and does not desire for itself. A necessity [*besoin*] of one who no longer has necessities [*besoins*].[478]

In another way: "The ego [*Moi*] possesses a personal life, the atheist ego, in which atheism is consummated [. . . and] is surpassed [*dépassé*] in desire [*Désir*], which has its basis in the presence of the Other. *Desiring* is the desire of a being who is *already* happy: *desiring* is the unhappiness [*malheur*] of being happy."[479] This is not only a criticism of drives; it is also a critique of rationalism, even perhaps of Socratic reason itself, but more subtle, more complex, and more radical in character:

> Ontology subsumes the Other in the same. . . .[480] Here, theory[481] becomes committed to a path that denies metaphysical *desiring* [*Désir*], and also denies the marvels of exteriority, where this *desiring* [*Désir*] dwells. Meanwhile, theory with exteriority as a reference . . . has a *critical* [*critique*] intention that does not repress the Other in the same as ontology does, but instead puts the Other into question.[482] . . . We call this *calling into question* of my spontaneity, in the presence of the other, *ethics* [*éthique*]. . . .[483] Metaphysics, transcendence, a place of hospitality for the Other within the same, for the Other in place of myself, that is to say as an ethics that fulfills the critical essence of knowing [*l'essence critique du savoir*]. And this is how *criticism* precedes dogmatism, just as *metaphysics* precedes ontology.[484]

So Levinas proposes, on the one hand, and in the first place, (a) a "*creative* drive" associated with alterity, which launches totality all over again, as well as the reproductive drives of self-preservation (that of the same, of egoistical *psychologism*) and even the Dionysian narcissistic drives themselves (egoistical *éros* or basic constituted cultural need);[485] and on the other hand, and secondly, (b) corresponding "*critical* reason."

[261] I think that in order to make Levinas's thinking comprehensible in full, we have to begin from a double scenario that, in fact, delimits the three key moments of his life (in terms of his most important works). Let us see how this phenomenological adventure takes him to the level of precise and fine distinctions by means of a honed instrument of analysis, but at the same time let us explore *the limits* of this instrumentality, especially Levinas's philosophy of history and philosophy of politics.

The first moment (up until 1961) (the first scenario) encompasses three important phases.[486] The first is that of his preparation at Strasbourg and

Freiburg, in direct contact with Heidegger (in the former city) and Husserl (in the latter), influences clearly apparent in his doctoral thesis.[487] Without a doubt, the translation into French of the *Cartesian Meditations*[488] that Husserl would read in Paris, could not have failed to introduce him to the question of *"the Other."*[489] During the 1930s his preparation continued. During the next phase, the Second World War broke out, and he went through his "experience" in the concentration camp. In 1947, he published *From Existence to the Existent*: "The research I had initiated before the war has been resumed, and in large part was written while in captivity [*captivité*]."[490] His theme is not abstract, neutral existence. It is instead that of "the existent," an "entity," "the instant," the "fatigue" of corporeality, all that which ontological phenomenology ignores: *"Desire [désir]*, to the extent that it implies a relationship with the world, amounts to a distancing between the ego and the desired one. . . . In the world, the Other is certainly not treated as a thing, but is never separated from other things. . . . The relationship with nudity is the true experience . . . of the alterity of the Other [*alterité d'Autrui*]."[491] His theme is that which is still "existent" but without the world yet (before and after the world). In dreams, the "unconscious [*inconscient*]"[492] has no world nor "light" nor "consciousness," but there is something "existing" in the space of an "instance." This sentient existing body is vulnerable rather than something that "comprehends being": "The suffering of this moment lingers like a scream, whose echo will resonate forever in the eternity of space."[493]

In 1946, Levinas occupies himself with the material that will appear in *Time and the Other*,[494] where time again and again he seeks to go beyond the cognitive position, the "intention" of phenomenological knowledge, the ontology of "one is" (in the "Oneself" of the world), and in the face of an "I am"[495] alone in the face of the Other, in a "face to face" (first as a feminine being). The Other shatters the sameness and its solitude. *Éros*[496] is a window, but an ambiguous one, since the "primacy of the same," egoism, can also be "narcissistic."[497]

[262] In effect, the first scenario, apparent in *Totality and Infinity*, published in 1961, describes to us as the point of departure a "psychologism" that is prior to the phenomenon of understanding in a Heideggerian world (corresponding to B in figure 14, always from a starting point at A). At a point *prior to* that of "being-in-the-world," the preontological[498] *metaphysical conditions of possibility* can be analyzed phenomenologically, and could be summarized as characterized by "sensibility":[499] there is a preliminary opening to the world already cognizable as a bodily reality that can be traumatized and made vulnerable. But such a living "sensibility" that enjoys pleasure, that eats and inhabits (in a home with warmth and security), is constituted as an ethics because of its "face-to-face" experience with the

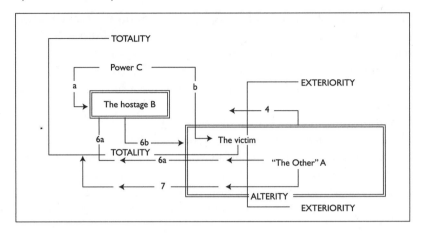

Figure 14. Relevant moments of Levinas's perspective on philosophical reflection.

NOTES: The numbers have the same meanings as in figure 12 (numbers missing from the series are *moments* to which Levinas has not devoted any special attention).

Totality: System 1 in figure 12; 4: ethical criticism of Totality from the perspective of the exteriority of the Other; 6: the "interpellation" of the Other (6a) upon participating in Totality (6b); 6b: "metaphysical desire"; 7: critical-ethical analysis of Totality; a: persecution inflicted by power (C) upon the "just innocent," the hostage; b: the traumatic action (originated by C), which is also borne by the victim, the Other (A).

Other, from the standpoint of its "re-sponsibility" before the Other's "face [*visage*]":

> The being that is *expressed* is imposed upon me, precisely calling to me from its misery and nakedness without my being able to close my ears to its call. . . . *To leave human beings without food is a fault for which there are no attenuating circumstances; the distinction between that which is voluntary and involuntary has no place here* says Rabbi Yochanan. In the face of the hunger of human beings responsibility must be measured *objectively*. . . . .
> In the overall unveiling of the self [Heidegger], as the basis of knowledge and as a sensation of being, there is a *preexistent* relationship with the entity which expresses itself [the Other]; at the ontological level the ethical [precedes].[500]

But the "interpellation" of the face of the suffering Other is only possible because I am "sensibility," a priori corporeal vulnerability. In *Totality and Infinity* the horizon of ontology, of the comprehension of the self, of theory, of the "being-in-the-world" are not only preceded time and again by a preontological a priori ("sensibility") but also by a postontological a posteriori ("exteriority"), but both terms expressive of the same framework of tensions. From the standpoint of a sensible corporeality *prior to* reason as the comprehension of self and cognizant of the entity as an *ideatum* (that speaks or conceptualizes), ethics (and "metaphysics" in the sense in which Levinas employs the term) describes human corporeal psychologism in a much richer way than as the mere subjectivity of a reason in the process of being apprehended by knowledge, and which is linguistically intramundane, which always lives, enjoys and possesses an "affectivity like that of the ipseity (*ipseité*) of the ego."[501] Those *who enjoy* the food that they eat are not to be found either at the level of representation or of knowledge. "Pleasure [*jouissance*] as a means through which life refers to *content* is not a form of intentionality to be considered in the Husserlian sense."[502] "The love of life does not love being, but rather being's *goodness*."[503] Goodness has to do with *satisfaction* primarily, before truth. This is how Levinas proceeds to analyze the "ontological categories of the existent" in affections (how one receives that which causes "impact": affectivity as passivity in the face of traumatization) prior to the Heideggerian "inhabitation," "possession and work," "economy," and so on. It is from the standpoint of this *precedence* that the self opens up to the world, and bursts forth into it immediately, as the *subsequent*, the postontological, from the hospitality of that psychologism which is situated in the exteriority of the world's horizon, the "face and sensibility" of the Other from the perspective of its transcendent quality.[504] Its appearance is not just a manifestation but a revelation; its apprehension is not just comprehension but hospitality; before the Other, reason is not representative but instead lends a sincere ear to the word: "The incomprehensible character of the presence of the Other is not described negatively. . . . The formal structure of language announces the ethical inviolability of the Other. . . . The fact that the face [of the Other] brings about a relationship with me by means of its discourse does not situate it within the same. He or she remains absolute in the context of this relationship."[505] The same reason and language surge forth from the "face-to-face" relation with the Other, prior to representation: "Reason is given life in language. . . . The *primary form of rationality*, that which is first intelligible, that which has the initial meaning, is the infinite form of the intelligence that is manifested (that is to say, which speaks to me) from within its face."[506] But what we paid attention to from the beginning as philosophers of the peripheral world in crisis was the way in which Levinas situated the problem of "asymmetry": "The presence of the face comes to me *from beyond the world* [and] implicates me in terms of human fraternity, does not crush me[507] . . . as does that which presents itself as fearful. . . . The Other, who *commands me* upon the basis of its transcendence, is also the foreigner, the widow, and the orphan with regard to whom *I am obligated*."[508]

[263] The "will" for Levinas is neither deficient nor arbitrary, nor egotis-

tical and thrust into a suicidal death. When the Other appears in an asymmetrical position (an asymmetry that, to the extent that we are speaking of a victim, comes "from above" and from a "superior" level of hierarchy in ethical terms, and which thus obliges me), the will is then impacted prior to any decision as "re-sponsible" (as he or she who above all takes on the burden of the Other"): "The will is free to assume its re-sponsibility in the sense that it wishes to, but it is not free to reject this re-sponsibility in itself, and cannot be free to ignore the world in the sense that the face of the Other introduces it. It is in the *hospitality of the face that the will opens itself up to reason* . . . . That which is absolutely new is the Other."[509] Levinas concludes, amid numerous analyses that I have set forth in other works, by showing us the terror of a reason that has been enclosed by totality; a reason such as that of Modernity, among others: "At the opposite pole of the subject who lives in the infinite time of fertility [in the face of the Other], is the isolated and heroic self, which is produced by the strong forces of the state. He faces death with pure valor whatever the cause for which he dies."[510] Levinas had experienced in his own flesh Nazism's *fanatical heroism*; similarly, I have experienced in Latin America the fanatical heroism of the ideologues of "Western Christian civilization" with its "dirty wars" and its military dictatorships, such as that of Pinochet (imposed by the United States, which portrays itself as the global leader of "democracy"), which are the necessary foundations of a peripheral capitalism in crisis.

This is how we come to the second Levinas (1961–74), with his second scenario, who from 1963 onward[511] demonstrates a clear grasp of the subject: "The Other produces this ethical movement in the conscience, which also undoes the structure of the good conscience of the same . . . which is the *desiring* [*Désir*]. . . . It is as a result of this inassimilable development, and of this transcendence, that we have described the link that has been reestablished between the ego and the Other as the idea of the infinite."[512] Slowly, Levinas begins to develop new categories, such as those of the passage from the position of "obsession" to that of the "hostage."[513] In 1974, in his book *Of Another Way of Being, or Beyond Essence*, we see that a new scenario has been outlined. Now, following Rosenzweig,[514] Levinas radicalizes the situation that serves as a basis for his phenomenological analysis. In a taxi, before he was to speak at a conference in Louvain in 1972, I asked him: "What is *exposition*?" And Levinas, opening up his shirt with two hands, ripping open his buttons, and exposing his chest, exclaimed: "It's like when you *expose* yourself before a firing squad!" The new scenario is more dramatic than the first, and he situates himself within it from another perspective. Now the interpellated is someone who is being "persecuted" because of the Other, the victim; that is to say, the interpellated one has substituted him- or herself as if he or she were the victim, as a "hostage [*otage*]"[515] (B in figure 14). This takes us back to the ancient question about giving one's life to "pay the ransom" for the life of a slave. It is the issue of the "redemption" of the Other in the face of the power of the system (C),[516] a system in which one "bears witness" to one's own "obsession" for the victim (A):

> The re-sponsibility[517] previous to dialogue . . . , the obsessive persecution [*obsession persécutrice*] . . . where the identity becomes individuated as unique,[518] without having recourse to any system of reference, amid the impossibility of escaping without deprivation, from the Other's assignment. The re-presentation[519] of oneself is already captured in its imprint. The negation of one's self[520] is nothing but evasion, not even abstraction; it is a more concrete expression of the concrete than that of the coherence of totality, since, in the face of everyone's accusation, the re-sponsibility for all goes all the way toward substitution [*substitution*]. The subject is hostage. Obsessed by re-sponsibility, . . . accused by that which Others do or suffer. . . . The singular character of oneself is the very fact of bearing [*porter*] the lack of the Other. . . . The persecution which is transformed into expiation.[521]

The "hard core" as a point of departure is always such when subjectivity's ultimate content becomes "sensibility" which is expressed in "pain":

> Pain is the other side of the skin, is nakedness, is that most naked form of dispossession; an existence grounded in the imposition of sacrifice—a sacrifice which is borne rather than offered, precisely because it is restricted to adversity or to the pain which is afflicted—and which is without contradiction. The subjectivity of the subject is vulnerability, exposure to being affected, sensibility, passivity more passive than all passivity, a time which cannot be recovered, a diachronicity which cannot be encompassed by patience, an expansion that must always be expanded, an exposition that must be expressed, and thereby said, and given.[522]

[264] Pain is the beginning of creation, of the new, and "without this madness in the confines of reason, the *one* will be reconstituted, and in the heart of its passion, the *essence* will recommence. The ambiguous adversity of pain!"[523] Levinas, nonetheless, will not remain trapped in a sensitivity[524] that is vulnerable,[525] nor in an affectivity[526] whose content is psychologism,[527] which is fundamentally that of the *conatus* essendi,[528] since the corporeal as-itself "exposes itself"[529] always and necessarily in the face of totality, the system, and, being linked again to the Other, discovers without intending to, or without deciding to do so when in "proximity," the unexpected "face to face": "It is the contact with the Other. To be in contact: not to invest in the Other nor to annul its alterity nor to suppress myself in the face of the Other. In contact itself, to be touching and that which is

touched separate themselves, as if that which is touched were to distance itself, yet remains always present, having nothing *in common* with me. As if its singularity, which is thereby not capable of being anticipated and, as a result, cannot be represented, did not respond except to its designation. This is in itself [*tóde tí*]."[530]

But now the properly *ethical* step is taken. Everything previous to this has been preparatory. The Other, that sensitive corporeality (like the ego of the psyche), appears in contact not only as a face but as a victim. Here Levinas arrives at his most important point in the currents of contemporary thought: "The face of the one who is closest to me [who I find in proximity] implies an unavoidable re-sponsibility, which precedes all free consent, all agreement, all contracts. He escapes all representation; he is the defection itself of any characterization as a phenomenon. . . . The unveiling of the face is nakedness, without form, an abandonment of one's self, aging, death; something which is more naked than nakedness itself: *poverty, the skin which is being stripped*; the skin which is being stripped: imprints of oneself.[531] And arriving at what had not been said before in Western thought, he writes about the re-sponsibility that permits him to pass from statements of fact ("This victim cannot live in this system") to normative statements:

> It is the obsession for the Other, for the one closest to me, who accuses me of the fault that I have not freely[532] committed, which drags the ego toward the itself here [*en deçá*],[533] above all conscious of itself, and which strips me completely naked. Must I refer to this *here* [*en deçá*] as *creatureness*[534] where the being has lost its footprints, a *here* which is more ancient than the intrigues of egoism tied to the *conatus* of the being?[535]

But this "here [*en deçà*]" is tied, as if passing right over the horizon of being, of the world, and of the system—directly to the "beyond [*au delá*]" of the Other, whom I "recognize" in the face and am "forced" by, into an irresistible "re-sponsibility," "obedience,"[536] and "obligation": "Obedience prior to any hearing of the command . . . . An anarchic affliction[537] that intercepts me like a thief, through the networks of conscience, a trauma that has absolutely surprised me, an order that has never been represented, . . . this unheard-of obligation."[538]

This re-sponsibility that ethically obliges one on behalf of the Other as victim, as in Benjamin's messianism (but more deeply), is described by Levinas as follows: "It can be called prophetic, this turning back in which the perception of the *mandate*[539] coincides with the discernment of the meaning of the very mandate carried out by one who has obeyed it.[540] This prophetic turn is the psychism of the soul: the Other in the same. . . . Obedience prior to the hearing of the mandate, the anachronism of inspiration

and of this prophetism is, according to the irrecoverable time of reminis-
cence, more paradoxical than the prediction of the future by an oracle."[541]

[265] Levinas has thus written the ultimate contents of ethics as such:
the "on-behalf-of-the-Other" as a responsibility that obliges. And reason?
Does he not thereby fall into an irrationalism that, in some manner, is the
precursor of French postmodernism? To the contrary, Levinas clearly demonstrates the importance of rationality, but does not tire of seeking to show
its *origin* and *meaning*. Reason, rationality, intentionality, the order of the
being and the world, language, "that which has been said [*le dit*]," all emerge
from a framework that has already been described and all are ultimately
turned on their heads within it. The intention of Levinas's work can thus
be defined in the following way: "Flowing from a sensibility interpreted as
a proximity *rather than as a form of knowledge*—seeking contact and sensibility in language, behind the circulation of information into which it develops, we have sought to describe *subjectivity as irreducible to consciousness
and to its categorization in themes*. Proximity appears as a relationship with
the Other which cannot be distilled into an *image* nor expressed in such
thematic categorization."[542] For a rationalist this could appear to be unfor-
givable. But Levinas has a vision of rationality that is positive *but critical*
(like Marx, Horkheimer, and Freud). Between the hostage and the victim
appears the "Third,"[543] who opens him- or herself up to the world, to the
comprehension-of-being, to the system, to totality, to justice (or injustice).[544] Ethical reason—which is the only sustainable reason—is born out
of a sense of re-sponsibility for the Other: "Re-sponsibility for the Other
or for communication,[545] is an adventure that contains all the discourses of
science and of philosophy. Because of this, this re-sponsibility *is the rationality of reason itself* or its universality, the rationality of the peace."[546]

[266] As can be seen, we are at moment 7 of figure 12, but now immersed
in an unexpectedly radical dimension. The notion of "re-sponsibility" for
the "Other" (indicated by the "interpellation," moment 6), does not oblige
me merely to search for the causes of the victimization I am confronted
with in the system or totality at issue, which is the properly critical moment
of Levinas's ethics. Levinas generalizes this fact, and ultimately says that the
"world," "knowledge," "consciousness"—all of the order of wisdom—are in
reality a response to this "re-sponsibility which obligates":

> From the re-sponsibility to the problem. The problem is framed from the
> perspective of proximity itself, which, on the other hand, to the extent it
> is immediate, is not problematic. The extra-ordinary engagement of the
> Other with respect to a Third party invokes control, a search for justice,
> the involvement of the society and of the state, comparison and possession,
> thought and science, commerce and philosophy, and from that point on,

anarchy and a search for the beginning. Philosophy is that measure given to the infinity of the *being-for-the-Other* in proximity and understood as the wisdom of love.[547]

Marx demonstrates that after various transformations all capital is ultimately the accumulation of surplus value. In the same way, Levinas wants to suggest that all of the horizon "of the truth,"[548] "the order of wisdom," beginning with Heidegger's "world" (science, knowledge, philosophy), and all of the institutions of all of the historical systems were (and continue to be) *ethical at their origin*: re-sponses to the search for a solution to the "problem" posed by the unjust pain suffered by a victim for which I am (we are) responsible a priori. And so we have to take a final step; in the *diakonía*[549] of ethics it is philosophy itself that must ultimately be redefined: "Philosophy: the wisdom of love at the service of love. . . . Philosophy serves as justice which categorizes difference into themes and reduces the thematic to difference. . . . In an alternating movement, like he who leads skepticism towards the refutation which reduces it to ashes, and which is reborn from these ashes,[550] philosophy justifies and *criticizes* the laws essential to the city's very being."[551] But I have extended the discussion too far.[552] I would have liked to explore here the thought of Michel Foucault, which is a clear expression of a philosophy that is conscious of the "exclusion" of the victims; or to have addressed the "postmodern" tradition, that despite its label undertakes a criticism of the modern system from its overall *acritical* affirmation of capitalism, and that embodies a surface criticism of rationality that leaves the victims absolutely opaque, shrouded, from within the horizon of a systematic rationality which ultimately goes unquestioned. But because this chapter is already long, I will not pursue these threads here.

§4.5. The Critical Criterion and the Material or Ethical-Critical Principle

[267] Now, although we find ourselves at the very core of all of the ethics of liberation, in a sense this is not the most arduous theoretical question that we have had to confront in this book. To the contrary, although we are "at the heart" of this critical *Ethics*, it nonetheless can be applied just in terms of its foundations. The most difficult of the ethical principles (and one that I will return to and explore in more detail in the future, in order to further develop and expound on its foundations) is that of the universal material principle (which has thus far only been addressed in chapter 1, and which I have touched on only at certain moments of the subsequent chapters). If this principle is accepted (that of the morality and feasibility part I of this book), then here I could then draw out the necessary conclusions, since the foundation is a reasoned one that has been empirically enriched

by the diverse levels of the overall argument which we have traversed in the course of this work).

Upon the basis of the affirmation of life we can thus found the non-acceptance of the impossibility of reproducing the life of the victim, from where we can touch the source from which we may (and must) use criticism against the system that is responsible for such negativity.

a. The Critical Criterion

[268] In the first place, abstractly and universally, a criterion of a critical nature (theoretical, practical, instinctual, etc.) of any norm, action, micro-structure, institution, or system of ethics begins from the premise of the *real existence of the "victims,"* whoever they might be, at this stage of the argument. That which does not permit them to live is what may be subjected to criticism, from this perspective. For their part, the victims are inevitable. Their inevitability derives from the fact that it is empirically *impossible* that any norm, action, institution, or system of ethicity *could be perfect* in its implementation and consequences. A perfect system is *empirically impossible*, although anarchocapitalism, for example, makes this claim (Hayek's view, for example, has as its premise the model of a market institution characterized by "*perfect* competition"), as does anarchist direct action (which presupposes the future existence of "perfect ethical subjects" as the active agents of a society without institutions). To demonstrate the truth of this argument I could refer to Karl Popper's argument in *The Misery of Historicism*. A perfect system would demand an infinite intelligence able to implement it at infinite velocity. Since this is impossible, any system will inevitably produce "victims," who are those who bear the unintentional negative effects, imperfections, errors, exclusions, dominations, injustices, and so on of the empirically imperfect and *finite* institutions of existent systems. That is to say, the "fact" that there are victims in any and all systems is a categorical conclusion, and it is because of this that criticism is equally inevitable.

The re-cognition of the Other, *as an other*, and as a victim of the system that produces him or her—and which goes beyond the Hegelian recognition studied by Honneth,[553] and the simultaneous re-sponsibility that Levinas identifies as that of a "face-to-face" character, and which subjects the system[554] or totality to critical questioning—is the point of departure for the criticism that follows.

The empirical question, and along with it the question regarding the sense of all this, comes later: Who are the victims, why are they victims, in what concrete factual circumstances do they exist, and so on and so forth? But the critical criterion counts as a necessary point of departure. This is not a matter of a "value judgment," or of "preference" or of a "subjective" nature. It is an "empirical judgment of fact":

      1. Here lies[555] someone who is poor, a victim!

This is a "descriptive statement" with a truth claim, which demands a new type of validity and also involves a judgment in terms of feasibility. This statement indicates that "consciousness" has already been acquired of a "negation in the first instance" (moment 1 of figure 12)[556] as a critical exercise of preoriginary ethical reason and of the drives that could overcome the mere reproduction or preservation of the prevailing system. To empirically detect a victim is to bear witness to "negativities": poverty, hunger, trauma, pain, pathologies, and many other dimensions of "negativity." Theoretical reason captures the empirical content, and undertakes the formulation of a judgment. The reproductive drives[557] face a contradiction: if the institutions at issue embody the repetition of successful actions to avoid pain and stave off death, and thus enable the attainment of happiness, the "victims" are the absolute contradiction of these efforts, since, despite their condition as effects of this system, they nonetheless suffer pain and their death is hastened.[558] In the face of the "fact" of the victim, the drives of reproduction ("psychologism" as egoism in Levinas, or the "death instinct" in Freud), and even the Nietzschean narcissistic pleasure principal, have their limits. The "*désir* of alterity"—Levinas's *désir métaphysique*—is the only possible transcendental impulse, since it is more than Dionysian: it is the dimension of the myths of Egyptian Osiris-Moshe, if we want to identify it in terms of the world of metaphors, and Nietzsche brings us into it.

      Now, in contrast with part I of this *Ethics* ("Foundation of Ethics"), and as I have already stated above, what we are dealing with here is not the dialectics of "content (substance)/form" but that of "affirmation/negation." Critical thought is in the final instance *material* and *negative* (according to Horkheimer and Adorno, and all of the authors addressed in chapter 4). But "negativity" emerges, presents itself, is discovered (this is the process of "conscientization") from "positivity" as the point of departure (this is what Marx and Levinas were able to perceive). This is why we will begin from the *affirmative* moment (what I have referred to in other works as the "*ana*-lectical" moment), in order to open up the path toward "negativity" from there.

a1. *The critical-positive condition of possibility*

[269] The condition of possibility of knowing the primary or originary "negation" that is suffered by the victim consists in an a priori "affirmation" from which the "negation" is removed. This condition cannot be other than that which we have already explored in part I. Criticism of the existing system is not possible without the "re-cognition [*Anerkennung*]" of the Other (of the victim) as an autonomous, free, and dis-tinct subject (not only as

one who is equal or di[f]ferent).[559] The "re-cognition" of the Other, as a result of the exercise of *preoriginary ethical reason* (which we have addressed above),[560] precedes criticism and argument (discursive or dialogical reason); it is also at the origin of the process and is already the affirmation of the victim as a subject, who is *negated* or ignored in the system as an object. In Luhmann's definition of the system, the Other appears as the same: never as an Other, never as a subject. This is the opening toward the revelation of the Other as an accepted interpellation in Levinas's preontological sense. But the step that takes us further still is the simultaneous response to that re-cognition as re-sponsibility, even before the victim's call to solidarity. The victim's very face of hunger, the ethical re-cognition of her or his corporeal pain "traps" us in re-sponsibility: "we take up the burden" before we can reject or assume it. This is the origin of criticism.

The first condition of possibility of criticism is, then, the *re-cognition*[561] of the dignity of the other subject, of the victim, from a definitive dimension: *as a living human being*. This act of "knowing" human beings from the perspective of life,[562] this act of "re-cognizing" them, is to know them "from" the vantage point of their traumatic vulnerability. The return to their empirical negative state and "re-cognition" *"as victims"* (that is to say, with a deficit of life in some dimension, or with the nonfulfillment of an impulse or drive with respect to their self-preservation), is the analectical moment of the dialectic and one that permits us to subsume everything achieved in part I of this *Ethics*. The victim *is a living human being* and has his or her own unfulfilled demands in terms of the reproduction of life within the system. The re-sponsibility for the Other, of the victim as victim, is equally a condition of possibility, because at their place of origin the destitute do not have the ability to stand up for themselves. Mutual re-sponsibility (in the first place between the victim and others in the same condition) is, as we shall see, the second moment of this condition of possibility.

Thus I have indicated—but only indicated—the material or positive conditions of possibility (moment 2 in figure 12) *from which* critical negation may proceed.

a2. *The critical-negative aspect*

[270] The criterion of criticism is properly "negative": the discovery of the negativity of the victim *as victim*. There are as many negative dimensions as there are levels of ethics.

The negative criterion, which is either material or a reference to content, is the fact of the *impossibility of the reproduction of the life* of the victim. This material-negative aspect which affects the victim is reflected, as a result of the exercise of critical consciousness, upon the system (norm, action, institution, etc.), and the victim "judges" it from the perspective of its results as a *nontruth* as the untrue. Nietzsche, for his part, criticizes the "Socratic truth" in general (although he should have criticized only the "truth" that states that it is possible to live in a system that produces victims who cannot live, which is by the same token contradictory or deceitful). But the Nietzschean proposition of a "will to power" is not a sufficient criterion for discernment, because of its narcissism. The existence of the victim is always a material refutation or "falsification" of the *truth of the system* that produces such victims. In the same way, the reproductive drives or those of self-preservation are put into question as well, since institutions make, as I have noted, the claim of avoiding pain and defending against death.[563] Here we discover the meaning of the doubts articulated by many different forms of skepticism (even that of the postmodernists) against reason itself (to the extent that it is a dominating force), of exclusionary dominant ideologies, of fetishism (discovered by Marx), and of positions critical of the imposition of cultural values (as in Nietzsche), or those that have been introjected repressively by means of the superego (detected by Freud). The criterion of enunciated falsification refers back to the semantic content of the practical judgment and is such (false) if it leads to death, to the negation of life, to that which makes a victim of the victim. The death principle, which is the foundation of all of the pathology of the drives, denies the Other *as an other*, and simultaneously the idea of taking up the Other's burden, situating oneself in the place of the co-responsible hostage, as one re-sponsible for the Other within the system: to "risk the loss of one's face" for the Other, in substitution for his or her suffering. The victims themselves, before any one else, re-sponsibly re-cognize other victims as victims and do so in a manner that is critical, communitarian, and motivated by solidarity. In this way the critical community of victims[564] emerges prior to the explicit "interpellation"[565] of others. But such a re-sponsible re-cognition, for its part, although it affirms the Other, does so from the standpoint of a pre-existing negativity: the fact of being a victim in the suffering of her or his corporeality (a primary material negativity).

b. The Critical-Ethical Principle

[271] This is the core of the ethics of liberation, the deontological point of departure as such. The "factual" anthropological criterion ("descriptive judgment") permits us to lay the foundation for the ethical or normative statement ("judgments of *what-ought-to-be*"), at a level different from the one where the so-called naturalist fallacy can be situated in formal logical terms. In effect, the synthesized result of the material criterion takes concrete form in a "judgment" or "statement of fact":

2. This action or mediation[566] *that does not permit the victims to live* at the same time denies them their dignity as subjects and excludes them from the discourse regarding their condition.

The question posed earlier by Leibniz ("*Unde malum?*") reemerges here. The "evil" is not the "material" or the "other" co-originary principle as has been thought since Plotinus, and even in a Gnostic, Kabbalistic tradition that continues all the way up to Böhme or Schelling, and in some sense to Kant and Hegel: the principle of determination (the *principium individuationis*) appears to be something like the "original evil" within these traditions. For the ethics of liberation, by contrast, the possibility of evil is to be found simply in human finiteness; that is to say, in the *impossibility* of a perfect knowledge and drive or impulse (love). As I have said, Popper was correct in his argument against the concept of perfect planning,[567] which I apply here in another context, when he said that it is *impossible* to assume that the production of a norm, action, institution, or ethical system could have an infinite intelligence functioning at infinite velocity at its command. By the same token I believe it is impossible to conceive of a drive with an *absolutely* free tendency of its own, bound only to reality itself (that of the Other and that of nature, in a kind of *absolutely perfect* version of Levinas's *désir métaphysique*. *Since this is impossible*, a human being has to decide practically between different forms of knowledge and drives of norms, and even ethical systems, which are never completely apprehensible by reason, and which are not the plenary origin of *perfect* happiness (as is Nirvana, for example). Human beings must decide, even intersubjectively, in the ambiguous space between (a) *perfect* knowledge and drives (which are empirically impossible) and (b) the clear negation of life (which is ethically impossible).

A wide spectrum of knowledge and drives, each of them finite, imperfect, opens up between these two extremes, among which are to be found *the possibility* of error (both practical and theoretical error as the "totalization" of the system over and above the reality of life) and of instinctual egotism determined by the self-referential character of the instincts of self-preservation under the sway of the death principle; in a word: "evil." This type of "evil" becomes the basis of choices among mediations that produce victims, to a large degree unintentionally,[568] and that accumulate in the course of its history; this is our focus. The evil is discovered by the inversion[569] undergone by the prevailing *ethical system* that has been established, or by the norms, actions, or institutions, and so on, which although they claim to comply with the ethical principles necessary to put the "goodness claim" into effect (as outlined in chapters 1 through 3), nonetheless produce victims. This evil is the hidden cause that produces victimization (and which does so in terms of the traditional common sense of the dominant groups and from the perspective of noncritical social science, such as that of Weber or Popper; it is worth recalling here that the latter was criticized by Adorno in a famous polemic). This concealment of evil is a process of fetishization, of the formulation of the basis for the claimed *truth* of the system's untrue character. The "criticism of fetishism" is thus an inversion of the inversion: the discovery of the *nontruth* of the system from the perspective of its victims. The unveiling of this "foundation [*Grund*]" (which *grounds* the death of the victims) is the manifestation of its being. With Levinas, ethics criticizes this ontology. Marx criticizes the valorization of value that becomes the essence of capital, as a critique of the capitalist economy. This is the task of criticism as a moment of the struggle for life. To insist on legitimizing (rationally and instinctually) the traditional fulfillments of the system (the "good," values [Scheler], laws [Kelsen], virtues [MacIntyre], etc.) that produce victims, translates the good into "absolute evil" (as indicated by Adorno), as the effect of properly human action rendered possible by its finite character, but realized in its totalization. This is the process of fetishistic divinization of the system first perceived by Feuerbach. To re-sponsibly re-cognize the victim as an autonomous subject in her or his suffering corporeality, as *an Other* in the face of the system, subverts "evil" and lays the foundation that makes possible a process of liberation.

b1. *The negative critical-ethical aspect*

[272] The ethical principle is founded upon the criterion discussed above. Now it is no longer a matter of passing from the human "living being" given by nature, life given over to its own responsibility, and because of this a passage to the mere "ought-to-be" of living ethics (at a material level different from an ethics at the abstract logical-formal level, at which the "naturalist fallacy" is situated, a question dealt with in §1.5). Instead, what I am addressing is the passage from the *"living-inability-to-be"* of the Other, of the victim, in the face of a system that negates his or her life, to the *"ought to be"* of the living victim being liberated under the principle of co-responsibility for the life of the Other in the face of a system in power. Let us begin with the following statement:

3. He or she living in misery is an effect of system X.
4. I re-cognize this victim as a human being with his or her own dignity and as *Other* than the system X.

The deontological step emerges instead immediately in the context of responsibility (which is what Levinas's analysis focuses on):

5. This re-cognition situates me/us as those re-sponsible for the victim in the face of system X.

The properly critical-ethical act or action has its origin in the fact of the negativity of the Other re-cognized as someone *Other than* the system: because she or he is a victim; because he or she is hungry; because I can obtain no profit from this person's existence: a priceless re-sponsibility. The victims are asking for my solidarity from the "exposition" (exposure) of their suffering corporeality. They ask, they plead, *they demand* of me ethically to intervene. This is the commandment, analyzed by Levinas, that demands a transition from statements of fact to a normative material statement:

> 6. I am impelled by an *ethical duty*, because I am co-responsible for[570] this victim, to take up this victim's burden as my own.

And this "taking-up-of-the-burden" is *prior to* the decision to assume or not assume that co-responsibility. The *assumption* of re-sponsibility comes later, and is already ethically assigned; if I do not assume such co-responsibility I do not thereby escape responsibility for the death of the Other, who is my/our victim, and regarding whose victimization I am/we are complicit causes, at a minimum because the victim is a human being assigned to the communitarian co-responsibility of the shared vulnerability of all living beings. I am/we are re-sponsible for the Other because he or she is a human being, "an intersubjective sensibility." Moreover, this is not a matter of re-sponsibility (as in §1.5) for one's own life; now it is solely a matter of re-sponsibility for the negated life of the Other that lays the foundation for a normative statement: because I ought to produce, reproduce, and develop human life in general, there is more of a reason to produce, reproduce, and develop the negated life of the victim of an oppressive system. What is at the heart of all this is the ethical negation of an empirical negation. The passage from the formulation of the basis for the factual judgment ("There is a negative effect, a victim!") to the normative judgment ("I must responsibly take up the victim's burden as my own and put the system responsible on trial"), is now justified.

This is not a matter of a re-sponsibility for an Other before whom we are innocent. In truth we are always situated, even before the negative judgment of the system (norm, act, etc.), as agents in the context of the mediations that produce victims. By taking up the victim's burden as my/our own, we turn back upon itself a guilt of our own (even if it is unintentional) in order to remedy its effects. In any case, when we assume such co-responsibility a crisis results: someone is "risking the loss of his or her face," *in the face of the system*. This is the *krísis* par excellence: the "final judgment" (like what Benjamin describes in the work of Paul Klee), from the "tribunal [*kriterion*]" of history[571] (from the place of the victims), which *takes measure of the goodness* of every norm, act, institution, or system of ethics. This is the source of the following statement:

7. Since I am co-responsible in the face of system X for this victim, *I must* (this is an ethical obligation) *criticize* this system because it causes this victim's negativity.

The judgment of the system with a "no" is preceded by a "no" to what causes victims. If "this" victim did not exist "this" criticism would not be necessary, nor the assumption of re-sponsibility for it. But even this "no" to the causing of more victims is preceded by having assumed them under my/our co-re-sponsibility. This is why it is understandable why the most ancient and venerable imperatives of humanity were always *negative* in character. Since I am co-responsible for the Other I must protect his or her life. In the face of the violence that threatens it we shout, "Hands off, I am its protector!" I am the adoptive parent who takes charge of the orphan and cries out, "Do not kill this child, because it's like this orphan was actually my own son!" This is exemplified by the three fundamental ethical precepts of the Quechua world (that of the Incan empire before the European invasion of Peru), which were stated in negative terms: "*Ama lulla. Ama kella. Ama sua.*"[572] These three negative precepts aim to avoid causing victims, loss of equilibrium, and injustice, and their meaning can be summarized in the following terms:

8. You shall so act that your praxis causes no victims, because we are co-responsible for their death, and thus we would be appropriately subjected to criticism for failing to prevent it!

Wellmer's[573] proposition about the force of the universal imperative as a prohibition of a nongeneralizable maxim should be recontextualized in this framework.

[273] The critical-ethical principle, first in its negative aspect (and as a demonstrative judgment on the nonreproduction of life), and then positively (as the co-responsible assumption of Others as victims, so that they cease to be such, or as a necessary condition for the demand that life be permitted to develop, to grow), and as that upon which the judgment of the system should be based, can be approximately stated as follows: those who act in a manner consistent with the critical-ethical principle have recognized the victim as an autonomous human being, as an Other *who is other than* the ethical systems, to whom has been denied the possibility of living (in its totality or in one of its moments); whose re-cognition simultaneously reveals a co-re-sponsibility for the Other as a victim, that *obligates* us to take up their burden as our own in the face of the system, and first and foremost, to *criticize* the system (or relevant aspect of the system) that causes this victimization. The ultimate subject of such a principle is then the community of victims themselves.

Who could be opposed to such an ethical principle? Or to state it another way: against whom would such a principle stake its claim? Evidently, in the current historical era we are alluding to contemporary "conservatives," such as Peter Berger with his "perfect plausibility,"[574] or the Karl Popper of *The Open Society and Its Enemies*. In Popper's view, the open society's "enemies" are utopians (of the anarchist type), because they claim to be criticizing (in whole or in part) the best society possible, which according to conservatives is the one that really exists. In effect, conservatives judge that the existing society cannot be either criticized or replaced by any better future society, with the result that any overall criticism (the "holistic" approach that has been repudiated so many times) of the present system (the best existing system) is impossible, unfeasible, or worse, destructive. There is no alternative! This kind of "conservativism" in instinctual terms is governed by the "death instinct" (since all past times were better) or by the drives of pure reproduction (Nietzsche's "Apollonian" adversary), and rejects the possibility of a new creative moment (not just Nietzsche's narcissistic desire of pleasure, but most radically the desire of creative-transformative alterity found in Levinas's *désir métaphysique*). It must be shown that such "conservatives" fall into a performative contradiction, because they do not understand that every model of society needs criticism, and, after the passage of centuries, a fundamental change of structures is necessary so that another kind of more qualitatively developed society can emerge. In addition, conservatives have fallen into a pathology governed by the "death principle," as I have noted above—the governing principle of all pathologies as such, as an issue left unresolved by Freud. As Freud argued, this tendency to go ever backward, all the way to the origin of things, radically toward the inorganic, implies a state of being dominated by the assurance that all change is impossible (and thus one attains happiness in the infinite peace of the original time of Schopenhauerian Nirvana); it is, in the strictest sense, a kind of necrophilia (love of death). For the conservative-dominator "all past time was better" because it is the foundation of the present that enables the dominator's "ability to live." For the victims, the future is the time of hope; struggle is necessary in order to improve their state of being, because the present is dominated by the negation that they suffer and that makes it impossible for them to live. Criticism is the beginning of the struggle.

Those who comply with the ethical duty of assuming the burden of the victim as their own in the face of the system, exercising the duty of criticism, end up confronting the structures that produce victims, and because of this their mere re-sponsibility manifested in criticism (which delegitimates) cannot fail to be followed by persecution of one kind or another inflicted upon them, as Levinas described in phenomenological terms when he spoke of the process of *substitution* by which the hostage took the place of the victim. Whoever assumes this kind of re-sponsibility with the victim in the face of the system is persecuted by the power that produces such victims. And it is in that place, when they have exercised the power of criticism as re-sponsibility, that they will be caught as prey, as a "substitute" victim who "bears witness" (*martys* in Greek) *within* the system, and who thereby stands in for the absent presence of the victims.

b2. *The positive critical-ethical aspect*

[274] If one assumes the re-sponsibility of "losing one's face" on behalf of the victim by using the sharp tool of criticism, this action is not undertaken so that the victim continues to be negated. This re-sponsibility must be played as "criticism" and as "transformation" of the causes that brought about the victim's suffering *as a victim*. Marx, in thesis 11 of his *Theses on Feuerbach*, wrote the famous line that now has its assigned place in the complex architecture of the process of building this ethics of liberation, as the positive moment of the critical-ethical principle: "Philosophers thus far have done nothing but *interpret* . . . , but the point now is *to transform* [*verändern*]."[575]

To merely "interpret" is to search for meaning from the neutral point of an uncommitted observer. "Transformation" begins with the commitment of the observer within the structure of the action: the first moment is the assumption of the very co-responsibility of criticism. Further moments will come, but they are subsequent. Within the architecture of the ethics of liberation, the achievement of re-sponsibility must be analyzed in light of the completion of the general orientations and "transformative" demands (of every norm, action, microstructure, institution, and ethical system, in the abstract; and of the criteria and principles for action, concretely and empirically in everyday life) so that victims could cease being so, in both monological and communitarian terms. The ethical obligation of "transforming"[576] the reality that produced victims flows from the perversity of their very existence (it is "evil" that there are victims), from our re-sponsibility (so many times reiterated here) for the fulfillment of the full potential of the life of the victims, and in fulfillment as well of the duty of the critic. The "transformation" will be possible thereafter and should be undertaken in all of the constitutive moments of the critical "goodness claim" (in terms of critical materiality, formality, and feasibility).

Here we enter into another appropriate field for the ethics of liberation. I have repeatedly stressed our concern for the "production, reproduction, and *development*" or "*growth*" of the life of each human subject in community. But what arises here is that the demand is not just for "reproduction" (according to the desires of self-preservation and the narcissism of pleasure associated with the will to power over and against the Other as victim) but also, and simultaneously, the insistence upon qualitative "development."

We can find the essence of the life that grows or dies in this demand; it cannot be fixed in stable immobility. Nietzsche, once again, clearly discovered what was necessary to "grow," and defined this objective from the perspective of the narcissistic drives of Dionysian pleasure. Zarathustra poses the challenge of the need for radical transformation. Nonetheless, his demand is insufficient. In effect, in order for there to be justice, solidarity, and goodness in the face of the victims, it is necessary to "criticize" the given order so the *impossibility of living* for these victims is transformed into *the possibility of living* and of living better lives. But in order to accomplish this end it is necessary to "transform" the prevailing order, to make it grow, to create a new one. And here Zarathustra is insufficient for an ethics of liberation, since the objective is not to annihilate the weak, as Nietzsche seemed to favor. To those poor masses of slaves or of the miserable, members "of the herd," Platonism for the people, the religion of masochistic ascetics—these have to be re-cognized as Others, and from the basis of the re-sponsibility of assuming their burden, to criticize the system, in order to co[l]laborate in solidarity with these excluded victims, who have the right to be part of future better systems. A truly creative drive is necessary, the production of a new order, the resurrection of the excluded and victimized, as with Osiris, the liberatory struggle of the slaves or victims, as with Moses (the Egyptian),[577] that would express itself first in de-constructive criticism. Nietzsche, before his definitive defection, thought he had the experience of being the "Anti-Christ." In effect, in his limited discovery of the affective world, and seeking to transcend the order of the "happy herd," a transcendence that consisted of generating something new, he sought too to discover creative desire, but finally fell into the dominating, war-mongering will to power, with a narcissistic drive. But in a purely ethical philosophical reflection, to the contrary, in forgiving[578] the Roman soldiers who tortured him, that Nietzschean Anti-Christ, the historical Jesus of Nazareth,[579] demonstrated the re-cognition and re-sponsibility for the impoverished masses of the Empire, in a critical negation wielded against the priesthood in the temple, against the destitution of the law in the hands of the Pharisees, and against the collaboration of many in Israel with the Empire, all of which is the negation of all masochism, thereby placing himself in the messianic tradition of Benjamin, of those who struggle for the creation of that which is historically, socially, and politically *new*, from the perspective of a criticism that brings them ultimately to death as the punishment that is the persecution of the system. In the final cry of the one who was crucified, we can discern the peace finally attained in the fulfillment of an agonizing creative responsibility for the Other.

[275] In effect, the obligation to "criticize" the norm, action, institution, or ethical system (in part or in whole) indicates, precisely, that the material

universal principle of the ethics of liberation is not just the reproduction of life (as reproductive reason or drives of happiness of the same type), but also the *development* of human life in history (from the creative drives— which are put at risk on behalf of the Other in order to confront pain and death—and critical reason, which becomes skeptical of the nontruth of the system that generates victims). In this way, the ethics of liberation demands a richer description than the habitual one of the *order* of the drives and of the *types* of rationality. Critical-ethical reason, which is both material and negative, has to, in the very *act of criticism* itself, be related not just with happy reproduction but more fundamentally with the *growth* of the life of each human subject in community motivated by alternative drives. It is an ethical principle of "qualitative progress" defined by new criteria, which differ from those of Modernity, being not purely technological or quanti- tative but instead referring to the sustainability of norms, actions, institu- tions, and systems of ethics that are capable of permitting and developing human life—and the life of other species linked in their dignity to the core dignity of human life, in what would constitute an ecological ethics and not merely folkloric, ambiguous, naturalistic, and in the end not critical of the capitalism which it serves.

c. The "Application" of the Critical-Ethical Principle

[276] Who is re-sponsible for this "application"? Given everything that has been said, we can understand that it is the community constituted by the victims who re-cognize each other as dignified, and affirm them- selves as those self-responsible for their liberation; they are the ones charged with the application in the first instance as a critical-ethical principle. As in the preceding cases, the moral "procedures" of application are formal: they are the *means* by which the criticism and the necessary transformation are undertaken. The formal-moral critical principle—the theme of chap- ter 5—and the liberation principle—addressed in chapter 6—take up pre- cisely this task regarding the "application" of the critical-ethical material principle.

CHAPTER 5

The Antihegemonic Validity
of the Community of Victims

[277] The ethics presented in this work is an ethics of life. The *critical consensus* of the victims promotes the development of human life. What we have before us is, then, the question of a new criterion of discursive validity, the *critical* validity of liberating reason. I will now make a decisive step. The moment has come to gather the different findings of this work together and to move forward without major theoretical difficulties. I will open paths not yet traveled by contemporary ethics. I believe that the method I have been pursuing will be shown to lead to important conclusions. The originality of this method and its results, like everything so far discussed, is tied to the Latin American "experience" from which this approach emerges—and which, in my view, has universal validity.

Rousseau portrayed in *Émile* the prototype of bourgeois revolutionary education—solipsistic, for an orphan without family and community, methodical, without a basis in medieval cultural tradition or monarchical aristocracy, taking place within the paradigm of consciousness and under the solipsistic orientation of a tutor; in contrast, Paulo Freire, the anti-Rousseau of the twentieth century, shows us an intersubjective community formed by the victims of the "Émiles" in power. This community is against the old hegemony. It reaches critical validity in dialogue, and in the process brings about the emergence of historical actors ("social movements" of diverse types) who fight for the re-cognition of their new rights and for the re-sponsible fulfillment of new institutional structures—cultural, economic, political, and so on. In short, what we find in Freire is the emergence of "ethical-critical consciousness" (monological and communitarian, with a re-sponsible and creative superego) as a progressive "conscientization" (*concientização*). In negative terms, this "conscientization" has to do with what makes "originary negation" (see chapter 4) emerge as a structural moment in any ethical system that creates victims. These are the same victims who initiate the exercise of critical-discursive reason by themselves. In positive terms, the victims gradually discern, by virtue of the creative (liberating) imagination, utopian-feasible alternatives of transformation. These alternatives represent future systems where the victims could live. It is at this point that I will examine the links between theory and praxis; between philosophy, the critical social sciences, and militancy; and between the avant-garde and the communitarian-historical subject (leader, movements, and people). I will differentiate between mere emancipation or reformism and real transformation or liberation. The validity of the praxis of liberation (discussed in chapter 6) is grounded on a previous moment that I discuss in this chapter.

An important consideration is that the different moments and modes of reason—the ontological moment (horizon of being) or systemic autoreferent moment (chapters 1–3), practical-material reason, formal or feasible-instrumental reason, the reproductive drives of self-preservation, discursive reason, and so on—are not negated but *subsumed*. I deny, however, their claim of sufficiency and situate them within a discourse (and reality) that mobilizes them in an environment in which they acquire fluidity. The totality is subsumed (denied and assumed) and transformed from the exteriority of the victims. The same occurs with all kinds of rationalities and drives. "Evil" consists of the conservative stubborn adherence to *impeding* the critical "development" of the moment that has been reached (and that generates victims). It is not a question of ontological or theoretical-critical reason, but of an ontological reason transcended practically and internally by an ethical-critical reason. Out of its own contents, but equally innovated by new aspects originating from the exteriority of the victims (a new beginning and yet a continuity in the best aspects of the ancient system: *subsuming*, ethical-critical reason throws itself again to new, future moments of fulfillment. We have here a whole philosophy of history that admits ruptures (of what is definitively irrecoverable because it is a direct cause of victimization and that, for that reason, should be deconstructed; in its paroxysm it is revolution). But it equally admits analectic or analogical continuity (recuperation of what can be recovered under the radical transformation of the new horizon created in an intersubjective manner in the time of repression and liberation, or "messianic time," as Benjamin would put it, of the critical community of the victims).

§5.1. Rigoberta Menchú

[278] First, according to my method, let's hear the words of the victim. Let's read a dramatic text:

> My life does not belong to me.[1] I've decided to offer it to a cause.[2] They can kill me at any time,[3] but let it be when I'm fulfilling a mission, so I will know that my blood will not be shed in vain, but will serve as an example to my companions.[4] The world I live in is so evil,[5] so blood-thirsty, that it can take my life away from one moment to the next. So the only road open to me is our struggle.[6] . . . I am convinced that the people, the masses are the only ones capable of transforming society.[7] It's not just another *theory*.[8]

Discourse ethics has largely dealt with the issue of intersubjective validity. Since I have not established the meaning of a *critical*-discursive reason, discourse ethics will remain our interlocutor for now. However, the horizon of discourse ethics, marked by the loss of the material and negative moments characteristic of its formalism, makes it impossible to discover and analyze a properly *critical*-discursive reason. Indeed, for discourse ethics, the minimum real conditions for the possibility of a valid discussion are the *survival* of the real community of communication[9] and the symmetric participation of all those who may be affected. But, when we consider what I call *principium exclusionis* (the empirical impossibility of not excluding someone from the discourse), the idea of *all the "possibly" affected* becomes ethically problematic. As I will insist later, the problem is that it is not even possible to discover the existence of the affected (they are affected by the "impossibility" of their participation). Indeed, *all* the affected *never* could be real participants (not even by representation). This impossibility is not a matter of empirical difficulty, like, for instance, not being able to invite everyone. The factual nonparticipation to which I refer is an *inevitable* and nonintentional exclusion. There will always be (and it is impossible for there not to be) affected people excluded from any *real* community of *possible* communication. This leads us to a contradiction: (a) even though all the affected always have (an implicit) right to argumentative participation in the real community of communication, (b) nevertheless, there is always some kind of exclusion to affect people.

Exclusion is "always" empirical, and the inevitability of its existence is apodictic: *it is factually impossible* that there are no people affected by exclusion. Only in a perfect community of communication (without excluded people), to use Popper's argument again, would there be no one affected and excluded. For this community to exist, however, we would need an infinite intelligence operating at an infinite velocity. But even if this were possible, we would be able to see only those who are actually excluded. We would be unable to see those who may be excluded in the future (already incipient in nonintentional and invisible present relations of domination). That is to say, at any particular point in time we cannot be aware of all the Others who are excluded in the present, but who will be discovered *as excluded* in the future and who suffer in anticipation the agreements reached by the community of communication. For instance, women were "affected" for millennia in regard to the question of "parental authority."[10] Since there was no awareness of the situation, they were factually "excluded" from the discussion. The same is true of people discriminated by racism, about generations who will be affected by the ecological problems, and so on.

[279] These considerations offer a fresh perspective on the problem of validity, or to what I also refer to here as the morality of the agreement (*Verständingung*). "Agreements" are not only provisional and falsifiable. At an ethical level they also exclude affected people. That is to say, "agreements" have a constitutive "finitude" limitation. "Procedurally," the first question that "participants" in a real and hegemonic community of communication should ask is, Who may we have left "outside"—without re-cognition? But this question can never be fully answered, even if it is considered by the best critical consciousness possible.

Moreover, one must consider that it is necessary to recognize each "participant" as a *dis-tinct* (not only *equal*) ethical subject. The participant must be considered as an *Other* in relation to the autoreferential system. The Other represents the always possible beginning of "disagreement" (or origin of new discourse). The possibility of "disagreement" means that one allows the Other to "participate" in the community with the right for the factual "irruption" of this Other as a *new* Other,[11] as a dis-tinct subject of enunciation. This respect and re-cognition of the Other as *an other* is the original ethical moment[12] par excellence that I am analyzing. It is entailed by any "explanation" (epistemologically, as in Thomas Kuhn, for instance) or by any "consent" reached at without coercion. "Respecting" the dignity and "re-cognizing" the *new Other's* ethical self (as autonomous and distinct)[13] is the original ethical act *kath'exokhén*. At this level, it is also rational and practical. This act implies "making space for the Other" so that she or he can intervene in the argumentation *not only as an equal*, with rights in effect, but as a free person, *as an Other*, as a subject of *new rights*.

[280] The essential difference on this point between discourse ethics and the ethics of liberation is found in the very point of departure. While discourse ethics begins with the community of communication, the ethics of liberation departs from the excluded-affected from such a community. These are the victims of noncommunication. As a result, discourse ethics is practically situated in a position where the fundamental moral norms become "inapplicable" (*Nichtanwendbarkeit*) *in "normal" situations of asym-*

metry (*not particularly exceptional situations*).[14] The ethics of liberation, on the other hand, locates itself precisely in the "exceptional situation of the excluded," that is to say, in the very moment when discourse ethics discovers its limitations. Albrecht Wellmer writes: "Revolutions against unjust claims should be considered *exceptional* moral situations; revolutions against unfair claims should be considered situations of moral exception; in this way, the bases of a reciprocity understood morally have been abolished, because the moral duties of one cannot have correspondence with the moral claim of the other."[15] These limit situations are central to the ethics of liberation. By "limit situations" I mean, for instance, the multiple ordinary asymmetrical processes of domination of women, discrimination against certain races, suffocation of peoples and indigenous cultures, and oppressive pedagogical processes. Consider also the situation of the majority of people in states without law or rights, and the peripheral or colonial world, which, by definition, is in a position of disadvantage under the military violence of the United States (in the present). We also have to recall the "dirty" wars of Argentina, Brazil, Chile, and others, and criminally orchestrated counterrevolutions like the one launched in Nicaragua in 1979, and so on. The concrete principle "Allow the excluded-affected person or victim to participate in the discussion!" has a procedural logic of its own, different from the dominant, merely discursive logic. The conditions of asymmetry that represent "situations of *exception*" for the application of discourse ethics become "*normal* situations" of the grounding of norms for liberation ethics. As we will see later, liberation ethics is able to constitute symmetry[16] *among the victims themselves*.

[281] In his book, *Nuevo punto de partida de la filosofía latinoamericana*, J. C. Scannone writes:

> Latin American liberation philosophy made critical use of conceptualization and developed it . . . in order to formulate in philosophical terms the Latin American *experience* of the *poor person* . . . ; before taking up the question of being, one needs to pursue the ethical-historical questioning of questioning itself. But the risks of remaining alone in the elaboration of that problem led to its taking a dialectical form . . . which brought about criticism as well as the reinterpretation of its forms and categories. This reinterpretation was possible by virtue of the *positive* expression of the new horizon of meaning opened up by Latin American history and symbols.[17]

As a way of overcoming the limitations of the point of departure that he indicates, Scannone suggests that we perform a double movement: first, a critique of the transcendental character of Apel's community of communication from the perspective of an ethical-historical community, which leads to the "we" of the Latin American people as subject.[18] Second, this "we" should be taken to "be" in the sense of the Spanish "estar": "nosotros estamos."[19] This "new" point of departure would allow one to go beyond the *philosophy of liberation*: "All things considered, in my judgment, the focus on the *dependency-liberation* opposition ran the risk of leaving insufficiently thematized the properly *positive* elements of Latin America. I refer to what cannot be reduced to the determinative negation of the negation, that is, to dependency and oppression. There was the risk of talking about the *positive* elements abstractly, . . . without treating them in light of their novelty through a hermeneutics of Latin American history and culture."[20] "Popular wisdom," the hermeneutics of symbols (with a strong influence from Ricoeur), would be the *new* point of departure.

I think that, with this move, Scannone relapses into ontology. He now relies on the world, on the totality, in a mere community of communication. The abstract "to be" (even the "we are") is just another "world." It is a "concrete form of life" (*Sittlichkeit*) (Hegel) without universal criteria to explain the reasons for the poverty (nonlife) of the people, and without critical criteria to pursue the dialogue among asymmetrical cultures and to determine the feasibility of the needed transformations. Scannone falls back into the point of view that was overcome by liberation philosophy at the end of the sixties.[21]

What are the reasons for this "relapse"? From a historical point of view, we find the horrible repressions by dictatorships since 1973. From a political point of view, we must consider the influence of populist Peronism. Many philosophers thought, with extreme and risky faithfulness, that it was a way of "being with the people." From a philosophical point of view, the abstract "to be" (*estar*) and the abstract "we are" (*nosotros estamos*), which offer resistance from the wisdom of the symbols of our people, become ambiguous when they are not related to the "formal capitalist system," which either includes the people (as oppressed subjects) or excludes them. It is clear that we need to "pass through" a "rereading" of Marx. These abstractions appear as just another "world" to which it is possible to apply the critique Habermas made of Taylor.[22] If, on the contrary, popular culture ("we are" [*nosotros estamos*] in the wisdom . . .) is situated as the Others oppressed by the system and as excluded-affected persons or victims, everything takes a different form. In this case, wisdom follows the dynamics of liberation, and it is not delimited by the efforts for self-preservation. It does not collapse into forms of complicity aimed at achieving bare survival—a passive resistance in which the "feast" becomes only a false, sublimating alienation.

[282] The complete and *positive* affirmation of one's own culture today, in the current world system, is impossible without two previous moments: (1) the discovery, primarily by the victims themselves, of the oppression and exclusion that weighs on their culture, and (2) the critical and autoreflexive awareness of what is valuable in this culture. Take, for instance, an

exceptional narrative testimony. A Venezuelan journalist (an "organic intellectual") produced a book, *Me llamo Rigoberta Menchú y así me nació la conciencia*, that told the story of the Guatemalan indigenous leader Rigoberta
Menchú, winner of the 1992 Nobel Peace Prize.[23] Her subject is (a) a dominated woman, (b) a poor peasant, (c) a Mayan—from a people conquered
five hundred years ago, (d) a person of colored skin or race, and (e) a native
of a peripheral Guatemala exploited by North American capitalism. Here
are five well-articulated and simultaneous forms of dominations.

The first part of this splendid narrative tells the life experience of a
woman in the culture of the Maya nation. Even though the story is told
from the perspective of an acritical popular wisdom that takes unjust suffering as pertaining to "the nature of things," the story is "self-affirming."
Conscientization does not begin, however, until chapter 16: "We'd start discussing and heaping insults on the rich who'd made us suffer for so long. It
was about then I began learning about politics."[24]

This critical-monological *conscientization* is rapidly transformed into a
communitary act[25] of reaching "agreement" or consensus. The ethical moment, which is the *radical* "point of departure" for any liberation ethics,
begins in chapter 17: "Yes, I was very confused. I went through a sort of
painful change within myself.[26] It wasn't so difficult for the rest of them
at home to understand what was real and what was false.[27] But I found it
very hard.[28] What did exploitation mean for me?[29] Why do they reject
us?[30] Why is the Indian not accepted?[31] And why was it that the land used
to belong to us?[32] Our ancestors used to live here. Why don't outsiders accept Indian ways? This is where discrimination lies!"[33] Here, the process
I described in chapter 4 appears in stages in the narrative. "Rigoberta and
her people" have always had their culture; they have treated it with disdain and nobody had taught them to value it; they have suffered a dreadful
oppression and exclusion.[34] Suddenly, the ethical-critical conscientization
emerges; it is made possible by the *affirmation* of the value of the victims
by the victims themselves. A struggle for liberation with an ethical awareness of their condition as victims begins out of that affirmation. The affirmation arises from a dialectical process whose horizon of comprehension
is the relation dominator/dominated, or system/exclusion. Scannone believes that it is possible to *affirm* one's own culture as valuable (as Arturo
Roig points out frequently), but he forgets that this affirmation should
proceed from the dialectic oppressor/dominated as victims. Without the
explicit discovery of this negative relation[35] one would inevitably fall into
an ambiguous and nonethical ontology. This ontology would be full of
wisdom but not critical. It would be a "concrete form of life" (*Sittlichkeit*)
without criteria for liberation. One would fall again into the preliberation
Ricoeurian hermeneutics.

[283] The testimony of Rigoberta Menchú shows that the "point of de-

parture" is complex, but that it nonetheless occurs before and beyond ontology, the world, and the *dominating* being or dominator, that is, the *hegemonic* community of communication. The point of departure is the victim, the Other, not simply as another "equal person" in the argument community, but, ethically and apodictically, as Other in some negated-oppressed (*principium oppressionis*) and affected-excluded (*principium exclusionis*) aspect. The new point of departure originates in the *ethical experience* of "exposition" in the face-to-face: "My name is Rigoberta Menchú," or the "Here I am!" of Levinas (opening one's shirt to bare one's chest before the firing squad).

Ontological ethics departs from the always already presupposed world; discourse ethics departs from the always already presupposed community of communication; the Latin American philosophy of the "we[36] are" departs from a knowledgeable, popular culture that is affirmed and analyzed from a hermeneutical standpoint. The ethics of liberation does not negate the previous moments, but it has a preferred point of departure: the "exteriority" of the ontological horizon ("reality" beyond the "comprehension of being"), beyond the community of communication, or beyond a wisdom that is ingenuously *affirmed* as autonomous (while it is, in contrast, concretely and historically repressed, destroyed in its creating nucleus, marginal, reproducible only with difficulty,[37] features that, when they are ignored, lead to an "illusion" of a folklorist type). The point is to clearly point out three kinds of "affected" recipients or referents:

a. The affected person, *as the excluded* in any discussion, who will suffer the effects of a valid agreement reached by the hegemonic community. For the ethics of liberation, the awareness of being "affected" (as excluded) is the result of a liberating process of *conscientization*. The radical immemorial time is, then, the situation in which the affected is *not aware of being affected*. Such is the situation of the slave who believes to be a slave by "nature." I have already quoted this text: "For years and years we harvested the death of our people in the fields of Chiapas.[38] Our men and women walked in the dark night of ignorance"[39]

b. The affected person, *as oppressed*, or the victim who is "exploited" intrasystemically, who suffers in the same way as (a). Examples include "peasants," who, according to Marx, create surplus value as salaried workers of the countryside; or women in the context of patriarchal chauvinism.

c. Those who are affected but who are not directly enmeshed in a relationship of domination, who nonetheless are materially excluded (there are, in effect, degrees of exteriority and being subsumed in a systemic sense). At this level, we find the "poor" (Marx used the term *pauper*), or those who cannot reproduce their life. The "poor" person is, for example, no longer a serf under a feudal system, but is also not yet a salaried worker (*pauper ante festum*). Poor persons may have lost their positions as salaried workers and become jobless (*pauper post festum*). We think here of available jobs and of current marginal urban masses. The poor are victims in all three determinations.

[284] The ethical and ontological analysis pursued by Heidegger, Taylor, or McIntyre, may be and should be also applied to the "world" of the affected, exploited, or excluded victims. The "world" of the victims must not be exclusively viewed as a pure negativity, formal exteriority without content, or as the Other formally exterior to the existing world, system, or hegemonic community. It is necessary to pay attention to their reality in a *positive* way.[40] For this reason, I believe that the task of Heidegger, Taylor, or Scannone makes sense: the Other should be "authentic" in his or her cultural exteriority. Hermeneutics makes sense even when it takes the Other as its object. Rigoberta Menchú tells us about the customs of her family (chapter 1), the ceremonies of birth (chapter 2), Nahuatl—as the "other-me," the double of each human being—(chapter 3), the land (chapter 4), the city as viewed by the Indian (chapter 5), planting cults (chapter 9), "mother earth" (chapter 10), marriage ceremonies (chapter 11), and community life (chapter 12). To narrate all this is necessary because victims, the oppressed and excluded Other, are not empty formal objects. They are, on the contrary, subjects who live in a world full of meaning, with a memory of their ventures, with a culture, and with the community of the "we-are-existing" (*nosotros-estamos-siendo*) as "re-sistant" reality. We are, then, "with Scannone," but it is necessary to go "beyond Scannone." The reason for this is made clear in Menchú's narrative. Suddenly, the story takes a different meaning as Menchú confronts a series of horrible "experiences": the death of her friend who was poisoned by a fumigation (chapter 13), her position as "servant" in the capital (chapter 14),[41] the imprisonment of her father, who later died in a fire set by the army at the Spanish Embassy, which had been occupied peacefully by peasants (chapter 15). A process of reflection begins in the light of these incidents. Menchú recalls, as if she were judging her own past critically:

> I started thinking about my childhood, and I came to the conclusion that *I hadn't had a childhood at all. I was never a child. I hadn't been to school, I hadn't had enough food to grow properly, I had nothing.*[42] I asked myself: "How is this possible? *I compared it*[43] to the life of the children of rich people I'd seen. How they ate. Even their dogs. They even taught their dogs to recognize only their masters and reject the maids. All these things were jumbled up in my mind, I couldn't separate my ideas.[44] That's when I began making friends from other villages.[45] . . . I asked them: What do you eat? How do you make your breakfast? What do you have for lunch? What

do you eat for supper?' . . . I have to tell you that I didn't learn my politics at school.[46] I just tried to turn *my own experience*[47] *into something which was common to a whole of people*.[48] I was also very happy when I realized that it wasn't just my problem. . . . That there were rich and poor and that the rich exploited the poor—our sweat, our labor. That's how they got richer and richer. The fact that we were waiting in offices,[49] always bowing to the authorities, was part of the discrimination we Indians suffered.[50]

An impressive, veridical story! It deserves to be read and commented on carefully.[51]

[285] Let us explore now the questions at the bottom of all this: What *kind of rationality* opens the Other *as an other* to us? What *kind of rationality* opens that Other even in her or his exteriority, before, in, and after the functional moments of the systems—for example, propositional systems (analytic), argumentative or pragmatic systems (Apel and Habermas), textual systems (Ricoeur), instrumental systems (Weber or Popper), political systems (Rawls), economic systems (criticized by Marx), and so on. I referred to the reason that discerns the mediations for the reproduction and development of the life of the human subject as "practical-material reason." But even more precisely I referred to a *specific kind of rationality* (different from discursive reason, strategical reason, instrumental reason, emancipating reason, hermeneutical reason, and so on) that "re-cognizes" the excluded victim, the Other as other than the prevailing system of communication. I called this "ethical-preoriginary reason." "Ethical-preoriginary reason" is the first rational moment, prior to any other use of reason, by virtue of which we have the *experience* (empirical and material, which makes it the same as the "practical-material reason") of re-sponsibility-for-the-Other. This experience occurs prior to any decision, commitment, linguistic expression or communication about the Other. "Ethical-preoriginary reason" allows us to be stirred by an "obsession" or "re-sponsibility for the Other." This responsibility is a priori. It is always presupposed by any propositional or argumentative linguistic expression in every communication, in every consensus or agreement, in every praxis. "Re-sponsibility for the Other" is the illocutionary moment in the origin of every "speech-act": "*I* tell *you* that . . .*"; it is the constitutive intention prior to the "act-of-work," to any work division, and to any claim of effectiveness in respect to the feasible or in regard to the co-solidarity with the Other.[52] It is the "saying [*Dire*]" previous to anything "said (*dit*)" (including argumentation); it is the moment of "being exposed" in one's skin before the Other;[53] it is the first moment, where we find the "very rationality of reason."[54] The source of critique is found in the practical moment of the "ethical-preoriginary reason," which establishes the mode of "being-for-the-Other" as an a priori re-sponsibility in the "face-to-face" of "proximity."[55]

[286] Discourse ethics begins with a community that presupposes certain "claims" in serious or authentic communication. These "claims" are grounded on the basic ethical norm, which makes reference to "an in-principle unlimited community of communication, *of people who recognize themselves reciprocally as equals.*"⁵⁶ The basic ethical norm on which the validity claims of pragmatics are grounded consists in this "re-cognition" of *people as equals*. The "encounter" with the victim as the Other, as an *ethical subject* in the originary "re-cognition," is the a priori of every ethics. This is what Levinas calls *proximité* or "face-to-face." Setting up this relation or encounter is the exercise of "ethical-preoriginary reason *par excellence.*" "Discursive reason," and more exclusively even "discursive-*critical* reason," are grounded on "ethical-preoriginary reason."⁵⁷ One only discusses something (practical or *theorical* moment of reason) because the Other is recognized as an autonomous ethical subject. Out of respect for the Other, one contributes to the discussion with rational arguments in order to reach an agreement, instead of using violence (irrational moment). If I am right on this, it is clear, then, that discursive reason is a moment founded upon "ethical-preoriginary reason." "Ethical-preoriginary reason" is, in short, the "for-the-Other" of practical reason taken as the origin or primary source of reason (previous to every argument and communication). Even the "validity claims" of discourse are founded on "ethical-preoriginary reason," which is prediscursive. Since the victim should become an ethical subject in a relation of symmetry, what is intersubjectively valid must be also agreed upon argumentatively by the Other. In this sense, ethics is, for Levinas, first, preoriginary, philosophy: "Ethics, understood as *exposure* and the extreme *sensibility* of one subjectivity in the face of another, becomes transformed into morality and toughens its skin as we pass into the political world of the impersonal *third person*—the world of government, institutions, courts, prisons, schools, committees, and so on. But the norm that should continue to inspire and structure the moral order is the ethical norm grounded in relations among human beings. . . . This is why ethical philosophy should continue to be considered the primary philosophy."⁵⁸

"Ethical-preoriginary reason" is prior to and opens up the "space" of "communicative action." It does this by making possible the "encounter" with the Other, which finds its extreme ethical limit of exteriority in the space of the "affected-excluded Other." The re-sponsibility for subverting the structures that hide the victim from communicative processes and from argumentative procedures is the originating-originary. "Ethical-preoriginary reason" is at the origin of the liberation of the victim, the poor, and all those who are excluded, because it un-covers the face that has been covered over by the "functional part" of the autoreferent system. It then re-cognizes the excluded as an ethical subject with dignity. This Other is re-cognized, not only as an equal, but as other than the dominant community, that is, as the possible *subject* of the process of liberation who aims to form part of the *new*, real, possible, and future community.

Analectical affirmation, beyond the horizon of the world and the dominant community of communication, is the fruit of "ethical-preoriginary reason." This mode of reason is exercised, first and foremost, by the dominated or excluded Others, who re-cognize themselves in community as the affected Others: Menchú, the indigenous peoples of the Americas. . . . This is not a mere empirical example; we are dealing here with a narrative that allows us to analyze "formal" situations, which are universal and form part of every possible system, world, or community of communication.[59]

[287] After the victims have become aware of their situation, there are other necessary, posterior, and diachronic moments in which the oppressed and excluded fight for full "participation" in the "future" community of communication. This "future" community is anticipated by the community of the victims themselves and their allies. For many years, liberation ethics insisted on the "interpellation" by the Other of a receptive person (who has the ears to hear) as the origin of the process of liberation. I have referred to this in the system as "*ethical* consciousness."[60] Since there is a *previous* process, I must propose a new development. The coming into awareness of the existence of the Other (*toma-de-conciencia del Otro*) as oppressed and excluded[61] initiates the process of re-cognition and the *first solidarity* (among the Others themselves as victims; among the oppressed) that emerges out of the *originary re-sponsibility*[62] of the victims themselves as *subjects of the new history*. Menchú recounts: "The rich come from over there, where the *ladinos'* government is. It's the government of the rich, the landowners. We began seeing things more clearly and,[63] as I said, it was not difficult for us to understand that we had to join together in the struggle. . . . I began traveling to different areas, discussing everything. . . . That's why my little brothers and my brothers and sisters understood more clearly than I did."[64] When the victim dis-covers that she has been covered over, ignored, or affected-negated, she begins to gain awareness of her-self in positive terms. From here derives the relevance of the contribution of Scannone, or the application of the analysis of Ricoeur and Taylor to the culture of the poor or the victims. This discovery, however, is dialectically codetermined by the "awareness" (*conciencia*; *Bewusstein-Gewissen*: theoretical and ethical awareness) of the negative *relation* with the system:[65] the victims discover themselves (we-others) [*nos-otros*] as exploited, covered over, and excluded. When Menchú writes that "we began *seeing* things *more clearly*," she does not only mean "to see our own wisdom clearly," but also to see its "negation." Without the awareness of negativity, the usefulness and the need of the fight ("It was not difficult for us to understand that we had to join together in the struggle," as Menchú puts it), the organization ("I

began traveling to different areas"), and, of the project of liberation would not come to mind.[66] Since this pro-ject must be pursued in a democratic, symmetrical, and participative fashion on the march "with others," it is the fruit of critical-discursive reason (but, it will be, in addition, the fruit of a critical reason of instrumental feasibility). The proposal and definition of political and economic ends (the historical-possible utopia) makes clear that the pro-ject of liberation is also the effect of strategic reason. Instrumental reason also plays a role in the design of this project, since its construction involves technical, economic, scientific, and political mediations.

[288] Out of this negativity (which consists of being "affected" or excluded; "invisible" for those who are in the system), which becomes a *subject* through militant organization, the popular Other is now able, as transontological original "source," to "interpellate" those with "ethical conscience" or those who know how to hear in the current system: "I *interpellate* you on the basis of the justice that you should have accomplished for us!"[67]

When someone "in the system" is moved by the victim's explicit interpellation and accepts, in a reflective manner, taking "responsibility-for-the-Other," another moment of the pre-discursive "ethical-preoriginary reason" is accomplished. The new moment takes place this time in the intrasystemic hearer:[68] the dignity of the Other as ethical subject is recognized and his or her almost unintelligible word is "taken as true" (*für-Wahrhalten*). The connection between the affected who are not participants and those who participate in the hegemonic system, but who nonetheless abandon their position of domination by the affirmation of an "obsession" or "co-responsibility" for the Other, makes possible an advanced theoretical-critical explicative elaboration of the historical-communitarian subjects with full critical consciousness. The critical consciousness in question here is not only that which resides in the "common sense" of the victims, but also the scientific and philosophical critical consciousness of experts that emerges in the process of liberation.[69] This critical consciousness is decidedly something different from the ambiguous affirmation of exteriority, from the hermeneutics of the complicit popular culture, and from the impossible application of the ethical principle of discourse ethics, which remains foreign to all this because it presupposes symmetry among the affected.

§5.2. The Ethical-Critical Process of Paulo Freire

[289] Now I should distinguish clearly between different positions that offer resources for the possibility of theoretical-critical explanations. First, there is Jean Piaget's cognitivism. His position is articulated in the "center" of the world system. I call it cognitive because, even though Piaget takes

into account affectivity and the phenomenon of moral consciousness[70] (a theme that must not be confused with so-called critical thinking, which finds better treatment in the hands of Lawrence Kohlberg),[71] he remains at the level of formalist morality. Second, there are positions, like that of Feuerstein, that emerge in the "periphery" and that consider the social marginality of the child. There is also Vygotsky, who takes into consideration the constitutive sociohistorical and cultural context in a "postrevolutionary" moment of the "periphery." The third position introduces the properly ethical-critical and intersubjective-communitarian position of the historical subject who finds her- or himself in the process of *concientização* (critical consciousness), to use Paulo Freire's term, a process of denunciation and announcement that emerges in the context of an oppressed society at the periphery of global capitalism. Freire is an original thinker, an authentic "anti-Rousseau of the twentieth century," whose originality I will demonstrate here with a precise definition of the intersubjective dialogism of ethical-critical and discursive reason. This mode of reason includes the strictly *ethical* dimension of the negated material content. It cannot be, thus, characterized merely as a formal morality like that of Kohlberg and Habermas. Freire is not only an educator in the strict sense of the term. He is something more—an educator of the "ethical-critical consciousness" of the victims, of the oppressed, of the condemned of the planet who live in community. I hope it will be possible now to situate his contribution, and maybe also his limits.

a. From Piaget to Kohlberg

[290] Originally a biologist, Piaget locates the problem of knowledge[72] at the ontogenetic level, dividing the cognitive process of the child into different stages.[73] The first stage, which takes place just after birth, is characterized by the practice of "coordination of sensation and action through reflexive behaviors," in a developing sensorimotor scheme.[74] The most important of these behaviors is breast-feeding, in which infants come to distinguish the mother's nipple from other objects that they take into their mouths.[75] In the second stage, "habits" develop, and classical conditioning (as in the conditional reflexes of Pavlov) emerges. In the third stage, which begins when the infant is four and a half months old, the child discovers the relation between cause and effect through the manipulation of things in space. Only in stage four does the technical-practical intelligence emerge; at this point the infant can interact with a hidden object (e.g., raising a lid to find it). Stage five begins when the infant is about eleven to twelve months old, when the child reaches "directive groping": to bring closer, by tugging at the sheet, an object that is lying upon it. In the sixth stage,

the infant is able to search for a new object in order to use it as a means to complete an action. This is similar to Köhler's findings with chimpanzees. What we have here is, then, an increasing capacity for the "construction of the real,"[76] along with the development of affective[77] and moral[78] characteristics. Language, along with semiotic capabilities, appears approximately from the fifth stage onward. The emergence of language accelerates the development of the psyche. The "lexicon," its multiple "operations" and "logical" relations[79] (in phrases of two or more words that augment with increasing memory), make possible a growing repertory of "objects."

The first period culminates, as we have seen, in the emergence of language. This is early childhood.[80] The second period takes place from two to six or seven years old. At this point we find the beginnings of socialization, of interior language, of the sign system, of the systematic assimilation of one's own actions, and so on. The third period begins with school education. Here, socialization advances and formal rational operations develop. This period occurs between seven to eleven years old. Sexual maturity is achieved at adolescence, which is the fourth period. At this moment, the characteristic disequilibria of a greater degree of social integration are also produced.[81]

[291] Piaget's conceptions of affectivity and of moral judgment rely on the positions of Freud and Kant. Piaget takes from Freud the questions concerning the interiorization of the affective image of the father in the "superego," and from Kant the ideas of duty and respect.[82] The child, Piaget argues, following the studies of Bovet,[83] initially accepts exterior norms commanded by a higher authority out of respect. At this moment, there is an ambiguous combination of affection and fear. This is a position of heteronomy in which a guilty feeling is attached to the accomplishment of the command. Value and obligation: rules are sacred, as much in a game of marbles as in the moral world, which are identified with each other at this stage. It is only in the third stage, which begins at the age of seven years, that the differentiations between reality and rules, and between technical and moral rules emerge. There is at this moment an increasing sense of the difference between "justice" and "obedience." The child begins to ask about the legitimacy or "justice" of an "order" and observes contradictions in adults.

Piaget's method consists in situating the theoretical reflections of moral philosophy (especially Kant's) at an ontogenetical level with the use of evolutionary psychology. This approach has advantages as well as limitations. The moral theory on which it is based is *formal*, based only on principles, only on practical-cognitive reason.

This discussion provides the background to understand Kohlberg's later development of Piaget's approach.[84] Kohlberg is inspired not only by Kant, but also by Rawls. He stays within the parameters of the formal Piagetian conception of morals, yet he expands its horizons by situating moral development at a phylogenetic level.[85] This intervention is not free of an evident Eurocentrism. Both Habermas and Apel feel comfortable with this cognitivist, formal, and universalistic vision that includes the postconventional level.[86] The limitations of this view are, as we will examine in what follows, characteristic of *acritical* formalist positions, which are subsumed and overcome by Freire. Unlike Habermas and Apel, Freire takes into consideration the communitarian-intersubjective, ethical, material, and critical aspects of the problem.

[292] Kohlberg divides the process of the maturation of moral judgment into three levels (A, B, and C) and six stages. Level A, defined as *preconventional*, comprises the first two stages. In stage 1, rightness consists of strict obedience to mandates and authority. The motivation consists of avoiding punishment and harm. In stage 2, rightness is identified with the immediate satisfaction of needs. Level B, the *conventional* level, comprises stages 3 and 4. In stage 3, rightness is defined in terms of the respect and trust in the equals; motivated by the fulfillment of rules and expectations, one takes care of others. In stage 4, rightness is identified with the accomplishment of duties for the sake of order and the social welfare. In the *postconventional* level, or level C, moral decisions obey rights, values, or principles: stage 5 is characterized by the definition of rightness in terms of the defense of rights, values, or legitimate pacts, even at the point where they stand in opposition to the norms of the group; in stage 6, the stage of universal ethical principles, the act obeys universal ethical principles that must be held by everyone in the world.

The transition from one stage to another entails learning at an ontogenetic level. It also presupposes phylogenetic or historic and cultural conditions. This is made obvious by the fact that stages 5 and 6 are only achieved in European Modernity. For non-European or nonmodern universalist ethicists such as Nezahualcóyotl, Confucius, Aristotle, Avicena, and Thomas Aquinas, their "cultural world" appeared to them as the entire extent of the human.[87] It is Habermas who, also considering the work of R. Selman,[88] completes Kohlberg's model.[89] To the problems that emerge when the model is extended to adulthood and old age, I would add the contradictions found in its application to peripheral cultures in a postcolonial situation. But I do not want to develop this critique now. As it will be made obvious later, I am interested in subsuming Kohlberg's position while at the same time showing—like Habermas—the lack of what I would call the *levels of critique* that belong—when they can emerge—to each of the levels indicated above. Thus, for instance, we can observe, still located in stage 1, that the following situations can emerge. A mother orders her little daughter:

1. Take care of your toys!

Following the order, the little girl does not lend her toys to any of her girl friends, even if any of the girls wants to take them from her. It is clear that the command presupposes that she should not put at risk her toys in that way. But the mother can order:

2. Take care of your toys, but lend them to your friends!

The command includes at a material level a moment of solidarity that conforms the moral consciousness of the girl. But it could be that a boy of dark skin, mestizo, son of the gardener, whose name is Pedrito comes to play. If the mother said:

3. Take care of your toys, but share them with your friends, and especially with Pedrito!

she would have included in the command *negatively and materially* a "critical-ethical" moment of social solidarity. The girl would incorporate this command in her ethical conscience at the ingenuous formal level of the logic "punishment-obedience." Her ethical conscience will thus turn "critical" without any intention on her part. It is in this way that the Egyptian *Book of the Dead* could have included "ethical-critical" norms ("I gave bread to the hungry"),[90] right beside magical, mythical, and purely conventional exigencies. A high level of *ethical-material* critical consciousness ("criticality") can subsist along with ingenuous degrees of *moral-formal* critical consciousness. It can also precede more universalistic expressions of *formal* critical consciousness. Distinguishing between these two types of critical consciousness represents the central problem of the pedagogy (and the politics) of the formation of the ethical and moral judgment. As we will see in my analysis of Freire's work, a consciousness located at a material, magical, or an alphabetic level can acquire an extreme form of ethical-critical awareness. The critical consciousness of this individual may turn more acute than that of the most refined member of a postconventional society. Paulo Freire points this out. An educator and not a philosopher, Freire does not articulate in an analytical manner categories that give more precision to his theoretical and critical language.

In this way, we should go over the different levels and stages one by one. The ethical-critical moment in the *postconventional level* or stage 6 (but also stage 7) should be expressed as follows:

Ethical-critical stage 6: The *empirical application* of the ethical and universal principles should be guided by the effort to discover the victims *inevitably* produced at *a concrete level* by the fulfillment of those same principles. The application of the "dominating" universality will be considered untrue, invalid, and infeasible from the perspective of the victims.

It could be argued that this negative moment does not really add any-thing to stage 6. The negative moment is only concerned with a mistaken application of the universal principle. Demands for respect, re-cognition, and responsibility for the victim would be included in the exigencies of the universal principle. But, as we saw in chapter 4, the ontological posi-tion of the moral subject, who applies the universal principle of stage 6, inevitably becomes "blind" to that which transcends the concrete univer-sality of his world, system, culture, and so on. "The Other" becomes in-visible. The ethical-critical stages (from 1 to 6), on the contrary, represent necessary moments and procedures that *explicitly* develop the exigency to take account of "alterity," which lies beyond the current "universality." The ethical-critical stages lead to the deconstruction of the negativity of the current "universality" from the perspective of the victims. We will see how Freire manages to "teach" (since this is a matter of *learning*) the practice of the "ethical-critical consciousness." But, I will first prepare the way by ex-posing the work of two progressive psychologist educators.

b. Reuven Feuerstein and Lev S. Vygotsky

[293] Feuerstein's work follows a cognitivist and, to an extent, solipsis-tic line, within a paradigm of consciousness[91] with regard to the interven-tion of the educator. Yet, he is, at least to some extent, critical of Piaget's ontogenetic Eurocentrism. In contrast to Piaget, who for the most part studied the "European child," Feuerstein focused on the differentiation of children in disadvantaged social positions in Israel.[92] According to Feuer-stein: "Changeability is the character of characters, the only one that is permanent. . . . [W]hat I would like to make understood is that what human beings possess of stability is their ability to change, to be always open to change. . . . In the first place this changeability absolutely negates the possibility of predicting human development and the classification of people: you are five years old, you are categorized as retarded, and this is where you will stay for the rest of your life."[93] Going beyond Piaget or Kohlberg, Feuerstein develops a pedagogy by which those who are consid-ered "retarded" can, through the aggressive and methodic intervention of a teacher, "modify" their position and initiate a positive, unexpected phase of learning. Regarding one case, a colleague wrote to him: "Feuerstein, it is not worth the effort to bring the girl to Jerusalem. You won't be able to accomplish anything more. Without being able to read or write, without a constituted language, without knowing what day of the month it is, with-out guidance, without being able to handle her own needs . . . nothing can be done."[94] After nine months of pedagogical intervention, that girl was unrecognizable. She had absolutely modified her capacity to learn. "The

ability to be transformed is accessible in individuals above and beyond the etiology that determines their state of being."[95] For him, intelligence is not an innate "capacity," but a "process." "Everything depends on the number of connections or links established by the brain; these links may be enriched by educative action, always conditioned to the degree of interest and to the relation with the one who learns."[96] Following J. P. Guilford, Feuerstein indicates that intelligence presupposes knowledge, memory, convergence, divergence, and evaluation. From Piaget, Feuerstein takes the idea that the child organizes and adapts the experiences by assimilation. From Vygotsky, he learns the design of stimulation programs that facilitate the development of conceptualization. Intelligence is, for Feuerstein, plastic and changeable. It is a constructive moment in the always possible activity of the individual. Mental "retardation," deficiency in learning, failure at school, and the "syndrome of cultural deprivation" (a negativity of the victims) can then be diagnosed differently and receive other pedagogical treatment. The problem is an intergenerational incapacity of the *mediation* of learning: it is about giving a certain active capacity to the new generation. It is thus necessary to intervene in the cognitive and structural modifiability in order to modify the *potential for learning*. Knowledge depends on the *adaptation* of the learner, as well as on his or her self-image, the openness to change, the feeling of competition, the domination of his impulsivity, and on the overcoming of blocking. The *adapted* person acts with self-confidence; the "retarded" person lacks self-confidence.

Following Piaget's model of the organism's response to stimuli by adaptation (sor),[97] Feuerstein proposes a mediated learning experience.[98] The mediation consists of the teacher situating her- or himself between the stimulus and the child (the organism, or mso) in order to allow the child to use her or his capacities in an efficacious manner. The teacher should likewise mediate between the child and the response (mor). The aim is for the child to be no longer a passive and traumatized receptor and to be able to *perform* better.[99] With this approach individuals are supposed to correct the deficiencies of their cognitive structure. The theoretical basis for this effort is mediated learning.

[294] Lev S. Vygotsky[100] is a genetic-evolutionary psychologist who focuses on the sociohistorical constitutive moment in the psychic origin of the child. His research takes place in a peripheral country at a moment of great postrevolutionary creativity: the Soviet Union of the 1920s before Stalinist dogmatism.[101] Vygotsky also worked with illiterate children in central Asia in 1931 and 1932. This context served Vygotsky and Alexander Luria[102] as an interhistorical (rather than intercultural) laboratory. Vygotsky was a student of philosophy and law with interests in art and literature who became acquainted with psychology late in his education.

Angel Rivière comments: "If he returned to psychology it was precisely because he searched for a scientific explanation for the origin of the superior functions of *cultural creation*. In the same way that Piaget's interests in psychology . . . originated in a more primordial concern for the problem of the genesis of [theoretical] knowledge, those of the Soviet psychologist were born out of an interest for giving an account of the *genesis of culture*."[103] The main theme of Vygotsky's work was "consciousness," which was for him the place where perception and artistic creation take place. Vygotsky was not interested in phenomenological description (as in *Gestalt*). Even though he was acquainted with Piaget's production in the 1920s,[104] Vygotsky was opposed to a purely cognitive ontogenetic method, which subscribes to the "paradigm of consciousness." Instead, he successfully combined a comparative-genetic method[105] with an evolutionary-experimental one. Vygotsky believed, however, that the successive stages of consciousness indicate revolutionary qualitative changes. On this point he followed dialectical thinking. Moreover, he believed that biological evolution alone did not explain the process in its entirety and that it was necessary also to consider the constitutive articulation of the historic-social and cultural moment in the psyche of the individual: "The social dimension of consciousness is primordial in time and fact. The individual dimension of consciousness is derivative and secondary."[106] By situating the child in the "interpsychic" (*interpsikhicheskii* in Russian) horizon, Vygotsky superseded the characteristic solipsism of the psychogenetics of his time. The social is "internalized," even at the level of "interior language." Consciousness as well as the meanings of words and actions are defined as "units of psychological operation." "Mind" is always constituted "from society."

[295] Perhaps the most interesting part of Vygotsky's work is not his view of the acquisition of language as an independent[107] and always articulated moment—at least in the semiotic moment that begins when the infant is around twelve months old[108]—but his discovery of the "instrumental" competence of the child.[109] He was led to this idea by Wolfgang Koehler's experiments with primates: "We, too, are convinced that the study of thought development in children from different social environments, and especially of children who, unlike Piaget's children, work, must lead to results that will permit the formulation of laws having a much wider sphere of application."[110] That is to say, "Vygotsky defined the *activity* itself [*deyatel'nost*] as a unit of what cognitivists would call the *functional architecture of consciousness*. This activity is not conceived simply as a response or reflex, but as a system of transformation of the medium by the aid of instruments. That is to say, an activity understood as *mediation*."[111] With this formulation, Vygotsky was able to integrate the problems of the paradigm of consciousness, of language, and of the instruments that the child has to

hand. The organic or biological processes of the child, referred to as "onto-genesis," enter in conjunction with the process by virtue of which conceptual thinking, semiotic language, and instrumental mediations emerge, which is known as historical-cultural philogenesis. According to Vygotsky, the "principle of decontextualization of the instruments of mediation" (material or formal) is responsible for processes of abstraction in the three levels.[112] However, Vygotsky, like all cognitivists, did not give too much importance to the level of drives, which includes phobias, unconscious substitutions, and exaggerated feelings, among other things. He did not pay much attention either to the community as the place for the active participation of the teacher and the student. This can be explained by the fact that Vygotsky found himself in a society that lived in a "*post*revolutionary" moment. It was time, then, to organize the *new* educative institutions, and not to "denounce" any dominating negativity. For this reason, the student, the child, and the illiterate person could not be considered victims who were culturally oppressed. We note the differences with Paulo Freire. Vygotsky simply cannot aim to generate ethical-critical consciousness in the child. He attempts to explain instead the emergence of cultural consciousness, higher psychic processes, and the "historic-social and cultural formation of the mind" in a young Soviet Union. Vygotsky was also in a position of power.

c. *Concientizaçao* in Freire

[296] All the development psychologists or psychologist educators whose work has been outlined here have a feature in common: they are all cognitivists. Their cognitivism does not lie so much in that they examine the intelligence, since they also take motivations, affectivity, and moral judgments into consideration; it lies in that they all aim to augment, correct, or unblock intellectual performance, either theoretical or moral. Freud attempts to modify the orders of the drives when they degenerate into uncontrollable pathologies—is not psychoanalysis precisely a dialogical pedagogy? They all use the mediation of a teacher or psychoanalyst, directly experienced. The psychoanalyst is an *individual*, as is the person who is learning, who suffers from a psychic pathology. The pedagogical activity occurs in a social, cultural, political, and economical context taken as "given." Consequently, the educator or psychoanalyst is not concerned with its *transformation*. Paulo Freire's position is radically different.[113] When he realized that education is not possible without the self-education of the learner in the *process of his or her own liberation*,[114] he changed his pedagogy—if indeed one can call it such, since it is related to something more universal and radical.

There is no doubt that Freire's aims differ from those of the other psychologist educators mentioned before. This point, however, is not entirely clear, neither among the "scientific" psychologist educators nor among those who agree with Freire and who have tried to develop his pedagogy. In comparison with Freire, the psychologist educators of development and psychoanalysts are, first, *cognitivists*. That is to say, they focus on theoretical or moral intelligence, or in consciousness as the mediation of pathology. And since they do not develop a dialogical, linguistic theory, they could also be called *consciousness-ists*. They are also *individualists*, since pedagogy is conceived as an individual relation between the educator as an individual and the learners, even when they form a group. But mainly they can be referred to as *naive*, since they do not aim to transform reality or promote an *ethical-critical* consciousness in the pupil.

The main goal of Freire's educative tasks consists precisely in promoting this transforming and critical activity. Unlike all the other authors considered here, Freire defines the conditions of possibility for the emergence of *ethical-critical* reason (defined in chapter 4) as part of an integral educative process. As a result, the learner is not only a child, but also an adult and, particularly, the oppressed person, who is culturally illiterate. *Pedagogical action* is exercised within the dialogical intersubjective and communitarian horizon[115] through the real transformation of the structures that oppress the learner, whose emergence as a "historical subject" allows education to take place in the same social process. The transformation of the structures out of which the new "social subject" emerges is the central procedure of the subject's progressive education. His or her freedom is brought about and unfolds in liberating praxis. For Freire, pedagogy is not primordially about theoretical or moral intelligence, or about the regeneration of the affective order. Without losing sight of these problems, Freire aims, first and foremost, to educate the victims in the very historical, communitarian, and real process through which they abandon their condition as victims. "Just as the gnoseological circle does not end with the step of the acquisition of existing knowledge, but proceeds to the phase of the creation of new knowledge, so neither may *consciousness-raising* come to a halt at the stage of the revelation of reality. Its authenticity is revealed only when the practice of revelation of reality constitutes *a dynamic and dialectical unity with the practice of transformation* [!] *of reality*."[116] Put differently, "Reading the world is an act antecedent to the reading of the world. The teaching of the reading and writing of the world to a person *missing the critical exercise* [!] of reading and rereading the world is, *scientific, politically, and pedagogically defective*."[117] We find here a pedagogical Copernican revolution that is far from understood in its entirety. In this line Freire writes: "[It is necessary] to criticize arrogance, the authoritarianism of intellectuals of the

Left or Right, who are both basically reactionary in an identical way—who judge themselves the proprietors of knowledge: the former, of revolutionary knowledge, the latter, of conservative knowledge—to criticize the behavior of university people who claim to be able to 'conscientize' rural and urban workers without having to be 'conscientized' by them as well. . . . They impose or seek to impose the '*superiority*' of their academic knowledge on the '*rude masses*.'"[118] Many think that Freire's work cannot be characterized as pedagogy, or that it is not scientific. They believe that his work has only "social and political goals." To this Freire retorts: "As if it were, or ever had been, possible, in any space-time, that an educational practice could exist that was distant, cold, and indifferent to *social and political purposes*."[119]

[297] Let us look briefly at Freire's treatment of the problem of pedagogy. In conversation with some friends in a Center for Intercultural Documentation (CIDOC) meeting in Cuernavaca, where we met frequently to discuss issues in pedagogy on the initiative of Ivan Illich, and where Freire met Erich Fromm (who then lived in Cuernavaca), Freire pointed out:

> To speak of conscientization implies a series of preliminary steps. . . . Generally it is thought that I am the inventor of this odd expression, because of the fact that it is a *key concept in my ideas* regarding education. . . . But its origin is in a series of reflections that a team of teachers developed at Brazil's Institute of Higher Studies. . . .[120] The concept was coined by one of these teachers. . . . I recall among others a professor named Alvaro Vieira Pinto, a great philosopher, who wrote a book entitled *Consciousness and National Reality*. . . .[121] When I first heard the term *conscientization* I immediately glimpsed the depth of its meaning, since I was already absolutely convinced that education, understood as the practice of freedom, is an act of knowledge which implies approaching *reality* from a *critical* perspective.[122]

I will divide my discussion of Freire into brief subsections, in each of which I will continue to develop the main arguments of this work[123] and show in the process the importance of Freire's work for a critical ethics. I will also make clear its influence for numerous contemporary liberation movements in Latin America and Africa.

CI. The *"limit situation"*: the "point of departure."[124] Receiving inspiration from Jaspers while at the same time giving a new meaning to his position, Freire explains:

> Let us study for example the *desperate situation*[125] of the peasants of northeast Brazil. They have a consciousness characterized by great oppression which impedes them from achieving a full structural perception of the reality in which they are immersed. They are incapable of perceiving the full empirical dimensions of the desperate situation in which they live, as some-

thing which is constructed based upon the objective and concrete reality in which they exist. But despite this limitation, and precisely because they are human, they have the need to explain the reality in which they live. How do they undertake this initial process of questioning? What is the nature of the rationality that they create for themselves as part of this process? How should we analyze their oppressed consciousness in this case?"[126]

Freire refers to a "material,"[127] economic, and political point of departure.[128] Education begins from the "reality" *in which the learners find themselves.* This "reality" is defined by structures of *domination* that are responsible for making the learners *oppressed* subjects. While he was exiled in Chile, Freire reflected in his magnum opus of 1969[129] on the existence of a foundational contradiction: oppressors/oppressed. Why is it that Freire begins with the oppressed, marginalized, and illiterate? Because it is the *"learner"* found at the limit who needs to be educated like nobody else. Freire situates himself in the *maximum possibility of negativity*:[130] "Criticism and an effort to transcend these *negativities* are not only recommended but indispensable. . . . There have been different forms of negative comprehension, and consequently of critical understanding."[131] If, as Horkheimer indicates, negativity and materiality are the conditions of critical theory, here we have not only a "theory," but also a critical praxis with a greater degree of negativity and materiality. Negativity and materiality are not indicated here by German workers, but by Fanon's "wretched of the Earth"—landless peasants in northeast Brazil, about forty million of the poorest people in the world. In a similar vein, instead of a critical theory of scientists who *search* a historical "subject" we find here that the "historical subjects" themselves are in *search of* someone who can educate them.

   [298] c2. *Prise de conscience?*[132] In contrast to Piaget,[133] Freire indicates that *conscientization*, which begins as critical consciousness, is much more than a mere cognitive *prise de conscience* of the world: "This *prise de conscience* [acquisition of consciousness] is not yet *conscientization*. The latter consists of the deepening of the *prise de conscience* itself. It signifies then the *critical development* of the *prise de conscience*; conscientization implies going beyond the spontaneous level[134] of mere perception of reality, by a *critical level* that makes it possible for reality *to be grasped*[135] as a cognizable object in a relationship to the human being who assumes a position anchored in the search for knowledge."[136] *Conscientization* indicates the *process of popular political education.* The *pedagogy of the oppressed* is the preeminent pedagogy *(kath'exokhén)*, and being situated in the maximum degree of negativity can serve as a model to any other *possible* critical pedagogical process.

   c3. *Stage 1.* Freire refers to the negative point of departure in many ways: "naive consciousness," the "culture of silence," the "mythification of reality," and so on. He is concerned with the transition from "magical consciousness"—subscribed to widely or only by fanatics, but even by a modern and urban but naive person[137]—to "critical consciousness." The "naive consciousness" is an "intransitive consciousness,"[138] that is, a consciousness that is *in itself* but that cannot express itself or acquire self-awareness of it *for itself*. "*Critical* consciousness" emerges out of "*naive* consciousness"; before the "culture *of silence*" comes "discourse"; before the "mystification of reality" comes "demystification": "In their increasing proximity to the world, to reality, in their movement in the world and with the world, human beings experience an *initial moment* when the world and objective reality *is not accessible to them as a cognizable object* susceptible of being grasped by their *critical consciousness* . . . , a moment when its primary characteristic is *ingenuousness*."[139] However, this critical consciousness is risky. The oppressed are not prepared to assume it.

[299] c4. "*Fear of freedom.*" Like Fromm, who clearly inspired him (and in this Freire is a successor of the Frankfurt school's emphasis on material negativity), Freire argues that at the level of the drives, those who are oppressed "fear freedom."[140] It is "ontologically impossible" for the oppressed to be "subjects," to face their liberation. The victim or oppressed person is initially "blocked" and can adopt a critical attitude only with difficulty: "Not infrequently, training course participants call attention to 'the danger of conscientização' in a way that reveals their own fear of freedom. Critical consciousness, they say, is anarchic. Others add that critical consciousness may lead to disorder. Some, however, confess: "Why deny it? I was afraid of freedom. I am no longer afraid!"[141] Freire refers continuously to this "block" of the drives. The reason for this is that, as Levinas has pointed out, those who come to possess a critical consciousness face the possibility of losing their happiness by becoming a "hostage" of the oppressive system. They are persecuted in the name of the community of victims. It is in this way that we must understand the problem of overcoming the utilitarian conception of a "happiness" that "enslaves" in a false "vital security,"[142] or what Nietzsche highlights when he refers to the "herd" (Zarathustra risks putting his "happiness" in danger in the face of the creative "pleasure instinct").

c5. *The participation of the critical teacher.*[143] This topic is very complicated and I will return to it in §6.1, where I will explore Lenin and Gramsci's contribution to the problem. As Freire said, "The process of teaching cannot be separated from the process of learning. . . . Such experiences cannot be transplanted, and must be reinvented."[144] When Freire arrived in Guinea-Bissau, a country that had seen a recent revolution and needed to begin a pedagogical process, he wrote: "It becomes the duty of the educator to search out the appropriate paths for the learner to travel and the best assistance that can be offered so that the learner is enabled to exercise the role of Subject in relation to learning during the process of literacy education. The educator must constantly discover and rediscover. . . . The most important fact is the development of a critical attitude in relation to the object."[145] The teacher must begin by learning about the "content" brought by the learner: "What I have said, untiringly, is that we must not bypass—spurning it as 'good for nothing,'—what learners . . . bring with them in the way of an understanding of the world. . . . Their speech, their way of counting and calculating, their ideas about the so-called other world, their religiousness, their knowledge about health, the body, sexuality, life, death, the power of saints, magic spells, must be all respected."[146] The teacher must "learn" the world of the student. Only in this way would he or she be able to intervene: "Illiterate peasants do not have need of a theoretical context to attain a consciousness capable of grasping their objectively oppressive situation. . . . But what this attainment of a consciousness that emerges from immersion in the conditions characteristic of daily life does not provide them with is a rationality capable of explaining their conditions of exploitation. This is one of the tasks we have to assume (as educators) from a theoretical perspective."[147] Freire recognizes that it is the victims themselves who gain critical consciousness. Teachers contribute with the discovery of their condition as victims. That is to say, "consciousness" emerges from "within" the consciousness of the victim as it is unfolded by the teacher. "Consciousness" does not come into being from the "outside." Teachers are important because they contribute a higher level of critique.[148] They teach the students how to interpret objective reality in a critical way. For this, they need the critical social sciences. I will return to this point in the next subsection.

c6. *Stage 2: Ethical-critical consciousness*.[149] Thus we arrive at the point of the crisis par excellence, the moment when the oppressed make the leap to "critique," which, as we will see, is communitarian. How is it that the oppressed reach this first degree of "critical consciousness"? Freire believes that the theoretical analysis of the causes of oppression leads to an increasing awareness of the *objective* reality that produces oppression. Theoretical analysis allows the oppressed to acquire a minimum understanding of the problem at a reflexive, theoretical, and critical level:[150] "The critically transitive consciousness is characterized by depth in the interpretation of problems; by the substitution of causal principles for magical explanations . . . by soundness of argumentation."[151] Nothing is more distant from Freire than postmodern irrationalism. The oppressed need to make use of theoretical, explicative reason, which, in turn, must be oriented by the criteria provided by the economic and political content. It must also be governed by critical reason. This is the central moment of the process of *conscientization*. It is at this point that the oppressed begin to diagnose the "culture of domination" and what Freire calls the *"banking* pedagogy" that they have been subjected to in the process of their domestication and massification. This process creates a "dual consciousness" in which the oppressed confuse their own consciousness with the projected consciousness of the domi-nator—Memmi had already talked about this in *Portrait of the Colonizer.* "Dual consciousness" is the fruit of a pedagogy of domination, the "bank-ing pedagogy," of the system: "Narration (with the teacher as narrator) leads the students to memorize mechanically the narrated content. . . . The more meekly the receptacles permit themselves to be filled, the better stu-dents they are."[152] Here, Freire calls attention to the psychology-pedagogy of development, which, at its best, educates the theoretical *performance* of children—in order to make them disciplined members of the system that oppresses them. There is no authentic education without ethical-critical consciousness. It is for this reason that the teacher must insist, along with the student, "that the social structure is the result of human labor and that because of this, its transformation shall equally be the fruit of human striving."[153]

[300] c7. *The "historical subject" of "transformation."*[154] Freire frequently repeats that the "subject" of education is none other than the oppressed person her- or himself. *"Critical* consciousness" involves a self-reflective act by virtue of which the subjects discover their condition as oppressed and emerge as a *historical subjects.* These historical subjects are the *"peda-gogical* subjects" par excellence: *"Conscientization* is . . . a process which involves a critical insertion *into history.* It implies that all human beings must assume their role as *subjective makers* and remakers of the world; it demands of human beings that they create the conditions for their exis-tence *with the materials that life offers them."*[155] Education is a "material" ethical process: the theme, the medium, the objective, and the happiness achieved is *life.* Freire's pedagogy is situated in the "place" where ethical critique is possible. From that point of departure, one can assert that the *subject* is only a *subject* when he or she is the origin of the transformation of reality. Freire does not invent hypothetical examples so that Cambridge's democratic scholarly community can argue intelligently over them. Much to the contrary, for Freire pedagogy is a *very real,* concrete, and objective process: "To discover themselves as oppressed only begins to imply a true *process of liberation,* when this discovery of oppression *becomes transformed into a historical commitment* . . . , a critical insertion into history in order to make it. . . . *Conscientization* implies this critical insertion in the pro-cess of liberation, and thus necessarily implies a historical commitment to a process of transformation."[156] The *praxis* of "transformation" cannot be reduced to a pedagogical "experience." It is not pursued in order to learn, nor is it learned in the classroom through the exercise of theoretical "con-sciousness"; it takes place in the very praxis of the "transformation" of the

historical and "real reality."[157] It *unfolds* as a progressive "conscient-*ization*," that is, as an "action" through which one's ethical consciousness is transformed or, in short, as liberation. This idea evidently presupposes a theory of the "social subject." Although I begin its elaboration in §6.2, its full development will come in a future work on "liberation fronts" or "fields."

c8. *Communitarian intersubjectivity: ethical-discursive reason.*[158] Rousseau's definition of the modern pedagogical subject is found in *Émile*, about a young, male, solipsistic orphan who does not belong to any tradition. Rousseau was guided by a bourgeois *curriculum* designed to develop the technical and industrial spirit that was opposed to the *ancien régime*. In contrast, Freire's transmodern pedagogy of liberation is grounded on a *community* of oppressed *victims* who are immersed in popular culture and traditions, on the one hand, and illiterate and miserable, on the other. They are the "condemned of the Earth." In these conditions, which represent the maximum of possible negativity, the educators may very well find themselves in a desperate position. Freire thinks otherwise, and so he introduces in chapter 3 of his *Pedagogy of the Oppressed* "dialogism"—the discursive action of the community of subjects in its struggle for liberation[159]—as a method that allows the unfree to practice their freedom.[160] The process of *conscientization* continues and develops as an increasing movement of radicalization.

We might say that Freire, in anticipation of Habermas, subsumed the procedure of discourse ethics from a "dialogical" point of view. Freire would clearly differ with Habermas's conclusion that ethics "provides orientation as to contents, but only in terms of a procedure full of presuppositions that should guarantee impartiality in the formulation of judgments. Practical discourse is not a process for producing norms that have been justified, but instead is one suited for the testing of the validity of norms that have been postulated hypothetically."[161] However, when Habermas describes a possible stage 4½ in Kohlberg's classification, he opens a door for Freire's solution: "At this stage, the perspective is that of an individual standing outside of his own society and considering himself an individual making decisions without a generalized commitment or contract with society."[162] Are not the oppressed referred to by Freire in the position of social "exteriority" (as excluded victims)? And is their dialogue not a "dialogue . . . undertaken in search of programmatic content"?[163] Does Freire's critical thought not emerge from such "exteriority"? Does the process of participatory democracy that stands behind a new antihegemonic validity not become a mediation of the "*ethical-critical* consciousness" that aims to "transform the world"?[164] Dialogue, or, to be more precise, the exercise of dialogue, has a "content"; it has the exigency of overcoming the asymmetry in the dominator-dominated dialectic: "Dialogue cannot occur between

. . . those who deny others the right to speak their mind and those whose right to speak has been denied. Those who have been denied their primordial right to speak must first reclaim this and prevent the continuation of this dehumanizing aggression."[165] The dialogue of the community always has a "content": "Dialogue . . . is the encounter in which the combined reflection and action of the interlocutors are addressed to the world that is to be transformed . . . [T]his dialogue cannot be reduced to the act of one person's 'depositing' ideas in another."[166] Dialogue, "that is to say the word, with reference to the world that is to be transformed, is understood as a place of encounter between human beings for the purpose of undertaking this process of transformation."[167] Freire conceives dialogue as an "encounter" among subjects in which they reveal to each other mediations for the transformation of the world, or the *contents* that would make it possible for everyone to inhabit that world. Freire was writing from his long experience with the "movement for basic education" and with what was later known as "base communities." In these communities, the illiterate, the oppressed, and the poor learned to talk about their misery, their dreams.

[301] c9. *"Denunciation" and "announcement."* For Freire there is a negative moment and a positive moment. The negative moment refers to the critique of the system as the cause of oppression. The positive moment has to do with the declaration of "utopia":

> That which is *utopian* for me is not that which is unrealizable, and is not equivalent to something which is idealist in character. Utopia is the dialectical expression that unfolds in the acts of *denouncing* and *announcing*. This is the act of *denouncing* the dehumanizing structure[168] and the act of *announcing* the humanizing structure. . . .[169] What can the future hold for the oppressors, but the preservation of the present of their oppressor status? And what space can there be for the denunciation generated by the oppressed, but that of the denunciation of those who denounce? What space can there be for the pronouncements of the oppressors but the pronouncement of their myths, and what hope could there be for those who have no future? . . . This is what *conscientization* consists of: taking possession of reality, making it one's own.[170]

"Denunciation" emerges as a result of the dialectic collaboration between the dialogical community of the oppressed who are critically conscious and the educators (intellectuals and scientists with an interdisciplinary approach, among others).[171] Utopia, on the other hand, is the exercise of the imagination that creates alternatives: "At the moment when these [the oppressed] come to the point where they no longer perceive ['desperate situations'] as a *border between being and nothingness*, but instead grasp it as a *border between being and being as something-more*, their actions linked to this perception become increasingly critical in character . . . and that which is *viable but unwritten* is implicit within."[172] This new "viable" possibility is the project of liberation of the community that operates as the subject of transformation.

C10. *"Liberating praxis . . ."*[173] The basis of the process is transformative praxis: "From my perspective, we cannot liberate others, and human beings cannot free themselves alone either, because liberation is a *communal* process, which can only be achieved by experiencing together the reality which they must transform."[174] For Freire, "liberating praxis" is not a final act. It is rather the continuing action that relates subjects to one another in the community that transforms the reality that produces oppression. "Liberating praxis" is the air in which critical pedagogy breathes. The pedagogical act takes place only *within the process of liberating praxis*. This process does not refer only to a revolutionary act but to every humanizing transformative act in favor of the oppressed and in the interest of overcoming one's own condition of oppression.

Inspired by Hegel, Merleau-Ponty, Sartre, Marcel, Mounier, Jaspers, Marx, Lukács, Freud, and many others, Freire develops a distinctive discourse that responds to the reality of the victims in northeastern Brazil and in Latin America. He then extends his theory and pedagogical praxis to the situation first in Africa[175] and then in other peripheral and central countries. Freire articulates a planetary pedagogy that aims to make *ethical-critical consciousness* emerge. He is concerned not only with the cognitive or the affective improvement (of social victims among others), but also with the *production of an ethical-critical consciousness*. This ethical-critical consciousness originates in the victims themselves by virtue of their being the *privileged historical subjects of their own liberation*. The *critical* pedagogical act is performed by the subjects themselves and in their transforming praxis: liberation is thus the "place" and the "purpose" of this pedagogy. I would like to conclude this section with an expression by Freire: "The difficulty [of the link between the leaders and the oppressed] is that this category of dialogical action (like the others), cannot occur apart from the praxis."[176]

§5.3. Functionalist and Critical Paradigms

[302] We have been reflecting on the validity of the *critical* discourse of the community of victims, when the community of victims confronts the system that oppresses or excludes it and begins to analyze (politically, practically, scientifically)[177] the causes of its alienation.[178] An ethics of liberation (and the philosophy of liberation that follows it) must pay attention not only to the demarcation criterion of science in general, in relation to

nonscientific discourses (the problem of the "logic of explanation") but also to distinguishing the natural from the human or social sciences. In doing so, it must integrate hermeneutics and the logic of understanding in order to introduce the question of the *critical* social sciences and their logic of discovery to the debate.[179] The definition of the *critical* social sciences is intrinsically connected to their relation with the *social and intersubjective subject* who originates such critical discourses. The *critical* social sciences, including ethics, give rise to new scientific paradigms.[180] These new paradigms emerge as a result of innovative research programs that are developed in solidarity with the victims. They stand as rivals to the functional paradigms of the dominant system.

a. From Karl Popper to Imre Lákatos

[303] Epistemologists typically approached the question of the "demarcation" of scientific hypothetic and deductive knowledge through a clear definition of theoretical and explanatory rationality[181] that denied the scientific character of discourses without an empirical referent. Such was the practice of the Vienna Circle, who challenged the scientific character of rival theories or programs that did not fulfill the "strict" definition of science. Typical targets of their criticism were Marxism and psychoanalysis— both of them arguably *critical* epistemological types, as we will see.

Popper, who criticized the neopositivists, nonetheless radicalized their position and, against those who justified scientific claims inductively, challenged the adjudicatory claims of science: "Science is not a system of certain, or well-established, statements; nor is it a system which steadily advances towards a state of finality. Our science is not knowledge (*episteme*): it can never claim to have attained the truth, or even a substitute for it, such as probability."[182] Science consists of theories that "are nets that we cast out to sea to capture that which we call *the world* in order to rationalize, explain, and dominate it."[183] The instrumental and solipsistic character of reason, still within the paradigm of consciousness, remains clear. The criterion of demarcation of what constitutes science is purely negative, in that a theory's propositions are by definition basically falsifiable. A "theory is *falsified* if we accept basic statements that contradict it."[184] Put simply, Popper proposed that a theory could be refuted or discarded, falsified in its totality, by a "falsifying hypothesis"[185] corroborated by a "crucial experiment." Popper was thinking about a situation in which a theory could be falsified by a crucial falsifying experiment, in which there would be only a falsifiable theory. From this point of view and in light of our theme, a *critical* human or social science could not coexist with the hegemonic social science. *One* of them would be considered scientific and the other pseudo-science.[186] It would thus be ridiculous to talk about the scientific character of a *critical* human or social science.[187]

[304] For his part, Thomas Kuhn opened a new horizon of problems with the idea of the existence of paradigm shifts brought about in history by "scientific revolutions."[188] Against Popper and his "crucial experiment" Kuhn wrote: "Once it has achieved the status of paradigm, a scientific theory is declared invalid only if an alternate candidate is available to take its place. No process yet disclosed by historical study of scientific development at all resembles the methodological stereotype of falsification by direct comparison with nature. . . . The decision to reject one paradigm is always simultaneously the decision to accept another, and the judgment leading to that decision involves the comparison of both paradigms with nature and with each other."[189] Kuhn proposed that the "crisis" of one paradigm mediates its overcoming by another. He did not examine, however, the relation between the crisis of "normal" science and the horizon of ordinary life in relation to which a "shift" from a paradigm to another is possible. To his credit, Kuhn overcame Popperian solipsism. The historical reference of his account is intersubjectivity. This is made clear in the preface of his work where he said, "Fleck's work helped me understand that these ideas had to be established in the context of the sociology of the *scientific community*."[190]

Kuhn also superseded Popperian ahistoricism. In his work, we can see the emergence of a sort of sociohistorical and intersubjective subjectivity (like that of Peirce). Kuhn's conception of "normal" science, which is not so different from Popper's formulation, however, blocks possible innovations. Kuhn paid more attention to "the emergence of a discovery or of a *new* theory."[191] The extreme deductivism that characterizes the paradigms and that renders them irreducible to one another, on the other hand, gives support to the idea of incommensurability.

At one point in his argument, Kuhn made a comparison between political and scientific revolutions. Believing that political revolutions are merely "external" to scientific revolutions, however, he did not explore them carefully. "Political revolutions are inaugurated by a growing sense, often restricted to a segment of the political community, that existing institutions have ceased adequately to meet the problems posed by an environment that they have in part created.[192] In much the same way, scientific revolutions are inaugurated by a growing sense, again often restricted to a narrow subdivision of the scientific community, that an existing paradigm has ceased to function adequately."[193] Kuhn, like Anglo-Saxon epistemologists in general, paid hardly any attention to the human or social sciences. French epistemology, inspired by the work of Gaston Bachelard, Alexandre Koyré, or George Canguilhem, is more balanced in this respect. If Kuhn had reflected on the *status* of the human or social sciences he would have discovered that there is a relation between the emergence of "new" *critical* paradigms in historical-social moments of crisis. The science of economics, for instance, is born with the emergence of the triumphant bourgeoisie in the "center," in Scotland and England. The first *critiques* of the new science came into being with the discovery, in the same horizon, of the first negative effects. Engel's *The Situation of the Working Class in England* could have been written only there. In cases like this, one cannot ignore that both historical and epistemological "revolutions" occur "intermittently" in the intersubjectivity of a concrete community of communication,[194] and in the same factic horizon.

[305] Feyerabend[195] represents a different moment of epistemological critique. He opposes dogmatic simplifications that offer cumulative and lineal conceptions of science and ignore the conflicts, revolutions, multiplicity, and incommensurability[196] of the diverse theories referred to as scientific. In his view, historical, sociological, psychological, and aesthetic factors are not to be looked at with disdain; a simple internalist reconstruction of science and a subjectless conception of objectivism without history appears insufficient. For Feyerabend, knowledge can never be certain that it has gained access to reality; this is a relativism that is also epistemic.[197] Science is more like art than logic, with all its rigor.[198] Like art, science uses intuition, fantasy, and instinct, as is most obvious when discoveries occur, when the inductive method, criticized by Popper and defined by Ernst Mach[199] as a process of approximation or probability, dominates. Nothing is more ambiguous than the "progress" of science[200] at the time of nuclear warfare (which could destroy everything) and ecological danger,[201] which are effects of science and technology.

We may be able to perceive the meaning and rationality of Feyerabend's seemingly irrational position if we locate it in the horizon of my critical model.[202] Feyerabend's thought is clearly situated in what I would call a *critical epistemology*, which supposes an ethical moment of originary practical reason. We will see later how to subsume his position within a vision of the critical human or social sciences articulated around the victims.

[306] Lákatos's view, which extends Popper's efforts, is summarized in his own statement:

> (a) I defend the idea that the typical descriptive unity of great scientific achievements is not an isolated hypothesis but instead a *research plan.* . . .
> (b) Newtonian science, for example, is not only an overall framework consisting of four hypotheses (the three laws of mechanics and one regarding gravity). These four laws are merely the *hard core* of the Newtonian project. (c) But this hard core is tenaciously protected against refutations by means of a vast *protective belt* of auxiliary hypotheses. And (d), most im-

portantly, this research plan has a heuristics at its command, which is in effect a powerful mechanism for resolving problems which, with the help of sophisticated mathematical techniques, assimilates anomalies as they arise and even converts them into positive proofs.[203]

In opposition to Feyerabend and others who believe in justification by induction,[204] Lákatos does not think there can be knowledge based on *proved* propositions. Lákatos also rejects a conventionalist position, including that of Pierre Duhem, that exaggerates the criterion of simplicity. Refusing at the same time what he calls dogmatic or naturalist *falsationism*, Lákatos adopts a methodological *falsationist* position that aims to overcome what he calls the "naive" attitude (in part Popperian) and replaces it with a more "sophisticated" vision: "According to my methodology, great scientific achievements are in effect research programs which can be evaluated in terms of progressive and regressive transformations of a problem; scientific revolutions occur when one research program replaces or progressively overcomes another."[205] Lákatos does not believe that a theory could be refuted by a falsifier "crucial experiment." It never happens that way; no theory has been refuted by a single experiment. All theories are able to produce ad hoc explanations to the anomalies confronted by them, so they cannot be considered to be in irreversible "regression." A theory can thus survive centuries. Only later is it possible to discover the "crucial experiment" that refutes the theory by making it false. In fact, however, rival theories coexist. The criterion of demarcation that divides scientific from unscientific programs is no longer the falsification criterion, but a new one: scientific programs are those that discover new "facts" and which are "progressive." Scientific programs contain an excess, or *plus*, of content that is corroborated: "Progress is measured by the degree to which a series of theories is the basis for discoveries of new facts."[206] There are always thus a plurality of rival programs in competition, and the refutation of any theory is possible only after the emergence of a new and better rival theory.[207] In this way "the concept of theory . . . is substituted by the concept of a series of theories."[208]

Even though Lákatos remains in a Popperian horizon, he makes the definition of science more flexible and opens the possibility of referring to the *critical* human[209] or social sciences as scientific research programs tied to the antihegemonic community of victims. Indeed, this would be the moment to raise the question of two new demarcation criteria. On the one hand, there is the criterion that delimits the natural from the human or social sciences; on the other, the criterion of demarcation between what we call *functional* and the *critical* social sciences. Let us take a tentative look at the problem.

[307] Carnap proposed a "unified" program of the sciences, in which

all the sciences would be regulated in terms of the paradigm of the natural sciences, and of physics in particular. The rationality or scientificity of the different sciences would be measured in terms of the logicality of a possible mathematical formalization. The successive Carnapian projects failed. Methodological neopositivist reductionism left room for many more flexible positions.

For his part, Popper, with his proposal of conjectures and refutations within a methodologically "unified" project of the sciences, defined the problem of the social sciences on three levels: (a) situational logic, (b) fragmentary social technology, and (c) social engineering. Situational logic begins with "method zero," which consists of forming an ideal of the full rationality of the individual acting subject. Without attempting to describe any *subjective motivation* by the individual in actions defined by the relation between means and ends in an "objective situation," one notes the variations with respect to the model of impossibility provided by the ideal. This model would allow the "explanation" and "prediction" of certain effects (agent A works on B). The rationality involved here is merely instrumental, and, according to Popper himself,[210] who follows in part Hayek's economical model of the market, it cannot be falsified.

The second level, fragmentary social technology, allows short-term predictions whose lack of fulfillment can be attributed to involuntary repercussions or variables that were not presupposed. Fragmentary social technology aims for social gradualism combined with a constant corrective analysis. At this level, revolution is to be avoided since it represents absolute irrationality. Accordingly, the point of departure is the Anglo-Saxon "open society," which is considered the best possible structure and which can only be reformed.

The third level, social engineering, consists of the application of fragmentary social technology to existing or new institutions—which play the role of objects in the natural sciences—from the perspective of an extreme form of individualism. It also involves the attempt to give a technocratic form to politics or to depoliticize citizens. Since this elaboration is the result of instrumental reason, Popper cannot say anything about the ends or values that this social engineering implements or presupposes. *Ends* and *values* are given by the social tradition that is accepted by virtue of an irrational and conservative decisionism.

In reaction to this position, which sustains an ambiguous or nonexistent view regarding the criterion of demarcation between the natural and social sciences, a debate about "explanation" and "understanding" arose. Von Wright described the problem subtly in his own terms in 1971,[211] while Apel clarified his position in an extensive work on the issue.[212] Gadamer had already raised the problem of "understanding" from a hermeneutical horizon some years before.[213] In this light, it could be said that the criterion of demarcation includes a new determination: the human and social sciences use "explanation" (in the subject-object relation, the "object" here being the human in society) or "understanding" (in the subject-subject relation, which involves the interpretation of the intentionality of the other subject or subjects: "understanding" the motivations, values, coming into the "world" of another community).[214] The social sciences must know how to use the "explanation" of events, going back to the "causes," and intersubjective "understanding" in a complementary way. "Explanation" involves an examination of the "causes," while intersubjective "understanding" refers to the interpretation of the meaning of actions from the point of view of the concrete and evaluative motivations. This makes clear that the interest is not only observational but also participative.

b. From the Interest of the Victims: "Critique"

[308] I still have to clarify a third criterion of demarcation between the *functional* and the *critical* social sciences. Evidently, this criterion is defined in terms of the community of victims and emerges with the interpellation of the community of victims in their call for solidarity and for the re-sponsibility of "organic intellectuals" who are invited to collaborate responsibly in the scientific *critique* of the system that oppresses them. By virtue of this "interpellation,"[215] intellectuals come to occupy a "position" of exteriority or transcendental position with respect to the established social order. Intellectuals become, as Levinas would put it,[216] "hostages" by substituting themselves for the victims to the point of suffering persecution for them. In this sense, the position of the "disinterested viewer" becomes *doubly* foreign.[217] Whoever attempts to "explain," as a social scientist, the causes for the negativity of the victims is in some ways forced to invent *new paradigms, new explanations*, and even *new hermeneutic interpretations* (in the search for "understanding"). This necessity responds to the discovery of *new* and previously *unobservable facts* that form part of the world that social scientists enter by virtue of an ethical-practical decision, often also political, which opens new horizons to them.[218] Marx explicitly referred to this when he wrote:

> Political economy (understood as formal moralities) takes private property as its point of departure, but does not *explain* [*erklärt*] it. . . . [I]t does not provide us with any *explanation*. . . . It takes as its point of departure that which it should explain. . . . We must not place ourselves, as the economist who wants to *explain* something does, in an imaginary primitive situation [*Urzustand*].[219] This primitive situation does not explain anything, it simply transfers the question to a gray cloudy distance. It presupposes as a fact, as an event, that which it should deduce [*deduzieren*].[220]

In these cases, the praxis, interest, and objectual horizon[221] of the community of victims do not refer to an "external" moment in the "internal" development of science, especially human or social science. They become a *constitutive moment of the objectuality* of the "theory," paradigm, or program, and of the respective "facts." The hermeneutical or ontological condition of possibility for the objectivity of the object or fact (its "objectuality") is an "internal" moment of the development of the social sciences, even more so if they are critical.[222] Habermas points out: "The system of objective activities creates the factual conditions of the possible reproduction of social life and at the same time the transcendental conditions of the possible objectivity of the objects of experience."[223]

[309] In this way, all the problems of knowledge "find a rational solution in human praxis and in the conceptualization of this praxis."[224] Indeed, the act of knowledge inscribes itself in the total process of praxis in a real and concrete way, becoming an *"internal" moment* that carries out a very precise function. From Aristotle[225] to Kant,[226] the constitution of all praxis is tied to a *"practical* interest." Hence, we find Habermas arguing in 1968: "I term *interests* the basic orientation rooted in specific fundamental conditions of the possible reproduction and self-constitution of the human species, namely work and interaction. Hence these basic orientations do not to aim at the gratification of immediately empirical needs but the solution of system problems in general."[227] And in agreement with our position, Habermas adds: "Interests that are constitutive of knowledge can be defined exclusively as a function of the objectively constituted problems of the preservation of life that have been solved by the cultural form of existence as such."[228] Husserl argues that "the phenomenological problem of the relation of consciousness with objectivity [*Gegenständlichkeit*] possesses, above all, a noematic character."[229] The objectivity of the object, its noematicity, is given primarily at the level of prescientific everyday life and in relation to the above mentioned practical *interest*.[230] What happens is that "the conditions of objectivity of possible knowledge"[231] originate in praxis, like all worldly practices, since this "same interest depends upon actions."[232] That is to say, praxis as a fundamental totality that includes interest in its essence, opens up the horizon of objectivity. Thus, it is possible to understand that

> the objects of thought and perception as they appear to individuals prior to all *subjective* interpretation have in common certain primary qualities, pertaining to these two layers of reality: (1) to the physical (natural) structure of matter, and (2) to the form which matter has acquired in the collective historical practice that has made it (matter) into objects for a subject. The two layers or aspects of objectivity (physical and historical) are interrelated in such a way that they cannot be insulated from each other; the historical

aspect can never be eliminated so radically that only the *absolute* physical layer remains.[233]

The fact-object (o1 in figure 15) of two possible cognizant subjects (s1 and s2) may be the same, but the meaning that it has acquired in the intersubjective historical practices may be diverse.

[310] The considerations just outlined indicate that for any theory or scientific research program a rival theory or program can emerge. The rival theory discovers *new* facts and *objects*, and, therefore, needs *new explanations*. When the scientific community examines the world or the established horizon of facts, objects, and comprehensive explanations in light of the experiences of a community of victims, the oppressed, and excluded that has gained awareness of its negativity and has begun to formulate a possible future alternative, the *novelty* of the facts becomes *critical*. The "interest" behind the search for new alternatives, which becomes a liberation project, opens up a *new* horizon of facts and objects. The interest that makes possible the observation of these objects is thus liberatory and not only emancipatory.

[311] Let us consider an example of the *critical* human or social sciences that is still valid at the start of the twenty-first century. Marx writes in Notebook 6 of the *Manuscript of 1861–1863*: "All economists fall into the same error: instead of considering surplus value [o2 in figure 15] purely, as such, they approach it through the particularized forms of profit or rent [o1]. Subsequently . . . where those theoretical errors that arise out of the transfigured form that surplus value [o2] adopts as profit will be demonstrated."[234] The following observation from the *Grundrisse* is even more enlightening: "There is no difference for [David] Ricardo between profit [o1] and surplus value [o2], which demonstrates that he has not understood with clarity neither the nature of the first nor that of the second."[235] The "fact" of profit as gaining price from the market (o1) in classical political economy has a "new" meaning (arrow d) for Marx, who observes this fact from the perspective of the "new" paradigm (paradigm 2) of the *critical* science of economics. From the perspective of this paradigm, Marx can show the mistake of the "old" description: profit from the market is not the same as surplus value from production. The categorical confusion of surplus value-profit (ambiguity of the value price) allows us to mistakenly consider profit as the final surplus price over the cost price (in production) of the merchandise (from the market). Marx's response to the ethical interpellation of the oppressed,[236] and his re-sponsible commitment as an economist with the oppressed,[237] allows him to reach a new "understanding" that is possible by virtue of the new *critical* foundation. Marx is an organic intellectual who is engaged with the victim (s2 in figure 15). He assumes the victim's interests (i2) and his possible alternative (PL). With bravery and with

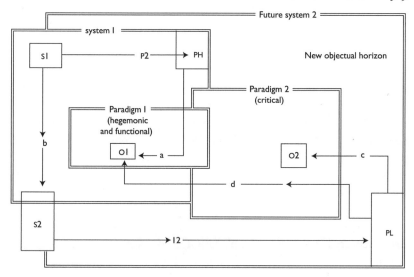

Figure 15. Comparison of rival paradigms (functional and critical).

NOTES: System 1: dominant (practical or scientific) subject or community; future system 2: practical interest of the dominant cognoscenti directed to PH (practical-functional project of system 1 [dominator]); a: constitution of O1—object-fact of paradigm I; b: praxis of domination; S2: the victim as (oppressed or excluded) practical or scientific cognizant subject or community; I2: practical interest of the cognizant victim directed toward PL (liberation project of future system 2 [possible alternative]); c: constitution of the new O2—new object-fact of the new paradigm II; d: falsification of the old O1. (See the discussion section titled "Dialéctica de toda filosofía con la praxis" [especially the figure on p. 27] in my article "Praxis y filosofía" [Dussel 1983b], where this point is analyzed in much more detail.) The human or social scientific "explanation" of a "fact" (arrow a to O1) of a dominant cognizant subject or community (S1) (I am tempted to use Noam Chomsky's notion of the "new mandarins" here [Chomsky 1969]) would be different from an explanation of the same "fact" from the scientific perspective that originates in the position of the victims (arrow d). Since the fundamental practical relation is defined by a horizon of interest different from the victim's, this "fact" (O1) "means" something different (and therefore requires a different "explanation" and "understanding") for the scientific paradigm of the dominant community (system 1) and for the oppressed (future system 2), because the relation of practical foundation begins from another horizon of interest, than the one of the victim (I2). For their part, the victims (S2) discover new "facts" (O2) within the new horizon of observation.

a theoretical focus, he first "attempts," and then, after painful research and using a *progressive* "scientific research program," he succeeds in "explaining" (arrow c), a "new" fact: surplus value (understood as the objectification of the living work of the worker) (o2) is the unpaid creation of the worker. Surplus value is an unobservable "fact" for the classical paradigm (paradigm 1) of the political economy of Smith or Ricardo. This political economy is practiced by a scientific community located within the unsurpassable "horizon" of capitalism (system 1).[238] On the contrary, Marx, who is practically or ethically moved (12) by the suffering of the worker,[239] *understands* the motivations and aims to *explain* in a rational or scientific manner the *cause* of victimization. Marx adheres to the most strict exigencies of the economical science of his time, but proceeds in terms of a *critical* social science—in the negative and material sense of Adorno. "Surplus value" is the *new* discovered "fact" whose "explanation" leads Marx to make it the essential moment or *key category* of the "firm nucleus" of the *new* critical theoretical framework: "[The capitalist] simply does not conceive of profit as a secondarily derived form of surplus value."[240] The *explanation* of this "new" fact can only be pursued within a paradigm that refutes the basic premises of the classical theory. This new paradigm makes evident the contradiction between the theory of labor value in relation to production, which has surplus value as its deductive consequence, and the theory of profit price in relation to the market, whose "source" remains without a deductive *explanation*. Refuting Smith from Smith's own perspective, Marx explains: "As Adam Smith actually develops the idea of surplus value, *although he does not do so explicitly*, under the form of a specific category, distinct from the different forms through which it manifests itself, he *confuses* it then directly with the most developed form of profit. And this defect directly passes from him to Ricardo and to *all* of his successors."[241]

[312] Marx's allusion to all of Smith's and Ricardo's successors clearly makes reference to his own critique of economists from J. Steuart[242] to the physiocrats and his contemporaries that he formulated in nine notebooks of more than 1,200 pages written between March 1862 and July 1863. With a rarely paralleled rigor, Marx refuted these economists' explanation of the "fact" of profit. He showed that they had not recognized the "new" fact of surplus value that a new paradigm of economics could explain. This new paradigm only took the nascent economy of "work value" to its logical consequences in order to "explain," as Marx often put it, the worker's *rate of exploitation*. Marx subsumes the old theory and redefines it in terms of the new paradigm. The new paradigm counts with a *plus* or an excess of content: it explains a previously unobservable fact that, as a result, could not have been "explained" by the old paradigm. This falsification would not be *accepted* by the functional and dominant capitalist political economy since

its criterion of "refutability" was flexible and self-protective. In which way was capitalist political economy able to declare itself immune to Marx's critique? It changed the general orientation of the scientific paradigm of economics. In fact, the impact of Marx's refutation was so strong that the subsequent functionalist science of economics did not "defend" itself with an ad hoc explanation; it had, in contrast, to abandon the theory of "labor value" as a whole in order to avoid the recognition of Marx's falsification. We see this only four years after the publication of *Capital* in Jevons's work in 1871. Marginalists, Keynesians, neoclassicists, and, even more, neoliberals, all of whom are moved by capitalism's interest (11),[243] would be unable to use the old paradigm (1) and to locate themselves in the same position (arrow a), both of which had been falsified. They would instead completely modify the research program, making the market their point of departure, by taking a theory of value price and changing it incrementally into a theory focused only on prices that avoids the so-called metaphysical category of value. They thus proceeded with an ad hoc elimination of the falsified part of their theory and with a modification of the rest in order to remain functional ("efficacious") to capital.

[313] We are now able to understand, changing to some extent Horkheimer's discussion of traditional and "critical theory,"[244] how it is possible for rival research programs to be going on at the same time: some of them respond to the dominant and functional bourgeois communities and aim for the "efficacious" fulfillment, in formal and instrumental terms (means-end), of the dominant system ("traditional theory"); while others respond to the groups of dominated or excluded people, and in this way become *critical* human or social (and philosophical) sciences with a "negative" aim: the hermeneutic understanding, explanation, or dialectical interpretation of the *causes* of the alienation of the victims ("critical theory"). The development of these *critical* human or social sciences takes place within the horizon opened up by the alternative positive formulations of the oppressed (possible projects). It is thus necessary to elaborate a pluralist, plastic, and flexible epistemology that could analyze the complex coexistence of multiple scientific functional and/or critical programs "within" and "in confrontation with" existing sociohistorical systems. We should recall that progressive *critical* programs that discover "new" facts and "new" theories are considered the innovations that become landmarks in the diachronic process of science. Orlando Fals Borda argued that in the current peripheral world of capitalism it is necessary to "convert the social sciences into an instrument of critical consciousness and in favour of cultural and political autonomy amid the struggle against misery and social inequalities. Our broadest objective is to place social sciences at the service of fundamental human rights and of the creation of authentic forms of economic, social,

and political democracy."[245] In their turn, the human or social sciences in close contact with groups of victims will elaborate new hegemonic epistemological paradigms that are functional to the new system. It is in this way that, following the establishment of the world system in the fifteenth century, the bourgeoisie transformed their struggles in the Middle Ages into a historical revolution and, in the work of Adam Smith, to a critical economics of the feudal world, and then turned itself immediately to the constructive and functional *explanation* of the emerging industrial order.[246] While with one hand the bourgeois revolution deconstructed the ancient order[247] in a negative[248] and scientific way, with the other it formulated an alternative of equality, liberty, and fraternity, as well as democratic republicanism.[249] The *critical* science of economics, that is, the transforming and revolutionary economics like that of Smith in the eighteenth century, was articulated as a *scientific theory* that emerged as a result of "militancy" in the process of the victims' liberation from the monarchical feudalism of the past. These victims were the European bourgeoisie vanquished in 1521 at Villalar, Spain, by Charles V, but who later were triumphant with Cromwell in England[250] and with the French Revolution in 1789.

[314] Another complex example is what happened to science in the context of real Soviet socialism,[251] which developed the sciences efficiently for some decades as steady rivals of the sciences in the "center" of capitalism (among the natural sciences were physics, astronomy, and neurology; and among formal sciences, mathematics, and logic). Under Stalinist ideology, however, the human or social sciences were less fortunate, and lost the *critical* posture that Marx had sustained in relation to capitalism. They thus collapsed into an acritical dogmatism that inhibited any sort of internal renovation.

Critical human or social sciences coexist with the dominant ones, and can refute the dominant human or social sciences with new *explanations* articulated from new paradigms. These new paradigms, however, can later turn *functionalistic*: out of the critical economics of Adam Smith emerged neoclassical or neoliberal marginalist thought; out of critical Marxist thought emerged a Soviet economics that helped sustain bureaucracy.

We cannot forget to include here the functional paradigm of the developed countries, that is, "Modernity," which is "managed" from the "center" of a cultural system.[252] European Modernity, which has existed since the fifteenth century, is the last of its kind, and the first of a new world system (which is to say the first of a truly "global" character). At a time when the victims of the dominant modernizing paradigm of globalization rise in dissent, the exploration of epistemological questions becomes particularly needed, as fundamental to clarify the logic of the antihegemonic critical intersubjectivity. This paradigm becomes part of everyday life as it is inscribed in culture, economics, politics, theory, and even science; on *average*, it becomes quasi-universal.

I have articulated a development with three moments: from the problem of the criterion of demarcation between (a) science and metaphysics (from neopositivism to Lákatos) I moved, second, to the demarcation between (b) the natural and the social sciences (in terms of the "understanding-explanation" debate), and then to a third moment of demarcation between (c) the critical and the functional human or social (and philosophical) sciences. This third level is frequently and correctly considered to be the place where the problem of "knowledge" and "power" appears.[253]

[315] The whole work of Michel Foucault is related to this theme. Habermas testifies to this in his choice for the title of a chapter dedicated to the work of Foucault: "The Critique of Reason as an Unmasking of the Human Sciences: Michel Foucault."[254] The mechanisms of "exclusion," according to Foucault, put discourses under the normalizing influence of an "omnipresent disciplinary discourse":

> "Discipline" may be identified neither with an institution nor with an apparatus; it is a type of power, a modality for its exercise, comprising a whole set of instruments, techniques, procedures, levels of application, targets; it is a "physics" or an anatomy of power, a technology. And it may be taken over either by "specialized" institutions (the penitentiaries or "houses of correction" of the nineteenth century), or by institutions that use it as an essential instrument for a particular end (schools, hospitals), or by pre-existing authorities that find in it means of reinforcing or reorganizing their internal mechanism of power (one day we should show how intra-familial relations, essentially in the parents-children cell, have become "disciplined," absorbing since the classical age external schemata, first educational and military, then medical, psychiatric, psychological, which have made the family the privileged locus of emergence for the disciplinary question of the normal and the abnormal).

Foucault's *critique*, aligned with the position "from the perspective of those excluded by society,"[255] allows us to discover many structures of domination as well as numerous ignored victims. I will consider this theme in a future study, at a different moment of liberation ethics, when I will write on the numerous "liberation fronts" or "fields" in the struggles for recognition.

Just as necessary as a discussion of the critical human sciences is a discussion of the problem of "skepticism." There are various kinds of skepticisms. Some are opposed to reason as such. This is not the case with liberation ethics. The "critic," who is allied with the victims, becomes a skeptic when he affirms the *nontruth* of the dominating system and opposes it to the *truth* of the possible alternatives of the victims. As we will see, the "critic" is a skeptic of dominating reason, but not of liberating reason. Hence, as Levinas indicates, skepticism is as old as philosophy, that is, of philosophy as critique: "At various times, truth,[256] [is] like respiration, a diachrony without synthesis that suggests the *destiny of skepticism* refuted and returning, legitimate child of philosophy, and which in some way strengthens it."[257] The *intersubjective critical validity* that is reached for by means of argumentative consensus and made possible by the discursive reason of the *symmetric* community of victims and the alliance of organic intellectuals (who use and recreate the critical social science and philosophies) is opposed in this way to the old hegemonic intersubjective validity. The symmetry among the victims, created by their arduous struggle for recognition and for the discovery of nontruth (even with the use of the scientific method), nonvalidity (through the formal participative-democratic process of the group of critically conscious and militant victims), and nonefficacy (technological, instrumental, or strategic feasibility that I discuss in chapter 6), opens the doors to positive creativity in the formulation of possible alternatives.

§5.4. The "Principle of Hope" of Ernst Bloch

[316] One could (with Habermas) reproach Bloch that "if utopia, based upon the experience of existing contradictions, must theoretically grasp the practical necessity of its transcendence, it must scientifically legitimate the interest that guides its knowledge."[258]

This criticism would hold if Bloch's work were situated at the level of the negative theoretical-analytical critique of the prevailing system,[259] as Marx thought (and as did Freire, in his moment of "denunciation"). However, Bloch's critics have not perceived that throughout his life he developed the *positive* critical moment of the liberation project.[260] In addition, his work revolved almost exclusively around the *instinctual, affective structure*, and not at the level of the scientific explanation of the project or program of liberation.

> His support and its correlation is a process that has not yet produced its *very content* [*Was-Inhalt*],[261] but that is always in process of becoming. A process that consequently finds itself in the hope and the objective presentiment of that which has not-yet-become [*Noch-Nicht-Gewordenen*], in the sense of the good-which-has-not-yet-become [*Noch-Nicht-Gutgewordenen*]. The consciousness of being on the front[262] sheds the best light upon this; the utopian function comes into play here to the extent that the conceptual activity that expresses the affect of expectancy, the presentiment of hope, is found in combination with all the dawns that arise throughout the world. The *utopian function* understands that which is explosive because it is itself explosive in a very concentrated form; its *rationality*[263] is the empower-

ment of a militant optimism. Item: the *content-of-the-act* [*Akt-Inhalt*] of hope is, to the extent that it is consciously clarified,[264] cognitively explained as the *positive* utopian function; the *historical content* of hope, recognized in representations, encyclopedically researched in real judgments [*Realurteilen*], is human culture[265] referred to its *concrete utopian horizon*. It labors in this knowledge as the effect of expectancy upon rationality, and as rationality in the affect of expectancy, the complex of *Docta spes*.[266]

The *place* of Bloch's philosophical production may be better understood after everything that has already been said in this work. Frequently considered to be metaphorical, ambiguous, and idealist, Bloch's work can now be seen clearly as situated *exactly* in the positive moment of projecting (as affect and reason) the possible, not-yet-realized alternatives. But Bloch's utopian position would be unintelligible if one did not approach it from the perspective of the *content* (*Inhalt* or *Material* with "a"). This is what remains obscure for the critics and commentators of Bloch's work.[267] For my part, I believe that Bloch's work is located at the level of the second ethics or *Ethics* II, if by *Ethics* I, which was discussed in part I, we understand "fundamental" ethics, and by *Ethics* II, the critical, postontological ethics.[268]

[317] Bloch's reflections show a radical concern for "content." In 1918, during his first exile to Switzerland, the young Bloch wrote: "I am. We are. This is enough. Now we must begin. Life has been given into our hands [*das Leben gegeben*]."[269]

As in every *material* ethics, the initial theme in Bloch's work is *life*. It does not matter that life does not become a universal criterion for Bloch, or that he was not *explicit* about founding an ethics in relation to this concept. What matters is that *life* is the initial theme in his work. In his masterpiece, *Principle of Hope* (1959), his reflection begins from the ontogenetic origin, from birth:[270] "I'm born, I move. From the very origin there is a search. One always implores, cries. One does not have what one wants. But we learn to wait."[271]

In the second chapter of this work (the "Grundlegung," or foundation), Bloch focuses on "anticipatory consciousness."[272] This is the beginning of the ontology of hope. This ontology is inserted in the tradition that was outlined in *Ethics of Liberation*, in chapter 1 and §4.3: "Who drives on within us? We move, are warm and keen. Everything living is aroused, and first of all by itself. It breathes, as long as it exists, and stimulates us. . . . That we are alive cannot be felt. The That which posits us as living does not itself emerge. It lies deep down, where we begin to be corporeal. . . . No living thing can ever escape from the That or urging, no matter how tired it may have become of this."[273] It would take a long time to follow Bloch's continuous exposition of themes step by step. These simple words, though, make clear the "point of departure" and the "foundation": we are living beings, and as a result we have "drives [*Triebe*]." Bloch analyzes these themes in the effort to delimit the *pathos* of "hope." I "tentatively" analyzed the themes that appear here in chapter 1: ethical-human beings delimit the scope of their reality out of their "*being*-alive" (living-*being*), which is the universal criterion of truth (and reality). By the very fact that "life has been given to us" — to our self-consciousness, autonomy, liberty, and responsibility — the universal material ethical imperative, which it is impossible to renounce, is enunciated: "You shall live!" Bloch analyzes the structure of drives, which is a feature of *material* ethics or the ethics of "content," and he relates this analysis to the rationality that verses on the "possible future." This rationality emerges in relation to a *negative* and a *positive* moment. The first refers to material scarcity;[274] the second to the affirmative alternative that aims to overcome the unbearable present. The "negativity" to which I refer here becomes clear in a passage found later in Bloch's account:

> Hunger [*Hunger*][275] cannot help continually renewing itself. But if it increases uninterrupted, satisfied by no certain bread, then suddenly it changes. The body-ego [*Körper-Ich*] then becomes rebellious, does not go out in search for food merely within the old framework.[276] It seeks to change[277] the situation which has caused its empty stomach, its hanging head. The No [*Nein*][278] to the bad situation which exists,[279] the Yes [*Ja*][280] to the better life that hovers ahead, is incorporated by the deprived[281] into *revolutionary interest* [*revolutionäres Interesse*].[282] This interest always begins with hunger, hunger transforms itself, having been taught [*belehrter*],[283] into an explosive force against the prison of deprivation.[284] Thus the self seeks not only to preserve itself,[285] it becomes explosive; self-preservation becomes self-extension [*Selbsterweiterung*].[286]

[318] I hope that it is possible to understand now why Bloch's work, along with this *Ethics* and the philosophy of liberation, are incomprehensible if one does not distinguish between the ethics of the system (Hegel's ontological *Sittlichkeit*, *Ethics I*) on the one hand, and critical ethics as trans-ontology or metaphysics (in Levinas's sense, *Ethics* II) on the other. The Heideggerian ontological *Sorge* or "pre-occupation" relates to the "being" of the world as a project (*Entwurf*).[287] It is like the bourgeois who ontologically "tends" to "being-in-richness" by the accumulation of surplus value. By contrast, in the case of salaried workers — whose lives are, as Marx would put it, "de-realized" by the market — when these workers are "hungry" (because their insufficient salary does not allow them to acquire the necessary means to "reproduce" their lives structurally and by the average standard of the prevailing system), they do not demand only to eat (like animals), or to have "being-in-richness" (after finding personal "salvation," leaving other workers hungry); instead, they wait to have "being-in-satisfaction," in a future system where they would be full participants in the community

of all those who are exploited and excluded today. Bloch locates the *positive content* of the drive for hope at the transontological level, that is, *beyond* the dominating totality. The transontological is the *analectic*. Hope is that "drive, or appetite" for a horizon toward which only those who are not satisfied move: "Hope, this expectant counteremotion against anxiety and fear *is therefore the most human of all mental feelings and only accessible to men, and it also refers to the furthest and brightest* [288] *horizon*. It suits that appetite in the mind which only the subject has, but of which, as unfulfilled subject, it still essentially consists." [289] The victim's "appetite" for the new and alternative project of liberation is "hope" as a transontological drive. [290] Bloch pursued a phenomenology of the drives like that of Max Scheler, whom he followed often, along with Freud: [291] "The *drives* [*Drängen*] express themselves in the first place as aspirations [*streben*]. . . . If the aspiration is felt it is transformed into longing [*sehnen*]. [292] When this *yearning* gains direction it *searches* for something: it becomes a *drive* [*Trieb*]. The instinctual drive for the object ("bread") is called "need [*Bedürfnis*]." When the "impulse" is "sensed [*gefühlt*]," we call it "passion [*Leidenschaften*]" or "affection." "Desiring [*wünschen*]" is a human appetite or affection that "tends towards an image of that which desire has sketched into its content." [293] The "representation [*Vorstellung*]" of that which is desired appears as what brings "satisfaction": "These representations incite desire to the same extent that the imagined, the anticipated, promise fulfillment. . . . This is how it should be." [294] But the desire of what is imagined is not "wanting [*Wollen*]." Wanting adds to desire the will to decide acting in relation to "preference."

[319] As always, behind every drive there is "the individual living body [*lebendige einzelne Körper*]" [295] or material corporeality. [296] Freud studied sexual instinct primarily, [297] and he was not interested in pressing needs like "hunger." [298] He thus left aside the most *material* aspect of "self-conservation [*Selbsterhaltung*]." "For Freud and his clients—as for almost all contemporary ethical thinkers, I would add—the concern about how to obtain food is one of the worries most lacking in basis," [299] says Bloch. "This is how psychoanalysis manages to ignore the cutting edge of hunger." [300] On the contrary, those with hunger "hope" to eat today. Hunger contains "the effects of awaiting . . . the daydreams of a better life." [301] "Dreams" are the space for the counterfactual anticipation of the "satisfaction of desires." Bloch gives us strength, especially at the beginning of the third millennium, to confront a generalized pessimism: "This is not a time to be without wishes, and the deprived certainly do not intend to be. They dream that their wishes will be fulfilled one day." [302] The hungry must escape from their negative situation. In order to do that it is necessary to create a new order. This creation takes place in three stages: "This premonition with its potential for work is intellectual productivity, understood here as *work forming*. More specifically, productivity extends threefold into the unarrived, grow-

ing in three directions: as incubation, as so-called inspiration, as explication."[303] Bloch describes the way in which the desired and possible future
is created. He is thus led to what he calls "utopian function [*utopische Funktion*],"[304] a function of the ethical-critical reason that is now positively and
not negatively situated—as was done in chapter 4. A nonexistent scenario
has to be created whose constitutive determinations are positively defined
in terms of the negation of the negativity of the victim—if there is hunger,
food; if there is homelessness, home; if there is illiteracy, education; if there
is nonsymmetrical political representation, real democracy; and so on. A *critique of utopian reason* would be in place here.[305] Bloch pursues this project
only tentatively, and mostly in relation to the drives, rather than in relation
to the types of rationality, the construction of ideal models, and so on.[306]

[320] The daydreams of the victims are conscious, open, and rational.
Bloch does not fall into irrationality. Hence, he integrates the "cold stream"
of Marxism, which does not allow us to fall into "the final image as an
illusion."[307] This "cold stream" fulfills the goals of the scientific moment,
which involves, as does Marx's work, a critical de-construction of the system of oppression and an analytical exploration of the feasibility of the
"possible."[308] The "warm stream" of Marxism, on the other hand, pays
attention to the drives and enthusiasm, the wait and the hope, the conquest of freedom toward the *novum ultimum* and the mystique (like the
Sorelian "myth" of Carlos Mariátegui) that inspires the attempt to build a
new society. There is no transformation without this aspiration. This point
is entirely clear for critical material ethics as it is also for the victims, the
oppressed, and the social movements of liberation. No matter how realist it
may be, pessimism promotes quietism and impedes movement. The "warm
stream" of Marxism—in the style of Mariátegui, Antonio Gramsci, Ernesto
"Che" Guevara, Subcomandante Marcos in Chiapas, and many others—
represents a necessary moment. Speaking first of the "cold stream," Bloch
writes:

> Its inexhaustible fullness of expectation shines upon revolutionary theory-
> practice as enthusiasm [*als Enthusiasmus*]; its strict, inescapable determina-
> tions demand cool analysis, cautiously precise strategy.[309] More precisely,
> by virtue of this, Marxist materialism becomes not only the science of
> conditions but at the same time also the science of struggle and opposi-
> tion against all ideological inhibitions and concealments of the ultimately
> decisive conditions, which are always economic.[310] To the *warm stream* of
> Marxism, on the other hand, belong liberating intention [*befreiende In-
> tention*][311] and the materialistically humane, humanely materialistic real
> tendency, toward whose goal all these disenchantments are undertaken.[312]

The "warm stream" *moves* the victims to the *possible* utopia. The point here
concerns the idea of feasibility,[313] which Bloch, unlike Hinkelammert, ap-

proaches as an ontological problem and not in terms of different forms of instrumental rationality. At this point, we find a sort of transontological "possibility," declared to be impossible by the conservative dominant system as Popper conceived it.[314] The "being" of the dominant system[315] is confronted with a counterfactual "not-yet." This is the coming-into-being of the utopian pro-ject as "possibility":[316] "There where nothing more can be done and nothing is possible, that is where life will have come to a halt."[317]

[321] Utopia cannot be reduced to a purely formal possibility, of either a logical or an empirical nature. Bloch is concerned with the "possible and real objective"[318] that presupposes "laying down the scientific-objective foundation, according to scientific knowableness [*wissenschaftlichen Bekanntheit*], which is incomplete under the conditions that objectively prevail at present."[319] Since "what is possible can equally transform itself into nothingness as it can into being"[320] the possible reality must strive to become a reality through waiting, courage, and hope. An extensive reflection on the eleven theses of Marx's *Theses on Feuerbach*[321] allowed Bloch to introduce a theme that will be addressed in chapter 6: the effective praxis of liberation. The "transformation" of the reality of oppression in light of the expected still unelaborated utopia is a practical and material process, that is, a process with content in which "the possibility that has been *theoretically elaborated*, has been converted in that way into *something for us*."[322] The material content of the action entails practical truth: "Just as every truth is a truth for a certain purpose, and there is no truth for its own sake, except as self-deception or whimsy, so too there is no complete proof of a truth from within itself as a truth that is merely theoretical. . . . Truth is not a theory relationship alone, but *a definite theory-practice relationship*."[323] The "truth" that Tarski understood only in terms of meaningful linguistic intelligibility in an abstract *language L*, and that Apel and Habermas conceived of in terms of intersubjective validity, is now interpreted in light of the ultimate horizon of reality, the real cosmos that serves as the horizon for the unfolding of the possibilities of human life. Human life is the practical criterion of truth, both *practical* and *theoretical*. Human life is first and foremost linked with *practical* truth insofar as *practical* truth aims to foment the reproduction and development of the life of every single ethical subject in community. It is also connected with *theoretical* truth, insofar as *theoretical* truth is an abstraction of any given dimension of the practical level. Bloch was a critical realist. From the unavoidable fact of "hunger," which Putnam was unable to render correctly in his relativization of "needs," Bloch determined:[324] "The hope of the goal, however, is necessarily at odds with false satisfaction, necessarily at one with revolutionary thoroughness; crooked seeks to be straight, half to be full."[325]

Day-dreaming is followed by "desired images in the mirror" (chapter 3 of *The Principle of Hope*, "Transition"), in which the bourgeois imagine their fictitious being. This is the alienated utopia of the dominating system. It is also its aesthetics, its refinement, its false *happy end*.[326]

[322] In his fourth chapter, Bloch expounds "the foundations of a better world."[327] What he wrote there is quite close to my own view: "Those who wait outside [*draussen*] are too numerous. Those who have nothing and accept it, lose even that. But the drive toward that which is lacking has no end. The absence of that about which we dream produces more suffering rather than less. And this prevents one from becoming accustomed to misery. That which always causes pain,[328] oppresses and weakens: it is the *must be* [*soll*], which has been suppressed."[329] This passage clearly evokes Bloch's "critical realism": there are no idealisms or value judgments. His ethics is based on "statements of fact": "that which causes pain" is the premise behind the grounding of the ethical-deontological: "*It should be suppressed*" (normative statement, or statement of "ethical obligation"). The premise of ethics is the intolerable, that which inhibits the flourishing of life. This "fact" makes reference to an "ought" or ethical obligation, because life "has been given to us" and, thus, we are re-sponsible for living it and for letting it be lived by others. Pain, on the other hand, *does not let us live*. We find ourselves now at the antipodes of Hume and his "naturalist fallacy."[330] Marx guides Bloch on this point: "[Marx] provides a basis for and corrects the expectancies of utopias achieved through the economy,[331] by means of the immanent transformations of the forms of production and exchange, and *thereby overcomes the thingified dualism between being what is and what must be, between experience and utopia*."[332] The "ought" can be anticipated. It is lived in the daydreams of the oppressed, which incorporate the criterion of critical rationality. The fourth chapter of Bloch's *Principle of Hope* focuses on this issue: Bloch searches for "dreamers" who are realists and who criticize utopias. Beginning with the medical utopias,[333] Bloch makes a journey through time and space,[334] from Solon and Diogenes to Plato and the Stoics, through the history of Israel, Augustine's *Civitas Dei*, Joaquin de Fiore, More, Campanella, Fichte, to the utopian socialists and Marx. Bloch then focuses on the "wakeful dreams," of humanity, from the "technical utopias," where not even the "magical past"[335] is undermined, to architectural and geographical utopias, and even the eight-hour workday.[336] Bloch shocks Stalinist Marxists with his discussion. Nothing human is foreign to him. The victims have always expressed hope, and it is thus necessary to record the historical traces of its presence.

[323] In the fifth chapter of *Principle of Hope*, Bloch outlines "desired images [*Wunschbilder*] of complete fulfillment."[337] Ethics is frequently linked with value judgments, with drives: "Even taste, about which subjectively there can be no arguing,[338] becomes unanimous the moment one

offers stones instead of bread . . . when it is a matter of the evaluation of plague bacilli or a matter of the negation of the good that death is."[339] Bloch makes explicit here the criterion of truth. Against his wishes, Bloch cannot escape from axiology. Even though he does not affirm any concrete "supreme good," he provides a schematic definition of it as that which is always hoped for, a final Identity, or the "Kingdom of Freedom." Bloch touches on the theme of my chapter 1: the life of each human subject introduces the ethical exigency of reproduction and development of life, while it also serves as the criterion of truth and becomes the *positive content* of any possible utopia. Bloch, however, *does not analyze this point in an explicit manner.* After making all the necessary arrangements for its definition, Bloch stays only at the threshold of a material universal ethics. This material ethics is characterized by a *content*, by an element of *negativity*, and by a drive for hope. By virtue of its *content*, which serves as an ethical criterion and principle, this ethics demands the respect of the life of every ethical subject. By virtue of its *negativity*, which is understood in relation to the material component as the impossibility of reproducing one's life or as hunger, this ethics uncovers the unethical character of the dominant world.

The impossibility of reproducing life is itself uncovered by ethical-critical reason, whose emergence is synchronic with the hunger for that "which is lacking." All of which moves ethics, by virtue of the drive for hope, toward the *positive future* content, the project of liberation or the possible utopia. The future utopia is the "possible" *development* of the life of every single subject in community (phylogenetically speaking as well). The subjects in question are primarily the victims, but also, *in the long run*, the oppressor, since whoever murders the victim commits suicide. Preventing murder is equally to preserve the life of the possible murderer, since he will not have then to commit suicide in the long run. Some of this is somewhat ambiguous. For instance, as Bloch puts it: "Nothing is good in itself if it is not desired. But nothing is desired unless it represents itself as good. The fact that an impulse is directed toward something presupposes the drive, but also that the object toward which it is directed be capable of satisfying it."[340] The first statement seems to be clear enough. Yet, nothing is good only by its being desired.[341] Desire only makes its object "satisfying"—in terms of an immediate means to life. But "satisfying" and "good" are not identical. Moreover, what does it mean for something to be represented "as good"? It would seem that Bloch is unable to distinguish throughout his whole work among the "practical truth" (mediation of life) that "satisfies" (desired by the drives but also a means for life), the instrumentally "possible" (objectively feasible), and the "good." As we have seen in part I of this work, (a) *the satisfying-truth* (the materiality of human life), (b) *the* intersubjectively *valid*[342] (the formal intersubjective consensus), and (c) *the feasible*[343] (the possible in terms of technical, and economic instrumentality), and so on—constitute, as ethical-operative fulfillment and synthesis, (d) *the good* (*el bien, das Gute,* the "goodness claim"). The object of hope or desire is not by itself "good." The "possible utopia" must fulfill the three conditions of the "future *good*" (or the so-called goodness claim) toward which the victims are disposed.

§5.5. The Critical-Discursive Criterion and the Principle of Validity

[324] These considerations allow us to avoid the inevitable aporia of discourse ethics: argumentation presupposes an empirically impossible perfect symmetry among the participants. Liberation ethics overcomes this aporia by discovering that the asymmetrically excluded victims of the dominant community of communication meet in a critical-symmetrical community. It would seem that this idea is a simple development of or deduction from discourse ethics. But this is not the case. Liberation ethics takes into consideration the fight for the re-cognition of the excluded victims who become re-sponsible subjects or actors of their own liberation because it counts for the material, the feasible, and the *critical* moments. In contrast, procedural morality, which stays in an acritical formal level, that of the intersubjectively dominant valid consensus, is not able to go beyond the "circle" of the ideal or empirical *single* community of communication. It is therefore impossible for discourse ethics to achieve empirical symmetry in argumentation. And without symmetry the moral validity of argumentation is impossible.[344] A much more complex liberation ethics considers ideal and empirical, dominant and nonhegemonic communication communities.[345] I believe that the ethics of liberation opens up in this way a new horizon and raises new issues in the elaboration of a critical-discursive and communitarian-antihegemonic reason. This new horizon is highly relevant for *new* social movements in civil society, for *critical* political parties, and for "emerging"[346] social subjects in civil society. Apel and Habermas were not able to see the *critical-communitarian* discursive possibilities of their own discourse.

It is convenient to recall here that *practical-material reason*[347] had a claim to practical truth. As we have seen, *practical-material reason* "refers" to *reality* at large, which is perceived in relation to the sphere of the production and reproduction of the life of every single human subject. "Knowing" how to differentiate through a judgment of fact between *venom* and *nourishment*, is taken by *practical-material reason* as a criterion of truth. For their part, the *drives for the self-preservation* of life make possible, through civilizing education, the systemic permanence of human life—reaching happiness as peace and security, as I have said before.[348] *Ethical-originary reason*[349] recognizes the Other, other human subjects, as its *alter ego*: as equals. This "recognition" has a material aspect: the *content* is the dignity[350] of the Other as a real subject. But, since argumentative-moral discursivity originates in the recognition of the dignity and equality of the other subject engaged in argument, "recognition" simultaneously becomes the means through which one makes a dialectical move (*übergehen*) to *discursive reason*. That is, "recognition" is not only material but becomes itself the ground of discursive reason,[351] which acquires intersubjective validity in the consensus through the symmetrical participation of Others who have been recognized and effectively treated as equals. Responsibility for the Other as equal makes itself present here. Finally, *instrumental and strategic reason* is subsumed by the *ethical reason of feasibility*,[352] which tends toward a utopia. It also formulates a feasible project and carries out the norm, act, institution or system of ethical life (the "good" or "bad") while being able to evaluate the consequences of its acts in an a posteriori fashion.

[325] The *critical* moment in question originates in response to the unintentional *negative* effects produced by the dominant norm, act, institution, or system of ethical life. The critical moment thus emerges as an ethics of *critical* "re-sponsibility."[353] First, *practical-material critical reason*[354] uncovers the inevitable negative effects or consequences of the current ethical order, which presents itself as true (at the practical level), valid, feasible, and thus, in its fulfillment, as "good" (making a "goodness claim"). Beginning with the victims,[355] it proceeds in a negative movement and becomes aware of the "untruth" of such an order (in which "life [at least that of the victims] is *not* possible"). The *drives for change* or pleasurable creation, which are not only Dionysian or narcissistic, as Levinas conceives of them, and whose reproductive dimension cannot be reduced to the "development" of the given order,[356] unblock affectivity and motivate the *risk* of "ethical critique." Taking place at the material level, *ethical-preoriginary* or *critical reason*[357] re-cognizes the victim not only as an *alter ego* (an Other "like me"), but *as other* (an Other *as other*; *alter ut alter*).[358] Here we find the re-cognition of the *alterity* of the Other, of the victim: as an ethical *autonomous* subject, it is other than the system that unintentionally produces or originates it. The autonomy of the victim's alterity questions the autoreferentiality of the system. A subject in the Luhmannian *Umwelt* distorts the autopoiesis of the dominating totality. *Ethical-preoriginary* or *critical reason* is presupposed by and provides the ground for *critical-discursive reason*.[359] The *critical community of victims*[360] originates in the re-cognition of the victims (by one another) as "other" than the dominating system. This community will reach a *new*, antihegemonic validity. We have now reached the topic of this section (§5.5): the exercise of critical-discursive reason. The

discovery of the "invalidity" of the consensus of the dominating system, which has asymmetrically excluded the victims from the procedures of valid consensus, marks the beginning of critical discursive reason's diachronic process. Since, at least at the beginning, the consensus of the victims will be against the dominant, illegal, and illegitimate—take as examples Washington in the United States and Hidalgo in Mexico—critique appears to be inherently dangerous.

a. The Critical-Discursive Criterion of Validity

[326] The *critical*, formal, and procedural criterion is a criterion of validity. It refers to the intersubjective participation of the excluded in a *new* community of communication of the victims. The crucial point here is the validity of ethical critique. We are focusing on the moment in which the critical agreement (empirical fulfillment of the rational consensus) concerning a statement of fact or descriptive utterance takes place (e.g., "We have been excluded from the discussion concerning the means that would eliminate our hunger"). This moment creates a *new* intersubjective validity for the victims. The approval of such a critical agreement presupposes the common "experience" of the suffering caused by "not-being-able-to-live." In negative terms, the critical agreement in question consists of a statement about the "invalidity" (to the victims at least) of the consensus of the hegemonic communication community (e.g., "The means that they decided to follow and that cause our hunger are invalid"). The criterion of invalidity (ethical fallibility) leads to the *new* elaboration of *critical* validity, which is grounded on the symmetry of the *new* consensual community, by virtue of the newly discovered "fact" of exclusion of the affected asymmetrically rejected. The diachronic process of critical consensus is also known as *conscientization*: the temporal unfolding of ethical-critical consciousness is part of the exercise of critical discursive reason. In this process, characterized by intersubjective solidarity, one learns in community how to argue against the dominant mode of argumentation.

The distinction between truth and validity claims[361] becomes especially relevant here. The "truth" of the dominant system is the "reference" or access to *reality* (I) as it appears in the horizon of the current system.[362] The symmetric participation of those who possess power in the system determines the intersubjective validity of such "truth." The victims, the excluded ones, discover that such a "truth" hides a *new* access to *reality* (II) from the possible alternative of liberation.[363] The "truth" of the dominant system appears then at this moment as "untruth," in Adorno's terms. The existence of the victim becomes a criterion of falsification. The dominant "validity" is likewise opposed to the *new critical validity* of the victims' community

of communication. By making it "in-valid" the existence of the victim becomes a criterion of invalidity. By means of consensus, the community of
victims gradually gives birth to a *new* practical paradigm[364] that has "critical" truth and validity. The new practical paradigm of interpretation, or
practical paradigm of critical hermeneutics, serves as the foundation for
new value judgments that aim to "develop" the life of every human subject
critically in relation to the *new* access to reality (II). The de-constructive
critique of current values (Nietzsche's *Umwertung*) paves the way to a creative construction of *new* critical values. Zarathustra's creative aesthetic appears here as a "will to life," and not as the narcissistic "will to power." The
new practical paradigm judges statements of fact (means-ends), along with
Weberian or Popperian values and ends. We have here a new horizon of critique that initiates the liberation pro-ject. It provides a new "comprehension" of what has been "grounded," and an innovative (critical) "explanation" of the "causes" of the negativity of the victims. It is nothing less than
an "ethical-critical conscience."

[327] We have thus arrived at a new place, that of critical intersubjectivity as a criterion for the new validity of the new critical consensus.
The analytical moments expounded by Apel or Habermas now need to
be rearticulated, taking into consideration the dialectic between the "old"
(dominant validity) and the "new" (*new* critical hegemonic validity). I propose to develop this theme in future works. At the moment, as before, I
only *situate* the architectural "place" of the issue.

The *critical* discursive criterion of validity consists, then, in the reference
to the intersubjectivity of the victims who are excluded from the decisions
that affect them (by alienating them at any level of their real existence). I
could preliminarily describe this criterion of validity as follows: there is
critical validity when the community of the excluded victims, having recognized each other as distinct from the oppressive system, symmetrically participate in the agreements about what affects them while at the same time
sustaining that critical consensus is grounded in rational argumentation
and motivated by the drive of co-solidarity. This critical consensus unfolds,
as it will be discussed in §5.5c, (a) *negatively*, as a way to comprehend and
explain the causes of alienation, and (b) *positively*, to anticipate creatively
future alternatives (possible utopias and projects).

There are three levels in the formation of the critical validity of the agreements: that of material critique ("The victim can *not* live"; this point was
initially treated in chapter 4); formal critique ("The victim has *not* been able
to participate discursively in any way in the matters that affect her," chapter 5); and instrumental critique ("What has been validated in the dominant system is *not* efficacious in regard to the victim's life"; this point will
be initially treated in §5.5c and more extensively in chapter 6).

b. The Critical-Discursive and Communitarian
Ethical Principle of Validity

[328] The formulation of the criterion ("is," *es*) allows us to make explicit or ground the normative principle ("ought to be," *debe ser*): whoever acts in an *ethical-critical* manner *should* (is deontically "obligated to" by re-sponsibility) *participate* (as a victim or "organic intellectual") *in a community of communication of victims* who, having been excluded, re-cognize each other as ethical subjects (as *other than* the dominant system), symmetrically accept argumentative reason as the ground of critical validity, and are motivated by a creating drive for solidarity in the alterity. Every critique or alternative project should then be the result of the symmetric community of victims' critical discursive consensus, which grants *critical* intersubjective validity. Subsequently, out of this critical intersubjectivity[365] the community will endeavor to (b1) "interpret," "comprehend," or "explain" the material, formal, or instrumental "causes" of the "negativity" of such victims, and (b2) critically "develop" the material, formal, or instrumental "positive" alternatives of the possible utopia and projects.

This communitarian process of the "ethical-critical conscience"[366] takes place first and foremost in the very subjectivity of the victim (ultimate monological origin of the always communitarian Freirean *concientizaçao*) from the victims' intersubjective horizon.

b1. *The negative aspect of the principle*

[329] The need for forming a victims' community of communication is the result of the awareness of "exclusion." Without a place in the dominant community of communication, the victims cannot participate in any community. Hence, some of them create a new community *among themselves* in a critical way. The awareness of unjust exclusion and, thus, critique (Freirean "denunciation") are the point of departure or negative aspect of the principle. The community or critical intersubjectivity of the victims begins its "work" of conscientization. The system of domination *is not* "true," "valid," or "efficacious" in regard to the life or the dignity of the victims. The critic, both the victim and the "organic intellectual," becomes a skeptic who is critical of the truth and validity of the system. The critique of the "great critics"[367] is thus something like the "return of skepticism," as Levinas described it.[368] They are skeptics of the "truth," "validity," and legitimacy of the prevailing system. The conservative thinking of all the ages is in agreement with Hegel: "The real is the rational; and the rational the real."[369] This identity presupposes (a) having an infinite intelligence (omniscient, divine), or, (b) as for Popper,[370] affirming the current system as the "best possible" (access to reality [I] and dominant reason are the same), declaring

alternatives (the new access to reality [II] would no longer be identical to the dominant system's rationality) impossible, and thus, "evil." Differently, for the victim, the "reference" to the reality of dominant reason (I) is not identified with the *new* "reference" to the future reality of critical reason (II). The difference between the "access" to reality from the perspective of the *present* and from the victims' possible *future* offers the "space" where critical reason can become skeptical of the functional exercise of dominating reason. It is nonetheless necessary to distinguish between (a) the skepticism of *reason as such*, which must be refuted in favor of the consistency of ethical discourse; (b) the cynic's *anticritical*, conservative, and antiutopian skepticism that denies the possibility of ethical-critical reason;[371] and (c) the *critical* skepticism of a dominant consensus that has turned invalid in the eyes of the victims. In this sense, the criterion articulated here is one of falsification, and as we will see in §5.5c2, one of judgment about the "inefficacy" of the dominant instrumental reason.

This is the precise architectural place in which the question of the origin of dissent and of the new consensus can be considered. Dissent, the interpellation as a "speech act" opposed to the consensus of the dominant community, emerges when the victim makes a "critical statement of fact" (ultimately a descriptive statement about the life or death of the victim) in regard to the system. Normally, such dissent is not listened to; it is denied, or excluded. *Critical* dissent becomes public only when it is supported by an organized community of dissenters (the victims) who struggle for recognition and who fight against the system's truth and validity in light of the impossibility of living and of their exclusion from the discussions that affect them. This community achieves symmetry in the fight for truth. Dissent thus has an ethical locus of enunciation. It consists of the exteriority that is generated by the new consensual communities of communication. This exteriority is now not only re-cognized, but also respected as real. Creative critical dissent is the origin of a new rationality, a new discourse. Dissent against the nontruth and nonvalidity of domination constitutes a new true and valid consensus.[372] So-called postmodern thought emerges in the intersection of the problem of dissent and the affirmation of critical "difference" ("dis-tinction").[373] Since the early 1970s, in *Toward a Latin American Ethics of Liberation*,[374] I have called attention to the diversity of the *field* of "difference" *within* the totality (an ontic difference for Heidegger and Levinas, and in the horizon of Hegel's "identity-difference"), as well as the concept of "dis-tinction"[375] as the Other, the alterity in exteriority— in this work, the victim. From this I have talked, before Lyotard, about a "postmodern philosophy,"[376] but even then using the term with a different meaning. When Rudolf Pannwitz, following an early Nietzschean tradition,[377] used the term "postmodern" in 1917, he formulated a neologism that was to have a long history.[378] Liberation ethics continually touches on aspects of postmodern thought, but it can never identify itself completely with it since, from its perspective, post-Modernity remains trapped in Modernity. This is due to the absence of a *critical* extradiscursive reference—the victims of both the globalization of Modernity and of post-Modernity as colonial domination.

b2. *The positive aspect of the principle*

[330] The demand of the "announcement" (Freire) includes the obligation for victims to imagine the procedural or moral moments that have to be transformed, using strategic, instrumental, and theoretical rationality. The search for consensus plays a crucial role in the invention and analysis of formal, democratic alternatives. Following a critical-democratic procedure is an obligation entailed by the principle of critical antihegemonic validity. Clairvoyant antidemocratic vanguardisms cannot be accepted.[379] This consensual approach allows for the emergence of social movements, autonomous organisms of civil society, and *critical* political parties. A philosophy of such "new social movements" would entail everything that has been gained so far.[380] Every single one of these *critical* "movements" refers to some negated material aspect, some excluded formal intersubjective dimension, or to moments in which the "efficiency" in the reproduction of the system impedes the production and reproduction of the life of every single ethical subject linked to the historical-social subjectivity of the emergent "movements." I will come back to this topic in the next chapter.

This formal critical principle can and must be grounded. As before, the discussion will take the form of an argument against a specific opponent, in this case, "dogmatics." Among them are (a) the conservative dogmatics in power, who tend to interpret themselves as the "possessors of eternal truth and values" that must be defended against the "destroyers" of tradition. This position represents a "traditionalist" or an antitraditional "fundamentalism." There are also (b) the dogmatic "vanguardists" of social movements or antidemocratic leftist political parties, who also think themselves to be "possessors of strategic, nonideological, enlightened truth" and who therefore think themselves to be different from the naive, spontaneous, or ignorant masses (e.g., Blanquism or Leninism). The argumentative strategy to oppose these diverse forms of "dogmatism" is similar. Reality can be accessed in different ways and never "gives itself" completely to finite knowledge. Hence, a finite subject cannot attain a definitive and perfect truth. Whatever was presented as true yesterday may appear today as false. One has to verify and validate it through argumentative confrontation.[381] Likewise, whatever has been found to be true and has gained intersubjective validity has to be validated again in light of objections, new findings, and new circumstances. The questioning of a statement's truth and validity does not imply relativism. It only demands the innovation of arguments, which are improved, innovated, or refuted only in the process of debate, in the confrontation of objections and critiques. Dogmatic persons commit a performative contradiction when they claim the nontemporality, and thus the dispensability, of a new defense, of any statement's truth and validity. The alleged dispensability of a refutation of a counterargument or reformulation of a claim indicates the loss of the historical condition of every expressed truth, the fossilization of a perspective that could have been superseded long ago, and the incapacity of distinguishing between a truth (with reference to reality) and the later intersubjective validity (which must be attained rationally by each community aiming to reach a consensus). Dogmatics believe that truth automatically grants validity. Or else, they conceive validity in terms of their own community's traditions, and believe that whatever is valid in this sense is true for any other community. Hence, it is not necessary for them to "doubt" the claimed validity and truth by defending them with *new* arguments, or to rationally innovate arguments to reach a new validity (in relation to their own and the other community). Traditional dogmatics (or fundamentalists) believe that truth is one and eternal, and that, as a result, there is no need for arguments that aim to reach a newly certified validity. Their irrationality consists of ignoring the need for renewing the actualization of the true "reference" to reality (which is historical) and the acceptability of validity. One only remains in truth by taking the risk of being refuted. Dogmatic vanguardists believe that since the professional and heroic group gives its life to the point of death, it has privileged access to the truth. They also believe that the consensus of the vanguardist community is an adequate anticipation of universality and that it is only a matter of time for it to be transmitted to the unenlightened masses. The contradictory irrationalism of this position consists of ignoring the possibility of a new access to the truth from the perspective of the victims themselves. This occurs, for instance, when the critical "expert" or scientist is oriented by the victim's experience and practical wisdom in the search for the truth. The dogmatic vanguardist also ignores that the dialectic of validity in the community of victims (naive at first) is nourished by the scientific *critique* of the experts. Their participation in the community leads to the enlightenment of the victims. The "enlightenment" of the base is the new point of departure (as in a growing spiral) for new developments. As we will see in the next chapter, the critical and militant community does not "possess" truth by virtue of its contacts with a "vanguardist community," but only in relation to its continuous articulation with the more ample organized and critical community of victims. The community of experts is "empty" without the critical community of victims; the community of victims is "blind" in respect to the "explanation" of its negativity without the community of experts. The Left should no longer propose a "democratic centralism" (a *contradictio terminorum*) but a participative critical-communitarian democracy.

c. Initial Discursive Tasks of the Critical Community

[331] If the previous points are correct, it is possible to say that the communitarian exercise of critical-discursive reason has two main tasks. The first is (a) the scientific critique of the current ethical totality (norm, act, institution or system), which is the negative moment or moment of critical de-constructive reason.[382] It is, to be sure, different from an uncritical de-construction that disarms or destroys discourses in order to uncover the "meaning," but not to "critique" the ethical untruth, invalidity, and the inefficacy of the prevailing system. The critical de-constructive reason here in question is that present in the scientific "critique" of Freud, Freire, and Marx. The second task, (b), is creative pro-jection by means of critical utopian-constructive reason. This is the positive moment of the critical task,[383] an expression of rationality that should be distinguished from mere utopian reason. Every system presupposes a utopian construction. Take, for instance, the notion of "equality, liberty, and fraternity" in the bourgeois revolution, or Hayek's idea of the "market that tends toward equilibrium." Critical utopian-constructive reason, in contrast, expressly anticipates what I have called for many years a "liberation pro-ject."[384] It is Freire's "announcement" or Ernst Bloch's "utopia" of hope. Let's take a brief look to these two tasks.

c1. *Negative explicative judgment*

[332] Strategic or instrumental reason becomes *critical* when it is subsumed by critical ethical and formal reason. It judges the inefficacy of the system, or the mediations that create victims. It also aims to provide a scientific explanation of the "causes"[385] of the alienation of the victims, with whom the scientist has been organically integrated. The principle's negative aspect, the duty of "denunciation," includes then the obligation of an explicit, scientific, explicative, rational-critical analysis of the "causes" or "fundament" of victimization. The negative aspect is something like the ethical presupposition of *critical* human or social sciences,[386] or like a new "ethics of science."

To demonstrate materially what impedes the victim to live demands a specific scientific development. Thus Marx pursued a critical scientific research program while he was organically integrated with the working class. With the category of surplus value, he provided an *explanation* of the *cause* of the worker's poverty in industrial capitalism.[387] I should now discuss in more detail the relation between the victims' own ethical-critical conscious-ness (of the English trade unions, for instance) and that of the intellectual "interpellated" by them. Scientists are at first only experts in the *standard* or *functionalistic* human or social sciences. The theoretical moment of co-solidarity with the victim propels them, to use Lákatos's words, to define a *new* "scientific research program." Co-solidarity involves the responsible embrace of the interest of the Other. The acceptance of the "interpella-tion" of the victim in the scientists' ordinary world precedes and orients this moment of theoretical co-solidarity. Scientists who become ethically re-sponsible for the victim impose on themselves the task of providing a theoretical explanation of the causes of the negativity of the alienated.[388] They thereby produce a *critical* human or social science. In this way, they fulfill what I would call the "third criterion of demarcation" (see figure 16). While the *first* criterion of demarcation (found in the work of Frege and Carnap up until Popper, Kuhn, Feyerabend, and Lákatos) distinguishes be-tween what is and what is not science; and the *second* (articulated around the "comprehension-explanation" debate as it takes place in the works of figures such as Dilthey, Gadamer, von Wright, and Apel) differentiates be-tween natural and human or social sciences; the *third* criterion of demarca-tion distinguishes, as it is defined in this work,[389] between the "functional" and the "critical" human or social sciences. The former operate in favor of the *internal* and autoreferential reproduction of the system (economic, political, related to gender, and so on), while the latter takes the form of "critical" human or social sciences, as, for example, psychoanalysis and the critique of political economy respectively. The "third" criterion of demar-cation *entails* really taking the side of the victims, assuming the many risks involved with this. This topic will be examined again in a different context in §6.3.

What is important to discuss in detail later is the constitutive role of the *ethical* "component" for the emergence of the *critical* human or social sciences.[390] Freud needs to put himself in the position of the repressed subject. He also needs to elaborate ethical categories, such as that of the "superego," and to defend the "participation" of the analyst when she or he confronts the patient's fears, repressed drives, and projections. Freud has to "manage" them in an ethical way. Referring to the alienating moment of the popular students, Freire, on his part, elaborates categories such as "*banking* education." Marx formulates the ideas of "*unpaid* work" and sur-plus value, which represent ethical categories par excellence.[391] Scientists are able to creatively "formulate" a "*critical* scientific research program" *from* an ethically, historically, and socially situated perspective. They are en-gaged "in proximity," face to face with the victim (as do Foucault or Levi-nas); otherwise they become hostages who take the place of the victims, as a substitute for the victims. Research originates in the re-sponsibility for

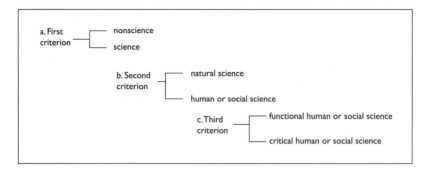

Figure 16. Three criteria of demarcation.

the Other as ethical option; re-sponsibility is the source or preoriginal moment: "If we were animals we could naturally turn our backs on the sufferings of humanity in order to focus on saving our own skin."[392]

Critical human or social science becomes part of the empirical practical reflection of the victims' community of communication, thus allowing the emergence of an *enlightened* critical-ordinary consciousness (see also figure 17).[393] A "scientific diagnostic of the state's pathologies," as Hermann Cohen demanded, now takes place.[394]

c2. The "possible utopia"

[333] There is a second task performed by strategic or instrumental reason when it is subsumed by critical ethical and formal reason, namely, the "anticipatory feasibility" or explicit formulation of the possible utopia as a program of action. This is the positive aspect of the principle, which is grounded on the obligation that emerges out of the victims' critical intersubjectivity.[395] The community or the victims' critical intersubjectivity begins to imagine utopia,[396] and by this imagination transcend the system: if the "current state of affairs" threatens life it is necessary to imagine "a world where it would be possible to live." "Hope" serves as motivation—life or pleasure drive, the Dionysian in Nietzsche corrected in terms of Levinasian "metaphysical desire"—for the *possible* future. This is the *possible* utopia. An alternative utopia that illuminates the way is needed. To arrive at it, a project and a detailed program must be made explicit.

Whoever aims to transform a given order, knowing the causes of the negativity of the victims, *should* (deontological moment) know how to imagine and formulate possible alternatives. A properly speaking *critique of utopian reason*,[397] which serves as a ground for Bloch's *principle of hope*, would consist precisely of this, the critique and proposal of alternatives. Negativity is the source of the positive alternatives. It is to the positive as a mold is to a sculpture. The nonfeasibility of the victim's life makes the apparent "efficiency" of the system appear now as nonefficient. Operating here is what could be called a formal-critical criterion of inefficiency. Capital "valorizes value." It accumulates increasing profit, but those who are excluded from the system get poorer and become the miserable majority. They are "de-realized." When I was writing this section, on August 9, 1996, the Argentinean CGT (General Confederation of Labor) launched a general strike for "bread and work." In the heavy repression of the seventies and eighties that occurred in the context of the "Dirty War," people asked for "peace." Today, people ask for the simple reproduction of life: food and employment. The formal autoreferential reproduction of the system (positivity) contradicts the possibility of reproducing the live of every human subject (negative aspect). Paying the national debt becomes a moral duty. The life or death of ethical subjects is not taken into account or forms part of the exigencies of globalization's capitalist ethics—as embodied, for instance, in the World Bank, or the International Monetary Fund. In contrast, and thanks to *critical* instrumental reason,[398] which develops the implications of the inversion of negativity, the *possible* liberation project and utopia give explicit articulation to a positive "content." The "hunger" of the

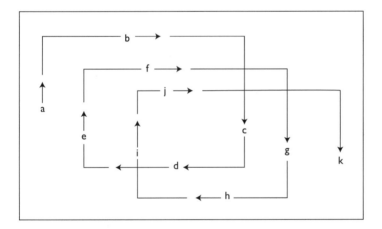

Figure 17. The organic integration of the militant-expert as a rising spiral.

NOTES: a: the critical community of victims, still ingenuous about the causes of its negativity, interpellates the expert; b: the expert pursues an innovative scientific research program in order to explain the negativity of the victim; c: the expert hands in the results of the investigation to the community of victims; d: the community loses some of its ingenuity and becomes "enlightened" (it not only studies the material, but develops and criticizes it); e: the community of victims returns the findings to the expert in a modified form after criticizing them; f: the expert modifies his research program to make it fit the situation better, and carries out new research projects, etc.

victim anticipates the future "nourishment" that will become a reality after the transformation of the ways in which the system produces and distributes "foods." It must be clear, then, that the positive "content" in question does not have anything to do with a nostalgic return to the past.

[334] The *possible* project and utopia that emerge out of a democratic and intersubjective discursive process and that count with the assistance of science and with techniques of different kinds, are different from: (a) the anarchist's impossible utopia; (b) the utopia of the current system; and (c) a merely regulative or transcendental idea (e.g., discourse ethics' ideal community of communication). This utopia has passed the test of feasibility, measured in terms of the ethical-material and moral-formal exigencies. For the ethical and moral alternatives to be empirically "possible," utopia, along with the alternatives proposed in every level, should be formulated by the consensus of the critical community as it discovers feasible and concrete alternatives. The critical community takes into consideration techniques, sciences, critical experts, and so on. The ethical and critical principle of transforming feasibility applies here. Utopia becomes first possible project, and then empirical program.

It would be equally necessary to discuss here the deontic dimension of the affective or motivational level of the life principle. The enthusiasm of hope and the drive for creation aim for the "development," and not only for the "reproduction," of human life. They are part and parcel of the responsibility for the life of the victims, who now appear as historical subjects with *enlightened programs* and *motivated by the struggle for re-cognition*. Bloch has partly explored this topic.

d. The "Application" (Effective Feasibility) of the Possible Project

[335] With a diagnosis of the alienation of the victims' community of communication and with a positive vision of its possible project there is still the need of a last step: a consideration of the real or a posteriori feasibility, which can be understood in terms of the notions of application or fulfillment. This is the topic of the next chapter.

As in previous cases, application is the task of the feasibility of operation; in this case it belongs to the area of what now strictly becomes the *critical* feasibility of the praxis of liberation. It is at this point that communitarian, critical, and creative "historical subjects" truly appear as subjects or actors. They emerge in certain moments and disappear after having accomplished their concrete function in a certain historical epoch. They then leave possibility for other emerging critical movements. They are not eternal "metaphysical" subjects, but, as we will see, they are *subjects or actors* who emerge "historically" in the "diagrams" of power.

CHAPTER 6

The Liberation Principle

[336] This is an ethics of life, a critical ethics from the victims. Now we shall discuss the creative and strategic liberating development of such life. Victims, when they irrupt in history, create new things. It has always been like this. It cannot be otherwise. In this last chapter, which represents a transition to other works, other *liberation fronts*,[1] many subjects that I can no longer discuss as fully as I would like press in on us. I shall therefore take a short cut, transversally, through some "questions"—only some of the possible ones—setting aside the remainder for future works.

First of all, I must raise the following question: Can we speak of "liberation" after the fall of the Berlin Wall in November 1989, the dissolution of the Soviet Union, the collapse of real socialism in Eastern Europe, or the defeat of Sandinism? Shall we try to struggle for liberation in times of the triumph of neoliberal dogmatism and transnational capitalism in the globalizing process? Shall we return to the subjects of 1903 or 1968, so far away for some and prior to the definite—for some—crisis of Marxism, ignored by philosophies such as discourse ethics, liberal political philosophy, and neopragmatism, not to mention the analytical metaethics of language or notions of the "end of history" as in Francis Fukuyama?[2] Taking all these aspects into consideration, I do feel that apparently anachronistic or "old-fashioned" problems, "overcome" by Western Europe, the United States, or Japan, are still present for the victims in the peripheral world of Africa, Asia, Latin America, and Eastern Europe; for the marginalized homeless, impoverished people in countries of the "center"; for ecologists, feminists, and excluded races. I wish to face certain objections honestly, and thus I shall begin my reflections by responding to an author who criticizes leftist thought. One of his biographers writes: "He wished to go against the current, clearly opposite to the dominant fashioned positions"[3]—"pour épater la gauche," I would add, in France when it was abuzz with Maoist Althusserianism in 1968. I refer to Michel Foucault, and my interest in him is that he positions us at the level of strategic and instrumental reason.

[337] Foucault in fact first worked at the historical-epistemological level of rupture (in the style of Bachelard and Canguilhem) in the order of discursive rules, of statements, of the "archive," of "words" (*mots*).[4] At the end of *The Archaeology of Knowledge*, however, a transition shows: "Might not this discourse be an *imprint* at the level of its *deepest levels of determination* . . . which upon speaking conjures not my death but instead grounds it more deeply, or better, annuls all interiority in this *exterior* which is so indifferent *to my life*, and so *neutral*, that it establishes no difference *between my life and my death*? . . . *Discourse is not life*: its time is not yours; in it you will not be able to reconcile yourself with death." Don't we find here the "cryptonormativeness"[5] of all Foucault's thought? In my opinion, in fact, in the works of the second stage,[6] the subject of "life" always appears as the last normative reference:[7] "What is vindicated and serves as an objective *is life, life*, much more than law, this is what is truly at stake in political struggles, even if these are dressed up in legal terminology. *The right to life, to one's body, to health, to happiness, to the satisfaction of one's needs* . . . these rights which are so incomprehensible to classical legal systems."[8] He now speaks of "biopower," of "biopolitics," of "the management of life," as that which is proper to the relationships of force that constitute power; most recently, he speaks of state power as the right to kill. Thus, he writes:

> We no longer await the arrival of the emperor of the poor, nor the apocalyptic kingdom. . . . [T]hat which we seek to vindicate and which serves as our objective, is *life*, understood in terms of basic needs, the concrete essence of human beings, the fulfillment of their virtualities, the plenitude of the possible. Little does it matter if a utopia is at issue; what we have before us is a struggle in the most real terms; *life as a political objective has in a certain sense to be taken literally and turned against the system that sought to control it.* Life then, much more than law, has become the objective which gives meaning to the gambles of political struggle . . . the right to life, to the body, to health, to the satisfaction of basic needs.[9]

Foucault thus "passes" from the formal order of language (the reductionist formalism of his first stage, which he now criticizes) to the material order (the level of production, reproduction, and development of the human corporeal life of each ethical subject). Against standard or Althusserian Marxism—dogmatic insofar as it rests on the proposition of an economicist "infrastructure" (which is not Marx's nor even Engel's position, for whom the ultimate reference ["last instance"] is the "production and reproduction of *immediate life*,"[10] as we have already seen)—Foucault rises rhetorically to an extreme position—denying economicism, the modern "metaphysical" subject, an exclusively globalizing history, and so on[11]—in order to redefine an "intermediate" material horizon.

[338] I shall place the "micro" level of subsystems,[12] microphysics (see figure 18), which deals with abstract categories,[13] between (a) the microphysics of the state, which is the level preferred by Marxism and—due to methodical demands—in the exposition of this ethics of liberation,[14] and (b) the individual level, properly speaking, of which Foucault becomes more aware toward the end of his life.[15] But, and this is the most interesting part for us, he discovers a more radical order than the discursive one: the material level of ethics, just as I have defined it. The order of power, of the "relationships of force," of "the bodies," of the "pleasures," is a material one.

"Power" is a "relationship of forces." "Forces" are actions in tension with other actions, which are self-sustained in "the management of life":[16] Foucault writes, "It could be said that the old right to *make* someone die or *let* someone live was replaced by the power to let *live* and to *reject* death. . . . [T]he care taken in avoiding death is connected less to a new anguish that would make it intolerable for our societies, than to the fact that the procedures of power have not ceased to distance themselves from it. . . . Now it is within life and throughout its development that power establishes its dominion; death is its outermost limit."[17] There is something like a "map" of asymmetric relationships of force, where the exercise of power involves the various extremes (forces 1, 2, n), and, although one can be "spontaneous" and the others "receptive," they all constitute a "diagram of power": thus, regarding gender, in a family situation, the feminine is ambiguously an accomplice of the disseminated forms of power, impossible without the

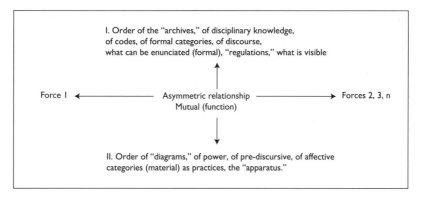

Figure 18. Fundamental orders in the microphysics of power.

cooperation of the latter, already immersed in gender's multiple and dif-
fuse relationships (not only "dual" for Foucault), from which disciplinary
knowledge, which "sees" and "talks," has already constituted the feminine
in a determined "place." Foucault shows the articulation between a "disciplinary knowledge"—in the hospital, prison, school, home, quarter, courts,
management, plants, and so on—that prepares "bodies" for the fulfillment
of their "functions" in the dispersed and plural distribution of power in the
"field" of the microphysics of institutional subsystems.

[339] Taking a closer look, however, one might see that Foucault focuses
his discussion on subsystems or institutions that "exclude" the Other[18]
(where we see a diffused type of "victim"), which place Others "outside"
(of power, of forces), in the "exteriority" (of what is visible,[19] of knowledge) of society, starting from a prior definition, presupposed in the order
of the reigning disciplinary knowledge, as sick, crazy, murderous, making
it possible to place a "limit" (the horizon of totality, as Levinas would say)
and "sever," or "protect" a watchful society from what is "watched" and
"negated":

> *Discipline* deploys a *relational power* which sustains itself by means of its
> own mechanisms and which, in the face of the clarity of its evidence, sub-
> stitutes for the uninterrupted game indulged in by the calculating gaze.
> Thanks to the mechanisms of surveillance, the *physics* of power, the domi-
> nation of the body, all is effectuated according to the laws of optics and
> mechanics, according to a complex game of spaces, lines, shadows, nets,
> degrees, and without recourse, at the beginning at least, to excess, to force,
> to violence.[20]

Anyway, we are always placed within a "paradigm of conscience" that has
not surpassed solipsism, although it situates it in the relational structure of
power (due to its "chiastic"[21] nature), from a linguistic turn as in French.
This paradigm is not yet pragmatic (not yet aware of the intersubjective
validity problem), is lacking still an explicit reference to the material level
(which discourse ethics lacks) under the control of a *strategic reason*. Microphysics is placed then within a "strategic field" of forces without subjects—
as the epistemology of the time demanded—from the power relationships,
which incite, induce, facilitate, expand, limit, impede, discipline.

To this point, my intention has been to recall what has been said, in
order to situate the level of strategic practical feasibility—which is in Foucault's "second period"—subject matter that I would like to discuss in this
chapter.

In fact, *strategic reason*, which is also subsumed by liberating reason,[22]
is placed in this level of microphysics of power. *Ethics of Liberation* has a
lot to learn from Foucault's analysis within the horizon of the practical-

critical feasibility of subsystems or of historical[23] "institutions." Thus, and not abandoning the microphysics of power, strategic reason, which handles power relationships, is left to be contained within the frame of the material (of content) possibility of production, reproduction, and development of human life: "Thereby arises the possibility of exploitation and domination. To monopolize and concentrate the material means *of life* is to destroy the possibilities *of life of another*, since that which is concentrated and wrested from others is not simply riches but instead the means necessary for life itself. . . . It is domination which makes exploitation possible and it is this which gives material content to domination. . . . No domination is definitive without the *manipulation of the distribution of the material means of life*."[24] Now we can pass from the level of material and formal reason (of previous chapters) to the level of feasibility of the horizon of life: to the practical-critical feasibility, to the practical-strategic critical action (the critical or liberation *praxis*) (see also figure 19). I have already discussed the horizon, which comprises social sciences and critical philosophy (*theory*). Now I must integrate ethical principles with this science and philosophy, a realm that is far broader than a mere "theory." To speak about the relationship between "theory and praxis" is an ambiguous simplification.

Among the various possible questions to be discussed in this chapter, and by way of indication, I shall deal with four, in order to treat through them the most ample and urgent "liberation question."

§6.1. The "Organization Question": From Vanguard toward Symmetric Participation — Theory and Praxis?

[340] "Liberating reason"[25] (which is properly employed as a final synthesis, first, of deconstructive-critical action and then, of constructive action, through the transformation of norms, acts, subsystems, institutions, or whole systems of ethicity) has, as an immediate component of that employment, critical-strategic reason — which is not instrumental reason but the reason of mediations at the practical (not technical) level. Strategic reason certainly intends "success" as an "end"; but, ultimately, and because it is now critical reason, it is an end that is a "mediation" of human life, in this case, especially of the victims, when there is a symmetrical participation of all those affected. The "success" of critical-strategic reason is no longer the formal "means-ends" of the prevailing system (e.g., "valorization of value" in capitalism), but the full development of life itself for all (especially of the victims, as we have indicated). Critical-strategic reason in its ultimate or concrete exercise *performs the transforming action*, starting from the exercise of the critical principles of practical-material and discursive-formal reason of critical scientific theories, of formulated alternative projects, of the use of

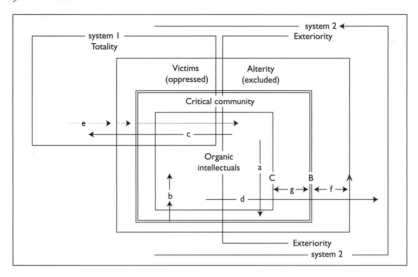

Figure 19. Some forces and subjects in the complex power relations in the organization of the critical community.

NOTE: A: victims in general (social movements, political parties, ethnicity, class, "peoples," "masses," etc.); B: organization as critical community (instance or "historical subject," *key element* of the ethics of liberation); C: critical community of "reference" (militants, professional politicians, experts, scientists, philosophers, etc.); a: centralizing relationship (from "top" to "bottom"); b: participating relationship (from "bottom" to "top"); c: reformist relationship (tendency to integrate to system 1); d: anarchist relationship (revolutionary radicalism in the immediate passage to system 2); e: repression by the system (against a critical community); f and g: mutual articulation among A, B, and C. Compare this figure with figure 12 [209].

critical-technical instrumental reason, in empirical reality, taking into consideration the "diagrams" of the "power relationships"—to use Foucault's terms, but, in our case, also including the macrophysics of power. It is the moment[26] in which praxis makes, from the horizon of concrete and critical ethical-practical *feasibility*, all that has been analyzed up to this point in this *Ethics*.

Let us now see, in the first place, the strategic question of the subject of transformation and the articulation of the "intellectual" with this historical subject.

a. The Proletariat's Self-Emancipation: Karl Marx

[341] Against the opinion of many, Marx's definition of the "intervention" of intellectuals in the historical transformation praxis evolved, in a clear form while he was still young. In fact, parting from Hegel, Marx be-

lieved that philosophy is something like the "form" that must be exerted upon "matter," first in politics, and gradually, upon the economic level. In his letters to Ruge, Marx showed the need for philosophy to change its interlocutor, which should be "suffering humanity,"[27] because liberal bourgeoisie did not have sufficient historical strength. Besides, "suffering humanity" is *passive*. Even in the *Economic and Philosophic Manuscripts of 1844* we still see a Marx who places theory externally with respect to material reality, a view that would change only with the revolt of the Silesian weavers,[28] in which, according to Marx, the recently discovered proletariat emerges as a social subject with its own conscience.[29] Marx writes: "The first duty of a thinking brain that loves truth, in light of the initial explosion of the Silesian workers' revolt, was not to situate itself like a *schoolteacher* in the face of such an occurrence, but instead to make the effort to study its specific character. It is clear that to do this demanded a certain amount of scientific acuity [*wissenschaftliche Einsicht*][30] and love for humanity [*Menschenliebe*],[31] while for the other procedure it was more than enough to employ well-trodden phraseology."[32] The Silesian insurrection showed Marx that it was not a political rebellion only, but a social one, since, as "human being is more infinite than the *citizen, human life* [*menschliche Leben*][33] is more infinite than *political life*."[34] We already see here a whole program of political philosophy. And he adds: "A social revolution must be situated within the *overall* horizon because . . . it implies a human protest *against the dehumanization of life*, because it takes *the point of view of a real individual* as its point of departure, because the *common essence*[35] whose division the individual is rising up against is the *true* common essence of humanity."[36]

[342] Marx stops thinking that philosophers are the form, the activity, the beginning of the process and, changing his "starting point," he now takes the proletariat itself: "It is only in socialism that a *philosophical people* [*philosophisches Volk*] can find its adequate expression for practice and therefore it is only in the proletariat that the *active element* [*tätige Element*] *of its own liberation* [*Befreiung*] can be found."[37] With the ambiguous term "a philosophical people" Marx is thinking of the liberation subjects, the "enlightened" people, conscious, self-conscious, self-liberating. They are no longer the former "*passive* elements" but are now "*active*." In *The Holy Family*, Marx deals explicitly with the subject under the title "The *Spirit* and the *Mass*":[38] "A few predestined individuals place themselves in opposition, as an *active* spirit, to the rest of humanity, which is the *mass lacking in spirit*, the *matter*.[39] The Hegelian conception of history presupposes an *absolute spirit*, which develops in such a manner that humanity is only a *mass*, which consciously or unconsciously serves as its foundation."[40] According to Marx, the masses, "the heart," the material, concrete, and practical, now have priority. He thus reaches a classic expression: "The proletariat *can and must*[41] liberate itself [*sich selbst befreien*]. But it cannot liberate itself

without abolishing its own conditions of life."[42] This allows us to understand the *Theses on Feuerbach*. The difficulty of its interpretation lies in the fact that one must presuppose everything mentioned up to this moment in this *Ethics*; namely, the critical and material principles, in the concrete level of strategic feasibility of relationships of power. Marx's "materialism"—against Feuerbach's individual, cognitivistic, static, and "functional" materialism—is anthropological (of living corporeality), critical or negative (depending on the circumstances of the victims), practical (insofar as this materialism is interested in the real "transformation [*Veränderung*]" of the conditions of these victims), and social (because it deals with subjects immersed in "social relationships").[43] Marx speaks about the "human activity [*menschliche Tätigkeit*]"[44] performed by the victims' own community (or those connected to them): "The coincidence between the transformation of circumstances with that of human activity or self-transformation [*Selbstveränderung*], can only be conceived of rationally as revolutionary praxis [*revolutionäre Praxis*]."[45] At this precise level, which is not that of a solipsistic and merely theoretical subject, but one of practical or strategic subjects in a *critical* position, for whom their own transformation praxis in the face of the system that excludes and dominates them is the condition of possibility for pronouncing a critical judgment (objective truth), Marx's thesis 2 should be read: "The problem as to whether *objective truth* [*gegenständliche Wahrheit*] can be attributed to human thought is a practical,[46] not theoretical problem.[47] It is in practice where a human being can demonstrate what truth is, that is to say reality[48] and power, the worldly grounding of his thought."[49] Marx has discovered the "starting point" of his praxis (the victims' critical community,[50] the proletariat in its moment and with its specific perspective), when responding affirmatively to the ethical interpellation of the same victims who are self-freeing themselves. In *The German Ideology*, Marx conceives such "critical community" as a historical movement under "communism's" generic domination: "*Communism* is not a state which must be implanted, but instead an ideal to which reality must be subjected. When I refer to communism what I am referring to is the *real movement* [*wirkliche Bewegung*] which subsumes the real state of things. The conditions of this movement are fragments of actually existing presuppositions."[51]

[343] But within such a "real movement," various organizations are discovered; and Marx speaks for the first time of a vaguely defined "communist party," which at its origin is something like an "opinion trend" within some labor parties,[52] especially against the so-called real socialism: "On the one hand then we have the really existing French Communist Party, with its literature . . . , the Chartists and the English communists, the National Reform association in the U.S., and in general the other parties active at

this time."[53] Such organizations of opinion within the political parties, as we can see, had their own "literature," their "ideas." "The existence of *revolutionary thought*[54] in a determined era already presupposes the existence of a revolutionary class."[55] In Paris and later in Brussels (and after 1846 in the Communist Correspondence Committee), Marx understood that the "strategic" struggle of liberation praxis (within the "diagram" of the macrophysics of power), not only in the hegemonic system but also in the realm of the community of victims, and of their various and contradictory organizations—with serious differences—demanded a tactical clarity (starting in the organization, "from the bottom")[56] and theoretical precision. "Communists," at that time, were opinion groups asserting that the community of victims (the working class, in this case) should free itself by the transforming praxis process (revolutionary, in this case) of the hegemonic system (capitalism under the power of the bourgeoisie). Marx began to discover that the transforming strategic or critical reason (according to him, revolutionary, at that time) demanded a "scientific"[57] precision, because "economists would like[58] workers to remain fixed in society as it is currently constituted and just as they describe it and reaffirm it in their manuals. Socialists instead want[59] workers to let the old society rest in peace in order to undertake the necessary transition towards the new society which they have prepared with so much foresight."[60]

[344] In 1847, the international opinion group ("communists") born from the "Communists League" or from the "Fraternal Democrats," from the European labor parties (Chartists and other English organizations, and also French or German parties), and among Americans, asked Marx and his friends to write the *Communist Manifesto*—something like a declaration for such groups of opinion within labor parties, which is clearly the result of well-defined critical positions.[61] The strategic structure of the *Manifesto* is developed in layers: the first being A, the community of victims (proletariat) is defined in relation to the prevailing system (bourgeoisie).[62] It is a first approach to the historical-economical "explanation" of the "causes" of the material negativity of the victims and of the internal contradiction that makes the prevailing system "impossible": "In this way the development of major industry tunnels the ground out from under the feet of the bourgeoisie, undermining the terrain upon which they have based their system of production and appropriation. . . . Their fall and the triumph of the proletariat are equally inevitable."[63]

A second layer is B, the community of victims (proletariat), where communists are situated.[64] Communists are an "opinion group."[65] Here the *critical-scientific* "communication community" makes *theoretical* definitions, in order to differentiate the "explication" of the group of communists from those of other proletariat movements in general. It must be stressed that since Marx had not yet discovered in his "explication" the existence of "surplus value," he could not provide radical enough theoretical reasons (fundamental, essential). There was a deep ambiguity in his exposition. In the third level, C, writers clarify in detail the *theoretical-strategic* differences of the various organizations within labor parties: reactionary socialists (feudal, petit bourgeois, "real socialism"), conservative socialists, and utopian socialists.[66] The *Manifesto* ends with a few considerations regarding the relationships of "communists" with all the opposition parties (including the bourgeois parties). Hence, it is a text on the level of critical-strategic reason, within the complex "diagram" of the macrophysics of power in a determined moment of Europe, that keeps in mind a specific victim: the salaried worker of European central capitalism in about the middle of the nineteenth century.

[345] When Marx was certain that the liberation of workers will be the result of the self-liberation of those workers, he started down a long road, defining *along the way* a strategy that would not get lost in the entanglements of ambiguous positions. LaSalle's "state socialism" became one of his main enemies.[67] Thus, when Marx was exiled in London, from August 24, 1849, the day in which he crossed the English Channel into England, although he never abandons the strategic action, he initiated a new *theoretical* stage, only understandable in light of the ethical-practical demands of a *critical-scientific* "explication"[68] of the "causes" that produce the misery of salaried labor in capitalism. Marx, from his strategic "experience" (from his commitment to the community of victims, being now aware that victims self-free themselves, but knowing the need to keep a *clear* "archive"—as Foucault would say—of the economical-material presuppositions of the "diagram" of power"), undertakes the task of redefining with extreme precision a "program of scientific investigation"—to express it in Lákatos's terms. This led him to go daily to the huge Reading Room of the British Museum (the best in the world in economic science at that time), and to de-construct all the existing *standard* economic science, in order to reconstruct it from the "interests" of the victims he cared about: the European and American proletariat. The result of his labor were the four editions of *Capital*:[69] critical social science, the beginning of a categorical launching of a "theoretical framework" to perform a scientific investigation of critical economy, theoretical references necessary for future social generations—until the capitalist system burns out—and also an "explanatory" horizon to frame strategic orientations within various macro- and microphysical "diagrams" of power at tactical levels.

b. Spontaneity, Organization, and Rosa Luxemburg

[346] Fifteen years after Marx's death, Rosa Luxemburg[70] appears on the scene, a brilliant Polish Jewish intellectual, very up-to-date with her consciousness of the three-dimensional power over her (as Jewish, female,[71] and Polish; this last because Poland, as a member of a nation dominated by other hegemonic countries—Russia or Central Europe—had since the sixteenth century been peripheral with respect to the new order of capitalism).[72] Her militant and critical scientific life had begun one year previously,[73] and from the beginning she showed great consistency, just as Marx had, between (a) socialistic principles and the explications of *critical* social sciences ("theory), on one hand, and (b) its analysis and *strategic* and *tactical* actions ("practice"), on the other. Her position on the "national question" in Poland, which would soon allow her to appear as a distinguished active leader in the social democrat congresses of the time, was a strict practical application of the critical-theoretical research of her doctorate thesis: neither the bourgeoisie nor the working class had anything to gain by the unity of the Polish nation—at least, not at that moment.

But Luxemburg's genius became evident in the intersection of concrete *strategic* and tactical praxis and *principles* (which must be differentiated from theory, even though Luxemburg did not do so explicitly). Criticizing the opportunists or reformists of the German Social Democrat Party, she asked herself: What makes them different from revolutionaries? And she answers that it is that one notes in them "[an] aversion to '*theory*' . . . since our *theory*, that is to say the *principles* [*Grundsätze*] of scientific socialism, impose a strict framework [*feste Schranken*] on our practical activities, both with reference to their *ends* [*Ziele*] and to the means of struggle (*Kampfweise*). Naturally those who pursue only practical *successes* [*Erfolgen*] soon wish to have their hands free, that is to say, to separate *praxis* from *theory*,[74] in order to operate freely from its constraints."[75] As one can see, the "theory"—which Luxemburg places in quotation marks—is in all its complexity something more: for the moment, it is a *set of "principles*."[76] Such "principles" are precisely, and in an abstract form, the principles already mentioned in this *Ethics*, namely, (1) the principle of production, reproduction, and development of human life in community, of each ethical subject; (2) the ethical-formal principle of discursive reason; (3) the principle of ethical fallibility; (4) the critical-material principle, and (5) the intersubjective-formal principle of critical validity. Such "principles"— *conditions of* ethical *possibility* of the norm, action, subsystem, institution, or ethical system, and the *frames* that frame such "possibilities"—are the ones that "impose strict referential frames [*feste Schranken*]," according to Luxemburg's writings—to our practical activity. That is to say, one cannot undertake "any action"—or use any means, or choose any ends, and so on—one can only decide, provide a discursive foundation, regarding only "those" actions that are "possible" (founded or applicable) within the narrow frame delimited by such principles.[77] In an amazingly accurate way—at the level of strategic organization[78]—Luxemburg points out that "principles" delimit and contain decision criteria "both regarding (a) the *ends* [*Ziele*] to reach, (b) as well as the *means of struggle*, and finally, (c) the *forms of struggle*." These three levels of strategic-instrumental reason define the horizon of mediations. This great political intellectual clearly describes the way in which strategic reason should be articulated with material, formal, and critical reason, constituting it as *critical-strategic reason*, that is, strictly ethical.[79] Now it can be understood that material-practical and critical reason "places" the *ends* of critical-strategic reason; from them it discovers means (not "any" possible means, nor "any" possible ends), and uses tactical methods for its concrete fulfillment that do not contradict the enunciated principles. Thus, neither is "any" method possible; since all of them fall within the "circle" of the allowed (or proper) possibilities by the former already defined principles.

[347] Critical-strategic reason is not strategic reason, which simply intends to reach the "ends" imposed by tactics or circumstances.[80] The latter would be Max Weber's position, for whom the "ends" are *inevitably* the ones of a given culture, of a present tradition, and as such they must be accepted—a position, on the one hand, "conservative" and, on the other, "irrational," since he cannot provide reasons based on ethical principles in favor of or against mere existing values or ends. Critical-strategic reason, by contrast, "does not have its hands free," like those who "only seek practical success [*Erfolge*]"—says Luxemburg. To seek an "end" and its fulfillment (the "success" of the action only) can be effective (it is what the successful person does), but it may well have nothing to do with a critical ethics (namely, the reproduction of life and the symmetrical participation of all humankind). If it is the case of liberating the victims, "success" (their effective liberation) will evidently depend upon the fulfillment of all their conditions of possibility, and thus, "freeing their hands," namely, severing praxis from theory, in order to act independently of it, cannot be possible. Luxemburg includes under the rubric of "theory"—just as Lukács and Habermas do; Habermas, for example, in his work *Theory and Praxis*—(a) all the principles enunciated in this *Ethics*; (b) any "explications" of "causes" or "foundations" of the negativity of victims (behavioral science, *critical* human or social sciences, which fulfill the "third criterion of demarcation" discussed in chapter 5); and (c) the liberation project (which includes strategic programs) intersubjectively decided by the critical community of victims[81] (both negatively as a "denunciation"[82] and positively as an "announce-

ment").[83] These three levels "frame" (d) the *ends* (of the strategic program); (e) the *means* (already defined in the program or to be defined while it is operating) discovered in community and consensually (in politics, "democratically"), which also "tie the hands" with regard to (f) the *methods*. Those whose actions fetishize or formally totalize the "ends" (and from them the "means" and "methods") without taking into consideration the principles, scientific explanations, and strategic programs consensually decided by the victims, may "sever *praxis*[84] from theory in order to act independently from it"—a phrase often repeated. Such "independence" of the "Machiavellian" action—put plainly, "Any means is adequate for the end"—is exactly this "severance" of a formal system (in the style of Max Weber or Luhmann, and what Marx called fetishized) from its discursive-formal, ethical-critical, material content (production, reproduction, development of human life, etc.). Critical ethics (liberation ethics) must know how to integrate all the enunciated principles in the choice of ends, means, and methods (see figure 20). This is, in fact, the whole problem of the "question of organization," from Marx, Rosa Luxemburg, Gramsci, Mariátegui, and so many others, just with regard to the critical-political sector; leaving aside feminist, ecological,[85] antiracist fields, and so on, although they all equally engage in the same kind of debate.

[348] When Lenin wrote *What Is to Be Done?* in 1902, in exile, against the oppression of czarism, with a strategic critical ("revolutionary")[86] party in mind, he had to consider realistically the need not to immolate organized workers in an unnecessary holocaust. His call for a "centralized professionalization" ("from top to bottom")[87] of avant-garde militants or intellectuals operating in the conspiratorial secrecy of clandestinity can

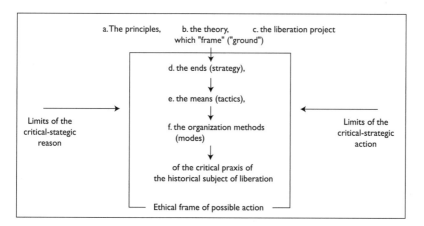

Figure 20. Ethical principles that frame (ground) reason or strategic action.

be understood as a suggestion placed in time and space. One must regret, nonetheless, that the strategies outlined in this 1902 text were deemed, from the 1930s onward, as the ideal template for the party's orthodox "organization"—applicable everywhere and under any strategic-tactical circumstance. One can thus understand, for reasons other than Lenin's, Rosa Luxemburg's strong reaction against young Lenin; an even more valuable reaction given the events from 1917 up to 1989—from the beginning of the Soviet Revolution up to its chaotic end. The failure of the revolution has not suppressed, however, the liberation process of the victims (even the liberation of classes or nations oppressed by capitalism) on planet Earth; it has, on the contrary, turned out to be a *higher lesson* about a principle of "organization" which, although it was very successful, in its final collapse demonstrated its initial inefficient ambiguity. Is the main principle not in fact the one indicated with such foresight by Luxemburg, which called for the *critical* articulation of "vanguard"[88] with the critical organized community of workers? Intellectuals must be very cautious in their interventions, when they "articulate" with the strategic actions of the "organized critical community" and with the critical community's interactions with the "masses,"[89] and carefully take into account the critical spontaneous[90] or self-regulated processes of the historical life of the victims.[91] Let us look, for example, at a short text, *Organizational Problems of Russian Social Democracy*,[92] where Luxemburg magisterially summarizes the main subject: "Whether the issue is organization or something else, opportunism has but *one single principle: the lack of principles* [*Prinzipienlosigkeit*]. It chooses its *methods* [*Mittel*] in accordance with the circumstances, if these *means* appear to be apt in order to achieve the *ends* [*Zwecken*] which are being pursued."[93] Luxemburg is describing nothing but the main ethical problem of critical-strategic reason; criticizing in advance Weber's conception of instrumental reason. Lenin, without being aware of it, and after giving a one-sided interpretation of opportunism (as in a core of intellectuals who tend to the "disorganization" of the masses in order to manipulate them), proposed a stern and unified party, disciplined under the centralized direction of a central committee.[94] Luxemburg shows that this type of organization is a response to a very dangerous "theoretical mistake" about the conception and the "subject" of liberating-strategic action of the last resort: the effectiveness of vanguard is the worst school (because it may arise from authoritarianism or an authentic internal repression) for the self-liberating creativity[95] of the masses, which does not mean spontaneity or irrational self-organization. Let us look further into this question, because although Lenin would later apparently correct his tactical position regarding the issue of organization (when he saw the spontaneous creativity of the masses in the 1905 Revolution), he never did change his view on what we could call the "subjectivity"[96] of the victims' organized critical community, a much undervalued conception.

[349] In fact, in *One Step Forward, Two Steps Back* (1904), Lenin answered Luxemburg that "discrepancies which separate one wing from the other currently are reduced, mainly, not with regard to the program,[97] nor to tactics,[98] but only to *"organizational problems."*[99]

For Lenin, clandestine[100] and professional revolutionary organization was different from revolutionary workers' organizations[101] and from workers' organizations in general.[102] After the 1905 Revolution, a spontaneous uprising of Russian workers, Lenin changed his tactical position,[103] but not his theory of organization—he always gave theoretical-formal priority for the self-aware movement to the vanguard, and to the masses, whether they belonged to the party or not, the role of something to be organized: "The conditions in which the activities of our party develop are changing radically. Freedoms of assembly, association, and press have been obtained."[104] Though Lenin indicates the need for "the total application of the democratic principle to our organizations," the relationship between intellectuals and members of the party,[105] which is the essential issue, is defined as follows: "The *relationship* between the functions of *the intellectuals* and the *proletarians* (the workers) in the Social Democratic workers movement can perhaps be most exactly expressed with the following general formula: the intellectuals effectively resolve issues *from the point of view of principles*, are effective at sketching out the general scheme, and are good at working out the need to do this or that, and it is the workers who *do and implant*[106] dry theory into life itself."[107]

[350] The "means" of the vanguard—the relationship between self-conscious[108] "intellectuals" who determine the "ends" and the organization and the working class who "perform" ("do, shape")[109]—could never have been expressed in a more Hegelian, conscious, formal way. So, for Lenin, "democracy" meant certain types of organization by consultation, by continuous dialogue, by mutual presence, but never by a constitutive-discursive relation based on the *same* foundational content for any decisions adopted. He confused ethical "principles" (the five already enunciated in earlier chapters of this *Ethics*) with a "theory" (the scientific-dialectical explication that would later be identified with a metaphysical, cosmological positivism) and with the fixing of strategic "ends" (of later Stalinism). He could never relate "organically" the original *critical* conscience,[110] albeit naive,[111] of the community of victims to the intellectuals, but he always thought in terms of a form-matter relation. Thus, "intellectuals" responsible for the "truth" (as reference to reality) would seek in the working masses (the party, the peoples, etc.) only intersubjective "validity" or "legitimacy" (induced "from the top"). The strategic interest in "success" (from

the intersubjective validity of the party following instructions imposed by the vanguard) would never give a space to respect and re-cognition of the dignity of the autonomy of the organic intersubjectivity, in an authentic discursive communication that could make an honest validity claim, from a truth discovered in relation to and within the "base."[112] For Lenin, the community of victims (as a workers' critical organization), had no direct privileged access to the "practical truth" that could serve as "frame" to the strategic or "scientific investigation program" of the intellectuals, or that could be developed as a social science or as critical programs. Just the same, for Lenin, the community of victims (to whom social scientists might deliver accounts of their investigations, not only to teach but to "verify" the pertinence of these findings and to reach mutual "validity," thus turning the interaction into a learning process)[113] cannot "judge" the results of a critical-scientific (abstract) explication from the foregoing concrete "frame" of practical truth to which it has access; instead, it should practically reduce its action to "perform" the decisions (of the Central Committee, the party's Congress, the postrevolutionary state, etc.).

[351] "Vanguardism" consists of this kind of overvaluation of the conscience and privileged level of the community of expert militants responsible for the central organs of the party or the state, from "the top-down":[114] namely, the bureaucracy. "Spontaneity," by contrast, would be a quasi-irrational trust in the self-regulative or creative power of the masses of victims[115] or in the organized and critical community of victims, without the benefit of sufficient scientific and ethical-critical "enlightenment." Luxemburg's and Antonio Gramsci's position are a balanced articulation between (a) the referral, as the *ultimate reference*, to the critical and organized community of victims and (b) the community of experts, scientists, and the militants who stand out (for their experience, practical-strategic intelligence, etc.), who provide the community of victims with (c) a development of its critical (now *enlightened*) consciousness. This new consciousness, like a spiral, constitutes a process of mutual development where the expert learns from the organized-critical base, and the base also understands, each time more profoundly, and in collaboration creating the "explications" of their negativity (denunciation) and the "construction" of possible alternatives (announcement). At the level of the political communities (and also in many other social movements), "democracy" is the discursive procedure of such mutual symmetric enrichment. Luxemburg writes in *The Mass Strike, the Political Party, and the Trade Unions*:

> The mass strike in Russia *has not been* the artificial product of a tactic[116] imposed by Social Democracy, but is instead a *natural historical fact on the ground* [*natürliches geschichtliche Erscheinung auf dem Boden*] in the context of the ongoing revolutionary process.[117] It is only the proletariat that can do

away with absolutism in Russia. But in order to accomplish this, the proletariat has need of a high degree of *political education* [*politischen Schulung*], *of class consciousness* [*Klassenbewusstseins*] *and of organization*. . . . These conditions can only be provided by the *living political school* [*lebendige politische Schule*] that arises in struggle and as the result of struggle, as part of the process of the revolution on the march. . . . But all of this can only have its origin in the struggle, in the development of the revolution itself, in the living school of events [*lebendige Schule der Ereignisse*], as a result of the clash between the proletariat and among the various sectors of the bourgeoisie, and of their continuous, *reciprocal friction* [*gegenseitiger Reibung*].[118]

Luxemburg interprets the "natural historical fact"—the "objective" circumstances—as coming from the spontaneous capacity of the Russian proletariat. Knowing that only *in the very same practical process* of deconstruction of the diagram of power, of the structures that cause the negativity of the victims—as Marx or Paulo Freire believe—do the victims learn, in the "school of events" of history, and thus increase their critical consciousness (the *latent* "class" consciousness becomes a *practical, active, clarified*,[119] *ethical, critical* consciousness of its own originary negation, through the revolutionary process). But, in order to achieve such critical consciousness, a "political education" and "organization" are required, to which only the party and the avant-garde permit access. Such "education" is produced in "friction," in the concrete contradiction, that is developed in the struggle when the proletariat acts. Hence, the excess of disciplinary organization from "top to bottom" creates conditions of passivity that hinders the creation of the sociohistorical subject and impedes access to "class consciousness." Rosa Luxemburg always kept a certain balance regarding this question. She is criticized by many as spontaneist, and Karl Liebknecht criticized her in 1915 for the position she took on the Socialist International, when she called it "too mechanical-centralist," of "extreme discipline," with very little "spontaneity," and for considering the masses "as instruments of action, not as carriers of will power; as instruments of the action decided by the International and not as wanting and deciding by themselves."[120]

[352] Let us now see, to conclude this section, a few central statements of Luxemburg's insight. In *Organizational Problems of Russian Social-Democracy*, she writes:

Social Democracy . . . advances in a dialectical contradiction, since it is only in the course of the struggle that it recruits the army of the proletariat and learns what tasks it needs to complete in the course of the struggle itself. The organization, the process of enlightenment, and the struggle itself are not separated mechanically from each other as in Blanquism,[121] but to the contrary are diverse aspects of a single process. For one thing, *beyond the general principles* [*Grundsätzen*][122] of struggle, there is no tactical plan developed in all of its details that the Central Committee can show to its troops as if they were in a barracks.[123]

This is followed by a famous Luxemburg formula: "Social Democracy is not connected to the organizational process of the working class, but is instead itself the *very movement* [*eigene Bewegung*] of the working class."[124] The critical community of victims[125] is for Luxemburg the "subject" of social democracy; the latter is the "enlightened" consciousness—the "philosophical people" according to young Marx. And demonstrating that the same workers were behind the Russian mobilization, she observes:

> In all of these cases the origin was in the *action* [*die Tat*] itself. . . . This phenomenon—the scant role played by the conscious initiative of the central organs in the elaboration of a tactical plan—is evident in Germany as elsewhere. . . . This is the emergence [*Ergebnis*] of an uninterrupted series of major creative acts [*schöpferischer Akte*] in the context of the class struggle with elemental frequency. *That which is unconscious precedes consciousness* [*schöpferischer Akte*], and the logic of the objective historical process[126] precedes the subjective logic[127] of its protagonists.[128]

Luxemburg clearly demonstrates that the self-regulation of the life of the community of victims has a "logic"—one of counteractions that know how to confront the rules of the system—nonintentional on the part of the actors (the community of victims) and their leaders, who should be very aware of the entire "objective historical process," of the "nonconscious" or nonintentional that they will never be able to dominate scientifically or in an enlightened manner. Thus, Lenin's Blanquist vanguard—with the excuse of fighting against the opportunism of the undisciplined Russian intellectuals—is theoretically wrong, because it takes a circumstance, interprets it incompletely, and intends "to make, from such framework, the absolute and universally valid abstract pattern." Luxemburg points out:

> The *academic*, being a social element with origins in the bourgeoisie and alien to the proletariat, can become an adherent[129] of socialism not based upon his or her *class sentiments* [*Klassenempfinden*],[130] but to the contrary, by overcoming them [*Ueberwindung*]. . . . This is why they are vulnerable to opportunistic oscillations to a much greater degree than the *educated proletarian* [*aufgeklärte Proletarier*]—to the degree that they do not lose their *living connection with their maternal social soil* [*lebendigen sozialen Mutterbonden*],[131] with the proletarian masses—which they find within in their immediate *class instincts* [*Klasseninstinkt*], which provides them with a more stable form of revolutionary support.[132]

[353] This is a definition of the enlightened community of victims as *the ultimate reference*, a statement of distrust of intellectuals when they "with-

draw" from this community, but also a decisive affirmation of the importance of "clarification [*Aufklärung*]" achieved through principles, science, the party. Anticipating history, she clearly sees what could happen if Lenin reached power:

> We cannot conceive of a greater danger for the Russian Socialist Party than the organizational plans proposed by Lenin. Nothing could more greatly submit a workers' movement that is still young to an elite of academics[133] who are avid for power than this hard bureaucratic crust of centralism in which the movement is imprisoned to reduce it to an automaton manipulated by a *Committee*. . . . The game of demagogues . . . would be much easier if during the current phase of struggle the spontaneous initiative and the political sense of workers' self-consciousness[134] had been coerced in their self-development and in their growth by the tutelage of an authoritarian Central Committee.[135]

In this passage, the elements that comprise a critical judgment of what was about to happen in the Soviet Union, from 1917 to 1989, are set forth. Liberation praxis can be achieved "only if social democracy becomes a strong and politically educated proletariat core."[136] But according to Luxemburg, Leninist theory was, unfortunately, very different:

> This is why the Russian *revolutionary Ego* [*"Ich" Revolutionärs*] makes haste with its pirouettes and once more declares itself to be the omnipotent master of history, this time in the person of His Highness the Central Committee of the Social Democratic workers' movement. This agile acrobat does not even glimpse the fact that *the only subject* [*das einzige Subjekt*] that fits the leading role is the *Mass-Ego* [*das Massen-Ich*] of the working class itself. . . . The errors committed by the real workers' movement are of a historical fertility and value which is incomparably greater than the *infallibility* [*Unfehlbarkeit*] of the best of the Central Committees.[137]

The foregoing insights already open the path toward the subject of the sociohistorical subjects of liberating transformation.

§6.2. The "Issue of the Subject": Emergence of New Sociohistorical Actors

[354] We must ask ourselves about the "subject" of the liberation praxis. Each ethical subject in everyday life, each concrete individual in all his or her acts, is already a possible subject of liberation praxis, insofar as he or she is a victim or solidary with the victim, and as such founds of norms, performs actions, organizes institutions or transforms ethicity systems. The ethics of liberation is a possible ethics regarding any action of everyday life.

What is specific about such ethics, however, its privileged referent, is the victim or community of victims that will operate as "subject/s" in the last instance.

The argumentative strategy of this section takes the following path. First (a), modern subjects "place" themselves; they are later criticized, but reappear in other horizons, because the Nietzschean and Heideggerian critique of the "subjectivity of the subject" critiqued an already reduced "subject" according to instrumental (formal) rationality. On the other hand, not paying attention to the subject (such that it would seem nonexistent) in analytic philosophy, as in Popper's epistemology or in Luhmann's theory of systems, is, in another form, an abstractive reduction. The way the French postmodern philosophers (in debt to Heideggerian critique and epistemology without a subject) handle, in addition, a new element: the critique of the "metaphysical" subject of Stalinizing Marxism, continuing the Althusserian (or structuralist) epistemological critique, but including the acceptance of a fragmentary "plurality" of "difference," of quasi-subjects without a claim of unity or universality—which already indicates a certain recuperation of the "subject" within the "pluralism" of Derridean *differance*. Finally, hermeneutics and "understanding," discourse pragmatics, and other current approaches recover the "subject" (with some reduction) from various sources.

For my approach to this question of the subject, I will show that (b) the "subject" of human life (constituted by her or his living "own-corporeality"), in the solidary re-cognition of the Other, the community, is—as *living* subject—the nonreplaceable truth and validity of ethics. In addition, I affirm (c), in an ethical reference as the ultimate relevant reference, the case of the victims (as *denied* subjects; as subjects who cannot live); who are subsequently revealed (d) as social (as communitarian subjects in the "diagram" of the micro or macrophysics of power) and historical (nonmetaphysical) intersubjective communities or movements, coexisting in a diversity that makes for difficult communication, but not incommensurable. If one goes deeper, moving toward growing complexity levels, into the profundity of each of these various historical subjects, one can find connections with the remaining, thanks to the function of a material-ethical reason of re-cognition and res-ponsibility for the Other, which "transversally" accedes to "universality" from the dis-tinct "diversity" (the other denomination of "difference" beyond the difference in the identity). Thus, Rigoberta Menchú's *feminine* "subject" (different by gender) is also the *Indian* subject (ethnicity), of a *dark color* (race), in devastated *lands* (ecological problems), *with no rights* (juridical exclusion), *no participation* in the dominated civil society (political), *poor* (economical), *peasant* (class), *illiterate* (formal culture), *Guatemalan* (a peripheral country), and so on. In each case, the "subjectivity" of the living *subject* has been "reduced" by a specific formality or refers to a performative systemic horizon, which can be seen abstractly (within formal "systems" as in Luhmann) and which are fetishized if one *judges* from them, as in the last instance, the *concrete living subject*, as only a "function" of the system. On the contrary, we must pass "transversally" from "the" concrete living subject (ultimate reference) to "all" possible functional subjectivities, as many levels of various systems of the subject that can intervene, *without the subject's being consumed by any of them* and *transcending* them always with a human living-ethical subject: as *the Other than any possible system*—"alterity" of all "totality," to express it in Levinas's critical metalanguage. I shall approach the subject, throughout this *Ethics*, only approximately.[138]

a. From Negation to the Reaffirmation of a Certain Type of "Subject"

[355] The negation of the "modern subject" is the horizon from which it is possible to affirm a new type of subjectivity—radically different, in our case. Heidegger's critique of the modern subject (certainly influenced by Nietzsche and Lukács) opposes the cognitive subjectivity of the subject prior and unilaterally reduced.[139] According to Descartes, the subject, the ego cogito, is a moment of a decorporealized soul, the function of which is mainly cognitive. In addition, our body is only a machine, purely quantitative, extensive. Our ego as soul is immortal; it cannot die. Without death, human life loses its vulnerability, its finitude; it stops being the criterion of truth; the logic of life no longer reigns in it; ethics becomes impossible: the angels or God are not governed by the ethics we are speaking about (which is an ethics of the living, within the horizon of death, always immediately possible), and even less by an ethics of liberation, which would be unnecessary under Cartesianism and, more than that, impossible. On the other hand, Kant's "transcendental subject," the *Ich denke überhaupt* (I think in general), takes a definitive step toward the dualism of Modernity, losing in its formalism the material criterion of the ethical content in human acts— remaining only with an empty *validity*. But it is Fichte who finally reaches the total self-referential foundation of the subject's subjectivity in the absolute Self: "We should employ the word Ego, as an absolute subject [*Ich, als absolutes Subject*].[140] I am I. The I is absolutely posed [*schlichthin gesetzt*].[141] The I as a Subject [*Subjekt*] and the I as an object [*Objekt*] of the reflection of the absolute subject.[142] The I does not proceed from a synthesis, upon the basis of which diversity could consequently become decomposed, but is instead derived from an absolute thesis: the I is an I-ness [*Ichheit*] in general."[143] The "I" is absolutely autonomous, it departs from itself to him/

herself. These are clear formulations of the "modern subject." In the *System of Transcendental Idealism* (1800), Schelling concludes that the I is the same Absolute (God before creation) who "places" the reality of the objective: "In the first place, the certainty of existence of external things [*der Aussendinge*] is a mere prejudice from which we should liberate ourselves in order to return to the foundation."[144] This foundation is the I's own "knowledge": "Self-consciousness [*Selbstbewusstsein*] is the absolute act through which everything is set forth for [*für*] the Ego."[145]

The paradigm of the "conscience" is its own foundation. Without a living corporeality as reference, conscience reflects on itself; self-reflective conscience is the starting point. All levels of the self-organization of the life of human corporeality, of social self-regulation, are mere unessential, external conditionings. Hegel continues in the same tradition, "negating" each level of objects until he reaches the final level or "result," "absolute knowledge," immediateness (*Unmittelbarkeit*) of theory and praxis in the truth where reason and reality are identical. Certainly, this is an ideal model, but it is logical and empirically impossible for a corporeal, finite, living subjectivity. It represents a complete destruction of the possibility of ethics in its dramatic sense.[146]

According to Husserl, pure subjectivity is the foundation of intentionality. Intention, as "consciousness of," is the correlate of *noesis-noema*, of a last reference "originary I [*Ur-Ich*]": *ego cogito cogitatum*. An estimating or axiological intention does not create the object, but reaches the practical object by constituting the correlate of the ethical *noesis*: value (axiological *noema*). Value has its ultimate foundation in pure transcendental subjectivity.[147]

Heidegger clearly and definitely shows in *Being and Time* that the subjectivity of the consciousness or the cognitive I always presupposes a priori the fundamental horizon of an ontological position of the Dasein (the human being as "Being-There") in the world. It is a critique of the subjectivity of the modern subject as cogito (ambiguous prehistory of postmodernism), which opens the founding feasibility of the everyday world for all subsequent human action: "Knowledge [*Erkennen*] does not create a *commercium* in the first instance between the subject [*Subjekt*] and the world, nor does this *commercium* emerge from an impact of the action of the world upon the subject. To know is a mode of Being-There [*Modus des Daseins*] founded upon the *Being-in-the-World* [*In-der-Welt-sein*]. This is the reason why the *Being-in-the-World* demands a hermeneutics as a prerequisite capable of providing it with a fundamental structure."[148] The modern relationship between subject and object has been "dislocated": before (Heidegger's much repeated *vor*) the explicit knowledge of the *ego cogito*, the subject is always in the empirical, everyday, concrete world, in the pre-cognitive feasibility. Thus, regarding the "who?" is-in-the-world, Heidegger says: "The *who* is that which maintains itself as something identical through the changes involved in varying manners of conducting itself and experiencing things, and with reference to such multiplicity. Ontologically speaking we can understand it as that which is *before our eyes*, in each case constantly in an enclosed space, like something situated *at the very foundation* in the sense I already indicated, as a *subjectum*."[149]

[356] For Heidegger, the "Being-There" is the *subjectum*, no longer the cognitive (*cogito*) "subject," but the subjectum of the "Being-in-the-world" as "understanding [*Verstehen*]" of the being that opens the horizon within which entities may be placed as ontic "objects" of a cognitive and speaking subject—the secondary and founded mode of the "Being-in-the-world" of ontological subjectum.[150] Heidegger even pointed out the issue of the ontological intersubjectivity—though it was not the starting point of his reflections: "The world of the Being-There is *a world-of-with* [*Mit*]. The *being is being-with-others*. The intraworldly *being in itself* of the latter is the *Being There-with*."[151]

In my work *Philosophy of Liberation*, published in the 1970s, I started the critique of modern subjectivity and defined myself in 1975 as "postmodern," in this strict sense. My critique is of the ontic cognitive subjectivity from the standpoint of a corporeal and concrete subject (as in Heidegger) who *is already in the world* when she or he "starts thinking explicitly," but always within an understood, "presup-posed" world.

[357] The way in which analytical philosophy (such as Frege's or Carnap's) or epistemology (especially Popper) criticizes the subject is very different. The first philosophy of the linguistic turn still fell within the paradigm of modern consciousness (that is, it presupposed a conscious I who theoretically and abstractly enunciates an intelligible proposition that has sense), and was naively solipsist (intersubjectivity as the level of constitution of the valid consensual "agreement" had not been addressed as a theme). It proceeded methodically at an "abstract" level—with intelligibility claims—thus leaving the subject outside its scope of observation, since "abstraction" means, precisely, not to care for the "concrete subject" who poses a proposition such as:

1. The wall is yellow.

But once the concrete subject of the enunciation had been "methodically" left *outside*, these philosophers apparently forgot their methodological abstraction and argued, with a self-contradictory metaphysical claim, that as far as the statement is concerned, it makes no difference whether the real subject exists or not. Since they abstracted the concrete subject from the statement—which is methodically correct and even necessary—they

Table 11. A Few Profundity Levels of Subjectivity

1. The modern subject (*ego cogito*): consciousness
2. The negativity of the subject in the system (Luhmann), in the epistemology of Popper, in the "diagrams" of power (Foucault), in the structuralism of Althusser, etc.
3. The ontological subject (*Dasein*) (Heidegger)
4. The discursive intersubjectivity (Habermas), the sociohistorical subject, etc.
5. The Freudian unconsciousness, the Levinasian subjectivity, etc.
6. The concrete human living subject.

may have an intelligibility criterion, but will never have a truth criterion,[152] which refers to the narrow space in which the objective reality is cut off from the *omnitudo realitatis* by the demands of concrete life and by the danger of death in the concrete *living subject*. The same thing is true of Luhmann's "systems theory," in which system, by definition, individuals (and the physical organic brains of people as subjects) necessarily form part of the "environment," but can never be "functional" parts of the system itself. The "subject" has been abstracted due to the methodological demands of the analysis (syntactic and semantic, of sense, of functionality in the system), but later on one no longer knows how to reintegrate it. In fact, something really different happens. Consider instrumental reason (means-ends), with its great efficiency or performativity, and analytic reason (theoretical subject-object), with its great formal precision or scientific standard,[153] as the *sole* type of rationality—hence denying empirical (and thus scientific) validity to any other type of rationality.[154] This analytical-instrumental reason reduces access to the status of objectivity (or reality) to mere empirical-descriptive judgments of means-end facts or natural-theoretical objects that can claim universal validity (facts or objects that can be quantified and validated—or falsified—by theories, frameworks, or research programs of the explanatory natural sciences; they are, at least, examples of "scientificity"). The case of Luhmann can clarify what is at stake here. I have already discussed a few of Luhmann's theses,[155] but I would like to go back to one of them, when he writes: "The chemical system of the cell is the brain's environment for the purposes of the brain, and *the consciousness of the person* is the environment of the social system for the purposes of the social system. No breaking down of neurophysiological processes could ever pinpoint specific cells as the key elements, just as no breaking down of social processes could ever lead to *consciousness*."[156]

[358] That the "human subject" is never a "functional" part of the system, but is instead its environment, is explicable—by Luhmann's definition of system (see also table 11). When the complexity of the environment rises, the system must reduce such environmental complexity by selection, and by organic self-adaptation it must raise its own complexity—if it cannot

THE LIBERATION PRINCIPLE 379

adapt, an entropic destruction process would start. The totality of the system operates as a nonintentional metasubject, cybernetically self-regulated, where no particular psychic, self-conscious subject could overcome or upgrade the system's own self-regulation. The problem arises when the system's perverse nonintentional effects start to show that self-regulated adaptation has become impossible for the system. Thus, for example, a growing number of victims manifests as a complexity beyond the system's response capacity. Under these entropy situations, the system would totally collapse. Luhmann does not deal with such questions. On the issue of "contradiction and conflict,"[157] Luhmann shows that, rather than critical consciousness, it is communication that confronts social-systemic "contradiction." Just as in human corporeality consciousness cannot overcome the contradictions of the organism (which are resolved in a self-organized process by the brain without the intervention of consciousness),[158] so, in an analogous manner, this would happen in society. Society also has its alarm systems or immunology systems (e.g., the system of law, with criteria such as fair/unfair, allowed/interdicted, or the "semantic of competence"[159]—with its own rules). For Luhmann, definitely, the self-conscious subject is in the environment; he or she is not a moment of the system as such.

Following on from these lines of thinking, in the France of the 1960s, and as a reaction to orthodox metaphysical Stalinism, with the "proletariat" as the only subject of history[160] (which is very far from Marx's own thought), and not without the influence of Lévi-Strauss's structuralism (which equally proposes mythical-anthropological a priori categorical "structures" with no subject), and from epistemologies that have no subject, we find Althusser. Althusser also formulated a Marxist reinterpretation "without subject"—his reductive differentiation of "ideology" and "science" allowed him to assign a radical primacy to an abstract theoretical epistemology.[161]

[359] Much more suggestive and complex, outstanding in many ways, is Foucault's archaeological, historical-epistemological analysis, who was a genealogist of the short term (from the eighteenth century in some investigations and from the nineteenth century in others) in his first work, and of the long term (in *The Care of the Self*[162] he places himself among the Greeks, as a passage toward Heidegger's ontology).[163] In the work of his last period, on health (diet), pleasure (*aphrodysia*), and survival (economics),[164] Foucault showed that a more concrete subject needed to be considered in sexual corporeality. In any event, he speaks more of the disciplinary act of subjectivation of the "places" of enunciation than he does of the subject per se.

Postmodern thought is a rich though ambiguous attempt, at various levels, to give a critique of the "philosophy of the subject"—of Cartesian

subjectivity. On the one hand, the subject disappears at the epistemological level of the performative system;[165] on the other hand is Foucault's critique, just outlined, of the "sovereignty of the subject."[166] But, here and
there throughout this critique, Foucault sketched a certain resurgence of
a fragmented "plurality," which can cross over, "transversally"—as Welsch
tries to do—the "places" of the enunciation of discourse, tales, narratives, texts.[167] Postmodern people are sensitive to such plurality of "difference";[168] modern thought, on the contrary, exaggerated a self-conscious
subject, subordinating the "unconscious" to such self-consciousness placed
at the "center," thus essentializing all the power in the exclusive macrostructure of the state, making the modality of domination operate with one
voice as violence, legalizing the teleological historiography, privileging the
enlightened vanguard in politics, and so on. Reaction to such reductions
must be taken in by critical thought, must be subsumed: it is necessary,
but insufficient, since the monological/communitary subjects make reference to certain "actors" that cannot be absolutely denied from the social or
systemic vital self-organization or self-regulation, or from the impersonal
structure of discourses or texts. Subjectivity must be redefined in a flexible,
complex, fluid, chiasmic form (not losing the various poles of the table,
the various "places" of enunciation, and reflecting on them in a tension
of mutual co-constitution). Thus, the question becomes more complex:
as Deleuze asked, "What are the new types of transversal and immediate
struggles, not simply those that are centralized and mediated? What are the
new functions of the *specific* or 'singular' *intellectual*, not simply of the 'universal' one? What are the new *modes of subjectivation* without identity, not
simply creators of identity?"[169] Or, as Alain Badiou would say, the intersubjective subject appears and disappears: "We call *subject* the support of a
fidelity, supporting the support of a process of truth. Subject, thus, by no
means preexists the process. It is absolutely nonexistent in a situation *before* the event. One can say that the process of truth *induces* a subject."[170]
In a previous work I emphasized that "person" is a relational concept:[171]
one can only become a person from the Other. In an analogous manner,
*inter*subjective subjects (monologic or communitary) appear and are constituted in the events that make them possible, and thus they exist as long
as the situation persists.[172]

[360] In addition, little by little the subject reemerges in other trends of
thought. In pragmatics,[173] philosophy of language overcomes the nonsub-
ject reduction of the consciousness paradigm (or of instrumental reason),
of the abstract propositional utterance of analytic philosophy, and makes
the passage to the community of communication of "speech acts," according to which, the simple statement

2. Snow is white,

without any empirical subject of enunciation, is transformed in a speech act to:

3. *I tell you* "the snow is white."

The illocutionary moment "I tell you [you]" establishes the proposition "snow is white" as concrete, practical and intersubjectively, in the practical relation of two subjects in communication. The *practical subject*, who had become invisible, reappears as another form of overcoming the modern and abstract solipsist subject: "In the paradigm of the intersubjective agreement what is fundamental is the performative attitude of those participating in interaction, who coordinate their plans of action agreeing among themselves about something in the world. In executing ego an action-of-speaking and in taking alter a position toward a situation, they both establish an interpersonal relation."[174] We have now passed to another level of the "subjectivity": the *inter*subjectivity of the "language games" of Wittgenstein in his second stage, which presuppose a determined "form of life" but also a certain form of "agreement" from tradition, from the presupposed consensus.[175] This new intersubjective "subjectivity" will be determinant for the ethics of liberation, as we shall see.

Levinas and Freud allow us to define the subject in a more complex manner than the modern form, which proposes a solipsist and instrumental paradigm of consciousness: Levinas—with his phenomenological conception of "subjectivity" as prior to Husserlian consciousness (to the *Urich*) and to the *subjectum* "which understands being" in the world (Heideggerian ontology), from the corporeality of pleasure ("closer") and as responsibility for the Other ("beyond");[176]—and Freud, with his more ample concept of subjectivity, which departs from the profundity of the realm which energetically pulses from a "before" (pre-) and "under" (sub-) consciousness,[177] the "id," and the "unconscious." I shall try to pass to an even more radical level of subjectivity that, subsuming every possible critical instance of the aforementioned modern reductionist subjectivity, does not "lose its footing" and still has the possibility of reaching the rock suggested by Wittgenstein "on which the shovel bends."

b. The Material Subject of Ethics: The "Living" Corporeal Subject

[361] Every cognitive act (*ego cogito*), every "place" of utterance, every system, the "world" of every *Dasein*, every discursive consensual intersubjectivity, every pre-, sub-, or unconscious, every subjectivity prior to the "world" presupposes always an a priori concrete, living human subject as the ultimate criterion of subjectivity—of reference to an actor in the last instance as *mode of reality*. The market, which seems to operate performatively

in a self-regulated form, is nothing but the complex cooperating structure of fulfillment of rules (private property, honoring agreements, acceptance of competence, etc.) of concrete living subjects (dispersed points in the market, corporeal cerebral poles existing within real, narrow frames of the vulnerability that are required for the reproduction of their lives. Thus the market[178] in London (although it may continue without interruption in New York and afterward in Tokyo, without "apparent rest")[179] must close its doors after eight hours of intense activity, simply because the stock market operators are tired, they must sleep, eat, regain "their strength" because night has fallen. This concrete life of the operators is not a mere "condition of possibility"; it is a constitutive, creative participation of that which "appears" as a self-regulated market. "Self-regulation" of the market is nothing but the creative empirical participation of many real subjects who comply with the "rules" of this formal system called the "market." It is obvious for every observer that without the concrete operators there is no market, but they are soon forgotten. The "stocks" or "stock market papers" that are purchased and sold belong to companies with "flesh-and-bone" workers, who will buy goods with their wages in order to be able to live. Corporeal drivers who have to feed themselves transport the materials used in such companies to the factories, and purchasers with concrete, vital, material human needs buy the products manufactured as merchandise. In all the moments of this cycle, the "human life of each subject" is the intrinsic constituent, the content of all that which "appears" as market. Hinkelammert observes:

> This mutual process of recognition between *naturally occurring* and *necessary* subjects transcends the bounds set by mercantile relations and their ability to judge. It also transcends language.[180] This transcendence occurs from within both mercantile relations and language. Nonetheless, it has to confront the limits of both in order to give them their authentic content. This real content, which applies its judgment to formal schemes of language and the market, is at the same time *subjective* in character. It is the fact that the *subject* is confronted with at the crossroads between life and death, which constitutes the reality of the world encountered by language and the market. But all of this relates to *a subjectivity* of objective validity, and most forcefully. This actor must comprehend him- or herself *as a subject in order to live.* But these judgments of fact, whose criterion of truth is of a life-or-death character, are at the same time judgments constitutive of *objective* truth. . . . Objective reality is *not something given independently* of the life of a human being.[181]

The concrete, living human subject is left by Luhmann in the environment of the system; according to Weber, no formal means-ends judgments of fact can be stated about him, not because he is a material moment. It would seem that Foucault, in his last stage—who discussed the corpore-ality of those excluded, the mentally ill, prisoners, sick people so well in his intermediate stage—comes as we have seen, to view the living subject as the ultimate reference.

[362] In fact, the *living human subject* is the starting point and con-tinuous reference, as well as the content of cognitive consciousness (since conscious "knowledge" is *a moment* of the production, reproduction, and development of the human subject's life), of the world (in a Heideggerian sense), of language, of cultural instruments and values, of all performative systems, of the discursive or communication community (we communicate and argue in order to "live better"): As Hinkelammert states, "The affirma-tion of life is not an end, but a project:[182] the project of preserving itself as a subject, which can have ends. The corresponding action is an action to avoid threats to the enjoyment of this life; it is a project."[183] One can state means-ends judgments of fact with performativity or systemic efficiency claims about formal systems, fetishized or not (capitalism, bank education, machist patriarchate, discriminatory racism, etc.). As such, the system has no subjects—in the sense of our definition—but operates with a holistic, functional, self-referential subjectivity. Its means-ends calculations—even scientific ones—cannot include, if it uses only the formal criterion, the life of the subjects that serve as the support, frequently invisible, of the various "functions" of the system. The death of workers, their impoverishment—as when companies, the "stock" of which rise in the market for having "ratio-nalized" their production, leave thousands of workers without a job[184]—is out of the calculations of the means-ends systemic relation. To reintro-duce, as a fundamental moment, a life-death reference (a "qualitative cal-culation," as critical ecology does, economic critique from the angle of the workers' life, etc.) means to take into consideration the *living subjects* that operate the performative systems as "functional portions of such systems." The critical judgment of fact (within the material frame of ethics) is uttered as the possibility of production, reproduction, and development of the life of the real subjects of the system and as a "measure" or criterion of their ends: if life is not possible, the instrumental reason that is exerted to make it impossible is ethically perverse.[185]

c. The Revelation of the "Denied Subject":
The Emergence of the Victim

[363] The subject appears most clearly in the systems' crisis, when the environment—to use Luhmann's words—becomes so complex that it can no longer be controlled or simplified. Thus, *in* and *before* the systems, in the diagrams of power, in the standard places of enunciation, all of a sud-

den, the Other appears, due to the critical circumstances—the Other, other than the system, the oppressed or excluded face, the nonintentional victim—as the effect of the performative logic of the rationalized formal whole, showing its irrationality in the denied life of the victim. A subject emerges, reveals himself or herself as the cry for which one must have ears to be able to hear: "Suddenly the voice [*Stimme*] of the worker is raised amid the din and agitation of the production process which had silenced it. . . .[186] In the marketplace, *you and I* only recognize one law, that of market exchange. . . .[187] What you gain in this manner in labor, I lose in the substance of work. . . . And *you rob me* daily."[188] In the victim, dominated or excluded by the system, the living, empirical, concrete human subjectivity is revealed, it appears as "interpellation" in the last instance: it is the subject who can no longer live and cries out in pain. It is the interpellation of the one who claims, "I am hungry! Please give me something to eat!" It is the vulnerability of the suffering corporeality—which the "*ego*-soul" cannot apprehend in its immaterial and immortal subjectivity—converted into the last open wound that cannot heal. Nonresponse to such interpellation means the death of the victim: it means that it must stop being a subject, in a radical sense—without any possible metaphor—to die. It is the last and first negative and material criterion of the critique as such—of the ethical consciousness, of reason, of the critical impulse.[189] The one who dies "was" someone: a subject, last real reference, ethics' definite criterion of truth. The Other is the possible victim and caused by my functional action in the system. I am re-sponsible. It is a concrete reference:

> The recognition between subjects that recognize each other mutually as natural and *needed* subjects is not yet the recognition of life *itself.* Such a recognition (in general) presupposes the constitution of objective reality by processes of recognition between subjects. This recognition implies that natural life, which is the same as human life understood in term of natural being, but also the objective reality of nature, is constituted by such recognition between subjects. Nonetheless, all of this does not imply the recognition of the human species as an object of survival. The human species *itself* as an object is an abstraction which in fact crushes the recognition that is achieved between subjects. This has to do with the recognition of the Other in a relationship between natural and needed beings. This recognition cannot exclude anybody. In this sense it is universal, yet *without constituting any kind of abstract universalism.* . . . The mutual recognition between subjects leads unavoidably to an option for certain subjects, which is to say, an option for those whose lives are more directly threatened. The criterion of truth is that of life or death . . . with the *victim* at the center. This has to do then with a state of being for the purposes of life, not with death. The criterion of truth is then the victim himself or herself.[190]

THE LIBERATION PRINCIPLE 385

Thus, we are speaking about the life of each subject, the last active refer-ence, as a self-regulated living organism, social and historical, but also as self-conscious, critical, without any reductionism (as when someone means to define what is essential to the subject as *cogito*), but neither with unilater-alisms (when all subject is denied, the *cogito* or the Kantian transcenden-tal subject with a whole other type of subjectivity, the "baby is thrown out with the bath water").

The *subject of the praxis of liberation* is the living, needy, natural, and, thus, cultural subject, and in the last instance the victim, the community of victims, and those who are co-responsibly articulated with it. The last "place" then of discourse, of critical enunciation, is the empirical victims, the lives of whom are in danger, as revealed in the "diagram" of power by strategic reason.

d. The Communitarian Intersubjectivity of the New "Sociohistorical Actors"

[364] The subjectivity of the *inter*subjective horizon of Wittgenstein's "language games" opens for us the broad space of what I will call the "socio-historical subject." In the tone of a self-critique, the former Althusserian Alain Badiou writes: "The *subject* of which I speak has no natural preexis-tence. . . ."[191] The subject of a revolutionary politics is not the individual militant nor the chimera of a *class subject*. It is instead a singular produc-tion, which had different names (sometimes *Party*, sometimes others).[192] Certainly the militant enters into the process of constituting this subject, whose limits are also transcended through this process (this is precisely the excess that makes him or her appear immortal)."[193] When "class" is inter-preted as a natural, substantive, unique, ultimate-reference subject, one falls into an inaccurate metaphysical conceptualization. Invested *inter*sub-jective "subjects" with a nonexisting substantial subjectivity turns them into justifiably criticized metaphysical subjects. But between (a) the nega-tion of such inappropriately substantiated metaphysical subjects, and (b) the negation of the subjectivity of each concrete living human subject, or (c) the negation of all subjectivity to intersubjective community, many misunderstandings prevail. I agree with the negation of (a), but not with the negation of the subjectivities in (b) and (c).

The *inter*subjective "subjectivity" is constituted from a certain commu-nity of life, from a linguistic community (as the world of the communicable life), from a certain collective memory of liberation efforts, from similar needs and forms of consumption, from a culture with some tradition, from concrete historical projects in which one tends in solidarity to hope. Partici-pants may speak, argue, communicate, reach consensus, be co-responsible, consume material products, desire common goods, desire utopias, coordinate instrumental or strategic actions, "and appear" in the public realm of civil society with a similar face that differentiates them from others. They are the "social movements," moments from a power microstructure, from institutions, from productive functional systems, social classes, ethnic groups, religions, whole peoples, nations, countries, states, and so on. There is a passage in Hegel, which, if we set aside for the moment its specific meaning in the original context, is still suggestive: "The global connection takes the shape of an organism formed by particular systems of needs, of instruments and labors, of ways of satisfying needs, of theoretical and practical culture, systems in which individuals take part, in order to constitute its different layers."[194] In a specific way I can take up again the problems set forth in §6.1: What type of sociohistorical subjectivity carries out what we can call the *liberation praxis* of the victims? The global and intersubjective community of each type of victim comes to the fore, as a potential, frequently contradictory, complex subjectivity, caught in a particular diagram of power, an *en soi* [*an sich*], which at the beginning is closed in itself, suffering, and, nonetheless, passive, noncritical, naive. The one dominated or excluded no longer has a critical-ethical consciousness. This is the starting point of ethical-strategic reflection. It is the community of victims in general,[195] always the fruit of a determined performative system, which has a profile of its own, a particular identity that affirms itself as difference before the other groups, movements, sociohistorical subjects. I am particularly interested in the emergence of new social movements in civil society or in history that, one way or another, are always communities of victims struggling for recognition and who come forward, "appear"—as the Zapatista Army of National Liberation appeared as if from nothing, unexpectedly, on January 1, 1994, in Chiapas, Mexico.

[365] José Carlos Mariátegui, Marxist thinker, anti-Stalinist *avant la lettre*, used realistic strategic reason and avoided the dogmatic categories that distort feasibility and obscure the objective reality of peripheral countries. He understood that a nonexistent proletariat could not be the sociohistorical subject of a long-dreamed-of revolution in Peru. His "hermeneutics" ("Seven Essays of Interpretation")[196] of the historical and economic Peruvian reality, places oppression in a community of victims, impressive for their number, culture, and poverty, but invisible even to left-wing thinkers at that time:

> The solution of the *problem of the Indian* has to be a social solution. Those who bring it about must be *Indian peoples* themselves.[197] This way of conceiving of the issue leads me to perceive a historical achievement in the celebration of the indigenous congresses. These events, whose importance was minimized by bureaucratic sectors[198] (within the left movement), *did*

not yet amount to or signify a program; but their first meetings signaled a path by bringing together indigenous peoples from different regions. . . . A people made up of four million human beings, once conscious of their numbers, can never despair of their future. The same four million, as long as they are nothing but an inorganic mass, a dispersed multitude, *are incapable of determining their historical destiny.*[199]

Seven years previously György Lukács had written something similar: "This unconsciousness about organizational matters is surely symptomatic of the movement's lack of maturity."[200]

In fact, the emergence of a new type of subject presupposes an ethical process of the passage from a level of passive subjectivity to other levels of higher self-consciousness,[201] in the *chiaroscuro* of the diagrams of strategic power. The community of victims starts from a "false consciousness,"[202] due to the phenomenon of "reification" in the cognitive process of these victims as oppressed people.[203] The so-called class consciousness—which in metalinguistical terms would be the "consciousness of the victim as victim"[204] (the ethical-critical consciousness of feminist women as dominated by machista patriarchalism, African Americans who suffer oppression at the hands of whites, and so on)—starts from a negative moment. Lukács says: "Class consciousness (that is to say, that of the victim) is, at the same time, considered abstractly and formally, a kind of *unconsciousness*, which reflects the characteristics of that class's economic, historical, and social situation."[205] It would be a minimum degree of subjectivity of the sociohistorical subject, that nonetheless must run a long way until becoming an agent subjectivity in history:

> The proletariat [that is to say, the victims] is, by its very existence, the criticism and the negation of these forms of [reified] existence, [but] until the proletariat itself has arrived at the point where this crisis has fully unfolded, culminating in a true class consciousness, . . . it will not advance, except in a negative sense, on the basis of what it is negating. When criticism fails to overcome its fragmentary quality, and until it succeeds in criticizing the *totality* in which it is enmeshed, it will not overcome the limits of what it negates.[206]

That is, in order to become a subject, it is necessary to make a self-conscious critique of the system that causes victimization.[207] Rigoberta Menchú claimed: "I was happy when I clearly saw that the problem was not only my problem," but rather "a general situation of the whole people."[208] The sociohistorical subject becomes a liberating subjectivity only when it is elevated to a critical-explicative consciousness of the cause of its negativity. Lukács tends to define such explicit consciousness like Lenin, and criticized Luxemburg: "She excessively valued the organic character of processes and undermined the importance of the conscious and consciously organized character of them."[209] Lukács then tended to construct the "party"[210] as the conscious, autonomous moment and exclusive coordinator of the community of victims,[211] negating the protagonist constitution of the sociohistorical subjectivity of the community of victims themselves. In other words, he in part minimized the organic and self-regulated nature of the community of victims in favor of a certain vanguardist consciencialism — especially by reducing to "theory" all the problematics of the "ethical principles," in relation to which the "ethical-critical consciousness" (class consciousness)[212] of the victims takes place.[213]

The "question of the subject" (in its intersubjective, sociohistorical sense, as emergence of the various subjects of new social movements in the diagrams of power), is then exactly the problem of the ethical-critical progress of the community of victims. "Social movements" are fluid or fragmented sociohistorical subjects who appear and disappear in well-defined junctures. I shall resume the subject in my future work on liberation fronts — since each of them, in the struggle for recognition, refers to one or various sociohistorical subjects.

We can conclude that the critique of the metaphysical modern subject leads us to deem certain systems, structures, or diagrams as "subjectless" — since real subjects remain in the invisibility of the "abstractions," "functions," or of the "relationships of force." However, right below them is the *Dasein*, the "being-in-the-world," but always already constituted from a community of life, from a language, of systems of cultural instruments, from the discursive intersubjectivity of the diverse sociohistorical subjects. These subjects, nonetheless, can be discovered by a reason that, by being universal (formally material and discursive), is, at the same time "transversal" (able to transition from the alterity of each "social movement" to others), given its material constitution. Thus, any woman, as I have already mentioned, is inevitably from a race, a class, a nation, a culture or ethnic group, and so on, by the demands in the last instance of the *living subject*, who fixes the framework of ethical feasibility.

§6.3. The "Reform-Transformation Question"

[366] We must now pass to a third issue. The organized (§6.1) sociohistorical subject (§6.2) — for instance, a feminist, a political party or union — acts strategically. When subjects act, their action is limited by certain frames or references and could be — for critical reason or for the ethics of liberation, but not for a *standard ethics* — a functional praxis of "reform" or critical liberation; I shall call the latter "transformation" (Marx called it *Veränderung*). "Reformist" action is action that fulfills the criteria and principles of

a "formal system in-force";[214] that is, it is a means within the frames of the *ends* of the instrumental reason of a given system. Hence, those who act under the capitalistic economic system modulate their praxis according to the criterion of increasing the "profit rate of capital"[215] (the company, the bank, etc.). Their action is perfectly rational or ethical, within the system's parameters. Just the same, a patriarchal or masculinist action that compels women to be "perfect housewives" also fulfills the values of such traditional gender practice, at least until recently in Western culture.

The problem appears in the conflict between (a) formal systems (insofar as they are abstract, means-ends, self-referential) that proceed according to the conscious acceptance of very few well-defined rules (already mentioned above), from the practice of which nonintentional effects start occurring, "behind the backs of the actors," and (b) the framework that is limited by the universal material-ethical and formal-discursive principles—that is, of the reproduction and development of the life of all the ethical subjects in this formal system and their discursive, symmetric participation. Formal systems are fetishized (they are self-identified with the reality, just like that) and become invisible to real subjects (the *living subjects*, who inevitably exert the few formal, consciously fixed rules, and who, in fact, by fulfilling such rules, set the structures of the system that "appears" self-regulated). Objective "tendencies" that are fulfilled when such conscious, fixed rules are observed cause nonintentional effects that produce, and "appear"—it is a mere appearance, not real—to the eyes of an external observer (and even to the eyes of the actors who make fixed rules but, obviously, without being aware of their nonintentional effects) to be necessary "social laws." Thus "it would seem" that the market regulates itself—as Hayek intends to demonstrate—or that capital self-produces value—an assertion that for Marx is the fetishist claim of the explication of the political economy given by Smith and Ricardo.

[367] In reality, such "social laws" are not (a) the natural laws that act by physical necessity (strictly natural laws, as the range of probability at the atomic level within which an electron must appear in photographs); nor are they (b) necessary social laws, similar to natural laws (dialectical materialism, for instance, as the standard Stalinist metaphysical historical determinism proposes, which Marx has nothing to do with); they are instead (c) sociohistorical "tendencies," not necessary as in nature and not the fruit of conscious acts either, but frameworks within which are possible, and within which occur, human acts, as a result of fulfilling the *fixed conscious rules* defined. The type of "determination" is not natural or necessary, nor conscious or chaotic, but a nonintentional regulation that limits actions, due to the fulfillment of the conscious fixed rules mentioned, which are now performed *as if* they were "necessary" (like nature) by the simple

fact of *not-being-conscious* (which is what we call "nonintentional"). "Nonintentionality" (or "nonexplicit consciousness") of the various agents in every point of the system, structure, or diagram of power, makes all the functions "appear" *subjectless* (as in the systems of Luhmann, Smith, or Ricardo). Modern philosophers, including those who developed discourse ethics (relying as a last resort on conscious and explicit argumentation), and formalist social scientists, claim that the system, market, or diagram operates only through the *conscious* acts of metaphysical *subjects* (the modern enlightened person says: "*I think* this as an object of the conscious knowledge"), for formal means-ends actions, in the style of Max Weber. They deny the self-regulation that should always be presupposed and respected, since consciousness (as neurobiology and psychoanalysis well know) cannot "intervene" *without any need* in such high-complexity systems. Life in general, with its *self-organization* processes, and social life in particular, with its *self-regulation* mechanisms (among which all nonintentional effects are found), cannot be replaced by merely conscious acts. The intent of the Soviet scientist Kantorovich,[216] to achieve "perfect or total planning"—criticized by Popper—is the extreme claim of *Modernity*: rationalization or total and perfect consciousness. Kantorovich dreams that someday human beings will rationally and consciously plan everything. This means taking to an extreme, and falling into performative contradiction, the tendency already initiated by Lenin, when he wrongly defined the relation in organization between the vanguard (conscious and in possession of the "truth": reason of the process) and the masses (spontaneous self-regulation despised as irrational and immature). Between the total spontaneity of the masses' nonintentional self-regulation and the leaders' hyperconscious vanguardism, we find all the *chiaroscuro* of conscious acts fulfilling fixed rules and the nonintentional effects that appear self-regulated (and which are postulated as empirically impossible to calculate due to their quasi-infinite complexity) and that are characterized as empirical frames that show as "tendencies" and as "laws" fulfilled without any "natural determinism"—"social laws," according to Marx.

But, to not accept the crucial and strategic importance of the intervention of *critical consciousness* would be a suicidal spontaneity, when the nonintentional *perverse* effects of the system (e.g., the growing impoverishment of current humanity as a nonintentional effect of the "prescriptions" of the International Monetary Fund and the World Bank, with their completely orthodox market neoliberalism) have become unbearable, evident, and dangerous to the reproduction of life of most human subjects. At this very moment, a critical conscious *intervention* becomes necessary, just as the intervention of the pilot is required in a ship correcting its course five degrees, thus avoiding collision with an iceberg that could destroy the ship. Machines (propellers as drives or self-regulated mechanisms) move the vessel. Nonintentional effects would send it straight towards self-destruction and make it crash into the iceberg, which, according to the foreseen "tendencies" is inevitable. In such cases, the critical consciousness must intervene, using its moral compass (the universal formal discursive and material ethical principles that establish the framework of the required ethical-conscious "correction"). This is the issue exposed by the community of victims (which operates nonintentionally), by its critical community (which operates as basic self-regulation and with a noncritical or naive consciousness), and by its core reference points of explicit critique, where consciousness reaches the "enlightened" level, thanks to specialists, strategists, scientists, "organic intellectuals," for example, in today's Brazil, both Paulo Freire (the scientist) and "Lula" (Luiz Inácio Lula da Silva, the worker leader who became a politician and head of a critical national party). Ethics, as we have seen, is realized when it shows and normalizes the compatibility of the nonintentional formal system with the production, reproduction, and development of the human life of each ethical subject with the right to discursive participation. If such compatibility is not achieved (e.g., when there is an increase in capital but a decrease in the life possibilities and democratic-discursive participation or the great majority of humankind) ethical-critical *intervention* becomes necessary.

[368] In this context we must understand the relation between "reform," "revolution," and "transformation." Rosa Luxemburg confronted "social reform" and "revolution"[217] in order to criticize the "reformists," who since 1879 had allied themselves with Eduard Bernstein, in the name of the "possible" internal change of the system. Reformists are those who, claiming to fulfill the revolutionary principles, have fallen into the "adaptability of capitalism."[218] Translated into an ethical language, reformists are those who act according to the criteria (that is, "adapt") of the formal or dominant hegemonic system (here, "capitalism"). All the arguments of the reformist form of reasoning aim to show that the critical diagnosis (in our case, Marx's) has been overcome by circumstances, and thus they start a detailed redefinition, from which the conclusion is derived that the formal system already in force can be reformed *from the inside*: Luxemburg commented, "It is clear that this current will maintain itself, that it will seek to destroy our principles [*Grundsätze*] and elaborate its own theory. Bernstein's book is precisely a step in this direction."[219] Luxemburg, confronting the reformists' intent to subsume the "principles" (ethical principles, the ethics of liberation would say) within the criteria of the capitalist formal system, was compelled to critically rethink Marxism, starting from the objections that reformists launched against Marx. On the other hand, being a "reformist" is not the same as being a traditional or "functional" intellectual of the

hegemonic system. Smith and Ricardo are bourgeois (even revolutionary, according to Marx), but they are not reformists. Reformists are those who, appearing as critics, have already adopted the criteria of the formal system they intend to criticize. Hence, theoretical confrontation is unavoidable. In fact, Luxemburg writes the second most important theoretical work in the Marxist tradition (after Marx's *Capital*) to refute such intent to incorporate Marx's critical thought into a merely functional interpretation of capital—as did E. Bernstein, Henryk Grossmann, even Karl Kautsky, and specially Otto Bauer, Serguéi N. Bulgákov, Mijaíl I. Tugán-Baranovski, and Eugen Böhm-Bawerk.[220] What should be stressed, for the purpose of my argument, is that Rosa Luxemburg was compelled to waste much of the time she was supposed to spend on the strategic concrete praxis, to deal with theoretical matters, not because of an abstract theoretical love of truth (as such), but because of the practical need to destroy arguments that justified the negation of the life of the victims and the exclusion of the workers from the capitalist formal system. Luxemburg's work is "*critical* social science," strictly speaking, since it is the fruit of a "scientific investigation program" developed for the purpose of *explaining* the cause of the material negativity of the victims, and that refutes the destructive or reformist theoretical work, which intends to deny the critique in Marx's thought regarding capital, namely, to "confuse" the explanation and the cause of the workers' alienation. Capital, says the reformist, is not impossible; it does not include a self-contradiction; crises are not signs of its failure, as Marx himself (they claim) demonstrated in his mathematical "charts" of reproduction: capital can self-produce and value itself indefinitely. Thus, Luxemburg fixes as the subject of her critical scientific program the core of the reformist argument: *the accumulation of capital*: "My work does not only have a *purely theoretical* interest, but also entails, in my view, some importance for *our practical struggle* against imperialism."[221]

[369] Luxemburg had to reach the most subtle abstract levels of Marx's discourse in order to demonstrate that the "mathematical examples" of the "reproduction charts" in the second book of *Capital*, are not an empirical description of what happens in the concrete reality—as reformists claim; they made a big methodological mistake, by confusing "the" *abstract* with "the" *real* concrete—but a pedagogical and abstract form of reflecting on reproduction as such. Luxemburg showed that, *concretely* and *empirically*: "Capitalism demands to be immersed in forms of noncapitalist production as a condition for its existence and development (for its broadened range of reproduction). It also has need of noncapitalist social sectors as markets in order to produce its surplus value."[222] Her theory—which is not that of the "principles" of socialism (ethical, at the time)—besides including in the horizon of her reflection the peripheral countries of capital-

ism (we must not forget that Rosa was born in Poland, a peripheral country of Western capital since the sixteenth century), serves as a frame in the "practical struggle against imperialism." She stepped out of the German national limit, becoming a thinker valid for the "world system," with its "center and periphery." The ethical principles frame the possible strategic action ("struggle") of critical intellectuals, organically articulated in the community of victims, though we must not confuse these principles with social critical and scientific theory, properly speaking. Struggle against reformism — not against capitalism, but against those who, having been critical and still claiming to be so, have abandoned their theoretical and practical solidarity with the community of victims, even though they may say the contrary — is ethical, theoretical, and strategic. Reformism adopts the criteria and principles of the dominant system — although it claims to be critical — and thus its strategy and tactic is "reformist" (it does not matter whether it is peaceful or violent; what matters is that it assumes the criteria and principles of the system in force), and creates a new theory with the peculiarity of using critical terminology, but within the interpretative horizon of the existing system, that is, it is no longer a *critical* but a *functional* social science: thus, after Luxemburg, the future German social democracy was born, capitalist according to its fundamental horizon, socialist according to its linguistic formulations. Critical thought must be clear about critical-ethical principles,[223] but it must also innovate or create more profound explanations (or an understanding from the base, or even, from interpretations) than the ones employed by the functional social sciences,[224] of the negativity of the victims (to provide reasons for the strategic struggle of the critical community of victims); it must also demonstrate scientifically and critically the *impossibility in the long run* of the dominating system, once its perverse nonintentional effects have become unsustainable, unbearable.

[370] But, for the ethics of liberation, in contrast with Luxemburg's ethics, the ethical action that is contrary to functional praxis (which is fulfilled *in* the system without contradiction) and to reformist praxis (which has a bad consciousness and wants to critically explain the reasons of its conformist action) is not "revolution" but "transformation." This is of the highest strategic (and even tactical) importance, because if the ethics of liberation intended to justify the goodness of a human act from "revolution" exclusively, it would destroy the possibility of a critical (or liberation) ethics *of everyday life*. Just as my friend Hans Schelkshorn, from Vienna, said when he criticized me orally, the ethics of liberation would seem valid only for revolutionary situations, which are absolutely exceptional, thus denying itself the possibility of becoming the foundation for everyday, common, ordinary action.

In fact, the criteria and principles that oblige the ethical subject to struggle even to the point of participating in a revolution (in favor of life and discursive solidarity with the victims, with the Other, with the majority oppressed masses), are the same that demand the "transformation" of every norm, action, microstructure, and institution. Only the *critical* "transformation" of a whole ethical system (a culture, an economic system, a state, a nation, etc.) can be called "revolution." Hence, revolution is nothing but the extreme moment of a complexity that starts at its lowest level with the transformation of a maxim of everyday life in reference to an insignificant possible action (e.g., from the very vulgar "I will spit on the floor!"); this must be "transformed" in some aspect, by the criterion and principle stated as the nonnegation of the Other, such that the fulfillment of the maxim of this action would lead to the diminishment of the life or symmetric-discursive participation of the victim (in the example, one should not spit on the floor because that would harm the person who has to do the cleaning, the victim, and not simply because of an aesthetic or hygienic demand—which are other valid reasons, such as cleanliness or the possible propagation of a virus, etc.). To "transform" means to change the course of an intention, the content of a norm; to modify a possible action or institution, and even a whole ethical system, due to the foregoing ethical criteria and principles, in the same strategic and tactical process. In the case of a sociohistorical subject, such as the proletariat mentioned by Luxemburg, the strategies and programs, tactics and methods, of the struggle are placed within a frame defined by the ethical-critical principles, the conclusions of critical social-scientific explanations, the practical experience of the corresponding group of leaders (many of whom are victims who became self-conscious, enlightened experts in liberation praxis), all of which are always discerned from the complex communitarian mechanisms of the discursiveness of those affected as symmetric democratic participants.

[371] Rosa Luxemburg criticized reformists as follows: "Reformist theory is confronted with a dilemma: either socialist *transformation* [*Umgestaltung*] is, as has been now conceded, the consequence of contradictions within capitalism, which means that as capitalism develops these too will mature within it, resulting inevitably in its collapse . . . ,[225] or its means of adaptation will actually avoid its collapse, and consequently will prepare it to survive by means of the suppression of its own contradictions."[226] "Reformists" do not add anything new to the twinned possible process; they are useless. Thus, for Luxemburg, the contradiction has to be stated as one of reform or revolution. In fact, the reformist "displaces the socialist movement's program from its material basis [*materiellen Boden*], and attempts to place it on its materialist basis."[227] If we translate this statement into the metalanguage of the ethics of liberation, we would say that the ethical

move of critical transformation occurs at the level of the material aspect of ethics (the reproduction of life and its *development*; materialism in a profound sense) and not merely at the level of the reproduction of the performative, formal system of instrumental reason (expressed ambiguously with the term "idealism," but better expressed as "functional formalism"). Luxemburg has an intuition about the ethical question when she writes:

> It is antihistorical, antiethical to represent the struggle for reforms as if it were a simple projection of the revolution and to reduce this in turn to a condensed series of reforms. A social transformation [*Umwälzung*] and a legislative reform (which is what the reformists seek to bring about) do not differ only in terms of their respective duration, but according to their distinct *essences* [*Wesen*].[228] The secret of historical *transformation* . . . is to be found precisely in the inversion of simple quantitative modifications (of the formal hegemonic system) in favor of a new qualitative order.[229]

In other words, reform and transformation are actions with different criteria and bases: the reformist action confirms the formal dominating system—claiming to be critical; the ethical-critical or liberating transformation has another "essence," because its reference, with its truth claim, is not the horizon of the self-referential formal abstract system (capital, for example), but the exteriority of the reality of the victims' lives (the denied life of salaried workers or of the unemployed, available as impoverished and marginal masses and "disposable," but always kept as a "reserve"). Consequently, the reformist is not the one who uses tactics in a more pacific, no longer violent form, or the one who simply avoids revolution's rupture, but the one who "elects another end [*anderes Ziel*]."[230] Such other "end" is an ethical action of a different kind, namely functional or reformist (of a very diverse nature due to its origin, mediation, and justification), which confirms the prevailing formal system. The transforming action, by contrast, judges and modifies the formal system from the life and re-sponsible discursiveness of any human subject, and, as the ultimate reference, of the victims. I must point out, however, that Luxemburg confuses ethical "transformation"—mostly revolutionary acts, though constituted with the same ethical criteria and principles—with "revolution." This is a very serious issue, because, in the eyes of the Luxemburgist, an ethically just act is either revolutionary or reformist. Whereas almost all ethically critical and just ("good") acts that are able to "transform"—starting from the victims, via a simple maxim (even if it concerns tiny details), up to different levels of the prevailing order—are not necessarily reformist or revolutionary. Revolutions, real and historic (not the ones dreamt of by anarchists or naive people), are the paroxysm of the transforming act; but not every ethical-critical transformation is, can, or should be intended, *hic et nunc*, to be only revolutionary. This is not reformism; it may still be a valid act of ethical-critical transformation. Today, at the turn of the twentieth century, during the time of Pax Americana's hegemony, which has no opposition, and under the military domination of the Pentagon, if the extreme left wing or alleged critics confuse "reformism" with nonrevolutionary "ethical-critical transformation" (since revolutions can be "anticipated" under exceptional conditions and for a short period of time, but they cannot be "invented"), they will only be able to condemn to disappointment or immorality all critical and honest women and men committed to various and numerous "liberation fronts," who at this time are not and cannot be revolutionaries—at least not in the political sense of aiming to seize state power to change deep socioeconomic structures—fronts such as environmentalism, feminism, antiracist struggles, and so on. In order not to fall in the "functional" praxis of the dominant formal systems, that is, into reformism, we must not lose the "compass"—of the pilot guiding the ship to avoid crashing into the iceberg. Says Luxemburg: "After the refutation undertaken by the socialist *critique* (that is to say that undertaken by means of critical-ethical principles) of capitalist society (and of all formal autonomous performative systems) . . . , when scientific socialism was abandoned, we lost our way."[231] Such a "compass" is equivalent to the ethical principles (the five mentioned up to this moment): they show the deep direction of praxis. The "helm" is the strategic-conscious guide, the critical, enlightened, living subject, who knows how to respect the mechanisms of vital self-organization and social self-regulation of the systems within which consciousness emerges to ethically redirect the process, without surpassing its limits. "Under the water," the keel (corporeality) is moved by drives (motors, etc.). The person at the helm presupposes them, does not replace them, she or he is under their command. We cannot accept the "modern subject," but neither can we accept the suicidal irrationality of denying the principles (the compass) and the critical conscience: an opportune spin of the helm can "transform" the course and save the life of the ship's crew. But an inopportune turn might destroy it just the same or even in a worse manner. So, we cannot accept the total market's rudderless ship; nor the ship of total planning which has no motor but advances by swings of the rudder. The ethics of liberation is much *more complex* than such simplifications; *sufficiently* complex, I hope, to avoid unilateral superficial approaches, but not *unnecessarily* complex either—for which some may criticize me. I know that an empirical perfect balance is impossible.

[372] *Critical* action then, "transforms" the process of praxis just as it would have if it had responded only to the criteria and principles (always present though not intentionally) of the formal system in force. Such "transformations" when taken together produce the moment of *develop-*

ment[232] that adds the new to the production and *reproduction* process of the life of every human subject. Mere "reproduction" (rational or instinctual, institutional and civilizing) can self-referentially close on itself, become fixed in its ways, in a totalitarian way totalize itself, become repressive (of real subjects, just as in Marx's notion of the often criticized alienation effect of unpaid work, in Freud's notion of the repression of the drives by the mechanisms of the superego, Foucault's prison "discipline"). Hence, the ethical principle is "transformative"; it develops life and not only maintains it. Such transformation is not a mere quantitative "progress" of the formal system. The critique of quantitative modern "progress," the formal efficiency of the instrumental reason of means and ends, the performativity of the fact as the ultimate goal—as Lyotard's proposal in *The Postmodern Condition* could be viewed—mastery of technical instruments, of numbers, of the efficient calculus, must not be eliminated completely, but subsumed within the criteria and principles of an ethics of the life of human subjects and their symmetric discursiveness. And it must be subsumed to be used in the "development" of human life and participation. What is required is cultural, economic, and political creativity, the reproduction and development of human life in the environmental cycle, the life possibilities of the victims in the face of autonomized performative systems, turned into the idols of progress by the progress of the ends or values *en soi*, without any reference to human life and discursiveness. I then deny—and this is the recoverable aspect of postmodernism—modern quantitative "performative *progress*" that is independent from the possibility of the life of each subject; however, I affirm the need for qualitative "efficient *development*" (performativity or critical-ethical feasibility) in favor of life, as the material content and co-responsibility of discursively participant moral subjects. If we take the life of the worker subject as a reference—to use Luxemburg's terminology—and not the capitalist formal system, we can understand that "in the history of the classes, revolution is the political creative act [*Schöpfungsakt*], while legislation[233] is the political expression of life in a society that has already emerged."[234]

Such development as a feasible critical-ethical transformation, is the *historical process of liberation*, not as mere enlightened emancipation (in the ambit of knowledge, science, and even critical theory), but as an emancipation integrated in an immensely more complex process, always also material, corporeal, cultural, of contents, with self-regulated moments and self-conscious interventions of critical discursiveness, the formal-materiality of which we call *liberation*. All the foregoing is always intersubjective, namely, involving particular subjects, who constitutively participate in a community of life and communication, as self-organized moments, but always open to the intervention of a critically conscious corrective of

Table 12. Types of Systemic-Functional or Critical-Transformative Acts

1 Noncritical systemic acts	
1.a "Functional" acts within the formal system	1.b "Reformist acts" that claim to be critical
2.a Critical acts of everyday "transformation"	2.b Revolutionary acts or acts of extreme "transformation"
2 Ethical critical acts or acts of "transformation"	

such self-reproduction whenever it becomes entropic. I am speaking of a historical process of the liberation of sociohistorical subjects, who have a memory of their past, of their already past liberation battles (forgetting is part of falling into an entropic self-regulation), who have projects and programs for a future fulfillment (when such communities of victims have reached a sufficient organization, namely, when the degree of sociohistorical subjectivity is such that they "emerge" as new historical subjects), who define their strategy, tactics, and methods of struggle to *transform* (at any level of practical complexity: from the norm to the ethical system) the social reality and subjectivity of each living human subject, having as the last critical-practical reference the victims of their specific intersubjective level (woman at the level of gender, people of color at the level of racial discrimination, human life on the earth at the level of the economic-formal systems that destroy the environment, etc.).

[373] What I have basically indicated throughout this work is, strictly, an introduction to a famous statement by Marx, in the eleventh of his *Theses on Feuerbach*: "Philosophers have only *interpreted* [*interpretiert*] the world in differing ways; but the point is to *transform it* [*verändern*]."[235] In this aphorism, Marx, as I have already mentioned, does not deny philosophy—as Korsch well observed—but points out that philosophy must stop being only a theoretical hermeneutics in order to develop as a discourse to found the real and practical "transformation [*Veränderung*]" of the world, as a "*critical-practical* [*praktisch-kritischen*] activity"[236] (also see table 12). Such philosophic discourse cannot be anything but a practical philosophy, and in the sense I have defined it here, strictly, a nonreformist *ethics of transformation*, an ethics of liberation. The Marxist Western tradition, from Lukács onward, deviated toward ontology, the critique of ideology, aesthetics, mere economic politics, and so on; it never intended to develop an ethics as the "first and practical philosophy" to discuss the criteria and principles to ground the required "transformation of the world" with its victims as the ultimate reference. This is what the ethics of liberation has intended since the end of the 1960s, in various forms.

Michael Walzer writes in *Exodus and Revolution*: "First, wherever you live is probably Egypt; second, there is always somewhere else that's better, a world that is more attractive, a promised land; and third, the way to get there is across the desert. There is no way to get there except by joining together and walking."[237]

§6.4. The "Question of Violence": Legitimate Coercion, Violence, and the Praxis of Liberation

[374] If the paroxysm of the strategic "transformation" (which focuses on the "ends" of action) of the totality of a formal performative system into another one, taking all the responsibility for the Other that this implies, is revolution, then the extreme tactical action in its ethical feasibility (the technical "means" of action), as the utmost danger, is a declaration of war. Hannah Arendt writes: "Wars and revolutions—as if only the facts had accelerated the fulfilling of Lenin's first predictions—have thus determined the physiognomy of the twentieth century."[238] Who would have said that only ten years ago? The twentieth century ended with the collapse of the major revolution of the century (the 1917 Soviet Revolution) and in some kind of mortal "quietude" without any possible revolution on the horizon. Is this the final hopelessness for dominated peoples, for most of human-kind, who are victims of a system that has unleashed, without any counter-weight after the end of the "Cold War," its legal violence, legitimate and lethal, against the disinherited? Has the "world liberal revolution" finally taken place[239] before the astonished eyes of the impoverished multitudes, excluded by their millions from the feast?

We are now at the level of means, of tactics, of instrumental reason, in order to consider the objective, but at the same time, ethical-critical feasibility of a possible way out from the situation of the victims at a world level.

Revolution and war are certainly dramatic facts, because, even if they were necessary, or even just, they cannot for those reasons avoid the use of instruments that could kill many people, inevitably causing suffering and hurting countless innocent victims. Revolution, as extreme transformation, is preponderantly a moment of strategic reason; war, as a limited mediation of tactics, is an instance of instrumental reason.[240] Arendt adds: "A theory of war or a theory of revolution can only be a justification of violence, but the glorification or justification of violence, as such, is no longer political but antipolitical."[241] I do not believe that problem should be posed in such form. A theory regarding such issues is not necessarily a justification of violence, although it has frequently been so, but, by contrast, it must be directed to show how coercion is transformed into violence when it loses legitimacy. The subject is extremely complex and, in order to come to a clear, possible conclusion, we must make a long detour, to create new analytical categories that allow us to reach the proper stance for an ethics of liberation.

[375] My argument will pursue the following strategy. First, I must define the right of every institutional system (political, economic, gender, racial, ecological, etc.) to have sufficient judicial and instrumental means, discursively agreed upon by those affected in symmetry with one another (that is, to define what is legitimate) to allow the reproduction and development of the life of each ethical subject in the respective systemic sector and thus, institutional sector. Any prevailing institution (with reference to the community life of everyone, and to what has been validly agreed upon) must be supported by a legitimate kind of coercion, which allows for guiding those not willing to comply with the validly accepted agreements. The ethical feasibility—to take a position contrary to anarchists—must be able to have the means to provide the institution, "the public," with objectivity beyond the mere subjective acceptance. This does not mean that "morality" is to be severed from "politics," as Kant believed to an extent, in his *Metaphysics of Customs*. The monological conviction of each member is necessary but not sufficient. Legitimate coercion is ethical, insofar as it is exerted fulfilling the demands of the material, discursive, formal principles of ethical feasibility: to guarantee the life of all those affected, who symmetrically participate in the decisions of ethically feasible mediations. If all the members of an institution were ethically perfect, as the anarchist dreams, no institutions would be necessary and, consequently, they would be intrinsically and from their origin, perverse. In such a case, coercion could never be legitimate, and coercion and legitimacy would be contradictory by definition. But, empirically, and given the impossibility of assuming such perfection, human life would be impossible, because any unjust member could oppress by force the rest, who would be innocent and defenseless, and could easily introduce the tyranny of his or her will, without any possible institutional limitation. Anarchists fall into a performative contradiction when they claim to do away with the coerciveness of institutions, thus making possible a worse form of coercion with no possible defense or participation of the innocent members who might suffer under this violence. Who could limit, oppose, and disarm the unjust member who would use force against the community?

But, to admit legitimate coercion does not mean to accept that domination is a part of legitimacy, as Max Weber presupposes. In addition, legitimacy is not only the consent that results from the best argumentation (best because of the symmetric discursive participation of those affected); it is also the acceptance of the institutional order insofar as it achieves the production, reproduction, and development of the human life of the members of such a system.

Table 13. The Difference between Legitimate Coercion and Violence

	a. Established Order (Legal)	b. Rebellion with/without Emergent Subject
1. Legitimate coercion	legal acts, legitimate	Liberation praxis, illegal and legitimate
2. Violence (use of illegal coercion)	legal repression, illegitimate	anarchist acts, illegal and illegitimate

The point is the acceptance of a legitimate and institutional coercive action, mutually agreed upon by consensus, for the empirical and ethical feasibility of the social functions of the system, and in order to have resources when some members do not comply with what has been freely, symmetrically, and validly decided. Such coercion, although it may include the use of force by means of instruments such as laws, courts, and also weapons, police organizations (not as torturers, but as respectful servers of civil order), places for the separation of uncompliant persons (humane institutions of ethical reeducation, not prisons like places of torture that pervert people), and so on, cannot be called violence. I would like this word ("violence") to be used with a well-defined ethical sense: as negative, perverse and, thus, never accepted justifiably. But violence must be defined in advance, clearly and univocally, differentiating it from other uses of force that are legitimate, legal, just, honest, and even meritorious, provided the heroism of the one using it in fulfilling his/her duty and as an ethical service to the community, to humankind.

[376] The ethical conflict starts when the victims of a prevailing formal system cannot live, or have been violently and discursively excluded from such a system; when sociohistorical subjects, social movements (e.g., ecological), classes (workers), marginal groups, genders (feminine), races (nonwhite), peripheral impoverished countries, and so on, become conscious, organize themselves, formulate diagnoses of their negativity and prepare alternative programs to transform the systems that are in force and that have become dominant, oppressive, the cause of death and exclusion. For such new sociohistorical subjects, the "legal" coercion of the system (which causes their negation and constitutes them as victims) has stopped being "legitimate." It has stopped being so, first, because the subjects have become aware that they had not participated in the original agreement setting up the system (and thus it stops being "valid" for them); and, second, because in such a system new victims cannot live (thus the system stops being a feasible mediation for the life of those dominated). To the critical consciousness that is communitarian and ethical, the community of life, the communication community of the victims, such coercion becomes illegitimate (see table 13). Any use of force against the new rights, which reveal-

ing themselves historically and progressively in the very eyes of the victims, will no longer be for them "legitimate coercion" but strictly violence: use of force against the right of the Other, without any validity or objective quality (being the destructive force of the "exclusive reproduction" of the system in force, not the reproduction and development of human life). When George Washington in the North American colonies and Hidalgo in New Spain rose against Britain or Spain, they had a clear ethical consciousness that, as victims of unjust colonialism, granted them the validity of the right of European monarchies before the *new validity* of the rights of the newborn right of the free originary United States or Mexico. The former legitimate coercion of Britain and Spain had become violence, and Washington's or Hidalgo's illegal-defensive coercion were not only acceptable to the victims but necessary for their self-defense as innocent victims (colonial peoples born in America and oppressed by Europeans) and, thus, completely ethical. Those who give their life in this struggle for the recognition of the dignity of innocent victims, in defense of those victims, shall be justly remembered by future generations, by history, as heroes. Heroism is the attribution to the subject of such a practice, by the community of victims, the re-cognition that this subject is the founder of a new ethic, of a new order, a new system, in Levinas's language, the new totality; those who produce bread for the hungry, clothes for the naked, shelter for the *homeless*—with all the ambiguity that this carries with it.[242] This is the subject of this section: *critical-empirical feasibility*, at which level, since it is predominantly a matter of instrumental reason (technical, scientific, military, etc.), the "means" are to be found. Maybe there is no harsher, colder, more pitiless means or instrument than a "weapon." It was created by hunters in the Paleolithic, because the human subject being omnivorous, needs proteins; thus they hunted animals with sharp tools that could penetrate the hide of such living beings (the membrane that separates the living from the non-living, starting with the amoeba and going up to the multicellular: the skin of mammals, the clothing of the naked, the walls of any house on earth, the borders of one's own country with other countries—the "line"). Soon the hunters turned in intraspecies aggression against other human beings, and warriors were born. With the huge institutional macrostructures of the urban Neolithic, professional militaries were born, and, with them, armies. With the industrial revolution, weapons were technologized, developed into machines, tanks, airplanes, and atomic bombs. What originally was devised as a means to promote human life (hunting) ended as a huge fetish, a military self-referential system (articulated to transnational capitalism) that automatizes itself and, now, more than ever, endangers not only human life but simply "life" on Earth. Instrumental reason has reached its totalization: what was made with our own hands (*fetiço* in Portuguese) has become an autonomous power (as Marx pointed out in 1844) and is turning against humankind to destroy life as a whole. But actually, humankind does not hold in its hands the structures of military power; they are held by very few countries and, since 1989, one in particular: the United States, which through its State Department runs the Pentagon, hominid power, for the first time in the history of millions of years of the *Homo* species concentrated in the domain of one economic-political military complex. From this concrete position we must think in the twenty-first century, at the gates of the third millennium, about the subject of ethical-critical feasibility and the liberation of the victims of planet Earth.

Let us look at these issues at several possible levels.

[377] One example can show the type of theoretical framework we need at this moment. As is well known, Mahatma Gandhi, in his struggle for the emancipation of India from British dominion used the tactical method of "war without weapons [*krishnalal sheidharani*]," or, more simply, the doctrine of "nonviolence"—which had for him an ontological-religious foundation. Martin Luther King managed to move in the same manner millions of African Americans, achieving a significant increase in their civil rights in the United States of America. Within the context of the ethics of liberation, the "efficiency" of this political tactic becomes perfectly comprehensible, which may be used only in certain well-determined situations (not by the dictatorship of a "state of right," that is, properly speaking, under revolutionary conditions). On certain well-determined occasions, when democratic respect of human rights exists, it is possible for new social movements to use nonviolence, since it is somewhat efficient. In fact, in order to achieve precise goals, one can produce a situation such that legal coercion (e.g., of the colonial metropolis or the state) "appears" clearly as violence (as nonlegitimate),[243] for instance, when a policeman confronts with his English soldier's gun the naked corporeality of the unarmed victim in a hunger strike in East India. Domination exerted daily against the victim, through unjust structures, now comes into broad daylight. *Legal coercion starts to lose legitimacy*; it starts collapsing morally. By contrast, the community of those who constitute the social movement, which because it is "new" is illegal—since it vindicates such emergent rights not yet positively sanctioned—becomes more and more aware of the ethical superiority of its cause and acquires a growing and mutual conviction of the legitimacy of the action that consolidates the self-recognition of the community's own dignity and mutual co-responsibility. Action, as can be understood, has a critical legitimacy against the coercive legality of dominant structures. This is the "friction" demanded by Rosa Luxemburg so that critical conscience of the masses could grow—though in her case, because it was a revolutionary action, the movement was not necessarily unarmed.[244]

Antonio Gramsci named such phenomenon the "hegemony"[245] crisis; it was the moment of the passage from "hegemony"—when there is sufficient consensus among all the members of a political system, an acritical acceptance, by the masses, of the bloc historically in power, of what is not questioned by any influential group—to "domination" as coercion or repression, as violence; this repression being an illegitimate action even if legal for a period of time, when the social bloc of the oppressed takes action.

[378] In fact, for Max Weber, the descriptive concept of legitimacy always includes some kind of domination, which makes it impossible for the concept to be transformed into a notion with ethical normative validity. Weber descriptively defines legitimacy as follows:

> Those who act in a social context may thus attribute *legitimate validity* to a determined order: (a) by the merits of *tradition*: understood as the validity of that which has always existed; (b) by virtue of an *affective belief* (particularly of an emotional character): the validity of that which is new and which has been revealed or of that which is exemplary; (c) by virtue of a *rational belief founded upon the basis of articulated values*: the prevailing of that which is held to be valued in absolute terms; (d) by the assumed merits of that which has been [*legally*] *enacted and instituted*, with a corresponding belief in its legality.[246]

As one can see, except for (d), three of these motives are "material" (tradition, affectivity, and values). The political "order" is "valid" when it is accepted by the tradition in force (the conventional order that has not entered into crisis), because it still motivates the members affectively (an example being "love for one's country"), because there is a consensual belief in cultural values, or a recognition of laws that are communitarily complied with. The "content of sense"[247] provides validity to order, namely, makes it legitimate. But such legitimacy is essentially unstable, because it exists "only as a probability, treated practically as such and maintained in important proportion."[248] All the foregoing is the result of order based on domination. Weber defines domination this way: "What we understand here by *domination* is a state of things by which the explicit will [*mandate*] of *one who dominates* or of *those who dominate* influences the acts of others [of *those who are dominated*], in such a way that to a socially relevant degree these acts occur as if the dominated had adopted the *content* of the dominator's mandate [*obedience*] for themselves and on their own account."[249] This is what constitutes legitimacy as a contradictory concept of impossible normativeness: legitimate is what is accepted as valid, but founded, in a social structure where most of the members (the dominated) fulfill the will of the other as if it were their own will, satisfying the dominator's interests, not their own. The concept of power then becomes central: "*Power* means the probability of imposing one's own will, in the context of a social relation-ship, even in the face of all resistance and whatever the basis of that proba-bility might be."[250] While such "probability" is maintained, domination is exerted and legitimacy is valid. Now, the ultimate institution of *legitimate* political order is the state, which has a monopoly on the use of physical co-ercion, "with the mission of compelling [the dominated] to observe such order or else be punished for their transgression";[251] holding dominion over life and death.[252]

[379] Habermas, in order to find a normality criterion to define legiti-macy ethically, starts from the Weberian rationalization process and de-velops it to an intersubjective level, showing legitimacy to be the consen-sual acceptance of a political order shared by members of a communication community who can engage in symmetrical argument: "Legitimacy signi-fies that the claim concomitant with a political order that it be recognized as rightful and just has good arguments to back it up; a legitimate order merits recognition. . . . What stands out within the context of this defini-tion is that legitimacy involves a debatable claim of validity whose recog-nition (minimally) depends (as well) on the stability characteristic of the order of domination [*Herrschaftsordnung*] at issue."[253] Thus, Habermas no longer has to found legitimacy in the mere conventional, affective, evalua-tive, and even legal positive order, and bases it on discourse ethic's norma-tiveness. But, just like Weber, he has to consider that domination is still a moment that is empirically unavoidable and a source of permanent crisis. The "crisis of legitimacy"—and the correlated necessary legitimizing pro-cess—seems to happen before "social disintegration," an effect of the colo-nization of "everyday life [*Lebenswelt*]" by economic systems, under the power of money and politically bureaucratized. This would be a crisis of rationality.

What is missing from Weber and Habermas—and also from Serrano—is an awareness that a relevant instance, one that can never be discarded, of a possible legitimate political order consists in the production, reproduc-tion, and development of the human life of each of its members, at a level that is acceptable or tolerable (in the consciousness of those dominated). The legitimacy crisis must also be articulated to a life reproduction crisis (the problem of the misery of those dominated and excluded), in order to develop a more profound concept of such legitimacy. In Latin America, Africa, Asia, and Eastern Europe, and among growing minorities in capi-talist "central" countries, the political order loses legitimacy when the misery of many becomes intolerable, unsustainable.[254] Legitimacy should thus be defined—in a basic and primary sense—as the *communitarian self-validation* granted to a political order (or to other practical systems), start-ing with the empirical capacity of such an order for (a) the reproduction and development of the life of the subjects (the material),[255] and (b) the symmetrical intersubjective participation in decision making by those affected (the formal); all of which should be possible (c) with efficient instrumental mediations (the feasible), thus creating a *fundamental consensus* of acceptance of the mentioned political order (or others).

The importance of the material instance (the whole issue of the material principle of ethics discussed in chapter 1) was not discussed by Habermas, nor by Foucault—although they do adequately place it at the level of the corporeality excluded from the diagram of power—because they stopped regarding political economics as a critical[256] social science; Habermas says: "Economic science is focused today on the economy as a subsystem of the society as a whole and sets issues of legitimacy[257] off to one side. In advanced Western societies, social conflicts have emerged in the last few decades that in many respects . . . are no longer unleashed in the spheres of *material reproduction*. . . . These conflicts emerge instead in the spheres of cultural reproduction."[258] The fact is that "advanced Western societies" (Europe and the United States of America) and Japan constitute approximately 15 percent of present humankind. For the remaining 85 percent "material reproduction" is still a relevant reference of legitimacy in every political order. This explains why all new social movements (and even political movements, movements of social classes, etc.) necessarily refer to the reproduction and development of human life, articulated to the intersubjective acceptability of the legitimating consensus.[259]

[380] The ethics of liberation is strictly interested in the moment when the legitimacy of the dominant order—in a Weberian sense—becomes *illegitimate*, at which point, the type of bureaucratic, instrumental, evaluative, traditional or exceptional charismatic domination is no longer valuable. Hiding in this type of charismatic Weberian domination is the kind of liberating action which, having been denied, struggles for the recognition of the new legitimacy, not itself charismatic—but not bureaucratic or traditional either. This is not a fourth type of domination but a different type of legality, which claims to be not domination but a "liberation" of any of the three types of legitimate domination set forth by Weber. He understands by "charismatic domination"[260] a specific type of recognition by "adepts"[261] among those "dominated," which is as based "upon the validity of the charisma" of the chief, caudillo, shaman, and so on, that is, on their "presumed charismatic qualities."[262] The charismatic leader "competes" with the other powers in the legitimate power market,[263] against traditional patriarchs and reigning values, against the legitimacy of bureaucrats, and against other charismatic leaders who are supernatural, all three types engaged in the struggle for "domination." Liberation praxis opposes these types of "legitimate" domination (each one of them *hegemonic* in their re-

spective classic stages, I would say, following Gramsci). The victims' lives and the critical communication community are not merely charismatic and are evidently antibureaucratic and antitraditionalist but rise up against the established system (legal and legitimate, traditional, bureaucratic, or charismatic, with its "witch doctors," its Hitler or fascisms, bourgeois nationalisms, or the new Christian or Muslim fundamentalist charismatic religions) to stand for other critical and intersubjective criteria of truth, validity, and feasibility; for other normative principles—those discussed in the previous five chapters of this ethics of liberation. The legitimacy crisis (which is, in fact, a slow delegitimating process) and the creation of a *new* legitimacy (against the forced process intended by the prevailing system in crisis) demand distinctions not made by Weber or Habermas, because of the narrowness of their frameworks. It is clear then, that the type of legitimacy on which liberation praxis is based, and which it affirms, does not correspond to any of the three types of Weberian domination, but to one located at another practical level: the legitimacy reached by new emerging social subjects, not founded, at least in the beginning, in any type of domination, but in an organization with some sort of internal discipline.

[381] Currently, for example, the neoliberal economic project, mainly inspired in F. von Hayek, which sets the theoretical framework for the International Monetary Fund or World Bank policies, produces victims in all postcolonial poor countries. Any social movements undertaken against such policies, such as the workers' strikes in Latin America's South Cone, under the direction of the Argentinean General Work Federation or the Brazilian Workers' Party, are actions called by sociohistorical subjects who go out to the streets to struggle for the recognition of the dignity of their endangered lives. Such actions acquire among their followers a growing validity and legitimacy against an order that starts losing legitimacy. The state that dismantles the former "benefactor state," by means of privatizations—which allows the *fictitious* financial capital of central countries to be "realized" in productive capital—and the monetary policies of economic recession, carries out a legal, but increasingly illegal coercion, of people who have no choice but to accept a political order that victimizes them with unemployment, hunger, and misery. These are the acts of a state that assumes the face of mere *violence*, namely, an illegitimate legal repression.[264] Thus, any critique that originates in the victims' material order delegitimizes the formal and apparently democratic validity, so any action of such social movements, in their liberation praxis, may never be deemed as violent, because they intend a legitimate coercion, though frequently illegal.[265]

Let me now develop the categories used so far. In the first place, the prevailing order has the right (legality) to the monopolistic exercise of coercion, because the public sphere (since Kant) cannot be left in the hands of the merely individual subjective decision.[266] In other words, in its *classic stage*, which Gramsci calls the "hegemony" moment,[267] the social, economic, political, and cultural order is well accepted by those who are dominated ones (in a Weberian sense), who do not yet have a *clear* consciousness of the domination exerted against them, or for whom the domination is tolerable (because the even more unbearable sufferings of the former system are still recent and remembered: for example, the suffering of servants under feudalism in relation to the free workers of European medieval cities). The legal political order is legitimate when it is materially acceptable (in that it sufficiently reproduces life) and has rational intersubjective validity (its arguments cannot be refuted with better or still inexistent arguments), and when it shows itself to be "efficient" compared with the previous order. Legitimate legality prevails without opposition. In modern European states, this classic moment coexisted with a "governmental state [*Regierungsstaat*]," based on the omnipresent sovereignty of the absolute king, the foundation of legality, in Karl Schmitt's words,[268] the self-legitimacy of the authority supports its legality. These definitions could lead to a conception of politics as the "centralization of power," the "isolation of individuals," claiming a certain "national" homogenization of all its members (with the disappearance of the autonomous private and market spheres,[269] thus giving rise to modern "totalitarianism"). By contrast, in the "state of right [*Rechtsstaat*]," discursively construed, there is an intersubjectively valid normativeness, based on the democratic rational principle of freely accepted consensus, which articulates the legal with legitimacy.

[382] The ethics of liberation entails an even more complex set of problems. The (positive) legal order and the (prevailing) legitimacy—in all the senses discussed—cannot but presuppose (and it is impossible that they do not presuppose it in some minimum degree at least) some degree of (material and formal discursive) negation of the victims. "From the victims' point of view" the problems of legality, legitimacy, coercion against rights, as well as many other issues, demand to be developed in their whole significance once again. Thus, to the prevailing positive legal order (notwithstanding its definition as such) one can now oppose the illegality (always unavoidable in the origin of the future order) of the *new* social movements of the critical community of victims, when these emerge, organized, within the prevailing order, which always presupposes them but had become accustomed to ignoring the victims, insofar as they passively "accepted" a domination exerted legally and legitimately against them. In the first place, the "irruption" of the victims—as emergence "from nothingness," in the Chiapas rainforests and mountains, of the "faceless" faces of Mayan Indians of the National Liberation Zapatista Army in Mexico—may produce a crisis in the system's legitimacy. At this moment a practical com-

plex event is produced, which has always been the subject matter of reflection for an ethics of liberation. The "legal and legitimate" (1a) actions of the "established order"[270] now face both "illegal" (from the standpoint of an established order: Miguel Hidalgo's illegality before the *Compilation of the Laws of the Kingdom of the Indies* of 1861) and "illegitimate" acts (from the standpoint of the hegemonic community, since the excluded ones have not been part of the basic agreements of the dominant groups). Coercion, now exerted against liberation praxis, against illegal actions (of Washington and Hidalgo), is "legal" and "legitimate"—in the eyes of, for example, British and Spaniard monarchs. But from the victims' rational and symmetric discursive intersubjectivity (the Creoles of New England or New Mexico), rebel actions ("liberation praxis," 1b) start becoming "legitimate" *for them*.[271] So, according to the victims, the system's legal "legitimacy" loses validity (becomes illegitimate) and its coerciveness (which used to be legitimate) turns into *violence*: mere use of force, coercion against the Other's legitimate rights (the Other who is now conscious of being an autonomous subject with *new* rights). The delegitimating process of the invisible domination of the former "classic" stage becomes unbearable from the perspective of the victims' consciousness (*concientização* in Portuguese).

[383] I will reserve the word *violence* (from Latin *vis* ["force"], used against the rights of the Other, in the sense of "violate") exclusively for the illegal and illegitimate rebellion of the anarchist[272] (2b), or legal coercion turned illegitimate (1b) (the coercion of the prevailing order, for instance, of the state as repressive agent, for example, the eighteenth-century British army against New England, the nineteenth-century Spanish army against New Spain, Augusto Pinochet's Chilean army against a defenseless peoples who had in Allende a legal and legitimate governor). Such coercion and violence is countered by the struggle for the re-cognition of new rights, of the establishment for transformation of norms, actions, institutions, or whole ethical systems, when they are the last possible resource of the critical communities of victims at their limit, and even if they use means "in equal proportion" to the contrary violence (propaganda vs. propaganda, fist vs. fist, nonviolent disarmed struggle vs. the weapons of the repressing system, and, in extreme cases, and when all other possible means have been exhausted, as in the case of Washington, Hidalgo, and many others, weapons vs. weapons). This is legitimate liberation praxis, the defensive co-action of innocent victims among the masses, who have no legal structures *yet* to justify their actions.[273]

The limit coercion in strategic transformations is, as the last resort, revolution. Here, by contrast with other forms of liberation praxis, we are dealing with war, which can be judged just or unjust. Once again, a certain semantic precision is required, in order to open paths toward the justification of liberation praxis. War is in the final analysis neither just nor unjust; it is simply the "field" or strategic structure, the "diagram" of macro forces where two or more armies confront each other. Armies fight *in* the war—in one or several battles, fronts, movements, positions—for just or unjust "causes."[274] The Spanish army with Cortés fought against Aztecs, claiming to liberate the Zapotecos, Otomíes, and other peoples under Aztec domination; the American army with Schwarzkopf fought against Iraqis, claiming to protect Kuwait against Iraq. But there are many armies in the battlefield: (a) the army of the dominated peoples that struggle for their emancipation (Zapotecs or Otomis, Kuwaitis or Panamanians;[275]) (b) the army of the new dominators (Spain or the United States), who achieve their goals (for the Spaniards, the Aztecs' gold and silver in the sixteenth century; for the Americans, the "black" gold, so strategic for the twenty-first century) because they now dominate (c) the former dominators (Aztecs, Iraqis). The "causes" of the armies are various; in case (b) it is domination for the long term; in case (c), the defense of their dominion over other peoples; finally, in case (a) it is the defense, properly speaking, of their sovereignty (Zapotecs, Kuwaitis). The two first "causes" cannot be fully legitimate; but the third one can. Just the same, Kurds nowadays fight against Turkey, Iran, and Iraq to obtain a territorial autonomy that was denied by British colonialism. Their struggle, like Washington's, Hidalgo's, or Fidel Castro's, is a legitimate liberation war.

[384] We are in the realm of ethical-critical feasibility, of tactical actions that must be directed at negating the causes of the negation of victims.[276] Let us consider, once again, this level from Rosa Luxemburg's insights, because they might be useful for us. After the 1905 Russian Revolution, Luxemburg addressed the question of general and national strikes by the masses; later, she commented on the social democracy crisis just before the First World War, when the Social Democrats voted on August 4, 1914, for funds for the Prussian army. Both decisions were tactical. The first was a novelty and subsequently would become legal; it is, to start with, liberation praxis. The second was legal (within the national order), and nonetheless with definite effects[277] for the unorganized community of the victims who fought and died in a war that belonged to their oppressors: they fought for a strange cause.

In fact, Engels had already stated, against Bakunin, that a national strike on the part of the masses was impossible because of their lack of organization and of a strike fund, and that such a strike was unnecessary, since if there existed sufficient force to call a general strike, power could be seized. Luxemburg replied: "The Russian Revolution [of 1905] has today submitted the argument set forth above to a complete revision. The Russian Revolution has for the first time in the history of class struggles made possible the fulfilment on a grand scale of the idea of a mass strike and as I will explore in further detail below, that of a general strike, thereby opening up a whole new era in the evolution of the worker's movement."[278] We are strictly at the social tactic level, within a political strategy. The mass strike is not an anarchist method; it is a social, trade union action that is always political. It is not voluntarily decided nor easily avoided. "It is a historical phenomenon," writes Luxemburg, "produced at a determinate moment, because of a historical necessity determined by social conditions."[279] In the "void of the abstract logical analysis"[280] everything is possible; but historical feasibility must respond to an "objective examination of the origins of the mass strike from the point of view of what is historically necessary [*geschichtliche Notwendigen*],"[281] but always within the framework of the ethically possible. A few reformists believe that strikes are tactical and not revolutionary, and in accordance with parliamentary practices, while anarchists believe that strikes are a revolutionary direct action. In fact, strikes are neither. When on January 22, 1905, two hundred workers walked in procession in Saint Petersburg in front of the czar's palace, an action that "ended in terrible butchery,"[282] it was the culmination of a process begun in 1896 with workers' strikes organized for merely economic relief, but which grew in number and became better organized: "This first direct general class action . . . resulted in an awakening for the first time of class sentiment and consciousness among millions and millions of human beings . . . *consciousness of the unsustainable character* of the social and economic existence they had endured under the chains of capitalism. This is the *spontaneous [spontanes]* origin of a general movement to shake off and break the chains."[283]

[385] This type of limit event, of serious crisis, is "the living school [*lebendige Schule*] of events . . . in continuous reciprocal friction [*Reibung*]."[284] Tactically, such actions (like a general strike) cannot be produced "just with organization,"[285] but only when "it transforms into a true popular movement [*Volksbewegung*]."[286] What in the German worker was just a "latent theoretical consciousness [*theoretisches, latentes*], . . . in the revolution, when the masses themselves appear on the political scene, class consciousness is practical and active [*praktisches, aktives*]."[287] But ultimately, as in the case of "nonviolence"—another tactic—all this is an "educational task [*Erziehungserk*],"[288] in the sense that the emerging historical subject, the critical community of victims, begins to develop a *critical-ethical intersubjective consciousness* (here, class consciousness) of the legitimacy of their liberating praxis. Tactical action is a mediation of strategic ends defined with reference to principles: "The issue is not to judge the specific case of the Waldeck-Rousseau cabinet," writes Luxemburg, "but instead *to deduce a rule of general conduct from our overall principles*."[289] Not any means (tactical "rule of conduct") for any end; nor any end (strategic "rule of conduct")

to realize the principles. On the contrary: principles are the basis for determining ends and means: all ends and means must correspond to the appropriate ethical syllogism. The "fundamental principles" (ethical-material and formal-discursive) are the framework where concrete general rules or tactics are located.[290] The general strike is possible based on such presuppositions, but not as the "ultimate" destructive "end"—the extreme anarchist position—but as a coactive means, so that workers may learn their main function within capital ("All capital is work," wrote Marx), and, for capital to discover the presence of a new sociohistorical subject with whom one has to sit at the "negotiating table"—even if it is not with discursive moral reason, at least within the agreements of instrumental or strategic reason.

[386] A second paradigmatic situation originated in the social democracy crisis with regard to war.[291] The German proletariat and the Social Democratic Party and, with it, the Second International, made a tactical error of definite consequence. Speaking of the International, Luxemburg wrote: "Its errors are as enormous as its tasks. It has no previously designed scenario that might be considered valid once and forever, nor any infallible guide that might show it the path that it should follow; no other teacher is available but that of *historical experience* [*geschichtliche Erfahrung*]. The painful path of its self-liberation [*Selbstbefreiung*] is not only paved by unlimited suffering but strewn with innumerable errors. It will only attain their *liberation* [*Befreiung*] if it is capable of knowing how to learn from its own errors."[292] When on August 4, 1914 the Social Democratic Party voted in favor of war bonds in Parliament, it entered into the dizzying maelstrom of German "imperialist nationalism"—which began with Bismarck and was expanding as a maritime power in the oceans, expanding too toward Turkey, and colonies of other continental powers, of Britain itself, through the efforts of Siemens, Krupp, Thyssen, the Deutsche Bank, among others. Unfortunately, "German social democracy was not only the strongest vanguard of the International; it was also its brain."[293] If in France in Marx's time the more critical process of the community of worker-victims was under way (though it received a mortal blow with the defeat of the Paris Commune in 1870), in Germany, from the end of the nineteenth century, social democracy was in the vanguard. The mistake of German social democracy in 1914 gave Russian Leninism—a consequence not clearly seen by Luxemburg at the time—the leading role as guide for socialist movements throughout the world, with regard to the tactical (and even strategic)[294] rules for fighting against world capitalism and within it. The defeat of the Third International in 1939 opened a new tactical scenario. In 1914, the German victims of the nationalist bourgeoisie, namely, the workers, should not have plunged "the murderous steel into the chests of their Russian, French, and English brothers."[295] By doing so, they provided the pre-

cedent for a repetition of the same act in 1939, when social democracy had stopped being a vanguard and had fallen into an eternal reformism.

As we have seen, liberation praxis as tactic and strategy, as the fulfillment of an ethical, critical feasibility, always walks a fine line between anti-institutionalist anarchism and integrationist reformism. Thus, one must be very clear about the criterion and the general principle of liberation praxis regarding the mediations taken to fulfill the strategic ends framed within prior ethical and formal-discursive general principles, so that with ethical-critical feasibility one can effectively negate the causes of negation of the victim, as a de-constructive struggle that demands appropriate means, in accordance with those against whom one struggles. But, as a vignette of the complex architecture of which I have just given a preliminary sketch, such praxis promotes constructive, possible, and demandable transformations: a new order based on a concretely designed program, which realizes progressively, *but never completely*, the possible utopia, the liberation project—all that Ernst Bloch hoped for.

§6.5. The Critical Criterion of Feasibility and the Liberation Principle

[387] Now I must undertake the last few steps of this ethics of liberation as part of a transition toward future works, which will have to develop the foundations for its principles within a much richer horizon (neither solely nor explicitly limited to a logical predicament or normative framework), and as applied to concrete tasks of liberation on various different fronts. The praxis of liberation is that which involves the possibility of action undertaken to transform subjective and social reality, with its ultimate point of reference always centered upon a particular victim or community of victims. The effective possibility of liberating victims is the criterion upon which the most complex principle of this *Ethics* is based. It is also the one principle that embraces all of the others at a more concrete, complex, real, and critical level.

The criterion of ethical-critical transformation is a criterion of *feasibility* with reference to the possibilities of liberation of the victim in the face of the dominant systems. From the perspective of the existence of the victim as the potential expression of an active, effectuating *capacity* (that which "is," that is given), the objective-systemic reality manifests itself in *opposition* to its full fulfillment (the "development" of human life in general). The system becomes apparent as a contradiction, since its claim to serve as a feasible means for the reproduction of life (like all such institutions) in fact ends up operating as the basis for the negation of these subjects, and of their life (as manifested in the victim's own self). The victims in and of themselves reveal the contradictions of the system, and of its impossibility of sustaining itself *in the long run*—in the absence of necessary transformations—of producing and reproducing the human life of those who have been affected by it (the victims), which is to say that it has thus exhibited a certain "inefficiency" (a problem of nonfeasibility) with reference to the existence of the victims. Whatever transformations are necessary are now visible as either *possible* or *impossible* (ethical-critical feasibility), and confront a certain systemic "inefficiency."

For its part, the liberation principle enunciates the *ought-to-be* that ethically obliges such transformation. This is a demand that must be fulfilled by the community of victims itself, under its own collective re-sponsibility, which has its origin, practically and materially, in normative terms, in the existence of a certain power or capacity (of *being*) possessed by those victims. Because *there are* victims of a certain capacity, *it is possible* and necessary to struggle in order to negate the inhuman negation of the pain of the victims, which is intolerable for an ethical-critical consciousness to bear.

The classic image of liberation expressed by a chain (the formal system that oppresses or excludes), which strong arms (the critical community of the victims) break at its weakest link, reflects everything I am seeking to describe here. The chains, which are material and made of metal, are the instrument that limits the freedom of slaves or prisoners, which must be "broken" (negativity) by a capacity that has the ability to act:²⁹⁶ the "force" of the arms must be proportional (a problem of feasibility expressed in their "success" in breaking the chains) to the resistance of the iron of the chains that bind. But at minimum victims must be *"capable"* of breaking the "weakest" links—a process that reflects the activation of a strategic and calculating instrumentality. All of this is indicative of the question of the critical feasibility of the praxis of liberation, of the "capacity" to transform reality upon the basis of factual or empirical "possibility," with the technical, economic, political, or cultural²⁹⁷ conditions necessary to bring about the changes required.

a. The Critical-Feasible Criterion for All Transformation

[388] What is at issue then is the confrontation between an organized social movement of the victims and a dominant formal system (for example, feminism in the face of patriarchy; wage labor, the poor, and those excluded by unemployment in the face of globalized capitalism; environmentalists confronted by the subsystems that destroy planetary life, etc.). My emphasis here is not on the justness or rationality embedded in a historical process or its underlying project, but instead on its empirical feasibility. It is not always someone who is just who is able to carry out an act of justice.

The criterion of feasibility of a potential process of transformation demands the consideration of empirical, technological, economic, political, or other relevant capacities or possibilities, with direct reference to the negation of the negativity of the victim, thanks to the practical calculus that fulfills the critical instrumental and strategic reasoning at issue. In other words, the criterion for assessing the possibility of transforming the formal system that produces victims is based upon a careful evaluation of the strategic-instrumental capacity of the community of victims to carry out that objective *in the face of* the prevailing power of the dominant system. This is not a matter, as in the case of mere ethical feasibility, of being "*capable*" of acting upon what has been decided in the face of the difficulties posed by *nature* (possibilities that are always scarce, as a mediation in the life of the ethical subject).[298] Now, instead, we are confronted with the *given existence* of a prevailing formal system, and of a norm, act, microstructure, institution, or complete system of ethics (which is the fruit of a *previously established* but now dominant ethical feasibility), whose bounds are determined by its capacity to produce victims (for example Levinas's "totality," Marx's fetishism of capital, or the institutional-cultural repression produced by Freud's drives); all of this demands a very special kind of caution.[299] Consider the following formulation of a diachronic pattern indicative of the moments that anticipate and follow upon the exercise of strategic-instrumental reason or of critical feasibility.

An initial aspect of "transformative" criticism engaged with everyday life would proceed as follows:

1. A victim X suffers M[300] negativity, which somehow puts his or her life in danger.
2. System Z produces M in X.
3. Subsystem Y[301] of System Z is the cause of M in X.
4. In order to negate M in X, Y must be avoided.
5. In order to avoid Y, and to transform Z, technical, economic, political, and pedagogical mediations of types A, B, C, etc. are necessary.
6. Mediations A, B, C, etc. are feasible *here and now*.
7. Ergo: Y can be avoided, and Z is thereby transformed.

Or another aspect might emerge (which I could describe as a "revolutionary" variant), which after step 4, above, would develop in the following manner:

5′. Y[302] cannot be avoided without completely destroying Z.
6′. In order to avoid M, and its cause (4), Z must be totally transformed into W (a new system).
7′. In W[303] victim X would no longer suffer[304] the effects of M.
8′. Mediations D, E, F, etc. can bring about W.

9′. Mediations D, E, F, etc. are feasible *here and now*.
10′. Ergo: W can be brought about.

The moments of critical exercise of the evaluation of the strategic-instrumental feasibility can be found in steps 6 and 9′,[305] taking into account that in order to be classified as evaluations of ethical-critical feasibility, they must be framed in a manner compatible with the material and formal discursive ethical principles described above.

We thus have three themes to consider: (a) the empirical-strategic factual judgment regarding the exercise of the concrete historical power of the system that dominates (whose weakest moment in times of crisis arises when it manifests its intrinsic impossibility externally, its contradiction taken to a point of collapse via entropy): (b) the capacity that the organized community of victims has to bring about empirically, with "success," through efficient "means," the strategic "ends" that it intends, taking into account the diagrams of power;[306] and (c) the objective[307] concrete conditions or conjunctures that provide a feasible basis for bringing about the transformations required, which can be partial or total, depending upon their importance in contributing to the origins of the negativity at issue with respect to the victim as the result of a norm, act, microstructure, and so on, even though such a result may not be intentional in character.

a1. *The critical judgment regarding the power of the order that dominates*

[389] This is a wide-ranging theme. Here I will describe its place in the overall architecture of the ethics of liberation. Everything suggests that the dominant system must in principle concentrate more power than the emerging sociohistorical subjects in a process of liberation. Nonetheless, the praxis of liberation does not initially demonstrate its feasibility upon the basis of its own power, but rather from the perspective of the fragility of every dominant system at its moment of crisis. The very existence of an organized and critical community of victims already reflects the system's crisis. When the dominant system becomes intolerable—the threshold of its "intolerability" is extremely variable—because of the existence of victims on a massive scale, its intrinsic impossibility (the *Krisis*, as Marx[308] understood it, which is embedded in the essence of capital but "appears" cyclically in its empirical crises) becomes a conscious reality in the critical consciousness of the community of victims. It is the task of critical social science to explain the (essential) impossibility of the dominant system and also to explain how its collapse can take hundreds of years.[309] This is the point at which the inevitably contradictory character of any historical system is revealed, precisely because it is historical (because it has an origin and a *limited duration*); in other words, the impossibility *in the long run* of perpetuating itself indefinitely. The "empirical principle of im-

possibility"[310] demonstrates the necessarily finite character of any system, beginning with its "basic enunciation," which is demonstrably false, along the lines of "This empirical system is infinite in its duration." Since such a case is impossible, critical social science, in conjunction with the victims' liberatory intention, is capable of developing a scientific agenda to demonstrate this impossibility. The victims of capital, for example, know, with Marx, that surplus value is accumulated as profit; but Rosa Luxemburg proved on her own that this process of accumulation is only possible if it subsumes noncapitalist wealth, through a prolonged structural process of primitive accumulation. Today it is necessary to demonstrate that capital is no longer capable of achieving its desired levels of surplus value (having subsumed all the possible noncapitalist wealth). This means that the fictitious bubble of globalized finance capital will increase geometrically until it bursts, once it is clear that it will never be transformed into any kind of productive industrial capital. The intrinsic impossibility of transnational capitalism has become increasingly apparent in the postwar era since 1945. This implies a new structural crisis (of an essential character, in term of its "possibility"), whose "existence" can be extended for some time. The liberation of the postcolonial and peripheral states as concrete and emerging historical and political subjects, should also imply an awareness of the "weaknesses" of the states at the "center" of the global system, which accumulate and manage global financial capital, underwritten by the military power of the Pentagon, which is the ultimate political instance of economic power. In a parallel sense, feminism recognizes the contradictions of patriarchy, and environmentalism those implicated in the destruction of life on the Earth, since all the prevailing systems that destroy life commit a variant of suicide upon reaching an absolute or impossible limit that cannot be surpassed.

This is to say, strategically, that it is necessary not only to explain theoretically and scientifically the "causes" that have induced the "negativity" experienced by the victim, but also to explain the "impossibility" of the system of domination at issue *in the long run*. This prediction is not a matter of mathematical or statistical predictability (where an empirical absence of confirming results here and now would imply a lack of scientific rigor or entail the falsification or scientific refutation of the prediction) but is instead one of a dialectical character. The massive presence of victims in the global periphery and even in the system's core, whose increasing misery is not taken into account, points to the impossibility of the system *in the long run*.

The "force" of the community of victims striving for liberation, who always appears to be weaker than their adversary, must instrumentally and strategically "calculate" their possibilities of movement amid the fissures of the dominant power that they confront. Not everything is lost. It would be true that they have lost only if their opponent were an eternal demigod without contradictions. If the system is finite, historical, and human in origin, liberation is possible and feasible, but the appropriate conditions must be awaited or created: "Just as the market appears to compensate for the lack of perfect knowledge, in the same way planning[311] appears in order to compensate the market's incapacity to achieve a level of economic equilibrium. Because of this, planning [which is possible, not perfect] does not appear as a claim of perfect knowledge, as Hayek implies, but instead as the result of the *impossibility of such knowledge*."[312] In the same way, criticism as an analysis of the impossibility of the system does not imply a claim to perfect knowledge of the system but instead a conviction about the predictability of its collapse because of the systemic explanation implied by its negative nonintentional effects (the victims). The impossibility of an absence of contradictions in the system (which would presuppose its supposed perfection for all eternity) should be an incentive for the researcher to detect the cracks through which the praxis of liberation might penetrate with objective feasibility. The struggle for life has a future in the face of the systems of death that are invariably permeated by internal contradictions. This must be demonstrated concretely and scientifically, but it is not a task suited to ethics, which can nonetheless contribute to this end from the spheres of activity of critical, interdisciplinary scientific communities, by providing minimal but strategic guidance.

a2. *The self-evaluation of the practical capacity of the community of victims*

[390] In the same way, the organized critical community of victims must be realistic with respect to an assessment of its own strengths and its possibilities of taking action. Gramsci's "philosophy of praxis" is situated precisely along this axis, which has to do with the matter of undertaking a successful transition from the "war of movement [that is to say of frontal attack] to the war of positions."[313] It is very difficult for the community of victims to confront the system of domination directly (in a war by strategic movements); instead it must often cloak its movements and efforts to organize itself and increase its levels of consciousness, appearing and disappearing as necessary (as part of the "war of positions"). These are all tactics that are part of a long-range strategy, which must take into account the inevitable weaknesses of an emerging sociohistorical subject. In any case, the "capacity" for effective action is not determined by the community of victims itself, but by circumstances external to it, which can be accelerated or accumulated by the organization—as we saw in §6.1, but these cannot be created by suicidal voluntarism. Once again, the critical discursiveness of the community of victims, in the context of a symmetrical democratic system, is the universal mediating instrument that enables the diagnosis

of the community's own strengths, its organization, and the conjunctures most favorable to it. In the end it is the community that is the sociohistorical subject of the actions that must be undertaken. Mistakes in judgment can be fatal (in terms of both overestimating and underestimating its strengths), but even errors can be learned from.

a3. *The objective conjuncture for the feasibility of transformative action*

[391] It is necessary to transform the causes of victimization by deconstructing them. The existence of victims is evidence of the need for new (transformed) norms, acts, microstructures, institutions, and ethical systems that might make the development of human life "possible" (through the reproduction of the life of the victims), as well as that of human discursiveness (through the symmetrical participation of the victims).

Hope in the possibility of utopia bridges the distance between its feasibility and the possibility of its fulfillment. This is a utopia of life that has the intention of overcoming the utopia of death. Of the latter Hinkelammert wrote: "The utopia of communism, as developed in the Soviet Union; the utopia of the Nietzschean society without hope, developed by Nazism; and the neoliberal utopia of the total market. All of these promise a better world beyond *all human feasibility*, and therefore beyond the human condition and the contingencies of the real world. . . . [N]one of these promises the most minimal *critique of the present*. To the contrary, they promise the creation of another world in the name of the celebration of present conditions."[314] These are utopias which justify the existence of victims. The community of victims should also imagine a utopia of a different character, one that opens up horizons of feasibility; this utopia is necessary but also insufficient—in order for it to become possible the community must have recourse to mediations that might enable their utopia through concrete projects and programs. These programs must be undertaken as the result of careful analyses developed by activists, experts, critical scientific researchers, and so on bearing in mind the real and objective circumstances that together define the context and range of possible proximate action. In this dimension, once again it is the symmetrically discursive and participatory democratic community of the victims that will make this analysis operational and will program the steps along which this overall process will proceed.

b. The Liberation Principle

[392] The liberation principle explicitly formulates the deontological moment or ethical-critical duty of transformation as a necessary condition for the reproduction of the life of the victim, and as an expression of the feasible development of human life in general. The principle subsumes all of the principles described earlier in this volume. It has to do with the

duty of intervening creatively in the *qualitative* development of history. The principle obliges fulfillment of the duty defined by the criterion I described previously; that is to say, it is obligatory as applied to all human beings, although it is often assumed as a responsibility by the critical community of victims, transformed by negative deconstruction and the renewed positive construction of the norms, actions, microstructures, institutions, or ethical systems that together produced the negativity of the victim.

As in the previous cases it is necessary to undertake a transition from the dialectical material grounding of a "factual judgment" (all of the statements given above from 1 to 7 and from 5′ to 10′) to a "normative judgment" (9 and 12′ below). This transition can be illustrated as follows:

> 8. Having recognized the dignity of the living human subject of X; assuming that X is a member of the same community; and furthermore that X wants to continue to live.[315]
>
> 9. Assuming that all who are part of this community share re-sponsibility for the life of X, as the expression of the demands of an unavoidable solidarity,[316] *ergo* Y *must* be avoided and A, B, C, n[317] must be activated.

This transition (from 7 [or 10′] to 9 [or 12]) of the criterion of critical feasibility (the real possibility of liberation) to the liberation principle (the "duty" that activates the underlying praxis) presupposes this transition in terms of all of the previously described principles.[318]

[393] In light of all of the above, the liberation principle can be described more or less as follows: one who operates in an ethical-critical manner *should* (is ethically obligated to) act to liberate the victim, as part (either by "location" or by "positioning," according to Gramsci) of the same community to which the victim belongs, by means of (*a*) *a* feasible *transformation* of the moments (norms, acts, microstructures, institutions, or ethical systems) *that produce* the material negativity at issue (which impede a certain aspect of the reproduction of life) or its formal discursivity (a certain asymmetry or exclusion with regard to participation) for the victim; and (*b*) *the construction*, through mediations with strategic-instrumental critical feasibility, of new norms, actions, microstructures, institutions, or even complete ethical systems, where such victims could live, as full and equal participants. What is at issue here as I have highlighted previously is a "qualitative historical advance"[319] or development. This obligation has a claim of universality; which is to say that it would exert its sway in every human act or situation. This *liberatory interest* is grounded in the regulatory idea of a society without victims (notwithstanding the empirical impossibility of such a society) and, concretely (and this *is* empirically possible) without *this specific* historical type of victim; each of these victims is empirically responsible for, and must struggle on behalf of, this society

without their kind of victim, in order to make their liberation possible. The *liberatory interest* thus has a driving force and opens up the horizon of this obligation, undertaken by *liberating reason* (practical-material[320] *ethical-critical* reason, characterized by a consensual, strategic, and instrumental discourse).

Furthermore, it must be taken into account that the practical positive fulfillment of this principle, or of its more aptly termed *praxis of liberation*, always has the critical community of victims as a referent for the construction of its sociohistorical subjectivity—whatever might be the visage with which it is revealed—and the community of victims always bears the burden of responsibility for this, as a self-liberating act undertaken by a specific sociohistorical subject.

b1. *The negative moment of the liberation principle*

[394] The ethical obligation of liberation is always imposed, in the first place, as a duty to take on the real deconstruction of the causes of the negativity of the victim. The most extreme action of this type is that of heroic figures who establish new ethical orders, often paying for this achievement with their lives (Joan of Arc in France, for example, or Miguel Hidalgo in Mexico, or Patrice Lumumba in the Congo). As part of this process they confront the legal violence of the system of domination that has lost its legitimacy (or which is gradually losing it in the eyes of the victims). Such leaders give their lives in exchange for more life: for the liberation of the victims. The praxis of liberation is the most "dangerous" of praxes because it confronts illegitimate *power* with the weakness of the indefensible human bodily reality (or of means that are always inferior though legitimate) of the victims. This is the core of the metaphoric story of David, the shepherd, and his battle against Goliath, the Philistine warrior. David battles in the name of life, and Goliath in defense of domination (which is the imposition of his law over that of the life of the Others, who are obedient to the law because of the risk of losing their lives to oppressive violence). It is the bravery of the just Semite, the poor shepherd (a guerrilla insurgent from the mountains)[321] armed with his humble, everyday slingshot in the face of the iron weapon of the professional Indo-European warrior. Inherent in this story is a metaphor regarding the weakness of whoever is imprisoned by the dominant system as a kind of hostage, as someone re-sponsible to its victims. I am speaking of a negative, deconstructive, necessary praxis that clears the terrain so that the foundations can be dug, and so that the walls (institutions) of a home can be raised upon them, where life can be produced, reproduced, and developed. In this way, a transition is made possible from a "war of positions" to a "war of movement," as Antonio Gramsci would put it.[322]

b2. *The positive moment of the liberation principle*

[395] To liberate is not only to break the chains (the negative moment described above) but also "to develop" human life (liberate in the sense of providing the subject with a positive possibility) by demanding that the institutions and the system open new horizons of transcendence beyond those of mere reproduction, as repetition, of "the same" — and, simultaneously, beyond the oppression and exclusion of the victims. Or it can also be, more directly, the effective construction of a possible utopia, the structures or institutions of a system where it is possible for the victims to live, and to "live well" (which is the *new* "good life"): to free the slave, to arrive at the culmination of the "process" of liberation as an action that brings about the effective liberty of the previously oppressed. This is a "liberation *for*" the *novum*, the success that has been achieved, the utopia that has been brought about.

This is not only the task fulfilled by the citizen who had to become a soldier to fight against oppression, to negate the negation (like the farmer named Washington; Hidalgo, the priest; Ché Guevara, the physician; or Mahatma Gandhi, the lawyer), but also the task that arises at the hour of the activist who has become a political leader and builder of new institutions. This is the constructive mode of the praxis of liberation, reflected in the legislators of a new legal system, of heroes transformed into rulers. It is necessary then to transform the sword into a ploughshare to make the furrows for the seed and produce bread for the hungry, whose hunger is satisfied by the happiness of knowing that the life now reproduced implies an increase in the conditions which make life possible.

To build a house for the *homeless* is an ethical duty demanded by the liberation principle; but it should be a house in which the victims have symmetrically participated in the design and in its actual construction. To build the new order is to effectuate the "Good II" (the "critical goodness claim"), assuming that the "Good I" was the fruit of the foundational part of this *Ethics* (see the end of chapter 3). The "Good II" — the reproduction of the life of the victims, with their critical-discursive participation and from the perspective of the precarious feasibility of their creativity — is the prevailing good, the fruit of the liberatory constructive actor of the past, which begins to be cemented in tradition and accumulates as custom, which prolongs itself much further beyond as oppression, and, finally, as violence against new victims (new because they are recent and different, never the same). This is the architectural space located in the positive liberating moment, which if I sought to address it in greater detail, as in previous cases, would lead me into detailed analytical expositions.

[396] The grounding of the liberation principle must be attempted in the face of its *conservative antiutopian* opposition, developed by Karl

Popper, who considered this utopia "impossible" (within the performative or efficiency criteria of the dominant system), even though it is critically "necessary" and "possible" from the perspective of the victims. This is the conservative antiutopianism explained by Hinkelammert. Between the *impossibility of the anarchist* attempt (of absolutely impossible feasibility) and the *impossibility of the conservative* declaration (which considers it impossible from the perspective of the self-referential dominant system), the praxis of liberation attempts to bring about *that which is possible*, that which is feasible under the given circumstances, in the interest of the victims, which may in fact coincide in material terms with the rebellious action of the anarchist (at the moment when the revolution breaks out) or with the systemic or functional action of the reformist (when the transformation in favor of the victim is coincidentally of identical character to that of the reformist with respect to the system),[323] but which is always distinguishable because of the criterion upon which it is based. In action that has the intention of bringing about liberation, the emphasis is on the transformation of norms, actions, microstructures, institutions, and ethical systems *from the perspective of the victims* and in favor of their life, and not because the institutions at issue are considered to be abstractly or intrinsically perverse (from the perspective of the anarchist) or systemically justified (from the perspective of the reformist).

c. Application of the Principle and Fulfillment of the *Novum*:
The New Goodness Claim

[397] In the face of the affirmation of postmodernists, who take their critique of the "modern subject" to the limit and end up negating *any* meaningful subject (which leaves the victims divested of the possibility of intersubjective strategic or tactical organization), and in addition renders such subjects incommensurable (to the extent that those who dominate need not render accounts to anybody regarding the effects of their domination, and cannot be recriminated ethically or rationally according to any argument), I affirm instead the need to concretely and positively recognize the living communal ethical *subject*. It is all the more necessary to historically and socially recognize the victims as *subjects* when they emerge as the victims of a self-referential system that negates them materially and formally; this must include the historical and social recognition of the *intersubjective* diversity of sociohistorical communities, particularly those consisting of the victims in the process of discovering and struggling for their *new rights*; *a diversity* that does not negate the universality of discursive and material reason, but instead renders it concrete and enriches it, uncovering the diverse and invisible "visages" of the Other, which must be articulated "transversally" in their wealth of alterity (what I described in the *Philoso-*

phy of Liberation as the *analectical moment* in the dialectical method, which flows from the "dis-tinct" positivity of the diverse alterity, in order to find universality in the depths of each diversity, in which the particularity of the alterity of other sociohistorical subjects is reflected). As I have noted, in the "visage" of Rigoberta Menchú a diversity of visages is transversally revealed: the "woman" and "indigenous" person, the "Mother Earth" of environmentalism, the poor "peasant," part of the "bronze" race native to the American continent, the "Mayan," the "young" woman subjected to the weight of gerontocracy, the "Guatemalan" and "activist" arising from a critical community of consciousness. A "visage" amid all of the "visages" of all the invisible Others: in each concrete victim there is also the presence of the universal victim, who is revealed as the epiphany of the visages of all the specific visages—as "universal" reason that is ethical-material, formal-discursive, critical-practical, articulated by the "transversal" reason that cuts across all the particular and distinct alterities: the "liberation fronts" of diverse sociohistorical subjects, within complex diagrams (spheres of the micro- and macrostructure of power) of forces that situate the monological and intersubjective subjects of living human bodily reality in its vulnerable materiality and amid its drives, of pathological discursivity, but with the interest of communicating with others from their own "places" of enunciation, attempting always to do what is possible to live communally, in order to live better in co-responsibility and collaboration.

[398] Let us situate ourselves in the architectural framework of this *Ethics* in terms of the "location" of the stage of argumentation at which we find ourselves, taking into consideration the statements set forth above, and proceeding from them. Let us move forward then with the effectuation of what is "due" (given that feasibility is ethical):

> 10. A, B, C, etc. are carried out and thanks to this Y is avoided.

Or alternatively:

> 13'. D, E, F, etc. are carried out and thanks to this W is effectuated (and Z is thereby avoided, which necessarily presupposed Y).

In both cases, "success" is obtained (as the fruit of the *"works [érgon]"* of the human being working upon his or her own self) through the exercise of ethical-critical "strategic-instrumental reason": the "good" (the "goodness claim") is thereby fulfilled. That is to say, Y is eliminated, or W is effectuated

> 11. (or 14'). Once Y has been eliminated,[324] X no longer suffers the effects of M, and X can satisfy—through the mediation of a positive structure—their necessities, reproduce their lives, live in happiness in community, etc.

The actual feasible operation, the praxis of liberation as transformative final actuality, is displayed in 10 and 13'. Now we have made the transition to the fulfillment of that which is "due" by "feasibly" bringing into reality the *novum* through the praxis of liberation in its own terms.[325]

Aristotle used to observe that natural and artificial (technical) beings had distinct ways of being ("by nature" or arising from "skilled work"). To the question, what is the "work [*érgon*] of a human being"?,[326] Aristotle responded that "the work particular [*tó ídion*] of the human being"[327] or "the human good" is "to bring about a presence in accordance with the habitual authentic mode of being."[328] In the context of an ethics of liberation, for its part, the "work" (or the fruit of the action according to the ethical principles that have been enunciated, according to the applicable practical, material, and formal discursive reason and equally to strategic and instrumental reasons that have been subsumed, *critically*, which is to say negatively and materially) consists of capturing the reality of every given system as the fulfillment of a process effectuated by a *former* victim. All of social reality, all of the contemporary "goodness claim"[329] was once a liberation project imagined by the heroes of the past (the Joans, Washingtons, Hidalgos, Lumumbas, or Castros). The only difference is the shift in perspective. In the "Good I" I observed only what leads to the production of this "claim" (chapter 3). Now, in the "Good II" (the *critical* goodness claim), I also consider every aspect of the struggle that allows the construction (the *development*) of the new project against the established, prevailing "Good I." The subject at issue is the community of victims (for instance, colonists in New England in 1776). The "Good I," the good in power, is ambiguous, almost anthropological. The Good II (in the explicit project of liberation, the "critical goodness claim"), is ethical *goodness par excellence*: to be "good" (just) is a dangerous task in which the negated reproduction of the life of the victim demands the sacrifice of the life of the critic, of the teacher of critical consciousness (Freire), of the critical scientist (Marx or Horkheimer), of the unblocking of mere reproductive drives (Nietzsche or Freud), of the already constituted "totality" which murders its victims and its hostages (Levinas). In these cases ethical action is dramatic, and implies the struggle for re-cognition, and of a war of movement for liberation.

But in the end, the *norm* of goodness is the one grounded in its validity according to the demands of moral-discursive reason, containing the practical truth that is governed by the demand of the production, reproduction, and development of the human life of each ethical subject and community, and by the feasibility of the strategic, practical, and instrumental technological requirements of the moment. But this *norm* is not yet "good" in itself, the "work" of ethics; it is instead a normative mediation.

The *good action* (the *praxis*) is the one that brings about the good norm in actuality and in accordance with not only the reproductive drives but also equally those that are creative or conducive to the development of human life. The "good action" is the concrete fulfillment of the "claim" but not of *goodness* itself.

The *microdiagrams* of power or of the *institutions* are nothing but stable systemic structures, where actions as forces are co-determined in the diachronic process of sociohistorical development. There are "good" institutions—or at least ones in good standing—and others that are corrupt, in crisis, repressive, and so on. In any case "institutions" are not in themselves the "good" either, *kath 'exokhen*.

A culture, an ethical system as a totality, the *Sittlichkeit* suggested by Hegel, is the ethical, concrete, and historical totality that provides a context for specific norms, actions, and institutions. It is "the given," the system that prevails, that is traditional; the "*material* good" par excellence for Weber, Popper, and the meta-analytical schools of ethics (which are conservative against their own will, since they lack the critical capacity characteristic of the cultures in which they are immersed, since they have removed the ladder that would allow them to arrive at their foundation). Nonetheless not even the "ethical" (as a concrete ethical totality) is the "good" as such either, but is instead, at most, the resources from which one may realize "goodness."

[399] Finally, the "good" is a moment of human subjects themselves; a mode of reality through which their *human* life can be found fully fulfilled according to the assumptions of human reality itself; a creative work which is the fruit of its self-re-cognition, re-sponsibility, and autonomy, and which is thereby grounded in community, having attained intersubjective validity (according to the monological accord of its own *frónesis*), motivated by the order of reproductive drives (which can end in the "death instinct") and innovative in character (the pleasure principle or "metaphysical desire"), but which can be summarized in a specifically ethical and critical moment: the supreme "good"[330]—by which all others are measured—is the *full reproduction*[331] of the human life of the victims. The "full reproduction" I am speaking of in this context means that the hungry eat, the naked are clothed, the homeless are housed, the illiterate write, those who have suffered experience enjoyment, the oppressed are equal to all, and that whoever uses time to live badly has free time; a time when the victims may contemplate beauty, live their traditions, dance the plenitude of their community's values, to be fully human at the superior levels of the spiritual creations of humanity. In a word: yesterday's victims are able to celebrate the re-cognition and re-sponsibility of their joyful communal corporeality. This is the "supreme good," a regulatory idea that is partially fulfilled in each good act, or in each ethical subject we describe as "good." But all of

this must be understood in light of the fact that this Good II, this "*critical* goodness claim" — the fruit of the liberation struggles of the victims — is gradually and imperceptibly established as an "*old* goodness claim," Good I; that is to say, and as I have already noted, the victims who were once homeless end up installing beautiful fences to protect their newly acquired comfort from others who are the new poor: their home is now their prison (the new "totality" conceived of by Levinas). No one can rest in peace in the "work" that has been achieved — because the mere fact of being there, in a specific time and space, in the context of specific institutions, produces rust and corruption — which produce others who are poor and constitute new victims.

A student of mine once objected that if new victims always appear, history was nothing but a tragic "eternal return *of the new*." My initial response would be to say that every human *novum* that is finite and historical, which can be falsified, which is mortal, and has a claim to "goodness" — in the best case — can become evil if discursive critical consciousness does not prevent it from falling into the temptation of affirming itself as that which is forever truthful, valid, and efficient. There is no "eternity" that could "return" as something "new." There is no eternity in the human being except that which is historical, and that which is newly emerging cannot be a "return," and conversely, that which is new cannot be eternal and cannot return. No. What is at issue here is the "historical emergence of the new" within a transmodern conception of the "*qualitative* progress of humanity." Each process of liberation (today we are experiencing the liberation of 50 percent of humanity, simply as a result of the process of women's liberation) achieves "success" (its "*work*"), but it is necessary to apply critical consciousness to such processes: any good action that is achieved is not perfection, and is only good in historical terms. The perfect society is logically possible but empirically impossible. The supreme good is a regulatory idea (a system without victims) but is empirically impossible. Does this make the effort worthless? No. It serves to help us criticize the domination that prevails in the reality around us and reveal the victims it produces, but it is not sufficient to enable historical achievement of the supreme good — Marx's "communism," conceived of as a "reign of freedom," was also a regulatory idea and not a "historical stage."[332] Because of all this, if the "good" is finite, if it is impossible to achieve a perfect work, then ethics teaches us to be attentively critical and in permanent struggle. Those who "install" themselves in the power of the "good" are already evil, and the prevailing good has already become transformed into that which is "not-good" (in a deliberate echo of Adorno's reflection regarding the *untruth* of the prevailing *truth*).

[400] The "good," as the fruit of the praxis of liberation, is the achievement of a difficult, arduous enterprise that is always ranged against superior

forces, and against the structures of those who exercise the power of the traditional and dominant "good." Because of this, its work is the fruit of the four cardinal virtues taken to their most extreme: unflinching strength, incorruptible and disciplined temperance (to the point of bearing torture without betrayal of a substitute who is held hostage), prudent intelligence regarding the feasibility of forces that are always greater, and justice that does not negotiate despite the loss of all hope for the helpless victim. This is the "war of movement" *in actu*. Those who carry it out in an exemplary manner, as an unsurpassable ethical reference, and in a creative, original manner, are those who will later be recognized as martyrs ("witnesses") of the future utopias, teachers of the heroes and heroines of new homelands.

The ethics of liberation is an ethics of a priori re-sponsibility on behalf of the Other, but it also implies an a posteriori responsibility (as in the work of Jonas) with regard to the unintentional negative effects of the structures of the systems that become manifest to the everyday consciousness of common sense: the victims. But, as I have insisted, and since this ethics of responsibility for consequences is an ethics that has material and formal principles, it is not reducible to good will or mere good intentions. The ethics of liberation is a radical ethics of responsibility, since what it is intended to address is the inevitable consequence of every unjust order: the victims. Its sense of re-sponsibility is not only systemic (Weber) or ontological (Jonas), but pre- and transontological (Levinas), because it assumes this re-sponsibility from the perspective of the Other, and from the standpoint of the victims.

[401] In the long run, the consequences of every norm, action, microstructure, institution, or system are intertwined in the chiaroscuro of infinite and indeterminable unintentional means that constitute the micro and macro moments of world history. The ethical meaning of any action, in its clearest and most absolute sense, capable of omnisciently judging any act, could only arise at the end of history, where everything done by all human beings would have meaning from the perspective of the totality of its circumstances (see also figure 21). That judgment is empirically impossible — though not mythically impossible: the "last judgment" of the Egyptian Osiris exists as an omniscient "eye" deep within the ethical conscience of each human being, applying a reflexive judgment to each instant before the public tribunal of all of humanity.[333] An ethics that seeks to judge concretely the content of the ethical meaning of any action without doubt or uncertainty is impossible. I have not sought to devise such a system. What I have attempted instead is to set forth the criteria and principles necessary to effect actions (a priori) and to judge them as "good" (or "evil") in abstract, in principle, in the final instance in light of their most relevant, inevitable, and evident consequence: because of their victims (a posteriori), and in

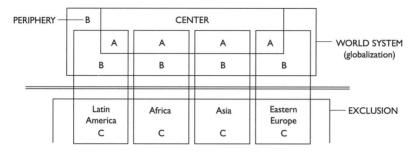

Figure 21. World system, globalization, and exclusion.

NOTE: A: presence of minorities from Latin America, Africa, Asia, or Eastern Europe in the central countries (Hispanics and Afro-Americans in the United States, Turks and Polish in Germany, Moroccans in Spain or France, etc.), or peripheral minorities that live as if at the center; B: actual peripheral structures in the three continents (the dominated); C: exclusion and impoverishment of the major part of the world population through the world system's globalization in Latin America, Africa, Asia, and Eastern Europe.

order to be critically responsible, and in solidarity to undertake once again the task of taking history to its next stage of development, as an expression of qualitative human progress, with the intention of assuring the reproduction of the life of victims and their discursive participation. These criteria and principles are enough to enable us empirically to reveal the negative nature of our actions or of the negative nonintentional acts and systems for which we are nonetheless responsible, given their consequences, and to remedy such effects by causing history to advance and to liberate these victims, which are *our* responsibility. The re-sponsibility for the vulnerable Other who suffers is thereby transformed into the "very rationality of reason itself"; into the "red light" that signals that something must be transformed so that it can become a "green light." In order for this to happen it is necessary for a process of liberation of the victims to be undertaken as part of the development of human life understood as the satisfaction of needs (from eating to aesthetic or mystical contemplation) and wants (corporeal, communal drives of joyful pleasure), of history as the qualitative progress of participatory and symmetrical community discourse, as achieved expressions of autonomy and freedom.

[402] In conclusion, I would like to recall the subtitle of this book: "In the Age of Globalization and Exclusion." This theme has been present throughout this *Ethics*, as an underlying current—not at the surface. My continuous references to neoliberalism, to Hayek, to the "center" and the "periphery," to capitalism, to the hegemony of the United States (particularly in military terms, through the Pentagon), all refer back to this theme.

This ethics of liberation, then, has sought to provide philosophical justification for the praxis of liberation by the victims in this age of history, at the end of the twentieth century and at the beginning of the third millennium, with particular reference to victims excluded by the contemporary process of globalization of capitalism as a world system.[334] This "five-hundred-year system," as it has been described by Frank and Chomsky, is that of Modernity which is coming to an end, and which is sowing terror, hunger, illness, and death, like the four horsemen of the Apocalypse, on the Earth and among the majority of humanity, those excluded from its benefits. This is the globalization of a *performative formal system* (the value that accumulates value, the wealth that produces wealth: D–D′, the fetishism of capital) which erects itself as the ultimate criterion of truth, validity, and feasibility and destroys human life, trampling the dignity of millions of human beings, denying recognition to the imperatives of equality, shirking its re-sponsibility for the alterity of the excluded, and assuming only the hypocritical legal obligation to pay the (fictitious) foreign debt of the impoverished nations of the periphery, at precisely the same moment as the indebted people perish: *fiat justiciam, pereat mundus* ("Let justice be done, even if it means that the world must perish"). This is murder on a massive scale, and the first steps toward collective suicide.

[403] It is because of all of this that I thought it necessary to unfurl the banner of a principle of absolute universality, which is completely negated by the prevailing system that is globalizing itself: *the duty to produce and reproduce each human subject*, which has urgent significance for the victims of this deadly system, which excludes ethical subjects and only includes the increase of values of exchange. This is a fetishist process that has led to a complete inversion: "We confront what appears to be a form of liberalism, which is quick to make concessions and to offer *human beings in sacrifice* [*Personen hinzuopfern*] . . . in order to keep *the thing* [*die Sache*] standing."[335] This was written by a young man in 1843 when he was still a bourgeois democratic radical. An ethics cannot be constructed reliably upon the basis of subjective value judgments that cater to personal taste. An ethics is built upon factual judgments—and the massive fact to which I have made recurrent reference in this book is the exclusion of the majority of humanity from the processes of development of Modernity and capitalism, which are systems that monopolize the reproduction and development of life, the enjoyment of wealth as a useful good, and participation in the discourses of deliberation about the decisions that benefit their interests (those of the Group of 7 or G-7) in the hands of their agents.

An ethics thereby becomes the last resort of humanity, which is in danger of becoming extinct as the result of its own actions. Perhaps only a solid co-responsibility with intersubjective validity, adequately grounded in the criterion of a life-and-death truth, can help us successfully navigate the tortuous path that is always close by. Such an ethics can make it possible for us to advance along the narrow edge, like acrobats on a high wire strung over the abyss of cynical ethical irresponsibility toward the victims or fundamentalist, death-loving paranoia that leads to the collective suicide of humanity.

Some Theses in Order of Appearance in the Text

Thesis 1

[404] (See figure 3.) I use the term "world system" to refer to the inter-regional system (if by "region" is understood a high culture or civilizing system) in its global or planetary, present phase, which is the result of four stages according to my interpretation:

a. In a first stage, the interregional system was only the structure of the relations of the Egyptian-Mesopotamian region (§I.1). India, China, and Amerindia (§I.2) were not yet directly connected.

b. In a second stage, the interregional system grew, covering from the Mediterranean and the north of Africa to the Middle East, India, and China, across the Eurasian steppes (the regions that were influenced by the Indo-Europeans). This "interregional" system was hegemonized or had as its connecting center the Persian or Hellenistic world of the Selec and the Ptolemaics[1] (§I.3).

c. In a third stage, the Christian, the first Byzantium, and Muslim world replaced the Hellenistic one and became the hinge of the entire system (from China and India to the Mediterranean) (§I.4).

d. In a fourth stage, peripheral Europe replaced the Turkish-Muslim world and came to constitute the first proper "world system" (§I.5), making Amerindia its first periphery.

In an abstract and simplified manner, I will for now use the terms "center" and "periphery" to refer to the cultural horizons of "life worlds" (see the second section of the introduction), which are determined by their "place" within the world system that has extended its reach since the end of the fifteenth century. The "center" of this system is constituted today by the countries of the North (Western Europe, the United States, and Japan). China and Russia maintain a special position. The rest is the "periphery."

Thesis 2

I will make a distinction between:

a. "Universal," which is an abstract category, in opposition to "particular."
b. "Global" or "planetary," which is a concrete horizon with respect to the world system that includes all the historical cultures (this is the level of "ethical life" that is not exactly the Hegelian concrete universal).

In this way, a "universal" morality (for instance, Habermas's proposal, §2.4, but also, in another sense, liberation philosophy's proposal) is located at a different level from either a "global" ethical life (for instance, the future project of a global culture that is negated by Modernity's aspiration to impose its particularity over all the cultures of the world system) or a global or planetary critical ethics (for example, the ethics of liberation).

Thesis 3

The *life* of which I speak is *human* life. By "human" we should understand the life of the human being at its physical-biological, historical-cultural, ethical-aesthetic levels, including even the mystical-spiritual level, and always within a communitarian horizon (see thesis 10). This is all far from either simplistic biologisms or cosmological materialism. The Egyptian symbol *Ankh*, which Osiris holds always in its hand, means "life." The *human life* of which we speak is not a concept, an idea, or an abstract or concrete ontological horizon. Nor is it a "way of life." Human life is a "mode of reality"; it is the concrete life of each human being from which reality is faced, constituting it from an ontological horizon (human life is the preontological point of departure of ontology) where the real is actualized as practical truth.

I reject as reductive the materialist (standard Marxist) or dominating conservatist vitalisms (Nazism for example; and even the Nietzschean narcissistic "will to power"). Human life has as an *intrinsic* constitutive rationality (because it is "human"), and the intersubjective and truthful exercise of rationality is an exigency of life itself: it is the "cunning" of life. Human life is never the "other" of reason; rather it is the absolute intrinsic material condition of rationality. For this reason it is required that we do not put reason above life (and life as irrational, as is the case with so many reductive rationalisms, because in this we fall into a contrary and mortal fallacy, insofar as it makes possible the death of the human subject, as is the case with irrationalist vitalism): neither reductive vitalisms nor reductive rationalisms. I will defend then that human life is the source of all rationality, and that material rationality has human life as criterion and ultimate "reference" of truth and absolute condition of its possibility. See Schnaedelbach 1983, chap. 5.

Thesis 4

I will make the following distinctions:

a. The "ethical" is material. It is the content of ethics (see thesis 10). See chapter 1.

b. "Morality" is formal or procedural, communitarian intersubjective. Discourse ethics (according to its definition) ought to be called the morality of discourse.

c. "Ethical life" (*Sittlichkeit*) is the concrete totality of the world, of the cultural horizon (this is the "morality" of my prior works; see Dussel 1986, sec. 10.2). See chapter 3.

d. "Ethos" is, in the Aristotelian sense, a system of virtues or cultural habits.

e. "Critical-ethical" indicates a moment proper to the ethics of liberation. Ethics is "critical" from the perspective of the victims, from the perspective of alterity. It is the "ethical" as such, or the face-to-face as encounter of practical subjects. See chapter 4. See also Kohlberg's (1981–84) incorporation of the critical within levels of moral consciousness [292].

f. The antidominant critical morality. See chapter 5.

g. I will also use "ethical," in its quotidian and pedestrian sense, which is equivalent to the practical.

Thesis 5

We must differentiate among four levels of ethical development:

a. The origin of the concrete ethical life and its *contents (material)*, which is as old as the history of humanity itself and that continues into the present.

b. The historical origin of prephilosophical *critical-ethical* categories (including those indicated in thesis 4e) that took place historically within the horizon of the first "interregional system," prior to Jasper's Axial Age. These are themes treated in §§I.1 and 5.2 [292].

c. The *formal* origin of moral philosophy, when it assumes its explicit classic formulation in Greek thought (implicit or initial in many peoples, including the Aztecs, for example, and certainly the Egyptian). The *formal* explicit beginning also depends on the maturity of the historical contextual ethical life, even in the case of the Greeks.

d. The autonomized origin of philosophy with respect to theology, from the first step toward secularization (Al-Kindi, Arabic, ninth century AD; see [23]), up to modern philosophy (from Descartes at least, in the seventeenth century).

It is evident that the contents of ethical life in peoples other than the Greeks can be (and in fact are) richer and more complex from a *critical-ethical* perspective (b) (which is what is of interest to an ethics of liberation) than in the

Hellenic-Roman world (c). The histories of ethics (and of philosophy) confuse the first three types of origins (and even project the idea of secularization as far back as the Hellenes) (c), and, for that reason, histories of philosophy always start with the Greeks (this is the Hellenocentrism that I want to criticize), assuming simultaneously the contents of material-ethical life (a). (See thesis 7a) and philosophically *formal* (here, c), generally abandoning the questions relating to the origin of the *critical-ethical* categories (b).

Thesis 6

Concrete ethical systems affirm the fact of human life. We have observed historically that this affirmation of life may follow concrete cultural roads:

a. The affirmation of human life as a creation of the singularity (*Einzelheit*) of the ethical subject, in the *"birth" as affirmation of life* ("this" subject is born), and for this reason it is an affirmation of terrestrial and corporeal life. Death is conceived as empirical death, but reaffirming life mythically as resurrection, reproduction, or survival of an ethical subject. This is the path of the Bantu, Egyptian, Mesopotamian and Semitic peoples (Jewish, Christian, and Muslim), among others (see §§I.1, I.4). These are holistic ethics of "carnality" (positivity of sensibility).

b. The affirmation of life that conceives of human *"birth" as the negation of life* (birth as *ensomátosis* and origin of evil), and for that reason it is a negation of the value of terrestrial and corporeal life, and that sees empirical death as the birth of true life (mythical immortality of the soul as return to the unity of the cosmos). This is the path of the so-called Indo-Europeans, among others (see §I.2). These are the dualist ethics of the "soul" (positivity) and of the "body" (negativity).

Thesis 7

I will distinguish between:

a. *Material* categories, those that originate and are used by a historical "ethical life" (for example, that of "alterity" or "exteriority" in the Egyptian-Mesopotamian world, §I.1). There are metaphorical categories of the world of quotidian life and the concrete vision of such a world (*Weltanschauung*).

b. Categories *formally* philosophical, those that are constructed by a methodical, philosophical, and rational discourse. (For example, the category of "alterity" was perhaps constructed philosophically and formally for the first time by Emmanuel Levinas in the middle of the twentieth century. Before, it had a material function in metaphorical, quotidian, mythical, or religious use, which was not strictly philosophical.)

Thesis 8

I propose that there are two paradigms of Modernity, in light of conceptual necessity and to achieve greater expository clarity.

a. The "*Eurocentric* paradigm of Modernity" (universally accepted, and which has an authorized exponent in Weber), which holds that Europe, due to an intrinsic superiority, expands in the modern age over other cultures, because of some type of technological superiority (technological, military, political, economic, religious, etc.) accumulated during the Middle Ages.

b. The "global paradigm of Modernity," which proposes that Europe, without having any proper superiority (even if it had it in some particular aspect, this was not the cause of Modernity), *because of the discovery of Amerindia in 1492* had at its disposition a geopolitical, economic, political, and cultural horizon that granted to it a *comparative advantage* (specifically over the Ottoman-Muslim and Chinese worlds). Henceforth and through the sixteenth and seventeenth centuries, Europe accumulated enough potential in order to overcome from the eighteenth century, and only from then on, the high Asiatic cultures. It is a Eurocentric mirage to "anticipate" to the European Middle Ages the evident European superiority (especially technological) over other peripheral cultures that was achieved in the eighteenth century. Europe certainly had superiority over Amerindia even in the fifteenth century (but not over the Ottoman-Muslim world or India, and, above all, not over China).

Thesis 9

I would like to distinguish clearly three phenomena:

a. *Origin of Modernity* (with Spain, beginning in 1492), insofar as the spread of the first "world system" gets under way.

b. *Crisis of the medieval paradigm* or of Europe as the secondary and peripheral culture of the Muslim world (which took place from 1492 and takes up the entire sixteenth century).

c. *Formulation of the new "modern theoretical paradigm"* that became explicit at the beginning of the seventeenth century (Galileo, condemned in 1616; Bacon, with the proposal for a new method in 1620; Descartes, who writes *Le discours de la méthode* in Amsterdam in 1536).

The majority of authors confuse the first moment (a) with the third (c), postponing the "origin of Modernity" until this last one or pushing it back as far as the Renaissance (fourteenth century), jumping over the Enlightenment (eighteenth century), and thus underscoring the "Eurocentric paradigm."

Thesis 10

The German "*Material*" (with "a") means "material," as "content" (*Inhalt*), which is opposed to "formal"; while "*materiell*" (with "e") means "material," of physical matter, which is opposed to, for example, "mental" or "spiritual." Marx's "materialism," obviously, is *Material* (with "a"), given that his problematics is that of an ethics of *content*. This was not the problematics of the "dialectical materialism" of nature (of Engels, or later Stalinism), which Marx never named in this way or dedicated any significant space to in his writings (Dussel 1985a, 36–37).

Thesis 11

In this ethics human survival or the "production, reproduction, and development of the human life of each ethical subject" (see §§3.5, 4.5, 5.1, and 5.2) will always be understood as the enunciation of the universal material criterion of ethics par excellence: the concrete human life of each human being as human life. This must be articulated in three moments:

 a. The moment of the *production* of human life at the levels of vegetative or physical, material (with "e" in German), and by means and *content* (with "a" in German) the higher functions of the mind (consciousness, self-consciousness, linguistic, valuing functions, with ethical freedom and responsibility, etc.), as a process that is continued in time by institutions through "reproduction" (historical, cultural, etc.). This is the horizon of practical-material reason. See thesis 17.11.
 b. The moment of the *reproduction* of "*human* life," through institutions and cultural values: human life of the historical systems of ethical life that are motivated by reproductive drives. See theses 17.4–17.7, 17.9, and especially 17.12. This is the horizon of "reproductive reason" (see figure 13, level 3 [245]).
 c. The moment of the development of this human life within the framework of the institutions or reproductive-historical cultures of humanity. Evolution or growth has given way to historical development. But, in addition, in critical ethics (chapters 4–6), the pure reproduction of an ethical system that prevents its "development" will require a transforming or critical liberating process. See thesis 17.8 and, especially, 17.13. This is the horizon of critical-ethical reason (figure 13, level 4).

 I will not therefore distinguish in this text between mere survival or material physical reproduction (eating, drinking, being in good health), and cultural, scientific, aesthetic, mystical, and ethical development. In *Ethics of Liberation*, the phrase "production, reproduction, and development" of the human life of the ethical subject will "always" refer not only to vegetative or animalistic aspects, but also to the "superior" aspect of the mental functions and the development of human life and human culture. The phrase indicates an a priori material criterion (in chapter 1 I deal with the question of ethical-originary reason). This criterion is anterior to every ontological or ruling cultural order (preoriginary ethical reason, a question dealt with in chapter 4). In this last case, a posteriori, it also fulfills the function of a critical material criterion of ethical judgments, whether they concern descriptive pronouncement or facts, or the cultural order or system of ethical life that are given as totality.

The "self-preservation" of the system will end up opposing the reproduction of human life.

Thesis 12

I will use the terms "value" (and "valorization") to refer to the position of *mediation as mediation* or that which is compatible with the criterion of truth, of survival, or the reproduction and development of the life of the human subject. Something "has" *value* in a weak sense, as (a) a sensory mediation (for an animal, and for this reason neurologists speak of "evaluation" by animals); and in a strong sense (b) a properly practical ethical-rational mediation (b1: universally, as a practical rational judgment of the object, or statement from the perspective of the possibility of the reproduction and development of human life; or b2: particularly, as cultural values). Ethical "values," in the first case, conceptually categorized (one has a concept of a "value"), *hierarchized* (in light of the greater or lesser compatibility, whether a basic need or not, of the reproduction-development of the life of the human subject), serve to evaluate the possibility of a medium, object, norm, act, institution, system of ethical life, and so on, in conformity or as a condition of the fulfillment of the indicated criterion of reproduction and development of human life. To "evaluate" is to know how to situate within a practical plexus, in a hierarchical order (or greater or lesser compatibility) the "possibilities" insofar as they are mediations for human life.

Thesis 13

I distinguish throughout the entire text (see especially §§3.5, 4.5, and 5.1–2) some words that may be confused:

a. "Practical truth" (*alétheia praktiké*). This is the *material content* of the normative ethical statements. Practical truth links to such statements, but does not constitute the "valid." This term is often confused with the "good."

b. The "valid" (*gültig*): this is never the "just." "Validity" (*Gültigkeit*) is the *formal* moment par excellence. It links to "practical truth" but is not defined in opposition to the "good" or "goodness."

c. The "good" or "goodness" (*agathón, das Gute*), "goodness claim." This is the practical *unity* of the act or praxis *factibly* fulfilled, which is always made up of a material content and has undergone a formal procedure, thus constituting ethical life. The good makes a "goodness claim" [*bondad*]; it opposes "evil." It does not oppose the "just" or the "valid," instead it subsumes them thus moving to a different level. The "goodness claim" is the synthesis of "practical truth," the "validity claim," and the "feasibility claim," as a real composite that includes the moments (a) and (b) and a process that fulfills the requirements of ethical feasibility (c).

d. The "just" proceeds from justice (*dikaiosyne, Gerechtigkeit*). "Just" (*right*) is used mistakenly (by John Rawls and Jürgen Habermas, for example) as that which is opposed to the "good," since "justice" can be formal (Habermas) or material (Rawls's second principle). I will never use it as a formal moment (in such a case I will use "valid").

e. "Rightness" (*orthotes, Richtigkeit*), as in the case of "rightness claim" (Habermas). This can be material (conformity with the customs or material values) or formal (conformity with the formal rules of consensus).

f. "Right" (*orthós, richtig*). We should use "right" as the correct and never as the "just." The term is very ambiguous, and therefore it is better to use "valid" (if it concerns the formal aspect) or "practical truth" (for the material aspect), reserving "right" for conforming with customs, or with all the drives or emotions (see thesis 17). One may speak of a "right" drive when the drive maintains conformity with the rational requirements of (a) and (b).

Thesis 14

Some types of material or "content" ethics, which are generally reductive:

a. Subjective material ethics (utilitarianism, etc.).

b. Material ethics reconstructive of history and culture (communitarianism, with Aristotelian and Hegelian traces).

c. Symbolic material ethics of culture (Scheler, Hartmann, Husserl, but equally Nietzsche, or in the intuitionism of numerous analytical axiologists of language, such as G. E. Moore).

d. Ontological-existential material ethics (Heidegger et al.).

e. Material-economic ethics (subjective-objective institutional and historical), such as that of Marx.

f. Material ethics that proposes a material universal principle as reproduction and development of human life (Hinkelammert, implicit in Marx and in some vitalists).

Thesis 15

Some formal ethics:

    a. Kant's transcendental morality and that of posterior Kantianism.

    b. The metaethics of the analysis of descriptive and normative statements of different types (analytical ethics); intuitionism of Moore, the emotivism of Stevenson, Ayer's ethics, and Hare's, etc. (MacIntyre 1966, 22 ff.; Moore 1968, 240–59; MacIntyre 1981; Habermas 1983; here §§3.1–2).

    c. Rawls's morality of procedural liberalism.

    d. Discourse ethics (Apel, Habermas, Wellmer).

Thesis 16

Some critical ethics:

    a. Out of political economy (Marx).

    b. Out of German philosophies and social sciences of the beginning of the twentieth century (the first Frankfurt school).

    c. Out of the affective and instinctual level (Schopenhauer, Nietzsche, Freud).

    d. Out of phenomenological thought, specifically Heideggerian (Levinas).

    e. In the face of the macrostructural theories of modern subjectivity (Foucault).

    f. In the face of Modernity (the postmodern).

  These are the critical ethics (presented in chapter 4) of the ruling systems (economic, rationalist, cultural, etc.). Each type of formal system of domination determines the type of critique.

Thesis 17

Some preliminary definitions: "With Freud against Freud" it is necessary to find a categorical framework that will allow us to interpret what is pathological, which Freud tries to explain with the "death principle," Nirvana, and the death drives, thus placing as foundation the instincts of life, which are divided into: (1) instincts of self-preservation (or reproduction of life), and (2) instincts of pleasure. Against formalist rationalism it is necessary to recuperate this libidinal dimension without discarding the rational. The "principle of reality" has its proper consistency and it is not possible to discard. The same should be said of the superego that is the "moral conscience," which is situated in the psychic apparatus and serves as a bridge to social institutions. The topology, economic and instinctual, needs to be broadened, and not be unnecessarily simplified.

Thesis 17.1: In the insects and lower mammalians *there is no consciousness* properly said; in some superior mammals or other mammals with highly developed brains there is consciousness but never full linguistic self-consciousness. The animal has no libido properly said; it is neither self-responsible nor free. In animals, instincts are specific, and necessarily regulated by the species, although sometimes there may be individual learning. There can be no libidinal repression because there is no spontaneity of the instincts or cultural institutions.

Thesis 17.2: Only in corporeality and the human brain is there libido, properly said. The metaphor of the primitive horde (the original father, his ritual killing by his sons or brothers, etc.) is illusory because at the origin there was a minimal degree of self-conscious libidinal spontaneity and therefore minimal possibility of repression, institutional memory, etc. At the origin there is need and no freedom, no libido, the impossibility of any repression whatsoever, and least of all paradisiacal happiness. Paradise is in the future, in a freer world, which struggles more against surplus repressions; it must, unfortunately, impose civilizing repressions never before experienced. If there is a "qualitative progress," it is in growing complexity, tension, and contradiction that are ever more difficult to control.

Thesis 17.3: The minimal appearance of spontaneity, but not of the libidinal-instinctual type that *sunders the psychic apparatus* and that allows also the beginning of the appearance of minimal psycho-social-historical institutions, also at their origin, which begin slowly to replace the structures of specific instincts. The growth of libidinal spontaneity is growth in the institutional complexity of the superego. Repression or the civilizing discipline of the superego grow in correspondence with the growth in libidinal spontaneity through the growing complexity of the brain, due to development in the cortex of phenomena such as consciousness, self-consciousness, language, or cultural history.

Thesis 17.4: Civilizing repression by the libidinal apparatus is proper to *Homo sapiens* and allows the permanence and slow transformation or substitution of specific animal instincts by cultural ones. For this reason, human libidinal instincts of self-preservation, of pleasure, and every type of aggressiveness and defense are different from those of animals.

Thesis 17.5: The phenomenon of *sociohistorical repressive domination* produces psychic "disturbance" in the libido proper to the civilized human being. The human being of modern culture suffers disturbances never before observed (e.g., the dramatic crisis of adolescence), which are proper to a civilization that, by making each subject individually responsible in the responsible and free resolution of his or her existence, and in allowing libidinal freedom, demands of it that it confront an enormous apparatus of dominating repression (modern European civilization as criticized by Freud, Horkheimer, or Marcuse).

Thesis 17.6: The instincts of pleasure or *éros* (as defined by Freud) ought to be accepted. The death instincts are properly defined within the structural pathology of Western-modern civilization with its repressive-domination of the libido (surplus repression); they should not be situated at the level of "normality," "humanity," human "nature," or similar because they are fundamental to a historical socio-civilizing pathology.

Thesis 17.7: The Freudian death instincts or death principle enter into play as "totalization" of the systems that repress the *instincts of life*. When a system closes upon itself, the instincts of self-preservation (which seek their own safety) reverse the atavistic phobia toward death, which inhibits the ability to confront pain; this pain is evaded (by the memory of failed acts) within the social institutions that postpone the immediate pain, requiring in its stead rigid discipline (the postponement of desire), which produces a certain repression of the libido. Punishment, conscious and anticipated disciplinary pain (domesticated, like the vaccine that produces antibodies) that is exercised over those who do not fulfill reasonable institutional norms in order to prevent death (given that this does not allow any proof: who dies, dies, and cannot learn for the next occasion), impresses upon the superego the consciousness of guilt: remembrance of pain inflicted as punishment, as a lesson and as the always imminent possibility of death. Punishment-guilt is a social institution that as such must be administered in such a way that it does not produce greater repression or trauma (like vaccines): it should be only an illness produced in order to prevent death. Its excess also produces sickness (no longer being able to control the intolerable tension). This is extreme or pathological culpability. The instincts of self-preservation or security reproduce life, giving it security and permanence. They repress in a gentle way. Their pathology is to want to reach absolute security by vanquishing death through heroic suicide (a desire of death, in which the healthy phobia of death transforms into its opposite: love of dying, the necrophilia of the death principle). But they can also be sadomasochistic, as actions that claim to vanquish pain by self-inflicting it. It is necessary to differentiate sadomasochism in the mere reproduction of the principle of creative pleasure.

Thesis 17.8: The *instincts of pleasure* or of life uninhibit the confrontation with pain in order to reach the objective of happiness. Instincts of pleasure allow the development of life, of the psychic apparatus, of historical institutions. They are also historical creation. Their pathologies are produced when— wanting to achieve the *necessary security* of pleasure, and since this requires to know how to confront pain in order to reach it—the shortest path is that of the masochist, who directly obtains pleasure in his or her pain (against the instinct of individual self-preservation); or, in the pain of the Other, the path of the sadist (against the principle of communitarian self-preservation). Analogously, suicide (in a different way, as in reproduction) is a pathology: the claim is to reach immediate and perfect pleasure, in the case of the suicidal hero (who in reality is not a hero, but someone who seeks his or her own pleasure in a supposed "heroism": the heroism of the extreme left or anarchism; pleasure of the perfect accomplishment of a duty that is fulfilled before a culpable ethical conscience, a deformed superego, who acts against ethical-real feasibility).

Thesis 17.9: The instincts of self-preservation engage in solidarity,[2] among other possibilities, with the victims of its own institutions created by these instincts for the reproduction of life itself. Victims are a contradiction that disorient the instincts: they are an effect of the phobia of pain and death (of the institutions), but are victims who suffer and die because of institutions that were created in order to prevent suffering and to postpone death. Who recognizes in the victim another ethical subject and assumes ethical-libidinal responsibility for him or her uninhibits having to confront pain (supersedes the instincts of *individually* self-referent self-preservation), and confronts in community the danger of being unfeeling toward victims themselves,[3] and inhibits *his or her* instincts of egoistic pleasure (which allows this individual to confront pain on behalf of the Other). The pathology at this level is a sadism that takes pleasure in the pain of the Other (against the instincts of *communitarian* self-preservation), since it achieves pleasure not by evading the pain of the Other but by producing it. The sadist presents a social danger to the life of the community, which is also the beginning of collective suicide.

Thesis 17.10: Still to be assessed is everything that refers to "resistance" (in the face of an attack) and "aggressiveness" in the face of a need, danger, and pain, and in the end, death. The instincts of resistance pair up with those of self-preservation, and the instincts of aggressiveness with those of pleasure. Instincts of resistance "support" with fortitude in order to prevent death or to confront pain; instincts of aggressiveness "assault" in order to supersede pain and to reach what is necessary for life (not necessarily pleasure).

Thesis 17.11: The material-ethical principle of life is closely related to, specifically, the moment of the *production* of life (with respect to the instincts of pleasure, still undifferentiated), and with truth that hides behind the danger present in the quest for what is required or necessary for human life.

Thesis: 17.12: The moral-formal principle of intersubjectivity enunciates a direct relation to the *reproduction* of life (with respect to the instincts of self-preservation as institutional security), and to validity that secures not falling into the *error* that kills.

Thesis 17.13: The critical-ethical principle has a direct relation to the development of human life in general and to the reproduction of the life of the victims (and for this reason, also with respect to the instincts of future communitarian self-preservation), as a requirement of the correction of surplus repression that may be suicidal for the entire community. It is *qualitative or progressive or creative development*—in Bergson's or Marx's sense. *It is the ethical moment par excellence.* It transforms educationally the superego, constituting a "sensibility" open to new ethical requirements of renewed life. The superego is necessary, but it must be an innovator and creator; there is no more radical and concrete possibility of criticism than assuming responsibility for the victims of the ethical system itself. This is the true part of the theoretical positions of Nietzsche and Freud.

Thesis 17.14: "Normality" is not a return to productive integration of oneself into a society free of repression, as Erich Fromm would seem to indicate.

Nor is it to remain in the quasi-anarchical position of Freud himself, of in-validating negatively, without a solution the civilizing process itself (*Civiliza-tion and Its Discontents*). Without admitting neo-Freudian revisionism, and preserving the critical thread in Freud and Marcuse, it is necessary to redefine the categorical framework in such a way that a critical view is allowed and that nonetheless opens the "feasible" possibility of "possible" human exis-tence (of the necessary institutions, of the human psyche and the necessary liberation when intolerable situations are reached under the empire of the death principle). In order to achieve this, it is necessary to indicate that "nor-mality" is knowing how to manage *tension, the inevitable contradiction*, always attempting a "certain" *always precarious equilibrium*: (a) between the instincts of self-preservation that seek their institutional security, (b) the instincts of pleasure that risk suffering in order to reach a new state of happiness. The in-stincts of communitarian self-preservation must know how to correct the in-evitable civilizing discipline so that not everything turns into domination, into so many excesses of avoidable and pathological institutions that, because they are unnecessary surplus-repression, turn unmanageable, socially (resulting in institutional injustices) or personally (mental illnesses).

Thesis 17.15: In this way no institutional system may present itself under the claim of being nonrepressive; instead, it will have to judge when it is intoler-ably dominating, in order to transform itself (partially or totally, a task that Freud says he is not called to in *Civilization and Its Discontents*).

Thesis 17.16: The psychoanalyst can then face "patients," those who are not able to manage the historical-institutional contradictions with their own li-bidinal psychic apparatus, which is tension with the instincts that attempt *nec-essary* functions but that easily turn pathological (into their opposites), given the complexity and lack of learning (individual and social) in the management of their and the communitarian libidinal structure. To "heal" the "sick" and to restore them to "normality," does not mean to *liberate them from all repres-sions and to return them to pristine libidinal freedom*. Such a pristine libidinal freedom did not exist in animals, either, or any human being. To "heal" and to return to "normality" is simply a practical-ethical knowing that allows being able to manage with *some success*, not exempt from failures that may be over-come, one's own libidinal apparatus, to a degree that would allow one's own life in the life of the community (libidinal, cultural, political, economic, etc.). The "line" that divides the "healthy" from the "ill" depends on so many fac-tors that it is a priori impossible to define it a priori, qualitatively and quanti-tatively. It is a question of allowing libidinal subjectivity to establish relations with the Other without having to rely any longer on the therapist or with the "therapeutical community"[4] (which is what is desirable: as with Alcoholics Anonymous, for example), knowing that the "normal" community is partly sick because of its tensions, but has therapeutic resources, such as that of the ancient wisdom of "common sense" (which may also be "sociohistorically sick") that we must know how to use "normally."

Thesis 18

I will differentiate among the following "claims."

a. The *intelligibility*, or meaningfulness, claim (the theoretical claim, in its analytical sense) is fulfilled when a proposition may be known, be conceptualizable, and be understood because it fulfills its definition (Tarski's "truth").

b. The *practical truth* claim of practical-material reason, in the sense of the present work as is presented in chapter 1: truth (always measured linguistically and intersubjectively) with reference to an objective reality as mediation of the reproduction of human life, or insofar as it is constituted from the perspective of the life-death criterion.

c. The *theoretical truth* claim of theoretical reason (understanding, or Kantian reason), inasmuch as it is an abstraction from the practical situation, and makes abstract reference to reality (always linguistically and intersubjectively mediated).

d. The *validity* claim proper, of discursive reason, in the sense of the reference to intersubjectivity, and not formally as truth.

e. The *rightness* claim, or claim of practical reason, insofar as it is evaluative, with reference to either cultural and ethical values, or norms.

f. The *ethical feasibility* claim of instrumental reason: the technological dimension, taking into account the material and formal ethical principles. Strategic feasibility is located at the political level (as the relation of the means to successful ends).

g. The *goodness* claim of practical reason (which synthesizes material, formal, strategic-instrumental rationality), as the practical position before a norm, act, institution, or system of ethical life, insofar as it fulfills the required ethical conditions (through an adequate application of the six principles articulated in the present work), and being able to give reasons for having accomplished said conditions.

h. The *liberation or critical transformation* claim of reality, of critical-strategic reason, which subsumes all prior claims from the perspective of the negatedness of the victims and with a view toward liberation.

Sais: Capital of Egypt

[405] I would like to describe here three short themes that emerged during my third trip to Egypt,[1] which took place in December 1994: (1) the so-called philosophy of Memphis; (2) chapter 125 of the *Egyptian Book of the Dead*; and (3) some commentaries regarding the city of Sais, the metropolis of the Athenian colony in the region which helped open up millenarian Egypt to the Greek periphery.

The Philosophy of Memphis

Memphis, in Greek (*Mennofré* in Egyptian), was probably founded by the legendary Menes, its first monarch, sometime before 3000 BC, and was responsible for the construction of the first great pyramids, not far from the place where they were ultimately erected. It reached its acme during the Third Dynasty (around 2700 BC) during the reign of the pharaoh Djeser. In the eighteenth dynasty (from 1580 BC onward) it was still the most cosmopolitan city in the Middle East. The city continued to be the religious capital of Egypt until the reign of the Roman emperor Theodosius, who did not proscribe the Coptic cults[2] until AD 389. The "philosophy of Memphis," whose mythical content should be situated at the beginning of the fourth millennium before Christ, is reflected in a text known from a version carved into granite[3] at the temple of Ptah in the days of King Shabaka (700 BC). According to James Breasted, "There is in the British Museum a sad deteriorated stone which in the opinion of this author contains the most ancient formulation of a philosophical vision of the world [*philosophical Weltanschaung*]."[4] Breasted concludes his reading and commentary by noting that "the Greek tradition regarding the origins of its philosophy in Egypt without a doubt contains more truth than it has been accorded in recent times."[5] In effect, the whole text is devoted to exploring the attributes of Ptah, the great god of Memphis: "Ptah, the great,[6] is the heart and tongue of the gods.[7] The Power of his heart and his tongue come into existence from within him [Ptah]."[8] The "heart" is Horus; the "tongue" is Thot. The "heart" (*leb* in Hebrew) is "life" (*Ankh*), the vital energy, the concreteness of the corporeality, flesh (*basar* in Hebrew), the "content" of the "tongue." In contemporary terms we could describe Horus as associated with the underlying affective drives and motor impulses, and with the ethical-practical consciousness that punctually and self-consciously "remembers" each act of the life of a human being and which is judged by Osiris— since it is also the "heart" of the dead that is placed on the scales of judgment in order to take a measure of its good works. Horus is "the creator of all works, of every artifact, of what is made by the hand, of what grows; what is inherent in the movement of every member in accordance with the mandate, and with the word."[9] We could say then that Horus is also akin to Ptah, recalling what Schopenhauer said: the Being is Will, Potency, Power. Ptah is Horus. But Ptah is equally Thot, the "tongue." This tongue is the origin of the Hebrew *dabar* and of the Greek *logos*, without a doubt—both cultures, the Hebrew and the Greek, are cultures of the periphery, of a secondary character, and heirs of Egyptian philosophical and ontological discoveries: "He [Thot] is the tongue, which repeats the designs of the heart.[10] Oh Thot . . . you fulfill my needs with bread and beer, and guard my mouth when I speak."[11] The "tongue" is the word, but the word understood as a "mandate" or "order," a practical, creative, productive word. It is that practical reason which has "projects," the thoughts that the architect[12] conceives in his or her mind before the structure has been built: "The Word is the creator of every food that can be transformed into an offering [to the gods]; the creator of that which is loved and that which is hated; the giver of life to the one who diffuses peace and of death to the one who is guilty.[13] It is Thot, the one who is imbued with wisdom, who is identical with Ptah, after he has created all things, every hieroglyphic, when the gods and villages have been formed."[14] He is the creative, organizing Word, the judge of the cosmos: "criterion (*criterion*)," law, and tribunal.

   Let these short reflections serve to indicate that it is necessary to break out of the Hellenocentric Prussian tunnel in philosophy, in order to open ourselves up to the wide horizon of philosophical suggestions of the cultures that humanity has developed, in all of their plurality and diversity. My sense is that Egypt, perhaps more successfully than the Greeks and the moderns, produced an ethics that was more balanced between the material (Horus) and the discursive (Thot), and that this might be capable of teaching us something. In the end, both the Greeks and the Semites (especially the Hebrews, the Christians, and the Muslims) are their descendants.

Chapter 125 of *The Egyptian Book of the Dead*

The Egyptian Book of the Dead is a collection of discrete texts, which, on papyri and in various different orders, were placed with the dead to serve to "re-call" their acts in life at the moment of Osiris's final judgment.[15] Osiris, after being crowned as the regional prince (he may originally have been a histori-cal figure), is murdered by his brother Set, who cuts his body up into pieces[16] and scatters them in different places, including the River Nile (his head ends up in Abydos). Isis recovers the parts of Osiris's body, and Anubis brings these parts together as one body and mummifies it. Set also attempts to kill his son Horus, son of Isis, who was Set's wife. Horus vanquishes his father (like a new Oedipus), and inherits the kingdom of Osiris. Meanwhile Osiris is resurrected in the afterlife. He has become thereby the first iconic figure of this kind to be raised from death and becomes the prototype for such a process, and the one who should be invoked by those seeking to emulate him. In the Ancient Em-pire the only persons who could be resurrected were pharaohs, high priests, and very notable personalities. The pyramids themselves embody the hope of an eternal "life."

During the Middle Period of the Empire (from 2060 BC), at the end of the eleventh dynasty, and following the period of anarchy that ensued in the wake of popular rebellions—motivated in part by the demand that the possibility of resurrection be extended to all, the possibility of resurrection becomes uni-versalized, but subject to the satisfaction of ethical demands made explicit in the *Book of the Dead*. *Ka*, the individual ethical consciousness, which has a memory and a sense of responsibility for its acts, a consciousness of an ethical-practical character, becomes recognized as the central component of the indi-vidual self (together with four other components).[17] This is the beginning of one of the most significant ethical myths in all of world history. Each indi-vidual subject, in life and later in death, in a completely individualized pro-cess,[18] has the ethical experience of bringing his or her life's work to fruition in light of the "judgment of Osiris" (all of this accompanied with an explicit self-consciousness, since the individual has "been seen" by an omniscient, in-corruptible, perfect, and internalized judge). And all of this within a context where it is assumed that "life" (*Anj* or *Ankh* in Egyptian) has been given indi-vidually by the gods to each human being, to be sustained eternally if the dead are found to be deserving of resurrection because of their good works. All the gods carry an *Ankh* (a kind of upside-down cross with a handle that enables the gods to grasp it) in their right hand.

I would like to highlight just a few aspects of the great ethical wealth of these texts, which relate directly to the central arguments of this book. My focus is on chapter 125 of the *Book of the Dead*. This long chapter is the ac-count of the presence of one of the dead in the great Hall of Maat (the Law of the universe), where the dead are brought to judgment in order to determine whether or not they possess the merits necessary for resurrection as "Osiris N."

(the dead have a name of their own). The chapter begins with the introduction of the one who is to be judged, followed by the familiar defenses presented by the subject of the judgment ("I did not commit any evil against human beings. I did not mistreat any person. . . .").[19] At a key moment of the text we read the following list of ethical criteria, which the dead person articulates *as the basis* for his or her publicly proclaimed claims to resurrection in the great Hall of Maat: "I satisfied God, providing him with what he desired. [1] I gave bread to the hungry, [2] water to the thirsty, [3] clothed the naked, and [4] provided a vessel for the shipwrecked."[20] And the gods, seeking to discern an individual identity facing them, ask: "'Who are you?' they say to me. 'What is your name?' they ask."[21] All of this indicates to us the depth of the concept of personal responsibility in Egyptian ethics, which will be inherited by Semitic thought—but not by that of Greece (with its insistence upon the universal immortality of the soul)—and through them into Jewish, Christian, Muslim, and modern thought.

One of the many historical resonances of the Egyptian contribution to universal ethics that I have cited above can be discerned twenty-three centuries after the origins of the Memphis school, in a Hebrew text included in Isaiah 58, where participants in the group of the third Isaiah write: "The fast that I desire is as follows: . . . to set free the oppressed, to break all the seals, [1] to break bread with the hungry, [4] to give shelter to the homeless poor,[22] [3] to clothe the naked, and not to close myself off from my own kind." All of the text of chapter 58 in Isaiah speaks to us of the demands of a concrete bodily reality that is recognized in all of its dignity.

Seven centuries after the text in Isaiah—more than twenty centuries ago, from our perspective, but itself almost thirty centuries after the classic origin of the Egyptian tradition in Memphis, at the moment of origin of that Egyptian city, some fifty centuries ago—the founder of Christianity referred once again to the ethical criteria set forth by Osiris as a basis for the Final Judgment with a view toward enabling the "resurrection of the dead." The great Hall of Maat is now a space close to Jerusalem. All of humanity is publicly present in the face of each individual human life that is subject to judgment. I am referring to Matthew 25. Instead of Ptah or Osiris, now it is the "Son of Man" who occupies the seat of judgment: "[1] Because I was hungry and you fed me, [2] I was thirsty and you gave me drink, [4] I was a stranger and you gave me hospitality, [3] I was naked and you clothed me." As can be observed, the logical order of the *Book of the Dead* (which will be referred to both by Christians and by Muslims as the *Book of Life*, because it contains the written record of every work that has been performed in the course of each human life) is more correct than that in the book of Matthew, since the latter makes it appear as if it made sense to clothe the body before putting a roof above it. In any case it is compelling to consider the close relationship in thinking between the founder of Christianity with the depths of Egyptian tradition—might this not have something to do with those accounts that claim that he was in Egypt for some period of time, while in flight from the political persecution of the Jewish government, which collaborated with the Roman Empire? (See also table 14.)

Table 14. The Order of the Four Ethical-Material Demands in Three Texts

Ethical Demand	Book of the Dead, Chap. 125	Isaiah 58:7	Matthew 25:35
1. To feed the hungry	first	first	first
2. To provide water to the thirsty	second	—	second
3. To give clothing to the naked	third	third	fourth
4. To provide a vessel or a roof for the stranger or the foreigner	fourth	second	third

It would therefore seem as if the text in Matthew has a closer relationship with the *Book of the Dead* than with the Hebrew book of Isaiah, judging both by the number of ethical demands included in each text (four in the two of them, and three in Isaiah), and because of their order (one variation in Matthew and two in Isaiah).

This entire book is an ethical-philosophical reflection regarding the meaning of these texts, which are perhaps the most *critical* ancient texts in all of humanity's memory. The ethics of liberation has no desire to appear to be some kind of novelty. It wishes instead to appear as the updated version of a millenarian tradition that has been trodden underfoot by the cynicism of globalizing capitalism, which struts about as if it were the maximum exponent of science and reason, when in truth it amounts to a decadent ethics of irrationality which is deaf to the pain of its victims.

The City of Sais: Founder of Athens

I came to Sais from Cairo, by train via Tantah, and from there to Basyun in the Nile delta by bus, heading north, until I arrived by taxi at a small dusty village called Sá-el-Hajar (or Hagar) in Arabic (Sais), which recalls little of its ancient splendor, close to old canals, somewhat to the south of the place where Champollion in 1822 found the Rosetta Stone, engraved with writing in Egyptian hieroglyphics, in the Greek phonetic alphabet and in demotic script (a simplified form of Coptic cursive writing). Nothing remains of Sais's former grandeur. Sais was capital of all Egypt during the twenty-sixth dynasty (from 666 to 524 BC, when the Persian invasion takes place) and was dedicated to the goddess Neith (whom the Greeks of Athens called Pallas Athena, but who at this time was an Egyptian goddess). Sais was a city that had already been named since the earliest dynasties, whose sailors and merchants founded Athens in Greece, one of its many Mediterranean colonies. Sametic I, son of Nicaeus, opened up the Egyptian market to the Greeks in 663 BC and employed them as mercenaries. In 568 BC Greek settlers were permitted to enter Memphis and the delta city of Naucratis was founded, so that the Greeks could engage in commerce. Sais existed until the fifteenth century AD, by then as a Muslim city. In 333 BC its residents received Alexander as their liberator from the Persians. From there Alexander went directly to the desert region west of the Nile to worship at the sanctuary of the Egyptian god Ammon, venerated as the most important god among the Macedonian Greeks. Of course Dionysus, who was so appreciated by Nietzsche, was an Egyptian god, but so was Apollo. Plato came to Sais, and it may be that his visit served him directly as inspiration when he wrote *The Republic*.

This is also where the Greeks studied mathematics, geometry, and astronomy, and where the pre-Socratics studied philosophy and many other disciplines, among which should not be forgotten what they learned from the mystical experiences of those who were dedicated exclusively to a contemplative life here (the "leisure" [*skholé*] that was so admired by Aristotle). In 311 BC it was governed by Ptolemy I, at the beginning of Hellenic domination. Sais, the ancient imperial capital, was thereby transformed from a metropolitan center of empire into the colony of one of its former colonies. I was there on December 9, 1994, with a spirit of non-Hellenocentric veneration, to remember that Greece was not the origin of the "love for wisdom" we have come to know as "philosophy"—that love that was certainly learned from Egypt, and by Athens from Sais, a center of African civilization that had strong influence from Bantu cultures, as well as those of the Camites and Semites, and none at all from the cultures of Indo-Europe, the West, or Europe.

Notes

Preface

1. See the introduction [1–8] and thesis 1 in appendix 1 [404]. All of the text of *Ethics* is organized by sections numbered in brackets placed at the beginnings of paragraphs, in order to facilitate cross-references within the manuscript.

2. This must be a case of the "impotency of what-must-be [*Ohnmacht des Sollens*]" (Habermas 1992, 78 ff. His hopes ride instead on the coerciveness of the "Rule of Law" grounded in ethical-democratic legitimacy with validity in the face of the political community (see Habermas 1992, and specifically the postscript [1994] in the English translation, 1996, 463 ff.).

3. Dussel 1973.

4. "Center" and "periphery" are recurrent analytical categories throughout this work (see thesis 1 in appendix 1, and §I.5 in this book).

5. "Globality," as I employ the term, is not abstract "universality," as can be seen in thesis 2 [404] (all the numbered theses cited in the notes may be found in appendix 1).

6. My dialogue with K.-O. Apel began in Freiburg that same November.

7. Throughout this book the term "victim" is employed strictly as an analytical philosophical category.

8. We will return to this theme, but let me already highlight that 20 percent of the wealthiest people on this planet consume 82 percent of the income produced by humanity; the poorest 80 percent consume only 18 percent of what is left, and the poorest 20 percent consume only 1.4 percent of such wealth (see *Human Development Report 1992*, 35). Furthermore, rebellions of the "poor" such as those of the indigenous communities organized in the Zapatista National Liberation Army (EZLN) based in the region of Chiapas in southeastern Mexico (whose uprising began January 1, 1994) reveal the fissures in the dominant system, which is not monolithic block without contradictions.

9. It is in that context particularly that I sought to demonstrate the "positivity" of the poor, of the widow and the orphan, based upon their ontological

content, in the spirit of Heidegger and Levinas, with their "positivity" understood as exteriority. Now my emphasis is on the development of an ethics of principles that is critical in its reception of Kant but has an architecture constructed in his tradition, particularly in the wake of the impetus derived from my debate with Apel.

10. See Merleau-Ponty 1945, 496 ff.

Introduction

1. See Schelkshorn 1992, 57–64.

2. The terms "ethical" and "moral," which lately have acquired new semantic variations, already need clarifying. In my earlier work (Dussel 1970–80) "morality" meant a determination of praxis (in the totality as "ethical life," or in the light of a project of liberation), while "ethic" indicated the transcendental-critical level (of the same ontological project discerned from the exteriority of the Other). See appendix 1, thesis 4 [404]. (All numbered theses cited in these notes may be found in appendix 1.)

3. See chapter 4.

4. Kohlberg's levels 5 and 6 (Kohlberg 1981–84), Habermas's commentary (1983, 135), or Apel's attempt at a "postconventional" morality (Apel 1988), are "conventionally" European, in a system of "late" and modern capitalism, in terminal crisis, partly contractualist, partly "Eurocentric," and finally, liberal or social-democratic. This is to say, these moments that would be impossible without the "material" determination of their own culture. It is in this sense that Charles Taylor's proposal makes sense.

5. See thesis 2.

6. See thesis 5.

7. See, for example, MacIntyre 1966; Taylor 1989, 115 ff.

8. We must consider with care the difference between *ethical* and *moral* "universality" (see thesis 4, a and b), and accomplished "criticalness" (indicated in thesis 2 and thesis 4, e and f).

9. The systems of "ethical life" (*Sittlichkeiten*) native to the American continent connected with the stage III interregional system only at the end of the fifteenth century. This is a good place to indicate that by affirming this I do not advocate a "diffusionist" position (cf. Blaut 1993, 11 ff.), which proposes "centers" from whence cultures originated, or, on the other extreme, the position of the absolute independence of cultural origins. My thesis is intermediate: there is autonomous creation (especially in the Amerindian cultures, of Asiatic Paleolithic origin and with recent Polynesian influences), but at the same time connection (with the Asiatic-African-Mediterranean interregional system). Before the linkage of America to the indicated system, there was no creating center of culture, but instead a center of linkage (which, following the expansion of Alexander the Great, was located to the north of Persia or Mesopotamia). The first periphery properly speaking in world history will be Latin America from the end of the fifteenth century.

10. For a general bibliography, see, for example, Berr 1955; Brenner 1983; Cambridge 1970–89; Dussel 1983a, 103–212; Dussel 1996a; Frank and Gills 1992; Franke et al. 1965; Kern and Lehnen 1952–61; Mann 1961–65; Toynbee 1934–59; Weber 1963.

11. See thesis 4e and §5.2 [292]. In the Egyptian, Mesopotamian, or surrounding Semitic world, the categories of "alterity" or "exteriority" (see chapter 4) began to gestate *materially*. Now it would be necessary to *formalize* them philosophically (this at least was Emmanuel Levinas's and the philosophy of liberation's effort). That is to say, a proper "ethical-critical" category (in the already indicated level e of thesis 4) can in fact be "applied" in a *Lebenswelt* (*material* application, as I will call it), and still not have been constituted yet as a *formal* philosophical category.

12. See Dussel 1969 (where I dealt with the theme of this paragraph); Dussel 1983a, 113–22; and Dussel 1966, secs. 14–15. In addition, see Armour 1986; Sources Orientales 1961, 15–141.

13. There are three possible models of a history of philosophy (and of ethics): (1) the German romantic "Aryan model," which sets out from the Greeks and which has been imposed in all the contemporary histories of philosophy; (2) the "ancient model," which thinks that philosophy began with the African Egyptians (this was the opinion of Herodotus, Plato, and Aristotle, as we will see); (3) and the one that I will adopt as a "global model," which grants importance to Egypt and the Middle East, in order to deal with new historical materials against the Hellenocentric thesis, which is the point of departure for modern Eurocentrism, and that is the main object of this present criticism.

14. Consider the suggestive proposal made by André Gunder Frank on the antiquity of five thousand years of the world system (Frank and Gills 1992). I, too, already in some of my earliest works, have set out from a similar hypothesis, but for different reasons (Dussel 1966, secs. 14 ff.). I will speak of an interregional system (and this is a fundamental correction to Frank's denomination, because he confuses "world system," which only appears in 1492, with "interregional system," which is the one that is five thousand years old). The world system is not five thousand years old but only five hundred. See also Blaut 1992, with an excellent bibliography, and those of Frank, and Amin (see Amin 1974 and 1989), among others.

15. Diop 1974. Consider James 1954 and Bernal 1991; in addition, Gray 1989; Harding and Reinwald 1990; and Masolo 1994, 21 ff.

16. The "desert" will be the first *material* metaphorical category that indicates "exteriority" as such (see thesis 7). This is the "place" par excellence of the "outside" of the civilized world; it is the barbarian, savage, the strange; but also the sacred, what is worthy par excellence.

17. Cornevin and Cornevin 1964, 33.

18. It should be taken into account that we are speaking of about 3200 BC; that is to say, about twenty-seven centuries before Socrates, Plato, or Aristotle. More time transpired between this Egyptian origin of the first postmythical and quasi-philosophical "rationalizations" than will transpire later between Socrates and us (only twenty-four centuries).

19. "Black" (*kmt*), as I already indicated, means civilized; "red" (*desret*) means primitive, barbarian, the inhabitants of the Mediterranean, the race that is today called "white" (Harding 1990, 45 ff.).

20. See Bleeker 1973; Boylan 1992; Festugière 1944–53.

21. See Breasted 1901; Sandman-Holmberg 1946; Sethe 1928. Egy-ptian or Co-pto means "the worshippers of Ptah" (Egi-ptah or Co-ptah). See appendix 2 on the city of Sais [405].

22. On the Egyptian origin of philosophy, see Bernal 1991; James 1954.

23. *Thot* (Hermes) was for the Hellenes the word or verb of God, the Wisdom created before all the centuries of the *Book of Wisdom* among the Hebrews, the creating Word (*dabar*) of Yahwe, the word of the Gospel of John, but similarly the *logos* of future Greek philosophers. In other words, Thot will have an ethical-practical development in the Semitic thought and *theoretikós* in the Hellenic tradition. In addition, Thot creates the entire universe through the means of *four* pairs of gods (the *ogdonda*), just as in the Mexican Toltec wisdom the *four* Tezcatlipocas ("smoked mirrors" as opposed to the "transparent mirror" Tezcatlanextia) are the mediation of the originating "duality" (*ometeotl*; the "divine") and the "temporal" (*tlalticpac*). The reflections of the pre-Socratics are already present in the Egyptian wisdom.

24. Plato, *Phaedo*, 274 d.

25. Herodotus recognizes that "almost all of the names of the Greek gods have an Egyptian origin" (*Histories* II, 50 [Herodotus 1954, 150 and 169]. It is well known, for example, that the goddess Neith from the Egyptian city of Sais is the same as the goddess Athena, for whom Athens was named: "The temple of Athens was founded by the daughter of Danaos, who touched the isle (of Rhodes) during the voyage of the children of Egypt" (*Histories* II, 182 [Herodotus 1954, 201]).

26. The Egyptians made a first "rationalization" of the mythical world through a numerical philosophy (like the later *Kabbala* and the Quechuas and Aymaras in the Inca Empire). The mythical-quotidian is thought through meaningful "numbers." With Socrates there began another type of rationalization, the linguistic-semantic rationalization of the concept that was first definitively formalized in Aristotle's *Organum*.

27. Aristotle, *Metaphysics I*, bk. 1, 981b, 22–26.

28. Armour 1986, 162.

29. See thesis 6a in appendix 1.

30. The formula of this resurrection is given in the following way: "Let the orders given in my favor be bestowed upon Ra's [the Sun's] entourage during the setting of the Sun! This must be so because Osiris N. [a construction that permitted the proper and singular name of the empirically dead to be inserted here], which is also who I am, will be revived after death, as Re, each day [exactly the same belief held by the Aztecs as to Huitzilopochtli]. And if, in truth, Re is born the day before, it is Osiris N. [who is I as well] who is also resurrected. All men rejoice because Osiris N. is resurrected": *Book of the Dead*, chap. 3, 1989, 4). This resurrection was referred to as "the emergence in daylight and life after death" (ibid.).

31. The Hebrew *néfesh* is a similar principle; it should not be confused with the Greek *psyche* (Dussel 1969, 22 ff.). On the topic, see Faulkner 1985; Otto and Hirmer 1966.

32. *Book of the Dead*, chap. 125. Chapter 125 is one of the most venerable ethical texts in all of human history. See Drioton 1922. In it we already find a set of ethical-critical *material* (see thesis 6) categories of great importance.

33. Existence, interpreted as being "before a tribunal" that must declare the human being as "just" (as "justified": *mâa-kheru*), opens up the whole field of the discovery of an individual self-responsible ethical subject. See Sources Orientales 1961, 24.

34. Budge 1911. Osiris is the divinity, the rationalized myth upon which is built a critical ethics of carnal corporeality.

35. The concept of *basar* in Hebrew indicated the totality of the ethical subject and in no way only the "body" (*soma* in Greek, as we will see). We find ourselves at a highly creative level of ethical-critical *material* categories (Dussel 1974a).

36. These *material* categories and ethical-critical principles are present, more than ten centuries later, in the critical thought of Israel (Isaiah 57:7), and, later after almost twenty centuries, in primitive Christian thought (Matthew 25:35–44). These ethical-mythical texts have nothing intrinsically theological for their consideration by philosophers. They are elements of a historical "ethical life" (*Lebenswelt*) and nothing else. In any event, they will be elements of what will be later called *ethical life* of the Muslim world and Europe (see §I.4), with sacralizations, secularizations, and dualist conceptions, but, in the end, as the ultimate "point of reference" of the life-world (Charles Taylor would say *sources*). See appendix 2 [405].

37. See Mellaart 1967, where we can read that the tenth level of the city Catal Hüyük (close to Konya in contemporary Turkey) can be dated as far back as 6385 BC.

38. Lara Peinado 1994, 11 ff. Perhaps the first text that we have concerning justice with respect to the victims might be the following: "He freed indebted families and forgave their debts . . . vowing solemnly to Ningirsu that he would never subjugate the orphan and the widow to the powerful" (Law 27 of the *Reforms of Uruinimgina*, 24–25).

39. See Klengel 1977.

40. *Hammurabi Code* 1986, 3. Once again we can discover ethical-critical categories of already greater radicalness.

41. Centuries later these categories and ethical principles will be used in Israel (e.g., Isaiah 1:23: "They neither defend the orphan nor take up the cause of the widow"; and in Deuteronomy 10:18–19: "Do justice unto the orphan . . . give him food and clothing; love the immigrant"). The "exteriority" of the widow, the orphan, the poor, and especially of the *foreigner* and *immigrant*, as the ethical demands of hospitality in the desert required, is fundamental to these systems of ethical life.

42. *Hammurabi Code* 1986, 42. In Babylon, since proof of each sale and buy was documented (on tablets, thousands of which have been found in archives discovered in the desert), the widow, for example, could inherit from her husband, and not, as before, be forcibly dispossessed of the goods of her deceased husband; the same with the son of his father, and so on.

43. In this way the "affected oppressed," who did not know how to read, were made aware of their written rights (since the code was "written" in the slab of stone erected at the entrance of each city of the empire this gave a public character to the norm). Here we have an impressive degree of "rationalization" of ethical life: "To do justice to the oppressed, I have written my precious words on my stela" (ibid., 43).

44. Gottwald 1981, 389 ff.

45. This is another metaphorical *material* category: "Egyptian" means the "system" that subsumes the "victims" and "alienates" it with unjust "labors." All of these are categories that can be philosophically *formalized* (which is what an ethics of liberation does).

46. 1 Samuel 13:3.

47. I am therefore indicating that Exodus, a book that I take as a narrative

with ethical content to be treated philosophically, is already a "rationalization" of what we could call the *oppressed/oppressor theoretical model* as a point of departure of a process *of liberation*. The people of Israel, the Christians, and the Muslims, will reread (thus allowing this text to fulfill its historical function; what Ricoeur would call "*le travail du texte*") these narrative texts as a practical "Diagram" and ethical norm of action: "I brought you out of Egypt, from slavery" (Deuteronomy 5:6); "You are witnesses to everything that (was) done in Egypt *against the Pharaoh*" (Deuteronomy 29:1).

48. Exodus 1:13–14. The concept "work," "labor" (*'abodáh*) has a technical (nature-person relation) and ethical sense (worker, servant, slave) in Hebrew. It is a central ethical-economic concept in an ethics of liberation since it includes "carnality" and "economics."

49. Thesis 1 should not be forgotten.

50. On the topic of this section generally, see Dussel 1966, secs. 18–20; Dussel 1983a, 123–56; Dussel 1993c, chaps. 6–8. On the third column of the Neolithic revolution, see Dussel 1966, sec. 16, 120 ff.: "The Pre-Aryan Hindu."

51. Dussel 1966, sec. 19, 122 ff.

52. Alfred Weber (1963) claims to articulate a world history of cultures without making any reference to the Amerindian Neolithic high cultures. For this reason, next to these four great "columns" of Afro-Asiatic cultures (Egypt, Mesopotamia, India, and China), I have added at the very least two more: the Mesoamerican Aztec-Mayan and the Incan Peru.

53. In any event, this reminds us of the second Taoist principle: "That essence [the Tao] had two immanent determinations, the *yin* concentration and the *yang* expansion which became manifest externally one day in the sensory forms of the sky (*yang*) and of the earth (*yin*)" (Lao Tzu, *Tao-Te Ching*, bk. 1, chap. 1; Wieger 1950, 18).

54. The Aztec "philosophers" were known as *tlamatinime* (León-Portilla 1979, 63–82).

55. "Divine Duality" (ibid., 154–78). Another representation: *Quetzal* (divine, beautiful feathers) *coatl* ("twin" or serpent). That is to say, this is another denomination of the "divine duality" but now symbolic, of the abstract nonsymbolic concept of *omeoteotl* ("duality" as such).

56. All of this is organized with dual symmetry, the Cuscan high (*Hanan*) and the low (*Hurin*), the four parts (two by two) of the empire: "Everything that belongs to the left is linked to the masculine, like being the Sun, or Imaymana Virachocha, and everything that is of the right is the feminine, like being the moon or Tocapo Viracocha" (Kusch 1970, 196–211).

57. See Krickeberg et al. 1961.

58. See López Austin 1990, 68.

59. This is true among the Aztecs as well as the Mayas or Incas (with minor variations). Humans did not inhabit the "four" prior worlds in time as such.

60. For the Aztecs the "human space" or terrestrial are made up of four levels: below the waters, on the earth, and on the moon and the sun). Over the four human levels there were nine heavens (astronomical-mythical). Beneath the waters there were nine lower worlds.

61. The hermeneutics of dreams is a universal practice in America, from Alaska to Patagonia. Among the Aztecs it reaches a high degree of rationalization. This is dealt with in a "book of dreams" (*temicámatl*), where the diverse types of dreams are codified and a universal content is assigned to them.

62. See the theme of the "negation of a nongeneralizable norm" (Wellmer 1986).

63. *Florentine Codex*, book 3, 67 (León-Portilla 1979).

64. Literally, "the ancient rule of life."

65. *Macehualli*: in Nahuatl, the human being deserved by Quetzalcóatl (León-Portilla 1979, 384).

66. This refers to the interregional system II. I have studied this question in detail in other works (Dussel 1966, secs. 25–30; 1975; 1974b, 105–37; 1973, 21–44; 1983a, 157–62), and for that reason I do not elaborate here. When I speak of "Indo-European," I want to indicate no more than a mere horizon of geographical contacts, mainly commercial (and religious-ritualistic), which produce linguistic contamination (many words in different languages have roots in common), and not to an "Indo-European" language, with a culture, and certainly not to a race or to a civilization proper. This is the phenomenon of the constitution of what I call the interregional system II (see table 1). China (and therefore Confucianism and Taoism) was also influenced by this geographical region, but it does not strictly form part of this cultural type.

67. See thesis 6b.

68. Beckwith 1987; Hambly 1966; Krader 1963; Stein 1974; consider also figure 1.

69. The first of these received the same denomination in different languages: Deipátyros among the Illyrians, Zeus pater among the Greeks, Jupiter (Diêspi-ter) among the Romans, and Dyaus pitah in Sanskrit. This is a celestial and divine being, "father" of the "day" (*dyâm* in Vedic, *diem* in accusative Latin), of light, "and being" as *tó fôs* for the Greeks (Rénou 1947, 315; Havers 1960).

70. See Frank 1992a.

71. Karl Jaspers (1963b, 15 fn.) proposes to us the existence of an "Axial Age" (*Achsenzeit*) in the mature period of this interregional system. Between the seventh and second centuries BC, we find Confucius and Lao-Tzu in China, the Upanishads and Buddha in India, Zarathustra in Iran, the pre-Socratics in Ionia in Hellas, as well as (although they belong to another cosmovision), the prophets of Israel. In a certain way, during this Axial Period the original ethical-rational nuclei would have been constituted up to today. "The Mythical age had ended, and with it placid tranquility and its naiveté" (ibid., 21).

72. In contemporary Indian philosophy, it is spoken of a "Brahamization" of the ancient cosmovision. That is to say, some would like making Brahamanic interpretation the only one that is proper to India. In fact, there were many other visions and philosophies in ancient India and the Asiatic southeast, materialist, atheist, skeptical, critical schools. Here I only recall the "dominant" current. This also holds for Buddhism, Manicheanism, etc.

73. See also Dussel 1974a, 61 ff.; Prümm 1960.

74. *Enneads*, V, 4, 1 (Plotinus 1924, vol. 5, 79–80).

75. Heraclitus, Fragment B 50 (Diels 1964, vol. 1, 161).

76. See König 1959–61, vol. 2, 581.

77. *Rig Veda*, X, 129 (Rénou 1936, 125).

78. *Chándoya-Upanishada*, 3, 14 (cited in Regamey 1961b, 116).

79. Bk. 1, chap. 1 (Wieger 1950, 18).

80. *Enneads*, VI, 6, 1.

81. Ibid., I, 8, 4. "Matter is the cause of the weakness of the soul and also of its vicious disposition. She is evil, or better yet, the origin of evil itself" (ibid.,

I, 8, 14). This is the theme of the "original sin" in Augustine, and later in Luther, which is foreign to the Semitic tradition.

82. Heraclitus, Fragment B 62 (Diels 1964, vol. 1, 164).

83. Heraclitus, Fragment 77 (Diels 1964, vol. 1, 168).

84. *Timaeus*, 34 c.

85. *Phaedo*, 245 d.

86. Ibid., 78 b–d.

87. *Republic*, X, 611 b.

88. *Phaedo*, 246 c; 248 a–c.

89. *Timeo*, 41 b and ff.

90. *Bhagavad-Gita*, 2, 18–20 (*Bhagavad-Gita* 1957, 21).

91. Quoted in Jaspers 1993, 146. The singular "I" as an aspiration to be oneself is the origin of suffering. To eliminate suffering requires that one eliminate the "I," to want, to love. Nirvana is "return" to the One, to Identity from the negated "difference." The body is "filthy matter (*kâmadhatu*)" for the Buddha; the soul (in its conscious form: *vijnâna*) is eternal (Regamey 1961a, 237).

92. Bar-Kônai, *Fihrist, Fragment of Turfân*, S 9 (quoted in Puech 1959, 497).

93. The empirical, corporeal, or appetitive will be for Kant what is "pathological," since the human being belongs to "two worlds"; that of the spirits and that of the souls with bodies. This "dualism" is at the base of recent extreme universalism and rationalist "formalisms"; which results in the ignorance of corporeality and therefore also of economics (see chapters 1 and 2).

94. *Enneads*, IV, 8, 4.

95. Ibid., II, 9, 6.

96. *Nichomachean Ethics*, bk. 10, 6–9 (Aristotle 1960, 1176a–1181b).

97. See Diogenes Laertius, X, 136 (1968, 112).

98. "Oh, Kauteya! Everything that exists returns after circling back to me, and this is how I bring new beings into existence in order to initiate a new cycle. I produce the multiplicity of existent beings upon the basis of my own nature, and everything is absolutely subject to it" (*Bhagavad-Gita*, 9, 7–8; 1957, 62).

99. Among those "things" we find the dominated, exploited, poor, excluded, women, discriminated races, etc., for whom this ethical life of the "soul" without a worthy body results in their *necessary* depreciation.

100. *Enneads* III, 6, 5.

101. See Dussel 1974b, 92–103.

102. *Ta-Hio*, 4–6 (Confucius 1865, 155 a–b).

103. That Buddhism, as I indicated, entered the dualist horizon of the "Indo-European" world, means, however, a true rebellion of the poor and dominated casts of Hinduism. Its impact in the Taoist-Confucian world will be of the same type. But, it is my opinion, the primitive Buddhism transformed, and for this reason it was not able to supersede the dualist horizon of the depreciation of carnal corporeality, perhaps because of this posterior deformation.

104. Dussel 1966, secs. 33–36; also, Amin 1989; Braudel 1978; Copleston 1964, bibliography, especially 591–617.

105. Asoka had unified the peninsula and imposed Buddhism in AD 232. Perhaps if an egalitarian Buddhism had been imposed, the later history of that continent would be different.

106. Recall table 1.

107. This is the meeting point of the Oriental pole (China) and the poles of

the South (India) and the West (Persian and Roman empires). The area extends from the cities of Bujara and Samarkand to the south of the Aral Sea, as far as the Tarim River (north of the Tibetan Himalayas), where the Silk Route from China divides: one road going south in the direction to India (crossing the Hindu Kush), and another west in the direction of Antioch, passing through Iran and Mesopotamia. See map 1.

108. See on this topic Dussel 1974a, 33–104.

109. Maimonides 1954, vol. 1, chap. 71, 340–44.

110. The young Max Weber indicated how a factor in the Christian expansion was its ethical presence in the *Sklavenkasernen* (Weber 1956a, 14).

111. The Hebrew text of their holy writings was translated into Greek by a Hebrew community in the city of Elephantine (located close to the first falls on the Nile, right in the midst of the "black," Bantu Egypt of the south) in the version of the Seventy.

112. Matthew 25:35–36. See appendix 2 [405].

113. Acts of the Apostles 2:42–46.

114. See Bloch 1959. Marx's expression "to each according to their needs" (*Kritik des Gothaer Programms*, in Marx 1956–90, vol. 19, 21), takes up the expression textually. Consider §5.4 of this *Ethics*.

115. Koran, 93:6–10. These texts are from the first period of Mohammed, when he criticized a rich merchant of Mecca (made wealthy on the commerce with the Persian and Egyptian region of the Byzantine Empire) who forgot the poor. Traditional ethics required sharing one's goods, but urbanized society did not want to fulfill the traditional precepts. It is for this reason that the prophet was expelled and had to make an escape (*hegira*) to Medina (where he established an egalitarian economic system without attenuations). Islam was born as a struggle for liberation and justice on behalf of the poor and excluded.

116. Tatian, 1954, I, 572.

117. It is interesting to note that "to be ready for an examination" of the expressed is, exactly, the "validity claim" or the attempt to reach intersubjective consensus in the hegemonic culture (Habermas 1984, on the "Theory of Truth"). These are questions that I will deal with in secs. 3.1–2.

118. Tatian 1954, 31–34 and 615–28.

119. Justin Martyr 1954.

120. When Hegel says that the "Germanic spirit" is the full realization of the "Christian principle" (*das christiliche Prinzip*) (*Vorlesungen über die Philosophie des Geschichte*, in Hegel 1971–79, vol. 12, 413–14), he seems not to be aware that this "Christian principle" is *Afro-Asiatic* (of the Egyptian-Mesopotamian Middle East) and has nothing Germanic or "Aryan" in it, nothing European or "Western." The "Germanic spirit" then is "eastern," African or Asiatic.

121. In AD 529 the last philosophical school of Athens was closed, and in AD 643, in Alexandria, the school of Constantinople was the most important intellectual center of its time—four centuries before the Islamic Bujara or Baghdad, and eight centuries before Europe's Paris.

122. See Dussel 1969; Gardet 1948 and 1967; Massignon 1922; Rahman 1979; Rondot 1963; Schacht 1974.

123. The coming centuries will remember the barbarians of the twentieth century, who dropped 100,000 tons of bombs on this memorable region.

124. Braudel 1978, 65.

125. "The windmills" of La Mancha, against which Don Quixote struggled,

come from the Muslim world and not from the Low Countries of Europe, which is evident—that is to say, the more technologically developed cultural horizon.

126. In Braudel 1978, 75.

127. *Islam* (absolute submission) thinks that the human being has established an "alliance" (*mithaq*) with Allah. This alliance has to be renewed in history consciously (*shahada*) in order to belong to the "community" (*umma*) (see Dussel 1969, 64–73: "Intersubjectivity in Islam"). The *dar al-Islam* (the "house of believers") is opposed to the *dar el-Harb* ("house of war"), the infidels, the barbarians, those who may be integrated in the *dar el-Salh* ("house of reconciliation"). The "slave" (*'abd*) becomes a "believer" (*mu'min*) when he submits to the lordship (*rububiyya*) of Allah. More than a "natural law" there is always the permanent and instantaneous will of Allah (Duns Scotus among the Christians held an analogous view of God): "Allah's law is the same that was. His decrees are immutable" (Koran 48:23). The most vehement debates took place over human freedom: the *mu'tazilies* affirm it, the Asarits (the position of Al-Asari, who died in AD 935/324 AH), denied it.

128. Carra de Vaux 1921–26; Gauthier 1923; Munk 1927.

129. The first translations of Aristotle were made into Syrian in Edesa, Mesopotamia, by Ephrem of Nisibis in AD 363. Invited by the Abbasids of Baghdad, the Christian Syrians translated Aristotle from the Greek to the Syrian, and other Greek philosophers to Arabic. In AD 832 a school of translators is established in Baghdad. Plato, Aristotle, Plotinus, Proclus, and others are translated.

130. Al-Farabi was born in Baghdad, where there had been a "House of Science" (a university) since the eighth century; he strongly affirmed "natural law" (*namous al-sabadia*) against irrational orthodoxy. He died in AD 950/339 AH.

131. The great Avicena (sometimes also spelled Avicenna; his name in the original Arabic is Ibn Sina), born in Bukhara, south of the Aral Sea, near the Oxus River (north of what is today Pakistan, a key location along the Silk Route toward China, not far from Samarkand); he died in AD 1037/428 AH.

132. The great commentator of Aristotle, Averroes (born in Cordoba, and died in AD 1198/595 AH), whom Thomas of Aquinas follows. He affirmed the eternity of the cosmos (Gauthier 1909; Renan 1861). To understand his exemplary work, see his commentaries on Aristotle, such as his *On the Soul* (Averroes 1953).

133. Jaeger (1952) has shown well that Plato's or Aristotle's *philosophy* (love of "wisdom") is *theologie* (not only as ultimate content, but also as fundamental intention). "The words, i.e., *theologians, theologie, teologein, theologikos* were created by the philosophical language of Plato and Aristotle" (10). For Aristotle, "prima philosophia" is "theology." For the Greek, "sage" and "theologian" are the same. This is also the case for Plotinus, especially for Proclus, and for the rest of the Neoplatonists.

134. The Greeks began *formal* philosophy (see thesis 5.c), but the Arabs made it autonomous from *theological* rationality (confused still with "positive revelation").

135. Al-Gazzali, born in Tus (south of Bukhara) and died in AD 1111/505 AH (Smith 1944).

136. Blaut informs us (1992, 2–3): "Medieval Europe was no more advanced or progressive than medieval Africa and medieval Asia."

137. See table 1 and map 1, region H.

138. See thesis 8.

139. Modernity in this view is a "substance" that is invented in Europe and that subsequently expands throughout the entire world. This is a metaphysical-substantialist and diffusionist thesis; it contains a reductionist fallacy.

140. The English translation does not translate an expression Weber uses here, "auf dem Boden," which means *within* its regional horizon. I want to establish that "in Europe" really refers to the development in Modernity of Europe as the "center" of a "global system," and not as an *independent* system, as if "only-from-within itself" and as the fruit of a solely *internal* development, as Eurocentrism claims.

141. This "we" refers precisely to Eurocentric Europeans.

142. Weber 1958, 13 (emphasis added). Some pages on, Weber asks: "Why did not the scientific, the artistic, the political, or the economic development there [China and India] enter upon that path of *rationalization* which is peculiar to the Occident?" (ibid., 25). In order to argue this, Weber juxtaposes the Babylonians, who did not mathematize astronomy, and the Greeks, who did (Weber does not know that the Greeks learned it from the Egyptians). Or, as he also argues, that science emerged in the West, but not in India or China, and so on—but he forgets to mention the Muslim world, from whom the Latin West learned Aristotelian "experiential," empirical exactitude (such as the Oxford Franciscans, or the Marcilios de Padua, etc.), and so on. Every Hellenistic, or Eurocentric, argument such as Weber's, can be falsified if we take 1492 as the ultimate date of comparison between the supposed superiority of the West and other cultures.

143. Hegel 1956, 341.

144. Following Hegel, Habermas in 1988, 27.

145. The world system or planetary system of stage IV of the interregional system of the Asiatic-African-Mediterranean continent, but now—correcting Frank's conceptualization—factically "planetary." See Frank 1990. On the world system problematic, see Abu-Lughod 1989; Brenner 1983; Hodgson 1974; Kennedy 1987; Mann 1986; McNeill 1964; Modelski 1987; Stavarianos 1970; Thompson 1989; Tilly 1984; Wallerstein 1974 and 1984.

146. On this point, as I already mentioned, I am not in agreement with Frank on using the term "world system" to refer to prior moments of the system; I therefore call these prior moments "interregional systems."

147. Wallerstein 1974–89, vol. 1, chap. 6.

148. Ibid., vol. 2, chaps. 4 and 5.

149. Ibid., vol. 3, chap. 3.

150. See Lattimore 1962; Rossabi 1982. For a description of the situation of the world in 1400, see Wolf 1982, 24 ff. For my vision of the situation of China, see Dussel 2007.

151. I have been to Mombasa and I have seen in the museum of this city, which is a port of Kenya, Chinese porcelain, as well as luxurious watches and other objects of similar origin.

152. There are other reasons for this lack of external expansion: the existence of "space" in the territories neighboring the empire, which focused all its power on "conquering the South" through the cultivation of rice and defending itself from the barbarian "North." See Wallerstein 1974, vol. 1, 80 ff., which has many good arguments against Weber's Eurocentrism.

153. For example, Needham 1961, 1963, and 1965. All of these with respect to

the control of ships, which the Chinese dominated since the first century AD. The Chinese use of the compass, paper, gunpowder, and other discoveries is well known.

154. Perhaps the only disadvantage was the Portuguese caravel (invented in 1441), used to navigate the Atlantic (which was not needed in the Indian sea), and the cannon. This last innovation, although spectacular, never had any real effect in Asia, outside of naval wars, until the nineteenth century. Cipolla (1965, 106–7) writes, "Chinese fire-arms were at least as good as Western, if not better."

155. The first bureacracy (as the Weberian high stage of political rationalization) is the Mandarin state structure of political exercise. The Mandarin are not nobles, nor warriors, nor an aristocratic or commercial plutocracy; they are *strictly* a bureacratic elite whose exams are *exclusively* based in the dominion of culture and the laws of the Chinese Empire.

156. William de Bary (1970) indicates that the individualism of Wang Yangming, in the fourteenth century, which expressed the ideology of the bureacratic class, was as advanced as that of the Renaissance.

157. Through many examples, Thomas Kuhn (1962) situates the modern scientific revolution, the expression of the new paradigm, with Newton (seventeenth century). However, he does not study with care the impact that events such as the discovery of America, or the roundness of the earth, empirically proved since 1520, and similar early advances could have had on the science and the "scientific community" of the sixteenth century, since the structuring of the first world system.

158. Needham 1963, 39.

159. A. R. Hall has the scientific revolution beginning in the 1500s (see Hall 1954).

160. Toward the end of the fourteenth century there begins a process of maturation of the entire interregional system, which was more urban and developed in China, India, and the Muslim world than in Europe itself. One may speak of a protocapitalist stage from China to the Mediterraan (Blaut 1993, 165 ff.).

161. Chaunu 1955–59, vol. 8, 50.

162. *Factically*, Colón will be the first modern, but not *existentially* (since his *interpretation of the world* remained always that of a Renaissance Genoese: a member of a peripheral Italy of the third interregional system). See O'Gorman 1957; Taviani 1982.

163. See Zunzunegui 1941.

164. Russia was not yet integrated as "periphery" in stage III of the interregional system (nor in the modern world system until the eighteenth century with Peter the Great and the founding of St. Petersburg on the Baltic).

165. Portugal already in 1095 has the rank of empire. In Algarve, 1249, the Reconquest concludes. Henry the Navigator (1394–1460), as patron, gathers the sciences of cartography, astronomy, and the techniques of navigation and construction of ships, which originated in the Muslim world (since he had contact with the Moroccans) and the Italian Renaissance (via Genoa).

166. Wallerstein 1974, vol. 1, 49–50. See Rau 1957; Verlinden 1953.

167. See Chaudhuri 1985.

168. My argument would seem to be the same as Blaut's (1992, 28 ff.), but in fact it is different. It is not that Spain was "geographically" closer to Amerindia.

No. It is not a question of distances. It is that and much more. It is a matter of Spain's having to go through Amerindia not only because it was closer (which was often a reason for expansion, especially with respect to Asiatic cultures, although this was not the case with the Turkish-Muslim empire that reached as far as Morocco), but because this was the required path to the center of the system—a question that is not dealt with by Blaut. Furthermore, though in a different way, my argument is also different to that of André Gunder Frank (Blaut 1992, 65–80), because for him 1492 is only a secondary internal change of the existing world system. However, if the interregional system, in its stage prior to 1492, is understood as the same system and not yet as a new "world system," then 1492 assumes a greater importance than Frank grants it. Even if the system *is the same*, there exists a qualitative leap (which, under other aspects, is the origin of capitalism proper; Frank denies importance to this leap because of his prior denial of relevance to concepts such as "value" and "surplus value," and he, therefore, attributes "capital" to "wealth" [use value with a virtual possibility of transforming itself into exchange value, but not into capital] that has accumulated in stages I–III of the interregional system). This is a grave theoretical question.

169. Dussel 1993c.

170. See ibid., appendix 4, where a map of the "fourth Asiatic peninsula" is reproduced (after the Arabian, Indian, and Malayan peninsulas); the map is certainly the product of Genoese navigations, where South America is a peninsula attached to the south of China. This explains why the Genoese Colón would hold the opinion that Asia would not be so far from Europe (South America being the fourth peninsula of China).

171. This is what I called, philosophically, the "invention" of Amerindia seen as India, in all of its details. Colón, existentially, neither "discovered" nor reached Amerindia. He "invented" something that was nonexistent: India in the place of Amerindia, which prevented him from "discovering" what he had before his own eyes. See ibid., chap. 2.

172. This is the meaning of the title of chapter 2 ("From the *Invention* to the *Discovery* of America") of my work *1492: El encubrimiento del Otro* (1993c).

173. See Amin 1970. This work does not yet develop a world system hypothesis; it would appear as though the colonial world were a *rear or subsequent* and *outside* space to European medieval capitalism, which is transformed "in" Europe as modern. My hypothesis is more radical: the fact of the discovery of Amerindia, of its integration as "periphery" is a *simultaneous* and *co-constitutive* fact of the restructuring of Europe *from within*, as center of the only new world system that is—only now and *not before*—capitalism (first mercantile and later industrial).

174. I have spoken of "Amerindia" and not of America, because it is a matter, during the entire sixteenth century, of a continent inhabited by "Indians" (wrongly called this because of the mirage produced by the interregional system in the third stage in the world system that was still being born. They were called Indians because of India, the center of the interregional system that was beginning to fade). Anglo-Saxon North America will be born slowly in the seventeenth century, but it will be an event "internal" to a growing Modernity in Amerindia. This is the *originating* periphery of Modernity, constitutive of its first definition. It is the "other face" of the very same phenomenon of Modernity.

175. Spain unified after the marriage of the Catholic king and queen in 1474, who immediately founded the Inquisition (the first ideological apparatus of the modern state for the creation of consensus). Spain moved forward with a bureacracy whose functioning is attested to in the archives of the Indies (in Seville), where everything was declared, contracted, certified, and archived; with a codified grammar of the Spanish language (the first grammar of a national language in Europe) written by Nebrija, in the prologue of which he warns the Catholic monarchs of the importance for the empire of having *only one language*; with Cisneros's edition of the Complutensian polyglot Bible (in seven languages), which was superior to Erasmus's because of its scientic rigor, the number of its languages, and the quality of the printing, began in 1502 and published in 1522; with military power that allows it to retake Granada in 1492; with the economic wealth of the Jews, Andalusian Muslims, Christians of the Reconquest, and the Catalans with their colonies in the Mediterranean, and the Genoese; with the artisans from the antique caliphate of Cordoba—Spain is far from being in the fifteenth century the semiperipheral country that it will become in the second part of the seventeenth century—the only picture of Spain that the Europe of the center remembers it by, as do Hegel and Habermas, for example.

176. The struggle between France and the Spain of Carlos V, which exhausted both monarchies and resulted in the economic collapse of 1557, was played out above all in Italy. Carlos V possessed about three-fourths of the Italian peninsula. In this way Spain transferred the links with the "system" through Italy to its own soil. This was one of the reasons for all the wars with France: for the wealth, the experience of centuries, were essential for whoever intended to exercise new hegemony in the system, and especially if it was the first "planetary" hegemony.

177. The vast imports of silver produced an unprecedented increase of prices in Europe, which resulted in inflation of 1,000 percent during the sixteenth century. Externally, this liquidated the wealth accumulated in the Turkish-Muslim world, and transformed even India and China internally (see Hamilton 1948 and 1960; Hammarström 1957). Furthermore, the arrival of Amerindian gold turned Bantu Africa into a continental hecatomb with the collapse of the kingdoms of the sub-Saharan savannah (Ghana, Togo, Dahomey, Nigeria, and others) that exported gold to the Mediterranean. In order to survive, these kingdoms increased the sales of slaves to the new European powers of the Atlantic, thus producing American slavery (see Bertaux 1972: "La trata de esclavos"; Braudel 1946; Chaunu 1955–59, vol. 8, 57; Godinho 1950). The whole ancient third inter-regional system is absorbed slowly by the modern world system.

178. All the subsequent hegemonic power has remained until the present on either side of the Atlantic: with Spain, Holland, England (and France partly), until 1945, and with the United States in the present. Thanks to Japan, China, and California of the United States, the Pacific appears for the first time as a counterweight. This is perhaps a novelty of the twenty-first century.

179. Wallerstein 1974, vol. 1, 45.

180. The "mouth of hell" referred to by the writer is the entrance to the mine.

181. This text has for the last thirty years warned me of the phenomenon of the fetishism of gold, of "money," and of "capital" (see Dussel 1993b).

182. *Archivo General de Indias* (Seville), Charcas 313 (see Dussel 1970, 1; this was part of my doctoral thesis at the Sorbonne in 1967).

183. Wallerstein 1974, vol. 1, 165 ff.: "From Seville to Amsterdam: The Failure of Empire."

184. Spinoza (1632–77), who lived in Amsterdam, was descended from an "Ashkenazí" family from the Muslim world of Granada, was expelled from Spain, and lived in exile in the Spanish colony in Flanders.

185. See Wallerstein 1974, vol. 1, 214.

186. See ibid., vol. 2, chap. 2: "Dutch Hegemony in the World Economy." Wallerstein writes: "It follows that there is probably only a short moment in time when a given core power can manifest *simultaneously* productive, commercial, and financial superiority *over all other core powers*. This momentary summit is what we call hegemony. In the case of Holland, or the United Providences, that moment was probably between 1625–1675" (ibid., 39). Descartes and Spinoza are the philosophical presence of Amsterdam, "center" of the world system (and—why not?—of the self-consciousness of humanity in its "center," which is not the same as a mere *European* self-consciousness).

187. See ibid., vol. 2, chap. 6. After this date, British hegemony will be uninterrupted, except in the Napoleanic period, until 1945, when it loses to the United States.

188. See Chaunu 1969, 119–76.

189. Europe had approximately fifty-six million inhabitants in 1500, and eighty-two million in 1600 (see Cardoso 1979, vol. 1, 114).

190. Wallerstein 1974, vol. 1, 103.

191. See Amin 1974, 309 ff.

192. Ibid., 312.

193. The colonial process ends, for the most part, at the beginning of the nineteenth century.

194. The colonial process of these formations ends, for the most part, in 1945 after the end of the so-called Second World War, given that the North American superpower requires neither military occupation nor political-bureacratic domination (which were proper only to the old European powers, such as France and England); what North America requires in its transnational stage, rather, is the management of the dominion of economic-financial dependence.

195. "Muslim" refers here to the most "cultured" and civilized Muslims of the fifteenth century.

196. I think that, exactly, to *manage* the new world system according to old practices had to fail because it operated with variables that made it unmanageable. Modernity *had begun*, but it had not given itself a new way to manage the system.

197. Later on, it will also have to manage the system of the British Isles. Both nations had very exiguous territories, with little population at their beginning, and with no other capacity than their creative "bourgeois attitude" toward existence. Because of their weakness, they had to perform a great reform of management of the planetary metropolitan enterprise.

198. The technical "factibility" will become a criterion of truth, of possibility, of existence; cf. Vico's "verum et *factum* conventuntur."

199. Spain, and Portugal also with Brazil, undertook as state enterprises (as world empire) (with military, bureacratic, and ecclesiastical resources, etc.) the conquest, evangelization, and colonization of Amerindia. Holland, instead,

founded the Dutch East India Company (1602), and later that of the Dutch West India Company. These "companies" (as well as the subsequent British and Danish ones, and others) were capitalist enterprises, secularized and private, which functioned according to the "rationalization" of mercantilism (and later of industrial capitalism). This indicates the different rational management of the Iberian companies, and the different management of the second Modernity (world system not managed by a world empire).

200. In every system, complexity is accompanied by a process of "selection" of elements that allow, in the face of increase in such complexity, for the conservation of the "unity" of the system with respect to its surroundings. This necessity of selection simplification is always a "risk" (see Luhmann 1988, 47 ff.).

201. See Dussel 1993c, chap. 5: "Critique of the Myth of Modernity." During the sixteenth century there were three theoretical positions before the fact of the constitution of the world system: (1) that of Ginés de Sepúlveda, the *modern* Renaissance and humanist scholar, who reread Aristotle and demonstrated the natural slave condition of the Amerindian, thus confirming the legitimacy of the conquest; (2) that of the Franciscans, such as Mendieta, who attempted a utopian Amerindian Christianity (a "republic of Indians" under the hegemony of Catholic religion), proper to the third Christian-Muslim interregional system; and (3) that of Bartolomé de las Casas, *the beginning of a critical counterdiscourse in the interior of Modernity* (in *De unico modo* [The only way] of 1536, a century before *Le Discours de la Méthode*, in which he shows that "argumentation" is the rational means through which to attract the Amerindian to the new civilization). Habermas, as we will see later on, speaks of counterdiscourse, and suggests that counterdiscourse is only two centuries old (beginning with Kant). Liberation philosophy suggests, instead, that this counterdiscourse begins in the sixteenth century, arguably in 1511 in Santo Domingo with Antón de Montesinos, and decisively with Bartolomé de las Casas in 1514 (see Dussel 1983a, 17–27).

202. Casas 1992, 31. I have placed this text at the beginning of volume 1 of my work *Para una ética de la liberación latinoamericana* (Dussel 1970–80, vol. 3 [1973]), since it synthesizes the general hypothesis of the ethics of liberation.

203. Frequently, in contemporary histories of philosophy, and of course of ethics, a "leap" is made from the Greeks (from Plato and Aristotle) to Descartes (1596–1650), who took up residence in Amsterdam in 1629 and there wrote *Le Discours de la Méthode*. That is, there is a jump from Greece to Amsterdam. In the interim, twenty-one centuries have gone by without any other content of importance. Studies are begun with Bacon (1561–1626), Kepler (1571–1630), Galileo (1571–1630), or Newton (1643–1727). Campanella writes *Civitas Solis* in 1602. Everything would seem to be situated at the beginning of the seventeenth century, the moment I have called the second moment of Modernity.

204. See Sombart 1902 and 1920.

205. See Troeltsch 1923.

206. See Habermas 1981b, vols. 1 and 2. Habermas insists on the Weberian discovery of "rationalization," but he forgets to ask after its cause. I believe that my hypothesis goes deeper and further back: Weberian rationalization (accepted by Habermas, Apel, Lyotard, and others) is the apparently necessary mediation of a deforming simplification (by instrumental reason) of practical reality in order to transform it into something "manageable," governable, given the complexity of the immense world system. It is not only the internal

manageability of Europe, but also, and above all, *planetary* (center-periphery) management. Habermas's attempt to sublate instrumental reason into communicative reason is not sufficient because the moments of his diagnosis of the *origin itself of the process of rationalization* are not sufficient.

207. The postmoderns, being Eurocentric, concur, more or less, with the Weberian diagnosis of Modernity. Specifically, they underscore certain rationalizing aspects or mediums (means of communication, etc.) of Modernity; some they reject angrily as metaphysical dogmatisms, but others they accept as inevitable phenomena and frequently as positive transformations.

208. Descartes 1985, "Discourse on the Method," part IV, 127.

209. See Dussel 1974a (at the end) and 1974b, chap. 2, sec. 4. Contemporary theories of the functions of the brain put in question definitively this dualistic mechanism.

210. Kant, *Träume eines Geistersehers* (1766), A 36 (Kant 1968, vol. 2, 940).

211. Thoughout this *Ethics*, I will expound on different "types of rationality," and I show the modern confusion or truncation of "practical" reason (that is to say, "ethical" reason) into mere instrumental or strategic reason (Dussel 1973, 161–62).

212. Galilei 1933, vol. 6:232.

213. See Dussel 1973.

214. Heidegger 1963c, 73.

215. See Bernal 1991.

216. Amerindia and Europe have a premodern history, just as Africa and Asia do. Only the hybrid world, the syncretic culture, the Latin American *mestiza* race that was born in the fifteenth century (the child of Malinche and Hernán Cortés can be considered as its symbol; see Paz 1950), have a history of five hundred years.

217. See, among others, Derrida 1964, 1967a, 1967b; Lyotard 1979; Marquart 1981; Rorty 1979; Vattimo 1985; Welsch 1993b.

218. This Spanish word *desarrollismo*, which has no equivalent in other languages (the word *Entwicklung* has a strictly Hegelian philosophical origin), points to the fallacy that claims the same "development" for the center as for the periphery, not taking note that the periphery is not *backward* (see Hinkelammert 1970a and 1970b). In other words, it is not a temporal *prius* that awaits a development similar to that of Europe or the United States (as a child does an adult); instead, it is the asymmetrical position of the dominated, the *simultaneous* position of the exploited (like the free lord and slave). The "immature" person (child) could follow the path of the "mature" (adult) and get to "develop" herself, while the "exploited" (slave) no matter how much she works will never be "free" (lord), because her own dominated subjectivity includes her relationship with the dominator. The "modernizers" of the periphery are developmentalists because they do not realize that the relationship of planetary domination has to be overcome as prerequisite for national development. Globalization has not extinguished, not in the least, the "national" question.

219. See Habermas 1981b, vol. 1, 72, and especially the debate with P. Winch and A. MacIntyre.

220. We will see that Levinas, "father of French postmodernism" (from Derrida on), is not postmodern and does not negate reason. Instead, he is a critic of the *totalization* of reason (instrumental, strategic, cynical, ontological, etc.). Liberation philosophy, since the end of the sixties, studied Levinas because of

his radical critique of domination. In the preface to my work *Philosophy of Liberation* (Dussel 1985b), I indicated that the philosophy of liberation is a postmodern philosophy, one that departed from the "second Heidegger," but also from the critique of *totalized* reason carried out by Marcuse and Levinas. It would seem as though we were "postmoderns" *avant la lettre*. In fact, however, we were critics of ontology and Modernity from the periphery, which meant (and which still *means*) something entirely different, as we intend to explain.

221. Up to now, the postmoderns remain Eurocentric. The dialogue with "different" cultures is, for now, an unfullfilled promise. They think that mass culture, the media (television, movies, etc.), will impact peripheral urban cultures to the extent that they will annihilate their "differences," in such a way that what Vattimo sees in Torino, or Lyotard in Paris, will be shortly the same in New Delhi and Nairobi; and they do not take the time to analyze the *hard* irreducibility of the hybrid cultural horizon (which is not *absolutely* an exteriority, but that will not be for centuries a univocal interiority to the globalized system) that receives those information impacts.

222. Santiago Castro-Gómez in his work *Crítica de la razón latinoamericana* (1996) criticizes all attempts, including mine, that aim to generalize rationally any methodological diagnosis or to formulate the question of feasible projects. In chapter 6, §6.2, I will return to this issue, and I will show the possibility of a *universal*, material, and discursive reason (strictly transmodern and postcolonial inasmuch as it allows one to judge from the *concrete life of peripheral peoples* of the modern, dominating world system) which may be related to the "transversal" reason (Welsch 1993b) of diverse, emergent historical-social subjects. To situate oneself so one sees from the perspective of the victims, from the perspective of exteriority, is not to "invert" modern reason (Castro-Gómez 1996, 16); rather, it is to open oneself up to a horizon unknown to it. See, for instance, the issues of neoindividualism, the culture of rock and roll, drugs, the consumption of fashion, the "softening" of political opinions (Follari 1991), pessimism due to the lack of alternatives, the turn toward the private and religion (Lechner 1990), the appearance of new social movements (Fals Borda 1987), and so on, which are only symptoms of a supposed postmodern culture. On this topic, see Maliandi 1993.

223. See Jameson's work (1991) on the "cultural logic of late capitalism as postmodernism."

224. In Stalinist real socialism, the criterion was the "increase in the rate of production"—measured, in any event, by an approximate market value of commodities. It is a question at the same time of fetishism. See Hinkelammert 1984, chap. 4: "Marco categorial del pensamiento soviético" (123 ff.).

225. Marx 1973, 410.

226. Ibid.

227. Pure necessity without money is no market; it is only misery, growing and unavoidable misery.

228. Marx 1987, vol. 1, 799. Here we must remember once more that *Human Development Report* 1992 already demonstrated in an incontrovertible manner that the richer 20 percent of the planet consumes today (as never before in global history) 82.7 percent of goods (incomes) of the planet, while the remaining 80 percent of humanity only consumes the 17.3 percent of said goods. Such concentration is the product of the world system we have been delineating.

229. Herbert Marcuse, "Liberation from the Affluent Society," in Cooper 1967, 181.

230. In the sense employed by Seyla Benhabib in *Situating the Self* (1992).

231. See what I have noted regarding the theme of the philosophy and praxis of liberation in §6.1b.

232. See Taylor 1989.

233. Ibid., 103. He tells us in the preface, "In part, it was because of the very ambitious nature of the enterprise, which is an attempt to articulate and write a history of the modern identity" (ix).

234. Ibid., x.

235. Although the same can be said of literary figures, theologians, and other cultivators of the human sciences.

236. I recall that Alphonse de Waehlens used to tell us in 1961 that "philosophy reflects, in the first place, on that which is not philosophical."

237. For Taylor the "*Self*" is both the *ego* and the *persona* (see all of part I, "Agency and the Self," in Taylor 1985a; 13–114; 1989, 25–51).

238. Ricoeur 1963.

239. I think that Taylor's works regarding Hegel (1975 and 1979) should have inclined him toward giving central importance to the concept of "ethical essence" (*Sittlichkeit*), in a "substantive" and not purely formal position in ethical matters, which is very convenient. But at the same time, he has absorbed Hegel's Eurocentrism. On this, see Dussel 1993c. Hegel came to the point of writing that "Europe is absolutely the center and the end" of universal history (Hegel 1955, 235). Commentators (including Taylor himself, 1975, 3 ff.) never refer to the Eurocentric manner in which Hegel refers disparagingly to Latin America, Africa, and Asia, and his way of justifying European colonialist violence: "Against the absolute right that the [dominating people in the world: *Weltherrschende*] has because it is the current bearer of the level of development of the World Spirit, the spirit *of other peoples has no rights at all (rechtlos)*" (Hegel, *Rechtsphilosophie*, sec. 347 [Hegel 1971, vol. 7, 506]).

240. This is the fundamental thesis of Dussel 1993c; its subtitle (translated) is "Towards the Origins of the Myth of Modernity."

241. I have made the distinction in my works between "concrete universality" (that which has been imposed by modern European domination in the world system; thus, in the periphery), with the "globality" or totality of concrete existent cultures. A "transmodern" project posits a new globality as a full realization of future humanity, where all cultures (not only those of Europe or North America) will be able to affirm their alterity, and not simply echo a process of "modernization" that implies the imposition upon them of the Euro–North American culture of the center or its apparent abstraction (an abstract Modernity that is in essence nothing more than the same Euro–North American Modernity from which some particularly jagged characteristics have been removed).

242. See "Vers une phénoménologie de l'*ego conquiro* (je conquiers)," in Dussel 1993c, French ed., 39 ff.: "Le *Moi (Self)-conquéreur* est la proto-histoire de la constitution de l'*ego cogito*; on est arrivé à un moment décisif de sa constitution comme subjectivité, comme *volonté de puissance*. . . . La conquête, c'est l'affirmation pratique de *Je conquiers* et la négation de l'Autre en tant qu'Autrui" (47).

243. See Todorov 1989.

244. Taylor 1989, 207.

245. Taylor indicates that colonialism or the domination of the periphery has only subsequent and quantitative effects: "This has obviously had tremendous importance for the *spread of these practices*"; but not as moments predating its constitution. Taylor does not comprehend the Eurocentrist significance of the phrases that I am about to quote, but does in any case recognize that these effects "won't figure in [his] analysis, except at the boundaries" (ibid.). Like Ginés de Sepúlveda he believes that Europe's dominion over the periphery "has had a crucial effect on the development of both [!] European and non-European societies, and the prestige [!] of the self-understandings associated with them has a fateful importance for the development of cultures" (ibid.). Thus it seems that, following Taylor, we must interpret all of this process of domination as a matter of cultural development. But what if the development of modern barbarity as reflected in slavery, colonialism, the structural underdevelopment of all of the cultures of the global South, were the focus of our attention, and what was actually most significant? Such conclusions as those drawn by Taylor are the product of a method that only takes abstract philosophical "ideas" into account (might this not be what some describe as *idealism*?).

246. Habermas 1988.

247. Ibid., 351.

248. Ibid., 353. Taylor prolongs Modernity a bit: "All of the modern era since the 17th century is frequently contemplated as the temporal framework of decadence" (1992a, 1).

249. Habermas 1988, 424–25.

250. The "entwicklungsideologische Fehlsschluss" (developmentalist fallacy).

251. Universities, endowed chairs, libraries, the publication of books, and so on, presuppose a level of economic development and an accumulation of wealth obtained in the peripheral colonial world that are the material conditions necessary to give rise to what Gramsci would call the "material apparatuses" of culture (as well as of philosophy, of course).

252. Clavijero was born in Veracruz (Mexico) and died in Bologna (Italy); he was forced into exile from Mexico in 1767, because of the expulsion of members of the Jesuit order imposed by the Bourbon dynasty. He mastered Spanish, Greek, and Latin, as well as Náhuatl (the language of the Aztecs or Mexicas) and Mixteco, which he learned in childhood. He was a professor at the school of San Gregorio in Mexico, in the cities of Puebla, Valladolid (later renamed Morelia), and Guadalajara. He undertook a thoroughgoing critique of the work of Buffon and De Pauw, defending the dignity of indigenous peoples in the Americas: "We were born of Spanish fathers and have no affinity or consanguinity with the Indians, and can expect nothing from their misery in compensation. Thus there is no other motivation but *our love of truth and our love of humanity* that causes us to abandon the advocacy of our own interests in order to defend those which are *alien* to us [those of the Other], with lesser danger of being in error" (from Clavijero's work *Disertaciones* V, on the "Physical and Moral Constitution of the Mexicans," in his *Historia antigua de México [Ancient History of Mexico]*, which he was compelled to translate from Spanish into Italian so that it could be published in Italy in 1780 [Clavijero

1976b, 503–24]). Clavijero also wrote *Historia de la Antigua y Baja California* (*History of Ancient Lower California*), published in Venice in 1789. See also Clavijero 1976a, and consider Leon-Portilla 1974. Clavijero chose a historical, hermeneutical-political approach to reconstruct the regional particularity of Mexico's peripheral character, which is why he wrote a pamphlet about the Virgin of Guadalupe (who became the emblem of Mexico's struggle for political emancipation from Spain). He also highlighted the possibility of a *positive* path for the reconstruction of Mexico's difference in the face of the abstract universality of the European Enlightenment; a truly "*positive* philosophy" akin to that of Schelling in his *History of Mythology* (Dussel 1974a, 116 ff.: "From the definitive Hegel to the old Schelling"). In effect, Clavijero wrote regarding these themes some fifteen years before Schelling published his work *The Positivity of Christian Religion* (1795–96).

253. This is the essence of Augusto Salazar Bondy's argument in his 1969 work *Existe una filosofía de nuestra América?* (Is there any philosophy in our America?).

254. See Todorov 1989.

255. This is why all of Clavijero's work in the eighteenth century, like that of the philosophy of liberation in the twentieth century, has as its point of departure the affirmation of an "identity" (that of the world of the Aztecs or Mexicas negated by the conquest led by a man of Modernity: Hernán Cortés), which is the negation of the modern "identity" as expressed in "modernization"; a modernization that presupposes the negation of the peripheral culture as an alien, distinct, other in-itself. The peripheral "Self" undertakes its process of construction beginning with the negativity produced by the "modern hegemonic self." All of this analysis by Taylor can be found in the first chapter of Taylor 1989. It is evident that all of the violent irrationality of the "modern self" with respect to the periphery, does not appear here—a violence that is justified in the name of civilization, which is what I have referred to as the "myth of Modernity." This "myth" has not been adequately uncovered or analyzed. See Dussel 1993c, lecture 5: "Crítica del Mito de la Modernidad" (Critique of the myth of modernity), which is a critique of both Lyotard and Habermas or Taylor; I begin at the "Great Debate" in Valladolid in Spain in 1550, where Ginés de Sepúlveda (a modern argumentative rationalist) contends with Bartolomé de Las Casas (the founder of the most explicit philosophical counterdiscourse in *global Modernity*, as part of a transmodern project grounded in the perspective of the Other in Amerindia, Africa, and Asia, the woman oppressed by patriarchy, the planet destroyed as a capitalist "medium of production," and so on).

256. In the sense of the "other face" of a coin, or of the "other side" of the Moon which, although we cannot see it, is a constitutive part of this satellite of the Earth.

257. I recall the concerns raised by the presidents of the International Federation of Philosophical Societies, Alwin Diemer (see Diemer 1981 and 1985) and Vincent Cauchy, regarding the matter of a dialogue between cultures. I had the occasion to address this issue in a talk given at the University of Dusseldorf, invited by Diemer. My travels in Africa since 1972 (to Senegal, Ghana, Zimbabwe, Tanzania, Kenya, and South Africa) alerted me to such issues. On the other hand, my travels in Asia since 1977 (to India, Thailand, Sri Lanka, Hong Kong, the Philippines, and China) guided me on the necessity of reinterpreting world history. My residence for two years among the Palestinians

(1959–61) (in addition to Israel, I have lived in Egypt, Syria, Lebanon, Jordan, and Morocco) provided me with the experience of daily life in the Arab world. I also lived in Europe for eight years as a student (1957–66) in Spain, France, and Germany (frequently traveling to, and later teaching in, Switzerland, Italy, Belgium, England, Austria, the Scandinavian countries, and so on, in addition to Hungary, Czechoslovakia, Yugoslavia, and Russia), all of which has provided me with a certain vision of Europe. My frequent stays in the United States (I have been a visiting professor for semesters or quarters in different universities such as Notre Dame in South Bend; also universities in New York; California State University in Los Angeles; Vanderbilt in Nashville; and Loyola University in Chicago) and my continuous travels to all of the Latin American and Caribbean countries have suggested many themes to me, which I have sought to address philosophically.

258. Latin America, Modernity's first periphery, received the impact of European conquest before any other culture. Its universities in Mexico City and Lima (whose classes were first held in 1553) are the first academic centers to teach modern philosophy (that of the first Modernity) in the peripheral world. This created a unique situation: premodern Amerindian philosophy existed only in very incipient form (see §1.2), unlike China, India, and the Islamic world in Asia; but at the same time, 450 years of university-based philosophy place Latin America in a situation different from that of Bantu Africa. See regarding this issue Dussel 1996b; Dussel 1977, chaps. 1 and 2; Fornet-Betancourt 1985; and in Zea 1957 and 1974 (in particular, "Latin American Philosophy as a Philosophy of Liberation," 32 ff.); Salazar Bondy 1968 (a work that concludes with the following words: "Today liberation is still a possibility. . . . Hispanic American philosophy also has this option before it, which is its own constitution as an authentic system of thought depends upon" (133); Roig 1981 (in particular, "De la historia de las ideas a la Filosofía de la Liberación" ("From the History of Ideas to the Philosophy of Liberation"); and Miró Quesada 1974 and 1981. The theme of a "Philosophy of the Americas" (substitute "Latin America" for the "Americas") was already espoused explicitly by the Argentine Generation of 1837 with Alberdi, and was reborn in the present with Salazar Bondy 1968, simultaneously with the problematic of the philosophy of liberation, of which this ethics of liberation is a component.

259. It is interesting to note, in order to understand the contemporary philosophical profile of some countries in Asia (for example, India), that there are abundant dimensions of reflection that are much less common in Europe or the United States. For example, in the *Poona Report* (Satchidananda Murty 1985, 32 ff.) we can see that among the 848 holders of doctorates or masters' degrees in philosophy in India, 283 focused on metaphysics, 157 on the philosophy of religion (more than 50 in these two specialities), only 83 on political philosophy and 79 on epistemology (10 percent each), 32 on logic, and 19 on the philosophy of science (about 5 percent).

260. For a quick overview of "African philosophy," see Nagl-Docekal and Wimmer 1992, 7–14; and Wiredu 1992. For Africa in general, see Gann and Duignan 1969–70; Masolo 1994; and Oliver and Atmore 1969.

261. See, for example, Olela 1979; also Masolo 1994, a recent work which must be taken into account. Some have highlighted the importance of a unitary vision of the human being (without the body/soul) duality in Bantu thought,

but we are reminded often enough that this was also the importance of Egyptian thought (this is set forth in §I.1).

262. Regarding this aspect, I have not seen in any of the philosophers I have named a reference to the transition in the hegemony of the world system from England to the United States as a cause of Africa's emancipation (the centrality of the world system dominated by the United States does not have need of the complicated and costly European colonial system: it is the product of a new simplification in modern "administrative" reason).

263. Beginning with the work of Placide Tempels (1949). Criticisms of this intention can be seen in Eboussi Boulaga 1968; Eboussi Boulaga 1977, 28 ff.; Hountondjii 1977, 11 ff. See also Nothomb 1969.

264. Elungu 1984, 31.

265. Kagame 1956. For a critical exposition, see Elungu 1984, 33 ff.

266. See especially the work of Odera Oruka 1991b. J. C. Scannone (1984, 1990, and 1993), in Latin America, has also sought to develop a "philosophy of wisdom" inspired by Rodolfo Kusch (1970 and 1986).

267. Elungu 1984, 55 ff.; Odera Oruka 1990, 17 ff. See especially Fanon 1963; Nkrumah 1971; Nyerere 1967.

268. From W. E. B. Du Bois (1868–1963) in Atlanta, New York, and Ghana to Marcus Garvey in Jamaica (1885–1940), until Dr. Price-Mars in Haiti (1876–1969). Later came pan-Africanism, African nationalism, Négritude (as espoused by Leópold Sedar-Senghor and Aimé Césaire) and African socialism (Nkrumah, among others). See the elaboration of this theme in Elungu 1984, 55–112. Odera Oruka (1991a, 87) argues that "complete freedom requires freedom both of the nation and their citizens."

269. This kind of imitative university-based philosophy (as in Asia and Latin America) is simply a preparatory course for the next historical stage; it is not properly a creative philosophy, but rather an informative one. I wanted to situate in this category all those African philosophers who are opposed to all philosophy centered in Africa and who believe that philosophy is simply universal, but without reference to the "world of life" (*Lebenswelt*). See Odera Oruka 1990, 18 ff. Regarding "professional philosophy" in Africa (where the term is given another meaning than that employed here): its most distant forerunner was Amo Guinea-Africanus (Amo-le-Guinéen), author of works such as *Dissertatio Inauguralis de jure Maurorum in Europa* (1729), *Dissertatio de humanae mentis apatheia* (1734), and *Tractatus de arte sobrie et accurate philosophandi* (1738), who lectured in Halle (where he was *Privatdozent*) and in Jena, in Germany; another contemporary of Kant with origins in the periphery (Hountondjii 1977, 139–70). This is equivalent, by analogy, to what Francisco Romero described in Latin America (after 1915) as the era of the founders or the second "philosophical normalization" (since the "first" took place in the colonial era, after 1553, as I have noted above). In any case, the variant of professional philosophy practiced in Africa is more honest: "African philosophy, as distinct from African *traditional world views*, is the philosophy that is being produced by contemporary African philosophers. It is still in the making" (Wiredu 1980, 36).

270. Elungu 1984, 113 ff. ("Les philosophies critiques"); further on he speaks of "African philosophy in a strict sense" (123–52).

271. Eboussi Boulaga 1977. The meaning of *Muntu* is something like "a

human being" (a kind of *Dasein*, as the term is employed by Heidegger, whose existence has been flung into the peripheral world of Africa, in its colonial, contradictory form, torn by contradictions). Eboussi Boulaga's work is divided into three parts: (1) the system of the global; (2) the symbolics of domination; (3) the consequences of the crisis. In the first he criticizes "ethno-philosophy" as a failed rhetoric ("The rhetoric fails because there is no community of discussion," 41).

272. For example: "Ontology is not only permanent, but murderous: it suppresses the false selves. . . . The end justifies the means, renders them just and sacred, labels itself as sacrifice" (ibid., 201).

273. Ibid., 16. "A philosophy that does not know from where it speaks, nor to whom, is hidden from itself and ends up playing a role which is arbitrary and irrational" (ibid., 23).

274. The Bantu "African-human-being."

275. "The world is asymmetrical. . . . Its secret is its strength; the secret of its strength is Western. . . . philosophy" (Eboussi Boulaga 1977, 35).

276. Ibid., 19.

277. Ibid., 18. "By identifying itself with the dominator, the *Muntu* denies its original self when it looks at itself in the mirror" (ibid., 21). See such magnificent texts as Memmi 1969 or Fanon 1963.

278. His criticism of ethnology is devastating ("The end of ethnology": "The essence of ethnology is connected to the hegemonic expansion of the West," 161 [Eboussi Boulaga 1977]: with the objective of substituting the Other, as center-subject of its world, in order to be able to describe it "from the outside." In a certain sense, Eboussi Boulaga invalidates all of Habermas's critique at the beginning of his cited work (Habermas 1981b, vol. 1, introduction, 2: "Some of the characteristics of mythical understanding and of the modern understanding of the world"; 72 ff.). Here it is important to note that Habermas always, when he wants to highlight the characteristics of "modern" rationality, compares it (even as he forgets China, India, the Islamic world, and Latin America) with a utopian "primitive man," who is the object of the study of ethnology. It would be very useful if writers such as Winch, Godolier, Lukes, Horton, Habermas, and others would carefully read and cite the works of *African philosophers* (who speak in the "first" person and not as "*outside* observers") of the stature of Eboussi Boulaga. It is already well past the time when the much-ballyhooed dialogue convening those who have been "*affected*" by and who are the *excluded* of the world system to join the "*hegemonic* community of (Euro–North American) philosophers." But this will still take quite a while, and is likely to be delayed for at least as long as the arrogance of the white man continues to have contempt for human beings (and their philosophy) among the periphery of Modernity.

279. See Eboussi Boulaga 1977, 42–66.

280. Ibid., 50.

281. Here Eboussi Boulaga writes: "The *language*. It is a manifestation of force, of original Power; it is a *kratofanía*. . . . That which is inside is exhibited on the outside, and the outside returns within" (ibid., 43). This brings to mind, for me, the Egyptian god Thot (see §I.1), the prehistory of the Greek *logos* and of the Semitic concept of *dabar*. This is the primordial experience at the origin of the Bantu people.

282. "Ethnicity is human nature as if it were an immutable destiny, as part of qualitative, distinctive necessities. Ethnicity espouses the rigidity of the species, within a fixed perspective" (ibid., 46).

283. "The individual does not exist anymore, and becomes transformed into an abstraction conceived through the prism of ethnicity" (ibid., 48).

284. Ibid., 51: "Because of this, everything that has value, that is imposed without discussion, is said to have its origin in the ancestors, and is categorized as sacred" (ibid.). "This is its foundation, that which is ontologically and logically prior to its existence" (ibid.).

285. Ibid., 54.

286. Ibid., 56. It would be worth including the rest of the text here as well, but it would unduly extend the length of this book. Eboussi Boulaga's work is well deserving of the kind of attentive reading with which one reads Aristotle's *Metaphysics*, Hegel's *Logic*, or Heidegger's *Being and Time*.

287. Eboussi Boulaga 1977, 64. "Divination . . . is reproduced within the symbolic order with the objective of eliminating and proclaiming the suppression of our body within the order of reality. . . . The global system is a magic wrought by the verb" (ibid.).

288. Ibid., 66.

289. Ibid., 229.

290. Ibid., 83 ff., part II of the work.

291. Ibid., 88.

292. Ibid., 220.

293. Ibid., 132 ff. In my opinion, in this respect the philosopher whose work I am addressing here does not sufficiently articulate pragmatics with economics in this context.

294. Ibid., 187.

295. Ibid., 152 ff.

296. Ibid., 221.

297. Youssough Mbargane Guissé (1979): "We have sought to demonstrate the African sources of philosophical tradition, deployed in combat upon the very terrain of the history of Eurocentrism" (174).

298. North American pragmatism had to wage a struggle for the recognition of the European philosophical community at the beginning of the twentieth century, as can be discerned in William James's talks in Edinburgh—which I will refer to later in this book. One hundred years later, Latin American philosophy finds itself in a similar position in terms of the demand for its due recognition. Today the *Latin American* philosophy of liberation has a similar task, but with a difference, because it is the expression of a discourse that has been conceived from a global perspective, a perspective distinct from that of James, given that his work emerged at the precise moment at the inception of the twentieth century, when the United States was *positioning* itself at the center of the already *ancient* world system (the modern system, which had been in existence since 1492). In contrast, Latin America, Africa, and Asia today seek to participate in the creation of a *new* world system. An exception to the trend exemplified by James is the recent work by David Cooper, *World Philosophies* (1996).

Part I

1. "Grounding," not in the ontological sense, but in a more radical sense, as what is "prior" to the "ontological"; but also prior to the metaphysical moment or the ethical in Levinas (see §4.4), given that in its beginning (human life), it is the pre-ethical: the material aspect of the ethical. It is the "*mode* of reality" of human life, which Levinas presupposes in his phenomenological analysis.

Chapter 1. The Material Moment

1. See theses 3, 10, and 11 in appendix 1.

2. I want at the outset to give the following warning. The "vitalistic" philosophical currents, especially the German ones, can lend themselves to bad interpretation. I want to make clear my distance from "vitalism" in the style of Ludwig Klages, Oswald Spengler, German Nazism, and Italian fascism, and its effects in Latin America and other horizons. I distance myself even from Nietzsche's vitalism (see §4.3). I want to be placed within a "Latin American" current (of the Native American, African, and Caribbean movements, and popular groups, and feminist movements), which struggles for the life of the ethical, human-corporeal, subject. This current agrees philosophically with a tradition that began with Karl Marx, passes through Freud, and could culminate with Franz Hinkelammert. It has nothing to do with reactionary pro vita groups. See again thesis 11 in appendix 1.

3. See thesis 10, appendix 1.

4. Here Kant uses *Materie*, in the sense of empirical "content."

5. Kant, *Kritik der praktischen Vernunft*, A 38 (1968, vol. 6, 127).

6. I will instead define the principle of material ethics as the demand (or obligation) of the production, reproduction, and development of the life of the human subject. Kant, it seems, refers only, and reductively, to something like "animal and vegetable life."

7. This anguish is today even more frightful than in Kant's time, since the majority of humanity sees itself thrown by the process of globalization into an impoverishment never seen before.

8. *Grundlegung zur Metaphysik der Sitten*, part I, BA 10 (Kant 1968, vol. 6, 23).

9. As we will soon see, the affective structure participates in the neurocerebral process of perceptive categorization, as well as in conceptual categorization and in the moment of self-consciousness or reflexive capacity of reason, in the constitution of the "objects" of knowledge of what could still be called a "theoretical reason." For this reason, the empirical as much as the conceptual universal always presupposes an "appetitive-evaluative" moment. The "affective" or "drive" moment toward what is satisfying achieves "pleasure," that is, satisfaction, in its fulfillment. The "evaluative" moment (see thesis 12 in appendix 1, §1.5c, and §4.3) is nothing less than the judgment of compatibility between an end, object, or practical statement (maxim) with the material principle of ethics that I articulate thus: whether or not it allows the production, reproduction, and development of human life. "Evaluate" will have at times

in this *Ethics* a strong sense (judgment enunciated from the universal material criterion of human survival), and at other times a weak sense (comparison with cultural values relative to a *particular* and concrete historical life world).

10. The material or practical truth criterion, the concrete life of the human subject, is the aspect of reality (a *mode of reality*) from whence emerge all "inclinations," and constitutes them with respect to their "content."

11. See, for example, Rabossi 1995; Rorty 1979, 17 ff.; Searle 1984, "The Mind-Body Problem," 13 ff.; or in Bunge 1988; Putnam 1988.

12. To clarify from the outset: I will use as examples, and without greater claims, some recent discoveries in neurobiology. I take into account Apel's criticisms of those that make "philosophical" use of neurobiology without taking note of the different levels (Apel 1991, passim). The *fact* of subjectivity by introspection, including philosophical reflection, *reflects* that it will never be a neurological *fact* for objective observation; but both "facts" have an identical material "support." Human "subjectivity" has an inevitable "cerebral" root as we will see. For this reason, I should not be accused of *standard* or naturalist materialism. After Darwin (with his "adaptation" of the "ethical codes" and "instinct of empathy," all of which would be guaranteed by the inheritance of acquired characteristics), passing through sociobiology, we arrive eventually at neurobiology. It is necessary not to claim to demonstrate how "altruistic" human life is at its exclusively genetic level. My query is of a different sort. See works in a Darwinist vein, such as those of Bertram 1988; Dawkins 1976; Wilson 1975 and 1978. For a general treatment, with bibliography, see Jonas 1982b and Paris 1994.

13. Maturana 1985. Niklas Luhmann owes to Maturana the fundamental concept of *autopoiesis* in his theory of social systems (Luhmann 1988, 60 ff.; 167 ff., 228 ff.).

14. For Zubiri, and with reason, the entire physical universe is only substantivity (Dussel 1977, 4.1.3–1.5; Zubiri 1963).

15. "The living" in our corporeality "has not died" for 4,000 million years. Each living being has its own, independent, substantivity (from the unicellular amoeba upward).

16. Maturana 1985, 28. It is worth noting the similarity between Maturana's observations with those of Zubiri, who also speaks of "closure" and the "self-sufficiency" of the "substantivity" of things, but properly living, and only in human substantivity is there maximal "self-sufficient closure" (Zubiri 1963, 220–48). See Dussel 1977, 4.1–4; Dussel 1984, 12 ff. I treat the question with reference to Putnam in §3.2.

17. Maturana 1985, 63 ff. Zubiri defines evolution in the following way: "The origination of specific essences by metaspecification is what we call evolution" (1963, 256). This definition deserves a long explication, but it underpins his entire book *On Essence* (ibid.).

18. Maturana 1985, 92.

19. The human nervous system is made up of more than 1,011 neurons, and "each one receives multiple contacts with other neurons and in turn is connected with many cells" (ibid., 105). We have millions of motoneurons, and tens of millions of sensory cells distributed through various parts of the body. To "feel" (in a membrane) pleasure or pain in the skin (think of the utilitarians) or hunger in the internal mucus membrane of the stomach (I am thinking here

of the phrase "I gave bread [to the hungry]" in the *Egyptian Book of the Dead*) is an effect of this immense "sensing" system of the corporeality of the ethical subject.

20. Maturana 1985, 138. The term "linguistic" has to be taken metaphorically or as only a beginning.

21. See Edelman 1989, 1992.

22. Edelman 1992, 79.

23. In other words, to know how to act when confronted by a virus or an object, or to know how to evolve, there is neither an a priori code nor knowledge of prior rules. It regards, rather, what lymphocytes do, when they act indiscriminately in producing antibodies. One of the antibodies is effective against the attack of the invading virus—the object of enquiry by immunology. This antigene reproduces itself without previous knowledge of its efficacy. It acts a posteriori. Edelman calls this knowledge as one acquired by "selection" (1992, 73–80).

24. At this exact moment, as is evident in the case of the human being, there exist as many institutions engaged in the technological production of things to satisfy human needs, as there are institutions of economic exchange and distribution. Thus the transition from "hunger" to "eating" is mediated by very complex institutions and to give an account of them all would, if I were to be exhaustive in the telling, include world history.

25. Damasio 1994, 116.

26. Zubiri 1986, 20 ff. I will return to this question later in this chapter and in §3.1.

27. "Perceptual categorization" is the "categorization" or generalization by comparison with other qualia or capturing of prior stimuli (moment 5 of figure 5). This "categorization" does not need any a priori order, nor genetic or innate rules of categorization. Each brain will flexibly encounter its own path of comparison or generalization and will localize in some approximately similar "places" in the brain (by topobiological compartments [see Edelman 1988], the "living sensations" or qualia, that is, relations of groups of neurons that can be "remembered" or "recalled"; this is what we call memory (system c of figure 5). This entire "organic" process is never exact, and each repetition ("new reentry") will be different in some aspect (this process of "new reentries" is indicated in figure 5 with arrows in both directions: ← →). This is not at all like a computer or a fixed mathematical equation.

28. The section of the brain that forms "maps" is the cortical region, not the limbic system or the base of the brain.

29. Edelman 1992, 89. Perceptual, as well as conceptual, categorization, does not act on the basis of representations or images, nor should one understand conceptualizing action in terms of the objectivist sense of Frege, Carnap, or positivism. As Noam Chomsky proposed (1968), categories are neither genetic nor fixed. They are generated by cerebral practices and are "kept" as recalling processes that "new *recalls*" (Edelman 1992, "Postscript," 232 ff.) bring about. When Heidegger speaks of the "understanding of Being" (*Seinsverständnis*) or the "understanding of the world" (*Weltverständnis*) he is perhaps expressing, as no philosopher before him, the cerebral phenomenon of *global mapping*; in other words, a general "mapping" of the totality of lived "experience," past-projective and present, as "possibilities" for life (human, linguistic-cultural, and historical). See Dussel 1970–80, vol. 1 (1970), secs. 1–6. "Existential under-

standing" is special. The "world" and the ontological "project" is a *télos* (not an "end," as the term is used by Max Weber), which includes practical and interpretative reason. The "understanding of the world" is the way in which the brain encompasses the totality of the experience of the ethical (and rational) subject in its millions of billions of relations of the neural base group, at the speed of electricity by "entries" and "exists" within a closed circuit. We have to remember, however, that reason has "no cerebral area specifically determined for intellection. . . . It is a species of unspecified cerebral activity" (Zubiri 1986, 493).

30. This "criterion of value" (which in reality is a "criterion of practical truth"; see thesis 13a) is what I am seeking to focus my reflections on at this stage, since the "criterion" that is attributable to the limbic system in genetic terms, and which is located at the base of the brain, will be subsumed by *values that are most properly conceived of as self-conscious and linguistic in character, and derived from ethical-cultural systems*, determined by what I will refer to as a "criterion of truth" from the perspective of survival (see thesis 11). In §1.1, when I speak of "value" it should be understood in the sense of normative statements with a claim to practical truth (see §§1.5, 2.5, and 3.5), and not only in the Weberian sense of cultural value. These statements are *factual* judgments that "judge" the compatibility of the content of concepts or judgments as mediations or not to the life of the ethical subject (see table 2 and figure 7, and §3.5c).

31. Edelman 1992, 90.

32. I call here "object" the synthesis that the brain produces that is neither a representation nor an image, as is traditionally thought. No homunculus could *see* this representation (otherwise we would regress infinitely). This was very well discerned by Rorty (1979), but unfortunately he does not describe positively how the brain proceeds strictly with categorization. The brain sees a color, smells a perfume, touches a texture, captures the perceptual content, and so on of the real thing in a "global" manner. In a second experience of the same thing, it "actualizes" the connection among groups of neurons that received the first impression (*qualia* for Edelman, *somatic marker* for Damasio), and "*recalls*" them by memory, reconnecting them. But, in this process of memorization the links between neurons are never repeated in the same way, but are instead reorganized and resynthesized, improving or forgetting some moment. This process is unlike what happens in a computer; it is not a process of mathematical identity; it is instead a "mapping" that allows the creation, plastically, of the vital and new.

33. If the human species, in its politics, economics, science, loses these criteria of "practical truth," it could disappear as a species (see §3.5), just as other creatures would. Ethics then becomes a question of life or death for contemporary humanity. Reductionist "formalism" (of Frege, Carnap, and Ayer, passing through Rawls and Hayek, and ending up with discourse ethics, as we will see) touches on this question at different levels.

34. In the way of: "*To feed the hungry* allows the reproduction of life." See below §1.5a.

35. See appendix 1, thesis 12, on "value."

36. In the human species, the formal moment of morality develops this moment rationally and intersubjectively as "application" of the concrete case of the criterion of survival (§2.5), or synthetically in the judgment of ethical feasibility (§1.5a).

37. I want to indicate here that the ancient philosophical problem of "values" is *situated* (see thesis 12). The question is, where may these so-called values be found? Their ontological status has always been dubious; they are found *mainly* in the limbic system and the base of the brain (also in the frontal lobe; see Damasio 1994, in the case of Phineas Gage, 3 ff.)—not in a *cosmos ouranos* as in Plato, nor in a simple metaphysical-cultural structure as in Scheler, nor in an indefinite way as in the axiological intuitionism of Moore—where, approximately and habitually, the exercise of judgments of compatibility with the criterion of life-death, or practical truth occurs. "Values" (types of accessing mediations departing from such a criterion) are found in the structural relations of neural groups (the product of perceptual and posterior conceptual categorization), which are situated in the organs of affective evaluation or specific "maps" of the cortex, and which determine the constitution of the "object" (or the remaining "judgments") insofar as they are "judged" with reference to whether they oppose or allow human survival, and this in different moments (perceptual, conceptual, consciously and practically decisive, self-conscious, linguistic, ethical-cultural, and historical institutional, and so on) of the human act (from vegetative moments up to political, economic, and artistic moments, to name a few, acknowledging the essential differences among them). As can already be suspected, I am speaking of a "criterion of *universal* truth" (not at all "capricious," chaotic, or moved only by "egoism"—human survival and egoism are opposed and have nothing to do with each other), which is inscribed instinctually and culturally in the same cerebral "affectivity" (which will destroy the whole Kantian argumentative strategy in §§1–6 of the beginning of book 1 of the *Critique of Practical Reason*).

38. "Classification is not the same as value, but instead it takes place on the basis of value. . . . Without a previous value, the selective somatic systems would not converge in their final behaviors" (Edelman 1992, 94).

39. Ibid., 163.

40. This neither presupposes nor produces any "representation" or "image" (ibid., 230; a correct critique against the "objectivism" of the first Vienna Circle and against rationalist reductionism). See §3.2.

41. We have to make a distinction between (a) the merely stimulaic "valuing" (of the animal, and that demands an immediate and necessary "response") and (b) the human "judging" or "valorizing" that "refers" to the possibility or impossibility of the reproduction and development of the life of the human subject (Hinkelammert 1984, chap. 4; which presupposes the actualization of the thing as real, as that which "is its own"—see Zubiri 1963 and 1981). This last "valorizing" is constitutive of the "concept" (always categorized *hierarchically* as leading or not leading to the reproduction or development of this human life) in the cognitive act itself, prior to every judgment of fact (means-ends). The properly "cultural" "valorization" (out of the cultural values of an ethical life) is a simultaneous moment but is grounded in the prior act. The material, ethical criterion of the reproduction and development of human life (preontological) is already executed in the conceptual categorization itself; when I express "poison" (as negative), "food" (as positive), "hunger" (negative), "wound" (negative), "health" (positive), and so on—before any abstract statement of fact, and, evidently, of a Weberian "judgment of value," which we will have to radically redefine—as words-concepts, they have already been "evaluated" with "reference" to human life.

42. Edelman 1992, 109–10.

43. Of mediations, objects, or statements already "judged" using the criterion of the truth of survival, in an "order" where those more compatible with survival (also cultural or ethical survival in the case of human beings) occupy the first place.

44. Edelman 1992, 119.

45. Eight million years ago, in the Rift Valley of East Africa, because of earth movements or climatic factors that caused dryness in the region, changing it from tropical jungle to plain dominated by shrubs, some primates gradually adopted an erect posture (Coppens 1975, 1994). This allowed, in addition to freeing up the development of the cerebral cavity (especially the cortical lobes) due to the decrease in the muscles in the neck, other fundamental phenomena: the development of the supralarynx system (which allowed the transformation of the phonetic and anatomical organs necessary for human speech; Edelman 1992, 126 ff.; these changes concern the *linguistic-pragmatic* dimension), and the liberation of the upper limbs, no longer required for moving on all fours (in other words, the development of the hands in front of a binocular visual field, which allowed in turn the prodigious technical-instrumental achievements of which I will give an account later: the *productive-economic* dimension).

46. Edelman 1989, 173 ff.; Edelman 1992, 130.

47. As we have seen, we cannot speak of an "innate grammar" in the way that Chomsky did early on—although, in any event, the cultural product of language should, clearly, also not be misunderstood as other than the global way in which the brain deals with the surrounding world.

48. "The behavioral configurations that, acquired ontogenetically in the communicative dynamic of a social medium, are stable through generations, I will designate as *cultural* behavior" (Maturana 1985, 133). At this point, beyond naive "evolutionism," a place is left open for the determination of a qualitative "jump" in life to a properly human life.

49. Ibid., 155. This would be a good place to offer a critical exposition of the fundamental thesis that begins with Bertrand Russell (1956, 192: "The analysis of apparently complex things . . . can be reduced to the analysis of facts which apparently refer to such things," which are expressed in "atomic propositions") and that leads to the Vienna Circle and Wittgenstein in his first phase. Wittgenstein would later write: "It is more than 16 years since I took up philosophy again, and was compelled to recognize serious errors [*schwere Irrtümer*] in what I had written in my first book" (the *Tractatus*) (1988, 12–13). In 1929, certainly having read Heidegger's *Sein und Zeit*, Wittgenstein set out on the path that would lead him to overcome the *reductionistic fallacies* of the first analytical school—and which, in the United States, meant a return to the theses of pragmatism, in many philosophers (West 1992, 182 ff.). In other words, the overcoming of the atomism of words and sentences, of the illusion that ordinary language and even transcendental and universal concepts could be abandoned, required, finally, the replacement of *abstract* semantic analysis with *practical* pragmatics (Apel 1973; Austin 1962; Searle 1969; see §§5.1 and 5.2).

50. See Derrida 1967a and 1967b.

51. Habermas 1981b, vol. 2, 7–170; Mead 1934, 135 ff.

52. Edelman 1992, 133–35.

53. For an introduction see Bloom and Lazerson 1988, 210 ff., and Miller 1983.

484 NOTES TO CHAPTER I

54. "Pleasure" and "pain" are properly felt in the skin, in the internal membranes of the organs, in the tissues that envelop muscles, and in the external membranes of the bones. It is the survival of the original membrane of the unicellular living organism that "remembers" the boundary between "inside" and "outside" of the living being, and which reacts to what is "foreign": if it makes "possible" the life of the organism, it is felt as "pleasure," if it is harmful, as "pain"—in principle.

55. Damasio 1994.

56. All of this could not be known by Benthamite utilitarianism.

57. Edelman would have written "structure of neural groups."

58. Damasio 1994, 131.

59. Ibid., 139.

60. Rorty proposes, as an example, a humanity of Antipodeans without "minds" (1979, 70 ff.: "Persons without minds"). In reality, this is an equivocation: if "mind" means something substantial, I am in agreement with Rorty. If "mind" is a higher function of the brain, then there can be no person without mind. The "mental functions" of the brain are, plainly and simply, presupposed and necessary for an ethics: conceptual categorization, existence of linguistic-cultural processes, and self-consciousness (which are the basis of freedom and responsibility). The question is not about "mind-body" but the existence of a "corporeality" in whose complex organicity the brain is given as an internal moment that has "mental functions." With this clarification we have circumvented a metaphysical anthropology of the substantial soul, but we have retained the necessary cerebral functions for an ethics in the strict sense.

61. Damasio 1994, 146–47.

62. All of this Levinas sought to analyze "phenomenologically" (see §4.4).

63. Here I cannot resist the temptation to refer to Levinas. Even Heidegger, analyzing the ontological *pathos* of existential "angst," places it in the general grounding of existence. It would thus be like a *background feeling* (which includes also the linguistic-cultural and historical "world"). This is the original *Befindlichkeit* (to find oneself). It is paradoxical that an "edifying" philosopher—to use Rorty's term—has analyzed, like few others, the cerebral-corporeal existence of the human being as a totality!

64. Damasio 1994, 150.

65. Ibid., 153.

66. Ibid., 154.

67. From the Greek, *anosognosia* means a complete lack of self-perception of one's body (of some part or its totality); ibid., 62–69.

68. See Kohlberg's studies, 1981–84, and Kohlberg and Colby 1987. See section 5.2a.

69. In figure 5, these items are numbered 2, 7, 13, the last of which ("General affective-evaluative mapping") should include, besides "general feeling," properly moral, ethical feeling (and cultural-historical, as we will see below).

70. Damasio 1994, 164. In chapter II ("A Passion for Reasoning"), Damasio describes the co-constitutive articulation of affectivity and reason: without affectivity there is no reason.

71. *Kritik der praktischen Vernunft*, A 39–40 (Kant 1958, vol. 6, 128).

72. This philosophical hypothesis, of magical mythical origin (which is behind a good part of the philosophies of the Enlightenment), is what makes the dualist, decorporealized, Puritan ethics so poisonous; an ethics that negates

sexuality, pleasure, the emotions, and the evaluative apparatuses, and which dominates women. It is a pathological syndrome that justifies systems of erotic, political, economic, cultural, and so on, domination, and which an ethics of liberation will radically discard. On unitary corporeality from a philosophical perspective, see Dussel 1969, 1973, and 1974a.

73. Searle 1984, 14; 1994, 27 ff.

74. Merleau-Ponty 1963, 202. See his splendid chapter "The Relations of the Soul and the Body and the Problem of Perceptual Consciousness" (ibid., 185–224).

75. Zubiri 1992, 334. Zubiri's thought would take us far, to spheres that neither Anglo-Saxon nor Germanic thinking are used to reaching in these days—or at least, not in the styles in vogue. Zubiri writes, "Feelings are, certainly, acts of the subject, but they are neither more nor less subjective than the intellections or volitions; they envelope formally a moment of reality" (ibid., 336). Zubiri distinguishes between feelings (the "passions" of classic philosophy) and the "will" (21–82). I will return to this theme later.

76. On this theme in *Being and Time*, sec. 31 (Heidegger 1963c, 142 ff.); also Schädelbach 1983, chap. 4.

77. Heidegger's approach is thus a point of departure, one that I moved beyond in *Towards an Ethics of Latin American Liberation*, written more than twenty-five years ago (Dussel 1970–80, vol. 1 [1970], chap. 1). Although "the Understanding [comprehension] of Being" was a cognitive moment, it was nonetheless also practical in character (a "pro-ject" [*Entwurf*], a *télos*, or "becoming" in the face of intelligence, and "*Sein-können*" ["being able" or capable] of laying the necessary foundation for the will and the appetitive faculty). Key discoveries regarding the science of the brain confirm for us this path of the unity of ethical corporeality.

78. Maturana 1985, 163. When Maturana links the biological-neural behavior of the brain with the linguistic horizon—understood here as a cultural product—he also lays the basis for overcoming a naive naturalism and provides a platform from which we can distinguish between that which "is" merely prelinguistic and cerebral (*global* perceptual management of the environment), and that which "ought to be," which emerges *explicitly* from the conceptual, linguistic, and self-conscious sphere of the ethical "good" (for instance, "justice," or the universal validity of the human act). For this reason, for Maturana and the neurologists I have mentioned, that which "ought to be" is the moment that is grounded on the biological-neural structure of the living human "being" (the fourth degree of unity is based on the third).

79. See Moore 1968, secs. 29 ff., 45 ff.

80. Ibid., sec. 31, 48.

81. When Moore speaks of "the correct estimation of values" (ibid., secs. 116, 192), he is dealing with an axiology that does not sufficiently challenge its ontological sense (see Dussel 1970–80, vol. 1, 126 ff.). It is for that reason necessary to take the time to reground it adequately, without contradicting the scientific results that I have thus far only sketched. Moore's critique of utilitarianism is semantically dubious (Rabossi 1979, 83–127), as it confuses descriptive statements with normative pronouncements (Habermas 1983, 60 ff.). Furthermore it is pragmatically insufficient (since it is a prepragmatic philosophy, and for that reason its semantics is reductionistic) and ethically irrelevant (because it does not touch on any ethical problem of any real importance, since as a meta-

ethics it defines itself as unable to deal with normative or empirical themes, such as the hunger of the majority of the humanity as the consequence of unjust political-economic systems). Later, Stevenson's emotivism (1945) or Hare's prescriptivism (1952) could be criticized in similar ways. See in this *Ethics*, sections 2.5, 3.1, and 3.2.

82. See table 8, level 1 [198].

83. This will be further developed in a future work on the foundations of the principles of an ethics of liberation.

84. Someone may write I "need" or "have to" instead of I "ought," but, as we will see, it is not a biological need but rather an "ethical" requirement forestalling suicide (of oneself or of the community) or homicide (of the other).

85. Kant himself, in another sense, as I have already noted, writes "to preserve one's life is a duty" (*Grundlegung zur Metaphysik der Sitten*, BA 10 [Kant 1968, vol. 6, 23]). What type of deontological requirement is this, and what does it mean for Kant? We will return to this point.

86. Again, "value" here is not meant in a cultural sense only, but also as the hierarchization according to a thing's distance or proximity (from being just allowed to being necessary) for the production and development of the life of the human subject. A "judgment of fact" is "valued"—and for that reason is required and can "measure" other judgments—inasmuch as it is compared to the criterion of survival or the criterion of practical truth.

87. A procedure for detecting the type of descriptive statements that ground normative ones would be to follow the reverse path in the constitution of statements. One could determine thus the descriptive statements (which are always and only anthropological and that refer to life) that would allow us to ground normative statements. If we set out from normative statements ("Thou shalt not kill"), we can discover several implied descriptive statements, among them, for example: "We are living human beings, and for that reason mortal." The life of the human being imposes—by the argumentation of practical-material reason, as grounded (although not by analytical formal deduction) on the criterion of life or truth—on each responsible and self-conscious subject as an "ought-to-be": "You are *responsible* for the care of human life, as much in yours as in that of others." This statement, as the prohibition of the nongeneralizable maxim, can be made concrete in "Thou shalt not kill" (Wellmer 1986). On every anthropological and descriptive statement (when these are fundamental determinations of the human "being" *as human*) can be grounded an "ought." The reductionistic fallacy (the "naturalist fallacy") consists in not distinguishing analytical (abstract), formal, and descriptive statements from material and anthropological (concrete) ones, which are able to ground an "ought." "The wall is yellow" is a statement from which no "ought" can be derived. However, from "I am a living human being and for that reason I must eat," can ground "I *have* to eat or I risk dying (if I cease to eat)," a path of action that cannot be *ethically* justified without falling into a performative contradiction. I will return to this topic.

88. In 1789 France had approximately twenty-nine million inhabitants, while the United Kingdom had only nine million. England enjoyed naval and commercial supremacy over the "world system," which it shared with France for a long time.

89. Modern "economics," the science of economics, developed in the Anglo-Saxon world. Not only Adam Smith (an ethicist), but also Bentham (1948),

John S. Mill (1981, vols. 2–5), and Henry Sidgwick (1901), wrote their respective "political economies." The theme is indicated by Mill at the beginning of his *Principles of Political Economy with Some of Their Application to Social Philosophy* (Mill 1965, vol. 2): "The requirements for production are two: work and appropriated natural objects. Work can be either physical or mental . . . muscular or conceptual . . . every type required by the human demand." In other words, the problem of "corporeality" (in the ethical subject, with preferences presented as demands) is clearly present in these ethics that understand *economics* in a capitalist sense.

90. Moore tells us: "These *universal* truths have always occupied a significant place in the reasoning of the metaphysical philosophers, from Plato all the way up to the present. The fact that they dealt directly with the difference between these truths and what I have described as *natural objects* constitutes their principal contribution to knowledge, and this differentiates them from another class of philosophers—the *empirical* philosophers—to which the majority of English philosophers have belonged" (1968, sec. 66, 111).

91. Bentham 1948, chap. 17, 4; 412, note. On this whole topic see Höffe 1972 and 1979 and MacIntyre 1966, sec. 12, 155; sec. 17, 220 ff.

92. Marx, "Reflections by a Youth upon Electing a Profession" (in Marx 1956–90, vol. 1, 594).

93. Marx, *Kapital*, chap. 23, 5 (Marx 1987, 588).

94. On utilitarianism, see Albee 1957; Glover 1990; Höffe 1972 and 1979; Quinton 1973. In Bentham, consider 1948 and 1983–89; in Mill 1981 and 1987. MacIntyre deals with the issue in his overall argument (1981, 62 ff.).

95. See the doctoral thesis of Germán Gutiérrez (1996), where he describes the "equanimous transcendental observer" in the market ethics of Adam Smith.

96. We will see in §4.3 how Hellenic-Roman stoicism, with its conception of the control of the instincts, gives expression to the reproductive sense of institutions by means of repetition, aspiring to security and peace, and profoundly conservative, though it may oppose slavery.

97. This is to say, the "discipline" of everyday life is practiced. In Europe this was accomplished by Calvinism or Protestantism; in the United Kingdom, by Scottish Presbyterianism (Hume and Smith, for example) and later on, by "Methodism" (as its name indicates: a disciplined "Methodism"). See Oestreich 1983. It would be interesting to draw a parallel between stoicism in the Roman (with *apátheia* as self-control) and the English Empires. In both cases it concerns the "self-discipline" of the elites of an empire that dominates over large "peripheries," and which requires of the "lords" an exemplar self-control (the *gentleman*), in order to manage the dominated subjects with efficacy from the "center." This would be the simply repetitive instinct of a "happiness" *criticized by Nietzsche, and different from the Dionysian or Zarathustran instinct for pleasure* (see §4.3).

98. See Taylor 1989, 159 ff.

99. For them, whether in the context of slave society (Aristotle), in Arabian mercantilism (Avicenna), or in the feudalism of the beginning of urban European society (Thomas Aquinas), that which is materially "just" refers to justice (*justitia, dikaiosyne*), that is, to "justice" (and not "right"), in the Hellenic, Muslim or Christian tradition (see thesis 13d). We will see later on the function of "*phronesis* (*prudentia*)" in the context of formal morality (that which is inte-

gral to the monological, private moment, at the procedural moment necessary to attain intersubjective or public validity).

100. See MacPherson 1964.

101. Locke 1975, bk. 1, chap. 28, sec. 5. In another text, he writes: "Then things are either good or bad only in relation to pleasure or pain" (ibid., bk. 2, chap. 20, sec. 2). He is referring to a criterion of the feasible constitution of the "goodness claim."

102. Hutcheson, *An Enquiry into the Origin of Our Ideas of Beauty and Virtue*, bk. 2, 3 (cited in MacIntyre 1966, 161).

103. MacIntyre 1988, 281 ff. It is interesting to note the importance that the *Scottish Enlightenment* had, since this was the product of a peripheral elite (ibid., 260) (Scotland lost its sovereignty in 1707), situated between the *dominating* English culture and the traditional culture of farmers who spoke the ancient Scottish language ("Gaelic Highlands"). The people who fostered the Scottish Enlightenment inscribed themselves within the Calvinist-Presbyterian tradition of the Scottish church, with an Augustinian and Aristotelian-scholastic background (ibid., 209). Figures such as Edmund Burke, Thomas Halyburton (with his work *Natural Religion Insufficient and Revealed Necessary to Man's Happiness*, Edinburgh, 1714), Robert Baillie, and Francis Hutcheson flourished in the industrial cities of Glasgow and Edinburgh, and had to confront the ambiguity of defending the cultural identity of their own culture or to incorporate themselves into English "Modernity." Scottish "moral philosophy" in the eighteenth century played thus a role in the bastion of a Scottish anti-English nationalism. The doctrine of divine predestination (rejected by the secularizing movement) and the defense of human freedom were central doctrines upheld by the Confession of Westminster.

104. "He accepted from Hutcheson in the first place and fundamentally the view that reason is inert at a practical level. It *cannot, by its very nature, move us to action*" (MacIntyre 1988, 285; and especially 300–325).

105. "Since vice and virtue are not discoverable merely by reason, or the comparison of ideas, it must be by means of some impression or sentiment they occasion, that we are able to mark the difference between them" (*A Treatise of Human Nature*, bk. 3, sec. 2 [Hume 1958, 470 ff.]).

106. See Broiles 1969.

107. *A Treatise of Human Nature*, bk. 3, sec. 1 (Hume 1958, 469). See part of the debate on the naturalist fallacy in Atkinson 1961; Camps 1976, 156–57; Dubois 1967; Hunter 1962; MacIntyre 1959; Rabossi 1979, 83 ff.; Sádaba 1989, 212–16; these works help us to situate the context of Moore's critique. See also Apel 1973, vol. 2, 362 ff.; Habermas 1983, 60 ff. MacIntyre (1981, 12 ff.) began with the criticism of emotivism. See §§2.5 and 3.2. I in turn will make the transition from being to ought, not at the logical-formal level of analytical-instrumental reason but at the level of practical-material reason (as a "grounding" and not as a "deduction"), which will require the development of new logical moments. I do not reject either logically or formally the impossibility of a "deduction"; rather, I declare it insufficient in order to explain the "passage" from "being" to "ought" in judgments of fact concerning *the life of the human being*, as explained above.

108. Bentham 1948, *Fragment*, preface, 3.

109. *Introduction to the Principles of Morality*, chap. 1, sec. 1 (Bentham 1948, 125). Bentham still wrote: "Frequently I have observed how the need to bring

about a connection which is sufficiently evident between the idea of happiness and pleasure, on the one hand, and the idea of utility on the other, ends up being purely functional in character, and even somewhat too efficient, thereby instilling resistance to the acceptance that these principles might have obtained otherwise" (ibid., note 1, 125).

110. *Treatise of Civil and Penal Legislation*, bk. 1, chap. 1 (Bentham 1981, 27).

111. Ibid., 28. The ultimate criterion is not "the life of each human subject in community" but pleasure.

112. Ibid. "A person's will can only be influenced by some *motive*, and whoever speaks of *motive* is in fact speaking of *pain* or *pleasure*" (ibid., chap. 7, 49).

113. In *Utilitarianism* (Mill 1957, 10).

114. Many objections may be made to this. In general, many emphasize the impossibility of "applying" the principle. We will see how this is exactly one of the advantages of consensual and formal moralities, but these are also "inapplicable" if they have not clearly subsumed the "material" aspect that we are addressing here (this will be the theme of chapter 2). Nietzsche's or Levinas's "instinctual" critiques agree that "happiness" (as a purely reproductive or repetitive principle: Socratic *ratio* or "the same") is not enough. A principle of "development" must also be added to the mix, which is of a creative (or Dionysian) nature, a "metaphysical desire" (see §4.4 of this *Ethics*, on Levinas), capable of putting one's happiness in question as an assumption of responsibility toward the victim. Utilitarian "happiness" is essentially conservative, and can turn dangerous when a people (such as the people of the United States) defends *its* happiness with increasing xenophobia through the negation of the victims it generates outside its borders.

115. As can be seen, Mill falls into an anthropological "dualism" when he places "pleasure" (which has a direct relation to corporeality) on a mainly "mental" plain (as "separate" from the body). Greco-Roman Epicureanism triumphs once again.

116. Mill vacillates, since speaking of the "majority" is something entirely indefinite. He becomes naive when he adds "uncostliness" to the list of advantages of mental pleasure, as if bodily pleasure could be the something of greater cost. We are facing a transformation that leads to the weakening of criteria.

117. Mill 1957, 11–12.

118. That a universal ethical principle is undemonstrable does not mean that it is not groundable. The grounding of a principle, as Aristotle taught, is performed through the reductio ad absurdum (today, pragmatically, by means of the "performative contradiction" inevitably enacted by the opponent).

119. See Rabossi's clarifications (1959, 112 ff.) to Moore's question, as well as MacIntyre 1966, sec. 18, etc.

120. In *Utilitarianism* (Mill 1957, 44). Mill himself is aware of some of the difficulties (and he is also unaware of many others), such as the impossibility of demonstration of the principle: "It is evident that this cannot be proven in the ordinary and popularly understood sense of the term. The problem of ultimate ends is not subject to direct proofs" (ibid.). He adds: "The art of music is good for the reason that it produces pleasure, among other things" (ibid.). Thomas Reid already reasoned (following Aristotle's doctrine of synderesis) that principles are not demonstrable. (See MacIntyre 1988, 331 ff.; also Dussel 1970–80, vol. 1 [1970], 81 ff., 171 ff., and Dussel 1973, 32 ff.: "Being as eudonomia"). One would still have to distinguish between merely "seeking pleasure," which is an

analytical statement, and "how to attain pleasure," which is, instead, a statement of an empirical character.

121. Mill 1957, 45, 49.

122. This point merits more specific analysis (see Otfried Höffe's works). Höffe criticizes utilitarianism for having fallen into the "naturalist fallacy." I offer a critique when I call this "transition" a "fallacy."

123. Mill 1957, 49.

124. For us, pleasure (or pain) and happiness (or unhappiness)—as the two extremes of the subjective repercussion of affectivity, from sensation (which is minimal) to the *background feeling* (maximal), as a *global mapping*—have to do with human corporeality, as a *subjective* and instinctual criterion of the effective survival of the subject: as is proven, corporeality "reacts" inward positively (from pleasure to happiness; or, in the case of a negative reaction, to warning) of a "right" (correct) functioning of the entire organism (vegetative, psychic, cultural, ethical). Every act with a goodness claim must make reference to the subjective aspects analyzed (pleasure, happiness). This criterion is *necessary*, but not *sufficient*. In the first place, I will attempt to rescue the fundamental intention, considering the possibility of a critical subsumption, and for this reason I may cease to point to the importance of attempting to discover the function of "pleasure/pain" or "happiness/unhappiness" as subjective components in the complex and mediated determination of the "goodness claim" of the human act. But subjectivistic "eudemonism" or "hedonism" are supremely ambiguous, with respect to determining the "goodness" of an act, precisely because many other criteria are necessary, principles or moments that allow one to overdetermine this "pleasure" and "happiness" inasmuch as they are "ethical." It is for this reason that utilitarianism proclaims, against Kant, that "pleasure/pain" or "happiness/unhappiness" (Höffe titles a chapter "Utilitarianism instead of Kant?" [Höffe 1993, 213 ff.])—in the way that sensation or subjective or instinctual resonance reflect the global affectivity of the complex components of the capacity of reproduction and development of the life of each ethical subject—refer to a constitutive ethical determination of the human act, and more specifically, when the negation of the corporeality is produced by unjust institutions (as pain or unhappiness) in the victims, that is, the oppressed (see in chapter 4).

125. Moore addresses this issue in the *Principia Ethica*, especially from sec. 14 (chap. 1), to sec. 65 (chap. 3) (Moore 1968), with reference to Bentham, Mill, or Sidgwick (Rabossi 1979, 106 ff.; Sádaba 1989).

126. Rawls 1971, from sec. 5, 22. On the critique of utilitarianism by Bentham or Mill, one may read Quinton 1973, 82 ff. (with the studies of John Grote, Henry Sidgwick, F. H. Bradley), and Glover 1990, which critiques Hare (33 ff. and 230 ff.), Ayer (48 ff.), Nozick (58 ff.), and Rawls (91 ff.). See again Höffe 1979 and Araújo de Oliveira's critiques (1995, 35–38).

127. The "value" of which I speak is as much value of "exchange" as value of "use." The "wish" of the buyer can produce neither (although it can decide the "final price of offer or demand," which is something entirely different).

128. William Jevons published *The Theory of Political Economy* in 1871 (Jevons 1957), only four years after the appearance of volume 1 of Karl Marx's *Capital*. Jevon's work began the "inversion" that is at the base of all contemporary capitalist economy (of "marginalism" and the philosophies that follow its steps). Jevons writes: "The science of Political Economy rests upon a few notions of an

apparently simple character. Utility, wealth, commodity, labour, land, capital are the elements of the subject. . . . The value depends entirely upon utility. Prevailing opinions make labour rather than utility the origin of value; and there are even those who distinctly assert that labour is the cause of value" (ibid., 1). The determination of value has as a ground the "pleasure or pain" (28), "feeling" (29), of the buyer of the commodity; the greater the pleasure or the "feeling" (or "need," but in a particular sense and linked to the market, as in "fashion," etc.), the greater "utility" a commodity has. In other words, it thereby has "value" (for me, for us, now and here). If there is a change in the "feeling," there is a change in the value (which is in turn determined by "supply and demand" and by the "availability or lack" of a commodity). For this reason, "pleasure and pain, unquestionably, are the ultimate object of economic calculus" (37), and the "degree of utility" determines the value (the "final degree of utility" is the point of departure for the future "marginalism"). Because of all of this, Jevons thinks, Smith was wrong when he thought that "labour was the first prize, the original money that bought everything" (52).

129. This is exactly Marx's point of departure (see §1.5 and chapter 4). Against utilitarianism or the later marginalism, Marx will show that the "desire" or "inclinations" (as demand) and "happiness" (as effect of consumption) of the buyer refer to the market (moment that is constitutive of the market) and presuppose the productive labor of the worker, whose life is objectified in the value of the commodity and does not return to the producer: the "*sur*plus value" is thus positioned as "*less* consumption," and for this reason as "*less* happiness" (the *un*-happiness of the worker). This point regards the application of a criterion not only of subjective happiness, positively applied (from the perspective of the buyer-consumer), but rather a criterion applied *objectively* and having double *negativity*, given (a) the distribution of *productive* subjects in the production of goods, with respect to the necessity of the reproduction of life or happiness of the workers themselves and (b) the distribution of the *consuming* subjects in the society (both rich and poor, which Rawls accepts as a "natural" fact, for the distribution of wealth in the previous production process). We will return to this theme.

130. See Dussel 1994c, where I respond to Apel's objections; here, I broaden that response to show the sense of Hume's formulation of the "naturalist fallacy." Furthermore, the "interpellation" of the "poor" (in this case, the experience of the "suffering" or "unhappy" subject as result of an unjust act or structure) is mediated in its intersubjective interpretation by the social sciences and philosophy, which are not neutral and should be critical in this case.

131. On the "model of impossibility," see §3.5 and chapters 4 and 5.

132. The utilitarian model limits its frame of reference to simply "the majority" (visible, possible), and not to the "totality" of the population.

133. Marx espouses a "model of impossibility" that is more complete than that of the utilitarians, since it includes objectivity, when he writes: "From each according to his ability, to each according to his need! [*Bedürfnissen*]" [the object of the distribution] (Marx, *Kritik des Gothaer Programms*, in Marx 1956–90, vol. 19, pt. 1 [1973], 21). That is to say, "the distribution of the means of consumption [which the utilitarians expound] is, at all times, corollary to the distribution of the appropriate conditions of production. . . . Vulgar socialism has learned from the bourgeois economists how to consider and treat matters of distribution without reference to the mode of production" (ibid., 22).

Utilitarianism is a subjective-material ethics that is not sufficiently material (it conceives of "happiness" as a matter of consumption, from the perspective of the market), and forgets the logic of production of the "objective goods"; and even fails to consider subjectively that, in the first place, that the one who is "unhappy" is the productive worker (from the factory itself) who cannot recover their objectified life in the object they have produced, which involves a problem of the ethics of bodily reality, as we shall see. In order to *overcome* this structure of injustice, "happiness" is not a sufficient motivation; instead it is necessary to possess an "instinct" (drive) which implies the willingness to risk one's own happiness for an other (see §4.4).

134. As Bentham wrote in his essay "The Psychology of Economic Man": "My notion of man is that of a being in pursuit of happiness, both in success and in failure, and in all of his acts will continue to pursue this end as long as he lives" (1954, 421). We can observe here how the "matter" of consumption is considered as a "source of pleasure" and not as an objectification of the life of the productive worker (an "objective" aspect that also attracted Marx's interest, as well as that of others). In his *Manual of Political Economy* Bentham wrote: "The wealth of any community is the sum of those portions of wealth that belong to the distinct individuals who compose the community" (1838–43, vol. 3, 33). Its finality is "1. subsistence; 2. pleasure; 3. security; 4. increased wealth" (ibid.). In other words, happiness for the greatest number implies the enjoyment of economic wealth. For his part, Mill also has an ethical-philosophical vision of the economy. In his *Principles of Political Economy*, he writes: "For practical reasons, Political Economy is inseparable from many other branches of social philosophy . . . [regarding] the philosophy of society" (1981, vol. 2, xcii). Mill is aware that "distribution" is a matter fundamentally related to "happiness." But both Bentham and Mill share a particular blindness with regard to the ethical logic intertwined with the production of such goods.

135. Bentham has an indirect awareness of the fact that it is the economy that determines that only those who dominate (*the ruling few*) can be "happy," while it is always the victims, the dominated, or the excluded, those who are "unhappy," and the subjects of "pain" to whom the "distribution" of happiness or pleasure (understood in terms of the consumption of goods that satisfy "necessities") should be accorded within a context of material justice anchored in their bodily reality. I will return to this theme when I explore Rawls's approach, with regard to his "second principle."

136. If "material" ethics is material because it is a matter of "contents," the most material moment in materiality is the structural, institutional objectivity of material goods as factors of "satisfaction," which "re-produce" "sur-vival." All of this is part of "material" ethics, which Anglo-Saxon ethics subsequent to utilitarianism forgot (intuitionism, emotivism, analytical philosophy, communitarianism, neocontractualism, etc.): *economic* ethics.

137. *The Theory of Moral Sentiments*, VI, ii, 3, 1 (Smith 1976, 235).

138. *An Inquiry into the Nature and Causes of the Wealth of Nations*, I, 2 (Smith 1985, 119).

139. See ibid., 6 (151).

140. Bentham, *Treatise on Civil and Penal Legislation*, chap. 12 (Bentham 1981, 75).

141. Ibid.

142. Chapters 6 ff.

143. For further reading regarding this matter, see §3.5.

144. With origins in a traditional "Tory" family, and having been a student at Oxford, Bentham was considered a traitor to his class because of his democratic commitments as an "English modernizer." But of course he never ceased to think from within a capitalist framework, which earned him violent criticism from Marx.

145. It seems that a text by Bentham regarding the Latin American colonies is still unpublished ("Rid Yourselves of Ultramaria") (Guisán 1992, 291).

146. Guisán 1992, 292.

147. It is interesting to read certain texts regarding the diversity among nations in which he writes: "The condition of those who are the poorest in different nations varies, as well as the proportions of magnitude and opulence of the classes that loom above those which are poorest" (*Principles of Political Economy*; Mill 1981, vol. 2, 19). And since "the laws . . . of distribution are partially human institutions" (ibid., 21), one could take utilitarianism as a point of departure for the study of the inequity of the world system in terms of the "distribution" of wealth on the planet, from an economic ethical-subjective perspective.

148. See Rodriguez Braun 1989.

149. There is also a neo-Aristotelianism in Germany, but I do not examine it here (see Shnädelbach 1986).

150. It is worth highlighting that each variant of "communitarianism" considers different "material" moments. For example, in MacIntyre, the "virtues"; in Taylor, "values" and the "authenticity" of one's own identity, but without reference to economic institutions (aspects that the utilitarians had at least considered, albeit unilaterally).

151. MacIntyre 1988, 348.

152. As we shall see, it is possible to carry out an intercultural dialogue based upon the universal material principle, which draws upon the "particular" moments of each culture, understood as "modes" of historical fulfillment of the "universal" material principle of ethics.

153. MacIntyre 1988, 348.

154. In other words, from the perspective of the peripheral and postcolonial world, the theme of "authenticity" espoused by Taylor can be reinterpreted as an affirmation of the alterity of ancestral cultures, which have been dominated throughout the modern colonial period.

155. All of this relates to the question of the universal material principle (see §1.5b and thesis 11 in appendix 1), which constitutes each culture from within, and which enables them to undertake dialogue because it is strictly universal, supracultural, and global.

156. MacIntyre 1966.

157. Ibid., sec. 1. The book concludes with the following passage: "One of the virtues of the history of moral philosophy is to demonstrate that . . . the same moral concepts have a history. To understand this is to free ourselves of all false absolutist pretensions" (sec. 18, 259).

158. This is characteristic of MacIntyre and Taylor's "Hellenocentrism" (not of Michael Walzer as we shall see), which I criticized in §I.7, because it discards everything I set out in §I.1 and much of §I.4. Instead they begin their histories with the "prephilosophical" world of the Greeks (for example, MacIntyre 1966, sec. 2, 15 ff.), without a grasp of the historical fallacy of "Eurocentric Helleno-

centrism" (and thereby fall into the trap captured by the popular saying "In the blacksmith's house, wooden knives prevail"). MacIntyre still lacks a *global* historical sensitivity.

159. Ibid., sec. 12, 164. MacIntyre repeats this argument in different variations in order to confront each formal, analytical, and ahistorical moral current: against Moore, Ayer, and others. "What I hope will emerge with still greater clarity is the function *of history* in relation to conceptual analysis" (ibid.). This matter still has importance in Europe and Latin America, where the philosophy of linguistic/conceptual analysis is frequently practiced in a dogmatic manner.

160. Ibid., 259.

161. Ibid.

162. MacIntyre 1981, in particular 11–35.

163. Ibid., 14 ff.

164. Ibid., 36 ff.

165. Ibid., 39.

166. Ibid., 56.

167. Ibid., 62 ff. MacIntyre not only criticizes Bentham and Mill but also demonstrates how Sidgwick (1930 and 1901) has to turn to "intuition" in order to recover some kind of foundation for his argument, thereby opening the way for his student Moore to continue "with his particular opacity of incorrect arguments in *Principia Ethica*" (ibid., 65).

168. Ibid., 66 ff. (Gewirth 1978).

169. This theme is recurrent in MacIntyre's writing (1981, 25–27, 30, 76–77, 88, 114, etc.), and is reflected in good examples by Carnap and Ayer (76).

170. Ibid., 79 ff., where he still confronts Quine (81).

171. Ibid., 88 ff.

172. Ibid., 110–11.

173. Ibid., 117 ff. "Aristotelianism is philosophically the most powerful form of pre-modern moral thought" (118).

174. MacIntyre's reconstruction is useful in reference to the Anglo-Saxon tradition. In Latin America we have often proceeded from the Aristotelian tradition (see Dussel 1970–80, vol. 1 [1970]; 1973, 1974, 1974b, 1975, etc.); in my own case, I have studied with Aristotelians in Argentina and with López Aranguren in Spain (López Aranguren 1968).

175. MacIntyre 1981, 233–35.

176. Ibid., 204 ff.

177. Ibid., 246 ff.

178. MacIntyre 1988. At the very inception of his history, MacIntyre (1966, sec. 1, 11; sec. 2, 19) has already suggested the importance of a history of the concept of justice (ever since the Greek *dikaiosyne*).

179. See §I.7.

180. MacIntyre 1988, 10–11 (where he recognizes that other traditions should be addressed, such as those of Islam, China, India, etc., and that his failure to do so reflects "the limitations of my enterprise"), or at 326.

181. Ibid., 336.

182. Ibid., 338.

183. Ibid., 346.

184. Ibid., 351.

185. Ibid. There is a positive aspect that we must not forget, since "no tradition has the right to accord itself a title of exclusivity; no tradition can deny the legitimacy of its rivals" (352), at least, not before it has authentically complied with the necessary conditions of argumentation and thereby arrived at some consensus. A humility that Europe has lacked throughout Modernity!

186. MacIntyre denies that he is a relativist (ibid., 370 ff.: "Tradition and Translation"), but, in any case, he makes no attempt to problematize material universality, except through the defective means of a world language, such as the English which is dominant within the "world system." His attention instead is fixed on demonstrating the *difficulties* of communication and the exercise of the *universality* of reason (from the perspective of the universal material principle and of the alterity of the Other: the victims), *without negating them*; this is one way to avoid falling into either ahistorical abstract formal universality or postmodern incommensurability. I will return to this theme throughout this *Ethics*.

187. See what I noted above (§I.2).

188. See Taylor 1975, 363 ff.

189. Taylor 1989, x.

190. See my criticism of axiology in *Para una de-strucción de la historia de la ética* (*Towards a De-Struction of the History of Ethics*), chap. 4 (Dussel 1973, 126 ff.). I think that Heidegger, in *Brief über den Humanismus* (Heidegger 1947), undertook in part and in an anticipatory manner a critique of this kind of ethics. I have studied Husserl's archives in Louvain, thanks to van Breda, and I have read Husserl's axiological manuscripts (see *Ethical Manuscripts of E. Husserl found in the Husserl-Archiv in Louvain*, in Dussel 1970–80, vol. 1 (1970), 193 ff. from F 1 20 (1890 ff.) to B I 16 (manuscripts dating from 1931 to 1934). Kant was the ethical philosopher most closely studied by Husserl, who focused in particular on the *Critique of Practical Reason*. I explored the work of Max Scheler (1954) and Nicolai Hartmann's (1962) critiques of formalism from the perspective of a "*material* ethics" in *Para una ética de la liberación latinoamericana* (1970–80, vol. 1 [1970]). Because of its "style" Taylor's philosophical position owes much to the axiologists, but as much also to ontological philosophers such as Aristotle, Sartre, and Heidegger, from the perspective of an Anglo-Saxon philosophy attentive to the paradigm of language. This amounts to something like an "axiological-existential-linguistic" amalgam.

191. Taylor should have addressed here the theme of "respect for *human* life," as a universal criterion that configures "all" cultures *from within* (and enables their criticism when they "kill" unjustly and institutionally). This criterion (and its corresponding principle) is universal and makes it possible for intercultural dialogue to be undertaken upon the basis of its material contents. In this way, incommensurability would have been overcome *from within*.

192. Generally, the *concrete* "content" of the "*good life*" is confused with the universal *necessity* of having to always sustain a priori a project of the good life (Aristotle's *eudaimonia*, medieval *beatitude*, Bentham's "happiness," Heidegger's *Seinsverständnis*, Max Scheler's "values," etc.) from the perspective of a universal demand for the reproduction and development of the life of each ethical subject in community. To sustain "one" or "another" good life in the face of another is something that is eminently debatable; but what cannot be subjected to debate is that *everyone always has an a priori good life* as a horizon

from which the debate can begin (Kant, Rawls, and Habermas are not exceptions, and in this MacIntyre is on the mark). The "good life" *is necessary* with respect to the concrete content of the act, but is not *sufficient* as an integral ethical principle. In addition, and with reason, MacIntyre observes that it is possible to fall into an ethical vacuum: "It is an illusion to suppose that there is a neutral foundation, some place for rationality as such, where sufficient rational resources are available for the independent research of all traditions" (MacIntyre 1988, 367). An ethics of liberation accepts (for example, with Apel) that there are "claims of validity" that are universal, in a formal sense, but that are not materially independent of any tradition; neither because of their point of departure (one always proceeds from a tradition of some kind); nor because of their destination in terms of their eventual application (in the context of a specific tradition); nor for failing to refer back to the universal material principle as a point of reference. MacIntyre is correct when he writes: "To pretend to be outside of any tradition is to be foreign to all research" (348). "The most absurd aspect of this kind of philosophy is its atemporal self" (369). But he is incorrect when he concludes: "A social universe composed exclusively of rival traditions . . . is one in which a certain number of incompatible contenders exists . . . in terms of their visions of the universe; each tradition is incapable then of justifying its pretensions in preference to those of its rivals" (348). What he lacks here is the articulation of a cultural horizon together with the universal material principle. (See further §1.5.)

193. Taylor 1989, 521.

194. Taylor 1992a, 1 ff.

195. Ibid., 25.

196. Ibid., 29 ff. In the context of an ethics of liberation, this "being true to one's self" is preceded by "being true to the victims, with a people oppressed and excluded" by the hegemonic identity (a communitarian historical moment).

197. Ibid., 33.

198. This is a matter addressed by George H. Mead (see works in bibliography).

199. Taylor 1992a, 45.

200. Ibid., 50.

201. Ibid., 66. In the context of the ethics of liberation, all of these themes are affirmed not from the perspective of an atomized "authenticity" but instead from that of the negated right to dignity of people belonging to communities that together comprise the majority of humanity, of the oppressed classes, of women dominated by patriarchy, of children without rights in the face of adult-dominated cultures, and so on. This is a frame of reference that is deeper, more extensive, more ethically relevant, than that of the "authenticity" described by Taylor in the countries of the hegemonic center, without denying its importance in its own terms.

202. Ibid., 117.

203. Ibid., 50.

204. Taylor 1992b.

205. "Furthermore, it is well known that since 1492 Europe projected an image upon these peoples, implying their inferiority and lack of civilization, and by force of conquest, even came to impose that image upon the conquerors

themselves" (ibid., 26). This is novel, but it is precisely upon the basis of such a hypothesis that the entire work *Sources of the Self* (Taylor 1989) should be expanded.

206. Taylor 1992b, 37. This is exactly the issue posed by *Ethics of Liberation* more than twenty years ago: the relevant other is the indigenous person (fifteen million dead at the start of Modernity), African slaves (three million enslaved between the sixteenth and nineteenth centuries), the nation of the periphery exploited by colonialism and neocolonialism (more than 80 percent of all of humanity), the workers dominated by a regime of wages and the production of surplus value (even in the countries of the hegemonic center), and so on. The Philosophy of Liberation, since 1970, explicitly espoused the need for a "dialogue" with *the other* in recognition of their significance (Dussel 1970–80, vol. 1 [1970], chap. 6: "El método de la ética" (The ethical method); "The visage of the oppressed Indian, of the oppressed mestizo, of the people of Latin America, is the theme of Latin American philosophy. This analectical or dialogical thought, because it arises from the revelation of the Other and seeks to reflect this reality in its thought, is Latin American philosophy itself, unique and new, the first truly postmodern philosophy capable of transcending modernity" (I wrote this in 1970; today I would describe it as "transmodern") (ibid., vol. 2 [1972], 162).

207. Taylor 1992b, 72–73. It is interesting that almost five hundred years after Bartolomé de Las Casas, a philosopher of the Anglo-Saxon world would repeat the same words, since in *De unico modo* [The only way], written in Guatemala in 1536, Las Casas sought to demonstrate that the indigenous peoples of the Americas had dignity and deserved to be treated *in the only human way* possible: with rational arguments and not with the violence of war (all the way from the Conquest of Mexico in 1519 up to the war in Iraq and the continuing sufferings of its people). See Dussel 1993c, lecture 5.3.

208. Taylor 1992b, 88. This is the heart of the argument developed in two other works by Taylor (1988a and 1988b).

209. Of the four works that we shall consider (Walzer 1977, 1979, 1983, and 1994), *Spheres of Justice: A Defense of Pluralism and Equality* (1983) is the one with the widest range. This book, because it came after the works of Nozik (1968) and Rawls (1971), should be considered a critical response to these.

210. Walzer 1983, 312–13.

211. It is interesting to note that when Walzer addresses the question of "need" (ibid., 25), he interprets the "productive" moment in one of the best-known quotations from Marx's works, as if it were "redistributive." In effect, "from each according to his ability" — the phrase from Marx's *Critique of the Gotha Program*, quoted earlier — is interpreted by Walzer in the following way: "Who among them has need [of employment] with greatest urgency?" (ibid.). For Marx, however, each worker *should* work to the limit of his or her *capacity*: the heart of the matter is a question of production. Distribution becomes relevant later, at the moment referred to by the phrase "to each according to his need." Of course these two aspects are intertwined and mutually determined, but one is material in character (the determining effects of production upon matters of distribution), and the other is practical-philosophical (that of distribution upon production). Marx writes: "If we assess these societies from an overall perspective, distribution appears to a certain extent to precede and

even determine production: it appears to be a kind of pre-economic [*anteöko-nomisch*] *fact*. A conquering people divides the country among the conquerors" (Marx, *Grundrisse der Kritik der politischen Ökonomie* [1857], in Marx 1974, 16). This is Walzer's position. But Marx goes on to say something more: "The organization of distribution [of objects and functions] is totally determined by the organization of production. Distribution itself is the result of production" (ibid., 15). This presupposition regarding the organization of capitalist production is not much evident in Walzer. What is thus necessary is a "*productive* justice" (which in Aristotle's view was "*legal* justice," in the broadest sense). See Dussel 1985a, 43 ff.

212. This can be seen, for example, when Walzer speaks of "*free exchange*" (1983, 21). Walzer understands the limits of neoliberalism. He criticizes this orthodoxy, noting that its proponents believe that "free exchange produces a market in which all goods are convertible into all others through the *neutral* medium of money. Neither dominant goods nor monopolies exist" (ibid.). Walzer demonstrates that "everyday life in the marketplace, the true experience of free exchange, is very different from what the theory suggests. Money . . . is in practice a dominant medium" (21–22). Nonetheless, his critique always stops short just when it should go deeper. He knows that "free exchange is not a general criterion," but admits that "the more perfect the market is, the smaller will be the inequalities of income, and the less frequent the failures" (116). But any market, no matter how "perfect," always supposes, and cannot fail to suppose, some kind of inequality, of dominant goods or some kind of monopoly, because "competition" necessarily implies inequality. A "perfect market" is logically impossible and is inconsistent (applying Popper's argument; Hinkelammert 1984, chap. 6). The concept of the "perfect market" contradicts the concept of "competition" (and that of "perfect competition," furthermore, is inconsistent), since such a scenario presupposes inequality, difference, struggle, and the possibility of destruction of other capitals (if there were perfect equality there would be immobility, quietude, equivalence, noncompetition). Furthermore, since Locke or Smith, we know that "money" is a medium of accumulation, by means of which those who possess it (the "rich," according to Locke or Smith) can purchase the labor power of the "poor" (who do not possess it). This means not only that it cannot be "neutral" but that those who possess it have unequal amounts of private property *as the result of historical and legal mechanisms* that cannot fail to congeal into structures with some degree of injustice or inequality, and which Walzer accepts as presuppositions instead of realities which must be analyzed.

213. Walzer 1983, xiii. This statement is acceptable as a "regulatory idea," but is *impossible* to implement as an empirical matter, although it is not contradictory in logical terms (it is consistent but not achievable), since no *empirically* existent society can claim not to practice some kind of institutional domination (however hidden), as we shall see in chapters 4 to 6. We would have to possess an infinite intelligence at infinite speed (to adopt Popper's argument [1973]; Hinkelammert 1984, chap. 5) in order to disprove the *Principle of Oppression* (*principium oppressionis*: there will always be victims and those who are dominated!). I will explore this in greater detail later in this book.

214. Walzer 1983, xv.

215. Pascal, *Penseés*, sec. 244 (Pascal 1954, 1153); Walzer 1983, 18.

216. I will take advantage of this distinction in a future work, where I will explore in greater detail various different "*fronts* of liberation" (in terms of these and other multiple *spheres* not addressed by Walzer), and which I will refer to as "fronts" because they involve "frontiers" of "struggle" for re-cognition.

217. See Walzer 1983, 6 ff. In each sphere there is a dominant good; in a "capitalist society it is capital which is dominant" (11).

218. Ibid., 13. It is interesting to note that for Walzer the model of "all revolutionary ideology" is expressed as follows: "The claim that some new good, *monopolized* by some new group, will replace that which is currently dominant: this is equivalent to claiming that the existent scheme of dominion and monopoly is unjust" (ibid.). Walzer is in error here. His reference to a new good that is "monopolized" by some new group should be replaced by a reference to its "consensual promotion," in order to remove the characterization of this valid claim as something which is ethically illegitimate. Walzer concludes: This "claim is not interesting in philosophical terms" (ibid.). Defined in Walzer's terms, it is not interesting; redefined as I am proposing here, it is precisely the crux of the ethics of liberation, and in this case not only is it interesting, but relevant to the vast majority of humanity, today (see chapter 5).

219. "Just as it is possible to describe a system of castes which fulfills the *(internal) parameters* of justice, it is possible to describe a capitalist system which meets the same goals" (ibid., 315). I agree with Walzer that all progress must flow from such "(internal) parameters," but there are moments in which the very foundations of a sphere or system in its totality must ripen to a point of crisis. Such a situation cannot be ignored either by the ethics of liberation (since it is *also* an ethics for normal times).

220. Ibid., 314.

221. Ibid., 321. For Walzer, then, to rule always implies a certain monopoly of that which is good, and a certain amount of domination. Compare the cited text with the following: "Those who can walk amid the darkness of the night [those who have wisdom] spoke: We have seen that this path of government that was once named by us [liberal democracy] is no longer a path which serves the majority, we see that it is the fewer increasingly who govern, and govern without obeying, as they seek to govern by commanding. And the power of command is passed back and forth among the few, without listening to the majority, the few rule by commanding, without obeying the commands of those who are in the majority. The few rule without reason. The word that comes from afar [from those who are wisest among the Mayan people] says that they rule without democracy, without the mandate of the people, and we can see that the irrationality of those who rule by command nourishes the unfolding of our pain and the suffering of our dead. And we can see that those who rule by commanding should be swept far away from us so that reason and truth can take hold again in our soil. And so we see that there must be a change, and *that those who rule should rule in obedience*, and we can see that the word that comes from afar to give a name to the reason for ruling, *democracy*, is good for both the many and the few" ("Communiqué from the Mayan Rebellion in Chiapas, Zapatista National Liberation Army, Democratic Elections," *La Jornada*, February 27, 1994, 11).

222. It is not materially sufficient, as we shall see, because it has not taken into account the universal material principle that we will explore later in this book in §1.5.

223. Here I will synthesize some positions set forth in greater detail in Dussel 1973.

224. *Nicomachean Ethics*, bk. 1, 12 (Aristotle 1960, 1102a 1–4). See Dussel 1973, 33 ff.

225. *Nicomachean Ethics*, bk. 1, 7 (Aristotle 1960 1098a, 16).

226. *Nicomachean Ethics*, bk. 1, 4 (Aristotle 1960 1095a, 19–21).

227. *Nicomachean Ethics*, bk. 10, 7 (Aristotle 1960 1177a, 12–18).

228. Aquinas, *De perfectione vitae spiritualis*, bk. 13, n. 634.

229. *Summa Theologiae*, pt. I–2, qu. 19, art. 10 (Aquinas 1950, 104). "It is impossible for someone to realize their good if their project is not convergent with the common good [*bene proportionatus bono communi*]" (ibid., qu. 92, art. 1, response 3 [Aquinas 1950, 419]).

230. See the exposition of this theme in Dussel 1974b, 64 ff.

231. In *Frühe Schriften* (Hegel 1971–79, vol. 1 [1971], 326).

232. Ibid.

233. Aristotle's *deutera physis*, the virtue of *héxis* (*Nicomachean Ethics*, bk. 2, 1 [Aristotle 1960, 1103a 18 ff.], in particular bk. 2, 6 [Aristotle 1960, 1106b 3 ff.]). The Hegelian *Sittlichkeit* is precisely that "second nature [*als eine zweite Natur*]" (*Rechtsphilosophie*, Hegel 1971–79, sec. 151, vol. 7, 301).

234. *Der Geist des Christentums* (Hegel 1971–79, vol. 7, 327).

235. *Grundkonzept zum Geist des Christentums* (Hegel 1971–79, vol. 1 [1971], 312). This formula, "*lebendige Gemeinschaft*," is employed by Marx in his exploration of religion: "der lebendigsten Gemeinschaft" (in Marx 1956–90, vol. 1, 600), and can be discerned at the roots of his *community paradigm*. I spoke on this topic at the Seminar on Marx in my debate with Apel, December 12, 1992, Goethe-Universität, Frankfurt: "Re-lektüre Marx aus Lateinamerika," Bremen Universität, Bremen, 1993.

236. I wrote in 1969: "Kant himself when writing his *Critique of Practical Reason* was not fully conscious of the fact that what he was writing reflected the thinking characteristic of the bourgeois *ethos* of an eighteenth-century Prussian. Could he have written, if he had possessed such a critical self-consciousness, that "neither in the world, nor in general outside it, is it possible to think of anything that can be considered to be good without restriction, except perhaps only as a good intention [*ein gutter Wille*]" (Dussel 1969, quoting *Grundlegung zur Metaphysik der Sitten*, BA 1)? Does this position reflect the tragic ethics of a chained Prometheus or of a blind Oedipus? Would these principles accept the ethics of Tlacaélel, the founder of the Aztec empire? Might it not be that this principle is only comprehensible within the Western Christian tradition, and in particular that of Spencer's pietism? (Dussel 1973, 9).

237. Kant himself recognized that "the question of how a law can be in itself and immediately the basis of the determination of will (what is, nonetheless, the essence of all morality) constitutes an unresolvable (*unauflöslich*) problem for human reason, and is identical to the question as to whether a free will is possible" (*Kritik der praktischen Vernunft*, A 128 [Kant 1968, vol. 6, 192]). Regarding the problem of the "Anwendung," see in ibid., A 119 ff., a question that I will address in the next chapter.

238. As we comment and critique Fichte, consider, for example, Hegel's own critique, *The Difference between Fichte's and Schelling's System of Philosophy* (1801): "Reason and freedom as a being-of-reason [*Vernunftwesen*] is no more

reason and freedom without a unique being [*Einzelnes*]. . . . If the community of reasoning-beings were essentially a limitation of true freedom, this would be in and of itself a tyranny. . . . In a living relation there can be no freedom except to the extent it implies the possibility of subsuming oneself and entering into a relation with others" (*Frühe Schriften*, in Hegel 1971, vol. 2, 82–83). To the contrary, in a "community subjected to the domination of understanding [*unter der Herrschaft des Verstandes*]" (ibid., 83–84), the "rational" or living moment is the transcendence of the limiting determination as domination.

239. See Taylor 1975, "History and Politics" (365 ff.) where he writes: "The problem with Kant's criterion of rationality is that, in order to achieve a radical autonomy, he has had to pay the price of emptying it of all content" (370). We shall see how an ethics of liberation subsumes the "contents" (which are universal from our perspective) of material ethics, from the standpoint of a formal, procedural morality that is critical and in the final instance engaged with the liberation of the oppressed or excluded. Hegel's critique is innovative *but insufficient*. A classic in this regard is the exposition of Hegel's critique of Kant (see in Benhabib 1986); see also a development of this question from the perspective of the ethics of discourse in Habermas 1991, 9 ff.

240. See Dussel 1995a.

241. *Rechtsphilosophie*, sec. 347 (Hegel 1971–79, vol. 7, 505–6).

242. See Schnädelbach 1983, chap. 6.

243. See Brentano 1969.

244. I had the good fortune to be able to conduct research in the Husserl Archives in Louvain, and was able to consult the lectures he gave on ethics between 1890 and 1934 (Manuscripts A II 1; F I 11, 14, 16, 20, 21, 22, 23, 24, 26, 28) at the Universities of Halle (1887–1901), Göttingen (1901–16), and Freiburg (1916–38). For a description of these, see Dussel 1970–80, vol. 1 (1970), 193–97.

245. See Hildebrand's most important works, *Die Idee der sittlichen Handlung* and *Sittlichkeit und ethische Werterkenntnis* (1969).

246. See Scheler 1954.

247. See Hartmann 1951.

248. See Hartmann 1952 and 1965 and Romero 1952.

249. *Grundlegung zur Metaphysik der Sitten*, BA 65 (Kant 1968, vol. 6, 60). For my part, like Marx, I cannot promote the idea of the value of a person: a person can have dignity, but not value.

250. Heidegger 1961, vol. 1, 488. I will return to this theme in §4.3b, with reference to Nietzsche.

251. "Wert ist . . . Ermöglichung, *possibilitas*" (ibid., 639).

252. It is interesting to recall here what I indicated in §1.1: the limbic system and the base of the brain, in which the *evaluative* neuro-biological and cultural centers are located, are (as Heidegger notes, following Nietzsche) "conditions of dominion that *life* imposes upon the *future development*" of the subject him- or herself as a participant in the community; I have identified this as the universal material ethical principle.

253. We will see in chapter 4 the essence of Nietzsche's position regarding values.

254. For a more detailed treatment in my work see Dussel 1973, 126 ff.

255. Scheler 1954, 68–69.

256. Here we can discern the metaphysical ingenuity of axiologies. Values

are conceptualized categorizations with hierarchical effects structured by cultural variants regarding the production, reproduction, and development of human life. It is life that is universal, not the values in themselves.

257. Scheler 1954, 68–69.

258. Ibid., 74.

259. See Ricoeur 1963.

260. In *Towards an Ethics of Latin American Liberation* (Dussel 1970–80, vol. 1 [1970]) I sought, precisely, to demonstrate the ethical-ontological meaning of Heidegger's existential analytics. Furthermore, my opinion regarding Heidegger's *Sein und Zeit* was that it was nothing less than a rereading of Aristotle's *Nicomachean Ethics*. Years later others have suggested the same interpretation (Volpi 1992).

261. Hans Schelkshorn analyzes this transition of the "comprehension of the self" as a "being-that-must-be" in my interpretation of Heidegger (Schelkshorn 1994, 388 ff.).

262. See in Sartre (1960) the same theme reiterated. I have addressed this matter at length in Dussel 1970–80, vol. 1, chap. 1: "El fundamento ontológico" (33–95).

263. See the works of Zubiri, from 1963 to 1992.

264. See López Aranguren 1968.

265. Zubiri 1986, 525. Formally, such moments (those of the "mental" and "neurological" fact, respectively) can be differentiated, not in material terms but in terms of their *contents*: "The human psyche and organism are essentially distinct: the human psyche cannot be reduced to that which is organic. . . . This is why the psychic notes of the human structure are essentially irreducible to those which are purely organic" (ibid., 57–59). Henri Bergson makes the same point, that the psychological cannot be reduced to the biological: "In reality, consciousness does not surge forth from the brain; but there is a relationship of correspondence between the brain and consciousness because they balance each other in a kind of equilibrium, one because of the complexity of its structure, and the other because of the intensity of its awakening" (Bergson 1912, 285).

266. Zubiri 1986, 54 ff.

267. Zubiri 1981. Here I would like to rely upon the more precise formulations I have ventured to explore in §1.1, originally proposed by Edelman (1989, 1992). These involve the inception of the process of "intellectual-cognitive categorization," which includes the simplest levels of consciousness, a certain degree of memory, linguistic moments, and self-consciousness itself. Zubiri proceeds through these levels in a somewhat general manner, given the period when he made these important contributions (since he writes of "nonspecific" moments or of "formalization," and not of the internal functions of the brain as such, including for example categorization).

268. Zubiri 1986, 23.

269. Ibid.

270. Ibid., 29.

271. Of course, this "suspension" is the product of complex connections of neurons among the centers of the brain, which enable the already indicated phenomena of "consciousness" and "self-consciousness," and the differentiation between "*Self*" and "*Nonself*." In this context, "reality" is the radical and initial grasping of self-legality, of that which comes prior to (*prius*) this grasp,

the very self of this "*Nonself*," of that which is grasped in the stimulus itself. All of this is linguistically codetermined.

272. Zubiri 1986, 391.

273. Ibid., 384.

274. Ibid., 71.

275. Ibid., 112.

276. Ibid., 406 ff.

277. Ibid., 399.

278. See in the index for this book, "truth," "life," "reality," "criterion of truth," and others related to this theme. Particular consideration should be devoted to §2.5, regarding the difference between truth and validity, and §§3.1–2, with regard to the difference between claims of truth, of validity, and of intelligibility (or the "meaningfulness" of a proposition). The points that I only suggest here will continue in those sections of the book.

279. See my trilogy (Dussel 1985a, 1988, and 1990b).

280. Marx understands the difference between *material* (with "a": *Inhalt*) and *materiell* (with "e") (see thesis 10 in appendix 1). For example, in his *Manuscripts of 1844* he writes: "regarding its *material* [*materiell*] wealth and its spiritual misery, all of the *material* [*Material*] for this formation" (Marx 1956–90, vol. 1 [1956], 542). In the first instance the reference is to "physical matter," and in the second, to "contents." My primary interest is in "matter" as the "contents" of ethics (my emphasis is on an ethics of *contents*).

281. "As a purely *formal* act [*formeller*] because it is abstract, because the human being only has value as an abstract thinking being. . . . In its abstract *form*, as a dialectic, this movement passes in this manner through *true human life*, but since this life is [for Hegel] an abstraction, an alienation of *human life*, that life is considered to be a divine process" (ibid., 584). In this passage, Marx criticizes Hegel, who has transformed his anti-Kantian "ethics [*Sittlichkeit*]" into a subsumed *(aufgehoben)* moment at the end of the formal process of thought that conceives of itself as absolute In-Itself: the materiality (content) that has been annihilated into the pure formality of Absolute Thought.

282. Ibid., 583.

283. Ibid., 584.

284. Ibid., 586. This "boredom [*Langweile*]" and nostalgia for content (*Sehnsucht nach einem Inhalt*) could be the exact definition of the contemporary ethics of discourse. The ethics of liberation is very different, in that it *assumes the risk* (on this, see especially §1.5) of seeking to formulate arguments that might serve to contribute in the spirit of solidarity toward "filling" the hands of the poor and the exploited with some "content" (some "bread" to feed their empty stomachs; not the "emptiness" of boredom, but instead the "emptiness" produced by the late capitalism anchored in the center of the world system). The hungry have another kind of "nostalgia for content," which is an inclination and an appetite: they want to eat, and we must demonstrate (beyond the naturalist fallacy, which is interpreted in purely formal terms) that they "have the right" to do so, that is to say that the "state of hunger" (of "being hungry," as human *beings*) encompasses a "*duty* to feed" them (something-that-must-be), even though (from a capitalist perspective) it is "not *possible*" or permissible to do so.

285. Ibid., 577–78. See the coincidence with Levinas (referred to in §4.4). Referring to the "nature" of Hegel Marx writes: "Nature understood as nature

. . . is nothing [for Hegel], a nothingness that is confirmed as nothingness, lacking in meaning or which has only the meaning of an exteriority that has been subsumed" (ibid., 587). Hegel has lost the sense of the "real" and has confused the reality of nature with the reality of the self-consciousness of Absolute Knowledge (where all that which is "real" or *existent* attains its fully realized "reality" *as something which is known*).

286. Consider level 1 of table 2.

287. For both the human being is an "I": an *ego cogito* for whom a body is indifferent (Descartes), or an *Ich denke* that did not require "inclinations" or bodily demands in order to determine the universal validity and *a priori* character of the act (as a morality).

288. This is level 1 of table 2.

289. This "continuous process necessary to prevent death [*um nicht zu sterben*]" is fundamental. As Sartre notes in the *Critique de la Raison Dialectique (Critique of Dialectical Reason)* (Sartre 1960, vol. 2), it is from the perspective of the "inability of choosing to die" ethically that the various different possibilities of "being able to live" can be framed. Life and its reproduction and development are the fundamental criterion of all material ethics. Marx develops this with great clarity throughout his *Manuscripts of 1844*. It would take quite some time to cite all of the related texts regarding this question.

290. Marx 1956–90, vol. 1 (1956), 515–16.

291. An animal responds immediately to a stimulus without possibility of distancing the stimulus from the response.

292. This is level 1 of table 2.

293. Marx 1956–90, vol. 1 [1956], 516. Marx perfectly noted the difference between "animal stimulus" and the human ability to "grasp reality" intelligently as part of the conditions which are confronted in life.

294. "No *free* and *spiritual* [*geistig*] physical energy is developed" (ibid., 514). "The given character of a species resides in the form of its vital activity, its generic character, and its *free, conscious* activity is the generic character of the human being" (516).

295. Ibid., 517. He might indeed be thinking of Schiller's concept of "beauty [*Schönheit*]," but not in a substitutive manner (as in Charles Taylor: aesthetics instead of ethics); rather, it involves subsuming aesthetics *in* ethics. This is what is referred to at level 4 of table 2.

296. The definitive Marx will differentiate between the "social [*gesellschaftlich*]" and that which pertains to "community [*gemeinschaftlich*]," but he is not there yet at this stage (Dussel 1985a, 87 ff.).

297. Note here that the "relationship with the Other" (Levinas's "face to face") is a material necessity (as to content) that is primary, real, ethical, and intersubjective (or more: it is the origin itself of intersubjectivity).

298. Here *material* with an "a," which is to say, as "content."

299. Marx is referring in an anticipated manner to the level of pragmatics, or to the level of language in general, which also always presupposes a "community." The ethics of content presupposes a community "of life"; pragmatics, a community of "communication" (the latter is a relevant dimension that unfolds as an expression of its *absolute* condition: the life of the subject who speaks, since a dead subject is unable to do so).

300. Here Marx, in a very precise manner, demonstrates the meaning of *theoretical rationality* in general and how practical rationality should be articu-

lated to it. "Theory" is an "abstraction" (which does not imply that it is "unreal"), and this is what explains its precision and "efficacy" (as an act of instrumental reason); the concrete real totality "from which" it abstracts itself is the community *of life*. The same thing occurs with the community *of communication*.

301. Marx 1956–90, vol. 1 (1956), 537–38. "Consciousness" and "reason" are moments of human life, and not vice versa.

302. Hess 1845, 2–3.

303. This is the whole matter of the contradiction between two ethical principles.

304. Hess 1845, 9. For Hess, since Christianity promises an individually resuscitated life, it lays the basis for egoism: "What God is for theoretical life, Money is for the practical life of an inverted world" (10). We can discern here that this theoretical horizon is that of Marx, which is theological-economical (Dussel 1993b, 46 ff.).

305. A redundancy that implies a defense against all forms of naturalism.

306. Nonintentional social structures and actions do not negate this statement, to the extent that they are responsible for themselves in the medium term and in the face of the critical consciousness that can describe nonintentionality from the perspective of the guilt that accompanies fetishistic praxis.

307. "Materials" (with an "a") among whose levels one can find spiritual needs (aesthetic, scientific, creative . . .): "be they of the stomach or of fantasy [*Phantasie*]" (*Kapital*, in Marx 1987, 69).

308. We have seen how for Marx the first "material necessity" (that of content) is the need for another subject: for intersubjectivity or for the community of life as a condition that presupposes other necessities. This was expounded anew, in a much more radical manner, in Levinas's ethical critique (see §4.4).

309. I intend to develop these questions in §§2.5 and 3.1–2.

310. We are situated here at level 1 of table 2. This theme is a determining one: the criterion for the reproduction and development of life is the "criterion of truth"; of *practical truth* (to the extent it has to do with *human* life), which is also theoretical (to the extent that it "opens" us up to the *omnitudo realitatis* "from the horizon" that life circumscribes as mediations of reproduction and development, see later in this book in §3.2. Otherwise, an "interest" (in the Habermasian sense: Habermas 1968a), which is ontological and anthropological (even psychological and psychoanalytical), and which is fundamental *from and in the name of life* motivates us to confront things in order to use them (technically), to know them (theoretically, from everyday life all the way to its elaboration in the sciences), and to value them (culturally) as "possibilities" of life. The appropriate "understanding of self" and of *Sorge* (ontological preoccupation) as understood by Heidegger, is an "opening which is implanted from the perspective of its previous range" (Dussel 1970–80, vol. 1 [1970], 42 ff., and note 54, 162–63, where I demonstrate that the horizon of the Heideggerian "being" must be transcended, and that that pre- or transontological range is "reality," in the same way in which "meaning" must be transcended as "truth"; see Dussel 1977, 2.2.3 and 3.4.7; and in §3.2 of this *Ethics*). The "circle" of reality that we discover in the real is not "*all* of reality," but instead the "reality that interests us"; only certain aspects are of interest, to the extent that they are integrated into the overall flow of our life (as biography, as the history of a culture, of humanity in our era, etc.).

311. It is dissolved as "objectivity" or as a manageable horizon by human beings. Human beings fulfill the fulfillment of the real prior (*prius*) to grasping it; in the absence of human beings it would be *impossible* to grasp what is real *as reality*, and what Hinkelammert describes as the "objectivity" of reality would become volatile.

312. Hinkelammert 1995c, 32. It is a "product" to the extent that only human beings fulfill their fulfillment *as reality* (this harking back of reality to the real can be given as a "product" of an intelligent act of a human being) (level 1 of table 2). But this is a "presupposition," because it is the human being who is capable of grasping the real (which precedes us); we do not "presuppose" the real *as real* (this is what we produce). Hegel confuses the "reality" *of knowledge* of the real, with "reality" of *the real* as such, with the "reality" of *the real* itself. But the *reality* "of the real" (which is grasped as something prior to knowledge) is not the *reality* "of knowledge" (which is the mediation which is necessary so that the real can become realized, furthermore, *as truth*).

313. In Dussel 1977, it was the living human being in the order of the "cosmos" as *omnitudo realitatis*.

314. Which I characterized in ibid. as the order of the world with respect to the "comprehension of being": that which is ontological.

315. This is located at level 3 of table 2.

316. Weber 1922, *Wirtschaft und Gesellschaft*, 24–25.

317. The human brain is characterized by certain parts of the cortex that are more developed than others, particularly those specialized in the recall of human "faces." The "face" of the Other (as expounded by Levinas) plays a radical role in ethics.

318. This "recognition" of the Other as equal is an act of original ethical reasoning, which is material and presupposes discursive reason (since argumentation, as we shall see, always assumes the recognition of the other as equal).

319. See §§2.5b and 3.5c.

320. Which I have denominated "material-practical reason" (with respect to the life of the subject) or "original-ethical" (with respect to the autonomy of the subject-Other as an other who is my equal). We shall see from chapter 4 onward that the mere "reproduction" of human life is not a sufficient criterion for ethics, which will demand, with the existence of the victim as criterion, the "development" of life as well. The "reproduction" of life is an absolutely necessary prerequisite, but is not sufficient.

321. Hinkelammert 1995c, 11–12.

322. The rationality that I have defined as practical-material (level 1 of table 2) with that which is instrumental (level 3), with which discursive reason must be articulated. See this discussion in §§2.5b and 3.5b.

323. Hinkelammert 1995c, 15–16.

324. See [78] above.

325. See, among others, Jonas 1982a.

326. See §6.2, where I address the "question of the subject." This is not a matter of the solipsistic modern subject, who is conscious, in a cognitive and abstract position, and so on.

327. These "normative statements" (determined by the ethical obligations or demands regarding the production, reproduction, and development of human life) (level 1 of table 2), and are not mere "value judgments" (those of Weber's instrumental reason or of metaethical analysis) (level 3 of table 2) or "normative

statements" only to the extent that they are valid with a claim of rectitude (such as for Habermas, since although they are differentiated from descriptive statements, they are articulated only with the cultural world) or are only grasped materially from the perspective of the established culture (as in the case of Charles Taylor) (level 2). These normative judgments can be deployed critically from the perspective of human life *in general* (materially and universally), or of particular cultural *values*, which are enunciated as "value judgments" or "value statements," and can equally judge the particular *ends* whose means occupy the formal "factual judgments" (for example scientific judgments or those involving mathematical calculations, etc.). Because of all this, we could denominate them as normative judgments or statements as to ethical reality, because it is from the reality of the life of the ethical subject that they are judged or revealed in terms of the compatibility (or incompatibility) of ends, values and "traditions" (as understood by Weber or Popper) with respect to the concrete human lives at issue.

328. What is the systemic murder of the Other (because of economic competition, arms sales, neglect of AIDS in Africa or among the poor) but the deployment of a habitual conduct whose logic ends up devouring humanity in a form of collective suicide?

329. In Latin, *ob*: that which lies in front of something; *ligare*: union, collection, or reconnection. This is the way in which the subject becomes "connected" to his or her obligation or duties.

330. Although leaving much more room for maneuver for decisions taken freely in terms of values or cultural norms, and so on, which are apparently self-regulated, and effectively nonintentional.

331. To make explicit that which is addressed here "ethically" would be redundant, since if the subject who acts is a human being, his or her acts necessarily have ethical dimensions. But in this case the redundancy is not excessive since it reinforces the intention of the statement.

332. Even in a postconventional culture, where each individual can rationally justify his or her decisions, and not simply play out the conventional moves for reasons of tradition, the project of critical argumentative intersubjectivity (as understood by Apel or Habermas) is already a project of the "good life" understood in postconventional terms, which can flourish in a historical culture, in a given moment, and so on.

333. Each culture's claim of universality (from the Eskimo to the Bantu all the way to the Mexicas or modern Europeans) reflects the presence of the universal material principle in all of them, which is contrary to ethnocentrism. Ethnocentrism or cultural fundamentalism is the attempt to impose on other cultures the universality that *my (our) culture* lays claim to, before it has been tested intersubjectively or in an intercultural context. A serious claim by any culture to universality should be tested by means of rational dialogue when two cultures confront each other. And when they confront each other historically, dialogue is possible from the perspective of each one's claim to universality, and materially, by applying the principle of content and regarding the production, reproduction, and development of the life of every subject of the culture, which animates each culture and all of them, and which enables them to materially discover the real articulations and places of convergence between them as they initiate a dialogue as *to how each culture concretely produces, reproduces, or develops human life*. The intersubjective discursive moment is exactly

the moment in the process which *formally* makes it possible for that dialogue to occur, but which does not negate the logic of the *material content* which defines the basis upon which the dialogue should proceed. All of this has been undermined by the *Eurocentrism of Modernity* as it has been inflicted upon the peripheral cultures of the world since the end of the fifteenth century up to the present (Dussel 1993c).

334. "The subject has an objective horizon [area 1 of table 2] which is that of life or death. This is each subject's objective limitation. In fact, the subject is a subject because it has such a limitation. This horizon enables the subject to be free of preconditions such as tradition and the world of life. Without this free space, which *transcends all traditions and all the worlds of life*, it would not be possible for there to be any traditions. We can have traditions only if it is possible for us to transcend them. That which cannot be transcended is not a tradition. The beating of the heart is repeated from generation to generation. But since it cannot be transcended it is not a tradition" (Hinkelammert 1995c, 34).

335. I hope to dedicate a work in the future to the *grounding of these principles*, where I will address the question of what such "grounding" means, in terms of laying a foundation for them. My position is not "fundamentalist" in character, but instead seeks to develop an argument from a "multifundamental" perspective: "Such a variant of anti-fundamentalism should perhaps in reality be denominated instead as a kind of *multifundamentalism* since instead of arguing that *no foundations exist*, what I propose is that there are many such foundations of various kinds and all of them form part of an open list" (Pereda 1994, 306).

336. Dussel 1996b. Each alternative involves a "practical truth" to the extent that it "refers" to life as such, as I have described.

337. Wittgenstein, *Notebooks 1914–1916* (1979, 91). And, in effect, what is in discussion here is not whether suicide is evil, but that it is not a basis upon which an ethical order can be founded. How can you found such an order upon death? What would the "dead" be like, who would be the subject of such an order? Suicide is the boundary that marks the limit beyond which all ethics is impossible; suicide is the radical negation of ethics. For its part, the principle of human life is not intrinsically ethical, but is instead the foundation of all possible ethical orders. *To negate* life is the evil; to *affirm* life is what is good. But life in itself is neither good nor evil. Life is beyond good and evil, as is suicide as such. Because one who commits suicide does not commit an evil act, but instead commits an act that results in the end of their existence: how could this be evil for them if they simply cease to exist? Suicide, without being evil, is the foundation for all evil; every evil contains some aspect of suicide within it, to the extent that it is an evil act, and if it becomes fully developed it ultimately leads to suicide. It is the same with Freud's "death principle" (see §4.3c).

338. See Henrich 1976.

339. See Blumenberg 1976.

340. For us the issue is not just the "reproduction of *social* life," but this and many other dimensions of the "*concrete* human life of each ethical subject in community."

341. Habermas 1981b, vol. 1, 526.

Chapter 2. Formal Morality

1. See Dussel 1973.

2. *Nicomachean Ethics*, bk. 6, 13 (Aristotle 1960, 1144b 28–30).

3. "This is why we call temperance *sofrosyne*, because it signifies a form of salvation [*sózousan*] from a concrete choice [*frónesin*]. That which she protects is the *hypólepsin*" (ibid., bk. 6, 5 [Aristotle 1960, 1140b 11–12]).

4. "The practical syllogisms [*syllogismoì tôn praktôn*] formulate their first principle in the following way: *Given that the* télos *is thus and the greatest good as well* [*tò ariston*], whatever it is" (ibid., bk. 5, 12 [Aristotle 1960, 1144a 31–32]). Note the reference here to "whatever it is"; this reflects the postulation of a universal ontological condition.

5. Aristotle 1960, 1144a 33–37. Along the way Aristotle recalls that formal practical validity (of a prudential character) should join with material goodness (the good). That which is "bad" is unable to formulate a "straightforward" argument ("distorting judgment") and thereby "incurs" a practical error.

6. "Deliberation [*bouleitikós*]" (*Nicomachean Ethics*, bk. 6, 5 [Aristotle 1960, 1140a 31]) is the concrete moment of practical argumentative reason, according to Aristotle.

7. Ontological grounding, in the case of Aristotle.

8. *Nicomachean Ethics*, bk. 6, 2 (Aristotle 1960, 1139b 5–6).

9. Ibid.

10. Aristotle 1960, 1139a 31.

11. Ibid., 1140b 6–7.

12. Ibid., 1140b 6. It is interesting to note here that for Aristotle a fully realized "good praxis" is a *télos* in itself—as if anticipating the Kantian formulation—to the extent that it fully expresses the ethical subject itself, as such.

13. "Ultimus finis nullo modo su electione cadit" (*Summa Theologiae*, pt. I–II, qu. 13, art. 3 [Aquinas 1950, 68]). The complete text reads: "What has been chosen comports itself as if it were the conclusion of the syllogism of that which is operative. The objective sought by its agents comports itself as a principle and not as a conclusion [*Unde illud cadit sub electione, quod se habet ut conclusion in syllogismo operabilium. Finis autem operabilibus se habet ut principium, et non ut conclusio*]" (ibid.). The "end" here is the ontological horizon, the "good life" in its most universal sense (that which is always supposed a priori and which aspires to be accepted as true and as an affirmation with universal validity).

14. Ibid., art. 5, 69.

15. Ibid., response 1.

16. The possible, amid the impossible and the illusory, occupies the full range of that which is ethically feasible (the focus of chapter 3 of this book).

17. "Per conscientiam applicator notitia synderesis . . . ad actum particularem examinandum" (*De Veritate*, qu. 17, art. 2, response [Aquinas 1964, 330]). The *syndéresis* (from the Greek, as rendered into Latin) is the habit of the first practical principles; the "intention [*intention*]" (*boûlesis* in Greek) is the tendency or inclination toward the ontological foundation or *télos*. All this can be reconsidered today and has analytical validity.

18. "Cum autem actus sit particularis, et synderis iudicium *universale* existat;

non potest *applicare* iudicum synderesis ad actum, nisi fiat *assumptio* alicuius particularis . . . Conscientia perficitur quasi quodam syllogismo particulari" (ibid.).

19. Ibid., qu. 24, art. 6 [Aquinas 1964, 445].

20. "Ratiocinari autem proprie est devenire ex uno in cognitionem alterius" (*Summa Theologiae*, pt. I, qu. 84, art. 4, response [Aquinas 1950, 406]). In more explicit terms, what the text suggests is that reasoning in the context of a practical choice is a transition from the principle to the acceptance of the conclusion: the concrete maxim.

21. Aquinas, *In X libros Ethicorum*, bk. VI, lect. 2, para. 1.137 (Aquinas 1949, 311).

22. It should be considered that the expositive method of the medieval *sumas* or *disputas*, which originated in the Islamic world, with their questions, articles, objections, theses, and responses to objections, all in the context of *argumentative debate*, created an atmosphere in medieval philosophy that was conducive to the intrinsic search for *intersubjective validity* among the community of scholars.

23. See examples of this from Espinas 1925 to Mesnard 1936, Couhier 1937, and others. Descartes's morality can be studied in his *Discours de la méthode*, pt. 3, and *Traité des passions*, as well as in many of his letters, for example Descartes 1935 (*Lettres sur la morale*). For the perspective of other rationalists, see Chevalier 1933, Delbos 1893, Thamin 1916, and others.

24. Malebranche 1707, 9–19.

25. Spinoza, *Ethica ordine geometrico demonstrata*, pt. 5, prop. 36 (1958, 266). This is clearly a rationalist expression, which, according to Kant, much too easily assumes an ethical *content*.

26. *Philosophia practica universalis*, vol. 2, sec. 9.

27. "The reflexive will expressed in happiness is the point of departure and law that governs moral life," Leibniz tells us, synthesizing all of his ethics (quoted in Chevalier 1933, 212).

28. "All of the spirits [*esprits*] . . . enter, armed with the virtue of reason and of eternal truths, in a kind of Society with God [*Société avec Dieu*], being members of the City of God" (Leibniz, *Principes de la nature et la grace*, sec. 15; see Dussel 1973, 113–14). Kant would write: "Leibniz considered the world to be the Kingdom of Grace if one's contemplation was limited to rational beings, and to their relations according to moral laws under the governance of a supreme good" (*Kritik der reinen Vernunft*, B 840, A 812 [Kant 1968, vol. 4, 682]).

29. In 1952, when I was a student at the University of Mendoza, I was struck by this "morality of resignation" which, in its worst sense, incited in the most illusory manner those who were "un-happy" not to despair. Marx demonstrated later that surplus value (the objectified surplus life that is not recovered by the worker) is a subtraction from happiness (objectified life that is not recovered, not paid for, and so, stolen: "This process of self-fulfilment through labour is at the same time a process of labor unrealized. Labor places something objectively, but this objectivity is put forward as if it were a *non-being* [*Nichtsein*] or as if it were a *being of its non-being*: capital" (*Grundrisse* [Marx 1974, 357–58]). This is the "un-happiness" that Kant justifies in moral terms. Kant was not conscious of this. But the "success" of his morality does not have its basis solely in the force of his argumentation in purely academic terms. It would "function"

perfectly in favor of capital in an exploited world of workers, precisely because it is "un-happily" exploited (today this phenomenon extends throughout the Global South). This morality demands that the poor and exploited be virtuous (as a result of which they will win a place for themselves in the Kingdom of God, as becomes clear if one undertakes a detailed reading of book 2, chapters 4 and 5, of the *Critique of Practical Reason*) and explains why being happy or unhappy ultimately has no moral relevance. The ethics of liberation instead seeks to demonstrate the *unhappiness of the poor*, of the exploited, of women repressed by patriarchy, and so on, that is the result (and one must be very clear about the material criterion necessary in order to judge it in these terms) of an unjust act which is perverse and ethically "evil." The *negation* of the happiness of the dominated is a critical ethical criterion (see more regarding this point in chapter 4), and is also a criterion of moral validity, in terms of its prohibition of a nongeneralizable maxim.

30. See Schilpp 1966.

31. *De mundi sensibilis atque intelligibilis forma et principiis* (*Von der Form der Sinnen- und Verstandeswelt und ihren Gründen*) (1770), sec. 9, A 11 (Kant 1968, vol. 5, 38–39).

32. In §1.1, particularly in light of the work of Damasio (1994), I have expounded this question as a relevant example from the neurobiological point of view. For an initial philosophical treatment, see Dussel 1970–80, vol. 1, 81 ff.

33. The rationalists, for their part, had equally lost the dimension of bodily reality along the way. The metaphysical ethics of rationalist "perfection [*Vollkommenheit*]," which Kant tended to refer back to, was already disembodied, abandoning "sensitive," "low," and "animal" emotions because of their supposed irrationality. The "material criterion" of human life, which can unite a "good life" (as historical "perfection") with the "tendencies" (emotions, affects, pleasure, happiness . . .) in a unitary universal anthropological understanding (as in contemporary neurobiology, and as in Marx from the *1844 Manuscripts* onward, Zubiri's feeling intelligence or intelligent feeling, Merleau-Ponty's phenomenology of perception, and many other similar contributions) would enable us to have a notion of "perfection" and an articulation with "sentiments" that was impossible for Kant. The result of this formalism is an irresolvable dilemma between Kant's formal morality (and its later variations as reflected in Rawls, Apel, Habermas, etc.) and material ethics.

34. See the definition of *bona, perfectio, beatitudo*, and *felicito* in Baumgarten's *Metaphysica* (sec. 787 [Baumgarten 1963, 322]).

35. *Untersuchung über die Deutlichkeit der Grundsätze der natürlichen Theologie und der Moral*, sec. 2, A 97 (Kant 1968, vol. 2, 771).

36. For example, see how Baumgarten structures his *Ethica* with obligation as his point of departure, from the beginning: "Ethica . . . est scientia obligationum hominis internarum in statu naturali" (sec. 2, A 3 [Baumgarten 1969, 5]).

37. There are two kinds of obligation: one where it is the means which compel the path toward happiness [*Glückseligkeit*], which has "problematical necessity"; or the other where it is the ends which compel the means [*Zweck*], which has "legal or immediate necessity." This last kind of necessity is that of the "immediate supreme rule [*unmitelbare oberste Regel*]" (Kant, *Untersuchung über die Deutlichkeit*, sec. 2, A 96 [Kant 1968, vol. 2, 770]).

38. Ibid.

39. Ibid., 771–72. "Hutcheson and others propose this sentiment to us

under the name of moral sentiment (*des moralischen Gefühls*)" (*Untersuchung über die Deutlichkeit*, sec. 2, A 98–99 [Kant 1968, vol. 2, 773]). Speaking of the will of God, he explains that it is a "material principle [*materialer Grundsatz*] of morality, although it is formally *(formaliter)* located under the above-mentioned formal (principle), which is the highest and most universal" (ibid., A 98).

40. *Nachricht von der Einrichtung seiner Vorlesungen in dem Winterhalbenjahre von 1765–1766*, A 12–13 (Kant 1968, vol. 2, 914).

41. *De mundi sensibilis . . .* , sec. 9, A 11 (Kant 1968, vol. 5, 38–39).

42. *De mundi sensibilis*, sec. 2, A 4 (Kant 1968, vol. 5, 18–19). The "body" in this sense is "material" (in German with an "a," as the ultimate *content*).

43. Kant 1968, vol. 5, 20–21. Baumgarten in his *Metaphysica*, sec. 640, writes: "ratio . . . est nexum rerum perspicientem" (Baumgarten 1963, 235).

44. During this period he writes: "The supreme principles of moral judgments are, in truth, rational, but are merely *principia formalia*. They do not determine any purpose; because of this it is *principia materialia* that arise in accordance with its form" (*Handschriftlicher Nachlass*, vol. 6 [Kant 1904, vol. 19, 120]).

45. With "a" in German.

46. *Grundlegung der Metaphysik der Sitten*, BA 3 (Kant 1968, vol. 6, 11).

47. *Kritik der praktischen Vernunft*, A 29 (Kant 1968, vol. 6, 193).

48. This claim is illusory, and many current ethical systems and moralities continue to fall for it. From my perspective, an ethics cannot be constructed on the basis of a "*single* principle," since a single principle can be *necessary but never sufficient*. Only a carefully developed architectural structure of principles can be sufficient, each of them necessary but not *unique*, as we shall see. Kant, to the contrary, writes that "the categorical imperative is, well, *unique*" (*Grundlegung der Metaphysik der Sitten*, BA 80 [Kant 1968, vol. 6, 69–70]).

49. I refer to this as inverted, because having cut the branch out from under him of everything material that he was sitting on, Kant still does not fall from the tree, because, as we shall see, he continues to affirm the formal development of his discourse made up of many presupposed yet inadvertent material moments (for example the dignity of the person, the Kingdom of Ends, the "common sense" that permits one to judge as "good" every act necessary for the generalization of the maxim, etc.).

50. If the entire material field of ethics had not been negated, it would have been necessary to "know" in depth the *content* of the world of daily life or of the ethical system at issue (including Heidegger's idea of a *Seinsverständnis*) as its essential constituent part, and not just as an absolute condition of possibility, and the material criterion of human life would have been discovered, and it would have been possible as well to "know" the practical material principle and its imperatives. This is to say that it would have been possible to propose a "knowledge" or rationality commensurate with the material order or with content along the lines of a universal practical truth prior to (or at least codeterminant with) the "formal" principle of intersubjective universality.

51. *Kritik der praktischen Vernunft*, A 161 (Kant 1968, vol. 6, 213). For a detailed comment, see Dussel 1973, 89 ff.

52. *Grundlegung zur Metaphysik der Sitten*, BA 80 (Kant 1968, vol. 6, 69–70).

53. *Kritik der praktischen Vernunft*, A 54 (Kant 1968, vol. 6, 140). See the earlier exposition in the *Grundlegung*, BA 52 (Kant 1968, vol. 6, 51).

NOTES TO CHAPTER 2 513

54. *Kritik der praktischen Vernunft*, A 56 (Kant 1968, vol. 6, 142).

55. *Grundlegung zur Metaphysik der Sitten*, BA 51, n. 50.

56. One might formulate the following question for Kant: How do I know ("knowledge" presupposed and prior to the formal principle, clearly) *materially* or judging by its content if this maxim is *good* or not, and whether or not it is generalizable? This is necessary, since I cannot inquire as to the validity of this concrete and individual maxim (which includes a reference to intersubjectivity) if I do not have, *always a priori* (historically and ontologically speaking), its material ethical content. This is so because intersubjective validity presupposes knowledge of the possible *goodness* or not of the maxim (of the practical *truth*), in each case, in order to enable the comparison with other situations and generalize it or not, and to be able to elevate it to the status of a universality of *content* without contradiction.

57. It is clear that that which is valid could not be validated without acceptance by all of an ethical *content* (the *truth*). Here we encounter the difficulty of the pure moral formality of validity. The material reference has to do with the "*truth*" (a complex, historical-ontological ability to reference the *reality* of the possibility of developing here and now, immediately or in the medium term, the concrete life of this human subject).

58. *Kritik der praktischen Vernunft*, A 122 (Kant 1968, vol. 6, 188).

59. Rawls's "original situation," as we shall see, is another "hypothetical situation." It is evident that the need to propose these "hypothetical models" indicates the impossibility of developing the formal morality at the purely formal level. The material must at least "hypothetically presuppose" this in order to proceed. A purely formal moral is impossible.

60. Concretely, the procedure would consist of "putting oneself in the place of other subjects" in order to demonstrate the moral validity of this maxim, or better, the noncontradiction with its possible universality, as in the examples of the *Grundlegung*, BA 53 ff. (Kant 1968, vol. 6, 52 ff.). It is interesting that Kant writes in the first example: "Soon we can see that a nature whose law implied the destruction of life itself [*das Leben selbst zu zerstören*] [which would work as a form of suicide] for the same reason that its determination must promote life [*zur Beförderung des Lebens*], would be contradictory and would not be able to subsist as nature" (ibid.). It is important to note that Kant here employs the first principle of *material* ethics (the "promotion of life [*zur Beförderung des Lebens*]," and furthermore *lays the foundation* for it correctly! This is to say that he who commits suicide destroys life based upon a rationality whose function is to preserve life. Kant here shows that he needs a *material* principle as a base in order to be able to generalize the maxim or not. How does he "know" that to "destroy life," as in suicide, is *bad*, and that to "destroy life" in a heroic act in the interests of one's homeland is *good*? Would it not be possible for a heroic people (like the brave Iberians who resisted the Romans) "to subsist like nature"? Charles Taylor, with reason in this regard, and even more so Franz Hinkelammert, could demonstrate to Kant his contradiction and his dead end.

61. *Kritik der praktischen Vernunft*, A 123 (Kant 1968, vol. 6, 189).

62. This is related, approximately, to part B (*Teil B*) of Apel's ethics, with many of its same anticipated difficulties. Its application without material criteria and principles is impossible, unless one has recourse to fantasy by means of hypothetical scenarios, as with Kant or Rawls. Among these scenarios are the "Kingdom of God," the "Kingdom of Ends," and all those of "rational faith"

(*Glaube*) (Dussel 1973, 104 ff.). Already in 1766 Kant had written: "The imma-terial substances (the souls) . . . can be immediately united to each other; they are capable of constructing together a great All that can be described as the im-material world" (*Träume eines Geistersehers*, A 30 [Kant 1968, vol. 2, 937]). And what about the bodies? Dualism as a point of departure, and the negation of material ethics, eventually demands a *great* deal of fantasy in order to bring us back to the real, the unitary, the carnal, the material as content, which were abandoned at the beginning, and all because the material question was posited *incorrectly* from the start. I have written elsewhere that an improvised take-off (from the material to the transcendental) predetermines an unfortunate land-ing (in the historical world of inequalities, of bodily necessities [*Bedürfnisse*], of economic and erotic domination, and so on, without any possibility of critical consciousness).

63. See Rawls 1951 and 1958 and Wolff 1977.

64. This idea, drawn from the concept of optimality or preferability devel-oped in Pareto's theory, suggests that when some obtain a benefit that contrib-utes to an increased benefit for all, those who do not experience such an in-crease in their levels of well-being "should not envy" those who benefit much more, since those with the greater benefit enable the others to acquire more benefits than before. In this context, the envious serve as impediments to the benefit of all.

65. The ingenious aspect of this solution relates to the power to determine "material" principles, once the material aspect of ethics has been dismissed as a point of departure (by the utilitarians, in their narrow and distorted view re-garding this, as we have seen). For Rawls, always, there will be *two* principles. It is interesting to recall that for him one of the defects of the utilitarians is their claim to *sustain only one principle*. Rawls admits the importance of more than one, but proposes that the first has priority over the second. This *prioritiza-tion* is not dialectical; from my perspective the different principles involved are intertwined and codetermining, and if one had to establish some order among them, it would be that which would result from subsuming them together; the liberation principle (the sixth) subsumes and presupposes the others, without negating their particular role and importance (see §6.5).

66. See Rawls 1967.

67. All of the modern "models," since Hobbes or Locke, are circular in their treatment of the "state of nature" (or now the "original situation"): their point of departure is the market and capitalist society, where the isolated indi-vidual (*Homo homini lupus*) competes without community. The models raise this abstract individuality in competition to the status of a hypothetical "state of nature." In this way they assign it the same abstract determinations that are already given in the market and the society that they claim to explain (or the same principles that they were supposed to decide). They then set up an abstract contract that is identical to the one assumed by existing society. Fol-lowing this operation, with this "model" (a mere ascendant idealization of existing society) in hand, they then return, to the very same society and its existing market and "demonstrate" that they can "explain" society by reference to this model. This is a tautological maneuver. Rawls proceeds in exactly the same fashion: he assigns the qualities of a liberal, individualist, and, according to the market, capitalist to those who participate, in the abstract, in a "game of chance" (which will later be redefined in terms of the "original situation")

in order to determine, with its participants, the principles and priorities of an ideal society. The whole process is tautological, empty, formalist, invalid, and circular (Hinkelammert 1984).

68. See Rawls 1971.

69. Ibid., chap. 3, secs. 20–30, 118 ff.

70. Ibid., 136.

71. Marx, as we have seen, wrote: "We will not place ourselves in an imaginary original situation, as economists do when they want to explain something [*Urzustand*]. Such an original situation explains nothing" (*The Manuscripts of 1844*, vol. 1 [Marx 1956–90, vol. 1, 511]).

72. Rawls 1971, chap. 2, sec. 10, 78.

73. "The principle of impartiality . . . maintains that it can be demanded that a person fulfill their role, and this is how the rules that govern an institution can be determined . . . ; and secondly, that the benefits of this agreement be accepted voluntarily" (ibid., sec. 18, 111–12).

74. Ibid., 58. "Formal justice is adherence to principle . . . obedience to system."

75. Ibid., sec. 11, 60–61.

76. See, among others, Apel 1988, 174 ff., 281 f., 285 ff., 406 ff.; Barry 1974; Daniels 1975; Dworkin 1977; Habermas 1991, 13 ff., 79 ff., 204 ff.; Habermas 1992, 80 ff.; MacIntyre 1988.

77. "The absolute value of liberty with respect to social and economic advantages, precisely as the lexicographic order of the two principles defines it" (Rawls 1971, chap. 2, sec. 11). His order, which consists of "one principle *above* another" (an inversion of the Stalinist order for the relationship between the economic base and the political superstructure, with its materialist economism, and which in the Soviet Union was in fact just a bureaucratic *formalism* that alienated the worker materially [with an "a" in German] though *in a different way* than did capitalism) is a formalist reification of politics. From my perspective, principles are codetermined without unilateral priorities. Utilitarianism posited a single subjective material principle (that of happiness); Rawls proposed the "absolute" priority of a formal principle (freedom). I do not believe that either position is acceptable. The whole matter of ethical principles must be articulated more consistently. See later stages of development of Rawls's approach, in Rawls 1982.

78. Rawls 1971, sec. 13, 75.

79. Ibid., sec. 11, 61.

80. "What then can justify such initial inequality in the expectations of life?" Rawls here asks himself the key question but fails to reply: "According to the principle of difference it would only be justifiable if the difference of expectations operates to the benefit of the representative person who is most poorly situated" (sec. 13, 78). Note that he has not responded as to why there is such inequality to begin with, only *that given* such inequality, it should be managed to the benefit of the most "poorly situated." But he has not explained *why* someone is so situated. This brings Adam Smith to mind, when he says that "in the primitive and noisy state of society, which precedes the accumulation of capital . . . the integral product of labour belongs to the worker . . . . But as soon as capital begins to accumulate in the hands of determined individuals, some of these [those who are the most favored in Rawls's scenario] tend to use it in order to engage the labour of working people" [a euphemism applied to those

Rawls describes as the most "poorly situated"] (Smith 1985, vol. 1, chap. 6, 150–51). This secondary "state of nature" continues to be "nature" from Rawls's perspective. Marx indicated: "On the one hand *it is forgotten* [this is exactly what the "veil of ignorance" does not forget] from the beginning (!) that the supposed exchange value, to the extent it is the objective base of the productive system as a whole, *already includes* (historically) the coercion [= nonfreedom] of the individual . . . . *It is forgotten* that all of this presupposes additionally a division of labour. . . . *It is not seen* that already the simple determination of exchange value and of money latently incorporates the contradiction between salaried labour and capital" (Marx 1974, 159 and 186). This is to say that Rawls confuses a particular *historical* relation internal to a capitalist market society with the nature of universality as such.

81. Rawls 1971, sec. 16, 98. In the English-language version included in the 1977 edition, a paragraph on p. 98 has been eliminated immediately before the text I have cited (see the 1971 edition: "Here it seems impossible to avoid a certain arbitrariness").

82. On the role of the critical social sciences, see §5.3, particularly §5.5c.1 [332].

83. Rawls 1971, sec. 17, 102.

84. How can a person who has not yet been born "deserve" something? This is obvious, which is to say redundant.

85. But this has an evil intention, to the extent it is clearly based on an ambiguity, which relieves the dominator of any responsibility for causing the injustice at issue (yet another illustration of the liberal who shuffles his cards too soon). Here we have to distinguish, as I indicated above, between (a) the proposition that individual birth as such is a matter of "luck"; and (b) the fact that the social structure *within which we are born* is a historical and social matter. The first, (a), is a matter of chance; the second, (b), is a matter of injustice and merits compensation, precisely *because* it is unjust. "To be born at the North Pole or in Chiapas [as the child of a person of indigenous origin] is not the same thing as to be born in New York City [as the child of Rockefeller]," as I wrote, in the sense of (b), ethical-social responsibility, in Dussel 1977, 1.1.1.2.

86. *Why* doesn't it follow? Rawls never explains this, instead assuming it to be proven a priori. This affirmation from the perspective of the materiality of the world of life, which is a presupposition (the ethical system characteristic of liberalism), invalidates his argument and hides its underlying premises and sources.

87. Rawls 1971, sec. 17, 102.

88. Aristotle, *Politics*, vol. 1, 12 (1960, 1254a 16).

89. That is to say, morally or formally, this current of thinking contributes notable clarifications and developments (formal and material, in the overall context of unitary and real complexity) that are, however, ethically irrelevant (to the extent that they imply or repeat what is given or what cannot effectively be applied), complicit (often inadvertently), or cynical (when they invalidate with skeptical arguments the "critical arguments" of those ethical thinkers who also integrate the material level, often with great difficulty because it is a very complex task, and not because of mere incapacity or lack of information or study).

90. Rawls 1971, chap. 9, sec. 81, 535.

91. Rawls 1993.

92. In ibid., 15 ff., 39 ff., 144 ff., etc.

93. This is the market to which the creation of conditions of balance and equality is consigned, unwittingly, given that the logic of the market is, precisely, the tendency toward imbalance (see Hinkelammert 1984, chap. 2, 53 ff., 62 ff.: "The categorical framework of contemporary neoliberal thought"). Hayek introjects the model of "perfect competition with a tendency toward equilibrium" (an inconsistent model—because if competition is perfect there can be no competition given that all of the competitors are equal—which cannot be implemented) in the empirical market. No scientific empirical study can demonstrate the "tendency toward equilibrium in the market"; to the contrary, the market produces only disequilibriums between nations, throughout the branches of capital, between regions, among social classes, and between individuals, because such "competition" destroys the weakest and *accumulates* capital in fewer and fewer hands. This is the clear "tendency" over the last two centuries.

94. Rawls 1993, chap. 4, sec. 42, 265.

95. On its formal aspects, see Ulrich 1993.

96. See Jay 1973. This point is explored later in §4.2.

97. Do I want to highlight here that Apel's rationalism is not that of an idealist, but rather that of an ethical thinker who feels responsible for what the Hitlerian irrationality of his homeland inflicted upon Europe and the world? (See "Return to Normality? Or have we been capable of understanding something specific after the national catastrophe?" in Apel 1988, 379 ff.). On Apel, see Cortina 1985, Hösle 1990, Schelkshorn 1994.

98. Apel 1950. It is interesting to note that a dual path can already be seen: on the one hand, his desire to clarify the problem of knowledge; on the other, since the Heideggerian *Sorge* (preoccupation), reflection has been implanted as the "constitution of meaning from the perspective of the interest of knowledge [*Erkenntnisinteresse*]," a theme that Habermas develops later (1968a).

99. See his essay of 1959, "Sprache und Wahrheit," in Apel 1973, vol. 1, 138–68.

100. See Apel 1980a. Apel begins to treat the theme of the construction of that which is valid intersubjectively from the perspective of language, from the discovery of the question of the "mother tongue" in Dante, up to the "institution of institutions" (language) of Vico.

101. Apel 1973, vol. 1 (1970), 223 ff.

102. See Apel 1994a.

103. See Apel 1981, which is a magnificent work of historical-philosophical reconstruction.

104. Apel 1973, vol. 2, 157 ff. Also Apel 1996, 1–67.

105. Apel 1973, vol. 2, 358–435. It could be said that in the last few decades Apel has developed the "intuitions" of this essay, to which it is always possible to return to productively.

106. Apel discards the project of an "anthropology" and discovers the "ethics that had already been proposed" in any community of communication, including the communication community of scientists, a question already posed in ibid.

107. This question continues to absorb Apel, for example, from Apel 1976

and 1980b, to Apel 1989, and in Apel 1996, 293–314. His critique of Albert 1968 is key. See also Hösle 1990, 123 ff.; Rojas, 1995, 39 ff.; Schelkshorn 1994, 285–380.

108. I believe that Habermas's essay "Was heist Universalpragmatik?" (1976) in Habermas 1984, 353–440, and the later Habermas 1981b, provided much material for Apel's reflection. In any case, the works of Austin 1962 and of Searle 1969 are determining factors in his work. See Apel 1994b.

109. We see a new turn in Searle's approach, when he writes: "Language is derived from Intentionality and not conversely" (Searle 1983, 5) or "We define speakers' meaning in terms of forms of Intentionality that are not intrinsically linguistic" (ibid., 160). This moves Apel to criticize the later Searle from the standpoint of the earlier Searle of *Speech Acts* (Searle 1969), in his essay "Linguistic Meaning and Intentionality: The Compatibility of the *Linguistic Turn* and the *Pragmatic Turn* of Meaning-Theory within the Framework of a Transcendental Semiotics" (in the original German, Apel 1990b). Habermas's essay "Intentionalistische Semantik" (1975–76) in Habermas 1984, 332–51, is an anticipation of this problematic. In "Pragmatic Philosophy or Language" (Apel 1994b, 231–53) Apel returns to this theme.

110. See Apel 1991 and 1994b.

111. The "descent" from the grounding or justification of the basic norm consists of successive steps through "deduction [*Ableitung*]" always and exclusively from the pure, formal, rational argumentative act. It is a formally coherent deductivism, but of an extreme kind (the fallacy of "formal deductivism"). The liberation of women dominated by patriarchy, for example, would be "deduced" exclusively from the moral obligation or demand of bringing about a symmetry between women and men for every discussion (argumentation) that might affect it. Can the act of loving another (erotically, humanly, orgasmically, ethically, respectfully, symmetrically) "be deduced" as an obligation only by concretely carrying out the conditions of a possible argumentation (or the application of a basic formal norm)? Is this not a rationalism that is too extreme, unilateral, and even superficial?

112. See "From Kant to Pierce: The Semiotic Transformation of Transcendental Logic" (in Apel 1973, vol. 2, 155 ff.).

113. See Austin 1962.

114. See Searle 1969.

115. See the differences in Habermas's position in Apel 1989, 1991, and 1994b. Regarding this theme, see Hösle 1990, 192 ff.; Wellmer 1986, 69 ff.

116. All of this is already expressed "intuitively" or generally in "The *a priori* of the Community of Communication," in Apel 1973, vol. 2, 358 ff.

117. Apel 1985, 235–36.

118. See Apel 1980b. After having contextualized fundamental material problems (of content), such as the ecological question or the survival of the human species (as illustrative of cases of planetary dimensions), his thought develops into a purely formal confrontation (regarding issues of validity) with analytical morality or epistemological positivism (all of part II in Apel 1980b): "scientific rationality blocks the genuine development of ethical reason" (ibid., 123).

119. Ibid., 146–47.

120. Apel cites Aristotle's *Metaphysics*, bk. 4, 1006a 6–18, a position that is transformed pragmatically and transcendentally; he also refers to the mono-

logical internalized position of Augustine in the *Etsi fallor, sum*, which we would equally have to transform into "performative self-reflexive contradictions," for example: "I declare here that it is possible that I do not exist" (Apel 1980b, 148).

121. Apel 1980b, 161.

122. Ibid., 161–62.

123. Apel 1988, 10. In a certain sense, this *Zwischenzeit* is, sadly, *all* of universal history, or—at least from my perspective—the epoch in which *all* of the ethics of liberation arises, since it is an ethics that seeks to think philosophically *from* the perspective of "asymmetry" as if it were "normality."

124. In Apel 1988, the analysis of this problem can be observed, flowing from the position of Max Weber, and particularly of Jonas 1982a. See Hösle 1990, 133 ff.; Schelkshorn 1994, 29 ff.

125. These consequences reach the limits of the horizons of humanity, as a possible "macro-ethics for humanity" (see the paper Apel presented in Hawaii in July 1989 [Apel 1992a], "The Need for the Apparent Difficulty, and the Eventual Possibility of a Planetary Macroethics of [for] Humankind." An ethics of responsibility would enable the transcendence of existing asymmetries as a basis for obtaining a future symmetry, as a condition of possibility necessary to enable the implementation of the basic norm of discourse ethics.

126. Apel 1985, 249.

127. Apel 1990a, 26.

128. "Do Hegel's Objections to Kant also Affect Discourse Ethics?" in Habermas 1991, 12.

129. Ibid.

130. I am referring here to all of those we might consider active fronts of struggles for liberation, from the perspective of a possible praxis of liberation. In this context, Apel can be described as a progressive social-democratic thinker, who is critical of reactionary, fundamentalist, and dogmatic movements. See the approach taken by *Ethics of Liberation* to the solution of this question in chapter 5.

131. Apel 1990b, 22.

132. Apel 1985, 260.

133. Ibid., 254.

134. Ibid., 260. On "application [*Anwedung*]," see Kettner 1992, 9–27; also Apel 1992a.

135. Apel 1990a, 32 and 38–39. "The reason for this is to imply that the conditions of application of the ethics of discourse have not yet been realized" ("weil die Anwendungsbedingungen der Diskursethik geschichtlich noc hicht realisiert sind") (ibid., 32). "The application of the principle of discourse ethics— for example, the practice of a discursive-consensual regulation of conflicts, strictly separated from the application of a rationality of strategic negotiation, can only be brought about approximately where the minimal basis for ethical relations exists and local law makes these possible" ("Die Anwedung des Prinzips der Diskurethik—z.B. die Praktizierung einer diskursiv-konsensualen Konfliktregelung, die von ver Anwendung strategischer Verhandlungsrationalität strict getrennt wäre—lässt sich nur da—approximativ—verwirklichen, wo die lokalen Verhältnisse der ittlichkeit und des Rechts dies von sich aus mitermöglichen"]" (ibid., 33). This formula is frequently reiterated: the application of the method is impossible if the necessary conditions do not exist.

136. See Apel 1985, 261.

137. In the peripheral world, the necessary minimum conditions for the production, reproduction, and development of human life frequently do not exist (because of poverty) among the possible participants in the real community of communication. In fact, under such condition there is often not even a rule of law.

138. See my discussion of this problem in Dussel 1994b, 87–92 [147–52].

139. See Hinkelammert 1994.

140. Of course, strategic reason (level 3 of table 2) is a mediating reason of feasibility, but not a material one (as Apel seems to suggest). Strategic reason is exercised "with respect to ends" (and this is why "judgments of fact" are stated from that perspective). But the ends (and even the ultimate cultural values) can and should be "put" forward, judged, and transformed from the perspective of "material ethical reason" or "original ethics"—as Levinas and I both refer to it, although my intention is to transform it radically. This "original ethical reason" (see level 1 of tables 2 and 8), *ante festum*, is what opens up the real conditions necessary for life in general and its human dimension in particular, and which make it possible for the ethical subject him- or herself to exist and to reproduce and develop human life. The fundamental "material ethical principle" (which is preontological), on the other hand, and *post festum*, is *internal* to each culture, which it can judge and transform. The "hypervalues" of Taylor are not the ultimate basis, but rather "mediations" (as Heidegger, Zubiri, and Marx each insisted in his own way) of the reproduction and development of human life. Given that these cultures are "modes" that can enable the reproduction and development of human life, when they "close" and produce victims and death (see chapter 4), the same principle that has given rise to them turns upon itself, from within these cultures (if it has internal resources, such as chapter 125 of the ancient *Egyptian Book of the Dead*, for example), or from the horizon of other cultures (by means of confrontation), in order to remind them of their mediating and *not ultimate* function.

141. Apel 1985, 261. Furthermore, to demonstrate the normative *truth* of the "final end" of an action is beyond the limits of all strategic or instrumental, or even discursive, reason, because it is the *content* of a "practical-material" or "original ethical" reason. The latter opens itself up to a space other than that of ends; it only opens that of ends to the extent that they are "possible," since it is not only the "condition of preontological possibility" of every end, value, act, norm, institution, and so on, but of the constitution of the *content* of the action. The point is the reproduction and development of the human subject as such. It is not the object of any possible "judgment of facts" that amounts to a formal means of feasibility (because it is not the object, nor is it the means for an end, nor the end of an action); it is a "normative judgment" or one with regard to life, "an ethical judgment of reality" that can criticize ends and values, and upon the basis of which a formal "judgment of facts" can be based as well as a "value judgment." It is a judgment that expresses the empirical impossibility of its negation; a judgment of facts of a type different from that of the judgments of facts in terms of means-end or value judgments, and which makes them possible. The "valuation" that the limbic cerebral system, from the perspective of the criterion of the life of the human subject him- or herself in the process of perceptual and conceptual categorization and of the values themselves, should be denominated "preontological ethical valuation"

or knowing how to situate the mediations (the same ends and values) for the reproduction and development of life of that human subject as such (to the extent it is life and it is human). To say "it is bad to steal" is not only to situate this act (a) as a negative mediation with respect to private property as an end (and in this case to make explicit the claim of intersubjective validity) but also, radically and at the same time, to situate it (b) as a nonmediation (a practical nontruth) for the reproduction and development of the life of the human subject as such. The first is a "value judgment" with the claim of rectitude based upon its characteristic as a value; the second is implicitly a "normative judgment," founded upon a "factual judgment," which lays the basis for the first (not with respect to an institution of property or to a modern culture, but to the life of the human subject as the ultimate absolute reference of the ethical possibility of property as such): "To steal from another ethical subject will not permit this subject to reproduce his or her life," in principle and to some concrete extent.

142. See "*Über ein vermeintes Recht aus Menschenliebe zum Lügen*" in Kant 1968, vol. 7, 635–43.

143. Apel 1985, 262.

144. Ibid. See Apel 1973, vol. 2, 431.

145. A "condition" is not the same as a "constituent" moment. The material level is the constituent *content* of the ethical act, not just its condition.

146. Apel 1985, 262. Apel had written several years earlier: "Starting from this (implicit) demand, contained in all philosophical argumentation, *two regulatory principles* can be *deduced*, in my judgment, regarding the moral strategy of human effort in the long run. In the first place, with each action and omission we must somehow try to ensure our *survival* [*Überleben*] [Why? I would ask Apel] as a human species that is also a real community of communication; in the second place, we must seek to achieve the ideal communication community *in reality*" (Apel 1973, vol. 2, 431). To know how to undertake the reflection necessary as to the "survival" of the subject (see §1.5) is the essence of the matter regarding the grounding of the material principle of ethics. Apel does not fully develop this argument; if he were to do so he would have to abandon his formalism. This is, precisely, the central point of a material ethics with a universal criterion. For Apel "survival" is approached as if it were a "condition" or "deductive" moment. From my perspective it is instead "*constitutive* of the content" of the reality of the act, to the extent it implies the fulfillment of the life of the subject of the argument, and also the place where its criterion is encoded.

147. Human life (which is more than mere survival) is the *material* determinant (because of its content) of the argumentation; and the argumentation *formally* determines human life.

148. Apel 1990a, 29.

149. In other words, Apel has a vision of universal history as a progression toward "enlightenment," or the creation of postconventional conditions of equality or ideal argumentative symmetry in the real communication community encompassed within the rule of law. This is a vision in which exclusive importance is given to what is formal, without any interest in exploring the actual contents that human life has produced and fulfilled (consumed, lived, enjoyed) in biographical, cultural, and historical terms, and above all it lacks the material criteria needed for determining the causes of asymmetries apparent in these contexts, or that might serve to differentiate functionalist versions

of the social sciences from critical ones, at the moment of having recourse to them in the processes of transformation necessary as part of the struggle to attain symmetry in the future (see §5.5c.1).

150. *Metaphysik der Sitten*, AB 36 (Kant 1968, vol. 6, 339). This "external level" is the "public sphere" that Habermas would later reconstruct as the intersubjective expression of the validity of agreement of the communication community.

151. In each debate, Habermas subsumes his critics instead of rejecting their arguments, and thereby enriches his own arguments through them.

152. Habermas 1976. See some of his works during this period: Habermas 1962, 1963, 1968a, 1968b, 1973, and 1982.

153. See McCarthy 1988.

154. See Adorno et al. 1969; Habermas 1982 (in the 1982 edition, Habermas reviews the trajectory from Karl Popper and Hans Albert to Niklas Luhmann).

155. Max Weber's influence is decisive, although Hegel is employed to signal the presence of a challenge broader than that engaged by Marx.

156. As Habermas told me personally in St. Louis in 1996.

157. Habermas 1963, 228. For an extensive treatment of Habermas's position regarding Marx, see Dussel 1990b, 319–33, which I will refer to here.

158. Habermas 1981b, vol. 1, 19.

159. Habermas 1963, 256–57. This text is of interest to Habermas because he repeats his reference to it in Habermas 1968a, 67 ff., although with different implications.

160. Marx 1974.

161. In the *Grundrisse* the question is not yet clear; for this we will have to await the *Manuscripts of 1861–63*. See Dussel 1985a, 291 ff.

162. Habermas, of course, does not pay any attention to the chronological order of the texts he cites, and at the time he is writing this does not yet understand the whole problem of the "archaeology of categories" in Marx.

163. At this point, Marx mentions *Arbeitsvermögen* and not *Arbeitskraft*.

164. True wealth [*wirklicher Reichtum*] is use value, not exchange value.

165. He calls it *Wertquelle* (Habermas 1968a, 46).

166. Ibid., 47.

167. Marx 1956–90, vol. 3, 44 (48); Habermas 1968a, 46.

168. He uses the word *Stoff*, not simply in its sense of physical matter but as something "with which" one works. Marx does not elaborate a "cosmology" or a "metaphysics of nature," but is instead interested in nature as the "material (or content) of labor." This is a theory of production and not of physics. Soviet materialism and Habermas, in this case, attribute to Marx what he is explicitly rejecting.

169. Referring to nature in Hegel, Marx writes: "Nature as nature . . . is nothing, a nothing that is confirmed as nothing, that lacks meaning or has only the meaning of an exteriority which has been subsumed" (*1844 Manuscripts* [Marx 1956–90, vol. 1, 206]; 663). Hegel here has lost his sense of what is the "real" and has confused it with the "reality of the concept" of nature, with the reality of the self-consciousness of being.

170. *1844 Manuscripts* (Marx 1956–90, vol. 1, 195).

171. If "ontology" is understood as the "totality" of the Being of capital: the valorization of value (Dussel 1990b, chap. 10). An ethical critique of "capital"

as a *totality* is what I have described as an "ethical judgment of reality" (regarding the system in its totality, prior to the understanding of ends contemplated by formal factual judgments, and to the values entailed in value judgments, as we saw in §1.5).

172. *Kapital* (1873), vol. 1, chap. 1, 2 ([Marx 1987, 76]); Habermas 1968a, 39. Habermas quotes another text: "Labor . . . puts the natural forces into motion that belong to bodily reality [*Leiblichkeit*], arms and legs, head and hands, in order to wrest power from the raw materials [*Naturstoff*] of nature in a form which is useful *for their own life* [*für sein eigenes Leben*]" *Kapital*, chap. 5, 192 ([Marx 1987, 215]).

173. This is an issue I addressed in §1.5.

174. What I am trying to say is that labor is the "actual condition" of a "content" that is even more fundamental: human life itself as an essential material and universal "condition" (and a "content") of all possible ethical systems. Apel's or Habermas's notions of "survival" are merely physical-animal.

175. Habermas 1968a, 9.

176. It is the significance of the "sur" in "*sur*vival": self-consciousness, which is the mind's superior function.

177. Marx 1987, 162.

178. Subsequently, he develops this critique of the paradigm of instrumental productivism and consciencism of Marx from the perspective of discursive reason (Habermas 1985, 95 ff.).

179. Habermas 1984, 353–439.

180. See Habermas 1981b.

181. See Habermas 1983 and 1991.

182. See Habermas 1988.

183. See Habermas 1985.

184. See Habermas 1992.

185. See Habermas 1995.

186. See "Discourse Ethics: Notes towards a Program to Develop Its Foundations," in Habermas 1983, 53–126.

187. See MacIntyre 1981 (in §1.3 of this book). Habermas, inspired by MacIntyre's communitarianism, accuses metaethical analytical philosophy of being skeptical: but, improving on MacIntyre's arguments, he employs them to situate his own pragmatic moral universalist position of normative statements with the claim of their own argumentative-rational validity of rectitude or correctness (*Richttigkeit*). Discourse ethics defines itself as a universal normative morality, which can be grounded and lay the foundation rationally for norms, and which is critical of analytical metaethics — because of its insufficiencies (for mistakenly delimiting the kind of statements upon which it is based) — and of material ethics, because it is incapable of universal reach.

188. Regarding a recent position in this regard, see Habermas 1991, 185–99.

189. Habermas 1983, 55–56.

190. Ibid., 60.

191. See Toulmin 1970.

192. Habermas 1983, 62.

193. Weber's "value judgments," which are mere matters of taste, have to do with the values already prevailing in a specific culture. Habermas speaks in this case of "judgments of value," material ones, of contents, which are not

the ones to which Weber is referring, since these are not susceptible to rational argumentation with the claim of consensual validity, but instead would be imposed simply and dogmatically because of the authority of tradition. For my part, I must insist upon a different description of these kinds of statements.

194. Here we must distinguish among the varying ways in which different languages describe these concepts. "Rectitude," "rightness," or "correctness" (*Richtigkeit*, *orthós* in Greek) can be "formal" or "material," so it is important to be precise. See thesis 13 in appendix 1.

195. *Principia Ethica* chap. 1, pt. A, sec. 2 (Moore 1968, 3). Habermas would not accept a metaethics of language, at a solipsistic, neutral (nonparticipative), assertive, and prepragmatic level. See Rabossi 1979 for a classification of ethical systems using an analytical vocabulary. His descriptions range from a descriptive ethics (which is empirical) to a normative one (which is traditional or metaphysical), and includes those that are analytical (the metaethics criticized here by Habermas; Rabossi 1979, 33 ff.), those which are objectivist or subjectivist (57 ff.), and so on. Rabossi gives special emphasis to criteria of classification 59 ff.). On intuitionism, see 72 ff.

196. Later, Habermas clarifies his understanding of the inference between theoretical and practical reason, in the face of Williams 1985 (Habermas 1991, 120–25).

197. Habermas 1983, 64.

198. Ibid., 64.

199. See Ayer 1958. Ayer falls into several different expressions of reductionism, for example, when he writes: "If I say, 'Stealing money is wrong,' I am formulating a statement that has no *factual* sense. . . . It is as if I had written: *Stealing money!!*" (Ayer 1958): "If now I . . . say 'Stealing money is wrong,' I produce a sentence which has no factual meaning—that is, expresses no proposition which can be either true or false. It is as if I had written 'Stealing money!!' where the shape and thickness of the exclamation marks show, by a suitable convention, that a special sort of moral disapproval is the feeling which is being expressed." Ayer would be correct if this were a solipsistic statement kept at a level of semantic abstraction; if it were not "factual." But pragmatically, *factually*, or intersubjectively when I say, "I affirm that to steal money *is evil*" (as a *speech act* in the sense suggested by Austin or Searle), with a propositional content affirming that it "is evil," I add something; I state something explicitly, and because of this I add semantic content, and the claim of an intersubjective defense with arguments that I propose as having the force of positive truth, or which I proffer openly with the claim that they have moral validity. Consider this theme, in terms of *descriptive* "speech acts," in Habermas 1984, chap. 2 ("Wahrheitstheorien," 127 ff.) and chap. 3 ("Was heist Universalpragmatik?" 353 ff.); Dussel 1993a, 33–66: "The Reason of the Other: *Interpellation* as a Speech Act."

200. See Hare 1952.

201. Habermas 1983, 65.

202. This would mean that ethical controversies could not be resolved by means of argumentation. In this he coincides with Albert (1980; see also Albert 1968).

203. Habermas 1983, 71. The difference between the claim of consensus and of norms, in the face of Rawls, is defined in Habermas 1991, 125–31.

204. Baier 1958.

205. Gert 1988.

206. See Singer 1961.

207. Habermas 1983, 76. This statement can be found in other parts of Habermas's definitive works.

208. See Habermas 1991, 137–42, in his defense against the criticism of "inapplicability" (*Nichtanwendbarkeit*) in Wellmer 1986.

209. Nonetheless, a monological moment is always concomitantly necessary; in other words, all the participants should each individually accept or not the proposed argument with its corresponding validity claim. Here, as we will see in §§2.5 and 3.1–2, we can find the point of convergence between the practical *truth* claim of the normative statement with the *validity* claim of the same statement, an issue that Habermas is unable to grapple with because of his consensualist position regarding truth as such.

210. Habermas 1983, 74.

211. From my perspective, the "reference" to "cultural values" is secondary; the primary "reference" is established with respect to human life as a practical or ethical criterion of truth.

212. Habermas 1983, 74.

213. There is an ambiguity here that he seeks to correct with the word "strict [*streng*]"; and this is so because the evaluative statements are also normative in character. The so-called normative statements articulated by Habermas are "moral or practical statements with *validity*" (or with "a claim of moral validity").

214. As I have emphasized elsewhere, "the just [*das Gerechte*]" here is employed incorrectly as a concept. Formal morality does not deal with the "just"—an ambiguity that has its origins in Rawls among others—but rather with what is "valid." "The just" or the "correct [*richtig*]" can be formal (valid) or material (to give each their due: which has to do with a content, with something supremely material [with an "a," as in German]). See thesis 13 in appendix 1.

215. These make an "intersubjective validity claim" that is traditional and customary, and not the product of argumentation. But, and this is something that Habermas is incapable of espousing (and that is fundamental to the ethics of liberation; see chapter 4), the traditional claims of cultural values can enter *into crisis* (from the perspective of the victims, the oppressed) and, in this case, the *dominant* morality must formulate its arguments in the face of the *criticism* of those who are skeptical regarding its premises and applications (and whose skepticism is focused on these values precisely *to the extent to which they are dominant*). All of this is precisely the problematic that is of interest to *critical* ethics. Discourse ethics has long abandoned this perspective.

216. Once again, what is said to be "strict" is in fact ambiguous.

217. Habermas 1983, 113–14.

218. Level 1 of table 2 or level 1 of table 9. This has to do with what I have described as "ethical judgments of reality": normative statements founded upon factual judgments with reference to the life of the ethical subject, from the perspective of the ethical demands of the reproduction and development of life of the human subject, beyond all culture, system, or "world" (in its Heideggerian ontological sense), and within each of these. See chapter 4.

219. For example, in the case of Habermas, I am critical of his lack of emphasis on economic factors in his analysis, and his failure to discern misery as a fundamental ethical problem. This refers in essence to the material critique of *Spätkapitalismus*—which is impossible from the perspective of a discourse ethics such as that devised by Habermas.

220. These are questions that I explore beginning in chapter 4 of this book, and particularly in §6.1b.

221. "*Critical* rationality" is fulfilled, then, from moment c toward a or b, and from moment d (because of the relationship of 4 "upward") toward c and b (relation 5). I address these questions in chapters 5 and 6.

222. Habermas 1983, 114. From the perspective of the ethics of liberation, the "normative validity of the norms of action" can equally be understood as "axiological preferences" of an antihegemonic critical ethical consciousness. For example, the statement "I should risk my life in the struggle for *justice* against capitalism in the world of the periphery" includes a mandatory component (as to what I "should do") and also an element of normative action, given the preference implied for a relevant "value" ("justice"), which is itself the result of a material economic analysis of a critical community that has discovered that a specific historical system impedes the reproduction of human life (a material principle and criterion). Here I articulate formal procedural reason with a demand regarding the material conditions necessary for human life.

223. See §2.5 [148 ff.], regarding the distinction between a (material) truth claim and (formal) validity.

224. For Habermas, these "orientations [*Orientierungen*]" are not tasks that correspond to moral philosophy. They certainly are assumed as such from the perspective of the ethics of liberation, but in a distinctly universal and abstract sense (not concretely, because then they would be themes appropriate for experts in the social sciences, in political parties or social movements, etc.). I address this point in §5.5.

225. Habermas 1983, 113.

226. Ibid., 118.

227. When Habermas provides the example "You shall not kill" or "It is commanded that you shall not kill" (ibid., 70) or *when he refers to suicide* (ibid., 110, 124 and 112, 127, for example), he draws closer to the theme I addressed in §1.5, but the person who claims to be laying the foundation for ethics should confront not the skeptic, but the cynic who justifies death or suicide.

228. See Henrich 1976.

229. Habermas 1981b, vol. 1, 532–33. Note how he is unable to comprehend how the self-conscious material reproduction of the human life of the human subject must always be integrated into intersubjective argumentation, in such a manner that he or she is not "blinded" nor *should* be. I will return to this question in chapter 4, in order to analyze the difference between the "first" and the "second" expressions of the Frankfurt school.

230. Principle "D" is the *"sole [einziges]* moral principle" (Habermas 1983, 103).

231. Habermas 1991, 24.

232. Ibid., 28.

233. This refers to the whole question of the nonexistent symmetry of real communication in the community, which is Apel's condition for application of his principle.

234. Habermas 1991, 29.

235. Ibid.

236. Ibid.

237. Habermas not only has no "privileged" access to this, but none at all, because the "moral" truth should be found on the material level that he has denied since the inception of his moral project.

238. Habermas 1991, 30.

239. Ibid., 44. The motivational and affective drives of desire are also discarded. The "hunger" of the victims *impels* them to struggle. Discourse ethics is not able to draw upon such "motivations," unlike the ethics of liberation.

240. Ibid., 22.

241. Especially notable here is his excellent reflection regarding how negation presupposes affirmation (whereby Habermas should know that the negation of the life of the victim, of the oppressed, presupposes its affirmation, as a previous act and as a universal positive material principle). See ibid., 166–76, contrary to Wellmer 1986 and others.

242. Ibid., 25.

243. Ibid., 176 (in the English MIT Press translation, 69). See also in ibid., 199–208 (88–95), in dialogue with McCarthy and Rawls.

244. As I noted in §1.3b, I cannot accept either Taylor's cultural-ontological conception of ethics, which causes him to fall into an incommensurable particularism (and which is incapable of discerning the universality of the spheres of human life as such), nor the "aestheticism" that he ultimately proposes. Aesthetics can have a liberatory quality, but not in the sense set out by Taylor.

245. I have learned and incorporated a great deal from Habermas, especially from his criticism of analytical ethics, as can be seen in the ideas I develop throughout *Ethics of Liberation*.

246. See, among other texts, Habermas 1983, 127 ff.; also Habermas 1991 (49 ff. in the English MIT Press translation); 113 ff. On Kohlberg, see Habermas 1981b and 1987.

247. Habermas 1983, 135.

248. Once again this critical approach to the "ethical judgments of reality" sees Kohlberg's universal moral principles from the perspective of the negation of the concrete production of the life of human subjects when they are victims. Consider the sphere of the alterity of the excluded with respect to the same formal universal moral principles.

249. Quoted in Habermas 1983, 135.

250. Wellmer 1986, 64–65.

251. Ibid., 102–3. "My thesis is that a universalist moral principle cannot be inferred, as Habermas [as well as Apel] intends, from *assumptions of normative content* in the context of argumentation" (ibid., 102).

252. Ibid., 106.

253. Ibid., 108.

254. See §1.5c.

255. Habermas 1983, 66. Also Habermas 1991, 130.

256. Note that from this point onward, a "moral truth" must be formal in character. This is why, in the strictest sense, we can never speak of a "moral" *truth* (but instead of moral "validity," because the matter of the "truth" will always be a matter of material or "ethical" content, at least for the purposes of the terminology employed in this *Ethics*.

257. Habermas 1991, 11.

258. Wellmer 1986, 71–72.

259. This consensus, evidently, would contribute a greater probability to the truth (*veritas*) character of reason, which we could describe as plausibility. It also reinforces a subjective sense of certainty, which is necessary for a non-omniscient social subject. Only an omniscient being could completely forego this complementary moment of truth.

260. Wellmer 1986, 70–71.

261. The truth is given, according to Habermas, in the sphere of descriptive statements, as a claim of providing or being able to provide reasons discursively if the occasion were to demand it because the statement at issue has become conflictive. In this manner, "an argument is the reason that impels us to recognize the claim of validity of the affirmation of a norm or the assessment of a value" (Habermas 1984: "Theories of Truth," 162). Truth and intersubjective validity have much in common, then. This argument would not directly and primarily claim to refer itself to some moment of reality (reality being considered too problematic), unless it is directed to the intersubjective validity claim (which would be equivalent, for Habermas, to the truth).

262. Wellmer 1986, 72.

263. Apel 1991, 48.

264. For my part, I do not speak only of "objective" truth, but also as to something that precedes it and that is more radical, in the sense suggested by Zubiri.

265. Apel 1991, 73.

266. Ibid. In other words, "no specific criterion of truth can serve by itself as a *sufficient* criterion for truth: neither the phenomenological evidence for correspondence, nor the integrability of the theory of coherence, nor the productivity in the practical contexts of life . . . ; and the ontosemantical-formal concept—which can be derived from Wittgenstein's *Tractatus* or from Tarski—regarding the *concordance between true propositions and the facts* (or of states of things that exist) is empty in terms of criteria of criticism, since the concept of *what has been done* or of the *state of things that exist* can only be defined, for its part, by means of recourse to the concept of a *truthful proposition*" (ibid., 73–74). It is something else altogether to study Apel's concept of truth. In any case, for Apel the coincidence between reality, truth, and validity can only be achieved fully in "the indefinite, ideal communication community" *in the long run*—a position criticized by Wellmer (1986, 81–102) and by Hinkelammert (1994, 123 ff.).

267. In chapter 3, we will return to this theme at several different points. At this point I would like to note that the question of "reference" can be found at the very center of a theory of truth. See initially Lafont 1993 and Tugendhat 1982.

268. Wellmer 1986, 203.

269. Always mediated intersubjectively and linguistically.

270. In other words, in truth there is a reference to reality that can be accessed communitarily. Truth has a "sociability" that is not identical to the "acceptance" of validity. Reality can be approached from the perspective of a community, through "enlightenment," not solely by "consensus," and from the perspective of the demands of life, always on the brink of death, as a criterion of that truth.

271. Wellmer himself does not discern the need to transcend formalism, since he agrees with Habermas when he affirms that "it is clear that the meaning of the *rational* cannot be derived by having recourse to *material* criteria of rationality anchored in *one* specific culture" (Wellmer 1986, 76). He does not grasp the possibility of a universal material sphere from which cultures can be developed organically and differentially, as I discussed in §1.5. He appears to be on the verge of opening himself up to this possibility, but in the end he is unable to make the leap due to his formalism, which (contradictorily) attempts to be more than merely consensualist in character: "This is why we can only proceed *negatively*; we cannot to the fullness of meaning, only to the elimination of what is nonsensical" (Wellmer 1986, 220). And what about the elimination of injustice, hunger, and misery? Our vision of an ideal society should also encompass "*material* conditions" and not merely "the *formal* conditions of a rational life" (ibid.).

272. The "community" is the concrete environment within which human subjects live; "intersubjectivity" is abstractly *the mode* in which subjects are constituted as such from the perspective of the subjectivity of others (in their minds, linguistically, historically, in reality). Someone can access reality monologically (or as a community) from the position of their intrinsic subjectivity, which is always a priori of an intersubjective character. The intersubjective constitution of the subject inevitably situates the validity of the consensus at the point of departure of truth; but truth and validity are two distinct and separate spheres precisely because of the difference between their points of departure and destinations. A monologue is not a solipsism; a solipsism is an intersubjective variation of a monologue. Furthermore, a monological design is evidence of the preexistence of an intersubjective consensus: it is impossible to dissent in the absence of a previous agreement that has been broken, otherwise what is at issue is not dissent but rather an original innovation.

273. See Wellmer 1986, 71.

274. We always presuppose constitutively a language or a "world," and so on, which are intersubjective moments (Apel 1994b).

275. Wellmer 1986, 76.

276. The dissent of the discoverer can be understood as an acceptance that what is truthful is that which is not valid *ante festum*, which is intertwined formally with validity and not with truth. Dissent is to validity what a nonverified hypothesis (but one that is intuitively grasped as truthful) is to truth; what has been proven to be invalid (invalid because it has been rejected after being subjected to probative argument) is equivalent to what is false but is not identical to it. To falsify is not to invalidate. I believe that Popper did not take this analytical distinction into account.

277. In the next chapter (§§3.1, 3.2, and 3.5), I will return to the theme of "truth" in the context of a debate with pragmatism and with positivist and analytical philosophy.

278. When I have referred to "culture" (for example, in my discussion of Hegel, MacIntyre, or Taylor), to some extent I have addressed it in the context of the analysis of an "ethical system" (*Sittlichkeit*), but without making explicit the validity of its intersubjective character, which has always been implicit; but now I am making it explicit, as part of my effort to subsume all of the achievements of discourse ethics into the architecture of the ethics of liberation.

279. *Nicomachean Ethics*, bk. 6, 2 (Aristotle 1960, 1139a 22–30).

280. Among other references see Habermas 1983, 62 ff., 70 ff. Wellmer notes that "in theoretical discourse what is fundamental is the validity of the statements and the extent to which they have been *threaded* together" (Wellmer 1986, 168); while in "practical discourse [it is] the *rectitude* of the actions" [that counts] (ibid.). The former has claims to being verifiable (such as mathematics, physics, history, etc.). The question is more complex, as we shall see, because the normative claim of practical *truth* seeks the *validity* of its statements in their *fabric* as well as in their *rectitude*.

281. Habermas 1983, 63.

282. I would say instead "in a *theoretical* sense."

283. Note here how Habermas does not completely reject the possibility that they might be "true or false" but never suggests *how* this could be so.

284. An impossible task if one is wedded to a consensualist doctrine regarding the truth. Furthermore, and as I have suggested above, a formal truth (= a morality) is contradictory; what is actually at issue is an *ethical*-material truth, or simply something that is not a truth at all, but instead a form of validity.

285. Which is what we are adopting here ourselves.

286. Habermas 1983, 66.

287. This claim is *practical* to the extent that one can argue regarding the statement's reference in the norm (because of its content) at the start of the process of the reproduction and development of human life. It is the norm that has *truth* in this context (because of its content) and which is *practical* (because it serves as a form of mediation for human life). In other words, "It is true that *p*" responds to criteria logically and rationally governed by rules with reference to the real (that human life which is made effective in a self-responsible way), and this can be argued rationally because of its content. For example, it can be demonstrated ethically that a neoliberal economy faithful to the tenets of Friedrich von Hayek simply *does not permit life to flourish* among those who cannot compete in the capitalist market. "It is valid that *p*," in contrast, is responsive to intersubjective demands or logical community rules of participation among those affected, in a symmetrical discussion (Wellmer 1986, 55 ff.).

288. This objective physical world is, nonetheless, the ecological "environment" of the life of the human subject, who then has an "ethical sense" with reference to the possibility of the reproduction and development of that human life.

289. This need to "accept" the *passage* from the factual to the normative judgment is grounded in an exercise of practical-material reason, which articulates the relationship between the "life" of the living human being, because of the *ethical* impossibility of suicide, and the unavoidable responsibility of pursuing the reproduction and development of that life: biological-cultural *necessity* is "imposed" upon us as an ethical *obligation*. Once again, because of the intersubjective process described, when the communication community inevitably decides—even in cases of heroic sacrifice of one's life for one's homeland—that the reproduction and development of life must continue, the "passage" from factual judgment to that which ought-to-be is realized as a moral "obligation" to be *fulfilled* in conformity with what has been agreed to as the result of argumentation, as moral subjects who are responsible for the agreements that have been arrived at in the context of community. This is an "obligation" arrived at by consensus.

290. "Rectitude" with respect to the way in which a particular culture gives concrete institutional form to the universal material principle "Thou shalt not kill."

291. See later the level of the "intelligibility claim" in figure 8.

292. For more on this theme, see §3.2 [172 ff.].

293. Wellmer 1986, 108.

294. See Dussel 1994b (2.3: "Originary ethical reason" [*Die ursprüngliche ethische Vernunft*]; 156 ff.). From the perspective of practical reason (given that originary ethical reason is one of its dimensions; level 1 of table 2 and level 3 of table 5) there must be an open attitude toward not ignoring any argument, not only for "theoretical" reasons (level 2 of table 5) but primarily for ethical reasons (level 3), since each argument contributed by a fellow human subject might express the needs or interests of that ethical subject. The recognition of and respect for another ethical subject (an essential ethical moment) is a constitutive moment in the acceptance of the argumentation of another (which is reflected in the way in which level 2 is subsumed into level 4), given the character of human rationality. In chapter 4 we will explore *pre*originary ethical reason that re-cognizes the Other *as another*, from the perspective of the work of Levinas: this is the very origin of *critical* reason, as another kind of material rationality, and will serve as a "bridge" between the "totality" (the civilizational system that reproduces itself) and the "liberatory *development*" that results from the effort of the victim (an Other as *another*) in order to establish the *novum* (new order).

295. The acceptance of the best argument (theoretical reason; level 2 of table 5) in the communicative act (discursive reason; level 4) is not separate from the recognition of the equal dignity of the person who expresses it (the recognition of originary ethical reason; level 3), but instead is morally founded upon them. Wellmer falls into a certain dualism when he writes: "without consideration of the person," because this person is always implicit (level 3 is presupposed in level 4, from where level 2 is subsumed) from the perspective of pragmatic considerations, or we would have fallen once again into an abstract objectivist and rationalist, prepragmatic fallacy. Wellmer is lacking the "bridge" or the exercise of originary ethical reason, and remains stuck at the theoretical level of truth (level 2), which is completely separated from the level of validity (level 4). The whole matter is much more complex than Wellmer acknowledges.

296. Practical-material reason constitutes reality from the perspective of the living human being as an *objective* reality, to the extent it serves as a form of mediation for life (practical *truth*).

297. At the formal level, we are speaking of instrumental or practical-strategic reason (level 4 of table 8 [198], which constitutes the "objects" of nature or of the everyday world of common sense (theoretical, analytical or scientific reason, etc.) from the perspective of *objective* reality as an ontological "totality" *opened up* by practical-material reason.

298. This "reference to persons" is their recognition as equals, but—contrary to Wellmer—not the "consideration of their arguments" but the opposite: the consideration of their arguments to the extent they are the expression of the dignity of a person recognized as an equal. In other words, I cannot discard "their" arguments—even though they might be erroneous in theoretical terms

from my perspective—in "consideration" of an overriding respect for their personhood. This is often referred to as "tolerance," as we shall see, without falling into truth-determining relativisms.

299. For now, this "must" implies a material demand that could appear to be pre-ethical in character, but, if we take into account that the material principle of ethics is universal, it could not be "taken for true" if it is something that puts human life in danger (something that might kill the ethical subject), and here too there would be an *ethical* demand that would be present, not just one in formal logical-analytical terms.

300. Here human life is the criterion of practical and theoretical truth.

301. This is a proper ethical demand, because the other ethical subject is part of the community of life and deserves respect for his or her dignity. This is the principle of autonomy, liberty, and alterity.

302. This kind of material solidarity is indicated at level 1.3 of table 10: it is the "welding together" of the community of life in the context of the community's reproduction of human life, as a moment that serves as a cultural complement to the group's instinct for self-preservation.

303. See level A of table 2.

304. Here, levels 1 and 2 of table 5 are confused.

305. Here, Wellmer is situated directly at level 4 but has failed to consider level 3 (that of recognition) and is also unable to grasp that the discursive moment subsumes the theoretical moment from the perspective of ethical implantation (the recognition of the Other as an argumentative subject), and in the name of such recognition *must* argue, not because of the relationship of the truth to the *content* at issue, but instead because of respect for the Other, and to the extent that there is a desire to obtain the acceptance of the Other.

306. Wellmer 1986, 108.

307. Ibid., 111.

308. This matter as to whether I should argue *at a certain time and at a certain place . . .* and so on depends on considerations of ethical "feasibility" (a question I address in §3.5) but the "circumstances" do not have anything to do with the "duty" to argue in general. I think that Wellmer does not clearly distinguish this aspect.

309. Apel's merit is to have attempted this. For the foundations of Apel's argument, see Apel 1976, 1980b, 1989; and Cortina 1985, 79–177. The performative contradiction of the sceptic is unavoidable. Now I must develop the argument taking into account Wellmer's objection and my proposal of distinguishing between the argumentative moment of the truth of the descriptive statement and the properly practical or moral validity that flows from the recognition of the ethical dignity of the other subject engaged in argumentation, which is always assumed in the anthropological descriptive statement (with reference to the reproduction and development of the human life of the ethical subject as such, and because of this with respect to the right of the subject affected to participate in the argumentation at issue). Normative statements have morally obligatory effects, precisely as Peirce's "logical socialism" expresses it, albeit in a still rudimentary manner. The performative contradiction in the face of veritably pure argumentation is different from that which emerges from the possible negation of the other argumentative subject in practical terms, because in moral terms to deny the possibility of argumentation is to negate the Other as a participant in argumentation. In this context, radical scepticism is

not only a contradictory form of irrationalism in performative terms but also constitutes an antimoral solipsism (which is also unethical). Wellmer denies that such a foundation could be laid for this argument (Wellmer 1986, 102 ff.); Habermas instead believes it is possible under certain conditions (Habermas 1983, 86 ff.).

310. The "criterion of relevance"—nonexistent in discourse ethics—is the criterion of truth: it is more relevant the closer it comes to the peremptory demands of the production, reproduction, and development of the human life of each ethical subject.

311. This community-based argumentation, practical discussion, or deliberation (which is not only solipsistic, as in the case of Estagirita or the neo-Aristotelians, since it subsumes and transcends mere monological *phronesis*, although it could be denominated an intersubjective-communitarian act of *phronesis*) is occupied materially with a statement whose "content" claims to be a *practical truth*. In other words, it must maintain within that ethical "content" a relationship (a) with the criterion regarding the production and development of the life of the human subject in general ("Let it be possible to live"); (b) with the criterion of "rectitude" regarding the current valorative-cultural demands of those affected that are sustainable or rational; and equally, it must be studied in detail in the future; and (c) with regard to the criterion of "rectitude" as to the inclinations or drives that are "adequate" (*Triebe*, which Freud has much to teach us about, in particular regarding the relationship between unconscious drives and the *Über-ich* (superego), which serves to articulate the repression of the libido with contemporary ethical-cultural norms and those that are latent in family history; see more on these issues in §§4.2–4). Aristotle also makes reference to these in the *Nicomachean Ethics*, where he refers to "[practical] truth in agreement with right desire [*te orexei te orthe*]" (Aristotle 1960, 1139a 27–32). Philosophical ethics can therefore provide some *orientations* that might guide practical discussion or deliberation in the context of community, in a manner articulated with those affected, with the leadership of relevant social movements, and with relevant experts (including critical scientists, among them), and so on, at a universal level and at the level of principles. An *ethical*-moral "discursive reason" (which is not purely formal as in discourse ethics) subsumes the ethical "contents," the "formal" procedural aspects, and subsequently confronts issues of practical "feasibility." We will explore the "discursive reason" that is practical, intersubjective, critical, and antihegemonic in chapters 5 and 6.

312. This is not fictitious, as is Rawls's "original situation," nor does it propose to delay the possibility of application of the formal moral principle to a distant future, once symmetry has been achieved.

313. *Kritik der praktischen Vernunft*, A 101 (Kant 1968, vol. 6, 174).

314. The "form" of a real "thing" is opposed to the "material," not to the thing as such. The contemporary debate between formalists (for example, those of the school of discourse ethics) and communitarians (Taylor, MacIntyre, and others) is often described mistakenly as a debate between "the just" and "the good" (for example, see Habermas 1991, 199–218), given that it is nothing else but a debate between differing formal moral demands and certain aspects of material ethics. The question of the "good," as such, has not yet entered into the discussion, since it lacks the necessary assumptions for its clear determination, as we shall see.

315. The difference between grounding and application can be seen in Wellmer 1986, 136 ff.

316. The practical *truth claim*, with the *validity* and *feasible claims*, constitutes the complex *goodness claim*.

Chapter 3. Ethical Feasibility

1. A one-story building requires a different kind of foundation than does a building of six floors. *Ethics of Liberation* must delve more "deeply" (as it becomes alert to nonobserved aspects) into certain moments that are necessary for it to "build upon" in the future. I must undertake extensive explorations of concepts such as "content," the "life of the human subject," and "truth" (in the previous chapter and especially here in chapter 3) because of the concrete demands of the global periphery, and because of the domination endured within it by women, the effects of the ecological destruction of the Earth, and in general because of the massive presence within it, in concentrated form, of the victims, the oppressed, and the excluded of our historical age.

2. This means then that these two, the "good" (*das Gute*) and the "just" (*richtig*), are not opposed to each other on the same level, as I have frequently argued.

3. At the beginning of the twentieth century, U.S. philosophers were discovering themselves to be the ones excluded from a *European* community of philosophical hegemony.

4. See, regarding pragmatism in general, and in particular regarding its most notable exponents: Ayer 1968, Scheffler 1974, West 1989, White 1973. The Gifford lectures laid the basis for James's book *The Varieties of Religious Experience* (1982). As a Latin American philosopher I have the consistent feeling, as I give talks or teach courses in the United States or Europe, that I am "experiencing" something very much akin to what James describes in the following passage: "It is with no small amount of trepidation that I take my place behind this desk, and face this learned audience. To us Americans [substitute Latin Americans, today], the experience of receiving instruction from the living voice, as well as from the books, of European [read: and U.S.] scholars, is very familiar. . . . . It seems the natural thing for us to listen whilst the Europeans [and philosophers from the United States] talk. The contrary habit, of talking whilst the Europeans [and those from the United States] listen, we have not yet acquired, and in him who first makes the adventure it begets a certain sense of apology being due for so presumptuous an act" (ibid., 2).

5. This book also has the intention of participating in the debate, to prove in that very act the existence of a philosophy of liberation (whose spinal column is an ethics), at the beginning of the twenty-first century, as a Latin American philosophy, which progressively has become conscious of being the strain that is currently "excluded" from the European-U.S. community of philosophical hegemony (since, during the past century, those from the United States have become accepted as full participants in the dominant circle).

6. See Jameson 1991.

7. See also the previously cited Almeder 1980, Apel 1991, Deladalle 1987, Fisch 1986, Misak 1991.

8. See, in addition to the overall bibliography, Putnam 1992a, 11 ff.

9. See among others Habermas 1981b, vol. 2, 7 ff.

10. See also West 1989, 69–111.

11. The same thing occurs in Latin America, although years later and with respect to other philosophical movements. See Gracia et al. 1985.

12. "Quine made American pragmatism something respectable in the post-war academic world" (West 1989, 184). Although Quine introduced analytical philosophy to the United States, he did it in a manner seasoned with pragmatist formulations and connected to Emerson.

13. See Bernstein 1971.

14. As we will see later in this book, issues related to the "praxis of liberation" should be situated in the context of this "Thirdness": from the material level of ethics (the first or primary stage) (chapter 1 of this book), through my reflections on the discourse of validity (secondary stage) (chapter 2), which leads to the process regarding the feasibility of the realization of this ethical system (third stage) (chapter 3). From the life world of this ethical system (at the first stage) arrives the antihegemonic intersubjectivity of the Other (chapters 4 and 5), in the form of the oppressed and the excluded who bear the burden of the crisis of the dominant system and who, because of that, enable a practical process of liberation (the third stage) (chapter 6). This is liberation understood as a process of mediation (third stage) in a situation of oppression in the world (primary stage), which is negated from the perspective of the critical and reflexive counterfactual anticipation of utopia as a future end (the secondary level).

15. Peirce 1978, lect. 3, §1.66. Peirce writes: "God the Creator is the point of departure of the universe, its absolutely Primary point. The end of the universe, God fully revealed, is the absolute Second. Each state of the universe at a measurable point of time is the Third" (Peirce 1931–60, vol, 1, 362). The Third is a process, a mediation; from the perspective of the ethics of liberation it is not mere liberty, but "liberation"; not consciousness but "consciousness-raising" (*concientización*).

16. Peirce 1978, lect. 4, sec. 2.104, 149.

17. Peirce 1931–60, vol. 5, 265.

18. When I use the term "American" in this context my intention is to include all Latin Americans as well. In effect, as I have already argued, the distinct characteristic of Latin American thought, since its origins in the fifteenth century (with important variations among its diverse components), is its mediating character, *as a process directed toward the future*. It would also seem as if the people of white North America as a Western extension of Europe—including even those of mixed race or the descendants of Africans who were sold as slaves—by denying the Amerindian peoples have their destiny in the future: they conceive of themselves, too, as part of a future-oriented process. Their lack of history leads them to stake their destiny on what might come. I think that Peirce, with his singular depth, expresses this most starkly. This is also what I associate with my childhood amid the immense semidesert steppes of Argentina in the mountainous regions of Mendoza.

19. In Peircian terminology this *Thirdness* is the mediation of the primary and secondary stages (*Firstness* and *Secondness*), as we have seen.

20. I would like to recall certain of Peirce's formulations. As early as 1868 he wrote: "The radical origin of the conception of reality demonstrates to us that this conception essentially includes the notion of *community* without definite

limits, and capable of an indefinite growth of knowledge . . . with sufficient time in the future [to do so]" [Peirce 1931–60, vol. 5, 311; 1955, 247]). And further: "But this would demand a conception of the identification of the interests of each one with those of the unlimited community" ("On the Doctrine of Chance" [Peirce 1955, 163]).

21. Peirce 1974, 45 ff.

22. Dewey himself (1920, 28 ff.) writes of Bacon as the person who defined the prototype of knowledge.

23. K.-O. Apel writes, in a creative synthesis: "It is precisely this which is assumed in the consensual theory oriented towards Peirce: that all available objective criteria of truth lay the foundation for the intersubjective validity of consensus, with the following consideration added: no specified criterion of truth can serve *by itself* as a *sufficient* criterion of truth: neither the phenomenological evidence of correspondence, nor that of integrability in the context of the theory of coherence, nor that of productivity in the practical contexts of life" (1991, 74–75). What is needed is a theory of mediated truth which is codetermined and not unilateral, and which thereby avoids falling into a reductionist fallacy. I will pick up this thread immediately.

24. The community of science itself demands a scientific ethic of "self-surrender" in favor of truth.

25. "On the Doctrine of Chance" (Peirce 1931–60, vol. 5, 354; 1955, 162).

26. Ibid.

27. See "Evolutionary Love" (Peirce 1955, 361 ff.).

28. Dussel 1970–80, vol. 1, 9: "Morality is not a branch of philosophy, but the primary philosophy itself." This relates to a quotation from Levinas 1968b, 281.

29. When you dig in the ground, at some point you hit hard granite, and it is impossible to dig further; one's shovel bends backward: ("mein Spaten biegt sich zurück") (Wittgenstein 1988, no. 217, 210–11).

30. Already in 1770 Kant expressed that only the Absolute has an intellectual intuition of the *Noumenon* ("die göttliche Anschauung . . . volkommen intellektuell/divinus intuitus . . . Archetypus"; *De mundi sensibilis atque intelligibilis* . . . , sec. 10, A 12 [Kant 1968, vol. 5, 40–43]). Human understanding possesses only a "symbolic knowledge" ("symbolische Erkenntnis/cognition symbolica," ibid., 40–41).

31. *Grundlegung zur Metaphysik der Sitten* [Groundwork of the metaphysic of morals], BA 105 (Kant 1968, vol. 6, 86–87).

32. Apel 1981, 19 ff. His early youth includes the period from his first reading of Kant (1855) until 1871.

33. In Kant, because of the omniscience of the *intellectus Archetypus* (God).

34. Peirce 1931–60, vol. 5, 257. He still writes: "Given that the meaning of a word is the conception that it transmits, what is absolutely unknowable has no meaning because it has no corresponding conception. As a result it is a word without meaning, and thus what can be expressed through any term such as *reality* is knowable to a certain degree, as well as the nature of knowledge, in the objective sense of the term" (ibid., 5.211).

35. I am not saying that Peirce has fallen into an absolute form of idealism, since he writes explicitly: "The essence of the realist's opinion is that it is one thing *to be* and another thing *to be represented*" (ibid., vol. 8, 129). But, as Apel comments: "Reality cannot be defined otherwise than as the correlate to the

consensus of an *unlimited community*. This is the only way in which the real's independence from being thought of can be understood as identical with the principle of cognizability of the real" (1981, 92). And this is confirmed when Peirce writes: "The only reality there could be would be conformity to the ultimate result of inquiry" (1931–60, vol. 5, 211).

36. "The radical origin of the *conception of reality* demonstrates that this conception includes the notion of *community*, without defined limits, and capable of indefinitely improving knowledge. And in this way these two kinds of knowledge—the real and the unreal—consist in the fact that, at some future sufficient time, the community will always want to continue the effort" ("Some Consequences of Four Incapacities" [Peirce 1955, 247]).

37. This is precisely what intersubjective validity consists of.

38. Peirce 1931–60, vol. 5, 407.

39. Ibid., 416.

40. Ibid., 430.

41. Apel 1991, 70. He continues: "That opinion must be, for us, *identical to truth*; which is to say an absolute and intersubjectively valid opinion also has to be—to the extent it embodies a non-demonstrable ontological relationship—an adequate representation *of the real*" (ibid.).

42. "How to Make our Ideas Clear," pt. 2 [Peirce 1955, 31].

43. See Zubiri's three volumes *Sensory Intelligence* (1981), *Intelligence and the Logos* (1982), and *Intelligence and Reason* (1983).

44. A broad term ("real") is used here deliberately, in order to avoid unnecessary distinctions at this point. The real is "actualized" in maps of neurons; this has nothing to do with any "correspondence," "similarity," or "equivalence" (homologous character), since we are not speaking of "representation" in this context. From Zubiri's perspective, activity in the brain (materially considered) and intellectual activity (in formal terms) are not the same things. The cerebral or neurobiological moment cannot then be identified with the subjective act. This means that the unity of the brain must be distinguished from subjectivity considered in philosophical terms.

45. Zubiri 1981, 233. This position might appear trivial or simply that of an ingenuous premodern metaphysics. Nonetheless, we have to approach these matters cautiously. Zubiri does not describe the intersubjective, linguistic, cultural, or ontological mediations of the real as expressed in cerebral "actuality." But he is very far from ignoring them, and it is not difficult to connect these two dimensions. In other words, this "actuality" is always intersubjective, linguistic, and so on. All of this must simply be analyzed explicitly. For example, Apel integrates the "evidence of the phenomenon" in a phenomenological sense (when I say, "The cat is on the carpet," and then turn my head and "see" the cat on the carpet) with the linguistic intersubjective level, without falling into the intentionalism of the "second" Searle (Apel 1991, 47 ff.; and in various places in Apel 1994b). In any case, because of his "consensualist conception of truth" (where truth and validity end up being confused *in the long run*), the "reference" to the real is not clear; there is only a glimmer of the perception of the "evidence of the phenomenon," in an eidetic world, and at the level of a "perceptual judgement referred to the evidence" (Apel 1991, 50). This is far from a clarification of the "reference" toward the "reality" of the real (which is not only perceptive evidence but first of all and most importantly an intellectual or rational act).

46. See in my *Filosofía de la Liberación* (*Philosophy of Liberation*, Dussel 1977) regarding the difference between "world" (understood as a totality of senses) and "cosmos" (*omnitudo realitatis*): 2.2.2–3; the question of the "being" and of "reality": 4.3; the problem of the "substantiveness" of real things: 4.1.2–4. In particular (contrary to secs. 43 and 44 of Heidegger's *Being and Time*), the theme of the "thing, entity, and meaning": 2.3.8, where the relationship between "sense-phenomena" (manifestation) and the "interpretation-of-the-real-thing" (discovery) is treated: 2.3.5. See also Dussel 1970–80, vol. 1.

47. Even in a hypothetical absolutely divine Intellect, or in some asymptotic future *in the long run*, truth is not and can never be the real, because by definition truth and the real are different. Furthermore, the real is cognizable *ad infinitum* but can *never* be completely "known" (as present or past). Reality and truth, by definition, and by means of empirical fulfillment, can never, ever coincide. They refer to two completely different dimensions. Reality is in reference to the *from-itself* of the real; truth instead is the actuality of the real within subjectivity. Here I differ from Peirce.

48. I may seem to be repeating here once again some thesis of ingenuous or trivial realism. But this is not so. Zubiri (anticipating the "deistic function" of the contemporary "referentialist" school [see Donnellan 1966; Kripke 1985; and Putnam 1975]) notes: "This is how each thing is present in its initial apprehension and is thereby the end-term of the *deictical function*, which is a merely nominal indication; it is *this*" (1963, 16). It is a "monstrative" function (from the Greek *deíktikós*; and not "de-monstrative": *apo-diktikós*). Only after Apel's "intensional" (with an "s") moment, or the cognitive and linguistic unfolding (which can be simultaneous) of the thing has been accomplished, do "we no longer have a *deîxis*, since this has been transformed into a true *denomination*, be it proper or specific in character. The *that*, understood in this way does not respond to the question of a deictic *quid*, but instead to that of a denominative *quid*: it is no longer *this*, but Pedro, a man, a dog" (ibid.) or a "baboo" (Apel 1994b, 155). Apel, in that magnificent article "Pragmatic Turn and Transcendental Semiotics," insists that there can be no prelinguistic access to a real thing. In a certain sense, *no*, but from the perspective of the totality of a world that is always linguistic in character we "confront" a real thing even at its most initial moment of being grasped by our senses; nonetheless, in another sense, *yes*, because even before the "initial protocol of identification" (ibid., 151; "This thing over there") the "*thing-there*" is already "a" *thing* that has become actualized in my subjectivity. Zubiri is placing himself at the very earliest stage of "ratification" of the actuality grasped by the brain (this is not psychologism or naturalism, but instead a matter of knowing how to situate subjectivity in a *new* way—though this would be something else to discuss with Apel) of the thing prior to the knowledge of its intensional (with an "s") "contents" and at the very first "*verifiable* intention," which is not solipsistic but which does not either "refer" *formally* (as a *verifiable* intention) to intersubjective validity. It is important to distinguish between a *verifiable* reference (toward the antecedent from-itself of the thing: reality) and the "reference" *to validation* (toward pragmatic intersubjectivity, which for Apel are identical because of his *consensual* theory of truth). It will be necessary to analyze all of this in detail in a subsequent work of ethics, and to enter into the debate with Searle 1983.

49. Zubiri calls it the "*field*." It is the "logos" (in Zubiri's terminology); it is also the second moment of "sensory intelligence," which unfolds an affirmation

or negation from the "field," a judgment: "The affirmation falls formally upon the unity of the *field* and of the individual, a unity of intelligence in the *field* of reality [. . . now that] the actualization of what the thing that has been grasped as real is *in reality*, that is to say, *among* others. Its intellectual action is an *affirmation*" (1982, 260). This judgment opens us up to a second kind of truth: "*dual* truth": "When the actualization is mediated, then the *truly* real which is in the affirmation becomes manifest, not as a pure and simple reality, but as something which is being in this or that reality *among others*. In the 'truthing' of reality in this differential mode resides what the other truth consists of: the dual truth. Truth which has been mediated" (ibid., see discussion from 255 to 392).

50. "Pragmatism's Conception of Truth": James 1943, 133.

51. Zubiri 1983, 222 ff. The concept of the "world" in Zubiri can be glimpsed in this text: "The *world* is not the complete assemblage of all things that are real (this would be the *cosmos* . . .) but is instead the mere character of reality, pure and simple" (ibid., 199). This "world" is not the "world" as understood by Hegel or Heidegger or Wittgenstein, nor as I understand it (Dussel 1977, index of themes). To have some clarity regarding Zubiri's distinctions see the figure for this note:

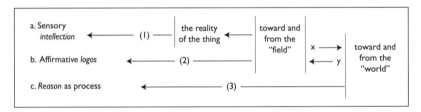

Figure 22. Three levels of intellectual perception of truth.

NOTE: (1) Real truth; (2) apophantic judgment; (3) truth as verification.

52. Among the proofs there is also a specific type when the reference is to a relationship between persons: "There is another kind of experience which consists not in doing the thing that demonstrates its own kind because of our provocation, but which consists instead of the effort to assist, to put it this way, the vision of the real which has been achieved *from its own interiority*" (Zubiri 1983, 249).

53. "Rational intellectual action," which is to say "knowledge," for Zubiri, "is a *searching beyond* the field toward its foundation, which is to say toward what it *could be* once made concrete in a worldly reality" (ibid., 258).

54. Ibid., 258.

55. Ibid., 263–317. Still Zubiri writes: "the sketched [hypothesis] as to the worldly *what*, precisely because it is worldly exceeds the field. This means in principle that the sketched contains more properties than the field does in reality. . . . Only a rational act of intellection that leads to the discovery of verifiable *new properties* has a strict scientific sense . . . . It is clear that neither a line of sufficiency nor a line marking the excess bounds are absolute verifications but instead go *toward a long-term point of verification* [this is the matter of the asymptote 'in the long run' as understood by Peirce and Apel, but subtracting from it Hegel's sense of 'infinite evil']. Each moment along the way does not

have any absolute value in itself except as a *provisional verification* [this is the matter of 'fallibility' as a syndrome akin to critical realism and not to consensualism]. Verification is an ongoing process of *going forth to verify*" (ibid., 270–71).

56. Ibid., 272.

57. Ibid.

58. "Thus I can verify that the vacillating *reason* of light leads to an interference, which is certainly verified in experience. . . . But what is it that it verifies? What is verified is the reality of interferences" (ibid., 272–73).

59. Ibid., 277. In concluding this figure Zubiri writes: "Verification is the *truthing* of the real in an act of inquiring intellection, which is expressed here in sketch form. To verify is to encounter the real, as a fulfillment of what we have sketched as to what the real might be: and in being an encounter in this fulfillment it becomes real [*facere*] in the intellection itself [*verum*]. And this is what *veri-fication* consists of" (ibid., 292). Or even more: "The ability to state a verification can be confirmed in conformity: the *verification is confirmed in the encounter*. Reason not only affirms but is confirmed in the encounter. Reason is not formally reason because it affirms, but instead the affirmation is formally rational because it constitutes the truth of the encounter in a constituent confirmation. The sketch is the affirmation of what *might be*. Rational intellection is the confirmation of what *might be* in and for what is. . . . It is verification as encounter" (ibid., 295–96).

60. Ibid., 297 ff.

61. Ibid., 302. Finally the reference to the passage from the sphere of the *field* to the *worldly* (the x arrow) is implanted as a problem from the perspective of the "worldly" horizon in the sketch: "The actuality of the real field can be found in its process of *becoming* worldly, but as a *pro-blem*. The worldly reality is the problem of the reality contained in this field" (ibid., 307). The root of the word "problem," in Latin, is the word *ballo*, which means to cast out: therefore a pro-blem is that which is cast out before (the "field") from the "world." "A problem is precisely the mode of actualization of the reality of the world" (ibid.). The process of verification on the march is a passage from that which has been affirmed (the field) x and problematized (transformed into a problem), from the perspective of the reality of the world. It is a matter then of resolving the "place" of the affirmed in the reality of the world. And because of this, "the identity of the logical and of the historical consists in the same actuality of reality as a problem. An intellection of the real as a problem is essential and constitutes an inquiring sketch regarding the measure of the real in the world of reality" (ibid., 309).

62. In which are also situated, of course, Mead or preferably Dewey—although always from the perspective of a theory of the truth that gives primacy to scientific-natural reason. See, regarding the political commitment of Dewey, Bernstein 1992, 232 ff. (to demonstrate his differences with Rorty; certainly an ethics of liberation could be closer to that of a "Deweyian pragmatist" than to that of the "aestheticism" of Rorty) or West 1989, 69 ff.

63. "Truth for us is simply a collective name for verification-processes, just as health, wealth, strength, etc. are names for other processes connected with life, and also pursued because it pays to pursue them. Truth *is made*, just as health, wealth and strength are made, in the course of experience" ("Pragmatism's Conception of Truth": James 1975b, 104).

64. For example, when Dewey speaks of Modernity with its "romantic sense of adventure into novelty," in which he includes everything from the Crusades to "the finding and opening up of North and South America" (1920, 38–39), and this latter aspect is perceived as an *"obvious external fact,"* which clearly indicates that he is not critical of "Eurocentrism." The United States then belongs to the same "tradition" of novelties. There is no rupture or consciousness of being something different than Europe. "North" America simply "has been opened up" to Modernity *before* "South America"—although historically the process was exactly the reverse, with the colonization of North America coming *later* than that of the southern portion of the continent—this is essentially my hypothesis set forth in §I.2 of the introduction—America is an object ripe for a romantic "finding and opening," and not the subject of a traumatic conquest or "invasion" that devastated the continent's Amerindian cultures, that included violent commerce in African flesh, and so on. Pragmatism is up to now the new and great philosophy of the "West," situated in the "hegemonic" region of the "center" of the world system at the beginning of the twenty-first century.

65. West 1989, 211 ff.

66. See Galbraith 1993.

67. It is worth highlighting the contribution of George H. Mead's reflections to several themes in this context. On the one hand, because of his mastery of the linguistic unfolding of sociological analysis (see Mead 1934), and in particular because of the concept of the "generalized other" (which enabled Seyla Benhabib to speak of women as a "concrete other"; Benhabib 1992, 9 ff.), from the perspective of a "philosophy of action" (Mead 1938; a matter which is not generally observed upon), from the standpoint of intersubjective communication: "Man is a rational being because he is a social being" (Mead 1934, 379).

68. Ayer 1958, 126, in the chapter "Critique of Ethics and of Theology."

69. Ibid., 130.

70. Still, it would be possible to add a fourth moment: that of "Being," which is the horizon or foundation of the reduced ambit of meaning, sense, or of the "state of the thing [*Tatsache*]," as totality. This is the correlative of the "world" (in the Heideggerian sense).

71. Putnam 1991, 41.

72. Reference is being made to the work of Tarski 1956, or 1977, 150 ff.

73. "Tarski does not consider any semantic notion—for example *to designate, represent, or to have reference to*—to be primitive (even though *to have reference to* is defined, in terms of non-semantic notions, in the course of his work). Thus, whoever accepts the notions of any language which is the object to be treated, and this could be chosen arbitrarily, can only understand *the truthful* as Tarski defined it for his object-language. *That which is truthful* possesses the same legitimacy as another scientific notion of the first order" (Putnam 1991, 10). This would be a perfect definition of linguistic "formalism"; a semantics that is "closed off" from a formal "world" that has been previously defined. In practical philosophy this concedes greater authority to a formalist metaethics. For his part, Apel attempts, from a horizon of intersubjectivity which has been redefined based upon Peirce (and directed *in the long run* to an ideal communication community, which is not only one of abstract, but of ordinary, language) which might attain a "consensus" regarding an "agreement" in which all might coincide; this is a pragmatic semantics that is also opposed to Tarski's

position (Apel 1991, 53–63), although it does exceed the limits of a "consensualist" theory of truth.

74. Tugendhat 1982, 121. In a certain sense, Tarski's example could be translated in the following manner: "The snow is white" has a *meaning* if and only if it "*makes sense*." Now this would no longer be tautological if we were inserted into the sphere of a defined language from the perspective of a specific "world" (of "being") understood as a determined totality of language *S*, as a totality of meaning and of 'states of being' [*Tatsachen*]" (see Wittgenstein, *Tractatus*, 1.1 [1969, 6–7]), which have been previously defined. But we would then not speak any longer of that which is "truthful" as in Tarski's definition, but instead of those things that are "meaningful" within the bounds of a defined language, since in this case "it is not necessary *to know* that there is a correspondence between the words and the extralinguistic entities necessary to understand our language" (Putnam 1991, "Reference and Comprehension," 130).

75. Here I am referring to W. A. Quine's expression in, for example, *Pursuit of Truth*, sec. 33 (1992, 122 ff.): "to preach the truth of a sentence *is the same as to preach the whiteness of snow; this is what correspondence* means in this example. The attribution of truth simply eliminates the commas. Truth must be put between quotation marks" (ibid., 123).

76. Putnam 1991, 17–18.

77. B1 is a "theory" in metalanguage.

78. Putnam 1991, 41.

79. Ibid., 42.

80. The criticism of the reductivist position is frequent in Putnam, for example in *Reason, Truth, and History* (Putnam 1981, 109 ff., 128 ff.); Putnam, 1990a, 13 ff., 103 ff.; and in Putnam 1992b, 164, we can read: "We need a theory of *reference by description* as much as a theory of primitive reference"; more recently, in Putnam 1994, "Truth and Reference," 316: "If there is a problem of conceptually analyzing our intuitive notion of truth, then Tarski's work does not speak to it." Finally, let us recall that "that *which is truthful* and the *reference* for a statement is captured by Tarski's logic, but that the same leaves the concepts of truth and reference *indeterminate*" (Putnam 1991, lect. 4, 61).

81. Putnam 1991, 42.

82. Carnap 1990, 25. In another text he writes: "When (within a determined language) [*A* in the chart] a word possesses a meaning [*Bedeutung*], it is usually said that it designates a *concept*; if this process of *attributing meaning* to it is only apparent and is truly possessed, we can speak then of a pseudo-concept" (Carnap 1965, 67). Hempel is in agreement with this when he writes that the "fundamental principle of modern empiricism is the idea that all nonanalytical knowledge is based on experience. . . . A sentence constitutes a cognitively *significant* affirmation and it can therefore be said that it is true or false only if it is either (1) analytical or contradictory, or else (2) capable, at least in principle, of being confirmed by experience. According to this criterion, the so-called empirical criterion of *cognitive meaning*, or of *cognitive potential for meaning*" (Hempel 1965, 115). Frege had referred to this question in his work regarding "sense and meaning [*Sinn und Bedeutung*]" (Frege 1980).

83. See Horwich 1990 and Martin 1959.

84. Lafont 1993. This question goes far beyond the issue I would like to raise here, but for those interested in the differing positions regarding the matter of "reference" (as *identification* [Frege, Russell, Strawson, Searle], as a *relationship*

of fulfillment [Quine], or as a *direct designation* [Kripke, Donnellan, Putnam]), see also the work of Runggaldier 1985.

85. In figure 8 in this book I seek to depict the "world" (or the horizon of "being") with *A*. I also want to highlight the problem of the "comprehension of being [*Seinsverständis*]." Since the sphere of "meaningfulness" of a language L can equally, and ultimately, be that of the ordinary language "closed in" upon itself, "Being" (as a horizon of the "world") is not the "reality" to which the "reference" is remitted to which I have alluded. Lafont indicates that the current of thought exemplified by Saul Kripke (1985), K. S. Donnellan (1966), and Putnam begins to change the meaning of the question from the perspective of the problem of the "direct reference" to a "reality" that I would like to radicalize.

86. Putnam 1987, 33.

87. Ibid.

88. Ibid., 35–36.

89. Ibid., 40.

90. Ibid., 32.

91. See Barret 1994, 157 ff. As Barret writes: "He also realized that when logicians and philosophers spoke of language they were speaking of *an abstraction*. There is nothing wrong with this. In order to speak of something *you have to make it abstract*. But when we do so we have to be careful not to lose sight of that which we have made abstract. Wittgenstein came to understand that this was exactly what the philosophers of language, himself included, had failed to do!" (159). This will be fundamental for §3.5, when I will explore *formal* factual judgments (and only those with "claims of efficacy" or feasibility, from the perspective of calculation) in the context of questions of feasibility, judgments of the Weberian type regarding means and ends, or those characteristic of applications of instrumental reason, distinct from those "factual judgments" regarding the reproduction and development of the life of the human subject, such as: "This is a poison, which is dangerous to life"—which is not a value judgment but a judgment of reality "with a practical truth claim."

92. Putnam 1987, lect. 1, 8 ff.

93. Ibid., 17.

94. "*Thing*" (*Ding* in German) would be the strict denomination of the real (see my *Philosophy of Liberation*, 2.3.8.1, 3.4.7.3–7.4, 4.1.4.1, etc., in Dussel 1977), as a "natural thing" (and not as a cultural artifact or "thing-with-meaning"). It is not yet an "object," "fact," or "state of things."

95. For Xavier Zubiri the totality of the galactic universe is "one sole *substantiality*" ("The material of nature in the restricted sense of being inanimate": Zubiri 1963, 238). A galaxy, a solar system, the sun or the Earth, a mountain, a river, a stone are mere subsystems or *singuli*. Objects of a language or "conceptual system," to speak in Putnam's terms, but not substantive "things."

96. The galaxies millions of light years away are not "observable" in their internal organization with the naked eye; viruses and atoms cannot be seen directly either. "Observability" based on the organs of the human body determines the possibility (feasibility) of *cerebrally constituting* certain "objects" *at hand*: the sun or stones (physical-natural subsystems), plants and animals in general (each one with its own substantivity), chairs and doors (things-with-meaning or artificial or cultural objects). Furthermore only the "objects" of common sense can be "constructed" *fully* by our brain: it is only from them

that we can sense aromas (because of our sense of smell), noise (because of our auditory system), softness (because of touch) . . . since the "construction" of the macro (a) or micro (c) "objects" is indirect and *incomplete*. Quine's opinion that the "true and ultimate nature of reality" can be detected through the conceptual system of physical science—such as atoms, electrons, and so on—has been invalidated (Putnam 1987, 90, n. 12).

97. Ibid., 77.

98. Ibid.

99. Ibid.

100. This question, posed in this manner, demands that we explore the significance of "world": is this only one more "conceptual scheme," a mere horizon of intelligibility of a given language (A in figure 8 or is it the totality of the reality of the real which we actualize in our brain as that which has *been given*, as a *prius* (but still without meaning!) (B)?

101. Ibid.

102. Ibid.

103. Ibid., 79.

104. This refers to Karl, a "savage" who could not speak.

105. Note that the "how" is not explained, but only the command "to eat": a necessity preexistent to every possible situation involving translation of another culture (be it Eskimo, Bantu, Aztec, or modern postconventional), as I explained in §§1.5 and 2.5 in this book with regard to the possibility of intercultural dialogue that takes its point of departure from "contents" (contrary to Habermas's pretension of only defining the formal logic of dialogue).

106. Putnam 1991, 54.

107. Putnam 1987, 79.

108. Ibid., 77.

109. I also believe this firmly, even more so than is reflected in James or Dewey.

110. Putnam 1987, 70.

111. Not only to eat or drink ("that which pertains to the stomach," said Marx), but to live in *comfort*, to acquire knowledge with rigor, to create artistically, to have mystical experiences ("that which pertains to fantasy"). All of this pertains to *human* necessities, also understood in their most sublime, spiritual, and creative sense.

112. See what I have written above regarding the "field" (one thing among others), as a kind of horizon in the face of judgment.

113. This will be a special part of the chapter of another work regarding these *ethical principles* and their foundations, which will unfold after the conclusion of *Ethics of Liberation*.

114. See my essay "A Conversation with Richard Rorty," in Dussel 1993a, 177 ff. Rorty's works (1979, 1982, and 1989) evidence a progressive and irreducible loss of a possible universalist reference. An ethics of liberation cannot fail to sympathize in the face of a skepticism directed at a reason *that dominates*, but nevertheless cannot accept that incommensurability impedes a North American from rationally analyzing the causes of his responsibility in the context of the contemporary world system. Rorty wants to have a "conversation" regarding the Gulf War; in the name of its victims we must formulate "arguments" instead regarding the responsibility of those guilty for having launched over 100,000 tons of bombs on the people of Iraq.

115. See especially "Truth and Knowledge: A Theory of Coherency," in Davidson 1992, 73–98. "Coherence" is certainly a *necessary* but not *sufficient* moment within a strong theory of the truth.

116. In my *Philosophy of Liberation* (Dussel 1977, 2.3.5.6) I used the same word: "A phenomenon or entity cannot be understood in its real constitution (2.2.7.4) (as a liquid) which can be interpreted through different senses (such as drinking and how to put out a fire). If it is *discovered* [in the sense employed by Lafont] in its formal constitution, the sense identifies a relationship [today we would speak of a *reference*] to reality [level B in figure 8] (which cannot be interpreted as "how to put out the fire" of alcohol, even though it is liquid); if it is constituted in its reference [today we should speak only of a *relationship* in this context] to the world, sense indicates that there is a relationship to the totality of the world" (level A of figure 8).

117. Lafont 1993, 245.

118. Some confuse truth with the validity claim (consensualists), others with the intelligibility claim (analytical formalists).

119. "Formalism," in its multiple dimensions, always, from its first moment, concerns itself with a certain "language L," "world," or "system" or horizon of "objects" that have been methodically rendered abstract from the plenitude of reality of the real so that they can be treated analytically. This first step is valid, and frequently necessary. It becomes invalid, however, and insufficient when it forgets, at the stage of a second moment, the previous abstractive movement, and falls into the claim that the original horizon that has been thereby reduced is "reality itself" (and because of this negates "all metaphysics," ordinary language, "objects" of common sense, or the possibility of "normative statements" based upon material "factual judgments"). The "truth" in this case does not abstractly have "reference" to the life of the human subject (the "reality"), in the final instance, and is confused with the "sense," "meaningfulness," or "coherency" of a reductive horizon; or, in another tradition, with intersubjective validity. One has fallen into the "reductivist fallacy" of the formalism of a "language L." In ethics, this produces various deviations with fatal practical consequences—above all when such "formalist theories" are in the hands of repressive entities or managers of the economy (as in the case of neoliberalism—an economic "formalism" that has fallen into that "reductionist fallacy"). At this level of the formal system, which has become autonomous (all of this unintentionally), it becomes transformed into a machine of terror, producing domination, injustice, and even torture, murder, and death.

120. Luhmann 1984. Regarding Luhmann, see Febraio 1975 and Izuzquiza 1990.

121. Habermas 1985, 444–45.

122. At minimum, see Parsons 1971 and 1978.

123. Giddens 1993, 99.

124. Habermas has dedicated many pages to Parsons (Habermas 1981b, vol. 2, 295–444).

125. Luhmann 1984, 100. See the recent exposition and critique undertaken by Habermas as to Luhmann (Habermas 1982, 369 ff.). With reason, Habermas criticizes the *automaticity* of his approach to the issue of self-regulation (from the perspective of instrumental reason and from that of a developed paradigm of untranscended consciousness), without mediation from the discursive rationality of intersubjective linguistic agreements (as to this point, as I

have suggested, I am completely in agreement with Habermas). Nonetheless, his critique is *necessary* but *insufficient*.

126. See, regarding everything I am in concurrence with in Luhmann's approach to the economy, Luhmann 1988 (which contains other relevant references to his work, whose point of departure is in economic analysis, in Luhmann 1971).

127. Luhmann retreats all the way back to a virtually Proudhonian position, which was aptly criticized long ago by Marx in the *Grundrisse*: "So this is how we have come to a fundamental problem. . . . Is it possible to revolutionize the relations of production by means of a transformation of the instrument of circulation? The falseness of such a fundamental premise is enough to demonstrate an equivalent misunderstanding of the internal connections between relations of production, distribution, and circulation" (Marx 1974, 42). Marx refers (this is the fundamental "reference") money to production, and this to human labor, and ultimately to its subjectivity in human corporeality (Dussel 1985a, 70 ff.).

128. Luhmann forgets about monopoly here: "Monopoly produces competition; competition produces monopoly" (Marx 1956–90, vol. 28, 458; Dussel 1988, 330 ff.).

129. All of this reminds me of the thinking of Friedrich von Hayek and Milton Friedman (Friedman and Friedman 1980, 1 ff.).

130. Remember the debate regarding the concept of "reference" in the foregoing paragraphs; the self-*referential* makes an abstraction of all "reality" *outside* the system. This is precisely and exactly what the reductivist formalism of every material aspect or content consists of.

131. As I have defined in §§1.5 and 2.5.

132. "System und Umwelt" (Luhmann 1984, intro., 22).

133. "Die Systemdifferenzierung" (ibid.).

134. Ibid., 24 ff.

135. Ibid., 25.

136. Ibid., 27.

137. Ibid., 30.

138. See figure 8, horizon A of the "world" or totality or meaningfulness with "sense," and everything expressed there with respect to "reference" to the world (for example, Wittgenstein) or reality (for example, Zubiri).

139. Mario Bunge has written in a similar vein in the prologue to his discussion of ethics in his *Treatise on Basic Philosophy*: "The ultimate goal of theoretical research, be it in philosophy, science, or mathematics, is the construction of systems, i.e., theories . . . because *the world itself is systemic*, because no idea can become fully clear unless it is embedded in some system or other, and because sawdust philosophy is rather boring" (Bunge 1974–89, vol. 8, v–vi). Here there is a confusion between the theory that ought to be "systemic" and "reality," which cannot ever be perfectly systematized. The "world" ("language L" according to Tarski) is systemic. For me the "world" is not "reality." For Luhmann the "reality" of the system is not completely systemic, because it is also the "environment," but he does not distinguish clearly among these.

140. Luhmann 1984, 36 ff.

141. Ibid., 7, 52.

142. Ibid., 98–99.

143. I have addressed this theme in §§3.1 and 3.2.

144. Note the convergence here between "objectivity" and "reality."

145. Luhmann 1984, 109.

146. Ibid., 11, 69–70.

147. Ibid., 244.

148. For an ethics of liberation, as we shall see in §3.5, human acts (which have a neurobiological basis) "unfold" intersubjectively and historically as institutions, as social, economic, and political systems, and so on. If there is an absolute break, the formal level of the systems becomes disconnected from its material content (the reproduction and growth of the life of the ethical subject: reproduction and growth that unfold in "systems," but are not fully contained within their bounds, and which are in the end only mediations, means-ends, values, etc.).

149. Luhmann 1984, 57–58.

150. Ibid., 70 ff.

151. Ibid., 115.

152. Ibid., 166.

153. Ibid., 171–72.

154. See ibid., 286 ff.

155. Chapter 7 (ibid., 372 ff.) is relevant to the effort intended to lay the foundation for the material ethical principle.

156. Ibid., 297.

157. Habermas 1982, 371.

158. Luhmann 1984, 599.

159. At the Free University of Berlin, Hinkelammert was named to the prestigious chair of political economy during the 1970s, but he was not appointed to any position by the Christian Democratic government in Berlin because of his political ties to the Popular Unity regime in Chile.

160. See Hinkelammert 1984.

161. It should be noted that this is already explicitly expressed in Hinkelammert 1970b, 32–33. Speaking there of the notion of "perfect competition" in the context of neoliberalism he wrote: "The result of this model is curious: equilibrium is only obtained if one assumes a complete mobility of all the factors of production and a perfect foresight as to everything that occurs in the whole market" (24). Both of these assumptions posit moments that are *empirically impossible*, as is therefore the supposed equilibrium of the market.

162. See Gómez 1995.

163. See Berger 1973.

164. Friedman 1966a and 1966b; Friedman and Friedman 1980; Hayek 1952, 1975, and 1979. For an ethical reflection from Latin America, see Rebellato 1995.

165. See Kantorovich 1968.

166. The anarchist has a model of impossibility or the formulation of a regulatory idea: "If *all of the members* of a society were ethically perfect, no institutional structure would be necessary." But since this is impossible, one can deduce: Some kind of institutional structure is always necessary in order to *discipline* (in Foucauldian terminology) the correspondent possible nonperfection. Which also leads to discovering the relevance of the ethical "ambiguity" of any institution (to which Levinas, Foucault, and the anarchists are so sensitive).

167. In other words, and applying what Hinkelammert reminds us of insis-

tently, *in the long run* the truth will never be obtained in an ideal "community of communication." To postulate a future convergence (between the reality, which is perfectly well known, the truth, and validity) is to postulate an impossibility. Peirce writes: "There I see nothing in the facts to forbid our having a hope, or calm and cheerful wish, that the community may last beyond any assignable date" ("On the Doctrine of Chances, with Later Reflections": Peirce 1955, 163). Might he not be falling into the "transcendental illusion"? See the critique of Apel in Hinkelammert 1994.

168. As I have already noted, it should be highlighted that, for example, Jürgen Habermas in his work *The Theory of Communicative Action* reflects on the work of sociologists (Weber, Mead, Durkheim, Parsons) but not on that of economists (Smith, Ricardo, Marx, Jevons, Marshall, Keynes, Von Hayek, etc.). Had he engaged some of the economists he would have had to achieve a greater degree of empirical complexity, regarding matters such as the reality of a "community of producers," the material reality of the human body from the perspective of a possible "transcendental fallacy" (in Hinkelammert's terms) such as "This person lives without food." This would involve an "economics" (as a component of an overall philosophical and ethical agenda) and it would have to be constructed materially as a "pragmatics." See Dussel 1993c, 145 ff.: "From Pragmatics to Economics."

169. See Hinkelammert 1990.

170. Hinkelammert 1984, 22.

171. Ibid., 24.

172. See Popper 1973.

173. Hinkelammert 1984, 29.

174. This can be found in chapter 6 of Hinkelammert 1984, 231–42. In chapter 4 I will pick up the thread of his argument, since at this point he transitions into the critical moment of exposition, which I prefer to set aside for now, for structural reasons in terms of the development of my argument.

175. Ibid., 236.

176. "Reality" is the sphere that the living subject confronts, and upon the basis of which he or she can proceed to carry out the "possible" transformations necessary in order to reproduce and develop human life.

177. "The principles of impossibility refer to impossibilities which conflict with human action" (Hinkelammert 1984, 231).

178. "Thus, the universal concept transcends any particular combination of observable cases" (ibid., 233).

179. "Unlimited reality transcends the limited reality of the facts which are observable through experience and the empiricism of the observer" (ibid.).

180. Hinkelammert describes reality itself as a "totality" (I instead reserve this term for the "given" or totalized system, as can be seen in chapter 4); in other words "totality" for Hinkelammert is Zubiri's *omnitudo realitatis*.

181. Hinkelammert 1984, 234. See Dussel 1985a, chap. 14.

182. From my perspective this is also the realm of "exteriority": that which lies beyond the world (the world as "totality" in Levinas's terms, understood as that which is observed from the perspective of the Heideggerian "comprehension of being"); this is the state of nonbeing (from Parmenides or in terms of Marx's understanding of capital) without ceasing to have the concreteness of reality (reality as "totality" from Hinkelammert's perspective, and as *omnitudo realitatis* for Zubiri, as I have suggested).

183. This is Zubiri's realm of verification; the third type of truth.

184. I am inserting here the determination that Hinkelammert introduces at a later stage of his argument.

185. Hinkelammert 1984, 237.

186. This "aspiration" is not postulating the equivalency of reality, truth, and validity *in the long run*, but is offered instead as an indication of an "impossibility."

187. Human life is the criterion of universal truth; technology is simply a *concrete* application of knowledge.

188. Hinkelammert 1984, 237.

189. Ibid.

190. In a convergence with the approach of "American" pragmatism to this question.

191. Examples of statements of *impossibility* include the following examples: (a) It is impossible to manufacture a perpetual motion machine (*perpetuum mobile*); (b) A person with perfect knowledge is impossible; (c) It is impossible for a person to be immortal; (d) It is impossible for a person to live without food; (e) It is impossible for a communication community to be perfect and completely free of violence; (f) It is impossible for a community to have unlimited productivity, and so on. The following statements have *falsifying* elements contained within them (employing Popper's terminology): (a) This is a perpetual motion machine; (b) This person has perpetual knowledge; (c) This person is immortal; (d) This person lives without food; (e) This community lives completely free of violence and its discourse is seamless; (f) This community has unlimited productivity, and so on. Example b is epistemological; while c, d, and f relate to the material aspect of ethics, and e to formal morality.

192. Hinkelammert 1984.

193. The "objects" or macro and micro *empiria*, which I have noted in my discussion of Putnam's work (§3.2), highlight the *technological* possibility of constituting "facts," "objects," and the like.

194. Hinkelammert 1984, 238.

195. In §2.5 I noted that every project regarding the reproduction and development of the life of human subjects is always lived from the perspective of a culture, a definition of "a life worth living," a conception of happiness, and so on, even in the case of "postconventional ethics" (Benhabib 1992, 11).

196. Even science and philosophy fail in the world of the periphery (Africa, Asia, Latin America) because of this kind of material conditioning or *matters of ethical content.*

197. Here I am speaking of conditions that are "ethically" feasible or "operative."

198. Hinkelammert 1984, 239.

199. In this case, again, "feasibility" is the ability to make something operable in terms of its ethical and material effective possibility.

200. This relates to formal technical-economic feasibility as such.

201. Hinkelammert 1984, 240.

202. Ibid.

203. Ibid., 241.

204. As we shall see, liberation in this context will take on characteristics much more precise than had been previously noticed. "Liberation" in this context will be understood as a praxis with critical ethical or transformative feasi-

bility, opposed both to the conservative (who believes that only that which is existent is possible, and negates the possible by confusing it with the impossible) as well as to the utopian (for example, the anarchist who believes that the impossible is possible). Liberation is a praxis that believes that the ethically feasible is possible beyond the horizons of the feasibility of the prevailing system of domination. The possibility of a transformation (of a norm, act, institution, or system, which might range from critical action in the context of daily life to the extraordinary dimensions of a revolution) must be "feasible," but this feasibility presupposes a project (which is neither anarchist, because of its impossibility, nor conservative, because of its antiutopian or antitransformative character; and which thereby opens up a wide range of possibilities, even though a specific utopia could be impossible as a regulatory idea). All of this then presupposes a "critique of utopian reason" as is suggested by Hinkelammert (1984).

205. See chap. 8 in Dussel 1990b.

206. This is what Habermas refers to as Marx's "productivism" (see Habermas 1985, app. to chap. 3: "Excursus Regarding the Aging of the Paradigm of Production"); even Hannah Arendt (1958, chap. 4, 136 ff.) and Seyla Benhabib (Benhabib 1986, who throughout her cited work attributes to Marx the employment of a "paradigm of labor" that is much too narrow from the perspective of the "philosophy of the subject"), fail to adequately identify the type of rationality exercised by Marx.

207. Only under capitalism does this become "I work *in order to* live" (with that end) (Marx 1956–90, vol. 1, 463).

208. Discursive reason, evidently, is *formally* founded on the basis of other kinds of rationality, with respect to the validity of their characteristic maxims. For its part, "originary ethical reason," as a kind of "bridge" between practical-material and discursive reasoning, affirms the freedom and autonomy of participants in ethical processes, and demands the participation of those affected in relevant processes of decision making and argumentation that might have an impact upon their interests, and so on, as I have noted previously.

209. For example in the near future, voting by citizens by computer might make it *possible* for regular plebiscites or consultations of "public opinion" to be conducted frequently and without inordinate costs. A much more *direct* democracy, one impossible in the days of Rousseau, could include millions of participants. *Technology* could thereby institutionalize levels of participation hitherto impossible and make them feasible or *empirically possible*. In a similar way, with computer models that can handle thousands of variables, it will be possible to plan (never perfectly, but to unsuspected limits of possibility that approximate perfection) with a speed (millions of operations in millionths of seconds) and complexity that would have been impossible just a few decades ago. This will make it possible to plan (to the minimum but strategic extent necessary) for the purpose of rationalizing critical economic and political decision-making processes.

210. See Ribeiro 1970.

211. Not in an everyday sense. In the context of limited material means it is necessary to take optimum advantage of the means necessary to carry out a particular end.

212. Weber 1922, part I, ch. 1, paragraph 2.

213. See Kant 1968, vol. 8, 233 ff.

214. Kant 1968, *Kritik der Urteilskraft*, B 21, A 21.

215. I italicize some of the words here for emphasis in order to highlight the "hypothetical" of the formulation "if . . . then."

216. Kant 1968, *Kritik der praktischen Vernunft*, A 122–23.

217. Kant provides the following example in this context: "If each one, seeking their own advantage, . . . considered themselves authorized to shorten their life, a complete tedium regarding its persistence would assault them" (ibid.).

218. Hinkelammert 1984, 238.

219. See Popper's argument (1973).

220. See Hinkelammert 1984, chaps. 4 and 5.

221. It is simply not "empirically" possible for a Bantu in the tropical forest of Africa or for an Eskimo in Alaska to advance the science of astronomy to the same degree as it is possible for a person to do from an observatory in California, simply because of the lack of the telescopes needed to "constitute" astronomic objects.

222. The Concorde was technically possible but surpassed the limit of economic profitability or possibility. It thus became a marker of the limits of economic possibility in the manufacture of airplanes.

223. I should note that when Wellmer (1986) objected to Apel and Habermas that the logical demands of argumentation should be distinguished from the moral demands of intersubjectivity and the how, when, and where of this process (that is to say, the effective circumstances necessary for its fulfillment), he passed inadvertently from the level of moral feasibility to that of ethical feasibility in terms of the "duty to argue here and now" *(hic et nunc)*. Of course the demands of feasibility cannot be deduced from material or formal demands, but these requirements of practical and valid intersubjective truth could once again intervene in the decision-making process regarding feasibility (and what follows it) in order that it might become transformed into "ethical feasibility." But as to the how, when, and where of the argumentation, another ethical principle (that of operability) responds effectively, which is no longer a theoretical principle with a claim of truth nor that of morality with claim of validity. It is a third principle that fixes (permits or obligates with duty) that *which-can-be-done* ethically, with a claim to becoming realized (operable).

224. Horkheimer 1967.

225. Marcuse 1964.

226. The "desirable" is determined within the range between that which is "permitted" and that which "must" be operable. That which is permitted is on the same scale as that which is a function of duty. When Moore distinguishes between the "desired" (because it produces pleasure or happiness) and the "desirable" (because of the intrinsic value of the object), he has confused the ethical desire for that which is permitted (which can be freely undertaken without incurring ethical fault) and that which it is a duty to desire (which cannot be avoided without incurring an ethical fault). That which is a duty but not desired must nonetheless be carried out even though it produces suffering; that which is permitted but not desired does not normally become a concrete reality, since normally no one is impelled to effect something that is neither desired nor required as an obligation.

227. It could be defined in the following way: Nothing that makes the life of the human subject impossible can possibly have a goodness claim.

228. That which is "ethical" here is the practical material and originary ethi-

cal reason, with reference to extradiscursive reality: the reality of the life of the other autonomous human subject in community.

229. I have already addressed the dialectical passage from the laying of the material foundation (from the perspective of the hungry beggar who would die unless we give him or her alms to buy food).

230. What is involved here is the passage from levels c to f of table 7. The order of mere empirical-technological possibility is subsumed in the scarcity of the properly ethical order as such: of judges c–e. This concrete "factual judgment" (statement 2 of figure 10) (if this means-end statement permits the reproduction and development of the life of the human subject in a specific situation), evidently, also requires subsumed statements of means and ends (including those which are scientific, technological, economical, and "common sense" in character); from time immemorial, at least explicitly since Egyptian-Mesopotamian civilization, there were decisions (maxims) which impeded life (see §I.1) and that demanded corrective (critical) judgments that become normative judgments.

231. This is the constitutive deontic moment of the principle.

232. This has to do with the model of impossibility.

233. See in chapter 5 this complex "spiral" of collaboration between the "expert" and the everyday citizen.

234. I have described this as "evaluation," in a universal and not in a particularist way (see §I.1 and thesis 12 in appendix 1).

235. We will explore this further from chapter 4 on, in terms of critical practical material reason and preoriginary (analectical) ethics, which for its part subsumes the practical-material reason I have been discussing here.

236. See the distinction I made prior to this *Ethics* (Dussel 1970–80, vol. 2 [1973], sec. 24, 52 ff.; Dussel 1973, at several points; Dussel 1977, 2.6.2; Dussel 1993a, which picks up the concept of "interpellation," in sec. 2.2.1) between "moral *consciousness*" (which is intrasystemic) and "*ethical* consciousness" (from the perspective of alterity) which now, in this *Ethics*, will be transformed into "*ethical* consciousness" (which was previously "moral" in character, since it has moments that are material, formal, and with regard to feasibility, as we have been discussing) and "*critical* ethical consciousness" (previously solely "ethical" in character), which I will discuss in greater depth beginning in chapter 4.

237. Regarding *phrónesis* at the political level, see Dussel 1973, sec. 66, 109 ff. In any case the monological exercise of *phrónesis*, instead of being negated, is now much better *situated*. Although there might be a valid intersubjective accord, obligation, or mandate, the "*monological* moral consciousness" of individual *phrónesis*, should continue being the ultimate tribunal of personal responsibility. Just as Wellmer noted that validity does not add a new reason or premise to the argument, in the same manner, the intersubjective accord does not nullify the personal responsibility of the monological *phrónesis* (which has nothing to do with neo-Aristotelianism). On the contrary, "due *obedience*" (of the Nazi generals toward Hitler, or of Argentine military officers during the dictatorship supported by the Pentagon during the decade that began in 1976) could be considered a basis for "innocence." Nazism had intersubjective "validity" (just like U.S. National Security Doctrine in Latin America, an ideology with its origin in the CIA and in U.S. military academies); nonetheless these "obedient" generals were justly tried and declared guilty. To judge them guilty is a strong argument in favor of the prevailing character of monological

phronesis, which "refers" back to their culpability: they each should have *disobeyed these orders* and confronted the majoritarian or massified validity of the "reason" of Nazism or of such CIA-backed dictatorships with their monological practical reason (individual *phrónesis*).

238. Wellmer distinguishes validly between the logical rules that obligate him to accept the best argument (the demand of theoretical truth) and the moral obligation of argumentation (the demand of intersubjective validity). In any case, we still have to distinguish "a duty to argue *in general*" and the "duty to argue *here and now*" (*hic et nunc*). In effect Wellmer is correct in that the *hic et nunc* cannot be deduced formally. It is necessary to consider the material level and that of feasibility in order to arrive at the "duty to argue or not, *hic et nunc*." The possibilities of fulfilling the demands of the *concrete* obligations of the context of the debate or the nonexercise of the obligation of arguing in general should pursue the fulfillment of the principle of ethical feasibility (which cannot be immediately deduced from the formal principle): perhaps, the duty to argue in general, because of concrete circumstances (means-ends, whose circumstance should be evaluated by instrumental reason, and should be assumed, as they are applied, through the search for compatibility with the life/death criterion, should be postponed *hic et nunc*, since *hic et nunc* is not appropriate with respect to the life or dignity of the party engaged in argumentation). The fact that it is not appropriate to argue the *hic et nunc* by no means negates the moral obligation embedded in the "duty to argue," since it should be available to be argued *when the possibilities or circumstances are favorable* (the effective ethical feasibility of argumentation). Given a more complex set of categories (including those of a material character), ethical reflection has greater possibilities of clarifying "ethical facts" that are inexplicable and even invisible from the perspective of formalism.

239. See the end of §2.1.

240. *Kritik der praktischen Vernunft*, A 123.

241. Ibid., A 100.

242. "That which is morally good is something which is ultra-sensitive from the perspective of the object, for which, consequently, nothing correspondent can be found in any sensitive intuition, and from this perspective the authority to judge according to the laws of pure practical reason appeared to be subjected to *special difficulties* founded upon the fact that there is a law of freedom that there is the pretension *of applying (angewandt)* to emergent events that occur in the feeling world and which thereby belong to nature" (ibid., A 120–21). For our part, as we have seen, the material principle can be found at the empirical level (of a judgment of a concrete fact: "The semantical content of this factual judgment is compatible—or incompatible—with the reproduction of the life of the ethical subject").

243. Ibid., A 119.

244. With the exception of "respect" (see ibid., A 126 ff.). The question of inclinations, affects, or drives (*Triebe*) will be addressed in §§4.3–4.4.

245. See Weber 1967 and 1982.

246. Weber 1922: "I describe as *materially rational* the degree to which the provision of goods within a group of people . . . that has a social action of economic character mediated or oriented by determined *postulates of value*" (64).

247. Ibid. "I refer to *formal rationality* as a *calculus* of management . . . that is technically possible and which is actually applied" (ibid.).

248. See table 2 (levels 2 and 3), figure 7 (at level a or subsumed at level c), and figure 10 (at the analytical or axiological level).

249. *Goodness, bonté,* and the opposite of *Bosheit* (in German there is no properly abstract sense of *das Gute,* but it could be *die Gute,* among other possibilities of approximation).

250. Aristotle 1960, *Politics,* bk. I.4, 1254a7.

251. Sec. 142 (Hegel 1971, vol. 7, 292).

252. All of this has been explored initially in my *Towards an Ethics of Latin American Liberation* (Dussel 1973, chaps. 1–2).

253. This is why it is not absurd that Hegel included world history at the end of his study regarding "ethicity." This is the quasi-infinite result of *all* human acts, intentional and unintentional, but it is also the product of its *consequences* in the strictest sense.

Part II

1. Adorno 1996, 346.

2. We refer to formulations such as those noted in the introduction to this book: "I caused no hunger. . . . I gave bread to the hungry, water to those who were thirsty, clothes to those who were naked and a vessel to the pilgrim" (*The Egyptian Book of the Dead,* chap. 125); "So that the strong do not oppress the weak, and in order to do justice to the orphan and the widow" (*Hammurabi Code,* epilogue).

3. Lukács 1959, 103 ff., following Engels's traditional position, considered Schelling the father of modern irrationalism because of his monarchist conservatism. I will show that the question is in fact more complex. Even Schopenhauer, Nietzsche himself, and of course Freud must be resituated within the history of rationality, although they themselves (consciously) sought to inaugurate traditions that were irrationalist (in the case of Schopenhauer), nihilist antirational (Nietzsche), or drive-based (Freud). I will attempt to show how a *universal critical-practical reason* moves all of this tradition, which is outlined in chapter 4.

4. I suggested all this in §I.1. We find the same among the indigenous peoples of the Americas (see §I.2).

5. See §I.3, regarding the so-called Indo-Europeans.

6. In philosophy, this unidimensionality of originary ontological thought prevails from Parménides to Hegel, and it was against this that Schelling rebelled.

7. See what I suggest regarding Peirce and Putnam in §§3.1 and 3.2.

8. Or "Being/comprehension-of-Being" in Heidegger.

9. See Dussel 1974b, paragraphs 22 ff., "Beyond Heidegger?," where I describe the positions of Zubiri, Sartre, and Levinas, which divide up "being" (the ontological, the "system" of domination, as totalized totality) of "reality" (as the *prius* "of Being," as the future dialectical totality, as the Other in a positive Exteriority). In the face of the ingenuous meaning of the "self-reality" identity, in neo-Thomism or in dogmatic or precritical philosophies, it is necessary to adopt a negative stance in a "postmetaphysical" era. But the affirmation of a *reality* "beyond" (*jenseits*) *being* (in the ontological Hegelian or Heideggerian sense) is something else. Schelling wrote in his *Exposition on the*

philosophical empiricism (1836) that for Descartes "every other *being* that is not identical with thought [*das mit dem Denken identische*] is doubtful" (Schelling 1927, vol. 5, 279), and for that reason only recognized "the objectual *being* [*vorhandene Sein*] as what was known" (ibid.), thus delegitimizing the "reality or real existence [*Realität oder wirkliche Existenz*]," with which "the existence of the corporeal world" (ibid., 280) is devalued. For Schelling, "being" should not be thought of as identical to "reality."

10. In this sense, all of the ethics reviewed to this point (those of a material, formal, or feasible character) that do not take the critical-ethical step that I will now outline, remain at the threshold of this ethics *as such*. These ethics or moralities are, because of this limitation, *ingenuous, complicit,* or *incomplete.*

11. In Greek there is a whole constellation of words like the verb *kríno* (to separate, distinguish, judge, condemn), and the noun *krísis* (separation, distinction, judgment, accusation, trial against), *kritérion* (tribunal of justice), *krités* (arbiter), that point semantically to what I want to underline here. This entire semantic constellation refers to (a) the *separation* of that which we are seeking to judge from the party who undertakes the judgment; (b) the constitution of someone *as judge* or arbiter who is equitable, distant, indifferent to the parties involved; and (c) the act of judgment in terms of *condemnation* or absolution. We are not speaking here of a theoretical critique (such as Kant's critique of pure reason), but rather of an *ethical* critique: not just philosophical, but, as a final reference, the real-empirical critique of a given norm, act, institution, or ethical system.

12. Which should be distinguished, for example, from the "critical theoretical reason" of a Hans Albert (see Albert 1968).

13. As we will see in Levinas's phenomenological analysis.

14. See Dussel 1973, chaps. 1–2.

15. As I indicated above, here "reality" appears once again. In the first part of this book (chapters 1–3), in the fundamental ethics, reality is that to which the truth "refers." Now, from within a "closed" system, "reality I" negates and conceals itself, and disappears behind the opaqueness of "being" (the foundation of the system negates reality without appearing to do so). Critical-ethical reason now refers to a new moment of "reality II," as a "metaphysical" moment (now with another meaning that is transmetaphysical), if by metaphysical is understood the ingenuous or dogmatic realist attitude (akin to that of the indicated neo-Thomism that Horkheimer found in the United States in the 1940s), such as the already noted fetishistic identification between the "being" of the system and "reality I." This metaphysical attitude must be surpassed, as I have said (see Habermas 1988, although some corrections should be applied). In this sense, critical-ethical reason is postmetaphysical. But a new "meta-physical" (with a hyphen to distinguish it from the prior) moment appears now, which Horkheimer himself defends (Horkheimer 1967), as we will see in §4.2; but as a *negation* of the identification of the "being" of the system and of "reality I," from "reality II."

16. In the sense of Hegel's *Wissenschaft der Logik*; *Der Grund* (Hegel 1971, vol. 6, 96 ff.).

17. Dussel 1974b, chap. 3; and Dussel 1977.

18. *Theodicy*, I, sec. 20 (Leibniz 1946, 121). If there were an Absolute there is no reason why its possible existence would contradict the fact of evil. To the contrary, because "evil" is the totalization of totality (closed system of domina-

tion), this "evil" consists precisely in what Marx defines as fetishism; that is to say, idolatry, the deification of the given system or the human negation of an Absolute (see Dussel 1993b). Leibniz did not possess categories sufficient even to pose the question.

19. Against Plotinus's view (see §I.3 in this *Ethics*).

20. This is the theme of my work (Dussel 1993c). This modern "myth" was not discovered by Horkheimer and Adorno, as we shall see.

21. In this book I present the international problem of an external debt that was irresponsibly "invented" by the United States and the nations of the "center" of the global capitalist system, because of the corruption of puppet governments, and charged to the account of an innocent and poor populace; it has been paid already many times over, and is suicidal in character.

22. Which is precisely Popper's *Open Society*.

23. And first of all in the face of its victims.

24. This "open society" is Popper's closed society.

25. Chapter 4; in Bergson 1969, 283–84. We will see in chapter 6 how some ambits that are "impossible" for the prevailing system (for antiutopians such as Popper), without being unfeasible antiutopias (a notion discarded in chapter 3), are nonetheless "possible" for the (liberatory) critic. The widening of the bases for "feasibility" is properly within Ernest Bloch's principle of hope, which I have subsumed within the framework of the critical instrumental *feasibility*, which is a component part of the principle of liberation (see §6.5).

26. Bergson 1969, 338.

27. Kant 1904–36, *Kants Gesammelte Schriften*, vol. 6, 53.

28. I have established sufficiently that the ethical demand or desire for the reproduction and development of the life of the ethical subject is a universal demand or drive.

29. Kant 1968, *Kritik der praktischen Vernunft*, vol. 6, A 46–47.

30. As we saw in §1.1, "pain" is a moment in the neurocerebral alarm system, stimulated by endorphins. The "materiality" of ethics can never be evaded.

31. We will see in §6.3 that the liberatory "*transformation*" will apply a criterion and principle distinct from that of the mere "reformist" modification of the system. From the latter perspective, the prevailing system is the foundation for actions taken, and the modifications are implemented so that the system can continue to reproduce itself indefinitely. Reformism is thus by nature conservative. Liberatory transformations are of a critical nature, although they might well be materially identical to those of the reformists.

32. Throughout this introduction to part II I will call this point on this level "moment 1," and so on for each moment successively thereafter (see figure 12).

33. From here on I expound the dialectics of negativity-positivity-negativity in new moments, which begin to be enunciated at this first level.

34. As I indicated above, this "consciousness" is not *Bewusstsein* (theoretical consciousness) but *Gewissen* (practical consciousness). For more than thirty years (since Dussel 1973, chap. 2) I have defined "moral consciousness" as practical consciousness (of the Aristotelian, Kantian, or Apelian variety) that "applies" principles that are universal (Kohlberg's Level 6) but always inadvertently those of the prevailing ethical system. I called "ethical consciousness" the ability of knowing how *to hear the voice of the Other* (from Levinas). Now I use "*ethical consciousness*" to apply to the material, formal principles of feasibility of a universal character, which in fact become confused with those of the

prevailing system (as I explore in chapters 1–3); "*critical-ethical consciousness*" has additional moments, 1 through 8, and continues to be relevant in moments 9 and 10. (See figure 12.) This *critical-ethical consciousness* has a temporal process as well, a time understood in terms of monological and intersubjective ethical consciousness, and is what Paulo Freire defines as *concientizaçao* (conscientization).

35. This "discovery" was formulated in the Semitic tradition; see the works of Walter Benjamin or Gershom Scholem, on a "Messianic" eruption. From moment 3 until 6—in terms of the constitution of a critical Messianic community—we are at the moment of Messianism as such. The ethics of liberation, which is strictly rational, does not need to express itself in terms of such metaphors and will simply define that "consciousness" as the critical-ethical consciousness itself.

36. In the first place, it is the cry that emerges as a roar from the pain of the victims, in their work, in their daily torment, or from the midst of their torture.

37. The interpellative act is complex, since it reproduces all of the previous stages: it must endow the victims with consciousness of their negated positivity, and negate the prevailing system that was until that moment affirmed by the victim. With respect to the negativity of the victim, the interpellation is an affirmative act; but it is a negative act with respect to the positivity of the system.

38. Now the interpellation negates the ethical character of the affirmative act of the member of the system (as functional), or affirms the necessity of being negative with respect to the system as a totality. This "interpellation" was in general analyzed as the *first moment* of ethics, both in Levinas and in my work of 1973. It has taken more than thirty years for me to discern clearly the moments that in fact take place before this one, in which the victims are the points of departure for the "interpellations." The ethical weight is now in the hands of the victims and not those of their co-responsible collaborators. From the perspective of the "interpellated," on their part, there are diverse moments that I will explore in due course, because this is a problem of the "interpretation" of the "content" of the interpellative statement or action itself. See my essay "*Interpellation* as a Speech Act" in Dussel 1993a, 33–65.

39. Once the criticism has been undertaken and made public, the ethical system defends itself. From that point on, a new kind of critical task must be undertaken. For example, if Marx undertook the critique of the capitalist system (of Adam Smith), today we must undertake the critique of the critics of Marx (e.g., of Hayek).

40. It is easy to speak of this topic but not so easy to confront the suffering of repression, persecution, torture, and even the death of those who dare undertake such a deconstruction.

41. It is in this moment that the "subversive" or actions that are invisible from the standpoint "of the prevailing system" are made visible, and the system then enters into a *crisis*. The *critique* (as a subjective practical-historical moment lived in community) erupts as a historical *crisis* (which could imply the transformation, through development, of a norm, action, or institution, and which implies a "revolution" if a *complete* ethical system is deconstructed; this would mean the emergence of a new paradigm, the full *destruction* of the *real structure* of the preceding historical moment [of feudalism with respect to the bourgeois revolution, etc.]).

Chapter 4. Ethical Criticism

1. "We Have Now Reentered History," EZLN (Zapatista National Liberation Army) (Chiapas, Mexico) communiqué, *La Jornada* (Mexico), February 22, 1994, 8.

2. It should be clearly understood that the "people" (*pueblo*) referred to in this context have nothing to do with the specter of the *Volk* that justifiably haunts German anti-Nazi consciousness. Here, the context for the term is how it is understood among Mexico's indigenous peoples, in terms of an identity based on a sense of belonging to a shared community. In Nahuatl, the language of the people commonly referred to as "Aztecs" (the term imposed by the Spanish on the Mexica or Nahua civilization), still spoken by millions today, the word "altepetl" was used to designate the "community" to which the indigenous people belonged. They have been oppressed by the conquest carried out in the name of Modernity ever since. In this sense, the concept of "pueblo" thereby acquires a positive critical meaning (Lockhart 1992, chap. 2).

3. Ibid.

4. This is the partial truth articulated by the utilitarians.

5. From a biographical perspective, although I have sought to explain this repeatedly in numerous dialogues over the years, I think that until now I have failed to a great extent, because I was not able to expound on the complexity of the intended theme at the moment when the process of criticism begins, from the perspective of a clear analysis of the multiple phases of earlier stages of the process.

6. See my response to Apel in Dussel 1995b.

7. David Aponte, "Mil quinientos millones *desesperadamente pobres*," *La Jornada*, January 3, 1996, 7.

8. This is the utopia of the prevailing system of domination, for example of the neoliberal economy that postulates a total market of perfect competition, a utopian myth that is inconsistent and theoretically impossible (Hinkelammert 1984).

9. The negation in the first instance is the process of alienation itself (Dussel 1970–80, vol. 3 [1973], sec. 23; vol. 2 [1972], 42 ff.; Dussel 1977, 2.5).

10. Moment 4 of figure 12.

11. This is the transcendentality of a Marx or Levinas, and not that of Kant: a place *beyond ontology* or the system, and not a place *beyond the material* or the content. Moments 1 to 3, which permit the critique to be undertaken, moment 4, which has already been referred to.

12. The "good" (the "goodness claim") thereby becomes equivocal: the "good" of the slave system of the pharaohs becomes a "system of domination" from the perspective of those enslaved. See Walzer 1986: "So pharaonic oppression, deliverance, Sinai, and Canaan are still with us, powerful memories shaping our perceptions of the political world" (149). Walzer acknowledges the debt he owes to Latin American liberation thought by citing our friend Severino Croatto (4). Nevertheless, he did not understand the oppression of the Palestinian people today.

13. See Dussel 1993a.

14. See Dussel 1985a and 1988 (especially chap. 4 regarding "criticism," 285 ff.) and 1990b (chap. 10, 429 ff., regarding "ethics").

15. We saw in §1.4 that the young Hegel undertook a criticism of Kant on the basis of the "positivity" of the Christian religion. In 1801, he initiated his criticism of Fichte; in 1804, that of Schelling (Dussel 1974b, 72 ff.). The Hegel of the phenomenology of the spirit arrives at a new conception, which subsumptively negates the positivity of the initial empirical experience of consciousness in order to elevate himself from being toward the absolute knowledge of *logic*, ultimately without any positive content. This is the end of the phase of his definitive *negativity*.

16. The importance of economics as a science has disappeared from the work of the "second" Habermas (see §2.4 of this book) because of its formalist reductionism. Only sociology (which can easily lose sight of the material as such) serves his ends now.

17. See my book *Method for a Liberation Philosophy* (*Método para una Filosofía de la Liberación*), chaps. 4 ff. (Dussel 1974b, 115 ff.) for further exploration of this theme. Consider the work of Friedrich Schmidt (1971) and the excellent work of Seyla Benhabib (1986), where she studies the problem of criticism in Hegel: as immanent critique (19 ff.), as antifetishistic critique (44 ff.), and particularly regarding the critique of Kant (70 ff.) and its actuality (279 ff.), although not specifically the theme of positivity and negativity.

18. Positivity is understood here as the origin of negativity that I have defined as "analectics" (a dialectics that is initially positive) (Dussel 1970–80, vol. 2 (1973), chap. 6; Dussel 1977, 5.3). Paradoxically, the first Frankfurt school discovered principally Hegel's critical *negativity* (the *negative* dialectic, as I will indicate; see Adorno 1966), but not *positivity* (analectics) and for that reason in the end it succumbed to a tragic messianism (Horkheimer or Adorno) or to a creative imagination without radical alterity (Marcuse). Walter Benjamin himself adopted a messianic antihistorical posture (messianic time erupts into certain unique and powerful ethical moments, which cannot be developed as a history of liberation).

19. Lukács opposed Schelling (Lukács 1959, 103 ff.), as I have already noted, because of his metaphorical ambiguity. In effect, Schelling demonstrated the difference between being and reality from the basis of a reflection at the level of theodicy. In *On the History of Modern Philosophy* he defines the totality of Hegelian thought in the following terms: "God, the Father, before Creation, is a purely logical concept, identical with the pure category of *being*. This God must manifest Himself because His essence includes a necessary process; this revelation or alienation [*Offenbarung oder Entäusserung*] of Himself in the World is God, the Son. But God must subsume [*aufheben*] or retract this alienation upon Himself; this is the negation of His pure logical self; a negation that is accomplished by means of humanity through art, religion, and most consummately in philosophy; this human spirit is equally the Holy Spirit, through which God for the first time acquires consciousness of Himself" (Schelling 1927–54, vol. 5, 198).

20. Schelling 1927–54, vol. 5, 199.

21. Ibid., 128, n. 1.

22. See ibid., 204 ff.

23. Ibid., *Einleitung in die Philosophie der Mythologie*, section I, 1; vol. 5, 753.

24. Schelling, lect. 1 (November 15, 1841), section XII (Schelling 1977, 161).

25. Schelling, lect. 1, section IX (Schelling 1977, 156).

26. Ibid., section XII (Schelling 1977, 172).

27. See this theme in Dussel 1974b, 116–28. In this sense, similarly, "God (the real and the creative) is *beyond* the Absolute Idea" (Schelling 1927–54, vol. 5, 744). See Scholem 1970.

28. Schelling 1927–54, vol. 6, 398.

29. Ibid., 407. Schelling writes that "negative philosophy tells us *about* what beatitude consists of, but does not help us achieve it" (*Einleitung in die Philosophie der Mythologie* section II, lect. 24, ibid., vol. 5, 749, note 4). Doesn't it seem as if we were hearing thesis 11 of Marx's *Theses on Feuerbach* here?

30. Habermaas 1963, chap. 5, 172 ff.

31. Hegel was equally inspired by Poltinus, Proclus, Pseudo-Dionysius, John Scotus Eriugena, Giordano Bruno, the Hindu mystics (he cited the Bhagavad-Gita in his *Logic*, basing himself on the studies of Schlegel) and especially the Islamic mystic Djalal-Ud-Din Rumi, who "places the unity of the soul with the One in particular relief" (Hegel, *Minor Logic*, in the *Enciclopedia*, vol. 3, bk. 3, part C, sec. 573 [Hegel 1971–79, vol. 10, 383–87]). This is the tradition that identifies Being with Thought, the "philosophy of Identity" for Schelling.

32. This doctrine originated in Egypt (where it began in Jewish thought, as in the case of Philo of Alexandria, along with hermetic Christian thought, such as the Corpus Hermeticum of Asclepius, studied in Festugière 1944–53, vol. 1 (1944), and Gnosticism (a position criticized by Ireneus of Lyon; see Dussel 1974a, 111).

33. In the school of Gerona it was taught that "nothingness was not *the* nothingness independent of God, but rather *his* nothingness. The transformation of nothingness into an entity is an occurrence that is consummated in God Himself; it is, as Azriel taught, the act by which divine Wisdom is manifested" (Scholem 1962, French trans., 448). The Infinite (*én Sof*: without limits), which is hidden and beyond all expression, produces everything in itself, and emerging from rest passes onward to realize itself ("Self-revelation is the great mystery of theosophy"; Scholem 1967, French trans., 233). The medieval book by an anonymous writer of Castille (Spain), the *Zohar*, states that in "the name (*Ashem*)" God has a left hand that judges and a right hand that forgives. It should not be forgotten that for the Egyptians the *name* of a god, of a pharaoh, or of a person is their ultimate essence: in the pyramids "the name" is surrounded by a sacred circle, because it not only names but *is* personal identity itself; someone who loses his or her name simply disappears, from the Egyptian perspective. In the same sense the Absolute creates itself from eternity toward Wisdom (*Bina*, a variant of the Egyptian Ptah), and this, among the attributes of God (the *Sefira*), is the basis of Creation. Isaac Luria, a Kabbalistic mystic (whose tomb I visited in Safed [Sfat] in Israel in 1960) believed that God *contracted in upon himself*, thereby producing the nothingness within which the universe was created (and didn't Isaac Newton believe that "empty space" was a *sensorium Dei*?). Schelling said that "in Him (in God) is the proto-force that *contracts*. . . . If in God there is love, there is also wrath, and this wrath or self-force in God is what gives love support, basis, and existence" (Schelling 1927–54, vol. 4, 331). See also "Tradition and New Creation in the Rite of the Kabbalists," in Scholem 1991, 130 ff.

34. Schelling 1927–54, vol. 4, 29.

35. See Dussel 1974b, 128 ff.

36. Already in 1827 the young Feuerbach had written of Hegel: "We certainly see in the Logic simple determinations like being, nothingness, some-

thing, other, the finite, infinity, essence, phenomenon . . . but these are in themselves abstract, unilateral, *negative* determinations" (*Zweifel* [Feuerbach 1959–60, vol. 2, 363]).

37. Feuerbach 1967, 35. In sec. 49 of his *Provisional Theses for the Reform of Philosophy* (1842), Feuerbach reflects about his two teachers: "Hegel represents the masculine principle of autonomy, of self-activity, in so many words, the idealist principle. Schelling, the feminine principle of receptivity, passivity— Schelling first admitted Fichte, then Plato and Spinoza, and finally J. Böhme— in short, *the materialist principle*" (ibid.).

38. Feuerbach 1967, 245.

39. Ibid., sec. 24, 282.

40. Ibid., sec. 32, 296.

41. Ibid., sec. 61, 318.

42. Ibid.

43. Dussel 1974b, 149 ff.; Wahl 1938; Fahrenbach 1968 and 1970.

44. Kierkegaard 1949, 71. This work of intuitive, not conceptual genius (the *Post-Scriptum*), which I had the pleasure of obtaining in Danish (*Aufsluttende uvidenskabelig Efterskrift*) during a visit to Copenhagen in 1975, merits separate treatment because of its extraordinary contemporary relevance; Adorno did not dedicate himself to it in vain. Since the work reflects a *critical* kind of thought, it must continuously counterpoint the *negative* and the *positive*. (See, for example, what is said about Lessing, sec. 2, 53, in the French translation.)

45. Ibid., 82.

46. Kierkegaard 1968, 60. All his work on aesthetics and ethics (Kierkegaard 1959) addresses this theme. The aesthetic is "enjoyment," the ethical is the "choice" of marriage, of work, of finiteness, the discipline of particularity in "universality" (ibid., 226 ff.).

47. Kierkegaard 1968, 87.

48. In the *Post-Scriptum* he writes "*Der Pathetiske,*" which is an "existential *pathos* [*den existentielle Pathos*]" (Kierkegaard 1949; Danish ed., 377, French trans., 261 ff.), which at a secondary level is "suffering [*Lidelse*]" (Danish ed., 421 ff.; French trans., 291 ff.).

49. Wahl 1938, 87–88.

50. "Et stakkels existerende enkelt Menneske" (Kierkegaard 1949: Danish ed., 175, French trans., 125). This would be, clearly, Levinas's position, following in the footsteps of the school of Gabriel Marcel or Jean Wahl and other Kierkegaardians or French existentialists. *De l'existence à l'éxistant* would be impossible without Kierkegaard.

51. "Det absolute Paradox, det Absurde, det Uforstaaelige . . . at fastholde dialektisk Uforstaelighedens *Distinktion*" (Danish ed. 555). "*Distinktion*" is not "*Differenz.*"

52. Kierkegaard 1949 (French trans., 380).

53. Ibid., 221.

54. "In existence it is necessary to begin with learning the relationship with absolute *télos* and by *denying* oneself all immediacy. . . . The immediacy of happiness has no contradictions; the immediate man is essentially happy" (ibid., 291–92). Unhappiness (pain), negativity is the immediate point of departure of the critique.

55. See the articles compiled in the "Anti-Schelling" of Engels (Marx 1956– 90, vol. 2, bk. 1, 161–221).

56. Ibid., 232.

57. Matter with an "a" in German: *content*.

58. Against Althusserianism, Engels writes strictly: "in letzter *Instanz* bestimmende Moment."

59. That is to say, of ethics in terms of its ultimate consequences, as world history.

60. Consider the coincidence with the *Egyptian Book of the Dead* and with similar texts of later Semitic thought (see §§I.1 and I.3 of this *Ethics*). To give food to the hungry, clothe the naked, and to give shelter to the homeless would appear to be a material-ethical demand that traverses a long tradition: from Egypt prior to the "Axis Age" of Jaspers until Engels, Marx, and the *Ethics of Liberation*.

61. Marx, *Der Ursprung der Familie*, 1884 prologue; in Marx 1956–90, vol. 21, 27.

62. This interpretation of the work of Marx culminates with *Capital*, and my three-volume commentary ends with a paragraph that asserts that "Das Capital is a book of ethics" (Dussel 1990b, 429 ff.). Now the true sense of this apparently inexact or exaggerated expression may be better understood. *Kritik*, as understood by Marx, is the exercise of *critical-ethical reason*: it is the epitome of the critical-ethical act (in its theoretical, abstract, and scientific moment). Its epistemological-economic precision provides critical *ethics* with a level of *quantitative* argumentability that is impossible for other social sciences. In a certain sense, the "rate of surplus value" (a quantifiable category) is a "rate of exploitation" (an ethical-qualitative category), as Marx liked to reiterate; the "rate of profit" is purely economic. But behind these categories there is an ethical and critical "position" that has often gone unperceived both by Marxists and anti-Marxists. We are situated here at moment 7 of figure 12: the "explanation" of the "causes" of the negation of the victims (see §5.3 [302] and §5.5c [332]).

63. It should be recalled that Osiris is represented in Egyptian hieroglyphic writing by an "eye": an eye that is secretly always in judgment.

64. "On Freedom of the Press," May 5, 1842; in Marx 1956–90, vol. 1, 60.

65. Marx opposed the idea of religion as the basis of the state (of the Christian state), just as Kierkegaard did in Denmark (Dussel 1993b, 36 ff.: "Critique of Christianity"). Marx writes in *The Jewish Question*: "The State that causes the Gospel to be preached in the letter of politics, in a letter other than that of the Holy Spirit, commits sacrilege, if not *in the eyes of men*, at least *in the eyes* of its own religion. . . . This State falls into a painful *irreducible* contradiction on the plane of religious consciousness. . . . This is why *criticism* [*Kritik*] is well within its rights when it obligates the State to invoke the Bible in order to recognize how twisted its consciousness is" (in Marx 1956–90, vol. 1, 359–360).

66. Marx 1956–90, vol. 1, 344.

67. Marx demonstrates all of his critical acuity when he writes: "In these customs of the poor [such as taking timber that has fallen from trees for firewood] therefore lies the palpitation of an instinctive legal sensibility, its legitimate and *positive* root and the form of customary law which here is all the more appropriate for its natural circumstances when the very existence of the poor (e.g. the victims) has up until now itself merely been a custom of bourgeois society, which still has not found an adequate place for itself within the circle of the State's overt organizational structure" ("Debates Regarding the Law Forbidding the Theft of Firewood" in "The Debates of the IVth Renan

Diet," in ibid., 257). That is to say the mere existence of the victims (moment 1 of figure 12) does not mean that they have a "place" in the dominant society (the society in which they have a place would be that of system 2 in figure 12). We are already at the material and economic level. Marx, furthermore, is aware that the victims cannot be merely mediations. The only thing that has "absolute value [*absolute Wert*]" (ibid.) for the members of the Diet is the firewood or the hares (that the peasants should not take). And Marx, unknowingly referring to a text by Bartolomé de las Casas, writes with ethical-critical clarity, demonstrating the "inversion [*Kehre*]": "Cuba's indigenous peoples understood that gold was a *fetish* for the Spaniards. They celebrated a feast in its honor . . . and then flung it into the sea. If they had assisted these sessions of the Diet in Renan, these savages would have understood that firewood was the *fetish* of the people of Renan. But in other sessions of the Diet they would also have learned that fetishism carries with it an animal cult, and they would have flung the hares into the sea to save *men*" (ibid., 147). For this *Ethics*, it is worth highlighting that Marx explicitly analyzed the phenomenon of "inversion": persons (ends) are taken as things, and things (firewood, hares, means) as ends. His is a critical-ethical judgment of norms, laws, actions, institutions, of a system of ethics (capitalism), where a critical-ethical criterion and principle are defined *explicitly*. This involves the deployment of mediations that are the *negation* in the first instance of human "personhood"; that is to say, the point of departure is the Kantian principle applied in a transsystemic and economic-material matter (moments 3 and 4 of figure 12).

68. See "Sobre la juventud de Marx (1835–1844)" in Dussel 1983b, 159–83. There are other essays in this work regarding the change in Marx's epistemological orientation (from a *politico*-philosophical [formal] critique to an *economico*-philosophical [material] critique at the end of 1843) (ibid., 36–53).

69. This is where Marx receives the "interpellation" of the victims themselves directed to a petty bourgeois intellectual radical, who is then transformed into what Gramsci would describe as an "organic intellectual" (moment 6 of figure 12). This intellectual's co[l]laboration would consist of a return to the origin and analysis from the moment of the "negation in the first instance" (moment 1), and the assumption of his or her co-responsibility with the negativity of the victims (moment 3), as well as the issuance of an ethical judgment against the system that causes such victims (moment 4), and then the initiation of the task assigned: *the theoretical-scientific and philosophical analysis of the system* from an ethical perspective, to the extent the system was the foundation of such oppression (moment 7); finally, in terms of the formulation of alternatives, which for Marx was the whole question of "socialism" (moment 8), his co[l]laboration includes the organization and practical activity of an emergent historical "subject" (the Communist Workers' Party of 1847 or that of the First International, later in London) (moments 9 and 10).

70. The "negation in the first instance," moment 1 of figure 12.

71. The praxis of liberation as such, moment 10.

72. See moments 1 and 3.

73. Marx 1956–90, vol. 1, 389–91.

74. The principle of "no private property."

75. It is through the praxis of liberation (moment 10) that system 2 is "born" (in terms of the figure 12).

76. Here Marx is situating himself precisely at moment 7 of figure 12: analy-

sis of the causes of the negation of the victim, where the victim and the co-responsible co-llaborators are articulated (experts, theoreticians, philosophers, etc.).

77. "Philosophers have done nothing but interpret the world in diverse ways, but the point is to *transform* [*verändern*] it" (in Marx 1956–90, vol. 3, 535).

78. "Contemplative materialism does not go any further . . . than to contemplate distinct individuals within bourgeois society" (ibid., thesis 9, 535). This would be the perspective of a scholar "within" "system 1" (figure 12), from within its horizon. But he or she who assumes as his or her own the "place" of the victims adopts a critical-ethical position (which is both practical and transformative, because it will tend to negate the negation of the victims *in reality*), and the theory articulates itself *within* a process of praxis—although it retains its specificities in terms of theory, science, and so on.

79. "*revolutionären, der praktisch-kritischen* Tätigkeit" (ibid., thesis 1, 533).

80. Moment 7, that is, the theoretical moment that articulates itself with an integral practical process seeking the liberation of the victims; from the moment that these become conscious of their state of oppression (moment 3), until through praxis reality is "transformed" (or liberated) (moment 10), creating a new system where it will be possible for them to live and participate freely. This is theoretical activity that is overdetermined from a practical ethical moment. It is the exercise of critical-ethical reason: to the extent that it is "ethics," it is practice.

81. "The problem of whether *objective truth* can be attributed to human thought is not a theoretical but a *practical* problem. It is by means of practice that man can demonstrate *truth*, that is, *reality*" (ibid., thesis 2).

82. This would be the philosophy that reflects on the themes treated in chapters 1–3 of this *Ethics*, that is to say at the level of the prevailing system of ethics.

83. See Engels's article in Marx 1956–90, vol. 1, 499 ff.

84. From the Greek *deiktikós*, not the "de-monstrative" *apo-diktikó*.

85. Passive in the German text. Marx used the word *Leiden*, which can be translated as "suffering" or "affliction," on two occasions (Marx 1956–90, vol. 1, bk. 1, 578), and it is the source from which Marx derives "the impassioned being [*leidenschaftliches Wesen*]," but also his conception of "passion [*Leidenschaft*]" as the "essential force of man that tends [*strebende*] energetically towards its objective" (ibid.). That is to say, Marx demonstrated in the *Manuscripts* the importance of "vulnerability" as an afflicted passivity and as a wounded necessity of real, physical corporeality, and thus as a *material* (*material* with an "a") moment of ethics, distinct from that of the *formal* aspects of morality. This is in turn the terrain of the "drives" (see §2.1).

86. Marx, *1844 Manuscripts*, vol. 3, 10 (Marx 1956–90, vol. 1, bk. 1, 545).

87. Ibid., 511. Marx adds: "It is evident that the more the worker immerses himself in his work, the more powerful is the strange, objective world that he creates in front of himself, and that *much poorer* that he becomes" (512).

88. Marx will speak of this "absolute poverty" in the *Grundrisse*, years later (Dussel 1985a, 139 ff.).

89. Marx 1956–90, vol. 1, bk. 1, 540.

90. Consider here how the "content" of the "life" of the worker, which should be under that worker's own free and autonomous responsibility, is now

determined in a manner "foreign" to him or her. The "content" is "negative." In order to "negate the negation" of the "content," this "content" would have to be first "affirmed" as the autonomous life of an alienated subject.

91. These "eyes" are the framework of critical ethical reason, as we shall see.

92. *1844 Manuscripts*, vol. 2; Marx 1956–90, vol. 1, 523–24.

93. The critique of the system (moment 4 of figure 12) becomes transformed into the expert's task of co-responsible co[l]laboration (moment 7).

94. See Wellmer 1986, 17 ff., on the prohibition of nongeneralizable norms. The negation of human life is the least generalizable thing that could be imagined. It is the nongeneralizable par excellence, and the basis of the prohibition You shall not kill.

95. Here we already have an entire position regarding the notion of "reality," the moment confronted by a type of rationality that I will call "pre-originary ethical reason" (following Emmanuel Levinas in this case).

96. The post-1857 Marx will say: of Capital.

97. Marx 1956–90, vol. 1, bk. 1, 512.

98. Ibid.

99. Note the metaphor: capital is "dead." Death itself is the objectification of human life: and "value," coagulated blood. "Blood" was "life" for the Egyptians and Semitic peoples of the Middle East. The "circulation of value" in capital is for Marx "the circulation of blood [*Blutzirkulation*]" (Dussel 1993b).

100. This "suffering [*leiden*]" is a point of great interest, and is the "*pain*" that the Utilitarians want to articulate with "*wrong*," but do not know how to.

101. Marx 1956–90, vol. 1, bk. 1, 472–73.

102. Ibid., 522. See Dussel 1993b, 213 ff.: "The Sacrificial Logic of Capital."

103. Note with caution that life for Marx is not an "end" in the sense of Weberian instrumental reason. It is an absolute condition, the horizon of possibility that "places" the ends within a framework.

104. "Auszüge aus Mills *Éléments d'economie politique*" (1843 or 1844), in Marx 1956–90, vol. 1, bk. 1, 463. Work would be life, as the actuality of life itself, in the case that life didn't function as an "end" but as an absolute condition: work, human action as the actuality of ethical human life.

105. *Materielle* with an "e": physical matter.

106. *Manuscripts of 1844* (Marx 1956–90, vol. 1, bk. 1), 537.

107. Regarding levels of abstraction see Dussel 1990b, 408 ff.; Ollmann 1993, 53 ff. ("V. Level of Generality"); and Rosdolsky 1968.

108. When I initiated my dialogue with Karl-Otto Apel in November 1989, I immediately understood that the formalism of discursive reason (discourse ethics) had to be assessed from the standpoint of the materiality of economic reason. Now I can suggest reasons that were then only intuitions.

109. See my paper "The Four Drafts in the Writing Process of *Capital* (1857–1880)," *First International Conference of Social Critical Reviews*, Eszmélet Foundation (Budapest), 1 [1991]: 165–82. See also Jahn 1983; Miller 1978; Wygotski 1978.

110. In terms of Hegelian categories, Marx shows that what he describes "positively" is a self-reflexive negativity, since it can operationalize anything truly positive.

111. *Grundrisse der Kritik der politische Oekonomie*, Notebook 2 (203; Marx 1974, vol. 1, 235). As we shall see, Marx carries out the inversion of the Hegelian

"theoretical nucleus" with Schelling in mind. It is strange that Habermas does not draw the conclusions that would be expected when he indicates that Schelling "proposes a *theology* while the other [Marx] analyzes the phenomena *economically*" (Habermas 1963, 215). See Dussel 1990b, 320 ff., where I explore Habermas's ambiguous position, which is especially noteworthy given that he is someone who knows Schelling's work very well. For my part, for more than twenty-five years I have sought to show how Schelling was at the root of certain key positions adopted by Marx (see Dussel 1974a, 116 ff.; and Dussel 1990b, 334–61).

112. *Grundrisse*, Notebook 2 (203; Marx 1974, vol. 1, 235).

113. Ibid., 183.

114. Chaps. 1 and 2 of *Kapital* of 1867 are later additions.

115. *Capital* (1873), sec. 2, chaps. 4, 3 (Marx 1987, 183). This "source [*Quelle*]" which is the source of the "creation [*Schöpfung*]" of value, is the theme derived from Schelling that I have referred to. What is really going on here is the transformation of creationist theology into creationist economics (something Habermas does not appear to have a clue about). It is worth repeating here for the purposes of emphasis: value is the foundation [*Grund*] or the being [*Sein*] of capital (in terms of Hegelian ontological terminology). But it so happens that the effect (the *thing*, the value) of its "creative source" (a *Quelle* found beyond and before the created foundation) is "living labor," which is violently subsumed from the *foundation* (the valorization of value, and creation of labor itself) as its mediation (fetishistic inversion). See Dussel 1990b, 357, n. 64. For example: "The *creation* [*Schöpfung*] of value is not represented as the *source* [*Quelle*] of surplus value" (*Grundrisse* [Marx 1974, 451]). Or: "The worker . . . has the possibility of beginning this act all over again, since its *constitution as a corporeality* is the *source* [*Quelle*] from which its use value always emerges again" (ibid., 194). This is the process of creating Capital, *ex nihilo, aus Nichts*.

116. See previous note.

117. *Grundrisse*, Notebook 2 (Marx 1974, 203).

118. See Dussel 1985a, 137 ff., where I undertake a precise commentary of all these texts.

119. *Grundrisse*, Notebook 2 (Marx 1974, 203). It would seem as if we were reading Kierkegaard: "from the individual himself [*des Individuums selbst*]."

120. A metaphor employed by Marx, by the *Egyptian Book of the Dead*, or later by Levinas. The reference is to the immediately naked corporeality of the skin: "The one, significantly, smiles arrogantly and advances impetuously; the other does so with hesitation, reluctantly, like the one that has taken *his own skin to the marketplace* and can expect nothing else but: that it will be tanned" (*Capital*, vol. 1, chap. 4 [1973]; Marx 1975, 191–92).

121. "The abstract existence of man . . . can precipitate itself daily from its plenary *nothingness* [*Nichts*] into *absolute nothingness* [*absolute Nichts*]," *1844 Manuscripts*, vol. 2 (Marx 1956–90, vol. 1, bk. 1, 524–25). The first "nothingness" (the plenary type) is that of the worker in his or her previous exteriority, in poverty, hunger, the danger of death if he or she is not "bought." The second "nothingness" (the absolute) is the effect of the "subsumption" of capital (active negation: alienation as such).

122. To the extent that it is a creative source of wealth.

123. Marx 1956–90, vol. 1, bk. 1, 524–25. To the extent that he or she is a

person in poverty in need of a wage. And it at this point, as a *living* being, that this person runs the risk of death. The impossibility of living refers back to the fundamental ethical-material principle (examined in §1.5).

124. See this theme in *Grundrisse*, Notebook 2 (Marx 1974, 151 ff.) and in Dussel 1985a, 109 ff. Marx returns to this theme in the definitive version of *Capital*: "What prevailed here was liberty, equality, property, and Bentham" (*Kapital*, vol. 1, chap. 4 [Marx 1987, 191]).

125. The critique of ideology is secondary; first we have to criticize its origin: the alienation in the real existent structures, of an economic character in this case (the second Frankfurt school confuses the criticism of ideology with the criticism of material structures).

126. *Manuscript of 1861–1863*, Notebook 1 (Marx 1976–82, pt. 1, 86).

127. Marx's ethical position is historically determined as a *Hegelianism that returns to Kant from Schelling* because of the demands of the practical and political commitment of his philosophy with the victims: the proletariat of the capitalist system as such. His is an *ethical philosophy with relevant scientific and economic categories* that are precise and unequivocal, and which enable the passage from a mere "interpretation" to the real, practical, and historical "transformation" of a given society, such as in the case of the ethics of liberation (the propedeutical moment of a philosophy of liberation).

128. Here we reach moment 4 of figure 13.

129. *Manuscript of 1861–1863*, Notebook 1, 83.

130. See, for example, in the *Manuscript of 1861–1863*, Notebook 4 (Marx 1976–82, pt. 4) (see Dussel 1988, 93 ff.).

131. Ibid.

132. This is definitively discovered in January 1863 (Dussel 1988, 270 ff.).

133. *Manuscript of 1861–1863*, Notebook 21 (Marx 1976–82, pt. 6, 142). Also Marx highlights here already the whole theme of the "exclusion" of the worker from the process of production, replaced in part by the machine, inaugurating the image of the *pauper post festum*: the unemployed.

134. Paradoxically, Marx, starting from a reflection centered on the machinery or material means of production, arrives at conclusions of a strictly ethical character.

135. See my essays "Living Labor and the Philosophy of Liberation" (in Dussel 1994c, 205–19) and "*Exteriority* in Marx" (in Dussel 1988, 365–72).

136. Recall what was said in §1.5.

137. See *Grundrisse*, Notebook 3, folios 21 through 40 of the original manuscript (Marx 1974, 227 ff.).

138. Regarding the page added to the second edition of the *Capital* of 1873, see Dussel 1990b, 188–93. The page is in Marx 1987, vol. 2, sec. 6, 3–4, and was later incorporated into the text of *Capital* itself, vol. 1, chap. 1, sec. 1, 1 (Marx 1987, 71–72).

139. When Marx wrote "values" as such, Engels added "commodity-values [*Warenwerte*]" (Marx 1956–90, vol. 23, 53, in the first, third, and fourth drafts of *Capital*). This means that Engels himself did not realize that what was at issue was a new discovery by Marx, which means that we have to clearly distinguish between "value" (as the hidden and essential "foundation") and "exchange value" (as the circumstantial "form of the appearance [*Ercheinungsform*] of value"): "Further investigation will lead us again toward exchange value as

a necessary *mode of expression* [*Ausdrucksweise*] or *form of appearance* [*Erschein-ungsform*] *of* value, which nonetheless we must consider *independently of that form*" (Marx 1987, vol. 2, sec. 6, 72). "Value" as such, in itself (*Wert*) is not "commodity value [*Warenwert*]": "value" is its "foundation" or basis in produc-tion, whereas "commodity value" is its circumstantial "form of appearance" in the market.

140. Marx 1987, vol. 2, sec. 6, 72. The metaphor of "crystallizations [*Krys-talle*]," and the formulations regarding (a) the economics of "abstract [*abstrakt*] human labor" and (b) the philosophical implications of "objectified [*vergegen-ständlicht*]" or "materialized [*materialisiert*]" labor speak to us of the strictly *material* level of ethics (*Inhalt* or *Material* with an "a") (see §1.5 of this book). That is to say, the *living* subjectivity (Marx's "*living* labor") becomes an ob-ject (instrument, thing), and becomes transformed into "content" or matter: "in production the person [*Person*] becomes objectified; [in consumption] the person makes the thing into a subject [*subjektiviert*]" (*Grundrisse der Kritik der politische Oekonomie*, vol. 1; Marx 1974, 11). "In the first [production], the pro-ducer is objectified as a thing [*versachlichte*]; in the second [consumption] the thing he creates is personified [*personifiziert*]" (ibid., 12).

141. In the face of Marxist groups such as that of *Monthly Review* in New York, and even that of Jacques Bidet of *Actuel Marx* in Paris, and others, who are of the opinion that the labor theory of value is not essential to understand Marx, we should point out that the *critical-ethical sense* of Marx's theoretical analysis is *absolutely negated* without that theory. Marx undertakes a rigorous description of the entire system of categories of bourgeois political economy in order to "explain" the cause of the negation of the worker (the victim of capital) which it produces (the impossibility of the reproduction of life); this cause would disappear into thin air without the labor theory of value. The final price, profit, competition, and the market are all characteristics of the "phe-nomenality of world," that of the surface, of the "forms of appearance," but are not the "essential foundation" where "value" is found to the extent that it is an objectification of human life. Without this key anthropological and economic link, critical ethics is impossible: we would not be able to see where theft and death arise, the *nonfulfillment* (which I will explain in §4.5) of the "ethical-material principle" (see §1.5).

142. To the extent that "value" is the objectification of human life.

143. *Capital*, vol. 1, chap. 17 (Marx 1987, 502).

144. Regarding "surplus value" see the *Manuscript of 1861–1863*, Notebook 3, folios 95 ff. (Marx 1976–82, pt. 1, 149 ff.); *Capital* (1873), vol. 1, pt. 3, chaps. 5 ff. (Marx 1987, 192 ff.).

145. *Manuscripts from 1844*, vol. 1 (Marx 1956–90, vol. 1, 549).

146. *Capital*, vol. 1, chap. 23 (Marx 1987, 562).

147. This "*moralische Degradation*" is the central theme.

148. *Capital*, vol. 1, chap. 23 (Marx 1987, 588).

149. See §3.5, and also §6.5.

150. Marx's earliest and most creative reflections about the crisis can be read in the *Grundrisse*, Notebook 4, folios 15 ff. (Marx 1974, 305–50), where he addresses the theme of the "process of devalorization [*Entwertungsprozess*]" (ibid., 354), since the crisis is a contradiction internal to the essence of capital that "appears" in moments of crisis: "In a crisis there is even a certain degree of *devalorization* or general annihilation of capital" (ibid., 350). Marx did not

believe that the end of capital was near, but rather that each crisis was over-come in part by creating the possibility of a graver future crisis. In these texts he already discovers, initially, the tendency toward the declining rate of profit as a central moment of the *impossibility of capital*. On this tendency, see Dussel 1990b, 79 ff.

151. See *Capital*, vol. 3, chap. 14 (Marx 1956–90, vol. 26, 242 ff.).

152. In this context, the original version of "dependency theory" must be reassessed in terms of the contemporary horizons of competition within the world capitalist system. See my discussion of the question of "center" and "periphery" in Dussel 1988, 297 ff. According to Marx: "Capital invested in foreign trade can produce a higher rate of profit, in the first place, because it competes with goods produced by other countries with *lesser facilities for production*, in such a way that the most advanced country sells goods at a price greater than their value, but cheaper than that of the countries who are its competitors [*Konkurrenzländer*]" (*Capital*, vol. 3, chap. 14, sec. 5; Marx 1956–90, vol. 26, 248). This has to do with "competition": "The most favored nation receives more labor in exchange for less labor" (ibid., 248). The national global capital of the countries of the periphery is in a structural, constitutive, permanent *crisis* because of the uninterrupted transfer of value. This is a theme which has motivated me to reread completely the Marx of section 2 of the *Karl Marx–Friedrich Engels Gesamtausgabe* (*MEGA*), in order to try to discover the causes of the poverty of peripheral countries, from which the philosophy of liberation emerges.

153. See §I.2.

154. This *Ethics* also "interpellates" the citizens (and the philosophers) of Europe and the United States, and tries to stimulate in them a sense of co-responsibility for the liberation of all of humanity.

155. We will return to this theme in §6.2. Alan Badiou speaks of the "subject as fidelity" to the event (see Badiou 1982). Without agreeing with his position, I think it is interesting to note that the "social subject" or "actors" appears and disappears: the social bloc of the oppressed, to speak in Gramsci's terms (for example, the people of Latin America during the process of their emancipation from Spain, which began in 1810) can "appear" *as a subject* in certain very precise conjunctural circumstances, and be directed by one of its class sectors (for example, the white Creole oligarchy) and disintegrate after completing a historical action (after 1824). Women can "emerge" as a subject, as a social movement, as "feminism," and so on.

156. Now Marx is an "organic intellectual." The lecture regarding "Wages, Price, and Profit" of June 1865 (on this subject see Dussel 1990b, 102 ff.), presented when Marx was deep into the elaboration of chapters 4 to 7 of part III of *Capital*, is an excellent demonstration of how an intellectual, who is deeply involved in the research of a critical topic, can illuminate the struggling worker (the victim) regarding situations that it is impossible for this victim to fully understand (for lack of expert scientific knowledge regarding the issue). Marx explains to the workers: "All of you are convinced that what you sell everyday is your labor. . . . And yet there is, nonetheless, no such thing as the *value of labor*" (Marx 1956–90, vol. 16, 134).

157. On these themes, see Dussel 1993b, 288 ff. and Dussel 1992. We are now at moment 8 of figure 12 (the subject that will be addressed in chapter 6).

158. *Capital*, vol. 1, chap. 17 (Marx 1987, 500).

159. See his text regarding "Marginal Notes to Adolph Wagner's Treatise on Political Economy" when he writes: "*Dignitas* comes from *dignus* and this from *dic*, which means to point out, show, indicate" (Marx 1956–90, vol. 19, 367). The worker must acquire "a sense of his own dignity" (*Capital*, vol. 1, chap. 5, n. 17 [Marx 1987, 209]).

160. First lines of *The Communist Manifesto* (Marx 1956–90, vol. 4, 461).

161. Letter dated April 30, 1867 (Marx 1956–90, vol. 30, 542). Marx's theoretical work, *Capital*, is the definitive "negative ethical judgment" (moment 4 of figure 12) of the capitalist system, for as long as this economic and cultural system survives.

162. In particular, I refer here to *History and Class Consciousness* (Lukács 1968), a work that influenced not only the members of the future Institute for Social Research of Frankfurt, but even earlier, Heidegger himself (who discovered in it the concept of *factibility*). Lukács, beyond the "economism" characteristic of the Second International, recovers Marx's philosophical vein," but does so primarily from Kant, specifically studying the *alienated* moment of the constitution of the "object" of knowledge as "commodity," and taking into account the category of "totality," later, from the standpoint of Hegelian dialectics. He will however become entangled in ontology (Dussel 1990b, 297 ff.). Adorno will recriminate him about this, especially in his last phase (Terulian 1986). In any case, Lukács lays the basis for doing philosophical work regarding the issue of the *reification* of bourgeois consciousness in general, and regarding the worker's own (theoretical, everyday) consciousness as well: "The worker recognizes himself and recognizes his own relationship with Capital in the commodity itself. To the extent that it will be impossible for him to raise himself above this function as an object, his consciousness will be of himself as a commodity, or, in other words, a consciousness of himself as reflected in a capitalist society based upon the production and sale of commodities" ("Reification and Proletarian Consciousness," 3; in Lukács 1968, French trans., 210). The proletariat itself can thus be, and is, alienated.

163. See Korsch 1978 (and Kellner 1981). I have addressed elsewhere Korsch's position (Dussel 1990b, 302 ff.), which clearly indicates the need to negate bourgeois or positivist philosophy and to practice a philosophy that must be more than a mere "system of abstract and anti-dialectical positive sciences" (Korsch 1978, 63). It was necessary to develop Marx's *implicit* philosophy, although Korsch did not say how.

164. Anti-Semitism and the critical history of workers' movements were the themes of the first research projects planned for the future institute. The charismatic Rabbi Nehemiah A. Nobel, together with Martin Buber, Franz Rosenzweig (who we will see influenced Levinas), Siegfried Kracauer, Ernst Simon, Gershom Scholem, and many others, had contact with the first members of the institute. The ethical tone of this research, not without influence of the Kabbalah (as we have seen above), has its origin in the Jewish households of its founders — the families of merchants, bankers, generally upper-middle-class, of Jewish people integrated into German culture — the best of Germany's "critical consciousness" before Nazism.

165. An Argentinian Jewish student who was a student in Germany, and who conceived in 1922 of the idea of founding a research institute. Max Horkheimer and Friedrich Pollock were born in 1895, Karl Wittfogel in 1896, Felix Weil and Herbert Marcuse in 1898, Leo Lowenthal in 1900, Theodor (Wiesengrund)

Adorno in 1903. To them we must add Walter Benjamin (1892), Erich Fromm (1900), and a few others.

166. Jay 1973, xi.

167. Moment 4 of figure 12.

168. Empirico-ontological criticism then, of system 1 of figure 12.

169. Jay 1973, xii.

170. See figure 12: Exteriority, or the sphere "outside" or "beyond" (we will see this later in Levinas) of the horizon of being, of system 1 (the ontological).

171. With the intervention of Erich Fromm and Wilhelm Reich.

172. For Kant, the purpose of criticism is to enable the victim to "emerge from" his or her "self-inflicted guilt of immaturity" (*aus seiner selbst verschuldeten Unmündigkeit*) (*What is Enlightenment?*, A 481; in Kant 1968, vol. 9, 53). Note with caution that Kant declares the victim's guilt to be *self*-inflicted. On the contrary, for Horkheimer the focus is on the need to criticize the relations *of domination*, as he indicates in "The Social Function of Philosophy" (1940) in Horkheimer 1970b: "In philosophy, in contrast with economics and politics, *criticism* does not imply the condemnation of anything whatsoever . . . but rather the intellectual effort, which is definitively *practical*, to refrain from accepting without reflection and as a simple habit ideas [here he is thinking of Kant], ways of acting, and *the dominant social relations.*" In this way, the criticism undertaken is *of the system of domination* and not just *of the immature victim and his or her "self-inflicted guilt"* (see the philosophical meaning of Kant's position in Dussel 1993c, sec. 1).

173. The arrival in New York, at Columbia University, at the beginning of the 1930s of a group of German Marxists, did not awaken suspicions. Why? Because they were not integrated into concrete social struggles in the United States. Once again, the institute had no articulation with a real social actor in the context of the United States. Thus they posed no danger to the prevailing system; and, in addition, they contributed to the task of finding reasons in the struggle against Hitler, a very high priority at that moment of history.

174. See Dussel 1970–80, vol. 1 (1973), from chapter 3 on.

175. See §5.3.

176. On the Frankfurt school overall, see Dubiel 1978; Held 1980; Jay 1973; and especially Habermas 1981b, vol. 1, 489 ff., 465 ff. (where he criticizes the "first" Frankfurt school for having been trapped in the "paradigm of consciousness"). In the second volume of Habermas 1981b (548 ff.), he indicates the themes dealt with by the school from the perspective of a "critical theory" of society, but does not see that this theory was always a renewed attempt of elaborating a *criticism* of (against) society itself. The "old" critical theory (as he calls it, and which is in reality the only "critical" Frankfurt school) had addressed various themes (six in all, ibid., 555), but in Habermas's account it is never explained what the "generative core" provides the link among them. Habermas could not expound that "core" because he lost sight of it long before. This core stems from a *material* concept of *criticism*, with the *victims* as a point of departure. Both of these aspects disappeared in the "second" phase of the Frankfurt school, because of its formalism (in negation of material ethics) and conformism (instead of criticizing Modernity, it seeks its "completion" (or "fulfillment"), and thereby is inevitably incapable of then criticizing the capitalism of the "core" or "central" countries). Its criticism is nothing but criticism of ideology; in addition, Marx's economic and material criticism and Freud's

criticism based on his theory of drives and focus on psychology are criticized in various ways, but not assumed or built upon. The *Lebenswelt* is necessary, but too weak, and *insufficient* as a critical criterion.

177. The text that we will comment on is in Horkheimer 1970b, 28–56.

178. Ibid., 12–28.

179. Note the "positivity" of system 1 of figure 12 as an "affirmation of the prevailing system."

180. System 2 of figure 12.

181. That which I have referred to as the "negation in the first instance" (moment 1).

182. That is to say, it demands an analytical explanation that can only be achieved at moment 7 (of figure 12), through the co-responsible co[l]laboration of the "intellectual" (scientist, expert, philosopher, etc.), which is Horkheimer's central theme.

183. This has to do with the "negative critique" of system 1 (moment 7), but also with the "positive construction of alternatives" (moment 8).

184. Here then, as I indicated above, Horkheimer speaks to us of *two* "realities": reality I of system 1, and the future reality II of system 2, as the fruit of the "praxis of liberation (*Praxis der Befreiung*)" (Horkheimer 1970b, 49).

185. Ibid., 35.

186. This is simultaneously moment 1 of figure 12 (misery) and its insufficiency (and as a result the demand of a critical-theoretical thought, moments 6 and 7). Consider this text from 1933: "Materialismus und Metaphysik," in Horkheimer 1970b, 76.

187. Moment 2 of figure 12.

188. But this is not so for the "second" phase of the school (Apel and Habermas) whose proponents "lose their footing" in terms of the material because of their reductionist formalism (purely pragmatic and discursive in character, as I showed in §§2.3–2.4). An authentically "critical" effort depends on the proportions of materiality and negativity found within it.

189. This formula, "erhalt, steigert und entfalter er das *menschliche Leben*," is almost exactly the same as the one I have adopted to express, in synthesis, the material criterion of this *Ethics* (see §1.5a). I replaced *Erhalten* and *steigern* with *produzieren* and *reproduzieren*, terms that are more biological and economic in character; and *entfalten* by *entwickeln* (which is more social, political, cultural, and aesthetic in character).

190. It is "the victims" who are indicated here (figure 12).

191. These are moments 2 through 7 of figure 12, from the moment at which the process begins whereby the victims become critically conscious of their conditions of oppression, until the process of theoretical and critical analysis of the causes of their negation in real, everyday life.

192. Moments 5 and 6, where the process of "conscientization" begins (a word and problematic unknown at this point to Horkheimer, and which Paulo Freire would discover in the contemporary misery of Brazil: from the periphery of world capitalism and of *Brazilian* capitalism itself, because the region of northeast Brazil where Freire did his initial work and undertook his first reflections is the "periphery" within Brazil).

193. Horkheimer 1970b, 31–32. A dual objective: that of formulating an alternative project (moment 8) or that of creating a new institutional reality (in part or in whole: system 2).

194. Ibid., 28.

195. We shall see that there is, in any case, a certain deficit, both in terms of the acceptance of the ethical or metaphysical *positivity* of the victims (a question I will address in greater detail in chapter 6), and in terms of the issue of the level of articulation to a "historical social subject"; because of this, there will be some inconsistency regarding the issue of feasibility or that of the construction of *positive* alternatives in the course of the praxis of liberation, as we will see in chapters 5 and 6.

196. We examined this displacement in §2.1 and thereafter, as a kind of anticipated critique of Apel and Habermas.

197. Adorno 1966, 30.

198. Marcuse will address the issue of this *"vernunftlosen Organismus"* in his key work *One-Dimensional Man*: "Nonetheless this society is irrational as a totality" (1968b, introduction, 11). In my own *Para una ética de la liberación*, vol. 1, sec. 15, I wrote in the context of the period when the Argentinian military dictatorship was closing in around me (shortly before a terrorist bombing incident at my home in Mendoza): "*This society*—Marcuse tells us—*is irrational as a Totality*, but the gravest aspect of all this is not its irrationality, but that it has no opposition and that it has orchestrated all kinds of controls so that such opposition could never appear"; I was thinking about the kind of persecutions that were going on at that very moment. "The *closure* of the political universe, *containment* of social change which is translated socially into the quieting down of all discourse. . . . The governing Totality produces a negative pseudo-philosophy (logical positivism): critical thinking is negated, because the world which is evidently dominant is assumed existentially" (see Dussel 1970–80, vol. 1 [1973], 117). In effect, fellowships and jobs at the research institutes and universities in Argentina were only granted to philosophers who posed no "problems" for the military dictatorship of the time, precisely because they were not "critical" in the sense understood by Horkheimer (or by the *Ethics of Liberation*). This history has not been written yet (something of this is related in my article "Una década argentina (1966–1976) and the Origins of the *Philosophy of Liberation*" in Dussel 1994c, 55–95). There are those who are skeptical of critical reason, in the name of epistemological precision and as a negation of "metaphysics." Precision is a necessary demand of serious philosophy, as is the critique of a naive metaphysics; but the critique of "critical" reason that makes it appear as if it were "imprecise" or "confused" (because it is committed to the search for *new creative arguments*) or "meta-physical" (because it affirms the *universality of reason and of the "reality" of the victims*) is something else entirely. How much we have suffered and continue to suffer in Latin America! We have dared to undertake these reflections because the first Frankfurt school also experienced life under a dictatorship in the context of the capitalism of the world's central economies; and we, in the context of dictatorship under the conditions of peripheral capitalism, whose repression is far from over, since it assumes diverse guises in the form of an expanding wave of neoliberalism (which began in Brazil in 1964, and which still persists into the first part of the twenty-first century).

199. Moments 9 and 10 of figure 12. "Emancipation" is the responsibility of the victims themselves ("My name is Rigoberta Menchú . . ."), with the co[l]-laboration of critical theory.

200. Note that "transformation" does not necessarily mean to undertake a

"revolution" of the system as a whole. The ethics of liberation is thus an ethics with validity for everyday life, but has a "criterion" distinct from that of a reformist perspective. In sum, we are dealing with Thesis 11 of Marx's essay on Feuerbach.

201. This *Ordnung* is system 1 in figure 12.

202. Moment 7.

203. Horkheimer 1970b, 28–29.

204. The same is true for Levinas and for this *Ethics of Liberation*. Marcuse, in his habilitation thesis regarding Hegel (see Marcuse 1970b) discovers "Life"—in relation to Dilthey and from the perspective of Heidegger—as the ultimate "content" of being, of Hegelian ontology. Later, perhaps not without some relation to the use of the concept of "life [*Leben*]" by Nazism, Marcuse will propose in its place the concept of "reason [*Vernunft*]" (especially in Marcuse 1967, and then in the context of his critique of Soviet Stalinism). Marcuse's theme throughout is "critical reason," which will always have a certain and excessive proximity to Hegel (once again without having discovered the whole question of Exteriority and its transontological positivity). It seems as if Lukács and Marcuse are not able to get beyond ontology. This is why, for Marcuse, Marx is the continuation of Hegel; he is not sufficiently aware of the discontinuities between them (Dussel 1990b, 304 ff.). Adorno, in contrast, is clearly critical of Hegelian ontology.

205. Adorno 1966, 7. "The author does not begin by developing that which according to the dominant opinion in philosophy would be the *foundation* [*Grundlage*], but instead first broadly develops many aspects which from that perspective appear to be well founded. This implies both a *critique* of the idea of laying such a foundation, and a greater priority being given to concrete thought" (ibid.). Lévinas addresses these aspects more clearly than Adorno, since the "criticism of fundamentals" that he alludes to must be undertaken not only from the perspective of the *concrete* (the material), but equally from that of an Exteriority (never discovered by the Frankfurt school) with a certain kind of *positive* character, a matter that in my *Ethics* (Dussel 1970–80, vol. 2 [1973]) I criticized as an ambiguity of this school. Adorno was correct in calling this "negative dialectics an anti-system" (Adorno 1966, 8). All of this is connected to a critique of ontology as it was practiced in Germany in this context.

206. Horkheimer 1970b, 29.

207. See "Exteriority" in figure 12, the "beyond" of system 1 (the prevailing system), but before system 2 (the future system). I will address this with some care in §4.4.

208. Horkheimer 1970b, 30.

209. Everything begins with "*zweispältigen Charakter.*"

210. Horkheimer 1970b, 28.

211. The nonacceptance of this "naturalization" is the nonacceptance of its "character of mere facticity": the new vision (which is the inversion of fetishism) of the prevailing system as a totality (moment 4 of figure 12).

212. See Marcuse 1964.

213. See Horkheimer 1967.

214. See Adorno et al. 1969.

215. See among others the works of Adorno 1970; Horkheimer 1982; Jay 1973, 173 ff.; Marcuse 1969. Here we should also include the Frankfurt school's studies on aesthetics, especially those by Walter Benjamin.

216. At this level, the school was better prepared than anybody else to take on this question, because it had directly suffered the implications of the Holocaust, and because it had taken important leaps forward in terms of its studies of authoritarianism (from the perspective of the subject) and of capitalist society (objectively, and even as a culture). See the exploration of this theme in Jay 1973, 143–72. The reflections of the Franfurt school are especially valuable from a Latin American perspective, because we have "lived" (and perhaps will "live" again) the experience of military dictatorships, orchestrated from the Pentagon—and characteristic of peripheral capitalism, and in particularly ferocious form in Argentina (my homeland of origin), Uruguay, Chile, Brazil, Central America, the Caribbean, and so on. The philosophy (and ethics) of liberation was born within the dark and horrific context of military repression. The dramatic nature of its language in the 1960s reflects this involuntary and hallucinatory reality. Removed from its context, Latin America's movement of critical philosophy can even seem to have a dramaticness that is "out of place."

217. Kellner 1984, 132.

218. Marcuse 1967, 8.

219. In this youthful work, Marcuse plays with words, as Heidegger did.

220. Marcuse 1928, 48.

221. The work by Habermas that I am referring to here (Habermas 1963, and especially Habermas 1968a) belongs to the last phase of the "first" Frankfurt school. Habermas had not begun his "pragmatic formalist" phase, in which discourse reason (a necessary but insufficient element) would win the upper hand and critical-material dialectical reason (also necessary but insufficient) would be superseded: in this *Ethics* my intention is to articulate both of these types of reasoning into an even broader and more complex framework. See §6.1.

222. Horkheimer 1970b, 33.

223. Ibid., 32. At moment 1 of figure 12, victims "experience" the pain of their negation in the first instance (from their alienation in terms of the content of their life); at moment 3 they become ethically conscious (from the affirmation of moment 2) of their state of negativity.

224. Horkheimer, for a European (such as Habermas), speaks about the past; for a Latin American, African, Asian—or East European—he speaks of the present and next future.

225. Horkheimer 1970b, 33.

226. We were even criticized for being "elitists" (Cerutti 1983) for having clearly demonstrated the moment when the critical conciousness of the philosopher, of the teacher, of the critical theorist intervenes in the "clarification" or "enlightenment" of the conciousness of the poor. I have written: "The ethics of liberation, which begins by being a philosophy of discipleship, humble in the face of the Other [the victims], faithful to his or her face . . . becomes the *norm* of existential everyday conduct. . . . The word of the philosopher is then in this context the *ethical conciousness* of a whole people: he or she stands in the place of the Other [the victims] in confrontation with totality and gives armor to their words with the cutting edge of the liberatory critical method" (Dussel 1970–80, vol. 2 [1973], sec. 39, 193).

227. Horkheimer 1970b, 33.

228. Ibid., 47–48.

229. Ibid., 49.

230. Ibid.

231. Ibid., 56.

232. Ibid., 49.

233. Rigoberta Menchú (Menchú 1985), among others, will serve us as a guide regarding this essential matter. "*And this was how my consciousness originated*: an analectical affirmation. This is ethical reasoning in the first instance" (Dussel 1994b, 156ff; 98 ff.). See §5.1.

234. I must confess that the difference between my *Ethics* of the 1970s (Dussel 1970–80) and that of the present is precisely this "perspective"; that is to say, I wish to focus for now on the "position" of the victim, in the first instance, and only later to move on to the description of "reactions" from the "perspective" of the scientist, philosopher, or expert "actually committed" to the struggle of the victims for their own liberation.

235. Horkheimer 1970b, 33.

236. See Cerutti 1983.

237. And this, conceding the point to Habermas, because of the failure to exercise democratic discursive reasoning in a process of dialogue "among the people" (as Mao would have said during that era), where the contribution of the intellectual or philosopher-critic could have entered into a dialectical process of analyzing and of being criticized; criticizing and advancing in a decision-making process, and so on. In this sense, Horkheimer was correct: "The thought of the intellectual himself, to the extent it is critical and propels things forward, forms part of the development of the masses" (Horkheimer 1970b, 33). I analyze all of this from the Latin American perspective, in the five volumes of my *Ethics* (Dussel 1970–80).

238. Horkheimer 1970b, 33.

239. As long ago as my first *Ethics* (Dussel 1970–80) I criticized Horkheimer, Marcuse, and Bloch for having "shut" themselves within Totality and not having the benefit of relying *positively* on the participation of Exteriority, of the Other. In Marcuse's Eros and Civilization "fantasy" (one's own, not that of the Other) is the creative motor force (Dussel 1970–80, vol. 3 [1973], secs. 42 ff.). For me it was always the *reality* of the victims from their perspective of negativity, resistant to and amid their Exteriority of Totality, who in their repressed libido, their nonnutrition, nonclothing, nonhousing, nonlearning, nonhappiness (e.g., their misery and suffering) (in the "noncapital" of Marx's living labor) obligate and demands ethically and *positively* that such negativities that are "absent" be included in the alternative project. This project is not merely the fruit of "my/our fantasy," but is rather already written *negatively* in the *really existent* needs of the victims. Because of this, "their *true* interests" are *already* their inverted interests reflected in their unfulfilled needs, and it is only by means of a *practical* articulated commitment that the critic (philosopher, scientist, expert) can come to discover them *theoretically*.

240. "Untrue" is the term chosen by Horkheimer in the original English-language prologue to Jay 1973.

241. Marcuse 1970a, 148.

242. These are the victims of conscientization (moment 3 of figure 12).

243. Habermas 1963, 228–29.

244. Habermas 1981a, 349.

245. "Thesis on the Philosophy of History," sec. 1, in Benjamin 1989, 177.

246. "Theological-Political Fragment" in ibid., 193.

247. Ibid.

248. It is necessary to consider these concepts in Franz Rosenzweig, especially, such as the "always durable pre-world [*immer während Vorwelt*]" (in Rosenzweig 1921, 1), and "redemption [*Erlösung*]" (ibid., vol. 2, 214 ff.).

249. Benjamin 1989, sec. 17, 190.

250. System 1 of figure 20.

251. Benjamin 1989, sec. 11, 184.

252. Ibid., sec. 13, 187.

253. Consider "the victim" in figure 12.

254. Benjamin 1989, sec. 12, 186. See Reyes Mate 1991, where he writes of the "reason of the vanquished" or "anamnetical" reason (a reason commemorative of the victims) (p. 209), but where it is never clear exactly what a "praxis of liberation" by the victims consists of. This is something like a critique of historical reason where the critique of utopian reason is absent.

255. "Theological-Political Fragment," in Benjamin 1989, 194.

256. "Thesis on the Philosophy of History," sec. 7, in ibid., 181.

257. We must situate ourselves at the "material," "content" level, as we have addressed it in chapter 1, but now negatively.

258. Benjamin 1989, sec. 6, 180.

259. Is there such a tradition? Does the praxis of liberation by the oppressed then constitute a "history"? For the ethics of liberation, this presupposes a strong and realistic sense of the concept of the critique of utopian reason, but this is something which is too weak in the Frankfurt school and in Benjamin.

260. Benjamin 1989, sec. 7, 182.

261. This is the first moment of the process of "conscientization" ("consciousness-raising") (moment 3 of figure 12).

262. Benjamin 1989, sec. 15, 188. The "great Revolution" is the messianic time, all the moments from 3 through 10 of figure 12, including the deconstruction of system 1, although the effective creative construction of system 2 will always be less clear (not only in Benjamin but in the entire Frankfurt school).

263. This is the *iom-yahweh* (Yahweh, the Messianic God) of the prophets of Israel (see Dussel 1969).

264. Benjamin 1989, sec. 18, 191.

265. Ibid., sec. 14, 188.

266. Ibid., sec. 17, 190.

267. Ibid., sec. B, 191.

268. I must confess that, as a historian, I have proposed and sought to undertake a history of Latin America "from the point of departure of the oppressed" since 1966, in the sense indicated here (see Dussel 1966, 1969, 1970, 1970–80, 1974a, 1975, 1983a, 1993c, and 1994c).

269. Benjamin 1989, sec. 3, 179.

270. Ibid., sec. 9, 183. With reference to Paul Klee's Angelus Novus.

271. Ibid., sec. 14, 188.

272. Ibid., sec. 16, 189. The specific reference here is to deconstruction (moment 9 of figure 12).

273. Ibid., sec. B, 191. Is not the "Messiah" the individual who becomes conscious of being a victim or who puts his or her own destiny "into play" on behalf of the victim and erupts into history as a liberatory discontinuity?

274. Ibid., sec. 6, 180. The Anti-Christ is system 1 as Marx's fetish, that which has been consecrated, the triumphant, that which prevails, that which is "legitimate" (as understood by Weber and Habermas).

275. Far from Germany, for sure, not from the Mexico that California belonged to before the U.S. occupation by force in 1848.

276. "By the Rivers of Babylon" in Cardenal 1969, 65. Cardenal's "river" is the one that flows by New York City (alongside Manhattan's Riverside Drive from 125th Street northward), and the singer of this song is a Puerto Rican. And now they are two Jewish refugees, German in origin, and not in Babylon but rather in California. The *pathos* of *The Dialectics of the Enlightenment* comes about as described by Benjamin (quoting Flaubert): "*Peu de gens devineront combien il a fallu être triste pour ressusciter Carthage.* The nature of this sadness is plain when we ask with whom the historicist historian enters into empathy. It is undeniable that the response is this: with the conqueror" ("Thesis on the Philosophy of History," sec. 7, in Benjamin 1989, 181). It is evident that in this case such empathy had millions who were dying in the concentration camps of the Holocaust as a counterpart. Habermas correctly indicates that "that state of mind, that attitude is no longer ours" (Habermas 1985, 130). But sadly, that attitude of those "exiles" is *precisely that of the ethics of liberation* (of those "exiled" in the context of Latin America, as the consequence of U.S. policy, and no longer because of Hitler as in the case of our colleagues from Frankfurt). In truth, Habermas is part of a generation that was the product of the German postwar "miracle." We belong instead to the generations of misery wrought by peripheral capitalism in Latin America, Africa, and Asia. Recently I received the news of the murder in Nairobi, amid the Kenya of a neocolonialist military dictatorship, of Professor Henry Odera Oruka (president of the African Philosophers' Association). And this "sadness" engulfs us. Habermas takes Horkheimer and Adorno's work as a mere argument, and its refutation seems to be out of place: for him, the authors of *The Dialectics of the Enlightenment* have fallen into a performative contradiction, since they have negated the rational foundation which their own critique is based upon.

277. Habermas 1985, 134–35, 140. After reading the text written by the exiled Horkheimer and Adorno and what Habermas criticized in it, it seems as if I had read *a different text*. In fact, Habermas does not possess the "code" necessary to understand the kind of reading I will propose and *his interpretation is completely wrong.* Horkheimer and Adorno's text is an impassioned—but critical—defense of *universal reason*, and is also a critique of a *reductionist reason* that is instrumental, quantitative, abstract, positivist, and antiethical in character, and which because of the negation of its presuppositions, its complicity, and its historical function remains trapped in myth (fetishism, according to Marx), which is precisely what it had hoped to transcend. It has become instead a "reproductive reason" that is *institutional,* and which suicidally and castratingly negates pleasure: "Pleasure [*die Lust*] . . . is permanently subjected [to the domination of] self-preservation" (Horkheimer 1970b, 32, 47). This is, as we shall see, Marcuse's theme in *Eros and Civilization.* But it is not a matter, as Habermas believes it to be, of a mere critique of ideology. It is rather a critique of ontology as a totality; a critique of the cynical and dominating reason that provides a *rationale* for system 1 in figure 12. All of the authors that I address to the end of chapter 6 write about the same (clearly, confusingly, coherently

or contradictorily): it is necessary to clearly situate their *intention*, to discover what it is they "want" to say first, in order to later respectfully and slowly see if it is possible to refute what "contradicts their intention" (with Horkheimer beyond Horkheimer, with Schopenhauer beyond Schopenhauer, with Nietzsche beyond Nietzsche). But a creative critique cannot be undertaken *from the outside* of the discourse being studied.

278. Horkheimer and Adorno 1971, 10 and 19. The inevitable "Eurocentrism" of the critics made it impossible for them to discover, for example, that in March 1492, with the expulsion of the Jews from Granada, and with Ginés de Sepúlveda (the "first" great modern philosopher), at the debate of Valladolid in 1550, the history of "modern reason" had begun, at the same time that the *first* modern critical reason was first undertaken by Bartolomé de las Casas (this is my argument in Dussel 1993c). The *worldwide* "myth" that inaugurates Modernity, at the moment of its globalization, was not perceived by Horkheimer and Adorno themselves—that of the civilizational superiority of Europe over all other cultures; its name is "Eurocentrism."

279. I remember that in Israel, in 1960, a Jewish cab driver showed me the number tattooed on his wrist at a Nazi concentration camp: a victim. The next day, an Arab Palestinian work companion (*khaver*), who was working as a construction carpenter in Nazareth, pessimistic in the face of discrimination and poverty, told me: "We are the Jews in Israel!" A victim, once again. Is not the "Intifadah" Moses (he who moves the slaves) all over again in Israel (Egypt of the Pharaohs)? This is the kind of *rememorative* "reading" suggested by Benjamin. Martin Buber was well aware of all of this!

280. Moment 7 of figure 12. The philosophers I have indicated have fulfilled all of the previous moments (from moment 4, as a *negative* critique of the "prevailing system" as a totality). They "extend" from the *most proximate victim* who suffers (the Jews), to the next closest example (the Proletariat), all the way up to the "universal victim": civilized humanity (and from there begins the possible reconstruction of the "institutions" of Greece itself).

281. The ethics of liberation is on the side of those who do not forget the *negative* (because of the negativity that weighs upon the periphery of the world system, in women, children, the aged, the immigrants, those who are not white, etc.), but without continuing their process at future positive moments (as we shall see in chapters 5 and 6, this latter stage is missing in the first Frankfurt school; and of course the "second" Frankfurt school misses this point entirely because of its blindness toward the *material* and the *negative*).

282. Horkheimer and Adorno 1971, 7.

283. The suicidal aspect of this ontological, totalizing, totalitarian pathology is expressed as follows: "Men expect that this world without exit will be converted into flames in the name of a Totality which is itself themselves and in the face of which they can do nothing" (ibid., 29, 44).

284. Ibid., 31. Please note carefully these distinctions (preservation, security, survival, reproduction, repetition, institutions, etc., the *negative* as repression) as opposed to others (pleasure, creation, novelty, rupture, criticism, etc., the *positive* as liberation). These will be the keys throughout chapter 4.

285. Habermas is unable to understand this.

286. "Contemporary Relevance of Schopenhauer," in Horkheimer 1970a, 89ff: "Schopenhauer's teaching has contemporary significance because of the

fact that it included an unequivocal denunciation of idols . . . amid its expression of that which it considered to be negative, and which is liberated by its very presence" (ibid., 109).

287. At our material beginning we speak always of the "*reproduction* of the life" of the human subject, and I have always repeated that this is *necessary but not sufficient*. See thesis 17 in appendix 1.

288. Horkheimer and Adorno are quoting from Spinoza's *Ethics*, vol. 4, prop. 22, corol. (Spinoza 1958, 191: "The tendency towards self-preservation is the first and only foundation of virtue").

289. Horkheimer and Adorno 1971, 29–31.

290. See my *Ethics* (Dussel 1970–80, vol. 1 [1973], chap. 1).

291. I should indicate, contrary to Horkheimer, that the concept "Western [*westlichen*]" manifests a "Eurocentrism" that I cannot accept: Greece is not "Western." It is the "Eastern" part of the Roman Empire, and is as much Islamic as Christian (in reality it is "something else"), since it was never part of Latin-Germanic Europe (at least until the origins of modern Europe). See Dussel 1993c, and in this *Ethics*, §§3 and 4.

292. "Conversation about Adorno," in Horkheimer 1970b (Spanish trans., 1973, 223).

293. "Means and Ends," pt. 1; in Horkheimer 1967 (Spanish trans., 1973, 15). This is instrumental reason.

294. Ibid. (Spanish trans., 16). This is, precisely, the material-practical and originary ethical reason I have referred to since chapter 1, and which has been ignored by the "second" Frankfurt school, and many others.

295. Hinkelammert speaks of "reproductive reason" because he conceives of it as referring to the reproduction of life *for all*, especially for the victims. Horkheimer and Adorno speak of the "reproduction" of the *system*, not of life itself.

296. On Nietzsche, see §4.3 [245–46] of this *Ethics*.

297. Horkheimer and Adorno 1971, 10.

298. Recall that point 6 was first addressed at [234].

299. The "praxis of liberation," that is.

300. We could say: self-contradictory in a performative sense. Here, Adorno gives us good arguments to provide a foundation for the so-called universal ethical-material principle: even suicide is argued for from the standpoint of a vision centered on life.

301. He is also, by the way, formulating what I will refer to hereafter as the "critical-ethical principle"; the duty to act in the face of the suffering unjustly borne by the innocent is the beginning of the process of "*Ethics* II," that of the *Ethics* itself.

302. Adorno 1966, 201. Here lies the partial truth of utilitarianism. Another reflection by Adorno along these lines, which could be applied to the case of the conquered indigenous peoples of the Americas or to enslaved Africans is: "In him an additional factor is made tangible which is part of what ethics consists of. The tangible, the corporeal, because it represents that which is abominable and made practical, in terms of all the unbearable physical pain to which individuals are exposed. . . . Morality does not survive except in the form of an unvarnished materialism. . . . The human layer, that which is somatic but distant from meaning, is the landscape of suffering which was embraced in the concentration camps without any consolation" (ibid., 365).

303. Marcuse 1981, 243.

304. See what I have written earlier about this matter (Dussel 1970–80, vol. 3 [1973], chap. 7).

305. In Horkheimer's 1936 essay regarding "Authority and the Family" (Horkheimer 1970b, 162 ff., 76 ff.). Freud is not cited, but his insights had already been incorporated into Horkheimer's approach. Adorno wrote on this theme in 1927 in "Der Begriff des Unbewussten in der Transzendentalen Seelenlehre"; cf. Jay 1973, 316; regarding this matter, 86 ff. The influence of psychoanalysis was clear in the institute through the work of Erich Fromm himself (a young, active, and militant Jew who enthusiastically recognized the importance of critical prophets such as Isaiah, Amos, and Osiah; see Fromm 1962, 5) and that of Karl Landauer and Fromm's wife Frida Reichmann. Since 1928, the figure of Wilhelm Reich (see Reich 1970) appears as part of Germany's scientific and political horizon. In one of the first texts where Fromm methodologically expounds the relationship between Freud and Marx, he manages to define a specific type of "victim": the primitive Christians interpreted from the standpoint of their class status in the Roman Empire (see Fromm 1963; written in Vienna in 1931). In 1932, Fromm published an article by Fromm which relates psychoanalysis to social psychology (in *Zeitschrift für Sozialforschung* 1, no. 3 [1932]), which is one of the foundations of the Frankfurt school's *Studien über Autorität und Familie* (1936). But Fromm had begun to "normalize" Freud before this. In the United States he opted for his own path distinct from that of his other colleagues at the Institute for Social Research, and his positive "integration" in a society in which "critical reason" had a lesser function and potential would not fail to influence his work. His noncritical optimism would distance him from the institute.

306. Horkheimer 1970b (1990: Spanish trans., 151–222).

307. Marcuse 1981.

308. The epilogue of Marcuse 1981, "Critique of Neo-Freudian Revisionism," is dedicated to him.

309. Marcuse 1938. See Kellner 1984, 154 ff.

310. Marcuse 1981, epilogue, 275.

311. Ibid., 50.

312. The material criterion of this *Ethics* (see §1.5a).

313. Marcuse 1981, 118–91.

314. See thesis 17 in appendix 1.

315. Freud and Marcuse did not perceive that Europe is not solely the fruit of Greece, and that the Egyptian-Mesopotamian tradition situates the libido differently (see §I.1 and I.3).

316. Marcuse 1981, 125. See what I have said earlier in Dussel 1970–80, vol. 3 [1973], sec. 44, 68 ff.

317. Marcuse 1981, 181.

318. Ibid., 205 ff.

319. Ibid., 240; quoting Benjamin, "Ueber den Begriff der Geschichte," in *Die neue Rundschau* (1950), 568.

320. See Dussel 1988, 159 ff.: "The only thing I have proved theoretically is the *possibility* of absolute rent, *without violating the law of value*" (letter from Marx to Engels, August 9, 1862, speaking of the *Manuscripts of 1861–63*, which he was writing at that moment; in Marx 1956–90, vol. 30, 274).

321. I think that it is only the very foundation of the pathology of modern Western culture itself, and not the libido of humanity (including other cultures) as such.

322. The "insurpassability" reveals the contradictory *tension*; the unstable "manageability" indicates the precarious "normality" of a certain "discipline" or inevitable repression (of all civilizational institutions) in danger of becoming pathological or being surpassed as a form of liberation. Liberation itself does not avoid a new state of unstable tension.

323. It is a question of "truth," not just of "validity," although as we shall see, they can and must be articulated to each other.

324. Horkheimer 1970b, 56.

325. "Reproduction" provides security and can kill in the mere repetition of domination, repression, and "civilizing" measures; "development" creates that which is new, but can fall into a destructive kind of anarchy, which also kills. This is a dialectics of the struggle for human life (vegetative, cultural, spiritual, human) in the face of pain and death.

326. See §I.1 and figure 13, levels I and II. Aristotle would write: "*Hoi dè tó alógon exon kai to alogon*" (Certain philosophers [believe there to be] the rational part and the irrational part)" (*Of the Soul*, bk. 3, chap. 9, 422–26); according to him the second part includes the "will [*boúlesis*]" (ibid., 432b 5) as a moment of the "instinctual" or "tendencial" (*órexis*) (ibid., b 7). Similarly, he recalls that for Parmenides "The first of all the Gods planted love [*érota*]" (*Metaphysics* bk. 1, chap. 4, 984b 27). For the Stoics there were three levels of the "affective" or "instinctive impulses": *ormé*, *epibolé*, and *órexis*, which in turn determined the four passions (*páthos*— "the passion of the arduous future": *epithymía*; the phobia in the face of a dangerous future: *phobos*; pain: *lúpe*; pleasure: *hedoné*). It is only the predominance of "hegemonic reason [*lógon hegemonikón*]" that enables "living in conformity with nature [*homologouménos tê physeis zén*]" or "with reason [*tô lógo*]," in order in this way to achieve the "negation of all passions [*apátheia*]." For the Epicureans everything consisted of the "avoidance of pain [*aponía*]," in order to achieve "pleasure [*khará*]," and with that, "imperturbability [*ataraxía*]."

327. I remember that at the Freiburg dialogue (1989) with K.-O. Apel (Dussel 1990a; Fornet-Betancourt 1990), Odo Marquart intervened, raising the issue of this renowned Aristotelian definition. Now I return to this theme in a certain sense.

328. The order of "being" is the order of the "world" (as both Heidegger and Schopenhauer understood it: the totality of sense or representation), and in an "intersubjective" (pragmatic-linguistic) sense, as well as where the "prevailing system" can arise as a given (the sociohistorical "being"). Schopenhauer attempts to reveal something "beyond" the "*world* as [a totality of] representation": the "thing-in-itself" as Will. The essence of the instinctive drives is identified as the Will, which is then confounded with reality itself and *which is then defined as irrational*. The Upanishads (which inspired Schopenhauer) with the One as the sole origin of everything have simplified these tensions. For my part, I believe that it is necessary to maintain the distinctions and the tensions: it is necessary to maintain the order of drives and of rationality and to know how to articulate them in a dialectical contradiction (see figure 13).

329. *The Quadruple Root of the Principle of Sufficient Reason*, in Schopenhauer 1961, sec. 42, 223 (German ed., Schopenhauer 1960–65, vol. 3, 7–191).

330. Ibid., sec. 43, 225.

331. Safranski (1991, 284) describes it as a "hermeneutics of existence."

332. Schopenhauer would carry out this discovery of the "experience" of self-awareness through the Indian Upanishads. He wrote: "The *higher consciousness* needs pain, suffering, failure in order to maintain itself awake in the same way a ship needs a ballast, without which the keel can never reach the depths" (Schopenhauer 1966, vol. 1, 380).

333. Ibid., vol. 2, 360.

334. Schopenhauer passes from the level of phenomena (the Kantian *Erscheinung*) to the "apparent" or illusory (*Schein*). The first is the horizon of knowledge, the second is already ethical in character; the deceitful or *illusory*: "The *Maya* of the Vedas . . . and the *phenomenon* of Kant are one and the same" (ibid., vol. 1, 380).

335. *Die Welt als Wille und Vorstellung*, in Schopenhauer 1960–65, vol. 2, sec. 19; vol. 1, sec. 164.

336. "When we consider the powerful and uncontainable impulse [*Drang*] with which currents of water flow into an abyss with a scrutinizing eye . . . it will not imply a great effort of our imagination to recognize . . . each component of this process as part of a single unity in all its parts—just like the first light of dawn bears the same name as that of the most intense rays at noon—here too the same label of Will [*Wille*] should be applied throughout, both as to that which describes what constitutes *the state of being in itself* [*das Sein an sich*] inherent in all the things of the world [*Welt*], as well as to the exclusive core of all phenomena" (ibid., vol. 2, sec. 23; vol. 1, 180–81; vol. 2, 26).

337. Ibid., vol. 4, sec. 54; vol. 1, 380; vol. 3, 12.

338. "The unlimited world, full of sorrow, becomes alien both in the past and in the future. . . . But a dark premonition beats in the most hidden folds of his consciousness that perhaps the world is not completely foreign to him and has a relationship with him from which the *principium individuationis* cannot free him" (ibid., vol. 4, sec. 63; vol. 1, 482; vol. 3, 69). It seems as if we are speaking here of what Freud referred to later as the "reality principle."

339. A central moment of "pain" is sexuality, where the genitals are "focus of the Will" for Schopenhauer, emblematic of the process whereby the species conquers the individual, and the animal emerges within the human.

340. "Egotism, that is the impulse to live and towards one's own welfare" (*On the Foundations of Morality*, sec. 14; in Schopenhauer 1993, 221).

341. Schopenhauer 1960–65, vol. 4, sec. 62; vol. 3, 64: "The State has been instituted, not against egotism, but against the disastrous consequences that result for all because of the multiplicity of individual egotisms." This is Hegel's conception of "civil society" (the *external* state). His ethical-social critical consciousness was nil, since he relates that in the worker's uprising of 1848—that was so important for Marx—he would generously supply the binoculars he used in the theater, so that an army captain and his soldiers, whom Schopenhauer welcomed into his own home, could aim more accurately through his window and shoot at the workers marching down his street (Safranski 1991, 443). He ferociously defended as well the inheritance handed down from his father, since it gave him the means to dedicate himself exclusively to the development of his philosophy; the social demands of the workers might have placed his own treasured private property into question. Thus are the petty

practicalities of a great ontologist, who Kierkegaard would justifiably criticize by putting his fingers in the wound of his ethical contradictions!

342. Schopenhauer 1960–65, vol. 4, sec. 22, 293–94. Here we see also the principle of *twa-twam asi* from the Upanishads in Sanskrit: "This is you."

343. Aesthetics permit us to elude the multiplicity of tensions and suffering induced by everyday life; music is especially effective in this regard (*Die Welt als Wille und Vorstellung*, in ibid., vol. 3, sec. 52; vol. 1, 358 ff.; vol. 2, 251 ff.) — the music that Schopenhauer so loved and which he contemplated in such ecstasy, with his theater "binoculars," which he lent to the captain in 1848.

344. "And since we have seen that such a self-suppression [*Selbstaufhebung*] of the Will has its origin in the domain of knowledge [*Erkenntnis*] and that is in itself independent of conscious will, it can be inferred from this that this self-suppression of the will, this excursion into the realm of freedom, cannot be obtained at will but rather emerges suddenly, as if it were a blow delivered from without" (ibid., vol. 4, sec. 70; vol. 1, 549; vol. 3, 106–7). It seems that in the end the road to salvation is a certain kind of "knowledge," as it was for the Hindus, Buddhists, Greek or Hellenists (see §I.3 in this *Ethics*). The "original sin" is "all of the will to live," all "affirmation of life"; "redemption" is the "negation of the will" (ibid., 550; 107).

345. Reformist "optimism" and the "hope" of the victims, in the manner of Bloch (1959 and 1977), must be distinguished from each other, as we shall see in the next two chapters of this *Ethics*, especially in §5.4.

346. To say that they are historic does not mean that they cannot be non-intentional. But the lack of personal consciousness does not permit the actions and institutions to evade responsibility, thanks to an ethics of critical responsibility, once the nonintentional consequences that the ethics of intention had set aside had been evaluated.

347. See Heidegger 1961, and "Nietzsche's Phrase: *God Is Dead*" in Fink 1969; Habermas 1985, chaps. 3–4; Heidegger 1963b, 193–246; Jaspers 1963a; Loewith 1964, passim; Müller-Lauter 1971; Savater 1993; Schutte 1984; Vattimo 1989a.

348. Nietzsche, *Die Geburt der Tragödie*, sec. 10 (Nietzsche 1973, vol. 1, 51). Regarding Socrates he says: "While in all productive men the instinct [*Instinkt*] is precisely the creative affirmative force [*schöpferisch-affirmative Kraft*], and the consciousness [*Bewusstsein*] a critical, demobilizing force, in Socrates the instinct is revealed as critical and the consciousness as creative: a true monstrosity *per defectum*!" (ibid., sec. 13, 64).

349. See Deleuze and Guattari 1972, 16 ff.

350. This is the Nietzschean construction of a sadomasochistic "Christ" who has more to do with a *conservative* pietistic Lutheranism (which Nietzsche perhaps experienced in his father's household) than with the historical Christ, who was involved, instead, in bringing the Dionysian tendency to its culmination as the expression of an Egyptian-Semitic and Babylonian tradition unknown to Nietzsche. In this tradition the "Dionysian" was the "Mosaic" (from the mythical *Móshe*, Moisés), liberator of the slaves "from Egypt" (a metaphor) (Gottwald 1981) — a paradigmatic economic (the slaves as *workers*), political, and historical (in terms of the liberation sought from Pharaonic *domination*) example of the pleasure instincts as a form of liberation. See my article "El paradigma del éxodo" in *Concilium* 209 (1987): 83–92. All of this "other tradition"

was unknown to Nietzsche's Hellenocentric racism (in this, he was a "victim" of German imperial ideology; his critical intentions were incapable of getting beyond this context), as we shall see later on.

351. Nietzsche opposed "happiness" (the first sphere of figure 13) to "pleasure" (the second sphere). This was perhaps his greatest discovery, which the ethics of liberation will make the nucleus of its reconstruction of the *entire structure of drives*.

352. Nietzsche, *Wille zur Macht*, sec. 696 (Nietzsche 1922–29, vol. 19, 145).

353. Ibid., sec. 703 (vol. 19, 150).

354. Ibid., sec. 704 (vol. 19, 151).

355. The transcendence of the "ego," the refutation of "freedom" and the "death of God" are three steps toward the *transcendence of metaphysics* in Nietzsche.

356. Level 1 of figure 13.

357. Nietzsche, *Menschliches, Allzumenschliches*, sec. 224 (Nietzsche 1922–29, vol. 8, 199).

358. Nietzsche, *Wille zur Macht*, secs. 657–58 (vol. 19, 115–16; vol. 4, 248). "Pleasure . . . is not only the feeling of Power, but the joy of creation and of that which is created; because all activity enters into our consciousness as the consciousness of a process of creative labor" (ibid., sec. 661 [vol. 19, 119; vol. 4, 250]). "The normal inability to satisfy our instincts, for example those related to hunger, to the sexual instinct, to the instinct of movement, do not contain in themselves anything which is depressive, and instead stimulate the sentiment of life" (ibid., sec. 799; 209; 308).

359. Level 1 of figure 13; level 1 of table 10 [257].

360. Level 2 of figure 13 and level 2 of table 10. See thesis 17 in appendix 1 at the end of this book.

361. The material principle obligates us not only to "reproduce" (levels 1 and 3 of figure 13) life, but equally to "develop it" (levels 2 and 4).

362. *Wille zur Macht*, sec. 715 (vol. 19, 158; vol. 4, 271). See the commentary to the concepts of *Erhaltungs, Steigerungs-Bedingungen* as *Dauer* of the "future [*Werdens*]" in Heidegger 1961, vol. 2, 101 ff.; Heidegger 1963b, 210 ff.; Heidegger 1947, 179 ff.; and in *Sein und Zeit*, Heidegger 1963c, 68, 99, 110, and 286.

363. Moment 1 of figure 12.

364. Moment 3 of figure 12.

365. "Power" understood as "Potential" (*Pouissance*).

366. Vattimo writes: "If this is the origin of consciousness, of language and grammar and philosophy which is implicit in these, above all with reference to the subject and the predicate, it will not be difficult then to see how the compulsive force of the rules of logic and of the fundamental principles of thought [which are structures of domination] from which we cannot escape" (1989a, 213). This would appear to be a totalizing ethics of reason, which must be the "irrationalism" criticized by Habermas.

367. Moments 4 and 7 of figure 12. This is a criticism not only of reason (level 3 of figure 13) but equally of the purely reproductive instincts, those "of the herd" (level 1).

368. Moment 4 of figure 12.

369. Nietzsche, *Wille zur Macht*, sec. 401 (vol. 19, 281). See Müller-Lauter 1971, 66 ff.: "Nihilismus als Wille zum Nichts." Of course, this "will to noth-

ingness" is wielded against the established order of values, initially, but lastly, in the face of the will to power as such, in the final leap into the eternal return of the same (as in Schopenhauer's ontology).

370. We are at moment 9, the deconstruction of system 1 of figure 12.

371. It is because of the "experience-decision" of the "eternal return of the same" that the past loses its inevitable "having been" and that the "self" tends no longer toward a future of self-fulfillment, rooting itself instead in an instantaneous account of the "present-eternity" that returns again and that dissolves the self and its fears, memory, and the *desire for vengeance*. This is similar to the "time-now" of Benjamin, but within a completely different tradition.

372. This would be something like moment 10 of figure 12.

373. See Heidegger 1961, vol. 1, 490–91.

374. By analogy we could relate this to moments 8 and 10 of figure 12, but in reality this is something completely different. As in Schiller, Schopenhauer, Taylor, and so many others, aesthetics transcend ethics and express the supreme moment.

375. The "will to power" was a will that could establish order (*befehlen*), a will to be lord (*Herrsein-wollen*).

376. Vattimo 1989a, 320.

377. *Zur Genealogie der Moral*, vol. 1, sec. 1 (Nietzsche 1973, vol. 2, 184).

378. Ibid., vol. 2, sec. 12 (vol. 2, 223–24).

379. Nietzsche at this point is completely correct, as we see in *Critique of Practical Reason*, in the section on the "perfect good," where Kant justifies the reward of "happiness" (the interest on the capital of good works?) that a "banker" God pays to the "immortal" soul, after its death, for the "virtue" of having had an *unhappy life* on "this earth"—the worst moral of resignation that we could ever imagine.

380. Ibid., vol. 2, sec. 24 (vol. 2, 281); "Der Wille zur Wahrheit." In another sense, for Marx, the truth of capital has fetishized everything (Lukács's concept of reification). For us, as we will see in chapter 5, the "*prevailing* truth" will be transformed (falsified) into a pure mask of appearances that hide true "reality" (beyond the horizon of the system of domination), from the perspective of the "*critical* truth" of the victims, when they become conscious of their condition and how to transform it.

381. And because of this, it must be negated in order to avoid such pain, and the only way to do so is via the pessimism of the "self-negation" of that will to live, submerging itself in the "nothingness" of Nirvana, where everything is *equalized* in a state of the eternal reproduction of the same: the "death principle" as a return of the inorganic in Freud.

382. As I have already indicated, this is addressed to a certain extent in system 1 of figure 12 and levels 1 and 3 of figure 13. Such an order would be the world of "consciousness" ruled by the "reality principle" that is introjected as Freud's "super ego" (reproductive practical reason; level 3 of figure 13), while the "pleasure principle" (level 2) opens up the horizon of "That." The first would be the "world of labor" (which expels the sadistic, incestuous, erotic, aesthetic and so on of Bataille), the imprisoning, excluding world that disciplines the body (Foucault). Habermas criticizes the self-referential character of Nietzschean discourse and how Nietzsche negates modern rationality. "Reason's Other" awakens in Habermas all of his passionate anti-irrationalism, which prevents him from giving due attention to the discovery of a "new continent" of ethics:

the *materiality* of the drives (*the Will to . . .*); Habermas's is a purely formalistic and external criticism (albeit from the perspective of discursive rationality). Here my interest is in entering into the understanding and "transformation" of the logic of drives. Habermas indicates: "*Forgetfulness of the Self* and *Expulsion* of the forbidden part are the two dialectical images that until today continue to inspire all those attempts that wrest the critique of reason from the thinkers of an Enlightenment which is in itself dialectical" (Habermas 1985, 128). What Habermas is incapable of seeing is that his own formalism has fallen into an "oblivion of the material," and that because of this he cannot uncover the theme of the "exclusion" of the victims (in the invisibility of the driven pain, which falls "outside" of the horizon of pragmatic-procedural philosophy).

383. Which brings to mind the Schopenhauer of "self-suppression [*Selbstaufhebung*]" of the "will to live," now only a will "to be happy."

384. There is no rationality in the "beyond" of that order (Nietzsche thereby denies the possibility of a critical-ethical reason, level 4 of figure 13), and for this reason falls into an irrationalist nihilism. The ethics of liberation, for its part, can deny the dominating rationality of system 1 (figure 12) (and also a purely reproductive conservative instinct) of the prevailing repressive order, but in the name of critical reason (and of the instincts of creative pleasure: level 3 of figure 13), establishing a liberating transcendence where rational moments persist (material, formal, and of critical feasibility). The philosophers examined in §4.3 have only privileged the overall critique of the rational system (moment 4 of figure 12) and are divided regarding the question of the critique of diverse spheres of drives. But in the context of Nietzsche: should Dionysus organize a future institutional order? Would it not become again an order that is Apollinarian or Christian masochist in character?

385. Level 1 of figure 13.

386. Level 1 of figure 13.

387. Level 2 of figure 13.

388. For this argument see M. Bernal's three-volume work, Bernal 1989. The "fall of Egypt and the rise of Greece" was produced in England with the racism of Locke and Hume up to that of Newton (*The Chronology of Ancient Kingdoms Amended*, 1690) (Bernal, vol. 1, 191), John Potter (1697) (Bernal, vol. 1, 195 ff.), and MacPherson (1762), or in France with Anne Robert Turgot. The latter initiated the metaphysical idea of "progress," which starting from China or Egypt arrived at Plato (still a quasi-Asiatic philosopher); it was only with Aristotle that the European age of empirical science began, which then continued with Bacon, Galileo, Descartes, and Newton. This is how the "Greco-Germanic syndrome" becomes inchoate (Bernal, vol. 1, 199–200). The Semitic experience (from the Acadians to the Arabs) is more complex and *ethically relevant* in the face of the Indo-European version (especially in its Greco-Hellenistic-Roman variant). See §§I.1 and I.3 of this *Ethics*.

389. It was reorganized in 1734, as the model for the universities of its day, assisted by the king of England and elector of Hanover, George II. The Scottish romantics arrived in Germany (Bernal, vol. 1, 215). Kristophe Hermann establishes in the *Acta Philosophorum* of 1715 that "although the Egyptians cultivated many studies, they were never philosophers" (ibid., 216). For him, the Greeks were the initiators of philosophy—against all of the tradition until the eighteenth century, including Herodotus, Thucydides, Plato, Aristotle, and all of the Hellenistic, Roman, medieval, and modern tradition until that century,

which believed that Athens was a colony of Egyptian Sais, and that philosophy had originated in Egypt (ibid., 98–120). "Isocrates admired the system of castes, the rule of the philosophers and the rigor of the *paidéia* (education) of the Egyptian philosopher/priests, that produced the *aner theoretikós* (contemplative man), who employed his superior wisdom for the good of the state. The division of labor permitted leisure (*skholé*) which by the same token made possible the *skholé*, learning. Above all he insisted that *philosophia* was and could only be a product of Egypt" (ibid., 104).

390. See Dussel 1993c, chap. 1: "Eurocentrism," and the excursus of chap. 6.

391. See Jaspers 1963b, 73.

392. Nietzsche, *Jenseits von Gut und Böse*, sec. 264 (Nietzsche 1973, vol. 2, 155).

393. See Bernal 1991, vol. 1, 21 ff. He indicates that around the middle of the fifteenth century BC (a thousand years before Socrates), during the eighteenth Egyptian dynasty, the cult of Dionysus must have begun in Greece. According to Herodotus, it was the Egyptians "who taught the Greeks the mystery and cult of Dionysus" (*Historia*, vol. 2, 49; Herodotus 1954, 150; Spanish trans., 169). Outside of one or two Greek gods, the remainder have their origin in Egypt or in the Semitic world. Apollo himself has his origin in Ra, Aten, or Tm, Egypt's young or old sun-god. "Semantically, the derivation of Apollo from *Hprr* would seem very good. *Hprr* was identified with *Hrmsht*, the Greek Harmachis, Horus of the Rising Sun. Horus had been identified with Apollo" (Bernal 1991, vol. 1, 68).

394. See appendix 2 regarding Sais.

395. See Bernal 1991, vol. 1, 98.

396. See, inter alia, Boylan 1922; Breasted 1901; Butler 1981; Diop 1978; Froidefond 1971; James 1954.

397. See appendix 1 in Dussel 1993c.

398. I examined Freud in Dussel 1970–80, vol. 3 (1973), 57–121 (published separately as *Liberacion de la mujer y erótica latinoamericana: Ensayo filosófico*, Nueva América, Bogotá, 1994). See Brown 1967; Deleuze and Guattari 1972; Fromm 1969; Lacan 1966; Legendre 1974; Lorenz 1994; Marcuse 1981; Mezan 1985; Mitscherlich 1971; Ortigues and Ortigues 1973; Reich 1970; Ricoeur 1965; Rozitchner 1972; and others.

399. For Freud, the "instinct of aggression is the descendant and chief representative of the death instinct" (*Das Unbehagen in der Kultur*, ch. 6 [Freud 1969, vol. 9, 249]). See Rozitchner 1972, 198 ff. I agree with Lorenz 1994, that the instincts of aggression are not necessarily rooted in the "death principle," but that to the contrary, intraspecies aggression between animals makes sense as a stage in the development of species life (in the human being, one has to know how to manage that aggressivity in an ethical, rational, and cultural manner, since it is the natural "unfolding" of the instinct understood as one that is "*cultural*" in character).

400. *Jenseits des Lustprinzips*, ch. 5 (Freud 1969, vol. 3, 250).

401. Level 2 of figure 13.

402. Freud is aware that it is a doubtful "hypothesis" (*Jenseits des Lustprinzips*, ch. 1 [Freud 1969, 217]): "spekulativen Annahmen." Regarding this, he writes later, with honesty: "I would be happy if all of my theoretical construction were demonstrated to be in error" (ibid., ch. 6 [253]).

403. If "end [*Zweck*]" means "finality" in terms of time, it is acceptable; if it

means that which is attempted, the content itself of the drive would be absurd, contradictory, and ultimately pathological. What is attempted (as an end) in life cannot be death, or we would be living beings who were perverted by nature: *total* pathology. Such logic would lead us to conclude that the "will to death," the foundation of all pathology, would be defined as natural in human terms or "normal." Might this not be instead a characteristic that Freud detects in his patients as an expression of the pathological structure of Western Modernity?

404. Freud 1969, vol. 6, 259. We should not be surprised that in this note Schopenhauer is cited, and shortly thereafter the myth of *Atman*, from the *Brihad-Aranyaka-Upanishada*, part I, chap. 4, para. 3 (ibid., 266, n. 2).

405. I first addressed this matter in Dussel 1970–80, vol. 3 (1973), in "Erótica latinoamericana," and will not repeat here what is said there.

406. The human being . . . senses the sacrifices that civilization imposes upon him to be an intolerable weight" (*Die Zukunft einer Illusion*, ch. 1 [Freud 1969, vol. 3, 296 ff.]).

407. Especially in *Das Ich und das Es*, ch. 3 (Freud 1969, vol. 3, 296 ff.).

408. Freud, *Jenseits des Lustprinzips*, ch. 1, 219.

409. Ibid., 220.

410. Ibid.

411. Ibid., vol. 2, 222.

412. Ibid., 226.

413. Phylogenetically for humanity and ontogenetically for each individual.

414. Freud 1969, vol. 2.

415. The Brazilian concept of Paulo Freire's pedagogy, "*concientizaçao*" is fully applicable here (in a solipsistic paradigm of consciousness that is lacking its intersubjective and communitarian elements).

416. Freud 1969, vol. 2, 230.

417. Level 1 of figure 13. See this "obsession with repetition" transformed by René Girard into a compulsion of imitation or mimetic impulse (Girard 1982).

418. Level 2 of figure 13.

419. Freud 1969, vol. 2, 232.

420. Marcuse 1981, vol. 2, 50. This *surplus repression* effectively has to do with *surplus value* in the structure of the cultural repression of labor in capitalism. For its part, it will modify the mere "reality principle" with a "principle of action," which will be the historical expression of that Freudian principle. In this way, the Egyptian or Aztec-Nahuatl "reality principle" is not equivalent to its modern bourgeois expression, for example, Freud does not have sufficient *historical* consciousness regarding his own categories of thought, and it is possible that he sought to universalize certain pathologies of modern Western culture as characteristic of human beings in general (Hinkelammert 1991, 11 ff.: "The Iphigenia of the West"). For his part, Marcuse—better than Reich—carries out the dialogue between Freud and Marx. I, instead, seek to liberate Marcuse from the Schopenhauer that still prevails in Freud, returning to the Nietzschean hope, modified first from Marcuse, and then from Levinas.

421. *Jenseits des Lustprinzips* 5, 246.

422. Freud continuously speaks of this matter, returning to the Heliocentric syndrome, and citing examples from Plato and Aristotle (ibid., 266); and at 267: when he speaks of the "regressive character of the instincts"; and then again at ibid., 270. The dominating European Modernity of capitalism (and of

the crisis of the Austro-Hungarian empire) coincides in this with the dominating Hellenic slaveholding society.

423. Ibid., 246.

424. Ibid., 247.

425. Ibid.

426. Ibid., 248.

427. If this expression were taken literally it would imply total irrationality, since in this case life itself would have no meaning at all.

428. *Jenseits des Lustprinzips*, 228.

429. Ibid., 251.

430. Ibid.

431. Ibid.

432. Ibid., 6, 261.

433. Ibid., 264.

434. Ibid., 7, 271.

435. *Das Ich und das Es*, 2.

436. Ibid., 3, 296.

437. Ibid., 301.

438. Ibid., 302.

439. Ibid., 5, 319.

440. Ibid.

441. Ibid., 325.

442. See Rozitchner 1972, an incomparable work of critical Freudian reflection regarding these works, from the perspective of "peripheral" capitalism, and in particular regarding Peronist populism ("the masses, place of historical elaboration," pp. 427 ff.), which is a basis for differentiating it from a "centrist" fascism.

443. *Die Zukunft einer Illusion*, I; Freud 1969, IX, 139.

444. Ibid., 140.

445. Ibid., 141.

446. Ibid., 2, 144.

447. Ibid., 147.

448. Level 1.1 of table 10.

449. Level 1.2 of table 10.

450. *Die Unbehagen in der Kultur*, 2 (Freud 1969, vol. 9, 208).

451. Ibid., 211. If happiness is "quietude [*Ruhe*]" it could be attained in the displeasure (*ataraxia* or *apátheia*) of the Hellenist or Roman ethicists.

452. Ibid. This takes us back to the aporia of Schopenhauer or Buddha: the only way to avoid suffering is death (liberation of the pleasure instinct under the dominion of the death instinct), but like the Manichean or Buddhist monks who employ the "most energetic and radical action through a different means, those who see the only enemy *in reality itself, as the origin of all suffering [die Quelle alles Leids ist]*, render existence itself intolerable, and as a result all relations must be broken if the intention is to be happy" (ibid., 213).

453. Note here how happiness and pleasure have been identified with each other as if they were equivalent.

454. Ibid., 214–15. In any case, we will return to this "principle of impossibility" which serves as a regulatory idea that indicates a possibility that has the sense of serving as a critical-utopian horizon (see Hinkelammert 1984, chaps. 5 and 6). Freud writes: "If culture imposes such weighty sacrifices, not only

in terms of sexuality but as to aggressive tendencies . . . , we will more easily understand why it is difficult for human beings to achieve a state of happiness in such a context" (ibid., vol. 5, 243).

455. Ibid., 4, 230.

456. Ibid., 233.

457. Ibid., 8, 250.

458. Ibid., 252.

459. Ibid., 270. But, as if with apparent regret, he writes at the end of the book (and perhaps of his entire life): "We can only hope [*erwarten*] that the other of the two celestial powers, that of the eternal *Eros*, unleashes its forces in order to be victorious in the battle with no less immortal adversary. But who could predict the final result?" (ibid.).

460. See §1.1 and especially the work of Damasio 1994.

461. The Apollonian horizon is the horizon of the death instincts when the "system" closes itself up in a self-referential way. I have used the Greek expression *anánke* to refer to necessity, repetition, cultural institution (Prometheus chained).

462. See Nygren's work *Éros et agapé* (1952).

463. Level 1 of figure 13, and 1 of table 10.

464. It is curious that all of the materialist and negative critics such as Lukács, Adorno, and so many others, developed only an aesthetics but not an ethics. I think this is due to the impossibility each encountered of discovering the theme of "alterity."

465. Regarding the theme of the other before Levinas see Laín Entralgo 1961; Theunissen 1965; Loewith 1969. Also see some recent work on Levinas by such authors as Bauman 1994, 47 ff.; Cohen 1994; Critchley 1992; Gibbs 1992; Olivetti 1992, chap. 4; and Taylor 1989, 185 ff.

466. In 1972, at Louvain, I brought together a group of students to dialogue with Levinas, and posed the following question to him: "And the fifteen million indigenous people killed in the conquest of Latin America, and the thirteen million enslaved Africans, are they also *the Other* of which you speak?" Levinas looked hard at me and said: "You must think about that." This is why I continued developing the philosophy of liberation that I had already begun to undertake. In this encounter, at the end, he revealed to us: "I look at all of you as if you were *hostages*." I did not understand what he was trying to say. A short time later, while reading the work that I have cited here, I understood his meaning: we, as young professors or students in Europe, obsessed by our Latin American victims, were perceived by Levinas to be hostages in the stead of our distant and oppressed peoples. I had thought that his statement might be an insult. Upon reading *Autrement qu'être* I understood that his had been an immense, unmerited judgment, brimming with hope.

467. Levinas 1974, v.

468. Levinas 1968b, 34. This is precisely level 2b of table 10.

469. In my work (Dussel 1970–80, vol. 3 [1973]) I called this the "alterity drive" or "love of justice" to the Other as an other, in the sense of an *ágape* beyond *éros*.

470. In this sense, for Levinas, the instincts of self-preservation and even those of pleasure constitute the I (*moi*) in its "egoism," as a "Totality" (all of the dimensions of table 10, from 1 to 2, excluding only 2b, which as a "window" opens up other ethical perspectives).

471. Level 2.2 of table 10. "To the subject who returns to himself, who according to the Stoic formula is characterized by *hormé* or the tendency to protect himself in his being [*connatus essendi*] . . . , we oppose Desire [*Désir*] to the Other who proceeds from a self that is already satisfied and that, in that sense, is independent and has no desire for his own self. Necessity [*besoin*] of he who has no needs [*besoins*]" (in Levinas 1964, 143). Levinas thus situates himself in the place that I have denominated as that of the "hostage," a satisfied member of the system who nonetheless receives the impact of the interpellation by the victims (moment 6 of figure 12), but is not exactly in the place of "the victim" (who is "the Other") of figure 14.

472. Levinas 1968b, 3–4: "Desire of the Invisible."

473. Once again, this is the difference between levels 2a and 2b of table 10.

474. Levinas 1968b, 233.

475. This is an "exit [*Ausgang*]" that is very different than that of the Kantian "exit" from the Enlightenment definition. This is not *solely a* matter of going beyond a precritical intellectual state of "self-referential guilty immaturity," but of an "exit" from the intramundane egoistic irresponsibility of the insignificance or neglect of the Other—for having "habitually" rejected their interpellation (level 6 of figure 14). See Levinas 1935 (*De l'évasion*), an early work by Levinas.

476. This is the *conatus esse conservandi* of Spinoza.

477. Consider that in the case of Nietzsche we are dealing with a notion of "happiness" as a state to be transcended, in this case by "pleasure [*Lust*]" (for Levinas, "narcissistic" and insufficient), and in Levinas by "Desire [*Désir*]" (non-erotic pleasure which is not narcissistic but instead transcendental: "for-the-Other [*pour l'Autre*]").

478. Levinas 1972, chap. 7, 45, 55.

479. Levinas 1968b, 34. This "unhappiness" is an ironic expression: he or she who is "called" to assume responsibility for the Other is propelled out of their quietude, peace, security . . . and plunged into the risky adventure (beyond the search for his or her own happiness) of the struggle for justice, "on behalf of the Other." Justice toward "the poor, the widow, and the orphan" that would be unthinkable for Nietzsche from his will for power. In Levinas, this would be "desire" (instead of a "will") for alterity.

480. "Le Même" is Totality, the Luhmannian system, the Heideggerian "world."

481. This would be Horkheimer's "traditional theory."

482. Moment 4 of figure 14. This is the same position of *Kritik* in Marx, Horkheimer, and the others named here.

483. Now perhaps it can be understood why I have described Marx's *Capital* as an "ethics": because it is a *criticism* of political economics (see Dussel 1988, all of chap. 14).

484. Levinas 1968b, 13. For the difference between "ontology" (Totality) and "metaphysics" (ethics, exteriority, the Other) see Dussel 1977, sec. 2.4.9.

485. Contrary to Nietzsche, discretely, Levinas writes: "Ontology as the first philosophy is a philosophy of power *(pouissance)*. It culminates in the State . . . . Universality is presented as something impersonal" (ibid., 16). "Heidegger, like all of Western history, conceives of the relation with the Other as playing itself out in the destiny of *sedentary* peoples, possessors and builders of the Earth. . . . The philosophy of power [*pouvoir*], the ontology, as the first philosophy does

not question the Same; it is a philosophy of injustice" (ibid., 17). In my work *El humanismo semita* (Semitic humanism) (Dussel 1969) I criticize this Indo-European "sedentary" tendency (see also *El humanismo helénico* [Dussel 1975]) from the perspective of the "nomadism" of the Bedouin and shepherds of the Arab desert. See in this *Ethics*, §I.1.

486. For these stages, see Costa 1996.

487. Levinas 1930.

488. Husserl 1966.

489. For example, Husserl writes (1966, 76): "I perceive the others (I perceive them as really existent) in a series of experiences that are at the same time variable and convergent." See Dussel 1970–80, vol. 1, 117, where I wrote that for Husserl "the Other as a transcendental *ego* is illusory, unreal, hypothetical."

490. Levinas 1947, 12. In Latin America we understand the point Levinas is making. In my *Philosophy of Liberation* I seek to undertake such clarifications.

491. Ibid., 59–61.

492. Ibid., 115 ff.

493. Ibid., 153–54. In the section "Time and the Other" (159 ff.) his future themes can already be found: "With the Other and in the Face of the Other" (161).

494. See Levinas 1983.

495. This is a Kirkegaardian theme, without a doubt.

496. Levinas 1983, 77.

497. Levinas 1967, 167 ff., in "L'idée d'Infini."

498. This "pre" who is so Levinasian attempts to place himself "before" and "below" the "world [*Welt*]" of *Sein und Zeit* (especially secs. 12–24, but also the criticism of "Being-with," sec. 26; in Heidegger 1963c, 52–114 and 117–25), but also that of the *Wissenschaft der Logik* of Hegel (especially vol. 2, chap. 2, 2: "Die erscheinende und die an sich seiende Welt" in Hegel 1971, vol. 6, 156 ff.). In the same manner, the "metaphysical" or "ethical" is the pre- and the post-ontological, in a postmetaphysical critical sense. In my first *Ethics* (Dussel 1970–80, vol. 3 [1973], 1–2), I situated myself predominantly in the "beyond [*Jenseits*]" and "after" the world; Marcio Costa (1996) very effectively demonstrates this "pre-," "before." Heidegger speaks of the "*vor-ontologisch*," but this "vor-" is simply the "everyday," the "factual," before asking oneself explicitly. Here instead is a "pre-" prior to the mere ontological everyday sense of the cognitive or "intentional" position of knowledge, as a "factual comprehension of being." "Before" the "comprehension [*verstehen*]" — a moment which is gnoseological in the ultimate sense — *there is [il y a]* a vulnerable corporeality, with a *Desire [Désir] already [déja]* constituted as a sensibility.

499. This is the theme of *materiality* in Marx and of the first Frankfurt school, set forth in works such as those of Damasio (1994), regarding emotions from a neurological point of view.

500. Levinas 1968b, 175.

501. Levinas 1961, 90 ff.

502. Ibid., 94 ff.: "Pleasure and representation."

503. Ibid., 118.

504. Ibid., 158 ff.

505. Ibid., 169.

506. Ibid., 183. It is through the "re-cognition of the Other" that the word is received (and also the argumentation): it is the preoriginary reasoning.

507. Such as the "will to power" of Nietzsche.

508. Levinas 1961, 190. This has to do with moment 6 of figure 14: the "interpellation" of the Other, but in the form of the victim, the poor, the oppressed, not as the Nietzschean "lord." "I am obligated" is the deontological moment of the normative statements with reference to the victims.

509. Ibid., 194. We are the "origin" of practical reason when it is obligated to argue seriously and in symmetry.

510. Ibid., 284.

511. In the essays "The Imprint of the Other," "Enigma and Phenomenon," and "Language and Proximity" (in Levinas 1967, 186 ff.).

512. "Le trace de l'Autre," in ibid., 196.

513. "Langage et proximité," in ibid., 233 ff.

514. The theme of the "ransom" or the "payment to free a prisoner of war," that is to say the "redemption" treated at length by Rosenzweig in vol. 2, book 3, of *The Star of Redemption* (Rosenzweig 1921, vol. 2, 152ff). A "hostage" or "prisoner" who is persecuted can offer him- or herself up to "redeem" a victim. In this case, the "just innocent" fulfills a "substitution" for the Other. I believe that this scenario is what Levinas has in mind (represented in figure 14). See the comparison with Rosenzweig in Cohen 1994 and Gibbs 1992.

515. I believe that Levinas's experience as a "prisoner" in a concentration camp is a clear "situation of reference." There, in the Nazi death camp, he was a hostage for his persecuted people, feeling conscious of guilt because he was a survivor. Obsessed by his fellow victims, he renders testimony with his critical-ethical philosophy, within the prevailing system, the evil of Being when it is closed off to the Other. This scenario must be kept in mind when we undertake the complete reading of *Autrement qu'être*. The matter of the hostage's internalization of the experience of bearing his or her process of substitution for the persecuted Other (the "many [*rabim*]") is represented in dramatic form in the four poems of the "Servant of Yahvé [*hebed yaveh*]" (Isaiah 42:1–53, 12), which coincidentally I wrote about in a student commentary in Paris (it can be found in an appendix to Dussel 1969, 127–70). I wrote then: "*The Servant* finds himself before a court in the situation of the *kidnapped object of a ransom*, in favor of the multitude (Isaiah 53:5–10; Psalms 143:2; Job 9:2; Genesis 15:6)" (ibid., 142). I explained that there were two polar extremes in this situation: "*My people [ámi]*, forgiven, the objects of mercy; *the multitude*, the indeterminate, that could be the objects of pardon. My people are a portion of the multitude who have been saved; the multitude is the symbol of all humanity—present or future—that *could be my people*" (ibid., 142). We will explore later in this book in greater detail how this diachronicity that flows from the "multitude" (a mere social bloc in contradiction with the established order; the community of victims) until we get to the "people" (a historical subject; the critical victims who have become conscious of their situation). The ethical question analyzed by Levinas has to do with the meaning and interpretation of Hebrew words such as *ga'ol* (translated in the seventies into Greek as *lu'tra*; in *Leviticus* 25:24–26) or *ge'ulah* (the price of the ransom for a piece of land); *padoh* (the freedom of a slave obtained by purchase); *peduím* (price of the purchase of a slave so that they could be freed) or *pidión* (the freedom of a slave); or even *hatsalah* (to save or liberate), from whence comes: "I have come down to free you [*lehatsiló*] from the power of the Egyptians," Exodus 3:8).

516. The "Third" is an observer: "The Third is other than the neighbor. . . . It

is important to find all the forms from the point of departure where the being, the totality, the state, politics, techniques, labor, are constituted in each moment *as their own centers of gravity*, and count as their only reference" (Levinas 1974, 200–203). Regarding the concept of "ransom (*nhl* in Hebrew)" or to "rescue" or "free" the prisoner of war or the slave (*pdh* in Hebrew, for example as in Leviticus 25:24–26 and 51–52). To redeem (redemption) is to "pay ransom" (the "money of the ransom [*Lösegeld*]"), which means to buy the freedom of the slave, free him or her, to save the victim. In Greek it was translated by the wisemen of Elefantina as *apolytrosis*.

517. This re-sponsibility, from *spondere*: "to take charge of" (in Latin) the Other, is prior to any decision. The responsibility of Hans Jonas (1982a) is the a posteriori responsibility for planetary life. Here instead the issue is of an a priori re-sponsibility, since we are situated in fact as if "we were in charge" of the victim who confronts us unexpectedly (someone begging for alms, or who lies injured on the road, a street child who cleans our car, a victim of repression, a woman punished by violence, a student unjustly treated by a teacher, etc.), and whose accusatory presence we cannot "shake off," and which triggers our obligation to "do something" for them. *Later* I can reflect regarding the matter, turn around and forget myself, or do something real for that victim: these intentional decisions or acts are a posteriori. Regarding responsibility, see Levinas 1974, 17, 18, 32, 60, 86, 112, and so on.

518. Here there is a veiled critical reference to Schopenhauer's *principium individuationis*. "We describe the being who has been conditioned in such a way that without being the cause in itself is the first factor with relationship to the cause as having a will. Psychism is his range of possibility. Psychism is developed as a form of sensibility, an element of pleasure [*jouissance* in French, *gozo* in Spanish], as a kind of egotism. In the egotism of pleasure [levels from 1 through 2a in table 10] the *ego* appears, as does the *will*. It is psychism and not material reality, which bears with it the origin of individuation. . . . Sensibility [*sensibilité*] is the very egotism of the Ego [*moi*]" (Levinas 1968b, 30).

519. In this case as a "re-flection" regarding itself.

520. The "one" is myself, but negated to the extent I am persecuted; looked for by first name and last in order to be eliminated (this was experienced by Levinas in Hitler's Germany and by so many of us during the Latin American dictatorships following the strategy that evolved from Henry Kissinger to George Bush).

521. Levinas 1974, 142–43. It is evident that the extremely rich subject matter of Levinas's ethics cannot even be indicated in these few pages, given their focus on developing our overall argument in this book.

522. Ibid., 64.

523. Ibid. Here Levinas touches that which cannot be said, and marks the moment of all "critical" thought—coinciding here with Marx, Horkheimer, Freud; see in ibid. 81, 93, and so on. It is interesting that, as in the Nietzschean "pleasure instinct," if the *desire* for the Other does not "bear the risk [*risque*], pain loses its own suffering" (ibid.).

524. See ibid., 17, 77.

525. See ibid., 78 ff.

526. But as that which is "affectable," as the recipient of the effect of a blow that causes a trauma in its physical corporeality (a "corporal state" in Damasio's words [1994]). See Levinas 1974, 83, 87, and so on.

527. See ibid., 86 ff.

528. See ibid., 4, 69, 91, 94, 100, 151, 163, and so on.

529. See ibid., 61, 63, and so on.

530. Ibid., 108–9.

531. Ibid., 112.

532. This is all the historical non-intentionality of the construction of the social structures that produce the system—and its victims.

533. This *en dejà* is a preontological meta-physical category; see ibid., 65–69, 95, 107, 117, 137, 148, and so on.

534. An opinion that is speaking of the extreme experience of the finitude of the human being as a living and suffering corporeality.

535. Levinas 1974, 117. Here, once again, he evidences his logic regarding Spinoza, Schopenhauer, and Nietzsche. In the "psycheism" of such sensibilities, it is egotism of the security in the reproduction of life which reigns (levels 1 and 2a of table 10); Levinas situates himself *as well* at level 2b (a *metaphysical desire*, which is not narcissistic).

536. See this theme in ibid., 16, 67, 69, and so on.

537. This category of *ana-arkhós* is in the *en decà*, as the "beyond within" of the being and of the world, the preontological.

538. Levinas 1974, 189.

539. Levinas is addressing *ordre* here, but not of "order" in a systemic sense, but in the sense of giving an "order" or the issuance of a "mandate."

540. The use of this *philosophical* category of Levinas in my first *Ethics* (see Dussel 1970–80, vol. 2 [1972]), elicited strong criticisms from those who misunderstood the heart of this matter (see Cerutti 1983 and Schutte 1993; the former criticizes the supposed "leap of faith" in these categorizations; the second repeats the same argument and adds others, such as indicating that "difference" is denied in my formulation, thus failing to understand that for Levinas the Other is not a mere "difference" in the "identity" in the Hegelian sense; and this is why I denominate as "distinction" the diversity of the Other with respect to intrasystemic "differences." I believe that in both cases the criticism is due to a hurried reading of Levinas's work as well as my own).

541. Levinas 1974, 190–92.

542. Ibid., 126. Is this an irrationalism? No, not if it is understood that the world of affectivity, corporeality, the materiality of the drives, "the enjoyment of life in itself while loving life [*complaisance en soi de la vie amant la vie*]" (ibid., 81) does not in any way negate reason as such, but instead marks out its limits: Not everything is rational, Levinas tells us, and he is "correct"—at least from the standpoint of an ethics of liberation, which implies the liberation of "victims," and not of those who are "satisfied." Heideggerian ontology, traditional phenomenology, the linguistic logics of sense and signification and even of intersubjective validity, and so on, are all philosophies of the "satisfied"— whose satisfaction is the undisclosed "point of departure" which is taken as a "reality" in itself and without question. To confront oneself with the "unsatisfied" (the victims, the poor, women afflicted by violence and abuse, and others) is to begin to ask oneself about this whole dimension that Levinas opens up *in a different manner* than Marx, Horkheimer, Freud, and their like, but in accordance with them at a much deeper level.

543. See ibid., 20, 96, 164, 165, 191, 200 ff.

544. "Justice cannot be justice but in a society where there is no distinction between those who are close by and those who are distant, but in which it is also impossible to take the part of those who are closest to us; in which the equality of all is measured by my inequality, and by the greater of my duties over and above my rights. The oblivion of one's self is what motivates justice. This is why it does not cease to be important to know whether the egalitarian and just state in which man develops his potential . . . has its origin in a war of all against all or from the irreducible responsibility of *one* for all and if this can be dispensed from friendship and from the face" (ibid., 203).

545. From the "communication" that has its origin in the "speech [*Decir*]" of the very same corporeal sensibility, which now develops as that "which has been said [*le dit*]," or language itself. Contrary to Apel or Habermas, communication is a second, not a primary, moment in this approach.

546. Levinas 1974, 205.

547. Ibid. As can be observed, Levinas dares here to invert twenty-five centuries of philosophy: philosophy should not be "the love of wisdom," but instead a "sophofilia": "the wisdom of love." It is love that moves all of the structures of carnality, sensibility, pain, and responsibility for the pain of the victim, and it is only from there that the "construction" (because there can be no "re-" construction of that which is *new*), of a new order (system 2 of figure 12) can proceed, as we will explore in chapters 5 and 6.

548. "But the question of the discernment of the meaning or significance, as a modality of the proximity, the justice, the society, and the truth that they demand, cannot be taken for being an anonymous law" (ibid., 205–6). The (ancient) "nontruth" of the system is clearly indicated to the extent that it is reconnected to the victim. For its own, the new "truth" is now possible as a fulfillment of the "signification" of one's responsibility for the Other.

549. This Levinasian "diachronicity" is understandable now in the context of critical thought, since the preceding character of sensibility and of the victim, *before*, opens up the sphere of rationality, *afterward*, through the assumption of the burden of responsibility.

550. See Levinas 1974, 210–18. The magnificent description of why skepticism is as old as philosophy, which permits us to see the nonrationalist affirmation *of reason* by Levinas, will serve as the basis in a future work where I will attempt to set forth the "foundation" for the ethics of liberation; a "foundation," that in Levinas's terms, would be reduced to ashes in order to rise up again in the ethical diachronicity of the struggle on behalf of the victims. Note statements of his such as this: "Language is already a form of skepticism. Is it not true that the coherent discourse that is entirely absorbed in that Which is Said is indebted for its very coherency to the State which violently excludes its subversive discourse? . . . The interlocutor who is not bound to *logic* is threatened with imprisonment or with being locked in an asylum where it has to bear the prestige of the teacher or the doctor's medication: in either case it is the violence or reason of the State that assures a universal dimension to logical rationalism and a submissive matter to the law. . . . This serves to remind us of the political character—in the broadest sense of the term—of all *logical rationalism*, of the alliance of logic with politics" (ibid., 216–17). Many "logical rationalists" were and are surprised, about how it could have been that it was precisely this philosophical current that blossomed during the recent period of

military dictatorships in Latin America, while it was the critical philosophers who were expelled from the universities (and even murdered). This is a history that must still be written!

551. Ibid., 210.

552. It would have been necessary to formulate several questions for Levinas. The first regards this matter of situating oneself in the place of the hostage, and less so in the place of the victim. The second, already noted by Rosenzweig, has to do with the critical point within Jewish tradition since the destruction of the temple of Jerusalem (a level that we have already considered in the context of Adorno or Benjamin): a weak philosophy of history, where it would seem as if the "just innocent" suffers passively without the possibility of transforming history itself. He is "the chosen one" who lives through Messianic eternity without respite and without escape: a people of Israel without a state (since Titus in AD 70 until 1948). What is Buber's or Levinas's position in the face of this? Situating ourselves at the end of the twentieth century: how do we judge the Intifada? Are not the poor, the foreigners, the strangers, those who are Other than the Totality, the Same, the terror of dogmatic ontology? On the other hand, is it possible for the "just innocent," the hostage, to begin to undertake a strategy of liberation (with instrumental and strategic reason, and with a critical and utopian reason in the manner of Bloch), like an Egyptian Moses leading his victimized people toward the new Promised Land? Why must the Messiah be only a sufferer (like the "suffering Servant" of Isaiah; see my essay "Universalismo y misión en los poemas del Siervo de Yahveh" in *Ciencia y Fé* [Buenos Aires], 4 [1964]: 419–63, reprinted in the appendix to Dussel 1969, 127–70), and not an architect of liberation and organizer of a new state "beyond the banks of the River Jordan"? Levinas is *necessary* in order to demonstrate the ultimate content of a material, positive ethics (the access to the carnality of the Other), which is also negative (critical) and inherent to the discourse of an ethics of liberation (moments 6 and 7 of figure 12), but he is also *insufficient* for that larger purpose.

553. See Honneth 1992. This subject was sketched out in [105].

554. System 1 of figure 12.

555. This is Levinas's *Ecce Homo*, in terms of the exposition of a vulnerable and painful corporeality.

556. The "moments" referred to in this chapter are in figure 12.

557. See levels 1 of figure 13 and table 10, respectively.

558. See thesis 17 in appendix 1.

559. I cannot reiterate here what I wrote prior to the dialogue with Apel (Dussel 1993a, sec. 1; 1994c, sec. 2.3; and 1995b, sec. 1, 116–19, etc.).

560. Mere "practical-material" reason crystallizes human life as a criterion of truth; "ethical-originary" reason is its unfolding, as the disclosure of a moment in which life becomes an ethical subject; the Other *as an equal* (studied in §§1.5 and 2.5); now "ethical *pre*-originary reason" with Levinas, is the same practical reason which "re-cognizes" the Other *not* "as an equal" *but rather* "as another"; in this sense the Other arises *before* (pre) the origin of the future system (system 2 of figure 12).

561. See Williams 1992.

562. Practical-material reason situates ethical-preoriginary reasoning.

563. See thesis 17 in appendix 1 to this *Ethics*.

564. Moment 5 of figure 12.

565. Moment 6a of figure 12.

566. We always speak of norms, acts, microstructures, institutions, or formal or material systems of ethics, and so on. In general, these "mediations" are *formal instrumental systems* in the ultimate sense (capital as criticized by Marx, the system analyzed by Luhmann, Levinas's Totality), which successfully reproduce themselves but kill the victims. The victims are those human beings who are unintentionally eliminated by such instrumental systems.

567. See Popper 1973.

568. Such "un-intentionality" not only confirms the correctness of Weber's ethics of responsibility, or of the discovery of "nonintentional" actions in Adam Smith's market, but of Marx's analysis of capital in *Capital*, the introjection of the super ego in Freud, and so on. This is the "Totality" of Levinas (system 1 of figure 12).

569. The clarity of the young Marx is astonishing with regard to glimpsing this "inversion." In a well-known article, during his petty-bourgeois period, when he was in fact critical of what was then known as communism, "The Law on Thefts of Wood" (from "The Debates of the IVth Renan Diet," in Marx 1956–90, vol. 1, 109 ff.) we can already see his first ethical-material intuitions: "In these customs *of the poor* there is therefore a palpable, instinctive juridical sentiment." He goes on to say: "A human being, a *living member of the community*, through whose veins runs its very blood." "The functions attributed to those who have being brutal as their mission, not only contradict the objective of protection, but also contradict that which refers to these *persons*." The only thing that has "absolute value [*absolute Wert*]" (ibid.) is firewood or jack-rabbits (the *means* that the peasants should not take possession of), and, unknowingly referring to one of Bartolomé de las Casas's texts, Marx writes the following with a clear critical-ethical consciousness, demonstrating the "inversion [*Kehre*]" of which I have spoken: "Cuba's indigenous people perceived that gold was the *fetish* of the Spaniards. They celebrated a feast in its honor . . . and later they flung it into the sea. If these indigenous people had attended these sessions of the Renan Diet, those savages might have seen the *fetish* of the deputies in the *firewood*. But during additional sessions of the Renan Diet they would have learned that *fetishism* brings with it a cult of the wild beast and would have flung the *jack-rabbits* into the sea in order to save *the men*." I commented on this in Dussel 1993b. But for the purpose of this *Ethics* it is worth highlighting that Marx specifically analyzes such "inversion": human beings (whose dignity is the point of departure for judging ends and values) are taken for things, and things (firewood, jack-rabbits, *means*) *as ends*. This is a criticism of Weberian instrumental reason, long before its time. It is a critical-ethical judgment of the norms, laws, actions, instruments, and system of ethics at issue (that of capitalism itself), wherein a critical-ethical criterion and principle is *explicitly* defined: the *affirmation* of mediations as the originary *negation* of the human "person," that is to say of the Kantian principle ("a person is an end"), which is applied critically (something Kant was not able to do because he had lost sight of the material horizon), and in a transsystemic and material-economic manner.

570. In the unavoidable sense indicated by Levinas, but also if we consider all of the necessary mediations, since every human being is also a moment within the complex structures of humanity in its process of development, and cannot declare him- or herself *completely* innocent of anything that befalls any

other human being. There is always some other kind of complicity (direct, indirect, conscious, or nonintentional) that implicates us with the negativity of the Other. It is a sign of "intelligence" or critical reason to know how to uncover this articulation.

571. This criterion is completely different from that of Hegel.

572. "Thou shalt not lie, Thou shalt not cease to work, Thou shalt not steal." See above [11].

573. See Wellmer 1986, chap. 1: "The Kantian Program."

574. See Hinkelammert's critique (1984, chap. 1).

575. Marx 1956–90, vol. 3, 535.

576. Moments 5 through 10 indicate the steps necessary for such a transformation (figure 12).

577. It is known that "Moses" must not have been a "Hebrew" or *apiru*, but instead a mythical Egyptian name within a hermeneutical account or explanatory narrative (Gottwald 1981, 35 ff.).

578. From a strictly philosophical point of view, the expression "Father, forgive them, for they know not what they do" (Luke 23:34), is presented as a statement that is critical of ideology and fetishism: those simple soldiers (as mediations for those responsible, who did not ask for forgiveness) *did not have a clear consciousness* of the *praxis* that they were carrying out into fulfillment. They did not know that they were torturing and killing someone who had been persecuted, and who was a hostage to the system (that of the Romans or that of the complicity of the Jewish elite and of the temple), and who had risen up critically on behalf of the poor and miserable oppressed people among the Jewish population. That "witness" from Galilee was a kind of Zarathustra, not as an expression of a narcissistic drive, but rather in terms of an alternative drive very superior to that imagined by Nietzsche, along a creative line of affirmation, and against a "law" that was "for man, and not man for the law"—the fundamental principle of radical social transformation. I have explored these themes in some depth in my work *Las metáforas teológicas de Marx* (Dussel 1993b).

579. The so-called Liberation Theology has interpreted Christ in a manner that does not contradict the transformative and liberatory drive of the victims, as a cultural phenomenon, and on a metaphorical plane that has its origin in Latin America and which did not exist in Nietzsche's time. "Christ as Liberator" is the "Anti-Christ" that Nietzsche pretended to be. Perhaps today Nietzsche would have been able to liberate himself from his vision of the masochistic and castrating Christ that had its origin in a certain variant of Lutheranism (and Catholicism) that he inherited from his father's native Germany.

Chapter 5. Antihegemonic Validity

1. Note again here the presence of "re-sponsibility," which is formulated in negative terms.

2. This is the "substitution" that Levinas discusses in his work.

3. The "alterity drive" or the "metaphysical desire" does not hesitate in facing pain. It relativizes one's own happiness and the conservation of one's own life and one's reproductive capacities.

4. This is the ethical and intersubjective pedagogical level of a life committed to saving the Other.

5. This is the negative judgment of the system (moment 4 of figure 12). The negation of the victim makes evident the ethical negation of the system.

6. "Struggle" takes the form here of "transformative praxis" and not only of a "struggle" for re-cognition. "Struggle" is the praxis of liberation.

7. Rigoberta Menchú introduces here the emergence of a "sociohistorical subject," a topic that will be discussed in more detail in chapter 6 and in future works. Menchú's declared "conviction" lies on her capacity to lean on or trust the liberating "subject."

8. It is not a *theory* like others. It is a practical theory that has come into being out of a praxis and that is intrinsically linked to that praxis. In short, it is a theory of liberation, precisely in the sense in which I am attempting to describe it in this work. The quotation in the text is from the testimony of Rigoberta Menchú, winner of the Nobel Peace Prize in 1992, as it appears in the account of Elizabeth Burgos, *Me llamo Rigoberta Menchú y así me nació la conciencia* (Menchú 1984, 246). [Translator note: The literal translation of this text is "My name is Rigoberta Menchú, and this is the way my conscience was born." The title of this narrative anticipates many of the themes that Dussel discusses throughout the chapter. That is the reason why he decided to include it in this note. The title of the English translation, *I, Rigoberta Menchú: An Indian Woman in Guatemala*, does not convey the issues that Dussel is interested in highlighting.]

9. The idea of the survival of the real community of communication brings up the issue of the reproduction and development of the participants' life. The examination of this theme was carried out in chapter 1. For discourse ethics, the question of survival is treated in terms of ontological conditions or presuppositions alone (the a priori *Leib*, and not in ethical terms). Discourse ethics has not been able to conceive life in terms of a universal ethical and material principle.

10. The authority of the father over his sons or daughters clearly implicated and affected the mother. However, she remained invisible as a subject with rights.

11. See my essay "The Reason of the Other: The *Interpellation* as Speech Act," in Fornet-Betancourt 1992, 106 ff.: "The Exteriority and the Real Communication Community" (Dussel 1993a, 42–48).

12. From an ontological point of view, it would seem that every possibility for critique is grounded on the material discussed in the first three chapters of this work. However, as both Marx and Levinas clearly saw, the *critical* moment (chapters 4–6 of this work) is itself on the base, serving as ground for and as origin of the future system (system 2 of figure 12). It is its pre-sub-position. Such a *future* system is any *present* system, which at one point in the past came into being by virtue of the alterity drive and by critical-liberating reason. Responsibility for the victims of a *past* system stands at the *origin* of the *present* reality. Both the alterity drive and critical reason (exercised in regards to the material, the formal, and the feasible) brought into existence the *present* institutional order. Chapter 4 describes the origin of all the existing social orders.

13. Slavery conceals the ethical subjectivity of the "slave" and, since the recognition of someone as an "ethical subject" is a prerequisite to considering that someone an "affected," it portrays the slave as an *unaffected-excluded*. Re-

cognizing the "slave" as an "ethical subject" is thus the "*radical* point of departure" for any possible discussion with the *former* slave or *new* Other who is now re-cognized as a "participant." Hegel treated the theme of intersubjectivity, and even that of the slave. See Honneth 1992 and Williams 1992. The first examines the issue in Fichte's work (27–71), and, chronologically, in all of Hegel's (73 ff.), while the latter also discusses Marx's position (230 ff.). But neither Hegel nor his commentators discover the "re-cognition" of the victim as a "re-sponsibility-for-the-Other" that is previous to any decision and that serves as a *critical* "point of departure" from the *exteriority* of the dominating system. The victim gains a critical mode of self-consciousness out of its material negativity and not out of the dominator's consciousness. Pain, as the vulnerability of "sensibility," is at the origin of the process. The "re-cognition of the Other" *as other* than the actual system of rights is the radical question.

14. If, in addition to the limits of "direct" applicability, one also considers that any application is "partial" and that it cannot proceed at all in abnormal situations of asymmetry where there are no rights, or where there is war, revolution, or intolerable social differences, it becomes clear that the fundamental moral norms can *never* be applied. This is what I mean by the "inapplicability [*Nichtanwendbarkeit*]" of discourse ethics' formal morality. How would it be possible to reach symmetry in a condition where one recognizes its inexistence, and thus, the impossibility of applying the basic moral principle? This situation of inapplicability is partly superseded by the solution provided in this chapter: the asymmetric victims promote the symmetry by critical intersubjectivity. This contribution shows the importance of liberation ethics.

15. "Natural right and practical reason," in Wellmer 1991, 29. Apel himself recognizes that "under finite conditions, the principle of moral development can never [*niemals*] attain—to the extent that it is a principle that implies a historically responsible application of ethics—moral reality, since it is not possible to endow *all human beings* with a new rational beginning upon the basis of the ideal validity of a discursive principle" (Apel 1988, 465).

16. The symmetry here in question is finite and only exists in reference to what becomes "conscious" for critical reason. The Bolivian miner who fights against his boss creates symmetry in the syndicate while at the same time dominates his partner, Domitila, when he comes back home: "Because, with such a small wage, the woman has to do much more in the home. And really that's unpaid work that we're doing for the boss, isn't it?" (Barrios de Churunga 1979, 34).

17. Scannone 1990, 88–89.

18. Ibid., III ff.

19. Ibid., 23 ff. Scannone draws from Rodolfo Kusch's works for his formulation of the problem. Among them I would like to highlight here *El pensamiento indígena americano* (Kusch 1970), where one can appreciate Kusch's philosophical anthropological approach. This becomes clear when, for instance, Kusch states: "In a situation like this we invoke *reason* and it leads us to the hydraulic bomb. What does the Indian grandfather invoke? It is surely not reason" (1970, 44). There is not a differentiation of types of rationality here; "reason" is instrumental, urban, middle-class, European. There is never a reference to capitalism. See in this line Carlos Cullen, *Reflexiones sobre América* (Cullen 1986–87). Even though it follows a Sartrean conception of the Other, which was superseded later by that of Levinas, and it never takes the perspective of the Indian,

Luis Villoro's *Los grandes momentos del indigenismo en México* (Villoro 1950) could also be taken as another example of this perspective. Here "the indigenous element [will only count] as a hidden principle of Myself" (225 ff.), the mestizo self.

20. Scannone 1990, 17.

21. I do not want to discard the value of the attempt to affirm popular Amerindian wisdom or later popular wisdom. This is a necessary task. I myself have contributed to it for many years ever since my *El catolicismo popular en Argentina*, vol. 4, *Antropológico* (coauthored with Ciro R. Lafón) (Bonum, Buenos Aires, 1969), 193–242, and *El catolicismo popular en Argentina*, vol. 5, *Histórico* (Bonum, Buenos Aires, 1970). Also in that time I wrote "Hipótesis para el estudio de Latinoamérica en la historia universal" (Dussel 1966), the fundamental theses of which appeared in "Cultura, cultural popular latinoamericana y cultura nacional," *Cuyo* (Mendoza) 4 (1968): 7–40. See also my "Hipótesis para el estudio de la cultura latinoamericana," in *América Latina y conciencia cristiana* (IPLA, Quito, 1970), 63–79.

22. See Habermas 1991, 90 ff. and 176–85. Even though he intends to supersede the issue of liberation, Scannone seems to have forgotten it. He takes popular forms of life and customs as *the eminent*, and forgets the oppressions, alienations, and exclusions suffered by the victims.

23. Menchú 1984. The Spanish term "conciencia" means both *Bewusstein* and *Gewissen* in German. Likewise, the Brazilian neologism *concientizaçao* refers to the "process of becoming" of a *theoretical* consciousness (*Bewusstein*), and to an *ethical* consciousness of responsibility (*Gewissen*) that takes place in a *critical* level. Semantically, this neologism gives exact expression to the "*conscientization*" (*Bewusstein-Gewissen werden*) that is implicit in the liberation process that is furthered by the affected, the oppressed, and the excluded.

24. Menchú 1984, 117.

25. Moments 4 and 5 of figure 12 come rapidly together. The protest against the system ("heaping insult on the rich") is moment 4.

26. Moment 3 of figure 12.

27. Observe here the extreme precision of this critical realism: truth is reality ("to understand what was real"), and the opposite is "false." See in connection with this theme §§2.5, 3.1, and 3.2.

28. Even in misery and pain, re-cognizing and taking "responsibility-for-the-Other" adds pain to the pain. In addition to hunger, unsafe conditions, and nomadism, there is now also persecution. This occurs when Menchú becomes a "hostage" of the soldiers by "substituting" herself for the pain of her people. For Benjamin, Rosenzweig, or Levinas she is a "messiah."

29. In this way one passes from an "ingenuous" level of consciousness to the state of inquiry that is characteristic of a *critical*-theoretical consciousness attributable to the "application" of "causes"; this is the first instance located at the level of the horizon of the political activist (which is not explicitly that of the scientist, philosopher, expert, etc.). One passes from a naive consciousness to the question of a critical-theoretical consciousness through the "application" of the "causes"; it is the first instance and at the level of the horizon of militance (which does not explicitly belong to science, philosophy, the expert, etc.).

30. Note the double question: oppression (exploitation) and exclusion (rejection).

31. Denied "participation."

32. One would have to ask this to Locke, Kant, Hegel, Habermas, and others.

33. Menchú 1984, 122.

34. Menchú had confronted oppression and exclusion since her brother died when he was two years old and his body rotted on a coffee farm because her family did not have the money to bury him properly. Other instances of this are the death of her best friend, who was poisoned after the farm's others fumigated the premises; when her father was burned alive in the Spanish Embassy; when her mother was tortured to death in front of her; when her brother is also tortured to death. This testimony provides an example of the experiences that serve as a "point of departure" for liberation ethics. Here is evinced the horror of the real reality that late capitalism produces in the skin of the world periphery.

35. Since Scannone does not point out the domination or exclusion (the negativity) that weighs over popular culture, he cannot indicate the necessary liberation (dialectical moment of overcoming) either. This judgment makes itself evident when one considers that while Scannone criticizes diverse "projects" (Scannone 1990, 150–64), he does not propose any project of liberation from the current situation. There is resistance but not liberation. This is similar to the way in which Leopoldo Zea (1978) concludes with a "thematic project" (by mestizos), and not with a liberation project grounded in the people (*proyecto popular*).

36. Scannone's play of words in Spanish is suggestive: "Nos-otros": "We-others." "We-others" is a community where each one is an "other" for all the others: "nos," all; "otros," for each one.

37. I am referring to the loss of its (political) "power," its capacity for economic undertakings, and its cultural tradition's hegemonic status. In the case of the Nahuatl people of the Aztec empire, the "*calmecac*" (school of the Tlamatinime) is not linked with *altepetl* (the "people") anymore. See lecture 6 of my *The Invention of the Americas* (Dussel 1993c).

38. These are Mayan indigenous people like Rigoberta Menchú.

39. In *La Jornada* (Mexico City), February 22, 1994, 8.

40. I have pursued the "hermeneutics of Latin American culture" from my studies in France in 1961 up to my formulation of the philosophy of liberation at the end of the 1960s and the beginning of the 1970s. I described the evolution of this part of my thought in "Hermeneutics and Liberation: Dialogue with Paul Ricoeur," more specifically in the second section, "Towards a Latin American Symbolics," in Dussel 1993a, 138 ff. (included in the English translation of 1996). This is the basis of my assertion that Scannone falls back on a hermeneutical moment. Scannone's ideas served as a point of departure for my lectures in Villa Devoto in 1968. Gera and Rodríguez M. were present there and immediately after that they began to use the category "culture" as a basis for analyzing national reality. I referred to this position later as "culturalism," since it was not capable of illuminating the way the dialectic between the dominator and the dominated played itself out in symbolic, ontological-cultural problems. The "ethical-mythical nucleus" ideologically and ingenuously assumes an allegedly autonomous world that cannot be affirmed without simultaneously discovering, with equal clarity, the principle of its own negation. But in addition, work is in itself the essence of culture—see my "Cultura latinoamericana y filosofía de la liberación: Cultura popular revolucionaria más allá del popu-

lismo y del dogmatismo," *Latinoamérica*, Anuario Estudios Latinomericanos (México) 17 (1985): 77–127; this essay is a critical response to Horacio Cerutti's simplifications regarding this topic; it also appeared in *Nueve ensayos sobre la Cultura* (Paulinas, Sâo Paulo, 1996). Marx and Freud are essential for understanding this. The absence of a critical rereading of their work may have the most devastating consequences, not only in Scannone or Cerutti, but also in terms of the formalism characteristic of discourse ethics.

41. This is exactly the moment of Menchú's "subsumption" into the capitalist system: incorporation of the exteriority of the indigenous ethnos as a *functionalistic* part of the self-referent and autopoietic system. This issue is not solved in works like Rodolfo Kusch's *América profunda* (1986; first published 1962), a work that is ahead of its time in important ways. He almost considers the problem in the chapter "Los objetos," 112 ff.: "The market and *being* are intimately linked. Perhaps, if the merchant disappears, so would the dynamic and expansion of a culture based in the urge to be someone. . . . Maybe one would need to substitute the exterior path of the city by an interior one and thus gain a wiser form of life" (123). The evil to be overcome is urban civilization: one must return to the telluric. A little Gandhi, a little of the Heidegger of the Black Forest, a little Nietzsche, postmodernism *avant la lettre*? Ultimately, a Rodolfo Kusch who reflects out of a strong, respectable, suggestive, ambiguous Amerindian anthropological experience.

42. Note the "negativities": "I had not had a childhood . . . , not . . . , not . . , I had *nothing*." How dreadful this conclusion, which claims justice in the world's tribunal of critical consciousnesses, to Osiris's metaphorical eyes!

43. Consider seriously the indigenous leader's originary ethical rationality, which is made evident in regard to the "comparison" of the *asymmetric* moments of the system/oppression-exteriority. Both Apel, who is situated in the hegemonic, epistemological, academic, formal world, and Scannone, who has forgotten the relational moment of internal material oppression or the moment of exteriority as exclusion, lack this.

44. Note here that at this stage she did not consider herself capable of putting her ideas in "order," and felt that she could not "express" them to others. Her process of "becoming conscious" "*conscientization*" was thus unavoidably "monological" in character—a soliloquy.

45. This is a fundamental moment (moment 5 of figure 12), the moment of the community's "face-to-face" relation in the exteriority of the system. We can see here the constitution of the excluded one's *symmetry*. I wanted to express this intuition in *Ethics and Community* (Dussel 1986) with the idea that the Other, the victims, the poor, constitute *empirical* communities out of the system. They *ethically experiment symmetric* human relations in these communities. It is out of this "empirical experience," out of this utopia (*ouk-topos*: that which does-not-have-a-place in the system) from which "critical-discursive reason" begins to work, now in the form of critical reason.

46. As we will see, here begins the emergence of a "historical subject."

47. This "experience" is more profound than the "experience" of consciousness (*Ehrfahrung des Bewusstseins*) in the introduction of Hegel's *Phenomenology of Spirit* (see Hegel 1971–79, vol. 3, 80). It is the "experience" of the emergence of a "new object" for consciousness, but from the standpoint or reality of critical exteriority. It is the first object that shows the "Totality of the self-referent dominant system" as oppressor, denier of life, exclusory of the victim who

gains consciousness. This is the experience of seeing a "new world" emerge: the future world from the point of view of the exteriority of the negated current world. It is the "experience" of "*conscientization*" as a process that begins creatively and critically.

48. Observe again the generalization or universalization of the particular empirical situation and the further universal conclusions drawn from it. This is part of the exercise of ethical-critical reason, which universalizes what will hold in the future.

49. What they experienced was "contemptuousness" from the officials.

50. Menchú 1984, 117–18.

51. We are now explicitly in moment 5 of figure 12. There is nonetheless a clear indication of moment 7, since we find here theoretical conclusions about "the structural origin of the victimization of the victims." This is the beginning of a critico-theoretical *rationality* that searches the "reasons" of negativity. Now it has to be related to the "organic intellectuals" in order to reach more *explanatory clarity*, but only after the demanded critical-rational universal path has begun. Nothing is further away from a folklorist or postmodern irrationalism. This path asks for principles, reasons, and for structural causes for the denial of life, for exclusion from argumentation, and for the inefficacy of feasibility. The mutual interpellation of the victims who gain critical-communitarian consciousness: the symmetry of those situated in an asymmetrical position. This is a solution to the aporia of discourse ethics. How to proceed with a discussion if there is always asymmetry? By putting the excluded victims in a critical community *of the oppressed themselves* where they discuss!

52. This is the theme of that strange and profound book by Levinas (1968b) in which he describes phenomenologically the "for-the-Other" (*pour Autrui*) of the subjectivity in terms of a quasi-intention. The "for-the-Other" makes him- or herself patent in situations such as the persecution by the Other in the system, or the condition of being hostage in the hands of the Totality.

53. It is interesting that Levinas insists upon "nakedness" in this context, understood as a vulnerability and sensibility reflected in one's skin (ibid., 94 ff.), in corporeality itself: "Such passivity is signified in what is said; and in what is said such passivity signifies and acquires significance; in this manner, it is also exposed in the response to . . . , being in question in the face of all questioning, in the face of all problems, without clothing, with no protection, immersed in nakedness (in all of its dimensions). . . . To be naked beneath one's skin, all the way onto the wound that brings death . . . (complete) vulnerability" (63). The same as in Marx, (and as he also understood this): "living labor," in the face of capital, once it is bought and sold, offers up its "immediate carnality [*Leiblichkeit*]"; this is how it becomes a form of subjectivity in labor. The worker thereby becomes transformed into a "total dispossession of this nakedness of all objectivity, this purely subjective existence of labor; labor understood as absolute poverty" (Marx 1956–90, vol. 1, 515–16; see [101] of this *Ethics*). In *Capital*, Marx returns to the metaphor employed by Levinas as to the "skin," which takes the form of the skin of an "innocent lamb" driven to slaughter or to shearing: "like someone who has taken their own skin to the market and cannot expect anything else but that it will in fact be stripped" (*Kapital* [1873], Marx 1987, vol. 1, end of chap. 4). It is in this sense that "living labor" is offered up, as "labor power itself becomes commodified, that labor

power which only exists in a living corporeality [*lebendigen Leiblichkeit*] and the carnality which is inherent in it" (ibid., 184).

54. Levinas 1974, 203. The "rationality" of reason is, ultimately, the "cunning" of life. "Reason" is the *intelligence* of knowing how to produce, reproduce, and develop human life. It gets "unblocked" and invested as "service work" (*habodah* in Hebrew) in favor of the victim. "Knowing" how to help the victim against the system is the practical intelligence of the Egyptian Moses, of Washington, of Hidalgo, of Menchú. It is the *maximum* of possible intelligence: it is creative reason, that is to say, critical-liberating reason. The scientific inventor participates in it theoretically.

55. See the category of "proximity" in my *Philosophy of Liberation*, sec. 2.1 in chap. 2 (Dussel 1977; English trans., 1985).

56. Apel: "Necessity, difficulty, and possibility of a philosophical foundation for ethics" ("Necesidad, dificultad y posibilidad de una fundamentación filosófica de la ética," in Apel 1986, 161).

57. Ethical-originary reason is exercised in respect of the Other *as equal*; ethical-preoriginary reason in respect to the Other *as other*. The latter form is even more critical than the former. They represent levels 1b and 6b of tables 8 [198] and 9 [208].

58. Kearney 1984, 65–66. On Levinas, see Critchley 1992 and Gibbs 1992. It is interesting to note that these authors, along with the French and German scholars who have recently written about Levinas, do not mention the "reception" of Levinas in the world periphery. This "reception" has taken place since the end of the sixties, with the philosophy of liberation, and precedes by much the discovery of Levinas in the "center."

59. Since they are regulative models of impossibility (Hinkelammert 1984), the universal (Habermas) or the transcendental (Apel) communities of communication do not admit the excluded affected. Liberation ethics also uses critical models (like Marx's, for instance) and presupposes a major complexity of the real.

60. See *Para una ética de la liberación latinoamericana* (Dussel 1970–80, vol. 2 [1973], 52 ff.): sec. 24. "La *conciencia ética* como oír la voz-del-Otro"; and *Philosophy of Liberation*, section 2.6.2 in chap. 2 (Dussel 1977), where I distinguish between a "*moral* conscience" that applies (*anwendet*) principles and an "*ethical* consciousness" that opens itself, as an exercise of "ethical-originary reason" (prediscursive), to the Other as other in the "face-to-face" encounter.

61. Moments 1–5 of figure 12.

62. The first moment of this a priori "re-sponsibility" is that of the Other in respect to the other members of the community of excluded-oppressed. The second one takes place between the "interpellation" and the one who accepts and assumes it *in the system* by taking responsibility for the Other as an ethical subject. There is also an "a posteriori responsibility," pointed out by philosophers like Hans Jonas or Apel, that consists of taking responsibility for the effects of the "agreements."

63. The symmetric community of the excluded victim's hermeneutical-political and ethical "clarity": "enlightenment."

64. Menchú 1984, 121.

65. Moments 3–4 of figure 12 show that the Other "is" negated, dominated, excluded: is-*not*-participant even though he is affected.

66. This "pro-ject" is not a "model of impossibility" like, for instance, Friedrich von Hayek's "perfect competition" or Habermas's "ideal community of communication." It is, on the contrary, a possible alternative, an ethical-strategic historical project where the "new" community of communication is counterfactually anticipated. In it the nonparticipants will be participants. It is important to consider that we are talking here about a "new" community and not simply about the "introjection" of the excluded in the "same" previous hegemonic community. See more on this on chapter 6.

67. See a pragmatic analysis of this "speech-act" in my essay "La *interpelación* del Otro," in Dussel 1993a, 33–65.

68. The point here has been narrated or metaphorically expounded in the pedagogical-theoretical construction of the mythical account of Moses ("son of the pharaoh": an intrasystemic hegemonic dominator), who hears the cry of the slave in Egypt. This story is not merely historical or mythical-religious. It was construed with highly critical *rational* categories. See Gottwald 1981. It seems that the *Apiru* were a group of slaves in the mountains of Palestine, who fought for their liberation against Philistine-Indo-European, Egyptian-Canaanite domination in times of the kingdom of El Amarna. This historical event propitiated a reflection that elaborated a *rational*, critical, ethical-political-economical "paradigm" of great coherence which is much more superior in these respects to the "paradigm" proposed by Hellenic culture (see §I.1 and Walzer 1979). The Hellenocentrism of the histories of ethics and philosophy is opposed to this. As has been pointed out, this Hellenocentrism serves as the foundation for the Eurocentrism of German romanticism at the end of the eighteenth century (Bernal 1991).

69. This is moment 7 of figure 12.

70. On the "psychology of development" and social pedagogy, see Schraml 1977.

71. It is interesting that instead of "ethical consciousness [*Gewissen*]," Habermas uses the term "theoretical-moral consciousness [*Moralbewusstain*]" (Habermas 1983). This term has a cognitivist (and not a properly ethical) "tone" that Kohlberg's English cannot offer. Consider the notion of *moral judgment* in Kohlberg and Colby 1987. With respect to conscience or "moral judgment," see Bruner 1984, 31 ff.: "Concepciones de la infancia: Freud, Piaget, y Vygotsky"; Hersh, Paolitto, and Reimer 1979; Peters 1984; Piaget 1932.

72. In the spirit of his time, Piaget felt compelled to demonstrate the child's capacity for the development of mathematics and formal logic as a prototype of knowledge (Bühler 1965). He indicates that before linguistic competence the child has "technical-practical intelligence," which Piaget describes as a defect (Piaget 1978, sec. 21). The use of instruments (*technical*-practical) is clearly different from the relation among subjects (*ethical*-practical) (Dussel 1984).

73. Piaget 1978, 17–23. Piaget ultimately conceives of intelligence as "instrumental reason." He integrates the linguistic, but not so clearly the intersubjective or communitarian moment. See also Piaget 1990, 123 ff.

74. See a discussion of this theme in my treatment of pedagogy, Dussel 1970–80, vol. 3 [1973], secs. 49–53, 132–98; *Ética*, 478–79.

75. For Edelman (1992; see also above [62–63]) regarding the process of encoding and perceptual categorization in the first place, which is different in each individual, and which is brought about by polymorphic types of criteria employed for purposes of classification (ibid., 234ff)., against the "objec-

tivism" of the Cognitivists (such as Searle, Putnam, Lakoff, and so on) (229), but also consistent with the approaches of Frege, Carnal, Russell ("in whose thought the analysis of mechanisms of human reasoning is undertaken logically," 232). Together these constitute a tradition in which Piaget himself must thus be inscribed.

76. See Piaget 1937.

77. There is a "nondualism," or nonawareness of the "I," in stages 1 and 2. Pleasant stimuli are looked for, while unpleasant stimuli are avoided. In stages 3 and 4, previously unknown feeling of distress emerge along with processes of differentiation. In stages 5 and 6, as a transference of the libido by the narcissist "I." Piaget draws this from Freud's work.

78. Paulo Freire asserts that he promptly used Piaget's work on "moral judgment" (Freire 1993, 23: "I address this matter at some length, using the excellent study by Piaget exploring the moral code of children [Piaget 1932], their mental representation of punishment, the proportionate relationship between the probable cause of punishment and its specific nature, and quote Piaget and defending a dialogical, loving relationship").

79. Here Piaget refers to Carnap, Tarski, and so on.

80. See Piaget 1969, 18 ff.; 1979, and 1985.

81. The point would concern the "second crisis of the Oedipus complex," which Piaget does not expound. In this complex, the diverse authorities, society, the state, and institutions replace the father.

82. See Hersh, Paolitto, and Reimer 1979; Piaget 1932.

83. See Bouver 1912.

84. See Kohlberg 1981–84; Kohlberg and Colby 1987.

85. Paradoxically, as a biologist Piaget could have elaborated a material ethic (Piaget 1969). He even touches the themes of "life and truth": "We will be told that the need for a differentiated organ is absurd, since the appropriate goal of all knowledge is to obtain truth, whereas the appropriate goal for life is simply to go on 'living'" (331). Piaget is not able to relate (because of "objectivist" presuppositions, Edelman would say) the "truth claim" with the universal criterion of any "truth," which is "life" itself (see [61], [98 ff.], [146 ff.], [165 ff.] and §3.2 [168–74]). Piaget is a biologist (material) with a formalist Kantian theory of knowledge.

86. See especially Habermas 1983, 4 ff.

87. Todorov shows that such a mechanism of "exclusion" continues working in Modernity (Todorov 1989). How could Modernity not recognize until the nineteenth century the "humanity" and the equal rights (even after the "Declaration of the Rights of Man" by the bourgeois French Revolution) of innocent African peasants sold as merchandise, as slaves, in America (where Washington did not have any scruples in buying and exploiting them) by "modern" English, French, Portuguese?

88. See Selman 1981.

89. They are summarized in square 7, where Habermas integrates the contribution of discourse ethics (Habermas 1983, 176–77).

90. See §I.1 [6].

91. I thank Rita Vergara for the material that she provided for this theme, particularly with respect to her work in her doctoral dissertation, "Educación de niños indígenas en México" (Universidad Pedagógica, México).

It would be interesting, although it would take us too long, to consider the

North American "critical thinking"—for example, Toulmin's works. "Critique" is in these cases, as I have noted before, purely theoretical or argumentative. The point is to educate the student in the "competence" of reasoning, creating new and needed arguments. This undoubtedly is a "creative" and "critical" attitude, but it does not reach the ethical-social level, or the level of the historical structures where the people who argue are present. Much less is this an ethical-critical attitude, one that emerges when the complicities with domination and the exigencies of solidarity with the victims are uncovered. "Critical thinking" is located at the level of *theoretical-argumentative reason* (level 2 of table 5), and could be at the very best rhetorical, but not discursive. The "ethical-critique" to which I refer uses "critical thinking," but only as an integral part of the exercise of ethical-practical (material) and discursive (pragmatical-argumentative) reason oriented by *ethical-critical* reason, which is negative, material, and historical—such as it is defined in chapter 4. Likewise, even though it is highly innovative and necessary, the "philosophy for children" (see Lipman 1992) does not pursue an ethical-critical education like that proposed by Paulo Freire yet.

92. See Feuerstein 1990; Feuerstein, Klein, and Tannenbaum 1991.

93. Feuerstein 1990, 7.

94. Ibid., 11.

95. Ibid., 12.

96. Ibid., 16.

97. Stimulus, organism, response: SOR.

98. Mediated learning experience: MLE.

99. See Feuerstein, Klein, and Tannenbaum 1991, 7 ff.

100. Vygotsky was born, like Piaget and some of the members of the Frankfurt school, in 1896. See Vygotsky 1979b and 1985; also see Siguán 1987 and Wetsch 1988.

101. Consider that, since the generation of scientists in which Vygotsky was included operated with some hegemony from Moscow in a *post*revolutionary period, it was a *constructive* consciousness and not a *critical anti*hegemonic one that primordially interested them. He resembles in this Piaget and Feuerstein (the former in the "center," and the latter in the stabilized and with no "revolutionary" horizon in the near future "peripheral" Israel). In the same way, Vygotsky is distanced from Freire who lives what is inevitably a *pre*transformative process in an intolerable Brazilian situation (even though nobody would consider today this situation "pre"-revolutionary, it had this physiognomy in the sixties).

102. See Luria 1976.

103. "El concepto de conciencia en Vigotsky y el origen de la psicología histórico-cultural," in Siguán 1987, 130.

104. See Piaget's comments on Vygotsky's work (in Vygotsky 1985, 199–215). Piaget asserts something that philosophers in the "periphery" are used to confronting: "It is not without sadness that an author [of the "center"] discovers, twenty-five years after its publication [most times nothing is discovered], the work of a colleague who has died in the meantime, when that work contains so many points of immediate interest to him which should have been discussed personally in detail" (Piaget 1962, 1). It is for this reason that Apel, guided by a sense of responsibility and solidarity, anticipated these type of laments, which I hope will be less frequent in the future as philosophy effectively reaches a worldly scope. Bakhtin is another intellectual, from the same generation of

Vygotsky, who has also escaped from that age of shadow and hiddenness of the thought from the "periphery."

105. See Wetsch 1988, 36 ff.

106. Vygotsky 1985, 48.

107. "Ontogenetically, the relation between thought and speech development is much more intricate and obscure" (English translation of Vygotsky 1985 [p. 41 in translation]).

108. See Vygotsky 1985.

109. See the "semiotic" (4.2) and instrumental "poietic" (4.3) moments in my *Filosofía de la liberación* (Dussel 1977).

110. Vygotsky 1985, 48 (English trans., 24).

111. Rivière 1985, 131.

112. See Wetsch 1988, 50 ff.

113. See Torres 1992. I thank Stella Araujo-Olivera for her support on this point.

114. One could compare Freire's position on this point with the North American pragmatists. While they rightly affirm that truth is reached in the *communitarian process of veri-fication*, Freire asserts that the process of critical education takes place only when the oppressed are educated in the very *practical process of liber-ation which transforms their reality*. Unlike the pragmatists, he does not posit learning as an intellectual process alone but as an integral process of *critical praxis*.

115. Since Freire's point of departure is an existing authentic community of the people, the dialogical intersubjective horizon is also different from "the Just Community of Cambridge" (Hersh, Paolitto, and Reimer 1979, 174–81; the example is of an elementary school as a community).

116. Freire 1993, 98–99.

117. Ibid., 78–79. Freire does not consider an analysis "scientific" if it lacks an "*ethical*-critical" dimension.

118. Ibid., 79.

119. Ibid., 80.

120. Freire published "Conscientização e alfabetização: Uma nova visão do processo" in *Revista de Estudos Universitarios* (Recife) 4 (1963): 5–23.

121. See Vieira Pinto 1961.

122. "Concienciar para liberar," *Contacto* (Mexico City) 8 (1971): 42; quoted in Torres 1992, 107.

123. I will compare them with the ten moments of figure 12.

124. Moment 1 of figure 12.

125. This is a key notion in his vocabulary.

126. Torres 1992, 108.

127. See chapter 1 of this *Ethics*.

128. See "A Sociedade brasileria em transiçao," in Freire 1980b, 39 ff.

129. See Freire 1994, 31–67.

130. Referring to Lucien Goldman, Freire talks about "maximum possible consciousness" ("Acción cultural liberadora," [1969], in Torres 1983, 22).

131. Freire 1993, 80–81.

132. Moment 3 of figure 12.

133. See Piaget 1985.

134. This sphere involves the order of the Heideggerian "world," the Luhmannian "system," the Habermasian "life world [*Lebenswelt*]," the Levinasian

"totality," and the consciousness turned fetish in the horizon of Marx's *Capital*. Piaget, Kohlberg, Vygotsky, and Feuerstein's work is situated in this sphere, without being able to supersede it.

135. This is a critical *Gegebenheit* from the victims, analyzed in chapter 4.

136. Torres 1992, 111.

137. "We wanted to offer the people the means by which they could supersede their magic or naive perception of reality by one that was predominantly critical" (Freire 1980b, 106; quotation from English translation, 44).

138. See Freire 1980b, 59.

139. Torres 1992, 109.

140. The "fear of freedom" is the first theme that Freire always repeated in his early work (Freire 1978b, 1980a, 1980b, and others). For Freire, "freedom" is not a point of departure, but a difficult goal that must vanquish obstacles, immense affective and traditional "blocks" created by punishment, domination, and the torture that oppressed people suffer.

141. Freire 1994, 21.

142. Ibid., 142.

143. Moment 6 of figure 12.

144. Freire 1977, 16–17.

145. Ibid., 18.

146. Freire 1993, 81. In 1973 I wrote in "Latin American Pedagogy": "The future liberating teacher, weak and blind, is taken by the hand through the darkness of the *new* world (the Other is a *reality*), by his son, the youth, the people. Only the trust in their word guides him and keeps him out of the error that comes from leaving the path that leads him to the Other. . . . The voice of the Other is ex-igency, urgent call to a liberating work" (Dussel 1970–80, vol. 3 [1973], sec. 53; III, 190).

147. "Concientización y liberación" (1973), in Torres 1983, 86.

148. "The task of the dialogical educator is, in working on the thematic universe reflected in a process of research with an interdisciplinary team, to turn it back to the human beings who produced these insights, not as a lecture but as a problem to be resolved collectively" (Freire 1994, 132).

149. Moment 3 of figure 12.

150. The explanation will have to be provided by a critical theory. As we will see later, the intervention of the "intellectual" or the teacher is indispensable. It is necessary to avoid both "vanguardism" and "spontaneism."

151. Freire 1980b, 61. "Critical consciousness, represents things and facts as they exist empirically, in their causal and circumstantial correlations" (English translation of ibid., 44).

152. Freire 1994, 72.

153. Freire 1979, 48.

154. Moment 5 of figure 12.

155. Torres 1992, 111.

156. Ibid., 112.

157. This expression appears in Marx's *Grundrisse*.

158. This is the central theme of this chapter.

159. Dialogism points to the procedural moral-formal and intersubjective moment that grants antihegemonic validity in relation to the ethical material contents of those who have become subjects of their own liberation.

160. Moment 5 of figure 12. It is a mutual conscientization that counts with

the participation of those who have been called. Moment 6 begins with the emergence of the educator of the ethical-critical consciousness.

161. Habermas 1983, 132.

162. Ibid., 197 (quotation from English trans., 183).

163. Freire 1994, 97.

164. Ibid., 99.

165. Ibid., 101.

166. Ibid.

167. Ibid. For Freire's thoughts on dialogue see Freire 1979, 68 ff.: "A organização do pensamento" (The organization of thought).

168. Moment 7 of figure 12.

169. Moment 8.

170. Freire 1994, 112–14.

171. The notion of "denunciation" has been largely discussed in chapter 4. Take, for instance, Marx's scientific "denunciation" of the capitalist system.

172. Freire 1994, 121.

173. Moments 9 and 10 of figure 12.

174. "Educación para un despertar de la conciencia" (1973), in Torres 1983, 43.

175. See Freire 1977.

176. Freire 1994, 223.

177. I am particularly interested in defining the epistemological status of the *critical* social sciences. My focus on epistemological issues will help locate the "place" of this problematic: the use of the human or social sciences by communities of victims (feminists, ecologists, antiracists; liberating pedagogy, critical economy of the dominant classes or the peripheral countries, and so on).

178. Wright 1971, chap. 2: "Causality and Causal Explanation" (57 ff.).

179. The logic of discovery includes inductive moments, which goes from the particular to a hypothetical generalization.

180. I use the notion of "paradigm" in a loose sense here, which comprises the theoretical as well as the practical and both the natural and the human or social sciences. The term can be used to refer to a theory, a group of theories, a scientific research program, or even an ideological formation—for example, when one refers to a capitalist, neoliberal, or socialist "paradigm," each of which may represent a different level of abstraction.

181. See Hempel 1979; Nagel 1978; Popper 1968; and others to be named in the following pages. Consider also Habermas's ambiguous position, "Analytical Theory of Science and Dialectic," in Adorno et al. 1969 (Spanish trans., 147 ff.).

182. Popper 1968, sec. 85, 278. "Yet, science has more than mere biological survival value." I readily agree with this since the reproduction of each ethical subject's life is *not only biological* but also cultural, aesthetic, and so on. "Although," Popper goes on, "it can attain neither truth nor probability, the striving for knowledge and the search for truth are still the strongest motives of scientific discovery" (ibid.).

183. Ibid., chap. 3.

184. Ibid., sec. 22.

185. Ibid.

186. For Popper, the *critical* human or social sciences are impossible. The reason for this is that, as his theory of "social engineering" makes clear, utopia appears in relation to the "open society" as regressive and impossible.

187. For a discussion and critique of Popper's position in relation to Hayek's neoliberal economy see Hinkelammert 1984 (chap. 5: "Popper's Methodology"). See also Gómez 1995.

188. See Kuhn 1962.

189. Ibid., 128–29.

190. Ibid., 11–12. It is evident that the "scientific community" is not only an "exterior" or sociological moment, but that it must be understood, as Apel does, as an always already given presupposition of science and ordinary language.

191. Ibid., 13.

192. It is interesting that only the dissatisfied dominant groups, and not the victims, are taken into consideration here.

193. Ibid., 149.

194. Moment 7 of figure 12. This moment occurs when the scientist joins (as a "committed" person, "militantly") the communities of victims who have "gained critical consciousness." This ethical-critical consciousness gives rise to the development of *critical* social science, which is born within a historical crisis and cannot be reduced to a "*proletarian* mathematic science." Freire's concept of "banking pedagogic" is negative and *critical*. It operates "within" the oppressed people's praxis of liberation, first in the northeast of Brazil and then elsewhere.

195. See Feyerabend 1987 and 1992.

196. See ibid., chap. 10: "Putnam on Incommensurability"; Feyerabend 1989, 265 ff. I think that it would be convenient in the context of that section to reintroduce the concept of "analogy." "Analogy" is different from reductive univocality and from incommensurabilist equivocality. It is, instead, a "similarity [*similitudo*]" in "distinction [*distinctio*]." See Dussel 1970–80, vol. 2 [1972], sec. 36: "The Analytical Method and Latin American Philosophy," 156 ff.

197. See Feyerabend 1989, chap. 1, 73 ff.

198. Ibid., chap. 4, 129 ff.

199. Feyerabend quotes Mach: "The psychological operation by means of which we obtain new explanations, and which frequently, though incorrectly, has been labelled as induction, is not a simple process but a very complex one. It is not a logical process, although logical processes can interpose themselves as intermediate and auxiliary links. *Abstraction* and *imagination* play an important role in the discovery of new knowledge. The fact that the method does not help much in these matters explains the mysterious [*das Mysteriöse*] air that according to Whewell characterizes the process of inductive discovery. The scientist is searching for a clarifying idea. At the beginning he does not know either the nature or form of the idea which he might encounter. But once the purpose and the path have been revealed, he is surprised at his discoveries, just as a person who has been lost in the forest suddenly finds a path between the thick bushes and glimpses an open landscape with everything clearly arrayed before him. The method can impose a certain order upon this process and improve the results only after the principal thing that is searched for has been found" (quoted in ibid., chap. 7, 200). Einstein agrees with this kind of reflection.

200. Ibid., chap. 5, 155 ff.

201. Through an elaborated and complex argumentation Feyerabend shows in "Galileo and the Tyranny of Truth" (ibid., chap. 9, 247 ff.) that the majority

of scientists today would agree more with Belarminus than with Copernicus or Galileo. A close reading of this chapter makes Feyerabend's position clearer.

202. See figure 15 ahead.

203. Lákatos 1989, 13; see ibid., 65–72, for more information on these four levels. Lákatos's own position is exemplified by his analysis of Bohr's case.

204. See Lákatos 1993, 13 ff.

205. Lákatos 1989, 144.

206. Ibid., 49.

207. "There can be no dissonance without a better theory eventually emerging" (ibid., 50). "Naturally, if dissonance is dependent upon the appearance of new theories, and of the invention of theories that anticipate new facts, then dissonance is not simply the relationship between a theory and an empirical basis, but rather a multidimensional relationship among rival theories. . . . . It can then be said that dissonance has a historical character" (ibid., 51). This passage is pertinent for my argument, since functionalistic research programs in the human or social sciences can coexist with critical programs.

208. Ibid., 65.

209. The French term is *sciences de l'homme* (see, for instance, Merleau-Ponty 1964, where he considers the issue in light of Husserl's work, especially in regard to psychology, linguistics, and history). They also refer to "empirical sciences of man" (*science empirique de l'homme*) — e.g., Strasser 1967, 253 ff. For other French perspectives, see Canguilhem 1968 and Bachelard 1972 and 1949. These perspectives are more in line with a conception of the sciences in terms of "understanding" (*comprendre, Verstehen, comprensión*) than with an Anglo-Saxon view of the scientific enquiry as "explanation" (*Erklärung*).

210. Gómez 1995, 166 ff. This assertion would put Popper in contradiction with his own methodology for the natural sciences.

211. See Wright 1971: "A teleological *explanation* of action is normally preceded by an act of intentionalist *understanding* of some behavior" (ibid., 132).

212. See Apel 1984, especially "The Complementarity of the Causal Explanation and the Hermeneutical Understanding of Social Sciences" (203 ff.). Apel had previously explored the issue in other essays; see, for instance, two articles in *The Transformation of Philosophy*, one originally published in 1964 ("The Development of Analytical Philosophy of Language and the Problem of the Science of Spirit," in Apel 1973, vol. 2, 28 ff.), and the other in 1971 ("The Communicating Community as Transcendental Presupposition of the Social Sciences" (ibid., 220 ff.).

213. See Gadamer 1960: "The expanding of the question of truth to that of understanding [*Verstehen*] in the science of spirit," where Gadamer discusses the problems of hermeneutics, interpretation, and "understanding" from Schleiermacher to Heidegger: "El lenguaje es el medio universal en el que se realiza la comprensión misma. La forma de realización de la comprensión es la interpretación" (pt. 3, 12; Spanish trans., 467).

214. See Winch 1958 and 1994 for work with significant consequences.

215. Moment 6 of figure 12.

216. See §4.4.

217. Strasser writes "disparition du spectateur désintéressé" (the disappearance of the disinterested viewer) (1967, 163). I refer to a double disappearance of the "disinterested viewer" because, while "understanding" requires an "entry" into the *life world* of the actor, there is now the need for a "departure"

from the ordinary life of the "dominant" or "hegemonic world" in order to undergo a new learning process in the *world of the victims* themselves. There is a "commitment" (*engagement* in Sartre's terms) that displaces the "interest for understanding" the Other in one's or any other system (as in Winch: participatory scientific-comprehensive intention), and that in turn elevates the need to "explain by understanding" the other *in his or her oppression*, victimization, and material negativeness (*ethical-critical* intention that gives rise to a new *critical* social scientific discourse).

218. Elsewhere (see Dussel 1970–80, vol. 2 [1972], chap. 6), I raised this issue in relation to the "interpretation" of the interpellation of the Other ("I am hungry, help me!"). This interpellation demands engaging by entering into the practical world of the Other: how can anyone "interpret" an interpellation if the world from which the interpellation is emitted is in-comprehensible to the one who receives the interpellation? Learning the world of the Other is the a priori of the "interpretation" of his or her cry of help. This is the problem of "interpellation as a speech act" (Dussel 1993a, 35; English trans., 21).

219. It would seem that Marx anticipates this by 150 years and refers to Rawls's "original position" or to discourse ethics' "ideal community of communication."

220. Marx 1956–90, vol. 1, 510–11.

221. See the "new objectual horizon"—field of "facts" or new observable objects; see figure 15.

222. I treated this topic before in "History and Praxis" (Dussel 1983b, 309–29); in "The Other's Reason: Exteriority and the Communication Community" (Dussel 1993a, 42 ff.): "I *propose* this new *explanation* (or understanding) X regarding fact Z, which has not been explained (or understood or observed as yet)"; in Fornet-Betancourt 1992, 106 ff.; and in "The Interpellation of the Poor from the Liberating Intention" (Fornet-Betancourt 1990; see the German translation, 85 ff. [diagram at 89]; especially 95 ff. [diagram at 100]). In *For an Ethics of Latin American Liberation* (*Para una ética de la liberación latinoamericana*), sec. 37 (Dussel 1970–80, vol. 2 [1972], 174 ff.), I situated this problematic around the issue of the "deduction of Totality and liberating praxis" because the Totality itself (system or paradigm 1 in this work) could be criticized ("deduced" from system 2–paradigm 2 as "false," "unjust"; here I could add "in-valid"): "Whoever takes the world, *physis*, as the only reality, implicitly accepts Totality but does not discover it as such, as Totality. In order to consider Totality a category it is necessary to criticize it from the Other, from the position of Alterity" (ibid., 175).

223. Habermas 1968a, 39 (English trans., 28). Rightly, Heidegger wrote "Knowledge [*Erkennen*] is a way of being-there *founded* [*fundierten*] on being in the world" (Heidegger 1963c, 62). For his part Husserl wrote, "The world is a world which is given in daily life [*Lebenswelt*] and which already has pre-scientifically the same structure as that of objective sciences. . . . The daily bodily reality [*lebensweltlicher*] which is concrete and which we live with is a real body itself, although not in the same sense, as that body which is the object of study in physics" (Husserl 1962, 142).

224. Marx, *These über Feuerbach*, sec. 8 (Marx 1956–90, vol. 3, 7).

225. See *Nicomachean Ethics*, bk. 1, 1 (Aristotle 1960, 1094a 1–2).

226. "It cannot be accepted that practical reason is subordinated to speculation and to the inversion of order, because in fact all *interest* [*Interesse*] is ulti-

mately practical in character, and even that of speculative reason is only conditioned, and is only completed in the course of its practical application" (*Kritik der reinen Vernunft*, A 219 [Kant 1968, vol. 6, 252]). As has been shown in this work, there are also material considerations or reasons about "content." For instance, speculative reason (of a scientific kind, for example) is a mediation of the reproduction and development of the life of every single ethical subject in community.

227. Habermas 1968a, 242 (English trans., 196).

228. Ibid. Habermas loses this "material" sense of ethics later and takes refuge in a "formal" procedural level. He did not know how to combine a "*material* ethics," which he believed to be particular, with a "*formal* morality," which he considers to be universal. I have exposed his reductionistic fallacy throughout this work. At that time he rightly pointed out that "knowledge-constitutive interests can be defined exclusively as a function of the objectively constituted problems of the preservation of life that have been solved by the cultural form of existence as such" (Habermas 1968a, 243 [English trans., 196]). Thus articulated, I completely accept Habermas's reflection. It is a shame that he did not realize that he needed a stronger formulation (e.g., the "reproduction of the life of every single ethical subject") in order to count with a *universal* ethical principle that transcends and constitutes each culture *from the inside*.

229. Husserl 1950, sec. 128, 315.

230. See arrow a in figure 15.

231. Habermas 1968a, 260.

232. Ibid., 261.

233. Marcuse 1964, 218.

234. Marx 1976–82, 333. See Dussel 1988, 110 ff.

235. Marx 1974, 450. See Dussel 1985a, secs. 13.3–13.4, 258 ff.

236. Moment 6a of figure 12.

237. Moment 6b.

238. Referring to Stuart, Marx writes "the rational [*rationelle*] expression of the mercantile monetary system" (*Zur Kritik der politischen Ökonomie [Manuskript 1861–1863]* [Marx 1976–82, 337]).

239. Moment 7 of figure 12.

240. *Grundrisse der Kritik der politische Oekonomie* (Marx 1974, 452). For a discussion of Marx's epistemological position in light of contemporary philosophical discourse see Dussel 1990b, chaps. 9 and 10. I also aim here to be faithful to Marx's historical discourse.

241. *Manuskript 1861–1863* (Marx 1976–82, 381). The *Manuscript* Notebooks 6–15 form what is mistakenly referred to as the fourth part of *Capital*; that is to say, the *Theories of Surplus Value*, which in fact are part of the *Manuscript*.

242. Marx writes: "Before the physiocrats of plusvalue [*Mehrwerth*] — profit, under the form of gains — was explained purely and simply on the basis of exchange, by the selling of merchandise for more than its value" (ibid., 333). I examined Marx's long critique in Dussel 1990b, 109–230. Marx's step-by-step refutation leads him to conclude that the capitalist political economy has reached an *irrational* conclusion: "This is how the Earth became transformed into a source of rental income, capital into a source of profit, and labor in a source of salary. . . . It is a kind of fiction without fantasy, a religion of vulgarity" (*Manuskript 1861–1863* [Marx 1976–82, 1450]). For Smith (the old paradigm refuted and subsumed by Marx), living labor represents the only source

of value, while rent, profit, and salary are conceived as three ways in which value *appears* in the market. Capital "inverts" these relations and turns "irrational": "Earth rent, capital interest are irrational expressions [Erde-Rente, Kapital-Zins sind irrationale Ausdrücke]" (ibid., 1515). Marx, who is organically integrated to the community of victims, the exploited and impoverished workers, is interested in *explaining scientifically* (in Lákatos's sense) the *cause* of that negativity. The political economy of the scientific community that exists among capitalists (or that is organically integrated to capital) commits "contradictions" and false developments. It does not take into consideration certain "facts" (like surplus value) while it provides ad hoc "explanations" of others (such as profit).

243. Since capitalism is a "functionalistic" economy, the "interest" of this scientific economy is that capitalism "works," grows, overcomes its crises, and develops.

244. "Critical theory" was an important project insofar as it brought to mind in Europe the need for "critique" in theoretical production in general. However, it was an ambiguous project, since it did not distinguish between, on the one hand, (a) human or social *sciences*, and (b) traditional theories, and, on the other, between them and (c) *critical* human or social sciences and (d) *critical* philosophies. These distinctions are important in order to avoid collapsing into an equivocal and indiscernible position: a quasi-science and quasi-philosophy as "critical theory." Habermas's critique of "critical theory" from the point of view of discursive rationality is partly valid (see Habermas 1981b, ends of vols. 1 and 2). However, his "reconstructive theory" lost *critical* sense (because it lost the "negativity" and the "materiality;" see §2.4) and epistemological clarity (in the sense of the *critical* human or social sciences and *critical* philosophy).

245. Fals Borda 1974, 31. Fals Borda also distinguishes clearly between *critical* and *functionalistic* social sciences: "With some very recent exceptions, the *pensum*, courses and research programs in university centers in developed countries (even in the Soviet Union) partly reflect this ecstatic orientation in which *order* and *functionality* are supreme norms" (ibid., 27).

246. For instance, Adam Smith discovered a "new" fact or object (O2 in figure 15): the market as the place where the "harmony" between the egoism of the citizen/producer of merchandise and the interest of the nation occurs. For Smith, this "harmony" was brought about by nonintentional actions seemingly orchestrated by the divine Providence of a redefined neostoicism. The "new" theoretical and ethical-economical paradigm replaced the old order founded on "conscious" and individual "virtues." According to the old paradigm, egoism was an evil. It portrayed the fulfillment of the market as the result of a hypocritical cynicism, and, ultimately it left market economy without an ethics. There was thus a need for a "new" ethical-economical paradigm, which Smith formulated in *Theory of the Moral Sentiments* (1976). See German Gutiérrez's excellent master thesis (Gutiérrez 1996).

247. Moment 7 in figure 12.

248. Since in this "negative" moment, when the victims have not yet achieved liberation, the scientific research program (e.g., Marx's) does not contribute many scientific "novelties," it would seem that it is "recessive." However, such purely negative *critique* serves as a foundation for the interpretation (understanding and explanation) of reality put forth by the "*critical* consciousness" *of the oppressed* in the very process of liberation. The *critical* science of eco-

nomics provides "reasons" to the oppressed and by this means "dismantles" (in a negative way) the hegemonic science. In moments like today, when neoliberal policies make themselves felt in the peripheral countries of capitalism (in places like Africa, Asia, and Latin America), Marxism, for instance, continues representing a progressive critical-scientific "reserve" for the ethical-political consciousness of the impoverished victims. Its scientific character may be measured by its "discovering," "comprehending," or "explicative" character concerning the causes for the poverty suffered by the victims, causes ignored by the hegemonic economic sciences functional for the "central" capitalism. It is a scientific program of investigation that serves an irreplaceable critical function, a creative reference even for the dominating economics—particularly in the contemporary crisis of internal critical theory of many paradigms that can only give ad hoc explanations in front of the ecological disaster or the growing misery among a good part of humanity.

249. Moment 8.

250. It took the modern bourgeoisie more than a century and a half (if we consider the Spanish "comuneros" who fought for their "jurisdiction," as the first vanquished bourgeois revolution in Modernity) to achieve its first political triumph in the control of a national state. Consider also that the first socialist revolution, the Russian Revolution of 1917, was defeated in 1989. But socialism continues in China, Vietnam, and Cuba. It continues existing as a reference of economic "rationalization" and makes possible the definition of the ethical-economical *limits* of the market, which turns global by exclusion.

251. It was the "Bolsheviks," and not the workers and the less numerous peasants with critical consciousness, who carried out the revolution of October 1917. The Bolsheviks were a minority, but they were nonetheless able to take power "in the name" (highly ambiguous "representation") of the "proletariat." The Leninist mode (see §6.1 ahead) of articulating the intersubjective relation "party-mass," which was never able to integrate a democratic consensus into its (inevitably perhaps, but equally tragic) bureaucratic system, greatly determined the outcome of the major revolution of the twentieth century.

252. Before the fifteenth century, the "intercultural" centrality was located, first *between* Egypt and Mesopotamia; then *between* the eastern Mediterranean Sea and Hellenistic Mesopotamia; and after that, in the Muslim Middle East around Baghdad or Samarkand (see introduction, §§I.1–7). "Peripheral" regions considered the dominant "cultural paradigm" of these "central" regions as *the most modern*. In their Middle Ages, the Latin people considered the Muslim world as the *most developed modern* society. But before the emergence of the first world system in the fifteenth century, the "central" regions of China, India, Mesopotamia, Latin Europe, and others (including Aztec and Inca civilization in the Americas) were considered to be the ones that "managed" the most developed information. They played the role of *regional Modernities*.

253. For the French school, see Salomon 1974. Salomon describes how the scientists collaborated with the French Revolution (Condorcet was the most famous among them, and he was, like others, also condemned by the Revolution itself), "where one sees the idea of progress as the basis of inspiration for a new relationship between science and political power" (27).

254. Habermas 1985, chap. 9.

255. Eribon 1989, 228, especially 286 ff.

256. The notion of "truth" here brings to mind the "truth" of the dominant order that becomes untrue for the victims. The victims' future truth will become equally untrue at some point . . . historical rhythm of progressive truth . . . breathing of the living.

257. Levinas 1974, 231 (quotation from the English translation, 1998, 183).

258. Habermas 1981a, 142.

259. Moment 7 in figure 12.

260. Moment 8.

261. This is the "positive" or constructive side of the *material* "content." The "negative" side consists, as we have seen before, in de-constructive critique.

262. As I mentioned earlier, I plan to write a book on liberation fronts.

263. Bloch does not forget the "rational" or even the scientific constructive moment.

264. It is a *diurnal* and prospective, and not a recessive, Freudian-*nocturnal*, or anamnetic (based on memories) creative imagination.

265. "Culture" is then subsumed. It is impossible not to do so. This is not, however, the fundamental moment.

266. Bloch 1970, 166. And he adds: "It was Marxism which for the first time scientifically discovered this topos, and has discovered it as part of the process of transition of socialism from utopia to science." The notion of "docta" indicates the rational-scientific constitution of the *possible future positive content*. One could apply here Marx's conception about consumption: "the foundation, tendential, the internal ideal [*den idealen, innerlich treibende Grund*]" (Marx 1974, 12). Bloch draws this "drive [*Trieb*]" from a careful reading of Marx's work. It was, in like manner, a radical modification of ontological *Sorge* (Heidegger's notion of "care") and of the affective or appetitive medieval *intentio*.

267. Consider here the discussions in part I of this work, particularly in chapter 1, concerning "*material* ethics." Cunico (1988, 237) has a reductive sense of this ethics (he refers to Scheler's virtue ethics). Also in a reductionist manner, he argues that Bloch has in mind "ideal models [*Leitbilder*]" and the "table of values [*Leittafeln*]" (238). And he is clearly mistaken when he remarks that Bloch's is "un'etica della perfezione in senso storico-dinamico" ("an ethics of perfection in an historical-dynamic sense") (239). Cunico does not become aware of all the "material" moments that I have mentioned already or those to which I will immediately refer.

268. Lukács and Bloch are not able to free themselves from an ontological concept of "totality" that impedes them to see, for instance, the moment of metaphysical alterity and exteriority, or ethical post-ontological moment elaborated by Levinas. At the same time, it is necessary to recognize that Bloch's work is not circumscribed by the hegemonic world, capitalism, or system 1 (in figure 12). Bloch's "militant optimism" distances him from the prevailing system. He joins the victims and conceives himself in a "metaphorical" inside the system with the oppressed, while also looking forward with hope to system 2 (project of liberation: PL in figure 12).

269. Bloch 1977, 11. In Bloch 1988, 2, we read: "Nobody lives simply because they want to. From the moment in which he or she is alive they *must* do so."

270. In German *regen* means to move, to make oneself noticeable, but also, to "be born."

271. Bloch 1959, secs. 1–2, p. 21 (Spanish trans., vol. 1, 3). "This 'knowing

how to wait' ontogenetically cuts across one's life, from childhood through old age" (English trans., 1986, vol. 1, 21–45).

272. Ibid., 47 ff. (Spanish trans., 27 ff.).

273. Ibid., sec. 9, 49 (Spanish trans., 29; English trans., 1986, vol. 1, 45).

274. Recall Horkheimer and Adorno's "material negativity" (see §4.2).

275. This "hunger" keeps appearing from the *Egyptian Book of the Dead* and Marx up to this *Ethics of Liberation*: it is a negativity of content, that of human corporeality.

276. This framework belongs to system I in figure 12. It is part of the "totality" of the system that produces "hunger."

277. This is the same *verändern* (transformation) that appears in Marx's eleventh thesis. For Freire, it is the "place" where the learning of "conscientization" occurs. It is the *praxis of the transformation* of the conditions that produce the victim (moments 9–10 in figure 12; see also §6.3).

278. This is the "negativity" of critique (moment 4 in figure 12).

279. This is the "good" of the current system's (Levinasian "totality," Marx's "capital," and so on) fundamental ethics, or *Ethics* I (a in figure 12).

280. The yes is the "positivity" of desiring (drives), imagining (creative imagination) and formulating scientific analysis and political realism of instrumental and strategic reason subsumed by the ethical reason of life and by moral consensual rationality. Bloch dedicates *all his life* as a theoretician to the exposition of this theme.

281. "Pain" marks the beginning of ethical-critical consciousness: see Rigoberta Menchú (§4.1).

282. "Revolutionary interest" gives expression to Heidegger's *Sorge*, but only in the sense of a "being-victim-in-the-world" and not of a being-in-the-world. The victim who is dominated or excluded aims to something that lies *beyond* the being of the world. For an extensive treatment of this theme see Dussel 1970–80, vol. 2 (1972), sec. 30: "Bondad moral de la praxis liberadora," 97 ff. In that text, I criticized Bloch for getting somewhat caught by the "totality" (99–102). "Revolutionary interest" has little to do with Habermas's quasi-theoretical "emancipatory interest," whose discursive and intersubjective but exclusively linguistic formalism does not allow it to be *critical* in an ethical, negative, or material way.

283. This is *critical reason* in its *utopian* moment, which goes against anarchist utopianism and Popper's antiutopian conservatism.

284. This "explosion" is the de-constructive "negativity" of the praxis of liberation in its *negative* moment (moment 9 in figure 12). In Freire's terms, it is the "transformation" that comes after the "denunciation" that causes "fear" in the oppressed.

285. This is Spinoza's *conatus*. It is the "reproductive" moment of the ethical principle. Levinas drew the limits of this drive for a happy reproduction of life with the idea of "*désir métaphysique [metaphysical desire]*." Consult thesis 17 in appendix 1 for a clearer idea on the complexity of this issue.

286. Bloch 1959, sec. 13, 84; (Spanish trans., vol. 1, 61; English trans., 1986, vol. 1, 75). It has already been established in the description of the ethical principle that there is a duty not only to "reproduce," *but also to develop* the life of every single ethical subject in community. Even though the victims cannot even reproduce their life, the fulfillment of the duty to reproduce their life gen-

erates a historical "development" — "qualitative progress" — that aims to make those victims excluded from the system full participants. The victims' very attempt to reproduce their life becomes an explosive expansion of the current system: the future development.

287. See Dussel 1970–80, vol. 1 (1970), chaps. 1–2.

288. It is a moment of diurnal rational consciousness.

289. Quotation translated into English from the Spanish translation of Bloch 1986, vol. 1, 61.

290. Both Bloch and Lukács conceive the project of liberation as a new future moment of the Totality. Ontological dialectics made them unable to see the radical novelty of the liberation project. This project emerges from the victim, who is partially *exterior* to ontology insofar as she is an *excluded* alterity. The victim brings about a moment of *rupture*, but also one of inclusion since he or she is included in the totality as oppressed. For this reason, the future pro-ject has a certain historical *continuity*.

291. See §1.4 [98].

292. Bloch 1959, sec. 10, 49–50 (Spanish trans., vol. 1, 29–30).

293. Ibid., 50 (Spanish trans., vol. 1, 30). The classics defined the "passions" as (a) lascivious (in the present) or (b) irascible (in face of a difficult future). They distinguished the former (a) in reference to a present (love or happiness) or an absent (desire) good (a1), and in reference to a present (hate or sadness) (a2) or absent (horror) (b). The latter are divided in relation to an arduous future that can (hope) or cannot (hopelessness) be reached (b1), and to an arduous evil in the future (b2) that can (audacity) or cannot (fear) be conquered. I wrote in 1973: "The third metaphysical position or original face-to-face virtue is to live today in anticipation of the joy of the Other's liberation, of those living in misery. *Hope* in the face of utopian reality transforms the ontological metatemporality into metaphysical or scatological historicity. It implies a process of overcoming the Heideggerian 'anticipation [*Vorlaufen*]' into a way of living death beforehand. To the contrary, hope is the anticipation of the most extreme position, not in the ontological but in the metaphysical sense, and not in the face of ontological negativity (nonbeing understood as death), but rather in metaphysical terms (that going beyond the self as a *logos* of totality: the Other, the primary negativity). Hope is not the expectancy of the fulfillment of the pro-ject of totality. No. Hope is a metaphysical or ethical virtue which is alterative, since it awaits liberation" (Dussel 1970–80, vol. 2 [1972], sec. 31, "El Ethos de la liberación," 118).

294. Bloch 1959, sec. 10, 50–51 (Spanish trans., vol. 1, 30–31).

295. Ibid., sec. 11, 52 (Spanish trans., vol. 1, 32).

296. Unfortunately, Bloch did not distinguish clearly between "material" as *content* and as physical reality. In order to found a *material* utopian reason, Bloch was forced, as a result of this imprecision, to develop (like Lukács) an ontology of physical matter (Bloch 1963 and 1972). He lost unnecessary time and energy in this task. Practical and historical ethical "materialism" consists of *the content of the living-cultural human corporeality in community.*

297. Bloch 1959, sec. 11, 55 ff. (Spanish trans., vol. 1, 35 ff.).

298. Ibid., sec. 13.

299. Ibid., sec. 13, 72 (Spanish trans., vol. 1, 50). Bloch notes that the Freudians, and I will also add contemporary ethicists, place a sign in front of their consulting offices: "Here economic or social problems are not addressed" (ibid.

[Spanish trans., 51]). Psychologist educators and "good" philosophers make the same remark when challenged by Freire or by liberation philosophy or the ethics of liberation.

300. Ibid.

301. Ibid., sec. 13, 85 (Spanish trans., vol. 1, 62).

302. Ibid., sec. 14, 86 (Spanish trans., vol. 1, 63–64; English trans., vol. 1, 77).

303. Ibid., sec. 15, 138 (Spanish trans. 110–11; English trans., vol. 1, 122).

304. Ibid., 161 ff. (Spanish trans., vol. 1, 131 ff.).

305. See Hinkelammert's attempt (1984).

306. Bloch analyzes the "utopian function" as "known conscious activity" against that which should not be; and in relation to interest, to ideology (false conscience), to cultural archetypes, to ideals, to symbol-allegories. Wonderful reflections that would lead us very far. Referring to the symbols he writes: "The pipe dreams that develop in the world are other allegories among these and living symbols which are given objective life. This is a clue we possess, since they also hold true in reality, and not only the allegorical and symbolic denominations of this reality; and these actual solutions to the puzzle exist *because the universal process is itself a utopian function, whose substance is that which is objectively possible*. The utopian function of conscious human modifications and planning only represent here the most advanced position, that which is most active, that which implies the function of being an author of that which has a place in the world" (Bloch 1959, 202–3 [Spanish trans., vol. 1, 168]).

307. Ibid., sec. 17, 236 (Spanish trans., vol. 1, 198).

308. "Real possibility is only the logical expression, on the one hand, of the conditionality which is *materially necessary*, and on the other hand, of that needed for *material* aperture (the inexhaustibility at the core of matter)" (ibid.). Since there are disturbing causes during fulfillment (moments 9 and 10 of figure 12), it is necessary to modify the process as one goes on.

309. Ibid., sec. 17, 239 (Spanish trans., vol. 1, 201; English trans., 1986, vol. 1, 208). Scientific analytic aspects of the argumentation (moment 7 in figure 12) in the process of creating future alternatives, as well as scientific rational and discursive ones.

310. Economy itself is, ultimately, a moment in the reproduction and development of the life of every single human subject in community.

311. Neither Apel nor Habermas can articulate this "intention" or "interest" because they do not locate themselves materially (via the "content") or negatively in a transontological position by taking sides with the victims. *Lebenswelt* as a discursive ambit is ambiguous: it can take place in the dominating system or in the community of victims. The two philosophers do not have categories that would allow them to define criteria to differentiate between these situations. The "liberating interest" of peripheral cultures (or nations of dependent capitalism) is opposed to the "emancipatory interest" of the dominant post-conventional modern central European (or North American) community, if the latter does not reach a properly speaking *ethical-critical* level.

312. Bloch 1959, 241 (Spanish trans., vol. 1, 202). Bloch means something different from Weber by the notion of "disenchantment [*Entzauberung*]." Weber is "disenchanted" and he "disenchants" any "hope" for the victims. Bloch and the victims' "disenchantment" concerns the oppressing system, not the "*possible* utopia."

313. See chapter 3, especially what was said about Hinkelammert in §3.4.

314. Since Bloch is not explicitly aware of the analectic moment (or moment of exteriority), he is not able to compare the system's "feasibility" (technical, economical, and so on) or "efficiency" with the "liberating feasibility" which *opens up* the horizon of the victims' hope toward the *ultimum novum*. Hegelian ontologism (as in Lukács) impedes Bloch to reach more clarity. That is the reason why he repeatedly refers to the Aristotelean *dynamis*, without considering that Aristotle was not able to envision the slave's *dynamis* against the slave system. Consider the case of Spartacus: the "possibility" of the victims is an "impossibility" for the dominating system, and it carries the "destruction" of the dominating "being"; for the dominator qua dominator it is "absolute evil."

315. System 1 in figure 12. Its ontological pro-ject (a in figure 3) is the current one (in system A).

316. Moment b in the future system B in figure 3.

317. Bloch 1959, sec. 18, 258 (Spanish trans., vol. 1, 217).

318. Ibid., 259 ff. (Spanish trans., vol. 1, 219 ff.).

319. Ibid., 261 (Spanish trans., vol. 1, 220). Bloch does not defend irrationalism. He comments here about the cognitive element of critique and the formulation of the possible utopia.

320. Ibid., 285 (Spanish trans., vol. 1, 240).

321. Ibid., sec. 19, 288 ff. (Spanish trans., vol. 1, 243 ff.). In Marx 1956–90, vol. 2, 1 ff.

322. Bloch 1959, 311 (Spanish trans., vol. 1, 263).

323. Ibid., 311 (Spanish trans., vol. 1, 262–64; English trans., 1986, vol. 1, 268).

324. See §3.2.

325. Bloch 1959, sec. 22, 391 (Spanish trans., vol. 1, 334; English trans., 1986, vol. 1, 336).

326. Ibid., secs. 23 ff., 395 ff. (Spanish trans., vol. 1, 337 ff.).

327. *Grundrisse einer besseren Welt*, secs. 33 ff., 521 ff. (Marx 1956–90, vol. 2, 7 ff.).

328. The point is to "explain" (also in a scientific and critical way) the *cause* of pain.

329. *Grundrisse*, sec. 33, 523 (Marx 1956–90, vol. 2, 11).

330. It is possible to accuse the analytical tradition of falling into what could be called a "Humean fallacy." This fallacy could be articulated as follows: "The self-responsible living *being* cannot serve as the material foundation of the imperative for the reproduction and development of human life." Hume and his followers are convinced about the impossibility of this "passage" because they are not aware of the possibility of a material foundation of practical reason. In this way they also dismiss the strong rationality of the ethical imperative that is grounded on the ethical exigency of the victim and that makes the denial of the victim's life irrational. Hume's proposal was "used" by Scottish and English early hegemonic capitalism. The one who "is" a slave (or a salaried worker) is not allowed to articulate the foundations of the imperative of his freedom (or nonexploitation). In Bloch's "daydream" the slave dreams "to-be-already-free" (hopeful anticipation that mobilizes praxis), a situation that finds its origins negatively in the slave's condition of "not-being-able-to-live."

331. It should have been said here: "By reference to the universal principle

NOTES TO CHAPTER 5   625

of life, of which economy is the moment of reproduction and development as *conditio sine qua* all the rest is impossible."

332. Bloch 1959, sec. 36, 725 (Spanish trans., vol. 1, 191).

333. Ibid., secs. 35 ff., 526 ff. (Spanish trans., vol. 1, 14 ff.).

334. Bloch hardly overcomes "Eurocentrism" even though he explicitly sets out to do so. Beginning with the Greeks and with a negative perception of the Egyptians that was linked to an Indo-Europeanist German interpretation that Bloch was not able to criticize, he later pursues a description of some positions that took place outside of Europe (ibid., sec. 53, 1417 ff. [Spanish trans., vol. 3, 311 ff.]). He offers a positive reinterpretation of Moses (ibid., 1450 ff. [Spanish trans., vol. 3, 341 ff.]). This interpretation will later make possible the emergence of a theology of hope in Bloch's own Tübingen by Jürgen Moltmann. In its turn, this theology influenced the later Latin American theology of liberation: "A people who have been enslaved: here lies the misery which provides the basis for prayer. And it is at this moment that a founder appears who ends the life of a representative of the governing tyranny: this is how suffering and rebellion can be found here at the very origins and together constitute the basis for faith upon the road towards freedom. . . . The Deus Spes is thus already prefigured and can be found in Moses" (ibid., sec. 53, 1453 [Spanish trans., vol. 3, 344]). However, Bloch's Moses is a "superfounder" with hardly any antecedents. His account lacks a historical orientation as he is unable to perceive that Moses is impossible without the fertile ground of Egyptians and Mesopotamians' ethical orientations. They already possessed critical elements that are still alive today. I was classified as a fideist or "theologian" for using these types of theoretical sources by scholars who claimed to articulate a strictly philosophical discourse (Cerutti 1983; Schutte 1993). My critics dismissed the liberating structure of *prephilosophical* religious myths like those to which Bloch referred, standing in opposition to a bourgeois Jacobin tradition. He writes: "*Deus spes* is found . . . positive" (Bloch 1959, 1464 [Spanish trans., vol. 3, 353]). See my article "Exodus as a Paradigm," *Concilium* 189 (1987): 83–92. It is possible to say that Bloch's work consisted in "mulling over" the idea (like Nietzsche's cow) of the slaves' exodus in Egypt. It would have been very useful for Zarathustra to know Moses, but the Indo-Europeanism of the German academy did not allow him to do it. See also Bloch 1970, 19 ff.

335. Bloch 1959 sec. 37, 729 ff. (Spanish trans., vol. 1, 196 ff.).

336. Ibid., secs. 38 ff., 767 ff. (Spanish trans., vol. 1, 229 ff.).

337. Ibid., sec. 43, 1089 ff. (Spanish trans., vol. 3, 7 ff.).

338. Putnam remained at this point (see §3.2).

339. Bloch 1959, sec. 54, 1567 (Spanish trans., vol. 3, 447; English trans., 1986, vol. 3, 1326).

340. Ibid., sec. 54, 1551 (Spanish trans., vol. 3, 347; English trans., 1986, vol. 3, 1312).

341. Aristotle ("The good [*agathón*] is that for which all have an appetite [*aphiesthai*]," *Nicomachean Ethics*, bk. 1, 1 [Aristotle 1960, 1094a 3]) and Thomas Aquinas thought that appetite and the good were correlative: one has an "appetite" for the "good [*bonum*]." This formulation is no longer acceptable today.

342. Bloch cannot perceive this aspect (of the intersubjectively valid) because he relies exclusively on a paradigm of consciousness and not on a linguistic-

intersubjective one. In politics, this aspect refers to the necessary intersubjective mediation of both democracy and the formulation of the future feasible utopian project.

343. Bloch perceives the ontological "possibility" of the good utopian future, but he does not elaborate on the ethical "feasibility" of the *present* good. Habermas criticizes Bloch on this point in the name of science. It would also be necessary to do it in the name of technology as well as in the name of strategic and instrumental reason.

344. This problem leads Apel to attempt to achieve symmetry "by other means"—as Karl Clausewitz would say. Apel uses a "complementary ethics" (an "ethics of responsibility"?) to do this. But an acritical "ethics of responsibility," such as that of Max Weber, ends up being cynical (Hinkelammert 1994). Liberation ethics does not need to be complemented in this way.

345. I pointed this out to Apel as early as our first encounter in Freiburg in 1989 (Dussel 1990a, figure, 69). Level 3b (the "community of communication that is possible in history") is the level of the critical community of victims (of those who are in the "exteriority" of the hegemonic system in vigor: level 2b. What was first an "intuition" now becomes a clear distinction at the level of categories.

346. See §6.2.

347. See table 8 [198], moment 1a.

348. Moment 1 in figure 13 [251].

349. Moment 1b in table 8.

350. The ethical subject possesses a supreme dignity in the "cycle" of the reproduction of life on planet Earth. As Kant wrote, a person is not a means; but, beyond Kant, a person is not an end either. A person is *an ethical subject who "proposes" (and "judges") the ends*. All living beings have dignity or value in terms of how they stand in relation to the production, reproduction, and development of *human life*, which, by virtue of its reality and (cerebral complexity) and ethical character (*eticidad*) (responsible self-awareness), is the ultimate referent of life as such. This is not an anthropocentric position. I aim only to locate human beings by virtue of their complexity in the central point of the "cycle of life."

351. Moment 2 in table 8.

352. Moments 3–5 in table 8.

353. Responsibility for the effects (as in Max Weber or Jonas 1982a) or a posteriori ontic responsibility, is different from the "re-sponsibility" for the victim that is *previous* to the organization of the new order—a priori transontological "re-sponsibility," in Levinas's terms. When the effect or "unintentional" result is not merely an "object," but the alienation or *negativity* of an ethical subject, anyone who becomes aware of the "effects" of his or her actions on the Other becomes *critical*. The subject is not responsible for the effects, because the effect is "unintentional." In cases like this, it is not even possible, from the perspective of the system, to become responsible because this requires intention. *Critical* "re-sponsibility" for the Other as victim is the "putting of the alienating *system* itself as totality *in crisis*." The simple Weberian responsibility for the consequences of the system only means to take charge, *"in" the existing system of ends and values* (which are not put in crisis, but *corroborated* as tradition), of the merit or punishment due to the act.

354. See table 9 [208], moment 6a.

355. From the "positive" field of the human subject's dignity.

356. See figure 13 [251], moment 2. The innovating order of the drives is co-constituted by critical reason (moment 4 in figure 13).

357. Moment 6b in table 9. Levinas refers here to a *pre*originary ethical reason ("une raison pré-originelle"; Levinas 1974, 212), which is located *before* and *below* ethical originary reason itself (moment 1b in table 8).

358. Neither Hegel nor Honneth (1992) clearly expound the "struggle for the recognition" of the Other *as other*.

359. Moment 7 in table 9.

360. See moment 5 in figure 12 [209].

361. This theme is examined in §2.5 [149–52] and in §§3.1–2 [168–78].

362. See, for instance, "system 1" (reality from the point of view of whatever is hegemoni(c) in figures 12 [209] and 15 [310].

363. See "system 2," or future system, in figures 12 and 15.

364. See "paradigm 2," or critical paradigm, in figure 15.

365. Critical intersubjectivity refers to the *critical community* (see moment 5 in figure 12) that plays the role of the "*sociohistorical* subject" of the praxis of liberation (see §6.2).

366. From early on in my work, I have distinguished the "ethical" or critical consciousness that "hears the cry of the poor" from the "moral consciousness" that simply takes care of applying the moral principles of the hegemonic system. See Dussel 1970–80, vol. 2 [1972], sec. 24, 52 ff.

367. See §§4.1–4.4 [213 ff.].

368. Levinas 1974, 21 ff. (English trans., 1998, 165 ff.). Levinas writes: "Skepticism, which traverses the rationality or logic of knowledge, is a refusal to synchronize the implicit affirmation contained in the saying and the negation which this affirmation states in the said" (ibid., 213 [English trans., 1998, 167]). The Said is expressed in the hegemonic system. Saying is, in contrast, the interpellation of the Other, of the victim as exteriority. The interpellation of the victim shows (diachronically or from the future) the noncoincidence of (a) the "truth" of "*dominating* reason, which is fixed in the past" (in "reference" to *reality*, as it is conceived from the point of view of the dominating system [1]), and (b) the "*critical* reason as the present" (with "reference" to *reality* as it is accessed from exteriority [system 2]). By virtue of the very contradictory and *negative* presence of the victims (the poor, the woman who becomes a sexual object, and so on), the hegemonic system that dominates turns illegitimate. Whoever inhabits the *new* world from the perspective of the victims discovers *new* objects, that is, to use Thomas Kuhn's terms, objects that could not be observed from the previous paradigm. For this reason, this subject becomes *skeptical* about the past moments of reason (which begin to be falsified). Skepticism always reemerges when there are radical historical changes. This is the skepticism of ethical-critical reason, which discovers the *untruth* of the dominating order. It does not accept the "truth" or the "*ratio*" of domination. Is not all this *ambiguously* found in Nietzsche or the postmoderns? The difference is that the ethics of liberation is able to demonstrate the untruth and the irrationality of the hegemonic order from the point of view of the critical truth and the new rationality of the victims. Postmoderns, in contrast, tend to "throw the baby out with the bath water."

369. Preface of the *Philosophy of Right* (Hegel 1971, vol. 7, 24): "Was *vernünftig* ist, das ist *wirklich*; und was *wirklich* ist, das ist *vernünftig*" ("What is reasonable is real, and what is real is reasonable").

370. See Popper 1967.

371. In a similar way, during the military dictatorship in Argentina, numerous philosophers aimed to demonstrate, with the use of reductive arguments (often inspired by philosophical analysis), the nonvalidity of any *critical* Latin American philosophy, which included psychoanalysts' and Marxists' positions as well as the philosophy of liberation.

372. Dussel 1990a, 89 (the *diagram* on the passage from situation 1 of argumentation to situation 2).

373. See, among others, Bauman 1994; Critchley 1992; Dews 1987; Habermas 1985; Lyotard 1979; Ross 1989; Vattimo 1985 and 1988; Welsch 1993a and 1993b.

374. Dussel 1970–80, vol. 1 (1970), sec. 14, "*Lo otro* como di-ferencia en la Totalidad" (103 ff.); sec. 15, "*Lo otro* como di-ferencia interna de la mismidad moderna" (108 ff.); sec. 16, "*Lo otro* como *el Otro* escatológicamente dis-tinto" (118 ff.). See also Dussel 1977, secs. 2.4.3–4, 2.5.3, 3.2.7.2, 4.1.8, and others. The development of this theme was part of a debate with Derrida and Deleuze in the 1970s.

375. Ofelia Schutte (1993) argues that I *deny* "difference"—in the feminist sense of "gender" as articulated by Benhabib 1987 and Benhabib and Cornell 1992. She does not take into consideration the diversity of the terminology in the text: I *deny* "difference" as *the other* (neuter, in the sense of an object) in Identity, while I strongly *affirm* "dis-tinction" as the Other (as someone or ethical subject) in the exteriority, in the alterity *as other*. Schutte's confusion could only be the product of not reading the text.

376. See Dussel 1977, end of the foreword.

377. See Welsch 1993b, 12–13.

378. I will consider a part of this topic in §6.2, discussing there the issue of the "locus of enunciation" of critical discourse: the victim as a dis-tinct, new, emergent *historical subject*.

379. See §6.1.

380. See §6.2.

381. See §1.4 [99] and in §§2.5, 4.1, and 4.2.

382. As a negative position, it is moment 7 in figure 12.

383. Moment 8 in table 9.

384. The "liberation pro-ject [*Entwurf*]" is ontological. However, since it unfolds *beyond* (in exteriority) the current system by affirming the negative aspects of the victim's position (defining, as part of the project, for instance, "food" in light of "hunger," and so on), I frequently refer to it as transontological. It is PL, the project of liberation, in figure 12 [209]. See Dussel 1970–80, vol. 2, secs. 22–25, 34ff; and Dussel 1977, sec. 3.1.9.

385. This could also be referred to as a dialectical "understanding" of the "foundation" of negativity or as a critical hermeneutical "interpretation" (like P. Ricoeur's *La simbolic du mal*, 1963).

386. The formal and the natural sciences may intentionally propose certain "objectives" for their "research program." This program serves as a *means* (having a "means"-to-"ends" relation and not an "exterior" one) for the unac-

complished needs of the victims. A *"proletarian* mathematics" does not have any sense as a direct propositional content. But one could perceive a more profound and indirect intention in its *ambiguous* formulation. It is possible to talk about an "ethical" choice of a given "objective" when, for instance, a mathematician decides to find the solution to certain equations that represent necessary formal mediations, for example, for the development of a special technique for poor peasants in Africa (one that requires the development of new scientific abstract approaches). This choice may modify or even innovate the old "research program." "Scientificism" consists in that *practical* attitude of the scientist which ignores and even explicitly denies the *inevitable* practical-concrete *link* of its "research program" with a "life world" ("form of life" in the second Wittgenstein's words), with a technology, with a real economic and political system. Denial, forgetfulness, or blindness in regard to such a "link" is the perverse moment par excellence of the scientist's *"uncritical* ethical consciousness," sustained under the pretenses of pure objectivity and neutrality. In this, a scientist is doubly at fault, as a human being and as a scientist.

387. See §4.1.

388. Scientists can also pursue the study of the impossibility of the system *in the long run* by virtue of the "intolerable" number of its victims.

389. See §5.3 [302–15]. See also Dussel 1996a, sec. 4: "Is a *Critical* Ethics Possible? The Three Criteria of Demarcation."

390. It is more than the simple "commitment" taken by an anthropologist in order to "understand" the concrete motivations of the agent "observed" (participative observation). See Winch 1994.

391. See Dussel 1990b, 429 ff.: *"Capital* is an ethics."

392. Letter of April 30, 1867, the same year in which *Capital*, bk. 1, to which it refers, appeared (Marx 1956–90, vol. 30, 542).

393. In the first moment, the community of victims' critical consciousness is *naive* (see §5.1); in the second moment, the co-solidary scientific community produces *critical human* or *social science* as an act of ethical re-sponsibility with the victim; and in the third moment, the victims themselves take on the critical-scientific results in their struggle for recognition: it is an *enlightened* practical and critical consciousness.

394. Cohen 1919 (English trans., 23).

395. Moment 8 in figure 12.

396. In like manner, there were three moments: (a) the militant's ingenuous utopian hope; (b) the participation of the community of re-sponsible scientists; and (c) the enlightened militant hope that is discussed in Bloch's work.

397. See Hinkelammert 1984.

398. The Frankfurt school's critique of instrumental reason ignored the necessary elaboration of a critical instrumental reason, which is part of the constructive process of the praxis of liberation. It intervenes in the formulation of a *feasible* alternative, as in the *real* construction of the new historical epoch. Perhaps the reason the Frankfurt school did not develop this dimension of the liberation project is that it was not part of any effective historical process of liberation before, during, or after the Second World War.

Chapter 6. The Liberation Principle

1. In volume I of my book *Politics of Liberation*, these "liberation fronts" will be called different practical *fields* (in a sense close to that used by Bourdieu).

2. See Fukuyama 1992.

3. Eribon 1989, 291. See Boyne 1990.

4. Foucault's first stage is the one in which he wrote his three classic works: Foucault 1972, 1966, and 1969.

5. See Habermas 1985, 331 ff. (Spanish trans., 337 ff.). "It is thus evident that a value-neutral analysis of the strong and weak points of an adversary is useful for someone seeking to undertake struggle against them: but why should this struggle be undertaken in the first place? *Why is struggle preferable to submission? Why should we oppose domination?* It is only by introducing some kinds of normative notions that Foucault could begin to respond to such questions" (333 [Spanish trans., 339]). "Dissent extracts its only justification by laying traps for humanist discourse without letting itself be trapped by it" (338 [Spanish trans., 332]).

6. See especially in Foucault 1975 and 1976.

7. Never defined, but always moving around the issue, without making a frontal attack. Such position, according to Habermas's critique, is deemed a "philosophy of life"—with all the reactionary ambiguity of such works for German thought, but not for us, provided the semantic precautions are taken (to which I have often referred when discussing the issue in this *Ethics of Liberation*).

8. Foucault 1975, 191 (Spanish trans.).

9. Foucault 1976, 175–76 (Spanish trans.). Part V of *The Will to Know* ("The Right to Die and the Power over Life") is important for the founding of the first ethical principle (see chapter 1 of this *Ethics*).

10. Engels's prologue to his work *The Origin of the Family, Private Property, and the State* (in Marx 1956–90, vol. 21, 27).

11. Foucault rejects as dogmatic the "postulates" of the French Left of that time: the "philosophy of the [*substantiated*] subject" (proletariat as *metaphysical* subject); the "location" as the center of the one uttering (which decentralizes and distributes in "space"); the "subordination" of the supra- to the infrastructure; "essentialization" (of a power possessed as attribute, especially by the state, which is exerted on a defenseless subject: the dominated one); the single voice of the "mode" (only "violence," etc.); the "legal" system (historiography with necessary laws); the uncriticized privilege of the "place" from which discourse is issued (as in the avant-garde), and so on. These negations do not mean that such levels should be *definitely* left aside. Foucault knows very well that it will be necessary to *reintroduce them, already "criticized"* in his subsequent discourse (many Foucauldians throw "the baby out with the bathwater"—Castro-Gómez, for example, in his intelligent 1996 work).

12. "Power is not an institution, and is not a structure, it is not a certain potency some are endowed with; it is the name given to a complex strategic situation in a given society" (Foucault 1976, 113, in the Spanish translation).

13. The opposition between totality and exteriority, system and victim could be deemed "dualism," but, as a method, it is only the "abstract" categorial consideration of "relationships" that get more complex in more concrete levels.

Thus the victim in the horizon of "gender" can be the woman, who must also be differentiated by culture, nation, class, historical situation, in order to allow a description at the *microphysical* level. The abstract is not at war with the concrete, and in this sense Foucault might be useful at the microphysical level, without our having to deny the macrophysical level (his own apparent negation, as I have mentioned, of the "style" of his rhetorical, polemic writing, located within the *narrow* horizon of a Eurocentric French philosophy, starting from the traumatic 1968 "experience").

14. In *liberation fronts* we place ourselves also at the level of the *microphysical*, when we reflect on "each" concrete liberation horizon (ecological, feminist, antiracist, of exploited classes, of the marginalized, etc.). The "victim" is not a "*metaphysical* subject," but the analogical (or metaphorical) denomination of "many" fronts struggling for recognition (whence alterity's diversity or "pluralism," more radical than the mere pluralism of difference *in identity*). The "poor" person of my first *Ethics* (Dussel 1970–80) was not a *metaphysical* subject either, but the analogical alterative realm of abstract exteriority, Levinas's "outside" (which is more clearly analyzed than Foucault's). The *erotic, the pedagogic, the political,* and so on, were more concrete realms, as an introduction to many microphysics (at that time we specifically discussed the "family," the "school," etc.).

15. For instance, in *Le souci de soi* (Foucault 1984).

16. In our architecture it would be something like the actions governed by the preservation instinct or reproduction drive. See level 1 of table 10 [257]. Foucault's spontaneity would be like the aggression (1.1.1) or receptivity instinct (resistance instinct, 1.1.2).

17. Foucault 1976, 167 (Spanish trans.). Before, power was exerted on death, now on life.

18. Strictly speaking, Foucault's thought is "critical" at the level of the microphysics of power. It would stop being critical if it negated macrophysics, with all its resulting consequences (e.g., a critique of global capitalism, with its multiple power relations, would be impossible; such a critique would be incomplete, as well, if it remained limited to a national scale, and would revert, against his will—and this happens specifically to many Foucauldians or postmoderns—to conservative and even reactionary positions: see Hinkelammert 1995c).

19. See Jay's wonderful work 1994 (on Foucault, 381 ff.; in Levinas, 543 ff.). The philosophy of Liberation distinguishes the ontological dimension of "seeing" from the uniquely ethical capacity of "hearing" (Dussel 1977, 1.1.5.1, 2.6.3.1); it insists, from the beginning, that the Other is beyond the "order of *vision*" (Dussel 1970–80, vol. 1 [1973], 121–22: the Other is not revealed "in the luminous order of the world, in the order of vision and of that which is limited to the eyes, in the realms of knowledge understood as *noeîn*, understanding, of that which is known, thought, or conceived of . . . , but which unfolds instead in another dimension defined upon the basis of what is enabled by the concept of *Alterity* . . . by means of the word, open to listening, with an attentive, evocative ear, where one's vocation from the perspective of *the Other* is revealed as a language").

20. Foucault 1975, 208 (French ed.).

21. See the concept of "schiasme" (chiasmus) in Mario T. Ramírez's doctoral thesis, "El quiasmo en el pensamiento de Merleau-Ponty," National Au-

tonomous University of Mexico, 1994 (by the same author, see Ramírez 1996). Chiasmus is the characteristic approach of Merleau-Ponty, a great phenomenologist, in which he asserts his thought in relation to two extremes always present and coimplicated.

22. This is the "critical-strategic-reason," between levels 8 and 9 of table 9 [208]. Mere axiological or evaluating reason can only be estimative; analytic or instrumental reason can be theoretical or technical. Strategic reason (in the action that seeks the practical success) includes analytic, axiological, and instrumental reason, but it takes all of them in order to determine the best "means" to reach the practical, strategic, political "end," within power relationships. They are utterances or norms with rightness claims, traditionally studied in a monological form as belonging to the *phrónesis*, now intersubjectively; when *critical*, reason has a validity claim from material negativity, since it assumes the perspective of the excluded—an issue not *explicitly* discussed by Foucault, but that would have led him into a performative self-contradiction if he had wanted to deny it: in fact, he took always "the side of" the sick, mentally ill, prisoners, and so on.

23. We always speak of five practical levels: (1) norms, (2) actions, (3) (Foucauldian) *microstructures*, (4) institutions (subsystems, realms, or concrete organizations) and (5) whole ethical systems (like, for instance, all the French "classical age" for Foucault). Foucault places himself preferably in the third level (not necessarily in institutions, which are frequently moments of minor subsystems)—just as Illich did in the 1960s in Latin America, in a notably creative form (see Illich 1971a and 1971b). When, for instance, Walzer (1983) and Rawls (1971) discuss "institutions," they do it in a completely "naive" way, if we compare their discussion with Foucault's sophisticated analysis.

24. Hinkelammert 1984, 242.

25. See at level 10 of table 9 [208]. "Liberating reason" is not "emancipating reason." The "liberating interest" must not be confused with "emancipatory interest" that is discursive or cognitive-enlightened" (in moment 8 of both levels of table 8 [195], and 7 and 10 of table 9).

26. Levels 9 and 10 of figure 12 [209].

27. Letters of February 10, 1842 (Marx 1956–90, vol. 27, 395 ff.).

28. See Marx, "Glosa crítica al artículo *El rey de Prusia y la reforma social*," *Vorwärts*, August 1844; in Marx 1956–90, vol. 1, 392 ff.

29. See Löwy 1979, 144 ff.

30. For us, it is the "*critical* social science," in a strict sense.

31. It is the moment of re-sponsibility for the Other, of "taking the side" of the Other as an ethical moment constitutive of the critique in a strong, negative and material sense (as we have shown in §4.1).

32. "*Functional*" social science. The source of the quotation is "Critical Notes," in Marx 1956–90, vol. 1, 405–6 (Spanish trans., vol. 1, 517).

33. It is the first criterion of this *Ethics* (see §1.5a). Marx writes: "This community, from which his or her own work is separated, is *life itself*, the physical and *spiritual* life, human morality, human pleasure, human essence" (Marx 1956–90, vol. 1, 405–6 [Spanish trans., 517]).

34. Ibid., 408 (Spanish trans., 519).

35. This is the "community of life" that we placed before Apel's mere "communication community" (see Dussel 1990a).

36. Marx 1956–90, vol. 1, 408 (Spanish trans., 520). Marx writes: "The revo-

lution in general—the *overthrowing* [*Umsturz*] of existent power and the *dis-
solutión* [*Auflösung*] of the old relations—is a *political act*" (ibid., 409 [Spanish
trans., 520]). What we have here is a first definition of the maximum limit of
the sociohistorical "transformation," as we shall see.

37. Ibid., 405 (Spanish trans., 517).

38. This is the title of chap. 6, 1a, in ibid., vol. 2, 82 ff. (Spanish trans., 1967,
144 ff.).

39. This is Lenin's final position (see §6.1 [349 ff.]).

40. Marx 1956–90, vol. 1, 89 (Spanish trans., 151).

41. "Feasibility" (can) and "normativeness" (must) are pointed out here. See
§6.5b1 [394 ff.] below.

42. Marx 1956–90, vol. 2, chap. 4, 38 (Spanish trans., 1967, 101–2). This is
Freire's pedagogical method.

43. Thesis 6; Marx 1956–90, vol. 3, 6 (Spanish trans., at the end of *La ideología alemana* [1970], 667).

44. Ibid., thesis 1, p. 5 (Spanish trans., 665).

45. Ibid., thesis 3, p. 6 (Spanish trans., 666). We can now understand that
Paulo Freire applies this principle to the pedagogical. As we shall see, Marx
confusedly identifies transformation ethics with revolution here.

46. The totality of the dominant system appears as "nontruth" for Adorno
(see §4.2), from the victim's practical position.

47. Intrasystemic, at level O1 of figure 15 [310] of "paradigm 1" within the
horizon of the standing or hegemonic "system 1."

48. I have insisted that life is the criterion of truth, and that reality appears
to the human being who is living from the demands of life itself. In addition, at
a strategic level, reality must answer to the feasibility criterion, of power—even
in a Foucauldian sense.

49. Marx 1956–90, vol. 3, 5 (Spanish trans. [1970], 666).

50. Moment B of figure 19 [339]. Does the concept of "movement" here
refer to a "social movement"?

51. Marx 1956–90, vol. 3, 35 (Spanish trans. [1970], 37).

52. Moment C of figure 19. Here "party" as a "group" *within* the workers'
parties (moment B), *within* the proletariat in general (moment A). See Löwy
1979, 187 ff.

53. "The real socialism," in Marx 1956–90, vol. 1, 453 (Spanish trans., 559–
60).

54. Revolutionary thought is, finally, the extreme limit of a critical—not
functional or reformist—"transformer thought" from the victims.

55. Marx 1956–90, vol. 1, 47, 51–52. It may be both moment A or B of figure
19.

56. Arrow b of figure 19. Marx writes: "Let us consider that a communist
congress would be premature at this point. Only once in all of Germany communist associations have been constituted and once these have gathered means
of action, only then will the various delegates of them will be able to meet in
a congress" letter of June 15, 1846). "We consider that a communist congress
would be premature as things currently stand. Only when communist associations have been established in all of Germany and when they have drawn
together such mediums for action, will it be feasible for the delegates of diverse
associations to meet together in congress" (Marx 1956–90, vol. 4, 21).

57. "*Critical* social science" (see §§5.3b [308 ff.] and 5.5c1 [332]).

58. "Scientists" *deduce* "wrong" tactics from their theories, according to Marx (a practical error of the strategic reason, from a *critical* position). That is, "theories" are relevant for the "strategy" of struggle within the "diagrams" of the *macrophysics* of power.

59. Now the politicians, within the tactics of strategic reason, are the ones who *deduce* practically "wrong" positions, according to Marx. For Marx, such "diagnosis" is false, because their "theory" is "false," but just the same, many "practical" premises are also "false." Thus we enter into the complex horizon of "liberation praxis," which is not a simplified opposition between "theory and praxis."

60. *Philosophy's Misery*, vol. 2, sec. 5, in Marx 1956–90, vol. 4, 179 (Spanish trans. [1970], 56–57).

61. This would be, as I have mentioned, at level C (communists), within the working-class parties (B) of (A) of figure 19. Even *among* the communists (C) there would still be a community of intellectuals, a critical-scientific community (the community expressed in "paradigm 2" of figure 15 [310] from the proletariats' "interest": (system 2), in which we must include Marx, Schapper, Bauer, Engels, Moll, and Wolff (the signers of the *Manifesto*; see "Das Komite" in Marx 1956–90, vol. 5, 2).

62. See Paragraph 1 (462 ff.; 27 ff.). It is level A of figure 19.

63. Marx 1956–90, vol. 5, 40. This type of formulation has been taken by *standard* epistemology as evidence of nonfulfillment of Marxist's "nonscientistic" prediction." Marx repeatedly indicated that capitalism has the possibility of overcoming its inherent contradiction, opening to horizons of greater contradictions, although, *in the long run*, its final crisis is inevitable, for the reasons pointed out. But the *strong* "scientific" movement is not the demonstration of "impossibility" of capitalism (before "functional" bourgeois and economists); it is, rather, the "explication" of the "cause" of negativity of the victims *before the victims themselves*.

64. Ibid., vol. 2, 474 ff. (Spanish trans., 41 ff.).

65. "The communists do not form a separate party opposed to other workers' parties. They have no interest in being separated from the proletariat groups" (ibid.).

66. Ibid., vol. 3, 482 ff. (Spanish trans., 51 ff.). Here "utopian" refers to the anarchist: trying the "impossible" (see §§3.4 and 3.5), or to those who use strategies (and tactics) that make "the historical transformation" equally "impossible" (Marx here thinks of the "revolutionary" praxis regarding groups that "repudiate all political action, and above all, revolutionary action"; ibid., 490 [Spanish trans., 59]).

67. Position defined in the sense of an "upside-down" organization (arrow a of figure 19). For Marx's strategic and tactical positions until the end of his life, see Löwy 1979, 236 ff.

68. *Explanation*, but within the tradition of understanding (*verstehen*) from the basis of a "well-founded-foundation"; more an "appearance-essence" than a process characterized by "cause and effect." See Wright 1971, chaps. 2 and 4; and Dussel 1988, chap. 14.

69. See Dussel 1985a, 1988, and 1990b.

70. See the ample biography in Nettl 1967. Cf. also Aubet 1962 and Gómez Llorente 1975.

71. See Nye 1994, 3 ff.

72. See Wallerstein 1974–89, vol. 1, chap. 6: regarding the "world system" he writes: "Russia outside, but Poland inside" (425, in the Spanish trans).

73. In 1897 she defended her doctoral thesis in political sciences, "Poland's Industrial Development," in Zurich (see Luxemburg 1979).

74. *Reforma social o Revolución*, 8; Luxemburg 1966, vol. 1, 128 (Spanish trans. [1967], 104). "Theory" here is also principle.

75. The strategic and practical level.

76. In this case they are called "of socialism." But in an ethics of liberation metalanguage, it is about the *ethical*, *moral*, and *critical* "principles"—valid in each liberation "front" with different content. It is the case of a rich diversity and not a mere incommensurable pluralism; a diversity "crossed" by a *transversal* reason (to use Wolfgang Welsch's terms).

77. See the relationship between the material and formal principles regarding *standard* feasibility (figure 10 [197]). Now not only do the first two principles frame the third one, but the first five principles frame the sixth one we are discussing, in the most complex form.

78. If I were to adopt the feminist, ecologist, antiracist, and so on, perspective, I would place it in the corresponding level of "organization" of the different social "movement." Luxemburg places herself in a preponderantly political level, while I place ourselves in the ethics of liberation metalanguage (which must be valid for the various concrete levels, among them, the political level).

79. This corresponds to level 9 of table 9 [208]. I pointed out there that (technical) instrumental reason and (theoretical) analytical reason are in the same realm of mediation as (practical) strategic reason, though many distinctions could be made along the way, since instrumental reason is exercised from within the framework of the formality of means and ends as a subject-nature relationship that must be materially technically transformed; while analytical reason is exercised as a form of abstract theoretical reason that grapples with objects or facts to be known; and strategic reason starts from the theoretically known, from the perspective of technical ends, and even from that of cultural values (be they ends or means: and in the latter case, when understood in terms of their exercise of axiological reason, level 8 of table 9) *to be implemented feasibly and critically* in the present with the purpose of advancing "success," understood in terms of effective efforts to obtain the liberation of the victims of a specific historical moment. This then implies another kind of exercise, interest, content, "object," etc. In any case I have sought to situate such forms of rationality solely at level 9 in order to restrict the range of classification of possible phenomena to be included.

80. Bebel wrote: "The right tactic is more important than the right program" (in *Vorwärts*, a publication of the Social Democracy Party of Germany, March 26, 1899).

81. Level B of figure 19 [339].

82. See §5.5b.2 [330 ff.].

83. See §5.5b.1 [329 ff.].

84. For Rosa Luxemburg these are the "reformists" in the style of Bernstein, who in the ethics of liberation metalanguage engage in "nonethical" acts (nor true, nor valid, nor critical feasible: whether they are norms, actions, micro-structures, institutions, or cultural ethicity).

85. In Germany, for instance, the debate between the (more reformist) *Realos* and the (more critical) *Fundi*.

86. The "revolutionary" is not strictly a criterion or ethical principle, or the only possibility of the critical praxis; but an extreme limit in the "transformation" process: the macro-political and economical transformation of a whole ethicity system. When a norm, action, subsystem, or institution is "transformed," and there is no revolutionary situation (which is exceptional), a critical criterion (ethical, as we shall see) can still be applied. The ethics of liberation does not necessarily and always propose *hic et nunc* "revolution" — which is an event that happens only once every many centuries in an ethical system — but demands "transformation" in all levels, from the most familiar, and on each occasion always starting from *one same criterion* and *ethical* principle (to be defined in §6.5), valid also for revolution.

87. Arrow a of figure 19 [339], where the "vanguard" (C) leads the proletariat organized as party (B), within the core of the proletariat as such (A).

88. Level C of figure 19, in arrow g.

89. Arrow f, of the relation of level B with A.

90. In fact, there would be an *a-critical* spontaneity of the masses of victims (in level A), which must be distinguished from the *critical* spontaneity of the victim's organized community (B). The masses' critical community (the party, the ecological movement, feminism, etc.) can reach, as I have noted, an *enlightened* criticism (when the expert's scientific critique is "assimilated" and subsequently "criticized" by the basis), without losing their "composure" or militant spontaneity (the last *key* resort of any liberation praxis, as we shall see below).

91. See in figure 17 [332], the mutually implicated relationship between the "expert" and the "critical militant."

92. See Luxemburg 1966–68, vol. 3, 83 ff. (Spanish trans. [1970], 41 ff.).

93. Ibid., 99 (Spanish trans., 57). It is exactly the case of the nonarticulation of "principles" and "ends," or of their identification in favor of the latter (figure 20).

94. Level C of figure 19.

95. Life itself, human life, the life of peoples, of the victims, has a great deal of self-regulated mechanisms that should not be overestimated (for this would be the irrational populist "spontaneism"), but nor should they be underestimated (for this would be the "consciencialism" of modern rationalism, of vanguards, of authoritarianism, of "democratic centralism" as *contradictio terminorum*).

96. I discuss the issue in §6.2.

97. Level d of figure 20, though it could also include part of the "liberation project" (concrete articulation of utopia as a regulative idea, *hic et nunc*).

98. Level e, the "means."

99. Lenin 1975, vol. 2, 295. Level f. According to Lenin, level f can be independent of the principles (a, b, and c), since, from his viewpoint, there is no reference to a possible ethics of liberation. "Theory" is subsequently developed by dialectic materialism, *but it is understood that "principles" should be exposed in an ethics*. Such is his fundamental mistake. By contrast, according to Luxemburg, the question of organization involves *all levels discussed* (from chapters 1 to 5 of this *Ethics*): the "question of organization" presupposes (ethical) prin-

ciples, theory (which she develops later in *The Accumulation of Capital*), and projects (programs from the socialist utopia).

100. Level B of figure 19, which includes the Russian Social Democratic Party.

101. Level C of figure 19 [339]: the "Bolsheviks."

102. Level A, among which some workers groups are "linked" to the party, while others are not, namely, the unorganized general workers mass.

103. In the 1907 *Prologue* (not included in the *Twelve-Volume Selected Works* I have been citing, edited in Moscow during Stalinism), Lenin makes the following correction: "It is only the participation of proletarian elements in the party . . . that will make it possible for all traces of an inbred circular mentality to disappear, which at present are nothing more than an obstacle. And the *principle of a democratic organization* proclaimed by the Bolsheviks in November 1905 in *Novaia Xzin*, when circumstances permitted open action, already constitutes, in the deepest sense, an irreversible rupture with what had decayed in the old circles" (quoted in Löwy 1979, 264).

104. "Concerning the Reorganization of the Party (1905), in Lenin 1961, vol. 1, 585.

105. Arrow g of figure 19.

106. "To mold" indicates the action of "*shaping*" "*matter*."

107. Lenin 1961, vol. 1, 593.

108. Level C of figure 19.

109. Figure 19, level B, arrow g.

110. Moments 3 and 5 of figure 12 [209].

111. Earlier I distinguished between (a) organized victims' *naive* critical conscience; (b) the explicit participation of the *critical* scientist, and (c) the way in which the victims' critical community, turning into an intersubjective community, becomes enlightened by the dominant systems' scientific and other instruments, and self-critical. But such articulation cannot be done in a Hegelian manner (as was proposed by Lenin), as a relation between the *active form* and the *quasi-passive matter*, but in an "organic" form, where "intervention" (as a certain "exterior" element) must be able to be "judged" by life, by the organized community of victims (last moment, level B of figure 19) according to the criterion of critical truth, discussed in chapters 1 and 4. Such a critical community may "accept" the expert's proposal (just as an organism "accepts" a vitamin) or may not (as when an organism "rejects" a virus). If such "intervention" is *accepted*, the community must integrate it into the structure of its now *enriched* life, which is transformed into a self-regulated substratum for a future greater life and strategic action. See figure 17 [332].

112. Lenin rightly shows that the "question of the truth" is related to the party (as the discovery, from exteriority, of the system's *nontruth* and the "openness" to a new reference to reality: the *truth* as critical, and thus, more universal than that of the prevailing system). But such reference to reality (from the horizon of life), also with strategic means, does not reach *only* vanguards, because it is the victims' organized community (the party, the social movement, etc.) that sets for the "scientific community," the experts' community, and so on, the "end" of its "critical-scientific research program": the explanation of the "causes" (foundations) of the negativity of the victims themselves ("interpellation" is prior [moment 6a of figure 12] to the intellectual's commitment [mo-

ment 6b] and to scientific "explanation" [moment 7]). Fidelity to such commitment is the only *guarantee* for intellectuals that they are on the "right track" (level B of figure 19 points out, as the *last resort*, the route of the *intelligentsia*, level C).

113. All the foregoing could be questioned if we consider, for instance, some 1917 texts, in which, at the time of the revolution, Lenin expresses full confidence in the masses: "There is no middle term. Experience has shown that there is not. Either all the power to the Soviets . . . or the land and property owners and capitalists will put a stop to everything" ("Uno de los problemas fundamentales de la revolución [One of the fundamental problems of the revolution]"; Lenin 1961, vol. 2, 288). But it can be noted that in this case, it is about the direct relation between the victims (level A of figure 19) and the standing system (I); but he does not speak about the organization of the party or the postrevolutionary state, but of a tactic to defeat the enemies *outside* the proletariat. The "proletariat's dictatorship" shall never mean a democratic symmetrical-discursive participation of real workers within the realm of the party or the postrevolutionary state.

114. Level C of figure 19.

115. Level A of figure 19.

116. Note the scorn expressed for vanguard's conscientiousness.

117. Luxemburg 1966–68, vol. 1, 199 (Spanish trans. [1970], 107).

118. Ibid., vol. 3; 158–59; 42–43.

119. Luxemburg uses the word *Aufklärung*: enlightenment, clearing. This can be deemed a contribution to Modernity; we know, however, that each culture (e.g., Muslim in the area of Baghdad, or Náhuatl in Mexico-Tenochtitlan) has its own "enlightenment": the *nucleus of reference* of culture's self-conscience wisdom. The European Enlightenment, obviously, is the enlightenment of the *first* world system's "center," with its specific degrees of development.

120. "To Rosa Luxemburg: Remarks Concerning Her Thesis for the International Group" ("A Rosa Luxemburg: Remarques à propos de son projet de thèse pour le groupe Internationale"), *Partisans* 45 (January 1969): 113 (quoted in Löwy 1979, 276).

121. Of which Lenin is accused.

122. According to Luxemburg, the "principles" always provide the framework and are immovable. Their place would be taken in Stalinism by the DIA-MAT, a positivist metaphysics that conceals a technologist and productivist project controlled by a dominant but minority bureaucracy: the culmination of a process that ignored the importance of democracy, and the symmetric participation and real spontaneous autonomy—though critical—of the organized base (level B of figure 19), which gave absolute priority, as the last resort, to the central "committee" (level C).

123. Luxemburg 1966–68, vol. 3, 88–89 (Spanish trans. [Luxemburg 1980], 46).

124. Ibid., 89 (Spanish trans., 47). Rosa comments that when Lenin asserts that "self-education is necessary in the spirit of organizational discipline" he is not making reference to the proletariat, but to some Social Democratic academics. "Lenin," says Luxemburg, "once again lets an excessively mechanical conception of organization slip in. . . . Lenin is thinking not only about the factory, but also about military barracks and in forms of modern bureaucracy and modern bureaucracy . . . and the obedience of the corpse of a dominated

class" (ibid., 90; 48). From this perspective the working class is a kind of raw, obedient, material that is finally unworthy of trust. When Luxemburg speaks of "barracks" (*Kaserne*) and "discipline" (*Disziplin*) one cannot help but think of Foucault, who must have read such texts during the time of the "scientific" version of French Leninism (dominated by the party's dogmatic elite), that was grounded in Althusser's conception of workers as vulgar and immersed in "ideology."

125. Level B of figure 19, which represents the last practical moment of liberation.

126. In fact, this is about intersubjectivity of the organized community (level B of figure 19) or of the community of victims in general (moment 5 of figure 12 [209]).

127. This is the case of the intersubjectivity of intellectuals or vanguards (level C of figure 19).

128. Luxemburg 1966–68, vol. 3, 92 (Spanish trans. [Luxemburg 1980], 50).

129. Such "being able to adhere [*gelangen kann*]" is key to the *acceptability* of the victim's interpellation (moment 6a of figure 12). It is the "ethical moment" par excellence, thanks to which the "scientific investigation program" of the critical social sciences can be developed (moment of the "epistemological third demarcation criterion").

130. This moment of the instinctual materiality of the petit-bourgeoisie's cultural subjectivity, for example, will last forever, one way or another, in those who "commit themselves" to the victims' liberation struggle. It is just what Leon Rozitchner discusses in *Freud and the Limits of Bourgeois Individualism* (Rozitchner 1972).

131. This formulation should make those who criticize the philosophy of liberation as "populist" think twice: some intellectuals "enlightened" in the European sense of that word are afraid of the popular—they are right not to fall into the irrational vitalism of the "spirit of the peoples," but they thereby lose something valuable, hewing to neither modern "consciencialism" nor liberal, elitist, or European "antipopulism." Luxemburg provides a complex balanced description, where each element is *necessary but not sufficient*.

132. Luxemburg 1966–68, vol. 3, 96–97 (Spanish trans. [Luxemburg 1980], 54–55).

133. Level C of figure 19.

134. Level B of figure 19.

135. Luxemburg 1966, vol. 3, 101 (Spanish trans. [Luxemburg 1980], 58).

136. Ibid., 102 (Spanish trans., 60).

137. Ibid., end; 105 (Spanish trans., 63).

138. The critiques directed to my work (e.g., Castro-Gómez 1996, 152) are unjustified, because to place oneself in the victims' perspective is not simply to "invert" Modernity: it is, to be exact, to opt for a *new* perspective, a level "three" (if "one" is domination, and "two" the dominated as dominated, then here one could simply "invert"—"three" would be access, by virtue of the victims' exteriority, to a *new postcolonial perspective*, in Mignolo's sense [1995a and 1995b]). The victim's exteriority is the *positivity* never included in the system because it is scorned, but, for that same reason, it is a guarantee of newness; this is the moment of the analectic positivity (see Dussel 1970–80, vol. 3 [1973] and 1977).

139. See the beginning of this *Ethics* §I.6 [36–41]. See also Dussel 1973, 75 ff.; Dussel 1974a, 33 ff.

140. *Grundlage der gesamten Wissenschaftslehre* (1794), vol. 1, sec. 3, D, 7 (Fichte 1971, vol. 1, 122).

141. Ibid., sec. 1, 7; Fichte 1971, vol. 1, 96.

142. Ibid., 97.

143. Ibid.; see Dussel 1974a, 43 ff.

144. Schelling, introduction to *System of Transcendental Idealism* (Schelling 1927, vol. 3, 344).

145. Schelling, *Allgemeine Anmerkung* (ibid., 630).

146. I made these points in Dussel 1970–80, vol. 3 [1973], sec. 1, 34 ff.

147. See ibid., 36 ff.

148. Heidegger, *Beginning and Time*, sec. 13; 62 (Heidegger 1963c, Spanish trans. [1968], 74).

149. Ibid., sec. 25, 114 (Spanish trans., 130).

150. I explained all these, in their practical dimension (as the same as Heidegger's), in Dussel 1970–80, vols. 1–5.

151. Heidegger, *Beginning and Time*, sec. 26, 118 (Heidegger 1963c, Spanish trans., 135). "The others [*die Anderen*] find us" in the world, but not primarily as "subjects *before the eyes*" (ibid., 119; 135). This "mode" of the others of coming "to our encounter" shall call for a specific hermeneutics. Starting from such indications, not subsequently continued by Heidegger, Levinas "shall de-found" the whole ontological "fundament" (see the explanation in §5.4).

152. See §3.3 [172].

153. Level 4 of table 8 [198].

154. In fact, they consider only a material rationality (Max Weber is an example) that has to do with values and "value judgment," merely subjective, individual, not universal.

155. See specifically §3.3 [181 ff.].

156. Luhmann 1984, 246 (Spanish trans., 190).

157. Ibid., 488 ff. (Spanish trans., 361 ff.).

158. Although, evidently, medical science and therapy are conscious "interventions" to correct nonintentional negative effects (sickness).

159. Luhmann 1984, 521 ff. (Spanish trans., 384 ff.). Because action is framed by rules concerning private property, inheritance, sanctions against robbery, the requirement to fulfill contracts and honor competence (*Konkurrenz*), these rules produce a logic that has its own immunity and that appears to the eyes of an external observer as a process in a self-regulated market. Actual self-conscious human subjects seem to be extraneous in this type of analysis.

160. The proletariat's "subjectivity" is "negotiated" in a totalitarian way by an unscrupulous bureaucracy.

161. See Althusser 1975a, 1975b, 1988, and Sánchez Vázquez 1978, among others.

162. See Foucault 1984, where he starts with Artemidorus's treatise on dreams (7 ff.).

163. "Passage" from level 2 to 3, of table 11.

164. See Foucault 1986.

165. As in the case of Lyotard (1989), who begins at the "system's performativity" (level 2 of table 11).

166. Peters Dews writes: "Moreover, contrary to the Frankfurt School, for

whom such contradiction between the illusory autonomy of the subject and his/her real slavery betrays the *preponderance of the objectified in subjects, which hinders them from becoming subjects* [quoting Adorno], for Foucault it suggests the desire to destroy the subject as *pseudo-sovereign*. The human being described by Foucault, whom he invites us to liberate, is already in essence, *the effect of a submission which is much deeper than himself* [quoting Foucault]" (Dews 1987, 161). (The quotation from Adorno is from his *Negative Dialectics*, English trans., 171; the first from Foucault is from "Revolutionary Action," English trans., 222; the second from *Discipline and Punish*, English trans., 30.)

167. Level 2 of table 11.

168. At this point I must agree that "Dussel fails to acknowledge the fact that the so-called *ethos of popular culture* is a text without borders, whose continuous process of writing cannot be directed from any center, since it has *as its subject a multiplicity of empirical actors who each read and rewrite in their own way*" (Castro-Gómez 1996, 168). I agree that a more complex analysis must be started, where the various enunciation "places" of popular culture discourses are discussed. But, just as the same Castro-Gómez accepts it, it has "*as subject* the multiplicity of empirical actors"—issue we shall discuss immediately, and thus "as a center" in the diversity of popular enunciation "places." This is a subtle question, it must be kept in tense complexity: neither metaphysical subject, or no-subject, subjective diversity as "diagram" (the popular diagram), intersubjectivity of Wittgensteinian "language games."

169. Deleuze 1991, 149.

170. Badiou 1995, 56. See Badiou 1982. We shall return to the issue when we deal with the sociohistorical subjects.

171. Dussel 1986, chap. 1. Of course, the "person" is not a "subject" in the strong sense. See Ricoeur 1990, 39 ff.

172. We are situated at level 2 of table 11.

173. See §§2.3–2.4 and §3.1.

174. Habermas 1985, 11, 346–46 and 354.

175. It would be level 4 of table 11.

176. See §4.4.

177. Level 5 of table 11.

178. One among so many formal systems, with its language-games, places of enunciation, forms of life, and so on.

179. The one that never rests is the fetish (*fetiço, made* by the hand of the systemic means-ends instrumental reason) of financial capital, like a great sacrificial Moloch that has a "fictitious subjectivity"; but subjects who negotiate this fetish in innumerable well-defined geographic "points" of the Earth in its destructive daily accumulation process are not fictitious but made of "flesh and blood."

180. That is, the "places" of enunciation in the power "diagram," for example, are empirical at a certain level (2 in table 11), but have as real "reference" material, corporeal subjects, who must produce, reproduce and develop their human life as a constitutive condition and fundamental position; if they die, there will no longer be any "place" of enunciation. If Indians are annihilated, the ethnic story of the American peoples will truly disappear—at least as an actual reality: the narrative of a dead language might be studied in the history of future linguistics.

181. Hinkelammert 1996, 42.

182. Even better than a project is the human *mode of reality*: we are not stones or Cartesian angels.

183. Hinkelammert 1996, 39.

184. The hunger or unemployment of dismissed workers does not become part of the company's "accounting books" or "computation." Nobody is "responsible" for the death of the unemployed.

185. I referred to this issue in chapters 1 and 4.

186. His/her invisibility is due to the cynical calculation of the functional instrumental reason in the fetishized system as a whole that becomes confused with reality itself. Workers are only a "means" and not "living human subjects." As humans, they need a salary to buy food, dress, house, and medicine for health. As subjects, above all, they deserve to be respected; their autonomy, freedom, and subjectivity should be re-cognized independently from the "system." They are not only an "end"—like the Kantian person—but also a subject who *places and judges the ends*.

187. These are the explicit and conscious "rules" of the functional system that subsumes human living subjects and "treats them" as "means," a reification considered by Lukács.

188. *Capital*, vol. 1, chap. 8; Marx 1956–90, 504; vol. 1, 660.

189. See chapter 4 on this issue. It is Levinas's main insight.

190. Hinkelammert 1996, 44–45.

191. If by definition it is an *inter*subjective it cannot have a "natural" existence. But the foregoing does not deny the existence of real "natural" subjects: each living human being.

192. The current "social movements" of civil society, but also classes, parties, institutions (universities, etc.), microstructures (family, etc.), and so on. Badiou's self-critique, fruit of an excessive culpability, is also excessive.

193. Badiou 1995, 56.

194. Hegel, *Rechtsphilosophie*, sec. 201 (Hegel 1971–79, vol. 7, 354).

195. Level A of figure 19.

196. It is an "interpretation" (hermeneutics) of concrete "reality."

197. The subjectivity of the victim must become the active subject of his or her own liberation.

198. The core of reference, of critical self-consciousness, which must "explain" negativity, has become lost in deviations already criticized by Luxemburg.

199. "The Indian Problem" (Mariátegui 1969, 55).

200. "Methodological Reflections on the Organization Question" (Lukács 1968, French trans., 334).

201. Such self-consciousness has nothing to do with Fichte's, Schelling's or Hegel's, but rather with Freire's "concientização," as an ethical-critical process (moments 1 to 7 of figure 12 [209]), the subject of which is the community of victims.

202. See Lukács, "Class Consciousness," 1 (Lukács 1968, French trans., 71 ff.).

203. "The Reification and Consciousness of the Proletariat" (ibid., 109 ff.).

204. Moment 3 of figure 12.

205. Lukács 1968 (French trans., 74).

206. Ibid., 102.

207. Moments 4 and 7 of figure 12.

208. Text quoted in [284] (Menchú 1985, 144).

209. "Methodological Reflections," 3 (Lukács 1968, French trans., 35).

210. Moment B of figure 19. "The Communist Party is, within Revolution, an *autonomous figure* of the proletariat class consciousness" (ibid., 371).

211. Moment C of figure 19.

212. Moments 5 and 7 of figure 12.

213. Lukács had difficulties when trying to write an ethics. See Lukács 1994. His *"Ethics"* remained unfinished, never written, due to difficulties or impossibilities? He was not aware that the relation was not "theory and praxis," but ethical principles that frame the strategic action—judging its compatibility, as ethical feasibility. His "aestheticisms" (just like Adorno's), to the detriment of an "ethics," bear on the issue here. "Alienated" work, according to Lukács, was to be criticized from the aesthetic utopia of nonalienated work, namely, artistic creation. Lukács did not see that "alienated" work, as an action of instrumental reason, could be de-alienated by an ethics, by the intervention of a critical reason that is material-practical and formal-discursive.

214. The *formal* "systemic" must be differentiated from the *formal* "discursive."

215. Under Stalinism praxis was keyed to a rise in the "production rate"—another type of systemic formal, instrumental fetishism—which did not have as criterion the life of workers, but the productive profitability of the system in the hands of the bureaucracy (which did not allow the discursive or democratic participation of workers themselves).

216. See Hinkelammert 1984, chap. 1b: "La teoría de la planificación económica perfecta [The Theory of Perfect Economic Planning]," 128 ff.

217. See Luxemburg 1966–68, vol. 1.

218. Ibid., chap. 2, 56 ff. (Spanish trans., 19 ff.).

219. Ibid. chap. 8; 28; 104.

220. See Rosdolsky 1968, chap. 30 (Spanish trans., 491 ff.); Dussel 1988, chap. 15.1, on the debate Rosa Luxemburg engaged in before the "reformists," 313 ff.; and Dussel 1990b, chap. 3, 86 ff., on the "reproduction of capital." It is interesting to note that when K.-O. Apel criticizes me (Apel 1992a), he finds support in these authors (see Hinkelammert's response 1996, 203 ff.) without noticing their argumentative weaknesses.

221. Luxemburg 1967, prologue, 9.

222. Ibid., chap. 17; 282. If Luxemburg were discussing the subject now, she would demonstrate that, as a product of the development of the "theory of dependence" in the "world system," world financial capital in 1977 had only 8 percent of its investment in industrial capital and thus urgently needed to be "realized" in processes of production. That is the reason why the "privatizations" of companies in welfare states among the peripheral countries, are like breaths of fresh air for stifled financial capital, which must become "real" in *new* productive companies. Just as surplus value in Luxemburg's time needed new possibilities for fulfillment in extended spheres of reproduction (or would instead vanish into thin air or lose its value), so it is with financial capital today. Capital is a self-contradictory structure, not only because of the decreasing rate of profit, which is "compensated" for (as Rosa Luxemburg suggested) by the subsumption of noncapitalist wealth through constant, recurrent processes of original accumulation (not only at the beginning or birth of the capital); the issue now is not how to *realize* surplus value, but how to realize the massive,

disproportionate interest accrued by financial capital, at a *fictitious* level. We need a new Rosa Luxemburg to explain the subject: *fictitious capital and its crisis of devalorization*, as a huge process inherent within current forms of globalization, which imply the impossibility of such "realization," whose principal nonintentional effect is the impoverishment of most of humanity. Capital increases, and living humanity decreases.

223. These were never enunciated as *ethical*, and this may be the greatest lack of historical Marxism, because it confuses (a) a required ethics of liberation (which does not have to be exactly as I explain it here, since there are many possible ways of stating it) with (b) dialectic or historical materialism as metaphysics or pure empiricist scientistic methodology.

224. "Reformist" theory is a "functional" social explanation with a terminology and apparent critical intention, therefore in need of people like Marx, Luxemburg, or the critical philosopher or scientist to demonstrate its invalidity: reformists appear as critics, pretending to refute critics, when in fact they remain functional for the system in force. Their "destructive" actions were extremely damaging; we would be better off with Smith or Ricardo, as Marx well showed—they were revolutionaries, not "apologists" like Malthus. But even the "apologist" is more honest than the "reformist."

225. That is, it is an empirical impossibility ("Capitalism is, due to its own nature, impossible") since it has constitutive contradictions; this is demonstrated in her work *The Accumulation of Capital* (Luxemburg 1967).

226. *Reform or Revolution*, chap. 1 (Luxemburg 1966–68, 55–56 [Spanish trans., 18]).

227. Ibid., chap. 5, 82 (Spanish trans., 49).

228. In another work she writes: "The difference lies not in the *what* [*Was*] but in the *how* [*Wie*]" (ibid. 82 [Spanish trans., 49]).

229. Ibid., chap. 8, 114 (Spanish trans., 88).

230. Ibid., 114; 89.

231. Ibid., 124–25 (Spanish trans., 100–101).

232. Luxemburg justly criticizes the "perspective espoused by Bernstein of "gradual" change of capitalism, and shows that it is necessary to discover in the "development [*Entwicklung*]" (ibid., 87 [Spanish trans., 54]) of capitalism the structure of its intrinsic contradiction. I have used the concept of qualitative "development"—in contrast to quantitative "developmentalism"—throughout this *Ethics* to indicate the creative moment that opens the "reproduction" of human life of all ethical subjects, and of their communities, to a qualitative moment of overcoming, enrichment, evolution. "Development" in this context does not oppose revolution, except that revolution is deemed a moment of *ethical* rupture, by means of which, fulfilling with the re-sponsibility for the Other (Levinas), it constructs for that Other a new material system (with contents), from his or her creative, discursive participation. The "development of life" in its critical moment can be a revolution; this does not prevent it being also an ethical-critical "transformation" of everyday life.

233. Which is the end of politics in reformist social democracy in our time.

234. Luxemburg 1966–68, 114 (Spanish trans., 88–89).

235. Marx 1956–90, vol. 3, 7 (Spanish trans., *Tesis sobre Feuerbach*, 668).

236. Thesis 1 in ibid., 5 (Spanish trans., 666). Note that Marx is speaking of action, of praxis, of a "*critical* activity [*Tätigkeit*]." This critical praxis is, exactly, liberation praxis, which is not a critical *theory*, but the practical (ethi-

cal) principles that frame the program of critical social sciences, articulated to strategies, tactics, and methods effectively performed in the *critical praxis*, in a critical or "transforming" action (which is not functional for the formal system in force or shamefully reformist).

237. Walzer 1986, 149. The quoted text is from Davies, 1982, 60.

238. Arendt 1990, introduction, 11. See Canovan 1992, 155 ff.

239. Fukuyama 1992, title of chap. 4, 64 ff.

240. War may use strategy and tactics, but, as such, it is a mediation of politics; it is a tactical-instrumental possibility of the use of force in its pure, maximum state, within the strategy of fulfilling or not the ends of a given political order. But, of course, the means (and in this case they are transformed into intermediate ends) may themselves have other means. When Clausewitz indicates that "war is politics by other means" (see Clausewitz 1973, vol. 1, chap. 1), that is because he is precisely proposing the passage from strategic reason (political) to instrumental reason (war).

241. Ibid., 19. See Walzer 1977.

242. Since the "house" of the *homeless* could soon be transformed into a new "prison." History goes on and new critics will deny the validity of this new "prison" that, before the eyes of the future ethical-critic shall be already "old-fashioned."

243. See table 13, passing from 1a to 2a. Violence "appears" here not only in the eyes of the victims, but also in the eyes of the victimizers as well and now with no escape.

244. Gandhi's approach is at the other end of the spectrum form from that of Ernesto Che Guevara, who in his "foquismo" (emphasizing the importance of "focal" points of guerrilla insurgency) proposed to channel revolutionary processes through armed struggle against the regular armies of states, which are in the hands of peripheral bourgeoisies (see Löwy 1979: "La dialéctica pueblo y guerrilla en el Che Guevara," 300 ff.). In a very preliminary form we could say that in the Cuban Revolution the process directed by Fidel Castro and Ernesto Guevara became clearly legitimate to the people, due to the intolerable character of the Batista dictatorship. On the other hand the variant of "foquismo" relied upon by Che in Bolivia never achieved legitimacy for the Bolivian people. It was a strategic and tactical "error" (which is easy to see *post factum*); its ethicity, just as political "self-critique," demands a posteriori judgments. The hero in the first example (the Cuban Revolution) committed a very clear strategic and tactical error in the second (Bolivia in 1967). The figure of the "heroic guerrillero" is not diminished, but that of the politician who must consider the ethical-critical feasibility of a concrete program is commensurately reduced. The Sandinista Front of National Liberation (FSLN) in 1979 undertook a new process of mass rebellion founded on a clear popular legitimacy. The same happened, within a framework of greater theoretical-practical complexity, with the Ejército Zapatista de Liberación Nacional (Zapatista Army of National Liberation) in 1994 in Mexico, although its legitimacy has a dual character: from the perspective of its grounding in indigenous peoples (its critical-ethnic community of origin), and from the perspective of Mexican "civil society." The latter is the target for the indigenous rebel communities' questioning of the basis of Mexico's contemporary forms of political domination as an expression of the movement's fulfillment of its obligations to its "base." From this perspective both nonviolence and armed struggle are tactical modes for the use of force

(coercion), which may have sound ethical foundations. But neither of these amount in themselves to *ethical or universal principles* that could be considered generally applicable.

245. See Gramsci 1975 and Buci-Glucksmann 1978.

246. Weber 1922, vol. 1, chap. 1, sec. 7. See Bendix 1979; Rabotnikof 1989; Serrano 1994.

247. Weber 1922, vol. 1, chap. 1, sec. 5.

248. Ibid., vol. 1, chap. 3, secs. 1, 3.

249. Ibid., vol. 2, chap. 9, sec. 1.

250. Ibid., vol. 1, chap. 1, sec. 16.

251. Ibid., sec. 6.

252. See all these in Serrano 1994.

253. Habermas 1976, 9; 271 (Spanish trans., 243). See Habermas 1992.

254. At the time of writing, in October 1996, Menem's government in Argentina, democratically elected for reasons present at the time of his election and with an ample majority, currently has the support of only about 10 percent of the electorate. The cause: an economic crisis with huge unemployment, recession, and poverty, due to measures adopted and demanded by the International Monetary Fund, the World Bank, and other organizations with neoliberal economic policies, the effects of which on the production, reproduction, and development of human life of the Argentine people has been felt immediately. The political order has fallen into a crisis of legitimacy. The General Confederation of Labour of the Argentine Republic has emerged as a powerful force together with other new social movements (such as the "Madres de la Plaza de Mayo," who demand information about their sons, who "disappeared" in a violent military repression, which continues today, as economic repression impoverishing the majorities, etc.).

255. The most developed, central countries (United States of America, those of Western Europe, etc.), as we have shown, tend to forget such an aspect in the definition of legitimacy. Nonfulfillment of such constitutive material turns *ipso facto*, "illegitimate" in "poor" countries, their political regimes, notwithstanding their formal intentions of being "democratic."

256. During a meeting in Saint Louis University (October 18, 1996), Habermas publicly recognized—in response to my veiled critique of the "loss of the material level" in his approach—the need to return to political economy, for the reasons I am now providing.

257. Habermas 1981b, vol. 1, introduction; vol. 1, 19 (Spanish trans., 19).

258. Ibid., vol. 8, 3 (Spanish trans., 2); vol. 2, 576 (Spanish trans., 555).

259. The material order determines, *due to its content* the (material or ethical, then) legitimacy; the formal discursive order determines it *by its procedure* (discursively moral-formal); the order of feasibility *by its efficiency* (formality of the instrumental reason). A state of affairs order that kills, that excludes or which is of an impossible empirical fulfillment, becomes inevitably illegitimate, in the short or long run.

260. See Weber 1922, vol. 1, chs., 1, 3, 4, secs. 10 ff. (193 ff.); vol. 2, chap. 9; vol. 3, chap. 6 (847 ff.), etc.

261. The "adept" believes in the leader for that leader's subjective qualities; in an irrational way adepts mean to adhere to the charismatic leader's "cause." But this is really about showing, as discussed in chapter 5, how liberation praxis provides for a type of legitimacy that is not based on domination

but on the intersubjective rational consensus (as Habermas), though from the critical community of victims (as Horkheimer, but not solipsist or conscience based, but communitarian and linguistic discursive).

262. Habermas 1981b, 193–94.

263. According to Pierre Bourdieu's remark: in the market of the "religious field"; here, in the "legitimate political field."

264. Figure 2a of table 13.

265. Figure 1b of table 13.

266. From an anarchist perspective, which as I have previously suggested presupposes perfect ethical subjects as its point of departure, coercive mechanisms of this kind may be considered to be perverse from their very origins as well as intrinsically. This is the basis for those expounding such an approach to launch active measures against all institutions simply because they exist. This is the kind of action we can situate at level 2b of table 13, action that from my perspective may be considered to be both illegal and illegitimate, since it is grounded solely upon the basis of agreement within the anarchist component of the overall community without any claim to be universally feasible in an empirical sense. It may thus also be classified as "violence" in terms of its literally subversive character, and as a form of rebellion with a negative character. The praxis of liberation has nothing to do with this kind of actions, which are *violent* in this sense.

267. Anderson states that "it is the cultural ascendancy of the dominant class which essentially guarantees the stability of the capitalist order. . . . Hegemony means ideological subordination" (Anderson 1981, 46). See Buci-Glucksmann 1978.

268. See Schmitt 1971 and 1990; and in Serrano 1996, 15–75. In this case the "legal" (norms) is based on the pure sovereign will of the state, of the one exerting power, that has the "legitimacy" (authority) beyond law. The will power has been fetishized.

269. According to Hannah Arendt (see Arendt 1958, 1978, and 1990), it is about having a rational criterion from which one can criticize such modern totalitarian systems. Arendt defended the democratic plurality, the recognition of the difference of individuals, groups, or societies in civil society, and also included a material criterion (from life [e.g., 1958, 13, and 96 ff. or happiness [1990, 3, and 115 ff.]). I shall return to Arendt in future works.

270. Consider table 13.

271. Rebel actions become legitimated in the eyes of these people for three reasons already noted: (a) because, among the Creoles in the colonies, the impediments to the reproduction and development of life are no longer tolerable; (b) because they have been excluded from the intersubjectivity that passes laws and resolutions; (c) because the monopolistic (political, economic, cultural, etc.) order of domination by European capitals has been found "inefficient" for the colonies.

272. Or to other irresponsible acts, which in the name of an impossible revolution propose suicidal acts.

273. The emerging liberation movements, after they have triumphed, may ratify and organize their legitimacy with a legal, constitutional order, with new rights and duties, with laws to ordain the main precepts. But the "legal" order, of right, is subsequent to the "seizure of power" by the community of victims, if it is ever triumphant. The legal is based on legitimacy, and legitimacy is based

in the order that allows the reproduction and development of the human life of each member of the community, who were previously excluded and can now symmetrically participate in the exercise of discursive rationality in all that affects them, making "possible" all the foregoing (ethical feasibility) by means of critical instrumental or strategic reasons. Kelsen forgets that a "constitution" is the effect of the legitimate subject who promulgates it, but who was inevitably illegitimate before. Juridical positivism is conservative; it takes the given as real.

274. The "cause" is, in fact, final cause.

275. Remember that Panama was created in 1903 by the United States so that a canal could be built linking the two oceans. At the same time Iraq was invading Kuwait, the United States was invading Panama. Iraq was attacked in the Gulf War; who could have attacked the United States? Cynicism occupies the place of reason and international justice. The Panamanian philosopher Ricaurte Soler wrote justified articles against the United States in *Tareas*, but very few people have read them.

276. Moment 9 of figure 12.

277. German socialist syndicalism of the Second International, till now, has never found its route to liberation. Its destiny is "reformist" — in the sense defined in §6.3.

278. Luxemburg 1966–68, 1; vol. 1, 137.

279. Ibid., vol. 2, 143.

280. Ibid.

281. Ibid.

282. Ibid., vol. 3, 147.

283. Ibid., 157.

284. Ibid., 159.

285. Ibid., vol. 6, 195.

286. Ibid.

287. Ibid., 197.

288. Ibid., 198. "From Rosa Luxemburg's perspective, a strike can never *fail*. It is only from a completely reformist perspective that one could argue that if concrete strike demands are not won then the whole effort has been in vain. To the contrary, she affirmed the educational value of strikes. . . . The wider and more intense the conflict, the greater the potential increase in consciousness and in levels of tactical preparation" (Gómez Llorente 1975, 96).

289. "A tactical question" (Aubet 1983, 110). Alexander-E. Millerand, a French socialist, was involved in the Waldeck-Rousseau bourgeoisie government, since 1899, thus was criticized by Luxemburg for being a "reformist."

290. See figure 20.

291. See Gómez Llorente 1975.

292. Luxemburg 1966–68, vol. 2, 21; Luxemburg 1980 (Spanish trans. [1972], 11).

293. Luxemburg 1966–68, vol. 2, 23 (Spanish trans., 14).

294. By mistake, as we have seen, a materialistic dialectics, as cosmologic metaphysics impeded to develop the "fundamental principles" of an ethics of liberation, what was needed, especially the second principle: the democratic formal discursiveness in the decision making (symmetrical, anti-bureaucratic, anti-totalitarian). This new mistake must be corrected in the future, as Luxemburg points out: "For the proletarian movement *self-criticism* [*Selbstkritik*] . . . is the air and light without which it is impossible to breathe. . . . What we are

witnessing is the *critique* and assessment of what has been accomplished over the last half century" (ibid., 21–22; 11–12). We must repeat such a critique at the end of the twentieth century.

295. Luxemburg 1966–68, vol. 2, 2; 33 (Spanish trans., 26).

296. In this context I am speaking of an ethical-liberating will for power, which subsumes and corrects Nietzsche's approach and renders feasible Levinas's *metaphysical desire*.

297. See §§3.4 [186 ff.] and 3.5 [189 ff.].

298. See §3.5 [190 ff.].

299. This is *phrónesis* (*prudence*) as a moment of the critical strategic-instrumental reason of the organized community of victims.

300. For example, cultural alienation or the misery of a wage laborer in peripheral capitalism.

301. Taking Paulo Freire's system of critical pedagogy as a reference: the banking system of education (Y) produces cultural alienation and a lack of critical consciousness (M) among students from poor backgrounds (X) in the educational system in general (Z).

302. In this case the example could be drawn from Marx: the surplus value (Y) of capital (Z), obtained as profit in the accumulation of peripheral capital, is the cause of misery (M) of the wage laborer (X).

303. This is the utopia that is possible, namely, the liberation project, mediated by concrete economic programs.

304. The future indicates the "hope" of negation of the negativity as a satisfaction of necessity.

305. Statements 5, 5′, and 8′ correspond instead to the decision regarding means and ends already established in the critical-discursive moments which in figure 12 were labeled as moments 7 and 8: when the critical organized community of the victims analyzed the positive (the possible utopia and its feasible program) and negative aspects (the causes of negativity) from a practical, scientific, and activist perspective.

306. "Power" here is understood not as the will of "being able to impose one's will"—the will of domination—even in the case of being creatively dionysiac, but rather as a will which "lets live" and which participates symmetrically in the relevant decision-making process.

307. These are what I have previously characterized as "objective revolutionary conditions." In the liberating metalanguage employed in this work I refer to them as the "empirical conditions" that can make a social transformation possible (at whatever level), understanding that voluntarism (the mere "desire" to change things) is not of much use, unless the fissures that are necessary to enable a real transformation in a dominant system do not arise empirically; otherwise the desired transformation may be impossible or doomed to foreseeable defeat.

308. See Dussel 1988, chap. 10, 200 ff.: "The *possibility* of a crisis and its *existence*."

309. "Really existing socialism" had the illusory dream of achieving a system without crisis (since it was incapable of defining at what level labor was alienated in a bureaucratically planned society), and because of this its first structural crisis produced its spectacular "collapse." If it had situated itself instead as a *historical* system (and not one that was supposedly transhistorical—this is the reason why it did not come up with a theoretical elaboration of how to behave

or adapt in the face of crises that were inevitable) perhaps it would have been able to successively overcome its crises and postpone its collapse, as capitalism has been able to do up till now. In any case, socialism is far from having disappeared from the present and future global agenda, though it occupies a discrete place on the periphery, for now.

310. See Hinkelammert 1984, chap. 5a, 161: "It is in this categorical form that Popper assumes the apodictic judgment as to the impossibility of perfect human knowledge, employing it in his theoretical analyses as a general empirical principle of impossibility."

311. The possible (not perfect) system of "planning," applying ethical as well as economic criteria, would include "correction" exercised by a strategic and scientific critical consciousness in the (apparently) self-regulated process of the market, which would avoid "causing" more victims. This would involve a conscious "intervention" that would correct the "impossibility" that the market might not produce disequilibrium (victims).

312. Hinkelammert 1984, 247.

313. Buci-Glucksmann 1978, 305.

314. Hinkelammert 1995b, 202: "The End of Utopia?"

315. All of this is also applicable for the other example, in the argument reflected in 5'–10', and would in this case be consistent with premise 11'. Furthermore, the argument can follow a negative path: "X is a living being; if X wants to *avoid death* it is necessary to proceed with mediations A, B, C, n" (or D, E, F, n).

316. In the final analysis, the "community" can be extended to include all of humanity, to which all of us inevitably "belong." This "demand" is derived not from a value judgment but rather from a factual judgment that underlies a normative judgment connected to the reproduction of life, which is always that of a community of life.

317. For the same reasons W should be attempted and mediations D, E, F, n of enunciation 12' should be attempted. Along the negative path, the conclusion would be: "If X does not want to die he (or she) *must.* . . ." This "must" is deontological, since the subject's life is his or her own responsibility, and if such subjects permit themselves to die they commit suicide; but this is ethically contradictory in performative terms, *ergo* . . . .

318. This is a matter addressed in §§1.5b, 2.5b, 3.5b, 4.5b, and 5.5b, where no simple formal deduction is undertaken in the manner of Hume, but rather a transition based on the grounding of material argumentation, which is appropriate in the context of material-*practical* reason.

319. The critique of the dominating reductionism implied by the measure of "*quantitative* progress" of Modernity (see above [37 ff.]) employed by postmodernists does not touch what I describe here as "qualitative progress" with reference to the "*quality* of life" of humanity.

320. Since the preoriginal ethical moment, when they assume re-sponsibility for the victim, in a "face-to-face" ethical and primary encounter, in the face of the Others in all of their vulnerability and trauma.

321. See Gottwald 1981.

322. In my first *Ethics* (Dussel 1970–80 [1973]) I have treated in some detail this kind of negative liberating action; it is the negation of the negation of the Other: the negation of alienation, the liberation of the prisoner or of the

slave (see ibid., passim, e.g.: "The movement that ruptures the prevailing order of domination opens a breach in the wall or horizon of the system through which the process of *destructive liberation* is fulfilled, which immediately (and from the beginning) is pursued as a *taking power*. This is the first moment, that of the liberation war or struggle" (ibid., "Latin American Politics," IV, sec. 66, 114: "The Morality of the Praxis of Political Liberation").

323. For example when a conservative changes something in the system in order to overcome a crisis, but with the intention of preserving it. Meanwhile the liberator can coincide materially with the content of this action, but as a transformation intended to negate some aspect of the alienation of the victim. In the first case, the action taken is functional to the system, and the change is cosmetic so that the "same" can stay the same; in the second case, the action carried out is a transformation with the intention of bringing about liberation, although on the surface its significant difference may not be immediately apparent.

324. In the second case, because of the achievement of W.

325. These are moments 9 and 10 in figure 12 [209].

326. *Nicomachean Ethics* bk. 1, 7 (Aristotle 1960, 1097b 24–25).

327. Ibid., 1097b 31–32.

328. "*enérgeia psykhés kat'aretèn*" (ibid., 1097a 16).

329. The "goodness claim" discussed at the end of chapter 3, with regard to the prevailing system. In other words, the United States today, the imperial power and policeman of planet Earth, is the fruit of a liberation process implemented by colonists in the eighteenth century; behind the United States is a necessarily historical story of the liberation struggle that constituted it.

330. In order to speak, as Kant did in book 2 of the *Critique of Practical Reason*, "Practical reason seeks . . . that which has not been conditioned and precisely not as a fundamental determinant of the will . . . but as an unconditioned totality of the object of pure critical reason, with the name of the *supreme good* [*höchsten Guts*]" (*Kritik der praktischen Vernunft*, A 194 [Kant 1968, vol. 6, 235]). From my perspective the "supreme good" is the "fundamental determinant of the will" (as a material moment) and also "the unconditioned totality of the object of practical reason."

331. By saying "full," I seek to include all the critical, material, and discursive moments and those of feasibility, in all of these dimensions. Furthermore, I have insisted throughout this book that the mere "reproduction" of the life of the victim is a "development" of the life of all of humanity as a whole, and even of the system that is obliged to "grow" and build a structure of such a character (internally or through some kind of innovative creativity) that it enables the victim to become an *equal* participant.

332. See Dussel 1992.

333. Is it possible to imagine a better method than this, which was the achievement of the wisdom of Memphis under the power of the pharaohs, and which thereby obtained the "introjection" within the ethical conscience of peasants, of exploited slaves, and also of the dominant classes of merchants, the military, and bureaucracies, of the oppressive rhythms of the dominant system?

334. I discussed this theme with Samir Amin in Manila in December 1996 (see Amin 1996).

335. Marx, "Regarding Censorship" (Marx 1956–90, vol. 1, 4).

Appendix 1. Theses

1. Ptolomeus III claimed to be "Lord of the Mediterranean and of the Indian Ocean" (to which one connected through the Red Sea).

2. As one can see, solidarity is equivocal. There can be internal solidarity among the members of a "mafia."

3. The victim is a social "alarm," a "red light" that something is "going badly." If a community does not inhibit its aggressiveness or insensibility before the victim's pain, it runs the risk of beginning to "fire" that logic over the "internal" members of the social whole (for example, neoliberalism unleashes the insatiable competition of all against all), which is the self-assassination of the social body; to kill the Other is already to begin suicide as community.

4. Here again the intersubjectivity that creates consensus is psychically and ethically necessary. For a time the "therapeutic community" replaces for a while the "hostile community" that causes the illness, allowing for the creation of a bridge for the reintegration of the sick into the "normal community" traversed by infinite tensions, which are never resolved, and that because of the principle of reality, are used by confronting them one against the other. Thus, in the bull games of Crete, the artist knew how to use the bull's strength (by letting the bull pass and by hanging on to it) and did not try—as the "ill" person does—to engage its horns.

Appendix 2. Sais: Capital of Egypt

1. My first visit was in 1976, en route to Dar-Es-Salaam (Tanzania), and my second in 1982, when I was traveling to Nairobi (Kenya).

2. In reality "Coptic" is a phonetic corruption of "Egyptian," which itself signifies a "worshiper of Ptah" (*egi-Ptah*), the principal god of Memphis.

3. This is the Shabaka Stone, no. 498, in the British Museum, measuring 92 x 137 cm, discovered in 1805 (Pritchard 1950, 4). On the same text, see Altenmüller 1975a; Breasted 1901; Junker 1941.

4. Breasted 1901, 39.

5. Ibid., 54.

6. Breasted writes *the great*. It seems as if we were listening to the exclamation of a contemporary Egyptian, during the call to daily prayer from the minaret of the village at the current site of Memphis: "Allah is Great!" Five thousand years of an uninterrupted tradition.

7. Breasted 1901, 44; Pritchard 1950, 379b.

8. Breasted 1901, 48.

9. Ibid., 45.

10. Ibid.

11. "A prayer to Thot," in Pritchard 1950, 379b.

12. Ptah was the patron of architects and bricklayers, the one who foresees the future work, who gives it existence in a blueprint before its existence in reality; he is the divine origin understood as a pre-vision of the universe before its creation. For the Hebrews Thot was the "Eternal Wisdom" that created the universe (of Solomon's book of *Wisdom*). For the Greeks he was the *nous*

or the original *logos* of the pre-Socratics, the idea that guides the formation of things. His "content" was Horus, but his practical-effectuating formalization is Thot. He is mathematics, astronomy, the wisdom that anticipates the cyclical flooding of the Nile (the return of Chaos), who, when the waters recede, gives shape to the "cosmos" (the eternal order subject to the designs of *Maat*: the natural-divine law that governs all things), the exact place in each field, each path "remembered" in exactitude of topographical geometrical readings. Thot "ordered" the universe, by means of an instrumental practical mandate of rationality.

13. Breasted 1901, 49.

14. Ibid.

15. Allen 1974; Altenmüller 1975b; Maystre 1937. The text I am citing from is in the bibliography under the listing *Book of the Dead* (under Faulkner).

16. This is a myth that is very similar to that of the Aztec (Mexica) Coyolxauhqui (the decapitated goddess whose blood fertilizes the earth) or that of Tupac Amaru in Peru (whose quartered limbs were placed by the Spanish dominating power at each of the four corners of "Tahuantinsuyo," the name of the indigenous realm of the Inca Empire).

17. The other components of the human being are *Pa*, the vital energy of life; *Ren*, the proper name (!) for each individual; *Aka*, the heart, which is the seat of motivations and practical reason; and each person's "*flesh*" (not the body).

18. Might this not be the origin of what we have come to understand as the experience and concept of an "I" or "personal self," which through the transmission of the Semitic tradition came to Modern Europe? Shouldn't Charles Taylor (see Taylor 1989) have looked for the origin of the *self* in Egypt and in the Athens of Plato, where it clearly cannot be found?

19. *Book of the Dead*, chap. 125, "Declarations of Innocence." Each of these is a universal negation of nongeneralizable maxims. Among them: "I did not add to the impoverishment of the poor . . . . I did not kill. . . . I did not steal with violence. . . . I did not tell lies" (ibid.).

20. Ibid., 209.

21. Ibid., 210.

22. It is interesting to observe how the "vessel" of the Egyptian Nile becomes a "roof" for the poor (which might be a shepherd's hut, a Bedouin's tent, or the "cottage" of a sedentary farmer). The essence here, of course, is the duty of hospitality.

Bibliography

[403] This bibliography lists only the sources cited in this work. Throughout *Ethics of Liberation* I often add emphasis in quotations, without noting the addition in each case; in other cases, the author's emphasis may be removed. The information within each listing follows the order given in the citations (first the original and then in some cases the translation, or simply the translation).

Abu-Lughod, Janet. 1989. *Before European Hegemony: The World System, AD 1250–1350*. Oxford University Press, New York.

Adorno, Theodor W. 1966. *Negative Dialektik*. Suhrkamp, Frankfurt (Spanish trans. *Dialéctica negativa*, Taurus, Madrid, 1975).

———. 1970. *Aestetische Theorie*. Suhrkamp, Frankfurt (Ital. trans. *Teoria estetica*, Einaudi, Turin, 1975).

———. 1994. *Minima Moralia*. Suhrkamp, Frankfurt.

Adorno, T. W., K. Popper, F. Dahrendorf, J. Habermas, and H. Albert. 1969. *Der Positivismusstreit in der deutschen Soziologie*. Luchterhand, Berlin (Spanish trans. *La disputa del positivismo en la sociología alemana*, Grijalvo, Mexico City, 1973).

Albee, Ernest. 1957. *A History of English Utilitarianism*. George Allen and Unwin, London.

Albert, Hans. 1968. *Traktat über kritische Vernunft*. Mohr, Tübingen (Spanish trans. *Tratado sobre la razón crítica*, Sur, Buenos Aires, 1973).

———. 1980. *Fehlbare Vernunft*. Mohr, Tübingen.

Allen, Thomas George. 1974. *The Book of the Death*. University of Chicago Press, Chicago.

Almeder, Robert. 1980. *The Philosophy of Charles S. Peirce*. Rowman and Littlefield, New Jersey.

Altenmüller, Hartwig. 1975a. "Denkmal memphitischer Theologie." In *Lexikon der Aegyptologie*, ed. Wolfgang Helck, vol. 1, cols. 1065–69. Otto Harrassowitz, Wiesbaden.

————. 1975b. "Totenbuch." In *Lexikon der Aegyptologie*, ed. Wolfgang Helck, vol. 6, cols. 641–43. Otto Harrassowitz, Wiesbaden.

Althusser, Louis. 1975a. *Curso de filosofía marxista para científicos*. Albert Roies, Editorial Diez, Mexico City.

————. 1975b. *Lenin y la filosofía*. Era, Mexico City.

————. 1988. *Para leer "El capital."* Siglo XXI, Mexico City.

Amin, Samir. 1970. *L'accumulation à l'échelle mondiale*. Anthropos, Paris.

————. 1974. *El desarrollo desigual: Ensayo sobre las formaciones sociales del capitalismo periférico*. Fontanella, Barcelona.

————. 1989. *Eurocentrism*. Monthly Review Press, New York.

————. 1996. "The Challenge of Globalization." *Review of International Political Economy* 3.2: 216–59.

Anderson, Perry. 1981. *Las antinomias de Antonio Gramsci*. Fontamara, Barcelona.

Anyanwu, K. C., and E. A. Ruch. 1981. *African Philosophy: An Introduction to the Main Philosophical Trends in Contemporary Africa*. Catholic Goos Agency, Rome.

Apel, Karl-Otto. 1950. *Dasein und Erkennen: Eine erkenntnis-theoretische Interpretation der Philosophie M. Heidegger*. Bonn Universität, Bonn.

————. 1973. *Transformation der Philosophie*, 2 vols. Suhrkamp, Frankfurt (Spanish trans. of vols. 1 and 2, *La transformación de la filosofía* by Adela Cortina, Taurus, Madrid, 1985).

————. 1976. "Das Problem der philosophischen Letzbegründung im Lichte einer transzendentales Sprachpragmatik." In *Sprache und Erkenntnis*, Festschrift for G. Frey, ed. B. Kanitscheider, 55–82. von B. Kanitscheider, Innsbruck.

————. 1980a. *Die Idee der Sprache in der Tradition des Humanismus von Dante bis Vico*. Bouvier, Bonn.

————. 1980b. "Notwendigkeit, Schwierigkeit und Möglichkeit einer philosophischen Begründung der Ethik im Zeitalter der Wissenschaft." In *Festschrift fur K Tsatsos*, ed. P. Kanellopoulos, Athens, 215–75 (Spanish trans. in Apel 1986, 105–74).

————. 1981. *Charles Peirce: From Pragmatism to Pragmaticism*. University of Massachusetts Press, Amherst (original, *Schriften II: Vom Pragmatismus zum Pragmatismus*, 2 vols., Suhrkamp, Frankfurt, 1967–70).

————. 1984. *Understanding and Explanation*. MIT Press, Cambridge (original, *Transzendental-Pragmatischer Sicht*, Suhrkamp, Frankfurt, 1979).

————. 1985. "¿Límites de la ética discursiva?" In Cortina 1985, 233–62 (original, "Grenzen der Diskursethik? Versuch einer Zwischenbilanz," in *Zeitschrift für philosophische Forschung*, Bd. 40, H. 1 [Jan.–Mar. 1986]: 3–31).

————. 1986. *Estudios éticos*. Spanish trans., Editorial y Alfa, Barcelona.

————. 1988. *Diskurs und Verantwortung: Das Problem des Übergangs zur postkonventionellen Moral*. Suhrkamp, Frankfurt.

————. 1989. "Normative Begründung der *Kritische Theorie* durch Rekurs auf lebensweltliche Sittlichkeit? Ein transzendental-pragmatisch orientierter Versuch, mit Habermas gegen Habermas zu denken." In *Zwischenbetrachtungen: Im Prozess der Aufklärung*, ed. A. Honneth, T. McCarthy, and C. Öffe, 15–65. Suhrkamp, Frankfurt (Spanish trans. in Fornet-Betancourt 1992 and again in Dussel 1994c, 207–53).

————. 1990a. "Diskursethik als Verantwortungsethik." In Fornet-Betancourt 1990, 10–40.

————. 1990b. "Ist Intentionaliät fundamentaler als sprachliche Bedeutung? Transzendental-pragmatische Argumente gegen die Rückkehr zum semantischen Intentionalismus der Bewusstseinsphilosophie." In *Intentionalität und Verstehen*, 13–54, Suhrkamp, Frankfurt (English trans. in *Foundations of Semiotics*, ed. A. Eschbach, J. Benjamin Publishing, Amsterdam, 1989).

————. 1991. *Teoría de la verdad y ética del discurso*. Paidos, Barcelona.

————. 1992a. "Die Diskursethik von der Herausforderung der Philosophie der Befreiung: Versuch einer Antwort an Enrique Dussel. [Part] I." In Fornet-Betancourt 1992, 16–53 (Spanish trans. Dussel 1993c, 97–133); "[Part] II," in Fornet-Betancourt 1994, 17–38).

————. 1992b. "Diskursethik vor der Problematik von Recht und Politik." In Kettner 1992, 29–60.

————. 1994a. "Narración autobiográfica del proceso filosófico recorrido con Habermas." In Dussel 1994, 192–206.

————. 1994b. *Selected Essays: Towards a Transcendental Semiotics*. Ed. Eduardo Mendieta. Vol. 1. Humanities Press, New York.

————. 1996. *Selected Essays: Ethics and the Theory of Rationality*. Ed. Eduardo Mendieta. Vol. 2. Humanities Press, New York.

Aquinas, Thomas. 1949. *In X libros Ethicorum Aristotelis ad Nicomachum expositio*. Marietti, Turin.

————. 1950. *Summa Theologiae*. Parts I and II. Marietti, Turin.

————. 1964. *De Veritate*. Parts I and II. Marietti, Turin.

Araújo de Oliveira, Manfredo. 1995. *Ética e práxis histórica*. Editora Atica, Sâo Paulo.

Arendt, Hannah. 1958. *The Human Condition*. University of Chicago Press, Chicago.

————. 1978. *The Life of the Mind*. Harvest Books, New York.

————. 1990. *On Revolution*. Penguin Books, London.

Arens, Edmund. 1995. *Die Anerkennung des Anderen*. Herder, Freiburg.

Aristotle. 1960. *Aristotelis Opera*. 2 vols. Ed. I. Bekker. De Gruyter, Berlin.

Armour, Robert A. 1986. *Gods and Myths of Ancient Egypt*. American University Press, Cairo.

Atkinson, Roland F. 1961. "Hume on *Is* and *Ought*: A Reply to MacIntyre." *Philosophical Review*, 70.2, April.

Aubet, María José. 1983. *El pensamiento de Rosa Luxemburg*. Ediciones del Serbal, Barcelona.

Austin, John. 1962. *How to Do Things with Words*. Harvard University Press, Cambridge (Spanish trans., *Como hacer cosas con palabras*, Paidos, Barcelona, 1988).

Averroes. 1953. *Averrois Cordubensis Commentarium magnum in Aristotelis De Anima*. Ed. F. Crawford. Cambridge University Press, Cambridge.

Ayer, Alfred Jules. 1958. "On the Analysis of Moral Judgements." In *A Modern Introduction to Ethics*, ed. Milton Munitz, 537–46. Free Press, New York.

————. 1968. *The Origins of Pragmatism*. Macmillan, London.

Bachelard, Gaston. 1949. *Le rationalisme appliqué*. PUF, Paris.

————. 1972. *La formación del espíritu científico*. Siglo XXIXXI, Buenos Aires.

Badiou, Alain, 1982. *Théorie du sujet*. Editions du Seuil, Paris.

————. 1995. *Ética: Um ensaio sobre a consciência do Mal.* Relume Dumará, Rio de Janeiro (original, *L'éthique,* Hatier, Paris, 1993).

Baier, Kurt. 1958. *The Moral Point of View.* Cornell University Press, Ithaca.

Barret, Cyril. 1994. *Ética y creencia religiosa en Wittgenstein.* Alianza, Madrid.

Barrios de Churunga, Domitila, with Moema Viezzer. 1979. *Let Me Speak! Testimony of Domitila, a Woman of the Bolivian Mines.* Trans. Victoria Ortiz. Monthly Review Press, New York.

Barry, Brian, ed. 1973. *Theory of Justice.* Oxford University Press, Oxford.

Bary, William T., de. 1970. *Self and Society in Ming Thought.* Columbia University Press, New York.

Bauman, Zygmunt. 1994. *Postmodern Ethics.* Blackwell, Oxford.

Baumgarten, Alexandri Gottlieb. 1963. *Metaphysica.* Georg Olms, Hildesheim.

————. 1969. *Ethica.* Georg Olms, Hildesheim.

Baumgartner, H. M., and J. Rüsen, et al. 1975. *Historische Objektivität.* Vandenhoeck, Göttingen.

Beckwith, Martin. 1987. *The Tibetan Empire in Central Asia.* Princeton University Press, Princeton.

Bendix, Reinhard. 1979. *Max Weber.* Amorrortu, Buenos Aires.

Benhabib, Seyla. 1986. *Critique, Norm, and Utopia: A Study of the Foundations of Critical Theory.* Columbia University Press, New York.

————. 1992. *Situating the Self. Gender, Community and Postmodernism in Contemporary Ethics.* Routledge, New York.

Benhabib, Seyla, Wolfgang Bonss, and John McCole, eds. 1993. *On Max Horkheimer.* MIT Press, Cambridge.

Benhabib, Seyla, and D. Cornell, eds. 1987. *Feminism as Critique.* University of Minnesota Press, Minneapolis.

Benjamin, Walter. 1989. *Discursos interrumpidos I.* Taurus, Madrid.

Bentham, Jeremy. 1838–43. *The Works of Jeremy Bentham.* Vols. 1–11. William Tate, Edinburgh.

————. 1948. *A Fragment on Government and an Introduction to the Principles of Morals and Legislation.* Blackwell, Oxford.

————. 1954. *Jeremy Bentham's Economic Writings.* Vol. 3. Royal Economic Society, London.

————. 1978. *Escritos económicos.* FCE, Mexico.

————. 1981. *Tratados de legislación civil y penal.* Editoria Nacional, Madrid.

————. 1983–89. *The Correspondence of Jeremy Bentham.* 9 vols. Ed. Stephen Conway. Clarendon Press, Oxford.

Berger, Peter. 1973. *Pyramids of Sacrifice. Political Ethics and Social Change.* Basic Books, New York.

Bergson, Henry. 1912. *L'évolution créatrice.* Félix Alcan, Paris.

————. 1969. *Les deux sources de la morale et de la religion.* PUF, Paris.

Bernal, Martin. 1991. *Black Athena: The Afroasiatic Roots of Classical Civilization.* Vol. 1. Rutgers University Press, New Brunswick.

Bernstein, Richard. 1971. *Praxis and Action.* University of Pennsylvania Press, Philadelphia (Spanish trans. Alianza Editorial, Madrid, 1979).

————. 1992. *The Ethical-Political Horizons of Modernity/Postmodernity.* MIT Press, Cambridge.

Berr, Henri, ed. 1955. *La evolución de la humanidad.* Vol. 1. Editorial Hispanoamericana, Mexico.

Bertaux, Pierre. 1972. *Africa: Desde la prehistoria hasta los Estados actuales.* Siglo XXI, Madrid.

Bertram, B. C. R. 1988. "Problems with Altruism." In *Current Problems in Sociobiology*, ed. King's College Sociobiology Group. University of California Press, Berkeley.

Bhagavad-Gita o Canto del Bienaventurado. 1957. Ed. J. Barrios Gutiérrez. Aguilar, Buenos Aires.

Blaut, Jim M., ed. 1992. *1492: The Debate on Colonialism, Eurocentrism and History.* Africa World Press, Trenton.

———. 1993. *The Colonizer's Model of the World.* Guilford Press, New York.

Bleeker, C. J. 1973. *Hathor and Thoth.* Brill, Leiden.

Bloch, Ernst. 1959. *Das Prinzip Hoffnung.* 3 vols. Suhrkamp, Frankfurt (Spanish trans. *El principio esperanza*, Aguilar, Madrid, 1977–80).

———. 1963–64. *Tübingen Einleitung in die Philosophie.* 2 vols. Suhrkamp, Frankfurt.

———. 1970. *Atheismus und Christentum.* Rowohlt, Hamburg.

———. 1972. *Das Materialismusproblem, seine Geschichte und Substanz.* In Bloch, *Gesamtausgabe*, vol. 7. Suhrkamp, Frankfurt.

———. 1977. *Geist der Utopie.* Suhrkamp, Frankfurt.

———. 1986. *The Principle of Hope.* 3 vols. Trans. Neville Plaice, Stephen Plaice, and Paul Knight. Basil Blackwell, London.

———. 1988. *Natural Law and Human Dignity.* MIT Press, Cambridge.

Bloom, Floyd, and Arlyne Lazerson. 1988. *Brain, Mind, and Behavior.* W. H. Freeman, New York.

Blumenberg, Hans. 1976. "Selbsterhaltung und Beharrung." In *Subjektivität und Selbsterhaltung*, ed. H. Ebeling, 144–207. Suhrkamp, Frankfurt.

———. 1996. *Die Genesis der kopernikanischen Welt.* 3 vols. Suhrkamp, Frankfurt.

Bolaji Idowu, E. 1975. *African Traditional Religion.* Orbis Books, New York.

Bouver, P. 1912. "Les conditions de l'obligation de conscience." *Année Psychologique*, number 23.

Boylan, Patrick. 1922. *Thoth, the Hermes of Egypt.* Oxford University Press, London.

Boyne, Roy. 1990. *Foucault and Derrida: The Other Side of Reason.* Unwin Human, London.

Braudel, Fernand. 1946. "Monnaies et civilisation: De l'or du Soudan à l'argent d'Amérique." *Annales ESC* 1.1: 12–38.

———. 1978. *Las civilizaciones actuales.* Tecnos, Madrid.

Breasted, James Henry. 1901. "The Philosophy of a Memphite Priest." *Zeitschrift für ägyptische Sprache und Altertumskunde* (J. C. Hinrischs'sche Buchhandlung, Leipzig) 39: 39–54.

———. 1939. *The Dawn of Conscience.* Charles Scribner's Sons, London.

Brenner, Robert. 1983. "Das Weltsystem: Theoretische und Historische Perspektiven." In *Perspektiven des Weltsystems*, ed. J. Blaschke, 80–111. Campus Verlag, Frankfurt.

Brentano, Franz. 1969. *Vom Ursprung sittlicher Erkenntnis.* Meiner, Hamburg.

Broiles, David. 1969. *The Moral Philosophy of David Hume.* Martinus Nijhoff, The Hague.

Bronger, H. A. 1949. *Hammurabi.* Servire, The Hague.

Brown, Norman. 1967. *Eros y Thanatos*. Mortiz, Mexico.

Bruner, Jerome. 1984. *Acción, pensamiento y lenguaje*. Alianza Editorial, Madrid.

Buci-Glucksmann, Christine. 1978. *Gramsci y el Estado*. Siglo xxi, Mexico.

Budge, E. A. Wallis. 1911. *Osiris and the Egyptian Resurrection*. 2 vols. Medici Society, London.

Bühler, K. 1965. *Psicología de la forma (Cibernética y vida)*. Ediciones Morata, Madrid.

Bunge, Mario. 1972a. *Causalidad*. Eudeba, Buenos Aires.

———. 1972b. *Ética y ciencia*. Siglo Veinte, Buenos Aires.

———. 1974–89. *Treatise on Basic Philosophy*. 8 vols. Reidel, Boston.

———. 1988. *The Mind-Body Problem*. Pergamon Press, New York.

Butler, Marilyn. 1981. *Romantics, Rebels and Reactionaries: 1760–1830*. Oxford University Press, London.

Cambridge University Press. 1970–89. *The Cambridge Ancient History*. 8 vols. Cambridge University Press, Cambridge.

Camps, Victoria. 1976. *Pragmática del lenguaje y filosofía analítica*. Península, Barcelona.

———, ed. 1989. *Historia de la ética*. Vol. 3. Crítica, Barcelona.

Camps, Victoria, et al. 1992. *Concepciones de Ética*. Trotta, Madrid.

Canguilhem, Georges. 1968. *Études d'histoire et de philosophie des sciences*. Vrin, Paris.

Canovan, Margaret. 1992. *Hannah Arendt: A Reinterpretation of Her Political Thought*. Cambridge University Press, New York.

Cardenal, Ernesto. 1969. *Salmos*. Lohlé, Buenos Aires.

Cardoso, Ciro F. S., and Héctor Pérez Brignoli. 1979. *Historia económica de América Latina*. 2 vols. Crítica, Barcelona.

Carnap, Rudolf. 1961. *La construcción lógica del mundo*. UNAM, Mexico (original, *Der logische Aufbau der Welt*, Leipzig, 1928).

———. 1963. *Filosofía y sintaxis lógica*. UNAM, Mexico.

———. 1965. "La superación de la metafísica mediante el análisis lógico del lenguaje." In *El positivismo lógico*, ed. A. J. Ayer, 66–87. FCE, Mexico City.

———. 1990. *Pseudoproblemas en la filosofía*. UNAM, Mexico City (original, *Scheinprobleme in der Philosophie*, Meiner, Leipzig, 1928).

Carra de Vaux, Bernard. 1921–26. *Les penseurs d'Islam*. 5 vols. Alcan, Paris.

Casas, Bartolomé de las. 1957–58. *Obras escogidas de Fray Bartolomé de las Casas*. Vols. 1–5. Biblioteca de Autores Españoles, Madrid.

———. 1992. *The Devastation of the Indies: A Brief Account*. Trans. by Herma Briffault. Johns Hopkins University Press, Baltimore.

Castro-Gómez, Santiago. 1996. *Crítica de la razón latinoamericana*. Puvill Libros, Barcelona.

Cerutti, Horacio. 1983. *La filosofía de la liberación latinoamericana*. FCE, Mexico City.

Chaudhuri, K. N. 1985. *Trade and Civilisation in the Indian Ocean: An Economic History from the Rise of Islam to 1750*. Cambridge University Press, Cambridge.

Chaunu, Pierre. 1955–59. *Séville et l'Atlantique (1504–1650)*. 8 vols. SEVPEN, Paris.

———. 1969. *Conquête et exploitation des nouveaux mondes (XVIe. siècle)*. PUF, Paris.

Chevalier, L. Le. 1933. *La morale de Leibniz*. Vrin, Paris.

Chomsky, Noam. 1967. *American Power and the New Mandarins.* New York (Spanish trans. *La responsabilidad de los intelectuales,* Ariel, Barcelona, 1971).

———. 1968. *Language and Mind.* Harcourt Brace Jovanovich, New York.

Cipolla, Carlo. *Guns and Sails in the Early Phase of European Expansion, 1400–1700.* Collins, London.

Clausewitz, Karl von. 1973. *De la guerra.* 3 vols. Editorial Diógenes, Mexico.

Clavijero, Francisco Xavier. 1976a. *Antología.* Sep-Setentas, Mexico.

———. 1976b. *Historia antigua de México.* Porrúa, Mexico.

Cohen, Hermann. 1919. *Religion der Vernunft aus den Quellen des Judentums.* Melzer Verlag, Darmstadt (English trans. *Religion of Reason out of the Sources of Judaism,* Ungar, New York, 1972).

Cohen, Richard. 1994. *Elevations: The Height of the Good in Rosenzweig and Levinas.* University of Chicago Press, Chicago.

Confucius [Confusio]. 1865. *La grande étude.* Vol. 1. Editions Migne, Paris.

Cooper, David, ed. 1967. *To Free a Generation: The Dialectics of Liberation.* Collier, New York.

———. 1996. *World Philosophies.* Blackwell, Oxford.

Copleston, Frédéric. 1964. *Histoire de la Philosophie: Le Moyen Age.* Casterman, Tournai.

Coppens, Yves. 1975. "Evolution des Hominidés et de leur environnement au cours du Plio-Pléistocène dans la Basse Vallée de l'Omo en Ethiopie." *Comptes Rendus Hebdomadaires de Scéances de l'Académie des Sciences* (Paris) 281: 1693–96.

———. 1994. "East Side Story: The Origin of Humankind." *Scientific American* (May): 88–95.

Cornevin, Robert, and Marianne Cornevin. 1964. *Histoire de l'Afrique des origines à la deuxième guerre mondiale.* Vol. 1. Payot, Paris.

Cortina, Adela. 1985. *Razón comunicativa y responsabilidad solidaria.* Sígueme, Salamanca.

Costa, Marcio. 1992. *Educaçâo et libertaçâo na América Latina.* Cefil, Campo Grande (Brazil).

———. 1996. *La ética como filosofía primera en Emmanuel Levinas.* UNAM, Mexico City.

Couhier, Henri. 1936. "Descartes et la vie morale." *Revue de Métaphysique et Morale* (January), 165–97.

Critchley, Simon. 1992. *The Ethics of Deconstruction: Derrida and Levinas.* Blackwell, Oxford.

Cullen, Carlos. 1986–87. *Reflexiones sobre América.* 3 vols. Rosario.

Cunico, Gerardo. 1988. *Critica e ragione utopica: A confronto con Habermas e Bloch.* Marietti, Genova.

Damasio, Antonio. 1994. *Descartes' Error: Emotion, Reason, and the Human Brain.* A. Grosset, New York.

Daniels, Norman, ed. 1975. *Reading Rawls.* Basil Blackwell, Oxford.

Davidson, Donald. 1981. *Essays on Actions and Events.* Clarendon Press, Oxford.

———. 1990. *De la verdad y de la interpretación.* Gedisa, Barcelona (original, *Inquiries into Truth and Interpretation.* Oxford University Press, Oxford, 1984).

———. 1992. *Mente, mundo y acción.* Paidos Ibérica, Barcelona.

Davies, W. D. 1982. *The Territorial Dimension of Judaism.* University of California Press, Berkeley.

Dawkins, D. 1976. *The Selfish Gene*. Oxford University Press, Oxford.

De Waehlens, Alphonse. 1961. *La philosophie et les expériences naturelles*. Nijhoff, The Hague.

Deladalle, Gérard. 1987. *Charles S. Peirce: Phénoménologue et sémioticien*. John Benjamins, Amsterdam.

Delbos, Victor. 1893. *Le problème moral dans la philosophie de Spinoza*. Alcan, Paris.

———. 1969. *La philosophie pratique de Kant*. PUF, Paris.

Deleuze, Gilles. 1962. *Nietzsche et la Philosophie*. PUF, Paris.

———. 1991. *Foucault*. Paidos, Mexico.

Deleuze, Gilles, and Félix Guattari. 1972. *Capitalisme et schizophrénie: L'Anti-Oedipe*. Minuit, Paris.

Derrida, Jacques. 1964. "*Violence et métaphysique*, essai sur la pensée d'Emmanuel Levinas." *Revue de Métaphysique et Morale* 69.3: 322–54, and 69.4: 425–43.

———. 1967a. *L'écriture et la différence*. Seuil, Paris.

———. 1967b. *De la grammatologie*. Minuit, Paris.

Descartes, René. 1935. *Lettres sur la morale*. Boivin, Paris.

———. 1953. *Oeuvres et lettres de Descartes*. La Pléiade, Gallimard, Paris.

———. 1985. *The Philosophical Works of Descartes*. Vol. 1. Trans. by John Cottingham, Robert Stoothoff, and Dugald Murdoch. Cambridge University Press, Cambridge.

Dewey, John. 1920. *Reconstruction in Philosophy*. Henry Holt, New York.

———. 1958. *Experience and Nature*. Dover Publications, New York.

Dews, Peter. 1987. *Logics of Disintegration: Post-structuralist Thought and the Claims of Critical Theory*. Verso, London.

Diels, Hermann. 1964. *Die Fragmente der Vorsokratiker*. 3 vols. Weidmannsche Verlag, Berlin.

Diemer, Alwin. 1981. *Philosophy in the Present Situation of Africa*. Frantz Steiner Verlag, Wiesbaden.

Diemer, A., and P. Hountondji. 1985. *Africa and the Problem of Its Identity*. Peter Lang, Frankfurt.

Diogenes Laertius. 1968. *Epikur*. F. Meiner, Hamburg.

Diop, Cheikh Anta. 1974. *The African Origin of Civilization: Myth or Reality?* Lawrence Hill, Westport.

———. 1978. *The Cultural Unity of Black Africa*. Third World Press, Chicago.

———. 1990. *Afrika: Mutter und Model der europäische Zivilisation?* Dietrich Reimer, Berlin.

Donnellan, Keith S. 1966. "Reference and Definite Descriptions." *Philosophical Review* 75: 281–304.

Drake, Stillman. 1957. *Discoveries and Opinions of Galileo*. Doubleday, Anchor Books, New York.

Drioton, Etienne. 1922. *Contribution à l'étude du Chapitre CXXV du Livre des Morts*. Bibliotèque de l'École Pratique des Hautes Études (Paris), Vols. 233–34.

Dubiel, H. 1978. *Wissenschaftorganisation und politische Erfharung*. Suhrkamp, Frankfurt.

Dubois, Pierre. 1967. *Le problème moral dans la philosophie anglaise de 1900 à 1950*. Vrin, Paris.

Duhem, Pierre. 1914. *Le système du monde: La cosmologie hellenique*. Vol. 2. A. Hermann, Paris.

Dussel, Enrique. 1966. *Hipótesis para el estudio de Latinoamérica en la historia universal*. Vol. 1. Universidad del Nordeste, Resistencia.

———. 1969. *El humanismo semita*. UDEBA, Buenos Aires.

———. 1970. *Les évêques latinoaméricains defenseurs et evangelisateurs de l'indien (1504–1620)*. Steiner Verlag, Wiesbaden.

———. 1970–80. *Para una ética de la liberación latinoamericana*. Vols. 1 and 2 (1970–72), Siglo XXI, Buenos Aires, 1973; vol. 3 (1973), Edicol, Mexico, 1977; vols. 4 and 5 (1974–75), USTA, Bogotá, 1979–80.

———. 1973. *Para una de-strucción de la historia de la ética*. Ser y Tiempo, Mendoza.

———. 1974a. *El dualismo en la antropología de la Cristiandad*. Editorial Guadalupe, Buenos Aires.

———. 1974b. *Método para una Filosofía de la Liberación*. Sígueme, Salamanca.

———. 1975. *El humanismo helénico*. EUDEBA, Buenos Aires.

———. 1977. *Filosofía de la liberación*. Edicol, México (English trans. *Philosophy of Liberation*, Orbis Books, New York, 1985).

———. 1983a. "Introducción general." In *Historia general de la Iglesia en América Latina*, vol. 1, 1–724. Sígueme, Salamanca.

———. 1983b. *Praxis latinoamericana y filosofía de la liberación*. Nueva América, Bogota.

———. 1984. *Filosofía de la producción*. Nueva América, Bogota.

———. 1985a. *La producción teórica de Marx: Un comentario a los Grundrisse*. Siglo XXI, Mexico City.

———. 1985b. *Philosophy of Liberation*. Orbis Books, New York, 1985.

———. 1986. *Etica comunitaria*. Ediciones Paulinas (English trans. *Ethics and Community*, Orbis Books, New York, 1988).

———. 1988. *Hacia un Marx desconocido: Un comentario de los Manuscritos del 61–63*. Siglo XXI, Mexico City (English trans. *Towards an Unknown Marx*, Routledge, London, 2001).

———. 1990a. "Die *Lebensgemeischaft* und die Interpellation des Armen." In Fornet-Betancourt 1990, 69–96.

———. 1990b. *El último Marx (1863–1882) y la liberación latinoamericana*. Siglo XXI, Mexico City.

———. 1992. "Re-lectüre Marx: Aus der Perspektive der Lateinamerikanischen Philosophie der Befreiung." In *Bremer Philosophica*, Universität Bremen, Studiengang Philosophie, 5.

———. 1993a. *Apel, Ricoeur, Rorty y la filosofía de la liberación*. Universidad de Guadalajara, Guadalajara (English trans. *The Underside of Modernity: Apel, Ricoeur, Taylor, Rorty and the Philosophy of Liberation*, Humanities Press, New York, 1996).

———. 1993b. *Las metáforas teológicas de Marx*. Verbo Divino, Estella, Spain.

———. 1993c. *1492: El encubrimiento del Otro—Hacia el origen del mito de la modernidad*. Nueva Utopía, Madrid (English trans. *The Invention of the Americas*, Continuum Publishing, New York, 1995).

———. 1993d. "Proyecto filosófico de Charles Taylor." *Signos: Anuario de Humanidades* (Mexico) 7.3: 15–60.

———. 1994a, ed. *Debate en torno a la ética del discurso de Apel: Diálogo filosófico Norte-Sur desde América Latina*, Siglo XXI, Mexico.

———. 1994b. "Etica de la liberación." In Sidekum 1994, 145–70.

———. 1994c. *Historia de la filosofía latinoamericana y filosofía de la liberación.* Nueva América, Bogota.

———. 1995a. "Hegel y el Estado." In *Laval Théologie et Philosophie*, Quebec.

———. 1995b. "La philosophie latinoaméricaine dans le xxme. siècle." In *Institut International de Philosophie* (Paris).

———. 1995c. "Die Priorität der Befreiungsethik gegenüber der Diskursehtik." In Arens 1995, 113–37 (original, "La ética de la liberación ante el desafío de la ética del discurso," *Signos* [Mexico] 7 [1994]: 241–75).

———. 1996a. "Globalization and Exclusion: From a Liberation Ethics Perspective." Saint Louis University, lecture.

———. 1996b. "Zur Architectonik der Befreiungsethik: Über materiale Ethik und formale Morale." In Fornet-Betancourt 1996, 61–94.

———. 2007. *Política de la liberación.* Trotta, Madrid.

———. 2010. *Politics of Liberation.* Vol. 1. SCM Press, Norwich, UK.

Dworkin, Roland. 1975. "The Original Position." In Daniels 1975, chap. 2.

———. 1977. *Taking Rights Seriously.* Harvard University Press, Cambridge.

———. 1986. *Law's Empire.* Belknap Press of Harvard University Press, Cambridge.

Eboussi Boulaga, Fabien. 1968. "Le bantou problematique." *Présence Africaine* 66: 5–40.

———. 1977. *La crise du Muntu: Authenticité africaine et philosophie.* Présence Africaine, Paris.

Edelman, Gerald M. 1988. *Topobiology: An Introduction to Molecular Embryology.* Basic Books, New York.

———. 1989. *The Remembered Present: A Biological Theory of Consciousness.* Basic Books, New York.

———. 1992. *Bright Air, Brilliant Fire: On the Matter of the Mind.* Basic Books, New York.

Einstein, Albert. 1977. *La física: Aventura del pensamiento.* Losada, Buenos Aires.

Elungu, P. E. A. 1984. *L'éveil philosophique africain.* Editions L'Harmattan, Paris.

Emerson, L. W. "MLE and American Indian Education." In Feuerstein 1991, 133–56.

Endress, G. 1982. *Einführung in die islamische Geschichte.* Beck, Munich.

Eribon, Didier. 1989. *Michel Foucault (1926–1984).* Flammarion, Paris.

Espinas, A. 1925. *Descartes et la morale.* Bossard, Paris.

Fahrenbach, Helmut. 1968. *Kierkegaards existenzdialektische Ethik.* Klostermann, Frankfurt.

———. 1970. *Existenzphilosophie und Ethik.* Klostermann, Frankfurt.

Fals Borda, Orlando. 1974. *Ciencia propia y colonialismo intelectual.* Editorial Nuestro Tiempo, Mexico City.

———. 1981. "El nuevo despertar de los movimientos sociales." In *Ciencia propia y colonialismo intelectual: Los nuevos rumbos*, 131–52. Carlos Valencia Editores, Bogota.

Fanon, Frantz. 1963. *Los condenados de la tierra.* Spanish trans. FCE, Mexico City.

Faulkner, Raymond O. 1985. *The Book of the Dead.* Limited Editions, New York.

Febraio, Alberto. 1975. *Funzionalismo strutturale e sociologie del diritto nell'opera di Niklas Luhmann*. Giuffré, Milan.

Festugière, R. P. 1944–53. *La révélation d'Hermès Trismégiste*. 3 vols. Lecoffre, Paris.

Feuerbach, Ludwig. 1959–60. *Sämtliche Werke*. Ed. W. Bolin and F. Jodl. 6 vols. Fromann, Stuttgart.

———. 1967. *Grundsätze der Philosophie der Zukunft*. Klostermann, Frankfurt (Spanish trans. *La filosofía del futuro*, Calden, Buenos Aires, 1969).

Feuerstein, Reuven. 1990. "La modificabilidad cognitiva y el PEI [Programa de Enriquecimiento Instrumental]." In *Metodología de la mediación en el PEI*, by José Martínez Beltrán et al., 7–14. Editorial Bruño, Madrid.

Feuerstein, Reuven, Pnina Klein, and Abraham Tannenbaum, eds. 1991. *Mediated Learning Experience (MLE): Theoretical, Psychosocial and Learning Implications*. Freund Publishing House, London.

Feuerstein, Reuven, Y. Rand, and M. G. Hoffman. 1979. *The Dynamic Assessment of Retarded Performers*. University Park Press, Baltimore.

Feyerabend, Paul. 1987. *Farewell to Reason*. Verso, London.

———. 1989. *Paul Feyerabend: Límites de la ciencia*. Ed. Diego Ribes. Paidos, Barcelona.

———. 1992. *Tratado contra el método*. Tecnos, Madrid.

Fichte, Immanuel Hermann. 1971. *Fichtes Werke*. 11 vols. Walter de Gruyter, Berlin.

Field, Hartry. 1972. "Tarski's Theory of Truth." *Journal of Philosophy*, 69.13: 347–63.

Fink, Eugen. 1969. *La filosofía de Nietzsche*. Alianza, Madrid.

Fisch, Max. 1986. *Peirce, Semiotics, and Pragmatism*. Indiana University Press, Bloomington.

Follari, Roberto. 1991. *Modernidad y posmodernidad: Una óptica desde América Latina*. Rei, Buenos Aires.

Fornet-Betancourt, Raúl. 1985. *Kommentierte Bibliographie zur Philosophie in Lateinamerika*. Peter Lang, Frankfurt.

———, ed. 1990. *Ethik und Befreiung*. Augustinus, Aachen (Spanish trans. in K.-O. Apel and E. Dussel, *Fundamentación de la ética y filosofía de la liberación*, Siglo XXI, Mexico City, 1992).

———, ed. 1992. *Diskursethik oder Befreiungsethik?* Augustinus, Aachen (Spanish trans. in Dussel 1994a).

———, ed. 1993. *Die Diskursehik und ihre lateinamerikanische Kritik*. Augustinus, Aachen.

———, ed. 1994. *Konvergenz oder Divergenz? Eine Bilanz des Gesprächs zwischen Diskursethik und Befreiungsethik*. Augustinus, Aachen.

———, ed. 1996. *Armut, Ethik, Befreiung*. Augustinus, Aachen.

Foucault, Michel. 1966. *Les mots et les choses*. Gallimard, Paris (Spanish trans. *Las palabras y las cosas*, Siglo XXI, Mexico City, 1986).

———. 1969. *L'archéologie du savoir*. Gallimard, Paris (Spanish trans. *La arqueología del saber*, Siglo XXI, Mexico City, 1987).

———. 1972. *Histoire de la folie à l'âge classique*. Gallimard, Paris (Spanish trans. FCE, Mexico).

———. 1975. *Surveiller et punir*. Gallimard, Paris (English trans. *Discipline and Punish: The Birth of the Prison*, trans. Alan Sheridan, Vintage, New York, 1979; Spanish trans. *Vigilar y castigar*, Siglo XXI, Mexico City, 1986).

————. 1976. *La volonté de savoir*. Gallimard, Paris (Spanish trans. *La voluntad de saber*, Siglo XXI, Mexico City, 1977).

————. 1984. *Le souci de soi*. Gallimard, Paris (Spanish trans. *La inquietud de sí*, Siglo XXI, Mexico City, 1987).

————. 1986. *El uso de los placeres*, Siglo XXI, Mexico City.

Frank, André Gunder. 1987. "The Shape of the World System in the Thirteenth Century." *Studies in Comparative International Development* 12.4 (Winter): 3–25.

————. 1990. "A Theoretical Introduction to 5000 years of World System History." *Review* (Binghamton) 13.2: 155–248.

————. 1992a. *The Centrality of Central Asia*. UV University Press, Amsterdam.

————. 1992b. "The Five-Thousand-Year World System." *Humboldt Journal of Social Relations* (Arcata, Calif.): 1–80.

Frank, André Gunder, and B. K. Gills, ed. 1992. *The World System: From Five Hundred Years to Five Thousand*. Routledge, London.

Franke, H., H. Hoffmann, and H. Jedin, eds. 1965. *Saeculum Weltgeschichte*. Vol. 1. Herder, Freiburg.

Frege, Gottlob. 1980. "Ueber Sinn und Bedeutung." In *Funktion, Begriff, Bedeutung*, ed. G. Patzig. Vandenhoeck & Ruprecht, Göttingen.

Freire, Paulo. 1971. "Concientizar para liberar." *Contacto* (Mexico) 8: 42–51.

————. 1976. *Education: The Practice of Freedom*. Trans. and ed. Myra Bergman Ramos. Writers and Readers Publishing Cooperative, London.

————. 1977. *Cartas a Guinea-Bissau*. Siglo XXI, Mexico City.

————. 1978. *Açâo cultural para a liberdade*. Paz e Terra, Rio de Janeiro.

————. 1979. *Educaçâo e mudança*. Paz e Terra, Rio de Janeiro.

————. 1980a. *Concientizaçâo: Teoría e prática da libertaçâo*. Editora Moraes, Sao Paulo.

————. 1980b. *Educaçâo como prática da liberdade*. Paz e Terra, Rio de Janeiro (English trans. *Education: The Practice of Freedom*, trans. and ed. Myra Bergman Ramos, Writers and Readers Publishing Cooperative, London, 1976).

————. 1984. *La importancia de leer y el proceso de liberación*. Siglo XXI, Mexico City.

————. 1993. *Pedagogía de la esperanza*. Siglo XXI, Mexico City.

————. 1994. *Pedagogía del oprimido*. Siglo XXI, Mexico City (original *Pedagogía do oprimido*, Paz e Terra, Rio de Janeiro, 1978 [1969]).

Freud, Sigmund. 1969. *Sigmund Freud: Studienausgabe*. 10 vols. Fischer, Frankfurt (Spanish trans. *Obras completas*, 3 vols., Editorial Biblioteca Nueva, Madrid, 1968).

Friedman, Milton. 1966a. *Capitalismo y libertad*. Rialp, Madrid.

————. 1966b. *Teoría de los precios*. Alianza, Madrid.

Friedman, Milton, and Rose Friedman. 1980. *Free to Choose*. Avon Books, New York.

Froidefond, C. 1971. *Le mirage égyptien dans la littérature grecque d'Homère à Aristote*. Ophrys, Paris.

Fromm, Erich. 1941. *Escape from Freedom*. Rinehart, New York.

————. 1962. *Beyond the Chains of Illusion*. Simon and Schuster, New York.

————. 1963. *The Dogma of Christ and Other Essays on Religion*. Holt, Rinehart, and Winston, New York.

————. 1969. *Ética y psicoanálisis*. FCE, Mexico City (original *Man for Himself*, Rinehart, New York, 1947).

Fukuyama, Francis. 1992. *La fin de l'histoire et le dernier homme*. Flammarion, Paris.

Gadamer, Hans-Georg. 1960. *Wahrheit und Methode*. Mohr, Tübingen (Spanish trans. *Verdad y método*, Sígueme, Salamanca, 1977).

Galbraith, John K. 1993. *La cultura de la satisfacción*. Ariel, Barcelona.

Galilei, Galileo. 1933. *Il Saggiatore*. In *Le opere di Galileo Galilei*, vol. 6, 197–372. G. Barbera, Florence.

Gann, L. H., and Peter Duignan, eds. 1969–70. *Colonialism in Africa, 1870–1960*. 2 vols. Cambridge University Press, Cambridge.

Gardet, Louis-Anawaqti. 1948. *Introduction à la théologie musulmane*. J. Vrin, Paris.

———. 1967. *Islam*. J. Vrin, Paris.

Gauthier, David. 1986. *Morals by Agreement*. Clarendon Press, Oxford.

Gauthier, L. 1909. *La théorie d'Ibn Rochd sur les rapports de la religion et de la philosophie*. E. Leroux, Paris.

———. 1923. *Introduction à l'étude de la philosophie musulmane*. E. Leroux, Paris.

Gert, Bernard. 1988. *The Moral Rules*. Oxford University Press, New York.

Gewirth, Alan. 1978. *Reason and Morality*. Chicago University Press, Chicago.

Gibbs, Robert. 1992. *Correlations in Rosenzweig and Levinas*. Princeton University Press, Princeton.

Giddens, Anthony. 1993. *Las nuevas reglas del método sociológico*. Amorrortu, Buenos Aires (Spanish trans. *New Rules of Sociological Method*, Hutchison, London, 1967).

Girard, René. 1982. *El misterio de nuestro mundo: Claves para una interpretación antropológica*. Sígueme, Salamanca.

Glover, Jonathan, ed. 1990. *Utilitarianism and Its Critics*. Macmillan, New York.

Godinho, V. M. 1950. "Création et dynamisme économique du monde atlantique (1420–1670)," *Annales ESC* 5.1 (January–March): 10–30.

Gómez, Ricardo. 1995. *Neoliberalismo y pseudo-ciencia*. Lugar Editorial, Buenos Aires.

Gómez Llorente, Luis. 1975. *Rosa Luxemburgo y la socialdemocracia alemana*. Cuadernos para el Diálogo, Madrid.

Gottwald, Norman. 1981. *The Tribes of Yahweh: A Sociology of the Religion of Liberated Israel, 1250–1050 BCE*. Maryknoll, New York.

Gracia, Jorge, Eduardo Rabossi, Enrique Villanueva, and Marcelo Dascal, eds. 1985. *El análisis filosófico en América Latina*. FCE, Mexico City.

Gramsci, Antonio. 1970. *Antología*. Manuel Sacristán, Siglo XXI, Mexico City.

———. 1975. *Quaderni del carcere*. 4 vols. Einaudi, Torino.

Gray, Chris. 1989. *Conceptions of History: Cheikh Anta Diop*. Karnak House, London.

Gruppi, L. 1976. "El concepto de hegemonía en Gramsci." In *Revolución y democracia en Gramsci*, 39–54. Fontamara, Barcelona.

Guisán, Esperanza. 1992. "Utilitarismo." In Camps 1992, 269–95.

Gutiérrez, Germán. 1996. "La ética en Adam Smith y Friedrich von Hayek." Ph.D. dissertation. Universidad Iberoamericana, Mexico City.

Habermas, Jürgen. 1962. *Strukturwandel der Oeffentlichkeit: Untersuchungen zu einer Kategorie der bürgerlichen Gesellschaft*. Luchterhand, Berlin (Spanish trans. published by G. Gilli, Mexico, 1986).

————. 1963. *Theorie und Praxis.* Suhrkamp, Frankfurt (Spanish trans. *Teoría y praxis*, Tecnos, Madrid, 1967).

————. 1968a. *Erkenntnis und Interesse.* Suhrkamp, Frankfurt (English trans. *Knowledge and Human Interests*, trans. Jeremy J. Shapiro, Beacon Press, Boston, 1971; Spanish trans. *Conocimiento e interés*, Taurus, Madrid, 1986).

————. 1968b. *Technik und Wissenschaft als "Ideologie."* Suhrkamp, Frankfurt.

————. 1973. *Legitimationsprobleme im Sprätkapitalismus.* Suhrkamp, Frankfurt.

————. 1976. *Zur Rekonstruktion des Historischen Materialismus.* Suhrkamp (Spanish trans. *La reconstrucción del materialismo histórico*, Taurus, Madrid, 1986).

————. 1981a. *Philosophisch-politische Profile*, Suhrkamp, Frankfurt (Spanish trans. *Perfiles filosófico-políticos*, Taurus, Madrid, 1984).

————. 1981b. *Theorie des kommunikativen Handelns.* 2 vols. Suhrkamp, Frankfurt (Spanish trans. *Teoría de la acción comunicativa*, 2 vols., Taurus, Madrid, 1987).

————. 1982. *Zur Logik der Sozialwissenschaften.* Suhrkamp, Frankfurt (Spanish trans. *La lógica de las ciencias sociales*, Tecnos-Rei, Mexico, 1993).

————. 1983. *Moralbewußtsein und kommunikatives Handeln.* Suhrkamp, Frankfurt (English trans. *Moral Consciousness and Communicative Action*, trans. Christian Lenhardt and Shierry Weber Nicholsen, MIT Press, Cambridge, 1993; Spanish trans. *Conciencia moral y acción comunicativa*, Ediciones Península, Madrid, 1985).

————. 1984. *Vorstudien und Ergänzungen zur Theorie des kommunikativen Handelns.* Suhrkamp, Frankfurt (Spanish trans. Cátedra, Madrid, 1989).

————. 1985. *Der philosophische Diskurs der Moderne.* Suhrkamp, Frankfurt (Spanish trans. Taurus, Buenos Aires, 1989).

————. 1988. *Nachmetaphysisches Denken.* Suhrkamp, Frankfurt (Spanish trans. Taurus Humanidades, Mexico, 1990).

————. 1991. *Erläuterungen zur Diskursethik.* Suhrkamp, Frankfurt (English trans. *Justification and Application*, MIT Press, Cambridge, and "Justice and Solidarity: On the Discussion Concerning *Stage 6*," *Philosophical Forum* 21. 1–2 [1989–1990]: 32–51; Spanish trans. *Escritos sobre moralidad y eticidad*, Paidos, Barcelona, 1991).

————. 1992. *Faktizität und Geltung*, Suhrkamp, Frankfurt (English trans. *Between Facts and Norms: Contributions to a Discourse Theory of Law and Democracy.* MIT Press, Cambridge, 1996).

————. 1995. "Reconciliation through the Public use of Reason: Remarks on John Rawls's Political Liberalism." *Journal of Philosophy* 92.3 (March): 109–31.

————. 1996. *Die Einbeziehung des Anderen.* Suhrkamp, Frankfurt.

Hall, Alfred Rupert. 1983. *The Revolution in Science, 1500–1750.* Longman, London.

Hamilton, Earl. 1948. *El florecimiento del capitalismo y otros ensayos de historia económica.* Revista de Occidente, Madrid.

————. 1960. "The History of Prices before 1750." In *International Congress of Historical Sciences* (Stockholm), 144–64. Almqvist and Wiksell, Göteberg.

Hammarström, D. Ingrid. 1957. "The Price Revolution of the Sixteenth Century." *Scandinavian Economic History* 5.1: 118–54.

Hammurabi Code. 1986. Ed. Lara Peinado. Tecnos, Madrid.

Harding, Leonard, and Brigitte Reinwald, eds. 1990. *Afrika. Mutter und Modell der europäische Zivilization?* Reimer, Berlin.

Hare, Richard Mervyn. 1952. *The Language of Morals*. Clarendon Press, Oxford (Spanish trans. *El lenguaje de la moral*, UNAM, Mexico City, 1975).

————. 1981. *Essays on Moral Thinking*. Clarendon Press, Oxford.

Hartman, Roberto. 1952. *La estructura del valor*. FCE, Mexico City.

————. 1965. *El conocimiento moral*. FCE, Mexico City.

Hartmann, Nicolai. 1962. *Ethik*. De Gruyter, Berlin.

Havers, W. 1960. "La religión de los indogermanos primitivos a la luz de su lengua." In König 1959, vol. 2, 645–94.

Hayek, Friedrich von. 1952. *Individualismus und Wirtschaftliche Ordnung*. Eugen Rentsch Verlag, Zürich.

————. 1975. *Los fundamentos de la libertad*. Unión Editorial, Madrid (English trans. *The Constitution of Liberty*, University of Chicago Press, Chicago, 1959).

————. 1979. *Law, Legislation and Liberty*. University of Chicago Press, Chicago.

Hegel, Georg Wilhelm Friedrich. 1955. *Die Vernunft in der Geschichte, Zweiter Entwurf* (1830). In *Sämtliche Werke*, ed. J. Hoffmeister. F. Meiner, Hamburg.

————. 1956. *The Philosophy of History*. Trans. J. Sibree. Dover, New York.

————. 1971–79. *G. W. F. Hegel Werke in zwanzig Bänden: Theorie Werkausgabe*. 20 vols. Suhrkamp, Frankfurt.

Heidegger, Martin. 1947. *Brief über den Humanismus*. Klostermann, Frankfurt.

————. 1961. *Nietzsche*. 2 vols. Neske, Pfullingen.

————. 1963a. *Die Frage nach dem Ding*. Niemeyer, Tübingen (Spanish trans. *La pregunta por la cosa*, Sur, Buenos Aires, 1964).

————. 1963b. *Holzwege*. Klostermann, Frankfurt.

————. 1963c. *Sein und Zeit*. Max Niemeyer, Tübingen (Spanish trans. *Ser y tiempo*, FCE, Mexico City, 1968).

————. 1967a. *Wegmarken*. Klostermann, Frankfurt (Spanish trans. "Carta sobre el humanismo," in *Sobre el humanismo*, 65–121, Sur, Buenos Aires, 1960).

————. 1967b. *What Is a Thing*. Trans. by W. B. Barton et al. Henry Regnery, Chicago.

Held, David. 1980. *Introduction to Critical Theory: Horkheimer to Habermas*. University of California Press, Berkeley.

Hempel, Carl G. 1965. "Problemas y cambios en el criterio empirista de significado." In *El positivismo lógico*, ed. A. J. Ayer, 115–36. FCE, Mexico City.

————. 1979. *La explicación científica*. Paidos, Buenos Aires.

Henrich, D. 1976. "Die Grundstruktur der Modernen Philosophie." In *Subjetivität und Selbsterhaltung*, ed. H. E. Berling. Suhrkamp, Frankfurt.

Herodotus. 1954. *The Histories*. Ed. Aubrey de Selincourt. Penguin, London (Spanish trans. *Los nueve libros de la Historia*, Biblioteca Edarf, Madrid, 1989).

Hersh, Richard, Diana Paolitto, and Joseph Reimer. 1979. *El crecimiento moral de Piaget a Kohlberg*. Narcea, Madrid.

Hess, Moses. 1845. "Ueber das Geldwesen." In *Rheinische Jahrbücher zur gesellschaftlichen Reform*, 1–15. C. B. Leste, Darmstadt.

Hildenbrand, Dietrich von. 1969. *Die Idee der sittlichen Handlung*. Buchgesellschaft, Darmstadt.

Hinkelammert, Franz. 1970a. *Dialéctica del desarrollo desigual: El caso latinoamericano*. Centro de Estudios de la Realidad Nacional, Santiago.

———. 1970b. *Ideologías del desarrollo y dialéctica de la historia*. Ediciones Nueva Universidad, Santiago de Chile.

———. 1984. *Crítica a la razón utópica*. DEI, San José de Costa Rica.

———. 1990. *Democracia y totalitarismo*, DEI, San José de Costa Rica.

———. 1991. *Sacrificios humanos y sociedad occidental*, DEI, San José de Costa Rica.

———. 1994. "Diskursethik und Verantwortungsethik: Eine kritische Stellungnahme." In Fornet-Betancourt 1994, 111–49.

———. 1995a. "Die Marxsche Wertlehre und die Philosophie der Befreiung." In *Für Enrique Dussel*, ed. R. Fornet-Betancourt, 35–73, Augustinus, Aachen (reprinted in Hinkelammert 1996, 89–234).

———. 1995b. *La cultura de la esperanza y sociedad sin exclusión*, DEI, San José.

———. 1995c. "Utopía, anti-utopía y ética: La *condición postmoderna* y la modernidad." In Hinkelammert 1996, 83–187.

———. 1996. *El mapa del emperador*, DEI, San José.

Hodgson, Marshall. 1974. *The Venture of Islam*. 3 vols. University of Chicago Press, Chicago.

Höffe, Otfried, ed. 1972. *Einführung in die utilitaristische Ethik*. Beck, Munich.

———. 1979. *Ethik und Politik: Grundmodelle und Problem der praktischen Philosophie*. Suhrkamp, Munich.

———. 1993. *Moral als Preis der Moderne: Ein Versuch über Wissenschaft, Technik und Umwelt*. Suhrkamp, Frankfurt.

Honneth, Axel. 1992. *Kampf um Anerkennung*. Suhrkamp, Frankfurt.

Horkheimer, Max. 1933. "Materialismus und Moral." *Zeitschrift für Sozialforschun* 2 (English trans. "Materialism and Morality," in *Between Philosophy and Social Science*, 15–48, MIT Press, Cambridge, 1993; "Materialism and Metaphysics," in *Critical Theory*, 10–46, Continuum, New York, 1982).

———. 1967. *Zur Kritik der instrumentellen Vernunft*. Fischer, Frankfurt (Spanish trans. *Crítica de la razón instrumental*, Sur, Buenos Aires, 1973).

———. 1970a. *Sobre el concepto del hombre y otros ensayos*. Sur, Buenos Aires.

———. 1970b. *Traditionelle und kritische Theorie: Vier Aufsätze*. Fischer, Frankfurt (Spanish trans. *Teoría crítica*, Barral, Barcelona, 1973; *Teoría crítica*, Amorrortu, Buenos Aires, 1990).

———. 1982. *Historia, metafísica y escepticismo*. Alianza, Madrid.

Horkheimer, Max, and T. Adorno. 1971. *Dialektik der Aufklärung*. Fischer, Frankfurt (Spanish trans. *Dialéctica del iluminismo*, Sur, Buenos Aires, 1970).

Horwich, Paul. 1990. *Truth*. Basil Blackwell, Oxford.

Hösle, Vittorio. 1990. *Die Krise der Gegenwart und die Verantwortung der Philosophie*. C. H. Beck, Munich.

Hountondji, Paulin. 1977. *Sur la "philosophie africaine": Critique de l'ethnophilosophie*. Maspero, Paris.

Human Development Report 1992. 1992. Development Programme, United Nations, Oxford University Press, New York.

Hume, David. 1958. *A Treatise of Human Nature*. Ed. L. A. Selby-Bigge. Oxford University Press, Oxford.

Hunter, Geoffrey. 1962. "Hume on *Is* and *Ought.*" *Philosophy* (April): 148–52.

Husserl, Edmund. 1950. *Ideen zu einer reinen Phänomenologie und Phänomenologischen Philosophie.* Husserliana vol. 3. Nijhoff, The Hague.

———. 1962. *Die Krisis der europäischen Wissenschaften*, Husserliana vol. 6, sec. 35. Nijhoff, The Hague.

———. 1966. *Méditations Cartésiennes.* French trans. by E. Levinas and G. Pfeiffer, Vrin, Paris.

Illich, Ivan. 1971a. *Libérer l'avenir.* Seuil, Paris.

———. 1971b. *Une société sans école.* Seuil, Paris.

Izuzquiza, Ignacio. 1990. *La sociedad sin hombres: Niklas Luhmann.* Anthropos, Barcelona.

Jaeger, Werner. 1952. *La teología de los primeros filósofos griegos.* FCE, Mexico City.

Jahn, Wolfgang, and Manfred Müller, eds. 1983. *Der zweite Entwurf des "Kapitals."* Dietz, Berlin.

James, George C. M. 1954. *Stolen Legacy: The Greeks Were Not the Authors of Greek Philosophy.* Philosophical Library, New York.

James, William. 1943. *Pragmatism: A New Name for Some Old Ways of Thinking.* Longmans, Green, New York.

———. 1975a. *The Meaning of Truth.* Harvard University Press, Cambridge.

———. 1975b. *Pragmatism.* Harvard University Press, Cambridge (Spanish trans. *Pragmatismo*, Daniel Jorro, Madrid, 1923).

———. 1976. *Essays in Radical Empiricism.* Harvard University Press, Cambridge.

———. 1982. *The Varieties of Religious Experience.* Penguin Classics, New York.

Jameson, Fredric. 1991. *Postmodernism, or The Cultural Logic of Late Capitalism.* Duke University Press, Durham.

Jaspers, Karl. 1963a. *Nietzsche.* Sudamericana, Buenos Aires.

———. 1963b. *Vom Ursprung und Ziel der Geschichte.* Piper, Munich.

———. 1993. *Los grandes filósofos: Los hombres decisivos: Sócrates, Buda, Confucio, Jesús.* Tecnos, Madrid.

Jay, Martin. 1973. *The Dialectical Imagination. A History of the Frankfurt School and the Institute of Social Research, 1923–1950.* Heinemann, London.

———. 1994. *Downcast Eyes: The Denigration of Vision in Twentieth-Century French Thought.* University of California Press, Berkeley.

Jevons, William. 1957. *The Theory of Political Economy.* Kelly and Millman, New York.

Jonas, Hans. 1982a. *Das Prinzip Verantwortung.* G. Wagner, Nördlingen (English trans. *The Imperative of Responsibility*, University of Chicago Press, Chicago, 1984).

———. 1982b. *The Phenomenon of Life: Toward a Philosophical Biology.* English trans. University of Chicago Press, Chicago.

Junker, Hermann. 1941. "Die politische Lehre von Memphis." *Abhundlungen der Preussischen Akademie der Wissenschaften* (Berlin).

Justin Martyr. 1954. *Diálogo con Trifón.* In Ruiz Bueno 1954, 300–548.

Kagame, A. 1956. *La Philosophie bantu-rwandaise de l'Etre*, Académie Royale des Sciences, Brussels.

Kant, Immanuel. 1904–36. *Kants Gesammelte Schriften.* 21 vols. Academia Prusiana, Berlin.

———. 1968. *Kants Werke*. 10 vols. Wissenschaftliche Buchgesellschaft, Darmstadt.

Kantorovich, L. V. 1968. *La asignación óptima de los recursos económicos*. Ariel, Barcelona.

Kearney, Richard. 1984. *Dialogues with Contemporary Continental Thinkers: The Phenomenological Heritage*. Manchester University Press, London.

Kellner, Douglas. 1981. *El marxismo revolucionario de Karl Korsch*. Premià Editora, Mexico City.

———. 1984. *Herbert Marcuse and the Crisis of Marxism*. Macmillan, London.

Kelly, Michael, ed. 1989. "Hermeneutics in Ethics and Social Theory." In *Philosophical Forum* (New York) 31: 1–2.

Kennedy, Paul. 1987. *The Rise and Fall of the Great Powers*. Random House, New York.

Kern, Fritz. 1952–61. *Historia Mundi, ein Handbuch der Weltgeschicht*. 10 vols. Leo Lehnen Verlag, Munich.

Kettner, Matthias. 1992. "Drei Dilemmata angewandter Ethik." In *Zur Anwendung der Diskursethik in Politik, Recht und Wissenschaft*, ed. Matthias Kettner, 9–27. Suhrkamp, Frankfurt.

Kierkegaard, Søren. 1949. *Post-scriptum aux miettes philosophiques*. Gallimard, Paris (original *Aufsluttende uvidenskabelig Efterskrift*, 2 vols., Gyldendal, Copenhagen, 1962).

———. 1959. *Estética y ética*. Nova, Buenos Aires.

———. 1968. *Temor y temblor*. Losada, Buenos Aires.

Klengel, H. 1977. *Hammurabi von Babylon und seine Zeit*. VEB Deutscher Verlag der Wissenschaften, Berlin.

Kohlberg, Lawrence. 1981–84. *Essays on Moral Development*. 2 vols. Harper and Row, Cambridge.

Kohlberg, Lawrence, and Anne Colby. 1987. *The Measurement of Moral Judgement*. 2 vols. Cambridge University Press, Cambridge.

König, Franz, ed. 1959–61. *Cristo y las religiones de la tierra*. 3 vols. BAC, Madrid.

Korsch, Karl. 1978. *Marxismo e filosofia*. Sugar Co Edizioni, Milano.

Krader, Lawrence. 1963. *Peoples of Central Asia*. Indiana University Press, Bloomington.

Krickeberg, Walter, H. Trimborn, H. Müller, and O. Zerries, eds. 1961. *Die Religionen des alten Amerika*. Vol. 7 of *Die Religionen der Menschheit*, Kohlhammer, Stuttgart.

Kripke, Saul. 1985. *El nombrar y la necesidad*. UNAM, Mexico City (original *Naming and Necessity*, Blackwell, Oxford, 1981).

Kuhn, Thomas. 1962. *The Structure of Scientific Revolutions*. University of Chicago Press, Chicago (Spanish trans. *La estructura de las revoluciones científicas*, FCE, Mexico City, 1975).

Kusch, Rodolfo. 1970. *El pensamiento indígena americano*. Cajica, Puebla (English trans. *Indigenous Popular Thinking in America*, trans. Maria Lugones and Joshua M. Price, Duke University Press, Durham, 2010).

———. 1986. *América profunda*. Bonum, Buenos Aires.

Lacan, Jacques. 1966. *Écrits I*. Seuil, Paris.

Lafont, Cristina. 1993. *La razón como lenguaje: Una revisión del Giro Lingüístico en la filosofía del lenguaje alemana*. Visor Dis, Madrid.

Laín Entralgo, Pedro. 1961. *Teoría y realidad del Otro*. 2 vols. Revista de Occidente, Madrid.

Lákatos, Imre. 1989. *La metodología de los programas de investigación científica.* Alianza, Madrid.

———. 1993. *Historia de la ciencia y sus reconstrucciones racionales.* Tecnos, Madrid.

Langer, S. K. 1967–73. *Mind: An Essay on Human Feeling.* 3 vols. Johns Hopkins University Press, Baltimore.

Lara Peinado, Federico, ed. 1994. *Los primeros códigos de la humanidad.* Tecnos, Madrid.

Lattimore, Owen. 1962. *Inner Asian Frontiers of China.* Beacon Press, Boston.

Laudan, L. 1984. *Science and Values: The Aims of Science and Their Role in Scientific Debate.* University of California Press, Berkeley.

———. 1986. *El progreso y sus problemas.* Encuentro, Madrid.

Lechner, N. 1990. *La democratización en el contexto de una cultura postmoderna.* FCE, Santiago de Chile.

Legendre, Pierre. 1974. *L'amour du censeur.* Seuil, Paris.

Leibniz, Gottfried W. 1946. *Teodicea: Ensayo sobre la bondad de Dios, la libertad del hombre y el origen del mal.* Claridad, Buenos Aires.

Lenin, V. I. 1961. *Obras escogidas.* 3 vols. Editorial Progreso, Moscow.

———. 1975–77. *Obras escogidas.* 12 vols. Editorial Progreso, Moscow.

León-Portilla, Miguel. 1974. *Recordación de Francisco Xavier Clavijero.* Porrúa, Mexico City.

———. 1979. *La filosofía náhuatl.* Universidad Nacional Autónoma de México, Mexico City.

Levinas, Emmanuel. 1930. *Théorie de l'intuition dans la phénoménologie de Husserl.* Vrin, Paris.

———. 1935–36. "De l'évasion." *Recherches Philosophiques* 5: 379–92.

———. 1947. *De l'existence á l'existant.* Vrin, Paris.

———. 1963. *Difficile liberté.* Albin Michel, Paris.

———. 1964. "La signification et le sens." *Revue de Métaphysique et de Morale* 2: 25–56.

———. 1967. *En découvrant l'existence avec Husserl et Heidegger.* Vrin, Paris.

———. 1968a. *Quatre lectures talmudiques.* Minuit, Paris.

———. 1968b. *Totalité et infini: Essai sur l'extériorité.* Nijhoff, The Hague (Spanish trans. *Totalidad e Infinito*, Sígueme, Salamanca, 1977).

———. 1972. *Humanisme de l'autre homme.* Fata Morgana, Montpellier (Spanish trans. *Humanismo del otro hombre*, Siglo XXI, Mexico City, 1974).

———. 1974. *Autrement qu'être ou au-delà de l'essence.* Nijhoff, The Hague (English trans. *Otherwise Than Being or beyond Essence*, trans. Alphonso Lingis, Duquesne University Press, Pittsburgh, 1998; Spanish trans. *De otro modo que ser o más allá de la esencia*, Sígueme, Salamanca, 1987).

———. 1976. *Noms propres.* Fata Morgana, Montpellier.

———. 1977. *Du sacré au saint: Cinq nouvelles lectures talmudiques.* Minuit, Paris.

———. 1982. "Sur la mort dans la pensée de Ernst Bloch." In *De Dieu qui vient á l'idée*, 62–76. Vrin, Paris.

———. 1983. *Le temps et l'autre.* PUF, Paris.

———. 1988. *A l'heure des nations.* Minuit, Paris.

———. 1991. *Entre nous.* Grasset, Paris.

———. 1998. *Otherwise Than Being or beyond Essence.* Trans. Alphonso Lingis. Pittsburgh: Duquesne University Press.

Libro de los muertos. 1989. Ed. Federico Lara Peinado. Tecnos, Madrid.

Lipman, Matthew, A. M. Sharp, and F. S. Oscanyan. 1992. *La filosofía en el aula.* Ediciones de la Torre, Madrid.

Locke, John. 1975. *An Essay Concerning Human Understanding.* Ed. P. H. Nidditch. Clarendon Press, Oxford.

Lockhart, James. 1992. *The Nahuas after the Conquest.* Stanford University Press, Stanford.

Loewith, Karl. 1964. *Von Hegel zu Nietzsche.* Kohlhammer, Stuttgart.

———. 1969. *Das Individuum in der Rolle des Mitmenschen.* Wissenschaftliche Buchgesellschaft, Darmstadt.

Lombard, Maurice. 1975. *The Golden Age of Islam.* North Holland, Amsterdam.

López Aranguren, José Luis. 1968. *Ética.* Revista de Occidente, Madrid.

Lorenz, Konrad. 1994. *Sobre la agresión: El pretendido mal.* Siglos xxi, Mexico City.

Löwy, Michael. 1979. *La teoría de la revolución en el joven Marx.* Siglo xxi, Mexico City.

Luhmann, Niklas. 1971. "Wirtschaft als soziales System." In *Systemanalyse in den Wirtschafts- und Sozialwissenschaften,* ed. K.-E. Schenk, 136–71. Duncker und Humblot, Berlin.

———. 1984. *Soziale Systeme: Grundriss einer allgemeinen Theorie.* Suhrkamp, Frankfurt (Spanish trans. *Sistemas Sociales,* Alianza Editorial, Mexico, 1991).

———. 1988. *Die Wirtschaft der Gesellschaft.* Suhrkamp, Frankfurt.

Lukács, György. 1959. *El asalto a la razón.* FCE, Mexico City.

———. 1968. *Geschichte und Klassenbezusstsein.* Luchterhand, Darmstadt (French trans. *Histoire et conscience de classe,* Minuit, Paris, 1960).

———. 1970. *El joven Hegel y los problemas de la sociedad capitalista.* Grijalbo, Barcelona.

———. 1972. *Zur Ontologie des gesellschaftlichen Seins.* Vols. 13–14 of *Werkausgabe; Ontologie-Marx,* vol. 86, and *Ontologie-Arbeit,* vol. 92, Luchterhand, Darmstadt, 1973 (Ital. trans. *Ontologia dell'essere Sociale,* Editori Riuniti, Roma, vol. 2, 1981; and *Prolegomini all'ontologia dell'essere sociale,* Guerini, Milano, 1990).

———. 1974. *Estética.* Vols. 1–4. Grijalbo, Barcelona.

———. 1994. *Versuche zu einer Ethik.* Akadémiai Kiadó, Budapest.

Luria, Alexander R. 1976. *Cognitive Development: Its Cultural and Social Foundation.* Harvard University Press, Cambridge.

Luxemburg, Rosa. 1966–68. *Politische Schriften.* 3 vols. Europäische Verlagsanstalt, Nördlingen (Spanish trans. *Reforma o revolución,* Grijalbo, Mexico, 1967; [of vol. 3 of *Politische Schriften*] *Huelga de masas, partido y sindicatos,* Grijalbo, Mexico, 1970).

———. 1967. *La acumulación del capital.* Grijalbo, Mexico.

———. 1979. *El desarrollo industrial de Polonia.* Siglo xxi, Mexico City.

———. 1980. "Problema de la organización de la socialdemocracia rusa." In *Teoría marxista del partido político,* Siglo xxi, Mexico City.

Lyotard, Jean-François. 1979. *La condition postmoderne.* Minuit, Paris (Spanish trans. *La condición postmoderna,* Cátedra, Madrid, 1989).

MacIntyre, Alasdair. 1959. "Hume on *Is* and *Ought.*" *Philosophical Review* (October): 451–68.

———. 1966. *A Short History of Ethics.* Macmillan, New York (Spanish trans. *Historia de la ética,* Paidos, Barcelona, 1991).

————. 1981. *After Virtue: A Study in Moral Theory.* University of Notre Dame Press, Notre Dame.

————. 1988. *Whose Justice? Which Rationality?* University of Notre Dame Press, Notre Dame.

MacPherson, C. B. 1964. *The Political Theory of Possessive Individualism: Hobbes to Locke.* Oxford University Press, London.

Maimonides. 1954. *Le guide des égarés.* Ed. S. Munk. Vrin, Paris.

Malebranche, Nicolas. 1707. *Traité de Morale.* Ed. E.Thorin. Paris.

Maliandi, Ricardo. 1993. *Dejar la postmodernidad: La ética frente al irracionalismo actual.* Almagesto, Buenos Aires.

Mann, Golo. 1961–65. *Propyläen Weltgeschichte.* 10 vols. Ed. Golo Mann and Alfred Heuss. Propyläen Verlag, Berlin.

Mann, Michael. 1986. *The Sources of Social Power: A History of Power from the Beginning to AD 1760.* Vol. 1. Cambridge University Press, Cambridge.

Marcuse, Herbert. 1928. "Beiträge zu einer Phänomenologie des Historischen Materialismus." *Philosophische Hefte* (Berlin) 1.1: 45–68 (English trans. "Contribution to a Phenomenology of Historical Materialism," *Telos* 4 [1969]: 3–44).

————. 1938. "Zur Kritik des Hedonismus." *Zeitschrift für Sozialforschung* 7.1–2: 55–89.

————. 1964. *One-Dimensional Man.* Beacon Press, Boston (Spanish trans. *El hombre unidimensional,* Joaquín Mortiz, Mexico City, 1968).

————. 1967. *Razón y revolución.* Universidad Central de Venezuela, Caracas.

————. 1968a. *El fin de la utopía,* Siglos XXI, Mexico.

————. 1968b. "Liberación respecto a la sociedad opulenta." In *The Dialectics of Liberation,* ed. David Cooper. Penguin Books, London (Spanish trans. Siglo XXI, Mexico City, 1969, 183–92).

————. 1969. *Ensayos sobre política y cultura.* Ariel, Barcelona.

————. 1970a. *Ética de la revolución.* Taurus, Madrid.

————. 1970b. *Ontología de Hegel.* Martinez Roca, Barcelona.

————. 1981. *Eros y civilización.* J. Mortiz, Mexico (original *Eros and Civilization,* Beacon Press, Boston, 1953).

Mariátegui, José Carlos. 1969. *Siete ensayos de interpretación de la realidad peruana.* Ediciones Solidaridad, Mexico City.

Marquart, Odo. 1981. *Abschied vom Prinzipiellen.* Reclam, Stuttgart.

Martin, Richard Milton. 1959. *The Notion of Analytic Truth.* University of Pennsylvania Press, Philadelphia.

Marx, Karl. 1956–90. *Marx-Engels Werke,* by Marx and Friedrich Engels. 43 vols. Dietz, Berlin (Spanish trans. *Obras fundamentales,* vol. 1, FCE, Mexico City, 1982; *Manuscritos del 44,* Alianza, Madrid, 1968; *La Sagrada Familia,* Grijalbo, Mexico, 1967; *La ideología alemana,* Grijalbo, Barcelona, 1970, including *Tesis sobre Feuerbach,* 665–68; *La miseria de la filosofía,* Signos, Buenos Aires, 1970; *Manifiesto comunista,* Claridad, Buenos Aires, 1967; *Crítica al programa de Gotha,* Colección Orbe, Madrid, 1970).

————. 1973. *Grundrisse.* Trans. Martin Nicolaus. Penguin, New York.

————. 1974. *Grundrisse der Kritik der politische Oekonomie.* Dietz, Berlin (Spanish trans. *Elementos fundamentales para la crítica de la economía política,* 3 vols., Siglo XXI, Mexico City, 1971–76).

————. 1975. *Works, Articles, and Drafts to March 1843.* Sec. 1, vol. 1 of *Karl*

Marx–Friedrich Engels Gesamtausgabe, by Marx and Friedrich Engels. Dietz, Berlin.

———. 1976–82. *Zur Kritik der politischen Ökonomie (Manuskript 1861–1863)*. 6 parts. Sec. 2, vol. 3 of *Karl Marx–Friedrich Engels Gesamtausgabe*, by Marx and Friedrich Engels. Dietz, Berlin.

———. 1985. *Works, Articles, and Drafts from August 1844*. Sec. 1, vol. 3 of *Karl Marx–Friedrich Engels Gesamtausgabe*, by Marx and Friedrich Engels. Dietz, Berlin.

———. 1987. *Das Kapital*. Sec. 2, vol. 6 of *Karl Marx–Friedrich Engels Gesamtausgabe*, by Marx and Friedrich Engels. Dietz, Berlin (Spanish trans. Siglo XXI, Mexico City, vols. 1–3, 1975–81).

Masolo, D. A. 1994. *African Philosophy in Search of Identity*. Indiana University Press, Bloomington.

Massignon, Louis. 1922. *La passion d'al-Hallaj*. Ceuther, Paris.

Maturana, Humberto. 1985. *El árbol del conocimiento: Las bases biológicas del entendimiento humano*. Editorial Universitaria, Santiago.

Maystre, Charles. 1937. *Les déclarations d'innocence (Livre des Mortes, Chapitre 125)*. Institut d'Archéologie Orientale, Cairo.

———. 1992. *Les grandes prêtres de Ptah de Memphis*. Vandenhoeck und Ruprecht, Göttingen.

Mbargane Guissé, Youaaouph. 1979. *Philosophie, culture et devenir social en Afrique noire*. Les Nouvelles Éditions Africaines, Dakar.

Mbiti, John. 1969. *African Religions and Philosophy*. Heinemann, London.

McCarthy, Thomas. 1988. *The Critical Theory of Jürgen Habermas*. MIT Press, Cambridge.

McNeil, William. 1964. *The Rise of the West*. University of Chicago Press, Chicago.

Mead, George H. 1934. *Mind, Self, and Society*. University of Chicago Press, Chicago.

———. 1938. *The Philosophy of the Act*. University of Chicago Press, Chicago.

———. 1981. *Selected Writings*. University of Chicago Press, Chicago.

Mellaart, James. 1967. *Catal Hüyük: A Neolithic Town in Anatolia*. Thames and Hudson, London.

Memmi, Albert. 1969. *Retrato del colonizado*. Ediciones de la Flor, Buenos Aires.

Menchú, Rigoberta. 1985. *Me llamo Rigoberta Menchú y así me nació la conciencia*. Siglo XXI, Mexico City.

Mendieta, Eduardo. 1995. "Discourse Ethics and Liberation Ethics." *Philosophy and Social Criticism* 21.4: 111–26.

Merleau-Ponty, Maurice. 1945. *Phénoménologie de la perception*. Gallimard, Paris.

———. 1960. *La structure du comportement*. PUF, Paris.

———. 1963. *The Structure of Behavior*. Beacon, Boston.

———. 1964. *La fenomenología y las ciencias del hombre*. Nova, Buenos Aires.

Mesnard, Pierre. 1936. *Essai sur la morale de Descartes*. Boivin, Paris.

Mezan, Renato. 1985. *Freud, pensador da cultura*. Editora Brasiliense, Sâo Paulo.

Mignolo, Walter. 1995a. *The Darker Side of the Renaissance: Literacy, Territoriality and Colonization*. University of Michigan Press, Ann Arbor.

———. 1995b. "Occidentalización, imperialismo, globalización: Herencias coloniales y teorías postcoloniales." *Revista Iberoamericana* (Pittsburgh) 170–71: 27–40.

Mill, John Stuart. 1957. *Utilitarianism*. Liberal Arts Press, New York.

———. 1981. *Collected Works of John Stuart Mill*. 5 vols. University of Toronto Press, Toronto, and Routledge and Kegan Paul, London.

———. 1987. *The Logic of the Moral Sciences*. Duckworth, London.

Miller, Jonathan. 1983. *States of Mind*. Pantheon, New York.

Miró Quesada, Francisco. 1974. *Despertar y proyecto del filosofar latinoamericano*. FCE, Mexico City.

———. 1981. *Proyecto y realización del filosofar latinoamericano*. FCE, Mexico City.

Misak, C. J. 1991. *Truth and the End of Inquiry: A Peircean account of Truth*. Clarendon Press, Oxford.

Mitscherlich, Alexander. 1971. *Auf dem Weg zur vaterlosen Gesellschaft. Ideen zur Sozial-Psychologie*. Piper, Munich.

Modelski, George. 1987. *Long Cycles in World Politics*. Macmillan, London.

Moore, George Edward. 1968. *Principia Ethica*. Cambridge University Press, Cambridge (Spanish trans. FCE, Mexico City, 1959).

Mudimbe, V. Y. 1988. *The Invention of Africa: Gnosis, Philosophy and the Order of Knowledge*. Indiana University Press, Bloomington.

Müller, Mandred. 1978. *Auf dem Wege zum "Kapital": Zur Entwicklung des Kapitalbegriffs von Marx in den Jahren 1857–1863*. Akademie Verlag, Berlin.

Müller-Lauter, Wolfgang. 1971. *Nietzsche*. De Gruyter, Berlin.

Munk, Salomon. 1927. *Mélanges de philosophie juive et arabe*. J. Vrin, Paris.

Nagel, Ernest. 1978. *La estructura de la ciencia*. Paidos, Buenos Aires.

Nagel, Thomas. 1975. *The Possibility of Altruism*. Clarendon Press, Oxford.

———. 1986. *A View from Nowhere*. Clarendon Press, Oxford.

———. 1987. "Moral Conflict and Political Legitimacy." *Philosophy and Public Affairs* 16.3: 215–40.

Nagl-Docekal, Herta, and Franz Wimmer, eds. 1992. *Postkoloniales Philosphieren: Afrika*. Wiener Reihe, Oldenbourg V., Vienna.

Needham, Joseph. 1954–85. *Science and Civilisation in China*. 5 vols. Cambridge University Press, Cambridge.

———. 1961. "The Chinese Contributions to Vessel Control." *Scientia* 96.98 (April): 123–28; (May): 163–68.

———. 1963. "Commentary on Lynn White's *What Accelerated Technological Progress in the Western Middle Ages?*" In *Scientific Change*, ed. A. C. Crombie, 117–53. Basic Books, New York.

———. 1966. "Les contributions chinoises à l'art de gouverner les navires." *Colloque International d'Histoire Maritime* (Paris): 113–34.

Nettl, J. P. 1967. Rosa Luxemburg. Kiepenheuer and Witsch, Koln.

Nietzsche, Friedrich. 1922–29. *Gesammelte Werke*. 23 vols. Musarion, Munich (Spanish trans. *Obras completas*, 5 vols., Aguilar, Buenos Aires, 1963–65; *Genealogía de la Moral*, Ediciones del Mediodía, Buenos Aires, 1967).

———. 1973. *Werke in zwei Bände*. 2 vols. Wissenschaftliche Buchgesellschaft, Darmstadt.

Nkrumah, Kwame. 1971. *Neo-colonialism: The Last Stage of Imperialism*. Panaf, London.

Nothomb, Dominique. 1969. *Un humanisme africain: Valeurs et pierres d'attente*. Lumen Vitae, Bruselas.

Nozick, Robert. 1968. *Anarchy, State and Utopia*. Basic Books, New York.

Nye, Andrea. 1994. *Philosophia: The Thought of Rosa Luxemburg, Simone Weil and Hannah Arendt*. Routledge, New York.

Nyerere, Julius. 1967. *Freedom and Unity/Uhuru na Umoja*. Oxford University Press, Dar es Salaam.

Nygren, Anders. 1952. *Éros et agapé*. 3 vols. Aubier, Paris.

Odera Oruka, Henry. 1990. *Trends in Contemporary African Philosophy*. Shirikon Publishers, Nairobi.

―――. 1991a. *The Philosophy of Liberty: An Essay on Political Philosophy*. Standard Textbooks, Nairobi.

―――. 1991b. *Sage Philosophy: Indigenous Thinkers and Modern Debate on African Philosophy*. African Center for Technology Studies, Nairobi.

Oestreich, Gerhard. 1983. *Neo-Stocism and the Early Modern State*. Cambridge University Press, Cambridge.

O'Gorman, Edmundo. 1957. *La invención de América*. FCE, Mexico City.

Olela, Henry. 1979. "The African Foundation of Greek Philosophy." In Wright 1979, 55–70.

Oliver, R., and A. Atmore. 1969. *Africa since 1800*. Cambridge University Press, Cambridge.

Olivetti, Marco. 1992. *Analogia del soggetto*. Laterza, Roma.

Ollman, Bertell. 1993. *Dialectical Investigations*. Routledge, New York.

Ortigues, M. C., and E. Ortigues. 1973. *Oedipe africain*. Plon, Paris.

Otto, E., and M. Hirmer. 1966. *Osiris und Amun: Kult und Heilige Stäten*. Munich.

Paris, Carlos. 1994. *El animal cultural: Biología y cultura en la realidad humana*. Crítica, Barcelona.

Parsons, Talcott. 1971. *The System of Modern Societies*. Prentice-Hall, Englewood Cliffs.

―――. 1978. *Action Theory and the Human Condition*. New York.

Pascal, Blaise. 1954. *Oeuvres complètes*. La Pléiade, Paris.

Paz, Octavio. 1950. *El laberinto de la soledad*. Cuadernos Americanos, Mexico City.

Peirce, Charles S. 1955. *Philosophical Writings of Peirce*. Dover Publications, New York (Spanish trans. *Mi alegato en favor del pragmatismo*, Aguilar, Buenos Aires, 1971).

―――. 1931–60. *Collected Papers of Charles Peirce*. Ed. C. Hartshonre, P. Weiss, and A. Burks. 8 vols. Belknap Press, Cambridge.

―――. 1974. *La ciencia de la semiótica*. Nueva Visión, Buenos Aires.

―――. 1978. *Lecciones sobre pragmatismo*. Aguilar, Buenos Aires.

Pereda, Carlos. 1994. *Vértigos argumentales*. Anthropos-Barcelona, and UAM, Mexico City.

Peters, R. S. 1984. *Desarrollo moral y educación moral*. FCE, Mexico City.

Piaget, Jean. 1932. *Le jugement moral chez l'enfant*. PUF, Paris.

―――. 1937. *La construction du réel chez l'enfant*. Delachoux et Niestlé, Paris.

―――. 1962. *Comments on Vygotsky's Critical Remarks Concerning "The Language and Thought of the Child" and "Judgement and Reasoning in the Child."* MIT Press, Cambridge.

―――. 1969. *Biologie et connaissance: Essai sur les relations entre les régulations organiques et les cognitifs*. Gallimard, Paris.

―――. 1978. *Psicología del niño*. Ediciones Morata, Madrid.

————. 1979. *Seis estudios de psicología*. Seix Barral, Barcelona.

————. 1985. *La toma de conciencia*. Morata, Madrid.

————. 1990. *La equilibración de las estructuras cognitivas*. Siglo XXI, Madrid.

Plato. 1982–86. *Plato*. 12 vols. Loeb Classical Library, Harvard University Press, Cambridge.

Plotinus. 1924–32. *Ennéades*. 9 vols. Les Belles Lettres, Paris.

Poiré, François. 1992. *Emmanuel Levinas*. Editions La Manufacture, Besançon.

Popper, Karl. 1967. *La sociedad abierta y sus enemigos*. 2 vols. Paidos, Buenos Aires (original *Die offene Gesellschaft und ihre Feinde*, 2 vols. [1945], Franke, Bern, 1977).

————. 1968. *The Logic of Scientific Discovery*. Harper Torchbooks, New York (Spanish trans. *La lógica de la investigación científica*, Tecnos, Madrid, 1980).

————. 1972. *Objective Knowledge*. Clarendon Press, Oxford.

————. 1973. *La miseria del historicismo*. Alianza, Madrid (trans. of German trans. *Das Elend der Historizismus*, Tübingen, 1974).

————. 1974. *El conocimiento objetivo*. Tecnos, Madrid.

Pritchard, James Bennett. 1950. *Ancient Near Eastern Texts*. Princeton University Press, Princeton.

Prümm, Karl. 1960. "La religión del helenismo." In König 1959, vol. 2, 157–212.

Puech, Henri-Charles. 1959. "La religión de Mani." In König 1959, vol. 2, 469–525.

Putnam, Hilary. 1975. *Mind, Language and Reality*. Cambridge University Press, Cambridge.

————. 1981. *Reason, Truth and History*. Cambridge University Press, Cambridge (Spanish trans. *Razón, verdad e historia*, Tecnos, Madrid, 1988).

————. 1987. *The Many Faces of Realism*. Open Publishing, La Salle (Spanish trans. *Las mil caras del realismo*, Paidos, Barcelona, 1994).

————. 1988. *Representation and Reality*. MIT Press, Cambridge.

————. 1990a. *Realism with a Human Face*. Harvard University Press, Cambridge.

————. 1990b. *Representación y realidad*. Gedisa, Barcelona.

————. 1991. *El significado y las ciencias morales*. UNAM, Mexico City (original *Meaning and the Moral Sciences*, Routledge and Kegan Paul, London, 1978).

————. 1992a. *Il pragmatismo: Una questione aperta*. Laterza, Roma.

————. 1992b. *Renewing Philosophy*. Harvard University Press, Cambridge.

————. 1994. *Words and Life*. Harvard University Press, Cambridge.

Quine, Willard Van. 1968. *Palabra y objeto*. Lavor, Barcelona (original *Word and Object*, MIT Press, Cambridge, 1960).

————. 1992. *La búsqueda de la verdad*. Crítica, Barcelona (original *Pursuit of Truth*, Harvard University Press, Cambridge, 1990).

Quinton, Anthony. 1973. *Utilitarian Ethics*. Macmillan, London.

Rabossi, Eduardo. 1979. *Estudios éticos: Cuestiones conceptuales y metodológicas*. Universidad de Carabobo, Valencia, Venezuela.

————. 1995. "La tesis de la identidad mente-cuerpo." In *La mente humana*, ed. Fernando Broncano, 17–42. Trotta, Madrid.

Rabotnikof, Nora. 1989. *Max Weber: Desencanto, política y democracia*. UNAM, Mexico City.

Rahman, F. 1979. *Islam*. University of Chicago Press, Chicago.

Ramírez, Mario Teodoro. 1996. *Cuerpo y arte para una estética Merleaupontiana*. Universidad Autónoma del Estado de Mexico, Toluca.

Rau, Virginia. 1957. "A Family of Italian Merchants in Portugal in the Fifteenth Century: The Lomellini." In *Studi in onore di Armando Sapori*, vol. 1, 715–26. Istituto Editoriale Cisalpino, Milan.

Rawls, John. 1951. "Outline of a Decision Procedure for Ethics." *Philosophical Review* 60: 177–97.

———. 1958. "Justice as Fairness." *Philosophical Review* 67: 164–94.

———. 1967. "Distributive Justice." In *Philosophy, Politics and Society*, ed. P. Laslett and W. G. Runciman, 58–82. Blackwell, London.

———. 1971. *A Theory of Justice*. Harvard University Press, Cambridge (Spanish trans. *Teoría de la Justicia*, FCE, Mexico City, 1985).

———. 1982. *The Basic Liberties and Their Priority*. University of Utah Press and University of Cambridge Press, Cambridge (Spanish trans. *Sobre las libertades*, Paidos, Barcelona, 1990). Reprint, as lecture 8 in Rawls 1993.

———. 1993. *Political Liberalism*. Columbia University Press, New York.

———. 1995. "Reply to Habermas." *Journal of Philosophy* 92.3 (March): 132–80.

Rebellato, José Luis. 1995. *La encrucijada de la ética: Neoliberalismo, conflicto Norte-Sur, liberación*. MFAL-Nordan, Montevideo.

Regamey, Constantin. 1961a. "El budismo indio." In König 1959, vol. 3, 213–78.

———. 1961b. "Las religiones de la India." In König 1959, vol. 3, 67–212.

Rehg, William. 1994. *Insight and Solidarity: The Discourse Ethics of Jürgen Habermas*. University of California Press, Berkeley.

Reich, Wilhelm. 1968. *La révolution sexuelle*. Plon, Paris.

———. 1970. *Materialismo, dialéctico y psicoanálisis*. Siglo XXI, Mexico City.

Renan, Ernest. 1861. *Averroès et l'averroïsme*. M. Lévy Frères, Paris.

Rénou, Louis. 1936. *Hymnes spéculatifs du Véda*. Payot, Paris.

———. 1947. *L'Inde classique*. Payot, Paris.

Ribeiro, Darcy. 1970, *El proceso civilizatorio*. Universidad Central de Venezuela, Caracas.

Ricoeur, Paul. 1963. *La symbolique du mal*. Aubier, Paris.

———. 1965. *De l'interprétation, essai sur Freud*. Seuil, Paris.

———. 1990. *Soi-même comme un autre*. Seuil, Paris.

Roazen, Paul. 1971. *Politik und Gesellschaft bei Sigmund Freud*. Suhrkamp, Frankfurt.

Rodríguez Braun, C. 1989. *La cuestión colonial y la economía clásica*. Alianza, Madrid.

Roig, Arturo. 1981. *Filosofía, universidad y filósofos en América latina*, UNAM, Mexico City.

Rojas, Mario. 1995. *Racionalidad y ética: Apel, Habermas, Hegel*. Facultad de Filosofía y Letras, UNAM, Mexico City.

Romero, Francisco. 1952. *Teoría del hombre*. Losada, Buenos Aires.

Rondot, R. 1963. *Der Islam und die Mahommedaner*. Schwaven Verlag, Stuttgart.

Rorty, Richard. 1979. *Philosophy and the Mirror of Nature*. Princeton University Press, Princeton (Spanish trans. *La filosofía y el espejo de la naturaleza*, Cátedra, Madrid, 1989).

———. 1982. *Consequences of Pragmatism (Essays: 1972–1980)*. Harvester Press, Brighton, England.

———. 1984. "The Historiography of Philosophy: Four Genres." In *Philosophy in History*, 49–75, Cambridge University Press, Cambridge.

———. 1987. "The Priority of Democracy to Philosophy." In *The Virginia Statute of Religious Freedom*, ed. M. Peterson and R. Vaughn, 257–82. Cambridge University Press, Cambridge.

———. 1989. *Contingency, Irony and Solidarity.* Cambridge University Press, New York.

Rosdolsky, Roman. 1968. *Zur Entstehungsgeschichte des Marxschen "Kapital."* Europäische Verlagsanstalt, Frankfurt (Spanish trans. *Génesis y estructura de "El capital" de Marx*, Siglo XXI, Mexico City, 1979).

Rosenzweig, Franz. 1921. *Der Stern der Erlösung.* 3 vols. Suhrkamp, Frankfurt (French trans. *L'étoile de la rédemption*, Seuil, Paris, 1982).

Ross, Andrew, ed. 1989. *Universal Abandon? The Politics of Postmodernism.* University of Minnesota Press, Minneapolis.

Rossabi, Morris. 1982. *China among Equals: The Middle Kingdom and Its Neighbors, 10–14th Centuries.* University of California Press, Berkeley.

Rozitchner, León. 1972. *Freud y los límites del individualismo burgués.* Siglo XXI, Buenos Aires.

Ruiz Bueno, Daniel. 1954. *Padres apostólicos.* BAC, Madrid.

Runggaldier, E. 1985. *Zeichen und Bezeichnetes: Sprachphilosophische Untersuchungen zum Problem der Referenz.* W. de Gruyter, Berlin.

Russell, Bertrand. 1956. *Logic and Knowledge.* Allen and Unwin, London.

Sádaba, Javier. 1989. "Ética analítica." In Camps 1989, vol. 3, 163–220.

Safranski, Rüdiger. 1991. *Schopenhauer y los años salvajes de la filosofía.* Alianza Universidad, Madrid.

Salazar Bondy, Augusto. 1968. *¿Existe una filosofía de nuestra América?* Siglo XXI, Mexico City.

Salmerón, Fernando. 1992. "Intuición y análisis." In Camps 1992, 153–76.

Salomon, Jean-Jacques. 1974. *Ciencia y política.* Siglo XXI, Mexico City.

Sánchez Vázquez, Adolfo. 1978. *Ciencia y revolución (El marxismo de Althusser).* Alianza Editorial, Mexico City.

Sandman-Holmberg, M. 1946. *The God Ptah.* Gleerup, Lund.

Sartre, Jean-Paul, 1960. *Critique de la raison dialectique: Théorie des ensembles pratiques.* 2 vols. Gallimard, Paris.

Satchidananda Murty, K. 1985. *Philosophy in India: Traditions, Teaching and Research.* Motilal Banarsidass, New Delhi.

Savater, Fernando. 1993. *Nietzsche.* UNAM, Mexico City.

Scannone, Juan Carlos, ed. 1984. *Sabiduría popular, símbolo y filosofía.* Guadalupe, Buenos Aires.

———. 1990. *Nuevo punto de partida de la filosofía latinoamericana.* Guadalupe, Buenos Aires.

———, ed. 1993. *Irrupción del pobre y quehacer filosófico: Hacia una nueva racionalidad.* Bonum, Buenos Aires.

Schacht, Joseph-Bosworth, C. 1974. *The Legacy of Islam.* Clarendon Press, Oxford.

Scheffler, Israel. 1974. *Four Pragmatists: A Critical Introduction to Peirce, James, Mead and Dewey.* Routledge and Kegan, London.

Scheler, Max. 1954. *Der Formalismus in der Ethik und die materiale Wertethik.* Francke, Berna.

Schelkshorn, Hans. 1992. *Ethik der Befreiung. Einführung in die Philosophie Enrique Dussels.* Herder, Freiburg.

————. 1994. *Diskurs und Befreiung: Studien zur philosophischen Ethik von Karl-Otto Apel und Enrique Dussel.* University of Vienna, Vienna.

Schelling, Friedrich W. J. 1927–54. *Werke: Münchner Jubiläumsdruck.* 6 vols. M. Schröter, Becksche Verlag, Munich (English trans. *On the History of Modern Philosophy,* Cambridge University Press, Cambridge, 1994).

————. 1977. *Philosophie der Offenbarung 1841/42.* Suhrkamp, Frankfurt.

Schilpp, Paul Arthur. 1966. *La ética precrítica de Kant.* UNAM, Mexico City.

Schmidt, Friedrich. 1971. *Zum Begriff der Negativität bei Schelling und Hegel.* Metzler, Stuttgart.

Schmitt, Karl. 1971. *Legalidad y legitimidad.* Aguilar, Barcelona.

————. 1990. *Politische Theologie.* Duncker und Humblot, Berlin.

Schnädelbach, Herbert. 1983. *Philosophie in Deutschland, 1831–1933.* Suhrkamp, Frankfurt (English trans. *Philosophy in Germany, 1831–1933,* Cambridge University Press, Cambridge, 1984).

————. 1986. "Was ist Neoaristotelismus?" In *Moralität und Sittlichkeit,* ed. W. Kuhlmann, 38–63. Suhrkamp, Frankfurt.

Scholem, Gershom. 1962. *Ursprung und Anfange der Kabbala.* De Gruyter, Berlin (English trans. *Origins of the Kabbalah,* Princeton University Press, Princeton, 1987; French trans. Aubier-Montaigne, Paris, 1966).

————. 1967. *Die jüdische Mystik in ihren Hauptströmungen.* Suhrkamp, Frankfurt (English trans. *Major Trends in Jewish Mysticism,* Schocken, New York, 1995).

————. 1970. "Schöpfung aus Nichts und Selbstverschränkung Gottes." In *Über einige Begriffe des Judentums,* 53–89. Suhrkamp, Frankfurt.

————. 1991. *La Cábala y su simbolismo.* Siglo XXI, Mexico City.

Schopenhauer, Arthur. 1960. *El mundo como voluntad y representación.* 3 vols. Aguilar, Buenos Aires.

————. 1960–65. *Sämtliche Werke.* 5 vols. Cotta-Insel, Stuttgart.

————. 1961. *La cuádruple raíz del principio de razón suficiente.* Victoriano Suárez, Madrid.

————. 1966. *Der handschriftliche Nachlass.* 4 vols. Deutscher Taschenbuch, Frankfurt.

————. 1993. *Los dos problemas fundamentales de la ética.* Siglo XXI, Madrid.

Schraml, Walter. 1977. *Introducción a la psicología moderna del desarrollo.* Herder, Barcelona.

Schutte, Ofelia. 1984. *Beyond Nihilism: Nietzsche without Masks.* University of Chicago Press, Chicago.

————. 1993. *Cultural Identity and Social Liberation in Latin American Thought.* State University of New York Press, Albany.

Searle, John. 1969. *Speech Acts.* Cambridge University Press, Cambridge (Spanish trans. Cátedra, Madrid, 1990).

————. 1983. *Intentionality.* Cambridge University Press, Cambridge.

————. 1984. *Minds, Brains and Science.* Harvard University Press, Cambridge.

————. 1994. *The Rediscovery of the Mind.* MIT Press, Cambridge.

Selman, R. L. 1981. *The Growth of Interpersonal Understanding.* New York.

Serrano, Enrique. 1994. *Legitimación y racionalización: Weber y Habermas.* Anthropos, Barcelona.

————. 1996. *Consenso y conflicto.* Interlinea, Mexico.

Sethe, Kurt. 1928. "Das Denkmal memphitischer Theologie." In *Untersuchungen*, 10, Hinrich, Leipzig.

Sidekum, Antonio. 1993. *Ethik als Transzendenzerfahrung: E. Levinas und die Philosophie der Befreiung*. Augustinus, Aachen.

———, ed. 1994. *Ética do discurso e filosofia da libertacâo*. Unisinos, Sao Leopoldo (Brazil).

Sidgwick, Henry. 1901. *The Principles of Political Economy*. 1883; Macmillan, London.

———. 1962. *The Methods of Ethics*. 1930; Chicago University Press, Chicago.

Siguán, Miguel, ed. 1987. *Actualidad de Lev S. Vigotsky*. Anthropos, Barcelona.

Singer, Marcos Georg. 1961. *Generalization in Ethics*. A. A. Knopf, New York.

Smart, John J. 1973. *Utilitarismo: Pro y contra*, with Bernard Williams. Tecnos, Madrid (original *Utilitarianism; Pro and Against*, Cambridge University Press, Cambridge, 1973).

Smet, A. J. 1975. *Philosophie africaine: Textes choisis*. 2 vols. Presses Universitaires du Zaïre, Kinshasa.

Smith, Adam. 1976. *The Theory of Moral Sentiments*. Clarendon Press, Oxford.

———. 1978. *Lectures on Jurisprudence*. Clarendon Press, Oxford.

———. 1985. *The Wealth of Nations*. Penguin Books, Harmondsworth, England (Spanish trans. *El orígen de las riquezas de las naciones*, FCE, Mexico City, 1984).

Smith, Margaret. 1944. *Al-Ghazali, the Mystic*. Luzac, London.

Sombart, Werner. 1902. *Der moderne Kapitalismus*. Duncker, Leipzig.

———. 1920. *Der Bourgeois*. Duncker, Munich.

Sources Orientales. 1961. *Le judgement des morts*. Seuil, Paris.

Spinoza, Baruch. 1958. *Ética demostrada según el orden geométrico*. FCE, Mexico City.

Stavarianos, L. S. 1970. *The World to 1500: A Global History*. Prentice Hall, Englewood Cliffs.

Stein, Mark Aurel. 1974. *On Ancient Central Asian Tracks*. University of Chicago Press, Chicago.

Stevenson, Charles L. 1945. *Ethics and Language*. Yale University Press, New Haven (Spanish trans. *Ética y lenguaje*, Paidos, Buenos Aires, 1971).

Strasser, Stephan. 1967. *Phénoménologie et sciences de l'homme*. Editions B.-Nauwelaerts, Paris.

Strawson, P. F. 1974. *Freedom and Resentment*. Methuen, London.

Susin, Luiz Carlos. 1984. *O homem messiânico: Uma introduçâo ao pensamento de Emmanuel Levinas*. Vozes, Petrópolis.

Tamayo-Acosta, Juan-José. 1992. *Religión, razón y esperanza*. El Verbo Divino, Estella (Spain).

Tarski, Alfred. 1951. *Introducción a la lógica*. Espasa-Calpe, Buenos Aires.

———. 1956. "The Concept of Truth in Formalized Languages." In *Logic, Semantics, Metamathematics*, 152–278. Oxford University Press, Oxford.

———. 1977. "Die semantische Konzeption der Wahrheit und die Grundlage der Semantik." In *Wahrheitstheorien*, ed. G. Skirbekk. Suhrkamp, Frankfurt.

Tatian. 1954. *Oratio adversus Graecos*. In Ruiz Bueno 1954, 572–630.

Taviani, Paolo Emilio. 1982. *Cristoforo Colombo: La genesi della scoperta*. Istituto Geografico de Agostini, Novara.

Taylor, Charles. 1975. *Hegel*. Cambridge University Press, Cambridge.

————. 1979. *Hegel and Modern Society*. Cambridge University Press, Cambridge.

————. 1985a. *Human Agency and Language: Philosophical Papers 1*. Cambridge University Press, Cambridge.

————. 1985b. *Philosophy and the Human Sciences: Philosophical Papers 2*. Cambridge University Press, Cambridge.

————. 1988a. "Language and Society." In *Communicative Action*, ed. A. Honneth and H. Jonas, 23–35. MIT Press, Cambridge.

————. 1988b. "Le juste et le bien." *Revue de Métaphysique et de Morale* 93.1: 33–56.

————. 1989. *Sources of the Self: The Making of the Modern Identity*. Cambridge University Press, Cambridge.

————. 1992a. *The Ethics of Authenticity*. Harvard University Press, Cambridge.

————. 1992b. "The Politics of Recognition." In *Multiculturalism and "The Politics of Recognitions,"* 25–74, ed. Amy Gutmann. Princeton University Press, Princeton.

Taylor, Mark. 1987. *Alterity*. University of Chicago Press, Chicago.

Tempels, Placide. 1949. *La philosophie bantoue*. Présence Africaine, Paris (English trans. *Bantu Philosophy*, Présence Africaine, Paris, 1969).

Terulian, Nicolae. 1986. "Lukács/Adorno: La riconciliazione impossibile." In *György Lukács nel centinario della nascita, 1885–1985*, 49–67. Quattro Venti, Urbino.

Thamin, R. 1916. "La traité de morale de Malebranche." *Revue de Métaphysique et Morale* (January): 93–126.

Theunissen, Michael. 1965. *Der Andere*. De Gruyter, Berlin (English trans. *The Other*, MIT Press, Cambridge, 1986).

Thompson, William. 1989. *On Global War: Historical-Structural Approaches to World Politics*. University of South Carolina Press, Columbia.

Tilly, Charles. 1984. *Big Structures, Large Processes*. Russell Sage Foundation, New York.

Todorov, Tzetan. 1989. *Nous et les autres*. Seuil, Paris.

Torres, Carlos, ed. 1983. *Entrevistas con Freire*. Gernika, Mexico City.

————. 1992. *La praxis educativa de Paulo Freire*. Gernika, Mexico City.

Toulmin, Stephen. 1970. *An Examination of the Place of Reason in Ethics*. Cambridge University Press, Cambridge.

Toynbee, Arnold. 1934–59. *A Study of History*. 12 vols. Oxford University Press, London.

Troeltsch, Ernst. 1923. *Die Soziallehren der christlichen Kirchen und Gruppen*. Siebeck, Tübingen.

Tugendhat, Ernst. 1967. *Der Wahrheitsbegriff bei Husserl and Heidegger*. De Gruyter, Berlin.

————. 1982. *Traditional and Analytical Philosophy: Lectures on the Philosophy of Language*. Cambridge University Press, Cambridge.

————. 1988. *Problemas de la ética*. Editorial Crítica, Barcelona.

————. 1993. *Autoconciencia y autoderminación: Una interpretación lingüístico-analítica*. FCE, Mexico City.

Ulrich, Peter. 1993. *Transformation der ökonomischen Vernunft: Fortschrittsperspektiven der modernen Industriegesellschaft*. Paul Haupt, Bern.

Vattimo, Gianni. 1968. *Schleiermacher filosofo dell'interpretazione*. Mursia, Milano.

———. 1985. *La fine della modernità: Nichilismo ed ermeneutica nella cultura post-moderna*. Garzanti, Milano.

———. 1988. *Le avventure della differenza*. Garzanti, Milano.

———. 1989a. *El sujeto y la máscara*. Ediciones Península, Barcelona.

———. 1989b. *Essere, storia e linguaggio in Heidegger*. Marietti, Genova.

Verlinden, Charles. 1953. "Italian Influence in Iberian Colonization." *Hispanic American Historical Review* 18.2 (May): 199–209.

Vieira Pinto, Alvaro. 1961. *Consciência et realidade national*. ISEB, Rio de Janeiro.

Viezzer, Moema. 1971. *"Si me permiten hablar. . .": Testimonio de una mujer de las minas de Bolivia*. Siglo XXI, Mexico City.

Villoro, Luis. 1950. *Los grandes momentos del indigenismo en Mexico*. Colegio de Mexico, Mexico City.

Volpi, Franco. 1992. "L'esistenza como *praxis*: Le radici aristoteliche della terminologia di *Esse e tempo*." *Filosofia '91*, 215–54. Laterza, Roma.

Vygotsky, Lev Semionovitch. 1979a. "Consciousness as a Problem in the Psychology of Behavior." *Soviet Psychology* (Moscow) 17.4: 3–35.

———. 1979b. *El desarrollo de los procesos psicológicos superiores*. Editorial Crítica, Barcelona.

———. 1985. *Pensamiento y lenguaje*. La Pléyade, Buenos Aires (English trans. *Thought and Language*, ed. and trans. Eugenia Hanfmann and Gertrude Vakar, MIT Press, Cambridge, 1962).

Wahl, Jean. 1938. *Études kierkegaardiennes*. Éditions Montaigne, Paris.

Wallerstein, Immanuel. 1974–89. *The Modern World-System*. 3 vols. Academic Press, New York (Spanish trans. *El moderno sistema mundial*, vol. 1, Siglo XXI, Mexico City, 1979).

———. 1984. *The Politics for the World-Economy*. Cambridge University Press, Cambridge.

Walzer, Michael. 1977. *Just and Unjust Wars*. Basic Books, New York.

———. 1979. *Exodus and Revolution*. Daniel Doron, New York.

———. 1983. *Spheres of Justice: A Defense of Pluralism and Equality*. Basic Books, New York (Spanish trans., *Las esferas de la justicia*, FCE, Mexico City, 1993).

———. 1986. *Exodus and Revolution*. Basic Books, New York.

———. 1994. *Thick and Thin: Moral Argument at Home and Abroad*. University of Notre Dame Press, Notre Dame.

Weber, Alfred. 1963. *Kulturgeschichte als Kultursoziologie*. Piper, Munich.

Weber, Max. 1922. *Wirtschaft und Gesellschaft*. Mohr, Tübingen (Spanish trans. *Economía y sociedad*, FCE, Mexico City, 1984).

———. 1956a. "Die sozialen Gründe des Untergangs der antiken Kultur." In *Soziologie: Weltgeschichtliche Analysen—Politik*, 1–26. Kröner, Stuttgart.

———. 1956b. "Vorbemerkung zu den Gesammelten Aufsätzen zur Religionssoziologie." In Weber 1956a, 340–56.

———. 1958. *The Protestant Ethic and the Spirit of Capitalism*. Trans. Talcott Parsons. New York, Charles Scribner's Sons.

———. 1967. *El político y el científico*. Alianza Editorial, Madrid.

———. 1982. *Escritos políticos*. Folios, Mexico City.

Wellmer, Albrecht. 1986. *Dialog und Diskurs*. Suhrkamp, Frankfurt (Spanish trans. *Ética y diálogo*, Anthropos, Barcelona, and UAM-I, Mexico City, 1994; English trans. *The Persistence of Modernity*, MIT Press, Cambridge, 1991).

———. 1991. "Derecho natural y razón práctica." In K.-O. Apel and A. Cortina et al., *Ética comunicativa y democracia*, 15–69. Editorial Crítica, Barcelona.

Welsch, Wolfgang. 1993a. *Aesthetisches Denken*. Reclam, Stuttgart.

———. 1993b. *Unseres postmoderne Moderne*. Akademie V, Berlin.

———. 1996. *Vernunft: Die zeitgenössische Vernunftkritik und das Konzept der transversalen Vernunft*. Suhrkamp, Frankfurt.

———. 1994. "Vernunft heute." In *Vernunfbegriffe in der Moderne*, ed. Hans Friedrich Fulda and Rolf Peter Horstmann. Klett-Cotta, Stuttgart.

West, Cornel. 1989. *The American Evasion of Philosophy: A Genealogy of Pragmatism*. University of Wisconsin Press, Madison.

Wetsch, James. 1988. *Vygotsky y la formación social de la mente*. Paidos, Barcelona.

White, Morton. 1973. *Pragmatism and the American Mind*. Oxford University Press, London.

Wieger, Léon. 1950. *Les pères du système taoïste*. Les Belles Lettres-Cathasia, Paris.

Williams, Bernard. 1972. "Utilitarianism." In *Morality: An Introduction to Ethics*, 89–107. Harper and Row, New York.

———. 1981. "*Ought* and Moral Obligation." In *Moral Luck*, 114–23. Cambridge University Press, Cambridge.

———. 1985. *Ethics and the Limits of Philosophy*. Cambridge University Press, Cambridge.

Williams, Robert. 1992. *Recognition: Fichte, Hegel on the Other*. State University of New York Press, Albany.

Wilson, Edward. 1975. *Sociobiology: The New Synthesis*. Harvard University Press, Harvard.

———. 1978. *On Human Nature*. Harvard University Press, Harvard.

Winch, Peter. 1958. *The Idea of a Social Science and Its Relation to Philosophy*. Routledge, London.

———. 1994. *Comprender una sociedad primitiva*. Paidos, Barcelona.

Wiredu, Kwasi. 1980. *Philosophy and an African Culture*. Cambridge University Press, Cambridge.

———. 1992. "On Defining African Philosophy." In Nagl-Docekal and Wimmer 1992, 40–64.

Wittgenstein, Ludwig. 1969. *Tractatus Logico-Philosophicus*. Routledge and Kegan, London.

———. 1979. *Notebooks, 1914–1916*. 2nd ed. Ed. G. H. von Wright and G. E. M. Anscombe. Blackwell, Oxford.

———. 1988. *Investigaciones lógicas*. UNAM, Mexico City, and Crítica, Barcelona.

Wolf, Eric. 1982. *Europe and the People without History*. University of California Press, Berkeley.

Wolff, Robert Paul. 1977. *Understanding Rawls*. Princeton University Press, Princeton.

Wolin, Richard. 1994. *Walter Benjamin*. University of California Press, Berkeley.

Wright, George Henrik von. 1971. *Explanation und Understanding*. Cornell University Press, Ithaca (Spanish trans. *Explicación y comprensión*, Alianza Universidad, Madrid, 1987).

Wright, Richard, ed. 1979. *African Philosophy: An Introduction*. University Press of America, Washington.

Wygodski, W. S. 1978. *Das Werden der oekonomischen Theorie von Marx*. Dietz, Berlin.

Zea, Leopoldo. 1957. *América en la historia*. FCE, Mexico City.

———. 1974. *Dependencia y liberación en la cultura latinoamericana*. Joaquín Mortiz, Mexico City.

———. 1978. *Filosofía de la historia Americana*. FCE, Mexico City.

Zubiri, Xavier. 1963. *Sobre la esencia*. Sociedad de Estudios y Publicaciones, Madrid.

———. 1981. *Inteligencia sentiente*. Alianza Editorial, Madrid.

———. 1982. *Inteligencia y logos*. Alianza Editorial, Madrid.

———. 1983. *Inteligencia y razón*. Alianza Editorial, Madrid.

———. 1986. *Sobre el hombre*. Alianza Editorial, Madrid.

———. 1992. *Sobre el sentimiento y la volición*. Alianza Editorial, Madrid.

Zunzunegui, J. 1941. "Los orígenes de las misiones en las Islas Canarias." *Revista Española de Teología* 1: 364–70.

Index

on feasibility, xvii, 181–85, 338–39, 419, 423, 506nn311–12, 528n66; on reproductive reason, 440, 580n295

Hispaniola, 44–45

History and Class Consciousness (Lukács), 570n162

history of ethical systems. *See* interregional systems

history of sociology, 176, 548n168

Hobbes, Thomas, 514n64

Holland. *See* Amsterdam

Holy Family, The (Marx), 361–62

Homer, 1

Honneth, Axel, 98, 279

hope. *See* principle of hope

Horkheimer, Max, 218, 570n165; on critical theory, 235–38, 243–47, 249, 331, 571n172, 576n239, 578nn276–77; on the Frankfurt school, 234; on material negativity, xvii, 217; on material reason, 245–47; on a new meta-physical (postmetaphysical) moment, 555n15; philosopher-critic perspective of, 240; on strategic-instrumental reason, 186, 188–89

Horus, 206, 250, 448, 652n12

Human Development Report, 470n228

human life, 342–43, 434, 479n19; Apel on, 127–28, 520n145; ethical subject and, 294, 373–88, 423–24; faculty of judgment in, 187–88, 191f; good in, 201–3, 554n249; late twentieth-century crisis of, 37–40, 470n228; performative systems of, 158; point of reference, 172–74; reproduction and development of, 397–99, 419–23, 425–27, 430–31, 438–39; self-preservation of, 245–47, 263–68, 368, 580n295, 591n470, 636n95; social interaction of, 59, 63, 66, 68, 108; truth in, 339; as universal principle of material ethics, 55–57, 92–93, 105–6, 187, 208, 436, 478n7, 507n328, 521nn146–47, 549n187. *See also* corporeality; victims/the Other

human nervous system: affective-evaluative brain of, 57–69, 478n7, 479n19, 480nn27–29, 482nn37–38,

482n41; perception of sensation in, 59–60, 64–65, 480nn27–29, 484n54

Humboldt, Wilhelm von, 169, 174, 219, 259

Hume, David, 72, 112; ethical "ought-to-be" of, 100; naturalist fallacy of, 340, 624n330

Husserl, Edmund, 89, 175, 201, 440; axiological work of, 495n190; Levinas and, 271, 593n489; on objectivity, 327–28; on subjectivity and intention, 376

Hutcheson, Francis, 70, 71, 112, 488nn103–4

I, Rigoberta Menchú: An Indian Woman in Guatemala (Menchú), 297–303, 601n8

Ibn Arabi, 77

Ibn Rushd, 22, 77

Ibn Sina, 22

identity, 380

Inca-Quechua culture, 10, 11–13

India, 3, 4–5, 9, 11f, 433; Axial Period of, 13, 459n71; Brahamization in, 459n72; British colonial era in, 467n194; contemporary philosophy in, 474n259; Hindu culture of, 13, 17, 23, 460n103; Muslim sultanate of Delhi in, 23; on the One, 14, 15; Sakas and Gupas of, 18, 23, 460n105

Indo-European system, 2–3, 13–17, 459n66; Alexandria and, 14; empirical death and, 16; the One and ethical life in, 13–17, 460n91; order and the status quo in, 16–17; Uranic gods of, 13, 459n69

Inquisition, 466n175

Institute of Social Research. *See* Frankfurt school

instrumental reason. *See* strategic-instrumental reason

intelligent feeling, 67, 485n75

International Committee of the Third World, xxii

international debt, 407, 556n20

International Monetary Fund, 407, 646n254

the theory of rent, 249; on truth and validity, 146; on the valorization of value, 284, 599n569; on vanguardism, 360–61

Mass Strike, the Political Party, and the Trade Unions, The (Luxemburg), 370–71

Mate, Reyes, 577n254

material critical-ethical principle. *See* critical-ethical principle

material critical reason, xviii–xix, 185, 190–91, 245–50, 278–90, 597n550, 598n560

material ethics, xix, 91, 198*t*, 435, 438, 440, 478n6, 492n136; of Aristotle's *eudaimonia*, 84–85; axiological practices of, 68, 81, 89–90, 485n81, 495n190; communitarian perspectives on, 77–85, 96, 493n150; criteria of practical truth in, 93–99, 108, 479n10, 481n30, 503n280; of Hegel's World Spirit, 87–89, 500–501nn238–39; of Heidegger and, 90, 502n260; normative judgment of obligation in, 99–106, 192; of Ricoeur and, 90; of Scheler and, 89–90; self-organizing brain in, 57–69, 478n9, 479n19, 480nn27–29, 502n267; Thomas Aquinas and, 86–87; universal material principle of ethics in, 104–7, 127, 507n333, 508n335; universal principle of human life in, 55–57, 92–93, 105–6, 478n7, 507n328, 521nn146–47; utilitarian perspectives on, 69–77, 488n103; of Zubiri's *prius* of reality, 90–92, 502n265

material principle of ethics, 104, 520n140; application of, 106–7; grounding of, 105–6, 127, 141

mathematics, 22

Matthew (Biblical book), 450–51

Maturana, Humberto, 58–59, 63, 67–68, 479nn16–17, 485n78

Mayan culture, 9–11

Mead, George H., 161, 496n198, 540n62, 541n67, 548n168

meaningfulness, 174–75, 446

meaning-sense, 167

Me llamo Rigoberta Menchú y así me nació la conciencia (Menchú), 297–303, 601n8

Memmi, Albert, 317

Memphis (Egypt), 6, 447–48

Menchú, Rigoberta, xvii, 374, 387–88; diverse visages of, 424; narrative of exclusion of, 293, 297–303, 601n8; on origination of consciousness, 576n233, 603n23

Mendieta, Eduardo, 468n201

Merleau-Ponty, Maurice, xxii, 67, 631n21

Mesoamerican (Mayan-Aztec) culture, 9–11

Mesopotamian period, 2, 3*t*, 4–5, 8–9, 11*f. See also* Egyptian-Mesopotamian system

messianic time, 241–43, 292

mestizos, 37, 469n216

metacellular organisms, 58–59

metaethics of liberation, xviii

Metaphysics of Customs (Kant), 400

Mexico: Chiapas revolt of, 298, 386, 408, 453n8, 604n38, 645n244; Hidalgo's revolt in, 402, 409, 421; Zacateca silver mines of, 31

microphysics of power, 356–59, 364, 631n14, 631n18, 632n23

Middle Ages, 18, 23–26

Mignolo, Walter, 639n138

Mill, John Stuart: on "greatest happiness" principle, 72–73, 489n120; on political economies, 76–77, 486n89, 493n147

Misery of Historicism, The (Popper), 279

Moabite people, 8–9

models of praxis, 211–14, 557n41. *See also* praxis of liberation

Modernity, 4, 437; Arab philosophical secularism in, 22–23; capitalist system of, 26, 30, 31, 36–37; center-periphery constructs in, 25–26, 31–40, 332–33, 355–56; central ethical question of, 33–40; counter-discourses from the periphery of, 41–52, 355–56, 468n201, 469n211, 473n257, 579n278; destruction of humanity by, 36–40, 470n228; Eurocentric paradigm of, 24–25, 30,

sophical secularism in, 22–23; Bantu community of Egypt in, 461n111; ethical-critical principles of, 457n36, 457n41; Exodus in, 9, 457–58nn47–48, 608n68; Hebrew liberating rationality in, 8–9; Jewish Kabbalah of, 219, 560nn32–33, 570n164; material critical reason of, 206; origins of philosophy in, 8–9, 456n23; prophets of, 459n71. *See also* Islam

Sendero Luminoso, 194

Sepúlveda, Gines de, 468n201, 472n245, 579n278

Serrano, Enrique, 405

Shabaka, King of Memphis, 447

Shaftesbury, Anthony, 70, 112

Short History of Ethics, A (MacIntyre), 79

Sidgwick, Henry, 486n89, 494n167

Silk Route, 4–5, 14, 18, 21–22, 460n107

Simon, Ernst, 570n164

simplification, 35–37

skepticism, 333–34, 346, 627n368

slavery, 32, 298, 601n13; Aristotle on, 118, 207; Exodus story of, 9, 457–58nn47–48; in Greek culture, 37; in Muslim culture, 462n127; in the Roman Empire, 19; of sub-Saharan Africa, 466n177, 497n206

Smith, Adam, 70, 71, 111, 548n168; Marx's critique of, 233, 330, 392, 617n242; political economics of, 75–76, 332, 486n89, 515n80, 599n568, 618n246

social engineering, 325–26

"Social Function of Philosophy, The" (Horkheimer), 571n172

socialism, 332, 619n250, 649n309

social laws, 389–90

social movements, 388. *See also* liberation movements of the twentieth century

Social System, The (Parsons), 176

social systems, 175–80

sociohistorical subject, 385–88, 421, 423–24, 601n7

sociology, 129–30, 176, 548n168

Socrates, 37, 455n18, 456n26

Sombart, Werner, 33, 35

Sources of the Self (Taylor), 41–42, 81–82

Southeastern Asia, 4–5

South-South dialogue, xxii

Southwestern Asia, 3*t*

Soviet Union: bureaucratic formalism of, 181, 373, 515n77; collapse of, xx, 77, 181, 355; Revolution of 1917 of, 368–69, 399, 619nn250–51; social sciences in, 332; Stalinist real socialism in, 73, 181, 379, 389, 470n224, 638n122, 643n215

Spain, 9, 25, 29; as first modern state, 30–32, 466nn175–78; Inquisition in, 466n175; management of new world system by, 33–35, 464n168, 467n199; silver and gold wealth of, 31–32, 466n177

Spencer, Herbert, 68

Sperandeo, Sebastiano, 12

Spheres of Justice (Walzer), 83–85

Spinoza, Baruch, 31, 111, 467n184, 467n186, 510n25

spontaneism, 240

Stalinism: praxis under, 643n215; real socialism of, 73, 181, 379, 389, 470n224, 638n122; social sciences under, 332

Steuart, J., 330

stoicism: *apátheia* of, 16; on control of instincts, 487nn96–97; love and virtue in, 80, 110–11. *See also* neo-stoicism

Strasser, Stephan, 615n217

strategic instrumental feasibility, 416, 446

strategic-instrumental reason, 186–96, 199–201, 343, 353, 358–60, 366, 424–25, 629n398

strategic practical feasibility, 358–59

Strawson, P. F., 133–34

strikes, 410–12, 648n277

structuralism, 379

subjectivity: reflexive facts of, 58*f*, 479n12; in utilitarian perspectives, 71, 72–73

subject of liberation praxis, 373–74, 601n7; intersubjectivity as sociohistorical subjects of, 380–81, 385–88,

critical-discursive criterion of validity and, 344–45; of the dominant order, 334, 620n256; ethical
principle of feasibility and, 186;
Hinkelammert and, 181–85; James
and, 165, 166, 171; Putnam and, 167,
168f, 543n95; in scientific contexts,
536n24; Zubiri and, 164–66. *See
also* intersubjective validity claim;
practical truth
Tsin dynasty, 17–18
Turan Tarim region, 18
Turgot, Anne Robert, 587n388
Twenty Theses on Politics, xi

Unidad Popular, 181, 547n159
United States: economic hegemony
of, 77, 417, 466n178, 467n187,
467n194, 475n262; international
debt and, 556n20; Iraq wars of, 410,
544n114, 648n275; military hegemony of, xx, 77, 160, 396, 403, 417,
429, 648n275; military violence of,
295; New Right Americanism in,
160, 260; original liberation project
of, 651n329; pragmatism of, 160–
67, 534nn3–4; Rawls and, 116–20.
See also Amerindia; world system
universal critical-practical reason,
554n3
universality, 108, 434, 507n333; Eurocentric assumptions of, 42–43,
471n241; Rawls and, 116–17; of
reason, 218
universal principles, xix; absolute universality as, 430; criterion of feasibility in, 187–90, 413–19; criterion
of intersubjective validity in, 106–8,
114–15, 128, 137–38, 140, 142–46,
151, 163–64, 175–76; criterion of
meaningfulness in, 174–75; criterion of practical truth in, 93–99,
141–42, 479n10, 481n30, 503n280;
critical-discursive principle of
validity in, 342–54, 427; ethical
principle of operability (concrete
feasibility) as, 190–203, 343, 403,
413–23; the liberation principle as,
126–27, 355–431; material critical-
ethical principle as, 185, 190–91,

245–50, 278–90, 580nn300–302,
597n550, 598n560; material principle of ethics as, 104–6, 278–79,
507n333, 508n335, 520n140; moral
principle of formal validity as, 142,
146–56; subsumption by the liberation principle of, 419–23; value of
human life as, 55–57, 92–93, 105–6,
187, 208, 436, 478n7, 507n328,
521nn146–47, 549n187
unreal utopians, 193–94
Upanishads, 14, 23, 459n71
Upper Egypt, 6–9
Uranic gods, 13, 459n69
Urinimgina, 8
Uruk, 8
utilitarianism, xvi, 69, 440, 580n302;
abstraction and reduction in, 70–
71; economic objectivity in, 70;
four dimensions of, 73; "greatest
happiness" principle of, 71, 72–75,
488n120, 490n124, 491n132; material consumption in, 74, 490–
91nn127–29, 491–92nn133–35; origins of, 70–71, 487n97; on political
economies, 75–77; as utopian illusion, 74–76
utopian thought: Bloch and, 334–35,
338–42, 352–53, 621n283; contradictions of world systems and, 217,
558n8; critical utopian-constructive
reason and, 350, 352–54; hope in
possibility of, 419, 649nn303–4;
Popper on, 194, 279, 283, 346, 390,
422–23, 650n310; of unreal utopians, 193–94; utilitarianism as,
74–76

validity, 167, 168f, 174–75, 425, 439,
440, 446; critical-discursive criterion of, 342–54; critical validity of
reason in, 291, 294; ethical principle
of feasibility and, 186, 189–90. *See
also* antihegemonic validity of victims; intersubjective validity claim
Valle, José del, 76
value ethics, 142
values/valorization, 439, 482n41; in
affective-evaluative systems, 61, 69,
482nn37–38, 482n41, 486n86; axio-

ENRIQUE DUSSEL teaches philosophy at the Universidad Autónoma Metropolitana, Iztapalapa, and at the Universidad Nacional Autónoma de México in Mexico City. He is the author of many books, including *Twenty Theses on Politics* (Duke, 2008), *The Invention of the Americas: Eclipse of the "Other" and the Myth of Modernity*, and *Philosophy of Liberation*. He is a coeditor of *Coloniality at Large: Latin America and the Postcolonial Debate* (Duke, 2008).